Issues in Contemporary
Literary Criticism

Issues in Contemporary
Literary Criticism

Edited by **GREGORY T. POLLETTA**

University of Geneva

Little, Brown and Company BOSTON

Preface

This anthology has derived from my experience teaching university courses in twentieth-century criticism and more general courses in literature studied by way of critical inquiry. I have composed the volume as a text-book for use in similar courses and I have attempted to bring the readings within reach not only of students who are specializing in the subject of criticism, but also of any student who is inquiring into literature by a critical mode of activity. My purpose is to show the activity of literary criticism in contemporary performance.

I have tried, of course, to choose critics of stature and representative selections of singular critical interest, but I have arranged them so as to facilitate an inquiry into the issues and concepts of contemporary criticism. The readings are ordered under five headings: The Place and Performance of Criticism, The Writer's Intention, The Literary Performance, The Reader's Response, and Literature's Relation to the World. In the introductions to these sections, I have sketched the general questions posed by the topic and then described the specific questions on which the individual selections turn as well as the particular views each critic brings to the inquiry.

The kinds of issues the critics engage and probe are: What is a literary text? An object, an act, the medium of an abstract and anonymous consciousness, a performance in words? If an object, of what sort? A mirror? With how many and what manner of planes? If not a mirror, what: a verbal icon, a linguistic construct, a well-wrought urn? How does literature differ from other verbal structures and modes of verbal action? Is literature privileged in its uses of language? Are critics elitist in their assumptions about the language, structures, and vocation of literature? Whom does literature benefit? What does it do to readers? How does it act in and upon the world? Are the structures of literature latent or manifest, deep or surface, implicit or explicit? Is structure the same as form? Is the form of a literary text open or closed? If a text is regarded as a closed verbal context, what is its relation to other texts by the same author? To other verbal contexts, such as a literary tradition? To other kinds of contexts? What is a context anyway?

Some issues are missing, to be sure, but those represented here are certainly among the presiding preoccupations of contemporary criticism. And although my own views are evident enough in the introductory commentaries, I have not promoted any one school or theoretical orientation or methodology, but have ranged freely over what is happening or at issue now in American, English, and Continental criticism.

For all my attention to issues and concepts, however, I am concerned more with the doing of criticism — criticism in performance. An arrangement of materials by issues, such as is common in textbooks for courses in aesthetics, risks making the speculative and conceptual override the performative aspects of the critic's jobs of work. But whatever the pleasures and value of criticism as pure speculation, I believe the student should be encouraged to see and feel it as an activity that directly modifies his experience of literature.

Accordingly, I have focused my commentaries on the conceptions of what literature is, how it is to be studied, and what ends govern a particular critic's performance — whether the performance is directed to theoretical or practical criticism. Moreover, I have emphasized the actual performance of the critic rather than the abstract issue. A general question such as "Is a poem a verbal object?", whether advanced as a theoretical proposition or assumed as a working principle in a critical analysis, can mean everything — or nothing. What counts, obviously, is how the critic shapes the issue. And it is the awareness of the process of shaping an issue, the sense of a critic at work on a text or a theoretical problem, that I have tried to foster by my commentaries.

I do not mean that the student should copy a particular critic's modes of work, or borrow his approach, or assimilate his ideas. There are no easy rules for critical inquiry, not even any simple way of saying what it is, but by watching attentively how one critic performs and then comparing his performance with other critics on the same issue or writer or text, we can begin to see what criticism is in action and to apprehend what is possible in the criticism of literature. With that kind of understanding a student can make up his own mind about any critical theory, method, or interpretation.

The teacher, however, may wonder whether an arrangement of material by issues is altogether fitting for these objectives. Does it not run the danger of cramping and circumscribing the selections? Why not let them stand and speak for themselves?

Georges Poulet's "Phenomenology of Reading," for example, touches on the topics of all five sections, and there is a certain arbitrariness in confining it to one section, perhaps caprice in placing it where I have rather than elsewhere. But the same objection would hold for any alternative design, since every arrangement implies a structure, and I have thought it preferable to arrange the selections by categories of issues than by the familiar alternative of theoretical orientations or critical approaches. The differences between the essays of Poulet, R. P. Blackmur, and Northrop Frye, as instances, are more meaningful and less arbitrary if we consider the issues they address in common than if we arrange them as illustrations of, respectively, "psychological," "formalistic," and "archetypal" approaches to criticism.

Nothing, of course, prevents the selections from being taken on their own and arranged in any order the teacher sees fit, but the presence of a particular essay in the company of others, far from jeopardizing its individuality, should work to exhibit its distinctive identity and power. As for my commentaries, and the question of whether they get between the reader and the selections as well as between the teacher and his students, they are only introductions; they leave most of what is of consequence in the essays to be revealed and discussed by each teacher with his own students. They are meant to make the selections accessible to inquiry and to set the stage for study and conversation in the classroom. They are designed to help the student become aware of what is at stake in a critical discussion, of what issues are in play, so that he may better be able to engage in that process of collaboration which, as several critics included here affirm, is singular to the activity of literary criticism.

I should like to acknowledge with thanks the help of Richard Poirier in compiling this anthology. As the publisher's reader of my original manuscript, his advice was uncommonly generous and constructive. The volume is better now than it would have been without his counsel, but he is, of course, blameless for whatever shortcomings remain.

I should also like to thank the other readers, Sylvan Barnet and Hazard Adams, for their helpful comments, and the members of the editorial and production staffs of Little, Brown and Company, especially Charles H. Christensen, Mrs. Jane Richardson, and Mrs. Deborah Otaguro, for their kind and expert assistance in guiding the manuscript into print.

Gregory T. Polletta

Contents

ix

II

The Writer's Intention   185

III

The Literary Performance   309

Issues in Contemporary
Literary Criticism

I

The Place and
Performance of Criticism

Contemporary literary criticism, both American and European, shows more variety, subtlety, and energy than any definition can encompass, but if one impulse is strongest, and new in its consequences for the place and performance of criticism, it is a reaching *beyond formalism*. Not "after" or strictly "against": *beyond*. Its objective is to challenge received ideas and an established tradition, but the phrase is ambiguous; the motive may be radical, to break clean with critical precedents, or reformative, to alter the tradition for the better. "What lies beyond formalist theory?" (p. 148) * is not solely an issue of finding an *antithetical* alternative, for although some of the best contemporary critics have repudiated formalist theory and can properly be called "antiformalists," others, equally committed to moving beyond established formalist theories, are just as revolutionary in the changes they are fashioning and yet must still be called "formalists."

The question obviously turns on how one identifies formalism. Geoffrey H. Hartman defines it "simply as a method: that of revealing the human content of art by a study of its formal properties" (p. 161). This is a fair statement, and by emphasizing method it avoids having to sort through countless specific schools, doctrines, and programs — the welter of formalisms and formal-

* Page numbers in parentheses refer to selections in this book; footnotes appear at the end of each part of the book.

1

ist theories in twentieth-century criticism.[1] Hartman gets at the heart of the contemporary controversy: whether the place of priority all formalists, whatever their individual differences, assign to the formal properties of the literary work is best for the performance of criticism and the study of literature. But to understand the present situation in criticism, the point from which the impulse to move beyond formalism springs, it might be better to begin with the specific movement that in America and England is usually associated with formalism and formalist criticism: the so-called New Criticism.

The New Criticism was anything but monolithic, and there are even grounds for doubting whether it ever was a "school," in the sense that a certain company of critics banded together to promote a common program. As it is usually described, however, the New Criticism was founded in the 1920's by T. S. Eliot and I. A. Richards, with borrowings from Kant, Coleridge, the French Symbolists, Benedetto Croce, T. E. Hulme, and Ezra Pound, among others; got its title in 1941 from John Crowe Ransom's *The New Criticism,* which was a study of, besides Eliot and Richards, William Empson and Yvor Winters; took on as partners Allen Tate, Cleanth Brooks, Robert Penn Warren, R. P. Blackmur, and as more distant associates, F. R. Leavis, Kenneth Burke, and Lionel Trilling; was consolidated by W. K. Wimsatt, René Wellek, and Austin Warren; and during the 1940's and 1950's attracted a legion of followers in English and American universities. The New Criticism gained a purchase in American universities with the publication in 1938 of Brooks and Warren's textbook, *Understanding Poetry.* After a period of fierce resistance from the entrenched forces in departments of literature, running battles with other varieties of criticism (psychoanalytical, Marxist, mythopoeic), and skirmishes with rival kinds of formalist criticism (chiefly the so-called Neo-Aristotelians based at the University of Chicago, led by R. S. Crane, Richard McKeon, and Elder Olson), the New Criticism steadily won adherents and influence until the late 1940's and the early 1950's, when it became firmly established as the dominant power in the teaching of literature in American universities. While never quite so strong, it became a major force in English universities, as well.[2]

However diverse and complex the concepts or modes of work of the New Critics were in actual performance, the motivation of their theories, their distinctive aim as critics, can be stated rather simply. It was to reorient the study of literature and the critic's jobs of work away from the poet or the reader toward the formal properties of the poem itself, and, further, away from the poem in its relations to historical causes or extrinsic structures of reality toward the poem as a verbal structure with its own mode of existence. As Cleanth Brooks wrote in 1962:

> . . . it is possible to restate the history of criticism in our time thus: We have been witnessing a strenuous attempt to focus attention upon the poem rather than upon the poet or the reader. Along with this stress upon the poem as a structure in its own right, has come the attempt to fix the boundaries and limits of poetry. Modern critics have tried to see what was meant when one considered the poem as an artistic document. . . . Poetry has a characteristic structure and yields a characteristic knowledge. It does not compete with, but exists alongside of and complements, scientific knowledge and historical knowledge.[3]

The main purpose of criticism is understanding the concrete literary work — a particular poem, play, or novel — the *text* as an object in its own right. Criticism begins with an artifact to be scrutinized, and however far it may wander into language, history, biography, and literary tradition, the excursion is always directed to the formal properties by which the human content of art is constituted and revealed. It follows that the descriptive and demonstrative modes — interpretation, explication, exegesis, analysis — that direct the mind toward apprehending the modes of language and form which constitute the text of a poem are given priority (not exclusive privilege) over such other modes as genetic, causative, affective, and evaluative. As Northrop Frye observes in "The Critical Path," the New Criticism "established itself as a technique of explication"; it "accepted poetic language as the basis for poetic meaning. On this basis, it built up a resistance to all 'background' criticism that explained the literary in terms of the non-literary" (p. 54).

The New Criticism has been the most influential and vigorous critical enterprise of the twentieth century in America and England. Moreover, it was spectacularly successful in changing the academic study of literature. Walter J. Ong has argued that the New Criticism was fully entitled to its name; it was genuinely new, the first really adequate criticism ever to exist. "English" did not enter the university until late in the nineteenth century, and it came first as a language of instruction to replace Latin and only later as an object of study, but even then it was the language that was studied rather than the literature. The first teachers of

English, themselves trained in the classics, approached English literature indirectly, treating it by a kind of extrinsic analogy to Latin and Greek. This philological disposition was the basis for the prevailing, virtually the only, mode of teaching literature when the New Critics began their work. They insisted on the primary importance of studying English as literature rather than as a corpus of philological or historical documents, and added the revolutionary principle of studying modern literature, the literature of one's own time. As Ong concludes:

> It really does not replace anything in particular. Insofar as it is new, it is simply the criticism which is generated when academic attention is turned first on the vernacular and then finally on contemporary productions in the vernacular. The New Criticism was the product of the first age when thousands of persons became intent on academic, and ultimately scholarly, analysis as penetrating and painstaking as academic procedure can make it, of the literary activity actually going on around them.[4]

All this is taken so much for granted that it may be hard for the student today to imagine what studying literature was like before the New Criticism. As René Wellek said in an address delivered in 1965:

> Present-day students seem completely unable to realize the situation of the early decades of the century in most English departments. Criticism was taboo, contemporary and even American literature was not taught at all, foreign literatures were largely ignored, texts were studied only as philological documents — in short, nineteenth-century positivism reigned unchallenged and supreme.[5]

About the mid- and late 1950's a reaction to the New Criticism developed against both its theories of criticism and its place in the academic study of literature. Many of its concepts were sharply revised or bypassed for newer critical theories. Attacks deplored the effect teachers who professed its methods were having on what students were made to read and the dispiriting manner of their study by explication. Indeed, the antagonism the New Criticism aroused has stemmed more from a sense of what was done in its name in the universities than from the performances of the original critics themselves. In any case, under the assault from these two quarters the prestige of the New Criticism declined and its authority in the universities waned. In 1960 René Wellek noted that the New Criticism had gone on the defensive, and in 1961 he declared it had "reached a point of exhaustion" — dying, as its mourners were given to say, of its very success.[6]

Obviously, however, the New Criticism cannot be written off that easily, nor can it be dismissed as a splendid but finished episode, having only historical interest and importance. Literary movements of any consequence don't simply expire; their effects will be felt long after their initial energies look spent. For one thing, many issues the New Criticism initiated or developed are very much alive; in fact, it has framed the terms on which arguments to these issues continue to turn. For another, some of the original New Critics, and many of their followers, are still active; W. K. Wimsatt, one might say, has become stronger and better over the years, not feebler. Moreover, some critics have extended and refined the theories of the New Criticism rather than rejecting them completely. Mark Spilka, for example, has taken exception to Wimsatt's notions, as his essay in Part II shows, but he has not broken with the New Criticism. "Our passion for the verbal object," Spilka says, "and for objective criticism, is right and central." And his proposal for a newer criticism is for "an advanced stage of critical practice, not of introductory methods" (p. 213). Finally, the New Criticism still has a strong grip on teaching and studying literature. Even the method of exegesis so often and so harshly censured — in Geoffrey H. Hartman's words, "our Whore of Babylon, sitting robed in Academic black on the great dragon of Criticism, and dispensing a repetitive and soporific balm from her pedantic cup" — has a secure place in contemporary critical practice. Ian Watt's explication of the first paragraph of James's *The Ambassadors,* included here, and John Frederick Nims's analysis of Robert Lowell's "Skunk Hour" have none of the defects that have been leveled at the New Criticism. They show what can be done with explication in the right hands. They are still valuable as models for the study of literature.

Nevertheless, even the most sympathetic observer must acknowledge that the New Criticism has become something to be resisted, opposed, or advanced beyond instead of the positive force it was in the 1940's and 1950's. Each assumption on the place and performance of criticism, every concept, the whole repertory of critical methods with which the New Criticism is identified has been challenged, rejected, or modified drastically in contemporary criticism. Some concepts, as following selections indicate, are based on completely foreign premises, but even those of critics who fit the terms of Hartman's definition of formalism are so different in tenor and effect as to be more revolutionary than revisionary. These critics are intent on fashioning, as an alternative to the New Criticism, a more complete and a more adequate method for revealing the human content of literature through the study of its formal properties. For them the question "What lies beyond formalist theory?" becomes "What formal properties other than those which preoccupied the New Critics should be investigated? In what order of inquiry? By what techniques? Toward what ends?"

Northrop Frye, for example, is the foremost theorist of literature writing in English since the 1950's, and whatever the kind and degree of his formalism, he is certainly no antiformalist. Ihab Hassan flatly labels him as a formalist, linking him to René Wellek, but Frye himself explains in "The Critical Path" why and in what ways he has tried to move beyond the formalism of the New Critics.⁷ His own course was guided by the desire to develop "the sense of context" that the New Criticism, in its attempt to push beyond the previous modes of documentary criticism, had ended by neglecting: "It simply explicated one work after another, paying little attention to any larger structural principles connecting the different works explicated." "Context" is a crucial term in contemporary criticism, and the relation between "text" and "context" an important nexus. Frye at first tried to arrive at his notion of context, not by reviving any documentary approach, for, like the New Critics, he was against explaining "the literary in terms of the non-literary," but by considering the single poem in the context of "the entire output of its author." Dissatisfied, he broadened his approach to include the study of "certain structural elements in the literary tradition, such as conventions, genres, and the recurring use of certain images or image-clusters." These "image-clusters" he came to call "archetypes."

Frye's concept of archetype has generated much misunderstanding because of the term's connection with Jung's "collective unconscious." Frye has repeatedly denied grounding his concept on that presupposition, but he continues to be classified as "a Jungian critic." In fact, Frye is more often called a myth critic than a formalist or structuralist. René Wellek, for example, asserts that "in the United States myth criticism can be described as the most successful attempt to replace the New Criticism," and he lists Frye among myth criticism's chief practitioners.⁸ But Frye is quite right in saying "the notion that I belong to a school or have invented a school of mythical or archetypal criticism reflects nothing but confusion about me." [9] However much he has discussed myths and archetypes he does not regard them as codes for the hidden messages in literature, as overlays of meaning or vehicles of content.

Myth, as Frye sees it, is less a specific content or story than a mold of form, a structural principle. "Myths," he says, "represent the structural principles of literature; they are to literature what geometrical shapes are to painting." And the reason for studying mythology, the concrete stories such as that of Ceres and Proserpina,

> is that mythology as a whole provides a kind of diagram or blueprint of what literature as a whole is all about, an imaginative survey of the human situation from the beginning to the end, from the height to the depth, of what is imaginatively conceivable.[10]

The mythic stories "come in certain conventional shapes," the anatomy of which Frye has examined with astounding scope and detail, arranging the shapes according to four "generic plots": romantic, comic, tragic, and ironic or satiric. The archetype is a ruling symbolic pattern of significance embodied in the mythic narratives. As Frye says in his essay on *Lycidas,* the archetype is "a literary symbol, or cluster of symbols, which are used recurrently throughout literature, and thereby become conventional" (p. 405). In another essay, he says:

> Myth *is* the archetype, though it might be convenient to say myth only when referring to narrative, and archetype when speaking of significance. In the solar cycle of the day, the seasonal cycle of the year, and the organic cycle of human life, there is a single pattern of significance, out of which myth constructs a central narrative around a figure who is partly the sun, partly vegetative fertility and partly a god or archetypal human being.[11]

A writer is drawn to myths because they illustrate the essential principles of storytelling and because the archetypal patterns embodied in the myths offer him models by which to shape his and his culture's vital concerns. One obvious problem, however, is how to make the myths plausible or credible or morally acceptable to a sophisticated audience — and the technique for accomplishing this Frye calls "displacement." [12] The precise contours of Frye's concepts of myth, archetype, and displacement can hardly be grasped in any brief summary, but a sense of his meaning can be derived from his essay on *Lycidas,* where, attending to "the primary business of the critic," he shows how myth acts "as the shaping principle of a work of literature."

In any case, Frye's theories of literature and his performance as a critic do not depend on how myth is treated in other disciplines — in anthropology, psychology, or comparative religion. Criticism, he makes clear in the "Polemical Introduction" to *Anatomy of Criticism,* should not be based on any presuppositions taken from outside literature. He starts with the assumption that "literature is not a subject of study, but an object of study," from which he derives the view that "criticism is a structure of thought and knowledge existing in its own right, with some measure of independence from the art it deals with." The direct experience of literature is not criticism, for that, "at first, is bound to be full of the subjective and private associations of stock response." Criticism is a structure constructed from "an inductive survey of the literary field" (p. 32), rather than from the concepts drawn from other disciplines. The first thing for criticism "to do with any literary experience, the first step in understanding it as literature, is to associate it with other literary experiences." Our literary understanding of a character, for example, "does not begin until we associate him with other literary characters." And "the more we know about literature, the more clearly its interconnecting structural principles appear." [13] The knowledge the critic builds from this investigation of interconnecting structural principles constitutes criticism as such, not the direct experience of literature. Hence, criticism is a systematic, even a scientific, discipline.

The real audacity in Frye's theories is less in the place he claims for criticism than in his conception of literature: "Literature," he says, "is not simply an aggregate of books and poems and plays: it is an order of words," [14] a total form, one vast structure. And that order is autonomous, separate from the orders of nature and of actual human life, though partaking of both: "when we speak of literature, we speak of a total imaginative form which is, in that context, *bigger* than either nature or human life, because it contains them, the actual being only a part of the possible." Literature is the most complete, the most satisfying order of all that is "imaginatively conceivable"; it is "a body of hypothetical thought and action."

> Literature, we say, neither reflects nor escapes from ordinary life: what it does reflect is the world as human imagination conceives it, in mythical, romantic, heroic and ironic as well as realistic and

fantastic terms. This world is the universe in human form, stretching from the complete fulfillment of human desire to what human desire utterly repudiates.[15]

Literature is made out of other literature, and its total structure is a vision of all that the imagination can conceive and create in human form.

Frye's formalism, then, is substantially different from that of the New Critics. He starts as they do with the conviction that "the structure and imagery of literature are central considerations of criticism," and he clearly shares their belief that a work of literature should not be related to anything outside of itself. But his conception of structure is singularly different, as he is not interested in discrete and autonomous poems but in the relation of the single text to the whole context of literature, and, perhaps most important for the performance of criticism, he is not pre-occupied with the verbal texture of particular works of literature.[16] He is not primarily a stylistic, or as he calls it, a "rhetorical" critic. Instead of the close attention to the play of language, the performance of the words in a particular poem, at which the New Critics excelled, Frye advocates backing away from the individual work until one is far enough to see its larger structural design rather than its local textural detailing. Frye explains the process in *Anatomy of Criticism:*

In looking at a picture, we may stand close to it and analyze the details of brush work and palette knife. This corresponds roughly to the rhetorical analysis of the new critics in literature. At a little distance back, the design comes into clearer view, and we study rather the content represented: this is the best distance for realistic Dutch pictures, for example, where we are in a sense reading the picture. The further back we go, the more conscious we are of the organizing design. At a great distance from, say, a Madonna, we can see nothing but the archetype of the Madonna, a large centripetal blue mass with a contrasting point of interest at its center. In the criticism of literature, too, we often have to "stand back" from the poem to see its archetypal organization. If we "stand back" from Spenser's *Mutabilitie Cantoes,* we see a background of ordered circular light and a sinister black mass thrusting up into the lower foreground — much the same archetypal shape that we see in the opening of the Book of Job. If we "stand back" from the beginning of the fifth act of *Hamlet,* we see a grave opening on the stage, the hero, his enemy, and the heroine descending into it, followed by a fatal struggle in the upper world. If we "stand back" from a realistic novel such as Tolstoy's *Resurrection* or Zola's

Germinal, we can see the mythopoeic designs indicated by those titles.[17]

And yet, however far this kind of structural analysis moves beyond the explication of the New Criticism, Frye is more concerned with description and demonstration than with affective, causative, or evaluative modes. "The fundamental critical act," he has affirmed,

> is the act of recognition, seeing what is there, as distinct from merely seeing a Narcissus mirror of our own experience and social and moral prejudice. Recognition includes a good many things, including commentary and interpretation.[18]

Indeed, one of the most controversial aspects of Frye's theories of criticism is his insistence that the critic should not be preoccupied with making judgments about individual writers and works of literature. Interestingly enough, this has vexed formalists even more than antiformalists. Frye has been accused of smuggling all sorts of value-judgments into his own criticism, and of failing to recognize judgment as indispensable for the critical activity, but such objections do not easily dispose of the reasons he offers for excluding or subordinating value-judgments to modes of recognition.[19] One aspect of his painstaking examination of this issue in the "Polemical Introduction" is among the more attractive and liberating features of his outlook on literature. Evaluation, he says, "always means that the critic wants to get into the concern game himself, choosing a canon out of literature and so making it a gigantic allegory of his own concern." [20] Critics, Frye believes, are always rearranging literature into a canon, a hierarchy, a great tradition reflecting their own values, which conspires to diminish the true order of words, the boundless total structure of all that is imaginatively conceivable which is literature. As Geoffrey H. Hartman has observed, Frye has had his greatest impact by demystifying and democratizing criticism; he has challenged the conviction "that literature is to be used as a training ground for elite judgment." [21]

R. P. Blackmur is usually identified as a New Critic, but he anticipated some of the dissatisfactions with explicatory criticism expressed by Northrop Frye and reflected in the essays by younger critics as diverse as Ihab Hassan, J. Hillis Miller, Susan Sontag, and Geoffrey H. Hartman. In fact, in "A Burden for Critics," published in 1948, he invokes the same context Hartman offers at the end of "Beyond Formalism": Blackmur says the New

Criticism "neither compares nor judges; it elucidates scripture." Later, Blackmur objected even more sharply. The New Critics shared, he said, a prodigious skill in analyzing the psychology of poetic language; but

> so attractive as well as necessary were the techniques of this skill in language that they led to excess analysis, excess simplification, and excess application, which is the normal pathology of a skill become a method and a method become a methodology.[22]

Blackmur was called a New Critic because he established an early reputation as a brilliant expositor of "the psychology of poetic language" in individual poems and poets. John Crowe Ransom, reviewing Blackmur's collection of essays on twentieth-century poetry, *Language as Gesture,* called him a "linguistic" critic whose studies were "technical": "the poems are examined along linguistic lines, procedural lines, strategical lines; whatever may be the gravity of the content." [23] But whatever the truth of this assessment, Blackmur's next collection, *The Lion and the Honeycomb,* shows him moving beyond "superficial and mechanical executive techniques" to include "the ulterior techniques of conceptual form" and finally the techniques of "symbolic form" that underlie and transcend the other forms.

In deepening and stretching his explorations, Blackmur left the New Criticism behind. René Wellek has charged that he progressively lost contact with any literary text — which is true enough if the text is conceived in Wellek's terms.[24] But in Blackmur's view a full understanding of the text needs an intimate response to and comprehension of all the verbal, personal, and cultural contexts that surround and are given life in the literary performance. "Bringing particular works of art to full performance" was Blackmur's constant concern, early and late in his career, and if he changed his focus and mind and method, he was motivated by a desire not to get outside of form, but to engage more completely "the forces that operate in the arts which are greater than ourselves and come from beyond or under ourselves . . . invokable forces, or raw forces, the force of reality, whatever reality may be, pressing into and transforming our actual experience."

Blackmur invites comparison with Northrop Frye on several counts. Blackmur is more quizzical about the place of criticism; he is preoccupied with the *burdens* that criticism, and the arts themselves, has had to assume. He is not nearly so rigorously schematic or systematic as Frye. Indeed, Frank Kermode has argued that Frye and Blackmur are polar opposites; Blackmur, he says,

> was essentially a very unsystematic critic and believed, dangerously but correctly, that criticism is mostly anarchic, though dependent on a difficult act of submission and then on the critic's having a mind with useful and interesting contents. The insights are quite unsystematic; their history is certainly not that of a "progressive" system.[25]

This quality of Blackmur's criticism may be less an incapacity for systematic rigor and terminological skill, as his detractors have charged, than an attempt, as Joseph Frank has described it,

> to avoid getting caught in his own dialectic — he is struggling to escape the ultimate treachery of language, which commits you to one position and one perspective when you are so agonizingly aware of all the others at the same time. To circumvent such treachery Mr. Blackmur defines his terms as sweepingly as possible, or he uses some emotive or metaphorical image to give the "feel" of what he means rather than any meaning which would hem him in too tightly.[26]

Blackmur's field of criticism is much smaller and more selective than Frye's. He is interested in the best literary performances, not the total order of words. But he is, in his own way, just as ambitious, for whatever his "program of work," as he calls it, may lack in anatomical sweep and precision, it more than makes up for in the scope of the critical problems it seeks to identify and explore.

Blackmur and Frye appear to be most at odds on the issue of the place of judgment in criticism. Actually, Blackmur is not vulnerable to most of Frye's strictures; he says explicitly that he is not concerned with ranks and hierarchies. Judgment, he declares, is "the last act in bringing particular works of art to full performance." He means by judgment, first, a quality of tact, specifically using one's critical skills judiciously; and, second, a quality of discerning "what happens in the arts — what gets into the arts," and what gets lost when certain literary forms are abandoned, in relation to the forces of human behavior, of language, of culture, of reality. The critic, Blackmur holds, must exercise "judgments upon the art of our time as an aid in determining the identity, the meaning itself, of present society." Judgment is the critical mode that tries to apprehend "the discovery of life which is art."

Perhaps the greatest difference between Frye and Blackmur is the point they seem to have most in common: the importance of form in literature. Blackmur shows a fondness for mottoes in "A Burden for Critics"; his own motto, which he quoted repeatedly, came from a saying of Croce's: "Art is a theoretic form of experience" (with the variations "feelings," "behavior," "life"). This is not that far from Frye's statement: "Literature is a body of hypothetical thought and action." Neither statement isolates the aesthetic fact from its human content, which is the charge behind all attacks on formalism, but for Frye the ordering process of literature absorbs and transfigures real human experience or action, whereas for Blackmur the theoretic form of art creates "the sort of order which is responsive to every movement of behavior and every pulse of inspiration: an order which gives room to fresh disorder whenever it occurs." [27] Blackmur's sense of theoretic form has more of the turbulence of actual human behavior that pulses in and around a literary work. "The fundamental act of criticism," Frye says, "is a disinterested response to a work of literature in which all one's beliefs, engagements, commitments, prejudices, stampedings of pity and terror, are ordered to be quiet." [28] For Blackmur the final purpose of form is "to bring into being — to bring into performance, for the writer and for the reader — an instance of the feeling of what life is about"; technical form, and the criticism of this and all the other forms of literature,

> is our means of getting at, of finding, and then making something of, what we feel the form of life is: the tensions, the stresses, the deep relations and the terrible disrelations that inhabit them as they are made to come together in a particular struggle between manners and behavior, between the ideal insight and the actual momentum in which the form of life is found.[29]

Blackmur would try to restore or emphasize that which Frye, for his own good and interesting reasons, would exclude or subordinate. The effect of the New Criticism and Frye's theories of criticism as well may be, as Geoffrey H. Hartman says, that "art turns out to be a mental purification of the impulses to action" (p. 760) — and this, as selections in Part IV will make clear, is a crucial issue in recent criticism. Blackmur, for all his commitment to form in literature, is closer to recent attempts to move beyond formalism on the issue than he is to his own contemporaries.

The most formidable challenge to American and English formalism comes from the so-called French New Criticism, which Leo Bersani describes in "From Bachelard to Barthes." The French

New Criticism is even less cohesive than its American counter-part; it covers so many varieties and schools of criticism that the only meaning the label may have is chronological. The French New Critics are united less by specific concepts or doctrines than by their opposition to the French academic criticism that pre-ceded them, the principal method of which was the *explication de texte* Ian Watt describes in "The First Paragraph of *The Ambassadors:* An Explication."

Two groups within the French New Criticism have had the most significant impact on contemporary critics in America and England. Bersani calls the older group "thematic," but it has other names: the "criticism of the Geneva School," "genetic criticism," and "the criticism of consciousness." It is exhibited here by Georges Poulet's essays. The other, which is called "struc-turalist," is part of the larger intellectual movement of "struc-turalism," and has been influenced by the Russian Formalists, active between 1916 and 1930; the structural linguistics of the Swiss linguist Ferdinand de Saussure (1857–1913) and of the so-called Prague School, of which a major figure is Roman Jakob-son; and the structural anthropology of Claude Lévi-Strauss. It is represented by the essays of Roland Barthes. There are crucial differences between the critics of consciousness and the struc-turalists, but the combined effect of their work has been to ques-tion radically, as Bersani puts it, the central piety of traditional criticism, American as well as European: the "belief in the existence of an analyzable literary object." And we may begin to gauge the differences between the two groups of French New Critics by saying that the critics of consciousness would stress the problematic nature of the *object,* whereas the structuralists would stress the problematic status of the *literary* object.[30]

The critics of consciousness replace a concern for the objec-tive structure of individual works with a concern for the subjec-tive "structure" of the mind or consciousness of the author as revealed in and by the whole body of his writings. Literature, for the Geneva critics, is a form of consciousness; in fact, as Poulet has said, the history of literature is a history of human conscious-ness. Whereas the American New Critics treated single poems or novels or plays as autonomous entities, the Geneva critics see each individual work of an author as an aspect of an ensemble of work, one composition. The complete oeuvre — poems, novels, plays, letters, diaries, autobiography, criticism, obiter dicta, every-thing written or recorded — is a revelation, an incarnation, of the author's essential self. The Geneva critics dissolve the boundaries and the particular contours of individual works as a way of getting at the *cogito,* the consciousness, the shaping spirit, or presiding mind of the author. "It is characteristic of a work," says Poulet,

> at once to create its structures and to transcend them, I should even say to destroy them. So the work of an author is certainly the collection of texts which he has written, but in the sense that as they follow one another, each replaces the last and reveals thereby a movement toward a liberation from structures.[31]

Literary criticism, therefore, is not an act of analysis or explication of the literary structures of a text, but rather an adventure into another person's consciousness by way of the total body of a certain author's texts. And the identity of the author's consciousness is neither formal nor biographical: the "author" is a literary, created subject, visible and real only in the "world," the inner space, of the oeuvre.

Georges Poulet expounds these notions in his "Phenomenology of Reading," and surveys the approaches of other critics identified with the criticism of consciousness. The selection ends with an anecdote that illustrates his conception of the critical process. Looking at an ensemble of Tintoretto's paintings at the Scuola di San Rocco in Venice, he was struck by

> the impression of having reached the common essence present in all the works of a great master, an essence which I was not able to perceive, except when emptying my mind of all the particular images created by the artist. I became aware of a subjective power at work in all these pictures, and yet never so clearly understood by my mind as when I had forgotten all their particular figurations.

Poulet's picture of the critical process resembles Northrop Frye's, in that they both back away from "the particular figurations" of the individual work. Like Frye, although for quite different reasons, Poulet and the other critics of consciousness derive their criticism from literature itself, without presuppositions, except for those which inhere in their conception of the phenomenology of reading. And again like Frye, they are relatively unconcerned with the verbal textures and linguistic techniques that preoccupied the American New Critics. They are indifferent to the work itself and interested instead in its larger design.

But here the resemblances end, for Frye's perspective is one of distance rather than "interiority," and what he sees in backing away from the particular work is altogether different from what the critics of consciousness seek to discern. Frye is still preoccupied with the structure and imagery of literature, with the literary constituents of genre, convention, and archetype, with the *forms* of literature, and not with the patterns of personal consciousness that literature incarnates or creates.

The basic difference is that the critics of consciousness, in principle if not completely in practice as Hartman argues in his critique of Poulet in "Beyond Formalism," simply do not observe the priority of place all formalists, including Frye, assign to the formal properties by which human content, whether it is human consciousness or something else, is revealed and constituted in a work of art. And that is why they are so disconcerting to American and English readers. The formalist tradition has become so native to our criticism, and so deeply ingrained, that the most peculiar and objectionable aspects of contemporary French criticism must seem to be, as Bersani says, "its neglect of the literary contexts of literary texts and its indifferences to judgments of literary value."

The views of the French structuralists are harder to grasp than those of the Geneva critics because their conceptual interests are more remote from literary criticism. As Bersani points out, Barthes does not go so far as to deny the *specificity* of literature — the differences between the structures of literary language and the structures of other organizing systems — but he "neglects formal and textual particularities in order to repostulate them within a general theory of human signs." Structuralism has followed about the same course as linguistics, both in America and in Europe, from the study of individual languages (or sign systems) to language in general (semiotics) to structures of mind. Hence, the structuralists have produced, as Bersani says, "very little that is 'critical' in the sense in which we have usually understood that word." Nevertheless, as Paul de Man and Edward W. Said have shown, the structuralists have raised issues that probe the act of critical inquiry itself, the very process of conceptualization that enables or hinders the performance of literary criticism.[32]

We might distinguish two aspects of the "structuralist activity," as Barthes calls it. One is constructive. Criticism is part of the sciences of man and therefore a department of an enterprise of analysis and fabrication that attempts, as Barthes says, to render the world intelligible. The structuralists are trying to find or reconstruct the configurations that shape man's linguistic and social behavior and account for the manner of its working; they are after a functional analysis of all forms of human behavior. Barthes particularly has been trying to develop a structural "semiology" that would analyze, across the boundaries of language, art, or science, how men make meaningful "signs." The structuralists are as firm in repudiating the "privilege of exterior objects" as Poulet and the other critics of consciousness, even though they are preoccupied with the structures of natural objects; the difference is that, as Barthes says, "the goal of all structuralist activity, whether reflexive or poetic, is to reconstruct an 'object' in such a way as to manifest thereby the rules of functioning (the 'functions') of this object." And that activity makes the *world* intelligible, whereas the dissolving of the object for the Geneva critics allows the *consciousness* incarnated in books to flow unimpeded and join with that of the reader. However Frye, too, is a structuralist, and he is preoccupied with rules of functioning. Moreover, he does not believe in the existence of reality somewhere "out there" that literature simply reproduces; nor does he think of the poem as a determinate thing. Unlike the French structuralists, however, he is concerned with recognition, of seeing what is there, in the total order of words that is *literature*.

The other aspect of the structuralist activity is a radical critique of the privileged status that has been accorded to literary language, the perceiving subject, the very act of consciousness itself. The French structuralists have attempted, as Paul de Man says, "a demystification of the belief that literature is a privileged language," which is part of their larger design to establish that

> there are no longer any standpoints that can a priori be considered privileged, no structure that functions validly as a model for other structures, no postulate of ontological hierarchy that can serve as an organizing principle from which particular structures derive in the manner in which a deity can be said to engender man and the world.[33]

The critics of consciousness begin with the conviction of a privileged consciousness as the center of what matters most in human activity, and they assume that language, for all its duplicity and interference, is the means by which the interior universe is constituted; literature is the vehicle by which reality is transmuted into a fictional equivalent. As Poulet says, the language of literature is the medium by which "I am freed from my usual sense of incompatability between my consciousness and its objects."

But the French structuralists have chosen to attack the very notion of the self as constitutive subject. Myths, Lévi-Strauss has argued, have no authors. The structure of human reality is in the interrelations of manifest entities or gestures, intersubjective forms (i.e., forms "common to every man as man, to priest and peasant, sophisticate and primitive"), the grammar and syntax of which reside in the culture, not in any particular self. The subject, Lévi-Strauss contends, is one of the prejudices of Western or historical man, and one of his mystiques, the product of his rational-visual bias of mind. Without the exclusivity of the "eye," we would have no fiction of the "I," and it follows that the phenomenological emphasis on the visual is only a product of the Romantic fiction of the "self." [34]

For the structuralists, as Edward W. Said has explained, any human investigation is actually bound up in the nature of language.[35] Language is man's principal means of signification, but as Barthes says, it is at once a problem and a model of order. Language is both the constricting horizon and the energizing atmosphere within and by which all human activity must be understood, but the effect of the structuralists' investigations, Said maintains, is to make us seem more the captives than the masters of language:

> In achieving a position of mastery over man, language has reduced him to a grammatical function. The world of activity and of human experience stands silently aside while language constitutes order and legislates discovery. According to Lévi-Strauss, "language, an unreflecting totalization, is human reason, which has its reasons and of which man knows nothing." Nearly every one of the structuralists acknowledges a tyrannical feedback system in which man is the speaking subject whose actions are always being converted into signs that signify him, which he uses in turn to signify other signs, and so on to infinity.[36]

The result of such a linguistic reduction is that "man the author is unceremoniously deposed." [37]

As Bersani shows, the structuralist attack on the privilege of the subject had already been undertaken by the American New Critics; they "deliberately refused to locate the *subject* of a text beyond its particular verbal organizations." Frye, too, has shifted the emphasis of criticism from personal expression to the structural forms in the total order of words that is literature. But neither Frye nor the American New Critics carried their views to the verge of *nullifying* literary texts.[38]

The implications of the structuralist critique are matters of spirited debate at the moment, and there is no telling how far or how permanently it will alter the assumptions about the place and performance of criticism we have taken for granted so long. Certainly the claims are genuinely radical, and profoundly unsettling to American critics who have a basic attachment to the native formalist tradition, as Murray Krieger, for example, shows in "Mediation, Language, and Vision in the Reading of Literature" (Part IV). Even such American critics as Bersani, Hartman, de Man, and Said, who have written about contemporary French criticism with a more sympathetic and intimate knowledge, and who are less clearly identifiable with any established formalist movement (as Krieger has been associated with American "contextualism"), have not been taken by the views of the French structuralists. Each critic has considered the premises and the motives of the structuralist activity seriously, and each has treated its exposure of the mystiques of literary study with understanding, but, without trying to restore one or another of the established native formalisms, all of them have sharply questioned the consequences of French structuralism for literary criticism. To take one fundamental issue: Hartman has said that "Continental criticism can be a lesson in how to subvert the specificity of literature," and his own criticism has shown the healthy effects of the astringent lesson.[39] But Bersani turns this around by raising the possibility that "a context is precisely the opportunity to allow a particular event to subvert a structure."

In any case, continental criticism has been a source of new energy for contemporary American critics. J. Hillis Miller, commenting on papers delivered at the Yale Symposium on Literary Criticism held in the spring of 1965, remarked that

> neither the new criticism nor archetypal criticism figured centrally, in spite of the fact that there was a paper on the work of Northrop Frye. There was hostility to neither, but a sense that their lessons can be taken for granted. For most of the participants part of the impetus for the next advances in literary study will come from one form or another of European criticism. Assimilating the best recent continental criticism, American scholars may come to develop new forms of criticism growing out of American culture as well as out of the encounter with European thought.[40]

The value of this encounter, as well as the evidence of its impact, can be seen in the essays by Miller himself, Ihab Hassan, Geoffrey H. Hartman, and Susan Sontag. To these critics conti-

nental criticism offers what the native formalist tradition has
excluded or submerged in priority: a concern with the human
content of art; an awareness of the problematic nature of things
taken too easily for granted; a passion for theory and pure speculation, or, as formalists like John Crowe Ransom and Frye have
offered that as well, for theories that answer better to present
moods and needs; a view of criticism more responsive to contemporary modes of literature, one strain of which is a subversion
of literary texts and holistic structures; and a regard for modes of
critical response that make criticism more of an adventure than
exegesis or analytical interpretation. This is not to say that the
contemporary critics are derivative, or that they are just treading
a few steps ahead in critical paths already cleared by their predecessors. They are raising new issues, not merely reopening closed
questions, recasting received opinions, or reappraising preceding
criticism. They are very much concerned with the limitations of
established concepts of criticism, to be sure, but they are not
simply reactive; they have their own views.

J. Hillis Miller's essay on William Carlos Williams clearly is
indebted to the criticism of Georges Poulet and the other critics
of consciousness — he has written informatively about their
work — but he makes an effort to reach beyond them as well.
Like them he believes, as he has said, that "the single poem or
novel is never enough" in literary study; the single work "can
never be made fully transparent or fully comprehensible if it is
kept in isolation." [41] In his essay on Williams he focuses on one
poem, "Young Sycamore," but he does not perform the typical
formalist explication. Rather, he examines the views of poetry
and human existence implicit in this and each of Williams's
poems, which "can only be discovered by that immersion in his
writing which must precede interpretation of any part of it." He
differs from the criticism of Poulet, however, in discussing the
grammar and syntax of the poem. Not that this brings him
closer to the verbal and textural analysis of the American New
Criticism; a comparison with Ian Watt's explication of the first
paragraph of *The Ambassadors* shows at once how differently
Miller conceives the language of a literary work. But other critics
of the Geneva School, Poulet acknowledges, attend as scrupulously as Miller does to the grammar and syntax of literature.
Miller's mode of criticism is distinguished by his attempt to render
the flow of consciousness in the words of Williams's poem, the way
the grammatical elements not only convey the consciousness of the

writer but shape its motions. Although in one sense Williams's poetry is static and spatial, instants of intense confrontation with objects made or seen, every moment contains a dynamic motion — and the pattern of Williams's verbs in "Young Sycamore," the *sequence* of its verbal forms, creates this movement, literally brings the sycamore into existence, not as a copy of a tree in nature, but as an imitation in words of the activity of nature. This sensitivity to temporal *form* is one of several qualities that marks Miller as an original critic rather than simply the American disciple of the Geneva School.

Ihab Hassan opens his essay here with his assumption that literature defines our concepts of criticism and then proceeds to argue that contemporary literature, because it is characterized by "unstructured and even random elements," undermines the idea of organic form on which formalist criticism in English is based. The literature being written now cannot be illuminated by formalist criticism: "contemporary letters can be judged as little by the standards of pure formalism as, let us say, Romantic poetry can be evaluated by the strict conventions of neo-Classicism." And beyond that: the forms of life embodied in contemporary literature herald not only a change in literary method, but in culture and consciousness; the crisis is not only of formalism or humanism, but of humanity itself. In a later essay, "Frontiers of Criticism: Metaphors of Silence," he is even more extreme. "The avant-garde," he says, finds "ingenious ways to destroy art, deny art," and these ("which often generate new kinds of art") he arranges into what he calls "five metaphors of anti-art": (a) art deprecates itself; (b) art cancels itself; (c) art becomes a game; (d) art orders itself at random — organic form becomes discontinuous form; the author does not impose *his* pattern on the material — he invites participation; and (e) art refuses interpretation.[42] René Wellek, addressing Hassan's arguments directly, deplores these developments in contemporary literature; he says that modern art, the avant-garde, or experimentation "has reached the zero point and is about to commit suicide."[43] Perhaps more important (besides the issue of whether the writers a critic chooses to call avant-garde are really those that matter) is the general question of the nature of the avant-garde itself and its claim to privilege in the criticism of literature, which Hans Magnus Enzensberger and Georg Lukács discuss in Part V. Murray Krieger tries to refute Hassan's critical notions in "Mediation, Language, and Vision in the Reading of Literature," but there is no denying Hassan's proposition that if criticism is to cope with what is genuinely new in literature (and the need to do that was established, after all, by the New Criticism), it must develop, to use a line from the poetry of Hart Crane which R. P. Blackmur liked to quote, "new thresholds, new anatomies."

Geoffrey H. Hartman is one of the best-informed and widest-ranging of younger contemporary critics. A superb performer as a critic, he also has a remarkable talent as both an expositor and an assayer of current theories of literature. He knows as few other American critics do the criticism that is being written today here and in Europe, but as he shows by his critique of Poulet in "Beyond Formalism," and of Frye and the French structuralists in "Toward Literary History," he has his own view of current needs in criticism and literary theory. In the Preface to the collection of his essays 1958–1970 Hartman says that "despite an allegiance to the Continental style of criticism," he feels strongly "what James called 'the coercive charm of form.' " Like many of his contemporaries he wants to advance beyond formalism, but he is not sure that it is possible to "get beyond formalism without going through the study of forms" (p. 161). Indeed, he does not reject the notion of literary form as organic and unified; his complaint is rather that "we have used it too reductively." His main objective has been less to reconcile the antithetical modes of continental antiformalist and Anglo-American formalist criticism — he is acutely conscious of how facile and flattening reconciliations can be — than to develop a sense of form that will be more adequate than existing methods to the problematic nature of art, culture, and human experience in all their intricate and perplexing relations. "In order to respect the formal study of art," he says, "I had also to go beyond formalism and to define art's role in the life of the artist, his culture, and the human community." [44] These objectives have led him to the difficult question of the relation of literature and criticism to history.

"Interpretation," Hartman says in "Beyond Formalism," "is bringing the poem forward into the present, which is acknowledging its historicity, which is grounding our terms in history." He takes exceptions to the formalist criticism of Cleanth Brooks and F. W. Bateson, as exhibited in their treatment of Wordsworth's Lucy poems, and the avowedly antiformalist criticism of Poulet, as exemplified in his essay on Henry James (included here in Part III), because they are both defective in understanding the relation of art to history. Brooks and Bateson offer "essentially unhistorical descriptions of style," and Poulet's "view of history is too formal": "he has not been able to situate James either in history or in the realm of values."

Hartman's positive effort in criticism has been, as he explains in "Toward Literary History," to fashion "a theory linking the form of the medium to the form of the artist's historical consciousness" (p. 760). His motive for the undertaking is that "it alone can provide today a sorely needed defense of art." Like Hassan and other contemporary critics Hartman is aware of the cultural crises that have made the burdens of literature and criticism something "more than the usual difficulty with inherited patterns or the desire to 'make it new.' " He is also aware that the Marxist and structuralist modes of continental criticism have put artistic form, and literature itself, under suspicion, as "ideologies to be exposed and demystified." His aim is to defend art against the artist himself as well as his other detractors by restoring a faith in two things: in form, and in the artist's vocation. His argument turns on the question: "How do we ground art in history without denying its autonomy?" And his solution is to expand, not to deny, the notion of form "until it cannot be narrowly linked to the concerns of a priestly culture or its mid-cult imitations." He wants a conception of form that moves literature beyond "elite modes of thought and feeling."

Hartman acknowledges that the New Criticism performed "a great service to the schools" by calling for a return to the text "and a new trust in the lights of a growing body of students drawn from all levels of society," but it could not resist the appeal of forms associated with an elitist conception of culture; it "retained many parochial and even aristocratic elements." [45] Hartman's views have explicit political overtones that coincide with the temper of militant anti-elitism which has profoundly affected the business and study of literature in American universities since the late 1960's, as Richard Poirier has described in his essay "What Is English Studies . . . ?" (in Part IV). Hartman has carried formalism far beyond that which has been associated with the three critics he mentions at the beginning of "Beyond Formalism," to a concern with "the role of arts in all culture" and with "larger structures of the imagination," even as he has remained "text-bound" and committed to the performance of interpretation.

Susan Sontag proclaims herself to be "against interpretation," by which she means what Hartman and other contemporary critics think of as "explicatory criticism." She does not go very far beyond what Blackmur urged. Nor is anything all that new in her argument that interpretation takes the sensory experience of the work of art for granted, whereas the "function of criticism should be to show *how it is what it is,* even *that it is what it is,* rather than to show *what it means,*" and thereby to recover our senses in the presence of art. But she is closer to contemporary critics on these issues, and on other points as well: she warns of the danger of taming works of art; she calls for criticism to be sensitive to contemporary needs and practice in the arts; she is wary of elite forms of art. She is not, however, an antiformalist, despite the provocation of the title of her essay. Like Hartman, she sees a need for a more adequate theory of form — more, not less, attention to form (p. 159). And here, in a footnote to this passage, she touches on one of the most interesting issues in contemporary criticism — the relation between spatial and temporal form.

Sontag says that our idea of form is spatial and we lack a criticism that can deal with the novel as a narrative, i.e., temporal form. The question of the two kinds of form has long intrigued aestheticians, especially in German philosophy from Lessing to Heidegger, but the issue has assumed a new importance in contemporary literary criticism. J. Hillis Miller, for example, has claimed that "literature is a temporal, not a spatial art, and should be described as such, in vocabulary proper to its temporality." [46] But Joseph Frank showed in a celebrated essay that much of modern literature, at least, aims deliberately at spatial form. When that essay was reprinted in 1963 Frank added a note commenting on Walter Sutton's attempt to refute his case. "Mr. Sutton's main argument," Frank says,

> is that, since reading is a time-act, the achievement of spatial form is really a physical impossibility. I could not agree more. But this has not stopped modern writers from working out techniques to achieve the impossible — as much as possible. [47]

Thus we have three elements in the problem: the temporality or spatiality of the constitutive form of the work of literature, the act of reading, and the act of criticism.

Northrop Frye has argued that whatever literary structure may be in itself, it must be spatial to the critic. In reading, he says, we attend to narrative movement. In criticism afterwards we can look at the work as a simultaneous unity and study its structure:

> When a critic deals with a work of literature the most natural thing for him to do is to freeze it, to ignore its movement in time

and look at it as a completed pattern of words, with all its parts existing simultaneously.[48]

But does literature work like that in the writing any less than in our reading? "Narration," William H. Gass has said, "is concerned with the coming on and passing off of words" — and the same may be true in varying degrees of all forms of literature, not just the novel. Words *move,* as much in writing as in reading, and the things words make — Gass calls them "concepts," but they can be other entities as well — "appear, accelerate, they race, they hesitate a moment, slow, turn, break, join, modify." [49] A main objective of contemporary criticism has been to get literature back in motion, in performance, in the act of criticism as much as in the acts of reading and writing.

Embedded in any discussion of the place and performance of criticism is the question of the nature of a critical *issue* itself and, because the word customarily implies argumentation, of what role argument plays in the conduct of critical inquiry. F. R. Leavis affirms in his essay in Part IV that criticism is a collaborative enterprise. In practice, however, criticism is frequently argumentative in character, often seeming as combative as any contact sport or as deliberate in its forensic proceedings as an action at law. Nevertheless, it may be quite misleading to conceive of argumentative issues as a paradigm for issues in literary criticism and argumentation as a model for the activity of criticism. It may be truer, or at least more fruitful, to see critical issues as occasions for inquiry, questions to be explored, rather than propositions to be defended or refuted.

Several selections in this volume, to be sure, are confrontations — two or more critics at odds over the same work or author or theoretical principle — but all of the essays have been chosen with an eye for conjunctions rather than strictly for a clash of opinions needing adjudication. The sense of contention seems sharpest in Part II, The Writer's Intention, where opposing views on a specific topic are so explicitly litigious that the entire section might almost be a case study in argumentation. But even here, where the critical exchange is ostensibly more antagonistic than collaborative, more may be gained by attending to the diversity of views under examination, and trying to grasp what is possible in criticism, than by laboring to resolve the conflict in positions.

In fact, one participant in the dispute, Frank Cioffi, asserts that it is an illusion to think of criticism as a mode of argumentation. Criticism, he says, is not producing and evaluating evidence but is an activity that inspires readers to expand and modify their awareness, their consciousness, of a particular work of literature, an author, or the act of writing. By this criterion the question, for example, of the "rightness" or "wrongness" of a critical interpretation, its "validity" or "invalidity," is less pertinent and meaningful than its power to make the reader apprehend more fully and sensitively the literature which is the object of the critical inquiry.

J. Hillis Miller's "The Antitheses of Criticism: Reflections on the Yale Colloquium" presents a full and percipient catalogue of present issues in criticism. But as we survey the whole range of contemporary criticism and the actual performances of the critics, we may wonder whether the dialectical principle suggested by Miller's title fits either the practice of contemporary critics or of criticism itself. However frequently criticism originates in polemical situations, and however often critical exchanges assume the character of an adversary proceeding, it is questionable whether the issues of criticism should be viewed as binary oppositions, as antitheses modeled upon the dialectics of argument.

Once we think of issues in strictly argumentative terms and frame them as antitheses, we are virtually committed to searching for some form of reconciliation. But the reader of criticism, and the critic himself, may find less value in conciliating oppositions than in expanding his sense of the possibilities of criticism — in stretching rather than simply correcting the assumptions and convictions we bring to an encounter with those other than we held beforehand.

Northrop Frye has said that he wishes we could throw away the notion of "reconciling" and use instead some such conception as "interpenetration":

> In criticism, as in philosophy, argument is functional, and there is bound to be disagreement. But disagreement is one thing, rejection another, and critics have no more business rejecting each other than they have rejecting literature. The genuine critic works out his own views of literature while realizing that there are also a great number of other views, actual and possible, which are neither reconcilable nor irreconcilable with his own. They interpenetrate with him, and he with them.[50]

This does mean that as readers we must inhibit the relish we take for the contest of criticism or for the fine energies displayed in a quarrel between critics; R. P. Blackmur, for example, always said that criticism is speculative *play*. Nor does it mean that we must be unconcernedly open-minded or value-free in our scrutiny; several critics in this anthology warn against the dangers of such postures. Rather, "interpenetration" is a disposition inviting us to attend to the great number of views of literature, "actual and possible," "neither reconcilable nor irreconcilable," exhibited by contemporary critics — the extraordinary range and depth of talents they bring to their inquiries into the issues in contemporary literary criticism.

NORTHROP FRYE

Polemical Introduction, Anatomy of Criticism

This book consists of "essays," in the word's original sense of a trial or incomplete attempt, on the possibility of a synoptic view of the scope, theory, principles, and techniques of literary criticism. The primary aim of the book is to give my reasons for believing in such a synoptic view; its secondary aim is to provide a tentative version of it which will make enough sense to convince my readers that *a* view, of the kind that I outline, is attainable. The gaps in the subject as treated here are too enormous for the book ever to be regarded as presenting *my* system, or even my theory. It is to be regarded rather as an interconnected group of suggestions which it is hoped will be of some practical use to critics and students of literature. Whatever is of no practical use to anybody is expendable. My approach is based on Matthew Arnold's precept of letting the mind play freely around a subject in which there has been much endeavor and little attempt at perspective. All the essays deal with criticism, but by criticism I mean the whole work of scholarship and taste concerned with literature which is a part of what is variously called liberal education, culture, or the study of the humanities. I start from the principle that criticism is not simply a part of this larger activity, but an essential part of it.

The subject-matter of literary criticism is an art, and criticism is evidently something of an art too. This sounds as though criticism were a parasitic form of literary expression, an art based on pre-existing art, a second-hand imitation of creative power. On this theory critics are intellectuals who have a taste for art but lack both the power to produce it and the money to patronize it, and thus form a class of cultural middlemen, distributing culture to society at a profit to themselves while exploiting the artist and increasing the strain on his public. The con-

SOURCE: "Polemical Introduction" is from *Anatomy of Criticism: Four Essays* (copyright © 1957 by Princeton University Press; Princeton Paperback, 1971), pp. 3–29. Reprinted by permission of Princeton University Press.

ception of the critic as a parasite or artist *manqué* is still very popular, especially among artists. It is sometimes reinforced by a dubious analogy between the creative and the procreative functions, so that we hear about the "impotence" and "dryness" of the critic, of his hatred for genuinely creative people, and so on. The golden age of anticritical criticism was the latter part of the nineteenth century, but some of its prejudices are still around.

However, the fate of art that tries to do without criticism is instructive. The attempt to reach the public directly through "popular" art assumes that criticism is artificial and public taste natural. Behind this is a further assumption about natural taste which goes back through Tolstoy to Romantic theories of a spontaneously creative "folk." These theories have had a fair trial; they have not stood up very well to the facts of literary history and experience, and it is perhaps time to move beyond them. An extreme reaction against the primitive view, at one time associated with the "art for art's sake" catchword, thinks of art in precisely the opposite terms, as a mystery, an initiation into an esoterically civilized community. Here criticism is restricted to ritual masonic gestures, to raised eyebrows and cryptic comments and other signs of an understanding too occult for syntax. The fallacy common to both attitudes is that of a rough correlation between the merit of art and the degree of public response to it, though the correlation assumed is direct in one case and inverse in the other.

One can find examples which appear to support both these views; but it is clearly the simple truth that there is no real correlation either way between the merits of art and its public reception. Shakespeare was more popular than Webster, but not because he was a greater dramatist; Keats was less popular than Montgomery, but not because he was a better poet. Consequently there is no way of preventing the critic from being, for better or worse, the pioneer of education and the shaper of cultural tradition. Whatever popularity Shakespeare and Keats have *now* is equally the result of the publicity of criticism. A public that tries to do without criticism, and asserts that it knows what it wants or likes, brutalizes the arts and loses its cultural memory. Art for art's sake is a retreat from criticism which ends in an impoverishment of civilized life itself. The only way to forestall the work of criticism is through censorship, which has the same relation to criticism that lynching has to justice.

There is another reason why criticism has to exist. Criticism can talk, and all the arts are dumb. In painting, sculpture, or music it is easy enough to see that the art shows forth, but cannot *say* anything. And, whatever it sounds like to call the poet inarticulate or speechless, there is a most important sense in which poems are as silent as statues. Poetry is a *disinterested* use of words: it does not address a reader directly. When it does so, we usually feel that the poet has some distrust in the capacity of readers and critics to interpret his meaning without assistance, and has therefore dropped into the sub-poetic level of metrical talk ("verse" or "doggerel") which anybody can learn to produce. It is not only tradition that impels a poet to invoke a Muse and protest that his utterance is involuntary. Nor is it strained wit that causes Mr. MacLeish, in his famous *Ars Poetica,* to apply the words "mute," "dumb," and "wordless" to a poem. The artist, as John Stuart Mill saw in a wonderful flash of critical insight, is not heard but overheard.[1] The axiom of criticism must be, not that the poet does not know what he is talking about, but that he cannot talk about what he knows. To defend the right of criticism to exist at all, therefore, is to assume that criticism is a structure of thought and knowledge existing in its own right, with some measure of independence from the art it deals with.

The poet may of course have some critical ability of his own, and so be able to talk about his own work. But the Dante who writes a commentary on the first canto of the *Paradiso* is merely one more of Dante's critics. What he says has a peculiar interest, but not a peculiar authority. It is generally accepted that a critic is a better judge of the *value* of a poem than its creator, but there is still a lingering notion that it is somehow ridiculous to regard the critic as the final judge of its meaning, even though in practice it is clear that he must be. The reason for this is an inability to distinguish literature from the descriptive or assertive writing which derives from the active will and the conscious mind, and which is primarily concerned to "say" something.

Part of the critic's reason for feeling that poets can be properly assessed only after their death is that they are then unable to presume on their merits as poets to tease him with hints of inside knowledge. When Ibsen maintains that *Emperor and Galilean* is his greatest play and that certain episodes in *Peer Gynt* are not allegorical, one can only say that Ibsen is an indifferent critic of Ibsen. Wordsworth's Preface to the *Lyrical Ballads* is a remarkable document, but as a piece of Wordsworthian criticism nobody would give it more than about a B plus. Critics of Shakespeare are often supposed to be ridiculed by the assertion that if Shakespeare were to come back from the dead he would not be able to appreciate or even understand their criticism. This in itself is likely enough: we have little evidence of Shakespeare's interest in criticism, either of himself or of anyone else. Even if there were such evidence, his own account of what he was trying to do in *Hamlet* would no more be a definitive criticism of that play, clearing all its puzzles up for good, than a performance of it under his direction would be a definitive performance. And what is true of the poet in relation to his own work is still more true of his opinion of other poets. It is hardly possible for the critical poet to avoid expanding his own tastes, which are intimately linked to his own practice, into a general law of literature. But criticism has to be based on what the whole of literature actually does: in its light, whatever any highly respected writer thinks literature in general ought to do will show up in its proper perspective. The poet speaking as critic produces, not criticism, but documents to be examined by critics. They may well be valuable documents: it is only when they are accepted as directives for criticism that they are in any danger of becoming misleading.

The notion that the poet necessarily is or could be the definitive interpreter of himself or of the theory of literature belongs to the conception of the critic as a parasite or jackal. Once we admit that the critic has his own field of activity, and that he has autonomy within that field, we have to concede that criticism deals with literature in terms of a specific conceptual framework. The framework is not that of literature itself, for this is the parasite theory again, but neither is it something outside literature, for in that case the autonomy of criticism would again disappear, and the whole subject would be assimilated to something else.

This latter gives us, in criticism, the fallacy of what in history is called determinism, where a scholar with a special interest in geography or economics expresses that interest by the rhetorical device of putting his favorite study into a causal relationship with whatever interests him less. Such a method gives one the illusion of explaining one's subject while studying it, thus wasting no time. It would be easy to compile a long list of such determinisms in criticism, all of them, whether Marxist, Thomist, liberal-humanist, neo-Classical, Freudian, Jungian, or existentialist, substituting a critical attitude for criticism, all proposing, not to find a conceptual framework for criticism within literature, but to attach criticism to one of a miscellany of frameworks outside it. The axioms and postulates of criticism, however, have to grow out of the art it deals with. The first thing the literary critic has to do is to read literature, to make an inductive survey of his own field and let his critical principles shape themselves solely out of his knowledge of that field. Critical principles cannot be taken over ready-made from theology, philosophy, politics, science, or any combination of these.

To subordinate criticism to an externally derived critical attitude is to exaggerate the values in literature that can be related to the external source, whatever it is. It is all too easy to impose on literature an extra-literary schematism, a sort of religio-political color-filter, which makes some poets leap into prominence and others show up as dark and faulty. All that the disinterested critic can do with such a color-filter is to murmur politely that it shows things in a new light and is indeed a most stimulating contribution to criticism. Of course such filtering critics usually imply, and often believe, that they are letting their literary experience speak for itself and are holding their other attitudes in reserve, the coincidence between their critical valuations and their religious or political views being silently gratifying to them but not explicitly forced on the reader. Such independence of criticism from prejudice, however, does not invariably occur even with those who best understand criticism. Of their inferiors the less said the better.

If it is insisted that we cannot criticize literature until we have acquired a coherent philosophy of life with its center of gravity in something else, the existence of criticism as a separate subject is still being denied. But there is another possibility. If criticism exists, it must be an examination of literature in terms of a conceptual framework derivable from an inductive survey of the literary field. The word "inductive" suggests some sort of scientific procedure. What if criticism is a science as well as an art? Not a "pure" or "exact" science, of course, but these phrases belong to a nineteenth-century cosmology which is no longer with us. The writing of history is an art, but no one doubts that scientific principles are involved in the historian's treatment of evidence, and that the presence of this scientific element is what distinguishes history from legend. It may also be a scientific element in criticism which distinguishes it from literary parasitism on the one hand, and the superimposed critical attitude on the other. The presence of science in any subject changes its character from the casual to the causal, from the random and intuitive to the systematic, as well as safeguarding the integrity of that subject from external invasions. However, if there are any readers for whom the word "scientific" conveys emotional overtones of unimaginative barbarism, they may substitute "systematic" or "progressive" instead.

It seems absurd to say that there *may* be a scientific element in criticism when there are dozens of learned journals based on the assumption that there is, and hundreds of scholars engaged in a scientific procedure related to literary criticism. Evidence is examined scientifically; previous authorities are used scientifically; fields are investigated scientifically; texts are edited scientifically. Prosody is scientific in structure; so is phonetics; so is philology. Either literary criticism is scientific, or all these highly trained and intelligent scholars are wasting their time on some kind of pseudo-science like phrenology. Yet one is forced to wonder whether scholars realize the implications of the fact that their work is scientific. In the growing complication of secondary sources one misses that sense of consolidating progress which belongs to a science. Research begins in what is known as "background," and one would expect it, as it goes on, to start organizing the foreground as well. Telling us what we should know about literature ought to fulfil itself in telling us something about what it is. As soon as it comes to this point, scholarship seems to be dammed by some kind of barrier, and washes back into further research projects.

So to "appreciate" literature and get more direct contact with it, we turn to the public critic, the Lamb or Hazlitt or Arnold or Sainte-Beuve who represents the reading public at its most expert and judicious. It is the task of the public critic to exemplify how a man of taste uses and evaluates literature, and thus show how literature is to be absorbed into society. But here we no longer have the sense of an impersonal body of consolidating knowledge. The public critic tends to episodic forms like the lecture and the familiar essay, and his work is not a science, but another kind of literary art. He has picked up his ideas from a pragmatic study of literature, and does not try to create or enter into a theoretical structure. In Shakespearean criticism we have a fine monument of Augustan taste in Johnson, of Romantic taste in Coleridge, of Victorian taste in Bradley. The ideal critic of Shakespeare, we feel, would avoid the Augustan, Romantic, and Victorian limitations and prejudices respectively of Johnson, Coleridge, and Bradley. But we have no clear notion of progress in the criticism of Shakespeare, or of how a critic who read all his predecessors could, as a result, become anything better than a monument of contemporary taste, with all *its* limitations and prejudices.

In other words, there is as yet no way of distinguishing what is genuine criticism, and therefore progresses toward making the whole of literature intelligible, from what belongs only to the history of taste, and therefore follows the vacillations of fashionable prejudice. I give an example of the difference between the two which amounts to a head-on collision. In one of his curious, brilliant, scatter-brained footnotes to *Munera Pulveris,* John Ruskin says:

> Of Shakspeare's names I will afterwards speak at more length; they are curiously — often barbarously — mixed out of various traditions and languages. Three of the clearest in meaning have been already noticed. Desdemona — "δυσδαιμονία," *miserable fortune* — is also plain enough. Othello is, I believe, "the careful"; all the calamity of the tragedy arising from the single flaw and error in his magnificently collected strength. Ophelia, "serviceableness," the true, lost wife of Hamlet, is marked as having a Greek name by that of her brother Laertes; and its signification is once exquisitely alluded to in that brother's last word of her, where her gentle preciousness is opposed to the uselessness of the churlish clergy: — "A *ministering* angel shall my sister be, when thou liest howling."

On this passage Matthew Arnold comments as follows:

> Now, really, what a piece of extravagance all that is! I will not say that the meaning of Shakspeare's names (I put aside the question as to the correctness of Mr. Ruskin's etymologies) has no effect at all,

may be entirely lost sight of; but to give it that degree of prominence is to throw the reins to one's whim, to forget all moderation and proportion, to lose the balance of one's mind altogether. It is to show in one's criticism, to the highest excess, the note of provinciality.[2]

Now whether Ruskin is right or wrong, he is attempting genuine criticism. He is trying to interpret Shakespeare in terms of a conceptual framework which belongs to the critic alone, and yet relates itself to the plays alone. Arnold is perfectly right in feeling that this is not the sort of material that the public critic can directly use. But he does not seem even to suspect the existence of a systematic criticism as distinct from the history of taste. Here it is Arnold who is the provincial. Ruskin has learned his trade from the great iconological tradition which comes down through Classical and Biblical scholarship into Dante and Spenser, both of whom he had studied carefully, and which is incorporated in the medieval cathedrals he had pored over in such detail. Arnold is assuming, as a universal law of nature, certain "plain sense" critical axioms which were hardly heard of before Dryden's time and which can assuredly not survive the age of Freud and Jung and Frazer and Cassirer.

What we have so far is, on one side of the "study of literature," the work of the scholar who tries to make it possible, and on the other side the work of the public critic who assumes that it exists. In between is "literature" itself, a game preserve where the student wanders with his native intelligence his only guide. The assumption seems to be that the scholar and the public critic are connected by a common interest in literature alone. The scholar lays down his materials outside the portals of literature: like other offerings brought to unseen consumers, a good deal of such scholarship seems to be the product of a rather touching faith, sometimes only a hope that some synthetizing critical Messiah of the future will find it useful. The public critic, or the spokesman of the imposed critical attitude, is apt to make only a random and haphazard use of this material, often in fact to treat the scholar as Hamlet did the grave-digger, ignoring everything he throws out except an odd skull which he can pick up and moralize about.

Those who are concerned with the arts are often asked questions, not always sympathetic ones, about the use or value of what they are doing. It is probably impossible to answer such questions directly, or at any rate to answer the people who ask them. Most of the answers, such as Newman's "liberal knowledge is its own end," merely appeal to the experience of those who have had the right experience. Similarly, most "defenses of poetry" are intelligible only to those well within the defenses. The basis of critical apologetics, therefore, has to be the actual experience of art, and for those concerned with literature, the first question to answer is not "What use is the study of literature?" but, "What follows from the fact that it is possible?"

Everyone who has seriously studied literature knows that the mental process involved is as coherent and progressive as the study of science. A precisely similar training of the mind takes place, and a similar sense of the unity of the subject is built up. If this unity comes from literature itself, then literature itself must be shaped like a science, which contradicts our experience of it; or it must derive some informing power from an ineffable mystery at the heart of being, which seems vague; or the mental benefits alleged to be derived from it are imaginary, and are really derived from other subjects studied incidentally in connection with it.

This is as far as we can get on the assumption that the scholar and the man of taste are connected by nothing more than a common interest in literature. If this assumption is true, the high percentage of sheer futility in all criticism should be honestly faced, for the percentage can only increase with its bulk, until criticizing becomes, especially for university teachers, merely an automatic method of acquiring merit, like turning a prayer-wheel. But it is only an unconscious assumption — at least, I have never seen it stated as a doctrine — and it would certainly be convenient if it turned out to be nonsense. The alternative assumption is that scholars and public critics are directly related by an intermediate form of criticism, a coherent and comprehensive theory of literature, logically and scientifically organized, some of which the student unconsciously learns as he goes on, but the main principles of which are as yet unknown to us. The development of such a criticism would fulfil the systematic and progressive element in research by assimilating its work into a unified structure of knowledge, as other sciences do. It would at the same time establish an authority within criticism for the public critic and the man of taste.

We should be careful to realize what the possibility of such an intermediate criticism implies. It implies that at no point is there any direct learning of literature itself. Physics is an organized body of knowledge about nature, and a student of it says that he is learning physics, not nature. Art, like nature, has to be distinguished from the systematic study of it, which is criticism. It is therefore impossible to "learn literature": one learns about it in a certain way, but what one learns, transitively, is the criticism of literature. Similarly, the difficulty often felt in "teaching literature" arises from the fact that it cannot be done: the criticism of literature is all that can be directly taught. Literature is not a subject of study, but an object of study: the fact that it consists of words, as we have seen, makes us confuse it with the talking verbal disciplines. The libraries reflect our confusion by cataloguing criticism as one of the subdivisions of literature. Criticism, rather, is to art what history is to action and philosophy to wisdom: a verbal imitation of a human productive power which in itself does not speak. And just as there is nothing which the philosopher cannot consider philosophically, and nothing which the historian cannot consider historically, so the critic should be able to construct and dwell in a conceptual universe of his own. This critical universe seems to be one of the things implied in Arnold's conception of culture.

I am not, therefore, saying that literary criticism at present must be doing the wrong thing and ought to be doing something else. I am saying that it should be possible to get a comprehensive view of what it actually is doing. It is necessary that scholars and public critics should continue to make their contributions to criticism. It is not necessary that the thing they contribute to should be invisible, as the coral island is invisible to the polyp. In the study of literary scholarship the student becomes aware of an undertow carrying him away from literature. He finds that literature is the central division of the humanities, flanked on one side by history and on the other by philosophy. As literature is not itself an organized structure of knowledge, the critic has to turn to the conceptual framework of the historian for events, and to that of the philosopher for ideas. Asked what he is working on, the critic will invariably say that he is working on Donne, or Shelley's thought, or the 1640–1660 period, or give some other answer implying that history, philosophy, or literature itself is the conceptual basis of his criticism. In the unlikely event that he was concerned with the theory of criticism, he would say that he was working on a "general" topic. It is clear that the absence of systematic criticism has created a power vacuum, and all the neighboring disciplines have moved in. Hence the prominence of the Archimedes fallacy mentioned above: the notion that if we plant our feet solidly enough in Christian or democratic or Marxist values we shall be able to lift the whole of criticism at once with a dialectic crowbar. But if the varied interests of critics could be related to a central expanding pattern of systematic comprehension, this undertow would disappear, and they would be seen as converging on criticism instead of running away from it.

One proof that a systematic comprehension of a subject actually exists is the ability to write an elementary textbook expounding its fundamental principles. It would be interesting to see what such a book on criticism would contain. It would not start with a clear answer to the first question of all: "What is literature?" We have no real standards to distinguish a verbal structure that is literary from one that is not, and no idea what to do with the vast penumbra of books that may be claimed for literature because they are written with "style," or are useful as "background," or have simply got into a university course of "great books." We then discover that we have no word, corresponding to "poem" in poetry or "play" in drama, to describe a work of literary art. It is all very well for

Blake to say that to generalize is to be an idiot, but when we find
ourselves in the cultural situation of savages who have words for ash and
willow and no word for tree, we wonder if there is not such a thing
as being *too* deficient in the capacity to generalize.

So much for page one of our handbook. Page two would be the place
to explain what seems the most far-reaching of literary facts, the distinction in rhythm between verse and prose. But it appears that a distinction
which anyone can make in practice cannot be made as yet by any critic in
theory. We continue to riffle through the blank pages. The next thing to
do is to outline the primary categories of literature, such as drama, epic,
prose fiction, and the like. This at any rate is what Aristotle assumed to
be the obvious first step in criticism. We discover that the critical theory
of genres is stuck precisely where Aristotle left it. The very word "genre"
sticks out in an English sentence as the unpronounceable and alien
thing it is. Most critical efforts to handle such generic terms as "epic"
and "novel" are chiefly interesting as examples of the psychology of
rumor. Thanks to the Greeks, we can distinguish tragedy from comedy in
drama, and so we still tend to assume that each is the half of drama
that is not the other half. When we come to deal with such forms as
the masque, opera, movie, ballet, puppet-play, mystery-play, morality,
commedia dell'arte, and Zauberspiel, we find ourselves in the position
of the Renaissance doctors who refused to treat syphilis because Galen
said nothing about it.

The Greeks hardly needed to develop a classification of prose forms.
We do, but have never done so. We have, as usual, no word for a
work of prose fiction, so the word "novel" does duty for everything, and
thereby loses its only real meaning as the name of a genre. The circulat-
ing-library distinction between fiction and nonfiction, between books
which are about things admitted not to be true and books which are
about everything else, is apparently exhaustive enough for critics. Asked
what form of prose fiction *Gulliver's Travels* belongs to, there are few
critics who, if they could give the answer "Menippean satire," would
regard it as knowledge essential for dealing with the book, although some
notion of what a novel is is surely a prerequisite for dealing with a serious
novelist. Other prose forms are even worse off. Western literature has
been more influenced by the Bible than by any other book, but with all
his respect for "sources," the critic knows little more about that influence
than the fact that it exists. Biblical typology is so dead a language now
that most readers, including scholars, cannot construe the superficial
meaning of any poem which employs it. And so on. If criticism could ever
be conceived as a coherent and systematic study, the elementary principles of which could be explained to any intelligent nineteen-year-old,
then, from the point of view of such a conception, no critic now knows

the first thing about criticism. What critics now have is a mystery-religion without a gospel, and they are initiates who can communicate, or quarrel, only with one another.

A theory of criticism whose principles apply to the whole of literature and account for every valid type of critical procedure is what I think Aristotle meant by poetics. Aristotle seems to me to approach poetry as a biologist would approach a system of organisms, picking out its genera and species, formulating the broad laws of literary experience, and in short writing as though he believed that there is a totally intelligible structure of knowledge attainable about poetry which is not poetry itself, or the experience of it, but poetics. One would imagine that, after two thousand years of post-Aristotelian literary activity, his views on poetics, like his views on the generation of animals, could be re-examined in the light of fresh evidence. Meanwhile, the opening words of the *Poetics,* in the Bywater translation, remain as good an introduction to the subject as ever, and describe the kind of approach that I have tried to keep in mind for myself:

> Our subject being poetry, I propose to speak not only of the art in general but also of its species and their respective capacities; of the structure of plot required for a good poem; of the number and nature of the constituent parts of a poem; and likewise of any other matters in the same line of inquiry. Let us follow the natural order and begin with the primary facts.

Of course literature is only one of many arts, but this book is compelled to avoid the treatment of aesthetic problems outside of poetics. Every art, however, needs its own critical organization, and poetics will form a part of aesthetics as soon as aesthetics becomes the unified criticism of all the arts instead of whatever it is now.[3]

Sciences normally begin in a state of naive induction [4]: they tend first of all to take the phenomena they are supposed to interpret as data. Thus physics began by taking the immediate sensations of experience, classified as hot, cold, moist, and dry, as fundamental principles. Eventually physics turned inside out, and discovered that its real function was rather to explain what heat and moisture were. History began as chronicle; but the difference between the old chronicler and the modern historian is that to the chronicler the events he recorded were also the *structure* of his history, whereas the historian sees these events as historical phenomena, to be connected within a conceptual framework not only broader but different in shape from them. Similarly each modern science has had to take what Bacon calls (though in another context) an inductive leap, occupying a new vantage ground from which it can see its former data as new things to be explained. As long as astronomers regarded the movements of heavenly bodies as the structure of astronomy, they naturally regarded their own point view fixed. Once they thought of movement as itself explicable, a mathematical theory of movement became the conceptual framework, and so the way was cleared for the heliocentric solar system and the law of gravitation. As long as biology thought of animal and vegetable forms of life as constituting its subject, the different branches of biology were largely efforts of cataloguing. As soon as it was the existence of forms of life themselves that had to be explained, the theory of evolution and the conceptions of protoplasm and the cell poured into biology and completely revitalized it.

It occurs to me that literary criticism is now in such a state of naive induction as we find in a primitive science. Its materials, the masterpieces of literature, are not yet regarded as phenomena to be explained in terms of a conceptual framework which criticism alone possesses. They are still regarded as somehow constituting the framework or structure of criticism as well. I suggest that it is time for criticism to leap to a new ground from which it can discover what the organizing or containing forms of its conceptual framework are. Criticism seems to be badly in need of a coordinating principle, a central hypothesis which, like the theory of evolution in biology, will see the phenomena it deals with as parts of a whole.

The first postulate of this inductive leap is the same as that of any science: the assumption of total coherence. Simple as this assumption appears, it takes a long time for a science to discover that it is in fact a totally intelligible body of knowledge. Until it makes this discovery, it has not been born as an individual science but remains an embryo within the body of some other subject. The birth of physics from "natural philosophy" and of sociology from "moral philosophy" will illustrate the process. It is also approximately true that the modern sciences have developed in the order of their closeness to mathematics. Thus physics and astronomy began to assume their modern form in the Renaissance, chemistry in the eighteenth century, biology in the nineteenth, and the social sciences in the twentieth. If criticism is a science, it is clearly a social science, and if it is developing only in our day, the fact is at least not an anachronism. Meanwhile, the myopia of specialization remains an inseparable part of naive induction. From such a perspective, "general" questions are humanly impossible to deal with, because they involve "covering" a frighteningly large field. The critic is in the position of a mathematician who has to deal with numbers so large that it would keep him scribbling digits until the next ice age even to write them out in their conventional form as integers. Critic and mathematician alike will have somehow to invent a less cumbersome notation.

Naive induction thinks of literature entirely in terms of the enumerative bibliography of literature: that is, it sees literature as a huge aggregate or miscellaneous pile of discrete "works." Clearly, if literature is nothing more than this, any systematic mental training based on it becomes impossible. Only one organizing principle has so far been discovered in literature, the principle of chronology. This supplies the magic word "tradition," which means that when we see the miscellaneous pile strung out along a chronological line, some coherence is given it by sheer sequence. But even tradition does not answer all our questions. Total literary history gives us a glimpse of the possibility of seeing literature as a complication of a relatively restricted and simple group of formulas that can be studied in primitive culture. We next realize that the relation of later literature to these primitive formulas is by no means purely one of complication, as we find the primitive formulas reappearing in the greatest classics — in fact there seems to be a general tendency on the part of great classics to revert to them. This coincides with a feeling we have all had: that the study of mediocre works of art remains a random and peripheral form of critical experience, whereas the profound masterpiece draws us to a point at which we seem to see an enormous number of converging patterns of significance. We begin to wonder if we cannot see literature, not only as complicating itself in time, but as spread out in conceptual space from some kind of center that criticism could locate.

It is clear that criticism cannot be a systematic study unless there is a quality in literature which enables it to be so. We have to adopt the hypothesis, then, that just as there is an order of nature behind the natural sciences, so literature is not a piled aggregate of "works," but an order of words. A belief in an order of nature, however, is an inference from the intelligibility of the natural sciences; and if the natural sciences ever completely demonstrated the order of nature they would presumably exhaust their subject. Similarly, criticism, if a science, must be totally intelligible, but literature, as the order of words which makes the science possible, is, so far as we know, an inexhaustible source of new critical discoveries, and would be even if new works of literature ceased to be written. If so, then the search for a limiting principle in literature in order to discourage the development of criticism is mistaken. The absurd quantum formula of criticism, the assertion that the critic should confine himself to "getting out" of a poem exactly what the poet may vaguely be assumed to have been aware of "putting in," is one of the many slovenly illiteracies that the absence of systematic criticism has allowed to grow up. This quantum theory is the literary form of what may be called the fallacy of premature teleology. It corresponds, in the natural sciences, to the assertion that a phenomenon is as it is because Providence in its inscrutable wisdom made it so. That is, the critic is assumed to have no conceptual framework: it is simply his job to take a poem into which a poet has diligently stuffed a specific number of beauties or effects, and complacently extract them one by one, like his prototype Little Jack Horner.

The first step in developing a genuine poetics is to recognize and get rid of meaningless criticism, or talking about literature in a way that cannot help to build up a systematic structure of knowledge. This includes all the sonorous nonsense that we so often find in critical generalities, reflective comments, ideological perorations, and other consequences of taking a large view of an unorganized subject. It includes all lists of the "best" novels or poems or writers, whether their particular virtue is exclusiveness or inclusiveness. It includes all casual, sentimental, and prejudiced value-judgments, and all the literary chit-chat which makes the reputations of poets boom and crash in an imaginary stock exchange. That wealthy investor Mr. Eliot, after dumping Milton on the market, is now buying him again; Donne has probably reached his peak and will begin to taper off; Tennyson may be in for a slight flutter but the Shelley stocks are still bearish. This sort of thing cannot be part of any systematic study, for a systematic study can only progress: whatever dithers or vacillates or reacts is merely leisure-class gossip. The history of taste is no more a part of the *structure* of criticism than the Huxley-Wilberforce debate is a part of the structure of biological science.

I believe that if this distinction is maintained and applied to the critics of the past, what they have said about real criticism will show an astonishing amount of agreement, in which the outlines of a coherent and systematic study will begin to emerge. In the history of taste, where there are no facts, and where all truths have been, in Hegelian fashion, split into half-truths in order to sharpen their cutting edges, we perhaps do feel that the study of literature is too relative and subjective ever to make any consistent sense. But as the history of taste has no organic connection with criticism, it can easily be separated. Mr. Eliot's essay *The Function of Criticism* begins by laying down the principle that the existing monuments of literature form an ideal order among themselves, and are not simply collections of the writings of individuals. This is criticism, and very fundamental criticism. Much of this book attempts to annotate it. Its solidity is indicated by its consistency with a hundred other statements that could be collected from the better critics of all ages.[5] There follows a rhetorical debate which makes tradition and its opposite into personified and contending forces, the former dignified with the titles of Catholic and Classical, the latter ridiculed by the epithet "Whiggery." This is the sort of thing that makes for confusion until we realize how easy it is to snip it off and throw it away. The debate is maintained against Mr. Middleton Murry, who is spoken of approvingly because "he is aware that there are definite positions to be taken, and that now and then one must actually reject something and select something else." There are no definite positions to be taken in chemistry or philology, and if there are any to be taken in criticism, criticism is not a field of genuine learning. For in any field of genuine learning, the only sensible response to the challenge "stand" is Falstaff's "so I do, against my will." One's "definite position" is one's weakness, the source of one's liability to error and prejudice, and to gain adherents to a definite position is only to multiply one's weakness like an infection.

The next step is to realize that criticism has a great variety of neighbors, and that the critics must enter into relations with them in any way that guarantees his own independence. He may want to know something of the natural sciences, but he need waste no time in emulating their methods. I understand that there is a Ph.D. thesis somewhere which displays a list of Hardy's novels in the order of the percentages of gloom they contain, but one does not feel that that sort of procedure should be encouraged. The critic may want to know something of the social sciences, but there can be no such thing as, for instance, a sociological "approach" to literature. There is no reason why a sociologist should not work exclusively on literary material, but if he does he should pay no attention to literary values. In his field Horatio Alger and the writer of the Elsie books may well be more important than Hawthorne or Melville, and a single issue of the *Ladies' Home Journal* worth all of Henry James. The critic is similarly under no obligation to sociological values, as the social conditions favorable to the production of great art are not necessarily those at which the social sciences aim. The critic may need to know something of religion, but by theological standards an orthodox religious poem will give a more satisfactory expression of its content than a heretical one: this makes nonsense in criticism, and there is nothing to be gained by confusing the standards of the two subjects.

Literature has been always recognized to be a marketable product, its producers being the creative writers and its consumers the cultivated readers, with the critics at their head. From this point of view the critic is, in the metaphor of our opening page, the middleman. He has some wholesaler's privileges, such as free review copies, but his function, as distinct from the bookseller's, is essentially a form of consumer's research. I recognize a second division of labor in literature, which, like other forms of mental construction, has a theory and a practice. The practitioner of literature and the producer of literature are not quite the same, though they overlap a good deal; the theorist of literature and the consumer of literature are not the same at all, even when they co-exist in the same man. The present book assumes that the theory of literature is as primary a humanistic and liberal pursuit as its practice. Hence, although it takes certain literary values for granted, as fully established by critical experience, it is not directly concerned with value-judgements. This fact needs explanation, as the value-judgement is often, and perhaps rightly for all I know, regarded as the distinguishing feature of the humanistic and liberal pursuit.

Value-judgements are subjective in the sense that they can be indirectly but not directly communicated. When they are fashionable or generally accepted, they look objective, but that is all. The demonstrable value-judgement is the donkey's carrot of literary criticism, and every new critical fashion, such as the current fashion for elaborate rhetorical analysis, has been accompanied by a belief that criticism has finally devised a definitive technique for separating the excellent from the less excellent. But this always turns out to be an illusion of the history of taste. Value-judgements are founded on the study of literature; the study of literature can never be founded on value-judgements. Shakespeare, we say, was one of a group of English dramatists working around 1600, and also one of the great poets of the world. The first part of this is a statement of fact, the second a value-judgement so generally accepted as to pass for a statement of fact. But it is not a statement of fact. It remains a value-judgement, and not a shred of systematic criticism can ever be attached to it.

There are two types of value-judgements, comparative and positive. Criticism founded on comparative values falls into two main divisions, according to whether the work of art is regarded as a product or as a possession. The former develops biographical criticism, which relates the work of art primarily to the man who wrote it. The latter we may call tropical criticism, and it is primarily concerned with the contemporary reader. Biographical criticism concerns itself largely with comparative questions of greatness and personal authority. It regards the poem as the oratory of its creator, and it feels most secure when it knows of a definite, and preferably heroic, personality behind the poetry. If it cannot find such a personality, it may try to project one out of rhetorical ectoplasm, as Carlyle does in his essay on Shakespeare as a "heroic" poet. Tropical criticism deals comparatively with style and craftsmanship, with complexity of meaning and figurative assimilation. It tends to dislike and belittle the oratorical poets, and it can hardly deal at all with heroic personality. Both are essentially rhetorical forms of criticism, as one deals with the rhetoric of persuasive speech and the other with the rhetoric of verbal ornament, but each distrusts the other's kind of rhetoric.

Rhetorical value-judgements are closely related to social values, and are usually cleared through a customs-house of moral metaphors: sincerity, economy, subtlety, simplicity, and the like. But because poetics is undeveloped, a fallacy arises from the illegitimate extension of rhetoric into the theory of literature. The invariable mark of this fallacy is the selected tradition, illustrated with great clarity in Arnold's "touchstone" theory, where we proceed from the intuition of value represented by the touchstone to a system of ranking poets in classes.[6] The practice of comparing poets by weighing their lines (no new invention, as it was ridiculed by Aristophanes in *The Frogs*) is used by both biographical and tropical critics, mainly in order to deny first-class rating to those in favor with the opposite group.

When we examine the touchstone technique in Arnold, however, certain doubts arise about his motivation. The line from *The Tempest*, "In the dark backward and abysm of time," would do very well as a touchstone line. One feels that the line "Yet a tailor might scratch her where'er she did itch" somehow would not do, though it is equally Shakespearean and equally essential to the same play. (An extreme form of the same kind of criticism would, of course, deny this and insist that the line had been interpolated by a vulgar hack.) Some principle is clearly at work here which is much more highly selective than a purely critical experience of the play would be.

Arnold's "high seriousness" evidently is closely connected with the view that epic and tragedy, because they deal with ruling-class figures and require the high style of decorum, are the aristocrats of literary forms. All his Class One touchstones are from, or judged by the standards of, epic and tragedy. Hence his demotion of Chaucer and Burns to Class Two seems to be affected by a feeling that comedy and satire should be kept in their proper place, like the moral standards and the social classes which they symbolize. We begin to suspect that the literary value-judgements are projections of social ones. Why does Arnold *want* to rank poets? He says that we increase our admiration for those who manage to stay in Class One after we have made it very hard for them to do so. This being clearly nonsense, we must look further. When we read "in poetry the distinction between excellent and inferior . . . is of paramount importance . . . because of the high destinies of poetry," we begin to get a clue. We see that Arnold is trying to create a new scriptural canon out of poetry to serve as a guide for those social principles which he wants culture to take over from religion.

The treatment of criticism as the application of a social attitude is a natural enough result of what we have called the power vacuum in criticism. A systematic study alternates between inductive experience and deductive principles. In criticism rhetorical analysis provides some of the induction, and poetics, the theory of criticism, should be the deductive counterpart. There being no poetics, the critic is thrown back on prejudice derived from his existence as a social being. For prejudice is simply inadequate deduction, as a prejudice in the mind can never be anything but a major premise which is mostly submerged, like an iceberg.

It is not hard to see prejudice in Arnold, because his views have dated: it is a little harder when "high seriousness" becomes "maturity," or some other powerful persuader of more recent critical rhetoric. It is harder when the old question of what books one would take to a desert island emerges from parlor games, where it belongs, into an expensive library alleged to constitute the scriptural canon of democratic values. Rhetorical value-judgements usually turn on questions of decorum, and the central conception of decorum is the difference between high, middle, and low styles. These styles are suggested by the class structure of society, and criticism, if it is not to reject half the facts of literary experience, obviously has to look at art from the standpoint of an ideally classless society. Arnold himself points this out when he says that "culture seeks to do away with classes." Every deliberately constructed hierarchy of values in literature known to me is based on a concealed social, moral, or intellectual analogy. This applies whether the analogy is conservative and Romantic, as it is in Arnold, or radical, giving the top place to comedy, satire, and the values of prose and reason, as it is in Bernard Shaw. The various pretexts for minimizing the communicative power of certain writers, that they are obscure or obscene or nihilistic or reactionary or what not, generally turn out to be disguises for a feeling that the views of decorum held by the ascendant social or intellectual class ought to be either maintained or challenged. These social fixations keep changing, like a fan turning in front of a light, and the changing inspires the belief that posterity eventually discovers the whole truth about art.

A selective approach to tradition, then, invariably has some ultra-critical joker concealed in it. There is no question of accepting the whole of literature as the basis of study, but a tradition (or, of course, "the" tradition) is abstracted from it and attached to contemporary social values, being then used to document those values. The hesitant reader is invited to try the following exercise. Pick three big names at random, work out the eight possible combinations of promotion and demotion (on a simplified, or two-class, basis) and defend each in turn. Thus if the three names picked were Shakespeare, Milton, and Shelley, the agenda would run:

1. Demoting Shelley, on the ground that he is immature in technique and profundity of thought compared to the others.

2. Demoting Milton, on the ground that his religious obscurantism and heavy doctrinal content impair the spontaneity of his utterance.

3. Demoting Shakespeare, on the ground that his detachment from

ideas makes his dramas a reflection of life rather than a creative attempt to improve it.

4. Promoting Shakespeare, on the ground that he preserves an integrity of poetic vision which in the others is obfuscated by didacticism.

5. Promoting Milton, on the ground that his penetration of the highest mysteries of faith raises him above Shakespeare's unvarying worldliness and Shelley's callowness.

6. Promoting Shelley, on the ground that his love of freedom speaks to the heart of modern man more immediately than poets who accepted outworn social or religious values.

7. Promoting all three (for this a special style, which we may call the peroration style, should be used).

8. Demoting all three, on the ground of the untidiness of English genius when examined by French or Classical or Chinese standards.

The reader may sympathize with some of these "positions," as they are called, more than with others, and so be seduced into thinking that one of them must be right, and that it is important to decide which one it is. But long before he has finished his assignment he will realize that the whole procedure involved is an anxiety neurosis prompted by a moral censor, and is totally devoid of content. Of course, in addition to the moralists, there are poets who regard only those other poets as authentic who sound like themselves; there are critics who enjoy making religious, anti-religious, or political campaigns with toy soldiers labelled "Milton" or "Shelley" more than they enjoy studying poetry; there are students who have urgent reasons for making as much edifying reading as possible superfluous. But a conspiracy even of all these still does not make criticism.

The social dialectics applied externally to criticism, then, are, *within criticism,* pseudo-dialectics, or false rhetoric. It remains to try to define the true dialectic of criticism. On this level the biographical critic becomes the historical critic. He develops from hero-worship towards total and indiscriminate acceptance: there is nothing "in his field" that he is not prepared to read with interest. From a purely historical point of view, however, cultural phenomena are to be read in their own context without contemporary application. We study them as we do the stars, seeing their interrelationships but not approaching them. Hence historical criticism needs to be complemented by a corresponding activity growing out of tropical criticism.

We may call this ethical criticism, interpreting ethics not as a rhetorical comparison of social facts to predetermined values, but as the consciousness of the presence of society. As a critical category this would be the sense of the real presence of culture in the community. Ethical criticism, then, deals with art as a communication from the past to the present, and is based on the conception of the total and simultaneous possession of past culture. An exclusive devotion to it, ignoring historical criticism, would lead to a naive translation of all cultural phenomena into our own terms without regard to their original character. As a counterweight to historical criticism, it is designed to express the contemporary impact of all art, without selecting a tradition. Every new critical fashion has increased the appreciation of some poets and depreciated others, as the increase of interest in the metaphysical poets tended to depreciate the Romantics about twenty-five years ago. On the ethical level we can see that every increase of appreciation has been right, and every decrease wrong: that criticism has no business to react against things, but should show a steady advance toward undiscriminating catholicity. Oscar Wilde said that only an auctioneer could be equally appreciative of all kinds of art: he had of course the public critic in mind, but even the public critic's job of getting the treasures of culture into the hands of the people who want them is largely an auctioneer's job. And if this is true of him, it is *a fortiori* true of the scholarly critic.

The dialectic axis of criticism, then, has as one pole the total acceptance of the data of literature, and as the other the total acceptance of the potential values of those data. This is the real level of culture and of liberal education, the fertilizing of life by learning, in which the systematic progress of scholarship flows into a systematic progress of taste and understanding. On this level there is no itch to make weighty judgements, and none of the ill effects which follow the debauchery of judiciousness, and have made the word critic a synonym for an educated shrew. Comparative estimates of value are really inferences, most valid when silent ones, from critical practice, not expressed principles guiding its practice. The critic will find soon, and constantly, that Milton is a more rewarding and suggestive poet to work with than Blackmore. But the more obvious this becomes, the less time he will want to waste in belaboring the point. For belaboring the point is all he can do: any criticism motivated by a desire to establish or prove it will be merely one more document in the history of taste. There is doubtless much in the culture of the past which will always be of comparatively slight value to the present. But the difference between redeemable and irredeemable art, being based on the *total* experience of criticism, can never be theoretically formulated. There are too many Cinderellas among the poets, too many stones rejected from one fashionable building that have become heads of the next corner.

There may, then, be such things as rules of critical procedure, and laws, in the sense of the patterns of observed phenomena, of literary practice. All efforts of critics to discover rules or laws in the sense of moral mandates telling the artist what he ought to do, or have done, to be an authentic artist, have failed. "Poetry," said Shelley, "and the art which professes to regulate and limit its powers, cannot subsist together." There is no such art, and there never has been. The substitution of subordination and value-judgement for coordination and description, the substitution of "all poets should" for "some poets do," is only a sign that all the relevant facts have not yet been considered. Critical statements with "must" or "should" in their predicates are either pedantries or tautologies, depending on whether they are taken seriously or not. Thus a dramatic critic may wish to say "all plays must have unity of action." If he is a pedant, he will then try to define unity of action in specific terms. But creative power is versatile, and he is sure to find himself sooner or later asserting that some perfectly reputable dramatist, whose effectiveness on the stage has been proved over and over again, does not exhibit the unity of action he has defined, and is consequently not writing what he regards as plays at all. The critic who attempts to apply such principles in a more liberal or more cautious spirit will soon have to broaden his conceptions to the point, not of course of saying, but of trying to conceal the fact that he is saying, "all plays that have unity of action must have unity of action," or, more simply and more commonly, "all good plays must be good plays."

Criticism, in short, and aesthetics generally, must learn to do what ethics has already done. There was a time when ethics could take the simple form of comparing what man does with what he ought to do, known as the good. The "good" invariably turned out to be whatever the author of the book was accustomed to and found sanctioned by his community. Ethical writers now, though they still have values, tend to look at their problems rather differently. But a procedure which is hopelessly outmoded in ethics is still in vogue among writers on aesthetic problems. It is still possible for a critic to define as authentic art whatever he happens to like, and to go on to assert that what he happens not to like is, in terms of that definition, not authentic art. The argument has the great advantage of being irrefutable, as all circular arguments are, but it is shadow and not substance.

The odious comparisons of greatness, then, may be left to take care of themselves, for even when we feel obliged to assent to them they are still only unproductive platitudes. The real concern of the evaluating critic is with positive value, with the goodness, or perhaps the genuineness, of the poem rather than with the greatness of its author. Such criticism produces the direct value-judgement of informed good taste, the proving of art on the pulses, the disciplined response of a highly organized nervous system to the impact of poetry. No critic in his senses would try to belittle the importance of this; nevertheless there are some caveats even here. In the first place, it is superstition to believe that the swift intuitive certainty of good taste is infallible. Good taste follows and is developed by the study of literature; its precision results from knowledge, but does not produce knowledge. Hence the accuracy of any critic's good taste is no guarantee that its inductive basis in literary experience is adequate. This may still be true even after the critic has learned to base his judgements on his experience of literature and not on his social, moral, religious, or personal anxieties. Honest critics are continually finding blind spots in their taste: they discover the possibility of recognizing a valid form of poetic experience without being able to realize it for themselves.

In the second place, the positive value-judgement is founded on a direct experience which is central to criticism yet forever excluded from it. Criticism can account for it only in critical terminology, and that terminology can never recapture or include the original experience. The original experience is like the direct vision of color, or the direct sensation of heat or cold, that physics "explains" in what, from the point of view of the experience itself, is a quite irrelevant way. However disciplined by taste and skill, the experience of literature is, like literature itself, unable to speak. "If I feel physically as if the top of my head were taken off," said Emily Dickinson, "I know this is poetry." This remark is perfectly sound, but it relates only to criticism as experience. The reading of literature should, like prayer in the Gospels, step out of the talking world of criticism into the private and secret presence of literature. Otherwise the reading will not be a genuine literary experience, but a mere reflection of critical conventions, memories, and prejudices. The presence of incommunicable experience in the center of criticism will always keep criticism an art, as long as the critic recognizes that criticism comes out of it but cannot be built on it.

Thus, though the normal development of a critic's taste is toward greater tolerance and catholicity, still criticism as knowledge is one thing, and value-judgements informed by taste are another. The attempt to bring the direct experience of literature into the structure of criticism produces the aberrations of the history of taste already dealt with. The attempt to reverse the procedure and bring criticism into direct experience will destroy the integrity of both. Direct experience, even if it is concerned with something already read hundreds of times, still tries to be a new and fresh experience each time, which is clearly impossible if the poem itself has been replaced by a critical view of the poem. To bring my own view that criticism as knowledge should constantly progress and reject nothing into direct experience would mean that the latter should progress toward a general stupor of satisfaction with everything written, which is not quite what I have in mind.

Finally, the skill developed from constant practice in the direct experience of literature is a special skill, like playing the piano, not the expression of a general attitude to life, like singing in the shower. The critic has a subjective background of experience formed by his temperament and by every contact with words he has made, including newspapers, advertisements, conversations, movies, and whatever he read at the age of nine. He has a specific skill in responding to literature which is no more like this subjective background, with all its private memories, associations, and arbitrary prejudices, than reading a thermometer is like shivering. Again, there is no one of critical ability who has not experienced intense and profound pleasure from something simultaneously with a low critical valuation of what produced it. There must be several dozen critical and aesthetic theories based on the assumption that subjective pleasure and the specific response to art are, or develop from, or ultimately become, the same thing. Yet every cultivated person who is not suffering from advanced paranoia knows that they are constantly distinct. Or, again, the ideal value may be quite different from the actual one. A critic may spend a thesis, a book, or even a life work on something that he candidly admits to be third-rate, simply because it is connected with something else that he thinks sufficiently important for his pains. No critical theory known to me takes any real account of the different systems of valuation implied by one of the most common practices of criticism.

NORTHROP FRYE

The Critical Path: An Essay
on the Social Context of Literary Criticism

The phrase "The Critical Path" is, I understand, a term in business administration, and was one that I began hearing extensively used during the preparations for the Montreal Expo in 1967. It associated itself in my mind with the closing sentences of Kant's *Critique of Pure Reason,* where he says that dogmatism and skepticism have both

SOURCE: Reprinted by permission from *Daedalus, Journal of the American Academy of Arts and Sciences,* Boston, Massachusetts, Volume 99, Number 2 (Spring 1970), pp. 268–276. This portion is Section I of the complete essay.

had it as tenable philosophical positions, and that "the critical path is alone open." It also associated itself with a turning point in my own development. About twenty-five years ago, when still in middle life, I lost my way in the dark wood of Blake's prophecies, and looked around for some path that would get me out of there. There were many paths, some well trodden and equipped with signposts, but all pointing in what for me was the wrong direction. They directed me to the social conditions of Blake's time, to the history of the occult tradition, to psychological factors in Blake's mind, and other subjects quite valid in themselves. But my task was the specific problem of trying to crack Blake's symbolic code, and I had a feeling that the way to that led directly through literature itself. The critical path I wanted, therefore, was a theory of criticism which would, first, account for the major phenomena of literary experience, and, second, would lead to some view of the place of literature in civilization as a whole.

Following the bent that Blake had given me, I became particularly interested in two questions. One was: What is the total subject of study of which criticism forms a part? I rejected the easy answer: "Criticism is a subdivision of literature," because it seemed obvious to me that literature is not a subject of study at all apart from some aspect of criticism. There seemed to me two possible larger contexts of criticism: one, the unified criticism of all the arts, which did not (and does not yet) exist; the other, some larger study of verbal expression which had not yet been defined. The latter seemed more immediately promising: the former was the area of aesthetics, in which (at least at that time) relatively few technically competent literary critics appeared to be much interested. But there was a strong centrifugal drift from criticism toward social, philosophical or religious interests, which had set in at least as early as Coleridge. I viewed this with some suspicion, because it seemed to me that an unjustified sense of claustrophobia underlay it. A critic devoting himself wholly to literature is often tempted to feel that he can never be anything more than a second-class writer or thinker, because his work is based on the work of what almost by definition are greater men. I felt, then, that a theory of criticism was needed which would set the critic's activity in its proper light, and that once we had that, a critic's other interests would represent an expansion of criticism rather than an escape from it.

The other question was: How do we arrive at poetic meaning? This question was closely related to the other question of context. When I first began to write on critical theory, I was startled to realize how general was the agreement that criticism had no presuppositions of its own, but had to be "grounded" on some other subject. The disagreements were not over that, but over the question of what the proper subjects were that criticism ought to depend on. The older European philological basis, a very sound one, had already been discarded, in most North American universities, for a mixture of history and philosophy, evidently on the assumption that every work of literature is what Sir Walter Raleigh said *Paradise Lost* was, a monument to dead ideas. I myself was soon identified as one of the critics who took their assumptions from anthropology and psychology, then still widely regarded as the wrong subjects. I have always insisted that criticism cannot take presuppositions from elsewhere, which always means wrenching them out of their real context, and must work out its own. But mental habits are hard to break, especially bad habits, and, because I found the term "archetype" a useful one, I am still often called a Jungian critic, and classified with Miss Maud Bodkin, whose book I have read with interest, but whom, on the evidence of that book, I resemble about as closely as I resemble the late Sarah Bernhardt.

In the last generation, of which I am now speaking, the accepted critical procedure was to take a work of literature, let us say a poem for short, and treat it as a document to be related to some context outside literature. One of the most obvious of these documentary approaches was the biographical one, where the poem is taken to be a document illustrating something in the poet's life. The golden age of this approach was the nineteenth century, and its strongest proponent was Carlyle, for whom great poetry could only be the personal rhetoric of a great man. The model great man was Goethe, who, for Carlyle, was to be admired not so much for the quality of his poetry as for the number of things he had been able to do besides writing poetry. Of course no one denies the relevance of the poet's life to his work: doubts arise only when the sense of that relevance is carried to uncritical extremes. In the first place, there are variations in the degree of its relevance: it is more important for Byron than for Wordsworth, more important for D. H. Lawrence than for T. S. Eliot. Secondly, when we have no real knowledge of a poet's life at all, it is better to leave it alone than to invent a biography out of fancied allusions in the poetry, as nineteenth-century critics so often did with Shakespeare, and as many are still doing with the sonnets.

In these days, a biographical approach is likely to move from the manifest to the latent personal content of the poem, and from a biographical approach properly speaking to a psychological one, which at present means very largely a Freudian one. All documentary approaches to literature are allegorical approaches, and this fact becomes even more obvious when poems are taken to be allegories of Freudian repressions, unresolved conflicts or tensions between ego and id, or, for another school, of the Jungian process of individuation. A considerable amount of determinism enters at this stage. It still seems unquestionable to many critics that literature has its origin in psychological processes, and that it can be explained only in terms that are ultimately psychological terms. But what is true of allegorical poetry is equally true of allegorical criticism; in both fields allegory is a technique that calls for tact. When the whiteness of Moby Dick is explained as a Lockian *tabula rasa,* or Alice in Wonderland discussed in terms of her hypothetical toilet training, or Arnold's "Where ignorant armies clash by night" taken as a covert reference to the copulation of his parents, one is reminded of the exempla from natural history made by medieval preachers. The bee carries earth in its feet to ballast itself when it flies, and thereby reminds us of the Incarnation, when God took up an earthly form. The example is ingenious and entertaining, and only unsatisfying if one happens to be interested in bees. Naturally such practices have produced a reaction from critics who see the futility of trying to base their professional scholarly competence on an amateur enthusiasm for something else. But I do not think it helps any merely to write cautionary treatises urging critics that they should be careful not to do too much various things that they are not effectively doing at all.

In any case, there will always be critics, probably the great majority, for whom the ultimate source of a poem is not the individual poet at all, but rather the social situation from which the poet springs, and of which he is the spokesman and the medium. This takes us into the area of historical criticism. Here again no one can or should deny the relevance of literature to history, but here again the relation is an indirect one, more relevant to some poets than to others. The historical subculture known as the history of ideas is more consistently rewarding, for ideas, like poems, cannot exist until they are verbalized. Here the allegorizing tendency in all such criticism shows up very clearly.

Once more, some historical critics, like the biographical ones, will want to go from manifest to latent social content, from the historical context of the poem to its context in some unified overview of history. Of these enlarged historical perspectives, Marxism is today the most widely adopted, and perhaps inherently the most serious. Here again, as with psychological criticism, the determinism in the approach, which includes a determination to find the ultimate meaning of literature in something that is not literature, is unmistakable. At the time of which I am speaking, there was also a conservative Catholic determinism, strongly influenced by Eliot, which adopted, as the summit of Western cultural values, the medieval synthesis of the period of St. Thomas Aquinas, and looked down benignantly on everything that followed it as a kind of toboggan slide, rushing through nominalism, Protestantism, liberalism, subjective idealism, and so on to the solipsism in which the critic's non-Thomist contemporaries were assumed to be enclosed.

All these documentary approaches, even when correctly handled, are subject to at least three limitations, which every experienced scholar interested in them has to reckon with. In the first place, they do not account for the literary form of what they are discussing. Identifying Edward King and documenting Milton's attitude to the Church of England will throw no light on *Lycidas* as a pastoral elegy with specific Classical and Italian lines of ancestry. Secondly, they do not account for the poetic and metaphorical language of the literary work. Documentary criticism in general is based on the assumption that the literal or real meaning of a poem is not what it says as a poem, but is something to be expressed by a prose paraphrase derived from the poem. Thirdly, they do not account for the fact that the unique quality of a poet is often in a quite negative relation to the chosen context. To understand fully Blake's *Milton* and *Jerusalem* one needs to know something of his quarrel with Hayley and his sedition trial, but one also needs to be aware of the vast disproportion between these very minor events in a very quiet life and their apocalyptic transformation in the poems. Similarly, one may write a whole shelf of books about the life of Milton studied in connexion with the history of his time, and still fail to notice that Milton's greatness as a poet has a good deal to do with his profound and perverse misunderstanding of the history of his time.

By the time I began writing criticism, the so-called new criticism had established itself as a technique of explication. This was a rhetorical form of criticism, and from the beginning rhetoric has meant two things: the figuration of language and the persuasive powers of an orator. New criticism dealt with rhetoric in the former sense, and established a counterweight to the biographical approach which treated poetry as a personal rhetoric. The great merit of explicatory criticism was that it accepted poetic language as the basis for poetic meaning. On this basis, it built up a resistance to all "background" criticism that explained the literary in terms of the non-literary. At the same time, it deprived itself of the great strength of documentary criticism: the sense of context. It simply explicated one work after another, paying little attention to any larger structural principles connecting the different works explicated. The limitations of this approach soon became obvious, and most of the new critics sooner or later fell back on one of the established documentary contexts, generally the historical one, although they were regarded at first as anti-historical. One or two have even been Marxists, but in general the movement, at least in America, was anti-Marxist. Marxists had previously condemned a somewhat similar tendency in Russian criticism as "formalism," because they realized that if they began by conceding literary form as the basis for literary significance, the assumptions on which Marxist bureaucracies rationalized their censorship of the arts would be greatly weakened. They would logically have to end, in fact, in giving poets and novelists the same kind of freedom that they had reluctantly been compelled to grant to the physical scientists. More recently, my Toronto colleague Marshall McLuhan has placed an extreme and somewhat paradoxical formalism, expressed in the phrase "the medium is the message," within the context of a neo-Marxist determinism in which communications media play the same role that instruments of production do in more orthodox Marxism. In him the centrifugal tendency in criticism which I spoke of a moment ago has expanded into a new mosaic code. Professor McLuhan formed his views under the influence of the conservative wing of the new critical movement, and many traces of an earlier Thomist determinism can be found in *The Gutenberg Galaxy.*

It seemed to me that, after accepting the poetic form of a poem as its literal meaning, the next step was to look for some context for it within literature itself. And of course the most obvious context for a poem is the entire output of its author. Just as explication, by stressing the more objective aspect of rhetoric, had formed a corrective to the excesses of biographical criticism, so a study of a poet's whole work might form the basis of a kind of "psychological" criticism that would operate within literature, and so provide some balance for the kind that ends in the bosom of Freud. Poetry is, after all, a technique of communication: it engages the conscious part of the mind as well as the murkier areas, and what a poet succeeds in communicating to others is at least as important as what he fails to resolve for himself. One soon becomes aware that every poet has his own distinctive structure of imagery, which usually emerges even in his earliest work, and which does not and cannot essentially change. This larger context of the poem within its author's entire "mental landscape" (to use a phrase often employed in a different connexion) is assumed in all the best explication — Spitzer's, for example. I became aware of its importance myself, when working on Blake, as soon as I realized that Blake's special symbolic names and the like did form a genuine structure of poetic imagery and not, despite his use of the word, a "system," to which he was bound like an administrator to a computer. I got another lead here from Yeats's early essay on the philosophy of Shelley's poetry, for by "philosophy" Yeats really meant structure of imagery.

There was another difficulty with new criticism which was only a technical one, but still pointed to the necessity for a sense of context. Whenever we read anything there are two mental operations we perform, which succeed one another in time. First we follow the narrative movement in the act of reading, turning over the pages to get to the end. Afterwards, we can look at the work as a simultaneous unity and study its structure. This latter act is the critical response properly speaking: the ordinary reader seldom needs to bother with it. The chief material of rhetorical analysis consists of a study of the poetic "texture," and such a study plunges one into a complicated labyrinth of ambiguities, multiple meanings, recurring images, and echoes of both sound and sense. A full explication of a long and complex work which was based on the reading process could well become much longer, and more difficult to read, than the work itself. Such linear explications have some advantages as a teaching technique, but for publishing purposes it is more practicable to start with the second stage. This involves attaching the rhetorical analysis to a deductive framework derived from a study of the structure, and the context of that structure shows us where we should begin to look for our central images and ambiguities. The difficulty in transferring explication from the reading process to the study of structure has left some curious traces in new critical theory. One of them is again in McLuhan, who makes it the basis for a distinction between the "linear" demands of the printed media and the "simultaneous" impact of the electronic ones.

I was still not satisfied: I wanted a historical approach to literature, but an approach that would be or include a genuine history of literature, and not the assimilating of literature to some other kind of history. It was at this point that the immense importance of certain structural elements in the literary tradition, such as conventions, genres, and the recurring use of certain images or image-clusters, which I came to call archetypes, forced itself on me. T. S. Eliot had already spoken of tradition as a creative and informing power operating on the poet specifically as a craftsman, and not generally as a cultivated person. But neither he nor anyone else seemed to get to the point of identifying the factors of that tradition, of what it is that makes possible the creation of new works of literature out of earlier ones.

And yet convention, within literature, seemed to be a force even stronger than history. The difference between medieval poets using Courtly Love conventions in the London of Richard II and Cavalier poets using the same conventions in the London of Charles II is far less than the difference in social conditions between the two ages. I began to suspect that a poet's relation to poetry was much more like a scientist's relation to his science than was generally thought. Literature and science, of course, differ profoundly in the way in which science is able to absorb the work of predecessors in a steadily growing body of knowledge, whereas literature shows no such progressive tendencies. We shall perhaps understand this fact more clearly as we go on. Apart from that, the psychological processes involved seem much the same. The scientist cannot become a scientist until he immerses himself in his science, until he attaches his own thinking to the body of what is thought in his day about that science, until he becomes less a man thinking about his science than a kind of incarnation of that science thinking through him. What is true of science is true of all academic disciplines. No scholar, *qua* scholar, can think for himself or think at random: he can only expand an organic body of thought, add something logically related to what he or someone else has already thought. But this is precisely the way that poets have always talked about their relation to poetry: from Homer to Rimbaud, poets have invariably insisted that they were simply places where something new in literature was able to take its own shape. The new critics had resisted the background approach to criticism, but they had not destroyed the oratorical conception of poetry as a personal rhetoric.

From here it is clear that one has to take a final step. Criticism must develop a sense of history within literature to complement the historical criticism that relates literature to a historical background. Similarly, it must develop its own form of historical overview, on the basis of what is inside literature rather than outside it. Instead of fitting literature deterministically into a prefabricated scheme of history, the critic should see literature as, like a science, a unified, coherent and autonomous created form, historically conditioned but shaping its own history, not determined by any external historical process. This total body of literature can be studied through its larger structural principles, which I have just described as conventions, genres and recurring image-groups, or archetypes. When criticism develops a proper sense of the history of literature, the history of what is not literature does not cease to exist or to be relevant to the critic. Similarly, seeing literature as a single created form does not withdraw it from a social context: on the contrary, it becomes far easier to see what its place in civilization is. Criticism will always have two aspects, one turned toward the structure of literature as a whole and one turned toward the other cultural phenomena that form its environment. Together, they balance each other; when one is worked on to the exclusion of the other, the critical perspective goes out of focus. If criticism is in proper balance, the "centrifugal" tendency of critics to move from critical to larger social issues becomes more intelligible. Such a movement need not, and should not, be due to a dissatisfaction with the narrowness of criticism as a discipline, but should be simply the result of a sense of social context, a sense present in all critics from whom one is in the least likely to learn anything. . . .

58

R. P. BLACKMUR

A Burden for Critics

When George Santayana made his apology for writing a system of philosophy — one more after so many, one more after a lifetime of self-denial — he put his plea for forgiveness on the ground that he was an ignorant man, almost a poet. No doubt there was some reservation in Santayana's mind when he made that plea; no doubt there is some in mine when I adapt it to myself. This essay does not introduce a system of criticism; it is only a plea that criticism take up some of its possibilities that have been in abeyance, or in corruption, for some time; and it may be that like Santayana's philosophy it will look like an approach to a system. If so, it is the system of an ignorant man, and there is nothing in it that does not remind itself at every turn that it is the kind of ignorance which goes with being almost a poet. Poetry is one of the things we do to our ignorance; criticism makes us conscious of what we have done, and sometimes makes us conscious of what can be done next, or done again.

That consciousness is the way we feel the critic's burden. By a burden, I mean both a weight and a refrain, something we carry and something that carries us along, something we have in possession and something that reminds us what we are. It is the burden of our momentum. In relation to it we get work done. Out of relation to it we get nothing done, except so far as we are swept along; and of course we are mainly swept along. The critic's job is to put us into maximum relation to the burden of our momentum, which means he has to run the risk of a greater degree of consciousness than his mind is fit for. He risks substituting the formulas of relation for the things related. I take it the critic is a relativist; but his relativism does not need to be either deterministic or positivistic, as in our time it usually is; he may rather be the relativist of insight, aspiration, vision. He is concerned with choice, not prescription, with equity, not law; never with the dead hand, always with the vital purpose. He knows that the institution of literature, so far as it is alive, is made again at every instant. It is made afresh as part of the process of being

known afresh; what is permanent is what is always fresh, and it can be
fresh only in performance — that is, in reading and seeing and hearing
what is actually in it at this place and this time. It is in performance that
we find out relation to momentum. Or put another way, the critic brings
to consciousness the means of performance.

Perform is a word of which we forget the singular beauty. Its meaning is: to furnish forth, to complete, to finish, in a sense which is influenced by the ideas clustered in the word *form*; so that *performance* is an
enlightening name for one of our richest activities, rich with extra life.
If it is the characteristic intent of the critic to see about the conditions of
performance, it is his characteristic temptation to interfere with those
conditions. He will find substitutes; he will make one condition do for
every condition; he will make precedent do for balance, or rote for authority; and, worst of all, he will impose the excellence of something he
understands upon something he does not understand. Then all the
richness of actual performance is gone. It is worth taking precautions to
prevent that loss, or at any rate to keep us aware of the risk.

The precautions of the past come down to us as mottoes; and for the
critic of literature in our time I would suggest three mottoes — all Latin
— as exemplary. *Omnis intellectus omniformis est*: every mind is omni-
form, every mind has latent in it all possible forms of the mind, even
one's own mind. The temptation is to make some single form of the
mind seem omnicompetent; omnicompetence becomes omniscience and
asserts for itself closed authority based upon a final revelation. *Omnis
intellectus omniformis est*. This is a motto of the Renaissance, and leads
us directly to a motto of the high Middle Ages, which preceded, or initiated, rather than followed, an era of absolute authority: *Fides quaerens
intellectus*. If the temptation of the Renaissance was to put one's own
version of the mind in first place, the temptation of the Middle Ages
was to identify God with either one's own knowledge of him or with
one's particular form of faith. *Fides quaerens intellectus* is a motto
meant to redeem that temptation; for it is faith alone that may question
the intellect, as it is only the intellect that can curb faith. The very
principle of balance, together with the radical precariousness of its nature, lies in the reversibility of this motto. Just so, the value of both these
mottoes is heightened by putting them into relation with a third, which
is classical in its time, and which has to do primarily neither with intellect nor faith but with the temptation of the moral sensibility. *Corruptio optima pessima*: in corruption the best is the worst. Here, in this
motto, is that hard core of common sense — Cochrane's phrase — of
which the Christian world has never got enough in its heritage from
classical culture. It reminds the moral ego of its fatal temptation to
forget that the ground it stands on is not its own, but other, various, and

equal. Surely we have made the best in us the worst when we have either pushed an insight beyond its field or refused, when using one insight, to acknowledge the pressure of all those insights — those visions of value — with which it is in conflict. If we do not see this, we have lost the feeling of richness, the sense of relation, and the power of judgment; and without these we cannot, as conscious critics, bring our experience of literature to actual performance. We should know neither what to bring, nor what to look for.

All this is generality; it applies to literature chiefly in the sense that literature is one aspect among many of the general human enterprise. The horror, for critics, of most aspects of that enterprise, is that they are exigent in action and will by no means stand still for criticism until they are done for. The beauty of literature is that it is exigent in the mind and will not only stand still but indeed never comes fully into its life of symbolic action until criticism has taken up the burden of bringing it into performance and finding its relation to the momentum of the whole enterprise. Both what constitutes performance and the very nature of relation — that is to say, what must be done and what may be taken for granted — change from time to time. It seems likely that one reason there has been so little great literature is that at most times so little has been required of it: how often has a Vergil felt obligated to create the myth of imperial culture? It is even more likely that the ability to cope with the task was wanting when required: how often has a Dante turned up to put into actual order all that had been running into the disorder of the rigid intellect and the arbitrary will? Ordinarily, past times have required little of literature in the way either of creating or ordering a culture. The artist's task was principally to express the continuity of his culture and the turbulence that underlay it. That is perhaps why we find the history of criticism so much concerned with matters of decorum: that is to say, with conformity, elegance, rhetoric, or metrics: matters not now commonly found or considered in the reviews. In our own time — if I may be permitted the exaggerations of ignorance and of poetry — almost everything is required of the arts and particularly of literature. Almost the whole job of culture, as it has formerly been understood, has been dumped into the hands of the writer. Possibly a new form of culture, appropriate to a massive urban society, is emerging: at any rate there are writers who write with a new ignorance and a new collective illiteracy: I mean the Luce papers and Hollywood. But the old drives persist. Those who seem to be the chief writers of our time have found their subjects in attempting to dramatize at once both the culture and the turbulence it was meant to control, and in doing so they have had practically to create — as it happens, to re-create — the terms, the very symbolic substance, of the culture as they went along.

I do not mean that this has happened by arrogation on the part of the writers; I mean they have been left alone with this subject as part of the actual experience of life in our time: which is always the subject which importunes every serious writer if he is honest and can keep himself free of the grosser hallucinations. The actual is always the medium through which the visitation of the Muse is felt. Perhaps a distinction will clarify what is meant. It is getting on toward a century since Matthew Arnold suggested that poetry could perhaps take over the expressive functions of religion. Possibly Arnold only meant the functions of the Church of England and the lesser dissenting sects. Whatever he meant, it did not happen, it could not and it cannot happen. All poetry can do is to dramatize, to express, what has actually happened to religion. This it has done. It has not replaced or in any way taken over the functions of religion; but it has been compelled to replace the operative force of religion as a resource with the discovery, or creation, of religion as an aesthetic experience. The poet has to put his religion itself into his poetry along with his experience of it. Think, together, of the religious poetry of George Herbert and of T. S. Eliot: of how little Herbert had to do before he got to his poetry, of how much Eliot is compelled to put into his poetry before he is free to write it. Consider too — and perhaps this is more emphatic of what has happened — the enormous mass of exegetical criticism it has seemed necessary and desirable to apply to Eliot's poetry and indeed to the whole school of Donne. This criticism neither compares, nor judges; it elucidates scripture.

Let us put the matter as a question. Why do we treat poetry, and gain by doing so, after much the same fashion as Augustine treated the scriptures in the fifth century? Why do we make of our criticism an essay in the understanding of words and bend upon that essay exclusively every tool of insight and analysis we possess? Why do we have to re-create so much of the poem in the simple reading which is only the preface to total performance? Do we, like Augustine, live in an interregnum, after a certainty, anticipating a synthesis? If so, unlike Augustine, we lack a special revelation: we take what we can find, and what we find is that art is, as Augustine sometimes thought, a human increment to creation. If this is so, how, then, has it come about?

We know very well how it has come about, and we come late enough in the sequence of our time so that we can summarize it in what looks like an orderly form — or at any rate a poetic form. It composes into something we can understand. We come late in a time when the burden of descriptive and historical knowledge is greater than any man or groups of men can encompass; when the labor by which our society gets along from day to day is not only divided but disparate and to the individual laborer fragmentary; and when, in an effort to cope with the burden of knowledge and the division of labor, we have resorted to the adulterative process called universal education.

As a natural effect of such a situation we have the disappearance or at least the submergence of tradition in the sense that it is no longer available at either an instinctive or a critical level but must be looked for, dug out, and largely re-created as if it were a new thing and not tradition at all. We have also a decay of the power of conviction or mastery; we permit ourselves everywhere to be overwhelmed by the accidents of our massive ignorance and by the apparent subjectivity of our individual purposes. Thus we have lost the field of common reference, we have dwindled in our ability to think symbolically, and as we look about us we see all our old unconscious skills at life disappearing without any apparent means of developing new unconscious skills.

We have seen rise instead a whole series of highly conscious, but deeply dubious and precarious skills which have been lodged in the sciences of psychology, anthropology, and sociology, together with the whole confusion of practices which go with urbanization. Consider how all these techniques have been developed along lines that discover trouble, undermine purpose, blight consciousness, and prevent decision; how they promote uncertainty, insecurity, anxiety, and incoherence; how above all they provide barriers between us and access to our common enterprise. Perhaps the unwieldy and unmanipulable fact of urbanization does more of the damage than the conscious techniques.

But this is not a diagnosis, it is a statement of sequence, a composition of things in relation. At the point where we arrest this sequence, and think in terms of what we can remember of our old culture, does it not seem plain to us what we have? Do we not have a society in which we see the attrition of law and rational wisdom and general craft? Do we not have an age anti-intellectual and violent, in which there is felt a kind of total responsibility to total disorder? Who looks ahead except to a panacea or a millennium which is interchangeable with an invoked anarchy, whether in the world or in the individual personality? Do we not above all each day wonderfully improve our chances of misunderstanding each other? These are the questions we ask of a living, not a dead, society.

They become more emphatic when we ask them about the schools of art and criticism which accompanied this shift in the structure of society. If we begin with Arnold's effort at the secularization of the old culture, it is easy to remind ourselves of the sequence which it began. Here it is, in very rough order. The hedonism in Pater, the naturalism of Zola, the impressionism of Anatole France, Art for Art as of the 'nineties, the naturalistic relativism of de Gourmont, the aestheticism of the psychologists, the rebirth of symbolism (as in Mallarmé and Yeats), the private mind, Imagism and Free verse, futurism, expressionism and expressive form, Dada and surrealism, dream literature, spontaneous or automatic form, anti-intellectual form, the school of Donne in English and American poetry, the stream of consciousness (that libel on Joyce), the revolution of the word, the new cult of the word. Some of these phrases will carry different meanings to different people; let us say that the general sequence runs toward some kind of autonomous and absolute creation and therefore total literalism.

That is on the positive side. On the negative side, every school on the list except Arnold's secularism, which was less a school than a plea for one, is an attack on disinterestedness of mind and imagination, though none of them meant to be so. And Arnold, who meant just the opposite, helped them at their business by seeing too much necessity in the offing. All of them either accepted or revolted violently against a predetermined necessity; none of them was able to choose necessity or to identify it with his will. None of them was apparently acquainted with the sense of our Latin mottoes. Their only causes were Lost Causes; their only individuals were atoms; they reflected their time, as schools must.

The world has about now caught up with these trains of ideas, these images, trends, habits, patterns, these tendencies toward either mass action or isolated action — equally violent whether in attraction or repulsion. It is a world of engineers and anarchs; rather like the Roman world when the impulse of Vergil and the Emperor Augustus had died out and the impulse of Benedict and Augustine had not yet altered the direction and aspect of the general momentum. It is a world alive and moving but which does not understand itself.

Of this world individual artists have given a much better account than the doctrines of their schools would suggest, and they have done so for two reasons. The arts cannot help reacting directly and conventionally to what is actual in their own time; nor can the arts help, whether consciously or not, working into their masterpieces what has survived of the full tradition — however they may contort or corrupt it. They deal with life or experience itself, both what is new and what is accumulated, inherited, still living. They cannot come *de novo*. They cannot help, therefore, creating at a disinterested level, despite themselves. That is why they constitute a resource of what is not new — the greater part of ourselves — and a means of focusing what is new, all that necessarily aggravates us and tears at our nerve ends in our friction with it. That is why Chartres Cathedral survives better than the schools of the Bishop of Chartres; though both were equally vital in their time.

Consider in this light what seem to be the masterpieces of our time. Consider the poetry of Eliot, Yeats, Valéry, Rilke; the novels of Joyce, Gide, Hemingway, Proust, Mann, Kafka; the plays of Shaw, Pirandello,

O'Neill; the music of Stravinsky, Bloch, Bartok, Ravel, Satie, Schoen-
berg; the paintings of Matisse, Picasso, Rouault, Marin, Hartley; the
sculpture of Maillol, Brancusi, Faggi, LaChaise, Zorach, Archipenko,
Moore. Think also, but at another level, not easy to keep in strict parallel, of the architecture of Leviathan: the railway station at Philadelphia, the Pentagon, the skyscrapers, the gasoline stations, the highway
systems, the East and West Side highways, apartment houses each a
small city, and the interminable multiple dwellings. Think too of the
beautiful bridges which connect or traverse eyesores: the Washington
Bridge, the Pulaski Skyway. Lastly, for architecture, think of the National Parks, with their boulevards running at mountain peak.

What an expression of an intolerable, disintegrating, irrational
world: a doomed world, nevertheless surviving, throwing up value after
value with inexhaustible energy but without a principle in sight. And how
difficult to understand the arts which throw up the values. Only Hemingway and Maillol in the roster above perhaps made works which seem
readily accessible when seriously approached. Shaw is as difficult as Joyce,
Mann as Kafka, if you really look into them. The difficulties arise, it seems
to me, partly because of the conditions of society outlined above as they
affect the audience and partly because of these same conditions as they
affect the artist at his work. The two are not the same, though they are
related. The audience is able to bring less to the work of art than under
the conditions of the old culture, and the artist is required to bring more.
What has changed its aspect is the way the institutions, the conceptions,
the experience of culture gets into the arts. What has happened is what
was said above: almost the whole job of culture has been dumped on
the artist's hands.

It is at this point that we begin to get at the burden of criticism in our
time. It is, to put it one way, to make bridges between the society and
the arts: to prepare the audience for its art and to prepare the arts for
their artists. The two kinds of preparation may sometimes be made in
one structure; but there is more often a difference of emphasis required.
Performance, the condition we are after, cannot mean the same thing to
the audience and the artist. The audience needs instruction in the lost
skill of symbolic thinking. The arts need rather to be shown how their
old roles can be played in new conditions. To do either, both need to be
allied to the intellectual habits of the time. Besides analysis, elucidation,
and comparison, which Eliot once listed as the functions of criticism,
criticism in our time must also come to judgment.

If we look at the dominant development in criticism in English during the last thirty years — all that Mr. Ransom means by the New
Criticism — with its fineness of analysis, its expertness of elucidation,
and its ramifying specialization of detail — we must see how natural,

and at bottom how facile, a thing it has been. It has been the critics'
way of being swept along, buoyed more by the rush than by the body of
things. It is a criticism, that is, which has dealt almost exclusively
either with the executive technique of poetry (and only with a part of
that) or with the general verbal techniques of language. Most of its
practitioners have been men gifted in penetrating the private sym-
bolisms and elucidating the language of all that part of modern poetry
we have come to call the school of Donne. With a different criticism
possibly another part of modern poetry might have become dominant,
say the apocalyptic school — though of course I cannot myself think so.
In any case, it was a criticism created to cope with and develop the
kind of poetry illustrated by Eliot's *Waste Land* and Yeats's *Tower*,
two poems which made desperate attempts to reassert the tradition
under modern conditions: Eliot by Christianity, Yeats by a private philosophy. Eminently suited for the *initial* stages of the criticism of this
poetry, it has never been suited to the later stages of criticism; neither
Eliot nor Yeats has been compared or judged because there has been no
criticism able to take those burdens. For the rest, the "new criticism" has
been suited for *some* older poetry, but less because of the nature of the
poetry than because of the limitation of the modern reader. For most
older poetry it is not suited for anything but sidelights, and has therefore made misjudgments when applied. It is useless for Dante, Chaucer,
Goethe, or Racine. Applied to drama it is disfiguring, as it is to the late
seventeenth- and all the eighteenth-century poetry. Yet it has had to be
used and abused because there has seemed no other way of re-creating
— in the absence of a positive culture outside poetry — a verbal sensibility capable of coping with the poetry at all. In a stable society with a
shared culture capable of convictions, masteries, and vital dogmas, such
a criticism might have needed only its parallel developments for the
novel and the play and the older forms of all literature; such a society
does not need much criticism. But in an unstable society like ours, precisely because the burden put upon the arts is so unfamiliar and so
extensive (it is always the maximum burden in intensity) a multiple
burden is put upon criticism to bring the art to full performance. We
have to compare and judge as well as analyze and elucidate. We have to
make plain not only what people are reading, but also — as Augustine
and the other fathers had to do with the scriptures — what they are
reading about.

Here I do not wish to be misunderstood. Critics are not fathers of a
new church. I speak from a secular point of view confronting what I
believe to be a secular world which is not well understood; and I suppose what I want criticism to do can as well as not be described as the
development of aesthetic judgment — the judgment of the rational im-

agination — to conform with the vast increase of material which seems in our time capable only of aesthetic experience. This is not to define a revelation or create a society. It is to define and explore the representations in art of what is actually going on in existing society. I see no reason why all forms of the word *aesthetic* cannot be restored to good society among literary critics by remembering its origin in a Greek word meaning to perceive, and remembering also its gradual historical limitation to what is perceived or felt — that is, what is actually there — in the arts. I have here the company of Bergson who thought that the serious arts gave the aesthetic experience of the true nature of what the institutions of society are meant to control. And in another way, I have more support than I want in the philosophy of Whitehead, who found that the sciences in new growth, far from giving us knowledge with relation among its parts, give us instead abstractions good for practical manipulation but conformable only to a mystery. As a consequence, his philosophy of organism, with its attribution of feeling relations everywhere, is an aesthetic philosophy; in which knowledge comes to us as an aesthetic experience.

We do not need to go so far as Whitehead. The sort of thing that is wanted here to go on with seems to show clearly in James Joyce, whose *Ulysses* is the direct aesthetic experience of the breakdown of the whole Graeco-Christian world, not only in emotion but also in concept. Or again, Mann's *Magic Mountain* is the projected aesthetic experience of both that whole world and the sickness which is breaking it down. And again, Gide's *Counterfeiters* is a kind of gratuitous aesthetic experience — a free possibility — of what is happening along with the breakdown. Lastly, Eliot's religious poetry is a partly utopian and partly direct aesthetic experience of the actual Christian life today. That is what these works are about, and they cannot be judged aesthetically until full stock has been taken of what they are about. For us, they create their subjects; and indeed it is the most conspicuous thing about them that they do so. On each of these authors — even Eliot in his kind of reference — the whole substance of his subject is a necessary part of the aesthetic experience of it. It is for that reason that we have to judge the subject as well as what is done with it. To exaggerate only a little, in the world as it is, there is no way to get a mastery of the subject except in the aesthetic experience. How do we go about doing so?

That is, how does criticism enlarge its aesthetics to go with the enlargement of aesthetic experience? Here we must take again the risk of generalization, and we must begin with a generalization to get what the sciences have done with aesthetics out of the way. If we do not get rid of them by generalization we cannot get rid of them at all, for in detail their techniques are very tempting. Let us say then that psychology turns aesthetics into the mechanics of perception, that scientific logic turns it into semasiology, just as technical philosophers had already turned it into a branch of epistemology. All these studies are trouble-makers and lead, like our social studies, to the proliferation of a sequence of insoluble and irrelevant problems so far as the critic of literature is concerned. Let us put it provisionally, that for the literary critic aesthetics comprises the study of superficial and mechanical executive techniques, partly in themselves, but also and mainly in relation to the ulterior techniques of conceptual form and of symbolic form. I do not say that one of these is deeper or more important than another, certainly not in isolation. But let us take them in the order given, and generalize a program of work.

By superficial and mechanical executive techniques I mean the whole rationale of management and manipulation through more or less arbitrary devices which can be learned, which can be made elegant, and which are to some extent the creatures of taste or fashion so far as particular choice is concerned. In some lucky cases they may be the sole preoccupation of the working artist, as in some unlucky cases they may be the one aspect of his work to which he seemingly pays least attention. In our own day they are troublesome to the extent that they are ignored in an abeyance from which they ought to be redeemed. It would seem to me, for example, that a considerable amount of potentially excellent verse fails to make its way because the uses of meter — in the sense that all verse has meter — are not well understood, though they are now beginning again to be played with: Mr. Eliot has just resorted to the metrics of Johnson and Milton. The critic who is capable of doing so ought to examine into the meters of his victims. Similarly, the full narrative mode is in little use by serious novelists, and the full dramatic mode is not in much more use; yet these are the basic modes of a man telling a story. If only because they are difficult, the critic ought to argue for them when he sees a weakness which might have been turned into a strength by their use. Again, and related to the two previous examples, there is a great deal of obscurity in modern writing which could be cleared up if writers could be forced (only by criticism) to develop a skill in making positive statement, whether generalized or particular, whether in verse or in prose. Statement may make art great and ought not to be subject to fashion.

And so on. The critic can have little authority as a pedagogue. The main study of executive techniques will always be, to repeat, in relation to the ulterior techniques of conceptual and symbolic form. By conceptual techniques I mean the rationale of what the artist does with his dominant convictions, or obsessions, or insights, or visions, and how they are translated into major stresses of human relations as they are actually experienced. Here we are concerned with the aesthetics of the idea in relation to the actual, of the rational in relation to what is rationalized. In Dostoevski, for example, we are interested in his conception of the Double only as we see what happens to it in the character of Versilov, or Raskolnikov, or Dmitri Karamazov. In Joyce's *Ulysses* it is not the Homeric pattern of father and son that counts, but what happens to the conception of intransigence in Stephen in concert and conflict with that transigent man Bloom. So in the later poems of Yeats, the concepts of the Phases of the Moon are interesting as they work or fail to work in the chaos and anarchy and order of actual lyric emotions. On a more generalized level, it is through concern with conceptual techniques that one notes that the European novels of greatest stature seem to follow, not the conceptual pattern of Greek tragedy but the pattern of Christian rebirth, conversion, or change of heart; which is why novels do not have tragic heroes. But examples are endless.

And all of them, as those just cited, would tend if pursued to lead us into the territory of symbolic techniques which underlies and transcends them. I am not satisfied with the term. By symbolic techniques I mean what happens in the arts — *what gets into the arts* — that makes them relatively inexhaustible so long as they are understood. I mean what happens in the arts by means of fresh annunciations of residual or traditional forces, whether in the language, culture, or institutions of the artist's society. I mean those forces that operate in the arts which are greater than ourselves and come from beyond or under ourselves. But I am not satisfied with the definitions any more than I am with the term. It may be I mean invokable forces, or raw forces, the force of reality, whatever reality may be, pressing into and transforming our actual experience. It is what bears us and what we cannot bear except through the intervention of one of the great modes of the mind, religion, philosophy, or art, which, giving us the illusion of distance and control, makes *them,* too, seem forces greater than ourselves. It is in the figure of Dante himself in the *Divine Comedy,* Faustus in *Faustus,* Hamlet and Lear in *Hamlet* and *Lear,* Emma Bovary in *Madame Bovary,* all the brothers in *The Brothers Karamazov.* It is in the conjunction of the gods of the river and of the sea with the Christian gods in Eliot's *Dry Salvages.* It is the force of reality pressing into the actuality of symbolic form. Its technique is the technique of so concentrating or combining the known techniques as to discover or release that force. It is for this purpose and in this way that the executive, conceptual, and symbolic techniques go rationally together: the logic, the rhetoric, and the poetic; they make together the rationale of that enterprise in the discovery of life which is art. But the arts are not life, though in the sense of this argument they may make a rationale for discovering life. Whether they do or not, and how far, is the act of judgment that is also the last act in bringing particular works of art to full performance. Because the arts are imperfect, they can be judged only imperfectly by aesthetic means. They must be judged, therefore, by the declaration and elucidation of identity in terms of the whole enterprise which they feed, and of which they are the play, the aesthetic experience. There is a confusion here that cannot be clarified for it is a confusion of real things, as words are confused in a line of verse, the better the line the more completely, so that we cannot tell which ones govern the others. The confusion is, that it is through the aesthetic experience of it that we discover, and discover again, what life is, and that at present, if our account of it is correct, we also discover what our culture is. It is therefore worthwhile considering the usefulness of a sequence of rational critical judgments upon the art of our time as an aid in determining the identity, the meaning in itself, of present society. Such a sequence of judgments might transform us who judge more than the art judged.

Here perhaps is a good point to sweep some bad rubbish into the bins. Critical judgment need not be arrogant in its ambitions, only in its failures. Nor is it concerned with ranks and hierarchies, except incidentally. What I mean by judgment is what Aristotle would have meant by the fullest possible declaratory proposition of identity. Again, the ideal of judgment — no more to be reached by critics than by other men — is theological: as a soul is judged finally, quite apart from its history, for what it really is at the moment of judgment. Our human approximation of such judgment will be reached if we keep the ideal of it in mind and with that aid make our fullest act of recognition. Judgment is the critic's best recognition.

Thus it is now clear that my purpose in proposing a heavy burden for criticism is, to say the least of it, evangelical. What I want to evangelize in the arts is rational intent, rational statement, and rational technique; and I want to do it through technical judgment, clarifying judgment, and the judgment of discovery, which together I call rational judgment. I do not know if I should have enough eloquence to persuade even myself to consider such a burden for criticism, did I not have, not this time as precautions but as mentors, my three Latin mottoes. *Omnis intellectus omniformis est. Fides quaerens intellectus. Corruptio optima pessima.* They point the risk, and make it worth taking.

IAN WATT

The First Paragraph of
The Ambassadors: An Explication

When I was asked if I would do a piece of explication at this conference, I was deep in Henry James, and beginning *The Ambassadors*: so the passage chose itself; but just what was explication, and how did one do it to prose? [1] I take it that whereas explanation, from *explanare*, suggests a mere making plain by spreading out, explication, from *explicare*, implies a progressive unfolding of a series of literary implications, and thus partakes of our modern preference for multiplicity in method and meaning: explanation assumes an ultimate simplicity, explication assumes complexity.

Historically, the most developed tradition of explication is presumably that which developed out of medieval textual exegesis and became the chief method of literary instruction in French secondary and higher education in the late nineteenth century. *Explication de texte* in France reflects the rationalism of nineteenth-century Positivist scholarship. At its worst the routine application of the method resembles a sort of bayonet drill in which the exposed body of literature is riddled with etymologies and dates before being despatched in a harrowingly insensitive *résumé*. At its best, however, *explication de texte* can be solidly illuminating, and it then serves to remind us that a piece of literature is not necessarily violated if we give systematic attention to such matters as its author, its historical setting, and the formal properties of its language.

Practical Criticism, on the other hand, as it was developed at Cambridge by I. A. Richards, continues the tradition of the British Empiricists. Inductive rather than deductive, it makes a point of excluding linguistic and historical considerations, so as to derive — in appearance at least — all the literary values of a work empirically from the words on the page. In the last thirty years the emphasis of Practical Criticism on the autonomy of the text has revolutionised the approach to literary studies, and has proved itself a technique of supreme value for teaching

SOURCE: Reprinted by permission from *Essays in Criticism*, Volume X (1960), pp. 250–274.

and examining students; I myself certainly believe that its use should be expanded rather than curtailed. Yet, at least in the form in which I picked it up as a student and have later attempted to pass it on as a teacher, both its pedagogical effects and its basic methodological assumptions seem to me to be open to serious question. For many reasons. Its air of objectivity confers a spurious authority on a process that is often only a rationalisation of an unexamined judgment, and that must always be to some extent subjective; its exclusion of historical factors seems to authorise a more general anti-historicism; and — though this objection is perhaps less generally accepted — it contains an inherent critical bias in the assumption that the part is a complete enough reflection of the literary whole to be profitably appreciated and discussed in isolation from its context. How far this is true, or how far it can be made to appear so by a well-primed practitioner, is a matter of opinion; but it is surely demonstrable that Practical Criticism tends to find the most merit in the kind of writing which has virtues that are in some way separable from their larger context; it favours kinds of writing that are richly concrete in themselves, stylistically brilliant, or composed in relatively small units. It is therefore better suited to verse than to prose; and better suited to certain kinds of either than to others where different and less concentrated merits are appropriate, as in the novel.

As for its pedagogical effects — and here again I have mainly my own past experience in mind — Practical Criticism surely tends to sensitise us towards objects only within a certain range of magnitude: below that threshold it becomes subjective and impressionist, paying very little attention to the humble facts of the grammar and syntax of the words on the page; while, at the other extreme, it often ignores the larger meaning, and the literary and historical contexts of that meaning.

As a practical matter these restrictions may all be necessary for the pupil and salutary for the teacher; and I mention them mainly to justify my present attempt to develop the empirical and inductive methods of Practical Criticism in such a way as to deal with those elements in a literary text whose vibrations are so high or so low that we Ricardian dogs have not yet been trained to bark at them.

It is mainly in these penumbral areas, of course, that the French *explication de texte* habitually operates; but its analysis of grammar and of the literary and historical background are usually a disconnected series of discrete demonstrations which stop short of the unifying critical synthesis that one hopes for. Until fairly recently the same could have been said, and perhaps with greater emphasis, about the German tradition of literary scholarship, with its almost entirely independent pursuit of philology and philosophy. More recent trends in *Stilforschung* however — of which Wolfgang Clemen's *The Development of Shakespeare's*

Imagery (Bonn, 1936), was an early example — come closer to, and indeed partly reflect, the more empirical Anglo-American models of literary criticism; while, even more promising perhaps for the study of prose, though seemingly quite independent of the influence of Practical Criticism, is the development, mainly from Romance philology, of what has come to be called "stylistics."

For my purposes, however, it remains not so much a method as a small group of isolated, though spectacular, individual triumphs. I yield to no one in my admiration for Leo Spitzer's *Linguistics and Literary History* (Baltimore, 1948), or for the continual excitement and illumination offered in Erich Auerbach's *Mimesis* (1946: trans. Willard Trask, Princeton, N.J., 1953); their achievements, however, strike me mainly as tributes to the historical imagination and philosophical understanding of the German mind at its best; I find their brilliant commentaries on words or phrases or passages essentially subjective; and if I am tempted to emulate the *bravura* with which they take off from the word on the page to leap into the farthest empyreans of *Kulturgeschichte,* I soon discover that the Cambridge east winds have condemned me to less giddy modes of critical transport.

Yet what other models are there to help one to analyse a paragraph of Jamesian prose? Some of the historical studies of prose style could, conceivably, be applied; but I am fearful of ending up with the proposition that James was a Ciceronian — with Senecan elements, of course, like everyone else. As for the new linguistics, the promises as regards literary analysis seem greater than the present rewards: the most practical consequence of my exposure to Charles Fries's *The Structure of English: An Introduction to the Construction of English Sentences* (New York, 1952), for example, was to deprive me of the innocent pleasure that comes from imagining you know the names of things. Structural linguistics in general is mainly (and rightly) concerned with problems of definition and description at a considerably more basic level of linguistic usage than the analysis of the literary effect of Henry James's grammatical particularities seems to require.

Perhaps the most promising signs of the gaps being filled have come from what are — in that particular area — amateurs: from Francis Berry's *Poets' Grammar* (London, 1958), or Donald Davie's *Articulate Energy* (London, 1955). But they don't help much with prose, of course, and they aren't basically concerned with grammatical structure in the ordinary sense; although Davie's notion that the principle of continuity in poetry is, after all, primarily grammatical and rational, at least lessens the separation between the stylistic domains of poetry and prose, and suggests some ways of studying how syntax channels expressive force.

Virtually helpless,[2] then, I must face the James passage alone as far as any fully developed and acceptable technique for explicating prose is concerned; but there seem to be good reasons why practical criticism should be supplemented by some of the approaches of French and German scholarship, and by whatever else will lead one from the words on the page to matters as low as syntax and as high as ideas, or the total literary structure.

I

Strether's first question, when he reached the hotel, was about his friend; yet on his learning that Waymarsh was apparently not to arrive till evening he was not wholly disconcerted. A telegram from him bespeaking a room "only if not noisy," reply paid, was produced for the
5   inquirer at the office, so that the understanding they should meet at Chester rather than at Liverpool remained to that extent sound. The same secret principle, however, that had prompted Strether not absolutely to desire Waymarsh's presence at the dock, that had led him thus to postpone for a few hours his enjoyment of it, now operated to
10   make him feel he could still wait without disappointment. They would dine together at the worst, and, with all respect to dear old Waymarsh —if not even, for that matter, to himself — there was little fear that in the sequel they shouldn't see enough of each other. The principle I have just mentioned as operating had been, with the most newly
15   disembarked of the two men, wholly instinctive — the fruit of a sharp sense that, delightful as it would be to find himself looking, after so much separation, into his comrade's face, his business would be a trifle bungled should he simply arrange for this countenance to present itself to the nearing steamer as the first "note" of Europe. Mixed with
20   everything was the apprehension, already, on Strether's part, that it would, at best, throughout, prove the note of Europe in quite a sufficient degree.[3]

It seems a fairly ordinary sort of prose, but for its faint air of elaborate portent; and on second reading its general quality reminds one of what Strether is later to observe — approvingly — in Maria Gostrey: an effect of "expensive, subdued suitability." There's certainly nothing particularly striking in the diction or syntax; none of the immediate drama or rich description that we often get at the beginning of novels; and certainly none of the sensuous concreteness that, until recently, was regarded as a chief criterion of good prose in our long post-imagistic phase: if anything, the passage is conspicuously un-sensuous and un-concrete, a little dull perhaps, and certainly not easy reading.

The difficulty isn't one of particularly long or complicated sentences: actually they're of fairly usual length: I make it an average of 41 words;

a little, but not very much, longer than James's average of 35 (in Book 2, ch. 2. of *The Ambassadors,* according to R. W. Short's count, in his very useful article "The Sentence Structure of Henry James" *American Literature,* XVIII [March 1946], 71–88).[4] The main cause of difficulty seems rather to come from what may be called the delayed specification of referents: "Strether" and "the hotel" and "his friend" are mentioned before we are told who or where they are. But this difficulty is so intimately connected with James's general narrative technique that it may be better to begin with purely verbal idiosyncrasies, which are more easily isolated. The most distinctive ones in the passage seem to be these: a preference for non-transitive verbs; many abstract nouns; much use of "that"; a certain amount of elegant variation to avoid piling up personal pronouns and adjectives such as "he," "his" and "him"; and the presence of a great many negatives and near-negatives.

By the preference for non-transitive verbs I mean three related habits: a great reliance on copulatives — "Strether's first question *was* about his friend"; "*was* apparently not to arrive": a frequent use of the passive voice — "*was* not wholly *disconcerted";* "a telegram . . . *was produced";* "his business *would be* a trifle *bungled*": and the employment of many intransitive verbs — "the understanding . . . remained . . . sound"; "the . . . principle . . . operated to." My count of all the verbs in the indicative would give a total of 14 passive, copulative, or intransitive uses as opposed to only 6 transitive ones: and there are in addition frequent infinitive, participial, or gerundial uses of transitive verbs, in all of which the active nature of the subject-verb-and-object sequence is considerably abated — "on his learning"; "bespeaking a room"; "not absolutely to desire"; "led him thus to postpone."

This relative infrequency of transitive verbal usages in the passage is associated with the even more pronounced tendency towards using abstract nouns as subjects of main or subordinate clauses: "question"; "understanding"; "the same secret principle"; "the principle"; "his business." If one takes only the main clauses, there are four such abstract nouns as subjects, while only three main clauses have concrete and particular subjects ("he," or "they").[5]

I detail these features only to establish that in this passage, at least, there is a clear quantitative basis for the common enough view that James's late prose style is characteristically abstract; more explicitly, that the main grammatical subjects are very often nouns for mental ideas, "question," "principle," etc.; and that the verbs — because they are mainly used either non-transitively, or in infinitive, participial and gerundial forms — tend to express states of being rather than particular finite actions affecting objects.

The main use of abstractions is to deal at the same time with many objects or events rather than single and particular ones: and we use verbs that denote states of being rather than actions for exactly the same reason — their much more general applicability. But in this passage, of course, James isn't in the ordinary sense making abstract or general statements; it's narrative, not expository prose; what need exploring, therefore, are the particular literary imperatives which impose on his style so many of the verbal and syntactical qualities of abstract and general discourse; of expository rather than narrative prose.

Consider the first sentence. The obvious narrative way of making things particular and concrete would presumably be "When Strether reached the hotel, he first asked 'Has Mr. Waymarsh arrived yet?'" Why does James say it the way he does? One effect is surely that, instead of a sheer stated event, we get a very special view of it; the mere fact that actuality has been digested into reported speech — the question "was about his friend" — involves a narrator to do the job, to interpret the action, and also a presumed audience that he does it for, and by implication, the heat of the action itself must have cooled off somewhat for the translation and analysis of the events into this form of statement to have had time to occur. Lastly, making the subject of the sentence "question" rather than "he," has the effect of subordinating the particular actor, and therefore the particular act, to a much more general perspective: mental rather than physical, and subjective rather than objective; "question" is a word which involves analysis of a physical event into terms of meaning and intention: it involves, in fact, both Strether's mind and the narrator's. The narrator's, because he interprets Strether's act: if James had sought the most concrete method of taking us into Strether's mind — " 'Has Mr. Waymarsh come yet?' I at once asked" — he would have obviated the need for the implied external categoriser of Strether's action. But James disliked the "mere platitude of statement" involved in first-person narrative; partly, presumably, because it would merge Strether's consciousness into the narrative, and not isolate it for the reader's inspection. For such isolation, a more expository method is needed: no confusion of subject and object, as in first-person narration, but a narrator forcing the reader to pay attention to James's primary objective — Strether's mental and subjective state.

The "multidimensional" quality of the narrative, with its continual implication of a community of three minds — Strether's, James's, and the reader's — isn't signalled very obviously until the fourth sentence — "The principle I have just mentioned as operating . . ."; but it's already been established tacitly in every detail of diction and structure, and it remains pervasive. One reason for the special demand James's fictional prose makes on our attention is surely that there are always at least three levels of development — all of them subjective: the characters' awareness of events: the narrator's seeing of them; and our own trailing perception of the relation between these two.

The primary location of the narrative in a mental rather than a physical continuum gives the narrative a great freedom from the restrictions of particular time and place. Materially, we are, of course, in Chester, at the hotel — characteristically "the hotel" because a fully particularised specification — "The Pied Bull Inn" say — would be an irrelevant brute fact which would distract attention from the mental train of thought we are invited to partake in. But actually we don't have any pressing sense of time and place: we feel ourselves to be spectators, rather specifically, of Strether's thought processes, which easily and imperceptibly range forwards and backwards both in time and space. Sentence three, for example, begins in the past, at the Liverpool dock; sentence four looks forward to the reunion later that day, and to its many sequels: such transitions of time and place are much easier to effect when the main subjects of the sentences are abstract: a "principle" exists independently of its context.

The multiplicity of relations — between narrator and object, and between the ideas in Strether's mind — held in even suspension throughout the narrative, is presumably the main explanation for the number of "thats" in the passage, as well as of the several examples of elegant variation. There are 9 "thats" — only two of them demonstrative and the rest relative pronouns (or conjunctions or particles if you prefer those terms); actually there were no less than three more of them in the first edition, which James removed from the somewhat more colloquial and informal New York edition; while there are several other "thats" implied — in "the principle [that] I have just mentioned," for instance.

The number of "thats" follows from two habits already noted in the passage. "That" characteristically introduces relative clauses dealing not with persons but with objects, including abstractions; and it is also used to introduce reported speech — "on his learning that Waymarsh" — not "Mr. Waymarsh isn't here." Both functions are combined in the third sentence where we get a triple definition of a timeless idea based on the report of three chronologically separate events "the same secret principle that had prompted Strether not absolutely to desire Waymarsh's presence at the dock, that had led him thus to postpone for a few hours his enjoyment of it, now operated to make him feel that he could still wait without disappointment."

Reported rather than direct speech also increases the pressure towards elegant variation: the use, for example, in sentence 1 of "his friend," where in direct speech it would be "Mr. Waymarsh" (and the reply — "He hasn't come yet"). In the second sentence — "a telegram . . . was produced for the inquirer" — "inquirer" is needed because "him" has already been used for Waymarsh just above; of course, "the inquirer" is logical enough after the subject of the first sentence has been an abstract noun — "question"; and the epithet also gives James an opportunity for underlining the ironic distance and detachment with which we are invited to view his dedicated "inquirer," Strether. Later, when Strether is "the most newly disembarked of the two men," we see how both elegant variation and the grammatical subordination of physical events are related to the general Jamesian tendency to present characters and actions on a plane of abstract categorisation; the mere statement, "Mr. Waymarsh had already been in England for [so many] months," would itself go far to destroy the primarily mental continuum in which the paragraph as a whole exists.

The last general stylistic feature of the passage to be listed above was the use of negative forms. There are 6 "noes" or "nots" in the first 4 sentences; four implied negatives — "postpone"; "without disappointment"; "at the worst"; "there was little fear": and two qualifications that modify positiveness of affirmation — "not wholly," and "to that extent." This abundance of negatives has no doubt several functions: it enacts Strether's tendency to hesitation and qualification; it puts the reader into the right judicial frame of mind; and it has the further effect of subordinating concrete events to their mental reflection; "Waymarsh was not to arrive," for example, is not a concrete statement of a physical event: it is subjective — because it implies an expectation in Strether's mind (which was not fulfilled); and it has an abstract quality — because while Waymarsh's arriving would be particular and physical, his *not* arriving is an idea, a non-action. More generally, James's great use of negatives or near-negatives may also, perhaps, be regarded as part of his subjective and abstractive tendency: there are no negatives in nature but only in the human consciousness.

II

The most obvious grammatical features of what Richard Chase has called Henry James's "infinitely syntactical language" (*The American Novel and its Tradition,* New York, 1957), can, then, be shown to reflect the essential imperatives of his narrative point of view; and they could therefore lead into a discussion of the philosophical qualities of his mind, as they are discussed, for example, by Dorothea Krook in her notable article "The Method of the Later Works of Henry James" (*London Magazine,* I [1954], 55–70); our passage surely exemplifies James's power "to generalise to the limit the particulars of experience," and with it the characteristic way in which both his "perceptions of the world itself, and his perceptions of the logic of the world . . . happen simultaneously, are part of a single comprehensive experience." Another aspect of the connection between James's metaphysic and his method as a novelist has inspired a stimulating stylistic study — Carlo Izzo's "Henry James, Scrittore Sintattico" (*Studi Americani*, II [1956], 127– 142). The connection between thought and style finds its historical perspective in John Henry Raleigh's illuminating study "Henry James: The Poetics of Empiricism" (*PMLA*, LXVI [1951], 107–123), which establishes connections between Lockean epistemology and James's extreme, almost anarchic, individualism; while this epistemological preoccupation, which is central to Quentin Anderson's view of how James worked out his father's cosmology in fictional terms (*The American Henry James*, New Brunswick, 1957), also leads towards another large general question, the concern with "point of view," which became a crucial problem in the history and criticism of fiction under the influence of the sceptical relativism of the late nineteenth century.

In James's case, the problem is fairly complicated. He may be classed as an "Impressionist," concerned, that is, to show not so much the events themselves, but the impressions which they make on the characters. But James's continual need to generalise and place and order, combined with his absolute demand for a point of view that would be plastic enough to allow him freedom for the formal "architectonics" of the novelists' craft, eventually involved him in a very idiosyncratic kind of multiple Impressionism: idiosyncratic because the dual presence of Strether's consciousness and of that of the narrator, who translates what he sees there into more general terms, makes the narrative point of view both intensely individual and yet ultimately social.

Another possible direction of investigation would be to show that the abstractness and indirection of James's style are essentially the result of this characteristic multiplicity of his vision. There is, for example, the story reported by Edith Wharton that after his first stroke James told Lady Prothero that "in the very act of falling . . . he heard in the room a voice which was distinctly, it seemed, not his own, saying: 'So here it is at last, the distinguished thing.'" James, apparently, could not but see even his own most fateful personal experience, except as evoked by some other observer's voice in terms of the long historical and literary tradition of death. Carlo Izzo regards this tendency as typical of the Alexandrian style, where there is a marked disparity between the rich inheritance of the means of literary expression, and the meaner creative world which it is used to express; but the defence of the Jamesian habit of mind must surely be that what the human vision shares with that of animals is presumably the perception of concrete images, not the power to conceive universals: such was Aristotle's notion of man's distinguishing capacity. The universals in the present context are presumably the awareness that

behind every petty individual circumstance there ramifies an endless network of general moral, social and historical relations. Henry James's style
can therefore be seen as a supremely civilised effort to relate every event
and every moment of life to the full complexity of its circumambient
conditions.

Obviously James's multiple awareness can go too far; and in the later
novels it often poses the special problem that we do not quite know
whether the awareness implied in a given passage is the narrator's or that
of his character. Most simply, a pronoun referring to the subject of a
preceding clause is always liable to give trouble if one hasn't been very
much aware of what the grammatical subject of that preceding clause
was; in the last sentence of the paragraph, for example, "the apprehension, already, on Strether's part, that . . . it would, at best, . . . prove
the 'note' of Europe," "it" refers to Waymarsh's countenance: but this
isn't at first obvious; which is no doubt why, in his revision of the periodical version for the English edition James replaced "it" by "he" —
simpler, grammatically, but losing some of the ironic visual precision of
the original. More seriously, because the narrator's consciousness and
Strether's are both present, we often don't know whose mental operations
and evaluative judgments are involved in particular cases. We pass, for
instance, from the objective analysis of sentence 3 where the analytic
terminology of "the same secret principle" must be the responsibility of
the narrator, to what must be a verbatim quotation of Strether's mind in
sentence 4: "with all respect to dear old Waymarsh" is obviously
Strether's licensed familiarity.

But although the various difficulties of tense, voice, and reference require a vigilance of attention in the reader which some have found too
much to give, they are not in themselves very considerable: and what
perhaps is much more in need of attention is how the difficulties arising
from the multiplicity of points of view don't by any means prevent James
from ordering all the elements of his narrative style into an amazingly
precise means of expression: and it is this positive, and in the present
case, as it seems to me, triumphant, mastery of the difficulties which I
want next to consider.

Our passage is not, I think, James either at his most memorable or at
his most idiosyncratic: *The Ambassadors* is written with considerably
sobriety and has, for example, little of the vivid and direct style of the
early part of *The Wings of the Dove,* or of the happy symbolic complexities of *The Golden Bowl.* Still, the passage is fairly typical of the later
James; and I think it can be proved that all or at least nearly all the
idiosyncrasies of diction or syntax in the present passage are fully justified by the particular emphases they create.

The most flagrant eccentricity of diction is presumably that where

James writes "the most newly disembarked of the two men" (lines 14–15). "Most" may very well be a mere slip; and it must certainly seem indefensible to any one who takes it as an absolute rule that the comparative must always be used when only two items are involved.[6] But a defence is at least possible. "Most newly disembarked" means something rather different from "more newly disembarked." James, it may be surmised, did not want to compare the recency of the two men's arrival, but to inform us that Strether's arrival was "very" or as we might say, "most" recent; the use of the superlative also had the advantage of suggesting the long and fateful tradition of transatlantic disembarcations in general.

The reasons for the other main syntactical idiosyncrasies in the passage are much clearer. In the first part of the opening sentence, for example, the separation of subject — "question" — from verb — "was" — by the longish temporal clause "when he reached the hotel," is no doubt a dislocation of normal sentence structure; but, of course, "Strether" must be the first word of the novel: while, even more important, the delayed placing of the temporal clause, forces a pause after "question" and thus gives it a very significant resonance. Similarly with the last sentence; it has several peculiarities, of which the placing of "throughout" seems the most obvious. The sentence has three parts: the first and last are comparatively straightforward, but the middle is a massed block of portentous qualifications: "Mixed with everything was the apprehension — already, on Strether's part, that he would, at best, throughout, — prove the note of Europe in quite a sufficient degree." The echoing doom started by the connotation of "apprehension" — reverberates through "already," ("much more to come later") "on Strether's part" ("even he knows") and "at best" ("the worst has been envisaged, too"); but it is the final collapse of the terse rhythm of the parenthesis that isolates the rather awkwardly placed "throughout," and thus enables James to sound the fine full fatal note; there is no limit to the poignant eloquence of "throughout." It was this effect, of course, which dictated the preceding inversion which places "apprehension" not at the start of the sentence, but in the middle where, largely freed from its syntactical nexus, it may be directly exposed to its salvos of qualification.

The mockingly fateful emphasis on "throughout" tells us, if nothing had before, that James's tone is in the last analysis ironic, comic, or better, as I shall try to suggest, humorous. The general reasons for this have already been suggested. To use Maynard Mack's distinction (in his Preface to *Joseph Andrews*, Rinehart Editions, New York, 1948), "the comic artist subordinates the presentation of life as experience, where the relationship between ourselves and the characters experiencing it is a primary one, to the presentation of life as a spectacle, where the primary relation is between himself and us as onlookers." In the James passage, the primacy of the relation between the narrator and the reader has already been noted, as has its connection with the abstraction of the diction, which brings home the distance between the narrator and Strether. Of course, the application of abstract diction to particular persons always tends towards irony,[7] because it imposes a dual way of looking at them: few of us can survive being presented as general representatives of humanity.

The paragraph, of course, is based on one of the classic contradictions in psychological comedy — Strether's reluctance to admit to himself that he has very mixed feelings about his friend: and James develops this with the narrative equivalent of *commedia dell'arte* technique: virtuoso feats of ironic balance, comic exaggeration, and deceptive hesitation conduct us on a complicated progress towards the foreordained illumination.

In structure, to begin with, the six sentences form three groups of two: each pair of them gives one aspect of Strether's delay; and they are arranged in an ascending order of complication so that the fifth sentence — 72 words — is almost twice as long as any other, and is succeeded by the final sentence, the punch line, which is noticeably the shortest — 26 words. The development of the ideas is as controlled as the sentence structure. Strether is obviously a man with an enormous sense of responsibility about personal relationships; so his first question is about his friend. That loyal *empressement,* however, is immediately checked by the balanced twin negatives that follow: "on his learning that Waymarsh *was not* to arrive till evening, he *was not* wholly disconcerted": one of the diagnostic elements of irony, surely, is hyperbole qualified with mock-scrupulousness, such as we get in "not wholly disconcerted." Why there are limits to Lambert Strether's consternation is to transpire in the next sentence; Waymarsh's telegram bespeaking a room "only if not noisy" is a laconic suggestion of that inarticulate worthy's habitual gloomy expectations — from his past experiences of the indignities of European hotel noise we adumbrate the notion that the cost of their friendly *rencontre* may be his sleeping in the street. In the second part of the sentence we have another similar, though more muted, hint: "the understanding that they should meet in Chester rather than at Liverpool remained to that extent sound"; "to that extent," no doubt, but to *any other?* — echo seems to answer "No."

In the second group of sentences we are getting into Strether's mind, and we have been prepared to relish the irony of its ambivalences. The negatived hyperbole of "not absolutely to desire," turns out to mean "postpone"; and, of course, a voluntarily postponed "enjoyment" itself denotes a very modified rapture, although Strether's own consciousness of the problem is apparently no further advanced than that "he could still wait without disappointment." Comically loyal to what he would like to feel, therefore, we have him putting in the consoling reflection that "they would dine together at the worst"; and the ambiguity of "at the worst" is followed by the equally dubious thought: "there was little fear that in the sequel they shouldn't see enough of each other." That they should, in fact, see too much of each other; but social decorum and Strether's own loyalties demand that the outrage of the open statement be veiled in the obscurity of formal negation.

By the time we arrive at the climactic pair of sentences, we have been told enough for more ambitious effects to be possible. The twice-mentioned "secret principle," it appears, is actually wholly "instinctive" (line 15); but in other ways Strether is almost ludicrously self-conscious. The qualified hyperbole of "his business would be a trifle bungled," underlined as it is by the alliteration, prepares us for a half-realised image which amusingly defines Strether's sense of his role: he sees himself, it appears, as the stage-manager of an enterprise in which his solemn obligations as an implicated friend are counterbalanced by his equally ceremonious sense that due decorums must also be attended to when he comes face to face with another friend of long ago — no less a person than Europe. It is, of course, silly of him, as James makes him acknowledge in the characteristic italicising of "the 'note' of Europe"; [8] but still, he does have a comically ponderous sense of protocol which leads him to feel that "his business would be a trifle bungled" should he simply arrange for this countenance to present itself to the nearing steamer as the first "note" of Europe. The steamer, one imagines, would not have turned hard astern at the proximity of Waymarsh's sacred rage; but Strether's fitness for ambassadorial functions is defined by his thinking in terms of "arranging" for a certain countenance at the docks to give just the right symbolic greeting.

Strether's notion of what Europe demands also shows us the force of his aesthetic sense. But in the last sentence the metaphor, though it remains equally self-conscious, changes its mode of operation from the dramatic, aesthetic, and diplomatic, to something more scientific: for, although ten years ago I should not have failed to point out, and my readers would not, I suppose, have failed to applaud, the ambiguity of "prove," it now seems to me that we must choose between its two possible meanings. James may be using "prove" to mean that Waymarsh's face will "turn out to be" the "note of Europe" for Strether. But "prove" in this sense is intransitive, and "to be" would have to be supplied; it therefore seems more likely that James is using "prove" in the older sense of "to test": Waymarsh is indeed suited to the role of being the sourly acid test of the siren songs of Europe "in quite a sufficient degree," as Strether puts it with solemn but arch understanding.

The basic development structure of the passage, then, is one of progressive and yet artfully delayed clarification; and this pattern is also typical of James's general novelistic method. The reasons for this are suggested in the Preface to *The Princess Casamassima,* where James deals with the problem of maintaining a balance between the intelligence a character must have to be interesting, and the bewilderment which is nevertheless an essential condition of the novel's having surprise, development, and tension: "It seems probable that if we were never bewildered there would never be a story to tell about us."

In the first paragraph of *The Ambassadors* James apprises us both of his hero's supreme qualities and of his associated limitations. Strether's delicate critical intelligence is often blinkered by a highly vulnerable mixture of moral generosity towards others combined with an obsessive sense of personal inadequacy; we see the tension in relation to Waymarsh, as later we are to see it in relation to all his other friends; and we understand, long before Strether, how deeply it bewilders him; most poignantly about the true nature of Chad, Madame de Vionnet — and himself.

This counterpoint of intelligence and bewilderment is, of course, another reason for the split narrative point of view we've already noted: we and the narrator are inside Strether's mind, and yet we are also outside it, knowing more about Strether than he knows about himself. This is the classic posture of irony. Yet I think that to insist too exclusively on the ironic function of James's narrative point of view would be mistaken.

Irony has lately been enshrined as the supreme deity in the critical pantheon: but, I wonder, is there really anything so wonderful about being distant and objective? Who wants to see life only or mainly in intellectual terms? In art as in life we no doubt can have need of intellectual distance as well as of emotional commitment; but the uninvolvement of the artist surely doesn't go very far without the total involvement of the person; or, at least, without a deeper human involvement than irony customarily establishes. One could, I suppose, call the aesthetically perfect balance between distance and involvement, open or positive irony: but I'm not sure that humour isn't a better world, especially when the final balance is tipped in favour of involvement, of ultimate commitment to the characters; and I hope that our next critical movement will be the New Gelastics.

At all events, although the first paragraph alone doesn't allow the point to be established fully here, it seems to me that James's attitude to Strether is better described as humorous than ironical; we must learn like Maria Gostrey, to see him "at last all comically, all tragically." James's later novels in general are most intellectual; but they are also, surely, his most compassionate: and in this particular paragraph Strether's dilemma is developed in such a way that we feel for him even more than we smile at him. This balance of intention, I think, probably explains why James keeps his irony in such a low key: we must be aware of Strether's "secret" ambivalence towards Waymarsh, but not to the point that his unawareness of it would verge on fatuity; and our controlling sympathy for the causes of Strether's ambivalence turns what might have been irony into something closer to what Constance Rourke characterises as James's typical "low-keyed humor of defeat" (*American Humor,* 1931).

That James's final attitude is humorous rather than ironic is further suggested by the likeness of the basic structural technique of the paragraph to that of the funny story — the incremental involvement in an endemic human perplexity which can only be resolved by laughter's final acceptance of contradiction and absurdity. We don't, in the end, see Strether's probing hesitations mainly as an ironic indication by James of mankind's general muddlement; we find it, increasingly, a touching example of how, despite all their inevitable incongruities and shortcomings, human ties remain only, but still, human.

Here it is perhaps James's very slowness and deliberation throughout the narrative which gives us our best supporting evidence: greater love hath no man than hearing his friend out patiently.

III

The function of an introductory paragraph in a novel is presumably to introduce: and this paragraph surely has the distinction of being a supremely complex and inclusive introduction to a novel. It introduces the hero, of course, and one of his companions; also the time; the place; something of what's gone before. But James has carefully avoided giving us the usual retrospective beginning, that pile of details which he scornfully termed a "mere seated mass of information." All the details are scrupulously presented as reflections from the novel's essential centre — the narrator's patterning of the ideas going forwards and backwards in Strether's mind. Of course, this initially makes the novel more difficult, because what we probably think of as primary — event and its setting — is subordinated to what James thinks is — the mental drama of the hero's consciousness, which, of course, is not told but shown: scenically dramatised. At the same time, by selecting thoughts and events which are representative of the book as a whole, and narrating them with an abstractness which suggests their larger import, James introduces the most general themes of the novel.

James, we saw, carefully arranged to make "Strether's first question," the first three words; and, of course, throughout the novel, Strether is to go on asking questions — and getting increasingly dusty answers. This, it may be added, is stressed by the apparent aposiopesis: for a "first" question when no second is mentioned, is surely an intimation that more are — in a way unknown to us or to Strether — yet to come. The later dislocations of normal word-order already noted above emphasise other major themes; the "secret principle" in Strether's mind, and the antithesis Waymarsh-Europe, for instance.

The extent to which these processes were conscious on James's part cannot, of course, be resolved; but it is significant that the meeting with Maria Gostrey was interposed before the meeting with Waymarsh, which James had originally planned as his beginning in the long (20,000) word scenario of the plot which he prepared for *Harper's*. The unexpected meeting had many advantages; not least that James could repeat the first paragraph's pattern of delayed clarification in the structure of the first chapter as a whole. On Strether's mind we get a momentously clear judgment at the end of the second paragraph: "there was detachment in his zeal, and curiosity in his indifference"; but then the meeting with Maria Gostrey, and its gay opportunities for a much fuller presentation of Strether's mind, intervene before Waymarsh himself finally appears at the end of the chapter; only then is the joke behind Strether's uneasy hesitations in the first paragraph brought to its hilariously blunt climax: "It was already upon him even at that distance — Mr. Waymarsh was for *his* part joyless."

One way of evaluating James's achievement in this paragraph, I suppose, would be to compare the opening of James's other novels, and with those of previous writers: but it would take too long to do more than sketch the possibilities of this approach. James's early openings certainly have some of the banality of the "mere seated mass of information": in *Roderick Hudson* (1876), for example: "Rowland Mallet had made his arrangements to sail for Europe on the 5th of September, and having in the interval a fortnight to spare, he determined to spend it with his cousin Cecilia, the widow of a nephew of his father. . . ." Later, James showed a much more comprehensive notion of what the introductory paragraph should attempt: even in the relatively simple and concrete opening of *The Wings of the Dove* (1902): "She waited, Kate Croy, for her father to come in, but he kept her unconscionably, and there were moments at which she showed herself, in the glass over the mantle, a face positively pale with irritation that had brought her to the point of going away without sight of him. . . ." "She waited, Kate Croy" — an odd parenthetic apposition artfully contrived to prefigure her role throughout the novel — to wait.

One could, I suppose, find this sort of symbolic prefiguring in the work of earlier novelists; but never, I imagine, in association with all the other levels of introductory function that James manages to combine in a single paragraph. Jane Austen has her famous thematic irony in the opening of *Pride and Prejudice* (1813): "It is a truth universally acknowledged, that a single man in possession of a good fortune must be in want of a wife"; but pride and prejudice must come later. Dickens can hurl us overpoweringly into *Bleak House* (1852–53), into its time and place and general theme; but characters and opening action have to wait:

> London. Michaelmas Term lately over, and the Lord Chancellor sitting in Lincoln's Inn Hall. Implacable November weather. As much mud in the streets, as if the waters had but newly retired from the face of the earth, and it would not be wonderful to meet a Megalosaurus, forty feet long or so, waddling like an elephantine lizard up Holborn-Hill. Smoke lowering down from chimney-pots. . . .

In Dickens, characteristically, we get a loud note that sets the tone, rather than a polyphonic series of chords that contain all the later melodic developments, as in James. And either the Dickens method, or the "mere seated mass of information," seems to be commonest kind of opening in nineteenth-century novels. For openings that suggest something of James's ambitious attempt to achieve a prologue that is a synchronic introduction of all the main aspects of the narrative, I think that Conrad is his closest rival. But Conrad, whether in expository or dramatic vein, tends to an arresting initial vigour that has dangers which James's more muted tones avoid. In *An Outcast of the Islands* (1896), for example:

> When he stepped off the straight and narrow path of his peculiar honesty, it was with an inward assertion of unflinching resolve to fall back again into the monotonous but safe stride of virtue as soon as his little excursion into the wayside quagmires had produced the desired effect. It was going to be a short episode — a sentence in brackets, so to speak, in the flowing tale of his life. . . .

Conrad's sardonic force has enormous immediate impact; but it surely gives too much away: the character, Willems, has been dissected so vigorously that it takes great effort for Conrad — and the reader — to revivify him later. The danger lurks even in the masterly combination of physical notation and symbolic evaluation at the beginning of *Lord Jim* (1900): "He was an inch, perhaps two, under six feet . . .": the heroic proportion is forever missed, by an inch, perhaps two; which is perhaps too much, to begin with.

It is not for me to assess how far I have succeeded in carrying out the general intentions with which I began, or how far similar methods of analysis would be applicable to other kinds of prose. As regards the explication of the passage itself, the main argument must by now be sufficiently clear, although a full demonstration would require a much wider sampling both of other novels and of other passages in *The Ambassadors*.[9] The most obvious and demonstrable features of James's prose style, its vocabulary and syntax, are direct reflections of his attitude to life and his conception of the novel; and these features, like the relation of the paragraph to the rest of the novel, and to other novels, make clear that the notorious idiosyncrasies of Jamesian prose are directly related to the imperatives which led him to develop a narrative texture as richly complicated and as highly organised as that of poetry.

No wonder James scorned translation and rejoiced, as he so engagingly confessed to his French translator, Auguste Monod, that his later works were "locked fast in the golden cage of the *intraduisible.*" Translation could hardly do justice to a paragraph in which so many levels of meaning and implication are kept in continuous operation; in which the usual introductory exposition of time, place, character, and previous action, are rendered through an immediate immersion in the processes of the hero's mind as he's involved in perplexities which are characteristic of the novel as a whole and which are articulated in a mode of comic development which is essentially that, not only of the following chapter, but of the total structure. To have done all that is to have gone far towards demonstrating the contention which James announced at the end of the Preface to *The Ambassadors,* that "the Novel remains still, under the right persuasion, the most independent, most elastic, most prodigious of literary forms"; and the variety and complexity of the functions carried out in the book's quite short first paragraph also suggest that, contrary to some notions, the demonstration is, as James claimed, made with "a splendid particular economy."

LEO BERSANI

From Bachelard to Barthes

France, as everyone knows, is the country of fashion. Intellectual jargons and artistic personalities are picked up as passionately and dropped as ruthlessly as the perpetually daring inventions of Givenchy and Saint Laurent. There is a hallowed myth about "the

SOURCE: From *Partisan Review,* Volume 34, Number 2 (Spring 1967), pp. 215–235. Copyright © 1967 by *Partisan Review.* Reprinted by permission of *Partisan Review* and the author.

French mind" which it would be useful to get rid of once and for all: the French, we have always been told, are critical and systematic. Nothing could be further from the truth. If indeed there is such a thing as a French style of thought, it could, I think, be much more accurately defined as impressionistic, theoretical, polemical and conformist. This combination of rather unattractive qualities makes some of us understandably suspicious of the intellectual revolutions which the French perennially announce. But there has, surprisingly enough, been something of a revolution in contemporary French criticism, or at least a considerable number of important works largely free of that arrogant frivolity which we recognize as the style of French cultural life.

But that style has naturally fed upon these works, and it therefore seems wise to prepare you for the discouragement you will surely feel if you decide to investigate what has recently been going on in French literary life. If, for example, you were to read the fashionable magazine *Tel Quel*, you might feel that most of the writers I will be discussing are hopelessly *démodés*. The "structuralists" quickly took over from the "thematic" critics. Georges Poulet, Jean-Pierre Richard and Jean Starobinski are, to be sure, still published and "respected" in Paris, but who would be naïve enough to think that they (or even Roland Barthes, raised in 1965 to martyrdom by Sorbonne Professor Raymond Picard's attack on his Racine book) are still "in," now that Michel Foucault has given us, with *Les Mots et les choses,* what has been called the most important work since *Being and Nothingness* or, better still, since *The Critique of Pure Reason?* But Foucault may already be last year's fare: a marvelously candid letter from Paris informs a friend of mine that the psychoanalyst Jacques Lacan, whose nine-hundred page *Ecrits* was recently published, "est vraiment le seul génie du moment." Who can keep up with these rapid changes of fashion? They are an inevitable part of cultural impressionism, which tends to be parasitic: the French make up for the lateness of their discoveries (for example, of Freud and of the Russian formalists) by the intensity and brevity of their fervor. It seems that French publishers are now interested in translating twentieth-century American criticism, and it is not inconceivable that in 1975 the literary revolutionaries of Paris will be carrying the banner of Brooks and Warren.

While the intellectual hierarchy in Paris may vary from year to year, there is, at any one moment, almost complete unanimity of opinion and interest from the base to the peak of the pyramid of power. The sharp disagreement among American critics a couple of years ago over *Herzog* and *An American Dream* would be inconceivable among the best French critics. How thrilling and improbable it would be to find in the pages of *Tel Quel, Preuves, Critique* or *La Nouvelle revue française* what strike me as simple and self-evident truths: for example, that Lucien Goldmann has an elephantine sensibility and is theoretically uninteresting once he stops paraphrasing Georg Lukács and René Girard; that the introduction and the essays on Corneille and Racine in Starobinski's *L'Oeil vivant* are extraordinarily dull; and that Barthes, by submerging the brilliantly impressionistic social criticism of *Mythologies* in the derivative theories of his *Eléments de Sémiologie* (where Saussurian terminology adds nothing *but* terminology to analyses of road signs and menus) has himself "signified" nothing more than his own evolution toward rococo banality.

The astonishing conformity of opinion about books and ideas which you find in French magazines is of course partly explainable in historical and geographical terms. The influence of New York in American cultural life is almost negligible compared to the monolithic power of Paris. There is simply no way to resist that power, no other center of diffusion; in France, Belgium and Switzerland, the attention of Paris is the *only* sign of success. And Paris is, after all, a rather small and provincial city; it takes a depressingly short time for people to get together and decide what's good and what's bad, to create, announce and impose various trends and fashions. As in all cultural oligarchies, differences of opinion are only sporadically tolerated. (The philosopher Paul Ricoeur is a notable exception to the structuralist chorus; two men long established in America, Serge Doubrovsky and Paul de Man, have provided almost the only other dissenting voices.) [1] Poulet and Starobinski teach, respectively, in Zurich and in Geneva, and it's difficult to believe that they sympathize with the most recent trends in French criticism. But the brutal fact of French cultural life is that if you attack what the centralizing, devouring and manifesto-mad in-group from Paris has decided to promote, you are liable to find that your only intellectual allies are a few Sorbonne scholars and the reviewers from *Le Monde* and *Le Figaro littéraire*.

What is generally taken for the French critical spirit is a highly deloped taste for attacking intellectual dwarfs. If the gods and temples of *la vie littéraire* change, the enemy is an immovable, permanently recognizable target. In structuralist terms (I'll spare you the diagrams that usually accompany structuralist analyses), it could be said that Parisian literary life is a diachronically feeble system: the opposition to what fashion excludes (the Sorbonne, the newspapers, bourgeois society) is hardly affected by the temporal changes in fashion (Richard → Barthes → Foucault). Now constant polemics against the most narrow-minded academicism is scant proof of a critical spirit. It is in fact largely gratuitous and incomprehensible except as a ritualistic act of self-congratulation. You would think from the hysterical sarcasm directed by some of the second-line new critics against the government and the press that they were being effectively persecuted, or at the very least that Frenchmen were being prevented from reading Roland Barthes and coerced into finding Pierre-Henri Simon of *Le Monde* a more exciting critic of literature. Certainly the journalistic reaction to Barthes's *On Racine* was a particularly unpleasant and even violent display of philistinism, and, as we know, official hostility toward intellectual life does not have to become real persecution in order to be felt as oppressive. But the distinction between the two, which the French prefer to ignore, is a useful one to make, if only as an aid in determining proper strategies of resistance. Furthermore, some of the attacks on the new critics surely express intellectual insecurity more than ideological hostility: Barthes, Blanchot and Richard are by no means always easy to read, and they are at least as much a threat to intellectual vanity as they are to bourgeois institutions. Perhaps profoundly indifferent to politics, the French (as we see in their comments on the United States) *immediately* see political intrigue everywhere; and nothing is more politically frivolous and ineffectual than the strident cry of "Right-wing plot!" at the drop of a reviewer's cliché. There can be a certain pleasure in that cry, and in Paris it is often part of a self-exciting and self-promoting game. American intellectuals, who tend, if anything, to be masochistically self-critical, would do well to remember this French aversion to self-criticism before they anxiously agree with the typically unexamined French view that America is the most conformist country in the world.

There is, happily, a much brighter side to the picture. The importance of what has been done in French criticism since the war can perhaps best be approached by a brief look at some of the assumptions it rejects. The central piety of traditional criticism is a belief in the existence of an analyzable literary object. Picard, in his anti–new-critical pamphlet, *Nouvelle critique ou nouvelle imposture,* at least has the merit of explicitly, if somewhat simplemindedly, defending this belief. We can't, he argues, say just anything about Racine's plays: "There is a truth about Racine on which we can all agree." You wonder why this exegetic Utopia had not been reached before the new critics. Never mind; the objective aspects of literature which will lead us directly to interpretive unanimity are the certainties of language, the implications of psychological coherence and the structural imperatives of the tragic genre.

I won't insist on the obviously simplistic notions of linguistic meaning and psychological coherence which are the most glaring defects of this critical credo. More interesting, as Barthes points out in his answer to Picard (*Critique et vérité*), is the question of the *kind* of interpretations sanctioned by an appeal to the supposedly objective criteria of a text's language and structure. It's a shame that Barthes didn't have a better reader of Racine to deal with. Picard's prejudices are so transparent, he is so anxious to save literature from what he fears are the incoherent obscenities of the unconscious, that he is continually closing his eyes to precisely the kind of evidence he accuses Barthes of neglecting. Thus, in order to preserve the hallowed notion of a "modest Aricie" in *Phèdre,* he simply ignores the accumulated brutality of eleven verses in which this sweet captive makes it abundantly clear that what draws her to Hippolyte is the prospect of making him suffer. Hippolyte is the appetizing object of attack in the play, the tender virgin whom both Phèdre and Aricie are out to rape. But for Picard, Aricie's love is simply there, an unmotivated, fleshless absolute, and if she mentions the pleasure of subduing Hippolyte, it's simply in order "to justify" (!) her feelings. In short, at its worst the religion of the literary object goes hand in hand with a shocking indifference to literary texts, and this for the obvious reason that Picard's critical objectivity only feebly conceals a view of literature as both banal and sublime, as a triumph of reason and order over a formless "source" called life.

The central issue between Picard and Barthes (which both see, but which Picard is unable to argue effectively) is the *specificity* of literary language. To what extent are its structures different from those of other organizing systems, from, say, those of dreams or of myths? Barthes doesn't deny literature's specificity, but it could be said that, like other new critics in France, he neglects formal and textual particularities in order to repostulate them within a general theory of human signs. The implications of this are more radical than it might at first seem. In what I have called the religion of the literary object, the uniqueness of literature may in fact be affirmed in order to deny it. The relation between literature and life, for many people far more perceptive than Picard about individual works, is thought of in terms of an absolute distance and, paradoxically, an identity of substance. On the one hand, the critic is not supposed to use the procedures and vocabulary of nonliterary disciplines; psychoanalysis and linguistics, for example, can't tell us anything about what is specifically "poetic" in a poem. The most interesting things we can say about literature are, in this view, inapplicable to anything outside literature. On the other hand, since literary creation obviously takes place within life, a connection has to be imagined between the two, and perhaps the only way to protect both the relevance and the remoteness of literature is to think of it as a sublimated copy of life. There is something which precedes the literary work and which the writer lifts up, transforms into what Picard calls the "superior order" of art. We end up, then, with a curious combination of ideas: the *processes* by which the writer constructs a verbal system of coherent meanings are irreducibly different from other semantic processes, but these processes have nothing to do with creating the *content* of meaning, which is given before the work is written and which the critic extracts as a "truth" about life.

The consequence of this view of literature's specificity is, as we have often seen, nothing less than the absorption of literature itself into a discussion of Life. For what can the critic actually talk about? An exaggerated respect for literature may, it seems to me, be exactly equivalent to an impulse to judge literary works on the quality of the life they presumably express. The peculiar position in which the literary work is placed by its being considered as an analyzable object about which certain very definite things can and cannot be said is one of an extraordinary devaluation (which is the hidden meaning of its sanctification) in comparison to every other activity in life. The remoteness of that "superior order" makes it particularly vulnerable to the most ruthless judgments. We are to believe that literature alone is knowable; but the distinctness of the object in literary criticism is, I suggest, an illusion created by the distance we arbitrarily put between ourselves and the work, a distance which makes it possible for us to think of our systematic interpretations of life as epistemological certainties. To put the case extremely, the discussion of literature is perhaps impossible as long as we continue to believe in the objective existence of literature. At least as far as modern literature is concerned, it's certainly no longer possible to think that we can define the particularity of literature in terms of the genres of fiction, drama or poetry; nor are most of us naïve enough to think that words in a literary work are any less ambiguous and symbolic than they are in ordinary conversation. The most intelligently stated objections to modern writing often frankly reveal what has perhaps always been behind our cherished notion of the privileged status of art: the desire to separate literature from life so that we may possess the supposed "meanings" and "values" of life in artifacts whose forms miraculously immobilize experience.

This would naturally be an unfair summary of modern American and English criticism, about which the French, as you might expect, are abysmally ignorant. The most convincing case for the existence of a discussable literary object has of course been made not in the halls of the Sorbonne, but in the studies of twentieth-century American critics. But the best textual critics, whatever complexities and ambiguities they may find in the literary object, have deliberately refused to locate the *subject* of a text beyond its particular verbal organizations. There is no "intention" behind an image outside the context in which it is used. The French critics' rejection of this premise accounts for what must seem to American readers like a scandalous indifference to "what the text says," by which we of course mean the immediate verbal environment. For the French the subject of a text is not the attitudes it demonstrably organizes, but rather an intentionality which contexts may obscure, or the working out of a structural coherence and intelligibility which only a kind of X ray of the text can reveal. The text is, so to speak, taken apart in order to be put together again, this time in a structure which, you might argue, is simply the critic's hypothesis. This is true, but it is beside the point: every interpretation is hypothesis, and the structuralist hypothesis at least has the merit of being a reenactment of that meaningful intention which, more than any specific meanings, may be the subject of literature.

The results of this approach for practical criticism should be clear. A character in a play or a novel, for example, is not explained in terms of his "lifelike" richness or moral and psychological probability, but is rather understood as a functional necessity in the creation of a coherent system. Thus, Barthes's interpretations of Racine depend on a redistribution of the contexts of specific dramatic statements. The originality of his approach is, as it were, in a fidelity to the "work" achieved by a certain neglect of the "text." In any "realistic" reading of *Britannicus* and *Phèdre,* Néron and Phèdre are objectively guilty of crimes. But when their guilt is seen in relation to the Racinian heroes' abortive attempts to break away from an authority both hated and loved, it could be thought of as an alibi, as a functional necessity in order to protect the "father" from being directly accused and to allow the "son" to remain in the dubious security of the tragic enclosure. Barthes's interpretive system is, as you can see, psychoanalytic, but he seeks no *causal* explanation of Phèdre's guilt outside of its place in the structure of what he calls *homo racinianus.* His study, like Richard's reconstruction of Mallarmé (although Barthes, unlike Richard, limits himself to Racine's works), is one of those original and disconcerting "portraits" of contemporary French criticism. He neither studies the plays in detail nor is he describing a biographical Racine. The "man" he portrays is nothing more than a certain type of structural coherence. Racinian psychology is a by-product of the peculiarly Racinian way of creating intelligibility.

There is, then, no "life" which is given and which Racine copies and formalizes. The parallelism between literature and life is in the act of creating meanings and not in the content of meanings. The immediate and most radical consequence of this view is the breakdown of the presumed differences of function between critical language and creative language. Both the critic and the poet are engaged in the fabrication of meaning. Criticism, as Barthes writes in his essay on structuralism, has the same mimetic and reconstituting role as art; as the artist makes the structures of natural objects intelligible, so the critic, in his "imitations" of the work, makes the structures of art intelligible. Now this clearly does not mean that the critic tries to sound like the writer he is discussing; a similarity of function is not an identity of styles. The failure to make this distinction undoubtedly accounts for works of modern literature in which the treatment of boredom, for example, is naïvely executed as an effort to be boring. The refusal in modern thought to consider discursive language as a privileged instrument which excavates "truth" from reality is more important than the frequently confused ways in which this refusal has been expressed. And the French have of course not been the only ones to insist that systems of communication participate in and perhaps even create the phenomena they describe. More specifically, their simultaneous reevaluation of both literature and criticism has led to a deliberate confusion between the two, and to a body of work which has very little that is "critical" in the sense in which we have usually understood that word.

These general remarks should help to explain what may seem the most peculiar and objectionable aspects of contemporary French criticism: its neglect of the literary contexts of literary texts and its indifference to judgments of literary value. Perhaps the most important early example of this kind of criticism is the work of Gaston Bachelard. Bachelard would be rather exotic fare for Anglo-Saxon readers. I can hardly hope, in a few lines, to convince you to look into a writer who reads in order "to vibrate phenomenologically," for whom "the reading of poets is essentially reverie," and who measures a poet's success by his ability "to induce the reader into a state of suspended reading." "Nous lisions," Bachelard writes admiringly in La Poétique de la rêverie, "et voici que nous rêvons." Reverie is a kind of half-conscious state in which human projects spontaneously express themselves in images of matter; either water, fire, earth or air is the "privileged substance" for each of the four "fundamental oneiric temperaments" which Bachelard sets out to classify in several of his works. "For certain souls, water is the matter of despair." Or: ". . . All tranquillity is a dormant water. . . . In front of dormant water, the rêveur adheres to the world's repose." The absorption of a reverie into a material substance is a participation in the life of that substance. It is the act by which imagination becomes the world, breaks down the duality between the self and the universe. Literature gives to these reveries "the exuberance of forms"; it is the "emergence" of imagination, the completion of human desires. But Bachelard is interested only in the "detached images" of poetry; the formal arrangements of a whole poem or novel are an obstacle to the reader's identification with "the poetic will," with the "élan" of reverie which is the source of poetry. The poetic image should, then, be the origin of the reader's reverie about origins.

By all ordinary standards of judgments, Bachelard's taste in poetry is often execrable. It is not always "to vibrate phenomenologically" that you make your eyes hurriedly leave the lines he quotes. But of course that's not the point. Our notions of literary quality are perhaps no more invulnerable to attack than Bachelard's "judgment" of an image on the basis of its reverie-provoking potency. The crucial element in his thought is what might be called a structuralist version of the old idea of poetry's inspirational power. The power of poetry is its ability to disappear, to make us participate so completely in the structures of the creating imagination that — like the poet himself who lives the lives of the elements — we no longer *see* the poem in our identification with the act that produced it.

Bachelard is the Freud of the French new critics, in the sense that he has provided them with a vocabulary in which to describe mental reality. Much of what is bizarre in the works of Poulet, Starobinski, the early Barthes (his essay on Michelet), and especially Richard derives from Bachelardian assumptions about the imagination's fundamental themes. Richard defines thematic criticism as a "critique abyssale," a "study of hidden physical or humoral sources." In *Littérature et sensation,* Richard treats Flaubert's ascetic attitude toward style as an escape from the fear of being drowned in undifferentiated liquid matter. Poulet constantly invites us to think of a writer's mind crossing intervals, concentrating itself on a point, diffusing itself along the periphery of a circle. And Barthes speaks of Michelet's Anglophobia as "supported by a feeling of nausea in front of an excess and stagnancy of blood," of his Germanophilia as deriving "from his delight in a ceaselessly flowing substance, in blood-milk. . . ."

These weird categories bring us to a dilemma in the new French criticism, and to a parting of the ways among some of the men involved. Bachelard's work is both abstract and psychologically concrete: he's more interested in a typology of the imagination than in particular imaginative products, but his classifications are entirely affective in content. His work thus opens out into the two directions which Barthes distinguishes in *Critique et vérité.* On the one hand, we can undertake the science of literature, which would attempt to describe the "signifying logic" of symbolic language itself, "the empty forms which allow us to speak and to operate." On the other hand, criticism, which deals with specific meanings, is bound to describe an individual signifying logic when it treats individual writers. The new critics, as I have said, are not interested in deriving a biographical personality from a literary work; there is no pregnant subject "behind" the writer's language. But even if the critic sees his job, as Barthes puts it, as one of producing a "new flowering of the symbols" of the work itself, as one of continuing the work's metaphors, he obviously does not merely reproduce the work, and he gives a greater intelligibility to literature by the language he *adds* to it. It is in this sense that all criticism is subjective: while the critic refuses to explain the work by causes external to it, he nevertheless creates a new relationship — between the work and the interpretive system in which he himself "speaks" the work.

What language will you choose to speak? I think that the themes chosen by the French critics in order to imitate what might be called the writer's path of coherence can best be understood as an attempt to formulate an acausal psychology. Their categories are most interesting — Bachelard makes the point explicitly — as an alternative to what the French seem to dread as the deterministic implications of Freudianism. The French managed to act for a long time as if Freud and psychoanalysis had never happened. Their indifference or ignorance was followed by protest (Sartre and Bachelard, for example), and they seem at present to have an uneasily sympathetic and not wholly knowledgeable relation to the methods of Freudian analysis. It's true that psychoanalytic criticism, like Marxist criticism, tends ultimately to formulate the relation between a writer's work and his life or his society not as a relation of parallel structures, but rather as one of cause and effect. Thus, Charles Mauron's often impressive "psychocritical" readings of Racine's plays are weakened by an appeal to Racine's life as, finally, a sanction for those readings, while Lucien Goldmann's generally unimpressive analyses of Pascal and Racine are supported by what Barthes rightly detects as the hidden economic determinism of the so-called structuralist approach in *The Hidden God*. Both methods are imitatively defective, and it could be shown, I think, that biographical and economic hypotheses actually make *un*intelligible structures of the texts Mauron and Goldmann discuss. That is, their various local interpretations fit together coherently only if you agree that the principle of Racinian coherence is independent of (but responsible for) Racine's creation of a coherent dramatic world. And an immanent, noncausal coherence is the only criterion on which structural criticism asks to be judged. The appeal to causes makes for a missing link in the structuralist chain.

The appeal of Bachelard's categories is that they presumably account for their own nature. He himself insisted on the absolute newness of the poetic image, on poetry as "a sublimation which doesn't sublimate anything." But thematic criticism has suffered badly from a Bachelardian and, in Poulet, a spatiotemporal vocabulary. The invention of a drastically simplified psychology is hardly a satisfactory escape from psychological causality. Those "humoral sources" are, after all, metaphors which have to be treated metaphorically, and not literally, if the critic's vocabulary is to "cover" the writer's work in its entirety. Any interpretive system is legitimate, writes Barthes, if it is capable of transforming *everything* in a work according to the laws of its own logic. But everything in a work simply does not yield to a system of sensory perceptions which are not, in any writer I know of, the final term of his intelligibility. Richard, who is a brilliant critic, gets further than anyone else with this method; the man who is least well served by his language, whose extraordinary sensitivity to literature is continually thwarted by his rigorously adhering to categories of only limited interest, is Poulet. The image of a circle may be recurrent in literature, but no interesting literary work can be adequately discussed in terms of its metaphors of "centers" and "circumferences." And even the categories of time and space in, for example, Proust can themselves be made intelligible only if they are placed in relation to other things in the work (jealousy and snobbery, which Poulet doesn't even mention), that is, considered as metaphorical terms of a larger system in which affectivity is infinitely more than geometric.

The principal interest of Poulet's and Richard's work is as models of abstract structuralist analyses with which they probably wouldn't like to be identified. While their *découpage* into a writer's language is unable to account for all that we respond to in a literary work, it could be argued that the very nature of their critical procedures makes explicit the real subject of literature. The direction of time in art, Poulet writes, is not from past to future or from future to past, but rather "from the isolated instant to temporal continuity," from discontinuous sensations to a structural coherence among sensations. Thus time for Poulet is not a chronological sequence but, instead, a process of connecting and differentiating among different "points," that is, the process of making lines and shapes, of giving form to *space.* Poulet's and Richard's constant use of false temporal transitions is both irritating and deceptive. We are always being told how things "begin" in a writer, what his mind is doing "now," how it moves from "now" to "then" to a "final moment." But these are, of course, anything but "moments"; Poulet and Richard use metaphors of temporal progress to point to the organizational potentialities of a mass of either undifferentiated or disconnected sensations. The progress of the critical essay thus illustrates the structural logic of the work; and the work's motivation is located in the very articulation of its coherence. Implicit in Poulet and Richard is the assumption that the work has been thoroughly described once the critic's metaphor has been exhausted, for the work seeks to express nothing more than the total intelligibility which is the object of criticism.

Time is nevertheless important in Poulet in that structures, as he writes in *Le Point de départ,* are never "radically objective"; their discovery is the writer's intention, and coherence can be only a gradual process. This interest in the subjective movement *toward* structures distinguishes the earlier French critics from the more recent structuralist critics, who have become intrigued by the possibility of finding structures entirely independent of individual histories and intentions. But already in Poulet and Richard one sees the possibility of that "science of literature" which Barthes speaks of and which would make literature superfluous, or which would at least, Barthes warns, leave aside, as a "residue," "genius, art, humanity." For if the *processes* of "signification" are the subject of literature, then the specific meanings of literary works can be thought of as obscuring the laws which make them possible. Even more radically, if the conditions for creating meaning are objective and universal, then literature — indeed all human expression — is endlessly tautological. As Philippe Sollers has announced, everything that has been written "is only a particular and limited case of writing (*écriture*)."

And so we find ourselves as nostalgic for absolute certainties as poor Picard. But of course the stakes are now higher. "There is a truth about literature or, even better, about the mind," the structuralists might say, "on which we can all agree." The master discipline of the new science would be linguistics. The structuralists have enthusiastically accepted the linguists' argument that the internal structure of every type of social discourse is organized on the model of the structure of language. The specificity of literature is that of a connotative discourse; its science would be the classification of those "figures" which are, as Gérard Genette writes, "the inner space of language," or the variously shaped spaces between a sign and its meaning, between a signifier (what the poet actually says) and the thing signified (the poet's virtual language). Criticism and linguistics thus meet on the common ground of rhetoric. The interest of Barthes and Genette in the science of rhetoric is nothing less than the ambition to establish an exhaustive code of literary connotations. Thus, peculiarly enough, the object returns, this time not as the text, but as the "literary function" itself. An illusion? That remains to be seen; any thorough critique of structuralism would probably have to be made within a more general critique of scientific ambitions to describe the programming of the brain. So far, at any rate, linguistic and rhetorical analyses of literature have been disappointing. It was in fact a Belgian linguist, Nicolas Ruwet, who, in a paper read at last October's symposium at Johns Hopkins on "The Languages of Criticism and the Sciences of Man," emphasized both the gaps in current linguistic analyses of literary texts (for example, the absence of a general theory of contexts) and warned against the danger of overvaluing, in criticism, a structuralist approach which may be only a transitional stage in linguistics itself. The well-known analysis which Lévi-Strauss and Jakobson have done of phonemic, syntactic and rhetorical structures in Baudelaire's "Les Chats" (such criticism can naturally be written by committees) manages to be the closest reading of a poem I have ever seen, while it makes the poem entirely invisible. But the delirium of the new "science" is precisely that: the annihilation of meaning, the destruction of literature as the very condition of an attempt to explain the possibility of either.

But the sanction for such interests does, to a certain extent, come from the history of literature itself. The destruction of literary texts is not an invention of contemporary critics; from Flaubert to Beckett, almost every important modern writer has been engaged in the subversion of his own meanings, in a more or less violent refusal to believe in or be limited by the expressiveness of his language. Beginning with *Bouvard et Pécuchet,* the masterpieces of monotony in modern art could be thought of as an attempt to say nothing at all within, however, a language that would never stop. More radical than the notion of universal structures which might finally be described independently of all local contents is the notion of the absolute neutrality and formlessness of a language which could never be spoken or described, a language which is merely the endless repetition of an infinite sameness.

No one has made that language the impossible subject of his work more explicitly than Maurice Blanchot, perhaps the most extraordinary voice — absolutely clear and absolutely enigmatic, unmistakable and devoid of personality — in modern literature. "The search of literature is the search for the moment which proceeds it." Where? Literally nowhere, that is, in the nature of language itself, which is not to refer to objects but to abolish them, which tempts us with the possibility of a pure and objectless designation. What Blanchot seeks to "hear" in literature is the "uninterrupted murmur" of an original, limitless, neutral language which the literary work in fact interrupts. It is, he suggests, perhaps only when literature is fragmented, discontinuous and incomplete that it can bring us back to that "pure point of the undetermined" which is its origin. By continually contesting the meanings which it cannot help but create, a work can thus evoke a kind of ideal meaninglessness, a vague and empty neutrality where, as Blanchot writes, being would be perpetuated as nothingness, as the absence of any *determined* being.

One feels that Blanchot is partly responsible for the vogue of deliberate obscurity among contemporary French writers. There is, it often seems, something competitively hermetic in their work: the writing in *Tel Quel* often makes Barthes seem as limpid as Voltaire, and Lacan has carried the day with a style which is, hopefully, the *ne plus ultra* of garbled impenetrability. Blanchot, however, is obscure without being difficult. There is nothing to "understand" in his work except the conditions in which understanding is irrelevant. It's nonetheless difficult to talk *about* Blanchot, which undoubtedly explains why Camus's unsuccessful attempt, in *The Stranger,* to write a book about which nothing could be said received much more attention than Blanchot's first book, *Thomas l'obscur,* published a year before Camus's novel. The "neutrality" of Camus's writing is an illusion; *The Stranger* has a philosophical and social thesis. Blanchot, on the other hand, is indifferent to negation and revolt. His work is an attempt to suggest a more "original," nondialectical mode of being. And the obscurity of his writing derives from this effort to approximate "the pure movement of dying" in literature and in being, to signify nothing more than the continual disappearing of significance.

Blanchot's enigmatic and poignant sentences seal the doom of their own meanings. His essays and récits almost *are* an uninterrupted murmur of an infinite sameness: a single Blanchot sentence contains the strategy, the model of his whole work. That obsessively repeated model is one of paradox (a silence which speaks, an interiority which is external), or rather of a juxtaposition of contradictory terms meant to affirm a reality beyond or before paradoxes and contradictions. The nonparadoxical paradox thus illustrates the extrinsic, arbitrary relation between language and meaning: language is the *possibility* of meaning, that is, the presence and absence of *all* meaning.

Blanchot's "literary criticism" has, inevitably, tended to tell us less and less about the writers he chooses to mention; what interests him in a work is how it refers to what is absent from the work. The "sympathy" between the writer and the critic is an impersonal anonymous identification. Since criticism and literature are occasions which violate the absence of occasions, ideally both would disappear in their common source. Thus, in its most extreme, most limited, and yet most intriguing form, modern French criticism would seem to envisage the perfectly sympathetic critical act as the consecration (and murder) of literature by an uninterrupted silence.

The perfect anonymity of the ideal critical act also makes it perfectly negligible, and in conclusion I would like to return from Blanchot's rarefied thought to the more livable achievements of recent French criticism. First of all, what disappears from criticism when it assumes a similarity of function between the critical and the creative acts, when it places itself alongside of literature rather than at a "critical" distance from it, are all judgments about the work's value. Now while I think that the refusal to judge implies a limited view of *all* meaningful activities, it is perhaps a healthy subversion of literature's falsely privileged status to assert that, in one sense, there are no bad books. More precisely, we can never judge art on the "truth" it supposedly contains; perhaps the most insidious form of censorship in criticism is an appeal to life as a sacred (and inhibiting) model for those operations by which all languages *invent* life. Any supposed statement about life is partial or distorting only in reference to other partial and distorting statements; and the interest of a language is more in its capacity for *conveying* meanings than in the hypothetical validity of the meanings it conveys. Furthermore, if the quality of life represented in a literary work is an essentially irrelevant basis of judgment, the best French critics remind us that, far from being indifferent to value, criticism in fact creates the work's value. The greatness of literature has, after all, never been anything more than an inference from the critical performances it inspires. By choosing to follow the writer's itinerary of signification, French critics have implicitly located the appeal of great literature not in the range of reality it covers or includes, but in a total intelligibility and structural coherence which allow us — and especially the critic of literature — to experience the exhilarating power of *making sense.*

But the structuralist view of meaning is, to say the least, extremely debatable. It is, I agree, important to point out that the "events" of all signifying systems are largely motivated by the patterns of intelligibility which those systems create. Form and content are not merely inseparable, as we have now been told *ad nauseam;* more exactly, form and structure can determine content, for the way in which a language is elaborated and constructed may actually establish the phenomena it describes. Thus, the determinations — and inspirations — of art are at least partly internal to the conditions in which art works in order to create meaning. Psychology, in literature and in life, may be a structural necessity, a function of intelligibility rather than a preexistent reality which language merely seeks to make intelligible.

But it is precisely this insight into the relation between meaning and the processes that create it which, I think, reveals the limitations of the structuralist approach. For what are the mental activities in which, so to speak, a rage for intelligibility actually creates content and determines meaning? Nothing could describe more accurately the way in which our dreams "signify." In dreams, events and people from our waking life lose their personalities in order to become pure functions. I have, in my past, created certain intelligible structures as a way of interpreting the world once and for all. And when I dream, my unconscious uses my boss to signify my mother and my brother to signify me for the sake of immobilizing my present experience in the security of those past structures. In the same way, neurotic behavior is a marvel of structural coherence: nothing that happens to the neurotic escapes the protective, deathlike order which he opposes to the structural *in*coherence of events in time. The unconscious is the original structuralist. Perhaps the greatest popular illusion about unconscious activity is that it is chaotic and incoherent; it strikes me as far more probable that its life is a tautology of beautifully and absurdly intelligible structures.

To the extent that literature, like all other human activities, expresses that unrelenting subordination of life to intelligibility which appears to characterize the unconscious, it is of course analyzable in structuralist terms. Much of the appeal of literature is undoubtedly in the almost magic spectacle it offers — and which Poulet, Richard and Barthes brilliantly reenact for us — of a mind in the process of reducing life to a purely formal expressiveness. The search for the structure of a literary work is analogous to the interpretation of dreams. What Barthes and Mauron discover is that Racine's situations (like the events of our conscious life in dreams) disguise a persistently distorting structure in which, for example, the psychological differences between Hermione, Oreste and Andromaque are less important than their place in an interpretive system where they all *function* as Pyrrhus's "father." Racine is of course the ideal subject for the structuralist demonstration: the rigid, repetitive intelligibility of Racinian violence is even further reinforced by some of the most fully rationalized, disciplining conventions in the history of literature.

But, as I have said, the demonstration is possible only if the literal sequences and contexts of events are ignored. And a context is precisely the opportunity to allow a particular event to subvert a structure. If we tend to spatialize the world in fixed patterns, we also adapt this tendency to innumerable occasions — in literature and in life — which we recognize as structurally unassimilable, which we can only "take in" and "attack" obliquely. That delicate adaptation defines our style, our tone and, in literature, the "voice" of a particular passage. An interest in tone, about which the French have absolutely nothing to say, is an interest in our astonishing capacity to question and be ironic about the theories and interpretations which make the world familiar to us. The French, proud of their reputation as the great nation of "style," no longer have anything to tell us about the enriching confusions which personal voice or style introduces into a structuralist system. Particular occasions, events in time, are the contents of literature, and it might almost be useful to reintroduce the notion of content in literary criticism to designate that which may indeed obscure the underlying structures, but which as a result makes a book or a life richer than the orders which it proudly but somewhat pathetically invents. Content immediately becomes a function of form only in our most frightened contacts with the world.

The best French criticism is, to be sure, a useful antidote to the naïve indifference to theory in the best Anglo-Saxon criticism. My own hesitation in this discussion between paraphrase and personal assertion undoubtedly reflects the difficulty I have found in bringing together very different critical perspectives in the writing of practical criticism. It would, I feel, be interesting to study literature as a struggle between self-immobilizing themes and structures and the pull away from such themes toward a greater variety of response to the world and to language. But I don't see how such a struggle could ever be described in terms of an exact science, and I see even less why we should sacrifice time, particularity, content and tone in order to make such a science possible. The French seem to have taken up the banner of a very primitive rage for intelligibility. But France has always been known as the country of reason, and it is perhaps only natural that it should be the Children of Reason who illustrate its derisions and its madness.

GEORGES POULET

Phenomenology of Reading

At the beginning of Mallarmé's unfinished story, *Igitur*, there is the description of an empty room, in the middle of which, on a table, there is an open book. This seems to me the situation of every book, until someone comes and begins to read it. Books are objects. On a table, on bookshelves, in store windows, they wait for someone to come and deliver them from their materiality, from their immobility. When I see them on display, I look at them as I would at animals for sale, kept in little cages, and so obviously hoping for a buyer. For — there is no doubting it — animals do know that their fate depends on a human intervention, thanks to which they will be delivered from the shame of being treated as objects. Isn't the same true of books? Made of paper and ink, they lie where they are put, until the moment someone shows an interest in them. They wait. Are they aware that an act of man might suddenly transform their existence? They appear to be lit up with that hope. Read me, they seem to say. I find it hard to resist their appeal. No, books are not just objects among others.

This feeling they give me — I sometimes have it with other objects. I have it, for example, with vases and statues. It would never occur to me to walk around a sewing machine or to look at the under side of a

SOURCE: "Phenomenology of Reading," translated by Richard Macksey, is from *New Literary History: A Journal of Theory and Interpretation*, Volume I, Number 1 (October 1969), pp. 53–68. Copyright by *New Literary History* and reprinted by their permission.

plate. I am quite satisfied with the face they present to me. But statues make me want to circle around them, vases make me want to turn them in my hands. I wonder why. Isn't it because they give me the illusion that there is something in them which, from a different angle, I might be able to see? Neither vase nor statue seems fully revealed by the unbroken perimeter of its surfaces. In addition to its surfaces it must have an interior. What this interior might be, that is what intrigues me and makes me circle around them, as though looking for the entrance to a secret chamber. But there is no such entrance (save for the mouth of the vase, which is not a true entrance since it gives only access to a little space to put flowers in). So the vase and the statue are closed. They oblige me to remain outside. We can have no true rapport — whence my sense of uneasiness.

So much for statues and vases. I hope books are not like them. Buy a vase, take it home, put it on your table or your mantel, and, after a while, it will allow itself to be made a part of your household. But it will be no less a vase, for that. On the other hand, take a book, and you will find it offering, opening itself. It is this openness of the book which I find so moving. A book is not shut in by its contours, is not walled-up as in a fortress. It asks nothing better than to exist outside itself, or to let you exist in it. In short, the extraordinary fact in the case of a book is the falling away of the barriers between you and it. You are inside it; it is inside you; there is no longer either outside or inside.

Such is the initial phenomenon produced whenever I take up a book, and begin to read it. At the precise moment that I see, surging out of the object I hold open before me, a quantity of significations which my mind grasps, I realize that what I hold in my hands is no longer just an object, or even simply a living thing. I am aware of a rational being, of a consciousness; the consciousness of another, no different from the one I automatically assume in every human being I encounter, except that in this case the consciousness is open to me, welcomes me, lets me look deep inside itself, and even allows me, with unheard-of licence, to think what it thinks and feel what it feels.

Unheard-of, I say. Unheard-of, first, is the disappearance of the "object." Where is the book I held in my hands? It is still there, and at the same time it is there no longer, it is nowhere. That object wholly object, that thing made of paper, as there are things made of metal or porcelain, that object is no more, or at least it is as if it no longer existed, as long as I read the book. For the book is no longer a material reality. It has become a series of words, of images, of ideas which in their turn begin to exist. And where is this new existence? Surely not in the paper object. Nor, surely, in external space. There is only one place left for this new existence: my innermost self.

How has this come about? By what means, through whose intercession? How can I have opened my own mind so completely to what is usually shut out of it? I do not know. I know only that, while reading, I perceive in my mind a number of significations which have made themselves at home there. Doubtless they are still objects: images, ideas, words, objects of my thought. And yet, from this point of view, there is an enormous difference. For the book, like the vase, or like the statue, was an object among others, residing in the external world: the world which objects ordinarily inhabit exclusively in their own society or each on its own, in no need of being thought by my thought; whereas in this interior world where, like fish in an aquarium, words, images and ideas disport themselves, these mental entities, in order to exist, need the shelter which I provide; they are dependent on my consciousness.

This dependence is at once a disadvantage and an advantage. As I have just observed, it is the privilege of exterior objects to dispense with any interference from the mind. All they ask is to be let alone. They manage by themselves. But the same is surely not true of interior objects. By definition they are condemned to change their very nature, condemned to lose their materiality. They become images, ideas, words, that is to say purely mental entities. In sum, in order to exist as mental objects, they must relinquish their existence as real objects.

On the one hand, this is cause for regret. As soon as I replace my direct perception of reality by the words of a book, I deliver myself, bound hand and foot to the omnipotence of fiction. I say farewell to what is, in order to feign belief in what is not. I surround myself with fictitious beings; I become the prey of language. There is no escaping this take-over. Language surrounds me with its unreality.

On the other hand, the transmutation through language of reality into a fictional equivalent has undeniable advantages. The universe of fiction is infinitely more elastic than the world of objective reality. It lends itself to any use; it yields with little resistance to the importunities of the mind. Moreover — and of all its benefits I find this the most appealing — this interior universe constituted by language does not seem radically opposed to the *me* who thinks it. Doubtless what I glimpse through the words are mental forms not divested of an appearance of objectivity. But they do not seem to be of a nature other than my mind which thinks them. They are objects, but subjectified objects. In short, since everything has become part of my mind, thanks to the intervention of language, the opposition between the subject and its objects has been considerably attenuated. And thus the greatest advantage of literature is that I am persuaded by it that I am freed from my usual sense of incompatibility between my consciousness and its objects.

This is the remarkable transformation wrought in me through the act of reading. Not only does it cause the physical objects around me to disappear, including the very book I am reading, but it replaces those external objects with a congeries of mental objects in close *rapport* with my own consciousness. And yet the very intimacy in which I now live with my objects is going to present me with new problems. The most curious of these is the following: I am someone who happens to have as objects of his own thought, thoughts which are part of a book I am reading, and which are therefore the cogitations of another. They are the thoughts of another, and yet it is I who am their subject. The situation is even more astonishing than the one noted above. I am thinking the thoughts of another. Of course, there would be no cause for astonishment if I were thinking it as the thought of another. But I think it as my very own. Ordinarily there is the *I* which thinks, which recognizes itself (when it takes its bearings) in thoughts which may have come from elsewhere but which it takes upon itself as its own in the moment it thinks them. This is how we must take Diderot's declaration "Mes pensées sont *mes* catins" ("My thoughts are *my* whores"). That is, they sleep with everybody without ceasing to belong to their author. Now, in the present case things are quite different. Because of the strange invasion of my person by the thoughts of another, I am a self who is granted the experience of thinking thoughts foreign to him. I am the subject of thoughts other than my own. My consciousness behaves as though it were the consciousness of another.

This merits reflection. In a certain sense I must recognize that no idea really belongs to me. Ideas belong to no one. They pass from one mind to another as coins pass from hand to hand. Consequently, nothing could be more misleading than the attempt to define a consciousness by the ideas which it utters or entertains. But whatever these ideas may be, however strong the tie which binds them to their source, however transitory may be their sojourn in my own mind, so long as I entertain them I assert myself as subject of these ideas; I am the subjective principle for whom the ideas serve for the time being as the predications. Furthermore, this subjective principle can in no wise be conceived as a predication, as something which is discussed, referred to. It is I who think, who contemplate, who am engaged in speaking. In short, it is never a *HE* but an *I.*

Now what happens when I read a book? Am I then the subject of a series of predications which are not *my* predications? That is impossible, perhaps even a contradiction in terms. I feel sure that as soon as I think something, that something becomes in some indefinable way my own. Whatever I think is a part of *my* mental world. And yet here I am thinking a thought which manifestly belongs to another mental world, which is being thought in me just as though I did not exist. Already the notion is inconceivable and seems even more so if I reflect that, since

every thought must have a subject to think it, this *thought* which is alien
to me and yet in me, must also have in me a *subject* which is alien
to me. It all happens, then, as though reading were the act by which a
thought managed to bestow itself within me with a subject not myself.
Whenever I read, I mentally pronounce an *I*, and yet the *I* which I
pronounce is not myself. This is true even when the hero of a novel is
presented in the third person, and even when there is no hero and nothing but reflections or propositions: for as soon as something is presented
as *thought,* there has to be a thinking subject with whom, at least for the
time being, I identify, forgetting myself, alienated from myself. "JE est
un autre," said Rimbaud. Another *I*, who has replaced my own, and who
will continue to do so as long as I read. Reading is just that: a way
of giving way not only to a host of alien words, images, ideas, but
also to the very alien principle which utters them and shelters them.

The phenomenon is indeed hard to explain, even to conceive, and
yet, once admitted, it explains to me what might otherwise seem even
more inexplicable. For how could I explain, without such take-over of
my innermost subjective being, the astonishing facility with which I not
only understand but even *feel* what I read. When I read as I ought, i.e.,
without mental reservation, without any desire to preserve my independence of judgment, and with the total commitment required of any
reader, my comprehension becomes intuitive and any feeling proposed to
me is immediately assumed by me. In other words, the kind of comprehension in question here is not a movement from the unknown to the
known, from the strange to the familiar, from outside to inside. It
might rather be called a phenomenon by which mental objects rise up
from the depths of consciousness into the light of recognition. On the
other hand — and without contradiction — reading implies something
resembling the apperception I have of myself, the action by which I
grasp straightway what I think as being thought by a subject (who, in
this case, is not I). Whatever sort of alienation I may endure, reading
does not interpret my activity as subject.

Reading, then, is the act in which the subjective principle which I
call *I*, is modified in such a way that I no longer have the right, strictly
speaking, to consider it as my *I*. I am on loan to another, and this
other thinks, feels, suffers, and acts within me. The phenomenon
appears in its most obvious and even naivest form in the sort of spell
brought about by certain cheap kinds of reading, such as thrillers, of
which I say "It gripped me." Now it is important to note that this possession of myself by another takes place not only on the level of objective
thought, that is with regard to images, sensations, ideas which reading
affords me, but also on the level of my very subjectivity. When I am
absorbed in reading, a second self takes over, a self which thinks and

feels for me. Withdrawn in some recess of myself, do I then silently witness this dispossession? Do I derive from it some comfort or, on the contrary, a kind of anguish? However that may be, someone else holds the center of the stage, and the question which imposes itself, which I am absolutely obliged to ask myself, is this: "Who is the usurper who occupies the forefront? What is this mind who all alone by himself fills my consciousness and who, when I say *I,* is indeed that *I?*"

There is an immediate answer to this question, perhaps too easy an answer. This *I* who thinks in me when I read a book, is the *I* of the one who writes the book. When I read Baudelaire or Racine, it is really Baudelaire or Racine who thinks, feels, allows himself to be read within me. Thus a book is not only a book, it is the means by which an author actually preserves his ideas, his feelings, his modes of dreaming and living. It is his means of saving his identity from death. Such an interpretation of reading is not false. It seems to justify what is commonly called the biographical explication of literary texts. Indeed every word of literature is impregnated with the mind of the one who wrote it. As he makes us read it, he awakens in us the analogue of what he thought or felt. To understand a literary work, then, is to let the individual who wrote it reveal himself to us *in* us. It is not the biography which explicates the work, but rather the work which sometimes enables us to understand the biography.

But biographical interpretation is in part false and misleading. It is true that there is an analogy between the works of an author and the experiences of his life. The works may be seen as an incomplete translation of the life. And further, there is an even more significant analogy among all the works of a single author. Each of the works, however, while I am reading it, lives in me its own life. The subject who is revealed to me through my reading of it is not the author, either in the disordered totality of his outer experiences, or in the aggregate, better organized and concentrated totality, which is the one of his writings. Yet the subject which presides over the work can exist only in the work. To be sure, nothing is unimportant for understanding the work, and a mass of biographical, bibliographical, textual, and general critical information is indispensable to me. And yet this knowledge does not coincide with the internal knowledge of the work. Whatever may be the sum of the information I acquire on Baudelaire or Racine, in whatever degree of intimacy I may live with their genius, I am aware that this contribution (*apport*) does not suffice to illuminate for me in its own inner meaning, in its formal perfection, and in the subjective principle which animates it, the particular work of Baudelaire or Racine the reading of which now absorbs me. At this moment what matters to me is to live, from the inside, in a certain identity with the work and the work alone.

It could hardly be otherwise. Nothing external to the work could possibly share the extraordinary claim which the work now exerts on me. It is there within me, not to send me back, outside itself, to its author, nor to his other writings, but on the contrary to keep my attention riveted on itself. It is the work which traces in me the very boundaries within which this consciousness will define itself. It is the work which forces on me a series of mental objects and creates in me a network of words, beyond which, for the time being, there will be no room for other mental objects or for other words. And it is the work, finally, which, not satisfied thus with defining the content of my consciousness, takes hold of it, appropriates it, and makes of it that *I* which, from one end of my reading to the other, presides over the unfolding of the work, of the single work which I am reading.

And so the work forms the temporary mental substance which fills my consciousness; and it is moreover that consciousness, the *I*-subject, the continued consciousness of what is, revealing itself within the interior of the work. Such is the characteristic condition of every work which I summon back into existence by placing my consciousness at its disposal. I give it not only existence, but awareness of existence. And so I ought not to hesitate to recognize that so long as it is animated by this vital inbreathing inspired by the act of reading, a work of literature becomes (at the expense of the reader whose own life it suspends) a sort of human being, that it is a mind conscious of itself and constituting itself in me as the subject of its own objects.

II

The work lives its own life within me; in a certain sense, it thinks itself, and it even gives itself a meaning within me.

This strange displacement of myself by the work deserves to be examined even more closely.

If the work thinks itself in me, does this mean that, during a complete loss of consciousness on my part, another thinking entity invades me, taking advantage of my unconsciousness in order to think itself without my being able to think it? Obviously not. The annexation of my consciousness by another (the other which is the work) in no way implies that I am the victim of any deprivation of consciousness. Everything happens, on the contrary, as though, from the moment I become a prey to what I read, I begin to share the use of my consciousness with this being whom I have tried to define and who is the conscious subject ensconced at the heart of the work. He and I, we start having a common consciousness. Doubtless, within this community of feeling, the parts played by each of us are not of equal importance. The consciousness inherent in the work is active and potent; it occupies the foreground; it is clearly related to its *own* world, to objects which are *its* objects. In opposition, I myself, although conscious of whatever it may be conscious of, I play a much more humble role, content to record passively all that is going on in me. A lag takes place, a sort of schizoid distinction between what I feel and what the other feels; a confused awareness of delay, so that the work seems first to think by itself, and then to inform me what it has thought. Thus I often have the impression, while reading, of simply witnessing an action which at the same time concerns and yet does not concern me. This provokes a certain feeling of surprise within me. I am a consciousness astonished by an existence which is not mine, but which I experience as though it were mine.

This astonished consciousness is in fact the consciousness of the critic: the consciousness of a being who is allowed to apprehend as its own what is happening in the consciousness of another being. Aware of a certain gap, disclosing a feeling of identity, but of identity within difference, critical consciousness does not necessarily imply the total disappearance of the critic's mind in the mind to be criticized. From the partial and hesitant approximation of Jacques Rivière to the exalted, digressive and triumphant approximation of Charles Du Bos, criticism can pass through a whole series of nuances which we would be well advised to study. That is what I now propose to do. By discovering the various forms of identification and non-identification to be found in recent critical writing in French literature, I shall be able perhaps to give a better account of the variations of which this relationship — between criticizing subject and criticized object — is capable.

Let me take a first example. In the case of the first critic I shall speak of, this fusion of two consciousnesses is barely suggested. It is an uncertain movement of the mind toward an object which remains hidden. Whereas in the perfect identification of two consciousnesses, each sees itself reflected in the other, in this instance the critical consciousness can, at best, attempt but to draw closer to a reality which must remain forever veiled. In this attempt it uses the only mediators available to it in this quest, that is the senses. And since sight, the most intellectual of the five senses, seems in this particular case to come up against a basic opacity, the critical mind must approach its goal blindly, through the tactile exploration of surfaces, through a groping exploration of the material world which separates the critical mind from its object. Thus, despite the immense effort on the part of the sympathetic intelligence to lower itself to a level where it can, however lamely, make some progress in its quest toward the consciousness of the other, this enterprise is destined to failure. One senses that the unfortunate critic is condemned never to fulfill adequately his role as reader. He stumbles, he puzzles, he questions awkwardly a language which he is condemned never to read with ease; or rather, in trying to read the language, he uses a key which enables him to translate but a fraction of the text.

This critic is Jacques Rivière.

And yet it is from this failure that a much later critic will derive a more successful method of approaching a text. With this later critic, as with Rivière, the whole project begins with an attempt at identification on the most basic level. But this most primitive level is the one in which there flows, from mind to mind, a current which has only to be followed. To identify with the work means here, for the critic, to undergo the same experiences, beginning with the most elementary. On the level of indistinct thought, of sensations, emotions, images, and obsessions of preconscious life, it is possible for the critic to repeat, within himself, that life of which the work affords a first version, inexhaustibly revealing and suggestive. And yet such an imitation could not take place, in a domain so hard to define, without the aid of a powerful auxiliary. This auxiliary is language. There is no critical identification which is not prepared, realized, and incarnated through the agency of language. The deepest sentient life, hidden in the recesses of another's thoughts, could never be truly transposed, save for the mediation of words which allow a whole series of equivalences to arise. To describe this phenomenon as it takes place in the criticism I am speaking of now, I can no longer be content with the usual distinctions between the signifier (*signifiant*) and the signified (*signifié*) for what would it mean here to say that the language of the critic *signifies* the language of the literary work? There is not just equation, similitude. Words have attained a veritable power of recreation; they are a sort of material entity, solid and three-dimensional, thanks to which a certain life of the senses is reborn, finding in a network of verbal connotations the very conditions necessary for its replication. In other words, the language of criticism here dedicates itself to the business of mimicking physically the apperceptual world of the author. Strangely enough, the language of this sort of mimetic criticism becomes even more tangible, more tactile than the author's own; the poetry of the critic becomes more "poetic" than the poet's. This verbal *mimesis*, consciously exaggerated, is in no way servile, nor does it tend at all toward the pastiche. And yet it can reach its object only insofar as that object is deeply enmeshed in, almost confounded with, physical matter. This form of criticism is thus able to provide an admirable equivalent of the vital substratum which underlies all thought, and yet it seems incapable of attaining and expressing thought itself. This criticism is both helped and hindered by the language which it employs; helped, insofar as this language allows it to express the sensuous life in its original state, where it is still almost impossible to distinguish between subject and object; and yet hindered, too, because this language, too congealed and opaque, does not lend itself to analysis, and because the subjectivity which it evokes and describes is as though forever mired in its objects. And so the activity of criticism in this case is somehow incomplete, in spite of its remarkable successes. Identification relative to objects is accomplished almost too well; relative to subjectivity it is barely sketched.

This, then, is the criticism of Jean-Pierre Richard.

In its extreme form, in the abolition of any subject whatsoever, this criticism seems to extract from a literary work a certain condensed matter, a material essence.

But what, then, would be a criticism which would be the reverse, which would abolish the object and extract from the texts their most *subjective* elements?

To conceive such a criticism, I must leap to the opposite extreme. I imagine a critical language which would attempt deliberately to strip the literary language of anything concrete. In such a criticism it would be the artful aim of every line, of every sentence, of every metaphor, of every word, to reduce to the near nothingness of abstraction the images of the real world reflected by literature. If literature, by definition, is already a transportation of the real into the unreality of verbal conception, then the critical act in this case will constitute a transposition of this transposition, thus raising to the second power the "derealization" of being through language. In this way, the mind puts the maximum distance between its thought and what *is*. Thanks to this withdrawal, and to the consequent dematerialization of every object thus pushed to the vanishing point, the universe represented in this criticism seems not so much the equivalent of the perceivable world, or of its literary representation, as rather its image crystallized through a process of rigorous intellectualization. Here criticism is no longer mimesis; it is the reduction of all literary forms to the same level of insignificance. In short, what survives this attempted annihilation of literature by the critical act? Nothing perhaps save a consciousness ceaselessly confronting the hollowness of mental objects, which yield without resistance, and an absolutely transparent language, which, by coating all objects with the same clear glaze, makes them ("like leaves seen far beneath the ice") appear to be infinitely far away. Thus, the language of this criticism plays a role exactly opposite to the function it has in Jean-Pierre Richard's criticism. It does indeed bring about the unification of critical thought with the mental world revealed by the literary work; but it brings it about at the expense of the work. Everything is finally annexed by the dominion of a consciousness detached from any object, a *hyper*-critical consciousness, functioning all alone, somewhere in the void.

Is there any need to say that this hyper-criticism is the critical thought of Maurice Blanchot?

I have found it useful to compare the criticism of Richard to the criticism of Blanchot. I learn from this confrontation that the critic's linguistic apparatus can, just as he chooses, bring him closer to the work under consideration, or can remove him from it indefinitely. If he so wishes, he can approximate very closely the work in question, thanks to a verbal mimesis which transposes into the critic's language the sensuous themes of the work. Or else he can make language a pure crystallizing agent, an absolute translucence, which, suffering no opacity to exist between subject and object, promotes the exercise of the cognitive power on the part of the subject, while at the same time accentuating in the object those characteristics which emphasize its infinite distance from the subject. In the first of the two cases, criticism achieves a remarkable *complicity,* but at the risk of losing its minimum lucidity; in the second case, it results in the most complete dissociation; the maximum lucidity thereby achieved only confirms a separation instead of a union.

Thus criticism seems to oscillate between two possibilities: a union without comprehension, and a comprehension without union. I may identify so completely with what I am reading that I lose consciousness not only of myself, but also of that other consciousness which lives within the work. Its proximity blinds me by blocking my prospect. But I may, on the other hand, separate myself so completely from what I am contemplating that the thought thus removed to a distance assumes the aspect of a being with whom I may never establish any relationship whatsoever. In either case, the act of reading has delivered me from egocentricity: another's thought inhabits me or haunts me, but in the first case I lose myself in that alien world, and in the other we keep our distance and refuse to identify. Extreme closeness and extreme detachment have then the same regrettable effect of making me fall short of the total critical act: that is to say, the exploration of that mysterious interrelationship which, through the mediation of reading and of language, is established to our mutual satisfaction between the work read and myself.

Thus extreme proximity and extreme separation each have grave disadvantages. And yet they have their privileges as well. Sensuous thought is privileged to move at once to the heart of the work and to share its own life; clear thought is privileged to confer on its objects the highest degree of intelligibility. Two sorts of insight are here distinguishable and mutually exclusive: there is penetration by the senses and penetration by the reflective consciousness. Now rather than contrasting these two forms of critical activity, would there not be some way, I wonder, not of practicing them simultaneously, which would be impossible, but at least of combining them through a kind of reciprocation and alternation?

Is not this perhaps the method used today by Jean Starobinski? For instance, it would not be difficult to find in his work a number of texts which relate him to Maurice Blanchot. Like Blanchot he displays exceptional lucidity and an acute awareness of distance. And yet he does not quite abandon himself to Blanchot's habitual pessimism. On the contrary, he seems inclined to optimism, even at times to a pleasant utopianism. Starobinski's intellect in this respect is analogous to that of Rousseau, yearning for an immediate transparence of all beings to each other which would enable them to understand each other in an ecstatic happiness. From this point of view, is not the ideal of criticism precisely represented by the *fête citadine* (street celebration) or *fête champêtre* (rustic feast)? There is a milieu or a moment in the feast in which everyone communicates with everyone else, in which hearts are open like books. On a more modest scale, doesn't the same phenomenon occur in reading? Does not one being open its innermost self? Is not the other being enchanted by this opening? In the criticism of Starobinski we often find that crystalline tempo of music, that pure delight in understanding, that perfect sympathy between an intelligence which enters and that intelligence which welcomes it.

In such moments of harmony, there is no longer any exclusion, no inside or outside. Contrary to Blanchot's belief, perfect translucence does not result in separation. On the contrary, with Starobinski, all is perfect agreement, joy shared, the pleasure of understanding and of being understood. Moreover, such pleasure, however intellectual it may be, is not here exclusively a pleasure of the mind. For the relationship established on this level between author and critic is not a relationship between pure minds. It is rather between incarnate beings, and the particularities of their physical existence constitute not obstacles to understanding, but rather a complex of supplementary signs, a veritable language which must be deciphered and which enhances mutual comprehension. Thus for Starobinski, as much physician as critic, there is a reading of *bodies* which is likened to the reading of *minds*. It is not of the same nature, nor does it bring the intelligence to bear on the same area of human knowledge. But for the critic who practices it, this criticism provides the opportunity for a reciprocating exchange between different types of learning which have, perhaps, different degrees of transparency.

Starobinski's criticism, then, displays great flexibility. Rising at times to the heights of metaphysics, it does not disdain the farthest reaches of the subconscious. It is sometimes intimate, sometimes detached; it assumes all the degrees of identification and non-identification. But its final movement seems to consist in a sort of withdrawal, contradistinction with its earlier accord. After an initial intimacy with the object under study, this criticism has finally to detach itself, to move on, but this time in solitude. Let us not see this withdrawal as a failure of sympathy but rather as a way of avoiding the encumbrances of too prolonged a life in common. Above all we discern an acute need to establish bearings, to adopt the judicious perspective, to assess the fruits of proximity by examining them at a distance. Thus, Starobinski's criticism always ends with a view from afar, or rather from above, for while moving away it has also moved imperceptibly toward a dominating (*surplombante*) position. Does this mean that Starobinski's criticism like Blanchot's is doomed to end in a philosophy of separation? This, in a way, must be conceded, and it is no coincidence that Starobinski treats with special care the themes of melancholy and nostalgia. His criticism always concludes with a double farewell. But this farewell is exchanged by two beings who have begun by living together; and the one left behind continues to be illuminated by that critical intellect which moves on.

The sole fault with which I might reproach such criticism is the excessive ease with which it penetrates what it illuminates.

By dint of seeing in literary works only the thoughts which inhabit them, Starobinski's criticism somehow passes through their forms, not neglecting them, it is true, but without pausing on the way. Under its action literary works lose their opacity, their solidity, their objective dimension; like those palace walls which become transparent in certain fairy tales. And if it is true that the ideal act of criticism must seize (and reproduce) that certain relationship between an object and a mind which is the work itself, how could the act of criticism succeed when it suppresses one of the (polar) terms of this relationship?

My search must continue, then, for a criticism in which this relationship subsists. Could it perhaps be the criticism of Marcel Raymond and Jean Rousset? Raymond's criticism always recognizes the presence of a double reality, both mental and formal. It strives to comprehend almost simultaneously an inner experience and a perfected form. On the one hand, no one allows himself to be absorbed with such complete self-forgetfulness into the thought of another. But the other's thought is grasped not at its highest, but at its most obscure, at its cloudiest point, at the point at which it is reduced to being a mere self-awareness scarcely perceived by the being which entertains it, and which yet to the eyes of the critic seems the sole means of access by which he can penetrate within the precincts of the alien mind.

But Raymond's criticism presents another aspect which is precisely the reverse of this confused identification of the critic's thought with the thought criticized. It is then the reflective contemplation of a formal reality which is the work itself. The work stands *before* the critical intelligence as a perfected object, which is in fact an enigma, an external thing existing in itself and with which there is no possibility of identification nor of inner knowledge.

Thus Raymond perceives sometimes a subject, sometimes an object. The subject is pure mind; it is a sheer indefinable presence, an almost inchoate entity, into which, by very virtue of its absence of form, it becomes possible for the critic's mind to penetrate. The work, on the contrary, exists only within a definite form, but this definition limits it, encloses it within its own contours, at the same time constraining the mind which studies it to remain on the outside. So that, if on the one hand the critical thought of Raymond tends to lose itself within an undefined subjectivity, on the other it tends to come to a stop before an impenetrable objectivity.

Admirably gifted to submit his own subjectivity to that of another, and thus to immerse itself in the obscurest depths of every mental entity, the mind of Raymond is less well equipped to penetrate the obstacle presented by the objective surface of the works. He then finds himself marking time, or moving in circles around the work, as around the vase or the statue mentioned before. Does Raymond then establish an insurmountable partition between the two realities — subjective, objective — unified though they may be in the work? No, indeed, at least not in his best essays, since in them, by careful intuitive apprehension of the text and participation by the critic in the powers active in the poet's use of language, there appears some kind of link between the objective aspects of the work and the undefined subjectivity which sustains it. A link not to be confused with a pure relation of identity. The perception of the formal aspects of the work becomes somehow an analogical language by means of which it becomes possible for the critic to go, within the work, beyond the formal aspects it presents. Nevertheless this association is never presented by Raymond as a dialectical process. The usual state described by his method of criticism is one of plenitude, and even of a double plenitude. A certain fulness of experience detected in the poet and relived in the mind of the critic, is connected by the latter with a certain perfection of form; but why this is so, and how it does become so, is never clearly explained.

Now is it then possible to go one step further? This is what is attempted by Jean Rousset, a former student of Raymond and perhaps his closest friend. He also dedicates himself to the task of discerning the structure of a work as well as the depth of an experience. Only what essentially matters to him is to establish a connection between the objective reality of the work and the organizing power which gives it shape. A work is not explained for him, as for the structuralists, by the exclusive interdependence of the objective elements which compose it. He does not see in it a fortuitous combination, interpreted *a posteriori* as if it were an *a priori* organization. There is not in his eyes any system of the work without a principle of systematization which operates in correlation with that work and which is even included in it. In short, there is no spider-web without a center which is the spider. On the other hand, it is not a question of going from the work to the psychology of the author, but of going back, within the sphere of the work, from the objective elements systematically arranged, to a certain power of organization, inherent in the work itself, as if the latter showed itself to be an intentional consciousness determining its arrangements and solving its problems. So that it would scarcely be an abuse of terms to say that it speaks, by means of its structural elements, an authentic language, thanks to which it discloses itself and means nothing but itself. Such then is the critical enterprise of Jean Rousset. It sets itself to use the objective elements of the work in order to attain, beyond them, a reality not formal, nor objective, written down however in forms and expressing itself by means of them. Thus the understanding of forms must not limit itself merely to the recording of their objective aspects. As Focillon demonstrated from the point of view of art history, there is a "life of forms" perceptible not only in the historic development which they display from epoch to epoch, but within each single work, in the movement by which forms tend therein sometimes to stabilize and become static, and sometimes to change into one another. Thus the two contradictory forces which are always at work in any literary writing, the will to stability and the protean impulse, help us to perceive by their interplay how much forms are dependent on what Coleridge called a shaping power which determines them, replaces them and transcends them. The teaching of Raymond finds then its most satisfying success in the critical method of Jean Rousset, a method which leads the seeker from the continuously changing frontiers of form to what is beyond form.

It is fitting then to conclude this inquiry here, since it has achieved its goal, namely to describe, relying on a series of more or less adequate examples, a critical method having as guiding principle the relation between subject and object. Yet there remains one last difficulty. In order to establish the interrelationship between subject and object, which is the principle of all creative work and of the understanding of it, two ways, at least theoretically, are opened, one leading from the objects to the subject, the other from the subject to the objects. Thus we have seen Raymond and Rousset, through perception of the objective structures of a literary work, strive to attain the subjective principle which upholds it. But, in so doing, they seem to recognize the precedence of the subject over its objects. What Raymond and Rousset are searching for in the objective and formal aspects of the work, is something which is previous to the work and on which the work depends for its very existence. So that the method which leads from the object to the subject does not differ radically at bottom from the one which leads from subject to object, since it does really consist in going from subject to subject through the object. Yet there is the risk of overlooking an important point. The aim of criticism is not achieved merely by the understanding of the part played by the subject in its interrelation with objects. When reading a literary work, there is a moment when it seems to me that the subject *present* in this work disengages itself from all that surrounds it, and stands alone. Had I not once the intuition of this, when visiting the Scuola di San Rocco in Venice, one of the highest summits of art, where there are assembled so many paintings of the same painter, Tintoretto? When looking at all these masterpieces brought there together and revealing so manifestly their unity of inspiration, I had suddenly the impression of having reached the common essence present in all the works of a great master, an essence which I was not able to perceive, except when emptying my mind of all the particular images created by the artist. I became aware of a subjective power at work in all these pictures, and yet never so clearly understood by my mind as when I had forgotten all their particular figurations.

One may ask oneself: What is this subject left standing in isolation after all examination of a literary work? Is it the individual genius of the artist, visibly present in his work, yet having an invisible life independent of the work? Or is it, as Valéry thinks, an anonymous and abstract consciousness presiding, in its aloofness, over the operations of all more concrete consciousness? Whatever it may be, I am constrained to acknowledge that all subjective activity present in a literary work is not entirely explained by its relationship with forms and objects within the work. There is in the work a mental activity profoundly engaged in objective forms; and there is, at another level, forsaking all forms, a subject which reveals itself to itself (and to me) in its transcendence over all which is reflected in it. At this point, no object can any longer express it, no structure can any longer define it; it is exposed in its ineffability and in its fundamental indeterminacy. Such is perhaps the reason why the critic, in his elucidation of works, is haunted by this transcendence of mind. It seems then that criticism, in order to accompany the mind in this effort of detachment from itself, needs to annihilate, or at least momentarily to forget, the objective elements of the work, and to elevate itself to the apprehension of a subjectivity without objectivity.

ROLAND BARTHES
Phèdre

To name or not to name, that is the question. In *Phèdre* it is language's very being that is put on the stage: the profoundest of Racine's tragedies is also the most formal; for the tragic stake here is less the meaning of language than its manifestation, less Phaedra's love than her avowal. Or more exactly: to name Evil is to exhaust it entirely. Evil is a tautology, *Phèdre* a nominalist tragedy.[1]

From the outset, Phaedra knows she is guilty, and it is not her guilt that constitutes a problem, it is her silence [2]: that is where her freedom is. Phaedra breaks this silence three times: before Oenone (I,3), before Hippolytus (II,5), before Theseus (V,7). These three outbursts have a mounting gravity; from one to the next, Phaedra approaches an increasingly pure state of language. The first confession is still narcissistic, Oenone is merely her maternal double: Phaedra disburdens herself to herself, seeks her identity, makes her own history; her confession is an epic one. The second time, Phaedra binds herself magically to Hippolytus by a performance: she *represents* her love, her avowal is dramatic. The third time, she confesses publicly before the person who by his mere being has instituted the transgression; her confession is literal, purified of all theatre; her language is totally coincident with the fact, it is a *correction:* Phaedra can die, the tragedy is exhausted. We are dealing, then, with a silence tormented by the notion of its own destruction. Phaedra *is* her silence: to break this silence is to die, but also to die can only mean *having spoken*. Before the tragedy begins, Phaedra already wants to die, but this death is suspended [3] : only speech will release this motionless death, restore to the world its movement.[4]

Phaedra, moreover, is not the only figure of secrecy; not only is her secret contagious, Hippolytus and Aricia also refusing to give any name to Phaedra's disease,[5] but further, Phaedra has a double who is also constrained by the terror of language: Hippolytus. For Hippolytus as for

SOURCE: From *On Racine* by Roland Barthes translated by Richard Howard. Original title *Sur Racine*, © Club Français du Livre, 1960, and Éditions du Seuil, 1963. English translation copyright © 1964 by Hill and Wang, Inc. Reprinted by permission of Hill and Wang, Inc. and Georges Borchardt, Inc.

Phaedra, to love is to be guilty before that same Theseus who forbids his son to marry as a consequence of the vendettal law, and who never dies. Further, to love and to speak that love is, for Hippolytus, the same scandal; once again the guilt of the emotion is not distinguished from its nomination. Theramenes speaks to Hippolytus exactly as Oenone speaks to Phaedra.[6] Yet as Phaedra's double, Hippolytus represents a much more archaic state of mutism, he is a regressive double; for Hippolytus' constriction is one of essence,[7] Phaedra's is one of situation. Hippolytus' oral constraint is openly given as a sexual constraint: Hippolytus is mute *because* he is sterile; despite Racine's worldly precautions, Hippolytus is the rejection of sex, anti-Nature; his confidant, by his very curiosity, attests to the monstrous character of Hippolytus, whose virginity is a spectacle.[8] Doubtless Hippolytus' sterility is directed against the Father; it is a reproach to the Father for the anarchic profusion with which he squanders life.[9] But the Racinian world is an immediate world. Hippolytus hates the flesh as a literal disease. Eros is contagious, one must disinfect oneself, avoid contact with the objects it has touched: Phaedra's mere glance at Hippolytus corrupts him,[10] his sword becomes loathsome once Phaedra has touched it.[11] Aricia, in this regard, is merely the homologue of Hippolytus: her vocation is sterility, not only by Theseus' decree,[12] but by her very being.[13]

Constriction is thus the form that accounts for shame, for guilt, and for sterility, and *Phèdre* is on all levels a tragedy of the imprisoned word, of life repressed. For speech is a substitute for life: to speak is to lose life, and all effusive behavior is experienced initially as a gesture of dilapidation: by the avowal, the flood of words released, it is the very principle of life that seems to be leaving the body; to speak is to spill oneself, that is, to castrate oneself, so that the tragedy is subject to the economy of an enormous avarice.[14] But at the same time, of course, this blocked speech is fascinated by its own expansion: it is at the moment Phaedra guards her silence most intensely that by a compensatory gesture she flings off the garments which envelop her and tries to reveal her nakedness.[15] We realize then that *Phèdre* is also a tragedy of accouchement. Oenone is truly the nurse, the midwife, who seeks to liberate Phaedra from her words at any price, who "delivers" language from the deep cavity in which it is confined. This intolerable confinement of the self, which is both mutism and sterility in the same impulse, is also, as we know, the essence of Hippolytus: Aricia will thus be Hippolytus' midwife as Oenone is Phaedra's; if Aricia is interested in Hippolytus, it is precisely in order to pierce him,[16] to make his words flow at last. Further, in fantasy it is this midwife's role that Phaedra would play for Hippolytus; like her sister Ariadne, untangler of the Labyrinth, she wants to unravel the skein, reel off the thread, lead Hippolytus out of the cavern into daylight.[17]

Then what is it that makes speech so terrible? First of all, it is because it is an act that the word is so powerful. But chiefly it is because it is irreversible [18] : no speech can be taken back. Surrendered to the *logos,* time cannot be reversed, its creation is definitive. Thus by avoiding speech, one avoids action,[19] shifting the responsibility for it to others; and if one has begun to speak out of an "involuntary distraction," it is no use breaking off, one must go on to the end.[20] And Oenone's ruse consists not in *retracting* Phaedra's confession, in annulling it, which is impossible, but in *reversing* it: Phaedra will accuse Hippolytus of the very crime she herself is guilty of; speech will remain intact, simply transferred from one character to the other. For language is indestructible: the hidden divinity of *Phèdre* is neither Venus nor the Sun. It is that god "terrible to perjurers" whose temple stands at the gates of Troezen, surrounded by ancestral tombs, and before which Hippolytus will die. Theseus himself is the true victim of this god: though he has been able to *return* from the Underworld, to recover the irrecoverable, he is the one who speaks too soon. Semidivine, powerful enough to dominate the contradiction of death, he nonetheless cannot unsay what he had said: the gods send back the word he has uttered, in the form of a dragon that devours him in his son.

Of course, as the panic drama of defenestration, of opening, *Phèdre* employs an abundant thematics of concealment. Its central image is the Earth; Theseus, Hippolytus, Aricia and her brothers [21] are all descended from the Earth. Theseus is a strictly chthonian hero, a familiar of the underworld whose asphyxiating concavity his palace reproduces;[22] a labyrinthian hero, he has been able to triumph over the cavern, to pass back and forth between darkness and light, to know the unknowable and yet to return, while the site natural to Hippolytus is the shadowy forest, where he nourishes his own sterility.[23] Confronting this telluric bloc, Phaedra is divided: through her father, Minos, she participates in the order of the buried, of the deep; through her mother, Pasiphaë, she is descended from the Sun. Her principle is a troubled vacillation between these terms. She ceaselessly suppresses her secret, returns to the interior cavern, but ceaselessly, too, a force drives her to leave it, to expose herself, to join the Sun; and ceaselessly she testifies to the ambiguity of her nature: she fears the light, yet invokes it; [24] she thirsts for the day, yet taints it. In a word, her principle is the paradox of a *black light,*[25] that is, of a contradiction of essences.

Now this contradiction has, in *Phèdre,* an absolute form: the monster. At first, the monstrous threatens all the characters; they are all monsters to each other, and all monsterseekers as well.[26] But above all, it is a monster, this time a real one, which intervenes to resolve the tragedy. And this monster is the very essence of the monstrous — in other words, it epitomizes in its biological structure the fundamental paradox of *Phèdre*. It is the force that bursts out of the depths of the sea, it is what pounces upon the secret, breaks it open, ravishes it, tears it apart, scatters and disperses it. To Hippolytus' principle of enclosure corresponds tragically — that is, ironically — his death by the dismemberment, the pulverization, broadly *extended* by the narrative, of a body hitherto essentially compact. Theramenes' narrative [27] constitutes, then, the critical point where the tragedy is resolved, that is, where the previous retention of all the characters is undone by a total catastrophe. So it is actually Hippolytus who is the exemplary character in *Phèdre* (though not the principal one); he is truly the propitiatory victim, in whom the secret and its explosion achieve their most gratuitous form. And in relation to this great mythic function of the broken secret, Phaedra herself is an impure character. Her secret, whose outcome is in a sense *tried out* twice, is finally released through an extended confession. In Phaedra, language recovers *in extremis* a positive function: she has time to die, there is finally an agreement between her language and her death, both have the same measure (whereas even the last word is stolen from Hippolytus). Like a sheet of water, a slow death creeps into her,[28] and like a sheet of water too, a pure, even language emerges from her; tragic time, that dreadful time which separates the spoken order from the real order, is purified, nature's unity is restored.

Phèdre thus proposes an identification of interiority with guilt; in *Phèdre* things are not hidden because they are culpable (that would be a prosaic view, Oenone's, for example, to whom Phaedra's transgression is merely contingent, linked to the life of Theseus); things are culpable from the very moment that they are hidden: the Racinian being does not release himself, and that is his sickness: nothing better attests the *formal* character [29] of the transgression than its explicit identification with a disease;[30] Phaedra's objective guilt (adultery, incest) is actually an artificial construction, intended to naturalize the suffering of the secret, to change form into content usefully. This inversion coincides with a more general movement, which establishes the entire Racinian edifice: Evil is terrible to the very degree that it is empty, man suffers from a *form*. This is what Racine expresses so well apropos of Phaedra when he says that for her, crime itself is a punishment.[31] Phaedra's entire effort consists in *fulfilling* her transgression, that is, in absolving God.

ROLAND BARTHES

The Structuralist Activity

What is structuralism? Not a school, nor even a movement (at least, not yet), for most of the authors ordinarily labeled with this word are unaware of being united by any solidarity of doctrine or commitment. Nor is it a vocabulary. *Structure* is already an old word (of anatomical and grammatical provenance), today quite overworked: all the social sciences resort to it abundantly, and the word's use can distinguish no one, except to engage in polemics about the content assigned to it; *functions, forms, signs* and *significations* are scarcely more pertinent: they are, today, words of common usage, from which one asks (and obtains) whatever one wants, notably the camouflage of the old determinist schema of cause and product; we must doubtless go back to pairings like those of *significans/significatum* and *synchronic/diachronic* in order to approach what distinguishes structuralism from other modes of thought: the first because it refers to the linguistic model as originated by Saussure, and because along with economics, linguistics is, in the present state of affairs, the true science of structure, the second, more decisively, because it seems to imply a certain revision of the notion of history, insofar as the notion of the synchronic (although in Saussure this is a preeminently *operational* concept) accredits a certain immobilization of time, and insofar as that of the diachronic tends to represent the historical process as a pure succession of forms. This second pairing is all the more distinctive in that the chief resistance to structuralism today seems to be of Marxist origin and that it focuses on the notion of history (and not of structure); whatever the case, it is probably the serious recourse to the nomenclature of signification (and not to the word itself, which is, paradoxically, not at all distinctive) which we must ultimately take as structuralism's *spoken sign:* watch who uses *signifier* and *signified, synchronic* and *diachronic,* and you will know whether the structuralist vision is constituted.

This is valid for the intellectual metalanguage, which explicitly em-

SOURCE: From *Partisan Review,* Volume 34, Number 1, (Winter 1967), pp. 82–88, translated by Richard Howard. Copyright © 1967 by *Partisan Review.* Reprinted by permission of the publisher and the author.

ploys methodological concepts. But since structuralism is neither a school nor a movement, there is no reason to reduce it a priori, even in a problematical way, to the activity of philosophers; it would be better to try and find its broadest description (if not its definition) on another level than that of reflexive language. We can in fact presume that there exist certain writers, painters, musicians, in whose eyes a certain *exercise* of structure (and not only its thought) represents a distinctive experience, and that both analysts and creators must be placed under the common sign of what we might call *structural man,* defined not by his ideas or his languages, but by his imagination — in other words, by the way in which he mentally experiences structure.

Hence the first thing to be said is that in relation to *all* its users, structuralism is essentially an *activity,* i.e., the controlled succession of a certain number of mental operations: we might speak of structuralist activity as we once spoke of surrealist activity (surrealism, moreover, may well have produced the first experience of structural literature, a possibility which must some day be explored). But before seeing what these operations are, we must say a word about their goal.

The goal of all structuralist activity, whether reflexive or poetic, is to reconstruct an "object" in such a way as to manifest thereby the rules of functioning (the "functions") of this object. Structure is therefore actually a *simulacrum* of the object, but a directed, *interested* simulacrum, since the imitated object makes something appear which remained invisible, or if one prefers, unintelligible in the natural object. Structural man takes the real, decomposes it, then recomposes it; this appears to be little enough (which makes some say that the structuralist enterprise is "meaningless," "uninteresting," "useless," etc.). Yet, from another point of view, this "little enough" is decisive: for between the two objects, or the two tenses, of structuralist activity, there occurs *something new,* and what is new is nothing less than the generally intelligible: the simulacrum is intellect added to object, and this addition has an anthropological value, in that it is man himself, his history, his situation, his freedom and the very resistance which nature offers to his mind.

We see, then, why we must speak of a structuralist *activity*: creation or reflection are not, here, an original "impression" of the world, but a veritable fabrication of a world which resembles the first one, not in order to copy it but to render it intelligible. Hence one might say that structuralism is essentially *an activity of imitation,* which is also why there is, strictly speaking, no *technical* difference between structuralism as an intellectual activity on the one hand and literature in particular, art in general on the other: both derive from a *mimesis,* based not on the analogy of substances (as in so-called realist art), but on the analogy of functions (what Lévi-Strauss calls *homology*). When Troubetskoy reconstructs the phonetic object as a system of variations; when Dumézil elaborates a functional mythology; when Propp constructs a folktale resulting by structuration from all the Slavic tales he has previously decomposed; when Lévi-Strauss discovers the homologic functioning of the totemic imagination, or Granger the formal rules of economic thought, or Gardin the pertinent features of prehistoric bronzes; when Richard decomposes a poem by Mallarmé into its distinctive vibrations — they are all doing nothing different from what Mondrian, Boulez or Butor are doing when they articulate a certain object — what will be called, precisely, a *composition* — by the controlled manifestation of certain units and certain associations of these units. It is of little consequence whether the initial object liable to the simulacrum-activity is given by the world in an already assembled fashion (in the case of the structural analysis made of a constituted language or society or work) or is still scattered (in the case of the structural "composition"); whether this initial object is drawn from a social reality or an imaginary reality. It is not the nature of the copied object which defines an art (though this is a tenacious prejudice in all realism), it is the fact that man adds to it in reconstructing it: technique is the very being of all creation. It is therefore to the degree that the goals of structuralist activity are indissolubly linked to a certain technique that structuralism exists in a distinctive fashion in relation to other modes of analysis or creation: we recompose the object *in order* to make certain functions appear, and it is, so to speak, the way that makes the work; this is why we must speak of the structuralist activity rather than the structuralist work.

The structuralist activity involves two typical operations: dissection and articulation. To dissect the first object, the one which is given to the simulacrum-activity, is to find in it certain mobile fragments whose differential situation engenders a certain meaning; the fragment has no meaning in itself, but it is nonetheless such that the slightest variation wrought in its configuration produces a change in the whole; a *square* by Mondrian, a *series* by Pousseur, a *versicle* of Butor's *Mobile,* the "mytheme" in Lévi-Strauss, the phoneme in the work of the phonologists, the "theme" in certain literary criticism — all these units (whatever their inner structure and their extent, quite different according to cases) have no significant existence except by their frontiers: those which separate them from other actual units of the discourse (but this is a problem of articulation) and also those which distinguish them from other virtual units, with which they form a certain class (which linguistics calls a *paradigm*); this notion of a paradigm is essential, apparently, if we are to understand the structuralist vision: the paradigm is a group, a reservoir — as limited as possible — of objects (of units) from which one summons, by an act of citation, the object or unit one wishes to endow with an actual meaning; what characterizes the paradigmatic object is that it is, vis-à-vis other objects of its class, in a certain relation of affinity and dissimilarity: two units of the same paradigm must resemble each other somewhat *in order* that the difference which separates them be indeed evident: s and z must have both a common feature (dentality) and a distinctive feature (presence or absence of sonority) so that we cannot, in French, attribute the same meaning to *poisson* and *poison;* Mondrian's squares must have both certain affinities by their shape as squares, and certain dissimilarities by their proportion and color; the American automobiles (in Butor's *Mobile*) must be constantly regarded in the same way, yet they must differ each time by both their make and color; the episodes of the Oedipus myth (in Lévi-Strauss's analysis) must be both identical and varied — in order that all these languages, these works may be intelligible. The dissection-operation thus produces an initial dispersed state of the simulacrum, but the units of the structure are not at all anarchic: before being distributed and fixed in the continuity of the composition, each one forms with its own virtual group or reservoir an intelligent organism, subject to a sovereign motor principle: that of the smallest difference.

Once the units are posited, structural man must discover in them or establish for them certain rules of association: this is the activity of articulation, which succeeds the summoning activity. The syntax of the arts and of discourse is, as we know, extremely varied; but what we discover in every work of structural enterprise is the submission to regular constraints whose formalism, improperly indicted, is much less important than their stability; for what is happening, at this second stage of the simulacrum-activity, is a kind of battle against chance; this is why the constraint of recurrence of the units has an almost demiurgic value: it is by the regular return of the units and of the associations of units that the work appears constructed, i.e., endowed with meaning; linguistics calls these rules of combination *forms,* and it would be advantageous to retain this rigorous sense of an overtaxed word: form, it has been said, is what keeps the contiguity of units from appearing as a pure effect of chance: the work of art is what man wrests from chance. This perhaps allows us to understand on the one hand why so-called nonfigurative works are nonetheless to the highest degree works of art, human thought being established not on the analogy of copies and models but with the regularity of assemblages; and on the other hand why these same works appear, precisely, fortuitous and thereby useless to those who discern in them no *form*: in front of an abstract painting, Khrushchev was certainly wrong to see only the traces of a donkey's tail whisked across the canvas; at least he knew in his way, though, that art is a certain conquest of chance (he simply forgot that every rule must be learned, whether one wants to apply or interpret it).

The simulacrum, thus constructed, does not render the world as it has found it, and it is here that structuralism is important. First of all, it manifests a new category of the object, which is neither the real nor the rational, but the *functional,* thereby joining a whole scientific complex which is being developed around information theory and research. Subsequently and especially, it highlights the strictly human process by which men give meaning to things. Is this new? To a certain degree, yes; of course the world has never stopped looking for the meaning of what is given it and of what it produces; what is new is a mode of thought (or a "poetics") which seeks less to assign completed meanings to the objects it discovers than to know how meaning is possible, at what cost and by what means. Ultimately, one might say that the object of structuralism is not man endowed with meanings, but man fabricating meanings, as if it could not be the *content* of meanings which exhausted the semantic goals of humanity, but only the act by which these meanings, historical and contingent variables, are produced. *Homo significans*: such would be the new man of structural inquiry.

According to Hegel, the ancient Greek was amazed by the *natural* in nature; he constantly listened to it, questioned the meaning of mountains, springs, forests, storms; without knowing what all these objects were telling him by name, he perceived in the vegetal or cosmic order a tremendous *shudder* of meaning, to which he gave the name of a god: Pan. Subsequently, nature has changed, has become social: everything that is given to man is *already* human, down to the forest and the river which we cross when we travel. But confronted with this social nature, which is quite simply culture, structural man is no different from the ancient Greek: he too listens for the natural in culture, and constantly perceives in it not so much stable, finite, "true" meanings as the shudder of an enormous machine which is humanity tirelessly undertaking to create meaning, without which it would no longer be human. And it is because this fabrication of meaning is more important, to its view, than the meanings themselves, it is because the function is extensive with the works, that structuralism constitutes itself as an activity, and refers the exercise of the work and the work itself to a single identity: a serial composition or an analysis by Lévi-Strauss are not objects except insofar as they have been *made*: their present being *is* their past act: they are *having-been-mades*; the artist, the analyst recreates the course taken by meaning, he need not designate it: his function, to return to Hegel's example, is a *manteia*; like the ancient soothsayer, he *speaks* the locus of meaning but does not name it. And it is because literature, in particular, is a mantic activity that it is both intelligible and interrogating, speaking and silent, engaged in the world by the course of meaning which it remakes with the world, but disengaged from the contingent meanings which the world elaborates: an answer to the man who consumes it yet always a question to nature, an answer which questions and a question which answers.

How then does structural man deal with the accusation of unreality which is sometimes flung at him? Are not forms in the world, are not forms responsible? Was it really his Marxism that was revolutionary in Brecht? Was it not rather the decision to link to Marxism, in the theater, the placing of a spotlight or the deliberate fraying of a costume? Structuralism does not withdraw history from the world: it seeks to link to history not only certain contents (this has been done a thousand times) but also certain forms, not only the material but also the intelligible, not only the ideological but also the esthetic. And precisely because all thought about the historically intelligible is also a participation in that intelligibility, structural man is scarcely concerned to *last;* he knows that structuralism, too, is a certain *form* of the world, which will change with the world; and just as he experiences his validity (but not his truth) in his power to speak the old languages of the world in a new way, so he knows that it will suffice that a new language rise out of history, a new language which speaks him in his turn, for his task to be done.

J. HILLIS MILLER

An Introduction to
William Carlos Williams

William Carlos Williams was born in Rutherford, New Jersey, in 1883. After medical training at the University of Pennsylvania, he spent the rest of his life, until his retirement in 1951, practicing medi-

SOURCE: "An Introduction to William Carlos Williams" is from *William Carlos Williams: A Collection of Critical Essays*, edited by J. Hillis Miller, copyright © 1966. Reprinted by permission of Prentice-Hall, Inc., Englewood Cliffs, New Jersey.

The poem "Young Sycamore" is from *The Collected Earlier Poems of William Carlos Williams*. Copyright 1938 by William Carlos Williams. Reprinted by permission of New Directions Publishing Corporation and Laurence Pollinger Ltd.

cine in Rutherford. He met Ezra Pound at the University of Pennsylvania, and later came to know Marianne Moore, Wallace Stevens, Louis Zukofsky, and other poets and artists. During a long lifetime he published several dozen books — poems, plays, stories, novels, essays, a book about American history, an autobiography. The complete body of his published poetry, with a few unimportant omissions, may be read in four volumes: *The Collected Earlier Poems, The Collected Later Poems, Paterson,* and *Pictures from Brueghel.* He died in 1963 at the age of seventy-nine.[1]

Though Williams' work received considerable attention during his lifetime, he has only gradually come to be recognized as one of the most important of twentieth century American poets, one deserving a place beside Pound, Eliot, Frost, and Stevens. His work registers a change in sensibility which puts him, along with other writers in America and abroad, beyond the characteristic assumptions of romanticism. Since these assumptions have for the most part been dominant in Western literature since the late eighteenth century, full understanding of Williams' work has been slow to develop. Though there is a recognizable kinship between that work and the work of certain other poets, artists, and philosophers of the twentieth century, Williams' presuppositions about poetry and human existence are his own. They are a unique version of a new tradition. What they are and the way they are implicit in each of his poems can only be discovered by that immersion in his writing which must precede interpretation of any part of it.

The difficulties of such interpretation may be suggested by consideration of the ways Williams' work fails to provide the reader habituated to romantic or symbolist poetry with the qualities he expects. Like a late eighteenth century reader encountering the *Lyrical Ballads,* many present-day readers of Williams "will look round for poetry, and will be induced to inquire by what species of courtesy these attempts can be permitted to assume that title." [2] Here is a characteristic text from "Collected Poems 1934":

> *Young Sycamore*
>
> I must tell you
> this young tree
> whose round and firm trunk
> between the wet
>
> pavement and the gutter
> (where water
> is trickling) rises
> bodily

into the air with
one undulant
thrust half its height —
and then

dividing and waning
sending out
young branches on
all sides —

hung with cocoons
it thins
till nothing is left of it
but two

eccentric knotted
twigs
bending forward
hornlike at the top [3]

Such a poem seems recalcitrant to analysis. The sycamore is not a symbol. "No symbolism is acceptable," says the poet (SE, 213). The tree does not stand for anything, or point to anything beyond itself. Like the red wheelbarrow, or the sea-trout and butterfish, or the flowering chicory in other poems by Williams, the young sycamore is itself, means itself. It is an object in space, separated from other objects in space, with its own sharp edges, its own innate particularity. The tree stands "between" the pavement and the gutter, but there is no assertion of an interchange between the three objects, no flow of an ubiquitous nature-spirit binding all things together. Things for Williams exist side by side in the world, and the poet here locates the sycamore by reference to the things closest to it.

The avoidance of symbolism in Williams' poetry is related to the absence of another quality — the dimension of depth. In romantic poetry, space frequently leads out to a "behind" or "beyond" which the poet may reach through objects, or which objects signify at a distance. In the Christian and Platonic traditions, things of this world in one way or another stand for things of the other world. Romantic poets inherit or extend this tradition, as in the thoughts too deep for tears which for Wordsworth are given by the meanest flower that blows, or as in the attraction of the "Far-far-away" for Tennyson, or as in Yeats's reaffirmation of the hermetic tradition in "Ribh denounces Patrick": "For things below are copies, the Great Smaragdine Tablet said." In Williams' poetry this kind of depth has disappeared and with it the symbolism appropriate to it. Objects for him exist within a shallow space, like that created on the canvases of the American abstract expressionists. "Anywhere is everywhere" (P, 273), and there is no lure of distances which stretch out beyond what can be immediately seen. Nothing exists but what stands just before the poet's wide-awake senses, and "Heaven seems frankly impossible" (SL, 147).

For this reason there is no need to go anywhere or do anything to possess the plenitude of existence. Each of Williams' poems, to borrow the title of one of them, is "the world contracted to a recognizable image" (PB, 42). The poet has that power of "seeing the thing itself without forethought or afterthought but with great intensity of perception" which he praises in his mother (SE, 5), and all his poems have the quality which he claims for "Chicory and Daisies": "A poet witnessing the chicory flower and realizing its virtues of form and color so constructs his praise of it as to borrow no particle from right or left. He gives his poem over to the flower and its plant themselves" (SE, 17). While a poem lasts nothing exists beyond it — nothing but the chicory, in one poem, or bits of broken glass on cinders, in another, or the young sycamore between pavement and gutter in another. Immediacy in space, and also immediacy in time. The present alone is, and the aim of a poem must therefore be "to refine, to clarify, to intensify that eternal moment in which we alone live" (SA, 3). "Young Sycamore" is written in the present tense. It records the instant of Williams' confrontation of the tree.

There can also be for Williams little figurative language, little of that creation of a "pattern of imagery" which often unifies poems written in older traditions. Metaphors compare one thing to another and so blur the individuality of those things. For Williams the uniqueness of each thing is more important than any horizontal resonances it may have with other things: "Although it is a quality of the imagination that it seeks to place together those things which have a common relationship, yet the coining of similes is a pastime of very low order, depending as it does upon a nearly vegetable coincidence. Much more keen is that power which discovers in things those inimitable particles of dissimilarity to all other things which are the peculiar perfections of the thing in question" (SE, 16). "Young Sycamore" contains a single figurative word, "hornlike," and though this word is of great importance in the poem, spreading its implications backward to pick up the overtones of words like "bodily" or "thrust" and suggesting that the sycamore has an animal-like volition and power (or perhaps, as Wallace Stevens has said, the lithe sinuosity of a snake), nevertheless the personification is attenuated. The poem is made chiefly of a long clause which in straightforward language describes the tree from trunk to topmost twig.

Such poetry provides problems not only for the analytical critic, but also for a reader concerned about the uses of poetry. Poetry of the romantic and symbolist traditions is usually dramatic or dialectical in structure. It often presupposes a double division of existence. The objects of this world are separated from the supernatural realities they signify, and the consciousness of the poet is separated both from objects and from their celestial models. A poetry based on such assumptions will be a verbal act bringing about a change in man's relation to the world. In uniting subject and object it will give the poet momentary possession of that distant reality the object symbolizes. Such a poetry is the enactment of a journey which may take the poet and his reader to the very bourne of heaven. Mallarmé's work provides a symbolist version of this poetry of dramatic action. He must avoid at any cost that direct description Williams so willingly accepts, and writes a poetry of indirection in which the covert naming of things is the annihilation of those things so that they may be replaced, beyond negation, by an essence which is purely notional, an aroma "absent from all bouquets."

Nothing of this sort happens in Williams' poetry. "Young Sycamore" does not go anywhere or accomplish any new possession of the tree. There is no gradual approach of subject and object which leads to their merger in an ecstatic union. The reader at the end is where he was at the beginning — standing in imagination before the tree. The sycamore and the poem about the sycamore are separate things, side by side in the world in the same way that the tree stands between the pavement and the gutter without participating in either. Romantic and symbolist poetry is usually an art of willed transformation. In this it is, like science or technology, an example of that changing of things into artifacts which assimilates them into the human world. Williams' poetry, on the other hand, is content to let things be. A good poet, he says, "doesn't *select* his material. What is there to select? It *is*." [4]

No symbolism, no depth, no reference to a world beyond the world, no pattern of imagery, no dialectical structure, no interaction of subject and object — just description. How can the critic "analyze" such a poem? What does it mean? Of what use is it? How can the poet justify the urgency of his first line: "I must tell you"? If the poem does not make anything happen, or give the reader something he did not have before, it seems of no more use than a photograph of the tree.

The answers to these questions can be given only if the reader places himself within the context of the assumptions which underlie the poem. Anywhere is everywhere for Williams not because all places are indifferent, so that one place is as good as another, each one confessing the same failure of mind, objects, and their meanings to become one. Quite the opposite is the case. His poetry can give itself to calm description because all objects are already possessed from the beginning, in what he calls an "approximate co-extension with the universe" (SA, 27). The co-extension need be only approximate because that concentration on a single object or group of objects so habitual to Williams confirms his identification with all things. In order to attain that concentration, other things, for the moment, must be set aside; but they are no less there, no less latently present in the realm of co-extension the poet has entered. A primordial union of subject and object is the basic presupposition of Williams' poetry.

In assuming such a union his work joins in that return to the facts of immediate experience which is a widespread tendency in twentieth century thought and art. This tendency may be identified in painters from Cézanne through cubism to abstract expressionism. It may be seen in poets like René Char, Jorge Guillén, Charles Olson, and Robert Creeley. It is visible in that transformation of fiction which has, most recently, generated the French "new novel," the *romans blancs* of Alain Robbe-Grillet or Nathalie Sarraute. It may be found in the linguistic philosophy of Wittgenstein in the *Philosophical Investigations,* and in the tradition of phenomenology from Husserl through Heidegger and Merleau-Ponty. Williams' poetry has its own unique structure and assumptions, but if any milieu is needed for it, this new tradition is the proper one. Though he understood the connection between his work and modern painting, and though he admired, for example, the poetry of Char, the similarities between his writing and other work should not be thought of in terms of "influences." The similarities are rather a matter of independent responses to a new experience of life.

Williams differs from other recent English and American poets in the timing of his acceptance of the new relation to the world. Yeats, Eliot, and Stevens, for example, also move beyond dualism, but this movement fills the whole course of their lives. It is accomplished only in their last work — in the explosive poetry of the moment in Yeats's "High Talk" or "News for the Delphic Oracle," or in the poetry of Incarnation in Eliot's "Four Quartets," or in the fluid improvisations, joining imagination and reality, of Stevens' "An Ordinary Evening in New Haven." Williams, however, begins his career with the abandonment of his separate ego. Only in the unfinished narrative poem written during his medical studies [5] and in his first published volume, the *Poems* of 1909, does he remain within the romantic tradition. Themes of spatial distance and of the isolation of the self are dominant there. With his next long poem, "The Wanderer," Williams takes the step beyond romanticism. The poem ends with the protagonist's plunge into the "filthy Passaic." He is swallowed up by "the utter depth of its rottenness" until his separate existence is lost, and he can say, "I knew all — it became me" (CEP, 12). This "interpenetration, both ways" (P, 12) is assumed in all Williams' later poetry. His situation may be defined as "the mind turned inside out" into the world (KH, 72), or alternatively, as the world turned inside out into the mind, for in the union of poet and river both his separate ego and the objective world disappear. An important letter to Marianne Moore describes this union of inner and outer and the "security" which resulted from it. It is, he says, "something which occurred once when I was about twenty, a sudden resignation to existence, a despair — if you wish to call it that, but a despair which made everything a unit and at the same time a part of myself. I suppose it might be called a sort of nameless religious experience. I resigned, I gave up" (SL, 147).

"Young Sycamore," like the rest of Williams' mature poetry, is written on the basis of this act of resignation. In the poem there is neither subject nor object, but a single realm in which all things are both subjective and objective at once: the tree, the pavement, the gutter, the poem, the poet. The reader is included too, the "you" of the first line. The poet's address to the reader assimilates him into the realm of interpenetration in what Williams calls "a fraternal embrace, the classic caress of author and reader" (SA, 3). In Williams' poetry there is no description of private inner experience. There is also no description of objects which are external to the poet's mind. Nothing is external to his mind. His mind overlaps with things; things overlap with his mind. For this reason "Young Sycamore" is without dramatic action and can limit itself to an itemizing of the parts of the tree. There is no need to do anything to possess the tree because it is already possessed from the beginning.

The imaginary space generated by the words of "Young Sycamore" is not that space of separation, primarily optical, which the reader enters, for example, in the poetry of Matthew Arnold. The poem creates a space appropriate to the more intimate senses whereby the body internalizes the world. Such a space is characterized by intimacy and participation. It denies the laws of geometrical space, in which each thing is in one place and is limited by its surfaces. So Williams describes, for example, that aural space in which each sound permeates the whole world, like the pervasive tone in "The Desert Music" which is everywhere at once, "as when Casals struck/and held a deep cello tone" (PB, 119). Or in "Queen-Ann's-Lace" he experiences a woman and a field of the white flower not as metaphors of one another, but as interpenetrating realities. The poet's body, for Williams, is the place where subject and object are joined, and so, in "Young Sycamore," the tree is described as though its life were taking place inside his own life. The poem is a characteristic example of Williams' minimizing of eyesight and his emphasis on the more intimate senses, hearing, tasting, smelling, and above all touch, that *tactus eruditus* (CEP, 63) which it is proper for a physician to have.

The assimilation of the world by the senses makes of the body a kines-
thetic pantomime of the activity of nature. "A thing known," says Williams, "passes out of the mind into the muscles" (KH, 71). "Young
Sycamore" affirms this possession not only in the tactile imagery of
"round and firm trunk" and "bodily," but also in the pattern of verbs or
verbals which makes up the framework of the poem: "rises," "undulant/
thrust," "dividing and waning," "sending out," "hung," "thins,"
"knotted," "bending." These words articulate the way the poet lives the
life of the tree.

The sequence of verbal forms also expresses the special way in which
"Young Sycamore" takes place in a single moment. The instant for
Williams is a field of forces in tension. In one sense his poetry is static
and spatial. The red wheelbarrow, the locust tree in flower, the young
sycamore, even all the things named in long poems like *Paterson* or
"Asphodel, That Greeny Flower," stand fixed in the span of an instant.
It is therefore appropriate that Book Five of *Paterson,* for example,
should be organized according to the spatial image of a tapestry. Nevertheless, there is in every moment a dynamic motion. "Young Sycamore"
exemplifies one of the most important modes of this in Williams' poetry:
flowering or growth. According to the cosmology of three elements which
underlies Williams' poetry,[6] things rise from the "unfathomable ground/
where we walk daily" (CLP, 23) take form in the open, and in that openness uncover a glimpse of the "hidden flame" (IAG, 204), the universal
beauty each formed thing both reveals and hides. This revelation takes
place only in the process of growing, not in the thing full grown. For
Williams the momentary existence even of a static thing like a wheelbarrow contains future and past as horizons of the present. In its reaching out toward them it reveals the presence of things present, that
"strange phosphorus of the life" (IAG, [vii]). His poetry is not primarily
spatial. Time, for him, is the fundamental dimension of existence. The
dynamic motion of the present creates space, unfolding it in the energy
which brings form out of the ground so that it may, for the moment,
reveal the "radiant gist" (P, 133). Though the young sycamore is all
there in the instant, from trunk to topmost twig, the poet experiences
this stasis as a growth within the moment. It is an "undulant thrust"
taking the tree up out of the dark ground as a bodily presence which
pushes on into the air, "dividing and waning," until it thins out in the last
two eccentric knotted twigs bending forward with the aggressive force
of horns.

A grammatical peculiarity of the poem may be noted here as a stroke
of genius which makes the poem a perfect imitation of the activity of
nature. When the undulant thrust from trunk to twigs has been followed
to its end the sycamore seems to stand fixed, its energy exhausted, the

vitality which urged it into the air now too far from its source in the dark earth. But this is not really true. The inexhaustible force of the temporal thrust of the tree is expressed not only in the cocoons which promise a renewal of the cycle of growth, but also in the fact that there is no main verb in the second clause of the long sentence which makes up the poem. The poem contains so much verbal action that this may not be noticed, but all these verbs are part of a subordinate clause following "whose." Their subject is "trunk" not "tree," and "trunk" is also the apparent referent of "it" in line eighteen. All the movement in the poem takes place within the confines of the subordinate clause. The second line, "this young tree," still hovers incomplete at the end of the poem, reaching out toward the verb which will complement its substantiality with an appropriate action. If the subordinate clause is omitted the poem says: "I must tell you/this young tree" — and then stops. This is undoubtedly the way the poet wanted it. It makes the poem hold permanently open that beauty which is revealed in the tree, just as, in one of Williams' last poems, "Asphodel, That Greeny Flower," the moment of the poem is the endless space of time between a flash of lightning and the sound of thunder:

> The light
> for all time shall outspeed
> the thunder crack.   (PB, 181)

"Young Sycamore" too prolongs indefinitely the moment between beginning and ending, birth and death. There is, however, a contradiction in what I have said so far about the poem. To say the poem "expresses" Williams' experience of the temporality of objects is more or less the same thing as to say it "pictures" or "represents" or "describes" this. Such a notion presupposes a quadruple division of existence. The poet is in one place and looks at a tree which is outside himself. On the basis of his experience of the tree he makes a poem which mirrors in language his experience. The reader re-creates the experience through the mediation of the poem. This is precisely the theory of poetry which Williams emphatically denies. Again and again he dismisses the representational theory of art. Like Charles Olson, he avoids all "pictorial effects" (ML, 9), all that " 'evocation' of the 'image' which served us for a time" (SA, 20). Poetry, for him, is "not a mirror up to nature" (SA, 91), "not a matter of 'representation' " (SA, 45), "nor is it description nor an evocation of objects or situations" (SA, 91). The poet must deny such notions of poetry if his writing is to be true to that union of subject and object he gains with his plunge into the Passaic. But if the sycamore is already possessed in the perception of it, of what use is the poem? And yet Williams says that the aim of poetry is "to repair, to rescue, to complete" (SL, 147). What can this mean? The answer is suggested by another passage from the letters: "To copy nature is a spineless activity; it gives us a sense of our mere existence but hardly more than that. But to imitate nature involves the verb: we then ourselves become nature, and so invent an object which is an extension of the process" (SL, 297). "Young Sycamore" is an object, like the tree itself, and it grows out of the poet's identification with nature. Like the tree again, the poem exists as an activity, not as a passive substance. For this reason it must be a dynamic thing, primarily verbal.

What it means to think of a poem as a thing rather than as a picture of something is revealed not only by Williams' constant poetic practice, but, most explicitly, in the prose sections of *Spring and All* reprinted for the first time in this volume. Words are for Williams part of the already existing furniture of the world. They are objects, just as the red wheelbarrow, the bits of green glass, and the sycamore tree are objects. As a painting is made of paint, or music of sounds, so a poem is "a small (or large) machine made of words" (SE, 256). Words differ from bits of green glass or a sycamore not because meanings are inherent in one case and ascribed in the other. Both a word and a tree have their meanings as inextricable parts of their substances. But the meaning which is intrinsic to a word is its power of referring to something beyond itself. Williams has no fear of the referential power of words. It is an integral part of his theory of imagination. On the one hand he rejects those poets who "use unoriented sounds in place of conventional words" (SA, 92). On the other hand he also rejects the notion that things depend on words. The thing "needs no personal support but exists free from human action" (SA, 91). To think of words as too close to the objects they name would be a return to that kind of description in which "words adhere to certain objects, and have the effect on the sense of oysters, or barnacles" (SA, 90). A further sentence from the prose of *Spring and All* expresses in admirably exact language Williams' way of avoiding these extremes: "The word is not liberated, therefore able to communicate release from the fixities which destroy it until it is accurately tuned to the fact which giving it reality, by its own reality establishes its own freedom from the necessity of a word, thus freeing it and dynamizing it at the same time" (SA, 93).

Here is a concept of poetry which differs both from the classical theory of art as a mirror up to nature and from the romantic theory of art as a lamp radiating unifying light. The word is given reality by the fact it names, but the independence of the fact from the word frees the word to be a fact in its own right and at the same time "dynamizes" it with meaning. The word can then carry the facts named in a new form into the realm of imagination. In this sense poetry rescues and completes. It lifts things up. "Words occur in liberation by virtue of its processes" (SA, 90), but as the words are liberated, so also are the facts they name: "the same things exist, but in a different condition when energized by the imagination" (SA, 75). The words of a poem and the facts they name exist in a tension of attraction and repulsion, of incarnation and transcendence, which is like the relation of dancer and dance. So John of Gaunt's speech in *Richard II* is "a dance over the body of his condition accurately accompanying it" (SA, 91). The poem about the sycamore creates a new object, something "transfused with the same forces which transfuse the earth" (SA, 50). In doing this it affirms its own reality, and it also affirms the independent reality of the tree. The tree is free of the poem, but not free of the poet, for both poem and tree exist with other things in the space of inwardness entered by the poet in his dive into the Passaic. This notion of a free play of words above things, different from them but not detached from them, is expressed concisely in another sentence from *Spring and All:* "As birds' wings beat the solid air without which none could fly so words freed by the imagination affirm reality by their flight" (SA, 91). Bird and air are both real, both equally real, but the bird cannot fly without the air whose solidity it reveals in its flight. So the poem about the sycamore both depends on the tree and is free of it. In its freedom it allows the tree to be itself, at the same time as it confirms its own independent existence.

Now it is possible to see why Williams makes verbs and verb forms the axis of "Young Sycamore." The poem is not a picture of the tree. It is an object which has the same kind of life as the tree. It is an extension of nature's process. In order to be such an object it must have "an intrinsic movement of its own to verify its authenticity" (SE, 257). The pattern of verbs creates this movement. "The poem is made of things — on a field" (A, 333), but words, like other things, exist primarily as energies, directed forces. Words are nodes of linguistic power. This power is their potentiality for combining with other words to form grammatical structures. When words are placed side by side against the white field of the page they interact with one another to create a space occupied by energies in mobile tension.

All Williams' ways with language go to make words act in this way: his rhythmical delicacy, that modulation of words according to the natural measure of breathing which culminates in his development in his last years of the "variable foot"; the separation of words from "greasy contexts" so that, as in the poetry of Marianne Moore, each word stands "crystal clear with no attachments" (SE, 128); the short lines which slow the pace, break grammatical units, and place ordinarily unnoticed words in positions of prominence so that their qualities as centers of linguistic energy may stand out (as in the seventh line of "Young Sycamore," three verbs or verb forms in a row: "is trickling] rises"); the emphasis on the syntax of simple sentences, the "grammatical play" of words which Williams praises in the work of Gertrude Stein (SE, 115). In "Young Sycamore," as in Williams' other poems, each word stands by itself, but is held within the space of the poem by the tension which relates it in undulant motion to the other words. As in the writing of Stein and Laurence Sterne, "The feeling is of words themselves, a curious immediate quality quite apart from their meaning, much as in music different notes are dropped, so to speak, into repeated chords one at a time, one after the other — for themselves alone" (SE, 114). The musical metaphor is important here. The space of the poem is generated by the temporal design of the words. In the time structure of the poem as it is read, as in the tense life of the tree thrusting from trunk to twigs, future and past are held out as horizons of the present in its disclosure.

Poems are more, however, than objects added to the store of objects already existing in nature. The words of a poem "affirm reality by their flight." Language is so natural to man and so taken for granted as part of his being that it is difficult to imagine what the world would be like without it. Though man is not human if he is completely bereft of speech, his language may become soiled or corrupted. Then it will no longer affirm reality, but hide it. It will become part of the "constant barrier between the reader and his consciousness of immediate contact with the world" (SA, 1). The theme of the degradation of language runs all through Williams' writing, from the prose of *Spring and All* and *The Great American Novel* through the analysis of American civilization in *In The American Grain* to the passages on the speech of urban man in *Paterson*: "The language, the language/fails them" (P, 20). Even though man's language is corrupt, the sycamore will still be there and will still be a revelation of beauty. The failure of language, however, means necessarily a failure of man's power to perceive the tree and share its life. The loss of a proper language accompanies man's detachment from the world and from other people. Authentic speech sustains man's openness to the world. It is in this sense that "we smell, hear and see with words and words alone, and . . . with a new language we smell, hear and see afresh" (SE, 266). As Williams puts it in a phrase, the poem alone "focuses the world" (SE, 242).

Language is the unique power man has to bring beauty out of hiding and in so doing to lift up, to repair, to rescue, to complete: "Only the made poem, the verb calls it/into being" (PB, 110). The radiant gist is present in the young sycamore, not projected there by the poet, but it is hidden from most men, for the language fails them. The poet's language brings into the open the revelation which is going on secretly everywhere. It uncovers the presence of things present. This presence inheres in things and in other people, and it also inheres in our speech:

"It is actually there, in the life before us, every minute that we are listening, a rarest element — not in our imaginations but there, there in fact. It is that essence which is hidden in the very words which are going in at our ears and from which we must recover underlying meaning as realistically as we recover metal out of ore" (A, 362).

These sentences define exactly Williams' aim as a poet: the attempt through a purification and renewal of language to uncover that rarest element which dwells obscured in the life before us. This notion of the function of poetry justifies the urgency of the first line of "Young Sycamore": "I must tell you." Only in proper language does man's interpenetration with the world exist, and therefore the poet *must* speak. The poem does not make anything happen or transform things in any way. When it is over the tree still stands tranquilly between the wet pavement and the gutter. But in letting the sycamore be, the poem brings it into existence for the reader, through the words, in that caress of intimacy which the first line affirms.

IHAB HASSAN

Beyond a Theory of Literature: Intimations of Apocalypse?

I begin with an assumption: that literature defines our concepts of criticism or else it defies them, and that life constantly challenges the pieties of both art and thought. What I shall attempt here, then, could not be considered an authoritative review of postwar criticism. It should be understood, rather, as a partial statement on the gathering mood of American criticism, an intimation of a trend which the facts of literary history in the past two decades (colored inevitably by my own sense of fact) may help to clarify.

The admission that I neither hold nor accept a definitive view of

SOURCE: "Beyond a Theory of Literature: Intimations of Apocalypse?" is from *Comparative Literature Studies*, Volume I (1964), pp. 261–271, and from *Comparative Literature: Matter and Method*, edited by A. Owen Aldridge (Urbana: University of Illinois Press, 1969), pp. 25–35. Copyright by Ihab Hassan and reprinted with his permission.

criticism should not be too shocking. In England, where the empiric temper prevails in the name of common sense or urbanity, and even in France, where questions of methodology yield to a lively concern with new writing, such an admission would seem fairly innocuous. It is otherwise in America. Among us, the notion that criticism must become a rigorous, quasi-scientific activity in order to justify its name still finds wide support. Not long ago — or is it really ages past? — most students of literature, myself included, recognized the elegance of René Wellek's formulation of the destiny of criticism: "the interpretation of literature as distinct from other activities of man." [1] Coming from Professor Wellek, the emphasis on interpretation rather than on literary theory seemed unduly self-effacing. Be that as it may, the formula appealed then to the common rage for order, and seemed also to aver the dignity of the humanities on terms that the age demanded. With the years, however, the formula seems, to me at least, to have lost in elegance as it has gained in naïveté. The breed of technicians it has unwittingly sanctioned may have found a truer consummation of their hopes in the laboratories of Oak Ridge. Literature as a distinct activity of man? Criticism as a distinct response to a distinct activity of man? What is man that we should be so little mindful of him, so arbitrary with the complexities of his mind? From Surrealism to Absurdism, literature itself suggests that a distinct aesthetic response may be defined only at the risk of deadly discrimination.

Yet my object is not to engage in polemics. The point can be stated with some equanimity: a new breed of American critics are anxious to assert themselves against the rigors and pieties they have inherited. Their mood is restless, eclectic, speculative; sometimes, it is even apocalyptic. Those who feel out of sympathy with them may wish to apply different epithets: romantic, primitivist, existential, amateurish, or plain anti-intellectual. (The usefulness of these tags, dispensed usually with contumely, is as doubtful as their accuracy.) Others, however, may recognize the creative possibilities of this new mood, troubled, vague, or disruptive as it may seem.

Evidence of the new mood is various though one senses behind it the enduring search for wholeness and vitality in the literary response. One senses, too, the paradoxical desire to appropriate literature to the dream life of men, and then again to implicate it in the widest sphere of their daily actions. Is not the secret task, for poet and critic alike, to participate in that magic process whereby the word is turned into flesh?

The critic therefore feels the need for commitment; he wants to testify. And what is to prevent him? The encounter with an authentic work of art is a bruising experience, full of strange knowledge and hidden pleasure, of the kind we usually spend a life-time resisting. The critic knows that he himself is on trial, and that the act of literary criticism is above all an act of self-judgment. Since his business is to speak of literature, speech in his case must ultimately take the form of self-revelation. But the need for self-revelation is not only a private or existential need. It is also a social function of the critic. "Is art always an outrage — must it by its very nature be an outrage?" Durrell asks.[2] The question haunts the critic even more than it does the oafish censors of our time. For should the critic insist on his dubious right to privacy or detachment, his deepest knowledge of literature would remain locked, a private outrage, an inner wound. Yet literature, we know, acts through language; it is a communal call, there where words and experience are one, as it is solitary subversion, where words begin to fail. In the act of testimony, therefore, the critic admits the *relevance* of the buried power of literature; he offers himself to the harsh task of mediating between society and vision, culture and anarchy. Only thus can be give to outrage wider reference, give it a meaning beyond itself. There is the risk, of course, that such mediation may rob both culture and outrage of their particular force. Yet from that loss a new life in history may be gained, a new consciousness of self and society may be born. This is precisely the gain, implicit in the discomforts of critical commitment, which Lionel Trilling, in his otherwise subtle essay, "On the Modern Element in Modern Literature," seems to ignore.[3]

Commitment, however, is but a single impulse of the new critical attitude; it simply prepares the ground for dialogue. Another impulse may be defined as the refusal wholly to objectify the work of literature. The art work, of course, has been long considered as an *object,* an object for dissection or knowledge, idolatry or classification. Yet the encounter between critic and work is neither entirely objective nor purely aesthetic; it may be a "dialogue" of the kind Martin Buber has proposed. In Buber's sense, the work of art resists identification with the insensible It; for the work demands answer and response, and it requires a meeting. Is it then so perverse to ask the critic, whether he subscribes to Buber's theology or not, that he "turn toward" the work and confess with Buber, "in each instance a word demanding an answer has happened to me"?[4] Nothing is mystical in this statement, nothing inimical to the spirit of poetry. The statement, in fact, points to some rather mundane questions which Walter J. Ong, theologian of another faith, happily raises. In his original essay, "The Jinnee in the Well-Wrought Urn," Father Ong states: "Creative activity is often . . . powered by the drive to accomplish, in terms of the production of an object of art, an adjustment or readjustment in certain obscure relationships with other persons." What does this mean? Quite obviously, it means that behind every work of art lurks and strains a human being; less obviously, perhaps, it means that the voice of the human creator, raging heart and feet of clay, is not entirely silenced in his art. The jinnee cannot be exorcised from the urn it inhabits, however shapely the latter may prove; the artifact still comes to life with voices unknown. And indeed this is what we, as readers, require. Once again, Father Ong sees the point clearly: "as a matter of full, serious, protracted contemplation and love, it is unbearable for a man or woman to be faced with anything less than a person. . . ." [5] This is precisely what critics, compelled by the difficult reciprocities of love, may now want to face: not an object but a presence mediated cunningly, incomprehensibly, by language. Such a presence is not simply human. It is the presence, moving and participating in reality, which Owen Barfield, in *Saving the Appearances,* has shown us to lie at the heart of the symbolic process. In facing such a presence, critics may hope to recover the primal connection with a universe mediated increasingly by abstractions. But they may also hope to recover something more modest: a spontaneity of judgment which reaches outward, reaches beyond itself. Holden Caulfield, we recall, was moved to call on an author whose work he had much enjoyed. In such naïveté there may be a parable for critics as well as an occasion for derision.

If some postwar critics are loth to consider the literary work merely as an object, they are equally reluctant to believe that contemplation is the sole reaction to it. Beyond testimony, beyond participation or dialogue, the critic now wishes to entertain the possibility that *action* may be a legitimate response to art. By this, of course, I do not mean that he rushes to the barricades after reading *The Conquerors,* or that he develops tuberculosis after reading *The Magic Mountain.* I mean that the experience of a literary work does not leave him unchanged. To the extent that he is altered in the recesses of his imagination, indeed of his being, to that extent he must act differently in daily life. For if literature is both cognitive and experiential, as we have been so often told, then how can new knowledge but prompt new action? We may have accepted the Thomist notion of *stasis* in art much too uncritically. The counterstatement is boldly presented in Sartre's essay, "Qu'est Ce Que la Littérature?" "Parler c'est agir:" Sartre claims, "toute chose qu'on nomme n'est déjà plus tout à fait la même, elle a perdu son innocence." Sartre continues: "L'œuvre d'art est valeur parce qu'elle est appel." [6] The appeal, above all, is to that act of self-definition which the work persuades its reader to perform, an act of definition and also of freedom. For in a sense, the work itself is "created" by the freedom of the reader to give it a concrete and, ultimately, personal meaning. The work, that is, finally enters the total existence of a man, not simply his dream life or aesthetic consciousness; and in doing so, it becomes subject to the total judgment of human passions. This is precisely what an existential writer of a different breed, Camus, meant when he wrote, "To create today is to create dangerously. Any publication is an act, and that act exposes one to the passions of an age that forgives nothing. . . ." [7] But if the writer must create dangerously these days, the critic cannot afford to criticize timorously. Dangerous criticism assumes that final and somewhat frightening responsibility which some critics naturally resist; namely, the willing suspension of aesthetic judgment in the interests of right action.

I quite realize the enormity of this assertion. For one thing, it brings the critic dangerously close to the posture of the censor — the commissar, the propaganda helot, the prurient chief of police — who requires that every work of art display its social credentials or else stand convicted. No doubt, the redemption of man is a more momentous task than the creation of beauty, and virtue and goodness are not to be scoffed at. Yet redemption, one suspects, does not lie in the grasp of regulators; nor does virtue depend on the degradation of art by power. How, then, can the critic hope to transcend the aesthetic domain of literature without seeming to capitulate to dogma or authority, without seeming to endorse a vulgar or repressive utilitarianism?

There are many answers to this question, though all are equally provisional, for in this as in other literary matters, tact not theory comes to our aid. We can begin, however, by making two observations. First, serious literature offers great resistance to political expediency; other forms of propaganda are far more effective. The basic affinity of modern literature particularly is with vision and outrage. By vision, I mean neither doctrine nor even revelation, but simply a concrete projection of the imagination into the conduct of life. Henry Miller has such an idea in mind when he says: "The role which the artist plays in society is to revive the primitive, anarchic instincts which have been sacrificed for the illusion of living in comfort"; or when he says again: "I do not call poets those who make verses, rhymed or unrhymed. I call that man poet who is capable of profoundly altering the world." [8] Both these statements reveal the artist's conception of himself as visionary actor; both attest to his hope that prophecy may find its incarnation, beyond language, in action. Emboldened by such statements — and they are by no means restricted to Miller — the critic may feel justified in participating in the action that the work initiates. This is to say that the critic becomes himself part of the devious process by which a writer's vision penetrates culture. The character of this devious process is closer to the character of pedagogy than of social reform. This leads me to the second observation. Since the process is indeed devious, subject to all the ambiguities of modern culture, the critic cannot really maintain a purely pragmatic, a purely political view of literature. This is salutary for the activist critic who finds in the visionary or subversive power of literature an inner check on his propensity for dogma, his penchant for expediency.

This critical ideal is not nearly as pretentious as it may sound; nor does it always require the critic to make his home in the midst of chaos. It may require him, however, to heed certain *thematic* questions which were once considered beneath notice. A number of critical works of the last decade reflect this emergent concern. In *The Tragic Vision,* for instance, Murray Krieger pertinently asks, "But how, if we limit ourselves to technical literary definitions, can we find for the tragic any meaning beyond that of Aristotle? The answer is, by moving from formalistic aesthetics to what I would term 'thematics.' " Krieger's analysis of that term cannot be summarized easily, but the implications of his method are stated succinctly enough. He concludes thus: "All of which is perhaps to say only that a literary theory must be adequate to the literary experiences for which it is to account and that we trust our way of experiencing literature only as it is adequate to the life out there, which cries for a way of being organized literarily that will yet leave it preserved intact." [9] If the insistence on "the life out there" does not necessarily force the critic into a study of "thematics," it does persuade him to dwell on precisely those formal matters that invoke the larger aspects of reality and may even engage religious thought. Thus the essays of James E. Miller, Jr., Karl Shapiro, and Bernice Slote, in *Start with the Sun,* explore the relation of Dionysian poetry to cosmic consciousness, mystery, and apocalypse. "Start with the sun:" Miss Slote ends, taking her cue from a noble phrase of Lawrence, "Perhaps then we may be absolved from the poetry of mirrors." [10] Parallel explorations of fiction lead R. W. B. Lewis, in his fine study, *The Picaresque Saint,* to distinguish between the generation of Proust, Joyce, and Mann, in whose world the aesthetic experience was supreme, and the generation of Silone, Faulkner, Camus, and Greene, in whose world "the chief experience has been the discovery of what it means to be a human being and to be alive." Lewis continues: "Criticism, examining this world, is drawn to the more radically human considerations of life and death, and of the aspiring, sinful nature of man." [11]

Perhaps I have spoken long enough of certain interests of postwar criticism, though I feel I have spoken of them only tangentially. If one were to search for the theoretical basis of these interests — a task which I must leave to more philosophical critics — one might be inclined to develop a view of literature that does not put the idea of form as its center. By this I do not simply mean a redefinition of the concept of form so that it may account, say, for the plays of Beckett or the novels of Burroughs. I would plead for a more radical view. From Kant to Cassirer, from Coleridge to Croce and down to the New Critics, the idea of organic form has been a touchstone of value and a cornerstone of theory in literary study. We assume, and indeed we believe, that the imagination incarnates itself only as an aesthetic order, and that such an order is available to the analytic mind. We believe more: that aesthetic order defines the deepest pleasures of literature and conveys its enduring attractions. I am not at all secure in these beliefs. Indeed, I am willing to take the devil's part and entertain the notion that "structure" is not always present or explicable in literary works; and that where it reveals itself, it is not always worth the attention we give it. Such works as *Hamlet* and *Don Quixote* are not diminished by the discovery that their form, whatever it may be, is less organic than we expect the form of great works to be. Even that supreme artifact of our century, that total structure of symbols, puns, and cross-references, that city of words full of secret alleys and connecting catacombs, even Joyce's *Ulysses,* may prove to the keen, fresh eye of a critic more of a labyrinth, dead ends and ways without issue, than Dublin itself which encloses the nightmare of history. This is precisely what Robert Martin Adams concludes in his fascinating study, *Surface and Symbol.* Adams inspects minutely the wealth of details in the novel, and finds that many of them serve to blur or confuse rather than to sustain patterns: "The close reading of *Ulysses* thus reveals that the meaningless is deeply interwoven with the meaningful in the texture of the novel. . . . It is a book and an antibook, a work of art particularly receptive to accident. It builds to acute and poignant states of consciousness, yet its larger ambition seems to be to put aside consciousness as a painful burden." [12] Nothing catastrophic to the future of criticism is presaged by this statement. Quite the contrary: criticism may derive new vitality from some attention to the unstructured and even random element in literature. For is not form, after all, best conceived as a mode of awareness, a function of cognition, a question, that is, of epistemology rather than ontology? Its objective reality is qualified by the overpowering reality of human *need*. In the end, we perceive what we need to perceive, and our sense of pattern as of relation is conditioned by our deeper sense of relevance. This is why the aesthetic of the future will have to reckon with Freud, Nietzsche, and even Kierkegaard, who have given us, more than Marx himself, compelling economies of human needs.[13]

I could not persist in suggesting the theoretical implications of postwar criticisms without falling into the trap which I have myself described. We do not always need a theoretical argument to bring forth a new critical attitude; we only need good critics. But perhaps we need, more than anything else, to regard literature in a more oblique fashion, regard it even in the slanting light of its own absurdity. We might then see that the theoretical solemnity of modern criticism ignores the self-destructive element of literature, its need for self-annulment. What Camus said of

his own work applies, in various ways, to all literature: the act of creation is akin to chance and disorder, to which it comes through diversity,
and it constantly meets with futility. "Creating or not creating changes
nothing," Camus writes. "The absurd creator does not prize his work. He
could repudiate it." And again: "The absurd work illustrates thought's
renouncing of its prestige and its resignation to being no more than the
intelligence that works up appearances and covers with images what has
no reason. If the world were clear, art would not exist." [14] Perhaps the
function of literature, after all, is not to clarify the world but to help
create a world in which literature becomes superfluous. And perhaps the
function of criticism, as I shall argue later, is to attain to the difficult
wisdom of perceiving how literature is finally, and *only* finally,
inconsequential.[15]

The foregoing remarks limn certain trends in postwar criticism; they
are not intended to define a school or movement. Still, I feel it wise to
anticipate some objections before concluding this mock survey.

It may be argued, for instance, that many of the attitudes I have
described are not so novel as I make them out to be. Richards' emotive
theories, Burke's concept of action, Leavis' cultural vitalism, Trilling's
depth-view of manners and imagination, Blackmur's metaphors of silence
in literature, and above all, Herbert Read's sympathy for the anarchic
spirit, certainly open the way to the speculations of younger critics. The
latter, however, still distinguish themselves by a certain quality of passion, a generosity toward the perversities of spirit, and a sense of crisis
in man's fate. Two recent books of criticism, R. W. B. Lewis' *The
American Adam* and Leslie Fiedler's *Love and Death in the American
Novel,* seem quite disparate in tone and method; yet both, I think, stand
in this respect closer to Lawrence's seminal work, *Studies in Classic
American Literature,* than to Matthiessen's *American Renaissance.*

Then again, it might be argued that my use of the terms, "form" and
"theory," appears tendentious; that, ideally speaking, neither of these
terms excludes larger commitments; and that, in any case, there are so
many concepts of "form" and "structure" in modern criticism as to make
a general condemnation of them irresponsible. I should like to think that
there are more wicked uses of irresponsibility than in the criticism of
criticism. What an ideal formalist theory may contribute to our appreciation of literature is not in dispute; what it has contributed in the past
by way of practical criticism is also very considerable. Still, do we not
all sense the growing inertness of the Spirit of criticism beneath the
weight of the Letter? One sometimes feels that in another decade or two,
the task of criticism may be safely performed by some lively computing
machine which, blessed with total recall, would never misquote as
some critics are reputed to do.

I speak, of course, hyperbolically. Perhaps I can make the point clearer, and sharpen thereby the distinction between two generations of critics, by referring to two eminent theoreticians of literature. Both René Wellek and Northrop Frye are men of vast erudition; both have shaped the course of literary studies in America. This, I think, is entirely as it should be; the timely authority of such works as Wellek and Warren's *Theory of Literature* or Frye's *Anatomy of Criticism* deserves nothing less. Yet at the risk of seeming ungracious, it is to their later, and perhaps lesser, works that I wish to refer. After all, the question still remains: what lies beyond formalist theory?

In *Concepts of Criticism,* Professor Wellek shows himself to be somewhat out of love with the directions of contemporary criticism. "It seems to me that in spite of the basic truth of the insight of organicism, the unity of content and form, we have arrived today at something like a deadend," he states.[16] His dissatisfaction, however, is of short duration. Professor Wellek sees the way out in the doctrine of "structuralism," evolved by the Prague Linguistic Circle — alas, now defunct! "Such a concept of the literary work of art avoids two pitfalls," Professor Wellek hopes, "the extreme of organicism which leads to a lumpish totality in which discrimination becomes impossible, and the opposite danger of atomistic fragmentation." [17] The way out, as it turns out, comes very close to the ancient ideal of the golden mean. This is judicious. But is it really judiciousness which prompts him in two later chapters, "Philosophy and Postwar American Criticism" and "Main Trends of Twentieth-Century Criticism," to deride all recent criticism? The brilliant and inventive concern with American literature in the last two decades is deplored as an example of "romantic historicism," and mythic and existential criticism are condemned as an instance of "the irrationalistic philosophies of Europe" adapted to the pragmatic temper of the United States.[18] Professor Wellek sadly concludes: "Only those who adhere to either the German idealist tradition, in the Kantian or Coleridgean version, or those who rediscover Aristotle, still keep a grasp on the nature of art and recognize the necessity of an aesthetic and the ideal of a study of literature as literature." [19] Having defined literature in formalist terms, it is no wonder that Professor Wellek *still* believes formalist theory to be the most rewarding view of literature. Thus is the rigor of tautology achieved.

The Well-Tempered Critic, which is not wrought in the massive architectural manner of Professor Frye's earlier work, is too urbane to be tautological. Its urbanity expresses a fine subtlety of mind in the final chapter of the book, and the subtlety itself disguises a somewhat chilly view of literature. Professor Frye acknowledges the distinction between the classic and romantic tempers in criticism, and proceeds to discover the correlatives of each. The classic temper, he informs us, is aesthetic, the romantic is psychological; the former views art as artifact, the latter as expression; the one derives from Aristotle, the other from Longinus. I do not quarrel with these distinctions, particularly when categorical distinctions make the very basis of the geometric edifices Professor Frye likes to erect. "The first step to take here," he argues, "is to realize that just as a poem implies a distinction between the poet as man and the poet as verbal craftsman, so the response to a poem implies a corresponding distinction in the critic." [20] For both Northrop Frye and René Wellek, we see, the critical act rests on the *separation* of certain human faculties from the continuum of felt life. There are few critics willing to speak professionally for the ancient female principle, acceptance and fusion, and the enveloping wholeness of things, few willing to speak for the fourfold vision of Blake. Yet carried far enough, distinctions become the source of the mind's alienation, the Cartesian madness of the West.

Again, Professor Frye views criticism not as the experience of literature but, more discretely, as an area of knowledge. This leads him to the hard-boiled conclusion, so repugnant to visionary educators, that "the values we want the student to acquire from us cannot be taught: only knowledge of literature can be taught." [21] Can knowledge be dissociated from value, and criticism forego its aspiration to wisdom? Apparently so. "The fundamental act of criticism is a disinterested response to a work of literature in which all one's beliefs, engagements, commitments, prejudices, stampedings of pity and terror, are ordered to be quiet," he continues.[22] Ordered to be quiet! Who listens, then, and who speaks instead? The imagination never demanded such frozen void, nor do the supreme fictions of the mind reject the earth they transmute. We have seen criticism gaze long enough on the world with the quiet eyes of Apollo. Shall we ever see it partake again of the sacred flesh of Dionysus?

I do not wish to suggest that the Dionysiac vision is bound to penetrate literary criticism the world over. I do sense, however, a movement in contemporary letters which must force us to revise our tenets or else accept the charge of theoretical isolationism in America. It is doubtful, for instance, that the plays of Beckett or Genet or Artaud, the novels of William Burroughs, Maurice Blanchot, or Alain Robbe-Grillet, the later stories of Salinger, the poetry of Charles Olson, Blaise Cendrars, or Dylan Thomas — and I cite these names quite at random — can be illuminated brightly by the critical terms of Professors Wellek and Frye. Nathalie Sarraute's latest book, *The Golden Fruits*, and Marc Saporta's "shuffle novel," *Number 1*, deny the conventional idea of structure. The first is a novel about a novel which cancels itself in the very act of reading; the second is a stratagem which accepts the principle of chance as an integral part of the literary experience. As for Burroughs' *The Soft Machine*, it applies — to what extent, no one will know — the "cut up method of Brion Gysin," a method which combines collage and montage.

If these works possess a form, it is probably a "non-telic" form of the kind recently reflected in painting and music.[23] Must we then dismiss such works as faddish freaks, of more interest to literary gossip than literary history?

In France, where criticism has been long associated with the spirit of lucidity, critics take a different stand. A quick look at some of their statements may persuade us that their view of literature is not too far from the view I have proposed. The common theme of Claude Mauriac's *The New Literature* is stated thus: "After the silence of Rimbaud, the blank page of Mallarmé, the inarticulate cry of Artaud, a literature finally dissolves in alliteration with Joyce. The author of *Finnegans Wake* in fact creates out of whole cloth words full of so many diverse overtones that they are eclipsed by them. For Beckett, on the contrary, words all say the same thing." [24] The theme of Roland Barthes' *Le Degré Zéro de L'Ecriture* is similar: the avatar of the new literature is absence. Barthes writes: "dans ces écritures neutres, appelées ici 'le degré zéro de l'écriture,' on peut facilement discerner le mouvement même d'une négation, comme si la Littérature, tendant depuis un siècle à transmuer sa surface dans une forme sans hérédité, ne trouvait plus de pureté que dans l'absence de tout signe, proposant en fin l'accomplissement de ce rêve orphéen: un écrivain sans Littérature." [25] Likewise, for Maurice Blanchot literature is moving toward "l'ère sans parole." This movement may lead to a form of writing that is incessant sound; or it may lead, as Blanchot states in *Le Livre à Venir,* quite in the other direction: "la littérature va vers elle-même, vers son essence qui est la disparition." [26] Both directions, we can surmise, end in the dissolution of significant form, the abdication of language. Is this silence at the heart of modern literature the definition of outrage, a subjective correlative of our terror? Or is the monstrous language of action, which Bachelard [27] believes to be pointing, beyond Lautréamontism, toward "une réintegration de l'humain dans la vie ardente . . . ," a closer correlative of that terror? We can only observe that from Sade and Lautréamont to Kafka and Beckett, the twin dark streams of poetry, the poetry of action and the poetry of silence, have been flowing toward some unknown sea wherein some figure of apocalypse, man or beast, still lies submerged.

Critics, however, are of many ilks, and for some the mantic role is as foreign as Elijah's. I wish to force no prophesies in the mouths of students of literature. Still, it is not unreasonable to ask that criticism evolve a method which takes deeper cognizance of the evolving character of life as of literature. The point is almost too obvious: contemporary letters can be judged as little by the standards of pure formalism as, let us say, Romantic poetry can be evaluated by the strict conventions of neo-Classicism.

The problem of criticism, however, must not be left to the indolent spirit of literary relativism. Indeed, the problem may not prove to be one of literary method at all. The problem of criticism is always the challenge of awareness, full awareness of human existence in time and in place, but also outside of both, in the dream world which antecedes all responsiblities. In the end, perhaps, the problem of critics and poets alike is one of human destiny. To say less is to confuse cowardice and modesty.

If there is an underlying theme in recent American criticism, it is the implicit theme of crisis, a crisis not merely of literary method but of literature itself, which means of culture and consciousness. The crisis, as Nicolas Berdyaev knew, is not the crisis of humanism but of humanity itself. In the past, periods of crisis have often bred visions of apocalypse.[28] Such visions may come our way again. They may even lurk in a critic's perplexity. Here is how Krieger put the question: "Or is it, perhaps, that the Kierkegaardian version is right and that our world has itself become the tragic visionary in its unbelief using self-destructive crises to force itself finally to confront the absurdities of earthly reality . . .? Which is to ask, fearfully and even unwillingly, whether we have not been beguiled by aesthetic satisfactions and whether the utterly stripped tragic vision may not after all be less illusory than the fullness which shines through tragedy." [29]

This is no time to sit in judgment on the world or to interpret its modern tragedy. From the Revelation of St. John the Divine to Norman O. Brown's extraordinary PBK address, entitled "Apocalypse," men have envisioned the destruction of the world and foreseen its resurrection. "Blessed and holy *is* he that hath part in the first resurrection: on such the second death has no power . . . ," St. John says.[30] But we are not at the first resurrection yet; we are not even beyond madness. Thus from Norman O. Brown: "The alternative to mind is certainly madness. . . . Our real choice is between holy and unholy madness: open your eyes and look around you — madness is in the saddle anyhow." [31] What task will criticism perform, wavering between holy and unholy madness? What bootless task?

Criticism is no country for old men of any age. Criticism, which was born to behold literature, must still do so and look beyond itself. Tact and rigor may attend all our words, but our words will avail nothing if man prevails not. What lies beyond criticism? D. H. Lawrence knew. This is what he says in his *Apocalypse:* "O lovely green dragon of the new day, the undawned day, *come come* in touch, and release us from the horrid grip of the evil-smelling old Logos! Come in silence, and say nothing. Come in touch, in soft new touch like a spring-time, and say nothing." [32]

SUSAN SONTAG

Against Interpretation

Content is a glimpse of something, an encounter like a flash. It's very tiny — very tiny, content.
WILLEM DE KOONING, *in an interview*

It is only shallow people who do not judge by appearances. The mystery of the world is the visible, not the invisible.
OSCAR WILDE, *in a letter*

The earliest *experience* of art must have been that it was incantatory, magical; art was an instrument of ritual. (Cf. the paintings in the caves at Lascaux, Altamira, Niaux, La Pasiega, etc.) The earliest *theory* of art, that of the Greek philosophers, proposed that art was mimesis, imitation of reality.

It is at this point that the peculiar question of the *value* of art arose. For the mimetic theory, by its very terms, challenges art to justify itself.

Plato, who proposed the theory, seems to have done so in order to rule that the value of art is dubious. Since he considered ordinary material things as themselves mimetic objects, imitations of transcendent forms or structures, even the best painting of a bed would be only an "imitation of an imitation." For Plato, art is neither particularly useful (the painting of a bed is no good to sleep on), nor, in the strict sense, true. And Aristotle's arguments in defense of art do not really challenge Plato's view that all art is an elaborate *trompe l'oeil,* and therefore a lie. But he does dispute Plato's idea that art is useless. Lie or no, art has a certain value according to Aristotle because it is a form of therapy. Art is useful, after all, Aristotle counters, medicinally useful in that it arouses and purges dangerous emotions.

In Plato and Aristotle, the mimetic theory of art goes hand in hand with the assumption that art is always figurative. But advocates of the mimetic theory need not close their eyes to decorative and abstract art.

SOURCE: From *Against Interpretation and Other Essays* by Susan Sontag (New York: Farrar, Straus & Giroux, 1965), pp. 3–14. Copyright 1964, 1966 by Susan Sontag. Reprinted by permission of Farrar, Straus & Giroux and Laurence Pollinger Ltd.

The fallacy that art is necessarily a "realism" can be modified or scrapped without ever moving outside the problems delimited by the mimetic theory.

The fact is, all Western consciousness of and reflection upon art have remained within the confines staked out by the Greek theory of art as mimesis or representation. It is through this theory that art as such — above and beyond given works of art — becomes problematic, in need of defense. And it is the defense of art which gives birth to the odd vision by which something we have learned to call "form" is separated off from something we have learned to call "content," and to the well-intentioned move which makes content essential and form accessory.

Even in modern times, when most artists and critics have discarded the theory of art as representation of an outer reality in favor of the theory of art as subjective expression, the main feature of the mimetic theory persists. Whether we conceive of the work of art on the model of a picture (art as a picture of reality) or on the model of a statement (art as the statement of the artist), content still comes first. The content may have changed. It may now be less figurative, less lucidly realistic. But it is still assumed that a work of art *is* its content. Or, as it's usually put today, that a work of art by definition says something. ("What X is saying is . . . ," "What X is trying to say is . . . ," "What X said is . . ." etc., etc.)

2

None of us can ever retrieve that innocence before all theory when art knew no need to justify itself, when one did not ask of a work of art what it *said* because one knew (or thought one knew) what it *did*. From now to the end of consciousness, we are stuck with the task of defending art. We can only quarrel with one or another means of defense. Indeed, we have an obligation to overthrow any means of defending and justifying art which becomes particularly obtuse or onerous or insensitive to contemporary needs and practice.

This is the case, today, with the very idea of content itself. Whatever it may have been in the past, the idea of content is today mainly a hindrance, a nuisance, a subtle or not so subtle philistinism.

Though the actual developments in many arts may seem to be leading us away from the idea that a work of art is primarily its content, the idea still exerts an extraordinary hegemony. I want to suggest that this is because the idea is now perpetuated in the guise of a certain way of encountering works of art thoroughly ingrained among most people who take any of the arts seriously. What the overemphasis on the idea of content entails is the perennial, never consummated project of *interpre-*

tation. And, conversely, it is the habit of approaching works of art in order to *interpret* them that sustains the fancy that there really is such a thing as the content of a work of art.

3

Of course, I don't mean interpretation in the broadest sense, the sense in which Nietzsche (rightly) says, "There are no facts, only interpretations." By interpretation, I mean here a conscious act of the mind which illustrates a certain code, certain "rules" of interpretation.

Directed to art, interpretation means plucking a set of elements (the X, the Y, the Z, and so forth) from the whole work. The task of interpretation is virtually one of translation. The interpreter says, Look, don't you see that X is really — or, really means — A? That Y is really B? That Z is really C?

What situation could prompt this curious project for transforming a text? History gives us the materials for an answer. Interpretation first appears in the culture of late classical antiquity, when the power and credibility of myth had been broken by the "realistic" view of the world introduced by scientific enlightenment. Once the question that haunts post-mythic consciousness — that of the *seemliness* of religious symbols — had been asked, the ancient texts were, in their pristine form, no longer acceptable. Then interpretation was summoned, to reconcile the ancient texts to "modern" demands. Thus, the Stoics, to accord with their view that the gods had to be moral, allegorized away the rude features of Zeus and his boisterous clan in Homer's epics. What Homer really designated by the adultery of Zeus with Leto, they explained, was the union between power and wisdom. In the same vein, Philo of Alexandria interpreted the literal historical narratives of the Hebrew Bible as spiritual paradigms. The story of the exodus from Egypt, the wandering in the desert for forty years, and the entry into the promised land, said Philo, was really an allegory of the individual soul's emancipation, tribulations, and final deliverance. Interpretation thus presupposes a discrepancy between the clear meaning of the text and the demands of (later) readers. It seeks to resolve that discrepancy. The situation is that for some reason a text has become unacceptable; yet it cannot be discarded. Interpretation is a radical strategy for conserving an old text, which is thought too precious to repudiate, by revamping it. The interpreter, without actually erasing or rewriting the text, *is* altering it. But he can't admit to doing this. He claims to be only making it intelligible, by disclosing its true meaning. However far the interpreters alter the text (another notorious example is the Rabbinic and Christian "spiritual" interpretations of the clearly erotic Song of Songs), they must claim to be reading off a sense that is already there.

Interpretation in our own time, however, is even more complex. For the contemporary zeal for the project of interpretation is often prompted not by piety toward the troublesome text (which may conceal an aggression), but by an open aggressiveness, an overt contempt for appearances. The old style of interpretation was insistent, but respectful; it erected another meaning on top of the literal one. The modern style of interpretation excavates, and as it excavates, destroys; it digs "behind" the text, to find a sub-text which is the true one. The most celebrated and influential modern doctrines, those of Marx and Freud, actually amount to elaborate systems of hermeneutics, aggressive and impious theories of interpretation. All observable phenomena are bracketed, in Freud's phrase, as *manifest content.* This manifest content must be probed and pushed aside to find the true meaning — the *latent content* — beneath. For Marx, social events like revolutions and wars; for Freud, the events of individual lives (like neurotic symptoms and slips of the tongue) as well as texts (like a dream or a work of art) — all are treated as occasions for interpretation. According to Marx and Freud, these events only *seem* to be intelligible. Actually, they have no meaning without interpretation. To understand *is* to interpret. And to interpret is to restate the phenomenon, in effect to find an equivalent for it.

Thus, interpretation is not (as most people assume) an absolute value, a gesture of mind situated in some timeless realm of capabilities. Interpretation must itself be evaluated, within a historical view of human consciousness. In some cultural contexts, interpretation is a liberating act. It is a means of revising, of transvaluing, of escaping the dead past. In other cultural contexts, it is reactionary, impertinent, cowardly, stifling.

4

Today is such a time, when the project of interpretation is largely reactionary, stifling. Like the fumes of the automobile and of heavy industry which befoul the urban atmosphere, the effusion of interpretations of art today poisons our sensibilities. In a culture whose already classical dilemma is the hypertrophy of the intellect at the expense of energy and sensual capability, interpretation is the revenge of the intellect upon art.

Even more. It is the revenge of the intellect upon the world. To interpret is to impoverish, to deplete the world — in order to set up a shadow world of "meanings." It is to turn *the* world into *this* world. ("This world"! As if there were any other.)

The world, our world, is depleted, impoverished enough. Away with all duplicates of it, until we again experience more immediately what we have.

5

In most modern instances, interpretation amounts to the phil-
istine refusal to leave the work of art alone. Real art has the capacity
to make us nervous. By reducing the work of art to its content and
then interpreting *that,* one tames the work of art. Interpretation makes
art manageable, comformable.

This philistinism of interpretation is more rife in literature than in
any other art. For decades now, literary critics have understood it to be
their task to translate the elements of the poem or play or novel or story
into something else. Sometimes a writer will be so uneasy before the
naked power of his art that he will install within the work itself —
albeit with a little shyness, a touch of the good taste of irony — the
clear and explicit interpretation of it. Thomas Mann is an example of
such an overcooperative author. In the case of more stubborn authors,
the critic is only too happy to perform the job.

The work of Kafka, for example, has been subjected to a mass ravish-
ment by no less than three armies of interpreters. Those who read Kafka
as a social allegory see case studies of the frustrations and insanity of
modern bureaucracy and its ultimate issuance in the totalitarian state.
Those who read Kafka as a psychoanalytic allegory see desperate revelations of Kafka's fear of his father, his castration anxieties, his sense of
his own impotence, his thralldom to his dreams. Those who read Kafka
as a religious allegory explain that K. in *The Castle* is trying to gain
access to heaven, that Joseph K. in *The Trial* is being judged by the
inexorable and mysterious justice of God. . . . Another *oeuvre* that has
attracted interpreters like leeches is that of Samuel Beckett. Beckett's
delicate dramas of the withdrawn consciousness — pared down to
essentials, cut off, often represented as physically immobilized — are
read as a statement about modern man's alienation from meaning or
from God, or as an allegory of psychopathology.

Proust, Joyce, Faulkner, Rilke, Lawrence, Gide . . . one could go
on citing author after author; the list is endless of those around whom
thick encrustations of interpretation have taken hold. But it should be
noted that interpretation is not simply the compliment that mediocrity
pays to genius. It is, indeed, *the* modern way of understanding something, and is applied to works of every quality. Thus, in the notes that
Elia Kazan published on his production of *A Streetcar Named Desire,*
it becomes clear that, in order to direct the play, Kazan had to discover
that Stanley Kowalski represented the sensual and vengeful barbarism
that was engulfing our culture, while Blanche Du Bois was Western
civilization, poetry, delicate apparel, dim lighting, refined feelings and
all, though a little the worse for wear to be sure. Tennessee Williams'
forceful psychological melodrama now became intelligible: it was *about*

something, about the decline of Western civilization. Apparently, were it to go on being a play about a handsome brute named Stanley Kowalski and a faded mangy belle named Blanche Du Bois, it would not be manageable.

6

It doesn't matter whether artists intend, or don't intend, for their works to be interpreted. Perhaps Tennessee Williams thinks *Streetcar* is about what Kazan thinks it to be about. It may be that Cocteau in *The Blood of a Poet* and in *Orpheus* wanted the elaborate readings which have been given these films, in terms of Freudian symbolism and social critique. But the merit of these works certainly lies elsewhere than in their "meanings." Indeed, it is precisely to the extent that Williams' plays and Cocteau's films do suggest these portentous meanings that they are defective, false, contrived, lacking in conviction.

From interviews, it appears that Resnais and Robbe-Grillet consciously designed *Last Year at Marienbad* to accommodate a multiplicity of equally plausible interpretations. But the temptation to interpret *Marienbad* should be resisted. What matters in *Marienbad* is the pure, untranslatable, sensuous immediacy of some of its images, and its rigorous if narrow solutions to certain problems of cinematic form.

Again, Ingmar Bergman may have meant the tank rumbling down the empty night street in *The Silence* as a phallic symbol. But if he did, it was a foolish thought. ("Never trust the teller, trust the tale," said Lawrence.) Taken as a brute object, as an immediate sensory equivalent for the mysterious abrupt armored happenings going on inside the hotel, that sequence with the tank is the most striking moment in the film. Those who reach for a Freudian interpretation of the tank are only expressing their lack of response to what is there on the screen.

It is always the case that interpretation of this type indicates a dissatisfaction (conscious or unconscious) with the work, a wish to replace it by something else.

Interpretation, based on the highly dubious theory that a work of art is composed of items of content, violates art. It makes art into an article for use, for arrangement into a mental scheme of categories.

7

Interpretation does not, of course, always prevail. In fact, a great deal of today's art may be understood as motivated by a flight from interpretation. To avoid interpretation, art may become parody. Or it may become abstract. Or it may become ("merely") decorative. Or it may become non-art.

The flight from interpretation seems particularly a feature of modern painting. Abstract painting is the attempt to have, in the ordinary sense, no content; since there is no content, there can be no interpretation. Pop Art works by the opposite means to the same result; using a content so blatant, so "what it is," it, too, ends by being uninterpretable.

A great deal of modern poetry as well, starting from the great experiments of French poetry (including the movement that is misleadingly called Symbolism) to put silence into poems and to reinstate the *magic* of the word, has escaped from the rough grip of interpretation. The most recent revolution in contemporary taste in poetry — the revolution that has deposed Eliot and elevated Pound — represents a turning away from content in poetry in the old sense, an impatience with what made modern poetry prey to the zeal of interpreters.

I am speaking mainly of the situation in America, of course. Interpretation runs rampant here in those arts with a feeble and negligible avant-garde: fiction and the drama. Most American novelists and playwrights are really either journalists or gentlemen sociologists and psychologists. They are writing the literary equivalent of program music. And so rudimentary, uninspired, and stagnant has been the sense of what might be done with *form* in fiction and drama that even when the content isn't simply information, news, it is still peculiarly visible, handier, more exposed. To the extent that novels and plays (in America), unlike poetry and painting and music, don't reflect any interesting concern with changes in their form, these arts remain prone to assault by interpretation.

But programmatic avant-gardism — which has meant, mostly, experiments with form at the expense of content — is not the only defense against the infestation of art by interpretations. At least, I hope not. For this would be to commit art to being perpetually on the run. (It also perpetuates the very distinction between form and content which is, ultimately, an illusion.) Ideally, it is possible to elude the interpreters in another way, by making works of art whose surface is so unified and clean, whose momentum is so rapid, whose address is so direct that the work can be . . . just what it is. Is this possible now? It does happen in films, I believe. This is why cinema is the most alive, the most exciting, the most important of all art forms right now. Perhaps the way one tells how alive a particular art form is, is by the latitude it gives for making mistakes in it, and still being good. For example, a few of the films of Bergman — though crammed with lame messages about the modern spirit, thereby inviting interpretations — still triumph over the pretentious intentions of their director. In *Winter Light* and *The Silence,* the beauty and visual sophistication of the images subvert before our eyes the callow pseudo-intellectuality of the story and some of the dialogue. (The most remarkable instance of this sort of discrepancy is the work of

D. W. Griffith.) In good films, there is always a directness that entirely frees us from the itch to interpret. Many old Hollywood films, like those of Cukor, Walsh, Hawks, and countless other directors, have this liberating anti-symbolic quality, no less than the best work of the new European directors, like Truffaut's *Shoot the Piano Player* and *Jules and Jim*, Godard's *Breathless* and *Vivre Sa Vie*, Antonioni's *L'Avventura*, and Olmi's *The Fiancés*.

The fact that films have not been overrun by interpreters is in part due simply to the newness of cinema as an art. It also owes to the happy accident that films for such a long time were just movies; in other words, that they were understood to be part of mass, as opposed to high, culture, and were left alone by most people with minds. Then, too, there is always something other than content in the cinema to grab hold of, for those who want to analyze. For the cinema, unlike the novel, possesses a vocabulary of forms — the explicit, complex, and discussable technology of camera movements, cutting, and composition of the frame that goes into the making of a film.

8

What kind of criticism, of commentary on the arts, is desirable today? For I am not saying that works of art are ineffable, that they cannot be described or paraphrased. They can be. The question is how. What would criticism look like that would serve the work of art, not usurp its place?

What is needed, first, is more attention to form in art. If excessive stress on *content* provokes the arrogance of interpretation, more extended and more thorough descriptions of *form* would silence. What is needed is a vocabulary — a descriptive, rather than prescriptive, vocabulary — for forms.[1] The best criticism, and it is uncommon, is of this sort that dissolves considerations of content into those of form. On film, drama, and painting respectively, I can think of Erwin Panofsky's essay, "Style and Medium in the Motion Pictures," Northrop Frye's essay "A Conspectus of Dramatic Genres," Pierre Francastel's essay "The Destruction of a Plastic Space." Roland Barthes' book *On Racine* and his two essays on Robbe-Grillet are examples of formal analysis applied to the work of a single author. (The best essays in Erich Auerbach's *Mimesis*, like "The Scar of Odysseus," are also of this type.) An example of formal analysis applied simultaneously to genre and author is Walter Benjamin's essay, "The Story Teller: Reflections on the Works of Nicolai Leskov."

Equally valuable would be acts of criticism which would supply a really accurate, sharp, loving description of the appearance of a work of art. This seems even harder to do than formal analysis. Some of Manny Farber's film criticism, Dorothy Van Ghent's essay "The Dickens World:

A View from Todgers'," Randall Jarrell's essay on Walt Whitman are among the rare examples of what I mean. These are essays which reveal the sensuous surface of art without mucking about in it.

9

Transparence is the highest, most liberating value in art — and in criticism — today. Transparence means experiencing the luminousness of the thing in itself, of things being what they are. This is the greatness of, for example, the films of Bresson and Ozu and Renoir's *The Rules of the Game.*

Once upon a time (say, for Dante), it must have been a revolutionary and creative move to design works of art so that they might be experienced on several levels. Now it is not. It reinforces the principle of redundancy that is the principal affliction of modern life.

Once upon a time (a time when high art was scarce), it must have been a revolutionary and creative move to interpret works of art. Now it is not. What we decidedly do not need now is further to assimilate Art into Thought, or (worse yet) Art into Culture.

Interpretation takes the sensory experience of the work of art for granted, and proceeds from there. This cannot be taken for granted, now. Think of the sheer multiplication of works of art available to every one of us, superadded to the conflicting tastes and odors and sights of the urban environment that bombard our senses. Ours is a culture based on excess, on overproduction; the result is a steady loss of sharpness in our sensory experience. All the conditions of modern life — its material plenitude, its sheer crowdedness — conjoin to dull our sensory faculties. And it is in the light of the condition of our senses, our capacities (rather than those of another age), that the task of the critic must be assessed.

What is important now is to recover our senses. We must learn to *see* more, to *hear* more, to *feel* more.

Our task is not to find the maximum amount of content in a work of art, much less to squeeze more content out of the work than is already there. Our task is to cut back content so that we can see the thing at all.

The aim of all commentary on art now should be to make works of art — and, by analogy, our own experience — more, rather than less, real to us. The function of criticism should be to show *how it is what it is,* even *that it is what it is,* rather than to show *what it means.*

10

In place of a hermeneutics we need an erotics of art.

GEOFFREY H. HARTMAN

Beyond Formalism

Five years ago, on this campus, F. W. Bateson attacked what he called "Yale formalism." His main targets seem to have been Cleanth Brooks, René Wellek and W. K. Wimsatt, and he has recently added Yale's "pseudo-gothic Harkness Tower" to this distinguished list. Bateson defined formalism as a tendency to isolate the aesthetic fact from its human content, but I will here define it simply as a method: that of revealing the human content of art by a study of its formal properties. This definition does not say that form and content are separable, nor does it infer that the human and the formal could not be caught and exposited as one thing by a great interpreter. It does suggest that the literary scholar establishes a priority which has procedural significance, and which engages him mediately and dialectically with the formal properties of the work of art. I do not know whether the mind can ever free itself genuinely of these procedural restraints — whether it can get beyond formalism without going through the study of forms. I am sure, though, that the faults of those whom Bateson calls formalists are due not to their formalism as such but rather to their not being formalistic enough; and that, conversely, those who have tried to ignore or transcend formalism tend often to arrive at results more abstract and categorical than what they object to. My argument on these points will develop in a twofold way: I want first to take up an interpretation by Mr. Brooks, and a comparable one by Mr. Bateson, to suggest that their faults are alike (that neither critic is enough of a formalist); and will then consider an essay by an avowed anti-formalist, Georges Poulet, to suggest that he is more formalistic than he thinks, and that where he is less so his work may fail to situate the writer. My conclusion is a sceptical one, or else critical in the

SOURCE: "Beyond Formalism" is from *Modern Language Notes*, Volume 81, Number 5 (1966), pp. 542–556. Copyright © The Johns Hopkins Press and reprinted with their permission.

Kantian sense: to go beyond formalism is as yet too hard for us; and may even be, unless we are Hegelians believing in absolute spirit, against the nature of understanding.

I

In "Irony as a Principle of Structure" (1949), Mr. Brooks interprets two of Wordsworth's lyrics on Lucy: "She dwelt among the untrodden ways" and "A slumber did my spirit seal." The essay is well-known, and I can limit myself to recalling what it says about Wordsworth. Mr. Brooks is anxious to show that irony is a general aesthetic structure, that it is found variously in the poetry of every school or period. Words-worth, as in the Lucy poems, is a challenge to his thesis: common feeling as well as common verbal usage prevent us from thinking of such poetry as "ironic." Yet Mr. Brooks' armed vision, examining poems as clear as water, reveals to us new animalcules of structure. The following comment on the second stanza of "She dwelt among the untrodden ways" is representative of his argument for the presence in the Lucy poems of something comparable to witty contrast:

> The violet and the star . . . balance each other and between them-selves define the situation: Lucy was from the viewpoint of the great world, unnoticed, shy, modest, and half hidden from the eye, but from the standpoint of her lover, she is the single star, completely dominating that world. . . . The implicit contrast is that so often de-veloped ironically by John Donne in his poems where the lovers, who amount to nothing in the eyes of the world, become, in their own eyes, each the other's world — as in "The Good Morrow" . . . or as in "The Canonization," where the lovers drive into the mirrors of each other's eyes the "towns, countries, courts" — which make up the great world; and thus find that world in themselves. It is easy to imagine how Donne would have exploited the contrast between the violet and the star, accentuating it, developing the irony, showing how the violet was really like its antithesis, the star, etc.

To this let me add a quotation from Mr. Bateson's analysis of what he calls the dreamlike or unreal quality of the same poem:

> Wordsworth's method here is to combine positive and negative ideas so that they cancel each other out. . . . A simple example of the method is the paradox propounded by the last two words of the poem's first lines. How can *ways* be *untrodden?* . . . There are two similar verbal contradictions in lines 3–4 and 9–10. . . . If it is possible to use language so loosely that *untrodden* need not mean "not trodden," that *love* cannot connote *praise,* and that *unknown* obtains a positive

sense ("known to a few"), *and yet be completely intelligible,* the neighbouring oppositions and collocations of grammar and logic also tend to become discredited. Both the private and the public worlds retreat into a common unreality for the reader, who emerges with the impression that the boundaries between them are less absolute and perhaps less important than the surface meaning of these three sentences had suggested.

The same structure of "contradictions" is said to appear in the antithetic yet merging images of violet and star.[1]

The two interpretations have a problem in common. Both puzzle over a style that is felt to be, in some sense, a *no style.* Bateson recalls matthew Arnold's comment that nature itself seemed to have written Wordsworth's poems for him. Yet Bateson interprets this as involving an attack on language as such. "In order to get at meaning behind language he has had to discredit and break down the ordinary apparatus of language." Hence those subversive qualifications. Yet to Wordsworth himself it surely seemed as if he were returning to, not breaking down, ordinary language: poetic diction is discarded for a natural diction. Unless "She dwelt among the untrodden ways" is a special case in Wordsworth's canon, Mr. Bateson's view is non-historical in that his understanding of the poet does not harmonize easily with the poet's understanding of himself.

Mr. Brooks' view is also non-historical in that no effort is made to relate the new and subdued style to the more overt style it replaced. Mr. Brooks suggests that there are at least two poetic modes centering on the art of contrast, and that Wordsworth's art differs from that of Donne or Marvell in favoring "simple juxtaposition with no underscoring of the ironical contrasts." But he does not connect these modes, or read one of them out of court by means of an Act of Uniformity. Thus we are left with two essentially unhistorical descriptions of Wordsworth's style. Mr. Bateson's is perhaps less formalistic, and more historical, in going directly from a formal feature to a generalization about the engagement of the poet in his society and in the language moulded by it. But we cannot check whether it goes genuinely from the one to the other. The only kind of ideal or "objective" interpretation is that in which we can cross-check our terms (rather than particular exegeses or conclusions) by relating them to the poet's own or to those prevalent in the poet's milieu. Interpretation is bringing the poem forward into the present, which is acknowledging its historicity, which is grounding our terms in history. To do this we must go beyond both Bateson and Brooks and describe as historically as possible the difference between the Wordsworthian "no style" and the stylish style it challenged.

Wordsworth's subtler mode serves to free the lyric from the tyranny of *point*. To recover what the pointed style implied is to review a considerable segment of literary history. The pointed style as it developed in seventeenth-century England is witty and antithetical: everything in it is sharp, nervy, *à pic,* and overtly so like a hedgehog. Metaphysical poetry, on which Brooks' poetics is ultimately based, although he has extended its range with the help of Coleridgean theses, is a particular development of the pointed style: indeed, its freest and richest efflorescence, even in prosody where "point" and "roughness" unusually combine. Neoclassicism pruned the hedgehog and smoothened the prosody. But both metaphysical and neoclassical style are essentially epigrammatic, and each mediates between two recognized, divergent traditions of the epigram. Scaliger had classified these as *mel* and *fel;* and tradition varied these terms as *sweet* and *sour, sugar* and *salt, naive* and *pointed.*[2] Short epigrams, writes Robert Haydn in his *Quodlibets* (1628)

> Short epigrams relish both sweet and sour,
> Like fritters of sour apples and sweet flour.

This may also, of course, reflect the Horatian *utile dulci.* Yet the condiments were not always so deliciously mixed. Because the sonnet had become identified with petrarquising poetry, or the sweet and honeyed mode, epigram was often contrasted with sonnet, as specialized in gall and the sour. Sir John Harrington, in his *Elegant and Witty Epigrams* (1618), sees it this way:

> Once by mishap two poets fell a-squaring,
> The sonnet and our epigram comparing,
> And Faustus, having long demurred upon it,
> Yet at the last gave sentence for the sonnet.
> Now for such censure this his chief defence is,
> Their sugared taste best likes his lick'rous senses.
> Well, though I grant sugar may please the taste,
> Yet let my verse have salt to make it last.

Those final lines, of course, are supposedly pointed and salty, like the concluding couplets in Shakespeare's sonnets — sonnets which, though essentially "sugared,"[3] attempted to marinate the style of love. By a natural development, since epigram and sonnet were not all that distinct, the pointed style often became the honeyed style raised to a further power, to preciousness. A new opposition is consequently found, not between sugared and salty but between pointed (precious, overwritten) and plain. Samuel Rowland gives us a bumbling sketch of that opposition at the turn of the century, when he describes an English *précieux ridicule* ordering his servant to fetch him his cloak:

> He utters speech exceeding quaint and coy:
> Diminutive, and my defective slave,

Reach my corps couverture immediately.
My pleasure's pleasure is the same to have,
T'ensconce my person from frigidity.
His man believes all's Welsh his master spoke,
Till he rails English, Rogue, go fetch my cloak! [4]

Wordsworth redeems the mother tongue from such precious and foreign artifice — but without railing. The Lucy poems, Lucy herself, are directed against something non-English: Lucy is no German-Gothic spook or French coquette. The style of the poems is a new and gentle plain style. Following Ben Jonson's example English poetry had tried to marry plain style to the sinew and maleness of point. The poems of Herbert, and especially those of Marvell, are an exceptionally successful blend of the naive and the pointed epigram.[5] Ben himself had chosen plainness as most appropriate for the epitaph, where things were to be expressed at once pithily and simply. Yet precisely the epitaph succumbed most often to the tyranny of point. Eighteenth century elegiac verse at best is smooth antithesis and elegant turn: at worst, striving for the simplicity of pathos, as in the verses on the Lady who passed away at Bath ("She bowed to the wave, and died") the expectation of point leads to splendid instances of the art of sinking. Lyttleton's epitaph on his wife illustrates the usual and perverse smoothness of eighteenth century elegiac lyricism. Here is Lyttleton's Lucy:

Made to engage all hearts, and charm all eyes,
Though meek, magnanimous; though witty, wise;
Polite, as all her life in Courts had been;
Yet good, as she the world had never seen. . . .[6]

And here is Wordsworth's:

A Maid whom there were none to praise
And very few to love
Fair as a star, when only one
Is shining in the sky
She lived unknown, and few could know
When Lucy ceased to be. . . .

Is this not a tender parody of Lyttleton's pointed inanities? Instead of a *catalogue raisonné* of mutually qualifying and even alliterative antitheses, Wordsworth's statements are almost tautological, or with a second clause so simple as not to qualify the first in any calculating (plus or minus) fashion. Lucy is in her grave, subtract one: but the difference, as Wordsworth says, is incalculable. His verbal style purifies the mannered lyric and particularly the elegiac epigram.

In the light of this abbreviated history of lyric style, what Brooks calls irony or paradox is not an independent structural principle but is mediated by literary traditions developing in contradistinction to each other. The sharper epigram, often satirical, but not inevitably so, prided itself on a continuous fireworks of pointed sentiments and phrases, while the honeyed epigram had to justify itself by parallel yet finer devices. These devices, when they are truly fine and not merely dainty, are hard to describe because they grow naturally out of language or thought. To define them by terms drawn from the rhetoric of the copious style is futile, since we have to do with relatively brief and intensely personal verses — with lyric poetry. The only historical procedure open to us is to see how the modern lyric liberates itself from the tyranny of the witty style. The quarrel of the epigrammatists is especially intense at the beginning of the seventeenth century, when the vernacular art-lyric is freeing itself from its subordination to music, emerging as an independent genre, and so finding its own resources, both of the mellifluous and the pointed kind. The initial dominance of that pointed style we are accustomed to call metaphysical is probably due to this war of independence, since point, combined with roughness of versification, was at farthest remove from the musicality of music. Both Sidney's and Shakespeare's sonnet series participated in this battle of sugar and salt. The battle did not cease with the independence of the lyric: the two modalities remained, now mixing, now antagonistic. We begin to recover in this way the historical terms that validate Brooks' description of Wordsworth's style as "juxtaposition without an underscoring of the ironical contrasts," and Bateson's more specialized observation on the subversive antitheses in "She dwelt among the untrodden ways."

Our conclusion was reached, however, by a "formalistic" exercise in literary history. While existential issues are not excluded they remain closely associated with literary technique. Whatever ideas a composer may have must be translated by a set of equivalences into musical phrase: so it is here with human concerns that express themselves as modifications of style. I would not be so naive as to equate formalism with an understanding of the history of style, but I do not see, whatever else may be added, that it can do without this understanding. And only now, I feel, are we in position to ask the kind of question that might indeed lead beyond a primary concern with style or form or even poetry. The history of style itself seems to urge us beyond formalism by asking: what is the point of *point*? Conversely, what is achieved by Wordsworth's creation of so pointless, so apparently simple a style?

The question may serve to clarify the modern and recurrent aspiration towards a "natural" style. It can be charged that neoclassical poetry, or lyricism Old Style, was a didactic and digital poetry, calculating, pointing, computing too much by fingers and feet. It knew its weakness, certainly; and much of the theory of the time cautions against false wit and excessive *pointe*. (Marjorie Nicolson has written about "The Breaking of the Circle"; it is also useful to consider "The Breaking of the Point.") Perhaps Wordsworth comes to reveal rather than teach, and so to free poetry of that palpable design which Keats still charged him with. All truth, said Coleridge, is a species of revelation.

Revelation of what? The question cannot be answered without a certain kind of pointing, as if truth were here or there, as if life could be localized, as if revelation were a property. Yet Wordsworth's concepts of nature, of natural education and of poetry, are all opposed to this reduction. Who knows, Wordsworth asks in *The Prelude,*

> . . . the individual hour in which
> His habits were first sown, even as a seed?
> Who that shall point as with a wand and say
> "This portion of the river of my mind
> Came from yon fountain?"

The error in such pointing is not only intellectual, due to that "false secondary power . . . by which we multiply distinctions"; it is also spiritual. Pointing is to encapsule something: strength, mind, life. It is to overobjectify, to overformalize. It implies that there is a fixed locus of revelation or a reified idolatrous content.

Yet pointing in this larger sense cannot be avoided: it seems inextricably tied to the referential nature of signs or the intentional character of thought. All Wordsworth can do is to emancipate the direction of the reference. The Lucy poems, taken as a sequence, remove the mimetic dependence of imagination on reality, or on any fixed order of "this then that." We cannot tell whether the poet is reacting to an imaginary thought or to an actual death, or which of the two came first. Lucy's death is reflective rather than reflected; it is, in fact, so strongly linked to the awakening consciousness as to be coterminous with the latter.[7] Lucy is a fiction integral to the mind: did she not exist she would have to be invented. Her mode of being, therefore, cannot be reduced to the imagined or the real by a temporal principle of anteriority or an ontological one of priority. Between the imagined and the real there is, in Merleau-Ponty's words, a "modulation of coexistence." Reflection becomes revelation and alters so radically the relation of consciousness to itself that Wordsworth sometimes denies primacy to his point of departure. Thought "hath no beginning." This is something Georges Poulet, to whom we now turn, and who loves beginnings, should interpret.

II

If it is hard to be a thorough formalist, it is equally hard to be a genuine anti-formalist. Georges Poulet's work may help to illustrate this.

What I say is critical of him, but I take it for granted that his work is sufficiently esteemed to withstand my barbs.

Poulet has not written on Wordsworth, though a long essay on Romanticism refers to him as well as including a section on Coleridge. I prefer to choose for analysis his essay on Henry James in *Les Métamorphoses du Cercle* (1961). Poulet's method is to place himself in a writer's consciousness. He can do this by ignoring all formal distinctions, as between part and whole, or preface, novel, journalistic comment, *obiter dicta*. He may be sacrificing lesser forms to greater, but this would have to be proved, not assumed. Chronological distinctions are also ignored: the method, in truth, approaches that of the synoptic reading of the gospels. In the case of the gospels there is of course a central event, a common mythos responsible for the clustering of the original stories and which outweighs their divergencies. It is not surprising that something similar to this center is assumed by Poulet as common to the biblia of the individual writers. This center is the artist's "cogito," a continuously generated relation linking thought to the world, the *I think* to the *I am*. This is the crux relation, as it were. It precedes or constitutes all other relations of time, space, imagery, action.

Henry James' cogito is defined in the following terms. "To become conscious of oneself and the world is to be conscious of a double expanse whose borders are impossible to reach and whose parts cannot be separated out. Everything is connected, continuous and growing, everything stretches out as an illimitably growing web. We search in vain to discover something that might be isolated." The problematics of the Jamesian consciousness derive from this situation in which form is impossible except as a self-constituted and always illusory act. In James the formalization of consciousness is the very center of the literary activity, and there are no forms to be transcended except those imposed by the individual consciousness on itself.

Poulet aims at nothing less than the rewriting of literary history as a history of human consciousness. (Of masters he acknowledges, among others, Marcel Raymond, Paul Hazard, the Abbé Bremond, and Gaston Bachelard.) But are there not as many consciousnesses or cogitos as there are individuals? Poulet admits the difficulty and proposes a solution. The only way to emerge from this infinity of individuals, and to gain something that can be called history, is to postulate a period consciousness in which contemporaries participate.[8] The problem faced is similar to that of Dilthey who also wishes to respect the uniqueness of the individual and was obliged to postulate a typology of world-views which subsumed, as a genus does its species, types of great men. In the absence of an explicit comment by Poulet it is difficult to decide whether his period consciousness is a heuristic device, or whether it is grounded in a Hegelian view of the development of the human spirit.

Poulet's predominantly thematic method helps him to periodize the cogito of each writer. The themes chosen by him are well-known: space, time, center-and-circle. It is less obvious, perhaps, that these themes play the same role in the periodization of consciousness as Lovejoy's unit-ideas in the history of ideas. Lovejoy sees the history of ideas developing as the continuous attempt to reconcile an original paradox or antinomy in the idea of God. Time and space yield similar paradoxes for Poulet who traces the reconciling strategies of individual writers. His work illustrates and enriches rather than revises the accepted historical outlines; and his history remains a history of ideas with expanded materials and a finer method. I do not mean to suggest that a critic must rewrite literary history, but it is a curious anti-formalism which strains at the gnat of genre distinctions and is obliged to swallow the camel of periodization. I am not sure that Poulet gives us more than a subtle and expanded Great Chain of Inner Being. A considerable achievement, certainly; but is it what Poulet intended?

The need to periodize, which I take as a residual formalism, can seriously and detrimentally influence Poulet's studies. Many observations on James, acute and interesting as they are, would be more adequate to someone else; to Butor, or Virginia Woolf, or Valéry. They rarely reach to the quick of James' consciousness, to that which makes him unmistakably Jamesian. Take this remark, for instance, on the passage of time: "Time," says Poulet, "is realized by substitution, not of one moment for another but of one place for another. It is as 'localized' a time as possible. James' novel becomes a succession of changes of locale." This is certainly true, and Butor in *La Modification* may only exploit the technique, yet the remark omits something more primitive and essential in James, his refinedly superstitious response to spirit of place. The fact is that there are few neutral places in the world of his novels: place is always impregnate with spirit, and spirit is characterized by intentionality. The displacement of a person, as from America to Europe, is the start of a spiritual adventure involving a gothic traversing of unknown areas of influence, not necessarily forbidden rooms, recesses and gardens, yet analogous to these. Place has presence or is an extension of a presence: and if people fall under the spell of others, it is because they cannot escape an intentionality that extends to place and haunts imagination like a ghost.

If Poulet loses by the formalism he must retain, does he gain by what he rejects? It is part of his anti-formalism to make no distinction between Coleridge's primary and secondary imaginations. The I AM implicit in every act of consciousness is also the I AM revealed by art. In art as elsewhere consciousness feels out or I-am-izes the world; and the relation, in the original cogito, of "I think *therefore* I am," is shown to be phenomenological rather than logical. All knowledge is personal knowl-

edge, a construction putting us in relation to the world and to ourselves. It is as if Cartesianism were the trauma or primal scene of the
history of consciousness which the individual mind progressively repeats. The structure of this repetition is what concerns Poulet, but he
does not link it explicitly to the manifest form of the work of art. This
omission, however fatal, gives him a certain initial advantage over the
formalist critic. By looking *through* form, as Blake claims to look through
rather than with the eye, Poulet gains his unusually intimate access to
the writer's mind. It does not matter to him whether he enters that
mind by door or window or through the chimney: he tells us what he
finds inside without telling us how he got in. Yet one thing he cannot
properly describe — the essential latency of what he finds, the quality
of art's resistance to intimacy. Art, says Wallace Stevens, *almost* resists
the intelligence. In Poulet the differential relation of form to consciousness is lost. Yet form represents the Other to the practising artist; it is
form he must I-am-ize. And the stronger his concern with form the more
difficult his task: here, if anywhere, is "the seriousness, the suffering, the
patience, and the labor of the Negative."

The essay on James shows how interesting yet unsatisfactory Poulet
can be on the subject of form. We have already noted his remark that
since, in James, life gives no single or definitive clue for its organization
the artist himself must cut the tangle and find a limiting view. Thus
"point-of-view" is not a technique to achieve interiority but a way of
limiting introspection in order to make character and plot possible. Consciousness as such appears to be no problem; the only problem is how to
represent it.

A difficulty of *representation,* however, is not yet a difficulty of *being.*
Poulet either assumes or does not make the connection. He writes as if
everything were a procedural rather than substantive matter; and he is
probably misled by James' casual style of self-commentary. It is admirable that James should talk in such objective if engaged fashion about
his art, but this will deceive no one truly respectful of his realized art:
of verbal style, plot as story, plot as pressure of story leading to discoveries, and thematic structure. Of these Poulet respects only one kind
of thematic repetition, the imagery of point and circle, and there he
misses the fact that "point" is by no means divested of sting, and wavers
between its neutral and its wounding sense. Things come to a "point"
with difficulty in James because that point is knowledge and knowledge
is still under its old curse: it is an originative wound, a seeing of the
evil mixed in with the good. Consciousness is the place at which being
reveals itself as wounded. James' problem is not that of facing as a
writer the plenitude of things and having arbitrarily to limit it: his
problem is not to be able to think of consciousness as disinterested, as a

free and innocent appetite. Its appetitiveness is what is curbed by the self-imposed convention of point-of-view, though the momentum of James' novels erodes all such curbs.

That the difficulty is one of being rather than of representation is reflected by everything so naturally excluded from Poulet's essay. He does not mention the central importance of marriage, and a Jamesian marriage, or an analogous contract, is what principally generates, as well as imposes form on, consciousness. If we respect the simplest themes and structural features of James' novels, we must decribe his cogito as follows. In the beginning the mind is conscious of a plot or secret marriage of some kind. Eventually, the mind is conscious of itself — of its own complicity or "secret marriage." Consciousness, in other words, is not at all free or disinterested. It is knowingly or unknowingly the result of a contract, as in *Faust*, of a conspiracy, as in the Fall, or of a covenant like the crucifixion. Such *liaisons dangereuses* implicate us, make us historical, and create in us a new and powerful awareness. From this perspective each novel is seen to be a story that exacts from its hero and often from the story-teller himself a contractual quid pro quo. Consciousness must be paid for, and the usual wages are sacrifice and death. Thus whatever stands greatly against consciousness is drawn into a plot whose acquisitive and inquisitive purposes blend; the plot tests, until it destroys, the illusion that there is innocence or disinterestedness. I find no way to reconcile this view with Poulet's benevolent conclusion: "The astounding peripheric activity of multiple consciousnesses has, in James, the effect of inflating reality by charging it with all the possibilities it implies. Truth is a center surrounded by a luminous halo of both infinite and finite possibilities." No wonder that Bachelard commended phenomenology as "une école de naïveté"! This is the expanse, not the expense, of vision. Consciousness here is purely a good, and its triumph a matter of mental technology. The shadow-side of James is elided.

It is not that Poulet cannot respect this side of a writer (see, for example, his important study of Pascal).[9] Perhaps his error might have been avoided by considering the form of the novels and of their sequence, yet I doubt it is directly caused by the absence of this check. The flaw seems to reside in too optimistic a view of the Progress of Consciousness. Poulet is certainly too optimistic regarding James. By unperplexing James' "consciousness of consciousness," or substituting a perplexity of representation for one of being, he harmonizes James with a stage in the history of consciousness that might have been reached. As long as the artist, moreover, is in phase with a supposed historical progress, the problem of evaluation need not arise, and Poulet prefers it that way. His view of history is too formal, and his understanding of the writer not formal enough. He has not been able to situate James either in history or in the realm of values.

III

I conclude with the following observation. The case against formalism was stated eloquently forty years ago in Trotsky's *Literature and Revolution*. "Having counted the adjectives," says Trotsky of the formalist, "and weighed the lines, and measured the rhythms, a Formalist either stops silent with the expression of a man who does not know what to do with himself, or throws out an unexpected generalization which contains five per cent Formalism and ninety-five per cent of the most uncritical intuition." Our modern formalist is more sophisticated than this literary quasi-scientist but the remedy would seem to be the same. What is needed for literary study is a hundred per cent of formalism and a hundred per cent of critical intuition. Like all counsels of perfection this one sets an impossible ideal. But I do not see why the study of forms should distract from genuine critical intuition, or why there should be competition between virtues. There are many ways to transcend formalism, but the worst is not to study forms. Even multiplying distinctions in the manner of Northrop Frye helps to free literary study because it frees the mind vis-à-vis literature. Categories and forms are man-made before they are authenticated by tradition, and if we think Frye proposes too many terms and Brooks too few, we may have to rethink the whole question of terminology in an arduous, perhaps philosophical way — in fact to examine the *term* aspect of terms.

Lest these comments seem too unobjectionable, I should add that there is good reason why many in this country, as well as in Europe, have voiced a suspicion of "Anglo-Saxon formalism." The dominion of Exegesis is great: she is our Whore of Babylon, sitting robed in Academic black on the great dragon of Criticism, and dispensing a repetitive and soporific balm from her pedantic cup. If our neo-scriptural activity of explication were as daring and conscious as it used to be when Bible texts had to be harmonized with strange or contrary experience: i.e., with history, no one could level this charge of puerility. Yet our present explication-centered criticism *is* puerile, or at most pedagogic: we forget its merely preparatory function, that it stands to a mature criticism as pastoral to epic. Explication is the end of criticism only if we succumb to what Trotsky called the formalist's "superstition of the word." To redeem the word from the superstition of the word is to humanize it, to make it participate once more in a living concert of voices, and to raise exegesis to its former state by confronting art with experience as searchingly as if art were scripture.

I ———————————————————————————————————

Notes

Introduction

1. See René Wellek, "Concepts of Form and Structure in Twentieth-Century Criticism," *Concepts of Criticism,* ed. Stephen G. Nichols, Jr. (New Haven, 1963), pp. 54–68.

2. For a full bibliography of the New Critics and the New Criticism see Walter Sutton, *Modern American Criticism: Humanistic Scholarship in America, The Princeton Studies* (Englewood Cliffs, N.J., 1963), pp. 98–151. See also: Joseph Frank, "R. P. Blackmur: The Later Phase," *The Widening Gyre* (New Brunswick, 1963), pp. 229–51; René Wellek, several essays in *Concepts of Criticism* and in *Discriminations: Further Concepts of Criticism* (New Haven, 1970); "A Symposium on Formalist Criticism," *The Texas Quarterly,* IX (Spring 1966), 185–268; Walter J. Ong, S.J., "Synchronic Present: Modernity in Literary Study," *In the Human Grain: Further Explorations of Contemporary Culture* (New York, 1967), pp. 17–42; Hazard Adams, *The Interests of Criticism: An Introduction to Literary Theory* (New York, 1969); Monroe K. Spears, "The Newer Criticism," *Dionysus and the City: Modernism in Twentieth-Century Poetry* (New York, 1970), pp. 197–228.

On the Neo-Aristotelians see Sutton, *Modern American Criticism,* pp. 152–74.

3. "Literary Criticism: Poet, Poem, and Reader," in *Varieties of Literary Experience,* ed. Stanley Burnshaw (New York, 1962), pp. 98–99; see also Brooks, "The Formalist Critics: My Credo, V," *The Kenyon Review,* XIII (Winter 1951), 72–81. For a critique of this essay see Kenneth Burke, "A Symposium on Formalist Criticism," op. cit., pp. 242 ff.

Brooks's views derive in large measure from T. S. Eliot's "Tradition and the Individual Talent" (1919), which, for the reasons W. K. Wimsatt explains in "Genesis: A Fallacy Revisited" (included in Part II), is the single most influential essay in twentieth-century criticism in English.

The New Criticism was called other names besides *formalist,* and the propositions implied in these other labels may help to clarify its concepts of criticism as well as the controversies they have generated:

(a) *Ontological:* John Crowe Ransom used this term in *The New Criticism* to signify a concern with the literary work as a creation having its own mode of being. For a discussion of Ransom's notion see Murray Krieger, *The New Apologists for Poetry* (Minneapolis, 1956).

(b) *Contextualist:* Literature creates an independent context, a verbal world whose language points inward rather than outward, referentially, to exterior contexts of meaning. The term and its concepts have been debated by Walter Sutton, "The Contextualist Dilemma — or Fallacy," *Journal of Aesthetics and Art Criticism,* XVII (1958), 219–29, and Murray Krieger, "Contextualism Was Ambitious," *Journal of Aesthetics and Art Criticism,* XXI (1962), 81–88.

(c) *Intrinsic:* The work itself contains all the material necessary for its critical understanding and evaluation. The distinction between intrinsic and extrinsic was established by René Wellek and Austin Warren in *Theory of Literature* (1949), but Wellek, in an essay published in 1960, denied that they were attacking all extrinsic concerns ("Literary Theory, Criticism, and History," *Concepts of Criticism,* p. 6).

(d) *Objective:* Literature is a certain kind of object, and the function of criticism is to analyze the modes of its working. W. K. Wimsatt defines the concept in essays included in Part II.

(e) *Organicist:* A work of literature is organically unified. Wellek's criticism is most completely identified with this notion, and it comes under sharp attack from Ihab Hassan in "Beyond a Theory of Literature: Intimations of Apocalypse?" (this section).

(f) *Symbolist:* This term has often been used to signify that the New Criticism was obsessed with hunting down images and symbolism to the neglect of the other constituents of literature, and in that sense it is little more than polemical name-calling. More meaningfully, however, Frank Kermode has argued in *Romantic Image* (1957), a chapter of which is included in Part V, that modern criticism is based on what he calls "a symbolist aesthetic." He has defined that aesthetic succinctly in a review of Northrop Frye's *Anatomy of Criticism:* "A poem is an anonymous and autonomous verbal structure; literal meaning cannot be rendered in other words; literary form is spatial; the intention is defined in the text" (*Puzzles and Epiphanies,* London, 1962, p. 72).

(g) *Technical or Stylistic:* Criticism must focus on the techniques of language and the performance of style in literary works. The New Critics were preoccupied with such matters, but so were a number of other quite different critics and schools of criticism. See René Wellek, "Stylistics, Poetics, and Criticism," *Discriminations,* pp. 327–43.

4. "Synchronic Present: Modernity in Literary Study," p. 33. The issue of basing criticism on contemporary versus classical principles of study was the subject of an important debate between F. R. Leavis and F. W. Bateson in vol. III (1953) of *Essays in Criticism.*

5. "Comparative Literature Today," *Discriminations,* p. 42.

6. "Literary Theory, Criticism, and History," *Concepts of Criticism,* p. 6; "The Main Trends of Twentieth-Century Criticism," ibid., p. 359; Robert Langbaum, "The Function of Criticism Once More," *The Modern Spirit: Essays on the Continuity of Nineteenth and Twentieth Century Literature* (New York, 1970), p. 11.

7. Murray Krieger, in his introductory essay to *Northrop Frye in Modern Criticism: Selected Papers from the English Institute 1965,* ed. Krieger (New York, 1966), argues that Frye is an utter alternative to the modern critical tradition represented by the New Criticism; see, e.g., p. 10.

8. "The Main Trends of Twentieth-Century Criticism," in *Concepts of Criticism,* p. 360.

9. "Criticism, Visible and Invisible," *The Stubborn Structure: Essays on Criticism and Society* (Ithaca, 1970), p. 81.

10. "Elementary Teaching and Elemental Scholarship," *The Stubborn Structure,* p. 102.

11. "The Archetypes of Literature," in *Fables of Identity: Studies in Poetic Mythology* (New York, 1963), p. 15.

12. See "Myth, Fiction, and Displacement," *Fables of Identity,* p. 36.

13. *The Well-Tempered Critic* (Bloomington, 1963), p. 148; on "stock response" see p. 132.

14. Frye has developed this notion in a number of his essays, especially in *Anatomy of Criticism.* For an interesting later treatment see "Speculation and Concern," *The Stubborn Structure,* pp. 38–55. W. K. Wimsatt assails the notion in his contribution to *Northrop Frye in Modern Criticism,* pp. 75–107.

15. *The Well-Tempered Critic,* pp. 149, 155.

16. Cf. Frye's statement in "Reflections in a Mirror," *Northrop Frye in Modern Criticism,* p. 139: "Mr. [John Crowe] Ransom's conception of 'texture' is one from which every critic has learned a great deal, but his view that structure, which means ultimately the study of such recurring principles of literature as convention and genre, is somehow less relevant to criticism, is something I have never understood. The principle that a work of literature should not be related to anything outside

itself is sound enough, but I cannot see how the rest of literature can be regarded as outside the work of literature, any more than the human race can be regarded as outside a human being."

17. *Anatomy of Criticism: Four Essays* (Princeton, 1957), p. 140. Cf. "The Archetypes of Literature," *Fables of Identity*, p. 13. W. K. Wimsatt, discussing this process in *Northrop Frye in Modern Criticism*, asks tartly: "Who really wants to see a painting that way? Perhaps a pure neo-Kantian 'formalist' in art criticism — a Clive Bell or a Roger Fry. Scarcely a critic who has literary interests in the verbal art of literature" (p. 91). For a similar criticism see Frank Kermode, "Frye Reconsidered," *Continuities* (London, 1968), p. 117.

18. "On Value-Judgements," *The Stubborn Structure*, p. 68.

19. Wimsatt takes Frye severely to task for his alleged equivocations on this score: "we must remain unsure, as he no doubt is unsure, whether he wishes to discredit all critical valuing whatever, or only the wrong kinds of valuing," *Northrop Frye in Modern Criticism*, p. 84. René Wellek, discussing Frye in "Stylistics, Poetics, and Criticism," *Discriminations*, p. 338, asserts: ". . . the idea of emptying the study of literature, on whatever level, of criticism in the sense of evaluation and judgment is doomed to failure. The mere fact that we select certain texts out of millions for investigation is a critical judgment, even though it may be inherited and accepted without examination. The selection was accomplished by preceding acts of judgment, on the part of readers, critics, and even professors. The study of any work of art is impossible without constantly choosing the traits we are to discuss, the angle from which we are to approach it. We weigh, discriminate, compare, portion out, and single out at every step." I. A. Richards has said even more forcefully: "not only with *literature,* under whatever definition we assign it, and with *style,* no matter what definition we assign it, but with X, unrestrictedly however defined, value-packed questions will enter" (*Style in Language,* ed. Thomas A. Sebeok [Cambridge, M.I.T. Press Paperback Edition, 1966], p. 433). But Frye knows that. In his "Letter to the English Institute" (he chose to absent himself from the proceedings), he declared: "I have never said that there were no literary values or that critics should never make value-judgments: what I have said is that literary values are not *established* by critical value-judgments"; and after he had read the papers by Wimsatt and the other participants, he readily admitted, in "Reflections in a Mirror," that his "approach to criticism does not make any *functional* use of value-judgments" (*Northrop Frye in Modern Criticism,* pp. 29, 135).

20. "The Critical Path: An Essay on the Social Context of Literary Criticism," *Daedalus,* 99 (1970), p. 325.

21. "Ghostlier Demarcations," *Northrop Frye in Modern Criticism,* p. 112. Cf. Frye's "Criticism, Visible and Invisible," *The Stubborn Structure,* p. 76.

22. *The Lion and the Honeycomb: Essays in Solicitude and Critique* (New York, 1955), p. 190. T. S. Eliot, in a lecture on "The Frontiers of Criticism" delivered in 1956, expressed similar misgivings about what he called "the lemon-squeezer school of criticism" (*On Poetry and Poets,* New York, 1957, pp. 113–31).

23. "More Than Gesture," *Poems and Essays* (New York, Vintage Books, 1955), pp. 103, 104.

24. "Philosophy and Postwar American Criticism," *Concepts of Criticism,* p. 326.

25. "Frye Reconsidered," *Continuities,* p. 118.

26. "R. P. Blackmur: The Later Phase," *The Widening Gyre,* p. 244.

27. "Between the Numen and the Moha: Notes Toward a Theory of Literature," *The Lion and The Honeycomb,* p. 305.

28. *The Well-Tempered Critic,* p. 140.

29. "The Loose and Baggy Monsters of Henry James: Notes on the Underlying Classic Form in the Novel," *The Lion and the Honeycomb,* p. 268.

30. For more information about the various modes and schools of the French New Criticism see: Donald Davie et al., eds., *Poetics. Poetyka. Poetika* (The Hague, 1961); Yves Bonnefoy, "Critics — English and French," *Encounter,* XI (July 1958), 39–45; "Critics Abroad," *The Times Literary Supplement,* July 26 and September

27, 1963 (published as *The Critical Moment* [London, 1964]); Germaine Brée and Eugenia Zimmerman, "Contemporary French Criticism," *Comparative Literature Studies,* I (1964), 175–96; "Issue on Structuralism," *Yale French Studies,* 36–37 (1966) (published as *Structuralism,* ed. Jacques Ehrmann [Doubleday Anchor Books, 1970]), especially Geoffrey Hartman, "Structuralism: The Anglo-American Adventure," 148–68; J. Hillis Miller, "The Geneva School," *Critical Quarterly,* VIII (1966), 305–21 (reprinted in *Modern French Criticism: From Proust and Valéry to Structuralism,* ed. John K. Simon [Chicago, 1972], pp. 277–310); Paul de Man, "The Crisis of Contemporary Criticism," *Arion,* VI (1967), 38–57; Eugenio Donato, "Of Structuralism and Literature," *Modern Language Notes,* 82 (1967), 549–74; Laurent Le Sage, *The French New Criticism: An Introduction and a Sampler* (University Park, Pa., 1967); Wallace Fowlie, *The French Critic, 1549–1967* (Carbondale, Ill., 1968); Peter Caws, "What Is Structuralism?" *Partisan Review,* XXXV (1968), 75–91; Sarah N. Lawall, *Critics of Consciousness: The Existential Structures of Literature* (Cambridge, 1968); David Paul Funt, "Newer Criticism and Revolution," and "The Structuralist Debate," *Hudson Review,* XXII (1969), 87–96, 623–46; Richard Macksey and Eugenio Donato, eds., *The Languages of Criticism and the Sciences of Man: The Structuralist Controversy* (Baltimore, 1970); Michael Lane, ed., *Structuralism: A Reader* (London, 1970); Joseph N. Riddel, "Against Formalism," *Genre,* III (1970), 156–72; W. K. Wimsatt, "Battering the Object: The Ontological Approach," in *Contemporary Criticism: Stratford-upon-Avon Studies 12,* ed. Malcolm Bradbury and David Palmer (London, 1970), pp. 60–81; and Seymour Chatman, ed., *Literary Style: A Symposium* (New York, 1971). The volume *Modern French Criticism: From Proust and Valéry to Structuralism* includes a "Selected General Bibliography" and comprehensive individual bibliographies after each essay.

On Russian Formalism and the Prague School see: Victor Erlich, *Russian Formalism: History, Doctrine,* rev. ed. (The Hague, 1965); *Russian Formalist Criticism: Four Essays,* trans. Lee T. Lemon and Marion J. Reis (Lincoln, Neb., 1965); Paul Garvin, ed., *A Prague School Reader on Esthetics, Literary Structure, and Style* (Washington, D.C., 1964); and several essays by René Wellek in *Concepts of Criticism* and *Discriminations.*

For an introduction to the ideas of Claude Lévi-Strauss see Edmund Leach, *Claude Lévi-Strauss,* in the series *Modern Masters,* ed. Frank Kermode (New York, 1970). See, also, George Steiner, *Language and Silence* (London, 1967), pp. 267–79; Edward W. Said, "The Totalitarianism of Mind," *The Kenyon Review,* XXIX (1967), 256–68; and E. Nelson Hayes and Tanya Hayes, eds., *Claude Lévi-Strauss: The Anthropologist as Hero* (Cambridge, 1970).

31. Quoted by Miller in "The Geneva Critics," *Critical Quarterly,* VIII (1966), p. 307.

32. See de Man's "The Crisis of Contemporary Criticism," esp. p. 44; Said's "Abecedarium Culturae: Structuralism, Absence, Writing," in *Modern French Criticism: From Proust and Valéry to Structuralism,* pp. 341–92.

33. Op. cit., p. 47.

34. On "intersubjective forms," see Hartman, "Toward Literary History," p. 758 this anthology. Cf. Joseph N. Riddel, "Against Formalism," p. 166. See Lévi-Strauss, "The Structural Study of Myth," *Journal of American Folklore,* 68, no. 270 (1950), 428–44; cf. Edmund Leach, "The Structure of Myth," *Claude Lévi-Strauss,* pp. 53–86.

35. "*Abecedarium Culturae:* Structuralism, Absence, Writing," p. 344.

36. Ibid., p. 350.

37. Ibid., p. 371.

38. Such comparisons raise the question of whether structure is the same as form, and whether the French structuralists are in fact "formalists." "It becomes difficult to see what distinguishes form from structure, something Barthes seems eager to differentiate," Yves Velan says in "Barthes," *Modern French Criticism: From Proust and Valéry to Structuralism,* p. 322. Said affirms, "Certainly the structuralists are formalists," and theirs is a formalist doctrine, but he tries to show how it differs

"from earlier modern formalisms" ("*Abecedarium Culturae*: Structuralism, Absence, Writing," pp. 370 ff.).

39. Quoted from Hartman's Preface to *Beyond Formalism: Literary Essays 1958–1970* (New Haven, 1970), p. xi.

40. "The Antitheses of Criticism: Reflections on the Yale Colloquium," *Modern Language Notes*, 81 (1966), p. 557.

41. Ibid., p. 564.

42. "Frontiers of Criticism: Metaphors of Silence," *The Virginia Quarterly Review*, 46 (1970), pp. 85–86.

43. "Comparative Literature Today," *Discriminations*, p. 50. Cf. Frank Kermode's discussion of contemporary art in "Modernisms," *Continuities*, pp. 1–32.

44. Except for page reference in parenthesis, all quotations in this paragraph are taken from Hartman's Preface to *Beyond Formalism: Literary Essays 1958–1970*.

45. Ibid., p. xii.

46. "The Antitheses of Criticism: Reflections on the Yale Colloquium," p. 570.

47. See his "Spatial Form in Modern Literature," first published in 1945, and reprinted in *The Widening Gyre*, the note appears on p. 60.

48. "Myth, Fiction, and Displacement," *Fables of Identity*, p. 21.

49. "The Medium of Fiction," *Fiction and the Figures of Life* (New York: 1970), p. 29.

50. "Letter to the English Institute," in *Northrop Frye in Modern Criticism*, p. 29.

NORTHROP FRYE, *Polemical Introduction*, Anatomy of Criticism

1. "Thoughts on Poetry and its Varieties," *Dissertations and Discussions*, Series I.

2. "The Literary Influence of Academies," *Essays in Criticism*, First Series.

3. This phrase expresses, not a contempt for aesthetics, but a conviction that it is time for aesthetics to get out from under philosophy, as psychology has already done. Most philosophers deal with aesthetic questions only as a set of analogies to their logical and metaphysical views, hence it is difficult to use, say, Kant or Hegel on the arts without getting into a Kantian or Hegelian "position." Aristotle is the only philosopher known to me who not only talks specifically about poetics when he is aware of larger aesthetic problems, but who assumes that such poetics would be the organon of an independent discipline. Consequently a critic can use the *Poetics* without involving himself in Aristotelianism (though I know that some Aristotelian critics do not think so).

4. I am indebted here to a passage in Susanne K. Langer, *The Practice of Philosophy* (1930).

5. Shelley, for example, speaks in *A Defence of Poetry* of "that great poem, which all poets, like the co-operating thoughts of one great mind, have built up since the beginning of the world."

6. "The Study of Poetry," *Essays in Criticism*, Second Series.

IAN WATT, *The First Paragraph of* The Ambassadors: An Explication

1. A paper given at the Ninth Annual Conference of Non-Professorial University Teachers of English, at Oxford on April 5th, 1959. I am very grateful for the many criticisms and suggestions made in the course of the subsequent discussion; in preparing the paper for publication I have taken as much account of them as was possible, short of drastic expansion or alteration. I also acknowledge my debt to Dorothea Krook, Frederick C. Crews, and Henry Nash Smith.

2. This was before the appearance of the English Institute's symposium *Style in Prose Fiction* (New York, 1959), which offers, besides two general surveys and a

valuable bibliography of the field, stylistic studies of six novelists, including one by Charles R. Crow, of "The Style of Henry James: *The Wings of the Dove."*

3. Henry James, *The Ambassadors* (Revised Collected Edition, Macmillan: London, 1923). Since there are a few variants that have a bearing on the argument, it seems desirable to give a collation of the main editions; P is the periodical publication (*The North American Review,* clxxvi, 1903); 1A the first American edition (Harper and Brothers, New York, 1903); 1E the first English edition (Methuen and Co., London, 1903); N.Y., the "New York Edition," New York and London, 1907–09 (the London Macmillan edition used the sheets of the American edition); CR the "Collected Revised Edition," London and New York, 1921–31 (which uses the text of the New York Edition). It should perhaps be explained that the most widely used editions in England and America make misleading claims about their text: the "Everyman" edition claims to use the text "of the revised Collected Edition" but actually follows the 1st English edition in the last variant; while the "Anchor" edition, claiming to be "a faithful copy of the text of the Methuen first edition," actually follows the first American edition, including the famous misplaced chapters.

1.4.   *reply paid* NY, CR; *with the answer paid* P, 1A, 1E.
1.5.   *inquirer* P, 1A, 1E, CR; *enquirer* NY.
1.5.   *Understanding they* NY, CR; *understanding that they* P, 1A, 1E.
1.10.   *feel he* NY, CR; *feel that he* P, 1A, 1E.
1.13.   *Shouldn't* CR; *shouldn't* NY; *should not* P, 1A, 1E.
ll.14–15. *Newly disembarked,* all eds. except P: *Newly-disembarked.*
1.18.   *arrange that this countenance to present* NY, CR; *arrange that this countenance should present* P, 1A, 1E.
1.19.   *"note," of Europe* CR; *"note," for him, of Europe,* P, 1A, 1E; *"note" of Europe,* NY.
ll.20–21. *that it would* P, 1A, NY, CR; *that he would,* 1E.

4. I am also indebted to the same author's "Henry James's World of Images," *PMLA,* LXVIII (Dec., 1953), 943–60.

5. Sentences one and four are compound or multiple, but in my count I haven't included the second clause in the latter — "there was little fear"; though if we can talk of the clause having a subject it's an abstract one — "fear."

6. Though consider *Rasselas,* chap. xxviii: "Both conditions may be bad, but they cannot both be worst."

7. As I have argued in "The Ironic Tradition in Augustan Prose from Swift to Johnson," *Restoration and Augustan Prose* (Los Angeles, 1957).

8. See George Knox, "James's Rhetoric Quotes," *College English,* XVII (1956), 293–97.

9. A similar analysis of eight other paragraphs selected at fifty page intervals revealed that, as would be expected, there is much variation: the tendency to use non-transitive verbs, and abstract nouns as subjects, for instance, seems to be strong throughout the novel, though especially so in analytic rather than narrative passages; but the frequent use of "that" and of negative forms of statement does not recur significantly.

LEO BERSANI, *From Bachelard to Barthes*

1. After devoting a sympathetic issue to structuralism, Sartre's *Les Temps Modernes* has just published two negative reviews of the anti-Sartrean *Les Mots et les choses.* Until now there has been little resistance from the source which might have made resistance interesting.

ROLAND BARTHES, Phèdre

1. *Quand tu sauras mon crime, et le sort qui m'accable,*
   Je n'en mourrai pas moins, j'en mourrai plus coupable. (I,3)

When you learn what my crime is, and the fate that overwhelms me, I shall die not less, but more guilty.

> — *Hippolyte? Grands Dieux!*
>   — *C'est toi qui l'as nommé.* (I,3)

Hippolytus? O gods!
You are the one who spoke his name.

2. *Phèdre, atteinte d'un mal qu'elle s'obstine à taire* . . . (I,1)

   Phaedra, stricken by a disease she refuses to name . . .

3. *Une femme mourante et qui cherche à mourir* . . . (I,1)

   A woman dying, and longing to die . . .

4. *Et la mort, à mes yeux dérobant la clarté,*
   Rend au jour, qu'ils souillaient, toute sa pureté. (V,7)

   And death, darkening my eyes, restores all its brightness to the day they tainted.

5. Hippolytus to Theseus:
   . . . Je devrais faire ici parler la vérité,
   Seigneur; mais je supprime un secret qui vous touche. (IV,2)

   I should let truth speak for me here, my lord, but I pass over in silence a secret that concerns you alone.

   Hippolytus to Aricia:
   . . . et que jamais une bouche si pure
   Ne s'ouvre pour conter cette horrible aventure. (V,1)

   . . . lips so pure must never part to utter this horrible table.

6. Theramenes to Hippolytus:
   Vous périssez d'un mal que vous dissimulez. (I,1)

   You are dying of a disease you insist on concealing.

7. Hippolytus' love for Aricia is a challenge to essence:
   Maintenant je me cherche et ne me trouve plus. (II,2)

   Now I seek and no longer find myself.

8. *Et même, en le voyant, le bruit de sa fierté*
   A redoublé pour lui ma curiosité. (II,1)

   And even as I saw him, the rumor of his pride magnified twice over my curiosity about him.

9. *Mais quand tu récitais des faits moins glorieux,*
   Sa foi partout offerte et reçue en cent lieux . . .
   Tu sais comme, à regret écoutant ces discours,
   Je te pressais souvent d'en abréger le cours . . .
   Et moi-même, à mon tour, je me verrais lié? (I,1)

   But when you recounted his less glorious deeds, his faith pledged and accepted in a hundred places . . . you know how reluctant I was to hear such things, how I often urged you to skip the recital . . . and now it is my turn to see myself corrupted.

10. *Je ne puis sans horreur me regardez moi-même.* (II,6)

    I cannot look at myself without horror.

11. *Il suffit que ma main l'ait une fois touchée,*
    Je l'ai rendue horrible à ses yeux inhumains;
    Et ce fer malheureux profanerait ses mains. (III,1)

    It is enough for my hand to touch his once, to make it horrible in his inhuman eyes; and this wretched sword would profane his hands.

12. *Il défend de donner des neveux à ses frères,*
    D'une tige coupable il craint un rejeton,
    Il veut avec leur sœur ensevelir leur nom. (I,1)

    He forbids her to bear children, nephews to her brothers, fearing a new branch of that guilty stock, and would bury the name with their sister.

13. *Tu sais que de tout temps à l'amour opposée* . . . (II,1)

    You know I have always opposed love . . .

14. *J'ai pris la vie en haine* . . . (I,3)

    I have taken a loathing to life . . .

15. *Que ces vains ornements, que ces voiles me pèsent* . . . (I,3)

    How these vain adornments, how these veils weigh me down!

16. *Mais de faire fléchir un courage inflexible,*
    De porter la douleur dans une âme sensible . . .
    C'est là que je veux, c'est là ce qui m'irrite. (II,1)

    But to bend an inflexible will, to awake pain in a sensitive soul . . . that is my desire, and what eludes me.

17. *C'est moi, Prince, c'est moi, dont l'utile secours*
    Vous eût du Labyrinthe enseigné les détours . . . (II,5)

    I am the one, Prince, whose help would have taught you the way out of the Labyrinth's meanders . . .

18. In *Phèdre,* a tragedy without marivaudage, words are never taken back: there are no "scenes."

19. *La charmante Aricie a-t-elle su vous plaire?*
    — Théramène, je pars, et vais chercher mon père. (I,1)

    Can it be that the charming Aricia has won your heart?
    — Theramenes, I am leaving, to seek my father.

20. *Puisque j'ai commencé de rompre le silence,*
    Madame, il faut poursuivre . . . (II,2)

    Since I have begun to break the silence, lady, I must go on . . .

    . . . *Ah! cruel, tu m'as trop entendue* . . . (II,5)
    No, cruel Hippolytus, you have heard too much already . . .

21. *Reste du sang d'un roi, noble fils de la Terre* . . . (II,1)
    Last descendant of a king, noble son of the Earth . . .

    . . . *et la terre humectée*
    But à regret le sang des neveux d'Erechtée. (II,1)
    And the drenched Earth reluctantly drank the blood of the nephews of Erechtheus.

22. *Il me semble déjà que ces murs, que ces voûtes* . . . (III,3)
    Already it seems as if these walls, these vaults . . .

23. *Nourri dans les forêts il en a la rudesse.* (III,1)
    He has the savagery of the forests where he was raised.

24. *Vous haïssez le jour que vous veniez chercher.* (I,3)
    You hate the very daylight you came to find.

25. *Je voulais en mourant* . . .
    . . . *dérober au jour une flamme si noire.* (I,3)
    By dying, I sought to cleanse the day of a flame so black.

26. Phaedra to Hippolytus:
Délivre l'univers d'un monstre qui t'irrite. (II,5)
Rid the world of a monster that pains you.

Aricia about Phaedra:
   . . . *Vos invincibles mains*
Ont de monstres sans nombre affranchi les humains.
Mais tout n'est pas détruit, et vous en laissez vivre
Un . . . (V,3)
Your invincible hands have rid humanity of countless monsters, but not all
are destroyed, you have left one alive . . .

Phaedra to Oenone:
   . . . *Va-t'en, monstre exécrable.* (IV,6)
Leave me, you loathesome monster.

Hippolytus about himself:
Croit-on que dans ses flancs un monstre m'ait porté? (III,2)
Was I born from some monster's womb?

Phaedra about Hippolytus:
Je le vois comme un monstre effroyable à mes yeux. (III,3)
I regard him as a monster hideous to my sight.

27. There is a fine commentary on Theramenes' narrative by Leo Spitzer, in
Linguistics and Literary History, Princeton University Press, 1948.

28. *J'ai voulu* . . .
Par un chemin plus lent descendre chez les morts.
J'ai pris, j'ai fait couler dans mes brûlantes veines
Un poison . . . (V,7)
I sought to go down among the dead by a slower path, I have taken a poison
that is flowing now through my burning veins . . .

29. Claudel seems to have observed this *formal* character of Phaedra's disease
when he says: "*Phèdre* is an atmosphere all to itself."

30. *Phèdre, atteinte d'un mal qu'elle s'obstine à taire* . . . (I,i)
Phaedra, stricken by a disease she refuses to name . . .

31. Preface, end of the first paragraph.

J. HILLIS MILLER, *An Introduction to*
William Carlos Williams

1. [Editor's note: At the end of *William Carlos Williams: A Collection of Critical
Essays* Miller provides a chronology of Williams' life and a complete list of his publications in book form.] The various volumes of Williams' poetry are now being published in England by MacGibbon & Kee Ltd.
2. Wordsworth's phrasing, in the preface to *Lyrical Ballads* (*The Poetical Works
of William Wordsworth,* ed. E. de Selincourt, II [London: Oxford University Press,
1952], 386).
3. The following texts of Williams' work have been used in this Introduction.
Each is accompanied by the abbreviation which will hereafter be employed in citations. KH — *Kora in Hell: Improvisations* (San Francisco: City Lights, 1957); SA
— *Spring and All* (Dijon: Contact Publishing Company, 1923); IAG — *In the
American Grain* (New York: New Directions Publishing Corporation, 1956); CEP
— *The Collected Earlier Poems* (New York: New Directions Publishing Corporation, 1951); A — *The Autobiography of William Carlos Williams* (New York:

Random House, 1951); SE — *Selected Essays* (New York: Random House, 1943); SL — *Selected Letters*, ed. John C. Thirlwall (New York: Ivan Obolensky, Inc., 1957); ML — *Many Loves and Other Plays* (New York: New Directions Publishing Corporation, 1961); *Pictures from Brueghel and Other Poems* (New York: New Directions Publishing Corporation, 1962); CLP — *The Collected Later Poems* (New York: New Directions Publishing Corporation, 1963); P — *Paterson* (New York: New Directions Publishing Corporation, 1963). "Young Sycamore" is from CEP, 332.

4. Introduction to Byron Vazakas, *Transfigured Night* (New York: The Macmillan Company, 1946), p. xi.

5. See the *Autobiography*, pp. 59, 60, for his description of this poem.

6. For a description of this elemental cosmology see pp. 328–36 of my essay on Williams in *Poets of Reality: Six Twentieth-Century Writers* (Cambridge, Mass.: Harvard University Press, 1965).

IHAB HASSAN, *Beyond a Theory of Literature: Intimations of Apocalypse?*

1. René Wellek, *Concepts of Criticism*, ed. Stephen G. Nichols, Jr. (New Haven, 1963), p. 343.

2. Lawrence Durrell and Alfred Perles, *Art and Outrage: A Correspondence about Henry Miller* (New York, 1961), p. 9.

3. Lionel Trilling, "On the Modern Element in Modern Literature," *The Partisan Review Anthology*, ed. William Phillips and Philip Rahv (New York, 1962), pp. 267 ff.

4. Martin Buber, *Between Man and Man* (Boston, 1955), p. 10.

5. Walter J. Ong, S.J., *The Barbarian Within* (New York, 1962), pp. 19, 25.

6. Jean-Paul Sartre, *Situations II* (Paris, 1948), pp. 72, 98.

7. Albert Camus, *Resistance, Rebellion, and Death* (New York, 1961), p. 251.

8. Henry Miller, *The Cosmological Eye* (Norfolk, Conn., 1939), p. 156; and *Time of the Assassins* (Norfolk, Conn., 1956), pp. 38 ff.

9. Murray Krieger, *The Tragic Vision* (New York, 1960), pp. 2, 244.

10. James E. Miller, Jr., Karl Shapiro, and Bernice Slote, *Start with the Sun* (Lincoln, Neb., 1960), p. 238.

11. R. W. B. Lewis, *The Picaresque Saint* (Philadelphia and New York, 1959), p. 9.

12. Robert Martin Adams, *Surface and Symbol: The Consistency of James Joyce's Ulysses* (New York, 1962), pp. 245, 253.

13. In recent criticism, certain works have already begun to reflect this particular concern. Besides the works by R. W. B. Lewis and Murray Krieger already cited, one might mention Geoffrey Hartman, *The Unmediated Vision* (New Haven, 1954), Ihab Hassan, *Radical Innocence* (Princeton, 1961), Frederick J. Hoffman, *The Mortal No* (Princeton, 1964), and Arturo B. Fallico, *Art and Existentialism* (Englewood Cliffs, N.J., 1962).

14. Albert Camus, *The Myth of Sisyphus* (New York, 1959), pp. 72 ff.

15. These heretical statements are developed more fully in my essay "The Dismemberment of Orpheus," *American Scholar*, XXXII (Summer 1963), pp. 463–84.

16. Wellek, p. 65.

17. Ibid., p. 68.

18. Ibid., pp. 333 ff.

19. Ibid., p. 342.

20. Northrop Frye, *The Well-Tempered Critic* (Bloomington, Ind., 1963), p. 123.

21. Ibid., p. 136.

22. Ibid., p. 140.

23. See Leonard B. Meyer, "The End of the Renaissance," *Hudson Review*, XVI (Summer 1963), pp. 169–86.

24. Claude Mauriac, *The New Literature* (New York, 1959), p. 12.

25. Roland Barthes, *Le Degré Zéro de L'Ecriture* (Paris, 1959), p. 12.

26. Maurice Blanchot, *Le Livre à Venir* (Paris, 1959), p. 237.

27. Gaston Bachelard, *Lautréamont* (Paris, 1963), p. 154.

28. H. H. Rowley, *The Relevance of Apocalyptic,* rev. ed. (New York, n.d.), pp. 150–78.

29. Krieger, p. 21.

30. Revelation xx.6.

31. Norman O. Brown, "Apocalypse," *Harper's* (May 1961), p. 47.

32. D. H. Lawrence, *Apocalypse* (Florence, 1931), pp. 233 ff.

SUSAN SONTAG, *Against Interpretation*

1. One of the difficulties is that our idea of form is spatial (the Greek metaphors for form are all derived from notions of space). This is why we have a more ready vocabulary of forms for the spatial than for the temporal arts. The exception among the temporal arts, of course, is the drama; perhaps this is because the drama is a narrative (i.e., temporal) form that extends itself visually and pictorially, upon a stage. . . . What we don't have yet is a poetics of the novel, any clear notion of the forms of narration. Perhaps film criticism will be the occasion of a breakthrough here, since films are primarily a visual form, yet they are also a subdivision of literature.

GEOFFREY H. HARTMAN, *Beyond Formalism*

1. *Wordsworth: A Re-Interpretation* (London, 2nd ed., 1956), pp. 31–33. As a curiosity I might add that the first person to draw attention to the contrast implicit in the violet-star image was Mary Shelley in *The Last Man* (1826). "[Wordsworth's] lines," her narrator says, "always appeared to me rather a contrast than a similitude." He goes on to compare two women, Perdita "a violet . . . cowering from observation" and Idris "the star, set in single splendor, ready to enlighten and delight the subject world."

2. See J. C. Scaliger, *Poetices Libri Septem* (Lyons, 1561), p. 171, Appendix pro Epigrammate. Scaliger associates the "honey" type of epigram with Catullus, and lists no less than four anti-types characterized by the terms "gall," "vinegar," "salt," and one that is outlawed "in qua foeditas est." He seems to distinguish, further, between a continuously pointed epigram ("consertam, densam, multiplicem") and a finer, more naturally developed kind ("species quaedam nobilis ac generosa . . . aequabilitate plena . . . ut sit venustas cum gravitate, & acumen cum lenitate"). For echoes of Scaliger, or further evidence of the prevalence of these categories, see Ben Jonson, *Epigrams* (1616), II and XLIX; also John Peter, *Complaint and Satire in Early English Literature* (Oxford, 1956), p. 297, and the valuable introductions in James Hutton, *The Greek Anthology in Italy* (Ithaca, 1935) and *The Greek Anthology in France and in the Latin Writers of the Netherlands* (Ithaca, 1946).

3. "The sweete wittie soule of Ovid lives in mellifluous and hony-tongued Shakespeare, witnes his *Venus* and *Adonis,* his *Lucrece,* his sugred Sonnets among his private friends, &c." Francis Meres, reprinted by G. G. Smith, ed., *Elizabethan Critical Essays* (Oxford, 1904), II, 317.

4. *Letting of Humor's Blood* (1600). See the highly instructive section on Epigrams in J. W. Hebel and H. H. Hudson, *Poetry of the English Renaissance 1509–1660.*

5. I have tried to broach the question of Marvell's epigrammatic style in *ELH*, XXXI (1964), 185 ff.

6. See also Wordsworth's *Essay on Epitaphs*, where this poem is quoted. For Dr. Johnson, on the road to Romantic sensibility, elegy and epigram came to stand in

opposition. His *Dictionary* (1st ed., 1755) defines elegy, inter alia, as "A short poem without points or affected elegancies," where point is defined as "A sting of an epigram; a sentence terminated with some remarkable turn of words or thought."

7. To interpret this link as expressive of the primacy of consciousness is to re-introduce the (now causal) notion of "this then that" and with it the magical view that Wordsworth's thought is symbolically killing Lucy off. See Bateson's thesis in *Wordsworth: A Re-Interpretation.*

8. Cf. J. Hillis Miller, "The Literary Criticism of Georges Poulet," *MLN* 78 (1963), 471–88.

9. *Études sur le temps Humain* (1949), chap. 3.

The Writer's Intention

Most of us take it for granted that a literary work means what its author meant, and that an inquiry into "intention" — the term used to signify what the author had in mind to do and say, his design or purpose in a particular work — is indispensable for criticism. T. S. Eliot, however, maintained just the opposite. He said that once a work has been composed, "what the poet meant it to mean or what he thinks it to mean now that it is written, are questions not worth the asking." Accordingly, as Eliot declared, "the poet's interpretation of his poem is not required." [1]

W. K. Wimsatt and Monroe C. Beardsley went further in their influential essay, "The Intentional Fallacy" (1945), by arguing that such inquiries are not only fruitless but illegitimate. The literary work is what matters in criticism, they say, not the man — and as soon as the work is finished it becomes autonomous, an object in its own right, formally separate from its origin in the mind of its maker and from its affective results in the minds of its readers. It becomes not only formally but semantically autonomous, assuming an independent life and meaning; "it is detached from the author at birth and goes about the world beyond his power to intend about it or control it." As an autonomous object, a self-contained verbal context, the literary work must be judged solely by criteria intrinsic to its own mode of being. Its meaning must be judged by the public contexts of the meanings of its words rather than by the personal contexts of what the words, and the things they stand for, mean to the author or the reader; and its success or value must be judged first and foremost by the articulation, intelligibility, and integrity of the parts that make up "the coherently expressive structure." Wimsatt and Beardsley label as "external" everything that lies outside "the semantics and syntax of the poem," everything that is "not part of the work as linguistic fact." The only evidence they allow as proper for critical interpretation and appraisal is "internal" — that which is drawn from the poem itself. The intention of an author, because it is "private and idiosyncratic" rather than public and objective, is valid neither for certifying the presence of a quality or a meaning in a given instance in his literary work nor for judging the value of that work. The critic cannot establish what a work says or does by appealing to what its author *meant* to say or do.

The anti-intentionalist views of Eliot and Wimsatt and Beardsley dominated American academic criticism of the mid-century, but they have been challenged by recent critics — directly by Mark Spilka, in a 1960 essay, and by Frank Cioffi, in a 1963 lecture; and implicitly, on suppositions about the relation of a writer to his work, by two recent schools of criticism: the "genetic criticism" of "the Geneva School," represented here by Jean Starobinski in his 1961 essay on Stendhal; and "the New Rhetoric" (described by Kenneth Burke, one of its originators, in "Rhetoric — Old and New," in Part IV), represented by Louis T. Milic in a 1967 essay. Wimsatt, in turn, has rebutted some of the specific objections of such critics and restated the argument against intention in "Genesis: A Fallacy Revisited," published in 1968.

Spilka accuses Wimsatt and Beardsley of failing "to accommodate the author's role as stylist." He questions their conception of the literary work as an impersonal and autonomous object. First, "Each verbal object lives in company with others like itself." A given work is part of the body of an author's writings, not a single or isolated creation, and because the common element that unites them, the personal identity that informs specific works yet at the same time stands outside them, is the stylist who creates them, the critic must range beyond the frame of the single object. Second, "All works of art exist within surrounding contexts." Biography and history, which Wimsatt and Beardsley proscribe as personal or external, "enter, not as background, but as contexts which add knowledge of the stylist"; they interfuse and bring to life the linguistic contexts of the "closed" form of the poem. Intention, the knowledge of the aims and the distinctive modes of work of the shaping stylist, is inextricable from critical judgment. If the author is banished in order to analyze his text, if the principle that a work means what its author meant is abandoned, "the critic will become the author, he will supply his own intention." And once the critic takes exclusive possession of the work the way is open for a willful arbitrariness and extravagance in interpretation. The very objectivity Wimsatt and Beardsley set as a standard for criticism becomes harder to achieve.

Cioffi, like Spilka, maintains that biographical information is perfectly valid in some cases because "there is an implicit biographical reference in our response to literature." Indeed, it is "part of our concept of literature." Cioffi, who happens to be more a philosopher than a literary critic, argues that any general thesis about the relevance of intention to critical interpretation fails to account for the heterogeneity of the situations in which questions of interpretation arise. "Literature is a motley," and Cioffi offers a massive array of cases to show this heterogeneity — from which he asserts that the thesis of Wimsatt and Beardsley fits only a fraction of the cases that actually occur in criticism and has nowhere near the general status they claim. More particularly, the distinction they make between internal and external evidence is misconceived. A text does not have an outline as neat and definite as the page on which it is printed. Besides, a reader's response to a text will vary with his knowledge, and "one of the things which he knows and with which his responses will vary is what the author had in mind, or what he intended." The difficulty in separating critical remarks about the poem from biographical ones about the author is "that you can't know which is which until after you have read the work in the light of them." And for Cioffi, a critical remark is not the same as it is for Wimsatt and Beardsley, one that elucidates or appraises the meaning of the words in a given work, but rather one "which has the power to modify our apprehension of a work." In fact, the very analogy of literary criticism with logical argument that Wimsatt and Beardsley assume — their notion of criticism as the production and evaluation of evidence — is an illusion.

Starobinski's method of criticism offers a novel approach to the problem of the relation of the person or self of the writer to his work. Wimsatt and Beardsley contend that criticism must confine itself to the "created self" or "poetic self" expressed in the text. "We ought," they say, "to impute the thoughts and attitudes of the poem immediately to the dramatic *speaker,* and if to the author at all, only by an act of biographical inference." Opposite to this, such intentionalists as Spilka and Cioffi say that because every poem expresses, whether directly or indirectly, the personality of its author, it is perfectly proper to impute what a poem says to its author and to proceed in criticism as the work is created — from the man to the work. Even if a writer disguises his identity or masks his presence by using "personae," he still says what he *has* to say because of what he *is.*

Starobinski suggests that it is pointless to proceed either from the work to the man or from the man to the work because the literary work, indeed any use of language, is not an instrument distinct from the subject using it — but rather the perceiving self incarnate. A poem or a novel is the form by which the author is able to view and grasp his sense, his consciousness, of existence. Shaping a given experience is not the reproduction of something "outside" the work but rather the discovery and fashioning of the self of the author. Literature is the means by which a man orders the separate and dispersed elements of his personality; it is the means by which the self takes shape and achieves its most complete, most authentic form of being. As Georges Poulet, a founder of the school of criticism with which Starobinski is associated, declares: "An author creates himself as he creates his work." [2]

This places the relation of the writer's biography to the authorial "I" in his work, and in fact the whole problem of intention, on a new footing. Instead of looking for an author who has a prior and separate existence, mind, self, and a speaker who lives in the closed form of the work with a mind and self of his own, and then comparing the two to see whether they match, Starobinski's method is an attempt to re-experience in reading the author's developing grasp and formulation of his own existence; the work's simultaneous emergence from unconnected pieces of raw material into a cognitive, structural, and formally cohesive whole; and, joining both of these, the making of a distinctive self as it grows and takes shape through the author's writings. The critic tries to apprehend intentions that are not immediately perceptible and that are not necessarily known by the author himself; indeed, the intentions are not fully discernible until his oeuvre is finished. And the oeuvre of a writer is neither a collection of texts nor a biographical record but the single expression of a human attitude toward existence. Criticism in this view is a retracing of the "genetic process," but the genesis it looks for is not some *moment* of conception, some beginning will, design, or cause, but an animating consciousness, a pattern of perceiving and ordering existence, a vision and a voice that makes a man what he is and no other person.

Starobinski is subjective (or, more precisely, he dissolves the categorical divisions between subjective and objective) and anti-formalistic. He is less concerned with the verbal medium of literature than with its existential and phenomenological character. Milic, by contrast, is rigorously objective and preoccupied with literary style. His primary interest is what Wimsatt has urged as the first task of criticism: the study of "the concrete and fully answerable character of words as aesthetic medium." In these respects Milic seems to be following Wimsatt and Beardsley's program of objective criticism.

But Milic is flatly opposed to "aesthetic impersonality." Moreover, he is concerned not with single and autonomous works, but with the totality of an author's style, the stylistic identity of his writing, the individuality of his "literary personality." For Milic and the other critics of the New Rhetoric, style is the expression of a writer's personality and writing is a process of choice in language and rhetoric. "An individual's style," Milic says, "is his habitual and consistent selection from the expressive resources available in his language . . . the collection of his stylistic options." This brings the critic closer to the study of the writing process itself. Wimsatt and Beardsley rule out that kind of study on the grounds that only finished objects are proper for criticism, but the New Rhetoricians hold that critical analysis ought to follow the constitutive process of composition — the way a writer fashions his expressive and cognitive intentions in language. The work itself in this view becomes not an impersonal artifact but a stylistic performance. And the habitual patterns of linguistic and rhetorical choice that the critic finds by looking beyond single texts enable him to identify and clarify the author's intentions in a given work. Milic is no less attentive than Wimsatt and Beardsley to the general linguistic resources, the public language, from which an individual style is a selection, but he restores the personal dimensions of the writer's performance that they exclude. His conception of the author as a shaping stylist, an individual expressing himself by making and taking choices in language and rhetoric, restores the author to the place of sovereign importance in the meaning as well as the composition of the literary work. Milic gives a new precision to the notion many of us accept without thinking: "the style is the man." [3]

Wimsatt, however, in "Genesis: A Fallacy Revisited," argues once again that the proper study of the critic is not the man behind the style but the style of the verbal artifact. "In this debate," he says, "there are two antithetically opposed sides, and probably always will be, corresponding to two aspects of literature and to two kinds of persons who come to the study of literature." And he restates his conviction that, although the verbal work of art is "made of intentions or intentionalistic material," once formed "it enters a public and in a certain clear sense an objective realm"; "if the art work has emerged at all from the artist's private world, it has emerged into some kind of universal world." Whatever the worth or validity of using literature for biographical study, it is from the "value, richness, design in the poem itself" that "we infer an artist and a skillful artist, and not the other way round."

Wimsatt modifies slightly his and Beardsley's earlier argument, but he does not budge from their basic position; his reason for re-entering the debate is less to accommodate the objections of their opponents than to re-examine the issue in the perspective of some "terms and focuses of recent literary criticism" (p 257). And the striking feature of his re-examination is how much the situation of criticism has changed during the interval. Wimsatt says that Frank Cioffi's critique neglected to consider "the contexts of literary scholarship and criticism which framed" his essay with Beardsley of 1945. The contexts have altered radically since then, but the problem of intention remains the same, he claims, and it is the reappearance of the intentional fallacy in recent frames of criticism that he impugns.

Wimsatt concentrates on the kind of argument, represented here by Mark Spilka, where no single explicit statement of intention is adduced "but where the author's life and canon or some parts of them are urged as a surrounding and controlling context for the poem or some details of it." This is true, he argues, "only to the extent that the poet is talking to himself." The poet's canon and life are too private a context for determining the meaning and being of a given poem; it depends more on the wider and public contexts of the language and culture. "The search for the author's generative intention as context of the poem," he concludes, "is a search for a temporal moment which must, as the author and the poem live on, recede and ever recede into the forgotten, as all moments do."

Whatever cogency these strictures may have against such revisionary formalists as Spilka, they are scarcely relevant to "genetic critics" such as Starobinski. Wimsatt does not discuss the Genevan "critics of consciousness" directly or in detail, but he does take glancing notice of J. Hillis Miller, representative of their views, linking him to the general attempt in recent criticism to reveal "the inner life of the author mainly on the evidence of the dialectic sequence of his works" (p. 259). The only difference he remarks is that "for Miller chronology is not important."

Wimsatt is more precise and explicit in a later essay where, defending once more the idea of the poem as a verbal object basic to his view of intention, he analyzes four approaches in the history of criticism to "the problem of distinguishing the poem as a separable and knowable object." [4] The first and second of these movements — (1) the nineteenth-century organicist theories of Kant, Goethe, Schelling, Coleridge, and Keats, and (2) the position elaborated by the American New Critics — established "the modern idea of the art work as a separately existent and in some sense autonomous or autotelic entity." The third is the criticism of the Geneva School and is a phase of "reaction and rejection." The fourth is structuralism.

The Geneva School critics, Wimsatt contends, batter the poetic object by negating its singularity. He cites J. Hillis Miller again as an example. In Miller's treatment of Gerard Manley Hopkins in *The Disappearance of God: Five Nineteenth-Century Writers* (1963), "perhaps the book's most ample illustration of the Genevan method transplanted to the literary experience of the USA," individual works "are pulverized and reassembled in a mainly *a*-chronological dialectic." [5] Wimsatt supports his arguments against this procedure by reference to Murray Krieger's "Mediation, Language, and Vision in the Reading of Literature" (Part IV). Like Krieger, though less sympathetically, he believes that the Geneva critics obliterate a given poem's "delicate mediate status between poet and reader." [6] Although these critics do not seek a temporal moment for an author's intention, Wimsatt concludes, the generative process they fabricate for the oeuvre of a particular author violates the ontological status of his given poems, plays, or novels. [7]

The structuralists are harder to cope with in these terms. In criticism as well as in other disciplines, the structuralist activity from the start has tried to substitute the study of functioning structures for genetic intentions. For example, Roland Barthes conducts his inquiry into Michelet, as Yves Velan has observed, "at the level of the work itself, ignoring the life which engendered the work and all meaning which the work does not furnish"; he "considers only the configuration of the forms by which the work is manifested." [8] Moreover, the structuralists have been preoccupied with language, although their conception of language is quite different in theory and less empirical in application from that assumed by Louis T. Milic.

In "Battering the Object: The Ontological Approach," Wimsatt neglects to mention that the Geneva critics are equally indifferent, strictly speaking, to "the life which engendered the work," but he acknowledges that the structuralists are committed to the study of the formal relations of verbal structures, and he believes that they offer "testimony in favor of the poetic object." [9] Hence he prefers their critical method to the "voyage into boundless consciousness" of Miller, Poulet, and Starobinski. Nevertheless, he is apprehensive at the "tyranny of the exhaustive theoretical claim" of the structuralists, and like Murray Krieger, he ends by defending the specifically literary aspects of the linguistic object. The poem, for Wimsatt, is a singular, separable, and knowable object — and the only object worth knowing to the literary *critic,* in and for itself, not in its generalized linguistic existence nor in the manifold contexts of its generative intention.

The last selection, a symposium published in 1964 on Robert Lowell's "Skunk Hour" by three contemporary poet-critics and Lowell's comments on their critiques, shows how the issues in arguments over concepts of intention actually figure in performing criticism. Wimsatt offers materials relating to William Blake's "London" as a demonstration of several possible approaches to "the structure of the argument" over intention (pp. 270 ff.), but this symposium has the advantage of including the author's own commentary on critical interpretations of his poem. Moreover, the exhibit is particularly apt for examining the nexus of issues having to do with the personal or impersonal character of literature because Lowell's poem is a notable example of "the confessional mode," a favorite form with many contemporary poets, in which the poet appears to speak of himself as he really is, openly and directly in his own person, without masks or screens of any kind. [10]

By questioning his critics' interpretations, Lowell implicitly raises the central issue of whether we must accord the author a privileged status in statements about his work. Are Lowell's remarks on the meanings he intended inadmissible or valueless in criticism of the poem? John Berryman argues that the line, "A red fox stain covers Blue Hill," is the poem's "hard" line, its most problematic. Does Lowell's testimony undermine or invalidate Berryman's critique? Does it save the quality of the line, if, in fact, the line needs saving? Does Lowell's commentary have a special power to modify our apprehension of the poem?

The symposium also raises the broader question of the relation between text and context that has dominated contemporary debate about intention. Into what sorts of contexts, personal or otherwise, do Lowell's critics try to place the poem, and what does his account contribute to establishing which of these are proper or helpful to criticism? Berryman, for example, discusses "Skunk Hour" in the context of other poems on suicide and the poet's madness, cites several cases of poets who killed themselves or went mad, and compares Lowell's poem on these topics with poems by Elizabeth Bishop and Hölderlin. Lowell acknowledges that these poets, though not the specific poems Berryman mentions, were "sources" for "Skunk Hour," but the question that emerges from this exchange is not so much whether Berryman has found the intentional moment of the poem, nor even whether he has described only an envelope of thematic affinities between poems, but whether he has located a context actually animating the words of the poem.[11] "Where," J. Hillis Miller has asked, "does the context of a poem stop?" and Wimsatt dismissively answers by arguing that the poem begins and ends within the compass of its internal structure.[12] But the question is far from simple or closed, for as the Genevan as well as other contemporary critics have shown, a poet's canon, life, and vision, even his consciousness of history and literary tradition, may be enfolded within a given poem to form its generative intention — that which shapes the singularity of its structure of language, consciousness, or experience, and makes it, as I. A. Richards said of poetry generally, "relatively inexhaustible to meditation."

W. K. WIMSATT
MONROE C. BEARDSLEY

The Intentional Fallacy

The claim of the author's "intention" upon the critic's judgment has been challenged in a number of recent discussions, notably in the debate entitled *The Personal Heresy*, between Professors Lewis and Tillyard. But it seems doubtful if this claim and most of its romantic corollaries are as yet subject to any widespread questioning. The present writers, in a short article entitled "Intention" for a *Dictionary* [1] of literary criticism, raised the issue but were unable to pursue its implications at any length. We argued that the design or intention of the author is neither available nor desirable as a standard for judging the success of a work of literary art, and it seems to us that this is a principle which goes deep into some differences in the history of critical attitudes. It is a principle which accepted or rejected points to the polar opposites of classical "imitation" and romantic expression. It entails many specific truths about inspiration, authenticity, biography, literary history and scholarship, and about some trends of contemporary poetry, especially its allusiveness. There is hardly a problem of literary criticism in which the critic's approach will not be qualified by his view of "intention."

"Intention," as we shall use the term, corresponds to *what he intended* in a formula which more or less explicitly has had wide acceptance. "In order to judge the poet's performance, we must know *what he intended*." Intention is design or plan in the author's mind. Intention has obvious affinities for the author's attitude toward his work, the way he felt, what made him write.

We begin our discussion with a series of propositions summarized and abstracted to a degree where they seem to us axiomatic.

SOURCE: "The Intentional Fallacy" is from *The Verbal Icon: Studies in the Meaning of Poetry*, by W. K. Wimsatt [Jr.] (Lexington: University of Kentucky Press, 1954), pp. 2–18. Copyright 1954. Reprinted by permission of the University of Kentucky Press.

194

1. A poem does not come into existence by accident. The words of a poem, as Professor Stoll has remarked, come out of a head, not out of a hat. Yet to insist on the designing intellect as a *cause* of a poem is not to grant the design or intention as a *standard* by which the critic is to judge the worth of the poet's performance.

2. One must ask how a critic expects to get an answer to the question about intention. How is he to find out what the poet tried to do? If the poet succeeded in doing it, then the poem itself shows what he was trying to do. And if the poet did not succeed, then the poem is not adequate evidence, and the critic must go outside the poem — for evidence of an intention that did not become effective in the poem. "Only one *caveat* must be borne in mind," says an eminent intentionalist [2] in a moment when his theory repudiates itself; "the poet's aim must be judged at the moment of the creative act, that is to say, by the art of the poem itself."

3. Judging a poem is like judging a pudding or a machine. One demands that it work. It is only because an artifact works that we infer the intention of an artificer. "A poem should not mean but be." A poem can *be* only through its *meaning* — since its medium is words — yet it *is*, simply *is*, in the sense that we have no excuse for inquiring what part is intended or meant. Poetry is a feat of style by which a complex of meaning is handled all at once. Poetry succeeds because all or most of what is said or implied is relevant; what is irrelevant has been excluded, like lumps from pudding and "bugs" from machinery. In this respect poetry differs from practical messages, which are successful if and only if we correctly infer the intention. They are more abstract than poetry.

4. The meaning of a poem may certainly be a personal one, in the sense that a poem expresses a personality or state of soul rather than a physical object like an apple. But even a short lyric poem is dramatic, the response of a speaker (no matter how abstractly conceived) to a situation (no matter how universalized). We ought to impute the thoughts and attitudes of the poem immediately to the dramatic *speaker*, and if to the author at all, only by an act of biographical inference.

5. There is a sense in which an author, by revision, may better achieve his original intention. But it is a very abstract sense. He intended to write a better work, or a better work of a certain kind, and now has done it. But it follows that his former concrete intention was not his intention. "He's the man we were in search of, that's true," says Hardy's rustic constable, "and yet he's not the man we were in search of. For the man we were in search of was not the man we wanted."

"Is not a critic," asks Professor Stoll, "a judge, who does not explore his own consciousness, but determines the author's meaning or intention, as if the poem were a will, a contract, or the constitution? The poem is not the critic's own." He has accurately diagnosed two forms of irresponsibility, one of which he prefers. Our view is yet different. The poem is not the critic's own and not the author's (it is detached from the author at birth and goes about the world beyond his power to intend about it or control it). The poem belongs to the public. It is embodied in language, the peculiar possession of the public, and it is about the human being, an object of public knowledge. What is said about the poem is subject to the same scrutiny as any statement in linguistics or in the general science of psychology.

A critic of our *Dictionary* article, Ananda K. Coomaraswamy, has argued [3] that there are two kinds of inquiry about a work of art: (1) whether the artist achieved his intentions; (2) whether the work of art "ought ever to have been undertaken at all" and so "whether it is worth preserving." Number (2), Coomaraswamy maintains, is not "criticism of any work of art *qua* work of art," but is rather moral criticism; number (1) is artistic criticism. But we maintain that (2) need not be moral criticism: that there is another way of deciding whether works of art are worth preserving and whether, in a sense, they "ought" to have been undertaken, and this is the way of objective criticism of works of art as such, the way which enables us to distinguish between a skillful murder and a skillful poem. A skillful murder is an example which Coomaraswamy uses, and in his system the difference between the murder and the poem is simply a "moral" one, not an "artistic" one, since each if carried out according to plan is "artistically" successful. We maintain that (2) is an inquiry of more worth than (1), and since (2) and not (1) is capable of distinguishing poetry from murder, the name "artistic criticism" is properly given to (2).

II

It is not so much a historical statement as a definition to say that the intentional fallacy is a romantic one. When a rhetorician of the first century A.D. writes: "Sublimity is the echo of a great soul," or when he tells us that "Homer enters into the sublime actions of his heroes" and "shares the full inspiration of the combat," we shall not be surprised to find this rhetorician considered as a distant harbinger of romanticism and greeted in the warmest terms by Saintsbury. One may wish to argue whether Longinus should be called romantic, but there can hardly be a doubt that in one important way he is.

Goethe's three questions for "constructive criticism" are "What did the author set out to do? Was his plan reasonable and sensible, and how far did he succeed in carrying it out?" If one leaves out the middle question, one has in effect the system of Croce — the culmination and crowning philosophic expression of romanticism. The beautiful is the successful intuition-expression, and the ugly is the unsuccessful; the intuition or private part of art is *the* aesthetic fact, and the medium or public part is not the subject of aesthetic at all.

> The Madonna of Cimabue is still in the Church of Santa Maria Novella; but does she speak to the visitor of to-day as to the Florentines of the thirteenth century?

> *Historical interpretation* labours . . . to reintegrate in us the psychological conditions which have changed in the course of history. It . . . enables us to see a work of art (a physical object) as its *author saw it* in the moment of production.[4]

The first italics are Croce's, the second ours. The upshot of Croce's system is an ambiguous emphasis on history. With such passages as a point of departure a critic may write a nice analysis of the meaning or "spirit" of a play by Shakespeare or Corneille — a process that involves close historical study but remains aesthetic criticism — or he may, with equal plausibility, produce an essay in sociology, biography, or other kinds of nonaesthetic history.

III

> I went to the poets; tragic, dithyrambic, and all sorts. . . . I took them some of the most elaborate passages in their own writings, and asked what was the meaning of them. . . . Will you believe me? . . . there is hardly a person present who would not have talked better about their poetry than they did themselves. Then I knew that not by wisdom do poets write poetry, but by a sort of genius and inspiration.

That reiterated mistrust of the poets which we hear from Socrates may have been part of a rigorously ascetic view in which we hardly wish to participate, yet Plato's Socrates saw a truth about the poetic mind which the world no longer commonly sees — so much criticism, and that the most inspirational and most affectionately remembered, has proceeded from the poets themselves.

Certainly the poets have had something to say that the critic and professor could not say; their message has been more exciting: that poetry should come as naturally as leaves to a tree, that poetry is the lava of the imagination, or that it is emotion recollected in tranquillity. But it is necessary that we realize the character and authority of such testimony. There is only a fine shade of difference between such expressions and a kind of earnest advice that authors often give. Thus Edward Young, Carlyle, Walter Pater:

I know two golden rules from *ethics,* which are no less golden in *Composition,* than in life. 1. *Know thyself;* 2dly, *Reverence thyself.*

This is the grand secret for finding readers and retaining them: let him who would move and convince others, be first moved and convinced himself. Horace's rule, *Si vis me flere,* is applicable in a wider sense than the literal one. To every poet, to every writer, we might say: Be true, if you would be believed.

Truth! there can be no merit, no craft at all, without that. And further, all beauty is in the long run only *fineness* of truth, or what we call expression, the finer accommodation of speech to that vision within.

And Housman's little handbook to the poetic mind yields this illustration:

> Having drunk a pint of beer at luncheon — beer is a sedative to the brain, and my afternoons are the least intellectual portion of my life — I would go out for a walk of two or three hours. As I went along, thinking of nothing in particular, only looking at things around me and following the progress of the seasons, there would flow into my mind, with sudden and unaccountable emotion, sometimes a line or two of verse, sometimes a whole stanza at once.

This is the logical terminus of the series already quoted. Here is a confession of how poems were written which would do as a definition of poetry just as well as "emotion recollected in tranquillity" — and which the young poet might equally well take to heart as a practical rule. Drink a pint of beer, relax, go walking, think on nothing in particular, look at things, surrender yourself to yourself, search for the truth in your own soul, listen to the sound of your own inside voice, discover and express the *vraie vérité.*

It is probably true that all this is excellent advice for poets. The young imagination fired by Wordsworth and Carlyle is probably closer to the verge of producing a poem than the mind of the student who has been sobered by Aristotle or Richards. The art of inspiring poets, or at least of inciting something like poetry in young persons, has probably gone further in our day than ever before. Books of creative writing such as those issued from the Lincoln School are interesting evidence of what a child can do.[5] All this, however, would appear to belong to an art separate from criticism — to a psychological discipline, a system of self-development, a yoga, which the young poet perhaps does well to notice, but which is something different from the public art of evaluating poems.

Coleridge and Arnold were better critics than most poets have been, and if the critical tendency dried up the poetry in Arnold and perhaps in Coleridge, it is not inconsistent with our argument, which is that judgment of poems is different from the art of producing them. Coleridge has given us the classic "anodyne" story, and tells what he can about the genesis of a poem which he calls a "psychological curiosity," but his definitions of poetry and of the poetic quality "imagination" are to be found elsewhere and in quite other terms.

It would be convenient if the passwords of the intentional school, "sincerity," "fidelity," "spontaneity," "authenticity," "genuineness," "originality," could be equated with terms such as "integrity," "relevance," "unity," "function," "maturity," "subtlety," "adequacy," and other more precise terms of evaluation — in short, if "expression" always meant aesthetic achievement. But this is not so.

"Aesthetic" art, says Professor Curt Ducasse, an ingenious theorist of expression, is the conscious objectification of feelings, in which an intrinsic part is the critical moment. The artist corrects the objectification when it is not adequate. But this may mean that the earlier attempt was not successful in objectifying the self, or "it may also mean that it was a successful objectification of a self which, when it confronted us clearly, we disowned and repudiated in favor of another." [6] What is the standard by which we disown or accept the self? Professor Ducasse does not say. Whatever it may be, however, this standard is an element in the definition of art which will not reduce to terms of objectification. The evaluation of the work of art remains public; the work is measured against something outside the author.

IV

There is criticism of poetry and there is author psychology, which when applied to the present or future takes the form of inspirational promotion; but author psychology can be historical too, and then we have literary biography, a legitimate and attractive study in itself, one approach, as Professor Tillyard would argue, to personality, the poem being only a parallel approach. Certainly it need not be with a derogatory purpose that one points out personal studies, as distinct from poetic studies, in the realm of literary scholarship. Yet there is danger of confusing personal and poetic studies; and there is the fault of writing the personal as if it were poetic.

There is a difference between internal and external evidence for the meaning of a poem. And the paradox is only verbal and superficial that what is (1) internal is also public: it is discovered through the semantics and syntax of a poem, through our habitual knowledge of the language, through grammars, dictionaries, and all the literature which is the source of dictionaries, in general through all that makes a language and culture; while what is (2) external is private or idiosyncratic; not a part of the work as a linguistic fact: it consists of revelations (in journals, for example, or letters or reported conversations) about how or why the poet wrote the poem — to what lady, while sitting on what lawn, or at the death of what friend or brother. There is (3) an intermediate kind of evidence about the character of the author or about private or semiprivate meanings attached to words or topics by an author or by a coterie of which he is a member. The meaning of words is the history of words, and the biography of an author, his use of a word, and the associations which the word had for *him,* are part of the word's history and meaning.[7] But the three types of evidence, especially (2) and (3), shade into one another so subtly that it is not always easy to draw a line between examples, and hence arises the difficulty for criticism. The use of biographical evidence need not involve intentionalism, because while it may be evidence of what the author intended, it may also be evidence of the meaning of his words and the dramatic character of his utterance. On the other hand, it may not be all this. And a critic who is concerned with evidence of type (1) and moderately with that of type (3) will in the long run produce a different sort of comment from that of the critic who is concerned with (2) and with (3) where it shades into (2).

The whole glittering parade of Professor Lowes' *Road to Xanadu,* for instance, runs along the border between types (2) and (3) or boldly traverses the romantic region of (2). " 'Kubla Khan,' " says Professor Lowes, "is the fabric of a vision, but every image that rose up in its weaving had passed that way before. And it would seem that there is nothing haphazard or fortuitous in their return." This is not quite clear — not even when Professor Lowes explains that there were clusters of associations, like hooked atoms, which were drawn into complex relation with other clusters in the deep well of Coleridge's memory, and which then coalesced and issued forth as poems. If there was nothing "haphazard or fortuitous" in the way the images returned to the surface, that may mean (1) that Coleridge could not produce what he did not have, that he was limited in his creation by what he had read or otherwise experienced, or (2) that having received certain clusters of associations, he was bound to return them in just the way he did, and that the value of the poem may be described in terms of the experiences on which he had to draw. The latter pair of propositions (a sort of Hartleyan associationism which Coleridge himself repudiated in the *Biographia*) may not be assented to. There were certainly other combinations, other poems, worse or better, that might have been written by men who had read Bartram and Purchas and Bruce and Milton. And this will be true no matter how many times we are able to add to the brilliant complex of Coleridge's reading. In certain flourishes (such as the sentence we have quoted) and in chapter headings like "The Shaping Spirit," "The Magical Synthesis," "Imagination Creatrix," it may be that Professor Lowes pretends to say more about the actual poems than he does. There is a certain deceptive variation in these fancy chapter titles; one expects to pass on to a new stage in the argument, and one finds — more and more sources, more and more about "the streamy nature of association." [8]

"Wohin der Weg?" quotes Professor Lowes for the motto of his book. "Kein Weg! Ins Unbetretene." Precisely because the way is *unbetreten,* we should say, it leads away from the poem. Bartram's *Travels* contains a good deal of the history of certain words and of certain romantic Floridian conceptions that appear in "Kubla Khan." And a good deal of that history has passed and was then passing into the very stuff of our language. Perhaps a person who has read Bartram appreciates the poem more than one who has not. Or, by looking up the vocabulary of "Kubla Khan" in the *Oxford English Dictionary,* or by reading some of the other books there quoted, a person may know the poem better. But it would seem to pertain little to the poem to know that *Coleridge* had read Bartram. There is a gross body of life, of sensory and mental experience, which lies behind and in some sense causes every poem, but can never be and need not be known in the verbal and hence intellectual composition which is the poem. For all the objects of our manifold experience, for every unity, there is an action of the mind which cuts off roots, melts away context — or indeed we should never have objects or ideas or anything to talk about.

It is probable that there is nothing in Professor Lowes' vast book which could detract from anyone's appreciation of either *The Ancient Mariner* or "Kubla Khan." We next present a case where preoccupation with evidence of type (3) has gone so far as to distort a critic's view of a poem (yet a case not so obvious as those that abound in our critical journals).

In a well known poem by John Donne appears this quatrain:

> Moving of th' earth brings harmes and feares,
>   Men reckon what it did and meant,
> But trepidation of the spheares,
>   Though greater farre, is innocent.

A recent critic in an elaborate treatment of Donne's learning has written of this quatrain as follows:

> He touches the emotional pulse of the situation by a skillful allusion
> to the new and the old astronomy. . . . Of the new astronomy, the
> "moving of the earth" is the most radical principle; of the old, the

> "trepidation of the spheres" is the motion of the greatest complexity.
> . . . The poet must exhort his love to quietness and calm upon his
> departure; and for this purpose the figure based upon the latter mo-
> tion (trepidation), long absorbed into the traditional astronomy,
> fittingly suggests the tension of the moment without arousing the
> "harmes and feares" implicit in the figure of the moving earth.[9]

The argument is plausible and rests on a well substantiated thesis that
Donne was deeply interested in the new astronomy and its repercussions in the theological realm. In various works Donne shows his familiarity with Kepler's *De Stella Nova,* with Galileo's *Siderius Nuncius,*
with William Gilbert's *De Magnete,* and with Clavius' commentary on
the *De Sphaera* of Sacrobosco. He refers to the new science in his Sermon
at Paul's Cross and in a letter to Sir Henry Goodyer. In *The First Anniversary* he says the "new philosophy calls all in doubt." In the *Elegy on
Prince Henry* he says that the "least moving of the center" makes "the
world to shake."

It is difficult to answer argument like this, and impossible to answer
it with evidence of like nature. There is no reason why Donne might not
have written a stanza in which the two kinds of celestial motion stood for
two sorts of emotion at parting. And if we become full of astronomical
ideas and see Donne only against the background of the new science, we
may believe that he did. But the text itself remains to be dealt with,
the analyzable vehicle of a complicated metaphor. And one may observe:
(1) that the movement of the earth according to the Copernican theory
is a celestial motion, smooth and regular, and while it might cause religious or philosophic fears, it could not be associated with the crudity
and earthiness of the kind of commotion which the speaker in the poem
wishes to discourage; (2) that there is another moving of the earth, an
earthquake, which has just these qualities and is to be associated with
the tear-floods and sigh-tempests of the second stanza of the poem; (3)
that "trepidation" is an appropriate opposite of earthquake, because each
is a shaking or vibratory motion; and "trepidation of the spheres" is
"greater far" than an earthquake, but not much greater (if two such
motions can be compared as to greatness) than the annual motion of the
earth; (4) that reckoning what it "did and meant" shows that the event
has passed, like an earthquake, not like the incessant celestial movement
of the earth. Perhaps a knowledge of Donne's interest in the new
science may add another shade of meaning, an overtone to the stanza in
question, though to say even this runs against the words. To make the
geocentric and heliocentric antithesis the core of the metaphor is to disregard the English language, to prefer private evidence to public, external
to internal.

V

If the distinction between kinds of evidence has implications for the historical critic, it has them no less for the contemporary poet and his critic. Or, since every rule for a poet is but another side of a judgment by a critic, and since the past is the realm of the scholar and critic, and the future and present that of the poet and the critical leaders of taste, we may say that the problems arising in literary scholarship from the intentional fallacy are matched by others which arise in the world of progressive experiment.

The question of "allusiveness," for example, as acutely posed by the poetry of Eliot, is certainly one where a false judgment is likely to involve the intentional fallacy. The frequency and depth of literary allusion in the poetry of Eliot and others has driven so many in pursuit of full meanings to the *Golden Bough* and the Elizabethan drama that it has become a kind of commonplace to suppose that we do not know what a poet means unless we have traced him in his reading — a supposition redolent with intentional implications. The stand taken by F. O. Matthiessen is a sound one and partially forestalls the difficulty.

> If one reads these lines with an attentive ear and is sensitive to their sudden shifts in movement, the contrast between the actual Thames and the idealized vision of it during an age before it flowed through a megalopolis is sharply conveyed by that movement itself, whether or not one recognizes the refrain to be from Spenser.

Eliot's allusions work when we know them — and to a great extent even when we do not know them, through their suggestive power.

But sometimes we find allusions supported by notes, and it is a nice question whether the notes function more as guides to send us where we may be educated, or more as indications in themselves about the character of the allusions. "Nearly everything of importance . . . that is apposite to an appreciation of 'The Waste Land,'" writes Matthiessen of Miss Weston's book, "has been incorporated into the structure of the poem itself, or into Eliot's Notes." And with such an admission it may begin to appear that it would not much matter if Eliot invented his sources (as Sir Walter Scott invented chapter epigraphs from "old plays" and "anonymous" authors, or as Coleridge wrote marginal glosses for *The Ancient Mariner*). Allusions to Dante, Webster, Marvell, or Baudelaire doubtless gain something because these writers existed, but it is doubtful whether the same can be said for an allusion to an obscure Elizabethan:

> The sound of horns and motors, which shall bring
> Sweeney to Mrs. Porter in the spring.

"Cf. Day, *Parliament of Bees*": says Eliot,

> When of a sudden, listening, you shall hear,
> A noise of horns and hunting, which shall bring
> Actaeon to Diana in the spring,
> Where all shall see her naked skin.

The irony is completed by the quotation itself; had Eliot, as is quite con-ceivable, composed these lines to furnish his own background, there would be no loss of validity. The conviction may grow as one reads Eliot's next note: "I do not know the origin of the ballad from which these lines are taken: it was reported to me from Sydney, Australia." The important word in this note — on Mrs. Porter and her daughter who washed their feet in soda water — is "ballad." And if one should feel from the lines themselves their "ballad" quality, there would be little need for the note. Ultimately, the inquiry must focus on the integrity of such notes as parts of the poem, for where they constitute special information about the meaning of phrases in the poem, they ought to be subject to the same scrutiny as any of the other words in which it is written. Matthiessen believes the notes were the price Eliot "had to pay in order to avoid what he would have considered muffling the energy of his poem by extended connecting links in the text itself." But it may be questioned whether the notes and the need for them are not equally muffling. F. W. Bateson has plausibly argued that Tennyson's "The Sailor Boy" would be better if half the stanzas were omitted, and the best versions of ballads like "Sir Patrick Spens" owe their power to the very audacity with which the minstrel has taken for granted the story upon which he comments. What then if a poet finds he cannot take so much for granted in a more recondite context and rather than write informatively, supplies notes? It can be said in favor of this plan that at least the notes do not pretend to be dramatic, as they would if written in verse. On the other hand, the notes may look like unassimilated material lying loose beside the poem, necessary for the meaning of the verbal symbol, but not inte-grated, so that the symbol stands incomplete.

We mean to suggest by the above analysis that whereas notes tend to seem to justify themselves as external indexes to the author's *intention*, yet they ought to be judged like any other parts of a composition (verbal arrangement special to a particular context), and when so judged their reality as parts of the poem, or their imaginative integration with the rest of the poem, may come into question. Matthiessen, for instance, sees that Eliot's titles for poems and his epigraphs are informative apparatus, like the notes. But while he is worried by some of the notes and thinks that Eliot "appears to be mocking himself for writing the note at the same time that he wants to convey something by it," Matthiessen believes that the "device" of epigraphs "is not at all open to the objection of not being sufficiently structural." "The *intention*," he says, "is to enable the poet to secure a condensed expression in the poem itself." "In each case the epigraph is *designed* to form an integral part of the effect of the poem." And Eliot himself, in his notes, has justified his poetic practice in terms of intention.

> The Hanged Man, a member of the traditional pack, fits my purpose in two ways: because he is associated in my mind with the Hanged God of Frazer, and because I associate him with the hooded figure in the passage of the disciples to Emmaus in Part V. . . . The man with Three Staves (an authentic member of the Tarot pack) I associate, quite arbitrarily, with the Fisher King himself.

And perhaps he is to be taken more seriously here, when off guard in a note, than when in his Norton Lectures he comments on the difficulty of saying what a poem means and adds playfully that he thinks of prefixing to a second edition of *Ash Wednesday* some lines from *Don Juan:*

> I don't pretend that I quite understand
> My own meaning when I would be *very* fine;
> But the fact is that I have nothing planned
> Unless it were to be a moment merry.

If Eliot and other contemporary poets have any characteristic fault, it may be in *planning* too much.

Allusiveness in poetry is one of several critical issues by which we have illustrated the more abstract issue of intentionalism, but it may be for today the most important illustration. As a poetic practice allusiveness would appear to be in some recent poems an extreme corollary of the romantic intentionalist assumption, and as a critical issue it challenges and brings to light in a special way the basic premise of intentionalism. The following instance from the poetry of Eliot may serve to epitomize the practical implications of what we have been saying. In Eliot's "Love Song of J. Alfred Prufrock," toward the end, occurs the line: "I have heard the mermaids singing, each to each," and this bears a certain resemblance to a line in a Song by John Donne, "Teach me to heare Mermaides singing," so that for the reader acquainted to a certain degree with Donne's poetry, the critical question arises: Is Eliot's line an allusion to Donne's? Is Prufrock thinking about Donne? Is Eliot thinking about Donne? We suggest that there are two radically different ways of looking for an answer to this question. There is (1) the way of poetic analysis and exegesis, which inquires whether it makes any sense if Eliot-Prufrock *is* thinking about Donne. In an earlier part of the poem, when Prufrock asks, "Would it have been worth while, . . . To have squeezed the universe into a ball," his words take half their sadness and irony from certain energetic and passionate lines of Marvel "To His Coy Mistress." But the exegetical inquirer may wonder whether mermaids considered as "strange sights" (to hear them is in Donne's poem analogous to getting with child a mandrake root) have much to do with Prufrock's mermaids, which seem to be symbols of romance and dynamism, and which incidentally have literary authentication, if they need it, in a line of a sonnet by Gérard de Nerval. This method of inquiry may lead to the conclusion that the given resemblance between Eliot and Donne is without significance and is better not thought of, or the method may have the disadvantage of providing no certain conclusion. Nevertheless, we submit that this is the true and objective way of criticism, as contrasted to what the very uncertainty of exegesis might tempt a second kind of critic to undertake: (2) the way of biographical or genetic inquiry, in which, taking advantage of the fact that Eliot is still alive, and in the spirit of a man who would settle a bet, the critic writes to Eliot and asks what he meant, or if he had Donne in mind. We shall not here weigh the probabilities — whether Eliot would answer that he meant nothing at all, had nothing at all in mind — a sufficiently good answer to such a question — or in an unguarded moment might furnish a clear and, within its limit, irrefutable answer. Our point is that such an answer to such an inquiry would have nothing to do with the poem "Prufrock"; it would not be a critical inquiry. Critical inquiries, unlike bets, are not settled in this way. Critical inquiries are not settled by consulting the oracle.

MARK SPILKA

The Necessary Stylist:
A New Critical Revision

The progress of the New Criticism is relatively simple to graph: a steady upward climb, from about 1930 to 1950, then a sudden levelling off for the next decade, with noticeable bumps and ruffles near the sixties. Though the success of the movement is undeniable, it seems to have lost its initial force and direction and now threatens to decline for lack of generative ideas. For critics trained in the fifties, however, it remains a major source of intellectual ferment. For this generation especially it functions as the formative approach to literature, more challenging and absorbing than other current theories. If the movement is to acquire new strength, these new adherents must provide it. The founding fathers have had their say; the unruly or subservient sons — Jarrell, Fiedler, Hyman, Stallman — have gone their different ways, and the fate of the movement lies with younger men. This being the case, the nature of its appeal for them is worth exploring.

Irving Howe has argued that criticism has become "a problem in mechanics, the tools, methods and trade secrets of which can be picked up, usually during the summer, from the more experienced operatives." (*Partisan Review*, XXI, 27–28). As a representative summer product, let me vouch for this as partial truth. For better or worse, the New Criticism does attract the novice with its methodology which resembles "mechanics" in its thoroughness and objectivity: but it also offers him a ready-made aesthetic, a set of easily mastered concepts which subtly redirect its method. This blend of theory and practice is called "explicative holism" by W. K. Wimsatt, who means by this the careful analysis of specific texts, considered as autonomous wholes (*The Verbal Icon* [New

SOURCE: "The Necessary Stylist: A New Critical Revision" is from *Modern Fiction Studies*, Volume VI (Winter 1960–1961), pp. 283–297, revised by the author in *Modern Criticism: Theory and Practice*, edited by Walter Sutton and Richard Foster (New York: Odyssey Press, 1963), pp. 328–334, and revised further by him for publication here. *Modern Fiction Studies*, © 1961, by Purdue Research Foundation, Lafayette, Indiana. Reprinted by permission of the Purdue Research Foundation and the author.

York, 1954], p. 237). The word "autonomous" is, of course, an abstraction, like "universal" or "eternal"; but, unlike these older aesthetic terms, it puts space around a novel, poem, or story, and lends solidity to the work within; it outlines and substantiates a forbidden realm of knowledge, and thus opens it to explication.

In a positivistic age this strategy has its merits: it gives literature some status in reality, without raising metaphysical issues; and it saves it from absorption into origins and effects, as mere history and impression. Like other useful metaphors — "organic form," "the verbal icon," "the objective correlative" — it grants imagined life to words upon a page. Nor is this merely to hypostatize the work for critical practice; instead the term connects us with realities which we all affirm, but are hard put to defend against the realities of science. The New Critics defend them for us in two ways: by their own objective method, which is itself "scientific" and hence competitive in function; and by covert and protective metaphors, like autonomy and organic form, which begin in biology but end in metaphysics, since they point to knowledge of a kind not reached by science. These knowledge-claims are seldom boldly asserted; but all the major formalists — Brooks, Warren, Tate, Ransom, Vivas — seem to assume them; in fact, there is considerable ground for calling formalism a disguise for spiritual concern with literature (cf. Richard Foster, *Hudson Review,* XII, 232–46). For my own generation this has always been the secret appeal of the movement: its promise of something like objective certainty about subjective truths — their order, worth and meaning — as revealed through verbal forms. We are even somewhat impatient with our elders here. As Hyatt Waggoner confirms, young men "are likely to feel that the new criticism does not attack value questions directly or determinedly enough, that it tries . . . too hard to be objective and so ends by keeping its largest assumptions out of sight" (*Criticism,* I, 219). We feel the need, in short, to re-examine those assumptions.

If it was once necessary to hide them, so that literature might appear as respectable and real as science, it seems important now to exhume them and to face their implications squarely. The movement, having won all major battles, has become its own worst enemy: its problems are internal, not external, and strategies designed to rout scientists and "old scholars" will not resolve them. The defect here is narrowness of a special order. To remove it, some recent theorists would buttress formalism with an eclectic or synoptic mixture of methods (cf. Waggoner, 211–25, and Northrop Frye, *Anatomy of Criticism* [Princeton, 1957]). Others would strike at theory itself: they would broaden the base of formalism by showing that quality in verbal art depends partly on external elements, like history and language, and on shared awareness of those elements (cf. Roy Harvey Pearce, *Kenyon Review*, XX, 554–91, and Walter Sutton, *Journal of Aesthetics and Art Criticism*, XVII, 219–29). This connection between *form* and broader contexts seems to me exactly right. New Critical narrowness is internal; it will not be cured by added methods; but the movement might transcend its limits, and achieve its promise, through expansion and revision of its formal concepts. Among them is the concept of the author, which bears importantly on such issues as autonomy, intention, response and objectivity. If we can connect the author *formally* with his works, rather than historically or biographically, we can begin to make some headway in connecting literature with life.

II

The concept of the author is conspicuous, in New Critical thought, by its absence. Sometimes this absence means an actual blank space on the page, as in experimental texts where poems appear by number only and poets' names are exiled to the index (e.g., Richards' *Practical Criticism* and Thomas and Brown's *Reading Poems* [New York, 1955]). But generally speaking, names are given their usual task of identification. New Critics are even well-informed about authors' lives and times, and will use such knowledge freely, if "unformally," when it adds to meaning. They are not averse to scholarship, per se, but to its critical sins. When they first reacted against those sins, they did so to excess and created latent troubles of their own. Still, the initial step was badly needed.

According to Roy Harvey Pearce, historians had so confused works with setting that works became for them "just dim spots on the historical horizon — so dim that it [didn't] seem worthwhile to distinguish one from another; so dim that critical explication [was] at best an adventure in uncontrolled impressionism" (562). To correct that trend, early theorists tried to isolate and brighten works by calling them autonomous and organic; then later theorists defined two kinds of fallacies, the intentional and the affective, which made for further isolation, if not for greater brightness. By these definitions it was wrong to derive standards of critical judgment from authors' aims or readers' feelings; it was right to derive them from the work itself, conceived as verbal object. Rigidity and exclusiveness began here, I think, with definitions which were clear on sin but vague on virtue, and which made extremely sharp distinctions between feeling and idea. What is the role of feeling, for instance, in literary judgment? Do we abandon it, with Wellek and Austin Warren, and settle for "the perceptions of emotions" (*Theory of Literature* [New York, 1956], p. 25)? Or do we translate "formulas of emotion," with Wimsatt and Beardsley, so that others may respond to them (Wimsatt, pp. 34, 37)? In either case, it seems to me impossible to have perceptions, much less formulas, without using actual feelings to confirm them.

Discernment and response work hand-in-hand, in critical practice, though with varying predominance and intensity; but for most of the New Critics these elements remain estranged. Literature, for them, embodies feeling, while criticism disembodies thought: witness Richards' spurious distinction between scientific and emotive use of language; or Eliot's odd belief that poets never "think"— they find emotional equivalents for thought; or Wimsatt's admonition that understanding and evaluation are as far apart for cognitive as for emotive critics. Yet feeling and idea are seldom disconnected in this manner; the interflow between them is psychological fact (cf. Lionel Trilling, *The Liberal Imagination* [New York, 1953], p. 273). When New Critics hold, to the contrary, that emotion plays no role in critical discernment, they invite affective chaos. For in their view we need never question our emotions nor doubt the purity of our perceptions: as objective critics, we have already eschewed subjective judgments; but if complete detachment happens to be impossible, such judgments must return without our conscious knowledge. In other words, the affective fallacy, as a warning concept, has not eliminated impressionism; it has simply driven it underground.

But our chief argument is with the intentional fallacy, which has led to much the same results. As everyone knows, authors are suspicious figures, victims of inspiration, drugs, drink, neurosis, vanity and self-deception; they are fallible, that is, and critics have rightly questioned their pronouncements of intention. Ideally, the work itself reveals *achieved* intention — the only kind which matters, since it indicates where judgment must begin. At this level of discussion, we might add one rule of thumb: if outside evidence corrects or assists objective judgment, there is no point in ignoring it, provided that achievement (not intention) is the test of relevance (cf. Waggoner, pp. 220–21, and Henry David Aiken, *Journal of Philosophy*, LII, pp. 742–53). This is common sense, and most New Critics would accept it. The real trouble lies elsewhere, in their failure to accommodate the author's role as stylist.

One critic, Wimsatt, does allude to the poet as "sayer," "maker," or "accomplisher" (pp. xviii, 263). His terms are undefined, however, and he never demonstrates their value. He seems almost to equate the poet with his finished work. More likely, he detaches him completely, since equation might suggest a formal bond, an interfusion, a personal invasion of an otherwise impersonal and autonomous realm. But isn't this a definition of style — that personal element which seems so tangibly *there,* in arts like painting, where we identify a Rembrandt or Renoir by visible characteristics, ways of arranging light, shadow, color and shape to achieve *organic wholes?* Such distinctive traits are less apparent in literature, but they do exist in Austen, Conrad or Fitzgerald novels, in poems by Wyatt, Milton, Hardy, Yeats. And if we mean by style two things — a characteristic use of language and (more difficult to define) a characteristic way of arranging experience for aesthetic ends — then these and other writers have recognizable styles. If we mean, beyond this double definition, that style adapts itself to theme, or to an author's working vision of existence, then it affects the very quality and form of single works, and, through it, authors too connect with works in formal ways. In this sense, authors are that common element which persists, even in changing aspects, throughout their whole production: they inform specific works yet at the same time stand outside them; they are the shapers, makers and accomplishers whom critics *must* consult if they would analyze organic wholes.

Because they have concerned themselves, so frequently, with single poems, and because their rescue work has made them concentrate on isolation, New Critics have forgotten that each verbal object lives in company with others like itself. We read the *novels* of Joyce and Lawrence, the *plays* of Shakespeare, the *poems* of Keats: we seldom stop with one creation. And because we familiarize ourselves with *works,* we see the common element which unites them, the personal dimension which informs them, the stylist who creates them. To ignore the stylist, it seems to me, is to ignore the very principle of form — the creative principle, which invests each work with its uniqueness. Style ought to be our foremost clue to that uniqueness, that achieved intention which we also call "organic form." We use such clues in practice, where knowledge of related works improves our grasp of single texts. But New Critics treat such knowledge as mere preparation for analysis: they do the same with history and biography, as if autonomy were absolute and all else relative and inert. Yet autonomy itself is relative: all works of art exist within surrounding contexts, on which their quality depends.

We say of poetry, for instance, that it suffers in translation, which violates the subtle interconnections of image, rhythm, sound and idea. This inviolateness demonstrates the autonomy of specific poems, but it also highlights their dependence on a given language, social and historical medium in which their very form inheres. In the same vein, Walter Sutton holds that poems depend for their effects upon reference to things outside the poems: they appeal to common experience and shared value; they proceed from and are received in contexts broader than themselves (pp. 226–29). The responsible critic must accept these broader contexts and account for their effect on form. His maxim here might run: no work of art is an island, entire of itself; no organism exists which is not dependent, in the most vital way, on its surroundings (a maxim drawn, incidentally, from Aiken and Sutton). When those surroundings consist of similar creations, their common maker reasserts his formal role. As stylist, he controls the quality of language, the arrangement of experience for aesthetic ends, the expression of a total vision. Accordingly, the critic must consult the general contours of his work, his phases and progressions, his favorite themes and methods, the kinds of problems which he can or cannot solve. Biography and history enter, not as background, but as contexts which add knowledge of the stylist. Intention now becomes involved with critical judgment, since the maker's aims are manifest in form, in conscious and unconscious fusion. In short, the total process is organic, from biography through art to judgment, if we confirm the author's role as stylist and the supporting role of felt response.

If, on the other hand, we minimize the author's role, as we persistently minimize response, the penalties are these: the critic will become the author, he will supply his own intention (plus his own emotions) and rewrite the story; and he will do this with impunity, since there is no stylist to rebuff him, no maker to deny his reading: he is, after all, an objective critic, a master of autonomous wholes, who contemplates his text within the vacuum which surrounds it, or at the most, within inert surroundings. Wimsatt argues against such penalties, saying that works belong neither to authors nor to critics, but to the public (p. 5); but if an author does *inform* (rather than own) his works, and no one grants his role, the critic will assume it. The temptation is too great, in an age when creativity is scarce and precious; critics are as apt to steal it as biographers were before them. Indeed, we might even see a wave of New Intentionalists and Impressionists, of critics who twist stories to their liking and seem insensitive to affective quality. Such critics will commit what I would call the Objective Fallacy: the belief in objectivity without recourse to feeling or informing style. But of course we all commit that fallacy these days, as critics and teachers reared on formalist doctrines. Whatever our critical talents, we all project assumptions into texts; we acquire the gloss of objectivity from method, from thorough sifting of evidence and from close analysis, which guarantee our virtue; when contradictions arise, ingenuity removes them — the mind has patterns to enforce which override the text, the searching heart, or that biographical myth, the creative writer. Because such lapses are so common, we must all learn how to avoid them, or more pertinently, how to strengthen the movement which unwittingly invites them.

III

What are we to say, for instance, when sensitive, intelligent formalists reveal the co-existence, in "After Apple-Picking," of nightmares with contemplative delights? . . . One is reminded here of Randall Jarrell's complaint of 1952, that "Criticism will soon have reached the state of scholarship, and the most obviously absurd theory — if it is maintained intensively, exhaustively, and professionally — will do the theorist no harm in the eyes of his colleagues" (*Partisan Review,* XIX, 193). Apparently that state has come to pass. The above-mentioned reading *is* maintained "intensively, exhaustively, and professionally"; it seems exemplary in thoroughness and objectivity, in modesty and detachment: yet the whole effect is of methodology gone berserk. Confronted by such a reading, we cannot merely explicate the same details more sensibly and rest our case. Inclusiveness and coherence, those touchstones of objective certainty, will not avail us: our opponents have achieved inclusive and coherent readings (give or take a few absurdities), and there is no way to refute them from the isolated text. Objective readings, equally exhaustive and consistent, merely cancel out when diametrically opposed, and objectivity itself reverts to armed impressionism. If we can grant, however, that texts extend to human contexts, through creation and response, we may begin to validate objective readings. We may show, for instance, how critics violate the stylist's mode of operation, distort his plain assumptions, neglect his characteristic weightings and arrangements, ignore the limits of his diction, or appeal to other works for *corroboration* — but never to define the author's vision; and we may expose their affective blindness, their insensitivity to tonal quality, and their own disguised impressionism. If, on the other hand, we neglect these aspects of creation and response, we have no way to combat exemplary madness — and no way to prevent its certain spread. Our passion for the verbal object, and for objective criticism, is right and central; but without provision for the stylist, and for the emotionally responsive reader, our claim to objectivity will collapse — indeed, is now collapsing.

I am speaking here of an advanced stage of critical practice, not of introductory methods; and I am speaking of an advanced stage of the New Criticism, which, in its early missionary zeal, produced a permanent body of objective readings and worked a vital revolution in the academies through stress on explication. There is a point, however, when an objective mode becomes defensive, becomes an evasion of those inner depths which justify its use, and which it first sought to preserve. At such a point methods can rigidify or turn destructive: adherents, in their sophistication, can abuse them with humane intentions, or use them to disguise their own impressions. We are all familiar with such readings, which destroy or cancel meaning through exhaustive ingenuity. To avoid them, or simply to counteract their damage, we need acts of critical imagination, attempts to reconstruct the terms of an author's vision, and to define its limits and capacities (cf. E. D. Hirsch, Jr., *PMLA*, LXXV, 463–79, for corroborative views). Such acts can only proceed, of course, through cumulative insights, drawn from tentative and wisely selective reading, and from scholarly research. Once these requirements are met, the return to single texts should be rewarding. The need for sheer intelligence remains, but granting this necessity, the process fosters several virtues: it operates by open and demonstrable assumptions, which, even if they are wrong, are nonetheless open; it broadens critical outlook and so overcomes myopic trends in current practice; and finally, it works on human as well as formal grounds, since the imaginative act embraces human contexts and forces judgment of the stylist's aims, powers, and values — his vision of significant life.

We must commit ourselves, I think, to such analysis as we explicate specific texts. We can do so with confidence, if we use imaginative reconstructions to support (rather than supplant) objective methods, and to reinforce their cognitive role — their role, that is, in revealing patterns of experiential truth. Once methodology rescued verbal works from science, and preserved them as forbidden realms of knowledge; now it threatens to destroy them, since we worship it as an end and forget its instrumental function. In our extreme objectivity, we have reduced the reading process to an experience of isolated forms. In itself this is harmless, since those forms are rich with qualitative knowledge, and to experience them has immediate value. But method, used in isolation, will eventually betray the reader and destroy that value; we *must* connect those forms with human contexts — with stylists and responsive readers — to keep their worth (indeed, their *sense*) intact. The need is urgent in a changing academic world. The mass influx of students, in the postwar period, has created teaching jobs for young New Critics, or, at the least, young "explicative holists." Together with the "old" New Critics, this group has met the American middle class head on, or met its brighter children, and has taught them how to read good literature. This is a unique achievement, unparalleled in critical history; there has never been a semi-popular movement which could so affect the quality of our culture. But if method is its burden, the duration of effect seems doubtful and its depth uncertain. The New Critics are not "empty formalists," as so often charged; at their worst, they are self-defeating formalists who continue to use tough-minded scientific attitudes to rescue art from science. The great irony here is to defeat oneself by imitating positivists. The great challenge is to be humanists — to acquire subjective knowledge through objective methods, and so change the quality of American culture.

FRANK CIOFFI

Intention and Interpretation in Criticism

If we adapt Wittgenstein's characterisation of philosophy: "putting into order our notions as to what can be said about the world," we have a programme for aesthetics: "putting into order our notions as to what can be said about works of art."

One of the tasks of such a programme would be to elucidate the relation in which biographical data about an author, particularly of the kind loosely known as knowledge of his intentions, stand to those issues we call matters of interpretation. I.e., the relation between questions like these:

Whether it is Goethe who is referred to in the first line of the first canto of *In Memoriam*.

Whether it is the poet who is speaking in the concluding lines of *Ode on a Grecian Urn*.

Whether Pope is "screaming with malignant fury" in his character of Sporus.

Whether Hamlet in his famous soliloquy is contemplating suicide or assassination.

Whether Milton's Satan in his speech in Book IV beginning "League with thee I seek" may be wholly or partly sincere.

Whether the governess who tells the story in James' *Turn of the Screw*, is a neurotic case of sex-repression and the ghosts not real ghosts but hallucinations.

Whether Wordsworth's *Ode: Intimations of Immortality* is "a conscious farewell to his art, a dirge sung over his departing powers" or is a "dedication to new powers"; and whether the "timely utterance" referred to in that poem is *My Heart Leaps Up* or *Resolution and Independence*.

SOURCE: "Intention and Interpretation in Criticism" is from *Proceedings of the Aristotelian Society*, new series, LXIV (1963–1964), pp. 85–106. Copyright © 1963 The Aristotelian Society. Reprinted by permission of the Honorary Secretary and Editor of The Aristotelian Society. The passages from W. B. Yeats' *Among School Children* are reprinted with permission of The Macmillan Company, Mr. M. B. Yeats, Macmillan & Co., Ltd., and the Macmillan Company of Canada Ltd., from *The Collected Poems of W. B. Yeats*. Copyright 1928 by The Macmillan Company, renewed 1956 by Georgie Yeats.

Whether we are meant to reflect that Othello becomes jealous very quickly on very little provocation.

Whether the Moses of Michelangelo is about to hurl the tablets of the law to the ground or has just overcome an impulse to do so.

Whether Shakespeare's Sonnet 73 contains an allusion to despoilt and abandoned monasteries.

Whether the image which floats before Yeats' mind in *Among School Children,* "hollow of cheek," is of an old woman or of one beautiful in a *quattrocento* way.

Whether the metaphors in Othello's soliloquy which begins "Steep me in poverty to the very lips" are deliberately inappropriate so as to suggest the disorder of Othello's mind.

Whether Ford Madox Ford's novel *Parade's End* is a trilogy or a tetralogy.

Whether on reading the line "in spite of that we call this Friday good" from *East Coker* we are to think of Robinson Crusoe's friend.

Whether Gertrude's marriage to Claudius was incestuous.

Whether Othello was black or brown.

Whether Pippit in Eliot's *A Cooking Egg* is young or old, of the same social status as the speaker or not and whether the connotations of the expression "penny-world" in that poem are sordid or tender.

Whether in *The Mystery of Edwin Drood* Dickens has deepened his analysis of Victorian society to include Imperialism; and whether John Jasper in that novel is a member of the Indian sect of Thugs.

Whether we should identify with Strether in *The Ambassadors* and whether the Ververs in *The Golden Bowl* are unqualifiedly admirable.

And statements like these:

That Eliot associates the Hanged Man, a member of the traditional tarot pack with the Hanged God of Frazer and with the hooded figure in the passage of the disciples to Emmaus.

That Hopkins said: The Sonnet on Purcell means this: 1-4 I hope Purcell is not damned for being a protestant because I love his genius, etc., etc. "Low lays him" means "lays him low," "listed is enlisted" etc., etc.

That Wordsworth wrote *Resolution and Independence* while engaged on the first part of the Immortality Ode.

That Henry James in 1895 had his faith in himself shaken by the failure of his plays.

That Donne's *A Valediction: Forbidding Mourning* was addressed to his wife.

That James was conversant enough with English ways to know that no headmaster would have expelled a boy belonging to a county family without grave reasons.

That A. E. Housman vehemently repudiated the view that his poem *1887* contained a gibe at the Queen.

That Swift was philanthropic and well-loved by his friends.

That Maude Gonne was an old woman when Yeats wrote *Among School Children*.

That Keats in his letters uses the word "beauty" to mean something much more subtle than is ordinarily meant by it.

That Eliot meant the lines "to Carthage then I came, burning, burning, burning . . ." to evoke the presence of St. Augustine and the Buddha, of Western and Eastern Asceticism.

That Abraham Cowley had had very little to do with women.

That ruined monasteries were a not uncommon sight in 1585.

That Henry James meant his later novels to illustrate his father's metaphysical system.

That Conrad in *The Arrow of Gold* presents an unrealistic and sentimentalised portrait of a woman.

That Wordsworth nowhere in his work uses the word "glory" to refer to his creative powers.

That Eliot told someone that Richards in his account of *A Cooking Egg* was "barking up the wrong tree."

That Tennyson shortly before his death told an American gentleman that he was referring to Goethe when he wrote "of him who sings to one clear harp in divers tones."

That there were no industrial mills when Blake wrote *Jerusalem*.

That in the book of *Exodus* Moses shattered the tablets of the law.

That Dickens wrote a letter at the time of the Sepoy mutiny advocating the extermination of the Indian people.

In this paper I have assembled and invented examples of arguments which use biographical claims to resolve questions of interpretation and confronted them with a meta-critical dogma to the effect that there exists an operation variously known as analysing or explicating or appealing to the text and that criticism should confine itself to this, in particular eschewing biographical enquiries.

By now any of you who are at all interested in this topic must have had the phrase "the intentional fallacy" occur to you. This phrase owes it currency to a widely anthologised and often-alluded to paper of that title by two Americans, Wimsatt and Beardsley. I want now to try to bring what they say in it into relation with the issue I have raised.

1

The first statement of their thesis runs: ". . . the design or intention of the author is neither available nor desirable as a standard for judging the success of a literary work of art." These words don't really mean what they say. They don't mean that an artist may have intended to create a masterpiece but for all that have failed to do so; for the authors go on to say of their thesis that it entails "many specific truths about inspiration, authenticity, biography, literary history and scholarship," etc., and none of these specific truths follows from the truism that knowledge of an artist's intentions cannot provide us with criteria for judging of his success. The charitable conviction that they mean more than this is borne out by a later statement of the thesis; this time to the effect that it is a thesis about the *meaning* of a work of art that they are concerned to advance: that certain ways of establishing this meaning are legitimate whereas others are not. So, presumably, what they intended to say is: "the design or intention of an author is neither available nor desirable as a standard for judging the meaning of a literary work of art." But no argument can profitably be conducted in these terms. For if a discrepancy should come to light between a reader's interpretation of a work and the interpretation of the author or his contemporaries, no way of determining which of these could be properly described as *the* meaning of the work could be produced.

What an author meant, by a poem, say, what his contempories took him to mean, what the common reader makes of it and what makes the best poem of it are usually concomitant and allow us to speak of *the* meaning without equivocation. If when confronted by instances in which this concomitance breaks down we appeal to only one of the ordinarily coincident features as if we had a settled convention behind us, the question becomes intractable. If the question is expressed instead as "How should this poem be read?" it at least becomes clearer what the issues are. So the thesis becomes, "The design or intention of an author is neither available nor desirable as a standard for judging how a work of literature should be read." But does any criticism of literature consist of the provision of standards by which you may judge how the work should be read? One of the pieces of criticism which the authors have provided in their paper as an illustration of how it should be done concerns Eliot's *The Love Song of J. Alfred Prufrock*. They say that when Prufrock asks, "would it have been worth while . . . to have squeezed the universe into a ball," "his words take half their sadness and irony from certain energetic and passionate lines of Marvell's *To His Coy Mistress*." This may be true and it may be helpful but nothing in it answers to the description of providing a standard by which the work may be read. What they have done or have tried to do is to produce in the reader a more adequate response to Eliot's lines by reminding him of Marvell's. If we bring their thesis in line with their practice it becomes: "The design or intention of the author is neither available nor desirable as a means of influencing a reader's response to a literary work." But since they give us an example of what they consider as irrelevant to criticism the fact that Coleridge read Purchas, Bartram, Milton and Bruce and this is not a fact about either his design or his intention it is obvious that they mean something rather wider than this, something which the expression "biographical data" would be a closer approximation to. This gives us "biographical data about an author, particularly concerning his artistic intentions is not desirable [I omit 'available' as probably just a sign of nervousness] as a means of influencing a reader's response to a literary work."

What any general thesis about the relevance of intention to interpretation overlooks is the heterogeneity of the contexts in which questions of interpretation arise. This heterogeneity makes it impossible to give a general answer to the question of what the relevance of intention to interpretation is. There are cases in which we have an interpretation which satisfies us but which we feel depends on certain facts being the case. It may involve an allusion and we may wish to be reassured that the author was in a position to make the allusion. In this case biographical facts act as a kind of sieve which exclude certain possibilities. Then there is the case where we are puzzled, perhaps by an allusion we don't understand, perhaps by syntax, and reference to the author's intention, though it does not guarantee a favourable response, may at least relieve this perplexity and make one possible. There are cases in which we suspect irony but the text is equivocal, and cases where we aren't sure what view the author wishes us to take of the situation he places before us. Then there are the most interesting cases, those in which the text seems unmistakably to call for a certain interpretation and this is found satisfying, but in which we learn with surprise that it has been explicitly repudiated by the author. Even within the same kind of context the author's intention will vary in relevance depending on the kind of question involved; whether it concerns the meaning of a word or the tone of a passage, the view to be taken of a character or a situation or the general moral of an entire work.

Why did Wimsatt and Beardsley think they had a general answer to the question of deciding what the response to a work of literature should be? This is what they say:

> There is a difference between internal and external evidence for the meaning of a poem, and the paradox is only verbal and superficial that what is (1) internal is also public. It is discovered through the semantics and syntax of a poem, through our habitual knowledge of the language, through grammars, dictionaries and all the literature which is a source of dictionaries, in general through all that makes a language and culture; while what is (2) external is private or idiosyncratic;

not a part of the work as a linguistic fact; it consists of revelations (in journals, for example, or letters, or reported conversations) about how or why the poet wrote the poem. To what lady while sitting on what lawn, or at the death of what friend or brother. There is (3) an intermediate kind of evidence about the character of the author or about private or semi-private meanings attached to words or topics by an author or by a coterie of which he is a member. The meanings of words is the history of words, and the biography of an author, his use of a word, and the associations which the word had for him are part of the word's history and meaning. But the three types of evidence, especially (2) and (3) shade into one another so subtly that it is not always easy to draw a line between examples, and hence arises the difficulty for criticism.

It is not clear from this account what the authors mean to exclude as illicit sources of interpretive data. Once the author's character and the private associations a word may have for him are admitted among these, along with all that makes a language and a culture, what is there left to commit fallacies with? Were it not that their illustrations give a much clearer impression of their attitude than their attempts at explicit formulation of it do, and show it to be much more restrictive, they could be suspected of advancing one of those enchanted theses which possess the magical power of transforming themselves into truisms at the touch of a counter-example. They say of a line in Eliot's *The Love Song of J. Alfred Prufrock:* "I have heard the mermaids singing each to each" that it bears some resemblance to a line of Donne's: "Teach me to heare Mermaides singing" so that the question arises whether Eliot's line contains an allusion to Donne's. They go on to say that there are two radically different ways of answering this question. The way of poetic exegesis and the way of biographical enquiry, and the latter would not be a critical enquiry and would have nothing to do with the poem. The method of poetic exegesis consists of asking whether it would make any sense if Donne's mermaids were being alluded to. The biographical approach would be to ask Eliot what he thought at the time he wrote it, whether he had Donne's mermaids in mind. The answer to this question would be critically irrelevant. It is not surprising that their example bears them out since it was hand-chosen, as it were. To expose its tendentiousness we need only take an example in which it was felt that a literary allusion would enhance the value of the lines. Let us take their own example of Marvell's *To His Coy Mistress,* familiarity with which they maintain enhances the value of certain lines of Eliot's. If we take the case of someone not familiar with Marvell's *To His Coy Mistress,* then the biographical claim that Eliot alludes to it in Prufrock would enhance its value for them. If on the other hand they merely applied the test of poetic exegesis and incorporated the allusion to Marvell's *To His Coy Mistress* into the poem without knowing whether Eliot was alluding to it, it is doubtful whether their appreciation would survive the discovery that he was not. If a critical remark is one which has the power to modify our apprehension of a work, then biographical remarks can be critical. They can serve the eliminative function of showing that certain interpretations of a work are based on mistaken beliefs about the author's state of knowledge.

2

We can illustrate this eliminative function of biographical data by taking the very case on which Wimsatt and Beardsley based their arguments as to its irrelevance. They quote a quatrain from John Donne's *A Valediction: Forbidding Mourning*:

> Moving of the earth brings harmes and feares,
> Men reckon what it did and meant,
> But trepidation of the spheares,
> Though greater farre, is innocent.

They then go on to criticise an interpretation of this quatrain which basing itself on the biographical fact that Donne was intensely interested in the new astronomy and its theological repercussions sees in the phrase "Moving of the earth" an allusion to the recently discovered motion of the earth round the sun. Wimsatt and Beardsley show the unlikelihood of this, not by disputing the well-authenticated facts concerning Donne's interest in astronomy, which would be to use a biographical method, but through an analysis of the text. They maintain that whereas the fear which is produced by the motion of the earth is a metaphysical, intellectual one, the fear which Donne is attempting to discourage is of the emotional kind which an earthquake is more likely to produce and that this accords better with the "tear-floods" and "sigh-tempests" of the poem's second stanza than the earth's motion. Let us concede that the authors have made it very plausible that Donne was alluding not to the heliocentric theory of the earth's motion but to earthquakes. The gratuitousness of the conclusion which they draw from this becomes apparent if we ask the following question: have they established that Donne was not referring to the motion of the earth round the sun as persuasively as our belief in Donne's ignorance of the heliocentric theory would establish it? Wouldn't this "external" fact outweigh all their "internal" ones?

At this point someone who finds my question unrhetorical is thinking to himself "dark satanic mills." It is true that the knowledge that the poem that prefaces Blake's *Milton* is not an expression of the Fabian sentiments it has been usually taken as being has not caused the traditional interpretation to be abandoned. I suggest that what we have in this case is something in the nature of a spontaneous adaptation of Blake's poem. It is unlike what we ordinarily consider an adaptation in not being conscious (initially at any rate) and not involving any physical change in the work adapted. Does the fact that this was possible in the case of Blake's lyric reflect adversely on it as poem? Does the fact that the melody of *God Save the Queen* could be fitted with new words and become the national anthem of a republican nation reflect on it? The combination of resolution and exaltation which characterises Blake's poem carries over into its adaptation; it functions like a melody. We should see cases like that of *Jerusalem* as continuous with more deliberate cases of adaptation. When Pistol tells *French* audiences that his "rendezvous is quite cut off," his Doll lies dying of Maladie of *Naples*.[1] Does anything follow as to the relevance or irrelevance of an author's intentions? Then neither does it in the case of *Jerusalem*. It would only follow if the discovery that a work was an adaptation made no difference to us. There is one sort of literature in which adaptation is a matter of indifference: jokes. Wilkes becomes Disraeli and Disraeli becomes Birkenhead. The two Jews become two Irishmen or two Chinese. But then, we speak of the author of a poem but not of the author of a joke. I am saying: we don't stand in the same relation to Blake's lyric after changing our conviction as to what he meant to convey as we did before. If the case were one in which the discrepancy between the author's interpretation and the reader's were one as to the very emotions expressed and not just the accompanying imagery our attitude would be very different. Frank Harris read A. E. Housman's poem *1887* as an anti-imperialist gibe and the expression "God Save the Queen" which recurs in it as a sarcastic jeer until Housman revealed otherwise. Thereafter he naturally found it difficult to do so in spite of his conviction both as to the superiority of his interpretation and its greater consonance with Housman's general outlook. ("How was I to know that someone steeped in a savage disgust of life could take pleasure in outcheapening Kipling at his cheapest?")

The following examples should make it clear how inept Wimsatt's and Beardsley's characterisation of the role of biographical data in critical discourse is. An example which seems to support their account is Leavis' reaction to John Middleton Murry's attempt to give the word "beauty" in the concluding couplet of Keats' *Ode on a Grecian Urn* a less limiting sense based on the use Keats made of the word in his letters.

> To show from the letters that "beauty" became for Keats a very subtle and embracing concept and that in his use the term takes on meanings that it could not possibly have for the uninitiated is gratuitous

and irrelevant. However his use of the word may have developed as he matured, "beauty" is the term he used and in calling what seemed to him the supreme thing in life "beauty" he expresses a given bent — the bent everywhere manifest in the quality of his verse, in its loveliness . . . and that "beauty" in the *Ode on a Grecian Urn* expresses this bent is plain, that it should is the essence of the poem, and there is nothing in the poem to suggest otherwise.

This may sound as if a general principle akin to Wimsatt's and Beardsley's is being employed, but that this is not so Leavis' practice elsewhere shows. For example,

> Hopkins' *Henry Purcell* is a curious special case, there can be few readers who have not found it strangely expressive and few who could have elucidated it without extraneous help. It is not independent of the explanatory note by Hopkins that Bridges prints. Yet when one approaches it with the note fresh in mind, the intended meaning seems to be sufficiently in the poem to allay at any rate the dissatisfaction caused by baffled understanding.

We must not be misled by the expression "a curious special case." Leavis' dealings with *The Waste Land* make it clear that the only question which arises in connexion with notes or other extraneous aids to understanding is not one of their legitimacy but of their efficacy. For example, Leavis says of *The Waste Land* that it "sometimes depends on external support in ways that can hardly be justified . . . for instance, the end of the third section 'The Fire Sermon.' . . . No amount of reading of the *Confessions* or *Buddhism in Translation* will give these few words power to evoke the kind of presence that seems necessary to the poem." Of another passage he writes: "it leaves too much to Miss Weston; repeated recourse to *Ritual and Romance* will not invest it with the virtues it would assume." On the other hand, of Eliot's note on *Tiresias,* Leavis remarks, "if Mr Eliot's readers have a right to a grievance, it is that he has not given this note more salience." "Power to evoke," "invest with virtues," these are not the idioms in which the probative value of statements is weighed.

Wimsatt and Beardsley are aware of the problem posed them by Eliot's notes to *The Waste Land* and make the suggestion that the notes should be considered as part of the poem. They thus become internal evidence, and may be consulted with a good conscience. Does it follow that since the effectiveness of certain lines in *Prufrock* depends on familiarity with Marvell's *Coy Mistress,* Marvell's poem should be considered part of Eliot's, or does this not follow because whereas we are expected to be familiar with Marvell's poem, familiarity with the contents of Eliot's notes is not expected of us? Then is this what the distinction between external and internal evidence comes to; the difference between what we can and can't be expected to know?, and how is it decided what we can be expected to know? Leavis has said of Quentin Anderson's book on Henry James, "thanks to the light shed by Mr Anderson, we can see in the peculiar impressiveness of Mrs Lowder of the *Wings of the Dove* a triumph of morality art." Is Mr Anderson's book also to be considered part of James' *Wings of the Dove* then?

No amount of tinkering can save Wimsatt and Beardsley's distinction between internal and external evidence. It isn't just that it's made in the wrong place, but that it is misconceived from the start. A reader's response to a work will vary with what he *knows;* one of the things which he knows and with which his responses will vary is what the author had in mind, or what he intended. The distinction between what different people know of an author before reading his work or what the same person knows on successive occasions can't be a logical one. When is a remark a critical remark about the poem and when a biographical one about the author? The difficulty in obeying the injunction to ignore the biographical facts and cultivate the critical ones is that you can't know which is which until after you have read the work in the light of them.

The assumption which stultifies their exposition is the conception of critical argument as the production and evaluation of evidence. They say that there are two kinds of evidence: that provided by poetic exegesis and that provided by biographical enquiry. But the examples they give of poetic exegesis seem not to be evidence but conclusions or judgments. For example, that the lines from *Prufrock* take half their sadness and irony from lines in a poem of Marvell's, or that the mermaids in *Prufrock* derive no benefit from a reminiscence of the mermaids in Donne. We could construe these statements as evidence, only by taking them as biographical statements about Wimsatt and Beardsley, but so taken they would stand in the same relation to critical judgment as biographical statements about Eliot. If a critical remark fails to confirm or consolidate or transform a reader's interpretation of a work it will then become for him just evidence of something or other, perhaps the critic's obtuseness. Biographical remarks are no more prone to this fate than any others.

3

In the sixth stanza of Yeats' *Among School Children* there occur the lines:

> Plato thought nature but a spume that plays
> Upon a ghostly paradigm of things;
> Solider Aristotle played the taws
> Upon the bottom of a king of kings.

Many editions give the first word of the third line "solider" as "soldier." This is due to a compositor's error, a transposition of two letters which went unnoticed because by a fluke instead of producing gibberish, it produced the English word "soldier."

The American critic Delmore Schwartz was thus led to advance his well-known interpretation to the effect that the expression "soldier Aristotle" alludes to a legend that Aristotle accompanied Alexander on his military expedition to India. Since there is obviously a contrast intended between the unworldliness of Plato and the down-to-earthness of Aristotle, Schwartz' military interpretation accords well with the rest of the poem. But in spite of this, now that we know of the error wouldn't we insist on the restoration of the lines as Yeats wrote them and regard the view that there is a military allusion in the lines as a mistake? It might be objected that this is not to the point because the case here is one of a discrepancy between what the author *wrote* and what we made of it and not between what he *meant* and what we made of it.

But can this distinction be upheld? Can't we imagine cases where the words were homophones? In such a case the only distinction between what an author wrote and a mistaken reading would be what he meant. In fact, we needn't imagine such a case. Hopkins' note on his poem *Henry Purcell* provides us with one: "One thing disquiets me: I *meant* 'fair fall' to mean 'fair (fortune be) fall': it has since struck me that perhaps 'fair' is an adjective proper and in the predicate and can only be used in cases like 'fair fall the day,' that is 'may the day fall, turn out fair.' My lines will yield a sense that way indeed, but I never meant it so." Is the possible meaning mentioned but rejected by Hopkins any more tenable than "soldier Aristotle"?

There is thus no doubt that there are cases in which knowledge of an author's avowed intention in respect of his work exercises a coercive influence on our apprehension of it. The question now arises: When doesn't it? My answer is, "When the issue is of a complexity comparable to that which would cause us to discount his avowed intention in respect of something not a work of literature." To put it another way, we tend to think that there are cases where we over-ride the author's intention and persist in an interpretation which he has rejected but where what we are really doing could less misleadingly be described as favouring one criterion of intention as against another. If we establish the existence of a discrepancy between the interpretation we give to a work of art, and that of the author, we haven't shown that the work has a meaning independent of what the author intends because what the author intends will now be the interpretation given to the work by us and his own statement as to its meaning an aberration. The notion of the author's intention is logically tied to the interpretation we give to his work. It's not just that our language works this way; but that our minds do. Confronted with a choice between saying that an effect so complex could have come about by accident and that the author was mistaken we would opt for the latter. The work will be considered more conclusive evidence of his intention than his own statements. The colour flows back.

Edmund Wilson's dealings with Henry James' *The Turn of the Screw* bring this out clearly. *The Turn of the Screw* was generally considered a superior ghost story until Wilson popularised the view that the ghosts were figments of the narrator's imagination and the work a study in thwarted Anglo-Saxon spinsterdom. He thought he had discovered that the text was skilfully ambiguous so as never unequivocally to imply the ghosts' objective existence. He was able to interpret some passages in James' preface to the book to similar effect. The publication of James' notebooks some years later, however, made it clear that James' conscious intention was to produce a ghost story. At the same time Wilson came to admit that the text itself was not completely reconcilable with his thesis that the ghosts were hallucinatory. Nevertheless, Wilson continued to insist that it was not a straightforward ghost story, but a study in the neurotic effects of repressed sexuality. His arguments for this provide an excellent example of what I have called the colour flowing back. Instead of simply enjoying a gratuitous effect for its own sake, Wilson convinces himself, on the basis of certain biographical facts about James, that at the time the book was written, his faith in himself had been shaken and that "in *The Turn of the Screw,* not merely is the governess self-deceived, but that James is self-deceived about her. The doubt that some readers feel as to the soundness of the governess' story are the reflection of doubts communicated unconsciously by James himself."

The real interest of this kind of example is that it brings out quite clearly what otherwise is not so apparent; that there is an implicit biographical reference in our response to literature. It is, if you like, part of our concept of literature. It is only when it is missing that we notice that it was always there.

I want now to deal with some notorious ostensible counterexamples. This is the fifth stanza of Yeats' *Among School Children:*

> What young mother a shape upon her lap
> Honey of generation had betrayed,
> And that must sleep, shriek, struggle to escape
> As recollection or the drug decide,
> Would think her son, did she but see that shape
> With sixty or more winters on its head,
> Compensation for the pang of his birth,
> Or the uncertainty of his setting forth?

There is an accompanying note to this poem which indicates that the phrase "honey of generation" is taken from an essay of Porphyry's and that Yeats has arbitrarily used it to refer to "the drug that destroys the recollection of pre-natal freedom." It is then, the shape upon the mother's lap, the child, which has been betrayed by being born. John Wain has put forward a reading according to which it is the mother who has been betrayed, and "honey of generation" is an allusion to the sexual pleasure which accompanies conception, and the desire for which has betrayed her. Doesn't this example show the irrelevance of intention? Not necessarily. It could be interpreted as a case where we take the poem as better evidence of what the poet intended than his own explicit remarks on the subject. To persist in an interpretation in spite of an author's explicit disavowal of it is not necessarily to show an indifference to the author's intention. For we may feel that he was mistaken as to what his intention was. A case which comes to mind is Goldsmith's withdrawal of the gloss he offered on the word "slow" in the first line of his poem, *The Traveller,* "Remote, unfriended, melancholy, *slow.*" Goldsmith said it meant "tardiness of locomotion" until contradicted by Johnson. "No sir. You do not mean tardiness of locomotion. You mean that sluggishness of mind that comes upon a man in solitude."

Though it might be true, as Wimsatt and Beardsley say, that critical enquiries are not settled like bets, neither need questions of intention be. I can't resort here to the argument I used in the case of Donne's *Valediction* and ask you to imagine what your attitude to Wain's interpretation would be if you were convinced that Yeats was ignorant of the fact on which it is based, since this fact, that sexual pleasure is an incentive to procreation, is not such as can be overlooked. Nevertheless, I want to maintain that we don't, if we accept Wain's interpretation, think it an accident that it should be possible to read the text as he does, but we feel that the ambiguity which makes it possible was the result of a connection in Yeats' mind between the expression "honey of generation" and sexual pleasure. (In fact this can be demonstrated.)

In order to convince you that an implicit biographical inference is at work even in Wain's interpretation, I want you to imagine the case altered in some important respects. Imagine that the reading according to which it is the mother who is betrayed, was also that of Yeats, and that there was no footnote referring to Porphyry's essay, of which Yeats was completely ignorant, but that a reader familiar with it and sharing its views on pre-natal existence, insisted on taking the expression "honey of generation" as an allusion to the drug which destroys the recollection of pre-natal freedom and, therefore, to the infant, and not the mother, as betrayed. Wouldn't our attitude to this interpretation be quite different from our attitude to Wain's? Wouldn't we feel it perverse? And since it can't be the text which makes it perverse but only the facts about Yeats as we have imagined them, doesn't our implicit biographical or intentionalistic approach to literature emerge quite clearly here?

Of course, there are cases where the pleasure we take in literature doesn't depend on this implicit biographical reference. Literature, as Wittgenstein probably said, is a motley. Nursery rhymes come to mind as the most notable example. But in general we do make such a reference. Eliot's attitude towards a line of Cyril Tourneur's illustrates this reluctance to take pleasure in what is accidental and unintended. The line is: "The poor benefit of a bewildering minute," which is given as "The poor benefit of a bewitching minute" in the texts both of Churton Collins and of Nicoll who mention no alternative reading. Eliot comments: "*it is a pity* if they be right for 'bewildering' is much the richer word here." It has been argued that if the folio text of *Henry V* was right and Theobald's lovely guess wrong so that Shakespeare made the dying Falstaff allude to a painting rather than babble of green fields most of us would persist in reading the traditional and incorrect version. We probably would but it would worry us; and if "a babbled of green fields" wasn't even Theobald's guess but a transcriber's or printer's unthinking error, it would worry us even more. The suspicion that a poetic effect is an accident is fatal to the enjoyment which literature characteristically offers. If the faces on Mount Rushmore were the effect of the action of wind and rain, our relation to them would be very different.

4

In the course of their criticism of the interpretation of Donne's poem which saw in it an allusion to the revolution of the earth round the sun Wimsatt and Beardsley remark, "But the text itself remains to be dealt with . . ."!

Where understanding fails, says Goethe, there immediately comes a word to take its place. In this case the word is "text." Let us appeal to the text. But what is the text? These critics talk of the text of a poem as if it had an outline as neat and definite as the page on which it is printed. If you remind yourself of how questions about what is "in the text" are settled you will see that they involve a great deal which is not "in the text." Though there are many occasions on which we can make the distinction in an immediately intelligible and non-tendentious way, where an interpretative issue has already arisen, the use of a distinction between internal, licit considerations, and external, illicit ones is just a form of question-begging.

What are we to say of attempts to support an interpretation by citing other works of the author? For example, Leavis on Conrad's *Heart of Darkness:* "If any reader of that tale felt that the irony permitted a doubt regarding Conrad's attitude towards the Intended, the presentment of Rita (in *The Arrow of Gold*) should settle it." Isn't this illicit? Isn't the common authorship of several works a biographical fact?

What of the use of previous drafts of a work for critical purposes? Leavis in commenting on Hopkins' *Spelt from Sybil's Leaves* is able to enforce his point that "Hopkins' positives waver and change places and he is left in terrible doubt" by showing that in a previous draft of the poem the word-order in the phrase "black, white; right, wrong" was conventionally symmetrical "black, white; wrong, right." The only doubt which might arise in connexion with Leavis' point is whether the word-order may have been altered to avoid a rhyme, but this is equally intentionalistic.

Marius Bewley supports his interpretation of James' *The Turn of the Screw* by pointing out that when James collected his stories for the definitive edition he put it in the same volume as one called *The Liar*.

Even if the anti-intentionalist thesis were qualified to accommodate all these there would still be a fundamental objection to it.

You must all have had the experience while reading of having the words suddenly undergo a radical transformation as you realised you had missed the end of a quotation, say, and mistaken the speaker. The more familiar the speakers the greater the transformation when you realised your mistake. Doesn't this illustrate the importance of implicit biographical assumptions in interpreting what we read? Here's an illustration: In Rudyard Kipling's *Loot* occur the lines:

> An' if you treat a nigger to a dose of cleanin'-rod
> 'E's like to show you everything he owns.

Hugh Kingsmill has quoted these lines as an example of Kipling's brutality and even Kipling's biographer, Edward Shanks, is embarrassed by them. Edmund Wilson, on the other hand, in his well-known essay on Kipling, says this about them: "Kipling was interested in the soldier for his own sake, and made some effort to present his life as it seemed to the soldier himself. The poem called *Loot,* for example, which appears to celebrate a reprehensible practice is in reality perfectly legitimate because it simply describes one of the features of the soldier's experience in India. There is no moral one way or the other." T. S. Eliot takes a similar line in his introduction to his selection of Kipling's verse.

How is this issue to be decided? By an appeal to the text? Isn't it rather our sense of Kipling which will determine the side we come down on? A sense built up not only from the other tales but from his autobiography and other sources as well? Don't these throw a "field of force" round the work? If it had been written by someone else wouldn't this make a difference to our apprehension of it? Isn't this like the case described by Wittgenstein in the *Philosophical Investigations*? "I see a picture which represents a smiling face. What do I do if I take the smile now as a kind one, now as a malicious one? Don't I often imagine it with a spatial and temporal context which is one either of kindness or of malice? Thus I might supply the picture with the fancy that the smiler was smiling down at a child at play, or again on the suffering of an enemy."

The difference of opinion between F. R. Leavis and Marius Bewley over James' *What Maisie Knew* is an excellent illustration of an interpretation depending on "the fiction I surround it with." Unfortunately it is too long to quote, but the gist of it is that Bewley finds the atmosphere of the book one of horror and its theme the meaning and significance of evil, whereas Leavis can detect no horror and sees it as an extraordinarily high-spirited comedy reminiscent of the early part of *David Copperfield*. Bewley in attempting to locate the source of their difference says that it has its "origin in areas not readily open to literary-critical persuasion" and "that the way one senses the presence of evil and horror in the novel may be due to one's conception of them outside the novel."

There is one aspect of our response to a work of literature to which biographical data seem to have particular relevance and that is our conviction as to an author's sincerity. It is certain that there are cases where biographical considerations are genuinely relevant and equally certain that there are cases where they are intrusions which we feel we ought not to allow to condition our response. But it is difficult to know where the line should be drawn. I suppose that we would all consider Beethoven's inability to get on with Scott's *Kenilworth* because "This man writes for money" as eccentric, though the decline in Trollope's reputation which followed his revelation as to his methods of composition and his business-like attitude towards his writing, show it is not rare. Perhaps these responses should be considered more as moral gestures, like refusing to hear Gieseking perform, rather than as aesthetic responses.

A good example of a response which is genuinely critical but which we would all consider misplaced is Johnson's criticism of Abraham Cowley's *The Mistress*:

> But the basis of all excellence is truth: he that professes love ought to feel its power. Petrarch was a real lover and Laura doubtless deserved his tenderness. Of Cowley we are told by Barnes, who had means enough of information, that whatever he may talk of his own inflammability, and the variety of characters by which his heart was divided, he in reality was in love but once, and then never had resolution to tell his passion!
>
> This consideration cannot but abate in some measure the reader's esteem for the work. . . .

Another, perhaps slightly less conclusive example is provided by Johnson's remarks on Cowley's poem on the death of Hervey . . .

> but when he wishes to make us weep he forgets to weep himself, and diverts his sorrow by imagining how his crown of bays, if he had it would *crackle* in the *fire*. It is the odd fate of this thought to be the

worse for being true. The bay leaf crackles remarkably as it burns, as therefore this property was not assigned to it by chance, the mind must be thought sufficiently at ease that could attend to such minuteness of physiology.

It might be argued that Johnson has indicated a source of dissatisfaction *in* the poem, the bay leaves image. But it is what this enabled him to infer about something *outside* the poem concerning Cowley which abated his esteem. If he could have been convinced that Cowley was ignorant of the propensity of bay leaves to crackle remarkably and the felicity of his image therefore fortuitous, Johnson would presumably have liked the poem better. But it would be a mistake to think Johnson simply absurd here. Suppose that the poem in question were Bishop King's *Exequy* and the biographical fact that he was never married and therefore never bereaved. Some of us would decide it didn't matter, some that it did and some would oscillate. This is an example of the more general dilemma which arises when an empirical concomitance on which we habitually depend and so regular that it has influenced the build of our concepts, disintegrates. Van Meegeren's *Disciples at Emmaus,* the poems of Ern Malley, Macpherson's *Ossian,* Chatterton's *Rowley,* all point the same moral.

   D. W. Harding raised a related issue in a vivid form some years ago. He wrote:

> We think of it (a work of art) as being a human product, as implicitly sanctioning and developing interests and ideals and attitudes of our own. That being so it does become disconcerting to find that for the author it satisfied certain impulses which we ourselves are glad not to possess, or which if we do possess we think better left unsatisfied. The same thing goes on in social intercourse of a simpler kind than literature. We enjoy the *bon mot* with which our friend disposes of a charlatan, but if we know that he is incidentally working off irrelevant spite against either the charlatan or the world in general the flavour of the remark is spoilt. The *bon mot* is as good as ever regarded as something impersonal, but as a human product it no longer gives us pure satisfaction — an element of distaste or regret comes in and makes our state of mind more complex. Many people find this more complex attitude extremely difficult to maintain . . . especially because in most actual cases the neurotic flaw can be detected in the work itself.

But once in possession of biographical data it is difficult to be sure what is "in the work itself." Leavis has suggested it is a pity much is known of Pope's life since the expression of spite, envy, venom and malice so often found in his work is a consequence of the distorting effect of this knowledge.

   What I have called "putting a field of force round a work," surrounding it with a web of associations, may be effective even when it doesn't deserve to be. But this kind of suggestibility is a risk all critical remarks run and not merely biographical ones. Would anyone have found the last few lines of Bishop King's *Exequy* productive of an effect of terror if Eliot had not said so? And would Eliot himself if he had not first come across them in Poe's *The Assignation*? It is the fact that we can speak of criticism which is effective but mistaken which makes the analogy with argument so tempting for there too we speak of conclusions seeming to follow but not following; so it seems that we can have specious criticism in the same sense in which we have specious argument. But this is an illusion. You don't show that a response to a work of literature is inadequate or inappropriate in the way that you show that the conclusion of an argument has been wrongly drawn.

Wittgenstein has some remarks in Part Two of the *Investigations,* which shed light on the nature of the intractability which characterises so much critical argument and make its prevalence less surprising. His remarks though concerned with the question of the genuineness of an expression of feeling have a more general application. He contrasts our judgments about sincerity with those about colour. "I am sure, *sure* that he is pretending: but some third person is not. Can I always convince him? And if not, is there some error in his reasoning or observations?" Though there are those whose judgment is better in such matters and rules for determining this, these do not form a system and only experienced people can apply them. There are consequences which distinguish correct from incorrect judgment, but these are of a diffuse kind and like the rules incapable of general formulation . . . "only in scattered cases can one arrive at a correct and fruitful judgment." It is not surprising, then, that "the game often ends with one person relishing what another does not."

CONCLUSION

What I have been saying is this: a conviction that a poet stands in a certain relation to his words conditions our response to them. That this should be so seems to me part of the "physiognomy" of literature (as Wittgenstein might have put it). We are not ordinarily aware of this as these convictions tend to be held in solution in "the work itself." It is only in exceptional circumstance that we crystallise them out as explicit beliefs and become aware of the role they play. Why should anyone wish to deny this? Because it is then only a step to the production of phantasy-theses like Wimsatt's and Beardsley's, "What is said about a poem is subject to the same scrutiny as any statement in linguistics or in the general science of psychology."

This in its turn has its source in the determination to tidy up the activity of reading and to reduce what it involves to a neat, logically homogenous set of considerations such as guarantee a readily communicable rationale. The idea of a work of literature as "a linguistic fact" or an "integrated symbol" is comparable to the notions of "a concept" in philosophy or "behaviour" in psychology in being the manifestation of an irresistible demand for discrete, coherent and enduring objects of investigation. But, "Literature is a motley."

JEAN STAROBINSKI

Truth in Masquerade

When a man puts on a mask or takes on a pseudonym, we feel challenged. That man eludes us. We, in turn, want to *know*, we decide to unmask him. From whom is he trying to conceal himself? What Power does he fear? What manner of Glance shames him? Once again we ask: what kind of face had he that he felt the need to dissemble it? And other questions follow immediately from the preceding ones: What does this new face in which he masquerades mean, what significance does he give to his masked demeanor, what is he now trying to simulate having dissimulated that which wanted to disappear?

Doubtless political precautions play some part in Stendhal's pseudonymity. For one thing, Fouché or the Terreur Blanche explain and justify César Bombet.[1] Customs officials, concierges (and jealous husbands) would have had good reason to open his letters or decipher the cryptic writing of his diary. There is indeed matter for concern. For this somewhat over-loquacious libertarian the danger is quite real, as proved by the registers of the Austrian police and the papal chancellery. But danger is only a pretext, almost an excuse. Stendhal's concern is disproportionate to the actual menace. Even far from any danger Stendhal still plays at wearing masks. And not only those masks that abet his disap-

SOURCE: "Truth in Masquerade" is translated by B. A. B. Archer from "Stendhal pseudonyme," *L'Oeil vivant* (Paris: Librairie Gallimard, 1961), in *Stendhal: A Collection of Critical Essays,* edited by Victor Brombert, © 1962. Reprinted by permission of Prentice-Hall, Inc., Englewood Cliffs, New Jersey and Editions Gallimard.

pearance and favor incognito. Stendhal's pseudonymity is not an escape into anonymity. It is an art of appearing, it is a deliberate altering of human relations. For Stendhal attempts to flee the system of nominal values only to dominate it and better to manipulate it.

One discerns here an act of protest. To take a pseudonym is, first of all, either out of shame or resentment, a repudiation of the name transmitted by one's father. A name, like the effigy whose heart (or "heart region") is pierced, contains in substance the life one wishes to annihilate. If a name is truly an identity, if through it the essence of a human being can be reached and brutalized, the refusal of a patronym is a substitute for patricide. It is the least cruel form of murder in effigy. Humiliated by his father, Stendhal avenged himself by calling him (notably in his letters to his sister Pauline) "the bastard." The insult is clearly aimed at the legitimacy of the name. In his filial hatred, Stendhal concocts the most extraordinary hypotheses for disclaiming any relationship with the Beyle family. One can see the development of a veritable system of filial interpretation: he feels himself far too unlike Chérubin Beyle to be his legitimate son; he is probably the secret heir to a more impressive lineage. The "myth of birth" (which plays its part in the *Chartreuse*) is a deep-rooted reverie of the young Henri Beyle. It is Stendhal himself who would be the bastard, but the defamatory accusation is hurled at the father.

Our name awaits us. It was there before we knew it, like our body. The common illusion consists in believing that our destiny and our reality are inscribed in it. Thus one confers upon a name the dignity of an essence. Stendhal in some ways plays along with this illusion. If he rejects the patronym Beyle, it is because he sees in it a predestination from which he intends to escape. That predestination binds him to France, to Grenoble, to the middle class, to the paternal universe of parsimony and sordid calculation. And because he envisages the risk of being tied to his name, he tries to offer himself greater possibilities by taking a new name. He would not have found pseudonymity necessary had he felt free in spite of his name, had he known how to accept his bourgeois and Grenoblois identity as a purely official convention that in no way prevented him from seeking all possible destinies.

In assuming a new name, he not only grants himself a new face, but a new destiny, a new social rank, new nationalities. (He is the last of the Cosmopolites of the eighteenth century, but also the first of the "good Europeans" of the nineteenth.) Some of the pseudonyms are German: Stendhal, for example, is the name of a Prussian town. On the other hand, since happiness can flourish only in Italy, the imagination of young Henri Beyle constructs a whole Italian genealogy for the maternal side of the family. His mother, of whom he was enamored, cannot possibly belong in Grenoble. His image of her is thus repatriated in the warm and voluptuous countryside of Lombardy. And so, with each trip outside of France, Stendhal has the impression of rejoining his true world; he enjoys living outside his country just as he enjoys living outside his name. His passion for traveling, his pleasure in flight coincide perfectly with his pseudonymity.

It is useless to enumerate Stendhal's pseudonyms; there are more than a hundred. Alongside this list one might draw up another of the pseudonyms Stendhal bestowed upon his friends, some of which — for the game is contagious — they adopted for their own use. This is the tangible sign of the "understanding" that sets them apart from the rest of the world. They know henceforth that they belong to an exclusive group. The *Happy Few* are a small society who cultivate the rational knowledge of the human heart. But these rationalists like to surround themselves with the prestige of concealment, even to the point of assuming in jest certain esoteric manners. Secretiveness, or the simulacrum of secretiveness, becomes part of their system, and their complicity is confirmed by pseudonymity. In every clandestine society, initiates receive a new name; Stendhal and his friends all but adopted an initiatory language.

Stendhal's pseudonyms are amazing in their diversity. Some of them are episodic and disappear immediately upon use. Others persist throughout Stendhal's lifetime: along with the stable pseudonyms are unstable ones. Some of the pseudonyms are intended to charm: Dominique, Salviati, are names of love, components of a more elegant and more amorous nature. The entire effect of these seductive identities resides in the tenderness of the name which magically invokes a trusting intimacy. In other cases, for greater eminence, he takes some princely name. But there are also pseudonyms for sheer amusement; names that are grotesquely middle-class to the point even of caricature — Cotonnet, Bombet, Chamier, Baron de Cutendre, William Crocodile. Some of these pseudonyms are for exhibition — funny, glorious, tender. Others are pseudonyms of escape, to render him invisible to or protect him from bothersome individuals.

Such prodigality in the use of pseudonyms makes one wonder what is a name. In obliging us to pose such a question, the masked egotist walks off with the first victory; he manipulates us and leaves us uncertain. We discover, in fact, that a man is never completely within his name, or completely behind his name, just as he is never completely within his face, or back of it. We can not persevere very long in either the realistic illusion or the nominative illusion. A name alternately appears as something full and something empty, in some cases fraught with great density of existence, in others reduced to a superficial and meaningless verbal convention. An entire life is concentrated in it as it is reduced to a symbol. But this symbol is only a symbol; we can learn nothing from it. We no longer know before whom we stand. This is what the egotist anticipated. "I am not where you expected to find me."

Pseudonymity is thus not only a rupture with parental and social origins, it is a rupture with others. Our identity, which binds us to our name, delivers us at the same time as hostages to other consciences. It offers us up defenseless to the judgment of others. The egotist, however, is out to retrieve himself. He destroys the name that makes him vulnerable in that part of himself which reflects the gaze of others. In so loosing the bond that delivers him, unarmed, to outsiders, he hopes to escape all injury to his pride.

If it is true that our name contains the uniqueness of our life while at the same time transmitting its symbolic description to other consciences, then the egotist's striving will be to preserve this uniqueness while simultaneously destroying or undermining the reciprocity of consciences. He certainly cannot prevent the world from using his name, but he can arrange for his name to cease designating him. He dreams somewhat ingeniously of being in the situation of seeing without being seen (a desire clearly expressed in certain pages of Stendhal's intimate writings).

A name is situated symbolically at the confluence of existence "for oneself" and existence "for others." It is an intimate truth and a public thing. In accepting my name I accept that there be a common denominator between my inner being and my social being. It is at this level that the pseudonym proposes to effect a radical disjunction. It purports to separate two worlds at the very point at which, through the intermediary of language, their union was made possible. Through this act, the egotist revolts against his membership in society. He refuses to be offered up to others, and at the same time he is given to himself. For him, the freedom to act is conceivable only under insubordination. That is why he has recourse to the pseudonym which unties his hands. The first requirement of egotistical individualism is the dissociation of personal existence from its manifestation to the world. *Noli me tangere* could be his motto. But there he reveals his basic weakness. What is he afraid of? In permitting too clear an identity to appear he is afraid of being too clearly understood, of being wide open, which means for him being annulled, ceasing to mean anything in the eyes of others. If he had enough confidence in himself, he would not seek in this way to establish his value on the mystery of his conduct. The egotist, who suffers from being misunderstood, suffers even more from being understood. Through fear of his person being reached by others, he will devote himself systematically to the separation of his person and his personation.

In the equation $I = I$, the name (in the eyes of others) acts as the equal sign. Confined to our name, our identity becomes alienated; it comes to us through and from others. But the egotist revolts against this identity that is imposed from the outside. Why should he not be the sole master of this oneness that makes him identical with himself? In giving himself a pseudonym he affirms his basic autonomy. Is he, however, progressing validly toward the possession of himself? He gives himself a verbal identity as exterior and contingent as that attributed to him by others, the only difference being that in place of others he confers it upon himself. A pseudonym eliminates perjury and allows the invocation of a plurality of I's as a splendid alibi.

Noblesse oblige, it is said. That which obliges is the name, the title. The egotist is irritated above all when feeling that his name, in constituting an obligation toward himself, established a necessary relationship with others. Only he is responsible whom one calls by his name and whom one summons to answer. But if my name no longer designates me, I am no longer obliged to respond, unless it be to him who still possesses the right and power to name me. "To me alone," says the rebel. Nothing prevents him from playing out the game still further by refusing to hold himself responsible to himself. From that point on he no longer carries his name, he is carried away by an imaginary name. Thus he can indulge in a feeling of dizzying propulsion in which the energy of movement seems to come entirely from the mask, rather than from the "real" being who dissembles behind the mask. The mask and the pseudonym generate a perfect dynamics of irresponsibility.

The pseudonymity of Stendhal has this quality of movement and, among other ends, aims at effecting a change on the social ladder. From Henri Beyle to Baron Frédéric de Stendhal is quite an advancement. The essence of Stendhal's pleasure does not lie in the fake nobility that he assumes, but in the movement itself. For movement is the law of pseudonymous existence, it is the *sine qua non* of its success. As a matter of fact, Stendhal just as willingly assumes ridiculous names which in no way enhance him. What is important is never to tarry in the invention, is to renew constantly the surprise that nonplusses others. The mask must be a procession of masks, and pseudonymity a systematic "polynymity." Otherwise the egotist is recaptured by others, the misunderstanding he sought to flee will only be aggravated and to his disadvantage. He must always be a few lengths ahead of the others. He must even dissemble whatever is systematic about his secret behavior. For to allow the perception of a system is to render oneself explicable and thus lose any benefit from the secret. A ridiculous undertaking indeed if he gives the impression of following a *system* of escape! He who is too ostensibly in search of mystery risks spoiling all his effects and never becoming an enigma to others. His imposture defines him once and for all. A certain manner of candid living, given to confession and perpetual avowals, is sometimes more effective than the use of a mask. Stendhal knew this very well. His confidences, with their qualifications and infinite contradictions, make him more mysterious than his strategy of impersonation.

Stendhal's indefatigable and elusive pseudonymity is totally different from the simpler pseudonymity of those who once and for all assume an advantageous name that will more readily consecrate their glory. Most of the writers and artists who take an unchanging and definitive pseudonym do not seek to disconcert the consciousness of others, but rather to install themselves in it with greater prestige. The name they choose, and which confers upon them a more impressive life, character, and destiny, is only intended to attract celebrity. Their purpose is merely to place on their side all the phonetic possibilities that seem indispensable to success. This temptation exists in Stendhal but counts for very little. Certainly he is enamored of glory; he wants to make a name for himself. But he also wants that name to remain on the outside and grant him the freedom to inhabit a thousand other names.

In the case of Stendhal, the theme of confinement must be underlined. A name, a body, a social status, all are prisons. But their doors are not so well locked that the dream of escape is impossible. Of course, one takes leave of one's name more easily than of one's body, and a pseudonym is a substitute for the desired metamorphosis. (This impatience with having to tolerate one's body can be found in almost every writer who has had recourse to a pseudonym. However different, Voltaire and Kierkegaard share a certain anxious attention to their bodies and their ailments. In this sense pseudonymity represents a manifestation of hypochondria.)

In order to express this imprisonment, the metaphor of the cell naturally appears. One sees chains, thick walls, high well-guarded towers. These images stubbornly recur in Stendhal's works. The heroes who are imprisoned and who escape — Julien at the seminary, Fabrice in the Farnese tower, Hélène Campireale in the convent, Lamiel and the Hautemares — seem each time to recreate an archetypal situation. The theme of *amour-passion* is curiously involved. Imprisonment corresponds to the birth of the highest form of love, which derives its power from its impossibility. Desire, then, implies distance and insurmountable separation. Octave, confined within the fatality of his impotence, loves Armance all the more ardently in that he can not abolish the impediment that keeps him from her. Octave, however, is loved in return, just as all the imprisoned heroes are loved in return in spite of the locks, or perhaps because of them. Extreme unhappiness thus meets extreme happiness. It is in this that one clearly sees the power of compensation that pervades Stendhal's fiction. If society avenges itself on the exceptional individual by imprisoning him, from his very high tower he can avenge himself on society by transforming his solitude into a contemptuous and hopeless happiness. The motif of high places, stressed by Proust as a fundamental theme in Stendhal, merges with the theme of confinement. These glorious prisoners need but one long look to dominate the world. In these heroes, who are visited by love in prison, one must recognize (among other things) the figurative transposition of Stendhal's secret desire — to be loved in spite of his ugliness, in spite of the prison that his body and age are for him; to love and be loved from afar through the power of a glance. Destruction does not threaten this love, either because it can never be consummated in possession and marriage and is consequently never exposed to destruction, or because even if consummated it always remains furtive and clandestine, thus lightening in an extraordinary way the importance of the body.

We have then to do with a man unhappy with what he is and discontent with his body ("Why am I myself?"), and who is torn between two conflicting desires: to affirm himself by an act of power which will impose on others his absolute singularity, or to metamorphose ceaselessly, to become other than himself, to split in two so as to become both an accomplished actor and an invisible spectator through some form of efficacious travesty. These two tendencies, which Stendhal's behavior manages to keep from becoming totally contradictory, are expressed in two affirmations that must be juxtaposed without any circumspection: "The only thing of value in this world is the self." However, in *Souvenirs d'égotisme,* one finds: "Will I be believed? I would wear a mask with pleasure, I would change my name with delight. The thousand and one nights I adore fill more than a quarter of my brain. Often I think of Angelica's ring. My supreme pleasure would be to change into a tall blond German and wander about Paris." [2] The desire to be oneself; the pleasure in conjuring up impossible sorceries to cease being oneself — this is the premise we must examine.

Scattered through the *Journal* and other autobiographical writings of Stendhal are a thousand references to the use of a mask and to the pleasure of "the feeling of living in many versions." "Look at life as though it were a masked ball" [3] is the advice Stendhal gives himself in his diary of 1814. The essential thing about this profession of faith is not the accusation directed against the comedy of society nor the excuse it provides for any disguise, but rather the intense complicity between pleasure and travesty. The significance of Stendhal's hypocrisy, even more than the pragmatic success of the scheme, is its elegance of means, the aesthetic achievement of "gamesmanship." Hypocrisy, in the masked ball, becomes the rule of the game. The struggle for power or fortune becomes part of the festivity, and through an ultimate return to gratuitousness, the hypocrite has no further ambition than the perfection of his own game. He need only indulge in the pleasure of being so completely outside himself.

In an almost pristine form, there exists in Stendhal's writings the admission of a profound relationship between the "principle of pleasure" and the desire for metamorphosis. It can be found in a curious piece that he wrote at the end of his life entitled *Les Privilèges du 10 avril 1840*. In it, he formulates his permanent reveries — at an age at which most people are concerned with their last will and testament — under the format of a contract with God. The text begins with the line "God has given me the following licence." Let us look at one of the articles.

> Article 3. — The *mentula*, like an index finger for rigidity and flexibility, this at will. Size, two inches longer than original, same thickness. But pleasure through the *mentula* only twice a week. Twenty times a year, the licencee may become whatever individual he wishes, provided that individual exists. One hundred times a year, he shall know for 24 hours the language of his choice.[4]

The desire for erotic power, the desire for metamorphosis, and the desire for command of a new language are strangely juxtaposed. According to good logic, such utterly different wishes should not appear side by side. But good logic is here mistaken and it is the imagination that is right. It freely improvises and, under diverse aspects, translates a unique affective inspiration. The desire for erotic power and the dream of metamorphosis, which appear simultaneously, express a twofold aspect of a single wish for power. What is involved in each case is the submission of sexual life and the body to conscious will. This body that he must accept as a contingent fact, Stendhal dreams of retrieving from contingency and of offering to himself freely according to the caprice of a totally voluntary act. As to the sexual mechanism, so wholly dependent on the involuntary system, so independent from the exercise of will, it too will be able to respond to some deliberate command. One sees in this the imperialism of will taking as object not the exterior universe or the cosmos, but the body itself, which becomes an obedient tool. In the text cited above, we discern two meanings in the desire to have control over his body in order to possess *another* body. For sexual possession and metamorphosis are, in fact, two ways of "entering into the body of another." Desire here provides a choice between two kinds of attainment. It imagines in turn the infallible triumph of an extroverted sexuality, and the narcissistic satisfaction of inhabiting a body that remains his own while becoming another.

In this refusal of the body in its reality and limitations, there is nothing to bespeak disincarnation. Stendhal exalts physical existence by imagining it liberated from any servitude. Having a body becomes wonderful as soon as one receives it from oneself. This chimera is very similar to the mythical dream of a portion of immortality. While inhabiting an opaque body over which we have no mastery we live in a manner of dubious cohabitation with death. For it is precisely through that element in our body which eludes our will that death reaches us. To become lord and master of our body would mean to avert the threat. All at once, every enslavement of the human condition disappears; one passes into the ranks of the gods.

Les Privilèges is a text dating from Stendhal's later years, and manifests a Faustian desire for rejuvenation within the completely pagan perspective of new beginnings that defy death. Metamorphosis, for Stendhal, is an opening onto the future. It is an acceleration of existence, but one that turns its back on death. (Notice that for Kafka metamorphosis is the exact opposite. It is the aggravation of the physical condition, the slowing down of existence. Energy stops and becomes paralyzed; the future is cut off and shrinks concentrically until it is reabsorbed in the unique manifestation of destruction.)

One finds in ancient mythology two opposing forms of metamorphosis. For Zeus, it is an instrument of aggression and amorous conquest. For Proteus, it provides the means of escape and inaccessibility. For Stendhal, conquest and escape are linked and figure as complementary attitudes. The desire to appear and disappear are to him both part of the same "complex." They are two ways of being significant in the eyes of others, and of not being annihilated by the gaze of others. Ashamed of his ugliness, Stendhal knows that he can not be loved and desired as he is. He dreams of being seen in an image other than his real one. By shrouding himself in mystery, and trying to remain enigmatic, he invents a maze of appearances in which the glance of others will henceforth lose its way. He will be sought beyond his body in a trompe-l'œil perspective. The mask, when perfect, tempts one to imagine a world behind the mask. Pure mirage, but one toward which the victim rushes, only to deliver himself to his seducer.

Stendhal knows still other ways of diverting the gaze of others from his ugliness, for example, by forcing others to look at themselves. By posing in society as "connaisseur of the human heart," he has occasion to unsettle his interlocutors, who experience with little equanimity the piercing look that scrutinizes and interrogates them. Through a reversal that constrains others to feel gazed upon, he ceases to be the person looked at. He then expects to fascinate more easily those whom he previously disconcerted by their own mystery. He reaches them through their narcissism.

Stendhal, according to his contemporaries, was a past master at grimaces. One need only recall the appearance, in the Ancelot's salon, of Monsieur César Bombet, merchant in nightcaps. The hours he spends before his mirror — arranging his dress or his toupee, dying his hair, manicuring his nails — are real sessions of makeup. They reveal a man preparing for the outside world like an actor for his audience. If Stendhal takes infinite pains over his elegance, it is because he understands that his ugliness can only be annulled by his carriage, through which his body ceases to be a thing and becomes a symbol. And when, instead of seeking elegance, he opts for some kind of grotesque derision, it is also to make one overlook his ugliness through comedy and buffoonery. He who provokes laughter has already been accepted. One is no longer aware of his unsightly nose, but notices rather whatever amusement he can provide by means of his nose. By thus exploiting his physiognomy (as his uncle Gagnon advised him) he attracts attention, but not to his ugliness. Hidden behind the mobility of his grimaces, his ugliness becomes almost unreal and clears the way for the pleasure of pleasing.

Let us continue our perusal of those remarkable *Priviléges du 10 avril 1840*. We shall find some examples of metamorphoses imagined by Stendhal, and will be surprised to discover that, after having wished for exquisite worldly elegance, he manifests the desire to be transformed into an animal. This is to provide him with the pleasure of elementary vitality.

> Article 5. — Beautiful hair, beautiful skin, fine hands that are never rough, fragrant and delicate odor. The first of February and the first of June each year, the clothes of the licencee shall become as they were the third time they were worn.
> Article 6. — Miracles in the eyes of all who do not know him: the licencee shall have the face of General Debell, who died in Santo Domingo, without any imperfection. He shall play perfect whist, écarté, billiards, chess, but shall never win more than 100 francs. He shall shoot, ride, and fence to perfection.
> Article 7. — Four times a year, he shall turn into whatever animal he wishes; and thereafter, turn back into a man. Four times a year, he shall change into whatever man he wishes; in addition, he shall be able to dissemble his life in that of an animal, which animal shall, in the event of death or impediment on the part of the first man into whom he was changed, be able to reinstate him in the natural form of the licencee. Thus the licencee shall, four times a year, and for an unlimited period each time, inhabit two bodies at once.

This double transformation, to perfection and animal, corresponds rather well to the tendencies in Stendhal's amorous life. In effect, his experiences in love were either far above or far below his station. One finds practically no middle-class ladies among his mistresses — they are duchesses or slatterns. Love has no attraction for him unless he feels called upon to transform himself. His first passions were for actresses with whom he fell in love while reciting lines from Molière and Racine. He loved them because they led him into the world of metamorphosis and because, more than any others, they gave him the pleasure he sought — pleasure that can flourish only in an atmosphere of theatricality. He assumed, after having made their conquest, that he would love them more and longer than other women. For with them he expected to continue the exercise of metamorphosis, even to the minutest details of daily living. Such living is the only kind not threatened by boredom, which takes over as soon as the power of metamorphosis wanes. It happens that Stendhal is bored from the outset by middle-class women since he has no need to transform himself in order to seduce them. As to the lady of high society, the creature idealized "à la Correggio," what matters is that she remain constantly inaccessible. For to conquer her is to have lost the need to surpass oneself. When metamorphosis becomes useless, love is also paralyzed, frozen in the ice of boredom. Distance and obstacles are thus essential to Stendhalian lovers, not only to give value to the conquest, but above all to necessitate a transformation of the individual, which itself constitutes satisfaction. Love for a woman already won can only endure by becoming clandestine or illicit — by obligating Fabrice and Julien to repeat constantly a masked exploit.

The passage quoted above invites another comment. Stendhal dreams of inhabiting two bodies at the same time. The metamorphosis he desires is not a depersonalization, but a multiplication of the self, a veritable "superpersonalization." Not only does he wish to become another, but to become many others.

Stendhal adopts a pseudonymous existence both as a means and an end. He enjoys it for its own sake, but also in view of the effect it produces and the advantage it nets his pride. This is to say that all through his many metamorphoses Stendhal is concerned with preserving his vigilant conscience that secretly collects the spoils of his masked demeanor. Though altering his appearance he is nonetheless determined to maintain permanent clairvoyance; he ceaselessly surveys — from the vantage point of a chief of staff — all the movements of the battle, in which only the simulacrum of his thoughts is involved. One's powers of observation must never falter or misinterpret, if one is watching for the desired effect. And so an invulnerable interior is erected, since it has become pure observation of the self and of others, and cannot be reached in turn by the gaze of witnesses. Having made of his face and body an instrument of which he freely disposes, he is no longer their captive. He no longer accepts them as a fatality. The mask (and the pseudonym) thus appears as the attainment of liberty. This liberty makes use of a body from which it has finally disengaged itself and which can be maneuvered at will. Here we have a true mechanism of release, one from which this man, who was always ashamed of his body's clumsiness, knew how to profit. One need only think of the use of the mask as an accessory to the dance, whether primitive rites or modern dancing, to see that the effect of release is a permanent feature of masquerade. Irony, so cherished by Stendhal, achieves the same disengagement and the same release. But irony is nothing other than the spiritual quintessence of the mask.

Behind the game that conceals appearances, Stendhal plans to keep his lucidity intact; a lucidity that harbors his true permanence and his inalterable identity. He conserves the functions necessary for seeing himself act. A highly alert self must be ever-present in order to savor this experience of successful activity, which is one form of the pleasure. This taste for metamorphosis in Stendhal is directly allied to the taste for action and energy. Doubtless there is in the first place an impediment to spontaneous action; doubtless the recourse to metamorphosis manifests the need to utilize devious means to rejoin the world. Whatever the case, metamorphosis for Stendhal is always basically voluntary and dynamic, as proved by *Les Privilèges du 10 avril 1840*. This distinguishes Stendhal from seekers of passive metamorphoses. I doubt that Stendhal would have enjoyed the narcotics that transform existence into something fabulous at the cost of submitting to passivity. The mid-nineteenth-century taste for hashish and opium corresponds to a sensibility that differs greatly from Stendhal's voluntarism. Metamorphosis can be experienced actively or passively — to be metamorphosed, or to metamorphose oneself. Stendhal chose to metamorphose himself actively. He is in such need of others that he can not abandon himself to a daydream in which he no longer confronts his rivals and adversaries.

We know that Stendhal's worldly ambitions were meagerly fulfilled. The fall of the Empire marked the end of his social success. His chances for advancement in the reactionary world of the restoration were slim. In spite of the subtlest of tactics, Stendhal ran into insurmountable limitations and barriers. Can one really quit one's body? Mephistopheles does not appear on the scene every day to strike a bargain. The world of the imagination is then free to provide all the triumphs if reality resists too stubbornly. But that would mean stopping the game, renouncing once and for all his claim to society. Stendhal does not consent to this. One avenue remains open for conquering the world, while at the same time allowing him to conjure his metamorphoses. It is literature, a devious route that Stendhal first thought of using to achieve success. It must be noted that Stendhal banked on social success before banking on literary success. At the time he decided to write, his primary aim was to gain prestige, not to create a masterpiece. In seeking literary fame he was out to rebound into high society. As a young man Stendhal's velleities for the theatre were specifically directed toward the kind of theatrical success that promises quick celebrity. His plagiarisms were a financial speculation, at the same time providing the pleasure of cheap metamorphosis. After purloining someone's book, Stendhal *ipso facto* is obliged to go into hiding to deny his theft — superb occasion to dissemble. This situation that he deliberately provokes permits him to justify his love of the mask. Travesty thus becomes indispensable. But success is not that easily attained. At a loss for another alternative, Stendhal finally decides to hand over his private dreams to the general public. It is his last trump and he is reluctant to play it too fast. Endowed with a little more artfulness and greater savoir-faire, Stendhal might not have resisted the temptation to become a successful hack writer, contemptuous of his audience yet flattering at the same time. Perhaps it was out of awkwardness and an inability to dissociate completely from himself — the same awkwardness that paralyzed him in the face of others and doomed to failure his political ambitions — that Stendhal remained attached to his dreams of happiness, to his desires, his intimate preferences. Stendhal's good fortune as a writer lies in his incapability of leaving himself. In the reveries of metamorphosis in which he becomes Julien, Fabrice, Lucien, Lamiel, he changes face, body, social status, even sex, but it is always to tell his own life story while introducing greater fortune and greater misfortune. Unlike Balzac, he does not pursue the secret lives of others. He begins his own life anew in another body, the way one starts a card game with a fresh deal. Stendhal's metamorphosis does not attempt to concretize the basic alienation expressed by Rimbaud's "Je est un autre." It aims not at a change of being, but at a change of contingency. That is how he can remain himself while giving himself the destinies of Fabrice or Julien, who recompense him for his failures. This is how he consoles himself for not having been appointed prefect. The vexation of living under "the most knavish of kings" finds its compensation.

Compensation for Stendhal consists not only in imagining his characters happy in love, but merely in imagining them alive. They live under his eyes, they are others and himself, they live for him by proxy but without compromising him. He keeps his distance from his invented brothers but guides them from afar. After a while he sees them emancipate, take surprising decisions almost against his own will as creator. They are truly alive since they act freely, and yet never cease acting for Stendhal's benefit. He thus obtains the desired pleasure. He lives outside himself, he really inhabits "two bodies at the same time" since his imaginary figures have active bodies and autonomous destinies. In addition, we notice that these characters themselves do not forget to masquerade in their turn. The desire for metamorphosis that suscitated them perpetuates itself in them. One could enumerate the successive costumes of Fabrice del Dongo: barometer salesman, hussard, rustic, laborer, priest, English eccentric, valet. . . . Thus freed from his body and his ennui, Stendhal henceforth belongs to his characters who lead him where they will. His inner development has completely infiltrated into the unforseeable development of these "others" who are nevertheless himself. He thus gives himself the illusion of living out his destiny outside himself, seeing all without being seen, as though watching from a darkened box the spectacle of ultimately attained happiness and power.

LOUIS T. MILIC

Against the Typology of Styles

A typology is a classification and a typology of styles is an arrangement of styles into categories, such as periods of time (Elizabethan, Restoration, Victorian or modern), kinds of influence or derivation, such as Euphuistic, Senecan, Ciceronian, or of impression, such as ornate, formal, learned, simple, plain and casual. Such classifications are based on the belief that groups of writers have styles that are alike and that any single member of such a group is typical of it. I am convinced that this model, which has a certain antiquity in literary history, is false and unnecessary. It cannot contribute anything to our understanding of literary style. Moreover, we can explain stylistic phenomena without the aid of such categories.

The assumptions on which I base my disagreement are the following:

1. A writer's style is the expression of his personality.
2. A writer must write in his own style.
3. A writer can be recognized in his style.
4. No writer can truly imitate another's style.

SOURCE: "Against the Typology of Styles" is from *Essays on the Language of Literature,* edited by Seymour Chatman and Samuel R. Levin (Boston: Houghton, Mifflin Company, 1967), pp. 442–450. Copyright 1967 by Louis T. Milic and reprinted with his permission.

5. The main formative influences on a writer are his education and his reading.

6. A writer's language is governed by the practice of his own time.

7. Language changes gradually with time.

There is nothing very revolutionary here. Much of it is summed up in Buffon's aphorism: "Le style, c'est l'homme même."

I shall illustrate my thesis by reference to Restoration prose. Let me begin by quoting an authority, Professor James Sutherland:

> . . . Can we talk . . . about "Restoration prose," or are the two words merely a convenient way of referring to the prose that was written in England between 1660 and the closing years of the century? For myself, I believe that there *is* a prose style that is characteristic of the Restoration . . . and that this style is the genuine expression of a particular and definite type of culture.[1]

Professor Sutherland's studies of English prose need no encomia. I have selected his work because it is quite representative of typological *Stilforschung* in its assumptions and superior to most in originality and scholarship. My intention in singling out his work is to point to some limitations of this tradition.

The problem that I am interested in discussing will come into focus if we ask where this prose is to be found. Here is his answer:

> The prose I have in mind was written to perfection by Dryden and Halifax; with individual variations by such men as Robert South, Bishop Burnet, and Jeremy Collier; by Etherege and Rochester in their letters; with further variations by Roger L'Estrange in his pamphlets and translations; by Walter Pope in his *Life of Seth Ward* and by Robert Wolsey in his Preface to Rochester's *Valentinian;* by Thomas Sprat in his *History of the Royal Society* and by Robert Hooke in his *Micrographia;* and by many other minor writers. I do not think I should seriously confuse the issue if I added Cowley in his Essays and perhaps Stillingfleet in his *Origines Sacrae.* But I have got to admit that if there *is* such a thing as Restoration prose, not all the writers living in that period wrote it. There are a few of the greatest prose writers of the time whom I obviously cannot possibly include: one of these is John Bunyan, and another is Clarendon, and for various reasons I would exclude Isaac Barrow, the Hon. Robert Boyle, John Evelyn, Richard Baxter, Thomas Rymer, and such eccentrics as Thomas Burnet, the author of *The Sacred Theory of the Earth.* And I don't know what to do with Samuel Pepys.[2]

This is a very select list, almost an eccentric one. It says yes to Dryden but no to Bunyan, yes to Burnet and no to Clarendon, yes to Collier and no to Rymer. It mentions Robert Wolseley [sic] and Walter Pope, who are rare birds indeed, and yet talks of minor writers. Moreover, it leaves out altogether John Dennis, Thomas Traherne, Andrew Marvell, William Congreve, Sir William Temple, Samuel Butler and John Locke, all of whom wrote prose of some distinction. Such a process of selection seems to suggest that writers of Restoration prose were not in the majority during the Restoration. In other words only some, perhaps a minority, of the writers of this time wrote Restoration prose. The typological criterion then is not merely chronological; there seems to be something else.

This new quality is sometimes called plain prose or the plain style. This well-known notion — that a change occurred in English prose style during the seventeenth century, in the direction of plainness or simplicity — has been present in the writings of literary historians for some time. A. A. Tilley, for example, in 1911, observed:

> Perhaps the most important literary achievement within this period is the creation of a prose style which, in structure if not in vocabulary, is essentially the same as that of today . . . possessing before all things, the homely virtues of simplicity, correctness, lucidity and precision.[3]

The change can be illustrated very simply. The most dramatic way to sense its real force is to read ten pages of Milton's polemical prose and to follow this with ten pages of Dryden's critical prose. To most modern readers, this is like coming out of a tunnel into the sunshine. The typical response is, How did this happen, that is, How did the English come to write so simply, so clearly, so informally after having written so much the other way? The implication of this form of the question is that before 1660 everyone wrote like Milton and after that date like Dryden.

To promote this feeling or impression into a theory, it is necessary only to group a few extreme cases around our two antagonists in order to produce two schools. On Milton's side, we put Browne, Clarendon, Taylor, Lancelot Andrewes . . . ; Dryden is teamed with Swift, Steele, Addison, Shaftesbury, Defoe. . . . Examples are easily come by. The following pair of citations would find few to disagree that the first of the two passages is less plain than the second:

> Not to insist upon the examples of Moses, Daniel, and Paul, who were skilful in all the learning of the Egyptians, Chaldeans, and Greeks, which could not probably be without reading their books of all sorts, in Paul especially, who thought it no defilement to insert into Holy Scripture the sentences of three Greek poets, and one of them a tragedian, the question was notwithstanding sometimes controverted among the primitive doctors, but with great odds on that side which affirmed it both lawful and profitable, as was then evidently perceived, when Julian the Apostate and subtlest enemy to our faith made a decree forbidding Christians the study of heathen learning: for, said he,

they wound us with our own weapons, and with our own arts and sciences they overcome us.[4]

For there is a perpetual dearth of wit; a barrenness of good sense and entertainment. The neglect of the readers will soon put an end to this sort of scribbling. There can be no pleasantry where there is no wit; no impression can be made where there is no truth for the foundation.[5]

The second is in fact three sentences of Dryden, but together they take up less than half the space of Milton's single sentence.

If the case were always so clear, we should have no problem in characterizing plain prose and I would have no argument. Matter, however, does not follow categories. So for example, Isaac Barrow, who is relegated to Professor Sutherland's NO list, is described in the *Cambridge History of English Literature* as noted for "the clearness and simplicity which under his influence began to mark the prose of the later seventeenth century." His general manner "is an anticipation of Addison." [6] To show the practical difficulties of this sort of classification, I shall give a passage from Robert South from the YES list as well as one from Isaac Barrow.

We are all naturally endowed with a strong appetite to know, to see, to pursue Truth; and with a bashfull abhorrency from being deceived, and entangled in mistake. And as success in enquiry after Truth affords matter of joy and triumph; so being conscious of error, and miscarriage therein, is attended with shame and sorrow. These desires Wisdom in the most perfect manner satisfies, not by entertaining us with dry, empty, fruitless theories, upon mean and vulgar subjects; but by enriching our minds with excellent and useful knowledge, directed to the noblest objects, and serviceable to the highest ends.[7]

Now for the second passage:

As nothing can be of more moment; so few things, doubtless, are of more difficulty, than for men to be rationally satisfied about the estate of their souls, with reference to God and the great concerns of eternity. In their judgment about which if they err finally it is like a man's missing his cast when he throws dice for his life; his being his happiness and all that he does or can enjoy in the world is involved in the error of one throw. And therefore it may very well deserve our best skill and care to enquire into those rules by which we may guide our Judgment in so weighty an affair both with safety and success.[8]

I wonder how many readers would be able to pick out the work of the Restoration prose writer from the other. Barrow's does not seem to be distinguishable from South's by means of the criterion of plainness. I am not suggesting that the *Cambridge History* is correct in placing Barrow in the plain group and Sutherland wrong in excluding him. I do not believe there is much evidence for either side and neither has offered anything like an incontestable or even a workable criterion. Calling it the plain style is not enough.

What is this plain style? According to Sutherland it is an English "simpler, less ornate, more colloquial, more practical." [9] A linguist might describe the syntax of Milton as nested or embedded and that of Dryden as linear. But neither of these descriptions will really help us when we come to average cases, such as those of South and Barrow, rather than extreme ones. The typological procedure is not very enlightening in this kind of problem. It tends to deal in impressionistic generalities, which may be adequate for getting a vague sense of the difference between two modes of expression but not adequate for analyzing the difference between two particular examples.

Whether one examines the claims of one set of theorists who try to account for the emergence of plain prose in terms of the influence of pulpit oratory, or whether one is willing to accept the views of those who attribute it to the influence of the Royal Society and its desire for scientific writing, or accepts the opinion that it derives from the conversation of well-bred aristocratic gentlemen, who prized easy informality, lack of affectation and a stress on the colloquial, does not matter very much. All three of these explanations and any others that may arise are attempts to explain with ingenuity what can be explained without it.

I am prepared to concede without any reservation that the English of nearly any writer of the eighteenth century sounds different from that of most writers of the seventeenth. I am also willing to grant that the writing of many writers of the Restoration is easier to read than that of the subjects of the early Stuarts. What I am not willing to grant is that we need a theory of types in order to explain this development. The matter can be explained quite satisfactorily with some of the axioms cited earlier. On the scientific principle that an economical explanation based on opinions generally held is better than one requiring a number of dubious assumptions, I would suggest that the typological explanation of the plain style represented by Professor Sutherland be dismissed. I shall summarize the grounds.

Consider what we need to believe in order to accept a typological explanation of Restoration prose. First, we must believe that there is a hypothetical entity called Restoration prose, whose characteristics can be defined only generally. Second, we must agree that this entity is the common property of a certain number of writers of that period but not of some others, admittedly first-rank writers, and not only the work of a minority but of that minority only in certain works which can be specified. Third, we are invited to agree that the writers who partake of the mystic entity represent a significant subculture within the society, one which presumably is closer to the real work of the society than those outside it, however great the writers excluded may be.

The last of these points, that the writers who are thus isolated represent a significantly dominant aspect of the culture, cannot detain us long. Both common sense and statistics tell us that lists of members of an in-group tend to be fallacious. The real members of the group may only be known to the truly *in* people, who keep their identities secret, like the Gray Eminence. Apart from the evident difficulty of at this distance assembling a group of writers who will constitute the spirit of the Restoration, it would seem even more hazardous to prefer the claims of one group over those of others. The courtiers no doubt had influence, but was it literary? The scientists, dissenters, the merchants, all had competing claims, not to mention the dramatists and the pamphleteers.

The constitution of the group representing the spirit of the Restoration raises insistent questions of logic. If Etherege and Rochester were members of the significant minority, why did this fact only make itself known when they wrote letters? Why was L'Estrange only *in* in his pamphlets and Cowley in his essays? More mysterious still, why was Walter Pope only part of the circle in a single *Life* and Wolseley in a preface to someone else's work? The inconsistency of such an argument requires no deep searching to detect.

The most interesting point is the first, the problem of describing the characteristics of Restoration prose. Description proceeds by the accumulation of detail, a sound procedure in dealing with style. But descriptions of style usually proceed by generalization, by abstraction of qualities from masses of detail. Style is difficult to handle simply because it is a mass of detail. To classify a particular set of such details by means of an abstraction is to make a claim that these details are more important than others, that they fall into a configuration and that this abstraction outweighs others that might be constructed out of the same materials. For example, when following the trend of modern comment we call today's prose colloquial or informal, we are constructing a category of informality with certain characteristics and are implicitly claiming that most of today's writing conforms to those characteristics. Both of these steps are more difficult than appears at first. Since we cannot examine all writing, how can we determine that today's prose is indeed informal? We cannot examine more than a fraction of it and that fraction may not be a true random sample. It is based on our preferences. The reader of the *Christian Century*, the *Journal of the History of Ideas* and *Victorian Studies* will get a different idea of the state of modern prose than will the reader of the *New York Times,* the *New Republic* and the *New Yorker* or for that matter the reader of *Playboy, Mad* and the *Evergreen Review.* Unless we take special precautions to be objective and cross-sectional, our evidence will be hopelessly biased and we shall be making generalizations which, however perceptive, will be inapplicable to more than a segment of the population.

The problem of criteria is even more difficult: how do we decide what makes a prose informal? Many critics do this intuitively. Without pointing to anything in the language, they say it sounds informal to them. This kind of impressionism is equivocal: another critic may say it does not sound informal to him. There is no way to settle so metaphysical a dispute. A better procedure is to particularize informality by means of a set of indicia. When they are present, the prose can be called informal; when they are absent, the reverse. Unfortunately, this leaves a great many cases unsettled, when some of the indicia are present and some not, when some sentences are informal and some are not. No consistent classification can emerge from this kind of disorder. Unless a policy on such questions is established in advance, no statements of description can be made with reliability.

In other words, one important objection to the typology of styles is the matter of method or procedure. It is *practically* impossible to make an accurate generalization about an abstraction so remote and inchoate as the dominant feeling or quality of the writings of a group of people expressing themselves on every subject during a period of forty years. The human animal is too various to be so categorized. Group personalities of this kind have no reality, any more than national languages have a character, as once was thought. Only individuals have personalities and therefore only individuals can have a style.

Style has many definitions but most of them are merely casual variations on a theme. On the basis of the uncontroversial axioms I offered at the beginning of this paper, I would now claim that an individual's style is his habitual and consistent selection from the expressive resources available in his language. In other words, his style is the collection of his stylistic options. Options or choices are not always exercised consciously; they are often habitual practices of which the practitioner is as unconscious as he is of the way that he bends his leg in walking or the way that he ties his shoelace. His reading, the way he has been taught to write, the bent of his mind have all influenced him in the direction of a particular uniqueness. To this may be added the ingredient of conscious rhetorical choice. The net effect is an individual style, which be it noted may be as individual among literary hacks as among literary geniuses. Milton and Dryden each write in their unique individual styles because of who and what they are. What divides them is personality; what unites them is chronology.

The language changes all the time, but it changes very slowly, at times so imperceptibly that it gives the illusion of being stable, so that speakers who become aware of changes raise passionate outcries about corruption and decay. All speakers are bound by these changes but not all writers are chronologically at the same point in time. At any given moment, there are writers imbued with the lexical choices and the syntactical options of a previous era. And there are some who are on the frontier of change, coining new words like any teen-ager. Thus the co-existence of several chronological states of the language at one time provides the medium within which the rich variety of individuals can express itself. Between these two poles, the changing language and the individual writer, all the facts of style can be satisfactorily accounted for.

The individual's style is the aggregate of his stylistic selections from the particular state of the language that he construes as the real one of his time. The consistent choices that he makes from it to serve his own expressive requirements constitute his style, his literary personality. It is evident that the writer's choices will be determined by certain fashions in education, in rhetoric and in literature, but the main tendency of writers in a given time is to be unlike rather than alike. The notion of period styles underrates this tendency and implies a uniformity of expression which is wildly at variance with the facts.

The writers of plain prose or what has been called the clear stream — Dryden, Addison, Swift, Fielding etc.[10] — are granted by this typology a uniformity which is quite foreign to their practice. A selection of passages might be made from the works of any single writer to support the claim that he prefers short sentences or long sentences, few adjectives or many and so on. Similarly, the plain style is not the prerogative of a given period; it is a rhetorical tendency which is present in all ages. A history of the plain style might be written showing that it arose in the sixteenth century and was practiced by writers from Bacon to E. B. White. The history of ornate prose would show a similar line, ending let us say with Churchill or Walter Lippmann.

The division of eighteenth-century prose into the clear stream and the ornate one oversimplifies the problems it is striving to solve. Most people in Johnson's time did not regularly write balanced Johnsonian prose, not even Johnson himself. Balanced prose, employing the devices of antithesis and parallelism, has been in some degree a feature of formal writing in all periods, including our own. It is my conviction that such classes as plain style, ornate style, balanced style, may only be useful to describe individual sentences, paragraphs or perhaps even whole compositions, whenever they may have been written. But when such classes are tied to chronology and culture, they imply more than can be justified by a strict examination of the facts.

The dominant modern style, according to some observers, is the plain or casual or informal style. Many teachers and writing advisors recommend the following of this model. Yet we know that many highly admired writers of the present day do not do so. Writers of great reputation practice more elaborate forms, not to mention the esoteric language of the social scientists.[11] Whatever may be the central characteristics of modern prose style, they are not likely to tell us much about modern writing because the average of a very large number tends to iron out interesting peculiarities. That is a great danger of excessive typology.

The typology of styles seems to have descended to us from the practice, standard in literary history, of grouping writers in schools of drama or poetry, such as the Georgic poets, the bourgeois dramatists, the graveyard poets, whose subject matter and formal manner coincided significantly. But types of styles, schools of styles, genres of styles, and periods of styles are not analogous entities. A writer's style emerges from the tension between the state of the language that he uses and the demands of his individuality striving to express itself with the same materials as other individuals and struggling against the restraining powers of fashion, tradition and rhetoric.

Rhetorical training conditions both the writer and the reader and in that way may come to affect the language itself. The rhetorical inversion of one era is the normal word-order of another. But the scope of rhetoric is limited and affects mainly the more visible outward aspects of the repertory of stylistic resources provided by a language. To be sure, some writers have more or less consciously emphasized certain rhetorical features in their writing (Gibbon, Johnson, Macaulay), but these are not by themselves significant. Rhetoric becomes significant when it can be related to the writer's unconscious expressive mechanism, when it represents the controlling power, both limiting and enabling, of outer form upon idea and meaning. In that sense, it becomes one of the contributing factors to the totality we call an author's style. The contribution of conscious rhetorical adornment to the total style of an author is put into proper perspective when his theoretical pronouncements about style are compared with his actual performance. When Swift tells us about his ideals of style, he is not giving an accurate description of what he actually does. His own practice is some distance away from what he thought he was doing or what he would have liked to do. In fact, in the words of one scholar, Swift was always struggling against a tendency to write in just the way he disliked.[12] If this is true, it surely refutes the arguments of those who would credit a writer with the power to alter his style at will, as if he had a wardrobe — or a stable — of different styles for different occasions.[13] The extent of his ability to adapt his style is probably limited to certain superficial aspects, among which are included rhetorical devices and diction.

In sum, the proper subject of stylistic speculation is the individual writer. To understand the style of the individual, we must concern ourselves first with the individual's writings and second with the linguistic resources from which his peculiar style is a selection. Typologies attract our attention to specious and minor similarities among authors. They are misleading because they take us away from what is really significant, the individual author's own peculiarity, his difference from his contemporaries, which is what is truly his style.

W. K. WIMSATT

Genesis: A Fallacy Revisited

It would appear that literary studies, and especially theoretical studies, are subject to endless metamorphic cycles, and if they sometimes make progress, they can also suffer regress. Why not? Poems are, on one view, more or less imperfectly recorded acts of personal agents, and in literary study they are open to boundless speculation by further persons, whose activity, though sometimes partly scientific and historical, is always driven by an aim of individual intelligence. There is no theoretical or critical term set up for the purpose of clarifying or recommending a given perspective which is not susceptible of being seen and used in an opposite light. There is no rational and methodological concept, no attempted translucent universal, which is not capable of being transformed, and very quickly, into an opaque historical gimmick — as if some poems could be "beautiful" in some special Platonic sense (after a certain date), or as if symbolism had begun to appear in poetry about the time of Baudelaire or Mallarmé, just as blood began to circulate in human bodies about the time of William Harvey or dreams to have significance about the time of Freud. These reflections, verging on the melancholy, occur as I survey some recent writings on the critical problem of the artist's life story, his inspirations and his intentions, in relation to his work of art.[1]

Whatever the truth in this debate, or the preferred side (if there is one, and I still think there is), it must be evident that there are two antithetically opposed sides, and probably always will be, corresponding to two aspects of literature and to two kinds of persons who come to the study of literature. To speak broadly and to avoid the simplicity of one-word labels (or to defer the economy of such labels), let us say that an art work is something which emerges from the private, individual, dynamic, and intentionalistic realm of its maker's mind and personality; it is in a sense (and this is especially true of the verbal work of art) made of intentions or intentionalistic material. But at the same time, in the moment it

SOURCE: From *The Disciplines of Criticism: Essays in Literary Theory, Interpretation, and History (Honoring René Wellek)*, edited by Peter Demetz, Thomas Greene, and Lowry Nelson, Jr. (New Haven: Yale University Press, 1968), pp. 193–225. Copyright © 1968 by Yale University. Reprinted by permission of Yale University Press.

emerges, it enters a public and in a certain clear sense an objective realm; it claims and gets attention from an audience; it invites and receives discussion, about its meaning and value, in an idiom of inter-subjectivity and conceptualization. If the art work has emerged at all from the artist's private world, it has emerged into some kind of universal world. The artist was not merely *trying to* do something worthy of notice in that world. He has done it. Artistic activity has produced a valued result. Some critics will wish to talk about just that result. Other critics, however, will not. These will be the critics who entertain an antithetic drive toward viewing the art work as mainly a token of its source, a manifestation of something behind it, that is, the consciousness or personality of the artist (or perhaps of the society in which he lived, or of himself as representative of that society). These critics, wishing to throb in unison with the mind of the artist, will wish to know all about that individual artist and as much as possible about his historic context. At the very least, they will wish to know not only the poem in question, but also his other poems, his essays, letters, and diaries, his thoughts and feelings,[2] and not only those which occurred before the poem and might in any sense have caused it, but (in the more recent idiom) all those which came after it at any time and are thus a part of the whole personality of which the poem is an expression, the system of contexts of which it is a part.[3]

It was against a background of triumphantly prevalent genetic studies in various modes, and in an effort to give assistance in what seemed a badly needed program to rescue poems from the morass of their origins, that my friend Monroe Beardsley and I published in a *Dictionary of World Literature* (1944) an article entitled "Intention" and then, in response to a critique of that article, a further development of our argument in the *Sewanee Review* (1945), an essay entitled "The Intentional Fallacy." Mr. Beardsley followed these articles thirteen years later with some very lucid pages in his volume entitled *Aesthetics* (1958). It seemed to me then, and it still seems, that Mr. Beardsley and I succeeded in formulating a clear, reasonable, and viable statement of the thesis that the intention of a literary artist qua intention is neither a valid ground for arguing the presence of a quality or a meaning in a given instance of his literary work nor a valid criterion for judging the value of that work. "The objective critic's first question, when he is confronted with a new aesthetic object," says Mr. Beardsley in 1958, "is not, What is this supposed to be? but, What have we got here?"

As I have already noted, however, literary students who love the poem's genesis have no trouble in answering such arguments and returning to that luxuriant pasture. It is enough to assert that biography has such and such joys of discovery and communion, and thus biography *is* relevant to the study of the poem.[4] Or to say that the poet's life itself, or even the style of face he wears, is a work of art parallel to his produced art works, and hence the poet's life *is* a thing of great interest to the literary student.[5] Or that the intention of the artist, revealed in the title of a work or some similar adjacent index, is often a clue which the artist himself seems to feel it prudent to supply to his public, or which the given viewer of a work finds it very helpful to notice, and hence the intention of the artist *is* sometimes "relevant" to the work.[6] One may even add that in some instances, like that of Mr. Beardsley's invention, the "cruller-shaped object of polished teak" said by the sculptor to symbolize "Human Destiny," the plight of the artist who wishes to convey that meaning will indeed be hopeless unless we grant him the privilege of telling us what he wishes. And therefore his intention is indeed relevant and valid.[7] Or, a critic may prefer to talk, not about the meaning of a poem, but about his own "responses" to it, which may be "conditioned" by his knowledge of the author's intentions, as these create a kind of "field of force round the work" or a "web of associations." If Housman says that he meant no irony at all, that, it would appear, will settle the question for this critic. If Eliot were to testify that he had never heard of Andrew Marvell, that too would settle a question. Such a critic's responses might apparently also be conditioned by his knowing what Mr. Leavis thinks about a problem — though what this may be, in the given instance, seems unhappily in doubt.[8]

The argument about intention is then, in a sense, hopelessly circular and reentering. There is no way to keep the simpler kinds of intention-hunters from jumping on the vehicle of literary inquiry, and nobody I suppose really wishes the power to legislate anything against them. But at the precise level of abstraction and definition at which Mr. Beardsley and I argued the question, I do not see that any notable revision is required, or even any very emphatic repetition. Let me try to make a useful reentry into the debate by first noticing a few related, parallel, or complementary terms and focuses of recent literary criticism, perhaps some of them obstructions to a right view of literary "intention."

The idea of poetic "impersonality" is, I believe, in the thinking of many students a close adjunct to, or required condition for, the kind of criticism which hopes to escape the 'intentional fallacy." Much difficulty seems to arise here, however, and this has probably been promoted to a large extent by the writings early and late of a poet-critic who did as much as any other single authority to establish in English studies of the mid-century a climate favorable to objective inquiry — T. S. Eliot, of course. In a review of his posthumously collected essays, *To Criticize the Critic,* I have already discussed this matter in the perspective of his later career.[9] It will be sufficient here to look back for a moment at his seminal essay "Tradition and the Individual Talent" (published during the fall and early winter of 1919 in the last two numbers of *The Egoist, An Individualist Review*). This celebrated early essay, despite its forceful suggestiveness, the smoothness and fullness of its definition of the poet's impersonality (or perhaps inevitably in achieving these qualities), was a highly ambiguous statement. Therein, no doubt, consisted something of its pregnancy. In this essay Eliot as poet and critic is saying two things about three ideas (man, poet, and poem) and saying them simultaneously. He is saying that a poet ought to depersonalize his raw experience, transcend the immediacy of the suffering man. At the same time, he is saying that the reader ought to read the poem impersonally, as an achieved expression, not personally, with attendant inquiries into the sufferings, the motives, the confusions of the man behind the poem. The idea "poet" as Eliot employs it in this essay is sometimes the antithesis of "man" and sometimes the antithesis of "poem." "The more perfect the artist, the more completely separate in him will be the man who suffers and the mind which creates." "Honest criticism and sensitive appreciation are directed not upon the poet but upon the poetry." The two meanings are inextricably interwoven in Eliot's rich and memorable sentences. But they are not one meaning, nor does either one entail the other. Eliot, at moments much later in his career, could be very clear about one half of his doctrine. "I prefer not to define, or to test, poetry by means of speculations about its origins; you cannot find a sure test for poetry, a test by which you may distinguish between poetry and mere good verse, by reference to its putative antecedents in the mind of the poet." [10] But this injunction against peeping into the poet's activity, if it is valid at all, must be equally valid whether that activity itself is, in the poet's own consciousness, personal or impersonal. In fact, the critical lesson is that from the poem itself we cannot really tell, and so far as we are critics interested in the poem itself, we do not care. Despite his double doctrine of impersonality, the notion of the poet has always been, for Eliot, deeply centered in that personal suffering man himself. "It is not in his personal emotions . . . that the poet is in any way remarkable or interesting. His particular emotions may be simple, crude, or flat." Poetry is an "escape" from personality. Yes, but of course "only those who have personality and emotions know what it means to want to escape from these things." [11]

The dubious notion of the poet's impersonal personality, deriving so pervasively in modern American criticism from the ideas of Eliot, has also been colored no doubt by Yeatsian occultist notions of the "self" and the "anti-self" or "mask" (the latter either "true" or "false"). [12] Which is the poet in a given poem expressing? His real self? A true mask? A false mask? A fascinating question — and a safe one, so long as the inquirer is aware that the area of his inquiry is at the moment biography, perhaps a very refined version of this art, but still biography. Perhaps it will be sufficient to say here, without a long excursion, that the thesis that biographical evidence does not establish meaning *in* poems is not the equivalent of a thesis that poems cannot contribute their own kind of meaning, and a very rich and subtle kind, to the writing of biography.[13] For whatever does get into a poem presumably is put there by the poet and reflects *something* in the poet's personality and life. It is for the biographer, in his particular insight and skill, to say what is reflected and in what relation to other things in the poet's life. Nowadays we are increasingly promised, or shown, the inner life of the author mainly on the evidence of the dialectic sequence of his works.[14] If anybody wishes to challenge this as sound biographical method (I at least have no specific wish to do so), it ought to be clear that he does not do so on the same principle as that on which a critic may refuse to decide the meaning or value of a poem on external auctorial testimony or other biographical evidence. Affirmation of a cause and affirmation of an effect are different in their entailments. If a poet sees red, he may well either write or not write a red poem. If he writes a red poem, it would seem to be a sound enough inference, though in some instances little more than a truism, that he has in some sense seen red.

Patrick Cruttwell, in a richly illustrated and nicely modulated essay of 1959, "Makers and Persons," [15] discriminates four degrees of "distance" between a "maker" (poet) and the "person" (man in whom the maker perforce quarries his stuff): (1) the degree or way of "simple transcript" (genuine or partly faked — Boswell, Pepys, Rousseau, Byron in letters and journals, Montaigne); (2) the "masked" way — "the making of a self which pretends not to be, but encourages the reader to think it is," the real person of the writer (Sterne-Shandy-Yorick, Conrad-Marlow); (3) the way of "mythologized" self-presentation — "transportation of the person into symbolic figures, references" (the master of this obscure and mysterious way is Mr. Eliot); (4) the "dramatized" way — here "the distance is greatest between maker and person" (clearest in actual stage drama — the Greeks, Shakespeare, "the ages of great drama"). After presenting these distinctions, Mr. Cruttwell traces, very interestingly and I believe correctly, the rise of the modern cult of personality, the author as "exhibitionist," from about the time of Boswell's *Johnson* (1791) through episodes in the career of Byron and in Victorian literary biography. Modern poets themselves have sometimes protested against the invasion of their privacy — in vain, and wrongly. The floodgates of the personal interest, once opened, cannot be forced back. Art betrays its creators, and properly. They betray themselves, once the public and the literary scholars have been put on the right track. In a closing short section on problems for contemporary critics, Mr. Cruttwell argues that it is time for critics to overcome any anti-biographical inhibitions which may have been induced by the ideas of "Eliot, Richards, Leavis and the Scrutineers" or by the "New Criticism" in America. Let the critics now permit themselves a renewed and healthy release in the satisfaction of the "curiosity" which poems must in fact surely arouse in them. Who is the critic, after all, who can say that his responses to poetry *are* pure? After we "have enjoyed" and have been "impressed" by a writer, by Wordsworth in his Lucy poems, for instance, then we undertake the "microscopic investigation." We want to know about Wordsworth's "incestuous feelings for Dorothy" and what he "intended" Lucy to "stand for." So, in spite of Mr. Cruttwell's effort to establish a *critical* direction for his essay, the argument swings round in fact to post-critical interests, moving *from* the recognized and presumably understood poem toward the "putative antecedents." Mr. Cruttwell has earlier noted that a certain "degeneration" in Sterne's management of his Tristram and Yorick masks may be explained by a parallel in Sterne's life. "His failure to hold his masks was a symptom of his person's insincerity and weakness. . . . He slid from one pose to the next, from bawdy to sobstuff and back again, not through choice but through weakness" (p. 491). But Mr. Cruttwell can also have his argument the opposite way, on a later page (503), where he argues that Byron aspiring to escape from his true personality in *Childe Harold* wrote untruthfully and badly, but when he abandoned his aspiration to purity and simply "wrote out his mood as it came to him" in the "shameless self-parading of *Don Juan*," he "wrote at his best." The lesson of these two examples seems to be that the biographically oriented critic will find a correspondence between life and work an explanation of either goodness or badness in the work, as he happens to find the work itself good or bad. On another page (494), Mr. Cruttwell expatiates upon the futility of trying to find Eliot's personal or secret motive in the epigraph from Marston prefixed to *Burbank with a Baedeker*. Mr. Cruttwell is severe on Eliot for his two-faced stance of impersonal secretiveness yet constant invitation to the reader to speculate about personal reasons (in the absence of clear public ones). I think there is some justice in the complaint. I have dwelt long on Mr. Cruttwell's essay, however, not only because it seems to me probably the richest and most informative in the recent resurgence of biographically oriented "critical" arguments, but because in its own ambivalence or thwarted struggle to arrive at a "critical" direction, it is in fact a larger rewriting of Eliot's original and seminally confused essay of 1919.

A kind of critical metamorphosis to which I alluded in my opening paragraph is well illustrated in the recent history of the very useful term "persona" in American criticism. This term seems to have gained currency during the mid-century because it was a convenient way of referring to something *in the poem* which could be thought of as a counterpart of the *im*personality which was supposed either to reside in the author or, more accurately, to be a perspective adopted by the critic. This economical employment of the term "persona" (along with certain related or nearly equivalent terms such as "fiction," "ethos," "mask," or "muse") might be illustrated near its zenith in Maynard Mack's essay of 1951, "The Muse of Satire," [16] distinguishing three "voices" (the *vir bonus,* the *ingénu,* and the heroic public defender) in the persona or speaker of Pope's formal verse satire. All three of these voices were to be taken *by a critic* dramatically, not biographically, rhetorically, not historically. Something like a sheer reversal from that kind of critical use of persona to a convenient reconfusion of questions about criticism and questions about biography may be witnessed in a very richly variegated essay of 1963 by Irvin Ehrenpreis, entitled "Personae." [17] An expression of grave concern that certain nameless "scholars" have been doing the wrong thing with persona (making it a "distinguishing property" or special kind of merit in Augustan poetry, rather than the universal and "inescapable part of language and communication" that it actually is) leads Mr. Ehrenpreis, not, as one might at first hope, to a purified image of the scholar-critic, but very quickly into an opposite sort of thing, an exceedingly dense involvement of poet and poem as man and mask, reality and "rhetorical pose." "One could never reveal the whole truth about oneself, even supposing that one knew it." "If there is any meaning in the concept of persona or mask, it must imply a difference between appearance and reality."

Like Mr. Cruttwell, whom we have cited above, and like most writers on W. B. Yeats, Mr. Ehrenpreis reminds us forcefully that, whatever the relation of persona to author, it is not a simple one either of likeness or of difference. Other recent writers, Maynard Mack in the essay already cited, and notably Wayne Booth in *The Rhetoric of Fiction* (1961),[18] have been stressing a somewhat different, if parallel, truth — that the relation of persona, internally, to other parts or aspects of the work, need not be simple. Persona is not in fact a sufficient conception for the *de*personalization of the poetic object as the critic attends to it. It is not as if the persona is always the simple focus for the expression of everything in the poem. Sometimes he betrays himself in contrast to some cooler or saner perspective. This is the kind of thing that happens obviously in a monodrama like Browning's *Soliloquy of a Spanish Cloister,* a miniature of the situation in a full-scale play or novel, where numerous personae contend within the ambit of an encircling and managing intelligence. Browning's *Soliloquy* is a steady sequence of not very delicate little antithetic jolts. "*Ave, Virgo!* Gr-r-r — you swine!" The ironies of Swift are a more plenary instance of such internal cunning. Mr. Ehrenpreis observes that in *A Modest Proposal* there are not two, but three mentalities or "styles" — that of the initially prominent "sensible projector" of the proposal, that of the "monster" looming behind him, and that of a directly speaking, bitter denunciator, all three of these, as we should expect in this essay, said to be styles of the author's own voice. (Here perhaps it is worth adding that while projector and monster are aspects of the same persona, the denouncer is part of a perspective, or, if one wishes, he is a second person, who has already manipulated the projector so as to reveal him as a monster.) But what I am trying to get back to here is the direction of argument. From the work to the author (when one wishes to be biographical) is not the same as from the author (outside the work) to the work. These directions remain opposites no matter how numerous and complicated a set of deflectors or baffles we set up between the two termini.

The fact is that we can, if we wish, learn with relative certainty from biographical evidence that some personae are close to or identical with the author and some are much different from him. Nobody would confuse the persona of Browning's *Soliloquy of a Spanish Cloister* with Browning himself. But almost everybody rushes to confuse the persona of Gray's *Elegy in a Country Churchyard* with Gray himself. In fact it can be shown on quite convincing biographical evidence that the melancholy poet who is the anonymous speaker of that poem is very close to the melancholy poet Thomas Gray — "me I; il Pensoroso." Nor is that correspondence, in biographical terms, an accident. The *Elegy* does seem to come out of the historic person Thomas Gray much more directly than many other poems come out of their authors. Nevertheless, the *Elegy* is not *about* the historic person Gray. The self-contemplative speaker remains anonymous. The poem itself, if it were anonymous, would be intact.

What, however, if the poem does happen to be a poem *about* that historic person the author, about himself, his friends, and his enemies? If the author of the *Epistle to Arbuthnot,* says Ehrenpreis, "were not the great poet of his age, if his relations with his parents were not well known to have been as he testifies, if Atticus and Sporus did not belong to public life, the force of the poem would dwindle" (p. 32). Yet with increase of information, let us notice, comes complexity — and doubt. The canny persona of Pope's satire bears scarcely the same simple relation to the gardener of Twickenham as the melancholy churchyard speaker seems to bear to the pensive fellow of the Cambridge college. Three distinct voices are assigned by Mr. Mack to that satiric persona. In what variously shaded relations to the man who is both behind the poem and the subject of the poem may be difficult to say. Pope could be scheming and mean, as well as friendly and noble. The main evidence for his piety to his father is in the poem. Perhaps we do not inquire too rigorously whether he was in fact so righteous, charitable, and simple as the poem would make him. If he was not, still "his make-up of being so is in itself a piece of greatness; and not to enjoy it is a piece of stupidity." [19] Perhaps we enjoy it the more for its being in part make-up. And we sense that this is so, or may well be so, in large part from internal evidence, from the perspective or management of the whole witty poem.

In accepting this kind of biographical claim, let us notice that it is a particular kind of claim, not of intention but of subject matter. Pope's sincerity or insincerity, his virtue or his meanness, his character and intention, as generators of the poem or as criteria of its merit, do not really come into question. The poet and his friends and enemies are present in the poem as historic figures, and furthermore as well-established historic figures in precisely the roles they play in the poem. Milton's sonnets 17, 22, and 23 and his other allusions to his blindness provide similar, easy, and unimpeachable examples. Here we enter the problem of the universality and significance of the protagonist — the stature of Samson the agonist compared to that of Hobson the carrier. Aristotle understood that it gives a certain kind of advantage if the man is important. After Milton and Pope, the world became increasingly convinced of the importance of every man. Still it is not true, it never has been true, that the simple meanings or wishes of any man, even of any important man, can generate or guarantee a significant poetic symbol. [20]

"It is not illusory appearances," says Ehrenpreis, "that the real person sets before us: it is the visible effluences, aspects, reflections — however indirect, of an inner being that cannot be defined apart from them. In order to understand any literary work, we must view it as a transaction between us and that inner being" (p. 31). "Only as a relationship between a real speaker and a real listener can meaning exist" (p. 37). Some years earlier, Father Walter Ong, in one of the best essays on the "personalist approach" that I know, *The Jinnee in the Well-Wrought Urn,* had written:

> Man's deepest orientation is personal. . . . Each work of art that bids for attention in an act of contemplation is a surrogate for a person. In proportion as the work of art is capable of being taken in full seriousness, it moves further and further along an asymptote to the curve of personality. [21]

Perhaps it does. Yet the argument against intentional reading need not suppose, and does not suppose, that the monkeys in the British Museum will in the foreseeable future, or in any future at all, type out *Paradise Lost.* [22] "The words of a poem come out of a head, not out of a hat," as we quoted long ago from E. E. Stoll. James Thorpe has recently demonstrated how much some literary works actually owe to editors and other agents of transmission and even to such chance activity as that of a compositor, who may by mistake introduce a word that conceivably is better than the author's. Mr. Thorpe's philosophy of textual criticism says, however, that we should restore the author's own word, and I say the same thing, though perhaps more simply on grounds of plain convenience than he wishes to. He believes that to accept the compositor's happy slip would be to put the aesthetic object not in the realm of "art" (intended or designed work), but in that of the now popularly received object made by "chance" (a spilled can of paint, words selected by throwing dice, sounds of traffic recorded at a busy intersection).[23] But it is possible and, as he shows, frequently is the fact that a designed work is the design of more than one head. A second completes the work of the first. In this instance, it would be ourselves, the editors, who, in assessing and adopting the accidental intrusion, were the very junior collaborators in the original author's designed and intended work.

In our frequent focus on the history of modern literature as outlined by Mr. Cruttwell, with its heavy personal underpainting, its vigorous cult of personal authentication, let us not forget the massive foundations of the world's literature — the Book of Genesis, the *Iliad*, the *Odyssey*, the works of Virgil, Dante, Chaucer, Shakespeare — which survive for us either anonymously or with the merest wisps or shadows of biography attached. These works, it is to be assumed, no less than those of Milton, Johnson, Byron, Keats, Yeats, or Joyce, speak to us with the "inner being" of "real speakers," as "surrogates" for persons.

It may promote clarity if at this point we try to map the structure of the argument we are engaged in according to the following types of statement which are our subject matter:

1. Historical, biographical: Thomas Gray was a melancholy poet, and he planned or meant or was likely to mean certain things.

2. Historical, poetic: The speaker of Gray's *Elegy* is a melancholy poet; he uses certain words and images and means certain things.

3. Methodological, explicitly evaluative: The resemblance, or correspondence, between the poet Gray and either the speaker or the perspective of the *Elegy* makes it a good poem or shows that it is good.

4. Methodological, interpretive: The character, mind, or habitual meanings of the poet Gray are a valid guide (or the best guide) to the meaning of the *Elegy*.

This arrangement introduces one distinction on which I have so far not laid any emphasis, that between statements of type 3 and those of type 4. Statements of type 3 (the explicitly evaluative) are more ambitious than those of type 4 (the simply interpretive), but I use this order because those of type 3 are on the whole less plausible, and I wish to dispose of them first. In our articles of 1944 and 1945 Mr. Beardsley and I did not labor this distinction. In his *Aesthetics* of 1958 Mr. Beardsley has separated the two issues very cleanly, in fact by a space of 428 pages, with I think, considerable increase of clarity for the whole discussion. At the same time, it is my own view (and this will emerge more clearly as I go on) that an argument about instances of type 4 (the interpretive) will very often, or even characteristically, bring in considerations of value.

Let me proceed to notice and comment upon certain graded instances of argument, first some relating to statements of type 3 (a, b, c), then some relating to type 4 (a, b, c, d, e, f). There is some value in a chart or a guided tour of a field of argument even when the cartographer or guide has to confess that he looks on many of the stopping points as only of historic interest. The point of maximum live concern for our debate, and the one toward which I am working, let me confess in advance, is 4f.

(3a) The poet wrote his poem with the aim of making money, of winning a prize, of pleasing a mistress, of impressing an employer or patron — or for some opposite or more ideal sort of reason. His work was either a "free" work in Kant's sense, or not free. "He achieved a result commensurate with such aims. Therefore. . . ." Such reasonings concern what some writers on our problem take pains to distinguish as secondary or ulterior intentions of the artist. We ought to be able to see these as obviously outside any real critical question. In like manner, we should find no trouble in putting to one side the common artistic aim of creating a masterpiece — or perhaps of not creating a masterpiece, but just of turning out a potboiler — or of having a "lark." [24] "He intended only to appeal to popular sentiment; therefore we should not. . . ." (Or, to translate this kind of motive into the key of interpretive argument and thus get it out of the way: "We know that he thought of this as his masterpiece; therefore it. . . .")

(3b) The poem is or says what the poet himself was or thought or felt; it is hence good — or bad. We have been close to this framing of the argument in our whole discussion of persona. We have seen both kinds of conclusion (bad, for Sterne; good, for Byron) in Mr. Cruttwell's essay. This form of the argument runs very readily into talk about "sincerity" and "inspiration" and "authenticity," topics which Mr. Beardsley and I noted with some care in our essay of 1945. In his *Aesthetics* (p. 457) he lists "expression," "sincerity," and "intention" together, under the general head of the "genetic," but, rightly I believe, he sees "intention" as focusing most or all of what can be handled with any precision in this area.[25]

(3c) The poet had a specific aim or plan in mind; he managed (whether inspirationally or rationally) to carry this out in the poem; thus he is a successful artist; his work is good art. This is the "Spingarn-Croce-Carlyle-Goethe" theory named by H. L. Mencken. We alluded to this theory in our article of 1944, and it was defended by Ananda K. Coomaraswamy in his critique of that article.[26] A successfully planned and executed murder was for Mr. Coomaraswamy no less a work of art than a poem or painting. Mr. Beardsley makes the helpful suggestion that here we may indeed be likely to assign a kind of merit, but it should be understood as referring to the artist himself (who was "skillful" enough to do what he aimed at doing) rather than to the work — which may be murder, a robbery, a libel, a silly lampoon. It would scarcely be feasible to illustrate all the kinds of evidence (or supposed evidence) that may be adduced for an author's plan outside his poem. I do not know how many kinds there may be, each no doubt with somewhat special problems. Let me adduce a single example, representative I believe, if in part synthetic. Edgar Allan Poe's *Philosophy of Composition* professes to tell us how he proceeded in writing *The Raven* — a poem of a certain ideal length, presenting the most melancholy, moving, and poetic subject conceivable, the death of a beautiful woman, and making use of the most effective poetic device conceivable, a certain simple and sonorous refrain, repeated in various applications. There can be little question that *The Raven* does manifest Poe's professed intentions so far as they are specific and can be made manifest. But to argue (as some proponents of "intention" have seemed in general to argue) that, because we can here prove that the artist achieved his intentions, we know that *The Raven* is a good work of art would seem a fairly obvious kind of fatuity. A critical enterprise that would more seriously recommend itself would surely be the inquiry whether the proposed subject and technique were actually the most poetic conceivable. One kind of objection to such an argument from Poe's intention (or one explanation for giving it up) might be to say that Poe's *Philosophy of Composition* is not a valid guide to his intention in the poem because it is an ex post facto invention and a tongue-in-cheek tour de force. Perhaps so. But here we catch ourselves moving from intention to intention — when does the witness mean what he says? — and we may be left with the generally not very satisfactory principle that an external statement of intention by an author has to be examined to see if it was written before the poem or after. So externality is invested with externality, and testimonies written before the poem might well have suffered by change of intention while the poem was being written.

Another sort of argument in favor of intention as a criterion of value might say: Well, what is meant is precisely the fullness of the executed plan as seen in the poem itself. We can see the author's *skill* precisely in this. To which we might retort: Yes, precisely. We see a value of fullness, richness, design in the poem itself. *From this* we infer an artist and a skillful artist, and not the other way round. We do not compare the poem with any blueprint of the author's mind.

Let us turn then and consider some phases of the intentionalistic argument relating to statements of type 4 in our plan, those of interpretation — the author's mind outside the poem as a key to his meaning inside the poem.

(4a) A few of the recent writers on the term "intention" have pointed out, as indeed Mr. Beardsley and I were careful to point out in 1944, that interpretations apparently based upon an author's "intention" often in fact refer to an intention as it is found in, or inferred from, the work itself.[27] Obviously the argument about intention (or about the author's intention outside the work) is not directed against such instances — unless in an incidental and general plea for clarity in the use of critical terms. Such arguments may extend to *conflicts* of intention, or shifts of design, in a given work. They may give rise to such notions as that of a "secret meaning" (or even an unconscious meaning) to be distinguished from an "overt meaning." "Milton was of the Devil's party without knowing it." That is, Milton's *Paradise Lost,* in spite of certain contrary indications in it, on the whole makes Satan a hero. This argument can be enlarged by appeals to Milton's own rebellious personality, his political and religious prose writings. Yet it can be carried on too, and sufficiently, within the poem itself. Actually the poem itself seems to be the chief or only evidence which Blake, the author of the assertion just quoted, has in mind. Another classic instance is Tolstoy's judgment that Chekhov, in his story *Darling,* while trying to ridicule the womanliness of a woman, succeeded (like Balaam trying to curse the Israelites) only in pronouncing a blessing. Tolstoy had behind him a tradition of Russian book-reviewing which looked for covert and risky political meanings in nineteenth-century fiction.

(4b) In another variation of the same interpretive argument, the author's intention is sometimes said to have at least an "advisory" force.[28] This seems hardly a claim that ought to be debated. No doubt the author is likely to be a good guide. Yet it cannot be that on principle he is an infallible guide. As a commentator on his own works he enjoys no prescriptive, or creative, rights. If he says there is red in his poem, we will look carefully in the expectation of *finding* it.[29]

(4c) A somewhat similar sounding, but actually different, argument says that the intention of the artist (as learned in titles of works, epigraphs, and the like) may sometimes be said to fill in certain details or aspects of a work actually missing from the work but presumably needed for its understanding and appreciation.[30] In our article of 1945, Mr. Beardsley and I discussed something like this under the head of the modern poet's penchant for esoteric allusion, and we suggested that titles, epigraphs, and notes such as T. S. Eliot wrote for *The Waste Land*, were in fact loosely attached parts of poems or annexes of half-assimilated materials. As such they seemed to raise some questions about the achieved integrity of the poems. The notes to *The Waste Land* are not a manifest virtue, rather something we accept and submit to being teased by, in view of the probable depths of the poem itself, and latterly in view of Mr. Eliot's reputation.[31] Taken literally, the argument seems to imply some deficiency in the work of art itself, some need of adjunct or aid. On the assumption that the work of art is on the whole, or basically, worthwhile, nobody would wish to rule out such help — any more than to deny a crutch to a lame man, or an extra stone to a sagging arch. Only note that the crutch must fit the man; the stone must fit the arch, and in fact the stone becomes part of the arch. These analogies seem closer to what is meant by such special invocations of artist's intentions than, say, the use of a strong glass to see a miniature painting or a strong light in a gallery. The glass and the light can find only what is already there.[32]

Certain external aids or annexes to poems, we have just assumed, do fit or are appropriate to the poems in question. More broadly, however, if we are to think of poems as having any built-in character or structure of their own at all, then the inquiry must run the risk of encountering inappropriately offered annexes, false clues, mistaken efforts of the energetic historian.

(4d) Certainly there are features of gross material or of structure in art works which not only do not call for the artist's intention to help their interpretation but will even strongly defy contradictory indications. If the artist makes a statue of granite, then it is granite, and an affidavit that he thought he was working in marble or intended to work in marble or would rather have worked in marble will not make any difference.[33] The same principle will hold if the artist writes in English but happens to think he is writing in French. Or if he defies some code of classic rules, though he happens to think he is observing them, or vice versa. The former, or conservative, self-deception may be illustrated in Corneille's retrospective defense of *Le Cid*. The general principle for literary criticism was put precisely by Samuel Johnson in his *Preface to Shakespeare:* "Whether Shakespeare knew the unities and rejected them by design, or deviated from them by happy ignorance, it is, I think, impossible to decide and useless to inquire." [34]

(4e) Problems of local semantics may be more difficult. But even here, the more explicit the conflicting auctorial testimony, the more likely it is to seem comic in the degree of its externality and irrelevance. A member of the London Literary Club, Anthony Chamier, better known as a statesman than as a litterateur, once asked Oliver Goldsmith "What he meant by *slow,* the last word in the first line of 'The Traveller,' 'Remote, unfriended, melancholy, slow.' Did he mean tardiness of locomotion? Goldsmith, who would say something without consideration, answered 'Yes.' " But Samuel Johnson happened to be present and cut in, "No, Sir; you do not mean tardiness of locomotion; you mean, that sluggishness of mind which comes upon a man in solitude." "Chamier believed then" that Johnson "had written the line as much as if he had seen" Johnson write it.[35] It is worth adding that one editor of Goldsmith, Austin Dobson, has observed, "It is quite possible that Goldsmith meant no more than he said." [36] But an earlier commentator, John Foster, says: "Who can doubt that he also meant slowness of motion? The first point of the picture is *that.* The poet is moving slowly, his tardiness of gait measuring the heaviness of heart, the pensive spirit, the melancholy of which it is the outward expression and sign." [37] The point of the present exposition is that Goldsmith, though undoubtedly in some sense closer to the generative intention of his own poem than the others, is not in virtue of that fact a better critic or interpreter. If Forster seems better than Dobson and better even than Johnson in this instance, the grounds of his judgment and ours must lie in the observable force and relevance of the word "slow" in the *context* of the first line of Goldsmith's pensive travelogue.

Mr. Beardsley has cited the nearly parallel instance of A. E. Housman's angry attempt to deny the irony at expense of state and church manifest in his poem for Queen Victoria's fiftieth anniversary. "Get you the sons your fathers got, And God will save the Queen." Here a statement made in retrospect and under provocation, a kind of profession of loyalty to a sovereign, stands in sharp contradiction not only to the cunning details of the poem in question but to the well-known skeptical and cynical cast of the poet's canon.

The two instances just adduced may seem a parody of the intentionalistic argument, but they are no more than a fair parody of that argument as often formulated. Simple, even extreme, examples have the advantage of revealing and clarifying principles.

A classic instance of an author's serious intention, antecedent to and simultaneous with the writing, yet doomed to defeat, is Chekhov's desire (revealed in his letters) to have his *Seagull* and *Cherry Orchard* produced as comedies — resulting only in Stanislavsky's successful and now well-established interpretation of them as tragedies — or at least as very cloudy "dramas." [38]

(4f) But let us now refine (or complicate) the argument a little with an example from the other end of a scale of explicitness in auctorial testimony — where no single explicit statement is adduced, but where the author's life and canon or some parts of them are urged as a surrounding and controlling context for the poem or some details of it. In our article of 1945, Mr. Beardsley and I wrote: "The meaning of words is the history of words, and the biography of an author, his use of a word, and the associations which the word has for *him,* are part of the word's history and meaning." But a critic who is habitually concerned with this kind of evidence, we added, will in the long run produce a far different sort of comment from that of the critic who is mainly concerned with the public linguistic and cultural elements of the poem.

We are now seeking a maximum or crucial instance where a poet's private or personal and habitual meaning (as inferred from external documents) clearly clashes with what he managed to realize in the public materials (linguistic and cultural) of his poem. Such instances are no doubt difficult to find, because poets by and large do manage to say what they mean. There is a sense in which, even when their words are "peculiar" or catachrestic, poets remain the "servants" of their language rather than its "masters." [39] In order to show a clear instance of the sort of conflict we are interested in, it may be necessary for the expositor himself to drive both sides of an interpretive difference, the intentionalistic and the nonintentionalistic — and thus perhaps to expose himself to the opportunism of the captious. But the following may serve at least to define the issue. The materials are well known, but not the interpretive problem as I shall urge it. William Blake wrote in a sketchbook:

An ancient Proverb

Remove away that blackning church
Remove away that marriage hearse
Remove away that man of blood
You'll quite remove the ancient curse [40]

These lines remained in the sketchbook, where they deserved to remain. They are a raw expression of certain soreheaded antinomian attitudes which are beyond doubt a part of Blake's biography at the period when he was writing the *Songs of Experience.* Blake also wrote in the same sketchbook a draft for his "song" *London,* which he worked over with much struggle, adding only as an afterthought, in several successive versions, the last black stanza.

I wander thro' each charter'd street,
Near where the charter'd Thames does flow,
And mark in every face I meet
Marks of weakness, marks of woe.

In every cry of every Man,
In every Infant's cry of fear,
In every voice, in every ban,
The mind-forg'd manacles I hear:

How the Chimney-sweeper's cry
Every black'ning Church appalls;
And the hapless Soldier's sigh
Runs in blood down Palace walls.

But most, thro' midnight streets I hear
How the youthful Harlot's curse
Blasts the new-born Infant's tear,
And blights with plagues the Marriage hearse.[41]

The concluding phrase repeats that of the second line of the *Ancient Proverb* and creates a crux on which I wish to focus. This dark city poem is about human "weakness" and "woe" as they may be observed in certain (uncertain) visual and auditory betrayals ("marks" and "cries") and in certain (uncertain) imputed human causes (charters, bans, mind-forged manacles). The word "ban" as it is used in the second stanza of the poem no doubt includes many kinds of legal or official yells, proclamations, summonses, prohibitions, curses — no doubt even marriage bans. At this point let us consult one of the best informed and most soberly reliable of recent Blake critics.

> The one thing needful in achieving this transformation [of the human spirit] is the removal of the mind-forged manacles of the institutional tyrannies — marriage, the church, and the king.
>
> "Every ban" . . . is a multiple clank of the awful trinity of king, priest, and marriage.
>
> It is the marriage hearse that breeds youthful (and thus potentially innocent) harlots, by creating the necessity for prostitution. If there were no marriage, there would be no ungratified desires, and therefore no harlots. Thus it is ultimately the marriage hearse itself and not the youthful harlot which breeds the pestilence that blights the marriage hearse.[42]

Mr. E. D. Hirsch, as I have said, is well informed about Blake and reliable, and I believe he gives us an accurate reading of a sort of intention which Blake probably did entertain, a phase at least of Blake's habitual mind as it may be supposed to stand at some distance behind the poem. Mr. Hirsch gives us a good and learned instance of the new cryptography in Blake reading. "If there were no marriage, there would be no ungratified desires, and therefore no harlots." One thing, however, which perhaps he does not notice, or perhaps does not worry about, is that these ideas are silly. (Why wouldn't there be *many* ungratified desires, as many at least as there were losers in stag combats, or wooers rejected, or pursuers eluded, or matings frustrated? and *many* harlots? and *many* whoremasters?) An admirer of Blake the poet might well be content to leave these ideas, if he could, on a back shelf in the doctrinaire part of Blake's mind. What if we actually do find them or manage to put them in the poem? Won't this make the poem silly? And, since interpretation and evaluation are at the very least closely related, won't we be in danger of reading the poem as a pretty bad poem? And isn't this poem, in fact, supposed to be a masterpiece, "one of the best city poems ever written"? Isn't it, in fact, a masterpiece? It will be worthwhile to look closely at the difference between the last stanza of the engraved poem *London* and the crude second line of *An Ancient Proverb,* which stayed in the sketchbook. Blake's struggle with *London* was in part a struggle to make the last line of the last stanza viable. The tough fact was that the word "marriage" in the history of English usage and culture was not the name of an evil. ("Let me not to the marriage of true minds admit impediments.") It was the name of a sacred institution and a first principle of stability for nearly every important value in a whole religiously and ethically oriented civilization and culture. The explosive force of the two violently juxtaposed terms at the end of the last line of *London* is a poetic fact. But this was not to be achieved by the easy way of simple supposition or assertion (though that may be a rationale which very well suits the aims of the biographical critic or cryptographer). Here the angry conscience of William Blake the doctrinaire prophet and activist clashed violently with the more tactful and skillful conscience of William Blake the poet, master and servant of the English language.[43] The latter conscience, apparently after a hard struggle, won and (perhaps without Blake's being fully aware of what happened — who knows?) saved him from engraving a poem with a lame, perhaps even silly and ruinous, last line. Let us imagine that some inquisitor of school curricula, reading Mr. Hirsch's gloss on *London,* were to file a protest against corrupting the minds of schoolchildren by the required study of this depraved poem. One sort of answer, from the defenders of the English curriculum, might be that it was good for children to hear all views and to be exposed to a liberal assault upon the mores in which home, church, and state were trying to educate them. But another answer that surely would not be long delayed would be to the effect that Blake's *London* in fact says no such thing. True, the English teacher or the school principal would say, the poem stresses charters and mind-forged manacles, but circumstances, real and symbolic (the cry of sweeps, the decay of churches, the blood of soldiers), are adduced to give specific topical color to the imputations. We are dealing with very concretely colored instances. And in the last stanza it is potently suggested that there is a very real and evil antecedent cause why the marriage bed turns to a hearse. For an initiate reading of the last stanza, consult the career of an eighteenth-century Londoner like James Boswell or Charles Hanbury Williams.

In sum, a critic who says that the "poem" means that "if there were no marriage, there would be no ungratified desires," ought to show that this

meaning actually operates in the poem or is generated by it — and is
not merely a concealed or balked idea entertained by the author as revolutionary person. I myself think the poem is better than that meaning,
and to judge from the contexts where the poem has often appeared and
from earlier critiques, it would seem that most readers have also thought
so.

> Yet even these [blackened churches and blood-stained palace walls]
> are less terrible than the hideous perversion of the fairest joy on earth,
> voiced in the midnight cry of the young harlot. Love itself and the
> beauty of marriage and birth are stained by this most cruel misery
> of all.[44]

I have set up this discussion of the poem as a frame of reference within
which a student may be able to see the direction in which his own mind
moves in search of evidence for the meaning and value of a poem. When
he can really see the difference between the directions and the results,
then let him decide.

Mr. Hirsch's method of reading *London* is not an isolated instance,
though his clarity in realizing what he is doing and his frankness in ad-
mitting it may be unusual. A new mode in historical studies, which I
would describe as a kind of attempted Vista-Vision intentionalism,
searches reasons for inferring an author's intention not only in the whole
canon of his own works and life record, early and late, but in motifs
selected from anywhere in the intellectual ambient of his era. Let me cite
a remarkable instance of this new mode in Paul de Man's essay of 1956,
"Keats and Hölderlin." [45] Here, with the pursuit of the poet as philoso-
pher-hero in full cry and the method of theme and analogy rampant, we
bring Keats's *Endymion* into line with his own later *Hyperion* and with
Hölderlin's novel *Hyperion* by the simple if eloquently disguised
method of arguing that throughout the poem Keats failed to say what
he meant. His interest in another kind of meaning was just too
much for him. Keats should have been writing, or he wished to be writing, about a very serious subject, the "eccentric road" of man's repetitive
search for recovery of "unity of being." But he wrote actually about love
(erotic love). "No wonder it becomes difficult to keep apart the passages
in which love is an actual experience, among others, from those in which
it is a symbol for something else. But only at the expense of this effort
[i.e., violence] can *Endymion* be given a thematic coherence which
Keats's *Hyperion* amply substantiates" (p. 36). We proceed to a reading
of *Endymion* which makes its point only at the expense of finding the
imagery "incongruous," "confusing," "bizarre," "stifled," "awkward" (pp.
37–38) — in short, utterly ineffectual (or inexpressive) and hence un-
poetic. This is Keats's *Endymion*. "A thing of beauty is a joy for ever."

Some of our critics have argued that Mr. Beardsley and I have examined the term "intention" in too restricted and too simply mentalistic a sense (intention in the mind of the artist); at the same time they have adduced statements by us that show that we do not in fact object to certain broader invocations of "intention" (in effect, "intention" as present and verifiable "intent" in works of art themselves). And they have praised other writers, or themselves, for taking the term "intention" in a broader (or at least other) and more "generous" sense.[46] One writer has pointed out that we selected an example which showed what we meant and tended to support our argument, and thus he considers our example "tendentious."[47] It is difficult to see how such arguments are better than obscurantist devices of one-upmanship. We took "intention" in a specific or limited sense, because it was just the difference between this sense and the broader (or other) sense that we believed to be often obscured in critical argument, with consequent concealed dilution of, or escape from, objective criticism. At the same time, we tried to make the idea of "intention" a focal point (and I still believe it was a well-chosen focal point) for a cluster of genetically oriented ideas (inspiration, expression, authenticity, sincerity, purpose, and the like). What might seem at first glance a merely verbal and ambiguous cluster turns out on acquaintance to be a dynamic pattern that is well treated with as much unity of vision as possible. It is my opinion that as criteria for criticism these ideas stand or fall together.

Both in our essay of 1945 and in our earlier dictionary article, Mr. Beardsley and I argued "that the design or intention of the author is neither available nor desirable as a standard for judging the success of a work of literary art." A recent writer on the same theme has accused Mr. Beardsley of having, in 1958, weakened this thesis by asserting merely that the "specific intention" of the artist outside the work is "practically never available" — thus, it would appear, making the question only empirical and forfeiting its "theoretical" and "philosophical" status.[48] What we meant in 1945, and what in effect I think we managed to say, was that the closest one could ever get to the artist's intending or meaning mind, outside his work, would be still short of his *effective* intention or *operative* mind as it appears in the work itself and can be read from the work. Such is the concrete and fully answerable character of words as aesthetic medium.[49] The intention outside the poem is always subject to the corroboration of the poem itself. No better evidence, in the nature of things, can be adduced than the poem itself. This observation seems to me less needed in meeting the directly evaluative form of the argument (see above, pp. 265–67) than in meeting the interpretive form which we have just been considering. The statement in our essay of 1945 should certainly have read: "The design or intention of the author is neither available nor desirable as a standard for judging either the meaning or the value of a work of literary art."

We have never said that the way of the objective critic could be smooth, easy, or perfect. Still we have tried to delineate one of the principles by which this critic will have to discipline his efforts unless he wishes to surrender to the flux, the gossip, the muddle and the "motley" for which philosophers like Dr. Cioffi, Professor Aldridge, and Mr. Cruttwell seem so earnestly to yearn.

It is true that verbal compositions do not subsist metaphysically, by or in themselves, as visual words on paper. The difference between "inside" the poem and "outside" the poem (to which some of our critics object [50]) is not like the difference between the printed words and the margin of the page. But neither are verbal compositions merely passing acts or moments of the human spirit, sounds heard then or now but not again. The words have their peculiar existence in their meaning, and that derives from and is determined by their context or their history. The study of poems in their public contexts of language and culture sees them in a spread-out and universalized relation to those contexts. It is a study of pattern and ideal and is the only study which is capable of discriminating between the cogently organized artistic structure (both concrete and universal) and the mere particularities of personal moments, accidental and nonce meanings. What kind of unity or entity is the most valid object of literary study? Roughly, there are three possible answers: the Age, the Author, the Work. Various kinds of interest in race, milieu, and moment (so familiar to academic literary criticism for more than two centuries) come under the first head. Studies of literary genre come here when they get out of hand, and also the more extreme instances of deference to the historical audience.[51] One kind of ultimate metaphysician in favor of the author may be found in Benedetto Croce, who hardly believes in the literary work at all, certainly not in works of any length, but sees the whole duty of the critic as the pursuit of the "poetical motive," the "poetic personality" which he can find anthologically here and there in writers like Goethe, Corneille, and Dante. A newer sort of canonical historicist, as we have seen, makes the idolatrous assumption that a given author's mind or vision during his whole career is necessarily a coherent whole or a dialectic development, as good an entity as, or better than, any one of his works. For the objective critic of literary works, an author has as much unity as he can demonstrate in any given work or in a part of a work. The whole for which the critic looks is the coherently expressive structure, large or small. The poet's canon and life are "the most essential part of the context of the poem" [52] only to the extent that the poet is talking to himself. The words which the poet writes in a given passage depend for their meaning in one sense on the personal context and the author's intention (his word as *parole*), but they depend also, in a sense more important to the critic, on the wider context of the language (his words as *langue*) and culture.[53] Otherwise they would never, here and now, there and then, make sense to anybody but the author himself. Authors characteristically graduate from earlier, naïve stages and write masterpieces. Characteristically also they write later weaker works. To appreciate *Lear* and *Hamlet* it is not necessary to take into account *A Comedy of Errors* or *Timon of Athens* (or such parts of the latter as Shakespeare wrote) or even *The Tempest*. The search for the author's generative intention as context of the poem is a search for a temporal moment which must, as the author and the poem live on, recede and ever recede into the forgotten, as all moments do. Poems, on this theory of their meaning, must always steadily grow less and less correctly known and knowable; they must dwindle in meaning and being toward a vanishing point. The best known and most valuable poem must be that written but a moment ago — and its best or only possible audience must be the author. But poems we know are not really like that. The most self-assured authors publish their works and hang upon public recognition. Shakespeare has more meaning and value now than he had in his own day. There is a sense in which even Homer, though we construe his language with pain and are not sure how many persons he was, has more meaning and is more valuable today than ever before.

RICHARD WILBUR
JOHN FREDERICK NIMS
JOHN BERRYMAN
ROBERT LOWELL

On Robert Lowell's "Skunk Hour"

ROBERT LOWELL

Skunk Hour

For Elizabeth Bishop

Nautilus Island's hermit
heiress still lives through winter in her Spartan cottage;
her sheep still graze above the sea.
Her son's a bishop. Her farmer
is first selectman in our village;
she's in her dotage.

Thirsting for
the hierarchic privacy
of Queen Victoria's century,
she buys up all
the eyesores facing her shore,
and lets them fall.

SOURCE: "On Robert Lowell's *Skunk Hour*" is from *The Contemporary Poet as Artist and Critic: Eight Symposia,* edited by Anthony Ostroff (Boston: Little, Brown and Company, 1964), pp. 81–110. Reprinted by permission of Richard Wilbur, John Frederick Nims, John Berryman, and, in the case of Robert Lowell's contribution, by permission of Farrar, Straus & Giroux. Robert Lowell's poem "Skunk Hour" is from the volume *Life Studies,* copyright 1958 by Robert Lowell, and reprinted with the permission of Farrar, Straus & Giroux and Faber and Faber Ltd.

The season's ill —
we've lost our summer millionaire,
who seemed to leap from an L. L. Bean
catalogue. His nine-knot yawl
was auctioned off to lobstermen.
A red fox stain covers Blue Hill.

And now our fairy
decorator brightens his shop for fall;
his fishnet's filled with orange cork,
orange, his cobbler's bench and awl;
there is no money in his work,
he'd rather marry.

One dark night,
my Tudor Ford climbed the hill's skull;
I watched for love-cars. Lights turned down,
they lay together, hull to hull,
where the graveyard shelves on the town. . . .
My mind's not right.

A car radio bleats,
"Love, O careless Love. . . ." I hear
my ill-spirit sob in each blood cell,
as if my hand were at its throat. . . .
I myself am hell;
nobody's here —

only skunks, that search
in the moonlight for a bite to eat.
They march on their soles up Main Street:
white stripes, moonstruck eyes' red fire
under the chalk-dry and spar spire
of the Trinitarian Church.

I stand on top
of our back steps and breathe the rich air —
a mother skunk with her column of kittens swills
   the garbage pail.
She jabs her wedge-head in a cup
of sour cream, drops her ostrich tail,
and will not scare.

RICHARD WILBUR

When I think of *Lord Weary's Castle,* I think of a prophetic poetry directed against what Yeats called "order and fixity." In the name of a revolutionary Christ, the poems attack — as Randall Jarrell once added it up — "everything that is closed, turned inward, incestuous, that blinds or binds: the Old Law, imperialism, militarism, capitalism, Calvinism, Authority, the Father, the 'Proper Bostonians,' the rich who will 'do everything for the poor except get off their backs.' " The focus of the book is on this century's New England, on the times and places which the poet has best known; but for what he feels Lowell finds historical cases and precedents as far back as imperial Rome, and analogies in many reaches of literature. The crammed, hopped-up lines make continual dazzling transitions between some particular scene or occasion and the whole field of Lowell's historical, religious, and literary awareness — transitions which seem free-associational because the logic is so compressed, and which might seem virtuoso if the prophetic urgency were not so strong.

Many of the poems build toward straight prophecy — "the world shall come to Walsingham," "The Lord survives the rainbow of His will" — and there are many others in which, though the poet or someone else may figure as a character, individual sensibility is less important and less examined than the world which the poem sees and denounces. Still, the direction which Lowell's poetry was to take may be found in such a modest, relaxed, and steadily viewed reminiscence as "Buttercups," or in the brilliant monologues of "Between the Porch and the Altar." The direction, of course, is from the prophetic to the dramatic, from the world to the individual who suffers it.

The dramatic verse of *The Mills of the Kavanaughs* retains, generally speaking, the crammed and racing character of the first book; but now the quick jumps, the surprising collocations, the wrenched rhythms, the sixteen-line sentences full of avalanching particulars, are justified not by prophetic fervor but by the states of mind which Lowell allots to his characters. Dwellers in the world which *Lord Weary's Castle* described, they speak out of rumination, or revery or dream, or even from the edge of death by oven-gas; they are authorized to think with an often vertiginous subjectivity.

"Skunk Hour" is another sort of dramatic poem altogether. It is one of a series, largely reminiscent, in which the poet sheds all his personae (including the prophetic) and speaks of and for himself. Paradoxically, this permits him to sound impersonal:

Nautilus Island's hermit
heiress still lives through winter in her Spartan cottage;

her sheep still graze above the sea.
Her son's a bishop. Her farmer
is first selectman in our village;
she's in her dotage.

The lines are short, the rhymes off-hand, the language specific and con-versational, the tone level. We are given a certain amount of verifiable gossip in simple declarative sentences, and it seems, so far, as if the poet were speaking directly and objectively to the reader. Not until halfway through the poem will we know for sure that this is selected informa-tion, evidence for something, and that we are eavesdropping on the thoughts of a troubled man alone in his house at night. Hence we make little, initially, of the bishop and selectman, and if we derive any sus-picion of attitude it is from two quiet ironies. The first, emphasized by a halting *enjambement,* is "hermit / heiress"; we expect a hermit to be mas-culine and poor, and so the conjunction is amusing, whether as deroga-tion or mere flippancy we don't yet know. The second irony lies in the line "she's in her dotage," which repeats the grammatical structure of the previous declarations but affects us as an abrupt let-down. The heiress and her sheep are "still" there as always, she "still" has a finger in church and state, but the vital persistence of her regime is, after all, illusory.

The form of action which her dotage takes, as described in stanza II, is wonderfully extravagant, and the neutrality of the language inclines us to see her as deliciously eccentric, an Unforgettable Character. Per-haps one also reflects that her behavior is anti-social, selfish, regressive, and life-denying, but the poem does not as yet encourage such judgments, and they seem illicitly overserious.

The humor grows more emphatic in stanza III, at the expense of a de-ceased conspicuous-consumer who looked, when alive, like a sporting-goods dummy, and whose death is a blow to the summer resort's economy and distinction. At the same time, we are half aware in this stanza of accumulating ideas of death and decay: to the addled heiress and the collapsing eyesores we must add the dead millionaire, the passing of summer, and the decline of a fishing port into a vacation town.

This last idea carries over into the next stanza, where fishnet, bench and awl are disnatured and trivialized by a homosexual decorator, who represents the town's new economy. (The motifs of death and decline will continue in the likening of cars to boats, in "hill's skull," "graveyard," "shelves," and the "chalk-dry and spar spire" of the church.) The last two lines of the stanza are mimicry: there's no money in his work, the decor-ator complains; marriage would be work, too, but at least one might be supported.

At this point the poem suddenly reveals itself as dramatic monologue, and its first half becomes in retrospect a morose private meditation on a selfish, loveless, and diseased environment. The thought of the decorator's sexual inversion makes the poet remember the prurient yearning with which, "one dark night," he spied on love-cars from his Tudor (two-door) Ford. This recollection, which argues against his mental balance, upsets him, and a car radio, passing his house in the night, moves him by a fragment of "Careless Love" to a paroxysm of balked desire. One thinks of a line from "After the Surprising Conversions" — "a thirst / For loving shook him like a snake."

"I myself am hell" (the one literary echo in the poem) is what Milton's Satan says "in prospect of Eden," and Lowell surely means us to think not only of Satan's imprisonment in self but also of his envious spying in the scenes of Book IV which immediately follow. Does the quotation aim to suggest that the poet's emotional imbalance makes him see the world falsely, that like Satan he "sees undelighted all delight?" I think not; the first four stanzas have seemed not a prophetic vision but a dour review of certain facts, and if these facts imply a diseased society — precisely the one summarized by Jarrell — their interpretation seems as much ours as the poet's. The diseased world is really there; the point is that the poet shares in a measure its addlement, "illness," deadness and aloneness, and cannot shuck off the self which the world has thrust upon him.

"Skunk Hour" has a pattern roughly similar to that of "In the Attic," the first section of Lowell's early poem "The First Sunday in Lent." "In the Attic" moves from a glimpse of the present world to a recollection which establishes the poet's complicity in that world, and finally to a prayer for man's regeneration. What replaces the prayer, in the structure of the later poem, is the poet's contemplation of a mother skunk and her kittens. What do the skunks stand for? Are they the equivalent of a prayer? They ramble appetitively at night, like the poet of "Skunk Hour" or like the husband of " 'To Speak of Woe That Is in Marriage,' " who "hits the streets to cruise for prostitutes." Their "moonstruck eyes' red fire" is wild and passionate. Yet their passionate lives are simple, as the "column of kittens" suggests; their eyes are not "homicidal," like those of the husband in "Man and Wife"; their wildness is natural and sane, and need not be "tamed by *Miltown*." To the poet, as he "breathes the rich air" on the back stoop, they stand for stubborn, unabashed livingness, and for his own refusal (in the teeth of society and of his own jangled nature) to cease desiring a world of vitality, freedom, and love.

Some have said that the poems of *Life Studies* are dilute and artless by comparison to Lowell's earlier work. They look so only if one has been so conditioned by the latter as to be irresponsive to new techniques from the same poet. "Skunk Hour" does not afford the reader a kinetic jag, does not dazzle him with its transitions, does not disarm his unbelief by a passionate violence. It cannot be read passively. As with the poems of Elizabeth Bishop (to whom "Skunk Hour" is dedicated), one must participate in the lines, discovering their implicit emotional value and generalizing from their relatively dead-pan specificities. It is up to the reader to connect "my ill-spirit" with "The season's ill," and to construe the relationship of "dotage" and "moonstruck" to "My mind's not right." There is art enough, and density enough, in "Skunk Hour"; it is a more flexible poetry than Lowell has ever written; it admits a greater range of feeling, and in particular it liberates the author's excellent sense of humor. With no disrespect to *Lord Weary's Castle,* I should argue that the later poetry, with its objectivity and its demand for collaborative reading, renders Lowell's vision of the world more probable and more readily shared. In any case, "Skunk Hour" is an extremely fine poem.

JOHN FREDERICK NIMS

A word about form: a regular basis of rhythm and rhyme gives us not something to conform to, but something to rebel against when rebellion is meaningful. In "free verse" the revolt is over before the poem begins — hence the sameness of so much of it. "Skunk Hour" has a solid framework, though the poet is continually quarreling with it, wrenching it out of shape for purposes of his own. His 6-line stanza has two pulsations of the meter in lines 1 and 6, four elsewhere. The rhythm is often "sprung"; the poet counts only his strongest syllables, sometimes disregarding conventional stresses. The syntactical unit may substitute for the foot, as in the long line of VIII, in which the four units are subject, prepositional phrase, verb, and object. Or the quaternion we soon come to feel in lines 2–4 may make us stress syllables rhetorically important ("shé búys úp áll" of II). In the norm-stanza, on which the poet rings many changes, lines 1 and 6 rhyme — this happens half the time. When it happens, the other rhymes form, typically, an internal quatrain, as in IV, V, and possibly III. (This A-BCBC-A opened many of the longer stanzas in *Lord Weary's Castle.*) Rhymes and off-rhymes run from stanza to stanza: "all" — "fall" — "yawl" — "skull" — "cell" — "pail," etc. One might well begin his reading with the cadence of IV, V, or VII in his head; this is the metrical norm varied in other stanzas. Since Mr. Lowell does not label his images, but sets them forth for us to interpret (not arbitrarily; the clues are definite), his poem will probably require many readings. The first four stanzas present three characters taken as typical of a time and place; two stanzas describe the emotional crisis to which the protagonist is brought by this and other evidence; two more stanzas resolve the crisis with the little drama of the skunks.

STANZA I

Our first character: an old lady of wealth who chooses to live alone, not without hardship. Both her son and her tenant are filling conventionally successful roles. Our "heiress" lives in the past; her sheep suggest the agricultural economy of days long gone by. Diction is plain, almost without adjectives. The heavy genitive place-name before its noun is rugged; conventional English calls for something like "the lonely heiress of Nautilus Island." The words "hermit heiress" go together only with strain. Not quite oxymoron — but " 'words that surprise each other' on finding themselves together." Looking as if they began with the same sound, whereas they do not, the words are something of a tongue-twister. In the lack of parallelism in the last two sentences, the same kind of ungainliness: it would seem that the period after "bishop" and the semicolon after "village" should change places. But, as things are, the blunt last line comes out more strongly. There is little exploitation of sound either as structural or as expressive, although five thin *i*'s in line 2 dramatize persistence. With "cottage," two straggling off-rhymes; "her farmer" has sounds in common with "hermit," a grotesque rhyme; "sea" dangles unrhymed until the following stanza. With its uncertainties, this is the least tightly organized of the stanzas, as if the poem had not yet found its focus.

STANZA II

Two stanzas for this portrait, whereas the wry little thumbnail sketches that follow are done in one apiece. A few loose screws, something ramshackle — not out of place in this description of dotage. Though her cottage is Spartan, the lady "thirsts": her wasteful and self-indulgent mania squanders half the stanza on the participle and its object. Much of the emphasis comes out in the play on form: the rhyme "privacy" — "century" is jingling and false: this kind of privacy does not go with this century. Or try reading "most of" instead of "all" — far more than a rhyme is lost. The 4-beat "she buys up all" insists grimly on her fanaticism, while the 2-beat last line, apparently paced the same, yet metrically twice as fast, has a runaway speed in comparison ("shé búys úp áll . . . and léts them fáll").

The aptness of observation here is confirmed by the matriarch's resembling a synthesis of three characters in Sarah Orne Jewett's Maine classic of 1896, *The Country of the Pointed Firs.* (1) Joanna Todd: "a sort of nun or hermit person lived out there for years all alone on Shellheap Island . . . she was a well-off woman . . . there was something mediaeval in [her] behavior. . . . I called her a great fool . . . some

other minister would have been a great help to her — one that preached
self-forgetfulness and doin' for others to cure our own ills. . . . 'Tis
like bad eyesight, the mind of such a person: if your eyes don't see right
there may be a remedy, but there's no kind of glasses to remedy the mind.
. . ." (2) Esther, the Dunnet shepherdess, who had given up school-
teaching years before to take care of sheep. "Esther had always been
laughed at for her belief in sheepraising when one by one their neighbors
were giving up their flocks. . . ." (3) Abby Martin, the "Queen's
Twin," who built her life around coincidental resemblances to Queen
Victoria. "If you want to hear about Queen Victoria, why Mis' Abby
Martin'll tell you everything."

STANZA III

The virtues of the old independent are positive ones. The summer millionaire, however, is all façade. She belonged to and endured in
the difficult country; he is a fair-weather friend of vacationland, an out-
sider in native costume, too new, too picturesque. L. L. Bean, Inc., the
Maine mail-order house, specializes in camping equipment, clothes for
sportsmen, etc. The millionaire would be flaunting items like their Men's
Sueded Country Jacket, "made of imported Holland Suede . . . buffed
to a rich nap similar to sueded leather . . . Two slash pockets concealed
in front pleats . . ." or their Moccasin Chukka, "hand burnished to a
deep ivory glow." The three accented long *e*'s of the third line project
him before us in all of his compulsive athleticism — a failure both as man
and millionaire. Financial straits are implied by the auctioning off of his
fast yawl — though the way "nine-knot yawl" wallows in its sluggish
sounds suggests that the "millionaire" only claimed it could make nine
knots an hour. Line 6 sprawls over the two accents we have come to
expect: "a red fox stain covers Blue Hill." A wild stain, fox-red, or like
the stains that "fox" old paper, or like the rash of illness — though probably just the autumn coloring on a hill whose name evokes more tranquil
tones. (Blue Hill is also a town in Maine.) Sarah Orne Jewett had dwelt
on the early autumn color: in September "the frost-bitten grass grew
close about [the house] like brown fur. . . ." The stain is symbolic, another symptom that shows "The season's ill" — a statement not unlike
Hamlet's "The time is out of joint." "Ill" — a languishing half-rhyme with
"fall" above it — means more than "sick": a certain archaic strangeness
shifts it from the physical to the psychical, the moral. Again Hamlet:
"Thou wouldst not think how ill all's here about my heart." And the fox:
what more appropriate totem for a figure of fraudulence? The rhyme: is
"yawl" a far-off rhyme with the middle of "millionaire"? Or with "fall" in

other stanzas? "Millionaire" then is an off-rhyme with "shore" above or "fairy" below.

STANZA IV

Mounting evidence that the season is ill. In I and II, a real, if limited and withered, excellence; in III, pretense of excellence; now in IV, a corruption of human nature itself. A false man who falsifies what he deals in; who turns the gear of honest labor into objets d'art. The fisherman's corks, garish with paint, hang in their fishnet; the cobbler's bench, complete with useless awl and given an unnaturally high finish, will serve as coffee table or "conversation-piece" for some collector. In III, the pleasure craft had been degraded by being put into service. Here the reverse: the workman's tools have become gewgaws. But the decorator's work is unfruitful in another sense too: it doesn't pay. Having falsified objects, he is willing to falsify his nature by selling himself into a marriage he can scarcely have the heart for.

This stanza, with its ironic feminine rhyme in lines 1 and 6, is the most regular yet. Rhythm, at first uncertain, moves here with assurance, with even a derisive sing-song in its regularity. A sense too of excessive neatness, emphasized by the rhetorical word-order of line 4. After this line the tone falls back into plainness, in the last line particularly, with its flat *a*'s after the richer *or*'s and *aw*'s that preceded. Again the stanza is mispunctuated: lines 3 and 5 should close with semicolons. But expressiveness overrides convention: the running together of 3 and 4 dramatizes the orange jumble, the silly muchness; the comma after 5 lets the last line come blurted out.

The poet has given us a threefold classification of twisted souls: the self-centered isolation of the old woman, destructive rather than charitable; the hollowness or fraud of the millionaire; and now, and in V and VI, disordered love. Fanciers of literary parallels will recall that the most famous cataloguer of transgressions has also given us threefold divisions in his *Inferno* and *Purgatorio*. Since "Skunk Hour" is, among other things, a study of the Puritan syndrome, we may wonder if the modern poet has not deliberately inverted Dante's hierarchy of evil — assuming there is, as there should be, an order of climax here. Would not Dante have found the perverted love of the homosexual (cf. Brunetto Latini) and the excessive love of the carnal (cf. Paolo and Francesca) less censurable than selfishness, hollowness, and fraud? It is Puritanical to find the sins of the body more heinous than those of the spirit — hence the careless lovers, whose plight in hell moved Dante to a very distraction of pity and sympathy (*"pietà mi giunse, e fui quasi smarrito"*), moves the present beholder to his murderous and suicidal range (in VI).

STANZA V

In V and VI, an emotional crisis of the protagonist, prepared by the data of I–IV and now precipitated by his recognition that the illness is not only in others or in the season, but in himself. Up to now, he has been merely the observer, fairly dispassionate, through whose eyes and whose voice we have been shown the world of the poem. Abruptly, he becomes not only perceiver but participant; he implicates himself as deeply as he does the millionaire or the decorator. It would be wrong to think of this "I" as the poet speaking; what speaks is as much a character as the others. Or even more, for this is the character the poem is really about; its action is the drama within the soul of a Puritan Everyman who is combined censor and voyeur, the God and Satan of his world.

The action moves briefly into a past tense, but its urgency soon swings it back to the vivid present. The time reference, which prepares us for a greater immediacy of experience, is also a curious echo. One of the great poems of western culture begins *"en una noche oscura . . . ,"* "One dark night. . . ." How consciously the American poet echoes the *Noche oscura* of St. John of the Cross we cannot be sure; but we do know that the Muse of the Unconscious — perhaps the only Muse — caught the echo and permitted it. St. John's poem, also in the first person, describes how a girl (*el alma*) steals forth one dark night for an ecstatic meeting with her Lover:

> I gave all I own,
> gave all, in air from the cedars softly blown.
>
> All, in wind from the wall
> as my hand in his hair moved lovingly at play.
> He let soft fingers fall
> and I swooned dead away
> wounded: all senses in oblivion lay.
>
> Quite out of self suspended —
> my forehead on the lover's own reclined.
> And that way the world ended
> with all my cares untwined
> among the lilies falling and out of mind.[1]

Such sweetness of passionate self-surrender is what the Puritan on his island psyche can never manage; his own dark night is a ghastly burlesque of the Spanish adventure, though he too finds release and reconciliation, among the skunks if not among the lilies.

The protagonist, with his morbid curiosity, goes forth. Fascinated by a carefree indulgence he despises, he rages at it and at himself. The manufacturer's name for his "two-door" model identifies the driver ironically with the pageantries of the past. His car goes up the "hill's skull" — again the misplaced genitive is a deliberate ugliness. Hill . . . Skull . . . as the words rub together we realize that the most famous hill in our tradition was named for a skull: Calvary, from the Latin *calvaria*. The experience, then, is some kind of emotional crucifixion for the speaker? He goes as voyeur, but his ambivalence refuses to let him contemplate, even in imagination, the lovers. His attention instead is displaced to the "love-cars" which "lay together." Love is debased to the mechanical, as in the seduction scene of *The Waste Land*. Headlights are dimmed, in token of light rejected. The cars are seen as ships — the ship image is already, through the yawl, a something bought and sold. "Hull to hull" sustains the ship imagery, contrasts "skull" and "hull" (car or flesh), and also suggests "hull" as husk, a container that contains only hollowness. Our lovers' lane is near a cemetery, another place of skulls. Moralists are fond of mingling images of the body alive and pleasure-loving, with the body dead and decayed, as in Hamlet's words to the skull: "Now get you to my lady's chamber, and tell her, let her paint an inch thick, to this favor she must come." The last line of the stanza again goes off on an abrupt tangent. The mind, attracted by what it condemns, seeing the careless lovers in terms of coupling mechanisms, is no less corrupt than what it contemplates. Yet it is still sound enough to perceive and agonize over a dilemma from which the only escapes are madness and suicide. "My mind's not right." For most of us, the line will carry Shakespearean reminiscences, perhaps of Lear's "I fear I am not in my perfect mind." But more particularly echoes of Hamlet, whose derangement also had its origin in sexual shock: he saw his very home "a couch for luxury and damnèd incest." The madness of young Ophelia and old Lear was sex-obsessed.

Technically, two things are interesting. The most unsettling experiences of the poem are expressed in mellifluous liquids. As if the attraction, forbidden disclosure in the imagery, had come out caressingly in the sound. And nowhere before has there been such recourse to metaphor. Indeed, there has been almost none. Successful metaphor, like an electrical discharge, comes from emotions at high enough tension to leap considerable distances — as they do in this stanza.

STANZA VI

"Careless Love," which the goatlike metal voice is bleating, is about seduction, pregnancy, desertion, violence:

When I wore my apron low . . .
You'd follow me through rain and snow.

Now my apron strings won't pin . . .
You pass my door and won't come in.

> Now you see what careless love will do . . .
> Make you kill yourself and your sweetheart too.

A theme-song and dirge, then, for the careless lovers in their cars. (The capital *L* of "Love," if deliberate, would seem to imply a deity heedless if not evil — deeper reasons for dismay.) Upon hearing the song, the protagonist's mind projects a schizophrenic monster of its own: an ill-spirit in the flesh itself. The hyphen hypostatizes the illness, makes it a morbid presence to be exorcised, by killing if necessary. This waking nightmare has brought the protagonist to the verge of murderous violence — his awareness of this, his endurance in that awareness, is his hell. The phantom sobbing in the blood is not mere ghost-lore; it has a basis if we remember that "spirit" means breath and that the red blood-cells carry breath. It is this breath, this life, which the sufferer, in his self-hatred, imagines himself strangling. "I myself am hell" — these words are spoken by Lucifer in Book IV of *Paradise Lost* as he makes his way toward the Garden of Eden for his "dire attempt" on Adam and Eve:

> "Mee miserable! which way shall I flie
> Infinite wrauth, and infinite despaire?
> Which way I flie is Hell; my self am Hell;
> And in the lowest deep a lower deep
> Still threatening to devour me op'ns wide,
> To which the Hell I suffer seems a Heav'n."

"In the lowest deep a lower deep" — the escape which Hamlet pondered in his torment. "Nobody's here" is the wish-fulfillment of the self-loathing, self-destructive soul — but here too we may have the Muse of the Unconscious at work. If V opens with an echo of the *Noche oscura,* VI may close with another echo. The fourth stanza of St. John's poem ends: *"en parte donde nadie parecía"* — "where nobody appeared." Not only the idea but its positioning hint a relationship. In the *Noche oscura* the emptiness is only apparent:

> where there waited one
> I knew — how well I knew! —
> in a place where no one was in view.

In "Skunk Hour" there is a saving presence also, not so much the little animals who now appear as a spirit of resolution in the suffering soul itself.

Broken syntax expresses the distraction. The 2-beat norm hurries the first line: "a car rádio bleáts" — the words come with a silly insistence after the grave line preceding them. They come also with a dissonant half-rhyme — followed by a further raucous dissonance in "throat." The emptiness of the last line gapes in the vacuous "hear" — "here." The only rhyme that rings out in this turbulence is "hell" in the strongly accented fifth line, a rhyme clinging also to the *el* of "myself."

STANZA VII

The only stanza run on from the preceding one without a sentence break is paradoxically the only one that opens with a sense of time elapsed. The observer has moved onward, progressed in place and state of mind. There must have been a tormented struggle between the distraction of V and VI and the health and quiet breathing of VII and VIII. We are not shown this conflict, but we know where the victory lies: the destructive urges have been resisted; the victor, calm of mind as clear of eye, is looking outward at the mother skunk and her column of kittens. Actual skunks, and yet also a little string of metaphors moving down Main Street in the moonlight, which for more than one poet has meant the enchantment of the imagination. The crisis of the poem was on a dark night; the love cars had refused illumination; Blue Hill had been obscured. But the skunks appear in the softest and dreamiest of natural light — light with its many connotations of hopes and truthfulness. Unlike the avid heiress, the millionaire living his lie, the decorator perverting what he touches, and the lewd pursuing the lewd, the skunks are engaged in a natural quest: the search for "a bite to eat." Most of the human types have been somehow furtive; the skunks go about their business openly, "determination's totem" and "noble little warriors," as Marianne Moore described them in "The Wood-Weasel." Their vigor stiffens the verse: this is the only stanza with internal couplets, aligned as smartly as the marching columns. They march on their "soles" — at least one classic dream-interpretation has "sole" for "soul"; poets, like dreamers and writers of hieroglyphs, respect the pun. A trochee in the iambic movement brings the weight down heavily on "soles." The next line is a series of solemn spondees with four long *i*'s, our most vibrant vowel sound, brightening the white stripes and lighting the eyes with fire, as if they were inspired by the mystical moon. In contrast with this natural vitality, the church has only its "chalk-dry and spar spire," chalky as death, or the dusty controversies that divided Trinitarian from Unitarian. The thinness of the spire and of the doctrine it stands for is mocked by the harsh jingle of "spar spire."

STANZA VIII

The image of the mother skunk and her young contrasts with the sterile human types seen earlier. Nonchalant but earnest, oblivious of all but her mission and her young — so she appears in the longest line of the poem, itself indifferent to the obligations of meter. The young skunks move in a "column," with almost institutional stability. But a real stability, unlike that of the "spar spire." Obstinate virtue, indomitable confidence — these come out of the final image; the skunk, disdainful of attack, drops her menacing tail, airily beautiful as ostrich plumes. Her solidity bulks in the muscular non-Latin vocabulary: jab, wedge, sour, scare. Some interpreters might relate the wedge and cup of these lines to the Lance and Cup of Grail legends — images that Miss Weston says are "sex symbols . . . originally 'Fertility' emblems . . . employed in a ritual designed to promote, or restore, the activity of the reproductive energies of Nature." We cannot insist this is "meant," but we are not bumbling in wrong directions if it occurs to us, for the "wood-pussy," sturdy head in the garbage, is certainly a rank, rich, fertile, unashamed physical essence, and, as such, enjoys the benediction of the moon. Meanwhile, the protagonist stands on top of his steps, breathing the rich air. The struggle he has been through, which may well have taken longer than one symbolic night, had brought him to some verge of turbulence. But, in the drama we did not see, he has mastered the vertigo, and (again using a dream-technique) sees himself standing "on top of" something arduous. In VI, his spirit was threatened with strangulation; now it is breathing easily an air rich with the musk of an animality not lewd and furtive, like that which so unsettled him, but frank and confident. Release is felt even in structure: after the strain and constriction of earlier stanzas, the last two move fluently to the close.

But what, basically, is the poem saying? Surely nothing so banal as that people are corrupt but skunks are noble. The greater the poet — one might hazard — the less interested in animals: the great poets, after all, are out for bigger game. No, the poem is not about skunks; it is a human drama, a sort of *Hamlet* or *Lear* in miniature. Shakespeare's heroes were shaken by a disillusionment that plunged them into a nausea of world-weariness, world-abhorrence. Each agonized to a kind of serenity, a kind of reconciliation, if only at the moment of death. "Skunk Hour" is about a similar ordeal. The protagonist, already disillusioned with humanity, finds himself, one dark night, involved in deepest horror. Somehow — and how could we be shown the process in so short a poem? — he struggles through. A strange sort of reconciliation, this amid the skunks — but a restoration of balance none the less. In the struggle he seems to have discovered that if pretense and meanness exist, so do candor and courage; he comes down from his hill's skull prepared to admit these qualities, looking for an image for them, as we do in dreams. And if, by a ruse of displacement, he acknowledges them in animals rather than in man, it may be because the earlier aloofness, the earlier suspicion, have not had time to wear away. One does not have to look far to find a man as brave as skunks are, a mother as maternal as they. It is certain qualities (they are human qualities) he has come to respect and is looking for; otherwise no number of wood creatures could have dragged him from his slough of despond. Whatever is received, say the Schoolmen, is received according to the manner of the receiver. More than that: we see what we seek to see. Without his change of mood, the protagonist might have seen the skunks quite differently:

> Flat-footed skunks that prowl
> In the lewd moon to stuff their gut;
> Up Main Street, stinking-proud, they strut,
> Little eyes reddened, jailbird stripes . . .

Just as, with more compassion, he might have seen a pathetic courage in the failing millionaire (as E. A. Robinson did in that type) or in the decorator with his desperate problem. But the skunks have served their purpose in triggering the release he was ready for.

The little animals have close relatives in modern poetry: the *"dos lindas comadrejas"* (two pretty weasels) in one of the greatest poems of the century, Antonio Machado's *"A orillas del Duero."* Largely in terms of an allegorized landscape, Machado had been deploring the degeneracy and inertia of his homeland, when suddenly the two weasels (which in my translation turn to mink) appear — lively, interested, and committed children of the earth. Church bells (from a spar spire) are heard and

> Now gather for their rosary-beads the grannies all in black —.
> Suddenly two lissom mink glitter from the rock,
> Look at me with jewel eyes, flash away, and come
> Back at once, so interested! [2]

Machado's poem ends less reassuringly than ours, because his eye turns sadly back to a darkening country and an empty road, whereas the final image in "Skunk Hour" is one of sturdy triumph.

JOHN BERRYMAN

Despondency and Madness

A title opaque and violent. Since it throws, at once, little or no light on the poem, we inquire whether the poem throws any light on it, and are under way. Our occasion is the approach of a crisis of mental disorder for the "I" of the poem — presumably one leading to the hospitalization, or hospitalizations, spoken of elsewhere in the volume, *Life Studies,* where it stands last. Mr. Lowell's recent poems, many of them, are as personal, autobiographical, as his earlier poems were hieratic; and it is certain that we are not dealing here purely with invention and symbol. One thing critics not themselves writers of poetry occasionally forget is that poetry is composed by actual human beings, and tracts of it are very closely about them. When Shakespeare wrote "Two loves I have," reader, he was *not kidding.*

Back to the title then. The Hour of the Skunk, I suppose, would be one of the most unprepossessing times of the day, far less livable than the Hour of the Bear, say, or the (Chinese) Month of the Dog. Noon is held a luckless time for Sikhs. Up and down India, when anything goes wrong for a Sikh near midday, all nearby Hindus and Moslems have a ball. Skunk hour: the poet's Sikh noon. The skunk is a small, attractive black-and-white creature, affectionate and loyal when tamed I believe, but it suffers (or rather it does *not* suffer, being an animal) from a bad reputation, owing to its capacity for stinking. (The poet, in the identification, knows; and suffers.) Cornered, it makes the cornerer wish he hadn't. Painful, in symbolization, is the fact that its sting, so to speak, can be drawn, its power of defending itelf removed — as the poet can be made helpless by what is part of his strength: his strangeness, mental and emotional; the helplessness of a man afraid of going mad is the analogue. The skunk is an outcast; this is the basis of the metaphor, and how a mental patient feels. I hate to call the associations complex, but they are, and with a poet so daring or offhand that he once arranged a masterly elegy around his literal translation of the gambling expression *"Rien ne va plus,"* we must take it. The skunk, its little weakness or weapon apart, is charming; cheer-up. But nobody likes; paranoia. It is not what it seems: the reality belies the benign appearance — as with the statesman Forrestal who supervises American industry's brawl-for-contracts with scrupulous honor and kills himself, or the poet, brilliant, famous, appearing, who goes off his rocker. We like, in mature professional life, to know who we are; which may be on the point of becoming out of the question for the "I" of the poem.

If the topic seems to anyone theatrical, may I mention suicides: two of the three or four most important early Soviet poets, Essenin and Mayakovsky; while Hart Crane and Vachel Lindsay (and for that matter Sara Teasdale — writing really well toward the end) who destroyed themselves here were not our worst poets. Poets in odd ages have killed themselves or gone mad, Poe and Dylan Thomas as clearly as Swift, Chatterton, Smart, Beddoes, and many have written about it from inside and outside, from Cowper's posthumous "The Castaway" to Miss Bishop's wonderful "Visits to St. Elizabeth's" and Rilke's *"Das Lied des Idioten."* It is better not to feel so strongly:

> We poets in our youth begin in gladness,
> But thereof comes in the end despondency and madness.

Wordsworth once said that if he had written what he most deeply felt no reader could have borne it, Coleridge that he gave up original poetical composition (but the fine, bleak "Work Without Hope" is late) because he was unable to bear it. One poem does not edge into the terror but starts there and stays there: Jon Silkin's "Death of a Son." This you will find in the Hall-Simpson paperback anthology of recent verse, and it is as brave, and harrowing, as one might think a piece could be. But Lowell's subject is different from all these others'.

His target is the dreadful aura — in epileptic analogy — the coming-on, handled by Hölderlin in *"Hälfte des Lebens,"* which may be the deepest European poem on this unusual theme. You feel you're going too fast, spinning out of control; or too slow; there appears a rift, which will widen. You feel *too* good, or too bad. Difficult subject. Perhaps there is a quarter-inch of mordant humor, by the way, very like this author, in the title: dogs have their day, even the skunk has an hour, characteristic. An inverted celebration. Take the poet's arrangements in three parts, and one critical problem will be to determine how they culminate in the halluci-natory intensity of the seventh stanza. We have the opening stanzas (*praeparatio*), then statement — understatement. ("My mind's not right"), then the skunks. One of the poem's desperate points is their *cyclical* approach, each night; as episodes of mental illness are feared to recur. The skunks too, can we wonder, replace him (they will survive as he goes or is taken off) as well as figure him. But we're getting too far ahead.

Very good poem, incidentally, and gets better, explored. Perhaps one of his absolutely best; early to say. Maybe the Faustus allusion is over-drawn. Who cares to hand grades to a writer who could first *make* the Ovid stanza in "Beyond the Alps" (I believed it appeared in the *Kenyon* version) and then delete it? The reader may not have come on this, so I put it in evidence.

> I thought of Ovid, for in Caesar's eyes,
> That Tomcat had the number of the Beast.
> Where the young Turks are facing the red east
> And the twice-stormed Crimean spit, he cries:
> "Rome asked for poets. At her beck and call,
> Came Lucan, Tacitus and Juvenal,
> The black republicans who tore the teats

And bowels of the mother wolf to bits.
Beneath a psychopath's divining rod,
Deserts interred the Caesar-salvaged bog.
Imperial Tiber, O my yellow Dog,
Black earth by the Black Roman Sea, I lie
With the boy-crazy daughter of the God,
Il duce Augusto. I shall never die."

Mr. Lowell once told the present writer that the stanza took him a hundred hours; it is worth every second of the time, and may be read, despite its author, for as long as things not formular are read.

I hear the first four stanzas of "Skunk Hour" as a unit. Grandiose figures — the senile aristocrat, the summer millionaire — from the past, outworn, gone, or not gone: the theme of the first stanza is Survival — but survival how? — doting; anti-gainfully employed (second stanza, and the "eyesores" "let fall" are the first prefigurings of the paranoid aspect of the skunk-symbol), living in the past. Relevance? — for re-reading (all poems are built of course for re-reading, but this more than most): the poet is afraid of outliving himself, going away, like Hölderlin, Swift, Maupassant. Destructive second stanza, but queerly abstract and arbitrary, anachronistic; as for "privacy," in the modern world (so the underground thought goes) unattainable, hospital life is unspeakably public — one is available without will to doctors, nurses, even (usually) other patients. The sheep have things easy, so to speak, and the radio "bleats" to the untense satisfied lovers in stanza VI; no human responsibilities, any more than the skunks are to have. The poem makes use of the animal-morality tradition without quite belonging to it. "Spartan" I reserve. "Hermit" and "winter" make nearly standard associations with madness.

Note that we have first a true aristocrat, irresponsible ("heiress" — mental illness can be inherited), then a pure money-figure; an ominous declension. (L. L. Bean: I haven't seen a catalogue for years, some boys at my school in Connecticut had them; they were beyond Sears Roebuck and even Alex Taylor for fascination — compare Abercrombie & Fitch, if they put out a catalogue.) Somebody rooted, but off; somebody rootless, gone. Blue Hill I take to be Blue Hill, Maine, where I never saw foxes but don't doubt that they flourish. This is the poem's hard line. "A red fox stain covers Blue Hill." Even the syntax is ambiguous — the stain may be red, or it may merely be that foxes stain with their numbers (a plague to farmers) Blue Hill. Is the sportsman accused of having shot foxes? — but this seems sentimental and improbable; or is the fox population said to have increased since he quit shooting foxes? — but this seems even more implausible. I can't feel the implied narrative is clear. Perhaps there is no implied narrative (but shouldn't there be, tied to the millionaire as the line is?) and we have a straight dream item: for the meaning is certainly to be found in the association backward to "Spartan." This is the boy who stole a fox which, hugged to him in public, ate his vitals, the stain spreading, until stoical he fell dead; clearly a figure for the poet, still unheard of, with his growing hidden wound. At this point "Blue Hill" becomes extra-geographical and macabre: the dying Spartan boy turning blue, the tall poet sad, "blue" (the use of a popular song presently makes this likely).

Now in a succinct modulation from blood (and courage) to pale "orange," appropriate to the "fairy," comes the decorator, to fix things up inside (as psychiatrists will try to do for the poet); miserable, though, things not going well. "Marry" is callous and fraudulent, a last resort. The three figures, on their descending scale, are fruitless. The useful put just to decoration (fishnet), deprived of function, looks on to the poet's fear. One will get, in the poem, no sense of his *doing* anything, only waiting, driving about, skunk-watching, sleepless. (In the opposite conversion, just before, the sporting being put to work, the yawl, I hear as the dominant affect: longing.) This is a late-summer poem, idle, apprehensive.

It's half over. Outworn, gone, queer; analogous figures, tangential all — the first *having been* central, the second having mattered to local revenue. The four stanzas are unemphatic, muted. But their quiet, insistent mustering of the *facts* of an extant world opens toward the danger of its being swept away, into delirium. I have seldom seen stanzas (and by this poet, composer of the Ovid stanza) so un-self-evident. He's holding his fire, let's say. Down-rhyme, casual, unlike earlier Lowell, suggests Miss Bishop's practice; to whom the poem is dedicated; though the heavy, fierce rhyming of "The Quaker Graveyard" will be admitted in the final stanzas. Money-wellness, however misused (compare Eliot's ruined millionaire, Adam, in the *Quartets* — the auctioning off of the boat does not suggest that this one is doing very well), seems important all through the three figures and winds up in a "rich" air, freedom, the poet's to lose. The "fairy," poor, is already sick with perversion.

Since, on the entrance of "I" in stanza V, he climbs a sort of Golgotha (Place of the Skull), I will observe that there is more Christian detail in the poem than might have been expected. There's the bishop (I see no assimilation here to Chekhov's overwhelming story, which however I haven't read for years), the Marlovian hell of stanza VI ("where we are in hell," as Mephistophilis says at line 554 of Tucker Brooke's criminal edition, and compare other texts in that corrupt play, which even Greg was unsatisfactory with), the Trinitarian Church, and even the interior decorator goes in for suspicious properties: a fishnet (Peter, but Peter was married), cobbling (but Christ is said — on the Synoptic evidence, see Guignebert's *Jesus*, p. 106 — to have been a carpenter). The detail is not, I think, systematic, and serves the purpose of a kind of hopeless casting about for aid; — unavailable, as in Hemingway's "A Clean, Well-lighted Place," in *The Trial,* in *Waiting for Godot,* you name it. I should say that Lowell works rather in parable-form than in forms of allegory. There is no point-to-point correspondence, the details are free. The (hoped for?) rescue-figures are simply sinister and pathetic, the senile old lady who lets houses decay, the unhappy homosexual who would like to fix up their interiors. Who knows where the bishop is?

In stanza V there is much more than: furtive love, furtive madness. But both come out loud and open in stanza VI, and the loss of the person, in its last line, leads to the oneiric vision of the skunks.

Their ceremonial line, for (their kind of) nourishment, may belong with the religious traces. They have taken over the world; the poet has a final instant of freedom at the start of the last stanza. "Moonstruck" and "ostrich" (I am lunatic, hidden — hidden?) then take over. We began with one mother (of a bishop) and wind up with another (of a column of little skunks) in a sort of greedy parody of the Eucharist; the ultimate help. Some of Lowell's early poems were savagely Marian. I would not call this poem at all friendly to Christianity, which appears to have failed the shelving (and to be shelved) man. We feed instead on garbage. The "cream" is sour. The last line equals: "I will, I *do* 'scare.'" It is man's right, foreseeing, to be frightened. But the stubbornness of the mother skunk, like that (merely in association) of the Spartan boy, make up a small counterpoise to the poem's terror.

We attend, so, to a sense of having been failed by the biological and mental and emotional (and religious) probabilities: not at all, or most, have to feel this way; many can believe. There is a staving-off, with dramatization, of self-pity; an implied (at the end) confession of fear. I have a feeling that the poem may look better fifty years from now, even better. Snatching at war-terms irritates one, as of writers; Baudelaire hated "avant-garde"; but it takes moral courage, at least, to write in this poem's direction.

I must pause, briefly, to admire its administration of Time. In general for it Time narrows: a vista of decades, "The season's ill," *one* night, and so down to the skunk hour. But I notice two substantial exceptions to the method. The second stanza opens a longer vista still than the first, with "century." And the "Hour" is *nightly,* expanding again into a dreaded recurrence. Most real poets work in this way, but Lowell decidedly rather more than most. I will now admit that I cannot like "my ill-spirit sob in each blood cell"; the expression is just what it should not be, rhetorical, exterior, especially with "hear."

For convenience in exposition, with a poem so personal, I have been pretending that "I" is the poet, but of course the speaker can never be the actual writer, who is a person with an address, a Social Security number, debts, tastes, memories, expectations. Shakespeare says "Two loves I have": he does not say *only* two loves, and indeed he must have loved also his children, various friends, presumably his wife, his parents. The necessity for the artist of selection opens inevitably an abyss between his person and his persona. I only said that much poetry is "very closely about" the person. The persona looks across at the person and then sets about its own work. Lowell's careful avoidance, in "Skunk Hour," of the grand style he was still wielding in the Ovid stanza, for instance, makes the distinction material here. This mysterious "I" that poets deploy can certainly never be defined, but a good recent stab at characterization was Mr. Ransom's in an earlier one of these symposia, about Roethke: "The true self or soul or mind of the highly compounded authorial 'I' . . ." I would call it virtually certain that Lowell had in mind and at heart during this poem not only his own difficulties whatever they may be or have been but the personal disorders to which other poets of his age and place have been furiously subject.

Another question raised with acuteness by the poem is how far it is fair to take associations. A characteristic vice of modern criticism is taking them too far. One of Randall Jarrell's remarks sticks in my head: "as people ought to know, very complicated organizations are excessively rare in poetry." I am in ringing agreement. Hurrah. But whether the dictum applies to Lowell's poems, or to an onslaught against the Old Testament and the New Testament like Thomas's "A Refusal to Mourn . . . ," seems to me very doubtful; as I think Jarrell concedes in his handsome, better than handsome, studies of Lowell. No rules will help, naturally, but can we seek guideposts? Suppose we try two: (1) When there is something imperfectly narrative, imperfectly dramatic, which obstinately *needs accounting for,* we allow ourselves, as readers, more liberty of interpreting than otherwise; (2) Where accident and coincidence seem implausible, we stick by the textual and psychological (even depth-psychological) probabilities. Both signs point to a connection of "Spartan" and "fox stain," though fifteen lines separate them. I have several times gone too far here, deliberately, in order to repudiate my (non-) findings. But I think we must allow, with some poets, for broad and complex areas of suggestion; and I would propose a third guidepost: (3) Whatever relates, however uncertainly, to the *ruling theme* of the poem deserves the reader's intimate attention. Thus, in the fifth stanza, the fact of its being a *dark* night may suggest in our tradition spiritual despair (St. John of the Cross), and the desolate "hull to hull" may look back to the "Nautilus," adventurous, submerged; or they may not. I have made no attempt to exhaust the poem. If we were a little longer civilized here, the poet would plainly be declared, in Japanese fashion, a National Cultural Asset, and exempted from coarse analyses of his subtle, strong, terrible poems.

ROBERT LOWELL

I. THE MEANING

The author of a poem is not necessarily the ideal person to explain its meaning. He is as liable as anyone else to muddle, dishonesty and reticence. Nor is it his purpose to provide a peg for a prose essay. Meaning varies in importance from poem to poem, and from style to style, but always it is only a strand and an element in the brute flow of composition. Other elements are pictures that please or thrill for themselves, phrases that ring for their music or carry some buried suggestion. For all this the author is an opportunist, throwing whatever comes to hand into his feeling for start, continuity, contrast, climax, and completion. It is imbecile for him not to know his intentions, and unsophisticated for him to know too explicitly and fully.

Three papers by three poets on another's poem! Perhaps they should be considered as short stories and variants on my original. I shall comment on them later; here, I only want to say that I learned much from them. Very little of what I had in mind is untouched on; much that never occurred to me has been granted me. What I didn't intend often seems now at least as valid as what I did. My complaint is not that I am misunderstood, but that I am overunderstood. I am seen through.

I am not sure whether I can distinguish between intention and interpretation. I think this is what I more or less intended. The first four stanzas are meant to give a dawdling more or less amiable picture of a declining Maine sea town. I move from the ocean inland. Sterility howls through the scenery, but I try to give a tone of tolerance, humor, and randomness to the sad prospect. The composition drifts, its direction sinks out of sight into the casual, chancy arrangements of nature and decay. Then all comes alive in stanzas V and VI. This is the dark night. I hoped my readers would remember John of the Cross's poem. My night is not gracious, but secular, puritan, and agnostical. An Existentialist night. Somewhere in my mind was a passage from Sartre or Camus about reaching some point of final darkness where the one free act is suicide. Out of this comes the march and affirmation, an ambiguous one, of my skunks in the last two stanzas. The skunks are both quixotic and barbarously absurd, hence the tone of amusement and defiance. "Skunk Hour" is not entirely independent, but the anchor poem in its sequence.

II. HOW THE POEM WAS WRITTEN

What I can describe and what no one else can describe are the circumstances of my poem's composition. I shan't reveal private secrets. John Berryman's pathological chart comes frighteningly close to the actual event. When I first read his paper, I kept saying to myself, "Why he is naming the very things I wanted to keep out of my poem." In the end, I had to admit that Berryman had hit a bull's-eye, and often illuminated matters more searchingly and boldly than I could have wished. Is his account true? I cannot decide, the truth here depends on what psychologists and philosophers one accepts. Berryman comes too close for comfort.

"Skunk Hour" was begun in mid-August, 1957, and finished about a month later. In March of the same year, I had been giving readings on the West Coast, often reading six days a week and sometimes twice on a single day. I was in San Francisco, the era and setting of Allen Ginsberg, and all about very modest poets were waking up prophets. I became sorely aware of how few poems I had written, and that these few had been finished at the latest three or four years earlier. Their style seemed distant, symbol-ridden and willfully difficult. I began to paraphrase my Latin quotations, and to add extra syllables to a line to make it clearer and more colloquial. I felt my old poems hid what they were really about, and many times offered a stiff, humorless and even impenetrable surface. I am no convert to the "beats." I know well too that the best poems are not necessarily poems that read aloud. Many of the greatest poems can only be read to one's self, for inspiration is no substitute for humor, shock, narrative and a hypnotic voice, the four musts for oral performance. Still, my own poems seemed like prehistoric monsters dragged down into the bog and death by their ponderous armor. I was reciting what I no longer felt. What influenced me more than San Francisco and reading aloud was that for some time I had been writing prose. I felt that the best style for poetry was none of the many poetic styles in English, but something like the prose of Chekhov or Flaubert.

When I returned to my home, I began writing lines in a new style. No poem, however, got finished and soon I left off and tried to forget the whole headache. Suddenly, in August, I was struck by the sadness of writing nothing, and having nothing to write, of having, at least, no language. When I began writing "Skunk Hour," I felt that most of what I knew about writing was a hindrance.

The dedication is to Elizabeth Bishop, because re-reading her suggested a way of breaking through the shell of my old manner. Her rhythms, idiom, images, and stanza structure seemed to belong to a later century. "Skunk Hour" is modeled on Miss Bishop's "The Armadillo," a much better poem and one I had heard her read and had later carried around with me. Both "Skunk Hour" and "The Armadillo" use short line stanzas, start with drifting description and end with a single animal.

This was the main source. My others were Hölderlin's *"Brod und Wein,"* particularly the moon lines:

> *Sieh! und das Schattenbild unserer Erde, der Mond,*
> *kommet geheim non auch; die Schwärmerische, die Nacht kommt*
> *voll mit Sternen und wohl wenig bekümmert um uns,*

and so forth. I put this in long straggling lines and then added touches of Maine scenery, till I saw I was getting nowhere. Another source, probably undetectable now, was Annette von Droste-Hülshoff's *"Am letzten Tage des Jahres."* She too uses a six-line stanza with short lines. Her second stanza is as follows:

> *'s ist tiefe Nacht!*
> *Ob wohl ein Auge offen noch?*
> *In diesen Mauern rüttelt dein*
> *Verrinnen, Zeit! Mir schaudert; doch*
> *Es will die letzte Stunde sein*
> *Einsam durchwacht.*
>
> *Gesehen all*

Here and elsewhere, my poem and the German poem have the same shudders and situation.

"Skunk Hour" was written backwards, first the last two stanzas, I think, and then the next to last two. Anyway, there was a time when I had the last four stanzas much as they now are and nothing before them. I found the bleak personal violence repellent. All was too close, though watching the lovers was not mine, but from an anecdote about Walt Whitman in his old age. I began to feel that real poetry came, not from fierce confessions, but from something almost meaningless but imagined. I was haunted by an image of a blue china doorknob. I never used the doorknob, or knew what it meant, yet somehow it started the current of images in my opening stanzas. They were written in reverse order, and at last gave my poem an earth to stand on, and space to breathe.

III. THE CRITICS

I don't think I intended either the Spartan boy holding the fox or Satan's feeling of sexual deprivation, while he watched Adam and Eve in the Garden. I may have, but I don't remember. The red fox stain was merely meant to describe the rusty reddish color of autumn on Blue Hill, a Maine mountain near where we were living. I had seen foxes playing on the road one night, and I think the words have sinister and askew suggestions.

I can't imagine anything more thorough than Nims's stanza-by-stanza exposition. Almost all of it is to the point. I get a feeling of going on a familiar journey, but with another author and another sensibility. This feeling is still stronger when I read Wilbur's essay. Sometimes he and I are named as belonging to the same school, what *Time* Magazine calls "the couth poets." Sometimes we are set in battle against one another. I have no idea which, if either, is true. Certainly, we both in different ways owe much to the teaching and practice of John Crowe Ransom. Certainly, his essay embodies and enhances my poem. With Berryman too, I go on a strange journey! Thank God, we both come out clinging to spars, enough floating matter to save us, though faithless.

II

Notes

Introduction

1. "Introduction" to Paul Valéry's *The Art of Poetry*, trans. Denise Folliot, *The Collected Works of Paul Valéry: Volume VII* (New York, 1958), p. xvii.

2. See Sarah N. Lawall, *Critics of Consciousness: The Existential Structures of Literature* (Cambridge, 1968), passim, esp. pp. 132–34.

3. For a fuller discussion of Buffon's aphorism see Milic's "Rhetorical Choice and Stylistic Option: The Conscious and Unconscious Poles," in *Literary Style: A Symposium*, ed. Seymour Chatman (New York, 1971), pp. 77–94. Wimsatt was a participant in this symposium.

4. "Battering the Object: The Ontological Approach," in *Contemporary Criticism: Stratford-upon-Avon Studies 12*, ed. Malcolm Bradbury and David Palmer (London, 1970), p. 62.

5. Ibid., p. 66.

6. Ibid., p. 70.

7. See Paul de Man, "Form and Intent in the American New Criticism," *Blindness and Insight: Essays in the Rhetoric of Contemporary Criticism* (New York, 1971), pp. 20–35, for an argument that Wimsatt is caught in a contradiction between his assumption of the ontological status of the work of literature and his view of the intentional fallacy.

8. Yves Velan, "Barthes," in *Modern French Criticism: From Proust and Valéry to Structuralism*, ed. John K. Simon (Chicago, 1972), p. 315. Velan goes on to

say: "If anthropology (for example) has been revitalized, it is because men like Lévi-Strauss have substituted for the notion of genesis, which had governed the social studies, the notion of structure, which was borrowed from linguistics."

9. Op. cit., p. 81.

10. See M. L. Rosenthal, "Robert Lowell and 'Confessional' Poetry," *The New Poets: American and British Poetry Since World War II* (New York, 1967), pp. 25–78.

11. See Harold Bloom, *Yeats* (New York, 1970), for a concept of "sources" and "influences" that moves beyond the positivistic methods of such study traditional in academic scholarship.

12. "Battering the Object: The Ontological Approach," p. 75. The question by Miller that Wimsatt quotes is from "The Antitheses of Criticism: Reflections on the Yale Colloquium," *Modern Language Notes*, 81 (1966), p. 560.

W. K. WIMSATT AND MONROE C. BEARDSLEY,
The Intentional Fallacy

1. *Dictionary of World Literature,* Joseph T. Shipley, ed. (New York, 1942), 326–29.

2. J. E. Spingarn, "The New Criticism," in *Criticism in America* (New York, 1924), 24–25.

3. Ananda K. Coomaraswamy, "Intention," in *American Bookman*, I (1944), 41–48.

4. It is true that Croce himself in his *Ariosto, Shakespeare and Corneille* (London, 1920), chap. VII, "The Practical Personality and the Poetical Personality," and in his *Defence of Poetry* (Oxford, 1933), 24, and elsewhere, early and late, has delivered telling attacks on emotive geneticism, but the main drive of the *Aesthetic* is surely toward a kind of cognitive intentionalism.

5. See Hughes Mearns, *Creative Youth* (Garden City, 1925), esp. 10, 27–29. The technique of inspiring poems has apparently been outdone more recently by the study of inspiration in successful poets and other artists. See, for instance, Rosamond E. M. Harding, *An Anatomy of Inspiration* (Cambridge, 1940); Julius Portnoy, *A Psychology of Art Creation* (Philadelphia, 1942); Rudolf Arnheim and others, *Poets at Work* (New York, 1947); Phyllis Bartlett, *Poems in Process* (New York, 1951); Brewster Ghiselin (ed.), *The Creative Process: A Symposium* (Berkeley and Los Angeles, 1952).

6. Curt Ducasse, *The Philosophy of Art* (New York, 1929), 116.

7. And the history of words *after* a poem is written may contribute meanings which if relevant to the original pattern should not be ruled out by a scruple about intention.

8. Chaps. VIII, "The Pattern," and XVI, "The Known and Familiar Landscape," will be found of most help to the student of the poem.

9. Charles M. Coffin, *John Donne and the New Philosophy* (New York, 1927), 97–98.

FRANK CIOFFI, Intention and Interpretation
in Criticism

1. The allusion here is to the fact that when Shakespeare's *Henry V* is performed in France, Pistol's reference to syphilis as "malady of France" is sometimes replaced by the expression "malady of Naples" ("la maladie Napolitaine"). The line of thought is that since our tolerance of such practices does not imply a general indifference to an author's intentions neither need our toleration of anachronistic readings of Blake's *Jerusalem*.

JEAN STAROBINSKI, *Truth in Masquerade*

1. Joseph Fouché was Minister of the Police during the Empire. The Terreur Blanche refers to the persecutions and political repression during the first years of the Restoration. César Bombet was one of Stendhal's many pseudonyms. [Note by Victor Brombert, editor of *Stendhal: A Collection of Critical Essays.*]
2. *Souvenirs d'égotisme* in *Oeuvres intimes,* ed. Pléiade (Paris: Librairie Gallimard, 1955), pp. 1449–50.
3. *Journal,* in *Oeuvres intimes,* p. 1041.
4. *Privilèges,* in *Oeuvres intimes,* pp. 1559 ff.

LOUIS T. MILIC, *Against the Typology of Styles*

1. James R. Sutherland, "Restoration Prose," *Restoration and Augustan Prose* (Los Angeles, 1956), pp. 1–2.
2. Ibid., p. 2.
3. "The Essay and the Beginning of Modern English Prose," *The Cambridge History of English Literature,* ed. Sir A. W. Ward and A. R. Waller (Cambridge, 1911), vol. VIII, p. 368.
4. John Milton, "Aeropagitica," *Prose Selections,* ed. Merritt Y. Hughes (New York, 1947), pp. 218–19.
5. John Dryden, "A Discourse Concerning the Original and Progress of Satire," *Essays,* ed. W. P. Ker (Oxford, 1900), vol. II, p. 81.
6. Vol. VIII, p. 296.
7. Isaac Barrow, "The Pleasantness of Religion," *Seventeenth-Century Verse and Prose,* ed. Helen C. White, Ruth C. Wallerstein and Ricardo Quintana (New York, 1952), vol. II, p. 178.
8. Robert South, "An Account of the Nature and Measures of Conscience," *Seventeenth-Century Verse and Prose,* vol. II, pp. 186–87.
9. *On English Prose* (Toronto, 1957), p. 57.
10. James Sutherland, "Some Aspects of Eighteenth-Century Prose," *Essays on the Eighteenth Century Presented to David Nichol Smith* (Oxford, 1945), p. 94.
11. A number of critics, including Cyril Connolly and Roland Barthes, have expressed concern about the modern stress on a plain, featureless prose.
12. Jonathan Swift, *An Enquiry into the Behavior of the Queen's Last Ministry,* ed. Irvin Ehrenpreis (Bloomington, 1956), p. xxxi.
13. This is the so-called *persona* theory. See, for example, Paul Fussell, Jr., "Speaker and Style in *A Letter of Advice to a Young Poet* (1721), and the Problem of Attribution," *Review of English Studies,* X (1959), 63–67.

W. K. WIMSATT, *Genesis: A Fallacy Revisited*

1. Two friends have specially contributed to this essay — Monroe Beardsley of course, who brought to my attention some of our critics in the journals and who read my early draft, and Donald Hirsch, whose differences from me, whether in conversation or in print (see p. 276 and note 53), have the unusual character of being always illuminative. His essay of 1960 in *PMLA,* which I cite below and argue with (notes 18, 21, and 53), is one of the best on the subject which I now attempt to reapproach.
2. I leave out his headaches and his gallstones, though there was a time when these too would have been important. For a rich and orderly assortment of artist's drives and motives, conscious and unconscious, during the creative process, see Monroe C. Beardsley, "On the Creation of Art," *JAAC,* 23 (Spring 1965), 291–304.
3. See n. 14.

4. See, for instance, Alfred Owen Aldridge, "Biography in the Interpretation of Poetry," *College English*, 25 (March 1964), 412–20: "I shall try to indicate a few reasons why biography serves to humanize poetry and therefore to heighten our enjoyment." "No purely esthetic criticism has ever stimulated the same public interest," the same "extraordinary sensation which has been caused by the recent announcement of A. L. Rowse's biographical study of Shakespeare — with its revelations" (p. 415). Or see John A. Meixner, "The Uses of Biography in Criticism," *College English*, 27 (November 1966), 108–13; or Carlos Baker, "Speaking of Books: The Relevance of a Writer's Life," *The New York Times Book Review* (August 20, 1967), pp. 2, 31.

5. Leslie A. Fiedler, *No! In Thunder: Essays on Myth and Literature* (Boston, 1960), pp. 312–18.

6. William H. Capitan, "The Artist's Intention," *Revue Internationale de Philosophie*, 68–69 (1964), 331–32. Cf. Joseph Margolis, *The Language of Art & Art Criticism, Analytic Questions in Aesthetics* (Detroit, 1965), p. 99, on stage directions and musical notations. Also see below, p. 268. Margolis is a writer who cheerfully piles up examples that tell in favor of Wimsatt and Beardsley and even quotes passages from them with which he cannot disagree and then with equal cheer somersaults to a guarded conclusion that they "must be mistaken," that "intentional criticism has, to some extent at least, a recognizable and not inappropriate place in the aesthetic examination of art" (p. 103).

7. Capitan, p. 332.

8. Dr. F. Cioffi, "Intention and Interpretation in Criticism" (from *Proceedings of the Aristotelian Society,* 1963–64), in *Collected Papers on Aesthetics,* ed. Cyril Barrett, S.J. (Oxford, 1965), pp. 161–83, esp. 168, 170–71, 172, 174, 175, 179–81. See M. C. Beardsley's review of this volume, with special attention to Cioffi, in *JAAC*, 26 (Fall 1967), 144–46.

9. *The Massachusetts Review,* 7 (Summer 1966), 584–90.

10. *The Use of Poetry and the Use of Criticism* (London, 1933), p. 140.

11. All the words quoted are from "Tradition and the Individual Talent."

12. See Richard Ellmann, *The Identity of Yeats* (New York, 1954) and *Yeats: The Man and the Masks* (New York, 1948). The article by A. O. Aldridge cited above confuses the poet's view and the critic's view throughout and refers to much literature which also does. In Slavic countries formalist critics during the 1920s defined a poem as "a deflection, not a reflection, of experience" (p. 412).

13. "We ought to impute the thoughts and attitudes of the poem immediately to the dramatic *speaker,* and if to the author at all, only by an act of biographical inference" ("The Intentional Fallacy" [1945], paragraph 7).

14. See Leon Edel, *Literary Biography* (London, 1957); J. Hillis Miller, *The Disappearance of God, Five Nineteenth-Century Writers* (New York, 1965) — De Quincey, Browning, Emily Brontë, Arnold, Hopkins. But for Miller chronology is not important.

15. *The Hudson Review,* 12 (Winter 1959–60), 487–507.

16. *Yale Review,* 41 (Autumn 1951), 80–92.

17. *Restoration and Eighteenth-Century Literature, Essays in Honor of Alan Dugald McKillop,* ed. Carroll Camden (Chicago, 1963), pp. 25–37.

18. See this large and interesting work passim, esp. chap. 8, "Telling as Showing: Dramatized Narrators, Reliable and Unreliable." See too Allan Rodway and Brian Lee, "Coming to Terms," *Essays in Criticism,* 14 (April 1964), 122; and E. D. Hirsch's very subtle and accurate distinction between "speaking subject" and "biographical person," as illustrated in the "secret awareness" of lying and the "truth-telling stance" ("Objective Interpretation," *PMLA,* 75 [September 1960], 478–79). See also some good paragraphs on the theme of person and poet in Harry Berger, Jr., "Cadmus Unchanged," a review of *Selected Letters of Robert Frost,* in *Yale Review,* 54 (Winter 1965), 277–82. For a range of examples and insights from a different area, see Victor Erlich, "The Concept of the Poet as a Problem of

Poetics," *Poetics. Poetyka. Poetika* (The Hague: Mouton & Co., 1961), pp. 707–17, and "Some Uses of Monologue in Prose Fiction: Narrative Manner and World View," *Stil- und Formprobleme in der Literatur* (Heidelberg, 1959), pp. 371–78.

19. H. W. Garrod, *Poetry and the Criticism of Life* (Cambridge, Mass., 1931), p. 83. Garrod refers to Arnold's "make-up" of being the greatest English critic.

20. See the excellent article, in effect about anonymous lyric personae, by Arthur K. Moore, "Lyric Voices and Ethical Proofs," *JAAC*, 23 (Summer 1965), 429–39. "Lyrics are vouched for simply — . . . through intelligible relationships to activities, conditions, occasions, lives, ideologies, and states of consciousness into which interest enters" (pp. 429–30). See the same author's later "Lyric Personae and Prying Critics," *Southern Humanities Review*, 1 (1967), 43–64.

21. *Essays in Criticism*, 4 (July 1954), 315, 319. And see below, n. 53, *langue* and *parole* as expounded by Hirsch, "Objective Interpretation," pp. 473–75.

22. One of the monkeys employed in this experiment once got through the whole poem all right, as far as the last word of the last book, but then he slipped and wrote, instead of "day.," "lxdz.," and the whole version of course had to be scrapped.

23. "The Aesthetics of Textual Criticism," *PMLA*, 80 (December 1965), 465–82, esp. 465–68, 475.

24. See Sidney Gendin's sensible short article, "The Artist's Intentions," *JAAC*, 23 (Winter 1964), 195.

25. Another term which Mr. Beardsley (pp. 457, 490–91) puts in this genetic group is "originality," which, like "skill" (see 3c, p. 266), is a merit which seems assignable more readily to the author than to his work. During the neoclassic age, in arguments comparing Homer and Virgil, the latter was sometimes said to have written doubtless the more perfect poem; the former got a good mark for originality. A 1966 Fairlane is a better automobile than a Model-T Ford, but not as original.

26. See Beardsley, *Aesthetics* (1958), p. 489. Dr. Cioffi (p. 164) dismisses this form of the intentionalistic argument with great unconcern. He is no doubt largely unaware of the contexts of literary scholarship and criticism which framed our articles of 1944 and 1945. On "skill," cf. Gendin, p. 195.

27. See, for instance, John Kemp, "The Work of Art and the Artist's Intentions," *The British Journal of Aesthetics*, 4 (April 1964), 150–51; Capitan, pp. 324–26; and Gendin, p. 193.

28. Henry David Aiken, "The Aesthetic Relevance of Artists' Intentions," *The Journal of Philosophy*, 52 (24 November 1955), reprinted in *Problems in Aesthetics*, ed. Morris Weitz (New York, 1959), pp. 299–300. Cf. Gendin, p. 194.

29. Kemp, p. 121, describes this situation very clearly.

30. Capitan, pp. 331–32.

31. See his extremely intentionalistic justification of these notes in a lecture on Dante in 1950: "I gave the references in my notes, in order to make the reader who recognizes the allusion, know that I meant him to recognize it, and know that he would have missed the point if he did not recognize it" (*To Criticize the Critic and Other Writings* [New York, 1965], p. 128).

32. The claim for artist's intentions as auxiliaries to works of art will no doubt mean somewhat different things for different kinds and instances of art. See, for instance, Beardsley, pp. 20–29; Capitan, pp. 327–33; Erwin Panofsky, "On Intentions," in *Problems in Aesthetics*, pp. 288–95, extracted from Panofsky's "History of Art as a Humanistic Discipline," in *The Meaning of the Humanities*, ed. T. M. Greene (Princeton, 1940).

33. See Beardsley, p. 20, on painting and sculpture, "the simplest descriptive level." Cf. Gendin, p. 194.

34. *Preface to Shakespeare* (1765), paragraph 59.

35. Boswell, *Life of Johnson*, 9 April 1778.

36. *Poetical Works of Goldsmith* (Oxford, 1939), p. 167.

37. *Goldsmith* (London, 1848), I, 369.

38. Beardsley, p. 24; Margolis, pp. 97, 189; David Magarshack, *Chekhov the*

Dramatist (New York, Hill and Wang, 1960), pp. 188–89, *The Seagull,* p. 273, *The Cherry Orchard.* "*The Seagull* is usually interpreted on the stage as a tragedy (a misinterpretation Stanislavsky was the first to impose on the play), and yet Chekhov always referred to it as a comedy" (p. 188). "Practically every producer . . . in spite of Chekhov's unmistakable intentions, regards the play as a tragedy" (p. 189). We are here concerned in part with nuances of local meaning, in part also with whole dramatic structure and import. The example of Chekhov might well have been adduced above under 4d.

Margolis, p. 96, quotes the instance, no doubt unusual in the annals of literature, of Melville's acknowledgment that Hawthorne had revealed to him allegorical meanings in *Moby Dick* which he himself had not specifically "meant."

39. Cf. T. S. Eliot, "What Dante Means to Me" (1950), in *To Criticize the Critic,* p. 133. The terms are Eliot's. Though he would concede that "some great English poets . . . were privileged by their genius to abuse the English language," yet the poets who have best served their language are the greatest, Virgil, Dante, Shakespeare.

40. Number XXXV of the Rossetti manuscript, in Joseph H. Wicksteed, *Blake's Innocence and Experience* (London, 1928), after p. 256, p. 261, and facing p. 285; cf. *Poetry and Prose of William Blake,* ed. Geoffrey Keynes (London, 1932), p. 96.

41. Keynes, p. 75; Wicksteed, after p. 244, and p. 252.

42. E. D. Hirsch, Jr., *Innocence and Experience: An Introduction to Blake* (New Haven, 1964), pp. 263–65.

43. The evidence of the Rossetti manuscript supports the biographical dimension which I introduce for the sake of dialogue with the biographically minded. The distinction between the doctrinaire man and the subtle poem would remain even if the poetic achievement had cost Blake no trouble at all.

44. Wicksteed, p. 190. "I do not doubt that he continued to accept marriage at its face value even after his mind had learnt to entertain the revolutionary suggestions of the rationalistic and antinomian circles he came to mingle in" (p. 215).

45. *Comparative Literature,* 8 (Winter 1956), 28–45, esp. 36–38.

46. Margolis, pp. 103 and 189, citing Isabel Hungerland, "The Concept of Intention in Art Criticism," *Journal of Philosophy,* 52 (24 November 1955), 733–42, and other sources.

47. Dr. Cioffi, p. 167.

48. Margolis, p. 103, quoting Beardsley, p. 490.

49. One of our critics, Emilio Roma III, seems to grasp this principle firmly enough and to accept it. ("The Scope of the Intentional Fallacy," *The Monist,* 50 [April 1966], 250–65, esp. 250–51, 256, 265). It is perhaps his main reason for recognizing a sort of "minimal" and "pitifully easy" meaning in our notion of the "intentional fallacy." But he believes that a distinction between what the speaker means and what the "sentence" means, urged very explicitly by Mr. Beardsley in 1958, is not to be found in our essay of 1945. Mr. Roma writes with the air (e.g., p. 254) of painfully spelling out what we said. "Style," he says, "is treated [by us] as though it had nothing whatsoever to do with content" (p. 265). To me at least, and I think to Mr. Beardsley, this can come only as a matter of surprise. How much of what we have written, in the essay of 1945 and elsewhere, is really understood by Mr. Roma?

50. Roma, pp. 251–52, 258, 262; Cioffi, pp. 167, 170 (on excluding "illicit sources" of interpretation). The word "motley" in our text just above is from Cioffi, pp. 176, 183, taken by him "probably" from Wittgenstein.

51. This may involve what Mr. E. D. Hirsch calls the "fallacy of the homogeneous past." "The homogeneous critic assumes that everybody in a given cultural milieu shares the same basic attitudes and beliefs. He is content to speak of the Greek Mind, the Medieval Mind, the Victorian Mind" ("Criticism versus Historicism," mimeograph of a paper read at the meeting of the Modern Language Association, December 1963).

52. Hyatt H. Waggoner, in *What To Say About a Poem, CEA Chapbook*, by W. K. Wimsatt, Jr., and others, ed. Donald A. Sears (College English Association, 1963), pp. 22, 32.

53. See Mr. Hirsch's exposition of Saussure's distinction ("Objective Interpretation," pp. 473–75), where *langue*, the "system of linguistic possibilities shared by a speech community," "contains words and sentence-forming principles, but it contains no sentences." A poem or any other verbal text containing sentences cannot then simply "represent a segment of *langue*" (as modern literary theorists are said to hold) but must be a *parole*, "a particular, selective actualization from *langue*," a determinate individual expression. "Only individuals utter *paroles*," and "a *parole* of the speech community is non-existent." "Meaning requires a meaner." When we come to the difficulty of the "bungled text," the "freshman essay," the malapropism (which, let me add, is the basic difficulty of poem and purpose made large and unavoidable), we solve it by saying that the author's text, failing to "represent the *parole* he desired to convey," "represents no *parole* at all." But such an intuitionist and absolute (or Crocean) conclusion does not sit well in the abstractive and scientific premises (of *langue* and *parole*) with which we have begun. If we are going to have "words" and "principles" conceived as prior to *parole*, we must face the possibility of their being badly put together. A "house" put together of ill-matched cardboard prefabrications would not be no house at all, or nothing, but simply a bad house.

Mr. Hirsch's *Validity in Interpretation* (New Haven, Yale University Press, 1967), which urges his views in greater detail and usefully reprints his essay of 1960, appeared only some time after I had completed the present essay. Mr. Beardsley, in an essay entitled "Textual Meaning and Authorial Meaning," has written what I consider a shrewd critique of the book, scheduled to appear in a symposium in *Genre*, 1, no. 2 (June 1968), a new quarterly issued from the University of Illinois at Chicago Circle.

RICHARD WILBUR, JOHN FREDERICK NIMS, JOHN BERRYMAN, ROBERT LOWELL, *On Robert Lowell's "Skunk Hour"*

1. From *The Poems of St John of the Cross* by John Frederick Nims (Grove Press, 1959). By permission of John Frederick Nims.

2. From *Knowledge of the Evening, Poems 1950–1960*, by John Frederick Nims. (New Brunswick: Rutgers University Press, 1960). By permission of Rutgers University Press.

III

The Literary Performance

Wimsatt and Beardsley contend that "the objective critic's first question, when he is confronted with a new aesthetic object is not, What is this supposed to be? but, What have we got here?" (p. 256). But they assume, of course, that the poem, play, or novel under inspection *is* an aesthetic object, and it is just this belief in the existence of an analyzable literary object that has been rendered problematic by many contemporary critics. Questions of how to get at what is here and what to do with it in criticism once it is apprehended, as well as the adequacy of the methods by which literature is confronted and studied, will depend on how the critic conceives the very subject of his inquiry. For Wimsatt a poem is a verbal icon, for Cleanth Brooks, a well-wrought urn, and for all the American New Critics the poem is an artifact — a work. Georges Poulet, on the other hand, sees literature as an act of consciousness. After delivering the "Phenomenology of Reading" at a conference in 1966, he said:

> I do not like at all the expression "work of art," detest it in fact, and usually avoid it. I do not think that once in the text I read before you I used the expression "work of art." I used very often the expression "a mental work" or "a mental object" in contradistinction with that kind of external object which can be a sewing machine.[1]

Robert Frost, to take yet another view, described literature as "a performance in words." However closely this can be made to fit

309

the terms of the other two conceptions, it has its own distinctions, and when applied as a critical principle, it will obviously change the focus of what qualities of a poem are studied. The critic will proceed in his criticism by different avenues of approach, different methods of investigation, and with different ends in mind according to whether he conceives literature to be a verbal artifact, a mental object, or a performance in words. These three views do not exhaust the ways of naming and describing literature, of course, but they cover the major divisions in contemporary criticism, and by playing one off against the others, we may measure the special powers as well as the limits of each.

Georges Poulet's essay on Henry James is characteristic of his procedure as a critic of the literary performance. The essay is part of *The Metamorphoses of the Circle,* in which Poulet proposes the circle as a figure for understanding the mind's sense of its own being, in the specific form of the "cogito" of certain individual writers and in the larger form of the consciousness of certain historical periods. The center of the circle is the mind's identity, the circumference its serial passage through time, and the area of the circle is the space the mind inhabits. James is distinct from the other writers Poulet considers because of the supersaturation of his awareness; he is overwhelmed by the plenitude of his perceptions; his mind "is submerged as much by the multitude of detail as by the enormity of the ensemble." Hence, although consciousness is an illimitable power for James, his problem is how to frame and encircle it, how to *represent* it, in such a way as to keep it single in focus but multiple in its irradiations, at once finite and infinite.

Poulet's essay invites comparison with Ian Watt's "The First Paragraph of *The Ambassadors:* An Explication." Watt clearly is more concerned with the verbal details of a single work, and he seems to make a more telling disclosure of how the words actually work in James's novels, even though he seems to be interested in some of the same things as Poulet. Watt, too, considers the multiple forms (he calls them "levels") of consciousness, he is equally intrigued by the question of point of view, and he even uses the circle figure in the statement that is crucial to his analysis of *The Ambassadors:* "All the details are scrupulously presented as reflections from the novel's essential centre — the narrator's patterning of the ideas going forwards and backwards in Strether's mind." Watt's main concern, however, is with those aspects of

James's performance that Poulet hardly mentions: vocabulary and syntax.

The critics of consciousness generally have been criticized for failing to give a sense of individual literary works. Because they avoid studying the formal relations that constitute the verbal existence of a novel, say, and because they seek to absorb the study of style into existential or phenomenological concerns, they are charged with seeing the particular work only as an abstract entity, an exhibit of some underlying method of perceiving the universe rather than as an individual structure of words.

But Poulet makes it quite clear in the "Phenomenology of Reading" why he is indifferent to those things that matter most to critics like Watt. He looks at what the words of a novel create — and these are not verbal structures but compositions or states of consciousness. "By looking *through* form," Geoffrey H. Hartman says in "Beyond Formalism," "Poulet gains his unusually intimate access to the writer's mind."

Hartman goes on to make some trenchant criticisms. Poulet, he says, is too optimistic regarding James and not acutely enough aware of the *costs* of consciousness, which is a presiding theme in James's fiction. Poulet's observations "rarely reach to the quick of James's consciousness, to that which makes him unmistakably Jamesian." But this failure, if it is that in fact, may not establish the inherent superiority of Watt's method of treating the language and the verbal structures of particular novels. Each critic's view of James enables him to see something the others have missed or obscured.

R. P. Blackmur's essay on Stendhal's *The Charterhouse of Parma* is also characteristic of his later criticism, and it shows how he enacted the program of work he described in "A Burden for Critics." The differences between Blackmur and the critics of consciousness may be seen by comparing his essay with Jean Starobinski's treatment of Stendhal in "Truth in Masquerade." He seems closer than either Starobinski or Poulet to the kind of concern Ian Watt shows for the language and fictional structures of a particular work, but their differences in critical performance are perhaps even more striking.

Watt says that his explication is an attempt to apply close analytical reading to forms of literature larger than the poem. The failure to consider the novel was a frequent charge against the American New Criticism. Blackmur himself made the complaint in "A Burden for Critics," and in his later work, some years before Watt called for this development, he turned his attention to the criticism of the novel.

Comparing the essays by Blackmur and Watt raises the question of whether Blackmur's criticism meets the criteria Watt sets for literary analysis, and in turn whether his performance doesn't reveal the narrow limits of such criteria. Blackmur's "analysis" is more an inspired looking and pointing, sharing with the reader his relish in Stendhal's literary performance (though he does venture into judging where his author falls short in his vision of human action); his "explication" is an inquiry into the contexts of experience and literature by which Stendhal's words and forms acquire meaning. Blackmur's general theme, which preoccupied him in all his later critical studies of individual novels is "the novelist's effort to convert behavior into manners" — "the expression of experience in theoretic form."

For both Poulet and Blackmur style is an essential aspect of their performance as critics. The style of explicatory criticism, in keeping with its aim of being objective, is usually self-effacing. This is not to disparage critics such as Watt and W. K. Wimsatt; they are crisp and lively writers. For the Geneva critics, however, literary criticism is itself a form of literature, and Blackmur, although he insisted on the radical separation of criticism from literature, was equally artful in his writing.

The risks in writing criticism as if it were a form of literature are obvious, and both Poulet and Blackmur have been criticized for the alleged fancifulness and opaqueness of their critical performances. But a related charge, that they get between the reader and the literary object, whereas the critic ought to be invisible, serving only to elucidate the work at hand, is altogether misleading, as their aim as critics is to make reading the recreation of the experience of a poem, play, or novel from its origin to its incarnation in form. They enact in their writing the intimate response that they conceive to be the very purpose of criticism. Bringing particular works of literature to full performance for Blackmur, and adventuring in the activity of a writer's consciousness for Poulet, is virtually identical with the animating experience that makes the literature they study. The art of intimacy, then, is the essence of their criticism.[2]

The style of Maurice Blanchot, as Leo Bersani shows in "From Bachelard to Barthes," is also essential to his performance as a critic. The textures of his prose and the shape of his interrogations are as artful in style and as much an enactment of his critical theories as the performances of Poulet and Blackmur. But although Poulet is concerned with the act of consciousness in an individual writer, and Blackmur, with bringing particular works of literature to full performance, Blanchot is preoccupied with the problematic nature of literature itself. If he deals with an individual writer or a particular work, as he does in the essay here on Kafka's *Diaries,* he is as much interested in the literary activity in general as he is in the author or the text. Literature is problematic for Blanchot in that it cannot simply be taken for granted; it is an activity hedged with contradictions, riddled by philosophic doubt, and torn between dreading and desiring its own destruction. The *exigency* of the work of art is an obsession in Blanchot's criticism.

The critical act, Poulet points out in his discussion of Blanchot in "Phenomenology of Reading," attempts to annihilate literature. But the end of this process, as Blanchot says, is one of "negative transcendence," by which he means that writing depersonalizes (rather than aggrandizes) the experience that went into its making. The writer does not create another world; he arrives at a world other than our own, at reality, which is not a form of being but being itself, whose qualities are silence, absence, and freedom. "Literature," Blanchot says,

> reveals itself as the power which frees, the force which removes the oppression of the world, that world "where everything feels choked," it is the liberating passage from "I" to "he," from the introspection which had been Kafka's torment to a loftier observation rising above mortal reality toward the other world, that of freedom.

But this is not a compensation for the author's misfortunes. Kafka's fidelity to the exigency of the work of art and his equal fidelity to the exigency of misfortune "saved him absolutely from that fictional paradise which is the delight of so many a weak artist whom life has disappointed."

Blanchot begins with the same conception of literature as the Geneva critics, that it is "the experience whereby consciousness discovers its being in its inability to lose consciousness," but he ends at precisely the obverse position, holding that literature is not consciousness as such, but rather its antidote, evolved within consciousness itself.[3] The writer seeks to pass into reality rather than into heightened consciousness. Instead of the plenitude of personal awareness Poulet admires in James, Blanchot finds in

Kafka a pure absence, a withering away of personal experience, that he may come, as W. B. Yeats said in a famous line in his poem "Meru," "into the desolation of reality." [4]

Blanchot's criticism is not easy to grasp, but reading his essay on Kafka shakes any complacency we may have in certain ideas about literature: that writing is making over the world in the image of the author's desire, that the purpose of writing is to enable the author to transcend heroically or even positively his misfortunes in the world, that language exists to refer to and evoke the presence of objects, and that literature is possible without question.

If anything is lacking in Blanchot's criticism it may be a sense of Wallace Stevens's notion that "poetry is the gaiety (joy) of language" — which Frost knew as the poet's "performance in words," and which Blackmur embodied in his conception of criticism as performance. It isn't that Stevens has a brighter outlook. Rather, for him, poetry is a *play* of language, an activity that is self-delighting and self-creating but not illusion-making. Moreover, it is a necessary activity: the poet's gaiety of language may be as much an exigency as any that Blanchot mentions. And that this principle can fit writers like Kafka as well as Stendhal may be seen in Blackmur's critical essays on Dostoevsky which treat both the exigency of the work of art and the author's gaiety (joy) of language. [5]

The essay on Baudelaire's "Les Chats" by Roman Jakobson, one of the most eminent linguists of this century, and Claude Lévi-Strauss, equally renowned in his field of anthropology, is a model of the structuralist activity described by Roland Barthes. Among other things the essay offers a new way to undertake the critical analysis of the language and structure of literature. Although it is based on only one of several systems of linguistics, with special advantages and limitations, the essay exemplifies what linguistics in its prodigious growth over the last several decades has added to the repertory of methods now available to the literary critic. The study of the language of literature has become a small though spreading department of linguistics proper, but even more important has been the increasing attraction of certain literary critics to the concepts and methods of contemporary linguistics. These critics have added new dimensions to the study of literary language, structure, and style. [6]

Linguistic criticism and linguistic stylistics — that is, linguistically oriented studies of literature — begin with the same assumption as the American New Criticism: that poetic language is the basis of poetic structure and meaning. As Roman Jakobson has said in a famous paper on "Linguistics and Poetics":

> Poetics deals with problems of verbal structure, just as the analysis of painting is concerned with pictorial structure. Since linguistics is the global science of verbal structure, poetics may be regarded as an integral part of linguistics.[7]

John Crowe Ransom described poetry "as a kind of language" and called Blackmur a "linguistic" critic, but the technical senses these terms imply derive from the tradition of rhetoric (specifically from the so-called figures of language, thought, and speech) rather than from the science of linguistics. The American New Critics showed little interest in the discoveries such linguists as Jakobson were making contemporaneously in grammar, syntax, phonology, morphology, and metrics.[8]

Indeed, what notice literary critics did take was more hostile than sympathetic. An early debate between critics and linguists, which took place in 1956 in the pages of Ransom's journal, *The Kenyon Review,* was conducted like a pitched battle. Several other encounters over the next decade, if anything, deepened the antagonism. When Seymour Chatman and Samuel R. Levin compiled their anthology *Essays on the Language of Literature* in 1967 they began by saying: "For some time now we have been hearing of the need to reconcile linguistic and literary studies." [9]

They were optimistic over the chances of a rapprochement. "Reconciliation is in the air," they declared, and recent work on the borders of the two fields of activity shows "how much they have in common, both technically and substantively." The articles they collected "suggest surprising harmonies, and exemplify how much is to be won by friendly relations, indeed, where possible, by collaboration itself." [10]

Certainly both sides have drawn back from the extreme view of the linguist that "as no science can go beyond mathematics, no criticism can go beyond its linguistics," and from the opinion of the literary critic that linguistics "can contribute little to the critical study of literature." [11] Nevertheless, the issues that divide the two are not at all easy to reconcile, and the differences between them continue to be matters of heated debate.

The linguists charge that literary critics are unanalytical and imprecise in describing the workings of language in literature. If critics treat style at all, the linguists allege, they do so impressionistically; that is, they attach metaphorical labels such as "crisp" or "lively," which have no clearly identifiable meaning, to certain verbal features they intuit in a work or a body of writing.

On such impressions they go on to fabricate specious generalizations about the style of an author or even a whole period. Louis T. Milic shows how prone literary critics are to this sort of thing in "Against the Typology of Styles" (Part II).

Other linguistic critics have gone further and contended that the attempt on the part of many literary critics to present their imaginative experience of the work is emotional self-indulgence, "just pages of the critic's emotional autobiography." [12] Georges Poulet would hardly feel wounded by such a charge as he does not regard literature to be "a kind of language," except in a negligible material sense. It might, however, vex such critics as Cleanth Brooks or W. K. Wimsatt, who have been arguing all along that the business of the critic is to be objective. But even these critics, though hardly impressionistic, are not truly analytical in the eyes of the linguist. Beyond all the name-calling the basic contention of the linguistically oriented critic is that criticism has failed to develop adequate analytical techniques to describe and explain the effects registered in the language of literature; these techniques can be found best, if not only, in formal linguistics. Richard Ohmann presents this view in "Generative Grammars and the Concept of Style," and he offers a model of linguistic analysis in "Literature as Sentences" (pp. 389–97).

Literary critics have attacked linguistic critics on several grounds: (1) their indifference to aesthetic value; (2) their neglect of the distinctive forms, conventions, and structures of fiction or poetry; and (3) their failure to account for why as well as how the properties of language function in literature, both in the ways a writer uses verbal structures and linguistic devices to catch and hold the attention of the reader, and the ways the language of literature works on the specific expectations of the reader (which may be as basic, and as distinct from what he expects in any other form of language, as the disposition to accept the very fictionality of literature).[13]

F. W. Bateson presents some arguments on all these issues in "Linguistics and Literary Criticism" (Part IV), but an even stronger case for the differences between the uses of language in literature and in other forms of speech has been made by critics who are better-versed in linguistics. Alphonse G. Juilland, for example, has argued (in an essay-review published in 1954) against the view that the linguistic techniques would be sufficient for stylistic analysis, because "all they can disclose are linguistic facts." Juilland quotes a statement by the linguists Archibald Hill and Harold Whitehall that "a work of literature is . . . a language act, like other language acts, but differentiated from them by characteristics of its own," but the nature of these "characteristics of its own," Juilland says, we do not know, and by definition they are not of a linguistic nature; hence the literary act is something more than any other language act.[14]

Roman Jakobson, however, has been preoccupied with this distinction. "Poetics," he says, "deals primarily with the question, *What makes a verbal message a work of art?*" The principal subject of poetics "is the *differentia specifica* of verbal art in relation to other arts and in relation to other kinds of verbal behavior." [15] And he himself has made the first serious effort to formulate a general hypothesis explaining the specific difference between the language of literature and other forms of language.

The two basic modes of arrangement used in all verbal behavior are, in Jakobson's hypothesis, *selection* and *combination*. Selection is based upon equivalence, a metaphorical relationship, either of similarity or dissimilarity. The speaker establishes his topic (subject) by choosing one among various available synonyms and then says what he wants to say about it (predicate) by another selection from another set of interchangeable words (paradigm). Combining these words (their contiguity) produces a sentence.

> If "child" is the topic of the message, the speaker selects one among the extant, more or less similar, nouns like child, kid, youngster, tot, all of them equivalent in a certain respect, and then, to comment on this topic, he may select one of the semantically cognate verbs — sleeps, dozes, nods, naps. Both chosen words combine in the speech chain. The selection is produced on the base of equivalence, similarity and dissimilarity, synonymity and antonymity, while the combination, the build up of the sequence, is based on contiguity.

In poetic structures, however, equivalence is promoted to the constitutive device of the sequence. Accordingly, as Jakobson states his hypothesis, *"the poetic function projects the principle of equivalence from the axis of selection into the axis of combination."* For instance, words are combined into rhythmic, alliterative, and rhymic sequences because of their equivalence in sound, which inevitably establishes semantic equations between these words; their respective meanings are consequently perceived as related by similarity (hence a metaphor or simile) or dissimilarity (hence an antithesis).

> In poetry one syllable is equalized with any other syllable of the same sequence; word stress is assumed to equal word stress,

as unstress equals unstress; prosodic long is matched with long, and short with short; word boundary equals word boundary, no boundary equals no boundary; syntactic pause equals syntactic pause, no pause equals no pause. Syllables are converted into units of measure, and so are morae or stresses.[16]

These theories are implicit in the structural analysis of Baudelaire's sonnet, and Jakobson and Lévi-Strauss are so painstaking and thorough that there seems to be nothing more to say about the poem. And yet a literary critic may wonder what their analysis has accomplished. Leo Bersani says that it is the closest reading of a poem he has ever seen, "while it makes the poem entirely invisible" (p. 99).

Michael Riffaterre has offered a long and searching critique of the essay in his article "Describing Poetic Structures: Two Approaches to Baudelaire's 'Les Chats,' " in which he concludes:

The sonnet is rebuilt by the two critics into a "superpoem," inaccessible to the normal reader, and yet the structures described do not explain what establishes contact between poetry and the reader. No grammatical analysis of the poem can give us more than the grammar of the poem.[17]

Riffaterre's argument is too intricate to summarize here, but a basic contention is that the analysis by Jakobson and Lévi-Strauss "scans everything with even hand and is therefore misleading." It does not *screen* the "pertinent structures and only pertinent structures." [18]

The same criticism is made by Nicolas Ruwet in his paper on "Linguistics and Poetics." He says that the most serious theoretical problem raised by the structural analysis of poetry is: "Which equivalences must be treated as pertinent?" All the equivalences might be pertinent from a poetic point of view, but, up to the present time, Ruwet asserts, "We possess no criterion which might permit us to choose, among the multitude of possible equivalences, those which are really pertinent in a given poem, for a given author, or in a given style. "A theory of context, both linguistic and non-linguistic" is needed to explain the "beauty" of certain poems as well as describe their phonic structures.[19]

And that would seem to bring us back to the issue of judgment in the criticism of the literary performance. Linguistic critics need be no more concerned with ranking poets and poems than literary critics, but they have to be concerned as much with discernment, knowing what to look for, recognizing what is per-

tinent, as with what to do once it has been found. Their formidable techniques of description and analysis must engage the
very kinds of questions Blackmur proposes in Part I. In a
recent encounter between linguists and literary critics, Helen
Hennessy Vendler made a famous issue out of her review of the
English linguist Roger Fowler's collection of *Essays on Style and
Language* (1966). She wrote:

> The linguist's training is in description, and Mr. Fowler, for in-
> stance, gives us an accurate description of [Francis] Bacon's "tri-
> partite scheme in his grammatical constructions," adding that this
> is "an effective but rare rhetorical scheme; compare the much
> greater popularity of schemes based on two- or four-fold grammati-
> cal repetition (Lyly and most other balanced or antithetical prose)."
> But the *critical* act is one which goes beyond this descriptive process
> and asks questions: "What is the effect here of threes in preference
> to twos or fours? Are there more threes elsewhere in Bacon? What
> do threes mean as an order for Bacon? Who else, like Bacon, has
> a liking for threes? Why?" Mr. Fowler, then, has not really been a
> critic here, though his analysis is useful pre-critical material.[20]

Vendler's remarks are incisive, but they may be questionable as
a general indictment, and too condescending, for she fails to
acknowledge what Riffaterre and Ruwet, with all their reservations about the limits of structural linguistics for literary criticism, demonstrate so conclusively: that linguistics has produced
critical descriptions of amazing acuteness and power. If it must
go further, as Ruwet says, in developing "a theory of context"
that will explain why literary performances affect us the way
they do, that is no less a task for the literary critic than for the
linguist.

Richard Ohmann's essay, "Literature as Sentences," is based
on a later stage of linguistic theory than Jakobson's. One difficulty
in fashioning a linguistically oriented literary criticism is that
linguistics is a rapidly changing field which has undergone several
revolutions in basic theory. The structural linguistics on which
Jakobson and Lévi-Strauss base their critical analysis of Baudelaire's poem seems to have been supplanted in favor (for the
reasons Nicolas Ruwet offers) by the so-called transformational
generative grammar associated with Noam Chomsky. Ohmann
believes that an effective theory of literary style must come from
an adequate theory of syntax which will take into account the
deeper structural features of language as well as its surface structures. In "Literature as Sentences" and other articles, Ohmann

has been trying to derive such a theory of style from the concepts, methods of investigation, and techniques of linguistic analysis developed by Chomsky and his followers.[21]

The selections by Robert Frost and William H. Gass offer a different view of the topic of literature as sentences. They may come as a relief after the forbiddingly technical exercises of linguistic criticism. They are important however, not because they are lighter reading, but because they help us to see an essential quality about the literary performance to which linguists, and literary critics too for that matter, have so far paid insufficient notice.

Frost says that "the voice of the imagination, the speaking voice must know certainly how to behave, how to posture in every sentence" the writer offers. A writer must string his words "on definite recognizable sentence sounds." And Gass (who knows Frost's notions) says that the sentence of a fiction must be sounded: "It has a rhythm, speed, a tone, a flow, a pattern, shape, length, pitch, conceptual direction."

More is at stake here than the proper method of analyzing these constituents of the form of a sentence. Frost and Gass make us aware of the need to engage the shape and flow of sentences in literature, the modes of their *performance,* the very process by which a writer makes sense. Linguists, to be sure, can describe the action of speech, the way sentences are voiced, with fine precision, but the functions listed by Gass are hardly to be contained within any existing analytical framework. Nor can they be parceled out to the study of rhetoric, as Ohmann proposes. If an analysis of how these functions interact comes from linguistics at all, it will have to wait until "the general theory of context" Ruwet mentions is developed. Meanwhile, Frost has shown us a crucial quality to look for in the literary performance, something no critic, linguistic or literary, should ignore.

Northrop Frye has been preoccupied with issues of structure and context, as is evident in his selections in Part I, and in his essay here on Milton's *Lycidas* he demonstrates these notions in critical performance. It is at once apparent how different his mode of "structural analysis" is from that of linguistic critics. He is concerned more with the functions of language than with its constituent structures. In fact, he is hardly interested in the language of literature at all — only in the forms and structures literature creates. His notion of context is equally distinctive. The contexts giving shape and meaning to individual works of literature are derived from the total form of literature itself rather than the specific contexts of the language act or the more general contexts of verbal behavior.

Frye makes a point of separating the figure of the poet in *Lycidas* from Milton's personal experience. The "I" of the poem, he says, "is a professional poet in his conventional shepherd disguise." Lycidas is a literary figure in a family of literary pastorals, whose next of kin are in Theocritus and Virgil, not in seventeenth-century Cambridge. Milton's only relevant personal experiences were his previous efforts in the pastoral convention. And, Frye says, "the only relevant feelings he had are concerned with his determination to do a good job with a pastoral elegy." [22] That may sound like a frivolous way of putting Milton's motive, especially if, comparing Maurice Blanchot's otherwise similar attempt to depersonalize literature, we lose all sense of the exigencies of the poet's misfortunes. But Frye is perfectly aware of the serious meanings of the poem. What he may be showing in his own way is that exigency of the poet's performance Robert Frost described.

M. H. Abrams's essay tracing the imagery of "the correspondent breeze" through the poetry of several English Romantic poets raises some sharp questions about archetypal criticism. His strictures may not really apply to Frye's critical practice, because Frye says explicitly in his essay on *Lycidas* that we should not think of myth "as some kind of Platonic idea existing by itself," but some of Abrams's observations about the relation of convention to a poet's individual performance put the issue in a different light. Abrams attempts to identify precisely what makes "the correspondent breeze, like the guilt-haunted wanderer and the Promethean or Satanic figure of heroic rebel" a "distinctively Romantic image." Frye can explain the transformations and displacements of such archetypes, but it is probably fair to say that he minimizes "the conventional framework of ideas or assumptions which form the background" of individual poems (such as *Lycidas*), whereas Abrams is intent on establishing the relation of the imagery of a poem to "the philosophical, political, and aesthetic preoccupations" of a specific historical period. Abrams gives a different perspective on what Frye has said is the central activity of criticism: "establishing a context for the works of literature being studied." [23]

To move from the studies of imagery by Frye and Abrams to Gaston Bachelard's treatment of "Drawers, Chests, and Wardrobes" is to confront, as happens in the encounter with the French

New Criticism on many issues, a set of assumptions almost entirely different from those of American and English criticism. "The language of metaphor," Frye says, following Aristotle, is "the distinctive language of poetry." But Bachelard argues that there is a "radical difference between imagery and metaphor," and it is the image, "the pure product of absolute imagination," "a phenomenon of pure being," which is the true source of poetry. An image is a matrix of energy rather than a figure of representation.

Images have contexts for Frye and Abrams, but for Bachelard they can be separated from their surrounding words for literary study. The image, he says, "has an entity and dynamism of its own." Furthermore, although it is "the concentration of the entire" psyche of its author, it has no past, no cause. It is by some mysterious process self-generating, and even the efforts of a psychoanalyst to give it cause or context are misguided. (One way to appreciate the uniqueness of Bachelard's treatment of the image is to compare his selection with Freud's famous essay, "The Theme of the Three Caskets.") It follows that the image can only be apprehended by "reverie," not explained; it "has no need of scholarship." [24] Studying patterns of images is common enough in American and English criticism, but the method used by Abrams, say, is altogether different from Bachelard's "topo-analysis of intimate space."

Actually, however, Bachelard shares some similarities with the American and English "Imagist" poets of 1910–1920. As Frank Kermode has shown (see Part V), these poets considered the image to be "the primary pigment of poetry." Still, the absorption of their principles into criticism produced something quite different from Bachelard's view. It may be hard to see the critical implications of Bachelard's theory of the image from this brief selection (especially if Leo Bersani is right in saying that "by all ordinary standards of judgment, Bachelard's taste in poetry is often execrable," p. 95) but a good example may be seen in J. Hillis Miller's essay on William Carlos Williams in Part I, which owes something of its method to Bachelard.

Denis Donoghue's essay on W. B. Yeats addresses itself to certain issues of symbolism in connection with Yeats's poetry. Yeats is usually thought of as a symbolist poet, for the reasons that Donald Davie offers (p. 438 ff.), but Donoghue argues that though Yeats "flirted with the theory of Symbolism," he came to commit himself to "an oral culture," the culture of his native Ireland, and to the traditions and modes of the voice. Yeats's characteristic poems, Donoghue says, are "human sounds rather than objects" — the products of his labors at making a language of poetry that, in Yeats's own words, would "coincide with that of passionate, normal speech."

"Voice" is an important concept in recent American and English criticism. (Leo Bersani suggests that one thing wrong with the French New Criticism is its indifference to "the 'voice' of a particular passage" in literature, p. 102). The term, Frost's "speaking voice," uses the metaphoric associations of "speaking" to describe how a writer "talks" to his "listener," the reader. In the sense closest to its literal meaning, voice is an awareness by the writer of how his words perform, how they sound — which suggests an attempt to achieve in writing the kind of presence and immediacy we achieve in talk by intonation, pitch, gesture, facial expression, and all the other resources of speaking. One extension of the figure goes beyond compensating in writing for the expressive advantages of speaking to suggest that every occasion for writing is a dramatic situation, a performance in which the writer chooses a role suited to what he is or wants to appear to be. Another extension applies the figure to style by proceeding on the question: What sort of person does the author reveal himself to be by the way he "talks"? Even where the author separates himself from a dramatic character (as T. S. Eliot described in a famous essay of 1953, "The Three Voices of Poetry"), we can still judge how the author means us to take that *persona* by the way he makes him talk.[25]

Donoghue uses "voice" to show how Yeats patterned his poetry on the traditions of speaking in Irish culture and literature, and, more generally, to describe Yeats's progress from the frozen objects of the symbolist aesthetic to poems which "choose the living world for text . . . poems of place, time, memory, voice, conflict, personality." Other critics of Yeats might argue that Donoghue gives too little weight to the vacillations and ambiguities in Yeats's reconciliation to "the temporal, the limited, the finite"; that he was more than occasionally tempted to write "a Supreme Fiction." But his treatment of Yeats's literary performance is an eloquent demonstration of criticism attending to Frost's "speaking voice" and Yeats's own love for "passionate, normal speech."

GEORGES POULET

Henry James

I have to the last point the instinct and the sense for fusions and interrelations, for framing and encircling. . . .[1]

"Consciousness is an illimitable power. . . ."[2] The moment that Henry James' thought begins to take cognizance of itself and of the world, it recognizes the infinite character of its task. This consists of representing. Now, everything is to be represented. The being who applies himself to reflect the objects of his experience, perceives that nothing is excluded from his experience. "Experience is never limited and it is never complete."[3] The universe is an immense spider web whose threads recross one another indefinitely and, at the same time, prolong one another. How to distinguish, how to choose in this multitude, vibrant, silken, iridescent, made up of repeated contacts, of subtle contiguities, of ceaselessly renewed relationships? Like the sea wave whose murmur, for Leibnitz, is made up of all the particular sounds produced by the droplets composing it, for Henry James, experience, the total of consciousness, is at every moment formed by a vertiginous ensemble of connected impressions, linked in a web of events so pressed together that the spirit exhausts itself counting them.

The exterior world is therefore a vast living expanse along which, from all sides, and lost to sight, a shiver runs and scatters. "Life is, immensely, a matter of surface. . . ."[4] But the inner world, that of depth, reveals an equivalent immensity and complexity. From his earliest youth, James found himself to be the ecstatic and overwhelmed victim of what he calls "the terrible fluidity of self-revelation . . .";[5] a fluidity the more torrential since it was without let-up, added to by an inexhaustible reservoir of remembrances. In his family they "professed amaze-

SOURCE: From *The Metamorphoses of the Circle,* translated by Carley Dawson and Elliot Coleman in collaboration with the author from *Les Métamorphoses du cercle* (Paris: Plon, 1961), (Baltimore: The Johns Hopkins Press, 1966), pp. 307–320. This essay is inscribed "To Jean Rousset." Reprinted by permission of The Johns Hopkins Press.

ment, and even occasionally impatience, at my reach of reminiscence.
. . ." [6] One might have been even more surprised by its fertility. Far
from being, as with Proust, a fortuitous time rarely rediscovered by the
working of involuntary memory, the past, with James, is always present
and goes on constantly, enlarging itself like a spot of oil in the consciousness; so much so that in the last analysis the great problem for James
is not to remember, but quite the contrary, to clear his thought by forget-
fulness. For in his consciousness, images of the past come in swarms.

Speaking of a book of reminiscences which he intended to write, James
states:

> (I found) discriminations among the parts of my subjects again
> and again difficult — so inseparably and beautifully they seemed to
> hang together. . . . This meant that aspects began to multiply and
> images to swarm. . . . To knock at the door of the past was in a word
> to see it open to me quite wide. . . .[7]

And further on he confesses:

> I lose myself, of a truth, under the whole pressure of the spring
> of memory. . . .[8]

Nothing is more significant in Henry James than this loss of self
caused by the very abundance of memories. If thought is disturbed and
gets lost, it is not through diminution, it is through plethora. The mass
of remembered images obstructs and overwhelms him. It adds itself to
that other mass, no less profuse, which is that of present perceptions. In
this prodigiously rich universe, in which, without respite, the mind sinks
down, without direction and without end, as in a virgin forest, it is submerged as much by the multitude of detail as by the enormity of the ensemble. An inextricable entanglement of associations impedes his vision
and slows his step. Henry James feels himself to be lost within himself,
as a disciple of Copernicus felt himself to be without a landmark in the
vastness of cosmic space. As Pascal saw the universe measurelessly enlarging itself around him, so James, at the extremity of his gaze, sees himself ramify, subdivide, and finally burst the perimeter of his experience.
To become aware of himself and of the world is to become aware of a
double expanse the limits of which it is no more possible to attain, as it
is not possible to separate the parts. Everything gets tied up together;
everything goes on, and develops in "one mighty loom spreading many-
colored figures." [9] It is in vain that one seeks to "isolate, to surround with
the sharp black line, to frame in the square, the circle," [10] some element
which cannot be isolated. The first representation of the real which one
finds in Henry James is thus an illimitable, inform, and unintelligible
actuality. Never has a thought shown itself, at first, so embarrassed by its
own luxury. Where shall one find a way out, an end, a remedy? One

needs at all costs an act of mind to stop short this proliferation which is both marvelous and fatal. Henry James gives himself limits, as one becomes a convert, as one emigrates, as one decides radically to alter one's life. For him, the formal order is an almost despairing way to escape from what he calls *"to work in terror, fairly, of the vast expanse of the surface."* [11]

> Therefore it is that experience has to organize for convenience and cheer, some system of observation — for fear, in the admirable immensity, of losing its way. [12]

To the admirable immensity will be opposed the system of observation which will establish limits there. The important business for the writer is to place boundaries where, naturally, there are none. For James, as for the classics, literature is a limited representation, therefore formal, therefore artificial, of what for him, is illimitable: "Really, universally, relations stop nowhere, and the exquisite problem of the artist is eternally but *to draw, by a geometry of his own, the circle* within which they shall happily appear to do so." [13] Thus, with James, the circle in no way plays the part of a theological or a cosmic symbol; it has nothing to do with the *being* of things. It is pure representation of an appearance. An arbitrary cutting-out accomplished by the artist in the great fluid mass of experience, it creates a cloister in whose shelter reality can be isolated, contemplated, and represented, without running the risk of melting into the universal multiplicity of phenomena. The terror inspired in Henry James by the admirable immensity has, for him, as effect, the immediate desire to elevate barriers. So this thought, spontaneously and initially one of the most formless possible, almost from the very first adopts the most rigorous formalism.

It is therefore of the utmost importance to discern by what processes formalization in Henry James is accomplished. Already there is the simple fact that thought constituting itself into a "central" consciousness carries with it a kind of circular disposition of the environing world. The mind is a search-light moving in space. On all sides it projects its rays. The universe builds itself concentrically from a central source of light.

Thus consciousness now does not appear any longer as an illimitable activity. It spreads out in the fields which it illumines, but in the very manner in which it proceeds, one must note, says James, "something that holds one in one's place, makes it a standpoint in the universe." [14]

A whole series of novels by Henry James represents with precision the modalities of a central point of view opening onto a peripheral world. "The first thing we do," says James, "is cast about for some center in our field." [15] And elsewhere, " 'Place the centre of the object in the young woman's own consciousness,' I said to myself, 'and you get as interesting and as beautiful a difficulty as you could wish.' " [16] From *Roderick Hudson* to *The Ambassadors*, it is easy to point out in the works of Henry James those novels in which the consciousness of a central character forms the *"middle light,"* [17] around which all the other elements, driven back to second place, must be content with playing the role of objects. Like Adolphe, like Julian Sorel, or Emma Bovary, certain of James' characters (Rowland Mallet, Newman, Caponsacchi, Isabel Archer, Maisy, Strether) see themselves given the almost exclusive importance due those beings by whose eyes what is to be is going to be perceived. The universe appears to be, if not an invention of their mind, at least the frame filled by their interpretative fancy, or the ensemble of elements whose cohesion and even intelligibility depend on their organizing power. With most of the French novelists of the nineteenth century, the central consciousness is more often psychological than aesthetic. It is the starting point from which are revealed, before anything else (except perhaps with Flaubert) the inner depths of the conscious being. It is quite otherwise with Henry James. If consciousness diffuses itself there, it is almost exclusively outside itself, in zones which are those of external life. James' consciousness, a surprising fact at the time, turns away from interiority. It is, so to speak, never the center of itself. It remains purely a point of view. A point of view which, most of the time, is that of a character whose investigating look, different from all others, holds the faculty of leaving on the objects which it contemplates, a nuance, a specific coloration, which is the stamp of its contemplative activity. Every look attests the entirely relative way of looking of a definite being. And the novel of which it is the center has as its goal to make this invariable individuality of point of view to appear in the variety of objects on which he exerts it. Moreover, behind the centrality of the principal character, there is still, with Henry James, another centrality, if one can so phrase it, even more withdrawn: that of the author himself. Every central character is for James a means of perceiving things according to the angle of incidence which a creature of his choice gives him. At the back of the consciousness of the character, there is therefore the consciousness of the novelist. It is like the consciousness of a consciousness. Occult, dissimulated into the background, it reigns no less everywhere. It is the center of the center. From the commanding point of view which it occupies, it silently imposes on its universe the interpretations of its thought and the choices of its will.

Among the essential aspects of the work one must therefore note the supremacy manifested by the center on the sphere in which it exerts its action. Often James represents this superiority under the form of a radiating consciousness, more noble or more delicate or more innocent than those of the beings in whose milieu it is placed. Around the lofty-minded soul are grouped the ordinary ones. "My problem," Henry James writes, in speaking of a novel which he titled *The Spoils of Poynton*, "has decently to be met — that of establishing for the other persons the vividness of their appearance of comparative stupidity, that of exposing them to the full thick wash of the penumbra surrounding the central light. . . ." [18] "It isn't *centrally* a drama of fools or vulgarians," he says elsewhere, à propos of another novel, *The Ivory Tower*, "it's only circumferentially and surroundedly so." [19]

James therefore takes his delight in disposing around a certain central purity a more or less dense crowd of secondary characters, comic or tragic. To the central light are opposed the penumbras which it cannot always penetrate. If in itself it shines with an invariable brilliance, it does not bring the same intensity of light everywhere. There is nothing more striking in Henry James than this power's limitation at irradiating light. Certain of his works are like a bursting of sunrays, fan-shaped, through a ceiling of clouds trying to prevent their display. The resistance opposed by opaque peripheral objects to the illuminating power of central fire is one of the most certain means by which the novelist manifests the calculated limitation of his universe.

But if the Jamesian novel is most often the expression of a radiating look or thought, that is to say of a movement which goes from the center to the circumference, it can as easily be the reverse. As in Flaubert's novels, so well-loved and criticized by Henry James, one sometimes finds with the latter the description of a peripheral milieu, which exerts pressure at the center of the action on the consciousness of the hero. Instead of being an essentially diffusive force, the central consciousness becomes then a simple receptive center. And the beauty of these tales consists then, exclusively, in the entirely passive relationship to which the mind submits relative to the environing world:

> That such an hour has its meaning, and that the meaning might be great for him, this of course *surged* softly in, more and more, *from every point of the circle that held him.* [20]

Sometimes the affluence of the peripheral element is so great that it covers over and submerges, at least temporarily, the central consciousness:

> The sense was constant for her that their relation was as if afloat, like some island of the south, in a great warm sea that made, for every conceivable chance, a margin, an outer sphere of general emotion; and the effect of the occurrence of anything in particular was to make the sea submerge the island, the margin flood the text. The great wave now for a moment swept over. [21]

A wave that now unfurls and now withdraws. Of whatever sort, how-

ever, the movements are which traverse Henry James' novels, they unroll
between two limits. On one side, there is a thought placed in a center,
on the other, a world having nothing any more of the illimitable. The
choice of a consciousness, for James, is the choice of a *form*. Thanks to
the point of view which it assumes, the consciousness, at the heart of the
work, becomes an authentic *"principle of composition."* [22] A finite world
finds itself linked with a thought which, itself, is finite. The universe no
longer is a fleeing infinity. The novel's space is that which is enclosed in
a visually and mentally determined field.

To the finite space, moreover, a *finite time* corresponds. We have already spoken of the diffluent character of memory with Henry James. It
extends everywhere, submerges everything. To the overflowing activity of
his memory, Henry James also opposes the same restrictions as to the
illimitable multiplication of his actual experiences. Instead of allowing
the influx of remembrances immeasurably to swell the temporal area of
consciousness, he assigns extremely narrow limits to it. Like his brother
William, Henry James reserves his attention to the "specious present," that
is to say to the small circle of duration which, at every moment of existence, barely encloses the feeling of the immediate past and of the imminent future. In short, life is a matter of actuality, as it is a matter
of outside interests. Let us put memory in the ante-room and leave it
there. "The ragbag of memory hung on its nail in my closet, though I
learned with time to control the habit of bringing it forth." [23]

The Jamesian novel therefore will frequently be divested of the past.
Its characters find themselves in relationships which more often than not
are the effect of present junctures. They take new positions because of
events which are themselves just as new. A matter of the surface and not
of depth, of a displacement in space and not in time. The Jamesian character has usually little duration; or rather, his duration unlike the one of
Flaubert's or Tolstoy's characters, has no temporal thickness. Between his
actual existence and the depth of his mind stretch no thick layers of
memories. The duration of these characters is comparable to that of celestial bodies; not that it is particularly long — it is rather the contrary
— but it consists, as the one of stars, in the successive localization of the
selfsame entity in different points of space. In a certain minute and a
certain year, it is here; in another moment and another year, it is there.
Its nature does not change. What changes is the relationship all other
points of space have with it. This makes for a complex calculus in which
time is of great importance, yet less than space. To go from Europe to
America, or from America to Europe implies, in this regard, a more significant mutation than to pass from adolescence to manhood. In any
case it is more calculable. It is also more easily contained within the precise limits the mind sets.

There is still another way in which Henry James can prevent himself from becoming lost in profundity. This is to assign to his character a past which is close to the present, a duration which is least removed from the world of the surface:

> I delight in a palpable imaginable *visitable* past — in the nearer distances and the clearer mysteries, the marks and signs of a world we may reach over to as by making a long arm we grasp an object at the other end of our own table.[24]

The near past is thus neither dangerous nor prolix. By reason of its shallowness it is almost flush with the present: it is without distance and without depth. Therefore it is not a true past. It is made one with places. It is within reach of the hand. — But then, what does one do with the real past? Ignore it? This is what, most often, James is content to do. But sometimes the demon of curiosity, and that other demon, more perverse still, which incites a novelist to choose as a subject what he fears most and in which he least delights, draws him down into the depths. This is what occurs in what is perhaps the most famous of Henry James' stories, *The Turn of the Screw*. But the fabulous past — impalpable, unimaginable, non-visitable — which one finds in it is actually less perilous for James than the real past, the historic past. Despite the precautions he takes and the limitations which he gives himself, the desire persists in him "to remount the stream of time, really to bathe in its upper and more natural waters. . . ."[25] This is what he attempted to do in *The Sense of the Past,* an unfinished and posthumous novel, in which he gives his hero a disposition most different to his own, one which renders the mind "oddly indifferent to the actual and the possible."[26] But this past, far away as its upper range may be situated, also seems close to him for it does not in fact differ basically from the close past; it is also a distanceless past enclosed within precise limits: "It was when life was framed in death," James says of his character, "that the picture was really hung up."[27] Death here, therefore, is not a new, illimitable dimension, given to the person who disappears. It is, on the contrary, the definite stoppage of existence, its placing in a determined frame. The same perspective is found in another of James' stories, *The Altar of the Dead.* An old man creates a cult for his departed friends. He thinks of them before a symbolic arrangement of candles placed in a circle on an altar. Now that their lives are finished it becomes possible, so to speak, to make up their sum total and to enclose them in a circumference of retrospective meditations. The past is therefore not an infinity. Limited by death, it forms the subjacent frame of the present, hence, a limitation.

The limitation imposed by the circle is, for that matter, not single but double. In a circle there is not only an external rim, traced by the circumference, but at its interior, a point-limit, which is the center. For certain intellects, such as Plotinus, Cusa, Boehme, Amiel, or Blanchot, it is true that the center is not a limitation. It is a sort of interior infinity, a species of abyss. For Henry James, on the contrary, the center is a stopping-point, the place where convergences encounter each other and get immobilized. As has been noted, the circumferential limitation can be formed by the assemblage of the exterior objects on which, by turns, is placed the attention issuing from the center. Nevertheless, since there are two limits, it is simple to invert them, and, reversing the perspective, to manage in such a way that the object of attention becomes the point of arrival of a movement of prospection and exploration (one would have to say of *in-spection* and of im-ploration) coming from the periphery. So everything changes, consciousness, from central, becoming peripheral, and the object contemplated, becoming the central objective. Let us imagine, therefore, in the heart of a novel, a certain object — animate or inanimate — a vase, a town, a woman, it doesn't matter what. What does matter, is that there is a mind which bends over it, envelops it, places it at the center of its attention. At first this watchful thought is still distant, or its attention is divided, or it is otherwise occupied. Little by little it becomes fixed and draws near. At last, drawn into the circle, it concentrates itself upon the object. No doubt Balzac earlier — and before him, Rousseau — had known how to describe a world made up of convergent covetousnesses, at whose center, held as between cross fires, a victim fought. But Henry James is the first novelist to perceive that every one of these lusts has its seat in an appropriately peripheric consciousness; he gave to certain of his novels the structure of a central object reflected in such a kind of consciousness. Perhaps, incidentally, there was no more natural gesture for the author of *The Portrait of a Lady* than to begin by withdrawing and give first place to that on which his attention was fixed. In his social and sentimental relationships one sees him at first keeping his distance, only coming forward after some time, and with a thousand precautions toward the interiority of others. This is what is made very clear in the following lines, taken from a letter of Henry James' to one of his women friends:

> I don't know — and how should I? — much about you in detail — but I think I have a kind of instinct of how the sidebrush of things that I do get in a general way a reverberation of, touches and affects you, and as in one way or another there seems to have been plenty of the stress and strain of life on the circumference (and even some of it at the center, as it were) of your circle I've not been without feeling (and responding to), I boldly say, *some* of your vibrations.[28]

As this curious epistolary text shows us, James preferably places himself at the tangential point of the circles projected by souls. It is in this point that, in his opinion, he can more easily detect the waves emanating from the lives of others. He it is who sympathizes from afar, who vibrates delicately at a distance. More than that, to add to the space which separates him from the object to which the most lively sympathy allies him, he deliberately places between himself and the object a kind of character-witness, whose double mission consists in observing the object in question, and dissimulating the presence of the author. "I have already betrayed my preference . . . for 'seeing my story,' through the opportunity and the sensibility of some more or less detached, but not strictly involved, though thoroughly interested and intelligent, witness or reporter, some person who contributes to the case mainly a certain amount of criticism and interpretation of it, . . . a convenient substitute or apologist for the creative power otherwise so veiled and disembodied." [29]

There are therefore in the exercise of the peripheral consciousness the same possibilities of *control* as in the functioning of the central consciousness. A certain spectator, behind whom the intentions of the author are hidden, does his job, which consists of observing and interpreting. He casts a more and more informed look toward some central mystery. It is he who spies, who foresees, who even explains and makes ready. The events take place as he had predicted, as though to show their submission toward an intelligence which has thought them, even before their accomplishment. Thus Jamesian thought gives itself over to a game of marvelous subtlety. At the center of action there is an object, and on this object an attention places itself. The attention observes the object in all the complexity of its relationships. Finally, it knows it, and from the moment it knows it, it is as if the object became its creature and began to obey its instructions.

But to come to this result, what inspections, what proceedings and preliminary conjectures! James' peripheral thought detests nothing so much as to *be abrupt* in the progressive knowledge of his object. Then, too, he does not go down to the object in a straight line, but on the contrary, multiplies around it circumvolutions of all kinds. In *The Wings of the Dove, The Golden Bowl,* and *The Sacred Fount,* which are among the most sinuous of his novels and those least in a hurry to come to the final and central termination of their career, the moment that Henry James succeeds in establishing his interpretive thought in the neighborhood of an object to be investigated, he makes it turn right around by a spiral movement which closes on its prey only with extreme slowness. A prey which can be, as in *The Spoils of Poynton,* an assemblage of inanimate things, but which can also be, as in *The Golden Bowl,* the image of a loved person, to which the mind constantly returns. It is this situation which is described in a passage in the latter novel, in which the love of a woman is compared to a garden in whose center an ivory tower is set:

> She had walked round and round it — that was what she felt; she
> had carried on her existence in the space left her for circulation, a

space that sometimes seemed ample and sometimes narrow; looking up all the while at the fair structure that spread itself so amply and rose so high, but never quite making out as yet where she might have entered had she wished.[30]

In the final analysis, however, Maggy will arrive at the foot of the ivory tower and succeed in entering it. The Henry James novel advances by a movement often almost imperceptible, but it never marks time, and its progression is one of an understanding that wishes to be patient and meticulous. And in a sense, as it approaches the center, it is true to say of the investigative thought, that it turns in a narrower and narrower circle. But in another sense, since its inquiries ceaselessly grow in number, the circle containing them seems to become more and more vast; the more so as the mind is not content to perceive what is, but *supposes* what *could be,* so that reality thus discovered is engrossed in all kinds of possibilities. Thus, the inquiring motion which envelops the object can appear, turn by turn, immense and narrow, similar in this way to the circles which imagination follows in certain dreams. It is a movement of this kind that in *The Sacred Fount* is witnessed by the reader when, lost in the thousand suppositions which some mysterious happening arouses in him, the indiscrete, fanciful, and perplexed observer, who with James is always the typical representative of the peripheric consciousness, walks at sunset in a park whose capricious avenues, perpetually leading back one into the other, represent fairly well the meanderings of his cogitations. And it is then that, like a decisive answer to the complicated network of his interrogative approaches, at the bottom of the perspective, there appears the very person who holds the key to the problem and around whom the fantastic frame of hypotheses has been built:

> This was the light in which Mrs. Server, walking alone now, apparently, in the grey wood and pausing at sight of me, showed herself in her clear dress at the end of a vista. It was exactly as if she had been there by the operation of my intelligence.[31]

How many times in a Jamesian novel the reader does become a witness to this perfect coincidence of objective reality and of the mind which conceives it, as though, to employ James' expression, one was the effect of the sorcery of the other! A cry of triumph seems then to spring to the lips of him to whom, one might say, it has only been necessary to think of something to have it realized. Now the mind, finally ceasing to turn around its object, can rejoin at one leap, at the center of its investigations, truth confirmed.

A truth which, moreover, at the very instant in which it reveals itself, appears as the managing principle of all which surrounds it.

More than any other of James' novels, *The Sacred Fount* seems to have as its aim the description of the phenomenon by which things distribute themselves around a center, while this makes its presence felt at the very heart of peripheric consciousness. For instance, in this novel, there is a particularly notable scene in which a group of guests one evening are listening to a musician. "It was the infinite that, for the hour, the distinguished foreigner poured out to us, causing it to roll in wonderful waves of sound, almost of colour, over our receptive attitudes and faces."

Let us be wary however of believing that the infinity of which James speaks here is the same as the illimitable multiplication of sentient experience of which, there at the beginning, there was question. Here what is specifically considered is an infinity, if one may so phrase it, ordained and set in a frame. On the one hand, it would seem that the music should diffuse itself indefinitely into a sky where colors and sounds harmonize; but on the other, this great excentric current is as though dominated and directed by the same central presence which we have seen in the preceding passage, since James takes care to add: "The perfection of that, enjoyed as we enjoyed it, all made a margin, a series of concentric circles of rosecolor (shimmering away into the pleasant vague of everything else that didn't matter), for the salient little figure of Mrs. Server, still the controlling image for me, the real principle of composition, in this affluence of fine things." [32]

Once more, center and principle of composition identify. But this principle no longer is the conscious subject surrounded by the objective world. On the contrary, it is an *objective principle* which is enveloped by the subjectivity of consciousness. Around the object, the mind gravitates, as a spectator turns around a statue which he wishes to admire from all angles. This is what James calls, "the planned rotation of aspects." [33] Instead of a plurality of environing things, there is a unique object on which the mind concentrates itself and whose essential simplicity is to some extent counterbalanced by the multiplicity of its aspects. From this point of view, the Jamesian novel is singularly like a poem by Mallarmé, it, too, being made of "circumvolutionary plays" and of "the exhibition of all its facets" by a mysterious entity in which one finally recognizes the center of all.

The Jamesian novel therefore tends, despite all the windings and arabesques which mask the center, to establish in this the simplicity of a unique object contemplated by a unique consciousness. It is in the simplicity of the central object that the principle of composition now wholly resides. But if this is so, it is not necessary that consciousness, where the object is reflected, should in itself be *one*. The unity of consciousness is only indispensable when the consciousness is the center, not when it is circumferential. With a kind of intellectual frenzy, Henry James explores the infinite possibilities open to the novel by the variation of successive points of view. A whole series of characters defile, in whose consciousness the author insinuates himself by turns, in order to contemplate with ever-differing eyes an object which, of itself, remains unalterably the same. This is what James calls "the law of successive aspects," of which a certain number of his novels are very precise examples. One can find in them the figuration of a new kind of time and space. Around an objective center is established a moving circle of points of view, from one to the other of which the novelist passes. Nothing changes, except the point of view. Time is therefore constituted by the substitution, not so much of one moment for another, as of one *point* for another. It is therefore as "local" a time as possible. The novel is a succession of localizations. One can compare it, as James does, to "the house of fiction (which) has in short not one window, but a million. . . . At each of them stands a figure . . . ," [34] or, again, to "a chest of drawers." [35]

Thus space in the Jamesian novel now appears as a circular field, divided into a multitude of adjoining compartments, in each of which exists a consciousness. The most perfect representation of this space is found in the Preface to *The Awkward Age*. Henry James tells us that, wishing to make the editors of a review understand the composition of this novel, he had drawn on a paper the following symbolic figuration: "*a circle consisting of a number of small rounds disposed at equal distance about a central object.*" "The central object," James explains, "was my situation, my subject in itself, to which the thing would owe its title, and the small rounds presented so many distinct lamps, as I liked to call them, the function of each of which would be to light with all intensity one of its aspects." [36] A surprising image, but marvelously exact, of what the novelist wanted to accomplish: a novel constituted of a plurality of consciousnesses, all aimed at the same object. One could also compare this space to that of an auditorium. Everything there is directed to unify in a center a sheaf of peripheric interests. While, in the real theater, the watching consciousness, passively united, submit to the magic of a central object which alone holds the power to engender variety, in Henry James' novel, on the contrary, it is the witness-consciousnesses, which constantly come to bestow on the central object new virtues and even new possibilities of existence; so that the object thus contemplated appears to live a thousand lives, brought to it, and suggested, by a thousand different looks, by a thousand new interpretations of the real. The astonishing peripheral activity of multiple consciousnesses has the effect, with James, of dilating the real and loading it with all the possibilities which he implies. The real is a center surrounded by a luminous halo of possibilities, at once infinite and finite.

R. P. BLACKMUR

The Charterhouse of Parma

One remembers that Stendhal ends this novel with its dedication: TO THE HAPPY FEW, a phrase which some think was borrowed from Shakespeare. Perhaps. The meaning is at any rate something precious, which when I am reading Stendhal I seem to share: as a kind of elation, a kind of promise; although I cannot explain it. Stendhal had another phrase, to which Baudelaire three times adverts, that beauty is the promise of happiness, and here is the pang that goes with the elation: promises worth making are never kept. But let me quote Baudelaire:

> La dualité de l'art est une conséquence fatale de la dualité de l'homme. Considérez, si cela vous plaît, la partie éternellement subsistante comme l'âme de l'art, et l'élément variable comme son corps. C'est pourquoi Stendhal, esprit impertinent, taquin, répugnant même, mais dont les impertinences provoque utilement la méditation, s'est rapproché de la vérité plus que beaucoup d'autres, en disant que le Beau n'est que la promesse du bonheur.

There is more, but I pause on the three adjectives, impertinent, teasing (or tormenting), and repugnant for Stendhal's mind or spirit, adjectives of which Stendhal would have been proud, whether for himself or his heroes, and proud with a fierce pride, too: the very pride which is *against* every form of resignation, the pride which we do not dare permit to possess us, but which Stendhal's heroes (and half his heroines) wonderfully and rashly appropriate. It is the poetics which Aristotle did not write for the Greeks, but which Lu Chi in his *Wen Fu* did write for the Chinese and for the non-Greek parts of ourselves, and from which I ensample this: "Lay hold of the mutinous soul by sounding its secret depths, pay homage to its vital fierceness as you search for the very self: reason screened and obscured begins to creep forth, thought comes screaming, forced out from the womb" (Part II, Section O, numbers 3 and 4). This is the poetics of hysteria, also that of Stendhal.

SOURCE: From *The Kenyon Review,* Volume 26, Number 1 (Winter 1964), pp. 211–231. Reprinted by permission.

Let us at least pretend for the length of these reflections that there is a verisimilitude in this notion.

Stendhal at once makes it easy for us to do so when he indicates that it is a high thing "to sin from motives of hatred and love," especially if in the presence of a sense of *puntiglio,* passion, and honor, with a contagion or contact of manners and hysteria. Thus the entry of the French army into Milan transformed effeminate manners into passion, caprice into violence. "To risk one's life became the fashion." *Puntiglio* is ultramannerly hysteria. It is naturally an explosive force, especially in a "land of crafty despotism." One wonders whether Stendhal is not making a substantive critique of *puntiglio* when he hinges this last phrase to the idea of caricature. Manners always tend to their own caricature; any given hysteria *is* a caricature of its source, whether of blindness, syphilis, or love.

Examples are almost continuous in Stendhal's opening pages. There is an activity in these chosen people which if it did not have the attractiveness of hysteria (one might say, or do, this oneself!) would be mere fret, which if it did not have the horror of *puntiglio* would be mere violence, and which if it did not have that quality of honor-in-action which goes with manners would be mere fustian: the movement of discommoded instinct — the movement, as we might say, of instinct out of place. Here is a good place to suggest that there is little question of "realism" in Stendhal, and that what we need to approach his books is a convention as remote from realism as Ben Jonson with his ballet of farce and force — as Congreve with his lilting surfaces shot with sudden piercing phrases. These men got plenty of the "real" into their works, but not in the conventions of realism. The avarice of Volpone is as real as the anger of Fabrizio, and the lovely lyric of Millamant's speeches is no less real, and no more, than Gina's manner of dealing with two of her lovers, Limercati and Canon Borda. I think these realities are close kin and the ways of conceiving them even closer, though there is little relation in the mode of treatment. Neither Jonson nor Congreve ever stuck so fast to the anecdotal as Stendhal, who, on the other hand, leaves in unaccountable and incomplete matters which neither playwright would have permitted. In Stendhal, only the emotion has its fragments tied together; its seat, source, and story never are. It is a rare thing for Stendhal to complete any scene or any action — But, to get back to Gina and her lovers.

When Limercati thought her wish that he revenge her husband's murder absurd, her "contempt for him killed her affection," but not her ingenuity. She rekindled his affection into a fire of desperation, and for three years he wasted himself in the country, returning every other month to Milan to talk about his past favors. Meanwhile Gina conducted what was to her a false affair with a certain Conte N—. "When she had made

quite sure of Limercati's despair," she told N— she did not love him, to
which he made answer: "If you will be so extremely indulgent as to continue to receive me with all the distinctions accorded to a reigning lover,
I may perhaps be able to find a suitable position." Gina's hysteria takes
up the slack of missing reality and helps her bite her own nose off. Limercati and Conte N— use their hysterias rather to protect themselves from
reality and at the same time as their only access to the coveted dream of
reality which Gina had opened for them. Gina is volatile in mind, passionate in soul, as no doubt were her lovers, but note the preposterous situations she finds convenient and even necessary to keep herself going
between one lover and the next. Consider Gina flinging water over the
head of Ascanio to get rid of him. Or better still consider Gina climbing
on a rock in the middle of Lake Como so she could "see herself assailed
on all sides by raging waves." When she fell in, Fabrizio saved her, and
Stendhal adds: "No doubt it is not a pleasant thing to feel oneself drowning, but the spirit of boredom, taken by surprise, was banished from the
feudal castle."

This is neither the caprice of Dostoevsky nor the gratuitous act of Gide,
but it springs from similar insight and impulse during the novelist's effort to convert behavior into manners.

Gina's treatment of Canon Borda is perhaps the best example in the
first part of The Charterhouse, if only because, in its three or four pages,
it is most nearly developed into a scene, and because in it we see clearly
the combination of hysteria, manners, and honor at the delicious edge of
farce. (The reader who wishes to laugh again will find the episode nearly
at the end of the fifth chapter.) Neither Gina nor the Canon is deceived
by the other, but each must pretend to be. After all, which of us has
not been caught up in an intrigue — merely because it was *possible* —
even though the real stake was quite outside the intrigue and might even
be imperiled by it? A woman has only to rest her weight wholly on one
leg and the thing is done, if the man has any sense of honor to his
manners. Even the window-shopper will sometimes break the glass.
Here nothing happens, but it might. It is Stendhal at his best. Actually,
all Gina wanted of the Canon was information as to what the police
meant to do to Fabrizio, and as a reward to him he was to bring it
to her in her box at La Scala; at quarter to 11 she and her friends
would send everyone away, close the door, and blow out the candles.
Then the Canon would come, a new aria in the opera. The time and
place were chosen because "this would be the least compromising course
for him." The least compromising is evidently the most conspicuous. Who
will *not* see the lights go out, the doors close, who will not know that
Gina is still there? Gina was the most beautiful woman in Milan, and her
box the most stared at. Surely the Friends of Santa Margarita (Gina's
name for the C.I.A. of the day) would not misunderstand.

In the light cast by Gina's relations with Limercati and Canon Borda, regard Fabrizio at Waterloo and at Romagnano, zenith and nadir of Fabrizio's Napoleonic period: in which he is shaped, out of which he is released upon the world. Speculation is garrulous if not endless; so a few hundred words will not be amiss before we say, like Stendhal at so many interesting places, "and so forth." In Stendhal's two large novels it is Napoleon up and down: that man as great as a man can be without virtue, that man more Stendhalian than Julien Sorel or Fabrizio del Dongo could ever be. In *The Red and the Black* it was the *Memoirs of St. Helena;* here it is Waterloo and reflections at Romagnano. There it was the myth-image of past glory. Here it is the débacle. The glory little Fabrizio had gained from his Latin genealogy plus what he had heard from his father about Napoleon gave him incentive, resolution, will, heroism — all blind, looking for a vision; and it is only the form of these which is broken down by his realization of the incongruity between Napoleon's proclamations and the muddle of his last battlefield. The force has been roused or precipitated in his characters, but only that. His ethos is not yet his fate. He is one of those who, lacking experience, resort to resolution; lacking purpose must needs be heroic; lacking choice must needs invoke will; lacking discrimination must needs lose temper. He is an early and promising member of the intellectual proletariat who now invest us. Stendhal's *La Chartreuse de Parme* is the immediate preface to Matthew Arnold's *Grande Chartreuse,* which is the more interesting since no two men could with more reason have more detested each other.

It is amazing how blank Stendhal makes Fabrizio, so blank that one suspects Stendhal's intellectual powers — so blank that one suspects a whole department of *literature,* a word which, as a lover of Stendhal but not a Beyliste, I firmly italicize. Must hope in that quarter be a form of paranoia? At any rate, Fabrizio gets glory from a genealogy and an empty mind from the Jesuits and good grades by Gina's bribery. But one should not overrate one's suspicions, which is telling without kissing. This may be what must happen in the novel of ideas. Fabrizio is the embodiment — perhaps the history — of an idea, but he cannot be said to show any instinct for ideas himself. One would not expect him to use ideas as regular weapons unless they became the medium of intrigue. One would say the same of any figure in Balzac. Novelists have not yet been forced to find or construct genuine public motives, which are not the same as those of our private chaos; a situation to which I do not object but which I think should be more generally recognized. Perhaps in Fabrizio the other sense of idea is the one at work: idea as image, as a thing seen with an eye that almost handles its sight: the idea of generosity, justice, heroism, glory, and love, something gallant as a possibility, but not at all something sacrificial or sacramental to grand action, as in Dante or Shakespeare.

Both courses of ideas are welcome; one needs only the right salutation. Consider: Fabrizio represents the ideas of ambition and career. For ambition, he is a charming figure of our common lot: which is to be one of those who have not yet (no matter how well along) found out what ambition is. He is one of those, we hopefully say, to whom, if he lives long enough, ambition *will come,* and when it comes will come as a freshet of relief in a dry season: as a solution and washing away of strains. Yet one doubts that Stendhal could have made one of his heroes live long enough for that: for such a hero would have lost, for the sake of one possibility, one genuine wager with the gods, his quickening sense of many possibilities. Without alternative games to play, he would have been merely swept along, his scream drowned in the flood.

No. In Stendhal there will always be games to play every time you open your shut eyes. Games, in Stendhal, are how you handle the incomprehensible; which is how it is we find Fabrizio playing an all-consuming game in the sudden vast waste of Waterloo: the game of pretense — the most reassuring pretense of all, the pretense that is better than truth — that one does not know what it is. If you have enough games — not cards but games — you can always play. You need no revelation, no rebirth, no permanent commitment, only a game. If he had thought of it, Stendhal would have attached to Fabrizio at Waterloo the idea of the *déraciné.* As it is, there is something of the *déraciné* in the Happy Few, those who read and plague themselves, and play the last resourceful game of inventing the games others cannot or will not play. But for Fabrizio, as for Julien, there will always be games to play. Let us look again at Waterloo where he talked by signs in order not to give away his bad French, and so of course made himself more suspicious than ever. The cloak and dagger are everywhere, so to speak, under every disguise. No wonder he did not know, this charming and ferocious boy, whether or not he had been in battle or even whether there had been a battle. At Romagnano, where he was exiled *because* he had been at Waterloo, though most of the time he rode all day, "he went three leagues on foot and wrapped himself in a mystery which he imagined to be impenetrable, in order to read the *Constitutionnel,* which he thought sublime. 'It is as fine as Alfieri and Dante!' he used often to exclaim." The curé was right who said of Fabrizio: "He is a cadet who feels himself wronged because he is not the first-born." All Fabrizio's hysterias are devoted to raising himself to the position of the first-born who is at the same time illegitimate. There is a special ambition in Stendhal: which is to *usurp* your own place, and find yourself a hero by the act of usurpation — and such fun, too! or (in Stendhal's phrase) "such delicious puerilities!" Consider, for a small example, the scene in the melancholy café at Romagnano where Fabrizio rushes on the stranger with his dagger: we do not know with what reason and we never learn the upshot. Stendhal merely observes that he had forgotten honor "and reverted to instinct, or, more properly, to the memories of his earliest childhood." That is to say, he had reverted to behavior without manners; or, better still, pure behavior had come up on him. It is a commonplace to say that all sorts of writers and artists anticipated Freud, and indeed Freud says so himself. To me, there is perhaps less distortion of actual life in the behavior of Fabrizio than in the insights of Freud. Each mastered hysteria in a different way.

This remark must not be taken by itself. One good context is to think of hysteria — whether deliberately, spontaneously, or arbitrarily undertaken, and whether as the result of a wound or a wish — as one of the mind's great modes of dealing with reality, whether to solicit it or to escape from it making little difference. Doubtless, like seeing visions, it is a dangerous mode, though universal and perennial. We are not concerned with therapy, but with the expression of experience in theoretic form (Croce's phrase for what lyric poetry gives to feelings) in novels and individual lives. The point seems to be that, as Eliot says, contradicting Arnold, mankind cannot bear very much reality. If reality strikes out at us, or if we need a modicum of reality for comfort and we cannot find it no matter where we look, then we respond with a heightened imitation. This is why a doctor of my acquaintance defined love as habit-hysteria. At any rate the imitation of reality in our response is often hysterical: in some sense inappropriate, incongruous, irrelevant, even self-destructive. Hysteria is never prudent. Only in great hands is it raised into final decorum, deep congruity, immediate relevance, and true creation. Your ordinary actor hams Shakespeare beyond need, your great actor finds his lines a being. Stendhal, one thinks, was not great enough; he had the impulse and the insight, but a kind of positive smallness of stature. Hence the intensity of the mere language and the "mere" action (words and acts seldom joined). Hence his heroes were boys, his heroines delicious women who never grew up either in sex or mind. Hence their hysterias were compelled to turn half to farce, half to *puntiglio,* with intrigue to keep the emotion going. That his books have been mistaken for works of rational imagination in the great sense is no fault of his; they excel in their own order. He recorded within his convention what a great many people, and these not the least lively, are actually like in their behavior, or wish they were like, or did not know, till they read Stendhal, that they might be like. Hysteria is for them the only acceptable substitute for reality because it is the only one really believed in while it lasts, really forgotten when it is gone, and really available when wanted in fresh supply. We make it for ourselves and it takes us over. I do not know that there is any other mode of imagination that for so many keeps life a continuing adventure. Surely it is related to what Lu Chi was talking about in the lines quoted at the beginning of these remarks.

Assuming that the quotation has been reread, does it not touch the quick in Stendhal? in Fabrizio? in Gina? in Mosca? Each of them is in search of reality, or of love, or of a way of getting along: each wants the reality to appear as a scream, the love to be a grand passion, the way of getting along to carry infinite risks. None of them can tolerate boredom, which is the presence of undesired reality, the condition, as Tolstoy puts it, of desiring desire. Each is unequal to his or her self-appointed task — not from incapacity of ideal, but from too much ideal, and also because the promptings of reality emerge as caprice and are regulated by an absence of good sense. As Baudelaire says, Stendhal is full of *caprice sans motif* — unless, as Baudelaire of all people must have known, the motive was to escape or prevent boredom.

Consider, with this in mind, how each of them dreads, and woos, the precipitation of reality through a word. Gina extinguishes the lights and shrieks when she learns from her maid the first sound of the word love. Fabrizio resolves never to utter the word to Gina, for then the thing between them would have a name. Mosca cannot permit himself the fatal word jealousy, though he is ravaged by that disease of love. Indeed, so curiously have these three persons constructed themselves that, had they been able on the sudden to speak simply, their simplicity would have appeared the outbreak of cynicism or hypocrisy, precisely as prudence takes for them the form of cowardice, and motive generally the form of fear. In short, being incapable of reality or love, yet desiring both, they are drawn to use the mechanism of intrigue — intrigue which is reputed to manage reality and to arrange love — to get them through their days and nights and even through their moments of crisis lest the crisis show its real nature with its name. A superb example is the last quarter of Chapter Seven where Mosca develops the jealousy he will not name in a series of unspoken soliloquies, first in the presence of the Prince his master, then alone with an anonymous letter, lastly as the *terzo incomodo* (Italian for when two is company three's a crowd) at Gina's apartments. There, she and Fabrizio are making that love which is not quite making love (the beauty which is the promise of happiness?) while he paces up and down before them, each pace a degree of madness. Suddenly he left, "calling out in a genial, intimate tone: 'Good-bye, you two! — One must avoid bloodshed,' he said to himself." And the next day he questions Gina's favorite maid. To this we may add as comment some characterized words spoken by Fabrizio but which seem to me to belong better to Mosca. Gina asks him if he wants to run away from her. " 'No,' he replied with the air of a Roman Emperor, 'but I want to act wisely.' " Nothing could have been further from Fabrizio's or Mosca's heart.

"With the air of a Roman Emperor." The Roman Emperor told everything but nobody would look at more than the statue of it. Let us think of Mosca della Rovere. It is like Mosca when we first meet him: an actor in a farce who is ashamed of the gravity of his position in the farce as a minister of state; that Mosca who said of his master, "he has fits of panic [des accès de peur] unworthy of a man, but these are the sole source of the favor that I enjoy"; that Mosca whose age and powdered hair made him a kind of Cassandra, hoarding in the avarice of his emotion all his anticipations of his visit to Gina in her box at the opera: only to find, as he went, that he had lost his desire, overcome by an "impulse of genuine shyness"; that Mosca looking woefully to old age "when" — I now locate the phrase I have already used — "when one is no longer capable of these delicious puerilities." Mosca, of course, is still quite young enough, but he speaks in lovable voice for those who are not. Mosca, it seems to me, has always the air of a Roman Emperor — of the thing itself, not of those hideous, eyeless statues which we cannot look at without looking away from — but he takes care to show that air as little as possible.

Instead, he uses intrigue: the entanglement of things (but not their mystery) in a manipulable form. Intrigue is the substitute for mystery in action. Intrigue is intricate like a mystification — she gave him an intriguing look. For many persons intrigue is the limit of belief; if a matter cannot be converted into intrigue, its existence is at best dubious. That in the end a given intrigue blows up, never mind: another intrigue is already on the way. And so on. We can make some comments and ask some questions. Intrigue is a formal means of transforming caprice into motive. To enter into an intrigue is the cheapest way to acquire momentum. To intrigue is to make use of manners as disguise, not as expression. With these propositions we may associate the following questions. Does intrigue control hysteria, or does it rather give hysteria opportunities? Does hysteria give intrigue something really to do, or does it rather make the hysteria real? We speak of course with reference to The Charterhouse of Parma, and we will come out best if our conclusions are not too firm. Intrigue is a neutral medium, a rhetoric that invites any action to an attractive lodging for the time being; then we move on. So it is with Stendhal; he moves on. These propositions and these questions (and others would have done as well or better) are dramatized and burlesqued with great local importance by Stendhal, but I do not think them (or any other frame of intrigue) central to his purpose or results. The local importance is quite enough, and critics who think otherwise have forgotten what fun intrigue is as a medium. That something else may show when the intrigue is dropped is another matter, and another matter still that what shows may have been going on all the time. Consider Chapter Thirteen, which contains the episode of Fausta: Stendhal was wrongly tempted to cut it from the novel.

We are in Bologna where (as I once read in an eighteenth-century English travel book) the women cannot help scratching themselves as they make their evening walks in the spring, and which was then as now famous for the beauty of its women and the excellence of its cooking; and when we are not in Bologna we are secretly in Parma: intrigue is the medium by which we move between, and move ahead, and move away — all in relation to a certain discovery which Fabrizio makes about himself. For here Fabrizio finds his second Waterloo in a manner even more foolhardy than he had found his first: in a sedan chair drawn by twenty thugs with torches. Where at the first Waterloo he had sought glory and had his horse taken away from him, here, with equal vanity, and with the special incentive of boredom, he had sought love and found, though he had played with ruse after ruse and pinched himself all over, that for him love did not exist. The body of a servant girl or of an actress more nearly met his 6 o'clock appetite than any love. He is indeed — so far — that man whose destiny it is to be lacking in one passion. So little does he have of it that he cannot even carry through the game of it to pass the time, much less to make of it a career. The hypocrisy by which honest lovers rise to their roles, or reimmerse themselves in their passions, is impossible to Fabrizio except as burlesque.

Stendhal was right to entrust the fate of Fabrizio in battle to a *vivandière*. Nothing could be fantastic enough to render glory unpalatable to a sixteen-year-old boy. Was he not right, too, in terminating the *willed hysteria* of Fabrizio's love for Fausta in a sedan chair followed by a duel as senseless and inconclusive as the fight at the bridge in the earlier episode? This Fausta, to whom Stendhal does not permit much existence, is part Siren and part Circe, but insufficiently either to hold or degrade Fabrizio. We see better than he that it is his aunt Gina alone who could accommodate him; and we see, also, why Stendhal has made Gina impossible for him to secure. Beauty is the promise of happiness.

There is something about our hero's name, Fabrizio or Fabrice, which is suggestive of the calamities that happen to him. He is a creature *made up* for the old great roles of Prelate, Soldier, and Lover, but who is yet — though placed at the heart of prestige, power, and opportunity — personally incapable of playing any of them. No wonder the omens for him are prison and crime — but always with the haunting possibility that Gina might in some impossible "yet" recreate him in her own image — at her own intensity — her own true ardency — of the force that now moves him only to affection; and even with that crime and prison must be the end. Stendhal envisages no other fate for his heroes than truncation.

It is in such considerations that we find the shape of this novel accru-
ing — an almost unearned increment — upon the psychological clusters,
deep gestures, and hysterias that eventually defeat themselves in action.
Was the world so changing for Stendhal that some part of his spirit could
not assent to it except through the comic repudiation of all the values
which he had encouraged so to survive in himself? It is this sort of question to which he constantly makes us return.

Fabrizio, certainly, has so far taken only a comic part in his occupa-
tions: the unseemly, fearful comedy of the thing, man, spirit incongruous with itself. Things must be kept moving, kept a little fantastically
beyond themselves in expression in order to be tolerable at all. If we
could arrest the flux, freeze the immediate, we might be overcome by the
intolerable illusion that the immediate was all. It is the awareness of this
possibility that leads to Stendhalian comedy.

If we take the series hypocrite and hysterical as needing a next member might it not be histrionic? He who pretends, he who induces force
beyond practicable incentive, is not he precisely histrionic — an actor
playing beyond himself just so much of life as he can pretend to or invoke? Does he not then create a new sort of reality for the moment,
which we rejoice in even while we do not believe in it? Or do we
go a step further? Is not the histrionic the most powerfully seductive of
all our native talents: our first squall of breath, our last moan or sigh?
Whenever the histrionic talent has taken us over, and we have come back,
we know well enough, though we do not know what it is, that we have
been in touch with reality itself, and have been in procession with it: the
heaviness, the light, the crying. Some of the religious call it speaking with
tongues, which would never do for Stendhal, but which is something like
in the ordinary world the effect of the soliloquies and the rash acts of Gina
and Mosca and Fabrizio. They are histriophones.

If the notion is at all apt, we should perhaps reverse the order of our
series and make it: histrionic, hysterical, hypocritical. This is, of course,
an aesthetic not a prudent order, mutinous, not assenting; it is the voice
of *midi-carême,* Halloween, saturnalia with *puntiglio* and a sense of
honor: a sense that perfect murder would approach perfect virtue. Our
civilizations are never properly ours, our proper reality shows best only
in our intercalary feast days. And so forth; there are many ways that
Stendhal's people make us say the same thing. . . . Considering that
civilization is a tissue of surfaces we slide off and of institutions that raise
or degrade us outside our proper reality, and considering that we cling in
our sliding to that civilization just the same — as if could we but sit still
we would be ourselves! — it is to be expected aesthetically and impera-
tively that we should find something *other* than that civilization, perhaps fatal to us without the civilization, to express ourselves in at least

symbolic action. I cannot put it more formally. It is the willy-nilly cry of the willies within, the cry of the individual affronted in his dignity. If you would like a companion to Stendhal in this matter think of William Blake. Had it happened that way Fabrizio could have known "The Marriage of Heaven and Hell" by heart. Though he would have spoken looking in an opposite direction, the voice is much the same. Each from the proper reality cried the proper freedom.

Not that Stendhal ignored other worlds and other imprudences. It was he himself who fired off the pistol in the concert, or as he should have said in Grand Opera, for the politics are operatic, or *opéra bouffe*. This would hardly need saying if there were not critics who think that Stendhal wrote genuine political novels. The genuine is something like what you find in Tacitus, Saint-Simon, and Anthony Trollope rather than Suetonius, Stendhal, and Disraeli; though if you think of the two sets together they cast strange lights on each other. In Stendhal the truth has been taken out of the issue; there is no sense of the mangled truth in continuing purpose, and of its vitality in corruption; only the personal stake remains. It is as if political gossip were political power, where at most it may sometimes disclose it and at worst obfuscate it. Yet in politics we know there are no *unnatural* vices: the stake is common and has values superior to any principle. Machiavelli tells us this, not Stendhal.

As a novelist, he is not required to. The sense of what is at stake may be very small in a novel or play and yet stand for everything. It may be very personal as in *The Possessed* or very generalized as in *St. Joan* and in either case carry great and lasting force. But I do not believe that Stendhal's more or less unconscious convention of grand opera without music will carry his novel as politics. Perhaps he did not intend it to do so; perhaps the politics only got in in the sense that any other trade or profession might have got in: to give occupation to the hero and provide the career ladder of success and disaster. To the contrary, I think Stendhal meant to express his sense of politics to the hilt or handle: his version of what actually goes on; he was treating political behavior exactly as he treated behavior in love. In other parts of his mind he may have thought differently, but in the novelistic part this is how it was: a pattern that beset him and a patter that he practiced.

Let us remind ourselves of the terms we have been deploying: *puntiglio,* honor, rashness, hysteria, intrigue, to which we now add the politics of grand opera to follow on the histrionic. It is a vocabulary which cannot be accused of jargon, but in which every word crosses a threshold into the crackling sensibility of Stendhal.

For the operatic politics consider Chapter Fourteen. Rassi and the Marchesa Raversi have managed to get Fabrizio sentenced to twenty years *in absentia,* not so much because they hate Fabrizio, and certainly not for justice, but in the course of the contest for power, position, and prestige in the Parmesan court. Gina and Mosca together manage to abridge the sentence to twelve years by bulldozing the Prince and playing upon him generally. They believe they have secured exoneration, but the Prince fools them — as a Prince should. In these efforts Mosca is guided partly by his own struggle for power but much more by his allegiance to Gina. Gina is guided entirely by her (false) image of Fabrizio and by the impetuously grasped possibilities which bristle in front of her. Since everywhere in the Grand Duchy of Parma power takes absolute forms it takes also *small* forms, small enough to be grasped. Corruption is available, and is indeed for those anywhere near the top the only path to action. Corruption is the cement of this society; or, if not the cement, the elastic plastic adhesive which when it snaps lets crime and violence in. Thus Gina heaves her bits of power about with the magnificence of possibility and the exaltation of intrepidity which go with madness. Consider these items taken from the twenty-odd pages of this chapter of absolute but precarious politics. La Raversi is *mad with joy* at the twenty-year sentence. Gina *breaks into song* at her own intention and is *in a transport of joy* when she pretends she will leave Parma. The Prince *reigned a quarter of an hour* (by keeping Gina waiting) and knows that Gina *will make everyone believe* her own account of things if she leaves Parma. Gina, like Fabrizio, speaks *with a Roman pride* and makes her peace with Mosca *with a merry glance*. "She had acted at random and for her own immediate pleasure" and "had fully believed" her own intentions. But when her servants applaud her new decision to remain at Parma, she responds "like an actress taking a *call*." Writing the archbishop, she signs her full name because "in the eyes of the middle classes the caricature looks like beauty." Similarly, the Prince worries how to insult his minister Rassi; and Rassi (whose power lies in crime) wants prestige to guarantee his crime. And similarly the banished Raversi forges Gina's writing to bring Fabrizio to jail.

It is a magnificent scene in which no one is implicated in anything but the part played, and in which the players are monsters of vanity and rancor. The secret of their energy is indicated by Gina's phrase about herself in one of her bad moments: "I can no longer form an *exaggerated* idea of anything in the world, I can no longer love." The exaggerated idea is the prompter of most of the behavior in this book, and it is applied with the logic of passion: "The profound interest which it feels in knowing the truth does not allow it to keep up vain pretenses, while at the same time the extreme devotion that it feels to the object of its love takes from it the fear of giving offence." This was written of Clelia in love with Fabrizio; but if you put for passion "exaggerated idea" you have the whole story. One of Clelia's own observations gives a further emphasis:

"What a terrible passion love is. . . . And yet all those liars in society speak of it as a source of happiness."

Stendhal's psychology of the exaggerated idea is accurate enough, if we correctly estimate its ignorance, and is sound for its purpose within that accuracy. It provides a usable form to take care of the view and practice of life which we call burlesque: the last term we shall add to our series. The question will be how much Stendhal's burlesque is a true mode of the imagination and how much is mere puerilization: a question which is only to be asked, by no chance to be answered.

If you do not like the word burlesque, you may use *Commedia dell'Arte,* which was played on certain evenings of the week at the court of the new Prince. Only the plot was put on the boards and each player was left to fill out lines and action with whatever could be improvised or apparently improvised at the moment. I say "apparently" because there were of course occasions when one or another player made cause to fit into his role speeches already invented and even rehearsed. So, for example, did the young Prince make love to Gina, when he knew ahead that he might play the role of lover opposite her that evening. I suggest that the structure of the whole novel is like the structure of the game at Court. It is Grand Opera with the music left out, and sometimes, in the heat of the moment, with the plot left out, too. But there is always improvisation, careless or planned.

Item. When Mosca met Gina he was already married; that was careless improvisation. But when the time comes to marry Gina, the existing wife is readily forgotten, which is planned improvisation.

Item. When Fabrizio takes up preaching he has ready on the footstool in his pulpit a paper containing the prayer for the unfortunate man, which he then reads as if to Clelia in her golden chair. This is planned improvisation.

Item. The whole formula of Clelia's oath never again to see Fabrizio (of course she could be with him in the dark) is like the posted plot in the game. Granted the medium, everything follows by improvisation: by what will do at the moment, so long as only a burlesque of the sentiments is in order. Stendhal cares nothing for sentiment, everything for sensibility.

Item. Many times in Stendhal when a matter or a scene reaches the point where it would, under other hands, cry out for development, Stendhal writes his customary "and so forth." This is the black-out, the bursting into song and dance in a musical comedy. For example, the Princess' letter to Gina to the effect that she will make her Grand Mistress of her court breaks off with "and so forth" when it reaches the point of burlesque.

Item. Gina's letter of instructions to Fabrizio for his escape from jail (in Chapter Twenty) is either superb burlesque or idiocy — like the escape itself.

Item. When Gina confronts herself with the magnificence of a lonely death for the sake of that wretch, Fabrizio, it is characteristic of Stendhal to report it in private monologue. No one hears it, nothing is done with it, no one answers. Perhaps in this case, perhaps in any *one* case, Stendhal is right, but he does a similar thing everywhere in the book. These monologues, these speeches, these truncated sentiments of which this book is so full, are addressed to no one. They are the life not lived, almost the thought not thought, the act never construed. They represent either what one should have said or what one might possibly say: meanwhile knowing in blood and bones the absolute impossibility of ever saying or thinking or doing.

Ordinarily we have burlesque as an adjunct of satire (as in Jonson, or Martial, or Aristophanes): to castigate or destroy something or to protect ourselves from it in exaggerated mockery; or we have burlesque as high jinks in the lower and still playful parts of our sensibility, where we let ourselves go along favored and indecorous lines, as in slapstick, in masquerades, in games played in the dark, in fantasies of impossibility; and we have our modern burlesque with its coarse chorus and coarser skits punctuated by strip-tease with drums, where, as it ought, the bawdy approaches the obscene, and things in general get as near the sewer as the gutter can get. (There was that other form, now dead, last exemplified by the early Marx Brothers, and seen in reminiscence only now and then in Danny Kaye.) All these are ordinary forms of burlesque, and have quite sufficiently their own meaning. Stendhal's burlesque is another thing; it neither castigates, nor destroys, nor plays with reality. Like the hysteria upon which it is founded, it is meant to get hold of reality, or, if not that, to make by improvisation from caprice a substitute for the missing reality. I do not believe in Gina's playfulness when she makes all her peasants drunk and has her reservoirs opened to flood the streets of Parma; but I do believe in the hysteria, the caprice, the improvisation, and I have a special attachment which is not the same thing as belief to the burlesque of life in which, under Stendhal's hands, this combination results.

That is, this burlesque is a pretty precious form of the actual — for many an irresistible hallucination of the actual, while it lasts. In the *Charterhouse* there is a wonderful forced-flowering of that talent for sudden explosions of almost pure behavior — for rash acts — for shots in the dark — for nightmares at noon — for fire-crackers at midnight — for practical jokes taken as the height of action — for anything done without consideration for others — the talent for all those things having fatherhood in the anarch in us we call caprice.

I suppose the great images which inhabit our literature with the vital authority of caprice are the *Tempest, Don Quixote,* and the *Brothers Karamazov* — with some good words to be said for *Pickwick Papers.* Stendhal is not in this line because of the immaturity of his sentiments and because he never explored the behavior he tapped. Note that there is no quarrel with the maturity of his emotions. Emotions are not susceptible of maturity, only of different degrees of depth, intensity, and hysteria. But going back to caprice: it is those springs in behavior which incline us to anarchy: that is to say, rebellion to tyranny, the sweet and fearful intuition of our own natures, or the immediate creation of an absolutely fresh order out of the old materials. Caprice is our unmediated recognition of the underlying chaos and our knowledge that all our orders are made out of chaos. Order is what we do with chaos, as unity is what we see in chaos. The usual fields for capricious action are love, politics, religion, war, and crime. (I speak of history, morals, daily life; and say nothing of the mathematics, symmetrical and otherwise, which make life possible.) In the works named above the caprice is from very deep levels of perception of the underhalves of our natures. In Stendhal, the caprice comes from a perception which penetrates very little, and only into the effects, of our under-nature. The underblows to him are only a sort of trade wind. For another useful comparison look a century ahead to André Gide and his gratuitous act: the mere act against, or sometimes within, society which liberates the actor from it, usually at the expense of some individual. Gide seeks after freedom as if it were a suicide that fails, and his moral stoicism is a prelude to an orgasm of the intellect. His caprice, his anarchy, is far more in what his reason does to his behavior than in what his sensuality — and the tender ache in him — does to his reason. He suffers from what strikes me as a great heresy: the belief that to *cultivate* sin gets you any nearer either to behavior or to reality. "And so forth." Well, Stendhal lies between.

Let us look at an example and have done. When Fabrizio (this known criminal, this casual murderer) became bishop-coadjutor with the succession secured, as it seems, to the archbishopric, and at the same time lost hope for the love of Clelia, he made out as near as possible to retire from the pomps and vanities of this wicked world in a wonderful huff. He wore black, went nowhere, valued nothing, put on his death face (as one puts on a smile) and was a very holy man indeed: with the sense strong in him that he owed nothing to anybody since his possessions had no value. At this time Mosca and Gina were in their chosen exile (made for the purpose of return) and Mosca called upon this innocent false-recluse for aid in the politics of Parma. Fabrizio suddenly realized rhetorically the sum of his debts to the Count and carried out the political mission faithfully and expertly. He stepped at once out of every character he had had and became a model of Richelieu or Mazarin at twenty-five. This is the caprice of Napoleonism if you like. But let us say also that it represents the conflict of capricious psychologies within the narrow frame of Stendhal's mind; he is right to mix burlesque with the serious adventure, it is the only mixture he knows, and if he can improvise fast enough it may work. We note that in Stendhal's version of the psychology of caprice, there are no committing acts — no perfidies to the self — which cannot be reversed, at least in the leading characters. Each is always free for a new dodge, another resumption without continuity or rationale; there are instead successive waves of infatuation. In the Stendhalian world, only the lesser persons, whom we see only sideways, off side, or in perspective, enjoy purpose, choice, or decision at a rational level; and it is a travesty of modern psychology to say that the heroes enjoy these qualities at a deep level. The hero's intent only unfolds itself through a succession of caprices, and his achievement (usually death or desuetude) only in the unity of accidents seen together. This is the heroism of the simple gratuitous act, the caprice of the fresh start. It is very inviting, as the wilful in us always is; but what it amounts to is submission to the goddess Fortuna. Stendhal shows that he knew this by submitting the boy Fabrizio to the care of the Abbé Blanés, the astrologer who burlesqued the future by means of the past. That the balance for Fortuna is Scientia, or knowledge earned in life, Stendhal chose not to know. Hence the emptiness of the psyche in Fabrizio (he had plenty of spirit) which led him to cultivate his infatuation for Clelia — after having *himself* made it impossible that it should come to anything but sex at midnight — by scattering *nosegays* in Clelia's *garden*. What else could he do?

It is for this reason, too, that boredom is taken to be the engine of action in the world at large. Caprice, as an invoked pattern of conduct, leads inevitably at the turn of the wheel to another boredom, and so to another caprice. It was a fatal caprice, says Stendhal, that led Fabrizio to want his illegitimate son for himself. So the child died, so Clelia died, and so in a year Fabrizio himself died. Yet there is the haunting memory of capricious acts which created moments of freedom; and those moments, for all their hysteria, are a burlesque of life itself. Almost, as we see in the lives of many people, they pass for life, and their beauty is indeed a promise of happiness. To create that illusion may not make a novelist immortal but it gives him lasting life.

MAURICE BLANCHOT

Kafka's Diaries: The Exigency
of the Work of Art

In many ways, Kafka was until 1912 like any young man in whom is awakening the desire to write, who recognizes his vocation there, and who also recognizes there certain exigencies but has no proof that he will be equal to them. If, until 1912, he did not devote himself to literature, he offered this excuse: "I can take nothing on myself as long as I have not achieved a sustained work that satisfies me completely." [1] This achievement, this proof, came to him during the night of September 22, 1912, the night he wrote "The Judgment" at one sitting, and which brought him decisively close to the point at which it seemed that "everything can be said, . . . for everything, for the strangest fancies, there waits a great fire in which they perish and rise up again." Shortly afterward he was confirmed in this by giving a reading of this short story for his friends: "There were tears in my eyes. The indubitability of the story was confirmed." (This need to read to his friends, often to his sisters, even to his father, what he had just written also belongs to the middle region. He never quite gave it up. It is not literary vanity — although he condemned it himself — but a need to crowd physically upon his work, to let himself be raised, drawn up by it, by making it spread out in the vocal space which his great gifts as a reader allowed him to create.)

From then on Kafka knew he could write. But this knowledge was not knowledge, and this power not his own. With rare exceptions, he never found in what he wrote the proof that he was really writing. It was at most a prelude, an approach-work or mission of reconnaissance. Of "The Metamorphosis" he says (January 19, 1914): "I . . . find it bad. Perhaps I am really lost," or later, "Great antipathy to 'Metamorphosis.' Unreadable ending. Imperfect almost to its very marrow. It would

SOURCE: "The Diaries: The Exigency of the Work of Art," translated by Lyall H. Powers, in *Franz Kafka Today,* edited by Angel Flores and Homer Swander (Madison: The University of Wisconsin Press, Paperback Edition, 1964), pp. 195–220. © Editions Gallimard. Reprinted by permission of Editions Gallimard.

have turned out much better if I had not been interrupted at the time by the business trip."

This last remark alludes to the conflict which Kafka encountered, and in which he was shattered. He had a profession and a family. He belonged to the world and had to belong to it. The world gives us time but controls it. The *Diaries* are, at least until 1915, shot through with remarks of despair where the notion of suicide recurs, for he lacked time: time, physical force, solitude, and silence. Certainly external circumstances were unfavorable: he had to work evenings or at night, his sleep was fretful, and he was exhausted by worry; but it would be vain to suppose that the conflict could have been removed by "organizing things better." Later, when illness brought him leisure, the conflict remained and became worse and of a different nature. There are no favorable circumstances. Even if one gives "all his time" to the exigencies of the work, "all" is still not enough; for it is not a matter of devoting one's time to working or of spending one's time writing, but rather of passing into another time where there is no more work, of reaching that point where time is removed, where one enters the fascination and solitude of the absence of time. When one has all the time in the world he has none at all, and the "friendly" external circumstances have reached the unfriendly point where circumstances cease to exist.

Kafka is unable, or unwilling, to write "in snatches," in the intervals of separate moments. This is what he discovered on the night of September 22 when, having written at a stretch, he grasped in all its fulness the unlimited impetus that moved him to write: "Only *in this way* can writing be done, only with such coherence, with such a complete opening out of the body and soul." And later (December 8, 1914): "Again I realized that everything written down bit by bit rather than all at once in the course of the larger (or even the whole) of one night is inferior, and that the circumstances of my life condemn me to this inferiority." We have here the initial explanation of all the abandoned tales whose impressive debris is revealed to us in the *Diaries* as they are presently available. Very often, the "story" extends no further than a few lines, at times it will quickly achieve coherence and density and yet stop at the bottom of a page, at others it continues for several pages, expanding and asserting its authority — and yet stops. There are many reasons for this, but primarily Kafka does not find in *his* time the extension which permits the story to develop as it would according to all directions; the story is never simply a fragment followed by another fragment; "how, starting with fragments, can I found a story capable of getting off the ground?" Thus, the story, not having been mastered, not having created the proper space in which the need to write is to be at once repressed and expressed, falls apart, wanders, steals into the dark night whence it came and there sadly holds prisoner him who was unable to bring it into the light of day.

Kafka needed more time, but he also needed less of the world. The world was first his family, whose constraint he bore with difficulty, never being able to free himself from it. It was next his fiancée and his fundamental desire to observe the law which requires man to fulfill his destiny in the world, have a family, children, and take his place in the community. Here the conflict assumes a new aspect, enters a contradiction which Kafka's religious position makes especially strong. When, on the subject of his engagement with F. B. — once broken but resumed — he examined, tirelessly and with ever increasing tension, "all that is for or against our marriage," he always came up against this exigency: "My sole aspiration and my sole vocation . . . is literature. . . . What I accomplished was only the result of being alone. . . . Then I'll never be alone again. . . . Not that, not that!" During his engagement at Berlin: "Was tied hand and foot like a criminal. Had they sat me down in a corner bound in real chains, placed policemen in front of me . . . , it could not have been worse. And that was my engagement; everybody made an effort to bring me to life, and when they couldn't, to put up with me as I was." Shortly afterwards, the engagement was broken but the aspiration remained, the desire for a "normal" life, a desire made heartbreaking by the torment of having wounded someone near to him. The story of his engagement has been compared — Kafka thought of it himself — to that of Kierkegaard's. But the conflict was different. Kierkegaard was able to give up Regina, he could renounce the ethical stage; access to the religious stage was not thus compromised, but rather made possible. But if Kafka forsook the earthly happiness of a normal life, he forsook also the steadiness of a just life, placed himself outside the law, deprived himself and, to a certain extent, deprived the law, of the basis and the foundation he needed to exist. This is the eternal problem of Abraham. What is demanded of Abraham is to sacrifice not his son alone, but God Himself: the son is the future of God on earth, for it is time which is really the Promised Land, the true, the only dwelling place of the chosen people and of God in His people. Now Abraham must, in sacrificing his son, sacrifice time, and time sacrificed will surely not be returned to him in the eternity of the hereafter: the hereafter is nothing but the future, the future of God in time. The hereafter is Isaac.

For Kafka the trial is rendered more burdensome by all that makes it lighter for him (what would Abraham's test be if, having no son, he were yet required to sacrifice that son? we could not take that seriously, we could only laugh; this laughter is the form of Kafka's sorrow). The problem is also such that it eludes us and eludes in its indecisiveness him who tries to solve it. The confusion is great, for Kafka seemed to identify with the exigency of the work of art that which could bear the name of his salvation. If writing condemned him to solitude, made his existence that of a celibate, without love, without bonds, if however writing seemed to him — at least frequently and for some time — the sole activity which could justify him, it was because, at all events, solitude was a threat to him within and without, it was because the community was nothing more than a phantom and because the law which still speaks through it (the community) is not even the forgotten law but the feigned forgetting of the law. Writing becomes once more, then, in the midst of distress and weakness, which are inseparable from this impulse, a possibility of fulfillment, a path without a goal perhaps comparable to that goal without a path which is the only one that must be reached. When he was not writing, Kafka was not simply alone, "as alone as Franz Kafka," as he said to G. Janouch, but in a sterile, cold solitude, a petrifying coldness that he called stunned dullness and that seems to have been the great threat that he dreaded. Even Brod, careful as he was to make of Kafka a man free of anomalies, recognizes that he acted at times like one absent or dead. So very much like Hölderlin in that both of them employed the same terms of self-criticism; Hölderlin: "I am numb, I am made of stone," and Kafka (July 28, 1914): "*I am more and more unable to think, to observe, to determine the truth of things, to remember, to speak, to share an experience; I am turning to stone. . . . If I can't take refuge in some work, I am lost.*"

"If I can't take refuge in some work. . . ." But why could this work save him? It seems that Kafka recognized precisely in this terrible state of self-dissolution in which he was lost for others and for himself, the center of gravity of the exigency of writing. At the point where he felt utterly destroyed is born the profundity which replaces destruction with the possibility of the greatest creation. A marvellous reversal, a hope always equal to the greatest despair, and it is easy to understand how from this experience he derived a motivating confidence which he would not willingly call into question. Work then became, especially in the early years, something of a means of psychological (not yet "spiritual") salvation, an effort towards a creation "that might be linked word for word to his life, a creation which he drew to himself so that it might draw him away from himself"; this he expressed in the most naïve and most forceful way in these terms (December 8, 1911): "I have now, and have had since this afternoon, a great yearning to write all my anxiety entirely out of me, write it into the depths of the paper just as it comes out of the depths of me, or write it down in such a way that I could draw what I had written into me completely." [2] However somber he might become, this hope never completely failed, and we always find, throughout all periods of his *Diaries,* entries of this kind (November 27, 1913): "The firmness, however, which the most insignificant writings bring about in me is beyond doubt and wonderful. The comprehensive view I had of everything on my walk yesterday!" At such moments writing is not an appeal, the expectation of grace or a dim prophetic fulfillment, but something simpler, more immediately urgent: the hope of not sinking, or more exactly of sinking faster than himself and thus recovering himself at the last minute. A duty more urgent, then, than any other, one which led him to write, on July 31, 1914, these remarkable words: "I have no time. General mobilization. K. and P. have been called up. Now I receive the reward for living alone. But it is hardly a reward; living alone ends only with punishment. Still, as a consequence, I am little affected by all the misery and am firmer in my resolve than ever. . . . But I will write in spite of everything, absolutely; it is my struggle for self-preservation."

However, it was the upheaval of war, but even more, the crisis brought about by his engagement, the movement and the deepening quest of writing, the difficulties encountered in it, it was his unhappy situation in general which little by little was to throw a different light on the existence of the writer in him. This change was never effected, resulted in no decision, was simply an indistinct perspective; but still there are certain indications: in 1914, for example, he was still striving passionately, desperately toward this single goal of finding a few moments to write, of getting a two-week leave which would be devoted solely to writing, of subordinating everything to this single, this supreme exigency — to write. But in 1916, if he asked for leave, it was to enlist. "The immediate duty is unconditional: to become a soldier." A project which would lead to nothing, but that didn't matter; the wish which was at its center shows how far Kafka already was from his "I will write in spite of everything," of July 31, 1914. Later he thought seriously of joining the pioneers of Zionism and going off to Palestine. He said as much to Janouch: "I dreamed of going to Palestine as a laborer or farm worker." — "You would give up everything here?" — "Everything, to find a life full of meaning in security and beauty." But since Kafka was already ill, the dream was just a dream, and we shall never know whether he could, like another Rimbaud, have given up his sole vocation for love of a wilderness where he would have found the security of a justified life — nor if he would have found it there. Of all the attempts he made to give his life a different orientation, he himself would say they were but blighted efforts, just so many radii of light, their tips bristling about the center of the incomplete circle that was his life. In 1922 he enumerated all of his projects in which he saw only failure: piano, violin, languages, Germanic studies, anti-Zionism, Zionism, Hebrew studies, gardening, woodworking, literature, attempts at marriage, the bachelor life, and he adds (January 23, 1922): "If I sometimes prolonged the radius a little farther than usual, in the case of my law studies, say, or engagements, everything was made worse rather than better just because of this little extra distance."

It would be foolish to single out from passing remarks the absolute affirmations they contain; and although he himself forgets it here, we cannot forget that he never stopped writing, that he wrote right to the end. But the fact remains that, between the young man who said to the one whom he considered as his future father-in-law: "I am nothing but literature, I cannot and will not be anything else," and the mature man who, ten years later, put literature on the same level as his little stabs at gardening, there is a great internal difference, even if externally the writing force remains the same or even seems to us to be more rigorous and precise toward the end, being the force to which we owe *The Castle*.

Whence comes this difference? To answer that would be to master the inner life of a man infinitely reserved, secretive even with his friends, and, moreover, rather inaccessible to himself. No one can pretend to reduce to a certain number of precise statements something which for Kafka himself could not achieve the transparency of a tangible utterance. And we should need, furthermore, a community of intentions, which is not possible. At least we shall doubtless commit no external errors in saying that, although his confidence in the powers of art often remained great, his confidence in his own powers, put to an ever greater test, also enlightened him about this test, about its exigency; enlightened him above all about what he himself demanded of art: no longer to give his person reality and coherence, not, that is to say, to save him from insanity but to save him from perdition; and when Kafka foresaw that, banished from this real world, he was perhaps already a citizen of another world in which he had to struggle not only for himself but for that other world, then writing appeared to him simply a means of struggling, at times deceptive, at times miraculous, that he could lose without losing everything.

Compare these two notes. The first is for January, 1912:

> It is easy to recognize a concentration in me of all my forces on writing. When it became clear in my organism that writing was the most productive direction for my being to take, everything rushed in that direction and left empty all those abilities which were directed toward the joys of sex, eating, drinking, philosophical reflection and above all music. I atrophied in all these directions. This was necessary because the totality of my strength was so slight that only collectively could they even halfway serve the purpose of my writing. . . . the compensation for all this is as clear as day. My development is now complete and, so far as I can see, there is nothing left to sacrifice; I need only throw my work in the office out of this complex in order to begin my real life in which, with the progress of my work, my face will finally be able to age in a natural way.

The lightness of the irony should not mislead us, of course, but the lightness, the jauntiness are nevertheless real and illuminate, by contrast, the tension of this other note, the meaning of which is apparently the same (dated August 6, 1914):

> What will be my fate as a writer is very simple. My talent for portraying my dreamlike inner life has thrust all other matters into the background; my life has dwindled dreadfully, nor will it cease to dwindle. Nothing else will every satisfy me. But the strength I can muster for that portrayal is not to be counted upon: perhaps it has already vanished forever, perhaps it will come back to me again, although the circumstances of my life don't favor its return. Thus I waver, continually fly to the summit of the mountain, but then fall back in a moment. Others waver too, but in lower regions with greater strength; if they are in danger of falling, they are caught up by the kinsman who walks beside them for that very purpose. But I waver on the heights; it is not death, alas, but the eternal torments of dying.

Three movements cross here: an affirmation, "nothing else [but literature] will ever satisfy me," — doubt of himself, linked with the inexorably uncertain essence of his gifts which "is not to be counted upon" — the feeling that this uncertainty (the fact that writing is never a power over which one has free disposal) belongs to whatever is extreme in the work of art, this central, mortal exigency which "is not death, alas," which is but death held at a distance, "the eternal torments of dying."

We may say that these three movements comprise, in their vicissitudes, the test which exhausted in Kafka his fidelity to "his sole vocation," which, coinciding with his religious preoccupations, led him to read in this unique exigency something further, another exigency which tended to subordinate it, or at least to transform it. The more Kafka wrote, the less sure he was of writing. At times he tried to reassure himself by thinking that "once you have received the knowledge of writing, it can never more fail or founder, but also, most rarely, something wells up which exceeds all measure." A weak consolation: the more he wrote, the closer he came to that extreme point toward which the work of art tends as toward its origin, but which he who senses it can only regard as the empty depths of the infinite. "I can't write any more. I've come up against the last boundary, before which I shall in all likelihood again sit down for years, and then in all likelihood begin another story all over again that will again remain unfinished. This fate pursues me" (November 30, 1914).

It seems that in 1915–16, futile as it may be to try to date a movement that eludes time, a change of perspective took place. Kafka took up again with his former fiancée. This relationship which led to a new engagement in 1917 then ended immediately afterward in the illness which revealed itself at that time, and plunged him into torments which he could not overcome. He discovered with increasing anxiety that he could not live alone and yet could not live with others. The guilt of his situation, of his existence, given over to what he called bureaucratic vices, meanness, indecision, and scheming, gripped and obsessed him. He had at all costs to escape this bureaucracy, and for that he could no longer count on literature, for that work was eluding him, for that work had its share in the imposture of irresponsibility, since the work demands solitude but is also annihilated by it — whence his decision: "To become a soldier." At the same time allusions to the Old Testament appear in the *Diaries,* and these cries of a doomed man are to be heard: "Receive me into your arms, they are the depths, receive me into the depths; if you refuse me now, then later." "Take me, take me, web of folly and pain." "Have mercy on me, I am sinful in every nook and cranny of my being. . . . Don't thrust me in among the lost."

Certain of his writings were once translated into French with the word "God" added. It does not belong there. The word "God" almost never appears in the *Diaries,* and never significantly.[3] That does not mean that these invocations in their uncertainty have no religious direction, but that one must preserve in them the force of that uncertainty and not deprive Kafka of the spirit of reserve which he always showed in regard to what was most important to him. These words of distress are dated July, 1916, and correspond to a visit he spent at Marienbad with F. B. A year later, however, he was again engaged; a month after that he was again spitting blood; in September he left Prague, but the illness was still moderate and was not to become threatening until (apparently) 1922. In 1917 he wrote the "Aphorisms," the only one of his writings in which spiritual affirmation (in a general form, not concerned with him in particular) escapes from the trial of a negative transcendence.

For the years that follow, the *Diaries* are almost completely lacking. Not a word in 1918. A few lines in 1919 when he was engaged for a few months to a young woman of whom we know almost nothing. In 1920 he met Milena Jesenska, a young Czech woman, sensitive, intelligent, capable of great freedom of mind and passion, to whom a fierce emotion attached him for two years — at first full of hope and happiness, but later given over to distress. The *Diaries* resume their importance in 1921 and especially in 1922 when the difficulties of this friendship, while his illness was growing worse, brought him to such a degree of tension that his mind seemed to oscillate between madness and the decision of salvation. At this point we must insert two long quotations. The first is dated January 28, 1922:

> A little dizzy, tired from the tobogganing; weapons still exist for me, however seldom I may employ them; it is so hard for me to lay hold of them because I am ignorant of the joys of their use, never learned

how when I was a child. It is not only "Father's fault" that I never
learned their use, but also my wanting to disturb the "peace," to upset
the balance, and for this reason I could not allow a new person to be
born elsewhere while I was bending every effort to bury him here. Of
course, in this too there is a question of "fault," for why did I want
to quit the world? Because "he" would not let me live in it, in his
world. Though indeed I should not judge the matter so precisely, for
I am now a citizen of this other world, whose relationship to the ordinary one is the relationship of the wilderness to cultivated land (I have
been forty years wandering from Canaan); I look back at it like a
foreigner, though in this other world as well — it is the paternal heritage I carry with me — I am the most insignificant and timid of all
creatures and am able to keep alive thanks only to the special nature
of its arrangements; in this world it is possible even for the humblest
to be raised to the heights as if with lightning speed, though they can
also be crushed forever as if by the weight of the seas. Should I not be
thankful despite everything? Was it certain that I should find my way
to this world? Could not "banishment" from one side, coming together
with rejection from this, have crushed me at the border? Is not
Father's power such that nothing (not I, certainly) could have resisted
his decree? It is indeed a kind of Wandering in the Wilderness in reverse that I am undergoing: I think that I am continually skirting the
wilderness and am full of childish hopes (particularly as regards
women) that "perhaps I shall keep in Canaan after all" — when all
the while I have been decades in the wilderness and these hopes are
merely mirages born of despair, especially at those times when I am
the wretchedest of creatures in the desert too, and Canaan is perforce
my only Promised Land, for no third place exists for mankind.

The second text is dated the following day:

Suffered some attacks on the road through the snow in the evening.
There are conflicting thoughts always in my head, something like this:
My situation in this world would seem to be a dreadful one, alone
here in Spindelmühle, on a forsaken road, moreover, where one keeps
slipping in the snow in the dark, a senseless road, moreover, without
an earthly goal (to the bridge? Why there? Besides, I didn't even go
that far); I too forsaken in this place (I cannot place a human, personal value on the help the doctor gives me, I haven't earned it; at
bottom the fee is my only relationship to him), incapable of striking
up a friendship with anyone, incapable of tolerating a friendship, at
bottom full of endless astonishment when I see a group of people
cheerfully assembled together (here in the hotel, indeed, there is little
that is cheerful; I won't go so far as to say that I am the cause of this,
in my character, perhaps, as "the man with the too-great shadow,"
though my shadow in this world *is* too great — with fresh astonishment I observe the capacity for resistance some people have, who, "in

spite of everything," want to live under this shadow, directly under it;
but there is much more than this to be said on the matter), or especially when I see parents with their children; forsaken, moreover, not
only here but in general, even in Prague, my "home," and what is
more, forsaken not by people (that would not be the worst thing, I
could run after them as long as I was alive), but rather by myself
vis-à-vis people, by my strength vis-à-vis people; I am fond of lovers
but I cannot love, I am too far away, am banished, have — since I am
human after all and my roots want nourishment — my proxies "down"
(or up) there too, sorry, unsatisfactory comedians who can satisfy
me (though indeed they don't satisfy me at all and it is for this reason
that I am so forsaken) only because I get my principal nourishment
from other roots in other climes, these roots too are sorry ones, but
nevertheless better able to sustain life.

This brings me to the conflict in my thoughts. If things were only
as they seem to be on the road in the snow, it would be dreadful; I
should be lost, lost not in the sense of a dreadful future menacing
me but in the sense of a present execution. But I live elsewhere; it is
only that the attraction of the human world is so immense, in an instant it can make one forget everything. Yet the attraction of my world
too is strong; those who love me love me because I am "forsaken" —
not, I feel sure, on the principle of a Weissian vacuum, but because
they sense that in happy moments I enjoy on another plane the freedom of movement completely lacking to me here.

To comment on these pages seems superfluous. What should be observed, however, is how, at that date, the privation of the world is inverted to a positive experience,[4] that of another world of which he is
already a citizen where he is of course only the smallest and the most uneasy, but where he also experiences overwhelming elevations, where he
enjoys a freedom whose value is sensed and whose prestige is acknowledged by men. Still, not to change the meaning of such images as these,
one must not read them from the common Christian point of view
(according to which there is this world and then the world of the hereafter, the only one which has value, reality, and glory), but always from
the point of view of "Abraham"; for, in every respect for Kafka, to be
excluded from the world means to be excluded from Canaan, to wander
in the wilderness; and it is this situation which makes his struggle
pathetic and his hope despairing, as though, cast out of the world into the
error of infinite wandering, he had to struggle ceaselessly to make of that
outside another world, and of that error the principle and origin of a new
freedom. It is a struggle unproductive, uncertain, in which what he
must conquer is his own loss, the truth of the exile and the return to
the very bosom of the dispersal. It is a struggle which will be compared
with profound Jewish speculations, when, especially after the Spanish

exodus, religious minds try to overcome exile by pushing it to its ultimate.[5] Kafka clearly refers to "all such writings" (his own) as to a "new
secret doctrine, a Kabbalah" which, "if Zionism had not intervened, . . .
might easily have developed" (January 16, 1922). And we can better
understand why he was at the same time Zionist and anti-Zionist. Zionism is the cure for exile, the affirmation that the earthly life is possible,
that the Jewish people has as a dwelling place not only a book, the Bible,
but the earth, and no longer dispersal throughout time. Kafka profoundly desired this reconciliation, desired it even if he was excluded
from it; for the grandeur of that just conscience has always been to hope
for others more than for himself and not to take his personal misfortune
as the measure of general unhappiness. "All that is magnificent, except
for me, and rightly so." But he did not belong to that truth, and
that is why he had to be anti-Zionist for himself, lest he be condemned
to immediate execution and to the despair of absolute impiety. It was to
the other shore that he already belonged, and his migration did not consist of going toward Canaan, but of going toward the wilderness, the
truth of the wilderness, of going ever further in that direction even when,
likewise unfortunate in that other world and still tempted by the joys
of the real world ("especially as far as women were concerned": this is a
clear allusion to Milena), he tried to persuade himself that he perhaps
still dwelt in Canaan. If he had not been anti-Zionist for himself (in
the figurative sense, of course), if there had been only *this* world, then
"the situation would be dreadful," then he would be doomed immediately. But he is "elsewhere," and if the strength of the human world's
attraction remained great enough to lead him back as far as its frontiers
and keep him there almost shattered, no less great was the attractive
force of his own world, the one in which he was free, the freedom he
speaks of in trembling, an account of prophetic authority which contrasts
with his usual modesty.

There can be no doubt that this other world has something to do with
literary activity: the proof of this fact is that Kafka, in speaking of the
"new Kabbalah," speaks of it precisely in connection with "all such writing." But the fact that the exigency of the truth of this other world henceforth surpasses in his eyes the exigency of the work of art, is not exhausted by it and but imperfectly accomplished in it, that also makes
itself felt. When writing becomes "a form of prayer," the suggestion is
that there are doubtless other forms, and even if, as a result of this
unhappy world, there were not, writing, from this point of view, would
cease to be the approach to the work of art, and become the anticipation
of the single moment of grace for which Kafka realizes he is waiting and
in which one no longer has to write. To Janouch's question, "So poetry
leads to religion?" he replied, "I will not say that, but certainly to

prayer," and contrasting literature and poetry he added, "Literature strives to place things in an agreeable light; the poet is compelled to raise them into the realm of truth, purity, and the eternal." A significant reply, for it corresponds to an entry in the _Diaries_ (September 25, 1917) where Kafka asks himself what joy writing can still hold for him: "I can still have passing satisfaction from works like _A Country Doctor,_ provided I can still write such things at all (very improbable). But happiness only if I can raise the world into the pure, the true, and the immutable." The "idealistic" or "spiritual" exigency here becomes categorical. To write, yes, still to write, but only to "elevate to infinite life that which is perishable and isolated, to the domain of law that which belongs to chance," as he said again to Janouch. But at once the question arises: is it possible? is he sure that writing does not belong to evil? and is not writing's consolation an illusion, a dangerous illusion that must be challenged? "Undeniably, there is a certain joy in being able calmly to write down: 'Suffocation is inconceivably horrible.' Of course it is inconceivable — that is why I have written nothing down" (December 20, 1921). And hasn't the humblest reality of this world a consistency which is lacking in the most powerful work of art? "Writing's lack of independence of the world, its dependence on the maid who tends the fire, on the cat warming itself by the stove; it is even dependent on the poor old human being warming himself by the stove. All these are independent activities ruled by their own laws; only writing is helpless, cannot live in itself, is a joke and a despair" (December 6, 1921). A grimace, the grimace of a face that recoils before the light, "a defense of nothingness, a guarantee of non-being, a breath of gaiety lent to nothingness," such is art.

However, if the confidence of his early years gives way to a yet harsher view, the fact remains that in his most difficult moments, when his very integrity seems threatened, when he is prey to the almost tangible attacks of the unknown ("how that spies upon me; on the way to the doctor's, for example, down there, constantly"), even then he continues to see in his work, not the thing which threatens him, but that which can help him, can open to him the decision of salvation: "The strange, mysterious, perhaps dangerous, perhaps saving comfort that there is in writing: it is a leap out of murderers' row; it is a seeing of what is really taking place. This occurs by a higher type of observation, a higher, not a keener type, and the higher it is and the less within reach of the 'row,' the more independent it becomes, the more obedient to its own laws of motion, the more incalculable, the more joyful, the more ascendant its course" (January 27, 1922). Here literature reveals itself as the power which frees, the force which removes the oppression of the world, that world "where everything feels choked," it is the liberating passage from

"I" to "he," from the introspection which had been Kafka's torment to a loftier observation rising above mortal reality toward the other world, that of freedom.

Why this confidence? One may well ask. And we may answer with the thought that Kafka belongs to a tradition in which what is highest is expressed in a book which is writing in the highest sense of the word, the Scriptures,[6] a tradition in which ecstatic experiments were conducted by means of a combination and manipulation of letters, in which it is said that the world of letters, those of the alphabet, is the true world of blessedness.[7] To write is to conjure up spirits, it is perhaps to free them against us, but this danger is part of the liberating power.[8]

Kafka was not, however, of a "superstitious" turn of mind; there was in him a cold lucidity which prompted him to say to Brod as they left the hassidic celebrations: "Really, it was almost like an African tribe, crude superstitions." [9] We should not, then, be content with explanations, perhaps well-founded but which, to say the least, do not let us understand why Kafka, so much aware that each of his steps led him astray, should abandon himself with such faith to that essential error that is writing. There too it would not be enough to recall that since his adolescence he was extraordinarily influenced by artists like Goethe and Flaubert, whom he was often ready to place above all others because they put their art above all else. Kafka doubtless never completely separated himself internally from his conception of art, but if his passion was from the beginning so strong and for so long seemed to him to be salutary, it is because, from the beginning and through "the sin of the father," he found himself cast out of the world, condemned to a solitude for which he did not have to hold literature responsible, he owed it rather his thanks for having illumined that solitude, for having made it fruitful — an opening to another world.

It can be said for him that his conflict with the father cast into the shadows the negative side of the literary experiment. Even when he sees that his work demands he wither away, even when more seriously he sees the opposition between his work and his marriage, he in no way concludes therefrom that there is in work a mortal power, an utterance which pronounces the "banishment" and condemns one to the wilderness. He does not draw this conclusion because, from the beginning, the world was lost to him, real existence was withdrawn from him or was never given to him, and when he speaks again of his exile, of the impossibility of escaping it, he writes (January 24, 1922): "It even seems to me as if I had not come by myself but had been pushed here as a child and then chained to this spot." Art did not bring him this misfortune, did not even contribute to it but, on the contrary, illumined it and was "the awareness of misfortune," its new dimension.

Art is first of all the awareness of misfortune, not its compensation. Kafka's inflexibility, his fidelity to the exigency of the work of art, and his fidelity likewise to the exigency of misfortune saved him absolutely from that fictional paradise which is the delight of so many a weak artist whom life has disappointed. Art does not have reveries and "constructs" as its objective. But neither does it describe truth: truth is to be neither known nor described, it cannot even know itself, just as earthly salvation demands to be accomplished and not questioned or imagined. In this sense there is no place for art: rigorous monism excludes all idols. But in this same sense, if art is not justified in general, it is so at least for Kafka alone; for art, like Kafka, is linked to what is "outside" the world, and it expresses the profundity of this outside which is without intimacy and repose — which arises when, even with us, even with our death, we have no further connection with possibility. Art is the awareness of "that misfortune." It describes the condition of him who has lost himself, who can no longer say "I," who in the same movement has lost the world, the truth of the world, who belongs to exile, to that *time of distress* when, as Hölderlin puts it, the gods are no longer and when the gods are not yet. This does not mean that art affirms another world, if it is true that it has its origin not in another world but in the other of every world (it is on this point, as will be seen — but in the notes which express his religious experience rather than in his works — that Kafka made or was ready to make the leap that art does not authorize).[10]

Kafka wavers pathetically. At times he seems to do all he can to make a home for himself among men "whose power of attraction is monstrous." He tries to become engaged, he takes up gardening, practices manual labor, thinks of Palestine, procures lodging in Prague to overcome not only the solitude but the independence of a man mature and alive. On this plane, the conflict with the father remains basic, and all the entries in the *Diaries* confirm it and show that Kafka hid from himself nothing of what psychoanalysis could reveal to him. His dependence on his family not only made him weak, stranger as he was to manly tasks (as he affirms), but since this dependence horrified him it also made unbearable to him all forms of dependence and, to begin with, the marriage which disgustingly reminds him of that of his parents,[11] the family life from which he would have liked to free himself but in which he would also have liked to involve himself; for there is the fulfillment of the law, the truth — that of the father — which attracts as much as it repels him, so that "really I stand before my family, and in its circle ceaselessly brandish knives to wound them, but at the same time to defend them." "This on the one hand."

But on the other, he sees ever more clearly — and naturally his illness aids him in this view — that he belongs to the other shore, that, banished, he must not evade this banishment or remain turned passively away, as if crushed against its frontiers, toward a reality from which he feels excluded and in which he has never even lived, for he is not yet born. This new perspective could simply be that of the absolute despair, the nihilism which is too easily attributed to him. How can we deny that distress was his element? It was his abode and his "time." But this distress was never without hope; this hope was often only the torment of distress, not that which gives hope but which prevents one from being satisfied even with despair, which makes one "while condemned to put an end to it, condemned also to defend himself right to the end," and perhaps then engaged to transform condemnation into deliverance. The essential thing in this new perspective, that of distress, is not to turn toward Canaan. Migration has as its goal the wilderness which is now the true Promised Land. "Is it over there you are leading me?" Yes, over there. But where is this "over there"? It is never in sight, the wilderness is even less sure than the world, it is never more than the approach to the wilderness and, in this land of error, one is never "here" but always "far from here." And yet, in this region where the conditions of a real dwelling place are lacking, where one must live in incomprehensible separation, in an exclusion from which one is in some way excluded, as one is there excluded from himself; in this region which is that of error because one does nothing there but wander endlessly, there subsists a tension, the very possibility of wandering, of going to the end of error, of approaching its limits, of transforming what is an aimless traveling into the certainty of a pathless goal.

We know that the story of the surveyor offers us the most impressive image of this step. From the beginning, this hero of inflexible obstinacy is described to us as having renounced this world forever, the life in which there is wife and children. From the beginning, then, he is beyond salvation, he belongs to exile, that place where he is not only not at home but where he is outside himself — in the "outside" itself, a region absolutely void of intimacy, where beings seem absent, where everything one thinks he has hold of slips away. The tragic difficulty of the undertaking is that in that world of exclusion and radical separation all is false and inauthentic as soon as one stops there; everything fails the moment one relies upon it; but yet the basis of this absence is always given anew as an indubitable and absolute presence; and the word "absolute" is here appropriate, this word that means separate, as if separation, experienced in all its severity, could be inverted into the absolutely separate, the absolutely absolute.

We must be explicit: Kafka, his mind always just and in no way satisfied with the dilemma of all or nothing which he yet conceives with more intransigence than anyone else, makes it felt that in this step outside the true there are certain rules, contradictory and untenable, perhaps, but which still authorize a kind of possibility. The first is given in the error itself: one must err and not be negligent as is the Joseph K. of *The Trial*, who imagines that things are going to continue as before, that he is still in the world, whereas from the first sentence he is cast out of it. Joseph's mistake, undoubtedly like that for which Kafka reproached himself at the time he was writing that book, is to want to win his trial in the world itself, to which he thinks he still belongs but in which his cold, empty heart, his life as a bachelor and office-clerk, his remoteness from his family — all character traits which Kafka found in himself — already prevent him from making headway. To be sure, his insouciance gives way little by little, but that is the very result of the trial, just as the beauty which illuminates the prisoners and makes them attractive to women is the reflection of their own dissolution, of the death which advances in them like a truer light.

The trial — the banishment — is doubtless a great misfortune, it is perhaps an incomprehensible injustice or an inexorable punishment, but it is also — this is true only to a certain extent, and that is the hero's excuse, the trap in which he lets himself be caught — a gift which it is not enough to challenge by invoking in hollow speeches a higher justice, but which, on the contrary, one must try to take advantage of according to the rule which Kafka made his own: "One must limit himself to what he still possesses." The "Trial" has at least the advantage of making Kafka realize what he really is, of destroying the illusion, the deceptive consolations which, because he had a good job and some indifferent pleasures, let him believe in his own existence, in his existence as a man in the world. But for all that, the Trial is not the truth; it is on the contrary a process of error like everything which is linked to the outside, these "external" shadows into which one is cast by the force of banishment; a process in which, if a hope remains, it is for him who advances, not against the current through sterile opposition, but in the very direction of error.

The surveyor is almost entirely free of the faults of Joseph K. He does not seek to return to the place of his birth: lost is the life of Canaan, erased is the truth of *this* world; he remembers it scarcely, if at all, in brief and pathetic moments. Nor is he negligent, but always active, never stopping, almost never becoming discouraged, going on from defeat to defeat with tireless movement which recalls the cold uneasiness of restless times. Yes, he goes with inflexible obstinacy always in the direction of extreme error, disdaining the village which still has some reality but wanting the Castle which perhaps has none, breaking away from Frieda who has some living reflections on her, to turn toward Olga, Amelia's sister, the doubly excluded, the rejected, and what is more, she who voluntarily, by a terrifying decision, chose to be so. Everything therefore ought to be for the best. But it is nothing of the kind, for the surveyor repeatedly falls into the mistake which Kafka terms the most serious, that of impatience.[12] Impatience at the heart of error is the essential fault because it mistakes the very truth of error, which imposes the law of never believing that the goal is near nor that one is approaching it: one must never have done with the infinite; one must never grasp, as the immediate, as the already present, the profundity of the inexhaustible absence.

Certainly that is inevitable, and such is the depressing character of a quest like that. He who is not impatient is negligent; he who gives himself over to the anxiety of error loses the insouciance which would exhaust time. Hardly arrived, without understanding anything of that test of exclusion in which he is, K. immediately sets out to reach the limit at once. He neglects the intermediaries, and that is doubtless a merit, the force of straining toward the absolute; but there emerges only the more clearly his aberration, which is to take for the limit what is only an intermediate step, a representation according to his "means."

We are surely every bit as mistaken as the surveyor is when we think he recognizes in the bureaucratic phantasmagoria the fitting symbol of a superior world. This figuration is only proportionate to impatience, the perceptible form of error, through which, for the impatient eye, the inexorable force of the wrong infinite is substituted for the absolute. K. always wants to reach the goal before he has got to it. This exigency of a premature ending is the principle of the figuration, it engenders the *image* or, if you like, the idol; and the curse which is attached to it is the curse which attaches to idolatry. Man wants unity at once; he wants it in separation itself; he pictures it for himself, and that representation, the image of unity, immediately constitutes the element of the dispersion in which he is lost more and more; for the image, as image, can never be attained, and it hides from him, moreover, the unity of which it is the image, and separates it from him by making itself inaccessible and by making unity inaccessible.

Klamm is not at all invisible: the surveyor wishes to see him and he sees him. The Castle, the supreme goal, is not at all out of sight. As an image it is constantly at his call. Naturally, looked at closely, these figures are deceptive, the Castle is only a heap of village shanties, Klamm a big ungainly man seated in front of a desk. All very commonplace and ugly. Therein also lies the surveyor's good luck; it is the truth, the deceptive honesty of these images: they are not attractive in themselves, they have nothing to justify the fascinated interest one shows in them, thus they remind one that they are not the true goal. But at the same time, in this insignificance is allowed to be forgotten the other essential truth — of knowing that all the same they are images of that goal, that they participate in its ineffable value, and that not to cling to them is already to turn away from the essential.

The situation can be summed up thus: it is impatience that makes the limit inaccessible by substituting for it the nearness of an intermediate figure. It is impatience that destroys the approach to the limit by preventing us from recognizing in the intermediate the figure of the immediate.

We must restrict ourselves here to these few indications. The bureaucratic phantasmagoria, that busy idleness which characterizes it, these double beings which are its performers, guardians, assistants, and messengers, who always travel in pairs as if to make us aware that they are but the reflections of each other and the reflection of an inaccessible whole, all this chain of metamorphoses, this methodical increase of distance which is never given as infinite but deepens indefinitely in a necessary way by the transformation of the goal into obstacles, but also of the obstacles into intermediate steps leading to the goal; all this powerful imagery does not represent the truth of the higher nor even its transcendence, represents rather the happiness and unhappiness of the figuration, of the exigency by which the man of exile is obliged to make from error a means of truth, and from what deceives him indefinitely the ultimate possibility of grasping the infinite.

To what extent did Kafka realize the analogy between this procedure and the movement by which the work of art itself tends toward its origin, that center alone in which it can be fulfilled, in the quest for which it achieves reality and which, once reached, makes it impossible? To what extent did he equate the trial of his heroes with the manner in which he himself tried, as an artist, to open a way toward the work of art and by the work of art toward something true? Did he often think of Goethe's words: "It is by postulating the impossible that the artist obtains the whole of the possible"? This evidence at least is striking: the fault that he punishes in K. is also that which the artist blames in himself. This is impatience. This it is which seeks to hasten the story to its conclusion before it has developed in all directions, has exhausted the measure of time that is in it, and has raised the indefinite to a true totality in which each inauthentic movement, each partially false image can be transformed into a steadfast certainty. An impossible task, a task which if completely accomplished would destroy the very truth toward which it tends, as the work of art founders if it touches the point which is its origin. There are many reasons why Kafka finished almost none of his "stories," which led him, after hardly beginning one of them, to lay it aside and try to pacify himself in another. That he often knew the torment of the artist exiled from his work at the moment when it asserts itself and closes up, this he admits himself. That he sometimes abandoned the story in the fear that if he did not abandon it he would not be able to return to the world, this he also admits, but he was not sure that this concern, though essential, had been the strongest in him. That he abandoned it often because every conclusion carries in itself the happiness of a definitive truth which he had no right to accept, with which his existence did not yet square, this reason seems also to have played a large role; but all these movements amount to this: Kafka, perhaps unconsciously, felt deeply that writing is surrender to the incessant and, through anguish, the anguish of impatience, the scrupulous concern for the exigency of writing, he most often refused himself that leap which alone permits completion, that happy and carefree confidence by which (momentarily) a limit is put on the illimitable.

What has been so improperly called his realism betrays the same instinctive effort to stave off his impatience. Kafka often showed that he had a ready genius capable of achieving the essential in a few strokes. But more and more he imposed on himself a meticulousness, a slowness of approach, a detailed precision (even in the description of his own dreams), without which man, exiled from reality, is soon doomed to the wildness of disorder and to the merely approximate of the imagery. The more one is lost in the outside, in the strangeness and insecurity of that loss, the more he must call on the spirit of discipline, meticulousness, and accuracy, and must be present in absence by the multiplicity of images, by their determined and modest appearance (free of fascination), and their vigorously maintained coherence. One who belongs to reality has no need for so many details which, as we know, in no way correspond to the form of a real vision. But he who belongs to the profundity of the limitless and the distant, to the misfortunes of the excessive, he is indeed condemned to the excess of measure and to the search for flawless continuity without gaps and incongruities. And condemned is exactly the word, for if patience, accuracy, and cool mastery are the indispensable qualities to keep one from getting lost when nothing remains for one to cling to, patience, accuracy, and cool mastery are also faults which, dividing the difficulties and extending them indefinitely, perhaps delay the catastrophe but certainly delay the rescue, constantly transform the infinite into the indefinite, as it is likewise measure which in the work of art prevents the limitless ever being achieved.

"Thou shalt not make unto thee any graven image, or any likeness of anything that is in heaven above, or that is in the earth beneath, or that is in the waters under the earth." Felix Weltsch, Kafka's friend, who has well described his struggle against impatience, thinks Kafka took seriously these words of the Bible. If that is so, let us try to imagine a man on whom such a fundamental commandment weighs heavily, who, on pain of death, knows himself cut off from images, and who suddenly finds himself exiled in the imaginary with no other abode or subsistence except images and the domain of images. He is then obliged to live on his death and is compelled, in his despair and to escape this despair — immediate execution — to make of his condemnation his only way of salvation. But was Kafka conscious of being this man? It is impossible to say. One sometimes has the feeling that the fundamental commandment, the more he tries to remember it (for it is in any event forgotten, for the community in which it has life is virtually destroyed), the more he tries to remember the religious sense which dwells hidden in this commandment, and that with an increasingly greater severity, by creating a void within him and about him so that idols will not be welcome there, the more he seems ready, on the other side, to forget that this commandment ought also to apply to his art. From this results a very precarious balance. This balance, in the illegitimate solitude which is his, allows him to be faithful to an ever stricter spiritual monism while giving himself up to a certain artistic idolatry, then engages him in purifying this idolatry by all the severity of an ascesis which condemns literary realities (failure to complete his works, aversion to all publication, refusal to believe himself a writer, etc.), which, moreover, and this is more serious, would subordinate art to its spiritual condition. Art is not religion, "it does not even lead to religion," but in times of distress — like ours, this time when there are no gods, a time of absence and exile — then art is justified, which is the intimacy of that distress, which is the effort to make manifest through images the error of the imaginary and, at the boundary, the elusive, forgotten truth which lurks behind this error.

That there is at first a tendency in Kafka to replace religious exigency with literary exigency, then, especially toward the end, an inclination to replace his literary experience with his religious experience, to merge them in a rather confused way by moving from the wilderness of faith into faith in a world which is no longer the wilderness but another world in which freedom will be restored to him — this is what the notes in his *Diaries* lead us to feel. "Do I live in the other world, then? Dare I say that?" (January 30, 1922). On the page which we have quoted Kafka recalls that according to him mankind never has any other choice than this: either to seek the Promised Land through the way of Canaan, or to seek it through the way of that other world which is the wilderness, "for," he adds, "there is no third world for mankind." There is none, to be sure, but perhaps one must say more, perhaps one must say that the artist, the kind of man that Kafka also wanted to be, through concern for his art and his quest for its origin, the "poet" is the one for whom not even one single world exists, since for him there exists only the outside, the shimmering of the eternal outside.

ROMAN JAKOBSON
CLAUDE LÉVI-STRAUSS

Charles Baudelaire's "Les Chats"

It may come as a surprise that an anthropological review should publish a study devoted to a French poem of the XIXth century; there is, however, a simple explanation. If a linguist and an ethnologist have seen fit to join forces in their efforts to try to understand what a Baudelaire sonnet is made of, it is because, independently, they have found themselves confronted with complementary problems. The linguist discerns structures in poetic works which are strikingly analogous to those which the analysis of myths reveals to the ethnologist. For his part, the latter cannot fail to recognize that myths do not consist simply of conceptual arrangements: they are also works of art which arouse in those who hear them (and in ethnologists themselves when they read them in transcription) profound aesthetic emotions. Is it possible that the two problems are but one and the same?

Admittedly, the author of this preliminary note has at one time described the myth as being in opposition to the poetic work (see C. Lévi-Strauss, *Anthropologie structurale,* p. 232), but those who have reproached him for this have not taken into account the fact that the very notion of opposition implies that the two forms were originally conceived of as complementary terms, belonging to the same category. The relationship outlined here does not in any way detract from the quality of discreteness which we first emphasized, that is, that each poetic work, considered in isolation, contains within itself its own variables which can be represented on a vertical axis, since it consists of superimposed levels: phonological, phonetic, syntactic, prosodic, semantic, etc. Whereas the myth, at least in the extreme, can be interpreted only on the semantic level, the system of variables (always an indispensable part of structural analysis) being supplied by the multiplicity of versions of the same myth, that is to say, a cross-section through a body of myths at the semantic

SOURCE: " 'Les Chats' de Charles Baudelaire," *L'Homme,* II (jan.–avril, 1962), pp. 5–21. English translation by Katie Furness-Lane for *Structuralism* edited by Michael Lane and published by Jonathan Cape Limited. This version edited, with Professor Jakobson's revisions, by Stephen Rudy.

level only. However, one should not lose sight of the fact that this distinction fulfills above all a particular practical need, in that it enables the structural analysis of myths to forge ahead even in the absence of a genuine linguistic base. Only by practicing both methods, even if it means forcing oneself to change fields abruptly, can one begin to some extent to decide the initial wager: that if either method can be selected according to the circumstances, it is because, in the final analysis, they can be substituted one for the other, without necessarily being completely interchangeable.   C. L.-S.

1. Les amoureux fervents et les savants austères
2. Aiment également, dans leur mûre saison,
3. Les chats puissants et doux, orgueil de la maison,
4. Qui comme eux sont frileux et comme eux sédentaires.

5. Amis de la science et de la volupté,
6. Ils cherchent le silence et l'horreur des ténèbres;
7. L'Érèbe les eût pris pour ses coursiers funèbres,
8. S'ils pouvaient au servage incliner leur fierté.

9. Ils prennent en songeant les nobles attitudes
10. Des grands sphinx allongés au fond des solitudes,
11. Qui semblent s'endormir dans un rêve sans fin;

12. Leurs reins féconds sont pleins d'étincelles magiques,
13. Et des parcelles d'or, ainsi qu'un sable fin,
14. Étoilent vaguement leurs prunelles mystiques.

If one can give credence to the feuilleton "Le Chat Trott" by Champfleury, where this sonnet of Baudelaire was first published (*Le Corsaire*, November 14, 1847), it must already have been written by March 1840, and — contrary to the claims of certain exegetes — the early text in *Le Corsaire* and that in *Les Fleurs du Mal* (1857) correspond word for word.

In the organization of the rhymes, the poet follows the scheme: *aBBa CddC eeFgFg* (upper-case letters being used to denote the lines ending in masculine rhymes and lower-case letters for the lines ending in feminine rhymes). This chain of rhymes is divided into three strophic units, namely, two quatrains and one sestet composed of two tercets, which form a certain whole since the disposition of the rhymes within this sestet is controlled in sonnets, as Grammont has shown, "by the same rules as in any strophe of six lines." [1]

The rhyme-scheme of the sonnet in question is the corollary of three dissimilative rules:

1. Two plain (couplet) rhymes cannot follow one another;
2. If two contiguous lines belong to different rhymes, one of them must be feminine and the other masculine;

3. At the end of contiguous stanzas feminine lines and masculine lines alternate: [4]*sédentaires* — [8]*fierté* — [14]*mystiques.*

Following the classical pattern, the so-called feminine rhymes always end in a mute syllable and the masculine rhymes in a fully sounded syllable. The difference between the two classes of rhymes persists equally in the current pronunciation which suppresses the "mute *e*" of the final syllable, the last fully sounded vowel being followed by consonants in all the feminine rhymes of the sonnet (*austères — sédentaires, ténèbres — funèbres, attitudes — solitudes, magiques — mystiques*), whereas all its masculine rhymes end in a vowel (*saison — maison, volupté — fierté, fin — fin*).

The relation between the classification of rhymes and the choice of grammatical categories emphasizes the importance of the role played by grammar as well as by rhyme in the structure of this sonnet.

All the lines end with nominal forms, either substantive (8) or adjectival (6). All the substantives are feminine. The final noun is plural in the eight lines with a feminine rhyme, which are all longer, either by a syllable in the traditional manner or by a postvocalic consonant in present-day pronunciation, whereas the shorter lines, those with a masculine rhyme, end in all six cases with a singular noun.

In the two quatrains, the masculine rhymes are constituted by substantives and the feminine rhymes by adjectives, with the exception of the key-word [6]*ténèbres,* which rhymes with [7]*funèbres.* We shall return later to the whole question of the relationship between these two particular lines. As far as the tercets are concerned, the three lines of the first tercet all end with substantives, and those of the second with adjectives. Thus, the rhyme which links the two tercets — the only instance in this poem of a homonymous rhyme ([11]*sans fin* — [13]*sable fin*) — places a masculine adjective in opposition to a feminine substantive — and it is the only adjective, and the only example of the masculine gender, among the masculine rhymes in the sonnet.

The sonnet is made up of three complex sentences delimited by periods, i.e., each of the two quatrains and the sestet. These three sentences display an arithmetical progression according to the number of independent clauses and of the finite verbal forms:

1. One single finite (*aiment*);
2. Two finites (*cherchent, eût pris*);
3. Three finites (*prennent, sont, étoilent*).

On the other hand, the subordinate clause in each of the three sentences has but one finite: 1. *qui . . . sont;* 2. *s'ils pouvaient;* 3. *qui semblent.* This ternary division of the sonnet implies an antinomy between both two-rhyme sentences and the final, three-rhyme sentence. It is counter-balanced by a dichotomy which divides the work into two coupled stanzas, that is, into two pairs of quatrains and two pairs of tercets. This binary principle, supported in turn by the grammatical organization of the text, also implies an antinomy, this time between the two initial subdivisions or stanzas of four lines and the two last stanzas of three lines. It is on the tension between these two modes of arrangement and between their symmetrical and dissymetrical constituents that the composition of the whole work is based.

There is a clear-cut syntactical parallel between the pair of quatrains on the one hand and the pair of tercets on the other. Both the first quatrain and the first tercet consist of two clauses, of which the second is relative, and introduced in both cases by the same pronoun, *qui.* This clause comprises the last line of its stanza and is dependent on a masculine plural substantive, which serves as accessory in the principal clause (³*Les chats,* ¹⁰*Des . . . sphinx*). The second quatrain (and equally the second tercet) contains two coordinate clauses, of which the last; complex in its turn, comprises the two final lines of the stanza (7–8 and 13–14) and includes a subordinate clause which is linked to the main clause by a conjunction. In the quatrain this clause is conditional (⁸*S'ils pouvaient*); that of the tercet is comparative (¹³*ainsi qu'un*). The first is postpositive, whereas the second, incomplete, is an interpolated clause.

In the 1847 *Le Corsaire* text, the punctuation of the sonnet corresponds to this division. The first tercet ends with a period, as does the first quatrain. In the second tercet and in the second quatrain, the last two lines are preceded by a semicolon.

The semantic aspect of the grammatical subjects reinforces this parallelism between the two quatrains on the one hand and the two tercets on the other:

I Quatrains	II Tercets
1. First	1. First
2. Second	2. Second

The subjects of the first quatrain and of the first tercet designate only animate beings, whereas one of the two subjects of the second quatrain and all the grammatical subjects of the second tercet are inanimate substantives: ⁷*L'Érèbe,* ¹²*Leurs reins,* ¹³*des parcelles,* ¹³*un sable.* In addition to these so-to-speak horizontal correspondences, there is a correspondence that could be called vertical, one which opposes the totality of the two quatrains to the totality of the two tercets. While all the direct objects in the two tercets are inanimate substantives (⁹*les nobles attitudes,* ¹⁴*leurs prunelles*), the sole direct object of the first quatrain is an animate substantive ([3]*Les chats*). The objects of the second quatrain include, in addition to the inanimate substantive ([6]*le silence et l'horreur*), the pronoun *les* which refers to *les chats* of the preceding sentence. If we look at the relationship between subject and object, the sonnet presents two correspondences which could be called diagonal. One descending diagonal links the two exterior stanzas (the first quatrain and the last tercet) and puts them in opposition to an ascending diagonal which links the two interior stanzas. In the exterior stanzas subject and object form part of the same semantic category: animate in the first quatrain (*amoureux, savants — chats*) and inanimate in the second tercet (*reins, parcelles — prunelles*). Conversely, in the interior stanzas, object and subject are in opposing categories: in the first tercet the inanimate object is opposed to the animate subject (*ils* [=*chats*] — *attitudes*), whereas in the second quatrain the same relationship (*ils* [=*chats*] — *silence, horreur*) alternates with that of the animate object and inanimate subject (*Érèbe — les* [=*chats*]).

Thus, each of the four stanzas retains its own individuality: the animate class, which is common to both subject and object in the first quatrain, is peculiar to the subject only in the first tercet; in the second quatrain this class characterizes either subject or object, whereas in the second tercet, neither the one nor the other.

There are several striking correspondences in the grammatical structure both of the beginning and of the end of the sonnet. At the end, as well as at the beginning, but nowhere else, there are two subjects with only one predicate and only one direct object. Each of these subjects, as well as their objects, has a modifier (*Les amoureux fervents, les savants austères — Les chats puissants et doux; des parcelles d'or, un sable fin — leurs prunelles mystiques*). The two predicates, the first and last in the sonnet, are the only ones accompanied by adverbs, both of them derived from adjectives and linked to one another by a deep rhyme: [2]*Aiment également —* [14]*Étoilent vaguement*. The second and penultimate predicates are the only ones that comprise a copula and a predicative adjective, the latter being emphasized in both cases by an internal rhyme: [4]Qui comme *eux* sont fril*eux;* [12]Leurs r*eins* féconds sont pl*eins*. Generally speaking, only the two exterior stanzas are rich in adjectives: nine in the quatrain and five in the tercet; whereas the two interior stanzas have only three adjectives in all (*funèbres, nobles, grands*).

As we have already noted, it is only at the beginning and at the end of the poem that the subjects are of the same class as the objects: each one belongs to the animate class in the first quatrain and to the inanimate in the second tercet. Animate beings, their functions and their activities, dominate the initial stanza. The first line contains nothing but adjectives. Of these, the two substantival forms which act as subjects — *Les amoureux* and *les savants* — display verbal roots: the text is inaugurated by "those who love" and by "those who know." In the last line of the poem, the opposite occurs: the transitive verb *Étoilent,* which serves as a predicate, is derived from a substantive. The latter is related to the series of inanimate and concrete appellatives which dominate this tercet and distinguish it from the three anterior stanzas. A clear homophony can be heard between this verb and the members of the series in question: /etɛsɛlə/ — /e de parsɛlə/ — /etwalə/. Finally, the subordinate clauses contained in the last lines of these two medial stanzas each include an adverbial infinitive, these two object-complements being the only infinitives in the entire poem: [8]*S'ils pouvaient . . . incliner;* [11]*Qui semblent s'endormir.*

As we have seen, neither the dichotomous partition of the sonnet, nor the division into three stanzas, results in an equilibrium of the isometric constituents. But if one were to divide the fourteen lines into two equal parts, the seventh line would end the first half of the poem, and the eighth line would mark the beginning of the second half. It is, therefore, significant that just these two middle lines stand out most obviously by their grammatical make-up from the rest of the poem.

Actually, in more than one respect, the poem falls into three parts: in this case into the middle pair of lines and two isometric groups, that is to say, the six lines which precede this pair and the six which follow it. Hence there emerges a kind of couplet inserted between two sestets.

All personal verb-forms and pronouns and all the subjects of verbal clauses are plural throughout the sonnet, except in line seven, *L'Érèbe les eût pris pour ses coursiers funèbres,* which contains the only proper noun in the poem and is the only instance of both the finite verb and its subject being in the singular. Furthermore, it is the only line in which the possessive pronoun (*ses*) refers to a singular.

Only the third person is used in the sonnet. The only verbal tense used is the present, except in lines 7 and 8, where the poet envisages an imaginary action ([7]*eût pris*) arising out of an unreal premise ([8]*S'ils pouvaient*).

The sonnet shows a pronounced tendency to provide every verb and every substantive with a modifier. Each verbal form is accompanied by a governed modifier (substantive, pronoun, infinitive) or by a predicative adjective. All transitive verbs govern only substantives ([2-3]*Aiment . . . Les chats;* [6]*cherchent le silence et l'horreur;* [9]*prennent . . . les . . . attitudes;* [14]*Étoilent . . . leurs prunelles*). The pronoun which serves as the object in the seventh line is the sole deviation: *les eût pris.*

With the exception of adnominal adjuncts, which are never accompanied by any modifier in the sonnet, the substantives (including the substantivized adjectives) are always modified by attributes (e.g., [3]*chats puissants et doux*) or by adjuncts (⁵*Amis de la science et de la volupté*); line 7 again provides the only exception: *L'Érèbe les eût pris.*

All five attributes in the first quatrain (¹*fervents*, ¹*austères*, ²*mûre*, ³*puissants*, ³*doux*) and all six in the two tercets (⁹*nobles*, ¹⁰*grands*, ¹²*féconds*, ¹²*magiques*, ¹³*fin*, ¹⁴*mystiques*) are qualitative epithets, whereas the second quatrain has no adjectives other than the determinative attribute in the seventh line (*coursiers funèbres*).

It is also this line which inverts the animate/inanimate order underlying the relation between subject and object in the other lines of this quatrain, and which is, in fact, the only one in the entire sonnet to adopt this inanimate/animate order.

Several striking peculiarities clearly distinguish line 7 only, or the last two lines of the second quatrain, from the rest of the sonnet. However, it must be noted that the tendency for the medial distich to stand out agrees with the principle of an asymmetrical trichotomy, which puts the whole of the second quatrain in opposition to the first quatrain on the one hand and in opposition to the final sestet on the other, thus creating a kind of central strophe distinct in several respects from the marginal strophic units. We have already shown that only in the seventh line are subject and predicate in the singular, but this observation can be extended: only within the lines of the second quatrain do we find either subject or object in the singular and whereas in the seventh line the singularity of the subject (*L'Érèbe*) is opposed to the plurality of the object (*les*), the adjoining lines invert this relation, having a plural subject and a singular object (⁶*Ils cherchent le silence et l'horreur;* ⁸*S'ils pouvaient . . . incliner leur fierté*).

In the other stanzas, both object and subject are plural (¹⁻³*Les amoureux . . . et les savants . . . Aiment . . . Les chats;* ⁹*Ils prennent . . . les . . . attitudes;* ¹³⁻¹⁴*Et des parcelles . . . Étoilent . . . leurs prunelles*). It is notable that in the second quatrain singularity of subject and object coincides with the inanimate and plurality with the animate class. The importance of grammatical number to Baudelaire becomes particularly noteworthy by virtue of the role it plays in opposition-relations in the rhymes of the sonnet.

It must be added that the rhymes in the second quatrain are distinguishable by their structure from all other rhymes in the poem. The feminine rhyme *ténèbres — funèbres* in the second quatrain is the only one which brings together two different parts of speech. Moreover, all the rhymes in the sonnet, except those in the quatrain in question, comprise one or more identical phonemes, either immediately preceding or some distance in front of the stressed syllable, usually reinforced by a supportive consonant: ¹*savants austères — ⁴sédentaires*, ²*mûre saison — ³maison*, ⁹*attitudes — solitudes*, ¹¹*un rêve sans fin — ¹³un sable fin*, ¹²*étincelles* *magiques* — [14]prun*elles* my*stiques*. In the second quatrain, neither the pair [5]volup*té* — [8]fier*té*, nor [6]*ténèbres* — [7]*funèbres,* offer any correspondence in the syllable anterior to the rhyme itself. On the other hand, the final words in the seventh and eighth lines are alliterative, [7]*funèbres* — [8]*fierté,* and the sixth and fifth lines are linked by the repetition of the final syllable of [5]volup*té* in [6]*ténèbres* and by the internal rhyme [5]*science* — [6]*silence,* which reinforces the affinity between the two lines. Thus the rhymes themselves exhibit a certain relaxation of the ties between the two halves of the second quatrain.

A salient role in the phonic texture of the sonnet is played by the nasal vowels. These phonemes, "as though veiled by nasality," as Grammont aptly puts it,[2] occur very frequently in the first quatrain (9 nasals, from 2 to 3 per line) but most particularly in the final sestet (22 nasals with increasing frequency throughout the first tercet, [9]3 — [10]4 — [11]6: Qui se*m*blent s'e*n*dormir d*an*s *un* rêve s*an*s f*in* — and with a decreasing frequency throughout the second tercet, [12]5 — [13]3 — [14]1). In contrast, the second quatrain contains only three: one per line, excepting the seventh, the sole line in the sonnet without a nasal vowel; this quatrain is also the only stanza where the masculine rhyme does not contain a nasal vowel. Then again, it is in the second quatrain that the role of phonic dominant passes from vowels to consonantal phonemes, in particular to liquids. The second quatrain is the only one which shows an excessive number of these liquid phonemes, 24 in all, as compared to 15 in the first quatrain, 11 in the first tercet, and 14 in the second. The total number of /r/'s is slightly lower than the number of /l/'s (31 versus 33), but the seventh line, which has only two /l/'s, contains five /r/'s, that is to say, more than any other line in the sonnet — L'*É*r*è*be les eut p*r*is pou*r* ses cou*r*sie*r*s funèb*r*es. According to Grammont, it is by opposition to /r/ that /l/ "gives the impression of a sound that is neither grating, rasping, nor rough but, on the contrary, that glides and flows, that is limpid."[3] The abrupt nature of every /r/, and particularly the French /r/, in comparison with the *glissando* of the /l/ is clearly illustrated in Mlle Durand's recent acoustical analysis of the two liquids.[4] The agglomeration of the /r/'s eloquently echoes the delusive association of the cats with Erebus, followed by the antithetic ascent of the empirical felines to their miraculous transfigurations.

The first six lines of the sonnet are linked by a characteristic reiteration: a symmetrical pair of coordinate phrases linked by the same conjunction *et*: [1]*Les amoureux fervents et les savants austères;* [3]*Les chats puissants et doux;* [4]*Qui comme eux sont frileux et comme eux sédentaires;* [5]*Amis de la science et de la volupté.* The binarism of the determinants thus forms a chiasmus with the binarism of the determined in the next line — [6]*le silence et l'horreur des ténèbres* — which puts an end to these binary constructions. This construction, common to all the lines of this "sestet," does not recur in the remainder of the poem. The juxtapositions without a conjunction are a variation of the same scheme: ²*Aiment également, dans leur mûre saison* (parallel circumstantial complements); ³*Les chats . . . , orgueil . . .* (a substantive in apposition to another).

These pairs of coordinate phrases and their rhymes (not only those which are exterior and underline the semantic links such as ¹*austères* — ⁴*sédentaires,* ²*saison* — ³*maison,* but also and especially the internal rhymes) serve to draw the lines of this introduction closer together: ¹*amoureux* — ⁴*comme eux* — ⁴*frileux* — ⁴*comme eux;* ¹*fervents* — ¹*savants* — ²*également* — ²*dans* — ³*puissants;* ⁵*science* — ⁶*silence.* Thus all the adjectives characterizing the persons in the first quatrain are rhyme-words, with the one exception ³*doux.* A double etymological figure links the openings of three of the lines: ¹*Les amoureux* — ³*Aiment* — ⁵*Amis,* in accordance with the unity of this crypto-stanza of six lines, which starts and ends with a couplet, each of whose first hemistiches rhyme: ¹*fervents* — ²*également;* ⁵*science* — ⁶*silence.*

³*Les chats,* who are the direct object of the clause comprising the first three lines of the sonnet, become the implicit subject of the clauses in the following three lines (⁴*Qui comme eux sont frileux;* ⁶*Ils cherchent le silence*), revealing the outline of a division of this quasi-sestet into two quasi-tercets. The middle "distich" recapitulates the metamorphosis of the cats: from an implicit object (⁷*L'Érèbe les eût pris*) into an equally implicit grammatical subject (⁸*S'ils pouvaient*). In this respect the eighth line coincides with the following sentence (⁹*Ils prennent*).

In general, the postpositive subordinate clauses form a kind of transition between the subordinating clause and the sentence which follows it. Thus, the implicit subject "chats" of the ninth and tenth lines changes into a reference to the metaphor "sphinx" in the relative clause of the eleventh line (*Qui semblent s'endormir dans un rêve sans fin*) and, as a result, links this line to the tropes serving as grammatical subjects in the final tercet. The indefinite article, entirely alien to the first ten lines with their fourteen definite articles, is the only one admitted in the four concluding lines of the sonnet.

Thus, thanks to the ambiguous references in the two relative clauses, in the eleventh and the fourth lines, the four concluding lines allow us to glimpse at the contour of an imaginary quatrain which somehow corresponds to the initial quatrain of the sonnet. On the other hand, the final tercet has a formal structure which seems reflected in the first three lines of the sonnet.

Animate subjects are never expressed by substantives, but either by substantivized adjectives, in the first line of the sonnet (*Les amoureux, les savants*), or by personal and relative pronouns, in the further clauses.

Human beings appear only in the first clause, in the form of a double subject supported by substantivized verbal adjectives.

The cats, named in the title of the sonnet, are called by name only once in the text, as the direct object in the first clause: [1]*Les amoureux* . . . *et les savants* . . . [2]*Aiment* . . . [3]*Les chats.* Not only is the word *chats* avoided in the further lines of the poem, but even the initial hushing phoneme / ʃ / recurs only in a single word: [6]/il ʃ ε r ʃ ε/. It denotes, with reduplication, the first reported action of the felines. This voiceless sibilant, linked to the name of the poem's heroes, is carefully avoided throughout the remainder of the sonnet.

From the third line, the cats become an implicit subject, which proves to be the last animate subject in the sonnet. The substantive *chats,* in the roles of subject, object and adnominal adjunct, is replaced by the anaphoric pronouns [6,8,9]*ils,* [7]*les,* [8,12,14]*leur(s),* and it is only to *les chats* that the substantive pronouns *ils* and *les* refer. These accessory (adverbal) forms occur solely in the two interior stanzas, i.e., in the second quatrain and in the first tercet. The corresponding autonomous form [4]*eux* is used twice in the initial quatrain and refers only to the human characters of the sonnet, whereas no substantive pronouns occur in the final tercet.

The two subjects of the initial clause of the sonnet have one single predicate and one single object. Thus, [1]*Les amoureux fervents et les savants austères* end up [2]*dans leur mûre saison* by finding their identity in an intermediary being, an animal which encompasses the antinomic traits of two human but mutually opposed conditions. The two human categories, sensual/intellectual, oppose each other, and the mediation is achieved by means of the cats. Hence, the role of subject is latently assumed by the cats, who are at one and the same time scholars and lovers.

The two quatrains objectively present the personage of the cat, whereas the two tercets carry out his transfiguration. However, the second quatrain differs fundamentally from the first and, in general, from all the other stanzas. The equivocal formulation, *ils cherchent le silence et l'horreur des ténèbres,* gives rise to a misunderstanding summoned up in the seventh line of the sonnet and denounced in the following line. The aberrant character of this quatrain, especially the perplexity of its last half, and more particularly of the seventh line, is thoroughly marked by the peculiarities of its grammatical and phonic texture.

The semantic affinity between *L'Érèbe* ("dark region bordering on Hell," metonymic substitute for "the powers of darkness" and particularly for Erebus, "brother of Night") and the cats' predilection for *l'horreur des ténèbres,* corroborated by the phonic similarity between /tenεbrə/ and /erεbə/, all but harness the cats, heroes of the poem, to the grisly task of *coursiers funèbres.* Does the line which insinuates that *L'Érèbe les eût pris pour ses coursiers* raise a question of frustrated desire or one of false recognition? The meaning of this passage, long puzzled over by the critics,[5] remains purposely ambiguous.

Each of the quatrains, as well as each of the tercets, tries to give the cats a new identity. While the first quatrain linked the cats to two types of human condition, thanks to their pride they succeed in rejecting the new identity put forward in the second quatrain, which would associate them with an animal condition: that of coursers placed in a mythological context. It is the only identification that is rejected in the course of the whole poem. The grammatical composition of this passage, which contrasts expressly with that of the other stanzas, betrays its peculiar character: unreal conditional, lack of qualitative attributes, and an inanimate singular subject devoid of any modifier and governing an animate plural object.

Allusive oxymorons unite the stanzas. [8]*S'ils* POUVAIENT *au servage incliner leur fierté,* — but they *can*not do so (*ils ne "peuvent" pas*) because they are truly [3]PUISSANTS. They cannot be passively taken ([7]PRIS) to play an active role, and hence they themselves actively take ([9]PRENNENT) a passive role because they are obstinately *sédentaires*.

[8]*Leur fierté* predestines them for the [9]*nobles attitudes* [10]*Des grands sphinx*. The [10]*sphinx allongés* and the cats that mime them [9]*en songeant* are united by a paronomastic link between the only two participial forms in the sonnet: /ãsɔ̃ʒã/ and /alɔ̃ʒe/. The cats seem to identify themselves with the sphinxes, who in their turn [11]*semblent s'endormir*, but the illusory comparison, assimilating the sedentary cats (and by implication all who are [4]*comme eux*), to the immobility of the supernatural beings, achieves the status of a metamorphosis. The cats and the human beings who are identified with them are reunited in the mythical beasts with human heads and animal bodies. Thus, the rejected identification appears to be replaced by a new, equally mythological identification.

[9]*En songeant,* the cats manage to identify themselves with the [10]*grands sphinx*. A chain of paronomasias, linked to these key words and combining nasal vowels with continuant dentals and labials, reinforces the metamorphosis: [9]*en songeant* /ãsɔ̃ . ./ — [10]*grands sphinx* /. . . ãsfɛ̃ . ./ — [10]*fond* /fõ/ — [11]*semblent* /sã . . ./ — [11]*s'endormir* /sã . . . . . ./ — [11]*dans un* /. ãzœ̃/ — [11]*sans fin* /sãfɛ̃/. The acute nasal /ɛ̃/ and the other phonemes of the word [10]*sphinx* /sfɛ̃ks/ recur in the last tercet: [12]*reins* /.ɛ̃/ — [12]*pleins* /. .ɛ̃/ — [13]*étincelles* /. .ɛ̃s . . ./ — [13]*ainsi* /ɛ̃s/ — [13]*qu'un sable* /kœ̃s . . ./ — [13]*fin* /fɛ̃/.

We read in the first quatrain: [3]*Les chats puissants et doux, orgueil de la maison.* Does this mean that the cats, proud of their home, are the incarnation of that pride, or that the house, proud of its feline inhabitants, tries, like Erebus, to domesticate them? Whichever it may be, the [3]*maison* which circumscribes the cats in the first quatrain is transformed into a spacious desert, [10]*fond des solitudes.* And the fear of cold, bringing together the cats, [4]*frileux,* and the lovers, [1]*fervents* (note the paronomasia /fɛ̃rvã/ —

/frilø/), is dispelled by the appropriate climate of the austere solitudes (as austere as the scholars) of the desert (torrid like the fervent lovers) which surrounds the sphinxes. On the temporal level, the [2]*mûre saison,* which rhymed with [3]*la maison* in the first quatrain and approached it in meaning, has a clear counterpart in the first tercet. These two visibly parallel groups of words ([2]*dans leur mûre saison* and [11]*dans un rêve sans fin*) mutually oppose each other, the one evoking numbered days and the other, eternity. No constructions with *dans* or with any other adverbal preposition occur elsewhere in the sonnet.

The miraculous quality of the cats pervades the two tercets. The metamorphosis unfolds right to the end of the sonnet. In the first tercet the image of the sphinxes stretched out in the desert already vacillates between the creature and its simulacrum, and in the following tercet the animate beings disappear behind particles of matter. Synecdoche substitutes for the cat-sphinxes various parts of their bodies: [12]*leurs reins* (the loins of the cats), [14]*leurs prunelles* (the pupils of their eyes). In the final tercet, the implicit subject of the interior stanzas again becomes an accessory part of the sentence. The cats appear first as an implicit adjunct of the subject — [12]*Leurs reins féconds sont pleins* — then, in the poem's last clause, they function as a mere implicit adjunct of the object: [14]*Étoilent vaguement leurs prunelles.* Thus the cats appear to be linked to the object of the transitive verb in the last clause of the sonnet and to the subject in the penultimate, antecedent clause, thereby establishing a double correspondence on the one hand with the cats as direct object in the first clause of the sonnet, and on the other with the cats as subject of its second clause.

Whereas at the beginning of the sonnet both subject and object were of the animate class, the two similar parts of the final clause both belong to the inanimate class. In general, all the substantives in the last tercet are concrete nouns of the same class: [12]*reins,* [12]*étincelles,* [13]*parcelles,* [13]*or,* [13]*sable,* [14]*prunelles,* whilst in all previous stanzas the inanimate appellatives, except for the adnominal ones, were abstract nouns: [2]*saison,* [3]*orgueil,* [6]*silence,* [6]*horreur,* [8]*servage,* [8]*fierté,* [9]*attitudes,* [11]*rêve.* The inanimate feminine gender, common to the subject and to the object of the final clause — [13-16]*des parcelles d'or* . . . *Étoilent* . . . *leurs prunelles* — counterbalances the subject and object of the initial clause, which both belong to the animate masculine gender — [1-3]*Les amoureux* . . . *et les savants* . . . *Aiment* . . . *Les chats.* [13]*Parcelles* is the only feminine subject in the whole sonnet, and it contrasts with the masculine [13]*sable fin* at the end of the same line, which in turn is the only example of the masculine gender among the sonnet's masculine rhymes.

In the last tercet, the ultimate particles of matter serve in turns as object and subject. A new identification, the last within the sonnet, associates these incandescent particles with the [13]*sable fin* and transforms them into stars.

The remarkable rhyme which links the two tercets is the only homonymous rhyme in the whole sonnet and the only one among its masculine rhymes which juxtaposes different parts of speech. There is also a certain syntactic symmetry between the two rhyme-words, since both end subordinate clauses, one of which is complete and the other, elliptical. The correspondence, far from being confined to the final syllable, closely brings the whole of both lines together: [11]/sãblə sãdɔrmir dãnzœ̃ rɛvə sã fɛ/ — [13]/parsɛlə dɔr ɛ̃si kœ̃ sablə fɛ/. It is not by chance that precisely the rhyme that links the two tercets evokes un sable fin, thus taking the desert motif up again, in the same position as un rêve sans fin of the grands sphinx appears in the first tercet.

[8]La maison, which circumscribes the cats in the first quatrain, is abolished in the first tercet with its realm of desert solitudes, true unfolded house of the cat-sphinxes. In its turn, this "non-house" yields to the cosmic innumerability of the cats (these, like all the personae of the sonnet, are treated as pluralia tantum). They become, so to speak, the house of the non-house, since within the irises of their eyes they enclose the sand of the deserts and the light of the stars.

The epilogue takes up again the initial theme of lovers and scholars united in Les chats puissants et doux. The first line of the second tercet seems to answer the first line of the second quatrain; the cats being [5]Amis . . . de la volupté, [12]Leurs reins féconds sont pleins. One is tempted to believe that this has to do with the procreative force, but Baudelaire's works easily invite ambiguous solutions. Is it a matter of a power particular to the loins or of electric sparks in the animal's fur? Whatever it may be, it is a "magic" power that is attributed to them. But the second quatrain opened with two collateral adjuncts: [5]Amis de la science et de la volupté, and the final tercet alludes not only to the [2]amoureux fervents but to the [1]savants austères as well.

In the last tercet, the rhyming suffixes emphasize the strong semantic link between the [12]étinCELLES, [13]parCELLES d'or and [14]prunELLES of the cat-sphinxes on the one hand, and on the other, between the sparks [12]MagIQUES emanating from the animal and its pupils [14]MystIQUES illuminated by an inner light and open to a hidden meaning. This is the only rhyme in the sonnet which is stripped of its supporting consonant, as if to lay bare the equivalence of the morphemes, and the alliteration of the initial /m/'s ties the two adjectives even closer together. [6]L'horreur des ténèbres vanishes before this double luminance, which is reflected on the phonic level by the predominance of phonemes of light timbre (acute tonality) among the nasal vowels of the final stanza (6 front versus 3 back vowels), whereas there was a far greater number of nasal vowels of grave tonality in the preceding stanzas (9 versus 0 in the first quatrain, 2 versus 1 in the second, and 10 versus 3 in the first tercet).

Due to the preponderance of synecdochic tropes at the end of the sonnet, where parts of the animal are substituted for the whole and, on the other hand, the animal itself is substituted for the universe of which it is a part, the images seek, as if by design, to lose themselves in imprecision. The definite article gives way to the indefinite article and the adverb which accompanies the verbal metaphor — [14]*Étoilent vaguement* — brilliantly reflects the poetics of the epilogue. The conformity between the tercets and the corresponding quatrains (horizontal parallelism) is striking. The narrow limits of space ([3]*maison*) and of time ([2]*mûre saison*) imposed in the first quatrain are opposed in the first tercet by the removal or suppression of boundaries ([10]*fond des solitudes*, [11]*rêve sans fin*). Similarly, in the second tercet, the magic of the light radiating from the cats triumphs over [6]*l'horreur des ténèbres*, which nearly wrought such deception in the second quatrain.

Now, in drawing together the parts of our analysis, we shall try to show how the different levels on which we touched blend, complement each other or combine to give the poem the value of an absolute object.

To begin with, the divisions of the text: Several can be distinguished which are perfectly clear, as much from the grammatical point of view as from the semantic relations between different parts of the poem.

As we have already pointed out, there is a primary division corresponding to the three parts, each of which ends with a period, namely, the two quatrains and the ensemble of the two tercets. The first quatrain presents, in the form of an objective and static picture, a factual situation or one that purports to be so. The second quatrain attributes to the cats a purpose which is interpreted by the powers of Erebus, and to the powers of Erebus, a purpose in regard to the cats, which the latter reject. Thus, in these two sections, the cats are seen from without, first through the passivity to which lovers and scholars are especially susceptible, and secondly through the activity perceived by the powers of Erebus. By contrast, in the last part of the sonnet this proposition is overcome by acknowledging a passivity actively assumed by the cats, no longer interpreted from without but from within.

A second division enable us to oppose the ensemble of the two tercets to the ensemble of the two quatrains, at the same time revealing a close connection between the first quatrain and the first tercet, and between the second quatrain and the second tercet. As a matter of fact:

1. The ensemble of the two quatrains is opposed to the ensemble of the two tercets in the sense that the latter dispenses with the point of view of the observer (*amoureux, savants*, powers of Erebus) and places the being of the cats outside all spatial and temporal limits.

2. The first quatrain introduces these spatio-temporal limits (*maison,*

saison) and the first tercet abolishes them (*au fond des solitudes, rêve sans fin*).

3. The second quatrain defines the cats in terms of the darkness in which they place themselves, the second tercet in terms of the light they radiate (*étincelles, étoiles*).

Finally, a third division is superimposed upon the preceding one by regrouping, this time in chiasmus, the initial quatrain and the final tercet, on the one hand, and on the other, the interior stanzas: the second quatrain and the first tercet. In the former couple, the independent clauses assign to the cats the role of syntactical modifiers, whereas from the outset the latter two stanzas assign to the cats the function of subject.

These phenomena of formal distribution obviously have a semantic foundation. The point of departure of the first quatrain is furnished by the proximity, within the same house, of the cats with the scholars or lovers. A double resemblance arises out of this contiguity (*comme eux, comme eux*). Similarly, a relation of contiguity in the final tercet also evolves to the point of resemblance, but whereas, in the first quatrain, the metonymical relation of the feline and human inhabitants of the house underlies their metaphorical relation, in the final tercet this situation is interiorized: the link of contiguity rests upon the synecdoche rather than upon the metonymy proper. The parts of the cat's body (*reins, prunelles*) provide a metaphorical evocation of the astral, cosmic cat, with a concomitant transition from precision to vagueness (*également — vaguement*). The analogy between the interior stanzas is based on connections of equivalence, the one turned down in the second quatrain (cats and *coursiers funèbres*), the other accepted in the first tercet (cats and *grands sphinx*). In the former case, this leads to a rejection of contiguity (between the cats and *l'Érèbe*) and, in the latter case, to the settlement of the cats *au fond des solitudes*. Contrary to the former case, the transition is made from a relation of equivalence, a reinforced form of resemblance (thus a metaphorical move), to relations of contiguity (thus metonymical), either negative or positive.

Up to this point, the poem has appeared to consist of systems of equivalences which fit inside one another and which offer, in their totality, the appearance of a closed system. There is, however, yet another way of looking at it, whereby the poem takes on the appearance of an open system in dynamic progression from beginning to end.

In the first part of this study we elucidated a division of the poem into two sestets separated by a distich whose structure contrasted vigorously with the rest. In the course of our recapitulation, we provisionally set this division to one side, because we felt that, unlike the others, it marks the stages of a progression from the order of the real (the first sestet) to that of the surreal (the second sestet). This transition operates via the distich, which by the accumulation of semantic and formal devices lures the reader for a brief moment into a doubly unreal universe, since, while sharing with the first sestet the standpoint of exteriority, it anticipates the mythological tone of the second sestet:

1 to 6	7 and 8	9 to 14
extrinsic		intrinsic
empirical	mythological	
real	unreal	surreal

By this sudden oscillation both of tone and of theme, the distich fulfills a function somewhat resembling that of modulation in a musical composition.

The purpose of this modulation is to resolve the opposition, implicit or explicit from the beginning of the poem, between the metaphorical and metonymical procedures. The solution provided by the final sestet is achieved by transferring this opposition to the very heart of the metonymy, while expressing it by metaphorical means. In effect, each of the tercets puts forward an inverse image of the cats. In the first tercet, the cats originally enclosed in the house are, so to speak, extravasated from it in order to expand spatially and temporally in the infinite deserts and the dream without end. The movement is from the inside to the outside, from cats in seclusion to cats at liberty. In the second tercet, the breaking down of barriers is interiorized by the cats attaining cosmic proportions, since they conceal in certain parts of their bodies (*reins* and *prunelles*) the sands of the desert and the stars of the sky. In both cases the transformation occurs via metaphorical devices, but there is no thorough equilibrium between the two transformations: the first still owes something to semblance (*prennent . . . les . . . attitudes . . . qui semblent s'endormir*) and to dream (*en songeant . . . dans un rêve . . .*), whereas in the second case the transformation is declared and affirmed as truly achieved (*sont pleins . . . Étoilent*). In the first, the cats close their eyes to sleep, in the second they keep them open.

Nevertheless, these ample metaphors of the final sestet simply transpose to the scale of the universe an opposition that was already implicitly formulated in the first line of the poem. Around the "lovers" and "scholars" terms are assembled which unite them respectively in a contracted or dilated relation: the man in love is joined to the woman as the scholar is to the universe: two types of conjunction, the one close and the other remote.[6] It is the same rapport that the final transfigurations evoke: dilation of the cats in time and space — constriction of time and space within the beings of the cats. But, here again, just as we noted earlier, the symmetry between the two formulae is not complete. The latter contains within it a collection of all the oppositions: the *reins féconds* recall the *volupté* of the *amoureux,* as do the *prunelles* the *science* of the *savants; magiques* refers to the active fervor of the one, *mystiques* to the contemplative attitude of the other.

Two final points: The fact that all the grammatical subjects in the sonnet (with the exception of the proper noun *L'Érèbe*) are plural, and that all feminine rhymes are formed with plurals (including the substantive *solitudes*), is curiously illuminated by a few passages from Baudelaire's *Foules* which, moreover, seem to throw light upon the whole of the sonnet: "Multitude, solitude: terms equal and interchangeable by the active and fertile poet. . . . The poet enjoys that incomparable privilege, that he can, at will, be both himself and another. . . . What men call love is very small, very restricted and very weak compared to that ineffable orgy, that blessed prostitution of the soul which gives itself in its entirety, its poetry and charity, to the unforeseen which emerges, to the unknown one who passes." [7]

In the poet's sonnet, the cats are initially qualified as *puissants et doux* and in the final line their pupils are likened to the stars. Crépet and Blin [8] compare this to a line in Sainte-Beuve: ". . . l'astre puissant et doux" (1829) and find the same epithets in a poem by Brizeux (1832) in which women are thus apostrophized: "Êtres deux fois doués! Êtres puissants et doux!"

This would confirm, were there any need to do so, that for Baudelaire the image of the cat is closely linked to that of the woman, as is shown explicitly in two other poems entitled "Le Chat" and pertaining to the same collection. Thus the sonnet — "Viens, mon beau chat, sur mon cœur amoureux" — contains the revealing line: "Je vois ma femme en esprit. . . ." The second of these poems — "Dans ma cervelle se promène . . . Un beau chat, fort, doux . . ." — squarely asks the question: "est-il fée, est-il dieu?" This motif of vacillation between male and female is subjacent in "Les Chats", where it shows through from beneath intentional ambiguities (*Les amoureux . . . Aiment . . . Les chats puissants et doux . . . ; Leurs reins féconds . . .*). Michel Butor notes with reason that for Baudelaire "these two aspects: femininity and supervirility, far from being mutually exclusive, are in fact bound together." [9] All the characters in the sonnet are of masculine gender, but *les chats* and their alter ego, *les grands sphinx,* share an androgynous nature. This very ambiguity is emphasized throughout the sonnet by the paradoxical choice of feminine substantives for so-called masculine rhymes.[10] The cats, by their mediation, permit the removal of woman from the initial assemblage formed by lovers and scholars. "Le poète des Chats," liberated from love "bien petit, bien restreint," meets face to face and perhaps even blends with the universe, delivered from the scholar's austerity.

RICHARD OHMANN

Literature as Sentences

Critics permit themselves, for this or that purpose, to identify literature with great books, with imaginative writing, with expressiveness in writing, with the non-referential and non-pragmatic, with beauty in language, with order, with myth, with structured and formed discourse — the list of definitions is nearly endless — with verbal play, with uses of language that stress the medium itself, with the expression of an age, with dogma, with the *cri de coeur*, with neurosis. Now of course literature is itself and not another thing, to paraphrase Bishop Butler; yet analogies and classifications have merit. For a short space let us think of literature as sentences.

To do so will not tax the imagination, because the work of literature indubitably *is* composed of sentences, most of them well-ordered, many of them deviant (no pejorative meant), some of them incomplete. But since much the same holds for dust-jacket copy, the Congressional Record, and transcripts of board meetings, the small effort required to think of literature as sentences may be repaid by a correspondingly small insight into literature as such. Although I do not believe this to be so, for the moment I shall hold the question in abeyance, and stay mainly within the territory held in common by all forms of discourse. In other words, I am not asking what is special about the sentences of *literature,* but what is special about *sentences* that they should interest the student of literature. Although I employ the framework of generative

SOURCE: From *College English,* January 1966. Copyright © 1966 by the National Council of Teachers of English. Reprinted by permission of the publisher and Richard Ohmann. The passage from "A Winter's Tale" is from *The Poems of Dylan Thomas.* Copyright 1946 by New Directions Publishing Corporation. Reprinted by permission of New Directions Publishing Corporation, J. M. Dent & Sons Ltd., and the Trustees for the Copyrights of the late Dylan Thomas.

grammar and scraps of its terminology,[1] what I have to say should not ring in the traditionally educated grammatical ear with outlandish discord.

First, then, the sentence is the primary unit of understanding. Linguists have so trenchantly discredited the old definition — "a sentence is a complete thought" — that the truth therein has fallen into neglect. To be sure, we delimit the class of sentences by formal criteria, but each of the structures that qualifies will express a semantic unity not characteristic of greater or lesser structures. The meanings borne by morphemes, phrases, and clauses hook together to express a meaning that can stand more or less by itself. This point, far from denying the structuralist's definition of a sentence as a single free utterance, or *form*, seems the inevitable corollary of such definitions: forms carry meanings, and it is natural that an independent form should carry an independent meaning. Or, to come at the thing another way, consider that one task of a grammar is to supply structural descriptions, and that the sentence is the unit so described. A structural description specifies the way each part of a sentence is tied to each other part, and the semantic rules of a grammar use the structural description as starting point in interpreting the whole. A reader or hearer does something analogous when he resolves the structures and meanings of sentences, and thereby understands them. Still another way to approach the primacy of the sentence is to notice that the initial symbol for all derivations in a generative grammar is "S" for sentence: the sentence is the domain of grammatical structure — rather like the equation in algebra — and hence the domain of meaning.

These remarks, which will seem truisms to some and heresy to others, cannot be elaborated here. Instead, I want to register an obvious comment on their relevance to literary theory and literary criticism. Critcism, whatever else it does, must interpret works of literature. Theory concerns itself in part with the question, "what things legitimately bear on critical interpretation?" But beyond a doubt, interpretation begins with sentences. Whatever complex apprehension the critic develops of the whole work, that understanding arrives mundanely, sentence by sentence. For this reason, and because the form of a sentence dictates a rudimentary mode of understanding, sentences have a good deal to do with the subliminal meaning (and form) of a literary work. They prepare and direct the reader's attention in particular ways.

My second point about sentences should dispel some of the abstractness of the first. Most sentences directly and obliquely put more linguistic apparatus into operation than is readily apparent, and call on more of the reader's linguistic competence. Typically, a surface structure overlays a deep structure which it may resemble but little, and which determines the "content" of the sentence. For concreteness, take this rather ordinary example, an independent clause from Joyce's "Araby": "Gazing up into the darkness I saw myself as a creature driven and derided by vanity." The surface structure may be represented as follows, using the convention of labeled brackets[2]: $^S[^{Adv}[V + Part\ ^{PP}[P\ ^{NP}[D + N]]]\ ^{Nuc}[N\ ^{VP}[V + N\ ^{PP}[P\ ^{NP}[D + N\ ^{Adj}[V + and + V\ ^{PP}[P + N]]]]]]]$.

The nucleus has a transitive verb with a direct object. In the deep structure, by contrast, the matrix sentence is of the form $^S[NP\ ^{VP}[V + Complement + NP]]$: "I + saw + as a creature + me." It has embedded in it one sentence with an intransitive verb and an adverb of location — "I gazed up into the darkness" — and two additional sentences with transitive verbs and direct objects — "Vanity drove the creature," and "Vanity derided the creature." Since "darkness" and "vanity" are derived nouns, the embedded sentences must in turn contain embeddings, of, say "(Something) is dark" and "(Someone) is vain." Thus the word "vanity," object of a preposition in the surface structure, is subject of two verbs in the deep, and its root is a predicate adjective. The word "creature," object of a preposition in the surface structure, also has a triple function in the deep structure: verbal complement, direct object of "drive," and direct object of "deride." Several transformations (including the passive) deform the six basic sentences, and several others relate them to each other. The complexity goes much farther, but this is enough to suggest that a number of grammatical processes are required to generate the initial sentence and that its structure is moderately involved. Moreover, a reader will not understand the sentence unless he grasps the relations marked in the deep structure. As it draws on a variety of syntactic resources, the sentence also activates a variety of semantic processes and modes of comprehension, yet in brief compass and in a surface *form* that radically permutes *content*.

I choose these terms wilfully: that there are interesting grounds here for a form-content division seems to me quite certain. Joyce might have written, "I gazed up into the darkness. I saw myself as a creature. The creature was driven by vanity. The creature was derided by vanity." Or, "Vanity drove and derided the creature I saw myself as, gazer up, gazer into the darkness." Contents remains roughly the same, for the basic sentences are unchanged. But the style is different. And each revision structures and screens the content differently. The original sentence acquires part of its meaning and part of its unique character by resonating against these unwritten alternatives. It is at the level of sentences, I would argue, that the distinction between form and content comes clear, and that the intuition of style has its formal equivalent.[3]

Sentences play on structure in still another way, more shadowy, but of considerable interest for criticism. It is a commonplace that not every noun can serve as object of every verb, that a given noun can be modified only by adjectives of certain classes, and so on. For instance, a well-defined group of verbs, including "exasperate," "delight," "please," and "astound," require animate objects; another group, including "exert," "behave," and "pride," need reflexive objects. Such interdependencies abound in a grammar, which must account for them by subcategorizing nouns, adjectives, and the other major classes.[4] The importance of categorical restrictions is clearest in sentences that disregard them — deviant sentences. It happens that the example from Joyce is slightly deviant in this way: in one of the underlying sentences — "Vanity derided the creature" — a verb that requires a human subject in fact has as its subject the abstract noun "vanity." The dislocation forces the reader to use a supplementary method of interpretation: here, presumably he aligns "vanity" (the word) with the class of human nouns and sees vanity (the thing) as a distinct, active power in the narrator's psyche. Such deviance is so common in metaphor and elsewhere that one scarcely notices it, yet it helps to specify the way things happen in the writer's special world, and the modes of thought appropriate to that world.

I have meant to suggest that sentences normally comprise intricacies of form and meaning whose effects are not the less substantial for their subtlety. From this point, what sorts of critical description follow? Perhaps I can direct attention toward a few tentative answers, out of the many that warrant study, and come finally to a word on critical theory. Two samples must carry the discussion; one is the final sentence of "The Secret Sharer":

> Walking to the taffrail, I was in time to make out, on the very edge of a darkness thrown by a towering black mass like the very gateway of Erebus — yes, I was in time to catch an evanescent glimpse of my white hat left behind to mark the spot where the secret sharer of my cabin and of my thoughts, as though he were my second self, had lowered himself into the water to take his punishment: a free man, a proud swimmer striking out for a new destiny.

I hope others will agree that the sentence justly represents its author: that it portrays a mind energetically stretching to subdue a dazzling experience *outside* the self, in a way that has innumerable counterparts elsewhere in Conrad. How does scrutiny of the deep structure support this intuition? First, notice a matter of emphasis, of rhetoric. The matrix sentence, which lends a surface form to the whole, is "# S # I was in time # S #" (repeated twice). The embedded sentences that complete it are "I walked to the taffrail," "I made out + NP," and "I caught + NP." The point of departure, then, is the narrator himself: where he was, what he did, what he saw. But a glance at the deep structure will explain why one feels a quite different emphasis in the sentence as a whole: seven of the embedded sentences have "sharer" as grammatical subject;

in another three the subject is a noun linked to "sharer" by the copula; in two "sharer" is direct object; and in two more "share" is the verb. Thus thirteen sentences go to the semantic development of "sharer," as follows:

1. The secret sharer had lowered the secret sharer into the water.
2. The secret sharer took his punishment.
3. The secret sharer swam.
4. The secret sharer was a swimmer.
5. The swimmer was proud.
6. The swimmer struck out for a new destiny.
7. The secret sharer was a man.
8. The man was free.
9. The secret sharer was my second self.
10. The secret sharer had (it).
11. (Someone) punished the secret sharer.
12. (Someone) shared my cabin.
13. (Someone) shared my thoughts.

In a fundamental way, the sentence is mainly *about* Leggatt, although the surface structure indicates otherwise.

Yet the surface structure does not simply throw a false scent, and the way the sentence comes to focus on the secret sharer is also instructive. It begins with the narrator, as we have seen, and "I" is the subject of five basic sentences early on. Then "hat" takes over as the syntactic focus, receiving development in seven base sentences. Finally, the sentence arrives at "sharer." This progression in the deep structure rather precisely mirrors both the rhetorical movement of the sentence from the narrator to Leggatt via the hat that links them, and the thematic effect of the sentence, which is to transfer Leggatt's experience to the narrator via the narrator's vicarious and actual participation in it. Here I shall leave this abbreviated rhetorical analysis, with a cautionary word: I do not mean to suggest that only an examination of deep structure reveals Conrad's skillful emphasis — on the contrary, such an examination supports and in a sense explains what any careful reader of the story notices.

A second critical point adjoins the first. The morpheme "share" appears once in the sentence, but it performs at least twelve separate functions, as the deep structure shows. "I," "hat," and "mass" also play complex roles. Thus at certain points the sentence has extraordinary "density," as I shall call it. Since a reader must register these multiple functions in order to understand the sentence, it is reasonable to suppose that the very process of understanding concentrates his attention on centers of density. Syntactic density, I am suggesting, exercises an important influence on literary comprehension.

Third, by tuning in on deep structures, the critic may often apprehend more fully the build of a literary work. I have already mentioned how the syntax of Conrad's final sentence develops his theme. Consider two related points. First, "The Secret Sharer" is an initiation story in which the hero, through moral and mental effort, locates himself vis à vis society and the natural world, and thus passes into full manhood. The syntax of the last sentence schematizes the relationships he has achieved, in identifying with Leggatt's heroic defection, and in fixing on a point of reference — the hat — that connects him to the darker powers of nature. Second, the syntax and meaning of the last sentence bring to completion the pattern initiated by the syntax and meaning of the first few sentences, which present human beings and natural objects in thought-bewildering disarray. I can do no more than mention these structural connections here, but I am convinced that they supplement and help explain an ordinary critical reading of the story.

Another kind of critical point concerns habits of meaning revealed by sentence structure. One example must suffice. We have already marked how the sentence shifts its focus from "I" to "hat" to "sharer." A similar process goes on in the first part of the sentence: "I" is the initial subject, with "hat" as object. "Hat" is subject of another base sentence that ends with "edge," the object of a preposition in a locative phrase. "Edge" in turn becomes object of a sentence that has "darkness" as subject. "Darkness" is object in one with "mass" as subject, and in much the same way the emphasis passes to "gateway" and "Erebus." The syntax executes a chaining effect here which cuts across various kinds of construction. Chaining is far from the only type of syntactic expansion, but it is one Conrad favors. I would suggest this hypothesis: that syntactically and in other ways Conrad draws heavily on operations that link one thing with another associatively. This may be untrue, or if true it may be unrevealing; certainly it needs clearer expression. But I think it comes close to something that we all notice in Conrad, and in any case the general critical point exemplified here deserves exploration: that each writer tends to exploit deep linguistic resources in characteristic ways — that his style, in other words, rests on syntactic options within sentences (see fn. 3) — and that these syntactic preferences correlate with habits of meaning that tell us something about his mode of conceiving experience.

My other sample passage is the first sentence of Dylan Thomas' "A Winter's Tale":

> It is a winter's tale
> That the snow blind twilight ferries over the lakes
> And floating fields from the farm in the cup of the vales,
> Gliding windless through the hand folded flakes,
> The pale breath of cattle at the stealthy sail,

And the stars falling cold,
And the smell of hay in the snow, and the far owl
Warning among the folds, and the frozen hold
Flocked with the sheep white smoke of the farm house cowl
In the river wended vales where the tale was told.

Some of the language here raises a large and familiar critical question, that of unorthodox grammar in modern poetry, which has traditionally received a somewhat facile answer. We say that loss of confidence in order and reason leads to dislocation of syntax, as if errant grammar were an appeal to the irrational. A cursory examination of deep structure in verse like Thomas', or even in wildly deviant verse like some of Cummings', will show the matter to be more complex than that.

How can deviance be most penetratingly analyzed? Normally, I think, in terms of the base sentences that lie beneath ungrammatical constructions. Surface structure alone does not show "the river wended vales" (line 10) to be deviant, since we have many well-formed constructions of the same word-class sequence: "machine made toys," "sun dried earth," and so on. The particular deviance of "the river wended vales" becomes apparent when we try to refer it to an appropriate underlying structure. A natural one to consider is "the river wends the vales" (cf. "the sun dries the earth"), but of course this makes "wend" a transitive verb, which it is not, except in the idiomatic "wend its way." So does another possibility, "NP + wends the vales with rivers" (cf. "NP + makes the toys by machine"). This reading adds still other kinds of deviance, in that the Noun Phrase will have to be animate, and in that rivers are too cumbersome to be used instrumentally in the way implied. Let us assume that the reader rejects the more flagrant deviance in favor of the less, and we are back to "the river wends the vales." Suppose now that "the vales" is not after all a direct object, but a locative construction, as in "the wolf prowls the forest"; this preserves the intransitivity of "wend," and thereby avoids a serious form of deviance. But notice that there is *no* transformation in English that converts "the wolf prowls the forest" into "the wolf prowled forest," and so this path is blocked as well. Assume, finally, that given a choice between shifting a word like "wend" from one subclass to another and adding a transformational rule to the grammar, a reader will choose the former course; hence he selects the first interpretation mentioned: "the river wends the vales."

If so, how does he understand the anomalous transitive use of "wend"? Perhaps by assimilating the verb to a certain class that may be either transitive or intransitive: "paint," "rub," and the like. Then he will take "wend" to mean something like "make a mark on the surface of, by traversing"; in fact, this is roughly how I read Thomas' phrase. But I may be wrong, and in any case my goal is not to solve the riddle. Rather, I have been leading up to the point that every syntactically deviant construction has more than one possible interpretation, and that readers resolve the conflict by a process that involves deep and intricately motivated decisions and thus puts to work considerable linguistic knowledge, syntactic as well as semantic.[5] The decisions nearly always go on implicitly, but aside from that I see no reason to think that deviance of this sort is an appeal to, or an expression of, irrationality.

Moreover, when a poet deviates from normal syntax he is not doing what comes most habitually, but is making a special sort of choice. And since there are innumerable kinds of deviance, we should expect that the ones elected by a poem or poet spring from particular semantic impulses, particular ways of looking at experience. For instance, I think such a tendency displays itself in Thomas' lines. The construction just noted conceives the passing of rivers through vales as an agent acting upon an object. Likewise, "flocked" in line 9 becomes a transitive verb, and the spatial connection Thomas refers to — flocks in a hold — is reshaped into an action — flocking — performed by an unnamed agent upon the hold. There are many other examples in the poem of deviance that projects unaccustomed activity and process upon nature. Next, notice that beneath line 2 is the sentence "the twilight is blind," in which an inanimate noun takes an animate adjective, and that in line 5 "sail" takes the animate adjective "stealthy." This type of deviance also runs throughout the poem: Thomas sees nature as personal. Again, "twilight" is subject of "ferries," and should thus be a concrete noun, as should the object, "tale." Here and elsewhere in the poem the division between substance and abstraction tends to disappear. Again and again syntactic deviance breaks down categorical boundaries and converts juxtaposition into action, inanimate into human, abstract into physical, static into active. Now, much of Thomas' poetry displays the world as process, as interacting forces and repeating cycles, in which human beings and human thought are indifferently caught up.[6] I suggest that Thomas' syntactical irregularities often serve this vision of things. To say so, of course, is only to extend the natural critical premise that a good poet sets linguistic forms to work for him in the cause of artistic and thematic form. And if he strays from grammatical patterns he does not thereby leave language or reason behind: if anything, he draws the more deeply on linguistic structure and on the processes of human understanding that are implicit in our use of well-formed sentences.

Most of what I have said falls short of adequate precision, and much of the detail rests on conjecture about English grammar, which at this point is by no means fully understood. But I hope that in loosely stringing together several hypotheses about the fundamental role of the sentence I have indicated some areas where a rich exchange between linguistics and critical theory might eventually take place. To wit, the elusive intuition we have of *form* and *content* may turn out to be anchored in a distinction between the surface structures and the deep structures of sentences. If so, syntactic theory will also feed into the theory of *style*. Still more evidently, the proper *analysis* of styles waits on a satisfactory analysis of sentences. Matters of *rhetoric,* such as emphasis and order, also promise to come clearer as we better understand internal relations in sentences. More generally, we may be able to enlarge and deepen our concept of literary *structure* as we are increasingly able to make it subsume linguistic structure — including especially the structure of deviant sentences. And most important, since critical understanding follows and builds on understanding of sentences, generative grammar should eventually be a reliable assistant in the effort of seeing just how a given literary work sifts through a reader's mind, what cognitive and emotional processes it sets in motion, and what organization of experience it encourages. In so far as critical theory concerns itself with meaning, it cannot afford to bypass the complex and elegant structures that lie at the inception of all verbal meaning.

ROBERT FROST

Sentence Sounds

. . . I want to write down here two or three cardinal principles that I wish you would think over and turn over now and again till we *can* protract talk.

I give you a new definition of a sentence:

A sentence is a sound in itself on which other sounds called words may be strung.

You may string words together without a sentence-sound to string them on just as you may tie clothes together by the sleeves and stretch them

SOURCE: "Sentence Sounds" is a portion of a letter dated 22 February 1914 from Robert Frost to John T. Bartlett from *Selected Letters of Robert Frost,* edited by Lawrance Thompson. Copyright © 1964 by Holt, Rinehart and Winston, Inc. Reprinted by permission of the estate of Robert Frost and Holt, Rinehart and Winston, Inc.

without a clothes line between two trees, but — it is bad for the clothes.

The number of words you may string on one sentence-sound is not fixed but there is always danger of over loading.

The sentence-sounds are very definite entities. (This is no literary mysticism I am preaching.) They are as definite as words. It is not impossible that they could be collected in a book though I don't at present see on what system they would be catalogued.

They are apprehended by the ear. They are gathered by the ear from the vernacular and brought into books. Many of them are already familiar to us in books. I think no writer invents them. The most original writer only catches them fresh from talk, where they grow spontaneously.

A man is all a writer if *all* his words are strung on definite recognizable sentence sounds. The voice of the imagination, the speaking voice must know certainly how to behave how to posture in every sentence he offers.

A man is a marked writer if his words are largely strung on the more striking sentence sounds.

A word about recognition: In literature it is our business to give people the thing that will make them say, "Oh yes I know what you mean." It is never to tell them something they dont know, but something they know and hadnt thought of saying. It must be something they recognize.

A Patch of Old Snow

In the corner of the wall where the bushes haven't been trimmed, there is a patch of old snow like a blow-away newspaper that has come to rest there. And it is dirty as with the print and news of a day I have forgotten, if I ever read it.

Now that is no good except for what I may call certain points of recognition in it: patch of old snow in a corner of the wall, — you know what that is. You know what a blow-away newspaper is. You know the curious dirt on old snow and last of all you know how easily you forget what you read in papers.

Now for the sentence sounds. We will look for the marked ones because they are easiest to discuss. The first sentence sound will do but it is merely ordinary and bookish: it is entirely subordinate in interest to the meaning of the words strung on it. But half the effectiveness of the second sentence is in the very special tone with which you must say — news of a day I have forgotten — if I ever read it. You must be able to say Oh yes one knows how that goes. (There is some adjective to describe the intonation or cadence, but I won't hunt for it.)

One of the least successful of the poems in my book is almost saved by a final striking sentence-sound. (Asking for Roses.)

Not caring so very much *what* she supposes.

Take My November Guest. Did you know at once how we say such sentences as these when we talk?

She thinks I have no eye for these.

———

Not yesterday I learned etc.

———

But it were vain to tell her so

———

Get away from the sing-song. You must hear and recognize in the last line the sentence sound that supports, No use in telling him so.

Let's have some examples pell-mell in prose and verse because I don't want you to think I am setting up as an authority on verse alone.

My father used to say —
You're a liar!
If a hen and a half lay an egg and a half etc.
A long long time ago —
Put it there, old man! (Offering your hand)
I aint a going [to] hurt you, so you needn't be scared.

Suppose Henry Horne says something offensive to a young lady named Rita when her brother Charles is by to protect her. Can you hear the two different tones in which she says their respective names. "Henry Horne! Charles!" I can hear it better than I can say it. And by oral practice I get further and further away from it.

Never you say a thing like that to a man!
And such they are and such they will be found.
Well I swan!
Unless I'm greatly mistaken —
Hence with denial vain and coy excuse
A soldier and afraid (afeared)
Come, child, come home.
The thing for me to do is to get right out of here while I am able.
No fool like an old fool.

It is so and not otherwise that we get the variety that makes it fun to write and read. *The ear does it.* The ear is the only true writer and the only true reader. I have known people who could read without hearing the sentence sounds and they were the fastest readers. Eye readers we call them. They can get the meaning by glances. But they are bad readers because they miss the best part of what a good writer puts into his work.

Remember that the sentence sound often says more than the words. It may even as in irony convey a meaning opposite to the words.

I wouldn't be writing all this if I didn't think it the most important thing I know. I write it partly for my own benefit, to clarify my ideas for an essay or two I am going to write some fine day (not far distant).

To judge a poem or piece of prose you go the same way to work — apply the one test — greatest test. You listen for the sentence sounds. If you find some of those not bookish, caught fresh from the mouths of people, some of them striking, all of them definite and recognizable, so recognizable that with a little trouble you can place them and even name them, you know you have found a writer. . . .

WILLIAM H. GASS

The Sentences of Fiction

For the purposes of analysis we can regard the sentences of fiction as separate acts of creation. They are the most elementary instances of what the author has constructed. Wittgenstein believed for a time that a proposition, in the disposition of its names, pictured a possibly equivalent arrangement of objects. This is a pleasant fancy, and plainly must be true . . . of fictions; though sentences in stories should do more than simply configure things. Each should contrive (through order, meaning, sound, and rhythm) a moving unity of fact and feeling.

Before us is the empty page, the deep o'er which, like God, though modestly, we brood. But that white page, what is it? Perhaps it is the ideally empty consciousness of the reader — a dry wineskin or a *tabula rasa*. And if, as authors, we think this way, then what we want is a passive mind and, as in love, an utterly receptive woman. Thus our attitudes, before the first act of creation, make a philosophical difference. What shall we sail upon it first?

> All known all white bare white body fixed one yard legs joined like sewn,

Beckett's "Ping" begins. An audacious first term: all. The sentence isolates its words; they slowly fall, slowly revolve, slowly begin to group themselves. We are in the hands of an ancient atomist.

> All known all white bare white body fixed one yard legs joined like sewn. Light heat white floor one square yard never seen. White walls one yard by two white ceiling one square yard never seen.

SOURCE: From "Philosophy and the Form of Fiction," *Fiction and the Figures of Life* (New York: Alfred A. Knopf, 1970), Section 3, pp. 12–18. Copyright 1970 by the University of Tulsa. Reprinted by permission of the University of Tulsa and the editor, Robert Scholes.

Stately monotonous strokes, like measured beats of a gong, occur within, but do not fill, this void. Though here the gong sometimes emits a ping. Truly, nothing is previous. Groups first formed form the first connections, and are repeated.

> Bare white body fixed only the eyes only just. Traces blurs light grey almost white on white. Hands hanging palms front white feet heels together right angle. Light heat white planes shining white bare white body fixed ping fixed elsewhere.

With what remarkable confidence, on the other hand, does Jane Austen reach for our responses. She does not form a chaos or create from nothing. Her pen moves through us; we part a bit and yield the paths of her design. How much we are expected to know already: manners, values, social structure. She thinks in far, far longer lengths; her silences are like the silences which occur in happy conversations; her spaces are interiors, tamed and quiet; she does not begin, she ends, in terror, and the metaphysical.

Let's descend into the sentence briefly, on a rope for our return. How amazing they can be, how strange. The shortest one can spell us back to infancy. ("A cow broke in tomorrow morning to my Uncle Toby's fortifications," for instance.) The meaning of a sentence may make a unity, comprise some whole, but inevitably its concepts are loosed one by one like the release of pigeons. We must apprehend them, then, like backward readers: here's a this, now a that, now a this. The sentence must be sounded, too; it has a rhythm, speed, a tone, a flow, a pattern, shape, length, pitch, conceptual direction. The sentence confers reality upon certain relations, but it also controls our estimation, apprehension, and response to them. Every sentence, in short, takes metaphysical dictation, and it is the sum of these dictations, involving the whole range of the work in which the sentences appear, which accounts for its philosophical quality, and the form of life in the thing that has been made.

In Beckett's sentences, quoted above, there is no subordination, but a community of equals — well, hardly a community either, though the primordial relationship of adjective to noun is not entirely suppressed. This is not the place to get lost in details, but we are all aware of the kind of influence Aristotle's subject-predicate logic had on his philosophy, and on all those which followed for quite a long time. The novelist's characteristic grammatical forms affect the building of his book at least as much, though we must be careful to notice not only his words' syntactical pasts, but their present syntactical functions. So some sentences are crowded with nouns; some contain largely connectives. Some sentences are long and tightly wound; others are as hard and blunt as a hammer. Some combine events of contrasting sizes, like a sneeze and the fall of Rome; others set dogs at bears, link the abstract and the concrete, quality and number, relation and property, act and thing. In some worlds the banjo and its music are two banjos, in others all the instruments dissolve into their music, that into a landscape or a climate, thus finally, through the weather, to an ear.

The Humean sentence will reduce objects to their qualities, maintain an equality between them by using nonsubordinating conjunctions, be careful not to confuse emotion and reflection with perception, but at the same time will allow their presence in the same onward flow. Everywhere, Hume makes his world out of lists and collections. Some novelists, like I. B. Singer, for example, drain the mental from their books as if it were pus in a wound. Thoughts are rendered as public speech; there is recourse to journals; incidents and objects are presented always as the public might see them; and even inner temptations — lusts, hates, fears — receive embodiment as visibly material demons.[1] Henry James's sentences are continuous qualifications, nuance is the core and not the skin; [2] and the average idealist, proceeding with a similar scrupulosity, treats his entire work as the progressive exploration and exposure of a single subject. It would suit him if there were no ordinary periods, no real beginning or real end, if every word were an analytic predicate of one ultimate Idea.

Imagine for a moment we are making up a man, breathing life into a clay lung.

> He stood in the mud: long, thin, brown in his doctor's gown of fur, with his black flapped cap that buttoned well under his chin and let out his brown, lean, shaven and humorous face like a woodpecker's peering out of a hole in a tree.

What is the shape of Achilles' nose? what color were his eyes? Achilles is what Achilles does; he has no secret wishes, secret dreams; he has no cautiously hidden insides. Shall we make our man on that model, out of deeds? or shall we see him through his station: prince or clown, clerk or plumber, servant or secretary, general or priest? Shall we dress him in his features as Ford here puts Magister Nicholas Udal in his clothes? Whether a man has thick lips or thin, crafty ones or cruel, we can always count on Ford to tell us, though in other men's fictions many are lipless. The colon contrives to give the qualities which follow it to Udal's whole muddy standing, not to Udal and his form alone. Observe what happens if we remove it, and at the same time alter the order of our apprehension of these details:

> *He was long, thin, and brown in his doctor's gown of fur, with his black flapped cap that buttoned well under his chin and let out his brown, lean, shaven and humorous face like a woodpecker's peering out of a hole in a tree. He stood in the mud.*

The original passage is packed with possessives, the dominant relation is that of ownership, but the Magister need not own everything. Can we feel the effect of progressively loosening these ties, the clothing first, and then the features?

> *He stood in the mud: long, thin, brown in a doctor's gown of fur, with a black flapped cap that buttoned well under his chin and let out his brown, lean, shaven and humorous face like a woodpecker's peering out of a hole in a tree.*

> *He stood in the mud: long, thin, brown in a doctor's gown of fur, with a black flapped cap that buttoned well under a chin and let out a brown, lean, shaven and humorous face like a woodpecker's peering out of a hole in a tree.*

Perversely, let us let him own his clothes but not his face.

> *He stood in the mud: long, thin, brown in his doctor's gown of fur, with his black flapped cap that buttoned well under a chin and let out a brown, lean, shaven and humorous face like a woodpecker's peering out of a hole in a tree.*

It is not simply that our understanding of Udal changes; our understanding changes because Udal has become a figure in a changed world.

We might at first be inclined to think that style is a form of perception; that each sentence reveals the way the writer looks at the world —

> for example, observe the differences between (1) We walked through the woods. The trees had leaves. The leaves were newly green. (2) We walked through the woods. New leaves greened the trees. (3) We walked the greening woods. (4) It seemed the greening woods walked while we stood.

— but strictly speaking style cannot be, itself, a kind of vision, the notion is very misleading, for we do not have before us some real forest which we might feel ourselves free to render in any number of different ways; we have only the words which make up this one. There are no descriptions in fiction, there are only constructions,[3] and the principles which govern these constructions are persistently philosophical. The same, for that matter, is true of narration, dialogue, character, and the rest. Just as the painter's designs help make his object, the lines of the novelist offer no alternatives, they are not likely interpretations of anything, but are the thing itself. . . .

NORTHROP FRYE

Literature as Context: Milton's Lycidas

I should like to begin with a brief discussion of a familiar poem, Milton's Lycidas, in the hope that some of the inferences drawn from the analysis will be relevant to the theme of this conference. Lycidas, then, is an elegy in the pastoral convention, written to commemorate a young man named Edward King who was drowned at sea. The origins of the pastoral are partly classical, the tradition that runs through Theocritus and Virgil, and partly Biblical, the imagery of the twenty-third Psalm, of Christ as the Good Shepherd, of the metaphors of "pastor" and "flock" in the Church. The chief connecting link between the traditions in Milton's day was the Fourth or Messianic Eclogue of Virgil. Hence it is common enough to have pastoral images echoing both traditions at once, and not surprising to find that Lycidas is a Christian poem as well as a humanistic one.

In the classical pastoral elegy the subject of the elegy is not treated as an individual but as a representative of a dying spirit of nature. The pastoral elegy seems to have some relation to the ritual of the Adonis lament, and the dead poet Bion, in Moschus's poem, is celebrated with much the same kind of imagery as Bion himself uses in his lament for Adonis. The phrase "dying god," for such a figure in later pastoral, is not an anachronism: Virgil says of Daphnis, for example, in the Fifth Eclogue: "*deus, deus ille, Menalca.*" Besides, Milton and his learned contemporaries, Selden, for example, or Henry Reynolds, knew at least as much about the symbolism of the "dying god" as any modern student could get out of The Golden Bough, which depends mainly on the same classical sources that were available to them. The notion that twentieth-century poets differ from their predecessors in their understanding or use of myth will not bear much scrutiny. So King is given the pastoral name of Lycidas, which is equivalent to Adonis, and is associated with the cyclical rhythms of nature. Of these three are of particular importance: the daily cycle of the sun across the sky, the yearly cycle of the seasons, and the cycle of water, flowing from wells and fountains through rivers

SOURCE: Copyright 1959 by Harcourt Brace Jovanovich, Inc., and reprinted with their permission from Fables of Identity: Studies in Poetic Mythology by Northrop Frye.

to the sea. Sunset, winter, and the sea are emblems of Lycidas' death; sunrise and spring, of his resurrection. The poem begins in the morning, "Under the opening eyelids of the morn," and ends with the sun, like Lycidas himself, dropping into the western ocean, yet due to rise again as Lycidas is to do. The imagery of the opening lines, "Shatter your leaves before the mellowing year," suggests the frosts of autumn killing the flowers, and in the great roll-call of flowers towards the end, most of them early blooming flowers like the "rathe primrose," the spring returns. Again, the opening invocation is to the "Sisters of the sacred well," and the water imagery carries through a great variety of Greek, Italian, and English rivers to the sea in which the dead body of Lycidas lies.

Lycidas, then, is the "archetype" of Edward King. By an archetype I mean a literary symbol, or cluster of symbols, which are used recurrently throughout literature, and thereby become conventional. A poetic use of a flower, by itself, is not necessarily an archetype. But in a poem about the death of a young man it is conventional to associate him with a red or purple flower, usually a spring flower like the hyacinth. The historical origin of the convention may be lost in ritual, but it is a constantly latent one, not only in literature but in life, as the symbolism of the scarlet poppies in World War I shows. Hence in *Lycidas* the "sanguine flower inscrib'd with woe" is an archetype, a symbol that recurs regularly in many poems of its kind. Similarly Lycidas himself is not only the literary form of Edward King, but a conventional or recurring form, of the same family as Shelley's Adonais, the Daphnis of Theocritus and Virgil, and Milton's own Damon. King was also a clergyman and, for Milton's purposes, a poet, so, having selected the conventional archetype of King as drowned young man, Milton has then to select the conventional archetypes of King as poet and of King as priest. These are, respectively, Orpheus and Peter.

Both Orpheus and Peter have attributes that link them in imagery with Lycidas. Orpheus was also an "enchanting son" or spirit of nature; he died young, in much the same role as Adonis, and was flung into the water. Peter would have drowned too without the help of Christ; hence Peter is not named directly, but only as "The Pilot of the Galilean Lake," just as Christ is not named directly, but only as "Him that walked the waves." When Orpheus was torn to pieces by the Maenads, his head went floating "Down the swift Hebrus to the Lesbian shore." The theme of salvation out of water is connected with the image of the dolphin, a conventional type of Christ, and dolphins are called upon to "waft the hapless youth" just before the peroration begins.

The body of the poem is arranged in the form ABACA, a main theme repeated twice with two intervening episodes, as in the musical rondo. The main theme is the drowning of Lycidas in the prime of his life; the two episodes, presided over by the figures of Orpheus and Peter, deal with the theme of premature death as it relates to poetry and to the priesthood respectively. In both the same type of image appears: the mechanical instrument of execution that brings about a sudden death, represented by the "abhorred shears" in the meditation on fame and the "grim two-handed engine" in the meditation on the corruption of the Church. The most difficult part of the construction is the managing of the transitions from these episodes back to the main theme. The poet does this by alluding to his great forerunners in the pastoral convention, Theocritus of Sicily, Virgil of Mantua, and the legendary Arcadians who preceded both:

> O fountain Arethuse, and thou honour'd flood,
> Smooth-sliding Mincius, crown'd with vocal reeds . . .

and later:

> Return, Alpheus, the dread voice is past
> That shrunk thy streams: return, Sicilian Muse.

The allusion has the effect of reminding the reader that this is, after all, a pastoral. But Milton also alludes to the myth of Arethusa and Alpheus, the Arcadian water-spirits who plunged underground and reappeared in Sicily, and this myth not only outlines the history of the pastoral convention, but unites the water imagery with the theme of disappearance and revival.

In pastoral elegy the poet who laments the death is often so closely associated with the dead man as to make him a kind of double or shadow of himself. Similarly Milton represents himself as intimately involved with the death of Lycidas. The theme of premature death is skilfully associated in the opening lines with the conventional apology for a "harsh and crude" poem; the poet hopes for a similar elegy when he dies, and at the end he accepts the responsibilities of survival and turns "Tomorrow to fresh woods, and pastures new," bringing the elegy to a full rich *tierce de Picardie* or major chord. By appearing himself at the beginning and end of the poem, Milton presents the poem as, in a sense, contained within the mind of the poet.

Apart from the historical convention of the pastoral, however, there is also the conventional framework of ideas or assumptions which forms the background of the poem. I call it a framework of ideas, and it may also be that, but in poetry it is rather a framework of images. It consists of four levels of existence. First is the order revealed by Christianity, the order of grace and salvation and of eternal life. Second is the order of human nature, the order represented by the Garden of Eden in the Bible and the Golden Age in classical myth, and which man in his fallen state can, up to a point, regain through education, obedience to law, and the habit of virtue. Third is the order of physical nature, the world of animals and plants which is morally neutral but theologically "fallen." Fourth is the disorder of the unnatural, the sin and death and corruption that entered the world with the Fall.

Lycidas has his connections with all of these orders. In the first place, all the images of death and resurrection are included in and identified with the body of Christ. Christ is the sun of righteousness, the tree of life, the water of life, the dying god who rose again, the saviour from the sea. On this level Lycidas enters the Christian heaven and is greeted by the "Saints above" "In solemn troops, and sweet societies," where the language echoes the Book of Revelation. But simultaneously Lycidas achieves another apotheosis as the Genius of the shore, corresponding to the Attendant Spirit in *Comus,* whose habitation is said to be a world above our own, identified, not with the Christian heaven, but with Spenser's Gardens of Adonis. The third level of physical nature is the world of ordinary experience, where death is simply a loss, and those who mourn the death have to turn to pick up their tasks again. On this level Lycidas is merely absent, "to our moist vows denied," represented only by the empty bier with its flowers. It is on this level too that the poem is contained within the mind of the surviving poet, as on the Christian level it is contained within the body of Christ. Finally, the world of death and corruption holds the drowned corpse of Lycidas, which will soon come to the surface and "welter to the parching wind." This last is an unpleasant and distressing image, and Milton touches it very lightly, picking it up again in an appropriate context:

> But swoln with wind and the rank mist they draw,
> Rot inwardly . . .

In the writing of *Lycidas* there are four creative principles of particular importance. To say that there are four does not mean, of course, that they are separable. One is convention, the reshaping of the poetic material which is appropriate to this subject. Another is genre, the choosing of the appropriate form. A third is archetype, the use of appropriate, and therefore recurrently employed, images and symbols. The fourth, for which there is no name, is the fact that the forms of literature are autonomous: that is, they do not exist outside literature. Milton is not writing an obituary: he does not start with Edward King and his life and times, but with the conventions and archetypes that poetry requires for such a theme.

Of the critical principles illustrated by this analysis, one will be no surprise to the present audience. *Lycidas* owes quite as much to Hebrew, Greek, Latin, and Italian traditions as it does to English. Even the diction, of which I have no space to speak, shows strong Italian influence. Milton was of course a learned poet, but there is no poet whose literary influences are entirely confined to his own language. Thus every problem in literary criticism is a problem in comparative literature, or simply of literature itself.

The next principle is that the provisional hypothesis which we must adopt for the study of every poem is that that poem is a unity. If, after careful and repeated testing, we are forced to conclude that it is not a unity, then we must abandon the hypothesis and look for the reasons why it is not. A good deal of bad criticism of *Lycidas* has resulted from not making enough initial effort to understand the unity of the poem. To talk of "digressions" in *Lycidas* is a typical consequence of a mistaken critical method, of backing into the poem the wrong way round. If, instead of starting with the poem, we start with a handful of peripheral facts about the poem, Milton's casual knowledge of King, his ambitions as a poet, his bitterness against the episcopacy, then of course the poem will break down into pieces corresponding precisely to those fragments of knowledge. *Lycidas* illustrates, on a small scale, what has happened on a much bigger scale in, for example, the criticism of Homer. Critics knowing something about the fragmentary nature of heroic lays and ballads approached the *Iliad* and the *Odyssey* with this knowledge in mind, and the poems obediently split up into the pieces that they wished to isolate. Other critics came along and treated the poems as imaginative unities, and today everyone knows that the second group were more convincing.

The same thing happens when our approach to "sources" becomes fragmentary or piecemeal. *Lycidas* is a dense mass of echoes from previous literature, chiefly pastoral literature. Reading through Virgil's Eclogues with *Lycidas* in mind, we can see that Milton had not simply read or studied these poems: he possessed them; they were part of the material he was shaping. The passage about the hungry sheep reminds us of at least three other passages: one in Dante's *Paradiso,* one in the Book of Ezekiel, and one near the beginning of Hesiod's *Theogony.* There are also echoes of Mantuan and Spenser, of the Gospel of John, and it is quite possible that there are even more striking parallels with poems that Milton had not read. In such cases there is not *a* source at all, no one place that the passage "comes from," or, as we say with such stupefying presumption, that the poet "had in mind." There are only archetypes, or recurring themes of literary expression, which *Lycidas* has recreated, and therefore re-echoed, yet once more.

The next principle is that the important problems of literary criticism lie within the study of literature. We notice that a law of diminishing returns sets in as soon as we move away from the poem itself. If we ask, who is Lycidas? the answer is that he is a member of the same family as Theocritus' Daphnis, Bion's Adonis, the Old Testament's Abel, and so on. The answer goes on building up a wider comprehension of literature and a deeper knowledge of its structural principles and recurring themes. But if we ask, who was Edward King? What was his relation to Milton? How good a poet was he? we find ourselves moving dimly in the intense inane. The same is true of minor points. If we ask, why is the image of the two-handed engine in *Lycidas*? we can give an answer, along the lines suggested above, that illustrates how carefully the poem has been constructed. If we ask, what is the two-handed engine? there are forty-odd answers, none of them completely satisfactory; yet the fact that they are not wholly satisfactory hardly seems to be important.

Another form of the same kind of fallacy is the confusion between personal sincerity and literary sincerity. If we start with the facts that *Lycidas* is highly conventional and that Milton knew King only slightly, we may see in *Lycidas* an "artificial" poem without "real feeling" in it. This red herring, though more common among third-rate romantics, was dragged across the study of *Lycidas* by Samuel Johnson. Johnson knew better, but he happened to feel perverse about this particular poem, and so deliberately raised false issues. It would not have occurred to him, for example, to question the conventional use of Horace in the satires of Pope, or of Juvenal in his own. Personal sincerity has no place in literature, because personal sincerity as such is inarticulate. One may burst into tears at the news of a friend's death, but one can never spontaneously burst into song, however doleful a lay. *Lycidas* is a passionately sincere poem, because Milton was deeply interested in the structure and symbolism of funeral elegies, and had been practising since adolescence on every fresh corpse in sight, from the university beadle to the fair infant dying of a cough.

If we ask what inspires a poet, there are always two answers. An occasion, an experience, an event, may inspire the impulse to write. But the impulse to write can only come from previous contact with literature, and the formal inspiration, the poetic structure that crystallizes around the new event, can only be derived from other poems. Hence while every new poem is a new and unique creation, it is also a reshaping of familiar conventions of literature, otherwise it would not be recognizable as literature at all. Literature often gives us the illusion of turning from books to life, from secondhand to direct experience, and thereby discovering new literary principles in the world outside. But this is never quite what happens. No matter how tightly Wordsworth may close the barren leaves of art and let nature be his teacher, his literary forms will be as conventional as ever, although they may echo an unaccustomed set of conventions, such as the ballad or the broadside. The pretence of personal sincerity is itself a literary convention, and Wordsworth makes many of the flat simple statements which represent, in literature, the inarticulateness of personal sincerity:

> No motion has she now, no force:
> She neither hears nor sees.

But as soon as a death becomes a poetic image, that image is assimilated to other poetic images of death in nature, and hence Lucy inevitably becomes a Proserpine figure, just as King becomes an Adonis:

> Rolled round in earth's diurnal course
> With rocks, and stones, and trees.

In Whitman we have an even more extreme example than Wordsworth of a cult of personal statement and an avoidance of learned conventions. It is therefore instructive to see what happens in *When Lilacs Last in Dooryard Bloomed.* The dead man is not called by a pastoral name, but neither is he called by his historical name. He is in a coffin which is carried the length and breadth of the land; he is identified with a "powerful western fallen star"; he is the beloved comrade of the poet, who throws the purple flower of the lilac on his coffin; a singing bird laments the death, just as the woods and caves do in *Lycidas.* Convention, genre, archetype, and the autonomy of forms are all illustrated as clearly in Whitman as they are in Milton.

Lycidas is an occasional poem, called forth by a specific event. It seems, therefore, to be a poem with a strong external reference. Critics who cannot approach a poem except as a personal statement of the poet's thus feel that if it says little about King, it must say a good deal about Milton. So, they reason, *Lycidas* is really autobiographical, concerned with Milton's own preoccupations, including his fear of death. There can be no objection to this unless Milton's conventional involving of himself with the poem is misinterpreted as a personal intrusion into it.

For Milton was even by seventeenth-century standards an unusually professional and impersonal poet. Of all Milton's poems, the one obvious failure is the poem called *The Passion,* and if we look at the imagery of that poem we can see why. It is the only poem of Milton's in which he is preoccupied with himself in the process of writing it. "My muse," "my song," "my harp," "my roving verse," "my Phoebus," and so on for eight stanzas until Milton abandons the poem in disgust. It is not a coincidence that Milton's one self-conscious poem should be the one that never gets off the ground. There is nothing like this in *Lycidas:* the "I" of that poem is a professional poet in his conventional shepherd disguise, and to think of him as a personal "I" is to bring *Lycidas* down to the level of *The Passion,* to make it a poem that has to be studied primarily as a biographical document rather than for its own sake. Such an approach to *Lycidas* is apt to look most plausible to those who dislike Milton, and want to see him cut down to size.

One more critical principle, and the one that I have written this paper to enunciate, seems to me to follow inevitably from the previous ones. Every poem must be examined as a unity, but no poem is an isolatable unity. Every poem is inherently connected with other poems of its kind, whether explicitly, as *Lycidas* is with Theocritus and Virgil, or implicitly, as Whitman is with the same tradition, or by anticipation, as *Lycidas* is with later pastoral elegies. And, of course, the kinds or genres of literature are not separable either, like the orders of pre-Darwinian biology. Everyone who has seriously studied literature knows that he is not simply moving from poem to poem, or from one aesthetic experience to another: he is also entering into a coherent and progressive discipline. For literature is not simply an aggregate of books and poems and plays: it is an order of words. And our total literary experience, at any given time, is not a discrete series of memories or impressions of what we have read, but an imaginatively coherent body of experience.

It is literature as an order of words, therefore, which forms the primary context of any given work of literary art. All other contexts — the place of *Lycidas* in Milton's development; its place in the history of English poetry; its place in seventeenth-century thought or history — are secondary and derivative contexts. Within the total literary order certain structural and generic principles, certain configurations of narrative and imagery, certain conventions and devices and *topoi,* occur over and over again. In every new work of literature some of these principles are reshaped.

Lycidas, we found, is informed by such a recurring structural principle. The short, simple, and accurate name for this principle is myth. The Adonis myth is what makes *Lycidas* both distinctive and traditional. Of course if we think of the Adonis myth as some kind of Platonic idea existing by itself, we shall not get far with it as a critical conception. But it is only incompetence that tries to reduce or assimilate a poem to a myth. The Adonis myth in *Lycidas* is the structure of *Lycidas.* It is in *Lycidas* in much the same way that the sonata form is in the first movement of a Mozart symphony. It is the connecting link between what makes *Lycidas* the poem it is and what unites it to other forms of poetic experience. If we attend only to the uniqueness of *Lycidas,* and analyze the ambiguities and subtleties of its diction, our method, however useful in itself, soon reaches a point of no return to the poem. If we attend only to the conventional element, our method will turn it into a scissors-and-paste collection of allusive tags. One method reduces the poem to a jangle of echoes of itself, the other to a jangle of echoes from other poets. If we have a unifying principle that holds these two tendencies together from the start, neither will get out of hand.

Myths, it is true, turn up in other disciplines, in anthropology, in psychology, in comparative religion. But the primary business of the critic is with myth as the shaping principle of a work of literature. Thus for him myth becomes much the same thing as Aristotle's *mythos,* narrative or plot, the moving formal cause which is what Aristotle called the "soul" of the work and assimilates all details in the realizing of its unity.

In its simplest English meaning a myth is a story about a god, and Lycidas is, poetically speaking, a god or spirit of nature, who eventually becomes a saint in heaven, which is as near as one can get to godhead in ordinary Christianity. The reason for treating Lycidas mythically, in this sense, is conventional, but the convention is not arbitrary or accidental. It arises from the metaphorical nature of poetic speech. We are not told simply that Lycidas has left the woods and caves, but that the woods and caves and all their echoes mourn his loss. This is the language of that curious identification of subject and object, of personality and thing, which the poet has in common with the lunatic and the lover. It is the language of metaphor, recognized by Aristotle as the distinctive language of poetry. And, as we can see in such phrases as sun-god and tree-god, the language of metaphor is interdependent with the language of myth.

I have said that all problems of criticism are problems of comparative literature. But where there is comparison there must be some standard by which we can distinguish what is actually comparable from what is merely analogous. The scientists discovered long ago that to make valid comparisons you have to know what your real categories are. If you're studying natural history, for instance, no matter how fascinated you may be by anything that has eight legs, you can't just lump together an octopus and a spider and a string quartet. In science the difference between a scientific and a pseudo-scientific procedure can usually be spotted fairly soon. I wonder if literary criticism has any standards of this kind. It seems to me that a critic practically has to maintain that the Earl of Oxford wrote the plays of Shakespeare before he can be clearly recognized as making pseudo-critical statements. I have read some critics on Milton who appeared to be confusing Milton with their phallic fathers, if that is the right phrase. I should call them pseudo-critics; others call them neo-classicists. How is one to know? There is such a variety of even legitimate critics. There are critics who can find things in the Public Records Office, and there are critics who, like myself, could not find the Public Records Office. Not all critical statements or procedures can be equally valid.

The first step, I think, is to recognize the dependence of value-judgments on scholarship. Scholarship, or the knowledge of literature, constantly expands and increases; value-judgments are produced by a skill based on the knowledge we already have. Thus scholarship has both priority to value-judgments and the power of veto over them. The second step is to recognize the dependence of scholarship on a coordinated view of literature. A good deal of critical taxonomy lies ahead of us. We need to know much more than we do about the structural principles of literature, about myth and metaphor, conventions and genres, before we can distinguish with any authority a real from an imaginary line of influence, an illuminating from a misleading analogy, a poet's original source from his last resource. The basis of this central critical activity that gives direction to scholarship is the simple fact that every poem is a member of the class of things called poems. Some poems, including *Lycidas,* proclaim that they are conventional, in other words that their primary context is in literature. Other poems leave this inference to the critic, with an appealing if often misplaced confidence.

M. H. ABRAMS

The Correspondent Breeze:
A Romantic Metaphor

Writing in 1834, Henry Taylor noted that Wordsworth's attacks on eighteenth-century diction had succeeded in making poetry, in some particulars, more plain spoken. But Taylor also remarked that in effect a new poetic diction had covertly replaced the old. If Romantic poets no longer refer to the nightingale by the Greek name, Philomel, some of them refer to it by the Persian name, Bulbul; Taylor cites one reader who said "he had learnt, for the first time, from Lord Byron's poetry, that two bulls make a nightingale." Worse still are the stock terms scattered

SOURCE: "The Correspondent Breeze: A Romantic Metaphor" is from *English Romantic Poets: Modern Essays in Criticism,* edited by M. H. Abrams (New York: Oxford University Press, 1960), pp. 37–53, revised from an earlier version in *The Kenyon Review,* Volume XIX (1957), pp. 113–30. Revised version copyright © 1960 by M. H. Abrams. Reprinted by permission of the author and *The Kenyon Review.*

through poetry "with a sort of feeling senselessness," such as "wild," "bright," "lonely," and "dream," and especially the variant forms of the word "breathing"; "to breathe," Taylor says, has become "a verb poetical which [means] anything but respiration." [1]

To this shrewd observation I would add that "breathing" is only one aspect of a more general component in Romantic poetry. This is air-in-motion, whether it occurs as breeze or breath, wind or respiration — whether the air is compelled into motion by natural forces or by the action of the human lungs. That the poetry of Coleridge, Wordsworth, Shelley, Byron should be so thoroughly ventilated is itself noteworthy; but the surprising thing is how often, in the major poems, the wind is not only a property of the landscape, but also a vehicle for radical changes in the poet's mind. The rising wind, usually linked with the outer transition from winter to spring, is correlated with a complex subjective process: the return to a sense of community after isolation, the renewal of life and emotional vigor after apathy and a deathlike torpor, and an outburst of creative power following a period of imaginative sterility.

Coleridge's *Dejection: An Ode,* written in 1802, provides the earliest inclusive instance of this symbolic equation. The poetic meditation is set in April, which turns out, as in Eliot's *Waste Land,* to be the cruelest month because, in breeding life out of the dead land, it painfully revives emotional life in the observer, mixing memory and desire. And as the poem opens, a desultory breeze makes itself audible on a wind-harp — an instrument whose eerie modulations sound through most of the writings with which we are concerned.

James Bowyer, Coleridge's schoolmaster and pre-Wordsworthian reformer of poetic diction, had vigorously proscribed the traditional lyre as an emblem for poetizing. "Harp? Harp? Lyre? Pen and ink, boy, you mean!" [2] But by the process already noted — we might call it Taylor's principle — the lyre of Apollo was often replaced in Romantic poetry by the Aeolian lyre, whose music is evoked not by art, human or divine, but by a force of nature. Poetic man, in a statement by Shelley which had close parallels in Coleridge and Wordsworth, is an instrument subject to impressions "like the alterations of an ever-changing wind over an Aeolian lyre, which move it by their motion to ever-changing melody." [3] The wind-harp has become a persistent Romantic analogue of the poetic mind, the figurative mediator between outer motion and inner emotion. It is possible to speculate that, without this plaything of the eighteenth century, the Romantic poets would have lacked a conceptual model for the way the mind and imagination respond to the wind, so that some of their most characteristic passages might have been, in a literal sense, inconceivable.

In Coleridge's *Dejection* the moaning wind-harp foretells a storm

which the lyric speaker in his lethargy awaits in the hope that, as in the
past, it may send "my soul abroad" and release the

> stifled, drowsy, unimpassioned grief,
> Which finds no natural outlet, no relief. . . .

The speaker reviews the afflictions that have made him take refuge in
"abstruse research," and have destroyed his inner joy and any possibility
of emotional commerce with the outer scene. Worst of all is the attendant
paralysis of his poetic power, the "shaping spirit of Imagination." But
even as the speaker inventories the conditions of his death in life, the
outer wind mounts to a storm of driving rain and compels the wind-harp
into loud and violent music. In implicit parallel with the wind-harp, the
poet also responds to the storm with mounting vitality — what he calls
"the passion and the life, whose fountains are within," once more break
out — until, in a lull of the wind, the poem rounds on itself and ends
where it began, with a calm both of nature and of mind. But the poet
has moved from the calm of apathy to one of peace after passion. By the
agency of the wind storm it describes, the poet turns out to contradict its
own premises: the poet's spirit awakens to violent life even as he laments
his inner death, achieves release in the despair at being cut off from all
outlet, and demonstrates the power of imagination in the process of
memorializing its failure.

   That the poem was grounded in experience is evident from Coleridge's
many letters testifying to his delight in wind and storms, which he
watched "with a total feeling worshipping the power and 'eternal Link'
of Energy," and through which he had walked, "stricken . . . with
barreness" in a "deeper dejection than I am willing to remember," seeking the inspiration for completing *Christabel*.[4] In one passage, written
some nine months after he had completed *Dejection*, we find a symbolic
wind again involving the revival of feeling and imagination, and leading
to the sense of the one life within us and abroad:

> In simple earnest, I never find myself alone within the embracement of
> rocks and hills, a traveller up an alpine road, but my spirit courses,
> drives, and eddies, like a Leaf in Autumn: a wild activity, of thoughts,
> imagination, feelings, and impulses of motion, rises up from within me
> — a sort of *bottom-wind*, that blows to no point of the compass, and
> comes from I know not whence, but agitates the whole of me. . . .
> Life seems to me then a universal spirit, that neither has, nor can have,
> an opposite. . . . where is there *room* for death? [5]

   Similarly with Coleridge's friend, Wordsworth: "Winter winds," Dorothy wrote, "are his delight — his mind I think is often more fertile in
this season than any other." [6] Of this phenomenon Wordsworth himself
gave remarkable testimony in the autobiographical *Prelude*. From the
beginning of this work, in fact, the recurrent wind serves unobtrusively

as a leitmotif, representing the chief theme of continuity and interchange between outer motions and the interior life and powers, and providing the poem with a principle of organization beyond chronology.

Earlier poets had launched their epics by invoking for inspiration a Muse, Apollo, or the Holy Spirit. Wordsworth's opening lines, which have an identical function, are:

> Oh there is blessing in this gentle breeze
> That blows from the green fields and from the clouds
> And from the sky. . . .

Released at last from the city and the oppressive weight of the past, the poet says "I breathe again"; but so, we find, is nature breathing, in a passage where the wind becomes both the stimulus and outer correspondent to a spring-like revival of the spirit after a wintry season, and also to a revival of poetic inspiration which Wordsworth, going beyond Coleridge, equates with the inspiration of the Prophets when touched by the Holy Spirit. There is even a glancing metaphoric parallel between the resulting poetic creation and the prototypal creation by divine utterance — for "Nature's self," as Wordsworth said later, "is the breath of God" (*Prelude*, 1805 ed., V, 222.)

> For I, methought, while the sweet breath of Heaven
> Was blowing on my body, felt within
> A corresponding mild creative breeze,
> A vital breeze which travell'd gently on
> O'er things which it had made, and is become
> A tempest, a redundant energy
> Vexing its own creation. 'Tis a power
> That does not come unrecogniz'd, a storm
> Which, breaking up a long-continued frost
> Brings with it vernal promises . . .
> The holy life of music and of verse. . . .

> To the open fields I told
> A prophecy: poetic numbers came
> Spontaneously, and cloth'd in priestly robe
> My spirit, thus singled out, as it might seem,
> For holy services. . . .

And a bit farther on comes the remaining element of the Romantic complex, the analogy between poetic mind and Aeolian harp:

> It was a splendid evening; and my soul
> Did once again make trial of the strength
> Restored to her afresh; nor did she want
> Eolian visitations; but the harp
> Was soon defrauded. . . .   (1805 ed., I, 1–105)

Later Wordsworth parallels Milton's reinvocations of his divine guides by recalling the "animating breeze" which had made a "glad preamble to this Verse," and now, made visible by the tossing boughs of his favorite grove, once again

> Spreads through me a commotion like its own,
> Something that fits me for the Poet's task.   (VII, 1–56)

Wordsworth's account of his mental breakdown in *The Prelude* runs broadly parallel to the autobiographical passages in Coleridge's *Dejection*. And at the nadir of his apathy, when he felt "utter loss of hope itself, And things to hope for," Wordsworth signalized his recovery by addressing again the correspondent breeze:

> Not with these began
> Our Song, and not with these our Song must end:
> Ye motions of delight, that through the fields
> Stir gently, breezes and soft airs that breathe
> The breath of Paradise, and find your way
> To the recesses of the soul!   (XI, 7–12)

"Spring returns, I saw the Spring return"; and even the influence of Dorothy is apprehended as a revivifying spring breeze —

> Thy breath,
> Dear Sister, was a kind of gentler spring
> That went before my steps.   (XII, 23–4; XIII, 244–6)

Time and again Wordsworth's most arcane statements similarly involve, as he put it in *The Excursion* (IV, 600), "the breeze of nature stirring in his soul." [7] In the *Intimations Ode,* "The winds come to me from the fields of sleep"; and in *The Prelude,* the poet listens to sounds that

> make their dim abode in distant winds.
> Thence did I think the visionary power;

or asserts that

> visionary power
> Attends the motions of the viewless winds,
> Embodied in the mystery of words.

The shell of the Arab, in Wordsworth's dream, which utters "A loud prophetic blast of harmony,"

> Had voices more than all the winds, with power
> To exhilarate the spirit. . . .   (1850 ed., II, 310–11; V, 595–7;
> 92–108)

Of the two "spots of time" — the indelible memories by which his imagination, having, like Coleridge's, been "impaired," was "nourished and invisible repaired" — one incorporated a woman with "her garments vexed and tossed By the strong wind," and the other "the wind and sleety rain" evoking "the bleak music of that old stone wall." The result is that to this very time, whether in winter storm and rain or when the summer trees rock

> In a strong wind, some working of the spirit,
> Some inward agitations thence are brought. . . .
> (1850 ed., XII, 208–332)

Wordsworth read his completed masterpiece to Coleridge in 1807, five years after the writing of *Dejection,* and when Coleridge's spirits were at their lowest ebb. In his memorial on that occasion "To William Wordsworth," Coleridge duly noted that Wordsworth had described the quickening effect within his mind of the springtime wind: of "vital breathings secret as the soul of vernal growth." Then, as he listened to those passages in which Wordsworth expressed his love and hope for Coleridge himself, suddenly the poet's solemn voice seized upon his friend as though it were itself a great wind which, like the literal storm in *Dejection,* fanned his torpid spirit, "whose hope had seem'd to die," into a momentary and painful rebirth. The episode is one of the most moving in literature.

> The storm
> Scatter'd and whirl'd me, till my thoughts became
> A bodily tumult. . . .
> Ah! as I listened with a heart forlorn,
> The pulses of my being beat anew:
> And even as Life returns upon the drowned,
> Life's joy rekindling roused a throng of pains —
> Keen pangs of Love, awakening as a babe
> Turbulent, with an outcry in the heart. . . .[8]

It is easy to multiply similar quotations, from these and other Romantic writers. Childe Harold, for example, found his spirit participating in the violence of an Alpine tempest, and drew a parallel with the violent explosion of his mind in poetry (Canto III, xcii–vii). And while De Quincey, a child of six, stood secretly and alone by the deathbed of a beloved sister, "a solemn wind began to blow"; as his "ear caught this vast Aeolian intonation" and his eye turned from "the golden fulness of life" outdoors in the midsummer noon to settle "upon the frost which overspread my sister's face, instantly a trance fell upon me. . . . I, in spirit, rose as if on billows. . . ."[9]

One poet, the most visionary and vatic of all these, demands special attention. Shelley's best known poem is addressed directly to the wind, in the form of a sustained invocation and petition. In the opening stanzas the Wild West Wind is at once destroyer and preserver because in the autumn it tears down the dead leaves and the seeds, but only so that in a later season another west wind — "thine azure sister of the spring" — may blow the clarion of resurrection, revive the seeds, and call out the buds to feed, like flocks of sheep, on the moving air, the wind itself. In the last stanza Shelley, like Coleridge in *Dejection,* cries out to the wind, in the autumn of his spirit, to blow through him as through a wind-harp — "Make me thy lyre, even as the forest is" — and to drive the withered leaves of his dead thoughts over the universe "to quicken a new birth." And in the coda, to the blast of the wind sounding this time the apo-calyptic trumpet of the general destruction and resurrection, the im-mense analogy is consummated between the effect of the wind on the unawakened earth, the singer's inspiration to poetry and prophecy, and the springtime of the human spirit everywhere.

> Be thou, Spirit fierce,
> My spirit! Be thou me, impetuous one! . . .
> Be through my lips to unawakened earth
> The trumpet of a prophecy! O, Wind,
> If Winter comes, can Spring be far behind?

Elsewhere the wind served Shelley repeatedly as a stimulus and symbol of inspiration, in his prose essays as well as his verse. *Alastor* opens with an invocation to the "Mother of this unfathomable world!"

> Serenely now
> And moveless, as a long-forgotten lyre . . .
> I wait thy breath, Great Parent, that my strain
> May modulate with murmurs of the air. . . .[10]

Shelley's use of the wind in *Adonais* is of particular interest. This poem follows the classic elegaic pattern — consonant also with the evolution of earlier Romantic poems of dejection — from despair to consolation; although Shelley's consolation involves a death wish:

> Die,
> If thou wouldst be with that which thou dost seek! . . .
> Why linger, why turn back, why shrink, my Heart?

The conclusion, however, is astonishing. Most of these poems begin with a literal wind which transforms itself into the metaphorical wind of inspiration. Shelley reverses the sequence. At the end of *Adonais* the inspiration he had evoked "in song" (that is, in his *Ode to the West Wind*) actually descends upon him; and what he feels is a tangible breath which rises to the violence of a literal storm of wind:

> The breath whose might I have invoked in song
> Descends on me; my spirit's bark is driven,

Far from the shore, far from the trembling throng
Whose sails were never to the tempest given;
The massy earth and spherèd skies are riven!
I am borne darkly, fearfully, afar. . . .[11]

II

Taken singly the symbolic equations between breeze, breath, and soul, respiration and inspiration, the reanimation of nature and of the spirit, are not peculiarly Romantic, nor in any way recent. All are older than recorded history; they are inherent in the constitution of ancient languages, are widely current in myth and folklore, and make up some of the great commonplaces of our religious tradition.

When Shelley, for example, made the West Wind the breath of autumn's being and a spirit, which became his breath and his spirit and blew, through him, the trumpet prophesying a universal resurrection, he may seem radically innovative. But from a philological point of view Shelley was reactionary; he merely revived and exploited the ancient undivided meanings of these words. For the Latin *spiritus* signified wind and breath, as well as soul. So did the Latin *anima,* and the Greek *pneuma,* the Hebrew *ruach,* the Sanskrit *atman,* as well as the equivalent words in Arabic, Japanese, and many other languages, some of them totally unrelated. In myth and religion, moreover, wind and breath often play an essential part in the creation both of the universe and of man. In the beginning the spirit, or breath, or wind (*ruach*) of God moved upon the face of the waters; and after forming man, God "breathed into his nostrils the breath of life; and man became a living soul." Even in the Old Testament breath and wind were given the added power of renewing life after death, as in Ezekiel 37:9: "Prophesy, son of man, and say to the wind . . . 'Come from the four winds, O breath, and breathe upon these slain, that they may live.'" Similarly Jesus said (John 3:7–8): "Marvel not that I said unto thee, Ye must be born again. The wind bloweth where it listeth . . . so is every one that is born of the Spirit." But God's breath in the Bible could also be a destroying storm (as in I Kings 19:11; Ezekiel 13:13), symbolizing the explosion of God's wrath as well as the gift of life or grace. In parallel fashion the Wind Gods of Greek and Roman myth were regarded as destructive, requiring propitiation; but they also — especially the West Wind, "Zephyrus," or "Favonius" — were held to possess an animating or impregnating power, a fact noted by medieval encyclopedists, and by Chaucer:

Whan Zephyrus eek with his swete breeth
Inspired hath in every holt and heeth
The tendre croppes. . . .

Shelley thus had ample precedent, pagan and Christian, for his West Wind, both breath and spirit, destroyer as well as preserver, which is equally the revitalizing Zephyrus of the Romans and the trumpet blast of the Book of Revelation, announcing the simultaneous destruction of the present world and a new life in a world recreated. The additional connection between wind and inspiration is, of course, implicit in the latter term, for "to inspire" once meant "to blow or breathe into," and when a man received the divine "afflatus" he received, literally, the breath or wind of a god or muse. According to classical belief, this supernatural breath stimulated the visionary utterances of religious oracles and prophetic poets. Eliphaz the Temanite, in the Book of Job (4:13–16), expressed a similar view: "In thoughts from the visions of the night . . . a spirit [or breeze: *ruach*] passed before my face. . . . There was silence, and I heard a voice." And on the day of Pentecost, in the Acts of the New Testament (2:1–4), "suddenly there came a sound from heaven as of a rushing mighty wind. . . . And they were all filled with the Holy Ghost, and began to speak with other tongues, as the Spirit gave them utterance."

One other historical item is pertinent. The Stoic concept of the World Soul — of the Pneuma, or Spiritus Sacer, or Anima Mundi — originally involved, in the literal sense of these names, the concept of a kind of breath, a divine gas, which infuses the material world and constitutes also the individual human pysche. The poet Lucan said that Apollo founded the Delphic oracle at a huge chasm where "the earth breathed forth divine truth, and . . . gave out a wind that spoke"; and he suggested that the Pythian priestess stationed there is inspired by inhaling the very breath of the World Soul.[12] It is noteworthy that the familiar Romantic Soul of Nature, or Spirit of the Universe, sometimes retained its primitive airy essence, homogeneous with the soul of man, as well as its power of quasi-literal inspiration. In *The Eolian Harp* Coleridge speculated that all animated nature may be but organic wind harps, diversely framed, through which sweeps "one intellectual breeze, At once the Soul of each, and God of all." Wordsworth in *The Prelude* invoked the "Wisdom," "Spirit," and "Soul" of the Universe,

> That givest to forms and images a breath
> And everlasting motion,

and also the "Soul of things," that in its love renews

> Those naked feelings, which, when thou woulds't form
> A living thing, thou sendest like a breeze
> Into its infant being! [13]

Shelley called upon the West Wind, the "breath of Autumn's being," to blow through him: "Be thou, spirit fierce, My spirit!" The Soul of the worlds, Emerson later declared in "The Over-Soul," "can inspire whom it will, and behold! their speech shall by lyrical and sweet, and universal as the rising of the wind."

III

In the Biblical commentaries of the Church Fathers it was commonly recognized that the moving air, the breath of the Lord, the Holy Spirit, the life and spiritual rebirth of man, and the inspiration of the Prophets in the Old and New Testaments were connected, if not literally, then allegorically, or by a system of correspondence, or by some other exegetical relation. Before the end of the fourth century, Saint Augustine had imported the spiritual breeze into the context of autobiography that is common to all the Romantic writings I have cited. In the central passage of his *Confessions* (VIII, xi–xii), Augustine described his tortured state as he hesitated at the brink of conversion, "soul-sick . . . and tormented," as he said, "hesitating to die to death and live to life." Then one day he retired into the garden next his lodging, and "when a deep consideration had from the secret bottom of my soul drawn together and heaped up all my misery in my heart, there arose a mighty wind, bringing a mighty shower of tears"; with the result that "by a light as it were of serenity infused into my heart, all the darkness of doubt vanished away."

Even the typical procedure in Romantic wind-poems of beginning with the description of a natural scene and then moving to inner correspondences had precedents in prose and verse. During the Middle Ages the mode of self-inquisition and spiritual inventory, of which Augustine's *Confessions* became a prime exemplar, led to the identification of a standard condition of apathy and spiritual torpor called "acedia," or "aridity," or "interior desolation," closely related, according to Cassian, to another state of the soul called "dejection" (*tristitia*).[14] The descriptions of this interior condition and of its relief were sometimes couched in natural and seasonal metaphors: winter, drought, and desert, as against spring, the coming of rain, and the burgeoning plant or garden. Coleridge echoed the technical language of theology when, in a letter of March 25, 1801, which was a prose rehearsal for *Dejection*, he described his "intellectual *exsiccation*," a state in which "the Poet is dead in me," his imagination "lies, like a Cold Snuff on the circular Rim of a Brass Candle-stick," and he remains "squat and square on the earth amid the hurricane." [15]

In the later Renaissance the alternation of aridity and freshness, in which spiritual and imaginative death and rebirth are equated with aspects of the natural scene, became a frequent topic in the meditations of the religious poets. An instance in George Herbert is the pair of poems called *Employment,* which inspired Coleridge's *Work Without Hope;* another is *The Flower,* also a favorite of Coleridge, in which we find a complex interplay between the death-in-life and revival of the soul, of the poetic faculty, and of a perennial plant.

> How fresh, O Lord, how sweet and clean
> Are thy returns! Ev'n as the flowers in spring,
>   To which, besides their own demean,
> The late-past frosts tributes of pleasure bring. . . .
>
>   And now in age I bud again,
> After so many deaths I live and write;
>   I once more smell the dew and rain,
>
> And relish versing. O my only light,
>   It cannot be
>   That I am he
> On whom thy tempests fell all night.

Henry Vaughan at times approximates still more closely the familiar Romantic pattern of inner depression and revival, paralleled to changes in the landscape in diverse weathers and seasons. And the role of the wind is made explicit in poems such as *The Storm and Mount of Olives* (2), but above all in *Regeneration.* "One day," he says in that poem, "I stole abroad." "It was high spring. . . . Yet was it frost within." After traversing a spiritual landscape and toiling up a purgatorial mountain, he entered a flowery grove reminiscent of several earlier pleasances, all of them wind-blown: Dante's Earthly Paradise, the garden which had been the setting of Augustine's conversion, and that favorite medieval symbol, the *hortus conclusus,* the closed garden, of the Song of Songs [16]:

> Here musing long, I heard
>   A rushing wind
> Which still increased, but whence it stirred
>   Nowhere I could not find. . . .
>
> But while I list'ning sought
>   My mind to ease
> By knowing where 'twas, or where not,
>   It whispered: Where I please.
>
> Lord, then said I, on me one breath,
> And let me die before my death!

The Romantic wind, then, is remote in kind from the pleasingly horrific storm dear to eighteenth-century connoisseurs of the natural sublime; and the confessional lyrics of dejection and recovery in which this wind plays its part are not (as common report would have it) in the tradition of the eighteenth-century poems of melancholy and spleen.

These lyrics are rather secularized versions of an older devotional poetry, employed in the examination of the soul's condition as it approaches and retreats from God. Secularized — yet the religious element remains as at least a formal parallel, or a verbal or rhetorical echo. Coleridge's finest odes, including *Dejection* and *To William Wordsworth,* use theological language and end in the cadence of a prayer. Wordsworth's poetic meditations commonly involve a presence whose dwelling is the light of setting suns. And even the pagan Shelley's *Ode to the West Wind* is a formal orison addressed to the Spirit and Breath of Autumn's Being.

IV

And now the question: What are we to make of the phenomenon of the correspondent breeze in Romantic poetry? These days the answer seems obvious enough, and it may have occasioned surprise that I have so long resisted calling the wind an "archetypal image." I should not hesitate to use so convenient a term, if it were merely a neutral way of identifying a persistent material symbol for a psychological condition. In the context of present critical theory, however, the term "archetypal" commits the user to implications which are equally unnecessary and undesirable. For example, in order to explain the origin and currency of the correspondent wind it would seem adequate to point to the inescapable conditions of the human endowment and of its physical milieu. That breath and wind are both instances of air in motion, and that breathing is a sign of life and its cessation of death, are matters evident to a casual observation, as are the alternations of inhalation and exhalation, despair and elation, imaginative energy and torpor, birth and death, in the constant environmental rhythms of calm and storm, drought and rain, winter and spring. If a connection between a universal inner experience and an omnipresent outer analogue has been made once, it will be made again, and may readily become a commonplace of oral and written tradition; there is no rational need to assume, as Jung does, that after leaving its mark on the nervous system the image goes underground, to emerge sporadically from the racial unconscious. But of course if we neutralize the archetype by eliminating dark allusions to "primordial images," or "the racial memory," or "timeless depths," archetypal criticism is drained of the mystique or pathos which is an important condition of its present vogue.

For literary criticism, moreover, the ultimate criterion is not whether a doctrine is a justifiable psychological hypothesis, but what it does when put to work interpreting a text. And from this point of view standard archetypal criticism can be charged with blurring, if it does not destroy, the properties of the literary products it undertakes to explicate. A mode of reading that persists in looking through the literal, particular, and artful qualities of a poem in order to discover a more important ulterior pattern of primitive, general, and unintended meanings eliminates its individuality, and threatens to nullify even its status as a work of art. For the result of such reading is to collapse the rich diversity of individual works into one, or into a very limited number, of archetypal patterns, which any one poem shares not only with other poems, but with such unartful phenomena as myth, dreams, and the fantasies of psychosis.

Maud Bodkin's influential book, *Archetypal Patterns in Poetry*, intelligent and extremely suggestive though it is, provides a radical illustration of this process. Miss Bodkin begins her study by considering the significance of the wind in Coleridge's *Ancient Mariner*, and of the contrast between the becalmed ship and, after the blessing of the water snakes, the storm which drives the ship into violent motion. In the Romantic poems I have discussed, the rising wind was explicitly paralleled to a change in the inner state of the lyric speaker. *The Ancient Mariner*, on the other hand, is explicitly a narrative about the actions and sufferings of an unfortunate sailor; yet Miss Bodkin has no hesitation in reading the change from calm to storm as a symbolic projection — by the author — of the mental states that Jung calls "progression and regression." This psychic sequence constitutes the "Rebirth archetype," which is also manifested by the vegetation god of ritual and myth, is echoed in the resurrection of Christ, reappears in dreams, and in literature constitutes the basic pattern, among other works, of *Oedipus, Hamlet*, the Book of Jonah, the *Aeneid*, the *Divine Comedy, Paradise Lost, Kubla Khan*, and *Women in Love*. Once unleashed, indeed, the archetype proves insatiable, and goes on to assimilate even subhuman phenomena: Miss Bodkin (page 75) detects the characteristic pattern of the Night Journey and Rebirth in the behavior of Wolfgang Köhler's experimental apes, who passed through a period of baffled bewilderment before the flash of insight which enabled them to reach their banana.

These are astonishing equations, but the logical procedure by which they were achieved is simple enough. It consists in treating loose analogy as though it were identity. This strategy, to be sure, has a singular virtue; it cannot fail. Only leave out enough of the qualities that make a poem, or any complex experience, distinctive, and it can be reduced to an abstract pattern — almost any abstract pattern, including, if that is our inclination, the pattern of the vegetational cycle of death and rebirth. But by what a prodigious abstraction of everything that matters is a literary ballad, *The Ancient Mariner*, shown to be identical in ultimate significance with tragedies, epics, novels, and lyrics, together with the basic formulae of myth and religion!

A procedure which ingeniously contrives to reduce all — or at least a great many — serious poems to variations upon a timeless theme is not much to the purpose of the literary critic, whose chief concern is with the particularity of a work; nor is it more useful to the literary historian, despite his greater interest in establishing literary types and the general qualities of a literary period. For example, we know that the use of the wind in Romantic poetry had ample precedent in myth, religion, and the poetry of religious meditation. Yet the correspondent breeze, like the guilt-haunted wanderer and the Promethean or Satanic figure of the heroic rebel, can justly be identified as a distinctively Romantic image, or icon. For one thing, there is no precedent for the way in which the symbolic wind was called upon by poet after poet, in poem after poem, all within the first few decades of the nineteenth century. For another, the fact that they explored the literary possibilities of myth and primitive thinking, and played secular variations on ancient devotional patterns, is itself characteristic of the Romantic poets. But above all, these writers exploited attributes of the wind which rendered it peculiarly apt for the philosophical, political, and aesthetic preoccupations of the age.

Thus Wordsworth's are, specifically, "viewless winds," which are "unseen though not inaudible," [17] and Shelley's wind is an "unseen presence." When Blake denounced "Single vision and Newton's sleep," and Coleridge warned repeatedly against "the despotism of the eye," and Wordsworth, recalling his joy "before the winds, And roaring waters, and in lights and shades," decried the "bodily eye" as "the most despotic of our senses," all attributed to an obsession with what is materially visible the diverse shortcomings of the eighteenth century, from its sensationist philosophy to its theory and practice of the arts.[18] The wind, as an invisible power known only by its effects, had an even greater part to play than water, light, and clouds in the Romantic revolt against the worldview of the Enlightenment. In addition, the moving air lent itself preeminently to the aim of tying man back into the environment from which, Wordsworth and Coleridge felt, he had been divorced by post-Cartesian dualism and mechanism. For not only are nature's breezes the analogue of human respiration; they are themselves inhaled into the body and assimilated to its substance — the "breezes and soft airs," as Wordsworth said, "find [their] way To the recesses of the soul," and so fuse materially, as well as metaphorically, the "soul" of man with the "spirit" of nature. Lastly, the Romantic wind is typically a wild wind and a free one — Shelley's "thou uncontrollable" — which, even when gentle, holds the threat of destructive violence. Wordsworth's "gentle breeze," greeted as messenger and friend by a captive "coming from a house Of bondage, from yon City's walls set free," soon, like the breeze in Coleridge's Dejection, mounts to "a tempest. . . . Vexing its own creation." These traits made the windstorm, as it had been earlier, a ready counterpart for the prophetic furor of the inspired poet. But they also rendered it a most eligible model for Romantic activism, as well as an emblem of the free Romantic spirit; and in an era obsessed with the fact and idea of revolution, they sanctioned a parallel, manifest in Shelley, with a purifying revolutionary violence which destroys in order to preserve.[19] The Romantic ideal, it should be added, is that of a controlled violence, of a self-ordering impetus of passion, which Coleridge described in *To Matilda Betham,* and once again by analogy to the wind:

> Poetic feelings, like the stretching boughs
> Of mighty oaks, pay homage to the gales,
> Toss in the strong winds, drive before the gust,
> Themselves one giddy storm of fluttering leaves;
> Yet, all the while self-limited, remain
> Equally near the fixed and solid trunk
> Of Truth and Nature in the howling storm,
> As in the calm that stills the aspen grove.

This sovereign order in rage is, I think, characteristic of the longer Romantic lyric at its best. The tide of the systematic derogation of that achievement seems to be receding, but it may still be worth registering the judgment that the Romantic lyric at its best is equal to the greatest.

GASTON BACHELARD

Drawers, Chests and Wardrobes

I always feel a slight shock, a certain mild, philological pain, whenever a great writer uses a word in a derogatory sense. To begin with, all words do an honest job in our everyday language, and not even the most ordinary among them, those that are attached to the most commonplace realities, lose their poetic possibilities as a result of this fact. But somehow, when Bergson uses the word "drawer," he does it disdainfully. Indeed, the word always appears in the rôle of a controversial metaphor,

SOURCE: "Drawers, Chests and Wardrobes" is from *The Poetics of Space,* translated by Maria Jolas (New York: The Orion Press, 1964), pp. 74–89. Copyright © 1964 by The Orion Press, Inc. All rights reserved. Reprinted by permission of Grossman Publishers.

giving orders and passing judgment, always in the same way. Our phi-losopher dislikes compartmented arguments.

This seems to me to be a good example for demonstrating the radical difference between image and metaphor. I shall therefore insist upon this difference before returning to my examination of the images of intimacy that are in harmony with drawers and chests, as also with all the other hiding-places in which human beings, great dreamers of locks, keep or hide their secrets.

Although there is a superabundance of metaphor in Bergson's writings, in the last analysis, his images are rare. It is as though, for him, imagina-tion were entirely metaphorical. Now a metaphor gives concrete sub-stance to an impression that is difficult to express. Metaphor is related to a psychic being from which it differs. An image, on the contrary, product of absolute imagination, owes its entire being to the imagination. Later, when I plan to go more deeply into the comparison between metaphor and image, we shall see that metaphor could not be studied phenome-nologically, and that in fact, it is not worth the trouble, since it has no phenomenological value. At the most, it is a *fabricated image,* without deep, true, genuine roots. It is an ephemeral expression. It is, or should be, one that is used only once, in passing. We must be careful, therefore, not to give it too much thought; nor should the reader think too much about it. And yet, what a success the drawer metaphor has had with Bergson's followers!

Contrary to metaphor, we can devote our reading being to an image, since it confers being upon us. In fact, the image, which is the pure prod-uct of absolute imagination, is a phenomenon of being; it is also one of the specific phenomena of the speaking creature.

II

As is well known, the drawer metaphor, in addition to certain others, such as "ready-made garments," is used by Bergson to convey the inadequacy of a philosophy of concept. Concepts are drawers in which knowledge may be classified; they are also ready-made garments which do away with the individuality of knowledge that has been experienced. The concept soon becomes lifeless thinking since, by definition, it is classified thinking.

I should like to point out a few passages which show the polemical nature of the drawer metaphor in Bergsonian philosophy.

In *L'Evolution creatrice* (1907, p. 5) we read: "Memory, as I have tried to prove,[1] is not the faculty for classifying recollections in a drawer, or writing them down in a register. Neither register nor drawer exists. . . ."

Faced with any new object, reason asks (see *L'Evolution creatrice,* p. 52) "in which of its earlier categories the new object belongs? In which ready-to-open drawer shall we put it? With which ready-made garments shall we invest it?" Because, of course, a ready-made garment suffices to clothe a poor rationalist. In the second Oxford conference of May 27, 1911 (later included in *La Pensée et le mouvant,* p. 172), Bergson shows the indigence of the image according to which there exist "here and there in the brain, keep-sake boxes that preserve fragments of the past."

In the Introduction to Metaphysics (*La Pensée et le mouvant,* p. 221) Bergson states that all Kant saw in science was "frames within frames."

He was still haunted by this metaphor when he wrote his essay entitled *La Pensée et le mouvant,* 1922, which, in many respects, summarizes his philosophy. On page 80 of the 26th edition, he says again that in memory words are not deposited "in a cerebral or any other kind of drawer."

If this were the occasion to do so, it could be demonstrated that in contemporary science, the active invention of concepts, necessitated by the evolution of scientific thinking, is greater than those determined by simple classifications that "fit into one another," as Bergson expresses it (*La Pensée et le mouvant*). In opposition to a philosophy that seeks to discover the conceptualistic features in contemporary science, the "drawer" metaphor remains a crude instrument for polemical discussion. But for our present problem, which is that of distinguishing between metaphor and image, this is an example of a metaphor that hardens and loses even the spontaneousness of the image. This is particularly noticeable in the simplified Bergsonism taught in the classrooms, where the polemical metaphor of the drawer in the filing cabinet comes back time and again in elementary analyses that set out to attack stereotyped ideas. It is even possible, when listening to certain lectures, to foresee that the drawer metaphor is about to appear. And when we sense a metaphor in advance there can be no question of imagination. This metaphor — which, I repeat, is a crude polemical instrument — together with a few others that hardly vary at all, has mechanized the debates that Bergsonians carry on with the philosophies of knowledge, particularly with what Bergson himself, using an epithet that passed quick judgment, called "dry" rationalism.

III

These rapid remarks are intended to show that a metaphor should be no more than an accident of expression, and that it is dangerous to make a thought of it. A metaphor is a false image, since it does not possess the direct virtue of an image formed in spoken revery.

A great novelist has used this Bergsonian metaphor but it was for the purpose of characterizing the psychology of an arrant fool, rather than that of a Kantian rationalist. I refer to Henri Bosco's *Monsieur Carre-Benoit à la campagne,* in which the drawer metaphor is presented in reverse: it is not the intelligence that is a filing cabinet; the filing cabinet is an intelligence.

The only piece of furniture, among all that he possessed, for which Carre-Benoit felt real affection was his solid oak filing cabinet, which he contemplated with satisfaction whenever he passed in front of it. Here, at least, was something that was reliable, that could be counted on. You saw what you were looking at and you touched what you were touching. Its proportions were what they should be, everything about it had been designed and calculated by a meticulous mind for purposes of utility. And what a marvelous tool! It replaced everything, memory as well as intelligence. In this well-fitted cube there was not an iota of haziness or shiftiness. Once you had put something in it, even if you put it a hundred or ten thousand more times, you could find it again in the twinkling of an eye, as it were. Forty-eight drawers! Enough to hold an entire well-classified world of positive knowledge. M. Carre-Benoit attributed a sort of magic power to these drawers concerning which he said that they were "the foundations of the human mind." [2]

It should not be forgotten that in the novel, this is said by a very commonplace man. But the novelist who makes him say it is an unusually gifted one. For with this filing cabinet he has succeeded in embodying the dull administrative spirit. And since stupidity must be turned to ridicule, Henri Bosco's hero has hardly spoken when, as he opens the drawers of the "august cabinet," he finds that the maid has used it as a place to put mustard, salt, rice, coffee, peas and lentils. His reasoning cabinet had become a larder.

Perhaps, after all, this image could be used to illustrate a "philosophy of having," since it may be taken both literally and figuratively. There are many erudite minds that lay in provisions. We shall see later, they say to themselves, whether or not we'll use them.

IV

By way of preamble to our positive study of images of secrecy, we began by examining a hastily formulated metaphor that does not really unite exterior realities with intimate reality. Then, in this passage from Bosco's book, we succeeded in getting a direct, characterological hold, based on a clearly outlined reality. Now we must return to our studies of the imagination, all of them positive. With the theme of drawers, chests, locks and wardrobes, we shall resume contact with the unfathomable store of daydreams of intimacy.

Wardrobes with their shelves, desks with their drawers, and chests with their false bottoms are veritable organs of the secret psychological life. Indeed, without these "objects" and a few others in equally high favor, our intimate life would lack a model of intimacy. They are hybrid objects, subject objects. Like us, through us and for us, they have a quality of intimacy.

Does there exist a single dreamer of words who does not respond to the word wardrobe? . . .

And to fine words correspond fine things, to grave-sounding words, an entity of depth. Every poet of furniture — even if he be a poet in a garret, and therefore has no furniture — knows that the inner space of an old wardrobe is deep. A wardrobe's inner space is also *intimate space,* space that is not open to just anybody.

But words carry with them obligations. Only an indigent soul would put just anything in a wardrobe. To put just anything, just any way, in just any piece of furniture, is the mark of unusual weakness in the function of inhabiting. In the wardrobe there exists a center of order that protects the entire house against uncurbed disorder. Here order reigns, or rather, this is the reign of order. Order is not merely geometrical; it can also remember the family history. A poet knew this [3]:

> *Ordonnance. Harmonie.*
> *Piles de draps de l'armoire*
> *Lavande dans le linge.*
>
> (Orderliness. Harmony.
> Piles of sheets in the wardrobe
> Lavender in the linen.)

With the presence of lavender the history of the seasons enters into the wardrobe. Indeed, lavender alone introduces a *Bergsonian durée* into the hierarchy of the sheets. Should we not wait, before using them, for them to be, as they say in France, sufficiently "lavendered"? What dreams are reserved for us if we can recall, if we can return to, the land of tranquility! Memories come crowding when we look back upon the shelf on which the lace-trimmed, batiste and muslin pieces lay on top of the heavier materials: "A wardrobe," writes Milosz,[4] "is filled with the mute tumult of memories."

Bergson did not want the faculty of memory to be taken for a wardrobe of recollections. But images are more demanding than ideas. And the most Bergsonian of his disciples, being a poet, recognized that memory is a wardrobe. The following great line was written by Charles Péguy:

> *Aux rayons de mémoire et aux temples de l'armoire* [5]
>
> (On the shelves of memory and in the temples of the wardrobe)

But the real wardrobe is not an everyday piece of furniture. It is not opened every day, and so, like a heart that confides in no one, the key is not on the door.

> — *L'armoire était sans clefs!* . . . *Sans clefs la grande armoire*
> *On regardait souvent sa porte brune et noire*
> *Sans clefs!* . . . *C'était étrange!* — *On rêvait bien des fois*
> *Aux mystères dormant entre ses flancs de bois*
> *Et l'on croyait ouir, au fond de la serrure*
> *Béante, un bruit lointain, vague et joyeux murmure.*[6]

> (The wardrobe had no keys! . . . No keys had the big wardrobe
> Often we used to look at its brown and black door
> No keys! . . . It was strange! Many a time we dreamed
> Of the mysteries lying dormant between its wooden flanks
> And we thought we heard, deep in the gaping lock
> A distant sound, a vague and joyful murmur.)

Here Rimbaud designates a perspective of hope: what good things are being kept in reserve in the locked wardrobe? This time it is filled with promise, it is something more than a family chronicle.

André Breton, with a single word, shows us the marvels of unreality by adding a blessed impossibility to the riddle of the wardrobe. In *Revolver aux cheveux blancs* (p. 110) he writes with typical surrealist imperturbability:[7]

> *L'armoire est pleine de linge*
> *Il y a même des rayons de lune que je peux déplier.*

> (The wardrobe is filled with linen
> There are even moonbeams which I can unfold.)

This carries the image to a point of exaggeration that no reasonable mind would care to attain. But exaggeration is always at the summit of any living image. And to add fantasy linen is to draw a picture, by means of a volute of words, of all the superabundant blessings that lie folded in piles between the flanks of an abandoned wardrobe. How big, how enveloping, is an old sheet when we unfold it. And how white the old table-cloth was, white as the moon on the wintry meadow! If we dream a bit, Breton's image seems perfectly natural.

Nor should we be surprised by the fact that an entity which possesses such great wealth of intimacy should be so affectionately cared for by housewives. Anne de Tourville says of a poor woodcutter's wife: "She had started rubbing, and the high-lights that played on the wardrobe cheered the heart." [8] An armoire radiates a very soft light in the room, a communicative light. It is understandable, therefore, that a poet watching the October light play over the wardrobe should write

> *Le reflet de l'armoire ancienne sous*
> *La braise du crépuscule d'octobre* [9]

(The reflection on the old wardrobe
Cast by the live coals of an October twilight.)

If we give objects the friendship they should have, we do not open a wardrobe without a slight start. Beneath its russet wood, a wardrobe is a very white almond. To open it, is to experience an event of whiteness.

V

An anthology devoted to small boxes, such as chests and caskets, would constitute an important chapter in psychology. These complex pieces that a craftsman creates are very evident witnesses of the *need for secrecy*, of an intuitive sense of hiding places. It is not merely a matter of keeping a possession well guarded. The lock doesn't exist that could resist absolute violence, and all locks are an invitation to thieves. A lock is a psychological threshold. And how it defies indiscretion when it is covered with ornaments! What "complexes" are attached to an ornamented lock! Denise Paulme [10] writes that among the Bambaras, the center of the lock is sculptured "in the form of a crocodile, or a lizard, or a turtle. . . ." The power that opens and shuts must possess the power of life, human power, or the power of a sacred animal. "And among the Dogons, in the Sudan, locks are decorated with two human figures representing the first man and first woman." [11]

But rather than challenge the trespasser, rather than frighten him by signs of power, it is preferable to mislead him. This is where boxes that fit into one another come in. The least important secrets are put in the first box, the idea being that they will suffice to satisfy his curiosity, which can also be fed on false secrets. In other words, there exists a type of cabinet work that is "complexualistic."

For many people, the fact that there should exist a homology between the geometry of the small box and the psychology of secrecy does not call for protracted comment. However, novelists occasionally make note of this homology in a few lines. One of Franz Hellens' characters, wishing to make his daughter a present, hesitates between a silk scarf and a small, Japanese lacquer box. He chooses the box "because it seems to be better suited to her reserved nature." [12] A rapid, simple notation of this kind may well escape the attention of the hurried reader. And yet it is at the very core of a strange tale, in which father and daughter hide the *same* mystery. This same mystery is heading towards the same fate, and the author applies all his talents to making us feel this identity of intimate spirits. Indeed, this is a book that should be added to a dossier on the pent-up soul, with the box for emblem. For it shows us that the psychology of reserved persons is not depicted by listing their negative attitudes, cataloguing their detachments or recounting their moments of silence!

Watch them, rather, in the moment of positive joy that accompanies the opening of a new box, like this young girl who receives implicit permis-sion from her father to hide her secrets; that is to say, to conceal her mystery. In this story by Franz Hellens, two human beings "understand" each other without a word, without knowing it, in fact. Two pent-up human beings communicate by means of the same symbol.

VI

In an earlier chapter, I stated that to say one "reads" a house or a room, makes sense. We might also say that writers let us read their treasure-boxes, it being understood that a well-calculated geometrical description is not the only way to write "a box." And yet Rilke has spoken of the pleasure he felt when he saw a box that closed well. "A box-top that is in good condition," he wrote, "with its edges unbattered, should have no other desire than to be on its box." [13] A literary critic will prob-ably ask how it was possible, in as well-written a work as the *Cahiers,* for Rilke to have overlooked such a "commonplace" as this. The objection will be overridden, however, if one accepts the germ of daydream con-tained in the gently closed box. And how far the word *desire* goes! I am reminded of an optimistic proverb according to which: "Every pot has its cover." The world would get along better if pots and covers could always stay together.

Gentle closing calls for gentle opening, and we should want life always to be well oiled.

If we "read" a Rilke box, we shall see how inevitably a secret thought encounters the box image. In a letter to Liliane,[14] Rilke wrote: "Every-thing that touches upon this ineffable experience must remain quite re-mote, or only give rise to the most cautious handling at some future time. Yes, I must admit that I imagine it taking place one day the way those heavy, imposing seventeenth-century locks work; the kind that filled the entire top of a chest with all sorts of bolts, clamps, bars and levers, while a single, easily turned key pulled this entire apparatus of defense and deterrence from its most central point. But the key is not alone. You know too that the keyholes of such chests are concealed under a button or under a leather tongue which also only responds to some secret pressure." What concrete images to express the "Open, Sesame" formula! And what secret pressure, what soft words, are needed to gain access to a spirit, to calm a Rilkean heart!

There is no doubt that Rilke liked locks. But who doesn't like both locks and keys? There is an abundant psychoanalytical literature on this theme, so that it would be easy to find documentation on the subject. For our pur-pose, however, if we emphasized sexual symbols, we should conceal the depth of the dreams of intimacy. Indeed, one is probably never more aware of the monotony of the symbols used in psychoanalysis than in such an example. When a conflict between lock and key appears in a night dream, for psychoanalysis this is a clear sign, so clear, in fact, that it cuts the story short. When we dream of locks and keys there's nothing more to confess. But poetry extends well beyond psychoanalysis on every side. From a dream it always makes a daydream. And the poetic daydream cannot content itself with the rudiments of a story; it cannot be tied to a knotty complex. The poet lives a daydream that is awake, but above all, his daydream remains in the world, facing worldly things. It gathers the universe together around and in an object. We see it open chests, or condense cosmic wealth in a slender casket. If there are jewels and precious stones in the casket, it is the past, a long past, a past that goes back through generations, that will set the poet romancing. The stones will speak of love, of course. But of power too, and fate. All of that is so much greater than a key and its lock!

The casket contains the things that are *unforgettable,* unforgettable for us, but also unforgettable for those to whom we are going to give our treasures. Here the past, the present and a future are condensed. Thus the casket is memory of what is immemorial.

If we take advantage of images to indulge in psychology, we find that every important recollection — Bergson's pure recollection — is set in its little casket. The pure recollection, the image that belongs to us alone, we do not *want* to communicate; we only give its picturesque details. Its very core, however, is our own, and we should never want to tell all there is to tell about it. This in no way resembles unconscious repression, which is an awkward form of dynamism, with symbols that are conspicuous. But every secret has its little casket, and this absolute, well-guarded secret is independent of all dynamism. Here the intimate life achieves a synthesis of Memory and Will. This is *Iron Will,* not against the outside, or against other persons, but beyond all the psychology of being "against." Surrounding certain recollections of our inner self, we have the security of an *absolute casket.*[15]

But with this absolute casket, I too am now talking in metaphors. Let's get back to our images.

VII

Chests, especially small caskets, over which we have more complete mastery, are objects *that may be opened.* When a casket is closed, it is returned to the general community of objects; it takes its place in exterior space. But it opens! For this reason, a philosopher-mathematician would say that it is the first differential of discovery. In a later chapter I plan to study the dialectics of inside and outside. But from the moment the casket is opened, dialectics no longer exist. The outside is effaced with

one stroke, an atmosphere of novelty and surprise reigns. The outside has
no more meaning. And quite paradoxically, even cubic dimensions have
no more meaning, for the reason that a new dimension — the dimension
of intimacy — has just opened up.

For someone who is a good judge of values, and who sees things from
the angle of the values of intimacy, this dimension can be an infinite one.

As proof, I should like to quote a marvelously perceptive fragment from
an article by Jean-Pierre Richard,[16] which offers a veritable theorem of the
topo-analysis of intimate space. Jean-Pierre Richard is a writer who
analyzes literary works in terms of their dominant images. Here he allows
us to relive the moment in Poe's story, *The Gold Bug,* when the casket is
opened. To begin with, the jewels found in it are of inestimable value.
They could not, of course, be "ordinary" jewels. However, the treasure
was not inventoried by a lawyer, but by a poet. It is fraught with "unknown and possible elements, it becomes again an imaginary object,
generating hypotheses and dreams, it deepens and escapes from itself
toward an infinite number of other treasures." Thus it seems that at the
moment when the story reaches its conclusion, a conclusion that is as cold
as a police record, it has lost nothing of its oneiric richness. The imagination can never say: was that all, for there is always more than meets
the eye. And as I have said several times, an image that issues from the
imagination is not subject to verification by reality.

Having achieved valorization of the contents by valorization of the
container, Jean-Pierre Richard makes the following penetrating comment: "We shall never reach the bottom of the casket." The infinite quality of the intimate dimension could not be better expressed.

Sometimes, a lovingly fashioned casket has interior perspectives that
change constantly as a result of daydream. We open it and discover that
it is a dwelling-place, that a house is hidden in it. To illustrate, there
exists a marvel of this kind in a prose poem by Charles Cros, in which
the poet carries on where the cabinet-maker left off. Beautiful objects
created by skillful hands are quite naturally "carried on" by a poet's daydream. And for Charles Cros, imaginary beings are born of the "secret" of
a marquetry casket.

"In order to detect its mystery, in order to go beyond the perspectives of
marquetry, to reach the imaginary world through the little mirrors," one
had to possess a "rapid glance, fine hearing, and be keenly attentive."
Indeed, the imagination sharpens all of our senses. The imagining attention prepares our attention for instantaneousness.

And the poet continues: "Finally I caught a glimpse of the clandestine festivity. I heard the tiny minuets, I guessed the complicated web
of entanglements that was being woven inside the casket.

"The doors open, and we see what appears to be a parlor for insects,
the white, brown and black floors are seen in exaggerated perspective." [17]

But when the poet closes the casket, inside it, he sets a nocturnal world into motion (p. 88).

"When the casket is closed, when the ears of the importunate are stopped with sleep, or filled with outside noises, when the thoughts of men dwell upon some positive object,

"Then strange scenes take place in the casket's parlor, several persons of unwonted size and appearance step forth from the little mirrors."

This time, in the darkness of the casket, it is the enclosed reflections that reproduce objects. The inversion of interior and exterior is experienced so intensely by the poet that it brings about an inversion of objects and reflections.

And once more, after dreaming of this tiny parlor enlivened by the dancing of figurines of another day, the poet opens the casket (p. 90): "The lights go out, the guests, composed of belles and their beaux, and a few aging relatives, disappear pell-mell, into the mirrors and along the corridors and colonnades, without giving a thought to their dignity, while chairs and tables and hangings evaporate into thin air.

"And the parlor remains empty, silent and clean." Serious minded persons may then say with the poet, "It's a marquetry casket, and that's all." Echoing this reasonable opinion, the reader who is averse to playing with inversions of large and small, exterior and intimacy, may also say: "It's a poem and that's all." "And nothing more." [18]

In reality, however, the poet has given concrete form to a very general psychological theme, namely, that there will always be more things in a closed, than in an open, box. To verify images kills them, and it is always more enriching to *imagine* than to *experience*.

The action of the secret passes continually from the hider of things to the hider of self. A casket is a dungeon for objects. And here is a dreamer who feels that he shares the dungeon of its secret. We should like to open it, and we should also like to open our hearts. The following lines by Jules Supervielle can be read in a dual sense: [19]

> *Je cherche dans des coffres qui m'entourent brutalement*
> *Mettant des ténèbres sens dessus dessous*
> *Dans des caisses profondes, profondes*
> *Comme si elles n'étaient plus de ce monde.*

> (Roughly I search in coffers that surround me
> Putting disarray in the darkness
> Of cases that are deep, deep
> As though they had departed this life.)

He who buries a treasure buries himself with it. A secret is a grave, and it is not for nothing that a man who can be trusted with a secret boasts that he is "like the grave."

All intimacy hides from view, and I recall that the late Joë Bousquet wrote:[20] "No one sees me changing. But who sees me? I am my own hiding-place."

It is not my intention, in this volume, to recall the problem presented by the intimacy of substances, which I have outlined elsewhere.[21] I shall, however, point out the nature of the two dreamers who seek the intimacy of man and the intimacy of matter. Jung has shown very clearly this correspondence between dreamers of alchemy (cf. *Psychologie und Alchemie*). In other words, there is only one *place* for the *superlative* element of what is *hidden*. The hidden in men and the hidden in things belong in the same topo-analysis, as soon as we enter into this strange region of the *superlative*, which is a region that has hardly been touched by psychology. And to tell the truth, all positivity makes the superlative fall back upon the comparative. To enter into the domain of the superlative, we must leave the positive for the imaginary. We must listen to poets.

DONALD DAVIE

On The Pisan Cantos

. . . It may be said that W. B. Yeats shares with the symbolist poets, and with a poet squarely in their tradition, such as T. S. Eliot, an imperious, appropriating attitude toward the perceived world. When swans get into Yeats's verse, the swan loses all its swanliness except what it needs to symbolize something in the person who observes it: "Another emblem there!" And the poet at the end of "Coole Park and Ballylee" says explicitly that this is also what has happened to Lady Gregory. Similarly, Frank Kermode has demonstrated how far "In Memory of Major Robert

SOURCE: From *Ezra Pound: Poet as Sculptor* by Donald Davie. Copyright © 1964 by Donald Davie. Reprinted by permission of Oxford University Press, Inc., and Routledge and Kegan Paul Ltd. The passages from W. B. Yeats' "In Memory of Major Robert Gregory" are reprinted with permission of The Macmillan Company, Mr. M. B. Yeats, Macmillan & Co., Ltd., and the Macmillan Company of Canada Ltd., from *The Collected Poems of W. B. Yeats*. Copyright 1919 by The Macmillan Company, renewed 1947 by Bertha Georgie Yeats. The passages by Ezra Pound are from Ezra Pound, *The Cantos*. Copyright 1948 by Ezra Pound. Reprinted by permission of New Directions Publishing Corporation and Faber and Faber Ltd.

Gregory" is concerned with Major Gregory, much less for what he is or was in himself than for what the poet chooses to make him stand for in his (the poet's) private pantheon. It is for this reason, to give an example, that Gregory's activities as a landscape painter are made so salient — so that Yeats may applaud this imperious attitude to the natural world at just the point where it would seem least likely, in landscape painting:

> We dreamed that a great painter had been born
> To cold Clare rock and Galway rock and thorn,
> To that stern colour and that delicate line
> That are our secret discipline
> Wherein the gazing heart doubles her might.

We attend to natural landscape, not for the sake of delighting in it, nor for what it may tell us of supernatural purpose or design, but so that the imperious personality, seeing itself there reflected, may become the more conscious of its own power — "the gazing heart doubles her might." As Marion Witt was first to show, Yeats intends here to relate Gregory's practice as a landscape painter with that of Samuel Palmer and Edward Calvert, the nineteenth-century artists who, true to the Blakean tradition, which was Yeats's tradition also, reject the discipline that is the scientist's as much as the artist's, exact and intent observation, setting up instead the discipline of the visionary, who sees through the perceivable to what lies beyond.

This is a matter not of mutually exclusive categories but only of where the emphasis characteristically falls. For examples of vivid and exact observation can, of course, be found in Yeats the visionary; and conversely Ezra Pound, who characteristically sees scientific observation as not at all at odds with the poet's kind of attention, also shows himself sympathetic to the Platonist John Heydon ("Secretary of Nature, J. Heydon," in Canto 91) who attends to natural appearances only so as to read them as "signatures" of the realm of essence. The point is best made, therefore, by quotation from Canto 83:

> and Brother Wasp is building a very neat house
> of four rooms, one shaped like a squat indian bottle
> La vespa, *la* vespa, mud, swallow system
> So that dreaming of Bracelonde and of Perugia
> and the great fountain in the Piazza
> or of old Bulagaio's cat that with a well timed leap
> could turn the lever-shaped door handle
> It comes over me that Mr. Walls must be a ten-strike
> with the signorinas
> and in the warmth after chill sunrise
> an infant, green as new grass,

has stuck its head or tip
out of Madame La Vespa's bottle

mint springs up again
in spite of Jones' rodents
as had the clover by the gorilla cage
with a four-leaf

When the mind swings by a grass-blade
an ant's forefoot shall save you
the clover leaf smells and tastes as its flower

The infant has descended
from mud on the tent roof to Tellus,
like to like colour he goes amid grass-blades
greeting them that dwell under XTHONOS XΘΟΝΟΣ
ΟΙ ΧΘΟΝΙΟΙ; to carry our news
εἰς χθονίους to them that dwell under the earth,
begotten of air, that shall sing in the bower
of Kore,   Περσεψόνεια
and have speech with Tiresias, Thebae

If we say that neither Yeats nor Eliot could have written this passage, we
should have in mind, not in the first place any question of poetic method
or strategy, but the quality of the sensibility, the sort of attitude and attention to the natural world, that is here displayed. It is not helpful to
recall Wordsworth and "a heart/That watches and receives," for this sort
of contemplation is as much an active participation of the mind as are
the more imperious operations of a Yeats.[1] One is reminded rather of
passages in Coleridge's and Ruskin's notebooks, in some of the letters of
Keats, in the essays and poems of D. H. Lawrence, above all in the writings of Hopkins. In fact, what lies behind a passage such as this (and
they occur throughout the Cantos, though seldom at such length) is an attitude of mind that is incompatible with the symbolist poet's liberation
of himself from the laws of time and space as those operate in the observable world. In order to achieve that liberation the poet had to forego
any hope or conviction that the world outside himself was meaningful
precisely insofar as it existed in its own right, something other than himself and bodied against him. There is all the difference in the world between identifying a swan with one's self, and identifying one's self with
a swan. It may be the difference between Shelley's "Ode to a Skylark"
(where the lark is important because it is identified with Shelley) and a
famous letter by Keats in which he identifies himself with a sparrow
(where the sparrow is important because Keats can identify himself with
it, and so explore an order of being other than his own.) Pound identifies
himself with the baby wasp as Keats with the sparrow. The wasp bur-
rows into the earth to greet the chthonic powers of under-earth, just as

Odysseus, in the *Odyssey* and time and again in the *Cantos,* must descend to the underworld to consult the Theban sage Tiresias. But at no point in the passage — not even if we remember how important for Pound, as for Lawrence, is such encountering of the chthonic powers of the loins and the libido — at no point does the wasp become a symbol for something in Pound's predicament, or for his ethical or other programs, or for his personality. The wasp retains its otherness as an independent form of life; it is only by doing so that it can be a source of comfort to the human observer:

> When the mind swings by a grass-blade
> an ant's forefoot shall save you

For, only if the ant is outside the human mind, can it, as we say, "take us out of ourselves" when we observe it and try to enter into its life. This quality of tenderness, and this capacity for sympathetic identification with inhuman forms of life, make up an attitude of reverent vigilance before the natural world, an attitude which, if it is no longer the attitude of the physicist, is still surely the habit of the biologist, in the field and the laboratory alike.

These are not the terms in which Pound is usually considered, partly because these are not the terms in which he talks of himself; nor is this lineage — Coleridge, Keats, Ruskin, Hopkins — the sort of family tree that Pound draws up for himself. Moreover, it is taken for granted that, if Pound has any claim on our attention at all, it is for what he has in common with Yeats and Eliot, not for that in him which distinguishes him from his old allies, whose names are so much more respectable. Yet it should be clear that if this sort of attention is not to be found in Yeats, it is unthinkable in Eliot, as in any man whose main interest in the external world is as a repertoire of objective correlatives for his own states of mind. "Old Possum's Book of Favourite Cats," for instance, is Eliot's one venture into light verse; and the assumption behind it, that cats cannot be taken seriously in poetry, seems arbitrary when set beside the seriousness on just this subject of Christopher Smart, for instance, or Baudelaire. Pound's cat, "Old Bulagaio's cat that with a well-timed leap/ could turn the lever-shaped door handle" ("lever-shaped" — the exact observation anticipating the natural question, "how?") is more alive, more of a cat, than any of Eliot's.

Almost from the first, sure enough, Pound has defined his poetry as radically opposed to symbolist poetry. He confesses to having learned from Laforgue and from Corbière, still more from Rimbaud; but these poets he obviously does not regard as "symbolist." He claims to have learned much more from the non-symbolist Théophile Gautier than even from Rimbaud — a claim that J. J. Espey, in his book on *Hugh Selwyn*

Mauberley, shows to be well founded. Pound puts it on record "que les poètes *essentiels* [as texts for English poets to study] se réduisent à Gautier, Corbière, Laforgue, Rimbaud. Que depuis Rimbaud, aucun poète en France n'a inventé rien de fondamental." [2] In 1918 he writes that "Mallarmé, perhaps unread, is apt to be sightly overestimated . . ." [3] and that "Imagisme is not symbolism. The symbolists dealt in 'association,' that is, in a sort of allusion, almost of allegory. They degraded the symbol to the status of a word. . . ." "Moreover," he says, writing in the period of the First World War, "one does not want to be called a symbolist, because symbolism has usually been associated with mushy technique" (*Gaudier-Brzeska,* p. 97).

Yeats and Pound were close and constant friends, and some of Pound's remarks on symbolism are beside the point because, like many people since, he takes Yeats as a typical symbolist; and this is far from the truth. In the Pisan Canto 83 there are two passages on Yeats. One of them, which follows almost immediately the page of sympathetic identification with the baby wasp, is Pound's hilarious account of the life at Stone Cottage, Coleman's Hatch, Sussex, where Yeats and Pound lived together at several periods between 1913 and 1916:

> There is fatigue deep as the grave.
> The Kakemono grows in flat land out of mist
> > sun rises lop-sided over the mountain
> > > so that I recalled the noise in the chimney
> as it were the wind in the chimney
> > but was in reality Uncle William
> downstairs composing
> that had made a great Peeeeacock
> > in the proide ov his oiye
> > had made a great peeeeeeecock in the . . .
> made a great peacock
> > in the proide of his oyyee
>
> proide ov his oy-ee
> as indeed he had, and perdurable
>
> a great peacock aere perennius
> > or as in the advice to the young man to
> breed and get married (or not)
> > as you choose to regard it
>
> at Stone Cottage in Sussex by the waste moor
> (or whatever) and the holly bush
> > who would not eat ham for dinner
> because peasants eat ham for dinner
> > despite the excellent quality
> and the pleasure of having it hot

well those days are gone forever
    and the travelling rug with the coon-skin tabs
and his hearing nearly all Wordsworth
    for the sake of his conscience but
preferring Ennemosor on Witches

did we ever get to the end of Doughty:
    The Dawn in Britain?
                    perhaps not
(Summons withdrawn, sir.)
(bein' aliens in prohibited area)
clouds lift their small mountains
   before the elder hills

The fineness of this is identical with the fineness of the passage on the wasp. The whole man, Yeats, is carried before us; we delight, as the poet has delighted, in his alien mode of being. His foibles, recorded with affectionate and amused indulgence — his way of *keening* rather than reading poetry, his "Gothick" interests ("preferring Ennemosor on Witches"), his preposterous snobbery ("because peasants eat ham for dinner") — do not in the least detract from, they only substantiate, the perception of his greatness. Out of this personality, with all its quirky eccentricities, comes something in the splendid Horatian phrase "aere perennius," more lasting than bronze, equal in its achieved conclusiveness to the metal singing-bird of Yeats's own "Byzantium" and to those sonnets by Shakespeare ("the advice to the young man to/breed and get married"), where Shakespeare himself makes the proud Horatian claim,

    Not marble, nor the gilded monuments
    Of princes, shall outlive this powerful rhyme;

It should be plain that this is very far indeed, in human terms, from Yeats's treatment of the Gregories, the Pollexfens, John O'Leary, Lionel Johnson, John Synge. It manifests a respect for the uniqueness and otherness of the other person, a flexibility of feeling incompatible with the Yeatsian private pantheon and his deliberately noble style, even in such a splendid poem as "The Municipal Gallery Revisited."

    The other passage on Yeats in Canto 83 is shorter, but more immediately apposite, for it considers Yeats specifically as a symbolist, and at this point not unfairly:

              Le Paradis n'est pas artificiel
    and Uncle William dawdling around Notre Dame
    in search of whatever
                  paused to admire the symbol
    with Notre Dame standing inside it

> Whereas in St Etienne
> or why not Dei Miracoli:
> mermaids, that carving,
>
> in the drenched tent there is quiet
> sered eyes are at rest

"Le Paradis Artificiel" is the title of a book by Baudelaire about drugs and the beautific hallucinations they induce. Pound's rejection of the assumption behind its sounds as one of the strongest of many refrains that knit the later cantos together; it reappears, for instance, in an especially moving way in the Rock-Drill Canto 92. Pound's repeated assertion that the paradisal is *real,* out there in the real world, is a conscious challenge to the whole symbolist aesthetic. Hugh Kenner's gloss on this passage makes the essential point: "Yeats' incorrigibly symbologizing mind infected much of his verse with significance imposed on materials by an effort of will ('artificiel'). . . ." [4] Yeats can see Notre Dame as an artifact, a presence created in masonry and sculpture, only inside the symbol, only for the sake of what it answers to in him, not for what it is in itself. He must always arrange the perspective, and project upon the object the significance he can then read out of it. For Pound, to whom, ever since his friendship with Gaudier-Brzeska, cut and worked stone has been an especially fruitful source of presences and inscapes, this attitude is intolerable. Only when he sees stone in and for itself, the artist's working of it only a drawing out of what was latent in the stone to begin with — only then, as in the sculptures of S. Maria dei Miracoli in Venice, can it save him as the ant's forefoot could save him. Only by contemplating it thus can the "sered eyes" (both "seared" and "fallen into the sere, the yellow leaf") come to be "at rest."

DENIS DONOGHUE

Yeats and the Living Voice

For better or worse the high poetry of this century has proceeded on Symbolist lines; the poetry we agree to call "modern" in a sense in which *Prufrock and Other Observations* is modern and *Three Taverns* is not. The modern poet deals with experience by treating it as a plane surface upon which selected images are placed in silent juxtaposition: he takes his bearings from the landscape painting or the visual field, where images are ranged about like flags on a military map. Visual metaphors, visual analogies; the crucial moment is the moment of vision, when all the images are held in focus by the poet's imagination. Indeed, it is characteristic of Symbolism to identify Imagination with Vision: it was Milton's alleged lack of visual imagination that distressed Eliot in a famous encounter. The Symbolist poet assumes that meaning is available as a visual pattern, often a pattern imposed by the imagination. This accounts for our sluggishness in coming to terms with poets who live by a different allegiance; as Whitman's allegiance — a point already urged — is contact, and Yeats's is action. Marshall McLuhan has argued that the invention of the printing press and the corresponding change from an oral to a typographic culture have specialized our modes of knowledge; our minds work by seeing meanings as we see black marks on a white page without hearing the sounds for which they stand. The evidence is not fully convincing; there are problems. But it is hard to refute. In our present context it would link silent reading, spatial analogies, the promotion of sight over its four sensory colleagues, the book as a solid object rather than a transcript of speech, the poem as a well-wrought urn.[1] There is clearly a direct relation between this aspect of Symbolism and the primacy of the "closed system" as the modern image of knowledge. If we feel that a certain play by Pinter or Albee is "untrue," that is, morally

SOURCE: "Yeats and the Living Voice" is from *The Ordinary Universe: Soundings in Modern Literature* (New York: Macmillan, 1968), pp. 125–45. Copyright © 1968 by Denis Donoghue. Reprinted by permission of The Macmillan Company and Faber and Faber, Ltd. Poetry by Yeats is reprinted by permission of A. P. Watt and Son, The Macmillan Company, M. B. Yeats. Lines from *The Waste Land* are from T. S. Eliot, *Collected Poems 1909–1962*. Reprinted by permission of the publishers, Harcourt Brace Jovanovich and Faber and Faber Ltd.

nasty, a libel against life, it is very difficult to say so; because the prevailing meaning of "true" is "consistent with its own terms." Truth is the law which obtains within a closed system. The play is true in that sense; but it may be damnably false, a travesty, in the old sense.

A further word about the assumptions of Symbolism. The traditional poets invariably assumed that the grammatical structure which we call the sentence was an excellent instrument for the representation of reality. Composing a sentence was an act of faith, in one sense; you dedicated yourself to the proposition that the mind could deal with experience in that way by directing a flow of energy through a subject, a verb, and an object. If this seemed too rigid, you could complicate the report by bringing one sentence to bear upon another. The Symbolist, by and large, rejects this belief. Valéry is a case in point. The assumption that generates all his writings on literature and art is that a bourgeois demon resides in grammar and syntax and must be defeated. Syntax and grammar are always on the side of the common man because they serve his purposes. The poet must therefore use all his sceptical intelligence to thwart this demon, twisting the language into configurations from which there is no "practical" escape. Valéry also argued that the daily forms of language try to impose themselves upon the poet by insinuating the attitudes they imply: again the true poet will defeat the attitudes by resisting the grammatical forms. There are several possibilities. He can pretend to take the attitudes seriously while using them as grist for his mill. He can deny commitment in the words by locating expressiveness in the "presence" which is the poetic form; in the *being* of the poem as a force beyond its *meaning*. He can exalt the uselessness of art. He can deflect the reader's attention from the stubborn reference of the words. He can push poetry toward the condition of music, thereby defeating the aims of the practical world. The ideal poetic language is a systematic deviation from the daily forms and it is carried on with subversive intent. The poet can also resort to parody: by pretending to speak in sentences he can parody the pretention of their structure, as Eliot does so often. When the visionary Tiresias says, near the end of "The Waste Land":

> A woman drew her long black hair out tight
> And fiddled whisper music on those strings. . . .

it would be foolish to ascribe even a notional existence to this woman or to conclude from the use of the past tense that she might have been encountered thus engaged in London or Vienna. If we take her as a domesticated version of the maenad in the "Ode to the West Wind" or perhaps as one of the mermaids in "Prufrock," this is as far as we should presume upon her reality. Indeed, the best comment upon her is that passage in *Modern Painters* in which Ruskin distinguishes between the true grotesque and the false grotesque which he finds in the griffin on the Temple of Antoninus and Faustina at Rome:

"A fine grotesque is the expression, in a moment, by a series of symbols thrown together in bold and fearless connection, of truths which it would have taken a long time to express in any verbal way, and of which the connection is left for the beholder to work out by himself; the gaps, left or overleaped by the haste of the imagination, forming the grotesque character." [2]

Ruskin goes on to say that this is the third form of the grotesque, "art arising from the confusion of the imagination by the presence of truths which it cannot wholly grasp." And he argues that this is a noble form. We should not doubt him. It would be unwise to assume that Eliot's imagination was confused by the presence of truths which it could not wholly grasp. The nobility of the figure is beyond dispute; its nature remains opaque. The black-haired woman is a correlative object and therefore an important point on an emotional map. She is not in any sense verifiable: she has emblematic status in the landscape of the poem, but no other status. She is an event within a closed system. The words set up a network of associations, organized with great daring, and the network is engrossing as rhythms may be engrossing, but it refers to nothing; it constitutes the only reality there is, for the life of the poem. To the extent that the words "work," we are the music while the music lasts. The bold and fearless connexion of the words has far more to do with their internal resources, the relation between one vowel and another, assonance, and so on, than with anything "there." So this poetry is not essentially different from the systematic deviations encouraged by Valéry's aesthetic. (Not by Valéry's own poems, incidentally.) In fact, it works on the same assumption, that the traditional grammar of sentences is merely a mental category, one of many, and that it has no special qualifications in the confrontation of human life. Poets like Valéry resent these categories and resist their bourgeois influence. For proof, they point to the chaos of actual life. Hence the Symbolist poet disengages his poem from all responsibility to quotidian life by making it an object, an icon, a mobile floating free and pure in air. He demands, in the medium of words, the same degree of freedom which is accorded, in stone, to Barbara Hepworth or Henry Moore. When he proceeds from one thing to another, the movement is subject to his own laws, and these are much more permissive than those of logic, syllogism, grammar, or plot. In "The Fire Sermon" when the woman puts a record on the gramophone and Eliot gives, as the next line, a famous sentence from *The Tempest,* "This music crept by me upon the water," the only law at work is that of association, one music calls to another from a different moral world. The meaning of the passage is whatever happens in the reader's mind when he holds these two situations together, simultaneously, for contemplation. The lines mean as a sculpture means, by constituting an autonomous event for which the artist takes full responsibility. We cannot say that the procedure is either right or wrong, but we can say that it is arbitrary. We can also say, more generally, that the characteristic hazard of the Symbolist poet is that, as Yeats said of someone, he is helpless before the contents of his own mind. If you make language as independent as possible; if you think of it as a poor relation to music and hope to improve it by cultivating musical manners; you can never do this as thoroughly as the musicians, and you are unlikely to do much better than the Pure Poets. Indeed, Symbolism is merely Pure Poetry writ a little larger. The characteristic Symbolist frustration is the discovery that music and poetry are different; that words will drag their daily reference into the purest mansions of your poetry.

The only other alternative, it would seem, is to acknowledge a reality not yourself, not your Supreme Fiction, a reality independent of your consciousness. You can even acknowledge that it was there before you came and may survive your departure. After these acknowledgements it is much easier to think of language as an instrument by which a man mediates between himself and a world not himself; an instrument in the service of a reality that is not linguistic. If you go so far you will probably value the mental categories and share the allegiance that frames a sentence. This constitutes an act of faith, and there is no point in minimizing its implications. In the third Book of *Endymion* Keats speaks of "the feud/'Twixt Nothing and Creation." If we hold this phrase beside the history of modern Symbolism we see that for the Symbolist poet there is, strictly, Nothing; or rather, nothing but the human imagination, the strictly creative power. So that the poet becomes God, creating out of nothing. Wallace Stevens's poem, "Another Weeping Woman," speaks of

> The magnificent cause of being,
> The imagination, the one reality
> In this imagined world. . . .[3]

and another Stevens poem, "Tea at the Palaz of Hoon," invokes ointment, hymns, and the sea only to say

> Out of my mind the golden ointment rained,
> And my ears made the blowing hymns they heard.
> I was myself the compass of that sea:
>
> I was the world in which I walked, and what I saw
> Or heard or felt came not but from myself;
> And there I found myself more truly and more strange.

This is Stevens in one of his extreme moments, and it does not prevent him from having other moments in which he makes at least a provisional act of realist faith. In the fifth part of "The Comedian as the Letter C" he arranges that Crispin will discover for himself that

> The words of things entangle and confuse.
> The plum survives its poems.

Crispin lays aside the rebellious thought, he will rest in the decision not to set up as God or to challenge God. But the tendency of Symbolist poetry is to assume, not that the plum survives its poems, but that the very existence of a plum depends upon the goodwill of the poet and the hospitality of the poem: the poet invents a plum and gives it housing room in his poem, as God created man from nothing but divine goodwill and made a world in which man might live. This is the real difference between the Symbolist poet and the poet for whom reality, such as it is, is "given." Stevens is the kind of poet who, when faced with an "either-or" situation, opted for "both"; he could not bear to relinquish any mode of the imagination, any possibility of the mind; hence he preferred a dozen provisional beliefs to the imperative of a single belief, largely because the first arrangement gave his imagination more work to do. . . .

Yeats's part in this dispute is our theme. True, he flirted with the theory of Symbolism and made some attempts to understand it with the aid of Arthur Symons, but it was always an alien tongue. Besides, he had his own way of clearing spaces in which he might live. In his later years he recognized that Symbolism was a foreign device and he rejected it, notably in some of his last letters to Dorothy Wellesley. His chief objection to it was that it tried to disengage itself from time and history. But I would argue that the force which kept Yeats from joining the modern Symbolists was the persuasion of a native culture which he loved and hated and only barely understood.

We need not make this a chauvinistic occasion. On the other hand it is clear that Symbolism and the Irish tradition run in opposite directions. For one thing, Symbolism is visual; Irish literature is oral. Symbolism creates a mystique of the Book; Irish literature transcribes a world of sound. Symbolism aspires to the fixity of the sculptured object, freeing itself from responsibility to people, places, and things; Irish literature is devoted to these, and content to survive in a long memory. In "Literature and the Living Voice" Yeats said:

"Irish poetry and Irish stories were made to be spoken or sung, while English literature, alone of great literatures, because the newest of them all, has all but completely shaped itself in the printing-press. In Ireland today the old world that sang and listened is, it may be for the last time in Europe, face to face with the world that reads and writes, and their antagonism is always present under some name or other in Irish imagination and intellect." [4]

That was in 1904, and it explains why Synge went to the Aran Islands, to listen, to move in a world of sound. It also explains why Joyce's greatest gesture of repudiation was not his leaving Dublin; it was his determination to put everything into a *book,* and to make that a more bookish book than any book had ever been.

Yeats was not prepared to do this. He wanted, after all, a relation to a specific people. In "All Souls' Night" he would invoke

> Such thought, that in it bound
> I need no other thing,
> Wound in mind's wandering
> As mummies in the mummy-cloth are wound . . .

but he knew that this security was available only to the dead and that the living are unappeased. And like Synge he chose the living world for text. Think how often he envied those strong, simple men like Thomas Davis and John O'Leary who spoke directly to the Irish people by offering them strong, simple images. Think how often this problematic poet tried to write a ballad, a strong, simple story to coax into life those capable of responding to it. That he never had a genuine touch for the ballad makes his devotion to it the more remarkable. As early as "The Ballad of Moll Magee," as late as "Colonel Martin" he reached for a direct relation to a simple audience. And think how often he revelled in those situations in which people are gripped by the same image: it might be a revolution, a speech, or a meeting of the Galway races:

> There where the course is,
> Delight makes all of the one mind,
> The riders upon the galloping horses,
> The crowd that closes in behind. . . .

Yeats would try to achieve a similar cohesion in his own poetry by offering his sense of life in massive archetypes; the fisherman, the beggar, the fool, the hermit, the hunchback, the saint, the lover. On those occasions he would take his bearings from the Irish folk-tales provided for him by Lady Gregory and Douglas Hyde, where charm, magic, and prophecy run together. In "Ideas of Good and Evil" he says: "Whatever the passions of men have gathered about, becomes a symbol in the Great Memory, and in the hands of him who has the secret it is a worker of wonders, a caller-up of angels or of devils." And to complete this he says: ". . . that literature dwindles to a mere chronicle of circumstance, or passionless fantasies, and passionless meditations, unless it is constantly flooded with the passions and beliefs of ancient times."

For this reason, he says further, the Celtic element has again and again "brought the 'vivifying spirit' of 'excess' into the arts of Europe." [5] The general argument may or may not be true. What we should emphasize is simply this; that Yeats found in Celtic folk-tales a great "excess," a free range of the imagination, a flow of passionate experience, incorrigibly temporal, which he feared was lost in modern literature. We tend to smile, these days, at Yeats's traffic with legendary heroes, and yet our smile is idle and a little vulgar. When Yeats spoke of magical events he invoked and praised all those possibilities of the spirit for which there is no other explanation than the passion that incites them; and it was the passion he revered. By comparison, he thought his own time puny and timid, the work of the counting-house, except when it flowered beyond prediction in a great act, like the Easter Rising in 1916.

If we agree that Yeats's poems are concerned with the possibility of a completely human life — which he often invoked as Unity of Being — then the importance of the Irish tradition to that concern becomes clear. The old Irish stories are the speech of person to person: once that convention is established there is no limit to the range of imagination, fantasy, recklessness. The stories transcend the bounds of realism as easily as they invent a character, but it is always a human invention, even when they revel in linguistic exuberance. Indeed, we can put this more directly. An oral culture commits itself to the human situation in a sense that Symbolism tries to evade. It assumes the integrity of the Person and the validity of temporal life: it has no interest in the inscrutable silence of Symbolism. What Yeats missed in modern literature, besides "excess," was "emotion of multitude," a resonance of feeling which is primitive and fundamental. The modern well-made play or poem could have everything necessary for high art, he said, except emotion of multitude: unless it somehow touched and stirred that deep, primitive sense of life, it was bound to be meagre, superficial.

I am arguing that Yeats sought emotion of multitude and excess and found them in Celtic legends and never released himself from the human images they sponsored. If he revered the aristocratic hauteur it was because this was the nearest gesture he could find in history to the excess he found in legend. This partly explains one of the chief differences between the poems of Yeats and of Eliot. If we think of characteristic poems by Eliot, we can easily imagine them as paintings, or sculptures, or string quartets: this is what we mean, after all, when we say in some desperation that "The Waste Land" has Cubist form. But Yeats's characteristic poems are cries, laments, prayers, stories, legends, rebukes; human sounds rather than objects. This does not mean that he neglected to "make" his poems. It means that the making of a poem, for him, largely consisted in making the sounds more and more responsive to a human occasion, real or imagined. In the "General Introduction to My Work" he said that he tried to make the language of his poems "coincide with that of passionate, normal speech." "It was a long time," he said, "before I had made a language to my liking; I began to make it when I discovered some twenty years ago that I must seek, not as Wordsworth thought, words in common use, but a powerful and passionate syntax, and a complete coincidence between period and stanza." [6]

We must try to be more specific about this. Yeats wanted a language capable of registering the full life of man; body and soul, matter and spirit. He might have wished for a better reality than the one proffered by his senses, but he laboured with the given, with "the sigh of what is." The human situation, to Yeats, is the place of long memory, where values are audible from generation to generation. This, indeed, is Tradition.

Tradition as Voice. Eliot spoke of Tradition as if it were a visual field upon which the great works of the past figure as "monuments"; it is his own word in "Tradition and the Individual Talent." The genuinely new work that makes a difference is then inserted, placed on the field, and it alters the map; the entire configuration is changed. A man takes intellectual possession of his tradition, then, by inspecting it and taking in a simultaneous impression of the monuments laid out on the ground. But Yeats thought of tradition in quite different terms; as a choir of voices in which the new voice is heard. The values of the past are not seen or inspected, they are heard, passed along through the generations in story, song, and rhyme. A race is unified because the passions of its people have gathered around a few images. The continuity of these passions is the emotion of multitude. This is what Tradition means, the concert of passions and the images that engage them. The individual talent is the "excess," the flare of personality.

This explains why Yeats resorted to the drama. There is no more accomplished form for the representation of human life as a fully engaged experience, with all the faculties working at full stretch. Drama is the imitation of an action, we are told; action, not vision or consciousness. It is committed to the body, to gesture, to the paradigm of conflict, to beginning, middle, and end. It cannot easily reduce itself to a single faculty; or if it does, the reduction is immediately clear. Drama works by the justice of rival voices; it does not favour the fixed point of view. (And we recall again from the "General Introduction" Yeats's remark: "I hated and still hate with an ever growing hatred the literature of the point of view.") But above all, drama presents human life in the image of bodies in animation: in that sense it is the most human art. We often think that Yeats's plays are impossibly rarefied: we think this until we see them well played, and then we find that except for the very earliest plays they are much more resilient, much harder than their literary reputation has suggested.

Indeed, it is quite wrong to think of Yeats's plays as if they were trans-

lations of Maeterlinck; just as it is wrong to think that his dealings with
the Japanese Noh drama were merely exotic intellectual excursions. The
fact is that he wanted a form of drama which would be simple, direct,
stark, and which would get rid of the "furniture" of the modern well-made
European play. He wanted to throw out the furniture, the mimicry, the
busy acting. But he was always certain that drama is true because it is
dynamic; it is the dynamic element which bridges the gap between consciousness and experience. This is what he had in mind in that passage
in "The Irish Dramatic Movement" in which he wrote:

"There are two kinds of poetry, and they are commingled in all the
greatest works. When the tide of life sinks low there are pictures, as in
the 'Ode on a Grecian Urn' and in Virgil at the plucking of the Golden
Bough. The pictures make us sorrowful. We share the poet's separation
from what he describes. It is life in the mirror, and our desire for it is as
the desire of the lost souls for God; but when Lucifer stands among his
friends, when Villon sings his dead ladies to so gallant a rhythm, when
Timon makes his epitaph, we feel no sorrow, for life herself has made
one of her eternal gestures, has called up into our hearts her energy that is
eternal delight. In Ireland, where the tide of life is rising, we turn, not
to picture-making, but to the imagination of personality — to drama, gesture." [7]

That was in 1904, the year in which the Abbey Theatre tried to restore "Cormac's ruined house."

I would bring a few things together at this point. Yeats's commitment
to an oral culture held him to people, place, and time. His commitment
to Tradition as Voice was a feeling for the roots of things, memory, familial metaphors, all those continuities which persist in change. His commitment to drama was an assent to time and limitation.

There is much to be said about these and other commitments, and
even more about their relation, one to another. I would emphasize only
one point. Eliot's poems, in which we share the poet's separation from
what he invents, tend to present the essential figure of life as paradox;
the simultaneous presence of incompatible things on the field of life,
these being resolved by the religious faith that transcends them. Yeats's
poems tend to present human life in the mode of drama, conflicts in place
and time; value resides in the conflict, not merely in the victory. Hence,
among other advantages, Yeats can free himself from the obsession with
the transience of things which is one of the burdens of a visual culture.
Eliot's poems concede that life may offer a few dazzling moments in
which time stands still, but everything else is, as one of his poems says,
"a waste sad time stretching before and after." In Keats's great Ode permanence is conceded to the nightingale's song; natural processes work
benignly, it seems, in favour of birds, while man languishes, worn down by

the hungry generations. This is very much the note of a visual culture. When Keats says of the nightingale's song:

> The voice I hear this passing night was heard
> In ancient days by emperor and clown. . . .

those to whom tradition is a "speaking" from father to son will protest that there are also human continuities audible in precisely this way from generation to generation. In visual cultures it is very difficult to feel the continuities from one generation to another, because so much feeling is overwhelmed by intimations of waste and decay. Within an oral culture it is easier to reconcile oneself to the temporal, the limited, the finite, because these are the very conditions of Voice. In this sense, "all lives that has lived." Indeed, the best "answer" to Keats's "Ode to a Nightingale" and its image of man's fate is Yeats's "Meditations in Time of Civil War." When Yeats looks at Sato's gift, the sword five hundred years old, he is just as deeply moved as any other qualified spectator from any culture, but he does not see it as an emblem of man's transience. In fact, the continuities figured in Keats's bird-song are shown as proceeding, in time, from father to son; so that instead of the temporal appearing a poor second to the permanent, its characteristic quality is a continuous splendour. Thinking of the sword, Yeats says:

> In Sato's house,
> Curved like new moon, moon-luminous,
> It lay five hundred years.
> Yet if no change appears
> No moon; only an aching heart
> Conceives a changeless work of art.
> Our learned men have urged
> That when and where 'twas forged
> A marvellous accompliment,
> In painting or in pottery, went
> From father unto son
> And through the centuries ran
> And seemed unchanging like the sword.
> Soul's beauty being most adored,
> Men and their business took
> The soul's unchanging look;

which means, I suppose, that men and their business or the productions of Time, if only they are sufficiently "accomplished," have as much of Eternity's splendour as we can conceive or desire: enough is enough.

This is not, in Yeats, a flood of sentimentality, because he knows that the cost of man's achievement is high. In "Two Songs from a Play" he says:

> Everything that man esteems
> Endures a moment or a day.
> Love's pleasure drives his love away,
> The painter's brush consumes his dreams;
> The herald's cry, the soldier's tread
> Exhaust his glory and his might:
> Whatever flames upon the night
> Man's own resinous heart has fed.

But if the price is high, Yeats is prepared to pay it; and even when he thinks of human life as a wound, he rarely irritates it. A typical moment is the little poem "Consolation," from the sequence "A Woman Young and Old":

> O but there is wisdom
> In what the sages said;
> But stretch that body for a while
> And lay down that head
> Till I have told the sages
> Where man is comforted.
> How could passion run so deep
> Had I never thought
> That the crime of being born
> Blackens all our lot?
> But where the crime's committed
> The crime can be forgot.

This tone is unusual in modern literature, which rarely forgives and never forgets the crime of death and birth. One has only to think of the energy D. H. Lawrence had to expend in driving his readers to acknowledge the law of temporal limits. Indeed, a good text to put beside Yeats's antinomies of day and night is Lawrence's *Apocalypse,* especially that part in which he gives a free-wheeling gloss upon the two "witnesses" of *Revelation.* He says that they are "rivals, dividers, separators, for good as well as for ill"; they are "the rivals within a man's own very nature," they give "the two alternate forms of elemental consciousness, our day-consciousness and our night-consciousness." They are witnesses to life, Lawrence says, because "it is between their opposition that the Tree of Life itself grows, from the earthly root." And all the time, he says, "they put a limit on man. They say to him, in every earthly or physical activity: Thus far and no further. They limit every action, every 'earth' action, to its own scope, and counterbalance it with an opposite action. They are gods of gates, but they are also gods of limits: each forever jealous of the other, keeping the other in bounds. They make life possible; but they make life limited." [8]

This is very much in Yeats's idiom; the acknowledgement of conflict within the single state of man, and at the same time the further acknowledgement that value resides in the conflict itself. Eliot, in these circumstances, would tend to resolve the dispute by direct appeal to a higher authority: Yeats made most of his poems from the dispute itself. Think how often, in Yeats's poems, the antinomies of day and night are featured as rival claims upon our feeling; in a poem like "Father and Child," for instance:

> She hears me strike the board and say
> That she is under ban
> Of all good men and women,
> Being mentioned with a man
> That has the worst of all bad names;
> And thereupon replies
> That his hair is beautiful,
> Cold as the March wind his eyes.

But a rivalry of this kind is resonant only when the human situation is acknowledged as valid, in and through and despite its transience. If the human situation is deemed illusory or a mere construction of the human imagination, such rivalries are meaningless.

We need a poem, to bring these speculations into order. And, after that, we must tackle those poems, two especially, which would seem to undermine my general argument about Yeats. For the first poem I choose "Coole Park, 1929," not one of Yeats's most imperious performances but for that reason one of his most characteristic poems. Like many of Yeats's poems it "moralizes" a landscape — the swallows, a sycamore, a lime-tree, the great house itself. We think of it as an eighteenth-century mode of poetry, and this is proper especially if we think of the tradition inherited from such poems as Jonson's "To Penshurst," the verse letters, and so on. In this tradition there is a direct relation between the ascription of beauty and the acknowledgement of truth and merit; as the handsome scene at Coole Park is the place of great deeds, the fine things done and thought and said within the house, "a dance-like glory that those walls begot." As in "The Municipal Gallery Revisited" and "In Memory of Major Robert Gregory," the "genius of the place" is given through the people who visited or lived there; Douglas Hyde, Yeats himself, Synge, Shawe-Taylor, Hugh Lane, and the great lady herself:

> They came like swallows and like swallows went,
> And yet a woman's powerful character
> Could keep a swallow to its first intent;
> And half a dozen in formation there,
> That seemed to whirl upon a compass-point,

> Found certainty upon the dreaming air,
> The intellectual sweetness of those lines
> That cut through time or cross it withershins.

The certainty found upon the dreaming air is the "accomplishment" invoked in "Mediations in Time of Civil War," a splendour flowing through the generations into a house, a person, a deed, a thought. And the lines cut through time not to destroy it but to mark its possibilities, like a flare. In a difficult poem, "Stars at Tallapoosa," Wallace Stevens posits lines "straight and swift between the stars" which have nothing at all to do with the sea-lines or the earth-lines; we think of them as pure acts of the mind, performed by man for his pleasure and because he must. But the lines that Yeats praises are continuous with the earth-lines and the sea-lines, they are these articulated in speech, grace, and accomplishment. And lest this be lost through a breach of tact or a failure of memory, Yeats introduces a qualified witness, of a later generation, to remember what should be remembered:

> Here, traveller, scholar, poet, take your stand
> When all those rooms and passages are gone,
> When nettles wave upon a shapeless mound
> And saplings root among the broken stone,
> And dedicate — eyes bent upon the ground,
> Back turned upon the brightness of the sun
> And all the sensuality of the shade —
> A moment's memory to that laurelled head.

The shade is Hopkins's "dapple," Whitman's "drift," Stevens's "Summer," the "dark declivities" in another poem by Yeats himself; it is the plenitude of things. And the sensuality is the "brown hair over the mouth blown," in a poem by Eliot, or the "love's play" in another poem by Yeats. And both the shade and the sensuality are in time and place.

We are given this through the speech of the poem; common speech sharpened to an aristocratic grace, in keeping with Yeats's belief that the best things in life come from the peasant and the aristocrat. It is a commonplace that the high literature of the twentieth century has set itself to undermine the assumptions of the middle class. This is one of the reasons for which many high poets have repudiated common speech. Yeats approved of the object but not the means. He criticized the middle class by showing its members a common speech tempered to a new strength. But he gave nothing away. He would not hand over to the "hot-faced bargainers and money-changers" the language they had wounded; he would show the healing properties of intelligence and grace. From the peasants he would learn "emotion of multitude"; from the aristocrats, "excess": and he would bring those values into a common speech which would shine with a new resilience. If the new speech rebuked the old speakers, all the better: this is what fine speech is made to do:

> You gave, but will not give again
> Until enough of Paudeen's pence
> By Biddy's halfpennies have lain
> To be 'some sort of evidence,'
> Before you'll put your guineas down. . . .

And later in the same poem:

> Let Paudeens play at pitch and toss,
> Look up in the sun's eye and give
> What the exultant heart calls good
> That some new day may breed the best
> Because you gave, not what they would,
> But the right twigs for an eagle's nest.

In pitch and toss the players look up at the pennies and then down at the ground. In another poem Yeats would praise the "lidless eyes that face the sun"; and the prefatory poem to *Responsibilities* says, "Only the wasteful virtues earn the sun." Whoever looks directly into the sun is an aristocrat of feeling if not of birth; the wasteful virtues are the fine "excess." So Yeats is using an uncommonly fine common speech to rebuke those who treat common speech as their own property and abuse it accordingly.

I have argued that "Coole Park, 1929" is a typical Yeats poem; what is true of this poem is true of the vast majority of his poems from "Adam's Curse" to the very last pages of the great book: these poems choose the living world for text, they are poems of place, time, memory, voice, conflict, personality. I do not find there a single poem in which Yeats releases himself from these obligations: he never composed a Supreme Fiction. That he occasionally wished to do so, I would not deny: the poems that spring to mind at once are, of course, the two Byzantine poems.

I have argued on another occasion [9] that the best way to read Yeats's *Collected Poems* is to think of it as dramatizing a great dispute between Self and Soul; Self being all those motives which tie one to earth and time, Soul being the freedom of imagination transcending the finite. The dispute was never resolved. Yeats would lend himself to one side or the other, but always with misgivings, knowing the cost of severance. This is my chief quarrel with those who would read the Byzantine poems as if they were written by Wallace Stevens: these poems are not parables about the free imagination; they are poems about the dispute of Self and Soul at a time when old age and approaching death seem to vote resoundingly for Soul.

"Sailing to Byzantium" begins with the old man leaving the world and human life, looking back at the sensuality of the shade; partly in wonder, partly in pathos, partly in self-pity. In the second stanza the Self is separated from Soul, as Dublin — shall we say — is separated from the "holy city of Byzantium." The third stanza is a prayer to the new household gods to destroy the antinomies of day and night, resolving everything now in "the artifice of eternity." (Yeats still knows the limitations of this device; if it is eternity it is also artifice.) The last stanza is a furious promise, as if in atonement for all the selfish motives of a temporal life:

> Once out of nature I shall never take
> My bodily form from any natural thing,
> But such a form as Grecian goldsmiths make
> Of hammered gold and gold enamelling
> To keep a drowsy Emperor awake;
> Or set upon a golden bough to sing
> To lords and ladies of Byzantium
> Of what is past, or passing, or to come.

I wonder if it has been noted what a curious song the bird is to sing; almost as strange as the motto given to us by the figures on Keats's Grecian urn. We are but of nature, in Byzantium, in eternity, and yet the burden of the song is "what is past, or passing, or to come"; Self-topics, with a vengeance. Kenneth Burke takes these lines to mean "that 'nature' becomes tyrannously burdensome, once the poet, having made himself at home in 'grace,' finds that it has been withdrawn." [10] Nature is his term, I think, for Self, and Grace for Soul. I read the passage differently, on the principle that Yeats never made himself at home in Soul and dragged the Self with him even into Byzantium. The last lines seem to be a turning-back to the world of time, joining up again, incipiently, with the sensual music of the first stanza.

In the later poem, "Byzantium," a poet, half in sickness, thinks of death. But since death is by definition beyond experience he cannot do much with it, so he finds relief and some dignity in an engaging fancy, the neo-Platonic décor of death. And because he is at least an amateur dramatist he wants to give his images the thrust of action and event; hence his recourse to Dante and the guides. For the time being, the chosen affiliations are identified with Value, and an attempt is made to disengage these from the "fury and the mire of human veins." The poet's choices are temperamental and suitably "aesthetic," but once entertained they keep the needs of the occasion at bay and work up an impressive energy. Because they have an imposing lineage they are self-perpetuating, and Yeats goes along with them. The feelings engaged call for the High Style, not because they carry the freight of doctrine but because the occasion is

featuring a ceremonial event, a large showing. Officially, Yeats is opting
for the moonlit dome, and he tries to work up a corresponding severity, if
not "disdain," for "all that man is." The second stanza begins,

> Before me floats an image, man or shade,
> Shade more than man, more image than a shade;

thus giving us the terms of an ascending sequence, spiralling toward
Byzantium. Later in the poem we will be given another set of terms, distinguished in precisely the same way: for man, shade, and image we are
now to read bird, handiwork, and miracle:

> Mircle, bird or golden handiwork,
> More miracle than bird or handiwork,

and in any event we are directed thus beyond the natural condition. But
this needs a certain pressure, and the second stanza includes one dangerously vatic moment which the style can barely hold: "I hail the superhuman; I call it death-in-life and life-in-death." But the meditative trance
continues with a second version of moonlit disdain. In the third stanza
the flames on the Emperor's floor are distinguished from their counterparts in the natural world, which otherwise they would dangerously resemble; similarly the dance and the "agony of trance." And then, thinking
of the dolphins that carry the human souls to the next world, Yeats "makes
the mistake" of adverting to their "mire and blood." Now immediately
the dispute of Self and Soul, which seemed to have been resolved by
transcendence, breaks out all over again. As I read the poem, this is the
saving stanza, as the poet turns his gaze back and out to the sea of human life and the pity of the whole thing rushes into the rhythm, "That
dolphin-torn, that gong-tormented sea." For me this act certifies the drama,
and without it I would assent to the play only sluggishly, for most of it
is indeed a performance, however impressive. This mode of poetry is not
the highest, because it can hardly have the sublimity of prophecy and
anything less, on such an occasion, is bound to be a little fanciful. "Byzantium" is a more spectacular poem than "Sailing to Byzantium," but it is
not as fine, as coherent or as just. This is not because the later poem is
more dependent upon its handsome symbols but because it commits itself
to it presumptive form at a stage somewhat short of moral understanding.
It is as if "Byzantium" were a very late draft for a poem never quite completed. Yeats is saying rather less than he seems to claim, making spectacular play with the heuristic possibilities of the symbols. The poem, in short,
is weak in moral syntax. Perhaps this explains our hesitation, if we hesitate. The play is spectacular but heady, somewhat hysterical. A chosen
tradition plays an important part in the poem, supplying most of the
symbols and most of the feeling, but the function of the traditional lore

is largely honorific and picturesque; most of it is present to make up a distinguished gathering. The tradition does not test, because there is not enough to test, not enough to criticize, not enough Fact to put to the measure of Value. The domes, bobbins, cocks, and dances reverberate imperiously, and Yeats draws wonderful music from these traditional instruments, but the tradition does not finally grapple with the individual talent. This is why "Sailing to Byzantium" and — to choose another — "Vacillation" seem to me better poems, poems of reality and justice.

To bring this discussion toward a conclusion, there is one important qualification which I should make. I am arguing that Yeats was a much more rooted poet than we have allowed, and he was much more rooted in the oral tradition of Ireland than we have been prepared to acknowledge. We often think that he was barred from the resources of Irish culture because he did not know the Irish language. And we think that the Irish tradition was itself severely damaged when Irish ceased to be the daily language of the majority of Irishmen. Admittedly, the Irish oral tradition was not a "going concern" at the beginning of the twentieth century: Yeats was not Homer, with all the resources of a native tradition immediately available to him, ready for his hands. And of course the continuity of the Irish oral tradition was gravely undermined by the reduction of the Irish language to minority status. But the loss of the language, though tragic, did not mean that Irish culture was totally destroyed, that Irish memory was broken, or that the old Irish world was blocked off. Partly as a result of work done by the nineteenth-century scholars, translators, folklorists, and anthologists, a great deal of the Irish tradition persisted. To put the matter bluntly: Yeats got from Irish sources what he needed for his poems; a sense of roots, a feeling of continuity, a sense of communal values issuing in speech and action, "the dialect of the tribe."

III _____

Notes   .

Introduction

1. "Discussion" (following "Criticism and the Experience of Interiority," another version of the "Phenomenology of Reading"), in *The Languages of Criticism and the Sciences of Man: The Structuralist Controversy,* ed. Richard Macksey and Eugenio Donato (Baltimore, 1970), p. 82.

2. See Edward Said's essay-review on Poulet and Blackmur, "Sense and Sensibility," *Partisan Review,* XXXIV (1967), 628–33.

3. Quoted in Sarah N. Lawall, *Critics of Consciousness: The Existential Structures of Literature* (Cambridge, 1968), p. 230.

4. Yeats is apposite because his concept of the "mask," along with Ezra Pound's notion of "persona" and Eliot's "impersonal theory of poetry," comes closest in English to Blanchot's idea of depersonalization. Cf., e.g., Eliot's statement in "Tradition and the Individual Talent," *Selected Essays 1917–1932* (New York, 1932), p. 10: "Poetry is not a turning loose of emotion, but an escape from emotion; it is not the expression of personality, but an escape from personality." On the resemblances between Blanchot and the three English poets see Geoffrey H. Hartman, "Maurice Blanchot: Philosopher-Novelist," *Beyond Formalism: Literary Essays 1958–1970* (New Haven, 1970), p. 109. For a full discussion of Blanchot's concept of depersonalization see Paul de Man, "Maurice Blanchot," in *Modern French Criticism: From Proust and Valéry to Structuralism,* ed. John K. Simon (Chicago, 1972), pp. 255–76.

5. See Blackmur's essays on Dostoevsky in *Eleven Essays in the European Novel* (New York, 1964).

6. See Thomas A. Sebeok, ed., *Style in Language* (Cambridge, 1960; Paper, 1966); Roger Fowler, ed., *Essays on Style and Language* (London, 1966); Seymour Chatman and Samuel R. Levin, eds., *Essays on the Language of Literature* (Boston, 1967); Donald C. Freeman, ed., *Linguistics and Literary Style* (New York, 1970); and Seymour Chatman, ed., *Literary Style: A Symposium* (New York, 1971).

7. In *Style in Language,* p. 350.

8. See René Wellek, "Trends of Twentieth-Century Criticism," *Concepts of Criticism,* ed. Stephen G. Nichols, Jr. (New Haven, 1963), pp. 349–51.

9. "Preface," p. vii. For the debate between critics and linguists see Harold Whitehall, Seymour Chatman, Arnold Stein, John Crowe Ransom, "English Verse and What It Sounds Like," *The Kenyon Review,* XVIII (1956), 411–77.

10. "Preface," p. viii.

11. The linguist's statement is that of Harold Whitehall in *The Kenyon Review* debate, p. 415; the critic's is that of F. W. Bateson, "Linguistics and Literary Criticism," p. 511, this book.

12. Roger Fowler and Peter Mercer, "Criticism and the Language of Literature: Some Traditions and Trends in Great Britain." *Style,* III (1969), p. 48.

13. On the larger implications of this third issue, in another but related context, see Edward W. Said's argument that the structuralist activity "cannot show us why structure structures; structure is always revealed in the condition of having structures, but never, as Jean Starobinski has observed, structuring, or in the condition of *being structured,* or failing to structure," "*Abecedarium Culturae:* Structuralism, Absence, Writing," in *Modern French Criticism: From Proust and Valéry to Structuralism,* pp. 378–79.

14. Alphonse G. Juilland, from "Review of Bruneau's *L'Époque Réaliste,*" in Chatman and Levin, pp. 382–83. For other defenses of literary criticism against linguistics see John Hollander, "From the Viewpoint of Literary Criticism: Opening Statement," and René Wellek, "Closing Statement," in *Style in Language,* pp. 396–407, 408–19.

15. In "Linguistics and Poetics," *Style in Language,* p. 350.

16. This and preceding quotations are from *Style in Language,* p. 358.

17. *Yale French Studies,* 36–37 (1966), p. 213; the article is reprinted in *Structuralism,* ed. Jacques Ehrmann (Doubleday Anchor Books, 1970), pp. 188–230.

18. Ibid.

19. In *The Languages of Criticism and the Sciences of Man: The Structuralist Controversy,* pp. 297, 302–303.

20. In *Essays in Criticism,* XVI (1966), p. 460. The review provoked a protracted discussion: F. W. Bateson, "Editorial Postscript," ibid., 464–65; Roger Fowler and

F. W. Bateson, "Argument II. Literature and Linguistics," *Essays in Criticism,* XVII (1967), 322–47, and "Argument II (continued): Language and Literature," *Essays in Criticism,* XVIII (1968), 164–82; and E. B. Greenwood, "Language and Literature," ibid., 477–78.

21. "Literature as Sentences" was challenged by John Russell, *College English,* XXVIII (1966), 170–71, on the grounds that "a traditional rhetorical analysis" could accomplish just as effectively and more intelligibly what Ohmann had attempted in his analysis of the sentence from Joyce's story *Araby,* but Ohmann, in his reply, 171–73, explained why traditional modes of analysis are "arbitrary at crucial points."

22. *The Well-Tempered Critic* (Bloomington, 1963), p. 148.

23. Frye, *The Stubborn Structure: Essays on Criticism and Society* (Ithaca, 1970), p. 88. Abrams challenges Frye's views directly in his review of *Anatomy of Criticism: Four Essays* in the *University of Toronto Quarterly,* XXVIII (1959), 190–96. Two of Abrams' points are worth noting: (1) "Unlike most other archetypal critics, Frye explicitly disavows the standard attempt to give a causal explanation for the recurrence of archetypes. . . . The patterns, Frye says, are simply there, 'however they got there.' Which brings up the questions: how do we know they are there? what is the evidence for the existence of an archetype?" (2) The patterns of events comprehended by Frye's archetypal analysis "can be made to coincide only on a high level of abstraction, and abstraction, as Frye says in another context, implies 'the leaving out of inconvenient elements.' Even if we grant, in the first place, that these heroines [Hermione, Esther Summerson, Pamela, and Belinda] are all Proserpine figures who act out a ritual death, when we have made that discovery, our task as practical critics has not even begun. For few works differs more radically from each other in constitution, characterization, qualitative feel, and emotional effect than do *The Winter's Tale, Bleak House, Pamela,* and *The Rape of the Lock,* and the job of the practical critic is to account for each work in its minute particularity."

On Abrams's first point see W. K. Wimsatt, "Northrop Frye: Criticism as Myth," in *Northrop Frye in Modern Criticism: Selected Papers from the English Institute 1965,* ed. Murray Krieger (New York, 1966), pp. 93 ff.

24. Quotations are from Bachelard's "Introduction" to *The Poetics of Space,* trans. Maria Jolas (New York, 1964).

25. For a full treatment of the conceptions of "voice" discussed in this paragraph see Walker Gibson, *Tough, Sweet and Stuffy: An Essay on Modern American Prose Styles* (Bloomington, 1966), and *Persona* (New York, 1969).

GEORGES POULET, *Henry James*

1. "Letter to Henry James Junior," November 1813, in *The Letters of Henry James,* ed. Percy Lubbock (New York, 2 vols., 1920), II, p. 347.

2. "Letter to Grace Norton," July 28, 1883, op. cit., I, p. 100.

3. *Partial Portraits* (London, 1888), p. 388.

4. Ibid., p. 207.

5. *The Ambassadors,* Preface, in the New York Edition of *Novels and Tales of Henry James* (New York, 24 vols., 1907–17), XXI, p. xix.

6. *A Small Boy and Others* (London, 1913), p. 73.

7. Ibid., pp. 2–3.

8. Ibid., p. 242.

9. *Essays in London and Elsewhere* (New York, 1893), p. 300.

10. *The Awkward Age,* Preface, *Novels and Tales,* IX, p. viii.

11. *Roderick Hudson,* Preface, *Novels and Tales,* I, p. viii.

12. Ibid., p. vii.

13. Ibid., p. viii.

14. "Letter to Grace Norton," July 28, 1883, op. cit.
15. *Notes on Novelists* (New York, 1914), p. 395.
16. *The Portrait of a Lady*, Preface, *Novels and Tales*, III, p. xv.
17. *The Spoils of Poynton*, Preface, *Novels and Tales*, X, p. xii.
18. Ibid., p. xvi.
19. *The Ivory Tower*, *Novels and Tales*, XXV, p. 340.
20. Ibid., p. 109.
21. *The Wings of the Dove* (New York, 2 vols., 1902), I, p. 29.
22. *Roderick Hudson*, Preface, p. xvi.
23. *A Small Boy and Others*, p. 73.
24. *The Aspern Papers*, Preface, *Novels and Tales*, XII, p x.
25. *The Sense of the Past* (London, 1917), p. 47.
26. Ibid., p. 47.
27. Ibid.
28. "Letter to Grace Norton," March 5, 1907, *Letters*, II, p. 69.
29. *The Golden Bowl*, Preface, *Novels and Tales*, XXIII, p. v.
30. *The Golden Bowl*, XXIV, pp. 2–3.
31. *The Sacred Fount* (London, 1901), p. 101.
32. Ibid., p. 131.
33. *The Reverberator*, Preface, *Novels and Tales*, XIII, p. vii.
34. *The Portrait of a Lady*, Preface, p. x.
35. *The Ivory Tower*, p. 148.
36. *The Awkward Age*, Preface, p. xvi.

MAURICE BLANCHOT, *Kafka's* Diaries: *The Exigency of the Work of Art*

1. Almost all the passages quoted in the following pages are taken from the complete edition of Kafka's *Diary*, which reproduces the thirteen quarto notebooks in which, from 1910 to 1923, Kafka wrote everything that mattered to him, events from his personal life, meditation on these events, descriptions of his dreams, narratives begun, broken off, begun again. It is, then, not simply a "diary," in the current sense of the word, but the very workings of the experience of writing, right at its very beginning and in the essential meaning which Kafka was led to give to the word. It is with this perspective that the *Diary* is to be read and examined.

Max Brod states that he has made only a few insignificant abridgments, and there is no reason to doubt this. On the other hand, it is certain that Kafka, at many crucial moments, destroyed a great part of his notes. And after 1923, the *Diary* is completely lacking. We do not know whether the manuscript destroyed at his request by Dora Dymant included the continuation of these notebooks: it is very likely. We have to say, then, that after 1923 Kafka is unknown to us, for we know that those who knew him best considered him quite differently from what he imagined himself to be.

The *Diary* (which is completed by the travel notebooks) reveals to us almost nothing of his opinions on the great topics which might have interested him. The *Diary* tells us of Kafka at that earlier stage where there are as yet no opinions and where there is hardly a Kafka. Such is its essential value. The book by Gustav Janouch (*Conversations with Kafka*, London and New York, 1953), on the contrary, enables us to understand Kafka in the free-and-easiness of more everyday conversation when he speaks just as well of the future of the world as of the Jewish question, of Zionism, religious ceremonies, and occasionally of his books. Janouch knew Kafka in 1920 in Prague. He wrote down almost immediately the conversations he reports, and Brod has confirmed the faithfulness of this echo. But in order not to be misled about the importance of these utterances we must remember that they were spoken to a very young man of seventeen, whose youth, naïveté, and trusting spontaneity touched Kafka, but also doubtless led Kafka to tone down his thoughts so as not to make them dangerous to such a young mind. Kafka, a thoughtful friend, was often afraid of worrying his friends by uttering a truth which was desperate only to himself. This does not mean that he did not say what he thought, but that he sometimes said what he did not profoundly believe.

2. Kafka adds: "This is not an artistic yearning."

3. However, on February 10, 1922, we read this note: "Neuer Angriff von G." This must doubtless be read: "New attack by God."

4. Certain letters to Milena also allude to what there was of the unknown for him in this terrible impulse (see the studies in the *Nouvelle N.R.F.*: "Kafka et Brod" and "L'echec de Milena," Oct. and Nov., 1954).

5. On this topic reference should be made to the book by G. G. Scholem, *Les Grands Courants de la Mystique juive*: "The terrors of Exile influenced the cabalist doctrine of metempsychosis, which at that time gained an immense popularity by insisting on the various stages of the exile of the soul. The most formidable fate which could befall the soul, much more horrible than the torments of hell, was to be 'rejected' or 'laid bare,' a state which excludes either reanimation or even admission into hell. . . . The absolute deprivation of a home was the sinister symbol of an absolute impiety, of an extreme moral and spiritual degradation. Union with God or absolute banishment became the two poles between which was worked out a system that offered the Jews the possibility of being under the domination of a rule which sought to destroy the forces of Exile." And this further: "There was an ardent desire to overcome Exile by aggravating its torments, in savoring its bitterness in the extreme (including even the night of Shekinah itself) . . ." (p. 267). That the theme of "The Metamorphosis" (as well as the obsessing fictions of animality) is a reminiscence, an allusion to the tradition of the cabalistic metempsychosis, can well be imagined even though we are not sure that "Samsa" is a recall of "Samsara" (Kafka and Samsa are related names, but Kafka challenges this comparison). Kafka sometimes states that he is not yet born: "Hesitation before birth. If there is a transmigration of souls then I am not yet on the bottom rung. My life is a hesitation before birth" (January 24, 1922). We must remember that in "Wedding Preparations in the Country" Raban, the hero of this youthful narrative, expresses in jest the wish to become an insect (*Käfer*) which could doze away in bed and escape the unpleasant duties of the community. The "shell" of solitude is like the image which would be brought to life in the impressive theme of "The Metamorphosis."

6. Kafka says to Janouch that "the task of the poet is a prophetic task: the exact word guides; the word which is not exact seduces; it is not by chance that the Bible is called the Scripture."

7. Thus also arises the pitiless condemnation (which touched his very self) that Kafka brings against the Jewish writers who use the German tongue.

8. "But what follows from this very fact: being a poet? This act of writing is a gift, a gift silent and mysterious. But its price? In the night, the answer bursts forth upon my eyes with a dazzling sharpness: it is the wages received from the diabolic powers which one has served. This abandon of obscure forces, this loosing of powers habitually held in leash, these impure embraces, and all the rest that still is carried on in the depths, does one still know anything about them, up above, when one writes stories, in broad daylight, in the glare of the sun? . . . Does the surface retain any trace of this? Is there perhaps yet another way of writing? As far as I am concerned, I know only this one, in the night, when anguish torments me on the verge of sleep" (cited by Brod).

9. But later on Kafka seems to have become increasingly more attentive to this form of devotion. Dora Dymant belonged to "an esteemed hassidic Jewish family." And Martin Buber perhaps influenced him.

10. Kafka does not avoid denouncing what is tempting, the tempting facility, in the too definite differentiation of these two worlds: "And moreover the division

466   III — NOTES

seems to me to be much too definite, dangerous in its definiteness, sad, and too tyrannical" (January 30, 1922).

11. We must at least quote this passage from the rough draft of a letter to his fiancée in which he specifies with the greatest lucidity his relationship with his family: "However, I am descended from my parents, am linked to them and my sisters by blood, am sensible of it neither in my everyday affairs nor, as a result of their inevitable familiarity to me, in my special concerns, but at bottom have more respect for it than I realize. Sometimes this bond of blood too is the target of my hatred; the sight of the double bed at home, the used sheets, the nightshirts carefully laid out, can exasperate me to the point of nausea, can turn me inside out; it is as if I had not been definitively born, were continually born anew into the world out of the stale life in that stale room, had constantly to seek confirmation of myself there, were indissolubly joined with all that loathsomeness, in part even if not entirely, at least it still clogs my feet which want to run, they are still stuck fast in the original shapeless pulp" (October 18, 1916).

12. "There are two cardinal sins from which all the others spring: impatience and laziness. Because of impatience we were driven out of Paradise, because of laziness we cannot return. Perhaps, however, there is only one cardinal sin: impatience. Because of impatience we were driven out, because of impatience we cannot return" ("Aphorisms").

ROMAN JAKOBSON AND CLAUDE LÉVI-STRAUSS,
Charles Baudelaire's "Les Chats"

1. M. Grammont, Petit traité de versification française (Paris, 1908), p. 86.
2. M. Grammont, Traité de phonétique (Paris, 1930), p. 384.
3. M. Grammont, Traité . . . , p. 388.
4. M. Durand, "La spécificité du phonème. Application au cas de R/L," Journal de Psychologie, LVII (1960), pp. 405–419.
5. Cf. L'Intermédiaire des chercheurs et des curieux, LXVII, col. 338 and 509.
6. M. E. Benveniste, who was kind enough to read this study in manuscript, pointed out to us that between les amoureux fervents and les savants austères, la mûre saison also plays the role of intermediary: it is, in effect, in leur mûre saison that they reunite to identify themselves également with the cats. For, continues M. Benveniste, to remain amoureux fervents in leur mûre saison already signifies that one is outside of the common fold, as are les savants austères by their vocation. The initial situation of the sonnet is that of a life outside this world (nevertheless life in the underworld is rejected) and, transferred to the cats, this situation develops from chilly seclusion to vast starry solitudes where science et volupté are a dream without end.
In support of these comments, for which we thank their author, we would cite another poem in Les Fleurs du Mal: "Le savant amour . . . fruit d'automne aux saveurs souveraines" ("L'Amour du mensonge").
7. Ch. Baudelaire, Œuvres, II (Bibliothèque de la Pléiade, Paris, 1961), pp. 243 ff.
8. Ch. Baudelaire, Les Fleurs du Mal (Édition critique établie par J. Crépet et G. Blin, Paris, 1942), p. 413.
9. M. Butor, Histoire extraordinaire, essai sur un rêve de Baudelaire (Paris, 1961), p. 85.
10. In L. Rudrauf's study, Rime et sexe (Tartu, 1936), the exposition of "A theory of the alternation of masculine and feminine rhymes in French poetry" is followed by a "controversy" with Maurice Grammont (pp. 47 ff.). According to the latter, "for alternation as established in the XVIth century based upon the presence or absence of an unstressed e at the end of the word, we have availed ourselves of the terms 'feminine' and 'masculine' because the unstressed e at the end of a word

was, in the majority of cases, indicative of the feminine gender: *un petit chat/ une petite chatte,* or rather one could say that the specific termination of the feminine, in contradistinction to the masculine, always contained an unstressed *e.*" However, Rudrauf expressed certain doubts: "But was it purely the grammatical consideration that guided the poets of the XVIth century in their establishment of this rule of alternation and in their choice of the epithets 'masculine' and 'feminine' to designate the two kinds of rhymes? Let us not forget that the poets of the Pleiade wrote their stanzas with an eye to song, and that song underscores, much more than does the spoken word, the alternation of a strong (masculine) syllable and of a weak (feminine) syllable. Consciously or unconsciously, the musical point of view and the sexual point of view must have played a role along with the grammatical analogy . . ." (p. 49).

Inasmuch as this alternation of rhymes based upon the presence or absence of an unstressed *e* at the ends of lines is no longer realized, in Grammont's view it has been replaced by an alternation of rhymes ending either with a consonant or with a stressed vowel. While fully prepared to acknowledge that "the final syllables ending with a vowel are all masculine" (p. 46), Rudrauf is at the same time tempted to establish a scale of twenty-four degrees for the consonantal rhymes, "ranging from the most brusque and virile end syllables to the most femininely suave" (pp. 12 ff.). The rhymes with a voiceless stop at their end form the extreme masculine pole (1°) and the rhymes with a voiced spirant are viewed as the feminine pole (24°) of Rudrauf's scale. If one applies this tentative classification to the consonantal rhymes of "Les Chats," one is conscious of a gradual movement toward the masculine pole, which results in an attenuation of the contrast between the two kinds of rhymes: [1]*austères* — [4]*sédentaires* (liquid: 19°); [6]*ténèbres* — [7]*funèbres* (voiced stop followed by a liquid: 15°); [9]*attitudes* — [10]*solitudes* (voiced stop: 13°); [12]*magiques* — [14]*mystiques* (voiceless stop: 1°).

RICHARD OHMANN, *Literature as Sentences*

1. I draw especially on Noam Chomsky, *Aspects of the Theory of Syntax* (Cambridge, Mass., 1965) and Jerrold J. Katz and Paul Postal, *An Integrated Theory of Linguistic Descriptions* (Cambridge, Mass., 1964).

2. Each set of brackets encloses the constituent indicated by its superscript label. The notation is equivalent to a tree diagram. Symbols: S = Sentence, Adv = Adverbial, V = Verb, Part = Particle, PP = Prepositional Phrase, P = Preposition, NP = Noun Phrase, D = Determiner, N = Noun, Nuc = Nucleus, VP = Verb Phrase, Adj = Adjectival.

3. I have argued the point at length in "Generative Grammars and the Concept of Literary Style," *Word,* 20 (Dec. 1964), 423–39.

4. Chomsky discusses ways of doing this in *Aspects of the Theory of Syntax,* chap. 2.

5. See Jerrold J. Katz, "Semi-sentences," in Jerry A. Fodor and Jerrold J. Katz, eds., *The Structure of Language* (1964), pp. 400–416. The same volume includes two other relevant papers, Chomsky, "Degrees of Grammaticalness," pp. 384–89, and Paul Ziff, "On Understanding 'Understanding Utterances,'" pp. 390–99. Samuel R. Levin has briefly discussed ungrammatical poetry within a similar framework in *Linguistic Structures in Poetry* (The Hague, 1962), chaps. 2 and 3.

6. Ralph Maud's fine study, *Entrances to Dylan Thomas' Poetry* (Pittsburgh, 1963), describes the phenomenon well in a chapter called "Process Poems."

WILLIAM H. GASS, *The Sentences of Fiction*

1. This is a central concern of my essay on Singer, "The Shut-In." [Notes are by the author and refer to other pieces in *Fiction and the Figures of Life.*]

2. See "The High Brutality of Good Intentions" and "In the Cage."
3. See "The Concept of Character in Fiction."

M. H. ABRAMS, *The Correspondent Breeze:*
A Romantic Metaphor

1. "Essay on the Poetical Works of Mr. Wordsworth," *The Works of Sir Henry Taylor* (London, 1878), V, 1–4.
2. Coleridge, *Biographia Literaria,* ed. John Shawcross (Oxford, 1907), I, 5.
3. *A Defence of Poetry, Shelley's Literary and Philosophical Criticism,* ed. John Shawcross (London, 1909), p. 121.
4. Letters of 18 Oct. and 1 Nov. 1800, *Collected Letters,* ed. E. L. Griggs (Oxford, 1956), I, 638, 643. Genius, Coleridge wrote in his Notebook in 1806, may "lie hid as beneath embers, till some sudden and awakening Gust of regenerating Grace . . . rekindles and reveals it anew." (Cited by George Whalley, *Coleridge and Sara Hutchinson* [London, 1955], p. 128).
5. 14 Jan. 1803, *Collected Letters,* II, 916. On October 20 of that year Coleridge wrote in his Notebook: "Storm all night — the wind scourging and lashing the rain. . . . I, half-dozing, list'ning to the same, not without solicitations of the poetic Feeling. . . ." (*The Notebooks of S. T. Coleridge,* ed. Kathleen Coburn [New York, 1957], I, Entry 1577).
6. 29 Nov. 1805, *The Early Letters of Wm. and Dorothy Wordsworth,* ed. E. de Selincourt (Oxford, 1935), I, 547.
7. In his "Prospectus" for *The Recluse,* Wordsworth wrote (*Poetical Works,* ed. E. de Selincourt and Helen Darbishire [Oxford, 1949], V, 3):

> To these emotions, whencesoe'er they come,
> Whether from breath of outward circumstance,
> Or from the soul — an impulse to herself —
> I would give utterance in numerous verse.

8. I have inserted a passage from MS W into the standard version from *Sibylline Leaves;* see *The Complete Poetical Works of Samuel Taylor Coleridge,* ed. E. H. Coleridge (Oxford, 1912), I, 403–407.
9. *Autobiographic Sketches,* chap. I: "The Affliction of Childhood."
10. *Alastor,* 41–6. In *A Defence of Poetry,* "the mind in creation is as a fading coal, which some invisible influence, like an inconstant wind, wakens to transitory brightness."
11. Cf. Dante's *Paradiso* II, 7 ff.:

> L'acqua ch'io prendo già mai non si corse;
> Minerva spira, e conducemi Apollo.

Shelley's passage has a weak counterpart in the conclusion to Tennyson's *Locksley Hall,* where the abrupt turn from despair to hope, accompanied by the welling of "ancient founts of inspiration," materializes in a sudden outer storm:

> Let it fall on Locksley Hall, with rain or hail, or fire or snow;
> For the mighty wind arises, roaring seaward, and I go.

Valéry's *Cimetière Marin* concludes with a similar turn:

> Le vent se lève. Il faut tenter de vivre.

12. *The Civil War,* V, 82–101. In a draft of *Epipsychidion* Shelley described "a Power" in mortal hearts,

> A Pythian exhalation, which inspires
> Love, only love — a wind which o'er the wires
> Of the soul's giant harp. . . .

(*The Complete Poetical Works,* ed. Thomas Hutchinson [London, 1934], p. 429).
13. 1805 ed., I, 428–31; and MS fragment in de Selincourt, *The Prelude* (Oxford, 1950), p. 508.

14. Cassian, *The Institutes of the Coenobia*, Books IX and X. And see Sister Mary Madeleva, *Pearl: A Study in Spiritual Dryness* (New York, 1925).

15. *Collected Letters*, II, 713–14; cf. I, 470–71 (12 Mar. 1799), describing his imagination as "flat and powerless," and his inner state "as if the *organs* of Life had been dried up; as if only simple BEING remained, blind and stagnant!"

16. For the winds in these gardens see Dante's *Purgatorio*, XXVIII, 7–21, 103–14; Augustine, *Confessions*, cited above; Song of Solomon 4: 12–16.

17. See above, and *The Prelude*, ed. de Selincourt, p. 3 n.

18. Blake, letter to Thomas Butts, 22 Nov. 1802; Coleridge, *Biographia Literaria*, I, 74, and *Coleridge on Logic and Learning*, ed. Alice Snyder (New Haven, 1929), p. 126; Wordsworth, *The Prelude* (1850 ed.), XII, 93–131.

19. See also Northrop Frye's comment on Blake's "the wind of Beulah that un-roots the rocks and hills" as an analogue both of inspiration and destruction, in "Notes for a Commentary on Milton," *The Divine Vision*, ed. Vivian de S. Pinto (London, 1957), p. 125.

GASTON BACHELARD, *Drawers, Chests and Wardrobes*

1. This refers to Bergson's *Matière et Mémoire*, chaps. II and III.

2. *Monsieur Carre-Benoit à la campagne*, p. 126.

3. Colette Wartz, *Paroles pour l'autre*, p. 26.

4. Milosz, *Amoureuse initiation*, p. 217.

5. Quoted by Albert Béguin in *Eve*, p. 49.

6. Arthur Rimbaud, *Les étrennes des orphelins*.

7. Another poet, Joseph Rouffange, writes:

> *Dans le linge mort des placards*
> *Je cherche le surnaturel*
>
> (In the dead linen in cupboards
> I seek the supernatural.)
>
> *Deuil et luxe du coeur*, ed. Rougerie.

8. Anne de Tourville, *Jabadao*, p. 51.

9. Claude Vigée, loc. cit., p. 161.

10. Denise Paulme, *Les Sculptures de l'Afrique noire*, Presses Universitaires de France, 1956, p. 12.

11. Loc. cit., p. 35.

12. Franz Hellens, *Fantômes vivants*, p. 126. Cf. the line in Baudelaire's *Les petits poèmes en prose*, p. 32, in which he speaks of "the egoist, shut up like a box."

13. Rilke, *Cahiers*, p. 266, French translation.

14. Claire Goll, *Rilke et les femmes*, p. 70.

15. In a letter to Aubanel, Mallarmé wrote: "Every man has a secret in him, many die without finding it, and will never find it because they are dead, it no longer exists, nor do they. I am dead and risen again with the jeweled key of my last spiritual casket. It is up to me now to open it in the absence of any borrowed impression, and its mystery will emanate in a sky of great beauty" (Letter dated July 16, 1866).

16. Jean-Pierre Richard, "Le vertige de Baudelaire," in the review *Critique*, nos. 100–101, p. 777.

17. Charles Cros, *Poèmes et Prose*, Gallimard, p. 87.

18. In English in the text.

19. Jules Supervielle, *Gravitations*, p. 17.

20. Joë Bousquet, *La neige d'un autre âge*, p. 90.

21. Cf. *La terre et les rêveries du repos*, chap. I, and *La formation de l'esprit scientifique*, contribution to a psychoanalysis of objective knowledge, chap. VI.

DONALD DAVIE, *On* The Pisan Cantos

1. Such reliance on the special Wordsworthian case tends to blunt the point of an otherwise admirably penetrating essay by Peter Ure, "Yeats's 'Demon and Beast,' " in *Irish Writing* (Dublin, 1955), which makes very much the point about Yeats that I have sought to make.

2. *Letters*, p. 293 (letter to René Taupin, 1928).

3. "French Poets," *The Little Review* (Feb. 1918); reprinted in *Make It New* (1934), p. 161.

4. Hugh Kenner, *The Poetry of Ezra Pound* (London, 1951), p. 210.

DENIS DONOGHUE, *Yeats and the Living Voice*

1. Marshall McLuhan, *The Gutenberg Galaxy* (London: Routledge and Kegan Paul, 1962), cf. Rilke; "Ur-Gerausch," *Das Inselschiff* (Leipzig), I (1919), 14–20, reprinted in Rilke's *Gesammelte Werke* (Leipzig: Insel–Verlag, 1927), vol. IV, pp. 285–94. Translated by Carl Niemeyer in Rilke's *Primal Sound and Other Prose Pieces* (Cummington, Mass.: Cummington Press, 1947), pp. 33–38.

"At a certain time when I was beginning to concern myself with Arabian poetry, in whose origin the five senses seem to have a more simultaneous and more equivalent share, it first struck me how dissimilar and sporadic is the contemporary European poet's use of these talebearers, only one of which — sight — overcharged with perception, continually engulfs him. How small in contrast is the contribution of the inattentive hearing, to say nothing of the indifference of the remaining senses, which, functioning discontinuously and apart, exert themselves only in their own conveniently confined territories. And yet the finished poem can come about only on condition that the world, simultaneously grasped by these five levers, appear under a given aspect upon that supernatural plane which is precisely the plane of poetry."

2. John Ruskin, *Modern Painters* (London: Allen, 1910), III, pp. 100–102.

3. Wallace Stevens, *Collected Poems* (London: Faber and Faber, 1955), p. 25. Reprinted by permission of Faber and Faber Ltd., and Alfred A. Knopf, Inc.

4. Yeats, *Explorations* (London: Macmillan, 1962), p. 206.

5. Yeats, *Essays and Introductions* (London: Macmillan, 1961), p. 185.

6. Ibid., p. 521.

7. *Explorations*, p. 163.

8. D. H. Lawrence, *Apocalypse* (London: Secker, 1932), pp. 146–49.

9. Denis Donoghue and J. R. Mulryne, ed., *An Honoured Guest* (London: Edward Arnold, 1965).

10. Kenneth Burke, *A Rhetoric of Motives* (New York: Braziller, 1955), p. 317.

IV
The Reader's Response

What part does our response as readers of literature play in the performance of criticism? Is criticism separate from the act of reading, continuous with it, or a transposition of one mode of activity to something quite different? What does a poem *do* to us in our reading, and how do we take account of that in criticism?

If we say, following Keats, that a poem is proved upon our pulses, that does not mean we can "prove" what a poem is by what it does to our emotions. The reality or intensity of a reader's response does not guarantee that the response itself has critical interest or cogency. Much of what happens in reading is accidental or trivial or strictly private, and little is gained by becoming more self-conscious in the act: watching how our pulses race and tire in the presence of a poem, or, to seem more precise, calibrating our heartbeat, the sweating or dryness of our palms, the ups and downs of our moods. The authenticity of our experience in reading, its fidelity to how the poem modulates our sensibilities, is more in question in criticism than any affective quality of the experience. The critic must be concerned with how literature *shapes* response.

But excluding the direct experience of reading can be as falsifying and diminishing of what a poem is as any of the easy errors at attempts at affective criticism. It may be difficult for the critic to explain precisely how a poem stirs us, and it may be even more difficult to define how a poem distances our feelings or moves us to action, but the questions cannot be ignored because the im-

471

pulses literature incites or orders or disturbs, all the energies it quickens in us, are as clearly a part of the total performance of literature as any of its constituent structures. Indeed, literature may be, as Richard Poirier argues, "manifestations of energy" rather than immobile artifacts, an activity of writing to be participated in rather than a collection of "objects" to be contemplated. Once again the critic's views of these issues will turn on how he conceives the nature of the poem, play, or novel that creates the effects he is trying to describe and explain.

For Georges Poulet, whose topic is the "phenomenology of reading," reading, like criticism, is an experience of "interiority," whereby we dissolve the boundaries between subject and object to enter the real being of literature. Books are objects, he says, but distinguishable from other objects in that their existence is not strictly exterior or material. Reading replaces "external objects with a congeries of mental objects in close *rapport* with my consciousness." Reading "is the act in which the subjective principle which I call *I,* is modified in such a way that I no longer have the right, strictly speaking, to consider it as my *I.* I am on loan to another, and this other thinks, feels, suffers, and acts within me." As we read, the poem, play, or novel "lives its own life within me; in a certain sense, it thinks itself, and it even gives itself a meaning with me." Criticism seems to be more reserved in its identification, less complete in its surrender to literature, than reading — criticism "does not necessarily imply the total disappearance of the critic's mind in the mind to be criticized" — but it aims at the same experience of interiority. Criticism, Poulet says, "needs to annihilate, or at least momentarily to forget, the objective elements of the work, and to elevate itself to the apprehension of a subjectivity without objectivity."

To the objective critic, however, the phenomenology of reading is prior to and outside the act of criticism. Even the critic prepared to allow the topic to be discussed would look askance at the emphases in Poulet's notions: that books have to wait for a reader *to come and deliver* them "from their materiality, from their immobility," that books *begin to exist* when the reader "makes them come alive in reading," that they are *dependent* on the consciousness of the reader. Not that Poulet is suggesting anything so simple as the solipsistic view that we create the things we perceive, that books have no existence without perception, for he is intent on dissolving the categories on which the notion of solipsism rests. Rather, he is saying that reading enables books to *assume* their rightful life. Even so, the objective critic must reject any suggestion of literature's dependency on the reader's response, and he will shrink from the unreserved intimacy between reading and writing upon which Poulet insists.

In fact, Wimsatt and Beardsley, just as we might expect, hold it a fallacy to give any prominence to the reader's response. In their 1949 essay, "The Affective Fallacy," which they offered as a companion to their earlier piece of "The Intentional Fallacy," they argued that this fallacy "is a confusion between the poem and its *results* (what it *is* and what it *does*)"; "it begins by trying to derive the standard of criticism from the psychological effects of the poem and ends in impressionism and relativism." The outcome of either fallacy "is that the poem itself, as an object of specifically critical judgment, tends to disappear." [1]

The initial distinction of their argument may seem too restrictive, for what a poem *is* cannot be separated that easily from what it *does,* but they go on to qualify the proposition:

> If the affective critic (avoiding both the physiological and the abstractly psychological form of report) ventures to state with any precision what a line of poetry *does* — as "it fills us with a mixture of melancholy and reverence for antiquity" — either the statement will be patently abnormal or false, or it will be a description of what the meaning of the line *is:* "the spectacle of massive antiquity in ruins." [2]

Wimsatt and Beardsley recognize as well as Poulet that a poem is not a material object. As Wimsatt says:

> The poem conceived as a thing in between the poet and the audience is of course an abstraction. The poem is an act. The only substantive entities are the poet and the audience. But if we are to lay hold of the poetic act to comprehend and evaluate it, and if it is to pass current as a critical object, it must be hypostatized. [3]

The poem, then, must be treated as if it existed in some exterior space, "out there" as objects do, in order that it may be contemplated and elucidated. Hence, reading, like the very making of the poem, must be absorbed in the act of criticism so that "the poem itself" as a certain verbal structure will receive most if not all our attention.

Leo Spitzer's essay, "Linguistics and Literary History," offers another perspective on the relation of reading to criticism, and in turn on the question of whether "the poem itself" is, or can be treated as, an objective entity. Spitzer was a renowned practitioner of literary or philological stylistics, as distinct from the linguistic stylistics discussed in Part III, and he asserts here that he is intent on arriving at the right critical interpretation of what is in the literary text, of what a poem *is*. Furthermore, he is thoroughly aware of the dangers in irrelevant and arbitrary personal associations by the "user" of the work of literature. "The poem needs a reader," he recognized, but "aesthetically, the work of art acts by itself, and may do so because its aesthetic content is self-contained in it and in him." [4] In order "to overcome the impression of an arbitrary association in the work of art, the reader must seek to place himself in the creative center of the artist himself — and re-create the artistic organism." (Although this seems identical with the critical program of Georges Poulet, the two critics were poles apart on at least one fundamental issue: Spitzer was overridingly concerned with the particular work of literature, with "the most individual, the least cataloguable features" of an individual poem or fiction.[5]) Spitzer's method for achieving the re-creation of the artistic organism is called "the circle of understanding," which is derived from the theory of hermeneutics (the methodology of interpretation, specifically the science of interpreting scriptural texts) associated with the nineteenth-century scholars Friedrich Schleiermacher and Wilhelm Dilthey.

In this view critical interpretation is not a simple matter of recording what is "out there," in the text, which the percipient receives passively and inertly. There is a give and take between what the critic brings to a given work — from himself, his knowledge of the author, his awareness of larger literary and historical contexts — and what the work speaking for itself, as it were, exhibits to him. In forming "the circle of understanding" the critic allows his intuitions to be shaped, his perceptions refined, and his starting assumptions modified by what the work makes him see. In a sense, the work interrogates the reader and critic. What he finds as he examines the contours of the literary object causes him to look back and reconsider his original assumptions — the notions and habits of mind that predispose him to certain interpretations and judgments about what he is reading. The real meaning or right interpretation of a text is arrived at, if at all, by a circular route in a succession of looks into the work and looks back into the presuppositions that direct critical scrutiny.

F. W. Bateson, in "Linguistics and Literary Criticism," considers the differences between the responses to the general language act, which is the subject of the linguist's study, and to the act of reading literature, which he holds to be the domain of the literary critic. Bateson rebuffs any moves toward reconciliation between linguistics and literary criticism, because, he argues, the premises and ideals of the two disciplines "differ *tota caelo;* they cannot and should not be compromised."

To define these differences he takes the famous system of *le circuit de la parole* of the linguist Ferdinand de Saussure, which traces the sequence of events when A addresses a remark to B, and transposes it to the literary process, the relation between author and reader. The linguistic cycle, Bateson claims, "must always tend to refer the phenomena of style *back* to their constituents in language . . . rather than *forwards* to the post-linguistic or strictly psychological phase." The literary critic, on the other hand, is concerned with the pre-linguistic elements in literary composition — with the psychological origins of literature — and with the post-linguistic consequences in reading, as well as with "the linguistic constituents of such devices as irony and metaphor." Beyond the nine stages encompassed by *le circuit de la parole* lies the stage Bateson calls the Emotional Response (which he says is the stage after "the experience released in the actual process of reading loses its first imaginative freshness"), and later yet the stage of the Critical Verdict. Hence it follows that "when literary criticism begins the originating linguistic stimulus is already very remote."

Bateson remarks that a dictum by René Wellek on "the superstition of behaviorism" may serve as the epigraph to his paper: "It [behaviorism] denies the evidence of introspection and empathy, the two main sources of human and humane knowledge." This is an old issue in arguments about criticism, which Leo Spitzer contends with in defending his conception of linguistics and literary history. Spitzer shows that he was frankly "mentalist" in his outlook; he dismisses the behavioristic technique of a step-by-step procedure for accumulating and classifying data in stylistic study, which would seem to be one element that separates his philological stylistics from linguistic stylistics.[6] But, interestingly enough, the sharpest attack on and the most cogent refutation of "behavioristic" linguistics has come not from literary critics but from other linguists. Contemporary transformational linguists following Noam Chomsky have been exploring what Chomsky has said is the "close relation between innate properties of the mind and features of linguistic structure."[7] It may be, therefore, that Bateson's strictures apply more to a body of theory and method that has been bypassed than to current linguistics.

Rhetoric has always taken as its province the effects of literature and other forms of discourse on an audience, and Kenneth

Burke discusses the role of "identification," the empathetic processes of both reading and writing, in "Rhetoric — Old and New."

Rhetoric is just about the oldest criticism there is. M. H. Abrams has observed, surveying the orientation of critical theories, that the "pragmatic" view of criticism — which derives from the traditions of classical rhetoric and is oriented less to the aims of the artist and the character of the literary work than "to the nature, the needs, and the springs of pleasure in the audience" — has been "the principal aesthetic attitude of the Western world." [8] Rhetoric has had a more ambiguous status in modern criticism. Critical theories based on the precepts of classical rhetoric have been displaced by other orientations, but as Northrop Frye points out in "The Critical Path," rhetoric from the beginning has meant two things: "the figuration of language and the persuasive powers of an orator" (p. 54), and he calls the New Criticism "rhetorical" because it was preoccupied with the figuration of language. The New Critics, however, were quite uninterested in the second aspect of rhetoric. Like Keats they "hated poetry that has a palpable design on us," and, like Yeats (who said "what is rhetoric but the will trying to do the work of the imagination?") they mistrusted anything in literature that suggested the persuasive offices of the old rhetoric. If they mentioned rhetoric at all in their criticism, it was with disdain or suspicion.

Burke, on the other hand, has always been fascinated by the subject, and though he began his career in association with the New Criticism, he moved beyond its preoccupation with literary verbal figuration to a concern with rhetorical "strategies" of all kinds: verbal and nonverbal, conscious and unconscious, individual and social, in literature and in all other forms of communication. Burke, however, is not trying to revive or renovate classical rhetoric. Like certain other contemporary critics, but in a unique way, he has been fashioning a New Rhetoric. [9]

"Persuasion," Burke says, is the key term for the old rhetoric, "and its stress was upon deliberate design." I. A. Richards, who is as much a founder of the New Rhetoric as of the New Criticism, has made the same point: "The old Rhetoric was an offspring of dispute; it developed as the rationale of pleadings and persuasion; it was the theory of the battle of words, and has always been itself dominated by the combative impulse." [10]

The key term for the New Rhetoric, Burke explains, is "identification," which at its simplest is a deliberate device, "as when the politician seeks to identify with his audience," but it can also be an end, "as when people earnestly yearn to identify themselves with some group or another." Beyond identification is "dialectic," where the mode of action is "co-operative competition." And beyond that is the stage of "consubstantiation," where, in literature, we take pleasure in "ingenious symbolic structures" and in "the very aspects of language we might otherwise fear" so that we are moved "in the purely poetic sense"; and where, in social or personal relations, we conciliate differences or transcend conflicts of interest. The direction of the process is an "ascent" from exploitation toward "gestures of unification, promise, freedom."

Like the French structuralist critics Burke has been constructing a unified theory of verbal and social behavior, and like Northrop Frye he loves terms, nomenclature, classifications, and system. But Burke's aim is a global theory of "symbolic action," all the forms by which human beings act on and communicate with each other; his effort at "anatomy," although no less ambitious than Frye's, has gone into categorizing the rhetorical strategies and symbolic modes (rather than structures) of "human relations in general" as well as in literature. Burke draws much of the terminology of his theories from metaphors of "acting" (both in the theatrical sense and that of "doing"), and one way of describing his enterprise is as a *dramaturgy* of nothing less than all human behavior, utterance, and action.

All this may seem to be remote from literary criticism. "The early Burke was a good literary critic," René Wellek acknowledges, but his later work "uses literature only as document or illustration"; Burke "combines the methods of Marxism, psychoanalysis, and anthropology with semantics in order to devise a system of human behavior and motivation . . . whose center is not in literature at all." [11] Wellek dismisses Burke's enterprise as criticism because it abandoned the differences between "literature and life, work and action." [12] But Burke's career is all of a piece, and his nuclear concern has always been with the reader's response. While he was still a literary critic (if he has ever been anything else) Burke offered a famous definition of literary form. "Form," he said in *Lexicon Rhetoricae* (1931), is "an arousing and fulfillment of desires. A work has form in so far as one part of it leads a reader to anticipate another part, to be gratified by the sequence." [13] Burke has extended this to more general modes of "symbolic action" than literature, so that his later work seems less specifically *literary* criticism, but he has never departed from the critical principle in his original definition of form.

Frederick Crews's essay, "Anaesthetic Criticism," proposes that literary criticism base itself on Freudian psychoanalytical theory.

This had been tried before in modern criticism, but while the New Criticism dominated the academic study of literature, psychoanalytically oriented criticism had very little prestige and was never taken seriously.[14] Crews offers a sophisticated new defense, and he is aware of the shortcomings of earlier efforts, but beyond his programmatic purpose he explains why he has been drawn to Freudian theory in the first place: as a way of engaging the process of reading literature more directly and adequately. "Psychoanalytical principles," Crews says, "bring into question the very possibility that a critic's relation to his texts could be fundamentally rational and disinterested."

The first part of the essay attacks Northrop Frye's conviction that the critic must not look outside literature for principles of understanding. But Crews widens his indictment, and finds his real target, by suggesting that Frye's theories have provided the academic establishment of English studies with a rationale for continuing its reactionary and repressive policies. Frye is an apologist for "the prevailing academic faith" who has kept the profession from responding to a situation of crisis in literary study. "The official custodians" of "professional critical training," "the curators of culture," the whole lot, or "many of them," everybody in charge of the academic study of literature, has exhibited, among other things, "an intolerance toward students who want to come to grips with their deepest responses."

American universities, Crews contends, are under the control of "anaesthetic criticism." A criticism, such as Frye's, "that explicitly or implicitly reduces art to some combination of moral content and abstract form and genre conventions" deadens response and denatures literature; "it insulates the critic and his readers from a threat of affective disturbance." Literary criticism should "make the reading experience more possible for us, but anaesthetic criticism assumes that this requires keeping caged the anxieties that the artist set free and then recaptured." "Someone who wants to look more closely into literature's buried contest between impulse and inhibition," Crews declares, needs "a method for interpreting his own responses." Psychoanalytical theory promises to be the best source for such a method: "The real value of literary psychoanalysis is that it can embolden us to be alone with books, to recognize our own image in them, and from that recognition to begin comprehending their hold over us."

The same concern about anaesthetic criticism is voiced by other contemporary critics who do not otherwise share Crews's convictions about psychoanalysis and politics. It is, in fact, one of the strongest motives for reaching beyond formalism, and can be seen in the essays by Hassan, Hartman, Sontag — almost every younger critic included in this anthology. As Leo Bersani enunciates the issue, previous American and English criticism was governed by "the desire to separate literature from life so that we may possess the supposed 'meanings' and 'values' of life in artifacts whose forms miraculously immobilize experience" (p. 92). Contemporary criticism has the common purpose of liberating in reading, criticism, and in literature itself the energies of experience.

Lionel Trilling, in "On the Teaching of Modern Literature," shows how difficult it is to get students to come to grips with their deepest responses. Trilling believes that "the university study of art is capable of confronting the power of a work of art fully and courageously," but he had misgivings about teaching modern literature because its very character is to assault and expose feelings we keep private or do not admit into consciousness at all. He has found at the end of the term "that almost none of the students have been taken aback by what they have read; they have wholly contained the attack." Trilling admits that his students might have revealed their true feelings better to another teacher, or that they have only been feeding him "what they conceive to be the proper response to the official version of terror" he delivered, and that "in ways and to a degree which they keep secret they have responded directly and personally to what they have read." In that case, however, we are left with some hard questions: How would one know that a true or significant response has taken place? Is the direct and personal response communicable? Is there something about the teaching situation that inhibits any real disclosure of that response? Do teachers have any business with what students actually experience in their reading? [15]

As it happens, Northrop Frye has commented on Trilling's essay and he uses it to support his convictions that literature, being an object rather than a subject of study, cannot be taught directly; that the body of knowledge which constitutes criticism is all that can be taught, not the direct experience of literature; and that there is a fundamental difference between the acts of reading and criticism. "All teaching," Frye says, "is a transposition of literature into criticism, of passion and power and anguish" — the salient features of modern literature — "into pattern and craftsmanship and the following of convention." [16] Criticism, then, "is a disinterested response," not because Frye is afraid of his or his students' feelings or because he wants to keep literary study pure of politics, but because anything other than that ends by imprisoning the very powers of literature it would liberate.

Trilling's essay, however, offers another view. It may not be too fanciful to say that his account exemplifies the whole career of the academic study and teaching of literature from the New Criticism to the present, both describing and suggesting the motives for the great changes that are taking place. "When the teacher has said all that can be said about formal matters," Trilling remarks, "he must confront the necessity of bearing personal testimony." He first taught his course in modern literature in as *literary* a way as possible, treating each work as "a structure of words," but he came to see that this went against the grain — his personal grain, the grain of the classroom situation, and the grain of the authors themselves: "Structures of words they may indeed have created, but these structures were not pyramids or triumphal arches, they were manifestly contrived to be not static and commemorative but mobile and aggressive."

Not only pedagogical method is at stake, but a recognition of what literature itself is, and a willingness to commit one's responses in academic talk about literature. To say, as Trilling learned from his experience, that "the literature had to be dealt with in terms it announced for itself" is to accept the risk of an encounter with books that may shock, bruise, and wound as well as order and pleasure the affective expectations each of us brings to our reading.

And it is on this last point that Trilling and other contemporary critics would part company with I. A. Richards, who of all the New Critics was the most interested in the reader's response and the ways literature patterns our impulses. The value of art, Richards holds, is therapeutic; it not only excites emotions but brings them into equilibrium. Poetry, he says, is "a means of ordering, controlling, and consolidating the whole experience." [17] René Wellek, echoing a charge other formalist critics leveled at Richards, says that the danger of such a psychological theory is that it loses sight of "the objective structure of a work of art," but Wellek's own conception of literature as a process of giving order to experience, although not therapeutic in its ends, is not that different from Richards's. "A work of art," he says, "is an object or a process of some shape and unity which sets it off from life in the raw." [18] Contemporary critics reject this idea of literature as "an immobile artifact," and although they are more sympathetic to Richards's conception of literature as an activity, they do not regard its purpose as simply bringing our impulses into order. "Art can divide as well as heal," Geoffrey H. Hartman says in "Toward Literary History" (p. 761); "its healing power may be complicated by its power to hurt."

Richard Poirier picks up several of the issues discussed by Crews and Trilling in "What Is English Studies, and If You Know What That Is, What Is English Literature?" He is, for example, equally concerned with the need for a direct and personal response to literature, and he agrees with their diagnosis of the "anaesthetic" condition of present academic study. "Much of the classroom study of literature," he remarks,

> appears unfortunately destined to make all energies of response subservient to structures, with emphasis on the coherence resulting from recurrence of patterns, and with a corresponding deemphasis on any discordant elements, except where these can be included as irony or as some as yet unidentified sub-subgenre.

Poirier is fully aware of the embattled state of English studies, and he addresses at length the demand for "relevance" that has been the cutting edge of the attack, but his purpose is less to deplore or applaud the crisis than to seize its opportunities for probing certain basic questions about what literary study is. If English studies must become more relevant, he says, it should first be made more relevant to English literature. But his conception of literature, which shows at once that he is not one more apologist for the status quo, is that it is an activity of language, the performance of writing — not a thing, a corpus of texts, a field or body of "works." A literary "work" should be construed as "another dimension of action, of performance with language as its medium."

This sets Poirier apart from both the radical critics of "the literary-academic establishment" and the traditionalists, "those who defend English as a humane scholarly discipline." Not that he is above the fray as an uncommitted or neutral onlooker. He clearly sides with the radical critics in indicting the classroom versions of the New Criticism and of Northrop Frye's "anatomy of criticism." But he is generous in acknowledging the power of the critics themselves and he sees the fault to be more in the packaging of their theories for use in teaching literature. Certain critical doctrines of T. S. Eliot, for example, have been molded "into a critical system designed to take care of what might be called discordant or dissident elements," with the consequence that literary study "asks the reader to exist importantly only when he can find himself in a structure"; however, this directly counters "the marvelously *unstabilizing* intelligence at work in his critical writing and in his poetry." Before the New Criticism was fashioned into a pedagogical instrument, Poirier says, it "was itself more complex and liberating than it is now made out to be." In fact Poirier is, if anything, even harder on the assumptions of the contemporary radical critics and the implications of their views for the academic study of literature. He sharply criticizes, for example, Herbert Marcuse's notions that literature is a kind of "world elsewhere," an essentially higher form of life, and that there is a necessary antagonism between literature and society.

Poirier argues that the adversaries in the struggle for control of English studies are closer than they would like to think. The most vocal critics are excited by the same illusions that bolster its most vocal defenders: "the illusion, first, of the necessity, and, second, of the enormous importance of literary studies." Both the radical critics and the traditionalists "believe in 'works' more than in 'writing,' in books rather than in those manifestations of energy one might call *écriture*." "Defenders and critics," he says, "share the same illusion about the power of literature as a series of finished works, rather than a feeling for the power, still generating in those works, of the retraceable acts of writing, composition, performance."

And Poirier makes his own plea for that program of study. Developing a capacity for "watching performances in language, the actions of words," as they take place in the writing of any period in English literature, developing "ways of treating *all* writing and *all* reading as analogous acts, as simultaneously unfolding performances, some of which deaden, some of which will quicken us," is the positive new step English studies must take if it is to survive both the assault of its radical critics and the defense of its trimming apologists. And one consequence of such a program is that English studies, instead of withdrawing from politics and the turbulent life of our times, may teach us "how to meet and know words under different kinds of social and historical stress."

Poirier notes that he has been trying to develop his own understanding of "the mysteries of performance," and in his other essays, collected under the title *The Performing Self,* he has elaborated these ideas and put them into practice. Two points emerge.

First, he is perfectly aware of the hazards of "performance." The word itself has dubious aspects. A performance may be a shapeless act — and more than that, an "act," a put-on, deceiving or exhibitionistic, something done just for show: as Yeats said, a mere "talking for effect." [19] Poirier knows this. In the title essay of his collection he notices places where the performances of Norman Mailer and Henry James (writers he has elsewhere written of with affection and admiration) fall flat or are merely talking for effect.

"Performance," Poirier says,

> differs from what is called a happening by virtue of the fact that it is an action which must go through passages that both impede the action and give it form, much as a sculptor not only is impelled to shape his material but is in turn shaped by it, his impulse to mastery always chastened, sometimes made tender and possibly witty by the recalcitrance of what he is working on.[20]

The same recognition is evident in the essay included here, for performance in writing, Poirier says, is "struggling, wrestling with words and meaning." Like Robert Frost, who inspired his interest in literary performance, Poirier draws his metaphors more from athletics than from acting. Writing is not just any activity, but a *contest,* and that sense of contending with its medium of language keeps the activity honest and saves "performance" from shapeless posturing.

Second, Poirier is not overwhelmed, as Trilling seems to be, by the costs and the agony of the exigency of the work of art. In 1963 Poirier interviewed Frost for the *Paris Review* series, *Writers at Work.* During this fascinating exchange Frost, discussing the first poem he ever wrote, remarked how so many writers talk "about what it costs them, what agony it is to write," and he said it is natural to wonder how he or any reader of his poem could "have a good time with what cost me too much agony" — but, Frost declares, what else did he want to communicate "but what a *hell* of a good time I had writing it." Poirier explores the rich implications of Frost's statement in his essay on "The Performing Self," and concludes:

> If the poem expresses grief, it also expresses — as an *act,* as a composition, a performance, a "making," — the opposite of grief; it shows or expresses "what a *hell* of a good time I had writing it." [21]

A reader's response ought to be shaped by the poet's pleasure in his performance at writing as well as by the terrible and dark meanings of the things said by the words of the poem.

Poirier offers a lovely tribute to F. R. Leavis, especially to that quality in his criticism of "bearing personal testimony" (and its necessary condition: that there be something worth hearing about in the experience) which Trilling came to value most in teaching literature. Leavis is a critic of overpowering personal conviction, who has a positively evangelical feeling for literature, and though he says in "Literature and the University" that criticism is or should be a collaborative enterprise, he has been anything but amiable or accommodating in his public critical disputes. Fiercely litigious whenever literary study or criticism has been called into question, abrasive in manner, his career has been marked by a series of stormy controversies.[22]

Leavis is often classified as a New Critic because he was influenced by Eliot and Richards in his early work and because he practiced the mode of close reading, but, as Poirier points out, Leavis has never "thought of his principal job as interpretation at all." In time Leavis came to be labeled a "moral" critic, in the tradition of Matthew Arnold's moralistic humanism, or a "sociocultural" critic, but it might be more meaningful to apprehend what Poirier describes as the informing motive of Leavis's concern with moral, social, and cultural issues — that "English literature, English culture, England itself can be found in the performed condition of the English language." "Language," Leavis says here, "is very largely the essential life of a culture" — not just the mirror or vehicle or analogue of it. And, in the particular sense he describes in this essay and enacts in his own criticism, literature "is a mode or manifestation of language."

Leavis makes the largest possible claims for academic study in "Literature and the University," but his defense will scarcely give much comfort to the "traditionalists" of English studies. Leavis does not view the university as a citadel of privilege, a bastion of accepted humanistic values, or a training ground for what he calls the "technologico-Benthamite civilization," but rather "as a centre of consciousness" of all that is vital and alive for the community, where "the human heritage, the cultural continuity" may be nurtured and *recreated*.[23] English studies is "the focal centre" of that endeavor — and literary criticism is the lens, precisely because it directs us to the essential task of renewing and creating literary culture rather than simply handing on the monuments of the past.

Creative response is at the heart of Leavis's ideas of the functions of reading, criticism, and the academic study of literature. "Practical Criticism," he says, is "a creative, or re-creative process." It is a more deliberate and complete "following-through of that process of creation in response to the poet's words . . . than any serious reading is." Criticism is concerned with establishing

the poem or novel "as an object of common access," and the end
of the cycle "is the establishing of a value":

> The process, the kind of activity of inner response and discipline,
> by which we take possession of the created work is essentially the
> kind of activity that completes itself in a value-judgment.

It is precisely on the implications of this point that Leavis's views
clash with those of several contemporary critics. Poirier points
out that Leavis makes a canon, a "great tradition," of his personal
preferences: "It is he who decides, dogmatically as well as deliberately, that [the poem] should be 'there,' along with the extent to
which it makes proper use of the resources of its language." And
that seems to be what Northrop Frye has been fighting all along.
Geoffrey H. Hartman compares him to Leavis explicitly on this
issue. Hartman says that Frye's achievement has been to challenge
the mystique, so forcefully promoted by Leavis, that "literature is to
be used as a training ground for the élite judgment." Leavis, Hartman asserts, is part of the historical movement by which English
studies assumed "the mantle of Classical studies" and claimed for
"English literature the same function of training the judgment," of
cultivating "a specific and judicious sensibility." [24]
Leavis is not afraid of being called an "élitist," and the absurdity of saying he is such, in the disreputable sense the term
has acquired in contemporary debate about English studies, is
proved by his whole long career of battling against social or educational class, caste, and privilege. But that may not count. The
issue is whether any critic who makes a canon of his preferences,
however well-intentioned his motives, will end by investing literary study with an élitist mystique. Leavis shows that the issue is
much more complicated than it seems, for in his stubborn insistence that we must select and judge what is or is not worth keeping, he puts the case on harder grounds than any self-serving
apologist for English studies can offer.
If comparisons like Hartman's are to be made, it should be
noted that Leavis has never recommended training a critical sensibility for its own sake. Nor has he, as Hartman alleges, "adapted
and refined the Classicist emphasis on the importance of judgment" — and least of all for the purpose the Classicist idea has
served in English education: to give students a general education
preparing them for the variety of skills needed to administer an
empire. Leavis has always been dead set against these uses of literary study. The whole point of critical training, as Leavis says in
the essay included here, is that "it is a re-creation in which, by a

considering attentiveness, we ensure a more than ordinary faithfulness and fulness" *to the poet's words.* Unlike Frye, Leavis believes that criticism is "wholly subservient" to the created work.

Frye himself has discussed Leavis's criticism and questioned Leavis's idea that "the poem is a determinate thing: it is *there,*" and "unappreciated, the poem isn't *there.*" Frye contends that by Leavis's insistence on the "thereness" of a poem "the work of art remains permanently a detached object of contemplation." [25] But this is not quite what Leavis says in "Literature and the University." Without a many-sided real critical exchange, he asserts, "the object, which we think of as 'there' in a public world for common contemplation, isn't really 'there.' " Not, of course, that its material existence is affected; Leavis means that a poem or novel will not come into its true and full life unless we make ourselves responsive to its powers by criticism. Like language generally, literature is

> really *there,* it really exists in full actuality, only in individual users; it is *there* only as its idioms, phrases, words and so on, with the meaning, intention, force in which their life resides, are uttered and meant by me (for example) and taken by you.

Our response as readers and critics, then, is not one of analyzing the factivity of literature, but actively engaging its real powers in performance.

Interestingly enough, Frye and Leavis, for all their deep differences, have some genuine affinities. After what Hassan, Crews, and other critics in this anthology have said about Frye, it may come as something of a surprise to find him affirming that "what criticism can do, to point beyond itself, is to try to undermine the student's sense of the ultimate objectivity of the literary work." "Literature," he declares, "is a power to be possessed, and not a body of objects to be studied" [26] — precisely the conception of literature Leavis has advocated from the start.

The differences between the two critics are not to be blurred, of course, in any easy reconciliation. In the same essay, for example, Frye contends that a literary work presents "an alien structure of imagination" which "must become possessed by and identified with the student," but "criticism cannot make this act of possession for the student; what it can do is to weaken those tendencies within criticism that keep the literary work objective and separated" — whereas Leavis believes that criticism is nothing if not the *act* of possessing and absorbing the powers of literature.

Moreover, even if Frye and Leavis agree in principle (or in phrasing) on this point, the question is which critic gives the more direct and immediate sense of its workings in actual critical performance. Does Frye's criticism convey as complete a sense of grasping and being possessed by the powers and energies of literature as that of Leavis — or, to extend the question, of Poulet, Blackmur, Poirier, or any of the other critics included in this anthology?

Murray Krieger resolutely reaffirms the need to treat the poem as an object in "Mediation, Language, and Vision in the Reading of Literature." Examining the problem of "language as mediation in literature," Krieger offers a tough defense of "the contextualist movement" of the New Criticism against its major antagonists in contemporary criticism, including Northrop Frye, the critics of consciousness, and the French structuralist critics, whom he sees as making several forms of a concerted "attack on the mediating properties of poetic structure and of the critical language seeking to fix that structure." Krieger divides the adversaries into "antimediators," who attempt an unmediated response to literature, and "over-mediators," who recognize the structural properties of literature but attempt an overgeneralized response.

Krieger belabors Ihab Hassan as an extreme representative of the critics who would decompose the poem as a verbal object. Hassan attempts to pass through the words of a literary work and the mediating properties of its formal structures to apprehend the nature, body, human consciousness, vision, or whatever inhabits and animates the text but is not imprisoned there. Krieger discusses the critics of consciousness as "serving a similar tendency to deobjectify and repersonalize literature." He respects their motives, but he believes their conception is against the nature of literature as a process of mediation.

On the other side are Frye and the French structuralists, overmediators, who burden the individual poem, play, or novel "with universalizing mediations." The over-mediator, Krieger says,

> is willing to freeze his object by spatializing its form, universalizing it by absorbing it into common formulas — models — broader than the work (or, in cases, broader than literature itself). This sense of the model is what is placed between the work and our private response, shaping both work and response to our awareness of that model.

The trouble with Frye's criticism, however, is that his system absorbs the discrete object, the poem, too completely, "causing total deprivation to the singular." And if Frye jeopardizes the individual work, the French structuralist critics, in their concern with homologous anthropological and general linguistic structures, threaten the specificity of poetic structures, that which makes them "peculiarly literary."

In the face of these attacks "contextualism" (see p. 173, note 3c and pp. 629–30) must devise new tactics of defense. "Explication for explication's (or ingenuity's) sake," and the conception of the poem as an immobile artifact on which this procedure for study has been based, must be abandoned, Krieger says. In its place he urges a view of the poem "as at once object *and* immediate," an object with the qualities and "the immediacies of consciousness" that is dynamic, free-flowing, and pulsing with life rather than static, fixed, and impersonalized. Literature, he declares, is "a live art and act" — but still an object.

Krieger's own performance is obviously an attempt at mediation. He is incisive about the theoretical issues at stake, and he has a sharp eye for the questionable aspects of the alternatives to contextualism, but we may be left wondering about the force of his expedient: whether, for example, the symmetry of his argument isn't too coercive. He says of the over-mediator:

> The deadening effect upon work and response is almost enough to send us, by way of reaction, to the dynamic vitality of the anti-mediator, except that we know that danger too.

By these terms the only position worth taking is one which mediates between the two indefensible positions. But the question, of course, is whether Frye or the structuralist critics discussed by Leo Bersani can be arranged in that fashion.

Even more important is whether Krieger hasn't advanced his case for contextualism by appropriating, by "co-opting," just about everything that is distinctive to the attack of its adversaries. Krieger says we must see the poem as "at once still moving and forever still." But if we take these words at face value, how much of the conception of the poem as an object can we retain? It is all very well to exhort criticism to achieve the sensitive nuances of response Georges Poulet, for example, brings to his reading, and at the same time insist upon the need to preserve a sense of the poem as an objective structure, but how compatible are these activities? Can we reconcile these contraries that easily? Do we have to? Krieger makes much of the paradoxical nature of literature, and in his own argument he relies heavily on paradox, which is, of course, a composition of contraries, but the risk of such formulations, as he himself acknowledges, is that they may be "a verbal mystique" rather than a real solution to the challenges the antagonists to contextualism have been propounding in contemporary criticism.

Nevertheless, Krieger is trying to contain the attack rather than reverting to a *status quo ante*. His defense of the poem as an object is hardly a form of "anaesthetic criticism." Like many of the contemporary critics he does battle with, Krieger is moved in his argument by the need to restore to criticism the immediate and manifold qualities we experience in reading literature.

LEO SPITZER

Linguistics and Literary History

. . . Since the best document of the soul of a nation is its literature, and since the latter is nothing but its language as this is written down by elect speakers, can we perhaps not hope to grasp the spirit of a nation in the language of its outstanding works of literature? Because it would have been rash to compare the whole of a national literature to the whole of a national language (as Karl Vossler has prematurely tried to do) I started, more modestly, with the question: "Can one distinguish the soul of a particular French writer in his particular language?" It is obvious that literary historians have held this conviction, since, after the inevitable quotation (or misquotation) of Buffon's saying: *"Le style c'est l'homme,"* they generally include in their monographs a chapter on the style of their author. But I had in mind the more rigorously scientific definition of an individual style, the definition of a linguist which should replace the casual, impressionistic remarks of literary critics. Stylistics, I thought, might bridge the gap between linguistics and literary history. On the other hand, I was warned by the scholastic adage: *individuum est ineffabile;* could it be that any attempt to define the individual writer by his style is doomed to failure? The individual stylistic deviation from the general norm must represent a historical step taken by the writer, I argued: it must reveal a shift of the soul of the epoch, a shift of which the writer has become conscious and which he would translate into a necessarily new linguistic form; perhaps it would be possible to determine the historical step, psychological as well as linguistic? To determine the beginning of a linguistic innovation would be easier, of course, in the case of contemporary writers, because their linguistic basis is better known to us than is that of past writers.

In my reading of modern French novels, I had acquired the habit of underlining expressions which struck me as aberrant from general usage,

SOURCE: Selections from "Linguistics and Literary History," in Leo Spitzer, *Linguistics and Literary History: Essays in Stylistics* (copyright 1948 by Princeton University Press; Princeton Paperback, 1967). Reprinted by permission of Princeton University Press.

and it often happened that the underlined passages, taken together, seemed to offer a certain consistency. I wondered if it would not be possible to establish a common denominator for all or most of these deviations; could not the common spiritual etymon, the psychological root, of several individual "traits of style" in a writer be found, just as we have found an etymon common to various fanciful word formations? [1] I had, for example, noticed in the novel *Bubu de Montparnasse* of Charles-Louis Philippe (1905), which moves in the underworld of Parisian pimps and prostitutes, a particular use of *à cause de,* reflecting the spoken, the unliterary language: "Les réveils de midi sont lourds et poisseux. . . . On éprouve un sentiment de déchéance *à cause* des réveils d'autrefois." More academic writers would have said "en se rappelant des réveils d'autrefois . . . ," "à la suite du souvenir. . . ." This, at first glance, prosaic and commonplace *à cause de* has nevertheless a poetic flavor, because of the unexpected suggestion of a causality, where the average person would see only coincidence: it is, after all, not unanimously accepted that one awakes with a feeling of frustration from a noon siesta *because* other similar awakenings have preceded; we have here an assumed, a poetic reality, but one expressed by a prosaic phrase. We find this *à cause de* again in a description of a popular celebration of the 14th of July: "[le peuple], *à cause de* l'anniversaire de sa délivrance, laisse ses filles danser en liberté." Thus, one will not be surprised when the author lets this phrase come from the mouth of one of his characters: "Il y a dans mon coeur deux ou trois cent petites émotions qui brûlent *à cause de toi.*" Conventional poetry would have said "qui brûlent pour toi"; "qui brûlent *à cause de toi*" is both less and more: more, since the lover speaks his heart better in this sincere, though factual manner. The causal phrase, with all its semipoetic implications, suggests rather a commonplace speaker, whose speech and whose habits of thought the writer seems to endorse in his own narrative.

Our observation about *à cause de* gains strength if we compare the use, in the same novel, of other causal conjunctions, such as *parce que:* for example, it is said of the pimp's love for his sweetheart Berthe: "[il aimait] sa volupté particulière, quand elle appliquait son corps contre le sien. . . . Il aimait cela qui la distinguait de toutes les femmes qu'il avait connues *parce que* c'était plus doux, *parce que* c'était plus fin, et *parce que* c'était sa femme à lui, qu'il avait eue vierge. Il l'aimait *parce qu'*elle était honnête et qu'elle en avait l'air, et pour toutes les raisons qu'ont les bourgeois d'aimer leur femme." Here, the reasons why Maurice loved to embrace his sweetheart (*parce que c'était doux, fin, parce que c'était sa femme à lui*) are outspokenly classified or censored by the writer as being *bourgeois;* and yet, in Philippe's narrative, the *parce que* is used as if he considered these reasons to be objectively valid.

The same observation holds true for the causal conjunction *car:* in the following passage which describes Maurice as a being naturally loved by women: "Les femmes l'entouraient d'amour comme des oiseaux qui chantent le soleil et la force. Il était un de ceux que nul ne peut assujettir, *car* leur vie, plus forte et plus belle, comporte l'amour du danger."

Again, it can happen that a causal relationship is implied without the use of a conjunction, a relationship due to the gnomic character adherent, at least in that particular milieu, to a general statement — the truth of which is, perhaps, not so fully accepted elsewhere: "Elle l'embrassa à pleine bouche. *C'est une chose hygiénique* et bonne entre un homme et sa femme, qui vous amuse un petit quart d'heure avant de vous endormir." (Philippe could as well have written "car . . . ," "parce que c'est une chose hygiénique. . . .") Evidently this is the truth only in that particular world of sensuous realism which he is describing. At the same time, however, the writer, while half-endorsing these bourgeois platitudes of the underworld, is discreetly but surely suggesting his criticism of them.

Now I submit the hypothesis that all these expansions of causal usages in Philippe cannot be due to chance: there must be "something the matter" with his conception of causality. And now we must pass from Philippe's style to the psychological etymon, to the radix in his soul. I have called the phenomenon in question "pseudo-objective motivation": Philippe, when presenting causality as binding for his characters, seems to recognize a rather objective cogency in their sometimes awkward, sometimes platitudinous, sometimes semipoetic reasonings; his attitude shows a fatalistic, half-critical, half-understanding, humorous sympathy with the necessary errors and thwarted strivings of these underworld beings dwarfed by inexorable social forces. The pseudo-objective motivation, manifest in his style, is the clue to Philippe's *Weltanschauung;* he sees, as has also been observed by literary critics, without revolt but with deep grief and a Christian spirit of contemplativity, the world functioning wrongly with an appearance of rightness, of objective logic. The different word-usages, grouped together (just as was done with the different forms of *conundrum* and *quandary*) lead toward a psychological etymon, which is at the bottom of the linguistic as well as of the literary inspiration of Philippe.

Thus we have made the trip from language or style to the soul. And on this journey we may catch a glimpse into a historical evolution of the French soul in the twentieth century: first we are given insight into the soul of a writer who has become conscious of the fatalism weighing on the masses, then, into that of a section of the French nation itself, whose faint protest is voiced by our author. And in this procedure there is, I think, no longer the timeless, placeless philology of the older school, but an explanation of the concrete *hic et nunc* of a historical phenomenon. The to-and-fro movement we found to be basic with the humanist has been followed here, too: first we grouped together certain causal expressions, striking with Philippe, then hunted out their psychological explanation, and finally, sought to verify whether the element of "pseudo-objective motivation" [2] concorded with what we know, from other sources, about the elements of his inspiration. Again, a belief is involved — which is no less daring than is the belief that the Romance languages go back to one invisible, basic pattern manifest in them all: namely, the belief that the mind of an author is a kind of solar system into whose orbit all categories of things are attracted: language, motivation, plot, are only satellites of this mythological entity (as my antimentalistic adversaries would call it): *mens Philippina*. The linguist as well as his literary colleague must always ascend to the etymon which is behind all those particular so-called literary or stylistic devices which the literary historians are wont to list. And the individual *mens Philippina* is a reflection of the *mens Franco-gallica* of the twentieth century; its ineffability consists precisely in Philippe's anticipatory sensitivity for the spiritual needs of the nation.

Now, it is obvious that a modern writer such as Philippe, faced with the social disintegration of humanity in the twentieth century, must show more patent linguistic deviations, of which the philologist may take stock in order to build up his "psychogram" of the individual artist. But does Philippe, a stranded being broken loose from his moorings, transplanted, as it were, into a world from which he feels estranged — so that he must, perforce, indulge in arbitrary whimsicality — represent only a modern phenomenon? If we go back to writers of more remote times, must it not be that we will always find a balanced language, with no deviations from common usage?

It suffices to mention the names of such dynamic writers of older times as Dante or Quevedo or Rabelais to dispel such a notion. Whoever has thought strongly and felt strongly has innovated in his language; mental creativity immediately inscribes itself into the language, where it becomes linguistic creativity; the trite and petrified in language is never sufficient for the needs of expression felt by a strong personality. In my first publication, "Die Wortbildung als stilistisches Mittel" (a thesis written in 1910), I dealt with Rabelais' comic word-formations, a subject to which I was attracted because of certain affinities between Rabelaisian and Viennese (Nestroy!) comic writing, and which offered the opportunity of bridging the gap between linguistic and literary history. Be it said to the eternal credit of the scholarly integrity of Meyer-Lübke that he, in contrast to the antimentalists who would suppress all expressions of opposition to their theories, recommended for publication a book with an approach so aberrant from his own. In this work I sought to show, for example, that a neologism such as *pantagruélisme,* the name given by Rabelais to his stoic-epicurean philosophy ("certaine gayeté d'esprict, conficte en mépris des choses fortuites") is not only a playful outburst of a genuine gaiety, but a thrust from the realm of the real into that of the unreal and the unknown — as is true, in fact, of any nonce-word. On the one hand, a form with the suffix -ism evokes a school of serious philosophic thought (such as Aristotelianism, scholasticism, etc.); on the other, the stem, Pantagruel, is the name of a character created by Rabelais, the half-jocular, half-philosophical giant and patriarchal king. The coupling of the learned philosophical suffix with the fanciful name of a fanciful character amounts to positing a half-real, half-unreal entity: "the philosophy of an imaginary being." The contemporaries of Rabelais who first heard this coinage must have experienced the reactions provoked by any nonce-word: a moment of shock followed by a feeling of reassurance: to be swept toward the unknown frightens, but realization of the benignly fanciful result gives relief: laughter, our physiological reaction on such occasions, arises precisely out of a feeling of relief following upon a temporary breakdown of our assurance. Now, in a case such as that of the creation pantagruélisme, the designation of a hitherto unknown but, after all, innocuous philosophy, the menacing force of the neologism is relatively subdued. But what of such a list of names as that concocted by Rabelais for the benefit of his hated adversaries, the reactionaries of the Sorbonne: sophistes, sorbillans, sorbonagres, sorbonigenes, sorbonicoles, sorboniformes, sorboniseques, niborcisans, sorbonisans, saniborsans. Again, though differently, there is an element of realism present in these coinages: the Sorbonne is an existing reality, and the formations are explainable by well-known formative processes. The edition of Abel Lefranc, imbued with his positivistic approach, goes to the trouble of explaining each one of these formations: sorboniforme is after uniforme, sorbonigene after homogène, while niborcisans, saniborsans offer what, in the jargon of the linguists, is called a metathesis. But by explaining every coinage separately, by dissolving the forest into trees, the commentators lose sight of the whole phenomenon: they no longer see the forest — or rather the jungle which Rabelais must have had before his eyes, teeming with viperlike, hydralike, demonlike shapes. Nor is it enough to say that the scholarly Rabelais indulges in humanistic word lists with a view to enriching the vocabulary — in the spirit of an Erasmus who prescribed the principle of copia verborum to students of Latin — or that Rabelais' rich nature bade him make the French language rich; the aesthetics of richness is, in itself, a problem; and why should richness tend toward the frightening, the bottomless? Perhaps Rabelais' whole attitude toward language rests upon a vision of imaginary richness whose support is the bottomless. He creates word-families, representative of gruesome fantasy-beings, copulating and engendering before our eyes, which have reality only in the world of language, which are established in an intermediate world between reality and irreality, between the nowhere that frightens and the "here" that reassures. The *niborcisans* are as yet an entity vaguely connected with the *sorbonisans,* but at the same time so close to nothingness that we laugh — uneasily; it is *le comique grotesque* which skirts the abyss. And Rabelais will shape grotesque word-families (or families of word-demons) not only by altering what exists: he may leave intact the forms of his word material and create by juxtaposition: savagely piling epithet upon epithet to an ultimate effect of terror, so that, from the well known emerges the shape of the unknown — a phenomenon the more startling with the French, who are generally considered to inhabit an orderly, clearly regulated, well-policed language. Now, of a sudden, we no longer recognize this French language, which has become a chaotic word-world situated somewhere in the chill of cosmic space. Just listen to the inscription on the *abbaye de Thélème,* that Renaissance convent of his shaping, from which Rabelais excludes the hypocrites:

> Cy n'entrez pas, hypocrites, bigots,
> Vieux matagotz, marmiteux, borsoufles,
> Torcoulx, badaux, plus que n'estoient les Gotz,
> Ny Ostrogotz, precurseurs des magotz,
> Haires, cagotz, cafars empantouflez,
> Gueux mitoufles, frapars escorniflez,
> Befflez, enflez, fagoteurs de tabus;
> Tirez ailleurs pour vendre vos abus.

The prosaic commentators of the Lefranc edition would explain that this kind of rather mediocre poetry is derived from the popular genre of the *cry* (the harangue of a barker), and overloaded with devices of the *rhétoriqueur* school. But I can never read these lines without being frightened, and I am shaken in this very moment by the horror emanating from this accumulation of *-fl-* and *-got-* clusters — of sounds which, in themselves, and taken separately, are quite harmless, of words grouped together, bristling with Rabelais' hatred of hypocrisy — that greatest of all crimes against life. A *cry,* yes, but in a more extensive meaning of the word: it is the gigantic voice of Rabelais which cries to us directly across the gulf of the centuries, as shattering now as at the hour when Rabelais begot these word-monsters.

If, then, it is true that Rabelais' word-formation reflects an attitude somewhere between reality and irreality, with its shudders of horror and its comic relief, what of Lanson's famous statement on Rabelais in general, which is repeated in thousands of French schools and in most of the Lanson-imbued seminars of French throughout the world: "Jamais réalisme plus pur, plus puissant et plus triomphant ne s'est vu"? Well, it is simply wrong. I have not time to develop here the conclusions which would round out the utterly antirealistic picture of Rabelais that stands out in his work; it could be shown that the whole plot of Rabelais' epic, the fantastic voyage of fantastic people to the oracle of the priestess Bacbuc (whose ambiguous response: *"Trinc!"* is just a nowhere word) as well as the invention of detail (e.g., Panurge's speech on debtors and lenders, in which the earthy Panurge drives forward, from his astute egoistic refusal to live without debts, to a cosmic, utopian vision of a paradoxical world resting on the universal law of indebtedness) — that everything in Rabelais' work tends toward the creation of a world of irreality.

Thus, what has been disclosed by the study of Rabelais' language, the literary study would corroborate; it could not be otherwise, since language is only one outward crystallization of the "inward form," or, to use another metaphor: the lifeblood of the poetic creation [3] is everywhere the same, whether we tap the organism at "language" or "ideas," at "plot" or at "composition." As regards the last, I could as well have begun with a study of the rather loose literary composition of Rabelais' writings and only later have gone over to his ideas, his plot, his language. Because I happened to be a linguist it was from the linguistic angle that I started, to fight my way to his unity. Obviously, no fellow scholar must be required to do the same. What he must be asked to do, however, is, I believe, to work from the surface to the "inward life-center" of the work of art: first observing details about the superficial appearance of the particular work (and the "ideas" expressed by a poet are, also, only one of the superficial traits in a work of art); [4] then, grouping these details and seeking to integrate them into a creative principle which may have been present in the soul of the artist; and, finally, making the return trip to all the other groups of observations in order to find whether the "inward form" one has tentatively constructed gives an account of the whole. The scholar will surely be able to state, after three or four of these "fro voyages," whether he has found the life-giving center, the sun of the solar system (by then he will know whether he is really permanently installed in the center, whether he finds himself in an "excentric" or peripheric position). There is no shadow of truth in the objection raised not long ago by one of the representatives of the mechanist Yale school of linguists against the "circularity of arguments" of the mentalists: against the "explanation of a linguistic fact by an assumed psychological process for which the only evidence is the fact to be explained." [5] I could immediately reply that my school is not satisfied with psychologizing one trait but bases its assumptions on several traits carefully grouped and integrated; one should, in fact, embrace *all* the linguistic traits observable with a given author (I myself have tried to come as close as possible to this requirement of completeness in my studies on Racine, Saint-Simon, Quevedo . . .). And the circle of which the adversary just quoted speaks is not a vicious one; on the contrary, it is the basic operation in the humanities, the *Zirkel im*

Verstehen as Dilthey has termed the discovery, made by the Romantic scholar and theologian Schleiermacher, that cognizance in philology is reached not only by the gradual progression from one detail to another detail, but by the anticipation or divination of the whole — because "the detail can be understood only by the whole and any explantion of detail presupposes the understanding of the whole." [6] Our to-and-fro voyage from certain outward details to the inner center and back again to other series of details is only an application of the principle of the "philological circle." After all, the concept of the Romance languages as based on one Vulgar Latin substratum, and reflected in them although identical with none — this has been reached by the founder of Romance philology, Diez, the pupil of the Romantics, precisely by means of this "philological circle," which allowed him to sit installed in the center of the phenomenon "Romance Languages," whereas Raynouard, his predecessor, by identifying one of the Romance varieties, Provençal, with Proto-Romance, found himself in an excentric position, from which point it was impossible to explain satisfactorily all the outward traits of Romance. To proceed from some exterior traits of Philippe's or Rabelais' language to the soul or mental center of Philippe and Rabelais, and back again to the rest of the exterior traits of Philippe's and Rabelais' works of art, is the same *modus operandi* as that which proceeds from some details of the Romance languages to a Vulgar Latin prototype and then, in reverse order, explains other details by this assumed prototype — or even, from that which infers from some of the outward, phonetic and semantic appearances of the English word *conundrum* to its medieval French soul, and back to all its phonetic and semantic traits. . . .

In the essays to follow I have made an attempt to apply the principle of the "philological circle" to various authors of different nations and periods, applying it in varying degree and manner and in combination with other methods. But these articles are conceived not only as illustrations of my procedure, but as independent contributions to the understanding of the writers treated therein: contributions which should prove readable for any cultured person interested in the style of works of art.[7] For if my procedure should have any value, this must be revealed in the new results, the scholarly progress, attained by its means: the philological circle should not imply that one moves complacently in the circle of the already-known, in a *piétinement sur place*. Thus each single essay is intended to form a separate, independent unit: I hope that the repetitions of theoretical and historical statements which are the unavoidable consequence of this manner of presentation, will be felt by the reader rather as recurrent *leitmotifs* or *refrains* destined to emphasize a constancy and unity of approach.

Before putting to the test the method of the "philological circle" already delineated, I should like to warn the reader that he must not expect to find, in my demonstration of this method, the systematic step-by-step procedure which my own description of it may have seemed to promise.[8] For, when I spoke in terms of a series of back-and-forth movements (first the detail, then the whole, then another detail, etc.), I was using a linear and temporal figure in an attempt to describe states of apperception which, in the mind of the humanist, only too often co-exist. This gift, or vice (for it has its dangers), of seeing part and whole together, at any moment, and which, to some degree, is basic to the operation of the philological mind, is, perhaps, in my own case, developed to a particular degree, and has aroused objections from students and readers — in Germany, where the synthetic capacities of the public are, in general, superior to their analytic capacities, as well as in America where the opposite obtains. A very understanding but critical ex-student of mine, an American, once wrote me: "To establish a behavioristic technique which would reveal the application of your method is, it seems to me, beyond your possibilities. You know the principles that motivate you, rather than any 'technique' that you rigorously follow. Here, it may be a memory from boyhood, there an inspiration you got from another poem; here, there and everywhere it is an urge in you, an instinct backed up by your experience, that tells you immediately: 'this is not important; this is.' At every second you are making choices, but you hardly know that you make them: what seems right to you must be immediately right. And you can only show by doing; you see the meaning as a whole from the beginning; there are almost no steps in your mental processes; and, writing from the midst of your thoughts you take it for granted that the reader is with you and that what is self-evident to you as the next step (only, it's not the next step, even: it's already included, somehow) will also be so to him."

These words, obviously, offer a picture of the limitations of a particular individual temperament. But much of what my correspondent says is given with the operation of the circle — when this is applied, not to routine reading, on the one hand, or to the deductions of schematic linguistics on the other, but to a work of art: the solution attained by means of the circular operation cannot be subjected to a rigorous rationale because, at its most perfect, this is a negation of steps: once attained, it tends to obliterate the steps leading up to it (one may remember the lion of medieval bestiaries who, at every step forward, wiped out his footprints with his tail, in order to elude his pursuers!).

Why do I insist that it is impossible to offer the reader a step-by-step rationale to be applied to a work of art? For one reason, that the first step, on which all may hinge, can never be planned: it must already have taken place. This first step is the awareness of having been struck by a detail, followed by a conviction that this detail is connected basically with the work of art; it means that one has made an "observation" — which is the starting point of a theory, that one has been prompted to raise a question — which must find an answer. To begin by omitting this first step must doom any attempt at interpretation — as was the case with the dissertation . . . devoted to the "imagery" of Diderot, in which the concept "imagery" was based on no preliminary observation but on a ready-made category applied from without to the work of art.

Unfortunately, I know of no way to guarantee either the "impression" or the conviction just described: they are the results of talent, experience, and faith. And, even then, the first step is not to be taken at our own volition: how often, with all the theoretical experience of method accumulated in me over the years, have I stared blankly, quite similar to one of my beginning students, at a page that would not yield its magic. The only way leading out of this state of unproductivity is to read and reread,[9] patiently and confidently, in an endeavor to become, as it were, soaked through and through with the atmosphere of the work. And suddenly, one word, one line, stands out, and we realize that, now, a relationship has been established between the poem and us. From this point on, I have usually found that, what with other observations adding themselves to the first, and with previous experiences of the circle intervening, and with associations given by previous education building up before me (all of this quickened, in my own case, by a quasi-metaphysical urge toward solution) it does not seem long until the characteristic "click" occurs, which is the indication that detail and whole have found a common denominator — which gives the etymology of the writing.[10] And looking back on this process (whose end, of course, marks only the conclusion of the *preliminary* stage of analysis), how can we say when exactly it began? (Even the "first step" was preconditioned.) We see, indeed, that to read is to have read, to understand is equivalent to having understood.[11]

I have just spoken of the importance of past experience in the process of understanding the work of art — but as only one of the intervening factors. For experience with the "circle" is not, itself, enough to enable one to base thereupon a program applicable to all cases. For every poem the critic needs a separate inspiration, a separate light from above (it is this constant need which makes for humility, and it is the accumulation of past enlightenments that encourages a sort of pious confidence). Indeed, a Protean mutability is required of the critic, for the device which has proved successful for one work of art cannot be applied mechanically to another: I could not expect that the "trick of the five *grands*" (which I shall apply to an ode of Claudel's) would work for the "récit de Théramène," or that proper names, which will serve as a point of departure in my article on Cervantes, would play any part in the study on

Diderot. It is, indeed, most trying for the experienced teacher to have to watch a beginner re-use, and consequently mis-use, a particular clue that had served the teacher when he was treating a quite different writer — as though a young actor were to use the leer of Barrymore's Richard III for his performance of Othello. The mutability required of the critic can be gained only by repeated experiences with totally different writers; the "click" will come oftener and more quickly after several experiences of "clicks" have been realized by the critic. And, even then, it is not a foregone conclusion that it will inevitably come; nor can one ever foretell just when and where it will materialize ("The Spirit bloweth . . .").

The reason that the clues to understanding cannot be mechanically transferred from one work of art to another lies in the fact of artistic expressivity itself: the artist lends to an outward phenomenon of language an inner significance (thereby merely continuing and expanding the basic fact of human language: that a meaning is quite arbitrarily — arbitrarily, at least, from the point of view of the current usage of the language — associated with an acoustic phenomenon); just *which* phenomena the literary artist will choose for the embodiment of his meaning is arbitrary from the point of view of the "user" of the work of art. To overcome the impression of an arbitrary association in the work of art, the reader must seek to place himself in the creative center of the artist himself — and re-create the artistic organism. A metaphor, an anaphora, a staccato rhythm may be found anywhere in literature; they may or may not be significant. What tells us that they are important is only the feeling, which we must have already acquired, for the whole of the particular work of art.

And the capacity for this feeling is, again, deeply anchored in the previous life and education of the critic, and not only in his scholarly education: in order to keep his soul ready for his scholarly task he must have already made choices, in ordering his life, of what I would call a moral nature; he must have chosen to cleanse his mind from distraction by the inconsequential, from the obsession of everyday small details — to keep it open to the synthetic apprehension of the "wholes" of life, to the symbolism in nature and art and language. I have sometimes wondered if my "explication de texte" in the university classroom, where I strive to create an atomosphere suitable for the appreciation of the work of art, would not have succeeded much better if that atmosphere had been present at the breakfast table of my students.

F. W. BATESON

Linguistics and Literary Criticism

Il y a toujours un qui baise et un qui tend la joue. Mysteriously, in the curious flirtation now being conducted in our groves of academe between the specialists in linguistics and their opposite numbers in literature, the amorous advances have hitherto come exclusively from the linguists.[1] We literary critics and theorists, though naturally flattered by these attentions from our once hereditary enemies, have remained puzzled and more or less passive in the exchanges. Are the gentlemen's intentions *quite* as honorable as they profess them to be? Simpering coyly we have, it is true, occasionally allowed ourselves to be coaxed into a brief and embarrassed cooperation, but it has always been with a noticeable lack of enthusiasm. Perhaps, on the other hand, the whole thing is a colossal misunderstanding.

In this essay I propose to limit myself to the recent linguistic invasion of the once specifically literary area of style, though some of the seeds of doubt I hope to sow may prove to have a wider relevance. If I have a methodological conclusion to offer it is, I am afraid, one of almost total skepticism. A linguist is certainly entitled to investigate works of literature for his own nonliterary purposes; what he must not expect, I suggest, is that criticism will derive any but the most marginal benefit from his findings. The premises and ideals of our respective disciplines — the linguist's of objective analytic description (analysis in order to describe), the critic's of intersubjective synthetic evaluation (synthesis in the service of value) — differ *toto caelo;* they cannot and should not be compromised.

The first question I am bound to ask therefore is whether "language," the apparent common denominator, has the same meaning for the linguist as for the literary critic. John Spencer for one, an English neo-grammarian

SOURCE: "Linguistics and Literary Criticism" is from *The Disciplines of Criticism: Essays in Literary Theory, Interpretation, and History (Honoring René Wellek),* edited by Peter Demetz, Thomas Greene, and Lowry Nelson, Jr. (New Haven: Yale University Press, 1968), pp. 3–16. Copyright © 1968 by Yale University. Reprinted by permission of Yale University Press.

who has recently edited a slim volume called *Linguistics and Style,* has no doubt about it. He begins his introduction as follows:

> Few literary scholars would suggest that literature can be satis-
> factorily studied without due attention to its medium, language. Nor
> would many linguists justify the investigation of literary language
> without guidance from those who devote themselves to the study of
> literature. There would, moreover, be a measure of agreement on both
> sides that the student of literature, whatever his particular interests,
> ought to be trained in the study of both language and literature. Yet,
> beneath this appearance of politeness and mutual esteem, discord and
> tension sometimes manifest themselves between what have become
> distinct disciplines.

That the "discord and tension" to which Mr. Spencer refers — and which R. H. Robins has also recently deplored as "a certain sense of rivalry and even at times of hostility expressed between literary pursuits and the study of language in linguistics today" [2] — may derive from a tendency of the two parties to force their own meaning of "language" on each other does not seem to have occurred to him. But the formula "language is the medium of literature" — which has a way of turning up whenever a linguist feels it necessary to justify his intrusion into literature — is an ambiguous one. After all, language is also the medium of conversation, of business, of scientific discourse, indeed of every aspect of human social intercourse. The immediate practical problem, however, is the kind and quantity of linguistic knowledge that is needed for the understanding and appreciation of, let us say, the plays of Shakespeare or the poems of Milton. If the literary student is a native of an English-speaking country, the quantity of additional linguistic knowledge that he will require can, I believe, easily be exaggerated.

The difference in historical premises is nicely, perhaps decisively, illustrated by the respective habits of linguist and critic whenever we read aloud or quote orally from any noncontemporary work of literature. A linguist will take it for granted, in classroom or lecture hall, that each phoneme in every word used by a Chaucer, Shakespeare, or Milton must be pronounced as far as possible just as it would have been by an educated Londoner of their time. To the critic, on the other hand, such detailed phonetic reconstructions appear an absurd affectation. The performance of one of Shakespeare's plays today as it was originally pronounced at the Globe is unthinkable to him, except as a philological curiosity. And the undoubted fact that Shakespeare himself would have considered the English used in a typical modern revival — or when quoted by a professor of English — to be grotesquely mispronounced does not worry the critic a bit.

The paradox that what is the "correct" pronunciation historically is not the "right" pronunciation critically is not affected by the notorious difficulty modern philologists find in agreeing upon exactly what vowel sounds Shakespeare and his actors employed. As long as English is a living language, the natural pronunciation of the works of Shakespeare and Milton — and indeed of any fifteenth- or sixteenth-century English writer (Chaucer is the borderline case) — will always be whatever English is current when they happen to be acted or read. The occasional exception in a rhyme or a pun only proves my general critical rule of continuous modernization.

An important theoretical principle is implicit in this paradox. It is right and natural for the native of an English-speaking country to pronounce the English literature of any period as if it had been written yesterday — whatever the historical evidence to the contrary may be — because English literature constitutes a cultural continuum. This is easily demonstrable. Thus it can never be an argument against the interpretation of this or that passage in Shakespeare that a usage is presupposed which did not exist in the English of Shakespeare's time. If the innovation was possible in later English it must also have been possible in Elizabethan English, because there is no essential discontinuity — apart from the introduction of certain new techniques and industries — between the culture of sixteenth-century England and that of later periods. Although the linguistic evidence will always be relevant, it cannot be the final determining literary factor in such cases. The determining literary factor is *stylistic effectiveness within the general cultural context*.

A simple example of this supra-linguistic principle is the Folio reading of *Macbeth*, II, ii, 63, "Making the Greene one, Red." To the obvious emendation, first proposed by Johnson, "Making the green, one red," C. J. Sisson has objected that "No contemporary instance has been cited of the use of *one* to mean 'totally' (however familiar it may seem today) and we may not without authority gloss *one red* as meaning *total gules*." [3] He therefore retains the Folio's comma, explaining "the green one" as Neptune. This is certainly a grammatically possible sense; the objection to it is that it gives a bathetic anticlimax (even if we do not assume colloquial reduction of "one" in Sisson's sense to " 'un" — "green 'un"):

> Will all great Neptune's ocean wash this blood
> Clean from my hand? No, this my hand will rather
> The multitudinous seas incarnadine,
> Making the green one, red.

After the polysyllables of the previous line, the three final monosyllables must clearly all receive the maximum possible stress. To a literary critic the proposition is self-evident. That no contemporary instance of "one" in this emphatic sense is available is completely irrelevant. If Shakespeare can coin the verb "incarnadine" in the previous line, a license Sisson does not seem to object to, why may he not also extend the use of "one" to mean "totally"? Both usages were what may be called potential English, and the exact date when either became a formal part of the language has a merely antiquarian interest. What the critic is concerned with is the sentence's cultural significance in the continuum of English literature *from the viewpoint of the present* — not because the twentieth century can see more, or more clearly, than earlier centuries (losses have to be balanced against gains), but because an Englishman who happens to live in the twentieth century is committed to it willy-nilly. To become accessible to us critically, the literature of the past must in fact be translatable into the present tense. When confronted therefore with obsolete words or forms in it our only concern *as critics* is to know what they mean in modern English. The principle applies as much to a reader's own literature as to his reading of a foreign literature — such as that of the Romans or indeed, as I have argued elsewhere, the Anglo-Saxons. If we are to identify empathically with Hamlet, Macbeth, and the others, they must in effect become our contemporaries and so speak our English. Provided that object is obtained, however approximately and imperfectly, a cultural continuity is assured.

The hypothesis of a literary continuum — in the English case perhaps beginning about 1200 A.D. with works like *The Owl and the Nightingale* (in which language, prosody, style, and genre are essentially those familiar in later English poetry) — is a necessary one if the concept "English literature" is to have any substantial meaning. And we are then bound in logic, as I have implied, to concern ourselves principally, if not altogether, with those features of the English language that are *common* to the literature since 1200 or thereabouts.[4] The differences, in other words, must as far as possible be ignored — not because they do not exist but because this degree of anti-historicism is the price that has to be paid for the continuing vitality of an English literary tradition. (A parallel case would be the general implicit agreement, found within any linguistic area, to ignore for ordinary daily purposes of communication all but the grossest differences of class or regional dialect.)

The literary irrelevance that I have imputed in the preceding section to "diachronic" (historical) linguistics applies equally to "synchronic" linguistics, i.e., the detailed analysis of a language at any one period in its evolution. But the nature of the objection is different. The point that needs to be made depends, as it happens, on considerations invoked in a classic passage in that fountainhead of modern descriptive linguistics, Saussure's *Cours de linguistique générale* (Paris, 1916). It will be remembered that Saussure's point of theoretic departure — the distinction between *langue* (the language system) and *parole* (the language occasion) — was based on an analysis of the sequence of events implicit in

"A" addressing a remark to "B." [5] The following diagram is a simplified summary of what Saussure called *le circuit de la parole*.

Psychological plane

An idea comes into "A" 's head.

The idea releases the appropriate "sound-image" associated with it (the idea is verbalized).

The "sound-image" detaches itself from the idea.

Physiological plane

"A" 's brain transmits the correlative nervous impulse to his vocal chords.

Physical plane

Certain sound waves pass from "A" 's lips to "B" 's ears.

["B" then repeats the processes undergone by "A" in an inverse order; i.e. whereas "A" 's contribution terminates on the physical plane, "B" 's begins on it, "B" then moving first to the physiological plane and ultimately to the psychological plane, where "A" 's three processes are reenacted in the opposite order.]

It will be seen that "A" 's last stage, which is "B" 's first, is the only one common to them both. It is at this physical level that words, in the ordinary sense, are interchanged, but the conventional series of sounds emitted by "A" derive, of course, from "A" 's four earlier processes, just as they only "make sense" for "B" at the end of his four later processes. In the following diagram I have numbered the separate stages so as to make the full temporal sequence clear.

Psychological Plane

1. An idea enters "A" 's head.
2. "A" 's meaning is verbalized in linguistic "sound-images."
3. The "sound-images" detach themselves from the meaning.

9. "A" 's idea enters "B" 's head.
8. The "sound-images" release their conventional meanings.
7. The sounds are mentalized as linguistic "sound-images."

Physiological Plane

4. "A" 's brain transmits the appropriate nervous impulse to the vocal chords.

6. "B" 's ears transmit to his brain the appropriate impulses set in motion by "A" 's sounds.

Physical Plane

5. A series of conventional sound waves (the phonemes) are directed from "A" 's lips to "B" 's ears.

Saussure's details, some of which I may have oversimplified, need not detain us. For literary theory the point of particular interest is "B" 's exact repetition of "A" 's psychological, physiological, and physical processes *in an inverted order*. Whereas "A" proceeds from a psychological phase to a physical phase, "B" reverses the process and proceeds from the physical to the psychological. There is also a reversal of direction even on the same level. Thus on the physical plane, as the sound waves leave "A" 's mouth to impinge on "B" 's ears, "A" "gives out" and "B" "takes in." It follows that even if communication is completely successful and "B" reproduces accurately at each phase the exact equivalent of what "A" has already contributed to *le circuit de la parole,* there is still this difference of direction. For "A" the sequence is toward increasing externalization, for "B" toward increasing internalization. Saussure's analysis is, of course, incomplete. In the give-and-take of everyday conversation, what "A" has to say to "B" is counterbalanced by what "B" has to say to "A." Question begets answer, as assertion begets either assent or contradiction. But once the cycle of speech is inflated into what may be called the literary cycle ("the *best* words in the *best* order"), and "A" becomes the author and "B" the literary audience, the typical situation has changed. The function of the author qua author is to externalize all the time, just as the literary audience — once the curtain has gone up or until the book is put down — is internalizing all the time. Whether (i) the author is his own reader or reciter, or (ii) a professional reader or reciter substitutes for him, or (iii) the auditor becomes his own reader or reciter, either aloud or sotto voce, does not affect this basic relationship. Even when we are reading a work of literature to ourselves we are not doing it to externalize a psychological condition of our own, as "A" or an author "expresses" himself; on the contrary, our object is still under normal circumstances simply to internalize somebody else's externalizations. We are patients, not agents. The point becomes a crucial one for literary theory when the terminal areas of the linguistic or literary cycle are subjected to a rather different mode of analysis from that of Saussure.

Since we are all readers I shall begin with "B" (who now typifies the literary audience). "B," then, begins his book by reading the first sentence on page 1. The fact that a visual process is superimposed on that of speech adds a further stage to the cycle of communication but does not affect the direction of the series of impulses; the writer is still externalizing, the reader still internalizing. Having identified the series of black marks at the top of the block of printed matter as so many letters, and the separate groups of letters as so many words, "B" is able to fill out mentally what Saussure called *le signifiant* in front of his eyes with *le signifié,* a process that requires him to recognize the grammatical relationships between the words in his sentence as well as their separate meanings. At this point, if he is a competent performer, he has "understood" the first sentence.

But what does "understanding" imply in this context? It is with this question that the distinction between speech, as it is normally practiced, and any form of literature, as the term is normally used, forces itself upon the theorist's attention. There are, no doubt, modes of speech which resemble literature in the silent acquiescence of "B" (but always "B" in a plural number) to sentence after sentence from "A." The preacher, the political orator, even the teller of a complicated story, or the narrator of an elaborate series of events, are all differentiated from the "A" of such typical speech phenomena as question and answer or assertion and counter-assertion. In these more elaborate situations the speaker becomes in effect indistinguishable from an author and the auditor from a theatrical spectator or the audience at a reading such as those Dickens used to give of his novels. "B" for once is now content to leave the role of externalization entirely to "A." Social custom does not allow or at least encourage him to answer back or challenge "A" — not at any rate until the speech is complete or the tale has reached its end. His only defenses against "A" 's eloquence are to walk out of the political meeting or to close his ears, physically or metaphorically, to what "A" is saying.

"A," however, in his role of prophet or entertainer, is always aware, consciously or unconsciously, of the possibility of "B" 's denial of *le circuit de la parole;* he has therefore developed his own counter-strategy, which is to *persuade* "B" to continue silent, interested, and attentive. The eloquence of the orator must now become so irresistible, the story must be told so amusingly or so excitingly, that "B" "cannot choose but hear." In other words, rhetoric is now added to speech. Unless rhetoric, in its most general sense, *is* added to speech, the prolongation of "A" 's role in the speech cycle will tend sooner or later to be resisted or refused by "B." A club bore cannot hold his audience, because his rhetoric is inferior or nonexistent, because he is innocent of the *ars dicendi.*

Literature is committed by the nature of its audience relationship to the superimposition upon speech of the specially heightened rhetoric that we call "style." Etymologically the word carries us back to the *stilus* of the scribe, just as "literature" itself implies a mode of speech recorded physically in *literae* inscribed by a *stilus.* In a written work, because a rereading or a reference back will elucidate the obscurities or ambiguities, the speech can be heightened, concentrated, elevated, coordinated. The speech rhythms in a poem have been specially regularized or diversified; the vocabulary is unusually varied or purified; certain unusual or artificial "figures" add color, balance, and subtlety to the word order; the subject matter has been sifted selectively; appropriate attitudes toward the audience and modes of presentation (the genres) have been distinguished and elaborated.

This, it will be agreed, is what literature looks like *ab extra* — to all of us, whether we are linguists or critics. It will be objected no doubt by a linguist that the traditional categories of prosody and stylistics are now being revised and reconstructed by descriptive linguistics with much more precise and up-to-date tools of external analysis. Why is it then, we retort, that so little of critical interest has so far emerged from modern linguistics? One answer, I suggest, stares us all in the face in the movements of *le circuit de la parole*. The linguist must always tend to refer the phenomena of style *back* to their constituents in language (stage 8 in Saussure's scheme in the second diagram above) rather than *forwards* to the post-linguistic or strictly psychological phase represented by Saussure's stage 9. Language after all is the linguist's business. But a realistic approach to the problems of style demands a two-way investigation — not only of the linguistic constituents of such devices as irony and metaphor, but also of their psychological origins and post-linguistic consequences. The essence of *le circuit de la parole,* as we have seen, is its temporal continuity: each phase in the series is being displaced at any one moment by its successor, as word follows word and sentence follows sentence. But, just as the separate letters of each word are immediately lost to sight in the reader's consciousness as he internalizes their total significance, so the separate words, phrases, clauses, and sentences disappear mentally once they translate themselves into the ideas or images that they symbolize. In Saussure's formula, "A" 's idea eventually enters "B" 's head, le *signifiant* having again become le *signifié*.

In the literary cycle, with the intervention of "style" between Saussure's stages 8 and 9, the process is more complicated. Reduced to its simplest linguistic terms, "style" can be described as a complex of verbal repetition, either overt or disguised. Thus meter is basically the abstraction from the verbal totality of certain syllable patterns which are then repeated; in an accentual system, for example, the "foot," consisting typically of any heavily stressed syllable preceded by any lightly stressed syllable (the iamb), does not become a "line" unless it is repeated several times. Other modes or levels of repetition are equally familiar. A sonnet, for example, superimposes on the pattern of syllable recurrence the further pattern of its special rhyme scheme. In the area of figures of speech the repetition is usually a partial duplication. Thus in puns, ironies, and metaphors two things are being said at the same time which are in some respects identical, though in others blatantly discrepant or contradictory. A similar combination of identity and difference characterizes such other stylistic devices or categories as connotation, balance, ambiguity, and symbolism. I need not retraverse what is familiar ground.

A crucial point, however, tends to be overlooked in linguistic investigations into the various aspects of style, namely, the effect of such repetitions on Saussure's stage 9. As the separate words and sentence merge in the reader's consciousness into the verbal combinations or patterns that he has learned to associate with literature, *le signifié* changes its nature with *le signifiant*. The context of literary communication is different from that of speech in four respects: (i) "A" (the author) is invisible and "B" (the audience) cannot influence him or answer back in any effective way; (ii) "A" 's act of communication may often not be completed until "B" has spent many hours or days turning many pages; (iii) "A" 's communication is not meant to be confined to a single "B" but may sometimes have millions of readers, all responding to it in more or less the same way. But the real crux is the fourth difference, which might be described as the new sense of order and significance that the accumulated repetitions of style add to Saussure's stage 9.

In the literary cycle stage 9 can perhaps be called the Aesthetic Moment. As the actual words and stylistic devices recede from the reader's consciousness their place is taken by an illusion of actual experience, one in which the reader shares though without being actively involved in it. An aesthetic distance, as we say, separates the human situation which the reader appears to be contemplating from such a situation in real life. Lessing put it succinctly in Chapter xvii of his *Laocoön*:

> The poet wishes not only to be intelligible, his representations ought not only to be clear and perspicuous; with this the prose writer may be content. But the poet desires to make the ideas which he awakens in us so vivid, that from the rapidity with which they arise we believe ourselves to be really as conscious of his objects as if they were actually presented to our senses; and in this moment of illusion we cease to be conscious of the means — that is, of the words — which he employs for this purpose.[6]

We can now return to Saussure's stage 1. In *le circuit de la parole* "B" 's process of internalization repeated in an inverted order the phases — physical, physiological, and psychological — of "A" 's externalization. The idea that came into "A" 's head in stage 1 finally reached "B" 's head in stage 9. If we substitute the literary cycle for the speech cycle a similar relationship must be expected to hold. But if stage 9 is the reader's Aesthetic Moment, what are we to call stage 1? The author's Aesthetic Moment? The author's "moment of illusion"? If the parallel with stage 9 is valid, stage 1 in the literary cycle will at any rate be both pre-stylistic and pre-linguistic. Let us call it the Creative Moment, meaning by the term very much what Coleridge meant by the Imagination and Shelley by Inspiration.

The assumption that an author's progress toward composition follows the same pattern as a reader's toward the Aesthetic Moment but in an inverted order has an important theoretical consequence. It means that literary creation externalizes itself first as style and only secondarily as grammar or language. In style we are nearer to the working of the creative imagination than we are at the linguistic level. It follows that in interpreting literature's stylistic phenomena we shall be well advised to pay more attention to the causes of literary creation, the sources of a particular imaginative act and their correlatives in the reader's part of the cycle, than with the consequences in language.

No doubt this advice will sound suspiciously vague and unpractical, but the parallel between Saussure's *circuit de la parole* and what I have called the literary cycle is once again reassuring. It would not be difficult to discover why under certain circumstances a particular idea came into "A"'s head (he is passing a shop with fresh strawberries displayed in the window) — or what "B"'s reaction might be when he understood what "A" was saying (the strawberries are five shillings a punnet). The simplest verbal exchange operates in a social or cultural context which is no less real for being tacitly taken for granted. And it will be agreed that the reader's end of the literary cycle presents no special theoretical difficulties. Stage 9 (the Aesthetic Moment) terminates with or soon after the reading of the particular work of literature. But that is not the end, as far as the particular work's particular reader is concerned. As the experience released in the actual process of reading loses its first imaginative freshness it will be followed by a stage 10, which may be called the Emotional Response. (For Aristotle catharsis clearly occurred *after* the tragedy had reached its end.) And a stage 11, that of the Critical Verdict, no doubt comes later still, in most cases many hours or days later. By the time this phase is reached the memory has had an opportunity to discard the trivial and irrelevant elements from the original aesthetic experience, and the emotional consequences can also be seen in a perspective of similar reactions. It follows that when literary criticism begins the originating linguistic stimulus is already very remote.

If the Saussurian formula of an inverted order is equally applicable to the author on this pre-linguistic level, we are presumably left with a creative equivalent of the Critical Verdict as the ultimate origin of a work of literature. Perhaps this origin is some sort of communal value judgment itching to express itself? And instead of the Emotional Response of the reader do we posit an Emotional Explosion within the author resulting from the general originating value judgment? I make these final equations with extreme diffidence. The creative process begins below the level of consciousness, and hypotheses about its origins naturally resist adequate formulation and confirmation.

Nevertheless literary theory must insist that its concern with the pre-linguistic in literary composition and the post-linguistic in the reading of literature is legitimate and essential. To exclude these areas from the literary process, as modern descriptive linguistics is compelled to do, is unscientific as well as arbitrary. The literary cycle is as much a fact of experience as *le circuit de la parole*. Moreover — to reintroduce a concept that I have already applied to "diachronic" linguistics — both the circuit and the cycle must necessarily be experienced as continuous, if the terms are to have any meaning. In other words, for linguistic or literary communication to take place between them "A" and "B" must already be in pre-verbal contact as human beings. The sound waves directed from "A"'s lips to "B"'s ears presume an existing rapport between "A" and "B." I am not invoking any Jungian collective subconsciousness here but the elementary fact that "A" will not greet "B" unless some social bond already connects them. I do not say "How do you do?" to a complete stranger. There is therefore a *social* plane preceding Saussure's psychological plane that is as much a part of *parole* as of *langue*. And what is true of *le circuit de la parole* is equally true obviously of the literary cycle; authors do not write for a non-audience.

Because of its latent premise of discontinuity, linguistics, whether historical or descriptive, can contribute little to the critical study of literature. Some recent attempts to provide linguistic interpretations of poems by Donne, Hopkins, and Larkin have been dismal examples of ingenious irrelevance. Let us therefore follow Socrates' example with the poets, crowning these linguistic invaders of literature with garlands of wool and anointing them with myrrh — *and sending them away to another city.*

KENNETH BURKE

Rhetoric — Old and New

On the assumption that writing and the criticism of writing have an area in common, this statement is offered in the hopes that, though presented from the standpoint of literary criticism, it may be found relevant to the teaching of communication.

Let us, as a conceit, imagine a dialogue between two characters: "Studiosus" and "Neurosis." Studiosus would be somewhat of a misnomer for the first figure, who represents a not very interested member of a fresh-

SOURCE: "Rhetoric — Old and New" is from *The Journal of General Education,* Volume V (April 1951), pp. 202–209. Reprinted by permission of *The Journal of General Education.*

man class taking a required course in composition; and Neurosis would be his teacher. Studiosus has complained bitterly of the work which the course requires of him, whereupon Neurosis delivers a passionate oration in defense of his subject (naturally without mention of a flitting fantasy he sometimes entertains, according to which he has been granted some *other* cross to bear).

Imagining his apology, we found it falling into three stages, that corresponded roughly to an Inferno, a Purgatorio, and a Paradiso. First would be an account of the abysmal problems that beset the use of language. Next would come a movement of transition, whereby the very sources of lamentation could, if beheld from a different angle, be transformed into the promissory. This would be the purgatorial stage. And, despite the mournfulness of our times, a glorious paradisiac ending seemed feasible, if we did a certain amount of contriving — but let us put off for a bit the description of this third stage, while we prepare for it by first giving the broad outlines of the other two.

The first stage would stress the great deceptions of speech. As with Baudelaire's sonnet on "Correspondences," it would note how men wander through "forests of symbols." Man a symbol-using animal. Expatiate on the fog of words through which we stumble, perhaps adding an image (the dog and the waterfall heard enigmatically beyond the mist). Here we would consider the problems of news: the *necessary* inadequacy of the report, even in the case of the *best* reporting; the bungling nature of the medium; the great bureaucratic dinosaurs of news-collecting; the added risks that arise from the *dramatic* aspects of news. (And to get a glimpse of what sinister practices we do accept as the norm, where international relations are concerned, imagine a prize fight reported in the style regularly used for news of international disputes: one fighter's blows would be reported as threats and provocations, while the other's were mentioned in the tonalities proper to long-suffering and calm retaliation regrettably made necessary by the outlandish aggressiveness of the opponent.)

We hoped next to work in a reference to what we like to call the "scene-act" ratio. That is, a situation may be so described that one particular kind of act or attitude is implicit in it (described not falsely, but with "honest selectivity"). For a complex situation may without untruth be so reported that exclusively pugnacious rather than friendly or meditative attitudes are evoked; or the exact opposite may be as true — a rhetorical function thus lurking beneath the level of the report's "factuality." And when each day's "reality" is "dramatically" put together for us by enterprises that comb the entire world for calamities, conflicts, and dire forebodings, such a documentary replica of the arena confuses us as to the actual *recipe* of motives on which the world is operating. The most critical consideration of all is thus drastically slighted, namely, the *proportions* of the ingredients in a motivational cluster.

Given the conditions of our talk, we should pass over this stage rapidly. But before going into the second or purgatorial stage, I'd like to pause for an aside. I submit that this is the situation, as regards the present state of literary criticism: When aesthetic criticism came in, there was a corresponding demotion of rhetoric. Rhetoric was exiled. And, emigrating, it received a home among various so-called "new sciences." (Anthropology, social psychology, sociology, psychoanalysis, semantics, and the like all took over portions of it. I would also include here psychosomatic medicine, concerned as it is with ways in which our very physiques are led to take on attitudes in keeping with the rhetorical or persuasive aspects of ideas — attitudes of such conviction that they are worked into the very set of nerves, muscles, and organs.)

I shall cite one example of the way in which the "new sciences" took over: Anthropology now considers, under the heading of "magic," many symbolic devices for the establishing of social cohesion. Under the earlier dispensation, these would have been considered as aspects of *rhetoric*. But here is the paradox: After these topics were exiled and renamed "magic," literary critics who borrowed the new terms were accused by purists of importing alien perspectives into their special discipline. Accordingly, by a "new" rhetoric, we mean one designed to restore structures maimed by the vandalism of the exclusively aesthetic (an aesthetic stress, by the way, that had also made positive gains, though they are not our concern at the moment).

If I had to sum up in one word the difference between the "old" rhetoric and a "new" (a rhetoric reinvigorated by fresh insights which the "new sciences" contributed to the subject), I would reduce it to this: The key term for the old rhetoric was "persuasion" and its stress was upon deliberate design. The key term for the "new" rhetoric would be "identification," which can include a partially "unconscious" factor in appeal. "Identification" at its simplest is also a deliberate device, as when the politician seeks to identify himself with his audience. In this respect, its equivalents are plentiful in Aristotle's *Rhetoric*. But identification can also be an end, as when people earnestly yearn to identify themselves with some group or other. Here they are not necessarily being acted upon by a conscious external agent, but may be acting upon themselves to this end. In such identification there is a partially dreamlike, idealistic motive, somewhat compensatory to real differences or divisions, which the rhetoric of identification would transcend.

But we are now ready for our second stage. For, if identification includes the realm of transcendence, it has, by the same token, brought us into the realm of transformation, or dialectic. A rhetorician, I take it, is like one voice in a dialogue. Put several such voices together, with each voicing its own special assertion, let them act upon one another in co-operative competition, and you get a dialectic that, properly developed, can lead to views transcending the limitations of each. At which point, to signalize his change of heart, poor Neurosis might now be renamed "Socraticus."

Socraticus could point out how the very lostness of men in their symbolic quandaries has led to the invention of miraculously ingenious symbolic structures — whereat the very aspects of language we might otherwise fear can become engrossing objects of study and appreciation; and works once designed to play upon an audience's passions, to "move" them rhetorically toward practical decisions beyond the work, can now be enjoyed for their ability to move us in the purely poetic sense, as when, hearing a lyric or seeing a sunrise, we might say, "How moving!" (We here touch upon the kind of heightened or elevated diction discussed in Longinus' *On the Sublime*.)

Considering the relation between rhetoric and dialectic, we come with Socraticus upon the Platonic concern with the Upward Way (linguistic devices whereby we may move from a world of disparate particulars to a principle of one-ness, an "ascent" got, as the semanticists might say, by a movement toward progressively "higher levels of generalization"). Whereat there could be a descent, a Downward Way, back into the world of particulars, all of which would now be "identified" with the genius of the unitary principle discovered en route. (All would be thus made consubstantial by participation in a common essence, as with objects bathed in the light of the one sun, that shines down upon them as from the apex of a pyramid. And the absence of such dialectic journeys on the grand scale should not be allowed to conceal from us the fact that we are continually encountering fragmentary variants of them. For instance, you may look upon a world of disparate human beings; you can next "rise to a higher level of generalization" by arriving at some such abstraction as "economic man"; and, finally, you can look upon these unique human beings simply in terms of this one attribute, thus "identifying" them with a unitary term got by a tiny rise toward generalization and a descent again from it.)

But the mention of the pyramid can lead us nicely into the third state, our Paradiso. Socraticus might now even change his name to "Hierarchicus" — and we might dwell upon the double nature of hierarchy. Thus there is the purely verbal ascent, with corresponding resources of identification (our notion being that a rhetorical structure is most persuasive when it possesses full dialectical symmetry — or, otherwise put, dialectical symmetry is at once the perfecting and transcending of rhetoric). But there is also another line of ascent; and this involves the relation between the dialectics of identification and hierarchic structure in the social, or sociological, sense (society conceived as, roughly, a ladder, or pyramid, of interrelated roles).

Here we would consider how matters of prestige (in the old style, "wonder," or in the terminology of Corneille, "admiration") figure in the ultimate resources of "identification." Here we would note how our ideas of "beauty," and even "nature," are "fabulous," concealing within themselves a social pageantry. Here would be the ultimate step in the discussion of the ways in which man walks among "forests of symbols."

Then, for the localizing of our thesis, we might have Neurosis-Socraticus-Hierarchicus cite Castiglione's *Book of the Courtier* as a neat instance of the merger of the two dialectical series: the verbal and the social pyramids. For it deals with questions of courtly ascent, while rising though four successive stages from the mere quest of personal advancement, to a concern with the insignia of the courtier as expert or specialist, thence to the cult of courtly sexual relations, and on to the vision of an *ultimate* courtship. In this fourth stage we move into a sacrificial order of motives, fittingly introduced in the dialogues by talk of death, so that, in contrast with the earlier analysis of laughter, there is now a solemn note. This fourth section deals, first, with the Socratic erotic, the love of truth, beauty, goodness, as seen in terms of the courtier who is now in a pedagogic role, aiming not at his own advantage but at the education of the prince in ways that will be beneficial to mankind as a whole.

After the pages on the courtier as educator of the prince, you will recall, through appropriate transitions the work rises to its exhilarating close, the oration by Cardinal Bembo, on Beauty as "an influence of the heavenly bountifulness." Here is, to perfection, the device of *spiritualization*. So, by the time the Cardinal is finished, we have gone from the *image* of beauty to the pure *idea* of beauty — we have united with ideal beauty: the courtly, truth, utility, goodness — finally we arrive at talk of the soul, which is given "to the beholding of its own substance," a substance angelic (the soul kindled by the desire to partake of the heavenly nature), whereat, with images of mounting and burning and coupling, we end on a prayer to "the father of true pleasures, of grace, peace, lowliness, and goodwill," and on talk of hopes to "smell those spiritual savors" — and lo! after the Cardinal has paused, "ravished and beside himself," we discover that the discussion has continued until dawn, so that the company, edified,

> saw already in the East a fair morning like unto the color of roses, and all stars voided, saving only the sweet Governess of Heaven, Venus which keepeth the bounds of night and day, from which appeared to blow a sweet blast, that filling the air with a biting cold, began to quicken the tunable notes of the pretty birds, among the hushing woods of the hills.

Since this work is so exalted in its closing pages, like the final rejoicing of a symphonic finale, we thought we should contrive to end our apology on that. For it would be something that even Studiosus might readily applaud; and in applauding the citation, he might seem to be applauding the speaker.

But at that stage, we grew uneasy. Even suppose our ruse had succeeded. What of the morrow? What had we considered, as regards particular, practical problems?

To meet that question, we should go back to a hint introduced, in passing, when we mentioned the earlier stages of Castiglione's book. For there the author considers at great length the approved devices whereby the courtier can translate his aptitudes into schemes, stratagems, advantage-seeking actions. Can we not, when looking at the resources of words, seek to categorize and describe in that spirit the kinds of role which, while they impinge upon the rhetorical devices considered in Books vii, viii, and ix of Quintilian, have also a more personalized dimension? These would fall across all the three levels we have considered in our little Human Comedy.

Aristotle treated rhetoric as purely verbal. But there are also areas of overlap (making for a kind of "administrative" rhetoric). Consider, for instance, Machiavelli's *Prince,* as seen in this light:

Machiavelli's *The Prince* can be treated as a rhetoric insofar as it deals with the *producing of effects upon an audience.* Sometimes the prince's subjects are his audience, sometimes the rulers or inhabitants of foreign states are the audience, sometimes particular factions within the State. If you have a political public in mind, Machiavelli says in effect, here is the sort of thing you must do to move them for your purposes. And he considers such principles of persuasion as these: either treat well or crush; defend weak neighbors and weaken the strong; where you foresee trouble, provoke war; don't make others powerful; be like the prince who appointed a harsh governor to establish order (after this governor had become an object of public hatred in carrying out the prince's wishes, the prince got popular acclaim by putting him to death for his cruelties); do necessary evils at one stroke, pay out benefits little by little; sometimes assure the citizens that the evil days will soon be over, at other times goad them to fear the cruelties of the enemy; be sparing of your own and your subjects' wealth, but be liberal with the wealth of others; be a combination of strength and stealth (lion and fox); *appear* merciful, dependable, humane, devout, upright, but be the opposite in actuality, whenever the circumstances require it; yet always do lip-service to the virtues, since most people judge by appearances; provoke resistance, to make an impression by crushing it; use religion as a pretext for conquest, since it permits of "pious cruelty"; leave "affairs of reproach" to the management of others, but keep those "of grace" in your hands; be the patron of all talent, proclaim festivals, give spectacles, show deference to local organizations; but always retain the distance of your rank (he could have called this the "mystery" of rule); in order that you may get the advantage of good advice without losing people's respect, give experts permission to speak frankly, but only when asked to speak; have a few intimates who are encouraged to be completely frank, and who are well plied with rewards.[1]

As an instance of more purely literary tactics, we might cite this passage from Demetrius' *On Style* [2]:

> In fine, it is with language as with a lump of wax, out of which one man will mould a dog, another an ox, another a horse. One will deal with his subject in the way of exposition and asseveration, saying (for example) that "men leave property to their children, but they do not therewith leave the knowledge which will rightly use the legacy." [This he calls the method of Aristippus of Cyrene.] . . . Another will (as Xenophon commonly does) express the same thought in the way of precept, as "men ought to leave not only money to their children, but also the knowledge which will use the money rightly."
>
> What is specifically called the "Socratic" manner . . . would recast the foregoing proposition in an interrogative form, somewhat as follows. "My dear lad, how much property has your father left you? Is it considerable and not easily assessed? It is considerable, Socrates. Well now, has he also left you the knowledge which will use it rightly?"

For some years, in tentative ways, somewhat on the side, I have been trying to decide on terms for categorizing various literary strategies, as seen in the light of these borrowings from Machiavelli and Demetrius. This is no place to display the lot. But I might cite a few brief illustrations. Here, for instance, are some cullings from my notes on what I tentatively call the "bland strategy":

> At one point in *The Idiot*, Ippolit accuses Mishkin of learning how to "make use of his illness." Mishkin, he says, has managed to offer friendship and money "in such an ingenious way that now it's impossible to accept under any circumstances." Mishkin's behavior has been "either too innocent or too clever." Ippolit is here in effect giving the formula for blandness. Blandness is ironic, in that the underlying meaning is the opposite of the one that shows on its face, while there is always the invitation to assume that the surface meaning is the true one.
>
> Diplomats often use it, when sending warships abroad in times of peace. Though the warships may be dispatched purely for purposes of threat, the enterprise can be blandly put forward as a "goodwill mission." Or a government may use troop movements as a threat, and blandly call attention to the troop movements by announcing that they are but part of a "routine action" and are not intended as a threat.
>
> A friend said: "I once had an uncle who was gentle enough, but enjoyed watching fist fights among children. Each Saturday he would

get a dollar of his pay changed into pennies; and calling the children of the neighborhood, he would toss the pennies one by one, while explaining unctuously: 'Just scramble for the pennies, and each of you can keep as many as he gets. But no pushing, no shoving, boys, and above all, no fighting.' While thus setting up conditions of the Scramble that almost automatically made for a fight, he could blandly call for peace, confident that war would come before he had tossed a dozen pennies."

Or there was the case of Joseph, who, without funds, had married a rich Josephine. At first, in all simplicity, he paid for his keep by being assiduously attentive. Then slowly over the years, a perverse, and even morbid blandness emerged in his treatment of her, unbeknownst to them both. Joseph began to plague Josephine with his worries for her welfare. He did not let her live a moment without the feel of a doctor's hand on her pulse. He was so attentive that no one could fail to comment on his devotion. And in her unexpressed and inexpressible desire to poison him, she felt so guilty that each day she became more sickly. Here was a situation worthy of the André Gide who wrote *The Immoralist*. Blandness could go no further.

Soon after our occupation of Japan in the last war, Japanese officials exploited a blandness of this sort. They confounded the victors by being painfully meticulous in their desire to co-operate. They never tired of asking for "clarifications" of military orders, so that they might obey to the last letter. They were even "scrupulous" in reporting their own violations and misunderstandings of any order. They were so assiduously anxious to please, that they made the conqueror sick of his own commands. For instead of resisting the regulations, they tirelessly brought up bothersome questions supposedly intended to "help put the regulations into effect."

An ironically bland kind of co-operation is said to have taken place during the German invasion of Czecho-Slovakia. The Nazis had been sending spies among the Czechs. These spies would spot anti-Nazi patriots by going to Czech cafes and talking "confidentially" against Hitler. Soon the Czechs learned of the ruse. Hence, next phase: Nazi spy comes to cafe where Czech patriots are gathered. In the role of *agent provocateur,* the spy talks against Hitler. Whereupon the Czechs virtuously pummel him "for saying such things against the Führer."

Given blandness enough, one person might co-operate another off the map.

Such stratagems, instances of which I have been collecting (still using a somewhat experimental terminology of placement, not logically schematized — at least not yet), sometimes apply to a rhetoric of human relations in general; sometimes they are confined to purely literary tactics. Many taken from the press fall halfway between a purely "verbal" and an "administrative" rhetoric. And many taken from books (thus from the realm of literature) at the same time have social relevance generally.

I might cite a few more places where concerns of this sort are observable.

In *The Making of Americans* Gertrude Stein came close to a systematic study of rhetorical devices in personal relations. Toward the end, for instance, when discussing how sensitiveness becomes transformed into suspicion, making a "simple thing" look like a "complicated thing," she writes:

> These then I am now describing who are completely for themselves suspicious ones, who have it in them to have emotion in them become suspicious before it is a real emotion of anything for anything about anything in them, these have it completely to be certain that every one is doing feeling seeing the thing that one is feeling doing seeing believing when such a one is not agreeing with them, when such a one is feeling thinking believing doing anything that such a one is doing that thing for a mean or wicked or jealous or stupid or obstinate or cursed or religious reason, it is not a real feeling believing seeing realizing, that this one having suspicion in him is certain.

She then gives the paradigm of an anecdote:

> One of such a kind of one once liked very well some one and then that one forgot to give this one five cents that this one had paid for that one and then this one hated that one, had no trust in that one for this one was certain that that one knowing that this one was too sensitive to be asking did not think it necessary to pay that one, he never could believe that any one forgot such a thing. This is an extreme thing of a way of feeling that is common to all of these of them.

The stress here moves rather toward the agent than the act (that is, in our terms, it is idealistic); but underlying it is clearly the concern with social tactics (which, one notes, her style is well adapted for stating in *generalized* form).

In a satiric epigram leveled at Cato the Censor, who had walked out of the theater in righteous indignation, Martial asks rhetorically: "Why did you come to the theater? That you might leave?"

In Aristotle's *Rhetoric* a similar pattern is considered when he notes,[3] as a "topic," that one person may make a present of something to another, in order to cause him pain by depriving him of it. Then Aristotle goes on to show how the device may be given cosmological proportions; he cites from an unknown author: "It is not from benevolence that the deity bestows great blessings upon many, but in order that they may suffer heavier calamities" — and whether or not this be a favorite device of the gods, it is certainly a device of a sort that should properly be fitted into a collection of strategies for characterizing the antics of the Human Comedy.

Proust's work is full of such concerns. The kind of closely interwoven relationships he deals with makes for tiny replicas of the stratagems used in the manipulating of mighty empires. Thus Proust notes that the servant Françoise and Aunt Eulalie are related as quarry to hunter, so that "they could never cease from trying to forestall each other's devices." And after describing the nature of their sparring, he concludes:

> a middle-aged lady in a small country town, by doing no more than yield wholehearted obedience to her own irresistible eccentricities, and to a spirit of mischief engendered by the utter idleness of her existence, could see, without ever having given a thought to Louis XIV, the most trivial occupations of her daily life, her morning toilet, her luncheon, her afternoon nap, assume, by virtue of their despotic singularity, something of the interest that was to be found in what Saint Simon used to call the "machinery" of life at Versailles; and was able, too, to persuade herself that her silence, a shade of good humour or of arrogance on her features, would provide Françoise with matter for a mental commentary as tense with passion and terror, as did the silence, the good humour or the arrogance of the King when a courtier, or even his greatest nobles, had presented a petition to him, at the turning of an avenue, at Versailles.

Nor was Françoise lacking in ability to wage the same kinds of warfare against underlings who were, in turn, subject to *her* jurisdiction. After referring to Fabre's descriptions of a wasp that paralyzes an insect and deposits its eggs in the victim, Proust continues:

> in the same way Françoise had adopted, to minister to her permanent and unfaltering resolution to render the house uninhabitable to any other servant, a series of crafty and pitiless stratagems. Many years later we discovered that, if we had been fed on asparagus day after day, throughout that whole season, it was because the smell of the plants gave the poor kitchen-maid, who had to prepare them, such violent attacks of asthma that she was finally obliged to leave my aunt's service.

We could well cite Mark Twain as a source for a rhetoric of such devices. His concern with ruses, stratagems, with the lore of gamblers, swindlers, and the like, is not so much *moralistic* as *appreciative*. His roving enterprisers are not merely salesmen; they are rogues and spellbinders, preferably given to selling poor stuff grandiloquently.

Typically, Twain quotes this example of spiritualization, from a "now forgotten book," about a "big operator":

> He appears to have been a most dexterous as well as consummate villain. When he traveled, his usual disguise was that of an itinerant

preacher; and it is said that his discourses were very "soul-moving"— interesting the hearers so much that they forgot to look after their horses, which were carried away by his confederates while he was preaching.

Deflection is a particularly important device. In a sense any slight bias or even unintended error in our vocabulary for describing reality serves as a deflection. Since even the most imaginative, intelligent, virtuous, and fortunate of men must err in their attempts to characterize reality, some measure of deflection is natural, inevitable. Deflection is so perennially effective when deliberately used, because it arises so spontaneously. The Freudian notion of "displacement" in dreams indicates how close it is to the roots of natural human evasiveness.

Thus a child, provoked when made to give his brother something that he wanted to keep, began crying bitterly because his brother hadn't said "Thank you." His brother promptly said "Thank you," whereupon the child cried all the louder, "because he didn't say it soon enough."

A variant of deflection is used constantly in jokes, where two infractions are involved, one important, one trivial, and laughter is elicited by shifting the stress to the trivial one when the important one was, of course, the real issue.

A typical kind of spontaneous deflection arises thus: Wherever there is control along with disorder, the control can be blamed for the disorder. But if controls are relaxed and there is disorder, the blame can be laid to the absence of controls. Since both the controls and the relaxed controls are matters of government, it follows that government can be blamed for everything.

There is no time now for us to consider the various formulations we have tentatively used in classifying the devices. But we would like to say a few words on one of these, already mentioned in passing. And it will bring our discussion to a close. This is the device of "spiritualization," or the *nostrum* (which transcends the conflicts of the *mine* and the *thine,* the *meum* and *tuum,* by raising them to resonant terms of *ours,* the *nostrum*). Here is a grand device, central to polemic, which is forever translating back and forth between materialist and idealist terms for motives.

Are things disunited in "body"? Then unite them in "spirit." Would a nation extend its physical dominion? Let it talk of spreading its "ideals." Do you encounter contradictions? Call them "balances." Is an organization in disarray? Talk of its common *purpose.* Are there struggles over means? Celebrate agreement on ends. Sanction the troublously manifest, the incarnate, in terms of the ideally, perfectly invisible and intangible, the divine.

In a society beset by many conflicts of interests and aiming with the help of verbal tactics to transcend those conflicts, the uses of spiritualization as a device are endless. Spiritualization is the device par excellence of the Upward Way — vibrant with the gestures of unification, promise, freedom. And so, ending upon it (by recalling snatches, fragments, of Castiglione's symphonic finale):

> ... beauty ... truth ... utility ... goodness ... [all grandly united] ... spiritual savors ... in the East a fair morning like unto the color of roses ... the sweet Governess of Heaven, Venus which keepeth the bounds of night and day ... the tunable notes of the pretty birds, among the hushing woods of the hills. ...

FREDERICK CREWS

Anaesthetic Criticism

L'homme s'affirme par l'infirmité. VICTOR HUGO

I

The critical essays in this book have in common an overt reference to hypotheses and rules of procedure that were neither derived from literature nor primarily meant to apply to literature. Such criticism can go wrong in several ways: by using weak hypotheses, by using strong and pertinent ones in too mechanical a fashion, or by warping literary evidence to meet presuppositions. The recourse to "extra-literary" theory is not in itself, however, a methodological error. The simple fact that literature is made and enjoyed by human minds guarantees its accessibility to study in terms of broad principles of psychic and social functioning.

This point would seem too obvious to dwell on, but it is widely resisted among the very group to whom it should be most axiomatic, professional students of literature. Most literary scholars observe an informal taboo on methods that would plainly reveal literary determinants. Such methods are considered intrinsically antihumanistic, and criticism systematically employing them is regarded as ipso facto shortsighted. Academic critics often circumvent the taboo by disguising or compromising their explana-

SOURCE: "Anaesthetic Criticism" is reprinted from Frederick Crews, ed., *Psychoanalysis and Literary Process* by permission of Winthrop Publishers, Inc. Copyright © 1970 by Winthrop Publishers, Inc.

tory inclination, thus earning a hearing at the expense of some consistency and clarity. But the prohibition itself deserves scrutiny, not only because it is intellectually indefensible but also because its operation has grave consequences for the teaching of literature.

The majority view of deterministic schemes was aptly conveyed by Northrop Frye, one of the most influential of living critics, as he gave assurance that his own theory of literature would not borrow its conceptual framework from sources outside literature itself. Any extrinsic system, he said,

> gives us, in criticism, the fallacy of what in history is called determinism, where a scholar with a special interest in geography or economics expresses that interest by the rhetorical device of putting his favorite study into a causal relationship with whatever interests him less. Such a method gives one the illusion of explaining one's subject while studying it, thus wasting no time. It would be easy to compile a long list of such determinisms in criticism, all of them, whether Marxist, Thomist, liberal-humanist, neo-Classical, Freudian, Jungian, or existentialist, substituting a critical attitude for criticism, all proposing, not to find a conceptual framework for criticism within literature, but to attach criticism to one of a miscellany of frameworks outside it. The axioms and postulates of criticism, however, have to grow out of the art it deals with. The first thing the literary critic has to do is to read literature, to make an inductive survey of his own field and let his critical principles shape themselves solely out of his knowledge of that field.[1]

Insofar as this statement pleads against replacing sensitive criticism with a crude ransacking of literature to illustrate hypotheses about other matters, it is beyond dispute. More is meant, however. Frye is asserting that the critic, if he is to retain his objectivity, must derive his principles "solely" from his inductive survey of literary works. The point recurs insistently in *Anatomy of Criticism* and is extended into a cautionary view of *all* "axioms and postulates," whatever their source:

> There are no definite positions to be taken in chemistry or philology, and if there are any to be taken in criticism, criticism is not a field of genuine learning. . . . One's "definite position" is one's weakness, the source of one's liability to error and prejudice, and to gain adherents to a definite position is only to multiply one's weakness like an infection (Frye, p. 19).

> The modern student of critical theory is faced with a body of rhetoricians who speak of texture and frontal assaults, with students of history who deal with traditions and sources, with critics using material from psychology and anthropology, with Aristotelians, Coleridgeans, Thomists, Freudians, Jungians, Marxists, with students of myths, rituals,

archetypes, metaphors, ambiguities, and significant forms. The student must either admit the principle of polysemous meaning, or choose one of these groups and then try to prove that all the others are less legitimate. The former is the way of scholarship, and leads to the advancement of learning; the latter is the way of pedantry (Frye, p. 72).

These lines seemingly welcome, but actually discourage, the use of explanatory ideas in criticism. "Polysemous meaning" is recognized only in order to close off the possibility that any one line of investigation might be fruitfully pursued to its end. To have a definite position, no matter how correct, is to be "infected" with weakness, prejudice, and error, whereas to be tolerantly indifferent toward all definite positions, presumably including mistaken ones, is "the way of scholarship." Frye is quite emphatic about this. "All that the disinterested critic can do," when presented with the "color-filter" of an externally derived critical attitude, "is to murmur politely that it shows things in a new light and is indeed a most stimulating contribution to criticism" (Frye, p. 7). Frye himself illustrates his recommendation by glancingly alluding to a variety of frameworks, always with an understanding that they lie beyond the true business of criticism.

Professor Frye's widely accepted imperative, *Do not stray outside literature,* must be seen as territorial rather than intellectual. The avowed idea is to avoid indebtedness to other people's specialties, "for in that case the autonomy of criticism would . . . disappear, and the whole subject would be assimilated to something else" (Frye, p. 6). Once this apprehension is grasped, one can predict the degree of Frye's actual hospitality toward different lines of study. Works can, for example, be safely classified according to their patent resemblances and differences, but in order to say how those features came into being we would have to talk about motives, and there would be no assurance that the motives in question would prove properly "literary." Beneath, let us say, the urge to write an epic or a masque we might come across other urges at once more private and more universal than the literary taxonomist could account for. Thus it is not surprising that Frye repeatedly admonishes the disinterested critic to beware of all psychological explanations.

But this causal vacuum cannot be sustained; a critic who forswears deterministic thinking will inevitably fall back on a covert, wishful determinism bordering on tautology. In Frye's case this is particularly clear. "Poetry can only be made out of other poems," he says, "novels out of other novels. Literature shapes itself, and is not shaped externally . . ." (Frye, p. 97). "The true father or shaping spirit of the poem is the form of the poem itself, and this form is a manifestation of the universal spirit of poetry . . ." (Frye, p. 98); ". . . the central greatness of *Paradise Regained,* as a poem, is . . . the greatness of the theme itself, which

Milton *passes on* to the reader from his source" (Frye, p. 96; italics in original); "the real difference between the original and the imitative poet is simply that the former is more profoundly imitative" (Frye, p. 97). Literature makes literature which makes literature; tradition itself is the fount of all inspiration and value. No questions need be asked about how the world's great stories gained their appeal, for the stories themselves are motivational forces. Indeed, Frye dares to hope that even the idea of the Oedipus complex will someday be exposed as nothing more than a misplaced compliment to the power of the Oedipus story: perhaps we shall decide "that the myth of Oedipus informed and gave structure to some psychological investigations at this point. *Freud would in that case be exceptional only in having been well read enough to spot the source of the myth*" (Frye, p. 353; italics added).

This vision of literature as its own progenitor is very far from being a unique indulgence. It is, in fact, a common fantasy among writers, a wish that art could be self-fathered, self-nurturing, self-referential, purified of its actual origins in discontent; and it is no less common among critics. Frye found a use for it in his brilliant study of Blake, virtually annihilating his identity as a critic while fusing himself with Blake's obscure private reality.[2] In that case a rapt surrender to the poet's wish for total imaginative control over the world provided an opportunity for valuable clarification. But such reverence for the all-sufficient text is obviously too narrow a foundation for a whole theory of criticism, and when Frye turns lawgiver he ends by providing an apology for more timid work, indeed for the most routine academic drudgery.

It is important to see that such a result is dictated by the very project of severing literature from its determinants. As Murray Krieger has shown, Frye follows the Arnoldian and Eliotic line of argument which makes artistic unity a substitute for the lost religious matrix, and which decides that in an age of dissociated sensibility this unity must be propped by a body of consciously appropriated belief.[3] Frye's novelty is to fortify the supposedly "anagogic" universe of a poem, not with overt dogmas, but with the rest of literature itself, considered as a great phalanx of works aligned by genre and period. The receding sea of faith has at least left *this* much behind. But as Freud said of Dostoevsky's final piety, lesser minds have reached the same position with less effort. Frye's emphasis on the autonomy of tradition and his simple equation of merit (as in *Paradise Regained*) with borrowed thematic content are all too congenial to critics who could never have written a page of *Fearful Symmetry*. While few professors would say outright that "literature shapes itself," fewer still have ventured beyond the confines of tradition and convention. Indeed, the fear of "going too far" with any hypothesis about literature has proved considerably stronger than the fear of arriving nowhere. Frye's suggestion that Freud himself may have made his name through motif-spotting, a talent we already encourage in our literary trainees, must be reassuring to scholars who would prefer not to raise any awkward questions.

Most literary curricula seem to rest on the assumption, implicit throughout *Anatomy of Criticism,* that the scholar-critic need only become conversant with a certain list of primary and secondary texts in order to begin contributing to knowledge. He should of course be trained in rhetoric and bibliography, but no mention is made of interpretive procedures for bringing some order into the wildly variant subjective responses evoked by any given work. Though first-rate critics like Wilson, Empson, Trilling, and Burke have not hesitated to make "extraliterary" sense of literature, the idea that we positively *ought* to do so is conceived as a threat to scholarly balance. The critic already knows what he is doing and will be all right if he can just keep himself from being drawn too much toward either what Frye has called "the myth of concern" or "the myth of detachment." (It was left for Northrop Frye to identify and endorse the ultimate English-department stance, detachment from the myth of detachment.)

Professor Frye claims that the mental process involved in literary criticism "is as coherent and progressive as the study of science," and he expects that his colleagues' efforts will be revealed as a unified scientific system, "the main principles of which are as yet unknown to us" (Frye, pp. 10–11). This discovery would, as he says, "certainly be convenient" (Frye, p. 11), and many academics will forgive him for going on to treat it as already established. Unfortunately, there seems to be no objective basis for this optimism. The history of literary study is transparently a history of intellectual and political fashion, never more so than in recent formalism and neo-religious moralism. Critics have arrived at no agreement whatever about the meaning of beauty, the criteria of value, or even the grossest facts about books and authors, such as whether Shakespeare was or wasn't stoical, whether Milton was or wasn't of the Devil's party, whether Blake was crazy or visionary or both, whether *The Golden Bowl* is an example of self-transcendence or of colossal arrogance and evasion. Unless one had decided in advance to find criticism "coherent and progressive," he would be hard pressed to justify calling it an intellectual discipline at all.

Such a justification would have to show that literary study, like other disciplines, is concerned with the differential evaluation of various styles of inquiry according to their relative success in making sense of the objects studied. But not only is this winnowing process singularly missing from criticism, it is condemned outright as needlessly zealous, intolerant, and unliterary. Each critic is free to adopt the "approach" that suits his fancy, and most of the approaches prove to be little more than analogical vocabularies lending an air of exactitude to whatever the critic feels like asserting. This is precisely why Professor Frye can urge us not to "choose one . . . and then try to prove that all the others are less legitimate." What does it matter whether we call ourselves Thomists or Aristotelians or phenomenologists, provided we don't take our method too solemnly or show impatience with our neighbor's? *Anatomy of Criticism* is in part a book of professional etiquette, expressing and inculcating the civility that makes literary eclecticism possible. That this civility is in practice anti-intellectual has gone unnoticed — a fact that begins to suggest the extent to which "English" has deafened itself to criteria of knowledge.

The tolerance of literary scholars for "polysemous meaning" is understandably strained by methods that claim to deal in causes and effects. It disappears altogether as soon as such a method is applied in earnest. A critic can allude to Marx now and then, but he had better not get too interested in exposing the class apologetics in cherished texts, much less in other critics' theories of meaning. Similarly, it is a badge of broad-mindedness to season a conventional argument with references to Freud, but the references will be calmly received only if they remain honorific. One may, to be sure, safely credit an author (even a pre-Freudian one) with having made use of "Freudian insights." This is not psychoanalytic discourse but a subtle prophylaxis against such discourse, for the fantasy materials that a Freudian would have ascribed to the unconscious source of the work itself have been promoted to the realm of conscious art, where all of us feel at home. To say that an author has endowed his hero with Freudian traits is no more psychoanalytic a statement than to say that he has evoked a pleasant landscape; in both cases the question of unconscious influence over the whole text is being avoided. And this avoidance is the minimal condition a critic must fulfill if he doesn't want to be regarded as unbalanced.

Thus there is less Freudian criticism extant than one might think, and most of it continues to be received either with hostile alarm or with those polite murmurs that Professor Frye advises us to utter in the presence of the single-minded. The reasons for this reception overlap with those explaining the virtual ban on Marxian analysis. Both Freud and Marx ask us to think about matters that not only partake of alien disciplines, but are profoundly unsettling in their own right. While Freud may seem politically less iconoclastic than Marx, his method is in one sense more radical; it leaves the critic with less ground on which to strike a righteous attitude. Psychoanalytic principles bring into question the very possibility that a critic's relation to his texts could be fundamentally rational and disinterested.

Resistance to such self-appraisal assumes many forms, but it almost never assumes the form of meeting Freudian propositions on evidential grounds. From Wellek and Warren's icy and confused chapter on "Literature and Psychology" in 1949 to the present day, it is next to impossible to find a clear and informed discussion of psychoanalysis by a critic who does not employ it.[4] One hears instead that the Freudian revolution was won long ago and that we needn't make a fuss over it now, or that psychoanalysis has been replaced by any number of better systems, or that it neglects creativity or communication or religion or society or existential anguish or aesthetic textures. Such half-truths are usually followed by a retreat to homespun moralized psychology or to nebulous, dignified, quasi-metaphysical concepts such as Jung's, which, far from seeking to "explain" religion and art, seek to declare their sublime immunity from explanation.

Indeed, Jung has proved a godsend for many critics troubled by the menace of psychoanalysis, for he spent the better part of a lifetime coping with that menace in seductive and readily adaptable ways. Even someone who applies Jung's system with unfashionable explicitness and persistence will find himself free to retain an elevated notion of literature. To invoke that system is of course a revealing mark of indifference toward evidence, for as Edward Glover demonstrated, Jung's hypotheses are logically unnecessary and mutually contradictory; his methodological stance shifted continually between claims of adherence to the strictest clinical principles and claims of rapport with ineffable mysteries; and for these reasons and others his version of neo-Platonism has made scant impact on any field of serious inquiry.[5] These, however, are points of small concern to the lapsed-religious humanist, whose own hopeful guesses about the uplifting value of literature are as fanciful as Jung's. Modern men in search of a soul can make wide allowance for one another's poetic leaps of faith.

This is not to say that critics who openly espouse Jungianism will escape the disapproval of their more cautious colleagues. The latter, failing to appreciate the circularity of Jung's mental journey, its intent of rescuing spiritual and cultural matters from destructive scrutiny, will find in the use of Jungian terms yet another instance of going too far. But because the offense is not so much empirical as social, it can be forestalled merely by using Jung's ideas without attribution or with suitable disclaimers. Token gestures of skepticism can become a means of escape from considerations of plausibility — as, for example, in Professor Frye's statement that the collective unconscious is "an unnecessary hypothesis in literary criticism" (Frye, p. 112), even while he has been developing an immanent and impersonal notion of creativity that seems to demand that very hypothesis.

Since good criticism appears to be largely a matter of sympathy, sensitivity, and pertinent learning, one might reasonably ask whether such vagueness over theory has much importance. Yet it does not seem too venturesome to propose that all scholars, even literary ones, could profit from being clear about what they believe and what they are doing. There is also a possibility that what many of them are doing is wrong both in its premises and in its educational impact. Behind the public façade of eclecticism there may lie a dogmatic avoidance of unacknowledged aspects of literary experience; behind the tactful withdrawal from theories, a disregard for knowledge; behind the celebration of traditional themes, an intolerance toward students who want to come to grips with their deepest responses.

These possibilities are in fact widely realized. The cardinal features of professional critical training as most of us know it are a suppression of affect and a displacement of attention from artistic process onto motifs, genres, literary history (conceived not as the study of how books are influenced by objective conditions, but as chronology, borrowings, gossip, and a disembodied "history of ideas"), and the busywork of acquiring the skills and attitudes needed for circumspect research.[6] Actual criticism, in the familiar sense of making a case for the superiority of some works to others, is frowned upon as amateurishly subjective. Since sheer acquaintance with the body of Anglo-American literature is supremely valued, emphasis is laid on "working up" the designated genres and periods without concern over how literature moves us. As Professor Frye says with some enthusiasm, after showing how we can trace the devices of pastoral elegy from the Bible and the early Church and Theocritus and Vergil through Sidney, Spenser, Shakespeare, Milton, Shelley, Arnold, Whitman, and Dylan Thomas, "we can get a whole liberal education simply by picking up one conventional poem and following its archetypes as they stretch out into the rest of literature" (Frye, p. 100).[7]

One could hardly wish for a more vivid statement of the prevailing academic faith; all that need be added is that nobody believes it except those who propagate it. By now the humanizing pretensions of traditional literary study seem to have been questioned by everyone but its official custodians. But so long as the field prizes gentility over principled inquiry, no critique of those pretensions is likely to have much headway; one always runs against the tacit agreement that curators of culture needn't bother with ideas except as indulgences of taste or fashion.

At present it is generally true that students who reject this consensus must either feign acceptance of it or drop out of school. The survivors and inheritors of literary training tend to be those best adapted to dull, safe, provincial work, while the more creative and inquisitive students, having squandered valuable years on the graduate regimen expecting that it *must* have something to do with the life of the imagination, are mastered at last by despair.[8] Nor is the despair confined to students. The occupational disease of "English," rarely acknowledged until recently, is a debilitating fear that literary scholarship as we have been practicing it is a useless and elitist pastime. If the fear is somewhat exaggerated, the exaggeration nevertheless springs from an entirely understandable bad conscience.

II

The answer, then, to the question whether it is antihumanistic to look outside literature for principles of literary understanding must be a further question: What is meant by humanism? The humanism that purports to defend classical and Judeo-Christian values by cherishing the texts in which those values supposedly reside is indeed jeopardized by extraliterary knowledge, but such a humanism amounts to little more than the confusion of a book list with an education, and its practical results are hardly worth preserving. Suppose, however, that humanism were taken to mean a concern for knowing (and protecting) man as an evolved species, embarked on a unique and possibly self-abbreviated experiment in the substitution of learning for instinct. In that case there would be no need to build walls between one discipline and all others out of fear that the alleged autonomy of one's specialty might be challenged. On the contrary: the search for universals underlying all cultures and traditions would be everyone's business, and proof that one category of human production, such as literature, is functionally consistent with others would be welcomed as significant.

The starting point of this humanism might be a comparison of man to the nearest primates. Such a comparison seems at present to indicate that man's emergence was accompanied by the suppression of much of his forerunner's patterned behavior, the prolongation of his infantile dependency, the postponement of his sexual maturity but also a rich complication and intensification of his sex life, and the diversion of part of this heightened sexuality into substitutive aims and bonds. The delay and detour of instinctual discharge, while not in themselves an explanation of man's capacity to form concepts and modify his behavior experientially, are almost certainly preconditions for it; yet this same interference with animal function dooms man to self-disgust and neurosis, even making normal mating a precarious achievement for him. Each individual must recapitulate for himself, as if it had never been done before, the species' accommodation to social discipline, and this accommodation is always grudging, never finally settled before the moment of death. A true appreciation of man's works would take note of the renunciations and risks they inevitably entail.

Many lines of study could contribute to such an appreciation, but the postulates of Freudian psychoanalysis would be bound to command interest, for they alone have weighed the motivational effects of man's emergence as a species.[9] This was not Freud's original intent, but it was what he stumbled upon, with a disoriented retreat to fabulous reasoning, when he grasped the astonishing sameness of the repressed unconscious across all recorded eras and civilizations. Whatever its therapeutic or even its conceptual disadvantages, only psychoanalysis has registered the psychic costs involved in man's prolonged dependency and his improvising of culture out of thwarted desire.

Man, in a Freudian view, is the animal destined to be overimpressed by his parents, and neurosis is comprehensible as "abnormal attachment to the past." [10] Freud discovered that human beings can neither freely accept nor freely deny the parental demand that sexual and aggressive urges be tamed. All men, he saw, struggle not only against unregenerate impulses but also against their guilt for continuing to harbor those impulses. The fantasies and modes of infantile striving corresponding to the earliest experiences of nutrition, social training, and genital assertion are never wholly overcome and are reactivated when later crises strain the adaptive resources that have been pieced together through a trauma-marked development. It is not so much man's mortality as his inability to keep from being haunted by his repressed longings that makes him "a baby who is afraid of being left alone in the dark." [11] The prevalence of mass as well as individual delusion, the tendency of groups to unleash murderous hostility against other groups that have been projectively designated as embodying banished wishes, the orgies of ascetic penance and the rages for spiritual or material perfection that occupy much of recorded history exemplify the more general rule that men, tormented by the persistence of what they have forsworn, necessarily *regress together*.[12] They do so at their best as well as at their worst. A pooling of fantasies to impose bearable contours on the world seems to be a minimal requisite for all human achievement, even the achievement of those who work alone. By sanctioning certain regressions a culture enables its members to *reculer pour mieux sauter*.

This perspective indicates that the primary function of art may not be instructive or decorative or sedative. Originating in what Ernst Kris called a "regression in the service of the ego," [13] art uses symbolic manipulations to reconcile competing pressures. The artist is someone who provisionally relaxes the censorship regnant in waking life, forgoes some of his society's characteristic defenses, and allows the repressed a measure of representation, though (as in strictly unconscious symptom-formation) only in disguised and compromised form. His social role and his own equilibrium dictate a sign of victory for the ego, if not in "happy endings" then in the triumph of form over chaos, meaning over panic, mediated claims over naked conflict, purposeful action over sheer psychic spillage. In this sense the making and the apprehension of art works reenact the entire human project of making a tenuous cultural order where none existed before.

Assuming for the moment that this view is right, we can see that much "impersonal" literary criticism and theory tends to isolate and redouble the defensive activity in literature while ignoring its barely mastered elements of fantasy, desire, and anxiety. A criticism that explicitly or implicitly reduces art to some combination of moral content and abstract form and genre conventions is literally an anaesthetic criticism. It insulates the critic and his readers from a threat of affective disturbance — a threat that is perfectly real, for there is no reason to suppose that a reader's ego will prove more flexible and capacious than the artist's was. All literary criticism aims to make the reading experience more possible for us, but anaesthetic criticism assumes that this requires keeping caged the anxieties that the artist set free and then recaptured. The effect is often to transform the artist from a struggling fellow mortal into an authority figure, a dispenser of advice about virtue and harmony. "They all swear by the name of the great invalid," Thomas Mann said of any major writer's admirers, "thanks to whose madness they no longer need to be mad." [14]

Someone who wants to look more closely into literature's buried contest between impulse and inhibition will require a method for interpreting his own responses. As a richly overdetermined compromise formation, an art work can only be obliquely and dialectically truthful; so, too, our reaction to it will be a compromise demanded not only by the work's conflicting signals but also by the habitual bias of our ego. The nearest approximation to critical objectivity would seem to consist of gauging those factors both theoretically and intimately and of applying in reverse the principles by which artistic effects came about. This involves open preconceptions about psychic structure, disposition, and defenses and an expectation that certain thematic strands will prove important to follow because of their probable roots in early psychic development. Perhaps the key anticipation of psychoanalytic criticism is that art will borrow some of its real internal unity from repressed material, which "proliferates in the dark" in producing linked derivatives.[15]

Such preconceptions can of course be stigmatized as reductionistic, but all systematic research is comparably governed; the only logical way of getting beyond common-sense impressions is to sharpen one's focus and then see whether new evidence has come into view and an intelligible order has been revealed. To apply deep-structural rules to literary analysis is no more intrinsically reductionistic than to apply them to the study of language.[16] The establishing of predictable patterns can become a basis for showing the intelligibility of expressions that seemed inert and arbitrary because the wrong questions were being asked about them. Thus the validation of a psychoanalytically oriented criticism rests on whether, at its best, it can make fuller sense of literary texts than could the most impressive instances of a rival criticism.

The likelihood of this result rests on the psychoanalytic anticipation that even the most anomalous details in a work of art will prove psychically functional. Being at bottom a theory of how conflicting demands are adjusted and merged, psychoanalysis is quite prepared for literature's mixed intentions, dissociations of affect from ideational content, hints of atonement for uncommitted acts, bursts of vindictiveness and sentimentality, and ironies that seem to occupy some middle ground between satire and self-criticism. In much literary commentary such phenomena are either overlooked or treated as nuisances to be forgiven or condemned, yet they are pervasive. ("A novel," said Randall Jarrell, "is a prose narrative of some length that has something wrong with it." [17]) The fact that we can be moved by literary elements that are rationally incoherent or formally clumsy is puzzling to the nonpsychoanalytic commentator — so much so that T. S. Eliot, finding no adequate manifest referent for the clogged emotionality he perceived in *Hamlet,* reluctantly declared the play an artistic failure. Freudian discussion, by contrast, can locate the universality of the play's appeal and show how its very indirection, paralysis, and strangely overcharged language are enlisted in the task of coping with a powerful, relatively unelaborated Oedipal fantasy.[18]

Of course such a demonstration can never be more convincing than the reader wants it to be. Although psychoanalysis is not the wholly self-validating system described by some of its detractors,[19] the very nature of its attempt to interpose metaphorical psychic agencies between unconscious activity and overt behavior renders it unamenable to logical proof. Only those of its concepts that are closest to naked observation can be experimentally tested, and the few experiments thus far undertaken, while generally supportive of the theory, hardly close off alternative interpretations.[20] The skeptic is free to say, with the instrumentalists, that Freudian theory is unscientific because its assertions cannot be verified; or to join the positivists who relegate emotive matters to the harmless and meaningless realm of "poetic truth"; or to take refuge among the behaviorists who ensure that nothing so complex and uncontrolled as a human mind can become an object of their attention. All these versions of what C. Wright Mills called "abstracted empiricism" [21] shrug off the conclusions of psychoanalysis instead of attempting to replace them with better ones.

Unfortunately, Freud's achievement is entangled in an embarrassingly careless scientific tradition. The slowness of psychoanalysis to purge itself of unsubstantiated folklore and outmoded concepts cannot be denied. We no longer hear much about the primal crime, phylogenetic memory traces, Eros and Death, the Nirvana principle, or the infant's "primal hating" of the world, but we still find analysts deriving character traits solely from the vicissitudes of drives, dealing in hydraulically conceived sums of libido, and reifying Freud's oversimple tension-discharge model.[22] The virtual hibernation of psychoanalysis during the current period of revolutionary gains in natural science is cause for dismay. Yet there is no rival set of concepts covering the important ground that Freud appropriated seventy years ago. The literary student can hardly undertake a revision of clinical theory, but for the present he must try to ascertain which are its most essential and best verified points.

The main uncertainty facing a Freudian critic, however, is procedural rather than theoretical. The very abundance of "Freudian materials" in literature prompts him to ask what he should make of them, and here the theory cannot tell him which way to turn. Is the artist sicker, or is he better off, than those of us who observe his regressive forays at a distance? Nothing is easier than to "prove," using certain of Freud's premises, that art is a purely symptomatic activity, or to "prove" with equally Freudian premises that "the artist is not neurotic." The truth is that a literary critic is in a disadvantageous position for making such judgments. A text may open its fantasy life to him but it cannot, like an analyst's patient, react to his presence or delve for still hidden evidence that would support or refute his interpretive hunches. Indeed, because the regressiveness of art is necessarily more apparent to the analytic eye than its integrative and adaptive aspects are, psychoanalytic interpretation risks drawing excessively pathological conclusions. When this risk is put together with the uncertainties plaguing metapsychology itself, one can see why Freudian criticism is always problematic and often inept.

This point has not been lost on psychoanalytic theorists of literature, who have looked for ways of putting Freudian discussion on a sounder logical and empirical basis. The results to date, however, have been somewhat quixotic. The only apparent means of ensuring against the literary equivalent of "wild analysis" is to suppress all interest in pathology, bypass ambiguities of theory, and concentrate on a circumscribed range of evidence. But as soon as this exchange of investigative freedom for a higher degree of certainty has been made, a trivialization seems to occur, and some of the spirit of psychoanalysis is lost. The very routine of one's method becomes a barrier to the deep involvement that should energize all criticism, Freudian criticism above all.

Not even the most coherent and ambitious attempt at a Freudian aesthetics, Norman N. Holland's *The Dynamics of Literary Response*,[23] avoids this pitfall. Holland assumes that literature, on the analogy of the dream and the joke, is essentially understandable as the disguising and discharging of an infantile fantasy — not, however, in the author's mind, which he deems too conjectural to bother with, but only in the reader's. "Literature transforms our primitive wishes and fears into significance, and this transformation gives us pleasure" (Holland, p. 30). If this is so, then something approaching scientific accuracy appears within the reach of criticism, for psychoanalysis tells us much of what we need to know about the two most relevant categories of understanding, namely fantasies and mechanisms of defense. Holland develops a theoretical model that does succeed in differentiating among our responses to various kinds of literature, from entertainments to works of calculated absurdity; this is a substantial contribution. Yet the effect is to promote a predictable form of discussion geared to the model's limited scope. Glossaries of readers' fantasies and defenses, illustrations of their possible combinations, and proof that any work can be assigned a spot in the scheme do not capture the literary enterprise much better than manuals of sex postures capture love. In both cases the inadvertently fostered attitude is resignation: Here we go again, what will it be this time?

This objection does not arise from the common but unreasonable demand that a theory "feel like" what it describes; all theories are of necessity abstract. The quest for total certainty, however, seems to inhibit the first requisite of good criticism and good psychoanalysis, the capacity to be moved. A literary work may impress us with a complexity and economy, an energy and restraint, a precision and reverberation whose ultimate reference is not simply to the "nuclear fantasy" correctly isolated by Holland, but to the whole state of mind evoked by the text. Instead of presenting a disguised infantile wish that acquires "significance," great literature typically invites us to undergo a symbolic process of self-confrontation in which infantile solutions are resisted even as they are indulged. We identify with the pain as well as with the release involved in this process. "Beauty," as Rilke said, "is nothing but the beginning of terror that we are still just able to bear." [24] A criticism that cheerfully catalogs the unconscious tricks we play on ourselves and equates literary power with a judicious recipe of wishes and tactics, introjection and intellection, cannot avoid becoming a new version of anaesthesia — a version using Freud's terminology but lacking Freud's sympathy for the way great artists court unconscious engulfment in order to recreate the conditions of a human order.

This is to say that literature registers and arouses conflict, and that no theoretical preparation can spare a critic the necessity of submitting himself to that conflict. Norman Holland would, I am sure, agree with this statement, yet in practice he empties psychic defenses of their shame and anxiety and treats them much like the formal devices of rhetoric. When this is combined with ground rules discouraging biographical inquiry and value judgments, psychoanalytic discussion becomes what Holland has called "The Next New Criticism," a mere consolidation and deepening of the formalistic close reading of recent decades.[25] Such a tactful presentation seemingly makes room for us Freudians in the kingdom of polysemous meaning, but in actuality no one is placated. Conventional scholars remain quite aware that psychoanalysis constitutes a threat to their style of reading, and they are scandalized by the very claims (for instance, that literature is after all much like joke-telling) by which Holland hopes to make Freudian criticism seem more agreeable.

Freudian criticism can become generally agreeable only by disavowing the idea of unconscious causation. Holland would never do this; he simply avoids authors' minds [26] and keeps his Freudianism well-mannered by showing magnanimity toward the shortcomings of "English." Yet those shortcomings must be directly challenged if "the connection between knowledge and the zest of life" [27] is to be preserved. Psychoanalysis would be yet another scholastic distraction from art if it were assimilated to the current ethos of academic departments. To move from collecting pastoral elegy motifs to collecting instances of phallic mothers would be a smaller step than most professors could imagine, a mere exchange of one indifferent taxonomy for another. The real value of literary psychoanalysis is that it can embolden us to be alone with books, to recognize our own image in them, and from that recognition to begin comprehending their hold over us.

The represented mind to which we respond in literary experience is not precisely the one we could infer from biographical data, but is improvised from what Keats called negative capability. This capability, however, is temperamentally limited by the persisting conflicts that must be managed in any creative process. The ego-state suffusing the work must borrow heavily from the "countercathected system" — that is, the cluster of defenses preventing inadmissible actions and expressions — that makes up the author's habitual character, and his career will escape redundancy only to the degree that he can vary his defenses. So, too, our ability to participate will rest on whether we can afford to trade part of our character-armor for an imagined equivalent. Fear of psychic dissolution, of surrender to the repressed, is thus the paramount obstacle both to creative freedom and to a reader's capacity for involvement.

It is in this light that we can grasp the significance of fixed genres, with their coded assurance that psychic activity will be patterned and resolved along familiar lines; the genre itself is a ready-made countercathected system. For this very reason, however, art that strives for originality is always restless within its formal borders and frequently generates new forms, which imitators are bound to misunderstand as embodying permanently valid principles of beauty.[28] While the works favored by posterity are not invariably those that defy tradition, their traditional elements always prove to have been adapted to a new vision of reality. This point is familiar in nonpsychological criticism; what psychoanalysis can show is that the new vision amounts to a reconciling of competing claims so as to fuse perception with the expression of conflict.

Criticism starting from an infantile fantasy instead of from this task of reconciliation will not be able to do justice to the cognitive aspect of literature, which is just as "psychoanalytic" as fantasy itself. The crucial difference between literary creation and symptom-formation resides in the extra demand we make of literature, that it confirm and extend our sense of truth. Whereas symptoms are rigidly stereotyped, are usually accompanied by guilt, and subtract from an individual's rapport with his surroundings, in the highest literary enjoyment we feel that our pleasure is being sanctioned by reality itself, whose principles have been set before us. This is an illusion, but the illusion can be practiced only by artists whose perceptiveness has not been obliterated by ego-needs. A work that flouts our conscious intelligence, as symptoms do, may have an "escape" interest but will be soon rejected for its crudeness or empty conventionality.

To recognize the importance of cognition is not, of course, to say that doses of unadulterated social or historical truth are found in literature and account for its power. Neutral-seeming literary material always conveys unconscious apologetics, and the latter turn out to be more compelling than any amount of faithful description. Hence the shallowness of criticism that evaluates books by their correspondence to approved political facts, and hence the folly of assuming that literature naïvely mirrors the conditions of the age in which it was written. Whatever historical knowledge we can glean from literature is knowledge of the way objective circumstances were apprehended by one sensibility at the sufferance of all other psychic demands. This awareness can be illuminating once its restricted province is understood, but here again the proper point of vantage is neither fantasy nor facts, but the negotiating ego.[29]

Regarded psychoanalytically, literary works are very far from being simple lessons or exhortations decked out in poetic language; yet they *are* messages of a cryptic and intricate sort. Since our common plight is to be forever seeking acquittal from the fantasy-charges we have internalized as the price of ceasing to be infants, we share an eagerness for interpsychic transactions that seem to promise such an acquittal, or at least an abatement of guilt by means of establishing a confessional bond. Rather than being merely an unconscious release within the author or a similar release within the reader, literary process establishes a transitory complicity between the two. The forms this tie can assume are various. Milton's sensuality is hedged with law while Keats's is proclaimed as an imperious right, but both authors are posing ways for us to assert a measure of libidinal freedom. Swift implicates us in his aggression while Hemingway asks us to believe that life is castrating; both allow us to feel that our misanthropic sentiments are neither so unique nor so unfounded as we might have feared. Stendhal admits to a certain hypocrisy but easily wins our agreement that this is the way of the world; Joyce's Stephen tells us that his, and our own, creative ego must brush every hindrance from its path. In each instance we are invited, not to experience a fantasy, but to share a posture toward questionable impulses, and in the act of sharing to diffuse responsibility and stake out some unconscious territory free from the taxation of conscience.

Among the countless possibilities for literary exchange, one relationship seems frequent enough to merit special emphasis. An author often places his reader in the role of parent and begs his absolution. By revealing what has been on his mind, mixing oblique confession with a reassertion of commitment to decency and reality and beauty, and by involving the reader in everything he discloses, the author claims the right to be accepted as he is. But since everyone remains filial on the deep level where literature is registered, the reader does not use the communication quite as it was meant; he welcomes the represented self-exculpation, not as applying to someone else, but as a subtle brief in his own defense.

The tendency of critics to exaggerate the moral, social, or realistic content of literature becomes more comprehensible in this light. Every critic is first a reader who turns the text to the purposes of his beleaguered ego. By transmuting the author into a paragon of conscience or documentary literalism he completes the covering of his tracks; the literary self with which he has identified has been placed beyond reproach. Not even psychoanalytic theory, with its open attention to such unconscious tactics, is a sufficient preventative against their use. By bottling and labeling the repressed contents that Freud thought were so noxious, a Freudian can preclude the self-risk that literature asks of us. Literary art is then revealed as benign parlor magic and nothing more.

"The charm of knowledge would be small," said Nietzsche, "were it not that so much shame has to be overcome on the way to it." [30] Any system of propositions tends eventually to dissipate that shame, either by evading anxiety-provoking matters or by assimilating them to the sense of the ordinary. The latter course is obviously preferable if a choice must be made, yet knowledge about literature has a curious way of ceasing to be wholly true when such a regularization has been accomplished; the loss of uncertainty is also a loss of humanity. This is the kernel of truth in the widespread but largely foolish worry that psychoanalysis will "ruin" our favorite books. While literature is not so easily destroyed by critical remarks, any critic can temporarily make an engaging text seem dreary — not, however, by revealing too much of it, but by revealing too little and claiming this to be the whole. The very success of psychoanalytic theory in anticipating predictable aspects of literature leaves the Freudian peculiarly vulnerable to this coasting on his assumptions. His unusual advantage of method must be matched by an unusual susceptibility to the restless life of art if psychoanalysis is not to become a narcotic in his hands.

LIONEL TRILLING

On the Teaching of Modern Literature

I propose to consider here a particular theme of modern literature which appears so frequently and with so much authority that it may be said to constitute one of the shaping and controlling ideas of our epoch. I can identify it by calling it the disenchantment of our culture with culture itself — it seems to me that the characteristic element of modern literature, or at least of the most highly developed modern literature, is the bitter line of hostility to civilization which runs through it. It happens that my present awareness of this theme is involved in a personal experience, and I am impelled to speak of it not abstractly but with the husks of the experience clinging untidily to it. I shall go so far in doing this as to describe the actual circumstances in which the experience took place. These circumstances are pedagogic — they consist of some problems in teaching modern literature to undergraduates and my attempt to solve these problems. I know that pedagogy is a depressing subject to all persons of sensibility, and yet I shall not apologize for touching upon it because the emphasis upon the teaching of literature and especially of modern literature is in itself one of the most salient and significant manifestations of the culture of our time. Indeed, if, having in mind Matthew Arnold's lecture, "On the Modern Element in Literature," we are on the hunt for *the* modern element in modern literature, we might want to find it in the susceptibility of modern literature to being made into an academic subject.

For some years I have taught the course in modern literature in Columbia College. I did not undertake it without misgiving and I have never taught it with an undivided mind. My doubts do not refer to the value of the literature itself, only to the educational propriety of its being studied in college. These doubts persist even though I wholly understand that the relation of our collegiate education to modernity is no longer an open question. The unargued assumption of most curriculums is that the real

SOURCE: "On the Teaching of Modern Literature" is from *Beyond Culture: Essays on Literature and Learning* (New York: Viking Press, 1965), pp. 3–30. Copyright © 1961 by Lionel Trilling. Reprinted by permission of The Viking Press, Inc. and Martin Secker and Warburg Ltd.

subject of all study is the modern world; that the justification of all study is its immediate and presumably practical relevance to modernity; that the true purpose of all study is to lead the young person to be at home in, and in control of, the modern world. There is really no way of quarreling with the assumption or with what follows upon it, the instituting of courses of which the substance is chiefly contemporary or at least makes ultimate reference to what is contemporary.

It might be asked why anyone should *want* to quarrel with the assumption. To that question I can return only a defensive, eccentric, self-depreciatory answer. It is this: that to some of us who teach and who think of our students as the creators of the intellectual life of the future, there comes a kind of despair. It does not come because our students fail to respond to ideas, rather because they respond to ideas with a happy vagueness, a delighted glibness, a joyous sense of power in the use of received or receivable generalizations, a grateful wonder at how easy it is to formulate and judge, at how little resistance language offers to their intentions. When that despair strikes us, we are tempted to give up the usual and accredited ways of evaluating education, and instead of prizing responsiveness and aptitude, to set store by some sign of personal character in our students, some token of individual will. We think of this as taking the form of resistance and imperviousness, of personal density or gravity, of some power of supposing that ideas are real, a power which will lead a young man to say what Goethe thought was the modern thing to say, "But is this really true — is it true for *me?*" And to say this not in the facile way, not following the progressive educational prescription to "think for yourself," which means to think in the progressive pieties rather than in the conservative pieties (if any of the latter do still exist), but to say it from his sense of himself as a person rather than as a bundle of attitudes and responses which are all alert to please the teacher and the progressive community.

We can't do anything about the quality of personal being of our students, but we are led to think about the cultural analogue of a personal character that is grave, dense, and resistant — we are led to think about the past. Perhaps the protagonist of Thomas Mann's story, "Disorder and Early Sorrow" comes to mind, that sad Professor Cornelius with his intense and ambivalent sense of history. For Professor Cornelius, who is a historian, the past is dead, is death itself, but for that very reason it is the source of order, value, piety, and even love. If we think about education in the dark light of the despair I have described, we wonder if perhaps there is not to be found in the past that quiet place at which a young man might stand for a few years, at least a little beyond the competing attitudes and generalizations of the present, at least a little beyond the contemporary problems which he is told he can master only by means of attitudes and generalizations, that quiet place in which he can be silent, in which he can *know* something — in what year the Parthenon was begun, the order of battle at Trafalgar, how Linear B was deciphered: almost anything at all that has nothing to do with the talkative and attitudinizing present, anything at all but variations on the accepted formulations about *anxiety,* and *urban society,* and *alienation,* and *Gemeinschaft* and *Gesellschaft,* all the matter of the academic disciplines which are founded upon the modern self-consciousness and the modern self-pity. The modern self-pity is certainly not without its justification; but, if the circumstances that engender it are ever to be overcome, we must sometimes wonder whether this work can be done by minds which are taught in youth to accept these sad conditions of ours as the only right objects of contemplation. And quite apart from any practical consequences, one thinks of the simple aesthetic personal pleasure of having to do with young minds, and maturing minds, which are free of cant, which are, to quote an old poet, "fierce, moody, patient, venturous, modest, shy."

This line of argument I have called eccentric and maybe it ought to be called obscurantist and reactionary. Whatever it is called, it is not likely to impress a Committee on the Curriculum. It was, I think, more or less the line of argument of my department in Columbia College, when, up to a few years ago, it would decide, whenever the question came up, not to carry its courses beyond the late nineteenth century. But our rationale could not stand against the representations which a group of students made to our Dean and which he communicated to us. The students wanted a course in modern literature — very likely, in the way of students, they said that it was a scandal that no such course was being offered in the College. There was no argument that could stand against this expressed desire: we could only capitulate, and then, with pretty good grace, muster the arguments that justified our doing so. Was not the twentieth century more than half over? Was it not nearly fifty years since Eliot wrote "Portrait of a Lady"? George Meredith had not died until 1909, and even the oldest among us had read one of his novels in a college course — many American universities had been quick to bring into their purview the literature of the later nineteenth century, and even the early twentieth century; there was a strong supporting tradition for our capitulation. Had not Yeats been Matthew Arnold's contemporary for twenty-three years?

Our resistance to the idea of the course had never been based on an adverse judgment of the literature itself. We are a department not only of English but of comparative literature, and if the whole of modern literature is surveyed, it could be said — and we were willing to say it — that no literature of the past surpassed the literature of our time in power and magnificence. Then too, it is a difficult literature, and it is difficult not merely as defenders of modern poetry say that all literature is difficult. We nowadays believe that Keats is a very difficult poet, but his earlier readers did not. We now see the depths and subtleties of Dickens, but his contemporary readers found him as simply available as a plate of oysters on the half shell. Modern literature, however, shows its difficulties at first blush; they are literal as well as doctrinal difficulties — if our students were to know their modern literary heritage, surely they needed all the help that a teacher can give?

These made cogent reasons for our decision to establish, at long last, the course in modern literature. They also made a ground for our display of a certain mean-spirited, last-ditch vindictiveness. I recall that we said something like, "Very well, if they want the modern, let them have it — let them have it, as Henry James says, full in the face. We shall give the course, but we shall give it on the highest level, and if they think, as students do, that the modern will naturally meet them in a genial way, let them have their gay and easy time with Yeats and Eliot, with Joyce and Proust and Kakfa, with Lawrence, Mann, and Gide."

Eventually the course fell to me to give. I approached it with an uneasiness which has not diminished with the passage of time — it has, I think, even increased. It arises, this uneasiness, from my personal relation with the works that form the substance of the course. Almost all of them have been involved with me for a long time — I invert the natural order not out of lack of modesty but taking the cue of W. H. Auden's remark that a real book reads us. I have been read by Eliot's poems and by *Ulysses* and by *Remembrance of Things Past* and by *The Castle* for a good many years now, since early youth. Some of these books at first rejected me; I bored them. But as I grew older and they knew me better, they came to have more sympathy with me and to understand my hidden meanings. Their nature is such that our relationship has been very intimate. No literature has ever been so shockingly personal as that of our time — it asks every question that is forbidden in polite society. It asks us if we are content with our marriages, with our family lives, with our professional lives, with our friends. It is all very well for me to describe my course in the College catalogue as "paying particular attention to the role of the writer as a critic of his culture" — this is sheer evasion: the questions asked by our literature are not about our culture but about ourselves. It asks us if we are content with ourselves, if we are saved or damned — more than with anything else, our literature is concerned with salvation. No literature has ever been so intensely spiritual as ours. I do not venture to call it actually religious, but certainly it has the special intensity of concern with the spiritual life which Hegel noted when he spoke of the great modern phenomenon of the secularization of spirituality.

I do not know how other teachers deal with this extravagant personal force of modern literature, but for me it makes difficulty. Nowadays the teaching of literature inclines to a considerable technicality, but when the teacher has said all that can be said about formal matters, about verse-patterns, metrics, prose conventions, irony, tension, etc., he must confront the necessity of bearing personal testimony. He must use whatever authority he may possess to say whether or not a work is true; and if not, why not; and if so, why so. He can do this only at considerable cost to his privacy. How does one say that Lawrence is right in his great rage against the modern emotions, against the modern sense of life and ways of being, unless one speaks from the intimacies of one's own feelings, and one's own sense of life, and one's own wished-for way of being? How, except with the implication of personal judgment, does one say to students that Gide is perfectly accurate in his representation of the awful boredom and slow corruption of respectable life? Then probably one rushes in to say that this doesn't of itself justify homosexuality and the desertion of one's dying wife, certainly not. But then again, having paid one's *devoirs* to morality, how does one rescue from morality Gide's essential point about the supreme rights of the individual person, and without making it merely historical, academic?

My first response to the necessity of dealing with matters of this kind was resentment of the personal discomfort it caused me. These are subjects we usually deal with either quite unconsciously or in the privacy of our own conscious minds, and if we now and then disclose our thoughts about them, it is to friends of equal age and especial closeness. Or if we touch upon them publicly, we do so in the relative abstractness and anonymity of print. To stand up in one's own person and to speak of them in one's own voice to an audience which each year grows younger as one grows older — that is not easy, and probably it is not decent.

And then, leaving aside the personal considerations, or taking them merely as an indication of something wrong with the situation, can we not say that, when modern literature is brought into the classroom, the subject being taught is betrayed by the pedagogy of the subject? We have to ask ourselves whether in our day too much does not come within the purview of the academy. More and more, as the universities liberalize themselves, and turn their beneficent imperialistic gaze upon what is called Life Itself, the feeling grows among our educated classes that little can be experienced unless it is validated by some established intellectual discipline, with the result that experience loses much of its personal immediacy for us and becomes part of an accredited societal activity. This is not entirely true and I don't want to play the boring academic game of pretending that it *is* entirely true, that the university mind wilts and withers whatever it touches. I must believe, and I do believe, that the university study of art is capable of confronting the power of a work of art fully and courageously. I even believe that it can discover and disclose power where it has not been felt before. But the university study of art achieves this end chiefly with works of art of an older period. Time has the effect of seeming to quiet the work of art, domesticating it and making it into a classic, which is often another way of saying that it is an object of merely habitual regard. University study of the right sort can reverse this process and restore to the old work its freshness and force — can, indeed, disclose unguessed-at power. But with the works of art of our own present age, university study tends to accelerate the process by which the radical and subversive work becomes the classic work, and university study does this in the degree that it is vivacious and responsive and what is called non-academic. In one of his poems Yeats mocks the literary scholars, "the bald heads forgetful of their sins," "the old, learned, respectable bald heads," who edit the poems of the fierce and passionate young men.

> Lord, what would they say
> Did their Catullus walk this way?

Yeats, of course, is thinking of his own future fate, and no doubt there is all the radical and comical discrepancy that he sees between the poet's passions and the scholars' close-eyed concentration on the text. Yet for my part, when I think of Catullus, I am moved to praise the tact of all those old heads, from Heinsius and Bentley to Munro and Postgate, who worked on Codex G and Codex O and drew conclusions from them about the lost Codex V — for doing only this and for not trying to realize and demonstrate the true intensity and the true quality and the true cultural meaning of Catullus's passion and managing to bring it somehow into eventual accord with their respectability and baldness. Nowadays we who deal with books in universities live in fear that the World, which we imagine to be a vital, palpitating, passionate, reality-loving World, will think of us as old, respectable, and bald, and we see to it that in our dealings with Yeats (to take him as the example) his wild cry of rage and sexuality is heard by our students and quite thoroughly understood by them as — what is it that we eventually call it? — *a significant expression of our culture*. The exasperation of Lawrence and the subversiveness of Gide, by the time we have dealt with them boldly and straightforwardly, are notable instances of the *alienation of modern man as exemplified by the artist*. "Compare Yeats, Gide, Lawrence, and Eliot in the use which they make of the theme of sexuality to criticize the deficiencies of modern culture. Support your statement by specific references to the work of each author. [Time: one hour.]" And the distressing thing about our examination questions is that they are not ridiculous, they make perfectly good sense — such good sense that the young person who answers them can never again know the force and terror of what has been communicated to him by the works he is being examined on.

Very likely it was with the thought of saving myself from the necessity of speaking personally and my students from having to betray the full harsh meaning of a great literature that I first taught my course in as *literary* a way as possible. A couple of decades ago the discovery was made that a literary work is a structure of words: this doesn't seem a surprising thing to have learned except for its polemical tendency, which is to urge us to minimize the amount of attention we give to the poet's social and personal will, to what he wants to happen outside the poem as a result of the poem; it urges us to fix our minds on what is going on inside the poem. For me this polemical tendency has been of the greatest usefulness, for it has corrected my inclination to pay attention chiefly to what the poet *wants*. For two or three years I directed my efforts toward dealing with the matter of the course chiefly as structures of words, in a formal way, with due attention paid to the literal difficulty which marked so many of the works. But it went against the grain. It went against my personal grain. It went against the grain of the classroom situation, for formal analysis is best carried on by question-and-answer, which needs small groups, and the registration for the course in modern literature in any college is sure to be large. And it went against the grain of the authors themselves — structures of words they may indeed have created, but these structures were not pyramids or triumphal arches, they were manifestly contrived to be not static and commemorative but mobile and aggressive, and one does not describe a quinquereme or a howitzer or a tank with estimating how much *damage* it can do.

Eventually I had to decide that there was only one way to give the course, which was to give it without strategies and without conscious caution. It was not honorable, either to the students or to the authors, to conceal or disguise my relation to the literature, my commitment to it, my fear of it, my ambivalence toward it. The literature had to be dealt with in the terms it announced for itself. As for the students, I have never given assent to the modern saw about "teaching students, not subjects" — I have always thought it right to teach subjects, believing that if one gives his first loyalty to the subject, the student is best instructed. So I resolved to give the course with no considerations in mind except my own interests. And since my own interests lead me to see literary situations as cultural situations, and cultural situations as great elaborate fights about moral issues, and moral issues as having something to do with gratuitously chosen images of personal being, and images of personal being as having something to do with literary style, I felt free to begin with what for me was a first concern, the animus of the author, the objects of his will, the things he wants or wants to have happen.

My cultural and non-literary method led me to decide that I would begin the course with a statement of certain themes or issues that might especially engage our attention. I even went so far in non-literariness as to think that my purposes would best be served if I could contrive a "background" for the works we would read — I wanted to propose a history for the themes or issues that I hoped to discover. I did not intend that this history should be either very extensive or very precise. I wanted merely to encourage a *sense* of a history, some general intuition of a past, in students who, as it seems to me, have not been provided with any such thing by their education and who are on the whole glad to be without it. And because there is as yet no adequate general work of history of the culture of the last two hundred years, I asked myself what books of the age just preceding ours had most influenced our literature, or, since I was far less concerned with showing influence than with discerning a tendency, what older books might seem to fall into a line the direction of which pointed to our own literature and thus might serve as a prolegomenon to the course.

It was virtually inevitable that the first work that should have sprung to mind was Sir James Frazer's *The Golden Bough*, not, of course, the whole of it, but certain chapters, those that deal with Osiris, Attis, and Adonis. Anyone who thinks about modern literature in a systematic way takes for granted the great part played in it by myth, and especially by those examples of myth which tell about gods dying and being reborn — the imagination of death and rebirth, reiterated in the ancient world in innumerable variations that are yet always the same, captivated the literary mind at the very moment when, as all accounts of the modern age agree, the most massive and compelling of all the stories of resurrection had lost much of its hold upon the world.

Perhaps no book has had so decisive an effect upon modern literature as Frazer's. It was beautifully to my purpose that it had first been published ten years before the twentieth century began. Yet forty-three years later, in 1933, Frazer delivered a lecture, very eloquent, in which he bade the world be of good hope in the face of the threat to the human mind that was being offered by the Nazi power. He was still alive in 1941. Yet he had been born in 1854, three years before Matthew Arnold gave the lecture "On the Modern Element in Literature." Here, surely, was history, here was the past I wanted, beautifully connected with our present. Frazer was wholly a man of the nineteenth century, and the more so because the eighteenth century was so congenial to him — the lecture of 1933 in which he predicted the Nazi defeat had as its subject Condorcet's *Progress of the Human Mind;* when he took time from his anthropological studies to deal with literature, he prepared editions of Addison's essays and Cowper's letters. He had the old lost belief in the virtue and power of rationality. He loved and counted on order, decorum, and good sense.

This great historian of the primitive imagination was in the dominant intellectual tradition of the West which, since the days of the pre-Socratics, has condemned the ways of thought that we call primitive.

It can be said of Frazer that in his conscious intention he was a perfect representative of what Arnold meant when he spoke of a modern age. And perhaps nothing could make clearer how the conditions of life and literature have changed in a hundred years than to note the difference between the way in which Arnold defines the modern element in literature and the way in which we must define it.

Arnold used the world *modern* in a wholly honorific sense. So much so that he seems to dismiss all temporal idea from the word and makes it signify certain timeless intellectual and civic virtues — his lecture, indeed, was about the modern element in the ancient literatures. A society, he said, is a modern society when it maintains a condition of repose, confidence, free activity of the mind, and the tolerance of divergent views. A society is modern when it affords sufficient material well-being for the conveniences of life and the development of taste. And, finally, a society is modern when its members are intellectually mature, by which Arnold means that they are willing to judge by reason, to observe facts in a critical spirit, and to search for the law of things. By this definition Periclean Athens is for Arnold a modern age, Elizabethan England is not; Thucydides is a modern historian, Sir Walter Raleigh is not.

I shall not go into further details of Arnold's definition or description of the modern.[1] I have said enough, I think, to suggest what Arnold was up to, what he wanted to see realized as the desideratum of his own society, what ideal he wanted the works of intellect and imagination of his own time to advance. And at what a distance his ideal of the modern puts him from our present sense of modernity, from our modern literature! To anyone conditioned by our modern literature, Arnold's ideal of order, convenience, decorum, and rationality might well seem to reduce itself to the small advantages and excessive limitations of the middle-class life of a few prosperous nations of the nineteenth century. Arnold's historic sense presented to his mind the long, bitter, bloody past of Europe, and he seized passionately upon the hope of true civilization at last achieved. But the historic sense of our literature has in mind a long excess of civilization to which may be ascribed the bitterness and bloodiness both of the past and of the present and of which the peaceful aspects are to be thought of as mainly contemptible — its order achieved at the cost of extravagant personal repression, either that of coercion or that of acquiescence; its repose otiose; its tolerance either flaccid or capricious; its material comfort corrupt and corrupting; its taste a manifestation either of timidity or of pride; its rationality attained only at the price of energy and passion.

For the understanding of this radical change of opinion nothing is more illuminating than to be aware of the doubleness of mind of the author of *The Golden Bough*. I have said that Frazer in his conscious mind and in his first intention exemplifies all that Arnold means by the modern. He often speaks quite harshly of the irrationality and the orgiastic excesses of the primitive religions he describes, and even Christianity comes under his criticism both because it stands in the way of rational thought and because it can draw men away from intelligent participation in the life of society. But Frazer had more than one intention, and he had an unconscious as well as a conscious mind. If he deplores the primitive imagination, he also does not fail to show it as wonderful and beautiful. It is the rare reader of *The Golden Bough* who finds the ancient beliefs and rituals wholly alien to him. It is to be expected that Frazer's adduction of the many pagan analogues to the Christian mythos will be thought by Christian readers to have an adverse effect on faith, it was undoubtedly Frazer's purpose that it should, yet many readers will feel that Frazer makes all faith and ritual indigenous to humanity, virtually biological; they feel, as DeQuincey put it, that not to be at least a *little* superstitious is to lack generosity of mind. Scientific though his purpose was, Frazer had the effect of validating those old modes of experiencing the world which modern men, beginning with the Romantics, have sought to revive in order to escape from positivism and common sense.

The direction of the imagination upon great and mysterious objects of worship is not the only means men use to liberate themselves from the bondage of quotidian fact, and although Frazer can scarcely be held accountable for the evergrowing modern attraction to the extreme mental states — to rapture, ecstasy, and transcendence, which are achieved by drugs, trance, music and dance, orgy, and the derangement of personality — yet he did provide a bridge to the understanding and acceptance of these states, he proposed to us the idea that the desire for them and the use of them for heuristic purposes is a common and acceptable manifestation of human nature.

This one element of Frazer's masterpiece could scarcely fail to suggest the next of my prolegomenal works. It is worth remarking that its author was in his own way as great a classical scholar as Frazer himself — Nietzsche was Professor of Classical Philology at the Univerity of Basel when, at the age of twenty-seven, he published his essay *The Birth of Tragedy*. After the appearance of this stunningly brilliant account of Greek civilization, of which Socrates is not the hero but the villain, what can possibly be left to us of that rational and ordered Greece, that modern, that eighteenth-century, Athens that Arnold so entirely relied on as the standard for judging all civilizations? Professor Kaufmann is right when he warns us against supposing that Nietzsche exalts Dionysus over Apollo and tells us that Nietzsche "emphasizes the Dionysiac only because he feels that the Apollonian genius of the Greeks cannot be fully understood apart from it." But no one reading Nietzsche's essay for the first time is likely to heed this warning. What will reach him before due caution intervenes, before he becomes aware of the portentous dialectic between Dionysus and Apollo, is the excitement of suddenly being liberated from Aristotle, the joy of finding himself acceding to the author's statement that "art rather than ethics constitutes the essential metaphysical activity of man," that tragedy has its source in the Dionysiac rapture, "whose closest analogy is furnished by physical intoxication," and that this rapture, in which "the individual forgets himself completely," was in itself no metaphysical state but an orgiastic display of lust and cruelty, "of sexual promiscuity overriding every form of tribal law." This sadic and masochistic frenzy, Nietzsche is at pains to insist, needs the taming hand of Apollo before it can become tragedy, but it is the primal stuff of the great art, and to the modern experience of tragedy this explanation seems far more pertinent than Aristotle's, with its eagerness to forget its origin in its achievement of a state of noble imperturbability.

Of supreme importance in itself, Nietzsche's essay had for me the added pedagogic advantage of allowing me to establish a historical line back to William Blake. Nothing is more characteristic of modern literature than its discovery and canonization of the primal, non-ethical energies, and the historical point could be made the better by remarking the correspondence of thought of two men of different nations and separated from each other by a good many decades, for Nietzsche's Dionysian orgy and Blake's Hell are much the same thing.

Whether or not Joseph Conrad read either Blake or Nietzsche I do not know, but his *Heart of Darkness* follows in their line. This very great work has never lacked for the admiration it deserves, and it has been given a kind of canonical place in the legend of modern literature by Eliot's having it so clearly in mind when he wrote *The Waste Land* and his having taken from it the epigraph to "The Hollow Men." But no one, to my knowledge, has ever confronted in an explicit way its strange and terrible message of ambivalence toward the life of civilization. Consider that its protagonist, Kurtz, is a progressive and a liberal and that he is the highly respected representative of a society which would have us believe it is benign, although in fact it is vicious. Consider too that he is a practitioner of several arts, a painter, a writer, a musician, and into the bargain a political orator. He is at once the most idealistic and the most practically successful of all the agents of the Belgian exploitation of the Congo. Everybody knows the truth about him which Marlow discovers — that Kurtz's success is the result of a terrible ascendancy he has gained over the natives of his distant station, an ascendancy which is derived from his presumed magical or divine powers, that he has exercised his rule with an extreme of cruelty, that he has given himself to unnamable acts of lust. This is the world of the darker pages of *The Golden Bough*. It is one of the great points of Conrad's story that Marlow speaks of the primitive life of the jungle not as being noble or charming or even free but as being base and sordid — and for *that* reason compelling: he himself feels quite overtly its dreadful attraction. It is to this devilish baseness that Kurtz has yielded himself, and yet Marlow, although he does indeed treat him with hostile irony, does not find it possible to suppose that Kurtz is anything but a hero of the spirit. For me it is still ambiguous whether Kurtz's famous deathbed cry, "The horror! The horror!" refers to the approach of death or to his experience of savage life. Whichever it is, to Marlow the fact that Kurtz could utter this cry at the point of death, while Marlow himself, when death threatens him, can know it only as a weary grayness, marks the difference between the ordinary man and a hero of the spirit. Is this not the essence of the modern belief about the nature of the artist, the man who goes down into that hell which is the historical beginning of the human soul, a beginning not outgrown but established in humanity as we know it now, preferring the reality of this hell to the bland lies of the civilization that has overlaid it?

This idea is proposed again in the somewhat less powerful but still very moving work with which I followed *Heart of Darkness,* Thomas Mann's *Death in Venice.* I wanted this story not so much for its account of an extravagantly Apollonian personality surrendering to forces that, in his Apollonian character, he thought shameful — although this was certainly to my purpose — but rather for Aschenbach's fevered dreams of the erotic past, and in particular that dream of the goat-orgy which Mann, being the kind of writer he is, having the kind of relation to Nietzsche he had, might well have written to serve as an illustration of what *The Birth of Tragedy* means by religious frenzy, the more so, of course, because Mann chooses that particular orgiastic ritual, the killing and eating of the goat, from which tragedy is traditionally said to have been derived.

A notable element of this story in which the birth of tragedy plays an important part is that the degradation and downfall of the protagonist is not represented as tragic in the usual sense of the word — that is, it is not represented as a great deplorable event. It is a commonplace of modern literary thought that the tragic mode is not available even to the gravest and noblest of our writers. I am not sure that this is the deprivation that some people think it to be and a mark of our spiritual inferiority. But if we ask why it has come about, one reason may be that we have learned to think our way back through tragedy to the primal stuff out of which tragedy arose. If we consider the primitive forbidden ways of conduct which traditionally in tragedy lead to punishment by death, we think of them as being the path to reality and truth, to an ultimate self-realization. We have always wondered if tragedy itself may not have been saying just this in a deeply hidden way, drawing us to think of the hero's sin and death as somehow conferring justification, even salvation of a sort — no doubt this is what Nietzsche had in mind when he said that "tragedy denies ethics." What tragedy once seemed to hint, our literature now is willing to say quite explicitly. If Mann's Aschenbach dies at the height of his intellectual and artistic powers, overcome by a passion that his ethical reason condemns, we do not take this to be a defeat, rather a kind of terrible rebirth: at his latter end the artist knows a reality that he had until now refused to admit to consciousness.

Thoughts like these suggested that another of Nietzsche's works, *The Genealogy of Morals,* might be in point. It proposes a view of society which is consonant with the belief that art and not ethics constitutes the essential metaphysical activity of man and with the validation and ratification of the primitive energies. Nietzsche's theory of the social order dismisses all ethical impulse from its origins — the basis of society is to be found in the rationalization of cruelty: as simple as that. Nietzsche has no ultimate Utopian intention in saying this, no hope of revising the essence of the social order, although he does believe that its pain can be mitigated. He represents cruelty as a social necessity, for only by its exercise could men ever have been induced to develop a continuity of will: nothing else than cruel pain could have created in mankind that memory of intention which makes society possible. The method of cynicism which Nietzsche pursued — let us be clear that it is a method and not an attitude — goes so far as to describe punishment in terms of the pleasure derived from the exercise of cruelty: "Compensation," he says, "consists in a legal warrant entitling one man to exercise his cruelty on another." There follows that most remarkable passage in which Nietzsche describes the process whereby the individual turns the cruelty of punishment against himself and creates the bad conscience and the consciousness of guilt which manifests itself as a pervasive anxiety. Nietzsche's complexity of mind is beyond all comparison, for in this book which is dedicated to the liberation of the conscience, Nietzsche makes his defense of the bad conscience as a decisive force in the interests of culture. It is much the same line of argument that he takes when, having attacked the Jewish morality and the priestly existence in the name of the health of the spirit, he reminds us that only by his sickness does man become interesting.

From *The Genealogy of Morals* to Freud's *Civilization and Its Discontents* is but a step, and some might think that, for pedagogic purposes, the step is so small as to make the second book supererogatory. But although Freud's view of society and culture has indeed a very close affinity to Nietzsche's, Freud does add certain considerations which are essential to our sense of the modern disposition.

For one thing, he puts to us the question of whether or not we want to *accept* civilization. It is not the first time that the paradox of civilization has been present to the mind of civilized people, the sense that civilization makes men behave worse and suffer more than does some less developed state of human existence. But hitherto all such ideas were formulated in a moralizing way — civilization was represented as being "corrupt," a divagation from a state of innocence. Freud had no illusions about a primitive innocence, he conceived no practicable alternative to civilization. In consequence, there was a unique force to the question he asked: whether we wished to accept civilization, with all its contradictions, with all its pains — pains, for "discontents" does not accurately describe what Freud has in mind. He had his own answer to the question — his tragic, or stoic, sense of life dictated it: we do well to accept it, although we also do well to cast a cold eye on the fate that makes it our better part to accept it. Like Nietzsche, Freud thought that life was justified by our heroic response to its challenge.

But the question Freud posed has not been set aside or closed up by the answer that he himself gave to it. His answer, like Nietzsche's, is essentially in the line of traditional humanism — we can see this in the sternness with which he charges women not to interfere with men in the discharge of their cultural duty, not to claim men for love and the family to the detriment of their free activity in the world. But just here lies the matter of Freud's question that the world more and more believes Freud himself did not answer. The pain that civilization inflicts is that of the instinctual renunciation that civilization demands, and it would seem that fewer and fewer people wish to say with Freud that the loss of instinctual gratification, emotional freedom, or love, is compensated for either by the security of civilized life or by the stern pleasures of the masculine moral character.

With Freud's essay I brought to a close my list of prolegomenal books for the first term of the course. I shall not do much more than mention the books with which I introduced the second term, but I should like to do at least that. I began with *Rameau's Nephew,* thinking that the peculiar moral authority which Diderot assigns to the envious, untalented, unregenerate protagonist was peculiarly relevant to the line taken by the ethical explorations of modern literature. Nothing is more characteristic of the literature of our time than the replacement of the hero by what has come to be called the anti-hero, in whose indifference to or hatred of ethical nobility there is presumed to lie a special authenticity. Diderot is quite overt about this — he himself in his public character is the deuter-agonist, the "honest consciousness," as Hegel calls him, and he takes delight in the discomfiture of the decent, dull person he is by the Nephew's nihilistic mind.

It seemed to me too that there was particular usefulness in the circumstance that this anti-hero should avow so openly his *envy*, which Tocqueville has called the ruling emotion of democracy, and that, although he envied anyone at all who had access to the creature-comforts and the social status which he lacked, what chiefly animated him was envy of men of genius. Ours is the first cultural epoch in which many men aspire to high achievement in the arts and, in their frustration, form a dispossessed class which cuts across the conventional class lines, making a proletariat of the spirit.

Although *Rameau's Nephew* was not published until fairly late in the century, it was known in manuscript by Goethe and Hegel; it suited the temper and won the admiration of Marx and Freud for reasons that are obvious. And there is ground for supposing that it was known to Dostoevski, whose *Notes from Underground* is a restatement of the essential idea of Diderot's dialogue in terms both more extreme and less genial. The Nephew is still on the defensive — he is naughtily telling secrets about the nature of man and society. But Dostoevski's underground man shouts aloud his envy and hatred and carries the ark of his self-hatred and alienation into a remorseless battle with what he calls "the good and the beautiful," mounting an attack upon every belief not merely of bourgeois society but of the whole humanist tradition. The inclusion of *Notes from Underground* among my prolegomenal books constituted something of a pedagogic risk, for if I wished to emphasize the subversive tendency of modern literature, here was a work which made all subsequent subversion seem like affirmation, so radical and so brilliant was its negation of our traditional pieties and its affirmation of our new pieties.

I hesitated in compunction before following *Notes from Underground* with Tolstoi's *Death of Ivan Ilyitch,* which so ruthlessly and with such dreadful force destroys the citadel of the commonplace life in which we all believe we can take refuge from ourselves and our fate. But I did assign it and then two of Pirandello's plays which, in the atmosphere of the sordidness of the commonplace life, undermine all the certitudes of the commonplace, common-sense mind.

From time to time I have raised with myself the question of whether my choice of these prolegomenal works was not extravagant, quite excessively tendentious. I have never been able to believe that it is. And if these works do indeed serve to indicate in an accurate way the nature of modern literature, a teacher might find it worth asking how his students respond to the strong dose.

One response I have already described — the readiness of the students to engage in the process that we might call the socialization of the anti-social, or the acculturation of the anti-cultural, or the legitimization of the subversive. When the term-essays come in, it is plain to me that almost none of the students have been taken aback by what they have read: they have wholly contained the attack. The chief exceptions are the few who simply do not comprehend, although they may be awed by, the categories of our discourse. In their papers, like poor hunted creatures in a Kafka story, they take refuge first in misunderstood large phrases, then in bad grammar, then in general incoherence. After my pedagogical exasperation has run its course, I find that I am sometimes moved to give them a queer respect, as if they had stood up and said what in fact they don't have the wit to stand up and say: "Why do you harry us? Leave us alone. We are not Modern Man. We are the Old People. Ours is the Old Faith. We serve the little Old Gods, the gods of the copybook maxims, the small, dark, somewhat powerful deities of lawyers, doctors, engineers, accountants. With them is neither sensibility nor *angst*. With them is no disgust — it is they, indeed, who make ready the way for 'the good and the beautiful' about which low-minded doubts have been raised in this course, that 'good and beautiful' which we do not possess and don't want to possess but which we know justifies our lives. Leave us alone and let us worship our gods in the way they approve, in peace and unawareness." Crass, but — to use that interesting modern word which we have learned from the curators of museums — authentic. The rest, the minds that give me the A papers and the B papers and even the C+ papers, move through the terrors and mysteries of modern literature like so many Parsifals, asking no questions at the behest of wonder and fear. Or like so many seminarists who have been systematically instructed in the constitution of Hell and the ways to damnation. Or like so many *readers*, entertained by moral horror stories. I asked them to look into the Abyss, and, both dutifully and gladly, they have looked into the Abyss, and the Abyss has greeted them with the grave courtesy of all objects of serious study, saying: "Interesting, am I not? And *exciting*, if you consider how deep I am and what dread beasts lie at my bottom. Have it well in mind that a knowlege of me contributes materially to your being whole, or well-rounded, men."

In my distress over the outrage I have conspired to perpetrate upon a great literature, I wonder if perhaps I have not been reading these papers too literally. After all, a term-essay is not a diary of the soul, it is not an occasion for telling the truth. What my students might reveal of their true feelings to a younger teacher they will not reveal to me; they will give me what they conceive to be the proper response to the official version of terror I have given them. I bring to mind their faces, which are not necessarily the faces of the authors of these unperturbed papers, nor are they, not yet, the faces of fathers of families, or of theatergoers, or of buyers of modern paintings: not yet. I must think it possible that in ways and to a degree which they keep secret they have responded directly and personally to what they have read.

And if they have? And if they have, am I the more content?

What form would I want their response to take? It is a teacher's question that I am asking, not a critic's. We have decided in recent years to think of the critic and the teacher of literature as one and the same, and no doubt it is both possible and useful to do so. But there are some points at which the functions of the two do not coincide, or can be made to coincide only with great difficulty. Of criticism we have been told, by Arnold, that "it must be apt to study and praise elements that for fulness of spiritual perfection are wanted, even though they belong to a power which in the practical sphere may be maleficent." But teaching, or at least undergraduate teaching, is not given the same licensed mandate — cannot be given it because the teacher's audience, which stands before his very eyes, as the critic's audience does not, asks questions about "the practical sphere," as the critic's audience does not. For instance, on the very day that I write this, when I had said to my class all I could think of to say about *The Magic Mountain* and invited questions and comments, one student asked, "How would you generalize the idea of the educative value of illness, so that it would be applicable not only to a particular individual, Hans Castorp, but to young people at large?" It makes us smile, but it was asked in all seriousness, and it is serious in its subtance, and it had to be anwered seriously, in part by the reflection that this idea, like so many ideas encountered in the books of the course, had to be thought of as having reference only to the private life; that it touched the public life only in some indirect or tangential way; that it really ought to be encountered in solitude, even in secrecy, since to talk about it in public and in our academic setting was to seem to propose for it a public practicality and thus to distort its meaning. To this another student replied; he said that, despite the public ritual of the classroom, each student inevitably experienced the books in privacy and found their meaning in reference to his own life. True enough, but the teacher sees the several privacies coming together to make a group, and they propose — no doubt the more because they come together every Monday, Wednesday, and Friday at a particular hour — the idea of a community, that is to say, "the practical sphere."

This being so, the teacher cannot escape the awareness of certain circumstances which the critic, who writes for an ideal, uncircumstanced reader, has no need to take into account. The teacher considers, for example, the social situation of his students — they are not of patrician origin, they do not come from homes in which stubbornness, pride, and conscious habit prevail, nor are they born into a culture marked by these traits, a culture in which other interesting and valuable things compete with and resist ideas; they come, mostly, from "good homes" in which authority and valuation are weak or at least not very salient and bold, so that ideas have for them, at their present stage of development, a peculiar power and preciousness. And in this connection the teacher will have in mind the special prestige that our culture, in its upper reaches, gives to art, and to the ideas that art proposes — the agreement, ever growing in assertiveness, that art yields more truth than any other intellectual activity. In this culture what a shock it is to encounter Santayana's acerb skepticism about art, or Keats's remark, which the critics and scholars never take notice of, presumably because they suppose it to be an aberration, that poetry is "not so fine a thing as philosophy — For the same reason that an eagle is not so fine a thing as a truth." For many students no ideas that they will encounter in any college discipline will equal in force and sanction the ideas conveyed to them by modern literature.

The author of *The Magic Mountain* once said that all his work could be understood as an effort to free himself from the middle class, and this, of course, will serve to describe the chief intention of all modern literature. And the means of freedom which Mann prescribes (the characteristic irony notwithstanding) is the means of freedom which in effect all of modern literature prescribes. It is, in the words of Clavdia Chauchat, *"se perdre et même . . . se laisser dépérir,"* and thus to name the means is to make plain that the end is not merely freedom from the middle class but freedom from society itself. I venture to say that the idea of losing oneself up to the point of self-destruction, of surrendering oneself to experience without regard to self-interest or conventional morality, of escaping wholly from the societal bonds, is an "element" somewhere in the mind of every modern person who dares to think of what Arnold in his unaffected Victorian way called "the fulness of spiritual perfection." But the teacher who undertakes to present modern literature to his students may not allow that idea to remain in the *somewhere* of his mind; he must take it from the place where it exists habitual and unrealized and put it in the conscious forefront of his thought. And if he is committed to an admiration of modern literature, he must also be committed to this chief idea of modern literature. I press the logic of the situation not in order to question the legitimacy of the commitment, or even the propriety of expressing the commitment in the college classroom (although it does seem odd!), but to confront those of us who do teach modern literature with the striking actuality of our enterprise.

RICHARD POIRIER

What Is English Studies, and If You Know What That Is, What Is English Literature?

Some measure of distortion is probably inescapable in any effort to "teach" literature in a classroom, a relatively new and strange thing to do anyway. Still, it's possible to be discriminating even about necessary distortions, and those occurring in the classroom study of literature increase in direct proportion, I suspect, to the claims made for its transforming the lives of teachers, students, communities and even, such is the ambition, the shape of history. What I'm referring to, in part, are current demands, not new for being current, that the enterprise of English studies be made more "relevant." The term is in itself a cause of confusion. For if English studies is to become more "relevant" to anything, shouldn't it be first of all made more "relevant" to English literature? And yet before that can happen, isn't it necessary to decide what English literature is (if you believe, as I don't, that it's a "thing") or what you want it to be (if you're convinced, as I am, that it's an invention and can be reinvented at convenience)?

Questions about "relevance" presume some agreement about the shape of that invention and therefore about the resources in it now to be committed in some new way. Yet prior to any plans for investment in "relevance" is the persistent problem of none of us knowing — I'm including myself as a teacher in these strictures — what there is to be invested. There's no agreement, as there is in most other academic disciplines, even about the possible sources of revenue — Smollett as well as Cleaver? — because there's no agreement about *how* we are to look at the terrain, much less how any resources are to be gotten from it. English literature doesn't exist independently of some mode of apprehending it. And what ideally should that be? "What is poetry," Gertrude Stein once asked, "and

SOURCE: "What Is English Studies, and If You Know What That Is, What Is English Literature?" is from *Partisan Review*, Volume 37, Number 1 (1970), pp. 41–58. Copyright © 1970 by *Partisan Review*. Reprinted by permission of *Partisan Review* and the author.

if you know what poetry is, what is prose?" Since she was, as I am, raising questions as a restraint against passing beyond them to larger ones,
she immediately adds that "there is no use telling more than you know,
no, not even if you do not know it." Few really intelligent people would
be anything but cautious in answering such questions, but then there
are remarkably few intelligent people, and not all of them are in departments of literature.

What I want to suggest is that all the elements in what is called English studies are, or ought to be, in motion, including the student and the
teacher. A beautifully liberating instability, a relativity rather than a "relevance," should be all we know and all we need to know about English
studies. And yet these inherent opportunities are generally disdained in
the interest of grandiosities and pomposities and large claims. Those
who defend English as a humanistic scholarly discipline, the traditionalists, as they might be called, are as implicated as those who want the
teaching or study of literature turned into a function of personal and
political redemption. It's no surprise that last year's dissidents are this year
being recognized, vocally as well as tacitly, as allies within the literary-
academic establishment. (The smarter traditionalists of the Modern Language Association know their butter well enough not to care, for awhile,
which side of the bread it's on.)

The most vocal critics of English studies are excited by the same illusions which bolster its most vocal defenders: the illusion, first, of the
necessity, and second, of the enormous importance of literary studies.
These illusions, shared in some degree by anyone involved in literary
study, are difficult but necessary to resist. They intrude themselves because the study is confused with the subject, the teaching confused with
the thing taught, the teacher, very often, with the author, whom he is
"making available" to the young and to himself. It's a heady experience,
after all, to have a direct line to Shakespeare, especially when it's assumed
there's only one. Because of these confusions, the study of literature is
supposed to have some effect on the quality of life. So, it can be argued,
is the study of sociology or the study of history, but English studies
blithely appropriates these subjects at its convenience, while at the same
time insisting on the invulnerability of its own materials. Enterprises in
the humanities, of which literary study is preeminent, have been considered especially valuable, then, in ways not unarguably belonging to
literature itself: as a conditioning of the sensibility with respect to what
are called "concrete" human situations; as a humanizing, civilizing influence in that it bears witness to the irresolvable perplexities of living in
time and to the magnificent thrusts of human energy as it tries to transcend time. A long held assumption about literature has become the presumption of literary study: that it makes us conscious of the heroism of
transcendence. Not merely the fictional hero but the writer himself, in

his acts of creation, tries to establish realms freed of the contamination and erosions of time, tries to create forms that will become fuller and more beautiful from the accretions of time.

Literary study has come increasingly to depend on this way of thinking about literature. Classroom teachers are not, however, responsible for inventing this view of literature and are only beginning to inquire into the premises behind it. Of the many sources, a notably eloquent one is Henry James, Jr., of the *Prefaces* and of "The Art of Fiction," and Henry James, Jr., is not at all popular (though Sr. may soon, for good reason, become fashionable) with those who cry out against the irrelevance and disgrace of literary scholarship. It's therefore instructive, in seeing, again, how apparently dissident factions are closer to the traditionalists than they'd like to imagine, to note in Herbert Marcuse a position somewhat analogous to the younger James's. For Marcuse, art and literature are essentially higher forms of life. They are attached to historical or daily life by virtue of a provocative alienation, a challenge to the way things really are. Art contains, he says, "the rationality of negation. In its advanced positions, it is the Great Refusal — the protest against that which is. The modes in which man and things as they are made to appear, to sing and sound and speak are modes of refuting, breaking and recreating their factual existence." However, he argues, society has found the means — in the mass production and distribution of high culture — to assimilate and coopt the essentially antagonistic contents of literature. Surely the invention of literary studies, the whole idea of making works of art available to a classless class, is a prime instance of this cooption.

My disagreement with Marcuse is two-fold — with his conception of literary works and, consequently, with his idea of the necessary antagonism between them and society, including that social unit, ideally operative, which is a class studying a book. As for the first, literature in Marcuse is a kind of "world elsewhere." And (as I've already tried to suggest in a work of that title) it never can be. Given the nature of language and its deterministic social forms, no book can, for very long, separate itself from this world; it can only try to do so, through magnificent exertions of style lasting only for the length of the exertion. We are left to admire the effort, to lament, if we wish, the evanescent achievement. So that I would have to argue also against Marcuse's theory of the dangers of the assimilation of literature and of its antagonistic contents. The dangers *are* the glory; they are inherent in the very shape and materials of literary works. The alleged "assimilation" is the prior condition of the existence of the work of art, the very act by which one man tries to address another: the prior assumption of the whole exchange being a shared need for the forms in which they communicate, or think they do.

This condition of literature opens the way to a vigorous form of literary study. Admiration for, exploration into the effort which is literature, the act which is writing — these are what is mostly now missing from the study of literature. Literary works only provisionally constitute what Marcuse calls "another dimension of reality." They should be construed more properly as merely another dimension of action, of performance with language as its medium. Thereby we escape the contradiction that the ultimate logic of thinking of literature as a form of reality, with an exonerated status, is that it shouldn't be taught at all, that teaching only assimilates it into life as presently arranged, democratitizes and thus degrades (and deradicalizes) it. However, it still is taught under the assumption of its being "another dimension of reality"; it is meddled with, made available through all sorts of cheapening and mechanical devices, as if its integrity could only be perserved by violating it. In a perhaps crude shortcut to clarification, let me suggest that no man proud of deflowering a virgin would continue, unless he were mad, to introduce her as one. English studies cannot do what it most often does to literary works and pretend that these works still belong unto themselves or to English literature. They belong, all marked up, to English studies. Talk about the ultimate heresy of paraphrase or claims that the mechanics of *topoi* gathering are merely procedural, the necessary preparation for other and more important work — these are only bits of conscience money that critics pay themselves and do little to ameliorate the profound impressions made on the minds of students and on teachers' minds by some of the insistent methods of literary study. Much of the classroom study of literature appears unfortunately destined to make all energies of response subservient to structures, with emphasis on the coherence resulting from recurrence of patterns, and with a corresponding deemphasis on any discordant elements, except where these can be included as irony or as some as yet unidentified sub-subgenre.

My attack is less on the so-called new criticism or on the "anatomy of criticism" or on relevance seekers than on classroom versions of these and on the consequences, personal, political and literary, that follow from the classroom. As for the "new criticism," it is being treated, unfairly, as the villain of the piece anyway, despite far too casual acknowledgments that it was needed at the time as an antidote to anachronistic historical methods. Before it was fashioned into an instrument, the new criticism was itself more complex and liberating than it is now made out to be, especially as practiced by Ransom (who had the misfortune to coin the title), by Tate, by Warren and by Brooks (who took on the responsibility for translating extraordinarily supple critical formulations into a terminology and method fit for pedagogical use). And besides, all of these men, along with others of the Southern Agrarian movement, talked a politics, in *I'll Take My Stand* and elsewhere, with many of the radical, indeed Marcusean overtones, that are the reverse of the politics now ascribed to them. Their positive inclination, still immensely beneficial, was to finagle students into the work and then ask them to care about what was happening to its (and to their) language. This inclination derived in part from the classical training of the mostly Southern advocates of this kind of analysis, and derived, too, from a taste for conversational piquancy, for what Frost calls "sentence sounds." It can be fancied that this taste developed easiest in the rather close, familial, noncosmopolitan societies which these critics also tend to favor as social organizations of life, groupings in which one might learn to "read" as much through the ear as through the eye. From the first — this care about the derivation of words — comes an emphasis on the culture encapsulated in language, preserved there and mined by digging for puns and connotations; from the second — a concern for heard speech — may come the emphasis on tone and dramatic situation in the reading of literature. Given other possible sources, from Richards, Graves, Empson, one can only guess about lines of emergence and development. The important point is simply that these notions were not necessarily political in origin and that their assumed political effect, once they became classroom practice, can't easily be translated into the political thinking of men like Robert Penn Warren.

All such cautions allowed, however, the history of these ideas, and of related ones of "objective correlative" and organicism, is less important than are the consequences of their having been packaged, with something like urgency, for distribution in class. I say "packaged" because there are other critics — Blackmur, Burke, Brower, Empson and Trilling are among them — whose work doesn't submit to methodologizing. Neither, for all his enormous influence, does Leavis, about whom I'll have more to say later. The history of literary criticism is, fortunately, not the same thing as the history of pedagogy, and it is to this last that I'm addressing myself. Indeed it isn't the fault of T. S. Eliot, or Coleridge, Emerson or even Longinus, that the idea of organicism, really several contradictory ideas, is of enormous pedagogical convenience. It's rather that organicism, as usually interpreted, promises that a student, by commendably energetic local attentions will, if his responses are "responsible to the text," put together a puzzle at the end. All the better if that puzzle can be completed in the fifty or sixty minutes of a classroom hour. The implications of this emphasis have been historically as well as politically important to literature. One result has been the promotion of those works lending themselves easily for illustration, and a corresponding evasiveness about the status of those that don't. Why do students know more about Donne than about Jonson, more of the relatively trivial than of the mysterious Marvell of "Upon Appleton House," more of Keats than of Shelley; why do they all, to the last million, seem to have read *Dubliners* instead of some collected stories of Lawrence? What "goes well," what "works" in class has had an enormous and rigidifying effect on the shape of literary history during the last twenty or thirty years. I doubt that most of those now crying for "relevance" are going to be any less utilitarian in the selection of the works and writers they promote. The list will simply be different. Like the new critics, but for other reasons, they, too, believe in "works" more than in "writing," in books rather than in those manifestations of energy one might call *écriture*.

To say that the implications of the classroom study of literature are political, simply means that any concern for language and for the structures of imagination is now in some sense inescapably so. English studies is susceptible, though by no means so directly, to the kind of analysis of methods to which the social sciences have been subjected by C. Wright Mills and Noam Chomsky. Because literary studies can't claim, as can history and sociology, a very direct transmission of its findings into political consideration, any inquiry into the politics lurking in its practices is necessarily both more tentative, however, and far more risky than even Chomsky's have proved to be. It is nonetheless a necessary inquiry, though one must be on guard against reductiveness or imputation of motive or self-righteousness. The nature of the conditions I'm describing means that no one is innocent and that all descriptions, in the effort to explore the implications of a practice, must in some sense be unfair to the practitioners. Those opposed to any political interpretation of English studies can claim, quite understandably, that their intellectual conduct in class or in literary journals or as members of literary-academic organizations is susceptible to political interpretation only if they have intended it to be. I hope I've suggested that they do have an argument: I happen not to think it a very convincing or a very self-inquiring one.

For that reason, I found the disagreement in 1968 about whether or not MLA should meet in 1969 in Chicago merely symptomatic of a larger and persisting one: that we are now in a cultural situation wherein political meanings get expressed even in the effort to evade them. Those who wish this were not so have the sympathy of those who regret that it is; but those whose response is some genteel pretention that they are serving themselves and civilization by merely "doing their own work" with literature as they have always done it are deluding themselves. The "same" work is different from what it was even a few years ago, for the reason that so much has changed around it. The framers of the MLA ballot designed to poll the members about a 1970 meeting in Chicago did not recognize the changed contexts for words that a few months earlier would have been neutral enough. They were appalled at the evidence that their language expressed intentions they hadn't at all meant to express.

How did it happen that their wording confused hotel space with political space and implied a primary concern with the former? The critics of the ballot were astonished, perhaps in my own case too self-righteously so, that anyone committed to the study of language could think it possible, in the fall of 1968, to say or write anything, especially on such a subject as Chicago, which would not invite political readings.

That's a small example of what's meant by saying that no one speaks as he once did and means what he once did: the word Chicago had been made a political word. It was no longer simply a geographic one. And it had been changed, that word, not by an Academy, but by the Mayor of Chicago. He had made a geographic designation into a politically dirty word and an association of language teachers was somehow supposed to ignore this fact about its own language. Anyone could have been angered by this without being aligned with the New University Conference (often described as a faculty version of SDS), its proposals or its politics, though the Chicago issue had the effect of greatly strengthening this grouping. Anyone could have responded as I did who simply acted upon what the MLA says it stands for — a devotion to literature and language. The exercise of which didn't require even the reading of politically "relevant" pamphlets but only, as a preclude to an encounter with political language, some intense and alive reading of any writing of any kind. It meant a developed capacity for watching performances in language, the actions of words. What the difference about Chicago revealed was a naïveté, especially in an organization with a declared "devotion" to language, about the necessity to treat language almost as an antagonist, to struggle, to fight for control of it, knowing that if you don't it can be given meanings that without your even guessing it will take control of you. The only condition for avoiding disruption in MLA was for all of its members to accept, as a necessary general condition, the very special condition by which Mayor Daley tried to prevent the expression of struggle and dissent in his city. One needn't have been a schoolboy Marxist to recognize the process.

Literary study might well consist of such "lessons" in how to meet and know words under different kinds of social and historical stress. The point would be that any given expression in words has to be confronted as if meant pointedly, personally for *you*, meant as a violation, pleasurable or otherwise, of the self you'd put together before this shape of words entered into it and before the self in turn, with all its biases, cautions, histories, moved reciprocally back into those words. Literary study should show how in this engagement words can sicken and befoul, heal and uplift us, and how precarious and momentary each such induced state can be. A class can watch how words suddenly get snatched from our possession and are so recast that we don't want to possess them any more. This active way of responding to language and to the structures of imagination that are made from it is not, alas, what goes on in the classrooms of our colleges and universities. There's little effort to show how words and what is shaped by them are transformed in their passage through various contexts.

There's a lot of talk about "context" to be sure, but the word refers most often to the "work," whatever that is imagined to be, or some part of it, or to the genre of the work or to the historical pressures of the time, whatever those are supposed to be. But what about the "context" wherein the cluster of words is received — that odd place known as a classroom with all those ratty chairs and an actor up front? What about that "context" which is the reader himself and the various other "contexts" he carries in him to the context of the campus and the classroom? "Contexts" swirl around and in and out of the writing being looked at and listened to even before we begin pretending that we can firm up a literary or historical context of an authorized kind.

We ourselves, each of us, insofar as we are composed in and by language, should be as much the subject of literary studies as is any literary work similarly composed. The confrontation of these two kinds of composition — that should be the substance of our work. It's murderously hard work, however, except for those who take for granted the self known as the reader or for those satisfied with the almost invariably slapdash compositions of a self put together for any given discussion of political relevance. It's terribly difficult to find out who one is during an act of reading or to help a student find out who he or she is. It's maybe harder now than ever before: there are so many assaults on human vulnerability that, to survive at all, we become invulnerable, and then in order to seem worthy to ourselves pretend, again, to vulnerability. Hence the danger, dangerous to one's continuing and fluid self-creation, in any simple effort to attain "relevance" in literary study. What is relevant to what and where do we begin to stabilize one element in order to let it somehow feel the force of another?

For anyone teaching literature the problem is especially complicated if, as nearly all of us have, he has been educated to see things through the gridiron of one theory or another, especially a theory that has been turned into a method. Take the habit of thinking of literature organically, along with implicitly high valuations of society which is also ideally organic. It is perhaps a necessary comfort and pleasure of the imagination, a game of making oneself at home with words and images. But it is an expensive game, and there are denials in it not everyone thinks any longer worthwhile. What's missing from the habit, of course, is yourself or, more properly, yourselves and some true part of the will toward disorganization and freedom from pattern. What, indeed, are patterns for, when, if technology is frightful, it also proves inspiring to the point of awe; or when the excitements offered in forms that compete with literature and that are dismissed by left-liberal litterateurs as camp or pop or worse, are sometimes better, in that they do more to and for us, than are some works set for literary survey courses; or when the brutality and violence against which the humanities are somehow supposed to promote a civilized abhorrence also exhilarate us to the extent that we then look back at literature itself and wonder how much of the best of it isn't really to some degree pornographic in its resourceful brutality. I mean that phrase very precisely as applied, let's say, to Shakespeare and James in their "use" of characters as merely one of many expressive, "compositional" resources. As against these liberating and confusing and contradictory realizations, literary study too often asks the reader to exist importantly only when he can find himself in a structure, a structure which exists at times even at the expense of some of the most exciting *writing* in a work.

Imagine, as an instance, someone saying that he admires the political activism of youth, but finds he cannot wholly understand it or participate in it. Why? Because, he says, youthful dissent is dominated by an emotion which is inexpressible; because it is in excess of the facts as they appear. This is not, as you might think, a quote from George Kennan. It is from T. S. Eliot in his formulation of the term "objective correlative." He is talking about what might be called by certain critics, equally satisfied with pacification, the *topoi* of SDS, namely Hamlet. It matters, but not much, that the idea of objective correlative is as old as Poe and probably derivative of Washington Allston's 1850 "Lectures on Art." Given what Eliot himself called in 1966, not many years ago, its "truly embarrassing success in the world," what matters most about the term is its effect on us and its effect, still, in helping promote simplistic and repressive notions of depersonalization, unified sensibility and organicism. (If any political equivalences are thought out of order here, consider the night in 1969 at the Village Gate when Norman Mailer, later to propose that New York City be broken up into organically functioning sections, opened his campaign with a staccatoed charge that New York City lacked "an objective correlative." Though Mailer felt it necessary to identify the author of the phrase, Jimmy Breslin was perhaps on that occasion more accurate in complaining, privately, that he hadn't known he was running on a ticket with Ezra Pound.)

In any case, the effect of Eliot's too easily appropriated critical terminology, as distinct always from the marvelously *unstabilizing* intelligence at work in his critical writing and in his poetry, is to insist that feelings be grounded, secured, made explicable within structures of "unified sensibility." Such terminologies are what the academy has chosen to extract from Eliot and to mold into a critical system designed to take care of what might be called discordant or dissident elements. The effort in classroom criticism has been to make the student find a design by which these elements, including his own offbeat reactions, can be accommodated. Otherwise forget them, at least in class. "At every stage," Allen Tate cozily suggests, "we may pause to state the meanings so far apprehended, and at every stage the meanings will be coherent." Of course they will, if the critic has decided beforehand that it is right and good that they should be. Coherence, as I've suggested, is a virtue, a comfort we hope for, look for, but why need it have become the primary criterion in literary study? So much so that the conception of literature is itself tied to an idea of "works," which can be coherent, rather than to a feeling for "writing," an act in which there are various and mysterious exertions of energy? The search for coherence has been mostly a disservice to the very classics in which modern critics have been most eager to find it: *Moby Dick, The Waste Land,* and *Ulysses.* Why not cultivate the protean reader to match that emerging type of ourselves which Robert Lifton calls "the protean man"?

I am afraid that such a man would be no more assisted by a literary education conducted along lines laid down by Northrop Frye than he would along those extrapolated from Eliot, at his most formulaic, the Southern Agrarians or even Arnold — there being in each case a different degree of "spatialization" of literature and of possible responses to it. Frye can be commended for many things, and one of these is his skepticism about the Arnoldian exaltation of great works of literature as religious or political creed. Instead, he proposes that culture be treated as "the total body of imaginative hypothesis in a society and its tradition." Note, however, that he still prefers to believe in the word "body" as applied to works of imagination, to believe in a corpus of work, however enlarged, as the subject of study. There is still to be a "field," in which, as Alvin Kibel has pointed out, the relations of literature to primal fantasies are logical and not chronological. Predictably, he distrusts literary study which tries, in conjunction with psychology and anthropology, to understand works of art as the expression not of a necessarily coherent self, but of an anarchic one, a self frustrated rather than helped in expressing itself by the dominant modes of civilization or by literary forms.

Frye can be a very liberating critic, both in range and perspective, as when he remarks that "in Shakespeare the meaning of the play is the play, there being nothing to be abstracted from the total experience of the play. Progress in grasping the meaning is progress not in seeing more in the play, but in seeing more of it." And yet, as Reuben Brower has shrewdly noted, "progress" in Frye means not something about the accumulated experience, the dynamic unfolding of experience in the reader and in the work, of flashes of life. He means instead a progress that distances us from the play, that takes us on a spatial excursion from "the individual plays to the class of things called plays," and then on "to the 'meaning' of the drama as a whole." Frye leaves even less room than do adherents of "understanding poetry" for measuring or even allowing an unmeasured response to the *activity* which is reading and writing, the energy generated in a reader by some corresponding expenditure in the writer.

Looking into modern criticism in English for someone who will help in this matter and who has had some influence on the classroom study of literature, I would suggest Leavis, not because he is alone — I've mentioned others — but because his claims for "relevance" have been so pronounced and so articulated. Along with Blackmur, quite unlike him in so many other ways, he has been exceptional in his superiority to any mere talk about meanings; he hasn't thought of his principal job as interpretation at all, as a search for significances and the complication of these by ambiguities, ironies and paradoxes. Of course Leavis likes to insist, notoriously, that what's going on as he confronts a poem is really "there" in it, and he's seriously deficient where Frye is most useful. While Frye is happy to treat the genre of any work as "an essential part of the critical context," the context for Leavis is nearly always only the language of the work itself, though by language he means not simply words on a page but the accumulations from literature each word carries with it.

Still, the impressive "relevance" of Leavis — a favorite word of his with meanings that are only rarely approximated in current uses of it — and the claims to "relevance" which he makes for certain writings are indistinguishable from a thirst for verbal confrontation and intensity, a thirst for what he calls "life." Life for him is evidenced in the very effort of expression, an effort the more powerful in writers aware of oppositions, in the resistant, time-ridden nature of language, to anything but the most fashionable and facile modes of expression. There's something Maileresque (and Mailer has some aperçus about Leavis in his review of Norman Podhoretz) in the degree to which Leavis imagines that the historical context really is himself as a reader and writer; however much the poem is "there," it is he who decides, dogmatically as well as deliberately, that it should be "there," along with the extent to which it makes proper use of the resources of its language; however much he locates a "great tradition" it is a tradition of his preferences, with quite outrageous exclusions, and with inclusions, when it comes to American literature, that are merely loveable. Above all he is present everywhere in his writing. There is a personality, tense with life, at work in his sentences, all of them full of quick insinuation, and with such aristocratic refusal of self-explication that, in their breathless, witty, suspended momentum, points are condensed and subordinated — as in his unsurpassed early pieces on Eliot — which his detractors still remain incapable of reaching. For him, English literature, English culture, England itself can be found in the performed condition of the English language, with its incommensurable resources. One reason he's feared and mocked is that few teachers know what to make of this sort of personal energy, know what life and learning it offers. Most teachers look in criticism for the goods, to put it bluntly, delivered up, wrapped for carrying to class. Literary study as practised by Leavis or by Blackmur, is, for them, far too contaminated by personal testimony; he insists on preferences because he lives in and of a particular time and thinks of writing as an act going on or being repeated in that time.

I have brought up Leavis and a few others only to suggest that there has been at least some activity within English criticism, though not of the kind that's most easily snitched, which can be an alternative to any simple and, to that extent damaging application of a criterion of "relevance." Insofar as the issue touches on popular culture there are also, of course, the estimable works of Raymond Williams and Richard Hoggart. By too simple a use of the word "relevance" I mean, for example, that after agreeing with Benjamin DeMott that "we have to move away from the idea that English is a body of knowledge," I can't go on to say with him, if *Time* magazine reports him correctly (and from his other statements on the matter in *Supergrow* I can assume it does), that "we have to produce readers who think of literature as a valuable resource for the exploration of life's problems." Actually, the readers I'd want to produce would be immediately bewildered by Mr. DeMott's language, since surely a reader's first concern is with the primary resource of literature, which is language itself. In what sense is literature a "resource" for exploration except through some ways of first exploring what goes on in language, any form of language, including conversation? There's very little evidence, I think, that people of conventionally achieved literary culture or people who produce literature are any better at "the exploration of life's problems" than are some, and not a few, who cannot read or write. Those who write simply ask us to take their language in that rather than in some other form. The form makes them neither better nor worse with respect to "life."

Most calls for "relevance" now being heard manifest a perfectly clear and familiar intention: namely, that English studies is, once again, to be no more than a conveyor belt for the transmission into life of those parts of English literature which can be considered relevant to it. What about any parts of English literature that can't be made "relevant"? Do such writings (let's say "Lycidas" as a pastoral poem, since Mr. Louis Kampf, now First Vice-President of MLA, seems almost as exercised, in "The Scandal of Literary Scholarship," by the damned irrelevance of pastoral conventions in the teaching of that poem as by the reported appearance of a new journal devoted to the study of Henry James, Jr.) — do such writings constitute literature even if they *are* irrelevant to life's problems? Or another question. If one work is relevant to more of these problems than is another, does it therefore have measurably more of literature in it? Mr. Kampf's faith in the possible saving consequences of reading literature in a relevant way is quite literally disarming: "What relevance," he asks, "has the physicist's love of Marcel Proust to his work on missiles? If the love were real, he would, I assume, stop working on them." I'm afraid I don't see why this should be so. If the suppositious physicist hadn't already stopped out of love for his family or his dog, why should he stop for Marcel Proust? Are we to believe that literature's relevance to life is finally a matter of its being more relevant *than* life? Nor does one need George Steiner's operatic pronouncements that the humanistic tradition of literature somehow failed to prevent the gas chambers. While I never knew of any presumptive relationship anyway, Steiner apparently did, so that he can discover that "We now know that a man can read Goethe or Rilke in the evening — and go to his day's work at Auschwitz in the morning." Anyone can propose such connections but they don't happen to be necessary ones. Literature and, by extension, literary studies may have enormous powers, but we don't know of what they consist or how they could fail or succeed, and neither do the champions, disappointed or expectant, of relevance.

Locating the relevance of a literary work to any life or to any issue is an extraordinarily difficult and precarious job, even for those who have shown some talent for it. As a motive for English studies it is becoming perhaps insurmountably difficult. The reason is that in every area of expression there is now at work an accelerated deterioration of language — the very assertion itself has become banal — a nearly total cynicism about the adaptation, in the pursuit of power and profit, of any vocabularies, even antagonistic ones, that suit one's purpose. The speeches of Vice-President Agnew are a brilliant example of this willingness to appropriate the rhetoric of your enemies in the act of defeating them. His talk on media could have been, with only a few changes, a New Left position paper; his talk on universities made me wonder, paranoically, if the remarkable lady who does his research and helps with his speeches, hadn't adapted some things I'd said about youth and universities in a piece called "The War Against the Young." I wasn't surprised by his credits to George Kennan or Irving Kristol or Walter Lacquer or Arnold Beichmann — and apparently neither were they — but it was genuinely frightening to note how language so nearly one's own, and of a quite other political complexion, could be adapted to an argument so pernicious as Agnew's and so remote in intention from mine. Herein is a lesson for those who like to imagine the power of the word or of literature: power as a property, power of the kind at Agnew's command, can do what it wants with language, and language can do pathetically little to it.

What, then, is anyone to do who thinks of himself as a custodian not so much of language in the abstract but simply of his own language? How can he begin to dislocate language into his own meaning? I am conscious, in adapting a phrase from Eliot, that literature has always been in some sense a struggle to do this — which is why the pastoral elements of "Lycidas" could, by the way, be made to seem quite relevant to contemporary problems of expression. No one can think, however, that the problem has become anything but desperate in the last twenty years. The "struggle for verbal consciousness," Lawrence insisted, "should not be left out of art." It should now be the central concern of the study of writing in what is called literature and of writing generally. "It is a very great part of life," Lawrence reminded us. "It is not superimposition of theory. It is the passionate struggle into conscious being." Locating, then watching, then describing and participating in that struggle as it takes place in the writings of any period could be the most exciting and promising direction of English studies. It points to where language and history truly meet. Literary study can thus be made relevant to life not as a mere supplier of images or visions, but as an activity; it can create capacities through exercise with the language of literature that can then be applied to the language of politics and power, the language of daily life. It's simply terribly hard to do this, however — to make this shift of muscularity of mind and spirit from one allegedly elevated mode of expression, where the muscles can be most conveniently developed, to another mode of expression both more inaccessible and considered so ordinary, so natural as to be beyond inquiry. And yet in this transfer of activity, and in the reciprocations that would follow from it, is the promise of some genuine interplay between different and multiplying cultural traditions.

If English studies is not in command of a field of knowledge it can be in command of a field of energy. I doubt that this function will satisfy the ambitions, especially the rhetorical ones, either of many of the critics of English studies in its present shape or of many of its defenders. The latter think English studies so much more than it is — the bastion of English literature and of the values in it; the former want it to be more than it ever legitimately can be — the bastion of political and moral health. Defenders and critics share the same illusion about the power of literature as a series of finished works, rather than a feeling for the power, still generating in those works, of the retraceable acts of writing, composition, performance. "What is the late November doing / With the disturbance of the spring," asks Eliot of "East Coker," in lines any poet would have been happy to have written, one imagines. Only we are then told "That was a way of putting it — not very satisfactory: / A pariphrastic study in a worn-out poetical fashion, / Leaving one still with the intolerable wrestle / With words and meaning. The poetry does not matter."

English studies cannot be the body of English literature but it can be at one with its spirit: of struggling, of wrestling with words and meaning. Otherwise English studies may go one of two ways: it can shrink, hopefully in a manner as distinguished and health-giving as that which accompanied the retrenchment of Classics departments; or it can become distended by claims to a relevance merely topical. Alternatively, it can take a positive new step. It can further develop ways of treating *all* writing and *all* reading as analogous acts, as simultaneously unfolding performances, some of which will deaden, some of which will quicken us. This will not sound like a simple prescription to anyone who has given much thought, as I am now trying to do, to the mysteries of performance, even why we think some and not other acts belong under the heading. There will be a need, at the more advanced stages of such study, to ask questions that are essentially anthropological in nature — about ideas of beginnings, about what Frank Kermode calls "the sense of an ending," about pacings and their relation to different concepts of time, about bulk and foreshortening, about "fun" and "excitement" and how such notions change over quite brief spans of an historical period.

Once on its way, this activity can be applied to performances other than those occurring in language — to dance and sports, as much as to film or popular music. English studies must come to grips with different languages of popular culture, with newspapers, political speeches, advertising, conversation, the conduct of the classroom itself. Until proven otherwise, none of these need be treated as if it were necessarily simpler than any other or than literature. The same hard questions for all, as Richard Hoggart would have it. Far from meaning that English studies would thereby slight what it calls literature in order to extend operations, what I propose would give literature a real fighting chance to prove, if intensely enough encountered, not its cultural superiority, whatever that might mean, but its superiority as a training ground for all other efforts in the struggle for expression. English studies need only become happily, consciously limited in what it sets out to do with literature instead of, as now, an unhappy pretender. We are a long way from the day hoped for by Emerson when we shall see at last "that the most private is the most public energy."

F. R. LEAVIS

Literature and the University

English literature in our time — I am concerned in these lectures with that. If I had said "in *my* time" it would have tended to have a different effect. For there have been great and rapid changes in the last forty years. This fact is an essential consideration for my particular theme, though not, perhaps, in the way I may be immediately taken to intimate: what would ordinarily be suggested by "literary history" is not my proposed business.

Change is insisted on in this passage from the front page of the *Times Literary Supplement* for May 19, 1966 — a passage that is a pregnant text for me, inviting me to define positively the nature of my preoccupation:

"It seems inconceivable that higher education could be both a large system and a comprehensive one, and yet universities remain essentially the same as they have been; indeed there is a lack of historical perspective about Lord Robbins's comments that implies an idea of an eternal university, that belies the evidence of rapid social change in their students — and their teachers. As for their other function, have universities always been the source of the best ideas in our civilization? Name a great novelist who was a don; apart from Housman, most poets, I think, have been outside the university net."

The article is a review of the report of the Franks Commission and of Lord Robbins's *The University and the Modern World,* a collection of his addresses. I don't want to defend Lord Robbins, and I should have liked to be able to say that my sympathies were with the reviewer, who is critical of Lord Robbins's assumptions and mode of thought. But I can't. The whole article is depressingly documentary — words the force of which (I mean the last two) will have come out, I hope, before long. It confirms my sense of the great need there is to get attention for the considerations I want to put forward — and it makes me feel (as I have felt from time to time during the last forty years) that I would rather discuss the function

SOURCE: "Literature and the University [: The Wrong Question]" is from *English Literature in Our Time and the University: The Clark Lectures 1967* (London: Chatto and Windus, Ltd., 1969), pp. 39–60. Reprinted by permission of F. R. Leavis and Chatto and Windus, Ltd.

of the university with a mathematician or a physicist than with an academic humanist, which is what I take the reviewer to be.

The aspect of change represented by the passage I have quoted that I want to emphasize regards the latter part of it, and it is one of which the author is unconscious:

> Have universities always been the source of the best ideas in our civilization? Name a great novelist who was a don; apart from Housman, most poets, thinkers and creators have been outside the university net.

It is no new thing for an academic humanist to be blind and blank and urbanely unconcerned in that way. What I have to dwell on is the frightening truth that the blindness and blankness and unconcern are today general. You don't, of course, settle the question, how important or unimportant have Oxford and Cambridge been to English literature in the past, by asking how many dons were great novelists or great poets and offering us Housman. You say nothing to the point. You merely show your lack of interest in the nature of a civilization, and in the conditions out of which a great literature grows and by which it is kept alive.

A literature grows out of a culture. A great poet, though he may have a profound influence on his native language by his supremely creative use of it (it developed and is kept living in creative use), didn't create it. Shakespeare had an immeasurably great influence upon English, but couldn't have done so had he not inherited in it a rich, supple and exquisitely vital language. The indebtedness of Shakespearian English to the universities (though Shakespeare was notoriously *not* a classical or an English don) was immense — a subject on which a first-year man reading 'English' could write at least a page or two, and which a maturer student of distinguished mind, choosing it for a piece of original work, could make very much more of than a language specialist — or a linguistician — is likely (I believe) to have provided for in his implicit canons of relevance, or to be predisposed to applaud, or to see the point of.

I will say no more on this head — and I have said nothing about the University Wits. I will only add that, not merely to Shakespeare, but to the subsequent creators of modern English literature it has mattered in most vital ways (and not merely materially) that England contained an educated class and an educated public. No one will contend that the universities had nothing to do with *their* existence.

The points I have made are obvious. I don't for a moment suggest that the writer in the *Times Literary Supplement* is inclined to question them, or to question that Oxford and Cambridge have had the greatest importance in English life and civilization. What I am calling attention to is the portentous significance of his being, when taking part in the debate, which isn't merely theoretical, about the urgent need to expand, multiply and modernize the universities, able to dismiss with such unconscious irresponsibility all suggestion that the universities have had a vital function in relation to English literature. In doing that — this is the truth for which I aim at getting a full and real recognition — he is lightly dismissing the function that, in our world (which becomes every year more completely what it is), only the university can perform. "Lightly" is the word: his article is an unconscious tribute to the potency of the technologico-Benthamite climate in which we live. The function of the university towards the sciences will in any case be performed — provision for *them* is in no danger of being neglected: the humane function, that which gives the sciences their human meaning and their *raison d'être*, can be left to — what? The Sunday papers? If the idea of the university is not understood in the university itself, and is not fought for, with fierce, informed and resolute conviction there, where in our world will it be, and by whom?

I have perhaps made it plain by now that my associated insistences — on the university and on English literature — are two emphases in the expression of the same basic concern. It is the concern that it was Arnold's distinction to have given expression to and that makes the conception of the function of criticism he stands for — *he* made it part of the English-speaking cultural heritage — a significant development. Contemplating, in an earlier phase of it than ours, the advance of industrial civilization, he saw that something new was happening to humanity, and that England and America in especial were exposed to a new kind of menace. It is that which he has in mind when he expresses his fear that England will become a "greater Holland." This is obviously a recoil from triumphant materialism, affluent and unleavened. Whether or not the way of expressing it is fair to Holland, there can be no doubt about the essential nature of the fear; the Arnoldian context — the immediate one and the general context of essays and pamphlets — makes it perfectly plain. It is that the massive and rapid growth of material civilization, the changes in human habit and the human condition brought about by technological advance, will entail a lapse of that creatively human response to economic fact, to the inescapable exigencies of life and material circumstance, which a cultural tradition *is* — is, while it remains a living power in the present.

Arnold saw, and said, that to preserve continuity — continuity of cultural consciousness — a more conscious and deliberate use of intelligence was needed than in the past. This is the meaning of the stress he laid upon poetic tradition (literature for him *was* poetry), and of his preoccupation with "centrality," with defining the idea of "authority" in matters of taste and judgment, and with standards. If we are inclined

to comment that his prescription, for all his command of urbane irony,
looks pathetically unrealistic in relation to the menace it has in view,
we should remind ourselves of a difference between his time and ours
that we tend to forget: in the England he was addressing there was a
large and immensely influential educated class. He himself comments on
this fact explicitly, as well as implying everywhere his awareness of it,
and his reliance on it. But, as his work in the field of education and
such essays as that on "Equality" testify, he was far from resting in a
complacent ease of mind about the cultural advantage England enjoyed
in the existence of this social class which shared (he accepted for his
purpose that description) the education and manners of the governing
class, and — or, if you like, and yet — supported the Victorian intellectual reviews. He was too generous and fastidious humanly to be satisfied,
and, moreover, with his eye on the inevitable coming economic, social
and political transformations, he saw the dangers inherent in that ambiguity, the "educated class" — or "educated classes."

It was the main concern of his life to promote in this country the
steps and the process that should create (this being their ideal aim) a
class of the educated — a class that could be definable and thought of as
essentially and unequivocally that, in dissociation from the idea of social
privilege, or social privilege as ordinarily cried out against, detested
and prized (even by Lord Snow). Or perhaps it would be better to say,
not thought of as class at all — though it is well to insist that there must
be a community of the "educated" that can never be a majority. No one
minds — even in America — there being an *élite* of athletes. To be both
brief and unambiguous in this matter is difficult, and perhaps I had
better add to what I have said that Arnold had no designs *against* the
actual "educated class" that had produced him and his ideals, and that
mattered so much to him and made it possible for him to energize with
hope. It mattered so much because it represented the possibility of an effective appeal to standards. And what I mean by this has so essential an
importance for my theme that I must now, even at the cost of some insistence on what ought to be truism — and at the cost of saying what
some here will have heard me say before, try to make it plain, if I can,
beyond any misunderstanding. In that attempt I have a more difficult
task than Arnold had — or, perhaps I had better say, was conscious of
having.

The word "standards" is not the less necessary because, like so many
of the most important words in our field of discourse, its use can't be justified by the kind of definition the prompt logic of the enemy demands. One
can't long discuss the study of literature and the unavoidableness of critical judgments *without* using it. And when I try to explain what "standards" are, what is their nature and authority as we, students of literature

and (therefore) critics, are concerned with them, my underlying and essential preoccupation is not merely or mainly theoretical, but brings together very intimately my disquiet at the actual state of criticism in the English-speaking world, my conception of what literary studies should be at the university, and my sense of the idea of a university as it needs to be fostered — and realized — in the technological age.

How, then, when the question of "standards" — the challenge to explain what they are, or the problem of exorcizing misconceptions — comes up in the way in which it does come up for the literary critic, how as a literary critic does he deal with it? How, as a literary critic, should he deal with it?

In this insistence on "literary critic" I have a reason: I wish to intimate that I am not proposing to attempt a philosophical discussion. I'm not much interested in establishing in any thorough-going theoretical way that the phrase "the standards of literary criticism," means something; that their basis must be this, and their nature that. On the other hand, I *am* very much preoccupied with vindicating literary criticism as a specific discipline — a discipline of intelligence, with its own field, and its own approaches within that field. And in particular I am preoccupied with insisting that there is an approach to the problem of "standards" that is proper to the field of literary criticism and to the literary critic as such — that you don't need to be a philosopher to make it.

Let me add at once that with this preoccupation goes — as, when it is seriously entertained, there must, I think, go — a concern for the critical function in contemporary actuality; for the function of criticism as, in sum, it is performed or not performed, and as it ought to be performed, here in our day in England. I indicate here one aspect of the difficulty of dealing with the problem of standards: you can neither separate it off, nor deal with it in the abstract. You can't profitably discuss the standards of criticism apart from the purposes and the methods, or apart from the actual functioning of criticism in the contemporary world. And apart from the ability to arrive at intelligent and sensitive judgments in the concrete — except, that is, as informed by critical experience — understanding of the nature of critical judgment in the abstract can amount to little. To consider the nature of "standards" involves considering the function of criticism in the full sense of that phrase, and apart from intelligence about the actual functioning in the world as we know it (where, that is, we have the closest access to the concrete), that consideration will hardly achieve a living strength, the strength of real understanding. Real understanding in fact, can't be a mere theoretical matter; it will entail real critical engagement in relation to the contemporary scene.

I am emboldened to say elementary things when I remember — and I remember because the pronouncement was directed against me and an endeavour, in which I was involved, to ensure that there should be a play of serious criticism upon the contemporary scene, that not so very long ago an Editor of the *Times Literary Supplement* pronounced, in a British Council publication: "There is . . . no desirable life of the mind of which literary reviews are an essential component, and in which fixed standards of criticism gain a kind of legal backing." To emphasize the force of "fixed standards" he spoke also of "imposing accepted values" — and spoke as if that were something I myself notoriously advocated. No one, then, who knows what "standards" are and what is the nature of critical authority *could* talk of "fixed standards" or of "providing them with a legal backing," and no one who understands the nature of a judgment could talk of "imposing accepted values." Essentially, as I've said before (I suppose) in a good many places — but the point has to be made and much hangs on it, a critical judgment has the form, "This is so, isn't it?" And the concurrence appealed for must be real, or it serves no critical purpose, and, if he suspects insincerity or mere politeness, can bring no satisfaction to the critic — to the critic *as* critic.

What, of its very nature, the critical activity aims at, in fact, is an exchange, a collaborative exchange, a corrective and creative interplay of judgments. For though my judgment asks to be confirmed and appeals for agreement that the thing is *so;* the response I expect at best will be of the form, "Yes, but ——," the "but" standing for qualifications, corrections, shifts of emphasis, additions, refinements. The process of personal judgment from its very outset, of course, is in subtle ways essentially collaborative, as my thinking is — as any use of the language in which one thinks and expresses one's thoughts *must* be. But the functioning of criticism demands a fully overt kind of collaboration. Without a many-sided real exchange — the implicitly and essentially collaborative interplay by which the object, the poem (for example) in which the individual minds meet, and, at the same time, the judgments concerning it, are established, the object, which we think of as "there" in a public world for common contemplation, isn't really "there."

What, under the head of Practical Criticism, we call analysis is a creative, or re-creative, process. It's a more deliberate following-through of that process of creation in response to the poet's words (a poem being in question) than any serious reading is. It is a re-creation in which, by a considering attentiveness, we ensure a more than ordinary faithfulness and fulness. And actually when one is engaged in analysis one is engaged in discussion, even if only implicitly. That is a point I made in saying that a judgment has the form, "This is so, isn't it?" One is engaged in discussion of . . .? — the poem, which is there *for* discussion only in so far as those discussing have each recreated it.

The discussion is an effort to establish the poem as something standing in a common world between those discussing, and thus to justify our habitual assumption that it does so stand. It's "there" only when it's realized in separate minds, and yet it's not merely private. It's something in which minds can meet, and our business is to establish the poem and meet in it. Merely private, on the one hand, and, on the other, public in the sense that it can be produced in a laboratory, or tripped over — the poem is neither: the alternatives are not exhaustive. There is a third realm, and the poem belongs to that. I take courage for this reminder, for this repetition, for this insistence on the elementary, because, as I hope to bring out with the appropriate cogency — it's at any rate the purpose of these lectures, a great deal more than literary criticism is involved, just as the *rationale* of literary criticism involves a great deal more than this term itself, with its limiting adjective, might seem to imply.

Also, I wanted to say: this is as far as the literary critic *qua* literary critic need go epistemologically or metaphysically. It's all very familiar — with the familiarity of things that are so fundamental, so necessarily taken for granted, that we don't ordinarily bother to recognize them. If difficulty should seem to be caused by the demand for full conscious recognition (which is necessary when it's a question of justifying the pretensions of criticism, and the implicit pretensions of literature and art in general, and all mature interest in literature and art) the critic can say: "But consider language." A language — apart from the conventional signs and symbols for it — is really *there*, it really exists in full actuality, only in individual users; it is *there* only as its idioms, phrases, words and so on, with the meaning, intention, force in which their life resides, are uttered and meant by me (for example) and taken by you. Do they then belong to the public world (you can't point to them), or are they merely personal and private? We know that the brisk "either-or" doesn't meet the case.

And language, in the full sense, in the full concrete reality that eludes the cognizance of any form of linguistic science, does more than provide an analogue for a "culture" in that full sense which very much concerns us, but eludes the immense body of important people who share Lord Robbins's outlook; it is very largely the essential life of a culture. And literature, of course, is a mode or manifestation of language.

What in all this I have been trying to bring into clear and full recognition is the collaborative-creative nature of criticism; and I have my eye now particularly on the word "standards." Criticism is concerned with establishing the poem — or the novel — as an object of common access in what is in some sense a public world so that when we differ about it we are differing about what is sufficiently the same thing to make differing profitable. But the establishing of the poem (or the novel) is the establishing of a value. Any reading of it that takes it *as* a work of art involves an element of implicit valuation. The process, the kind of activity of inner response and discipline, by which we take possession of the created work is essentially the kind of activity that completes itself in a value-judgment.

Of course, here again the enemy has his opportunity. Valuation isn't a simple idea, and the process of "valuing" isn't in simple analogy with putting a price on. "Value," in fact, is another of those essential words which, as needed for our purposes, don't lend themselves to the kind of definition necessary for effective defence against the indifference that, in a Benthamite and egalitarian world, so rapidly becomes overt hostility. I'm avowing that when I say that "value" is inextricably bound up with "significance." And so far from valuing being a matter of bringing up a scale, a set of measures, or an array of fixed and definite criteria to the given work, every work that makes itself felt as a challenge evokes, or generates, in the critic a fresh realization of the grounds and nature of judgment. A truly great work is realized to *be* that because it so decidedly modifies — alters — the sense of value and significance that judges. That is what is testified to in the commonplace that a great artist creates the taste by which he is appreciated.

"Creates" is the right word: in the effect on the public's power to respond and realize, the effect on taste — to accept that word for the moment (though it carries a most inadequate suggestion), creative genius achieves the completion of its distinctive work. D. H. Lawrence makes that point in the answer he gave to a question put to him, very near the end of his life, about the nature of the artist's impulsion — his drive: "One writes out of one's moral sense; for the race, as it were." On "moral" — and that it should carry, even for the use in which the critic finds it necessary, the odour of an unpleasant or bad word is a symptom of our time — the immediately relevant commentary again comes from Lawrence.

> The true artist doesn't substitute immorality for morality. On the contrary, he *always* substitutes a finer morality for a grosser. As soon as you see a finer morality, the grosser becomes relatively immoral.

It is when we feel that the radical criteria are notably challenged that the word "moral" comes up; it comes up *because* they are challenged, and is our response to the realization. About Lawrence one might say that his moral perception is a manifestation of his genius, being the fineness of his sense of life — his sense of the difference between what makes *for* life and what makes against it. But to say that is to invite the comment that it is a large proposition, and "life" is a large word. What is life? The advantage the critic enjoys when justifying such uses as he has to make of the word, and of his other indispensable terms, is that he has the work of a creative writer in front of him; he is preoccupied with referring as sensitively, faithfully and closely to that as he is able. The terms are prompted by the created thing, and he in turn gives them, for the reader, their charge of special meaning, their due specific force, by means, essentially, of a tact of particular reference to the given work as present — that is the aim — in the evoked experience of it, the evoked recall (a critical process that is, in its wholly subservient and instrumental way, itself creative).

From time to time, as I was preparing these lectures, I felt that I had overworked that last adjective and must both become more sparing of it and do some revisionary elimination. But prescription, I found, was one thing, and performance another; and, further, I found myself reflecting that my theme of its very nature entailed so much the kind of insistence directed by Blake against the cultural tyranny he associated with the names of Newton and Locke that to avoid a frequent use of the word was impossible. Blake was the human protest on behalf of life against the repression of creativity represented by the prevailing ethos of the 18th century — life, he insisted, was essentially creative in a way denied not only by the prepotence of Newton and Locke in the dominant spirit of "civilized" and final common sense, but by the very language — the modes and conventions of utterance — established firmly as belonging to the basic nature of things and the spirit of civilization, and accepted as natural. The emphasis Blake lays on art and the artist is one with his insistence on the creativeness of perception.

The civilization we live in presents a more formidable menace to life, and, in saying that, I see the justification of my reference to Blake in the force, peculiarly appropriate to my purpose, that the word "life" now has, thus associated with Blake's kind of insistence on an essential creativeness — "creativeness" itself being given the right charge of meaning. The generality of my proposition has, then (I hope), for those I am addressing, the directed point and the edge it has in my own mind. The menace, the sense of its lethal insidiousness, was (as so often) borne in on me with disturbing vividness quite recently, when I listened to a paper on Newman's *Idea of a University*. The paper was distinguished, informed by wide experience, and provocative of question and comment; but, as I knew, effective discussion of fundamentals is improbable, indeed almost impossible, in a large assembly. Nevertheless, since no one, when the time for discussion came, seemed anxious to speak first, I opened by saying briefly what I most wanted to say. It was roughly this:

"I didn't, Sir, like your dividing the business of the university under two heads: one, handing things on (the word 'tradition' came in here), and the other, creating new knowledge. It prejudices the upshot at the very beginning — unless challenged. What I am most concerned for that comes under your 'handing things on' is rather to be called 'maintaining a continuity,' and perhaps I can make clear the difference I have in mind by adding immediately that for 'continuity' you can substitute 'a life' — 'maintaining a life.' Consider the life of a language: a language is maintained in *use* — use by a community in response to changing conditions and a changing civilization, and the use that maintains it is creative."

The reader of the paper saw my point, but as I expected, it wasn't taken up in discussion. But towards the close a speaker who had shown himself notably articulate remarked, glancing back over what had been said, that I, he gathered, was a vitalist. I could only reply that I didn't see how that word helped. I felt, in fact, nonplussed; very few, it was plain, had taken my meaning, and I recognized that an attempt to convey it on that kind of occasion was an enterprise absurdly out of the question. No thought of any philosophy or intellectual system, of course, had been in my mind; I merely meant to evoke in my hearers a strong present sense of what they of course knew, and to insist on its crucial relevance.

But did they know it? Do people know it? They do and they don't. The problem of getting them to recognize it is very like the problem of getting people to recognize what they take for granted, what they implicitly assume, when they formulate and advance a critical judgment and engage in the critical discussion to which it leads.

The "handing-on," then, for which it is recognized (in a kind of way) that provision has to be made in the conception of a new university isn't a mere matter of handing on — handing over — tools, data, inert equipment, externalities to be taken possession of as such, conquered provinces, technical know-hows. In its vital nerve (and if it hasn't one, it's nothing), and most essentially, it's a matter of carrying on a vital continuity in which the promoters and executants are already involved in such a way that, but for their being so involved, there would have been no conception, no planning, and no point in founding a university. They have, that is, a common culture in which (say), for all their differences, agnostics, Catholics and diverse kinds of Protestants can work together for common human ends. Such a cultural tradition, like the language that is at the heart of it, has been formed and kept living — that is, changing in response to changing conditions (material, economic and so on) — by continuous collaborative renewal. The participants tend to be hardly conscious of the basic values and assumptions they share, but it is the sense of something basic shared that makes possible the assumption (for instance) that there is point in founding new universities.

The state, however, of being hardly conscious, or mainly unconscious, illustrated by the episode I have just related, won't do in the civilization that sweeps us on. Without a human effort of a kind the need for which

582   F. R. LEAVIS

Lord Robbins and his associates have given no sign of being aware of, an effort directed and sustained by intelligent purpose, the new universities — the universities in sum — will merely be a part of the process by which, whatever provision is made for philosophy, psychology and the social sciences, the world comes to assume invincibly, to the immense impoverishment of life, that a rising "standard of living" is a sufficient account of human ends. That is the significance of the uninhibited frankness with which Lord Robbins avows his solidarity with Lord Snow.

What, of course, I have virtually been saying is that the unprecedented civilization to which we are committed demands a new, or a more strongly positive, conception of the university and its function. The great and most menacing change brought about by the technological revolution is that it has almost destroyed the creative cultural process, of which the finer operation in that continuous renewal which maintained the human world of values and significances and spiritual graces is on the point of death; it has turned the business of human adjustment to changing material conditions into a reductive process, largely determined by business profit. The worker earns the wherewithal and the leisure to enjoy a higher standard of living by work that has little interest for him and little human meaning; it is something to be got behind him so that he can get away to live — before the telly, over the pools form, in the bingo hall, in the car. Technology, and the financial appetites, mechanisms and potencies produced by it, have determined his culture for him and saved him the trouble.

It wasn't my purpose to develop this particular branch of the theme; but I wanted to remind you that the facts it points to concern vitally, not merely the industrial workers directly affected, but all of us, including those of us whose business is with English literature — which achieved its greatness in another kind of human world. And I will now revert to that matter of "standards," which I left hanging in the air — a matter on which, as everyone knows, the technological revolution has a bearing. The term "standards" presents itself when there is question of getting recognition for the justice — or the absurdity — of judgments affirming (explicitly or implicitly) relative value and importance. It's a representative use, for instance, when I say that the general acceptance, in England, of Hemingway as a great writer, or the spectacle of an academic critic going out of his way to pronounce a Kingsley Amis novel a "serious study in amorality," would have been possible only in a period marked by a collapse of standards. We talk about "standards," in fact, at times when it is peculiarly hard to invoke standards with effect. And they can be "there" to be invoked with effect by the critic only in the existence of an educated public capable of responding intelligently, and influential enough to make its response felt. I need say no more by way of defining standards. They depend on, they are a manifestation of, that collaborative interplay in which the poem is established as something in which minds can meet, which maintains the life of a language, which creates the essential values and significances of the human world, which creates a culture.

When one speaks of the lapse of standards what one is pointing to is the fact that it is hard for the critic to believe in any decisive influence represented by any public his work can be supposed to imply. It isn't that there aren't many intelligent and cultivated persons about, enough to be a potential influence of great value, whose "yes, but ——," or whose "no," is of the kind the critic needs, but they don't form an effective public; they don't really form a public at all.

To bring out the force of that truth one can adduce the fact — it is at least very suggestive — that the whole of the English-speaking world can't, or won't, maintain, on ordinary business lines, a single serious critical journal. The related fact is that such performance of the current function of criticism as can be alleged is what we see in the review pages of the weeklies and the Sunday papers, and it certainly doesn't imply the existence of a public that entertains and exacts a serious conception of the critical function.

The theme is one I needn't enlarge upon. The relevance of the present alarm about the difficulty of keeping a newspaper going on a circulation of a mere million or two is plain. If the advance of technology and the conditions of a technological civilization mean that a "quality" newspaper must have an immense advertising revenue, then the editorial policy must be one that ensures an immense circulation, and the review columns that make the formal salute to literary culture will, judged as an offer to perform the function of criticism, be contemptible. And the reviewing in the "intellectual" weeklies will be indistinguishable in general quality from that in the Sunday papers. The same kinds of writer, very largely the same writers, write in both and are most of them in other ways actively engaged in the culture of the technological age; and as for the cultural standards of their smaller and superior public, the Sunday papers (like the review columns of the *Guardian*) in any case give us them.

Now there is no question of trying to reverse, or halt, the advance of technology. There can be no restoring the wheelwright's shop or the conditions of production that integrated work organically with a living culture and associated it in a major way with the creative human response. But that doesn't mean that we must, or should, leave the human heritage, the cultural continuity, to lapse and let technology henceforward dictate, unchecked by any human wisdom or human sense more mature than Lord Robbins's. There is a dreadful blank unconsciousness to be faced, as Lord Robbins unconsciously testifies; but there is also in humanity an instinct of self-preservation to appeal to — a sense of vital needs thwarted and starved by technologico-Benthamite civilization.

The university, in so far as it is more than a centre and nursery of the sciences, a technological institute, or a collocation of specialist departments, is the representative of that instinct, and the organ through which society has to make the sustained effort (one directed by collaborative intelligence and a full human responsibility) to keep those needs recognized and provide our civilization with memory and mature purpose. Although, as I pointed out in commenting on that odd and significant dismissive attitude of the writer in the *Times Literary Supplement,* the university has always had a major importance in relation to the country's cultural life — an importance (the immediate emphasis) for creative literature, its function was never so vital as it is now: living continuity used to be maintained in many ways in the functioning of the general life of society — in the life of the home, for instance, and of the local milieu, and there was not that destructive action on the creative heritage and the human positive response which characterizes the mechanisms of civilization in our time — characterizes them to such a tune that, in the resulting amnesia and passivity, the destructiveness isn't recognized as such. As things are now, if provision is not made for the focused and fostered insight, purpose and effort of continuity, the heritage is lost, abandoned to oblivion, and mankind faces a fate more certain than the feared nuclear cataclysm. I recall Mr Owen Barfield's recent comment — a retort to naïve neo-Wellsian euphoria — on that transatlantic world which confronts us with our own imminent future.

I had not thought death had undone so many

— a sentence that, with its dual context, you know. The only possible provision, the only possible organ, is the university — to recognize which fact is to recognize the context of organic life the university must have in the country at large, will draw its strength from, and will foster.

When I say that the university as a centre of consciousness for the community must have its centre in an English school, I don't mean anything of the kind that was meant when we were told, at Cambridge, forty years ago: "Poetry will save us." Nor do I mean that in some hierarchy of esteem English comes first. But the need is for a focal centre; and a focus of cultural continuity can only be in English. English literature, magnificent and matchless in diversity and range, and so full and profound in its registration of changing life, gives us a continuity that is not yet dead. There is no other; no other access to anything approaching a full continuity of mind, spirit and sensibility — which is what we desperately need.

MURRAY KRIEGER

Mediation, Language, and Vision in the Reading of Literature

I

It is a special opportunity, and a special challenge — on an occasion sponsored by The Johns Hopkins University — for me to discuss the problem of language as mediation in literature, a problem increasingly at the forefront of recent theoretical discussion. I hope it is not also a presumption for me to do so. For it is largely through the intellectual activities that have been going on at Johns Hopkins that theorists and critics in our country have become concerned about the very applicability of the term "mediation." This concern opens to a broader one: the critic is to concentrate on the person and his vision or self-consciousness that shines through the literary work, in contrast to the previous, New-Critical obsession with the persona and the "impersonal" vision objectively structured *in* the work. This has been the source and has supplied the nourishment for both so-called phenomenological criticism and structuralist criticism as these two movements have — in their different, if not totally opposed, ways — supplanted the so-called New Criticism or contextualism that went unchallenged for so long. It was Johns Hopkins that was this country's forum for Georges Poulet; and it is at Johns Hopkins that we find such productive younger protagonists of these movements as J. Hillis Miller and René Girard, with Paul de Man shortly to arrive as a brilliant reinforcement. No wonder commentators begin to be tempted to speak of the Hopkins school.

Let me admit that I offer myself as a new offshoot of that contextualist movement, now perhaps deservedly displaced among those doing our most adventurous theoretical probings; I hope to find a new life (or at least liveliness) for it by trying myself to do justice to the serious misgivings

SOURCE: "Mediation, Language, and Vision in the Reading of Literature" is from *Interpretation: Theory and Practice,* edited by Charles S. Singleton (Baltimore: The Johns Hopkins Press, 1969), pp. 211–42. Reprinted by permission of The Johns Hopkins Press. Selections from Murray Krieger, *A Window to Criticism: Shakespeare's Sonnets and Modern Poetics* (copyright 1946 by Princeton University Press), pp. 209–13. Reprinted by permission of Princeton University Press.

about language as mediation which critics like Poulet have shown to us all. Surely in these late days criticism can no longer dare to assume the validity or the value of its discrete analyses of literary works, or of its arguments defending the exhaustive study of unique forms as unique language systems. As the person of the poet threatens to undo the persona, so his consciousness threatens to undo the work's telic self-sufficiency: as the person threatens to undo the persona, so his body threatens to undo the word-as-body, so the world threatens to overwhelm the word.

> . . . the modern [poet] either does not acknowledge or does not know a mediator for his orphic journey. He passes through experience by means of the unmediated vision. Nature, the body, and human consciousness — that is the only text.[1]

These words are taken from *The Unmediated Vision,* a remarkable volume by Geoffrey Hartman (recently a close colleague and cohort of Paul de Man). It was fitting that in 1966 this early work of Hartman's was at last reprinted and that it appeared with a freshness that suggested original publication. It was not only fitting but seemed to be a necessary accompaniment to the recent flourishing of criticism directed at denying or overcoming the mediating nature of poetry in order to get us to the thing itself. Indeed, in view of all we thought we had learned since 1954 (its original date of publication), and from more recent European writings, we surprise ourselves with the reminder of its date and of its being composed by a young American scholar (though by one clearly indebted heavily to European sources).

We may remember also that our recent fantastic, Norman O. Brown, in his Neo-Freudian apocalyptic plea, *Life Against Death,* recognized in kinship that *The Unmediated Vision* was a revolutionary work of criticism which bypassed the word for the body. He saw that, for Hartman, the poem is no longer to be conceived as "other" or as object; it is to be absorbed into the poet's (and, ultimately, the critic's) self as subject. In the modern world, now bereft of all mediation — of the Christian miracle in which Word did become flesh — there can be no verbal text for our study; instead, "the only text," as Hartman tells us, is "nature, the body, and human consciousness."

It is just the notion of the poem as object, as an "insensible It," that — by way of reaction against it — impels the anticritical crusade of Ihab Hassan, literary follower of Norman Brown. Despite differences between the European phenomenological tradition behind Hartman and our native irrationalist, anti-establishment radicalism, this connection between Hartman and both Brown and Hassan reveals them serving a similar tendency to deobjectify and repersonalize literature. The similarity deserves to be noted, as it has not been, for it points to a common need in our theoretical climate. Neither Hartman nor other phenomenological critics are likely to travel with Hassan to the logical extreme of maintaining that action, rather than contemplation, is a "legitimate response to art" once a presence — not depersonalized — has replaced the coldly viewed object as the stimulus of that response. But one might well claim that such an extreme is a proper consequence of those aspects of the neo-romantic theoretical impulse which they share.

These attitudes toward literature, seemingly revolutionary to those of us who grew up under the unchallenged dominance of the would-be classicism of New-Critical analyses of discrete poems, achieve their force and the momentum of their influence through their being a moving alternative to that criticism. Ever since the earlier revolution in the academy effected by the New Criticism, the abundance of discrete critiques in our books, our journals, and our classrooms has prompted the wearied cry "Enough — and too much." So convergent has been the focus on the discrete work that we must have expected, as an inevitable humanistic reaction, the impatient demand to have literature returned to the humane matrix that fosters it and is in turn fed by it. As critical method, fed less and less from a source of theoretical justification, seemed more and more to feed on itself, it multiplied its increasingly mechanical operations and its consequently lifeless products. The living body of the poems it dealt with was made more and more into a corpse: the critic's role, no longer the humanistic one of renewing the vitality of our verbal heritage, was becoming the pseudo-scientific one of post-mortem, dissection become autopsy.

There has, then, been the inevitable reaction against this sort of critical establishment by those determined in their own ways to restore life to literature, to reassert the critic as midwife instead of as coroner. Some would destroy criticism itself by opposing mediation: by seeing its mediating function and the mediating function of poetry as suspect, as precluding life, draining that life from an object left on the dissecting table. This attack on criticism as it is restricted to single works is an attack on the objective hopes and disinterested pretensions of the critical exercise. Under attack here is the detached critic — the critic as analyst and judge — the critic coolly operating a mediating (meddling) enterprise. Distance between the critic and the work is to be destroyed as that which replaces human response with dehumanized analysis: distance creates the space for analysis and, consequently, the claim to a would-be scientific objectivity. But the critic's destruction of space or distance can be accomplished only by his following the precedent of the poet, who must be seen as destroying the distance an "impersonal" theory of creation would impose between him and his work. If the critic (or, rather, anticritic), thus dedicated to process rather than product, must deny the distance between the work and its author, then poetry, too, comes to be seen as the enemy of mediation, of the mediating nature of language. The poem is at war with discourse as mediator. The poem is that paradoxical discourse dedicated to denying its own nature. It is to transmit immediacy, obliterating its own presence, a presence that threatens to deaden immediacy by freezing its dynamic flow into a static object. Instead, the work melts into an instantaneous union of "unmediated vision," shared among work, author, and critic, an undemarcated flowing of the vision among the three. And the spectacular — even apocalyptic — breath of life returns to inspire, as it rehumanizes, our traffic with literature. Thus it is that the central and detached concern with the object as a self-defined structure comes to be rejected because of its flight from the human contact with the object, the human contact that not only comes before and after the object but becomes the object, by merging with it, giving it its life.

The attack on the mediating properties of poetic structure and of the critical language seeking to fix that structure has taken several forms. The so-called phenomenological critics here and in Europe, perhaps most extremely represented by Georges Poulet, who, as Hillis Miller has shown us, is not really phenomenological at all — such critics (let us rather call them critics of unmediated self-consciousness) blur the work into the author's consciousness and ours, substituting a pulsating "interior distance," as subjective as human time, for the flat contours of spatial form, searched out by conventionally "formalistic" critics. Poulet's conception of form as static and dead — as objective — makes his antiformalism explicit. The disregard for the single work as a discrete whole, as well as the impatience with the critic who painstakingly fusses over such works, must follow — and normally does. The "human" and the "interior" must be made to prevail over the scientific and the fixedly exterior if the vitality of literature is to be ever renewed instead of once and for all stifled. The results of such studies are brilliant, spectacular, even at times persuasively luminous — but not finally very transferable. They superciliously bypass the function of criticism as an educating process. Poems about poems, they impress the imagination more than the understanding.

A visionary critic like Harold Bloom has an even more open disdain for the discrete critique. Behind his treatment of the individual author (all of whose works constitute a single corpus) is an all-unifying, monolithic, transcendent vision that absorbs all works and their authors into itself. The breath of meaning, issuing from the organic life that moves these visions and makes them one, can be received only as we merge work with author (as creative imagination), merge authors into a "visionary company," and merge all with the sublime vision. Again the objective, as impersonal, as distanced, is rejected in the romantic denial of space, the romantic explosion of distinctions.

Ihab Hassan, we have seen, looks toward another sort of neo-romantic apocalypse, an unmediated breakthrough to body from which the Word is finally excluded. The flesh, then touched in its immediacy, can dispense with the falsely metaphorical illusion that claims the Word-become-flesh. And, when the re-won bodily realities of our instincts can rush in, the middleman of art need not — nay, dare not — enter. The writers who celebrate this "dismemberment of Orpheus," Miller and Beckett and a host of younger novelists, create an anti-art, an antiword, directed at the extinction of art, at total silence.[2]

To a great extent, then, the attack upon the poem as object and upon criticism as discrete analysis is an attack upon word-worship, upon the mediating function of language and our willingness to settle for the medium, for the empty carton with its generic label. It is also an attack upon form-worship and upon the entire post-Kantian mood of our criticism of the last century and a half. What mediates subjective experience for the more aesthetic of us is not so much mere words as the special forms created by words, the order-producing impositions that become fixed, static objects. In molding chaos, in taming outrage, in directing chance, in rendering the casual into the causal — in other words, by converting all the raw materials of a no longer mediated human subjectivity into the willed perfections of Aristotelian inevitability — humanity has allowed the formal impulse (licensed as an act of freedom by Kant, Schiller, and many who follow) to end by destroying human freedom. For it destroys the subjective freedom of the random, of the unstructured, of the indeterminate, in its service of the formal impulse that was to allow the person, as human, triumphantly to transform the subjective into the objective, thereby redeeming the irrational within himself. But, with its formative impulse, the human is seen as betrayer of its free person.

The formal and classic, then, must come to be seen as stasis, that which arrests the dynamics of temporality in the deadness of shape, of spatial thereness. The still classical *Stürm und Drang* antagonism to Lessing's *Laokoön,* for all its promise of freedom of mingling among the arts, ends by freezing literature into sculpture. Time's jagged unpredictabilities are rounded into place. This may have been enough for Kant and Goethe, Schiller and the post-Kantians — indeed it was their grandly humanistic dream — as they tried to replace the divine mediation by Christ with the human mediator, now granted divinely creative powers. But the modern, with a more radical sense of human freedom, negates them as Mann's Leverkühn negates Goethe's Faust and "takes back" the human hallelujah of Beethoven's *Ninth.* The very formative categories of Kant are rejected in the return to the unformed continuum of the raw "given."

Such a temperament views poetic form as the mediating element, as that totalitarian force that everywhere subdues the wayward to its overwhelming autotelic purposiveness, thus delivering death to our subjective freedom. For form, being contextual, ought to involve the rigorous marsh-aling of words, the systematic transformation of all that comes to it from without into the "new word" within, whose totality of definition is con-stituted by its every serving part. All indeterminacies are rendered deter-minate under an irresistible Hegelian functionalism. The all-unifying human imagination, our gift from Coleridge, and the Kantian and post-Kantian tradition behind him, has, like God, conquered chaos, has used its *fiat* to make it order.

But this sort of human god, imposed by Kant, Goethe, Schelling, Cole-ridge, or even Nietzsche upon a world no longer mediated by the divine-human paradox authored by the true God, is for Hassan or the early Hartman an inflated phantom bent on depriving the fleshly creature of his newly won freedom from the word, that presumptuous surrogate for body. His body, which he knows in its instinctive immediacy from the inside, no longer need yield to an outside transubstantiating authority. If God, author of mediation, is dead, then the man-god should embrace the truly autonomous, unchartable freedom of the immediate rather than try to impose his own mediation, his own ersatz cosmos in the microcosm of the poem. For the entire notion of cosmos, of microcosm and macrocosm as mutual reflections, is seen as existentially obsolete, whether God-made or man-made. Thus Hassan, looking at the (to him) false mediations of an outmoded literature that seeks perfect speech instead of total silence, characterizes such language as a series of equations which his apocalyptic prophet must shun: language equals sublimation equals symbol equals mediation equals culture equals *objectivity* equals abstraction equals death. As point-by-point apocalyptic alternatives, silence (as the identity of noth-ingness and the indiscriminate, chaotic all) has as its equations (instead of sublimation) indulgence, (instead of symbolism) flesh, (instead of mediation) outrage, (instead of culture) anarchy, (instead of objectivity) subjectivity, (instead of abstraction) particularity, (instead of death) instinctual life. And the antipoet, who writes his "antibook" for the anti-critic with his anti-aesthetic, cultivates the accidental, the indetermin-ate, the "unstructured or even random element in literature," refusing to absorb it into the authority of form, insisting on its persisting on its own out there, radically autonomous in its caprice, as testimony of its and our own capricious freedom, nurtured in the gratuitous act. Hassan himself tells us that "Apollonian Form finally becomes Abstract Authority" (with the capital letters their emblem of Abstract Authority). From here we can see his Dionysian alternative lurking. True life, in its chaotic subjectivity, has regained its primacy over the trim lines of art. Indeed, art is to obliter-ate itself into the unmediated terrors of existence, into the rites and mysteries of the orphic act. Orpheus, then, is to aid in his own dismem-bering. "Imitative form," which is — as Yvor Winters taught us — no form at all but a dissolution into the formlessness of raw experience, yields up all aesthetic pretensions to wallow in the mimetic surrender to human darkness. The *Dunciad* has indeed become the *Inferno*.

I have given myself perhaps too expansively to dealing with Hassan, since I have granted that he is immeasurably more extreme than our more influential antimediators. I thought it worth doing because in him I found the neo-romantic impulse against the formal or mediating principle in its purest form. It should be helpful with the less immodest claims of more subtle minds. As a matter of fact, Hassan himself, in his moments of retreat, of recognition of the not-altogether-abandoned poet, is such a more subtle mind. He can at times see the artist's need forever to turn on himself, finally to make even the random element somehow *his* random element, the antibook somehow part of his total (and totally absorptive) book. Thus the act converts to intellectual gesture. Hassan himself can intellectualize even to this extent:

> Literature recoils from the withering authority of the new Apollo, but it does not surrender itself wholly to the frenzy of Dionysus. It only *feigns* to do so. It employs self-irony and self-parody, as in the novels of Mann and Camus; it develops, as in the works of Beckett or Genet, forms that are antiforms. . . . Literature, in short, pretends to a wordy wordlessness and participates in the Dionysian denial of language not with its own flesh, but with the irony of its divided intelligence.[3]

This is a long way from Hassan's more extreme justification of total silence as the last refuge of "the freedom of language to seek some purposeless and indeterminate antiform," or of a language that "becomes indiscriminate, random, fluent beyond words" in its dedication to its "outrageous vision." [4] His more balanced view that has the poet resist total identity with Dionysus in a turning upon himself allows for the poet's turning of the antibook into *his* book. And, of course, this is a reintroduction of aesthetic mediation.

As such it would quite satisfy me as a critic dedicated to return at last to the poem as an object, though enriched by what those suspicious of the mediating nature of language have revealed about the death-threatening tendencies of the word. The would-be objective critic, who wants to defend his art against the skepticism of the antimediators by meeting it head-on, must begin by agreeing about the paralyzing consequences of mediation. He, too, must be suspicious of discourse as a mere medium, that which by definition precludes immediacy and which by its action freezes all flow. But, having shared the visionary critic's distrust of the medium, he must yet try to exempt poetry from its deadening powers. Having condemned mediation, he must yet save poetry. He can accomplish this only if he does not deny the poem as object, that is, only if he does not force an immediacy in the poem's relation to its creator by collapsing the poem into consciousness or vision. To make the poem a special object, one without the object's deadly there-ness, its spatial "fix," he must be prepared to ask, "When is a medium not just a medium? How can a medium be free of its pre-destined curse of mediation?" And he must be prepared to earn and to believe his answer: "When it can be the thing itself, holding the dynamism of flux in its coils." For the poem as discourse and thing is motion and is in motion. Yet it is motion in stillness, the stillness that is at once still moving and forever still.[5]

All these are theoretical problems steep and troublesome. As such they demand something beyond the unquestioning, blithe pursuit of discrete explication, the sort of explication that in its late days helped create, and justified, the anti-objective reaction which now demands that we take such theoretical troubles — or else abandon to the visionaries the maintenance of literature as a live art and act.

The theoretical task is easier when the opposition to recent criticism comes from those who would overmediate, those whose impatience with the tentative delicacies of analysis leads to crude interposings. For the tentative delicacies of the critic are his responses to the uniqueness of his objects, his efforts to fit his discourse to ever-new systems that defy his common measures. And it is this uniqueness — the critic's tribute to that unmediating medium, that space-eluding object — which the stubborn overmediator cannot wait to pause over. We have seen that, even if the critic must resist yielding to the antimediator who bypasses all form for uninhibited subjectivity, he still must try to preserve the special life of his object by fighting for its immediacy, for the medium *malgré lui*. But the overmediator is finally willing to freeze his object by spatializing its form, universalizing it by absorbing it into common formulas — models — broader than the work (or, in cases, broader than literature itself). This sense of the model is what is placed between the work and our private response, shaping both work and response to our awareness of that model. The deadening effect upon work and response is almost enough to send us, by way of reaction, to the dynamic vitality of the antimediator, except that we know of that danger too. But we know we must not surrender his sense of life to paint a frozen model.

When we sweep aside the recently fashionable language of structuralism with its models, we find this very instinct for universalizing the individual work which lay behind the pre–New Critical attitudes, whether socio-historical or biographico-psychological, this instinct which made the New Criticism necessary. The unregenerate overmediator, who preferred to learn nothing from the contextualist revolution, sounds pretty much like those who preceded that revolution, as he tries to adapt the work to extramural commonplaces. For example, the social concerns of Walter Sutton, which move him to keep the lines between literature and culture at once, continually, and broadly open, are not markedly different from the concerns which prompted Ransom, Tate, Brooks, and others — by way of reaction — to make their defense of poetry several decades back.[6] Against such arguments as Sutton's, based as they are on the failure to grasp the organismic assumptions, the New-Critical defense is still valid, although there is now the need to deepen its theoretical basis and extend its theoretical consequences.

Other more subtle forms of overmediation also threaten to preclude the criticism of the poem as a unique language system. They all have their attractiveness to the extent that we cherish the encyclopedist's pretentious hope of unifying our knowledge and our languages. (Nor should we give up the encyclopedist's universal dream of a logocentric utopia, except grudgingly.) But the cost to literature as authentic discourse is high. The structuralist — a Lévi-Strauss or a Jakobson — runs the risk that the peculiarly literary will slip away when poetic structures, general linguistic structures, and anthropological structures come to be juxtaposed, not only as analogous, but even as homologous. Again, the methodological issues may not finally be very different from those that brought the New Criticism into existence. It is just this fear of the overuniversalizing, overmediating tendencies of such latitudinarian structuralism which moves sympathetic observer-participators like Michael Riffaterre and Geoffrey Hartman to their critiques and qualifications.[7] Of course, these suggest structuralist efforts that would preserve the uniqueness of the poetic structure and resist the adaptation to generic models; but they would appear to abandon the distinctively structuralist ambition and would pose no real opposition or alternative to contextualism.

Another variety of structuralism — René Girard's — combines it with something very like Poulet's method of bypassing mediation, as we see the extremes (of antimediation and overmediation) meet. In his conclusion to *Deceit, Desire, and the Novel,* Girard finds that all novels end by becoming the same novel: he uncovers at last the "banal" structure hidden in the common conclusions of all novels.[8] But the structural uniformity is a uniformity in the discoveries of self-consciousness in that the single conclusion creates its conversion by having the protagonist at last turn upon his mediator, so that in the end all barriers, all mediation, between the vision of a character and his author (and, as Poulet would extend this, between the author and us) are destroyed. A single pattern creates an always similar breakthrough in which distinct entities merge into instantaneity and identity. Antimediation is found to be the single structural model for the novel. Perhaps Girard can serve to remind us that Poulet himself, for all his antiformalism, for all his antimediation that suggests antistructuralism, may strengthen the structuralist impulse by his methodological monism. His work always seems to lead to the glorious identity of consciousness shared by reader, poet, and work, to the collapsing of the distinct categories of time and space in the instantaneous union between every critic and author. The very overcoming of mediation becomes a universal principle of writers, each of whom moves toward becoming Mallarmé or Proust. Or, finally, there is Northrop Frye, who, like the structuralist, works from a model, though in his case it is restricted to a model literary universe; but the overpowering shadows cast by his many-faceted monolithic structure upon the little lonely work have by now often enough been lamented. The overmediation often shrieks its impositions, even as it excites us with the monolithic set of forms which structures the common human imagination and its common human dream.

Whatever the alternative critical attitudes that have followed upon the criticism which emphasized discrete analyses of poems as objects, these attitudes have been taken up in part as a reaction against that emphasis; but they have not removed the need for such a criticism and have not overcome the arguments in support of this need. Whether the anticontextualist proceeds from the desire to destroy the poem as a mediating object by seeing through it to the poet's immediacy, or from the desire to destroy the poem's immediacy by burdening it with universalizing mediations, he has not precluded the need to preserve the object as at once object *and* immediate.

But we have noted also the extent to which these responses have been generated by failures within the critical movement and by a flagging of its theoretical impulse to justify what it was doing. Its evangelical mission to save poetry dwindled into the Sunday sermon, moving routinely from text to text. It is this explication for explication's (and ingenuity's) sake that late defenders of criticism must not resort to, must move beyond. If Frye's totally absorptive system is seen as too universal, causing total deprivation to the singular, the critic of the discrete must resist the mere compilation of isolated perceptions as part of an endless bill of particulars. This critic must at least move back to the world from his internalized systems: what has turned inward must at last, and in a special way, open outward; the mutually reflecting mirrors (to borrow a metaphor I have used elsewhere) must be transformed to windows that capture a newly visioned reality. The "new word" that is the poem, still fully released from what the old words had been, yet returns to our common language to enrich it by renewing its powers of reference. And the critic must help, not only in defining that new word, but — perhaps more crucially, if less easily — in tracing its return to its culture and language, illuminating as it goes. If the critic stops with mere explication of the system, if he does not return it to its subtle function in the world of reference, its redefinitions of language and of vision; then he may be sure that his own role will be usurped by the impatient noncontextualist, who will open the language of the poem outward at once and without taking pains, who will make it serve the world of reference in a vulgar way that deprives poetry of those special powers which the critic of the discrete poem should be dedicated to serve and preserve. And he will deserve to be replaced.

It may very well be that only by his taking the theoretical issues very seriously can the critic prevent himself from succumbing to the myopia which his endlessly attractive objects induce in him. He is obliged, at considerable pain, to convert a terminal experience of a self-sufficient object into an instrumental occasion: he must ask "why?" and "to what end?" even as he accounts for the "finality" that asks no more. Again we see it is his double need, the need to see the paradoxical poetic medium at once as immediate and as that which mediates the general meanings of the world beyond. At stake is the nature of language generally. The poet may subvert that language, words in their general naming function, but only to save and serve the possibilities of *his* language, a language created *pour l'occasion* out of its own general incapacities. This is the stuff that the rarest of dreams, of visions, are made of — the rarest since, in their ultimate immediacy, they are not transferable, can occur nowhere but here in this work. And this work at once denies the power of its words, and yet, by its very being, denies that denial.

Sir Philip Sidney, in his *Astrophel and Stella* (considerably more than in his *Apology for Poetry,* where he more properly might have done so), often confronted this very problem of the uses and limitations of language as the poet must find it and refine it. Perhaps nowhere does he manage this confrontation more explicitly and more brilliantly than in "Sonnet 35" ("What may words say, or what may words not say"), a poem which I have treated elsewhere in detail.[9] In conclusion here I should like to use it only as a sort of allegory of the argument of this paper. For the movement of the sonnet springs (as its first line tells us) from the poet's awareness of the absurdities of language in it normal uses: his explicit distrust of language-as-names yields a special sort of antinominal system.

The poem proceeds under the reasonable control that produces and sanctions a series of outrageously irrational compliments, all governed by the initial confession of the incapacity of words. The paradoxes that follow are made up of words colliding with themselves in a desperate flight from meaninglessness. Each key word denies its own meaning, each abstraction obliterates itself by being itself in a way that identifies it with its opposite. With reason itself supervising the process, the very possibility of language has been precluded by the reason-defying perfection of Stella. Yet the unique immediacy of her presence, having negated language, has become its own language — the language of *this* poem — which has transcended the emptiness of language that functions only as mediation. Out of the mutual blockages of language, then, the poet has broken through to his own language, with meaning newly restored out of the accumulated verbalistic wreckage of conventional meanings. Further, such a language comes freighted with its rarities of vision, although I cannot pursue them here. Poems like these give us access to immediacies of consciousness as perhaps no other object does (and I say "object" pointedly now, seeing the object in its dynamic freedom).

Is our sense of language or of vision ever quite the same again? "What may words say, or what may words not say" indeed! By denying that words can say anything, these specially empowered words can say it all. My argument has been that it is clearly the role of criticism to listen closely to such words, hearing and overhearing all that they can affirm and deny, and neither to obliterate them in search of wordless vision nor to move through them to the stereotyped visions we had before this configuration of them, this poem, came along. And, while it listens this closely, what many things must it clearly become and continue to be the function of criticism to say? Dare one have the temerity to propose more precisely than these vague notions of mine suggest? In the second part of this essay I shall try to dare. But you will rightly remember that most theorists have uttered such fond hopes before, so that you will not expect too much. And I fear I may give you no more than you expect.

II

Through diverse critical traditions, through many centuries in the history of criticism, the veil has appeared as a metaphorical equivalent of the aesthetic symbol (a variety, perhaps, of the garment figure, although it lends itself to far more ambiguous adaptations). The mediating character of art has thus been implicitly recognized as it has — through the veil — entered the very vocabulary and primary conceptions of the critical theorist. And the ambivalent attitude toward the role and value of the veil, in its relation to whatever reality was claimed to be behind it, is clue to the ambivalence of attitude toward art's mediation itself.

It is all part of the problem — as old as criticism — concerned with the opposition between particularity and universality in art. Or, to convert to more theological terms, it is the opposition between the sensible and the intelligible, the earthly and the transcendently spiritual. It is the problem of the sin, as well as the saving virtue, of art, Augustine's concern over Dido slain, the awesome question that asks whether art, as particular embodiment, is an avenue to heaven or an earthly drag that blocks our upward path. Is the symbol the incarnate thing (i.e., spirit) itself, a substitute needed by imperfect man in his need to find a sensuous equivalent, or is it a perverse substitute that man in his lowliness lusts to place in his own way? Is it a sacred effigy of the true God or a profane idolatry? And so the several Platonisms, Neo-Platonisms, and anti-Platonisms have wrestled with one another through the centuries.

As orthodoxy and heterodoxy struggled through the Middle Ages and Renaissance to find a satisfactory formulation of the role of art, the fortunes of the veil (as synonym for art) fluctuated: now it was the false mediator, purveyor of illusion, of distortion, the obscuring element; now it was the indispensable threshold to the absolute — pure transparency itself. Thus it could be restricted to its frustrating function as replaceable surrogate in the thinness of allegory or it could be expanded to the rich double life of another sort of allegory offered by the typological *figura:* both the pointer and that to which it points, which it bears immanently within itself. But in neither case was there any question about the ultimate reality of that universal, transcendent realm, whether the veil is that which obscures it or is our sensuous access to it.[10]

It is not to be unexpected that, with the revolutionary inversions of the secular world in these last centuries, reality eventually is transformed into the irreducible particulars that are swept along in the flux of experience. This fluid reality is now seen to be veiled by the false, nonexistent universals projected by our anti-existential need for mediation. So, as particulars and the universal exchange places, the concrete sensuous "given" that formerly functioned as veil now is in *its* turn veiled as the universal is revealed as a fraud invented for our comfort. After all, one cannot make an ontology out of the projection of universals by the Kantian categories without anthropomorphically blundering into things-in-themselves; and the universals can claim no further metaphysical authority, no matter how heroic an imposition they may be by man, who in his quest for sanity refuses to surrender to the chaos of sense data. Kierkegaard extends this Kantian notion — after Hegel's vainglorious attempt to restore the illusion of final reality for these universals — to the existentialist extreme of denying all ontology, affirming only subjectivity, only the particular as absolute. Thus the veil of false universals now becomes the veil of Maya, seen by Schopenhauer and Nietzsche as the agent of will which the Bergsonian T. E. Hulme calls upon poetry to strip away. Poetry, then, becomes the antimediator, destroying the mediating universal. Kierkegaard had denied this possibility — as his condescending distrust of the aesthetic kept art within the universal, refusing to allow it existential immediacy. For Kierkegaard insisted on the formal incommunicability of the unmediated, accepting it as being by definition incommunicable, as beyond language. He is only a little more denying than Georges Poulet was to be, Poulet who (as we saw in Part I, above) finally must get beyond the aesthetic even if he does not quite go beyond language — as, for example, we saw Ihab Hassan bring us.

A principal aim of the first part of my essay was, similarly, to establish

598   MURRAY KRIEGER

that the universal, as the spatial, is the mediator, hence is the veil, but —
unlike Poulet — to put the aesthetic symbol on the other side, as the correlative (hopefully objective) of unmediated particularity. Though it is
itself a final object, yet it is to be intimately related to reality as existential
and to be differentiated from the universal in experience and language
even as the existential itself is.

Let me recapitulate: I granted that the phenomenological and existentialist manners of constructing our world of experience in its immediacy
require us to distinguish in our experience between the existential as unmediated and that selection from the existential (in accordance with some
principle of order) which creates the universal as the mediated. I granted
further that our antiobjective existentialist quest might lead us to transfer
this dichotomy between the unmediated and the mediated — between
consciousness and its objects — in our experience to a similar dichotomy
in language. If we did, we could emerge with poetry as a language of
"human time," of "interior distance," a subjective, antiformalistic celebration of the instantaneous flight that bypasses all mediation, with the rest
(the frozen world of fixed objects to be related to one another and speculated about) left to the non-poet. Thus the critic involved with unmediated
self-consciousness can allow distinctions in experience to reflect themselves
directly in language: there is either the language of objects (mediated)
or the language of Cartesian preobjective consciousness (unmediated),
the latter seeming to be almost an abdication from language as well as an
abdication from the formal obligations of poetic discourse. But can language do no more to bridge the gap, language released from its normal
bondage? What could a total indulgence in language allow that a total
abdication from it would not?

Given the distinction in experience between unmediated and mediated, can we rather distinguish in our language between the poetic (contextually conceived as unique systems) and any other (systematically
propositional or ordinary), claiming that only the poetic has access to the
existential, from which the latter has removed itself by its generic nature?
But, it can be argued by the critic of unmediated self-consciousness, the
poem also is a form and formula, a fixed object that in its frozen state
incapacitates itself from capturing the immediate. It, too, occurs in a
medium and, hence, it is mediate rather than immediate and thus is subject to the antimediator's rejection of it and flight from it. Such an argument can be answered, as I tried to answer it in Part I, only by referring
to the paradoxical nature of poetic discourse, which thus becomes at
once the source and mouth of meaning, at once a fixed form and yet,
through its dynamics of interrelations capturing stillness in movement,
attaining objective immediacy. It thus converts into a medium that is at
war with its role, language that subverts the normal behavior of language

in order to attain the character of sacred communion which symbolism has lost in the secular world.

So at least the argument would go that would seek to recover the poem as object without having it forgo the existential immediacy that the contextualist, no less than the antimediator, must seek to keep within the poem's unique domain. The veiling function of poetic language, so long viewed ambivalently, is now seen as systematically ambiguous, if not downright miraculous. But the heart of the problem remains, since all we have been offered is a verbal mystique that cannot pretend to be a solution. In what follows I shall see if I can press these issues further.

The very formulation of the problems would seem to preclude our progress. Once we adopt enough of the existentialist stance to distinguish firmly between the immediate and the mediate in experience, how can we hope to capture or transmit the immediate in the mediate forms of language? Does not the very use of language carry with it the abandonment of the immediate to the extent that we commit ourselves to our symbolic systems? How can we justify our belief that our symbols can do better? There is, then, the "given" in experience in its immediacy, and there is the fixed object. How can the latter embody the former without losing the former's existential immediacy? That is to ask, how does the "given" in experience find its way into the vision of the whole work considered as an aesthetic form, a spatio-temporal moving finality?

I am aware that, at a time when "visionary" critics are in the ascendancy, I cannot use the word "vision" as my central term without trying to set off my sense of it from the sense it has commonly been earning — especially when I see the force of its common meaning as separating it from the work's totality even as I try to identify the two.[11] I must see the work not as a projection of a pre-existing vision, formed in the self behind it, but as a dialogistic entity that comes into being out of the dramatic conflict of forces and language which constitutes its finished form. Thus it was that Leo Spitzer used "vision" as a pre-aesthetic category that characterized how the author saw rather than how the poem meant, reserving his aesthetic claims for what became of vision when the whole went to work on it by becoming a "work." Though in the spirit of Spitzer, I prefer to use "vision" for what comes out rather than for what goes in.[12]

But it is the construction upon the "given" which creates the forms of a vision that creates, and is created by, its form. So we, too, must begin once more with the "given." In my book *The Tragic Vision* I began with the common assumption that our routine (which is to say pretragic) existence depends upon the universalizing veils (that word again) that our social and moral necessities force us to hold between ourselves and the brawling chaos — the jumble of unique instances — that is actually out there (and within us) ready to show its Manichaean face to any who dare thrust the veil aside to look. And it is that forced confrontation of extremity — the unpalliated series of ineluctable consequences which practicality normally persuades us to shun — which creates the tragic existent and sets his tragic course on its way.

If we assume, then, the existential immediacy of the Manichaean face of reality as irreducibly there for the stricken existent, we assume also the multidimensionality of the unique particularity of this experience, now viewed without the universalizing veils that comfort automatically imposed. In its particularity this experience is thus inaccessible to the reducing or abstracting habits of our usual linguistic apparatus, of our rational — or at least propositional — responses which we have so well and universally learned. In its uniqueness (instantaneous because it is not just an instance, but an instant) it resists all but its own unrepeatable, flowing, unadaptable self. It is surely utterly closed, shut off, because nothing else is like it; nothing else can explain it, its conjunction of impossible coordinate or simultaneous aspects. But — and here is the Bergsonian paradox — it is also and at the same instant utterly open, because, being instantaneous, it is not even an entity; rather, denying itself any discrete instance, it flows into all other instantaneous non-instances and has them flow into *it*.

Well, then, inner experience is impervious to language, and we are trapped in the linguistic shadow-world of the subjective critic of unmediated self-consciousness (really observer and voice-catcher more than critic), in the manner of Poulet, the commentator who tries to match his introspective, impressionistic language to the elusive structures of mental experience before him. We have more than once noted his necessary antipathy to form as the objectifying enemy.[13] Such a literary observer tends to see an unavoidable dichotomy in the options open to all literary observers, so that each must choose either the subjective or objective aspect of the work.[14] For Poulet, the literary work is the representative of the author's thought if we but conceive this thought as physical place, a home for its constituted objects. Thus conceived, the work, like the thought, may seem to those of us not attuned to interior distances to be related most obviously to its objects, those things of the outside world which it presumably is *about*. Being most obvious, this relation gives rise to "objective" criticism as the most usual sort. But the work, again like the thought, with those entities which it houses so commodiously, is related more crucially, if less obviously, to the thinking subject, the self that has "redisposed" those objects now newly created by mind. This "interior distance" between subject and his thought or work, thus conceived, and the redisposition of the objects in accordance with the housing demands in this inner space, is the less obvious but more urgent sort of criticism which must be practiced if the study of literature is truly to be humanized. It thus brings to light the hidden, dark side of the moon, the Cartesian *Cogito*.

But we cannot help but notice that in his open antiformalism a literary observer like Poulet too easily disposes of all formal matters by ranging them on the side of the "objective" features, as if formal features were of the same order as the external objects that thoughts or works presumably are *about,* external objects to which, in other words, thoughts or works would seem to the naïve critic to refer, objects which — to use the most naïve notion — they would appear to "imitate." In his one-paragraph preface to *The Interior Distance,* Poulet blandly sees the "objective aspect" of literature as including "formal" elements (by which he seems to understand no more than generic elements, the "contours" leading us to "poems, maxims, and novels, plays") as well as what we have learned to call the referential elements, "accounts" or "descriptions" of "objects." And he promises to turn from both to the subjective side. It is a promise he keeps all too faithfully.

But, if he disposes of all formal matters by ranging them indifferently with what we used to call objects of imitation as equally "objective" features, then perhaps he should be reminded to "redispose" his notion of form (as, after Mallarmé, he has the mind in its "interior vacancy" redispose its world of objects) to make it (as our best critics have made it) more than flat categories so dully externalized. Must we choose between the ineffably subjective and the naïvely objective? If so, are we not being too unsubtle? The external object does not stand in the same relation to the poem as that poem's form does, unless we are restricting ourselves to what has long been an obsolete eighteenth-century notion of form as universal generic mechanics. Clearly, as such it is too flattened out and externalized ever to have a vital existence, ever to do more than deaden through abstraction the particular living work to which it was to apply itself.

What else has literary criticism been about since Coleridge and before, if not to work toward a notion of an organic form which would enable us to talk formally about a work without adapting it to stale generalities, but finding instead a form that is uniquely its own, expressive of its own unrepeatable characteristics? What else have these two essays of mine been about? This effort has led to examinations of the special properties of poetic discourse, its ways of meaning, which can permit it to open vistas of vision which normal discourse, by its very nature, seems determined to shut off. I have been pressing myself to show how the literary medium, though still only the words we all, like Hamlet, despise most of the time, manages to free the subjective, even while freezing it into a permanent form, to make the poem an *im*mediate object rather than a mediate one. For, if the medium is at war with itself in literature, if language refuses to serve as it normally does, its struggle serves the higher fidelity to language that shows him who can master this extraordinary medium how thoroughly it can master the most inward folds of our experience. But still, though a medium rendered immediate, a poem's language works to make the poem an *object* and to that extent external and communicable — and in need of more than subjective observation. The dark side of the moon *is* what we are given, but the firm mastery gives it to us in a way we can hope to secure — for ourselves and others. It is a formal way, though of course "formal" here has so many other-than-formal elements in it if we restrict the term to the archaically formalistic meaning Poulet at times reserves for it.

All of which returns us, but I believe newly armed, to the matter of vision and the way it gets into literature. For I have meant to be claiming throughout that we need not see our inner experience as being, after all, impervious to all language once we remember the inward immediacies that our great poets can force their language to embody. Suppose we begin with the special sort of "given" which I saw the tragic vision assuming about moral experience, and suppose we can characterize that "given" in its extremity as unadaptably unique, at once an indissoluble lump among innumerable other equally autonomous but dissimilar lumps in the stream of chaos, yet at the same time the stream itself, always becoming but never having become, and thus never hardened to lump; then we have begun by seeming to put such a "given" and such experience beyond the generic, freezing powers of language. We can recall my remarks concerning Ihab Hassan's assault on the word, his fear that subjective "outrage" may be fatally compromised by culture's dedication to a mediating "object," with the consequence of abstraction, death. For him this is the necessary and only consequence of the word and its order of beauty, since he does not allow language to be tortured into an object that preserves immediacy and existential vitality, an object that for all its fixed eloquence can preserve a discursive silence. For him, as we saw in the first part of my essay, language must be either eloquent or silent: eloquent in its service of an object for culture (thus violating our "outrage"), or silent in its obedience to outrage (thus deserting all objects).[15]

But I must go further, in order to qualify our fears about the existential incapacities of language, by acknowledging that we have been speaking only of the "normal" powers of language, so that we may find a very abnormal series of possibilities in the history of our greatest literary works.

The subjective flow of the self's awareness of its experience must somehow be preserved, even while being preserved in a fixed object. The death-dealing immobility of the spatial impulse must yield to the dynamic, moving vitality of the temporal, while yet creating that which must persist in an unchanging form: I maintain this need despite those newest critics who claim — against all objectivity — that dynamism must be retained in the ever-changing vitalism of our responses to our inner experience. Despite all that contemporary personalism and existentialism have taught us about objectification (the making into things) as the murderer of the unique, I would want the critic to claim to have found in the abnormalities of poetic language the one way of having his object without surrendering the immediacy of its data.

There is in the work, as in the "given" of the experience, both the instance and the instant or even instantaneous, with the strange etymological and semantic coincidence of opposition and identity between these: the absolute and irreducible instance, which demands discreteness, a continual awareness of and pausing over the boundaries that constitute it as discrete, cutting it off from all that is not itself; and the absolutely instant or instantaneous, which denies the existence of bounds, of the entity-hood of the moment, in order to get on with the movement, the flow of the moment becoming the next without pausing to be marked. It is the role of poetic discourse to undo the generic tendencies of discourse generally, and so to complicate its context with contingency as to create that language context as its own unique body. Moving dynamically in time, the poem must yet become transfixed into a spatial form.

Hence what I have elsewhere termed the ekphrastic principle becomes the poetic principle in that it invokes "still movement" (in both the Keatsian and Eliotic senses of "still") as the special grace with which poetry is to be endowed.[16] The critic's job is to locate (as it is the poet's job to produce) the spatial orders within the temporal: the circular principle within progression; the freezing principle within the free-flowing; the emblematic as the ekphrastic within that which resists all spatial fixity; the multiple reflections of a mirrorized world of internal relations within a seemingly semantic and syntactic set of relations which, like all language, wants to open outward toward all other language and its referents; the causal and yet — or therefore — the casuistic within the casual; the logical within the chronological; the still recurring within the still moving; the extremities of experience within the compromising muddles of the uncommitted middle. To the extent that our discourse seeks to follow its non-poetic, natural (which, paradoxically, is to say conventional) paths — its "naturally" conventional paths, as it were — it seeks either to be casual and free (in its unsystematic modes) *or* to be causal and frozen (in its non-poetic systematic modes). The poet must have it as both at once: he must create the language as *his* medium by fostering in it the multiple capacities that transform the word into terminal entity, body, effigy, emblem, even as it clearly seems to function in the semantic and syntactic ways that words have as their wont. So the "given" is found in the work, preserved in its density and contingency and not reduced to any conceptual formula, yet preserved and intact by being an utterly formed object once and for all for one and all. It has a form but is not a formula after all, is constitutive but not conceptual; that is, it gives the forms for our reality but not concepts about it.

If the poem, then (as, alas, all too many poems do), should reduce itself — as the straw-man formalist (attacked by Poulet) would have it — to fixity and only stand still, it would reduce itself to the frozen death of the spatialized discourse of non-poetic systems, losing the empirical dynamism of movement, the flowing vitality of experience in its subservience to universality, that Platonic archetype that levels particularity. But, if the poem should do the reverse, if — as a Poulet would have it — it should be still moving only in the sense of always moving, giving up the paradox of unmoving movement at the heart of the stillness of the Keatsian urn, then it would deny utterly its character as object in an unqualified yielding to the boundless, ceaseless flow of our experience; and we are no better off for art, an art that has given over all in worship of imitative form, form that decries form and cries for formlessness in imitating a formless welter of experiences.

My use of the term "vision" has been shown to be systematically distinct from that of our admittedly visionary critics who seek, in the literary work, signs (often related to signs found in other works) of the author's grasp of his reality as that constituted reality relates to the grasping self. For I seek no vision behind or before the work, though I do seek the vision that comes to be created in the work, *as* the work.[17] Perhaps, to borrow a tired notion from Eliot, it is that the visionary correlative I seek is objective, not subjective, although the fact that it is objective makes it no correlative but the thing itself. In its concern with vision my study is still within what I have called *thematics,* by which I have meant the formal study of an aesthetic complex which becomes more than formal because the complexities that it unifies, as unresolved tensions, reflect the tension of our pre-propositional and extra-propositional experience.[18]

If, unlike Poulet, I insist on the work — for all its elusive subjective churning — as an object, I nevertheless share his fear that the dead hand of objectification can destroy its unique voice by adapting it to alien structures or classes. But I believe I voiced my antistructuralist, Crocean antagonism toward the *over*-mediators sufficiently in the first part of my essay.

If my argument has persuaded us to define vision only in terms of the unique work that constitutes it, we still must seek a more precise description of how that work achieves that unique vision, its objective formulation of all in the "given" that in its dynamics resists formulation. This is to ask, how does the infinitely variegated flow of experience achieve an aesthetically transcendent unity? In the midst of experiental chaos, endlessly divisive, we look, as desperately as Gerard Manley Hopkins did, for an aesthetic inscape that will satisfy our thematic craving.

> All things counter, original, spare, strange;
> Whatever is fickle, freckled (who knows how?)

> With swift, slow; sweet, sour; adazzle, dim;
> He fathers-forth whose beauty is past change . . .

Of course, as secular theorists we allow the miraculous metaphor of poetic incarnation to substitute for his theological Word made flesh. We resist Hassan's impulse to obliterate the word in order to embrace the flesh directly, unmediatedly. As I have argued elsewhere, figuratively (that is, in terms of the *figura*) the Trinitarian paradox is the very model of the poet's farthest claim for metaphor as transubstantiating miracle, with its union-in-duality of tenor and vehicle.[19] So there is the aesthetic need and the thematic need to freeze experience in order most fully to feel its flow. With the subjectivity of experience behind and beyond, the work must be created formally as its emblem, a total object; and the work must be created existentially as its vision, the very word "vision" bestowing upon the work the spatial fixity of a thing seen.

How, then, is the poet to play the casual casuist? How is he to realize and master the muddled flow of the confused center of our experience through an aesthetic-thematic symbol? I speak of our experience in its subjective confusion as the "center of our experience" because it resists the purity of definition, the *a fortiori* clarity, of the polar extremes. Experience at its hard edges is no longer confused, though in its extremity it is not where we dare live it unless we are to become polar creatures, tragic existents, ourselves. For, as my examination of the tragic vision was to have demonstrated throughout, the existent cannot embrace at all costs either pole without having it transformed into its antagonist (as, for example, in the relation of puritanism to sensual debauchery in many works in this thematic genre). Better the safe sanity, the ethical probity — if the visionary blindness — of the inconclusive, compromised middle.[20] But the poet dedicated to aesthetic resolution has to unmuddle the middle through a casuistic play that leads him to summon up and cultivate the extreme. However uncommitted existentially, however aesthetically committed to dialogue alone, he vicariously nourishes the extreme. His method of capturing the extreme (and, with it, all the impurities of the middle he has bypassed and yet, like the alchemist, distilled) is that of converting the endlessly variegated muddle into the terms of his extended metaphor for it. The critic's hypothesis of the work's form is his best guess about what this extended metaphor is, based on all in the work which feeds it.

The repetitive patterns of a work, which give stillness to the movement by freezing freedom, must be read by the critic into his hypothesis of the work's form, as he makes it a reductive metaphor — an emblem, a constitutive symbol — for all the moving life and liveliness of the work. The metaphor, while excluding so much of the middle in its reductive, extremist purity, is in its emblematic fullness at the same time all-inclusive.

The hypothesis tests itself by its capacity to account for every aspect of the work, aesthetic and experiential, which is stuffed within it (if it is not being imposed by the overanxious critic). At once puritan and catholic, the reductive metaphor must gather within itself the all of middle existence which it passes by in its pursuit of extremity, as it must gather within its holistic form the varied possibilities sloppily assembled in its tenor. Thus it becomes exclusively all-inclusive — at once existentially (or thematically) and aesthetically (or formally).

It may be helpful at this point for me to quote at length from my extended discussion of the reductive metaphor as both single and double, closed and open, in *A Window to Criticism: Shakespeare's Sonnets and Modern Poetics*.[21]

> The author plays the casuist, dedicated to extremity, by committing himself in the work absolutely to a reduction of one sort of experience to another, to a transfer of properties of one to those of another, a transfer to which every element in the work lends itself totally. Experience of a normal sort — messy, pre-poetic, of mixed and uncertain tendencies, veering in this direction and in that, impure in its continual compromise with the totality of definition — is viewed under the aspect of an extremely delimited sort of experience that threatens, momentarily, within its context, to reduce all experience to itself and to read life within its own awesome terms as unbearable and — to a common-sense reason that needs life as mixed — as irrational, even impossible.
>
> Thus, in Mann's *Doctor Faustus*, for example, all forces lend themselves to reveal the generally accepted world of artistic dedication and controlled artistic creativity exclusively under the aspect of the world of disease, to reveal the world of decent austerity and harsh asceticism exclusively under the aspect of the world of license. But the total transfer of properties, the total reduction, is deceptive. The terms I have used in my hasty oversimplification of these worlds should indicate that even as the extremes are poetically equated they remain polarized. In furnishing us a very paradigm of the functioning of extremity, Mann allows no mediation between extremes, but forces one to support the other, even to reflect the other, finally to become a mask for the other. Mann's extreme necessarily bears its opposite within itself by the very nature of its seemingly singleminded purity. The ill-defined, mixed components of the life he deals with follow the path of their most dangerous tendencies to extremes that are at once polar and reversible, opposed and identical. For the equation of the two worlds, the reduction of one to the other, becomes a substantive metaphor. As such it turns on itself, asserting for common sense the duality of its terms, the distinctness of their properties, even as it works the miracle of transubstantiation. Everything in the work — character, incident, language, style — contributes to the collapsing of the broad and mixed world to the narrow and pure one and thus to the creation of the work

as a total metaphor, except that, even as the transfer becomes dramatically complete, the separateness of elements asserts itself to our rational, less totally committed selves.

I could go on from *Doctor Faustus* to discuss the reductive metaphors, at once transubstantiating and skeptically self-denying, in others of the novels I treated as fully tensional bearers of the tragic vision. For example, we can too briefly characterize Gide's *The Immoralist,* in which all forces lend themselves to transfer the drive to assert the freedom of the self from the bonds of ethical restraint to its appearance exclusively under the aspect of a total enslavement to the senses. Or Malraux's *Man's Fate,* in which all forces lend themselves to transfer the ethical drive to merge the self with social betterment to its appearance exclusively under the aspect of the demoniac drive to the violence of uninhibited self-expression. Or Melville's *Pierre,* in which all forces lend themselves to transfer the moral devotion to well-meaning self-sacrifice to its appearance exclusively under the aspect of a total perversion at the service of monstrous desires. Or Kafka's *The Trial,* in which all forces lend themselves to transfer the amoral routine of *quotidien* existence to its appearance exclusively under the aspect of blind and unmitigated, moment-by-moment guilt. Of course, the half-innocence in K.'s stumbling half-pursuit, his essential ignorance, proclaim the absurdity of this absolute transfer of properties even as they help us marvel at the nothing-left-out character of Kafka's contextual inclusiveness that allows him to "work" his metaphor. But so it is with all of these and other examples. Always the transfer is complete; the "aspect" under which we are forced to see *is* imposed exclusively. And yet, and yet. . . . The polarities rebound; the muddled center reasserts itself; despite our utter captivation by the Word, our sensible selves skeptically reassert the recalcitrant world that resists all transfer and insists on doggedly, dully remaining itself. Still, the magic is never quite dispelled. We have it and we do not, we believe it and we do not, are hypnotically trapped and yet move freely in and out.

I now return to the passage from *A Window to Criticism:*

> . . . I see Mann's version of extremity as a paradigm that allows us to consider the poet's casuistry more broadly, so as to turn it into a generic literary strategy that can serve us with lyrics as well [indeed, even more easily, thanks to the obvious manipulation of devices of control in the lyric. Recall my comments on *Astrophel and Stella* 35, with the transfer of categories between the particular breathing lady and personified abstractions of universal virtues]. To use another obvious example . . . I can cite Donne's lovers in *The Canonization,* whose absorption by earthly love — which is shown in its normal state to be woefully mixed and incomplete in its nature — we are forced to view under the aspect of the total and unworldly dedication that earns sainthood.

Everything in the poem, in the fullness of its contextual interrelations, works to bring off the equation, to complete the metaphor in its transfer of properties from tenor to vehicle (from earthly lovers to saints), even though the tenor and vehicle seem opposed to one another. Nevertheless this step-by-step extension of the metaphor carries along with it the covert guide of rationality that asserts the absurdity, even the speciousness, of this extension. It is not that the identity produced by the metaphor is being denied, since such a denial would lead us outside the context and its mutually dependent terms, but that the miracle can be asserted as miracle only by continually recognizing its impossibility, by continually acknowledging the intransigence of the materials and oppositions being mastered, though they are never destroyed.

Such a miracle of substantive identity should of course not be viewed as a propositional truth claim (A is B) any more than it is a dramatic demonstration of a propositional moral claim (A ought to be B). With its context totally working to create it, it is rather a total and totally committed incarnation, an effigy of mixed and intransigent experience which has been substantively transferred into, or rendered within, an extreme, unmitigated reduction of one pure and narrow aspect to whose sway all cooperates or conspires in order to make the transfer complete — even as the miracle asserts itself as such by urging an awareness of its denial. Like Shakepeare's Phoenix and Turtle, like my mirror and window, like the *in* and the *through* of contextualism, but perhaps most like Clarissa's scissors which the baron manipulates in *The Rape of the Lock,* the miraculous metaphor divides even while it joins. [That miraculous poem itself works, like the scissors, to divide as it joins, if we consider how thoroughly it creates its vision of the heavy prosaic world of flesh and blood under the aspect of the airiness of the pure world of absolute play.]

In its simultaneous performing of its dividing and joining functions, its opening-out and closing-in functions, the dual nature of the extremity that leads to miracle — but a special sort of miracle at once assertive and denying — can correct an unfortunate over-emphasis that has for good reason bothered students of recent criticism. From Aristotle onward, critics, in insisting on the unity of the literary work, have insisted upon its convergent movement toward a unitary, sharply pointed conclusion and conclusive meaning. The *Poetics* traces, in the development of the literary work, the gradual, inevitable elimination of the multiple probabilities with which it began until, when the climax turns the complication into the dénouement, only the one way that — though hidden to us and to the protagonist — has been inescapably there all along is left and is pursued to its end. It has been hard to improve upon this classic formulation in its convergent simplicity. Thus it could not help seeming dangerously perverse to find recent critics [perhaps our best or most extreme example here would be William Empson] rather emphasizing almost exclusively the divergent meanings of literary works. While also insisting upon unity, they dwell upon the *organic* nature of that unity, upon the *variety* which is being unified. They celebrate the ambiguous instead of the unilinear, the unresolved tensions among centrifugal forces instead of the crowning assertion of the all-dominating centripetal force. At their more reckless moments they may seem to be claiming for the work no more narrowly unified a precision than that of a shotgun blast. And yet they have on the whole been persuasive about the many voices with which even an apparently simple poem may often speak. I am suggesting that literary extremity and its miracle, with the completeness of their absorption of alien, resistant, and incomplete materials together with the completeness of the unbridgeable separateness of these elements, can allow for the combined emphasis on the divergent and convergent natures of literary movement and meaning, the density and plenitude on the one side, the rarity and the order on the other. It can insist on the centrifugal thrust of a work only while placing its control within the pressing and uncompromising union of its finest and most centered point. The impossible combination of identity and polarity can make a total view of the object possible: the perspective is reduced to a single point even as, at the same time, the range of possibilities multiplies endlessly — thus the consequence of the object as both single substantive world and as bodiless reflection of multiple worlds beyond.

The reductive metaphor can in its closedness open an *im*mediate access to reality's figures, which is to say the way reality becomes "figured" for us, "figured" in the double sense of Auerbach: at once the concrete symbol of the single instance, instantaneous, and — while holding to this character — the *figura,* its ultimate human meaning for us, its allegorical representativeness that exceeds itself, but only by thoroughly being itself. Hence we come upon the vision, but not any vision that preexisted the work in an individual psyche or in a culture's *"humanitas"* or in a normative structure held in potentiality for individual entities to fulfill; rather the vision that is attained figurally by cutting so fine a verbal figure *as* the work. Yet it *does* become the culture for the moment and for the minds that so constitute it metaphorically. The extremity of total transfer, of metaphor, becomes window to the reduced moment of vision which characterizes the reality created for a culture (created *as* the culture) by its most symbolically gifted seer-makers.[22]

The hypothesis of the work's reductive metaphor thus becomes the formal opening to the work's existential vision. All of its directionless (because all-directional) experience, all of its "dappled," "pied" beauty, utterly ungraspable, is reduced to the emblematic unity that enables us to grasp its movements in a vicarious moment of vision. We are given this way (which neither precludes nor contradicts other ways) of seizing upon it as an entity we may perceive in its discrete entity-hood. It neither precludes nor contradicts other ways, because it gives us no propositional claim about the experience, a claim that would reduce it in another way, a logical way that would cheat it of its uniqueness and integrity by making it serve a universal law, reducing it to cipher, an enslaved particular that is therefore particular no longer. Instead, the metaphorical, visionary grasp gives us the particularity which the *poiesis* helps us to see as *one*, but as no more than one and as translatable to no others. Thus the metaphor, as the formal enabling cause of our vision, its source and its mouth, in the self-enclosure of its extremity, resists all propositional extrapolation, its persistent drama countering every would-be propositional claim with its antagonistic anticlaim.

The very reductive and yet all-embracing nature of the metaphor claimed by the critic's hypothesis must shout the rational denial of its absolute nature, the denial it bears within itself. It must force us to see nothing less than an identity between the muddle of its tenor and the pristine extremity of its vehicle. But the equation it proclaims as a self-enclosing metaphor it must proclaim in awareness of our skepticism. To be metaphor it must insist on the miracle by which things change their nature, become other than themselves, their substance dissolving into other things. It must, with the unrelenting tightness of a total aesthetic control exercised with equal pressure everywhere within its domain, create the vision that sees the messy center of our experience *becoming* its own purified reduction at the hard edge. For our vision it assumes a guise that alters the thing itself, thus proclaiming, however irrationally, the destruction of discrete entities, the blurring of the bounds, the limits, that create the property and propriety of entity-hood. Thus it achieves the fullness of capacity that (in the late Sigurd Burckhardt's terms) corporealizes itself and so attains the totality of definition of metaphor.

But, despite all such seeming magic, discourse — even poetic — remains only discourse, no matter how bent it may seem to be on subverting its own common nature as an open structure that leads us in and out, relating to other discourses and to the world that comes before and after all discourse (or we so assure ourselves in the naïve realism that is our common sense of how things go with us). And we, as prosaic users of discourse (even as we are the victims of the subversive perfection of its involutions in poetry), stubbornly retain the openness of our relations to it and the world, persisting in an anti-Kantian confidence that sees us and our world as pre-existing our symbols. So there must be that in the poem which we find comforting to our anti-aesthetic resistances, our recalcitrance to the miracles of language fully, if too trickily, endowed. The poem's patterned turnings upon itself end by allowing a part of us to turn on *it*, or to turn it against its most contextual pretensions. Our more rational selves find hidden within the poem, for all that would make it a new word, the comforting assurances that our sense for distinction and for property — which is to say propriety — may yet be preserved. It is nothing less than the comforting assurance that it all has been but a verbal game; and we try to set at rest that apocalyptic challenge to make the word into the Word, which is to say the fleshly world.

But of course this challenge, so persuasively urged by the closing, all-reducing action of the all-inclusive metaphor, still remains to possess us. This is to say that the rational covert guide that threatens to undo the mask by revealing it as no more than mask undercuts the miracle of metaphor by proclaiming it not as equation but as miracle, with all the inspiration of awe — and of skepticism — which the notion of miracle engenders. It is no fact; it is no proposition; indeed, fact and proposition flatly deny it. It is but an *im*position upon our vision, sanctioned only by the daring leaps sponsored by the delicate play of language. As no more (but no less) than miracle, it can be held only in the teeth of all rational denials. For it goes without saying that, if we can believe in it as a rational possibility, it is no miracle. By definition its very existence for us as miracle depends upon that part of us which knows it cannot happen — except in a way that passes understanding, an understanding we cannot altogether yield up.

Thus it is that, even as the enclosing metaphor captures the motley variety of experience's soft center within the hard edge of its extremity, thereby reading all of life within its own closed visionary system, there is something else at work in the countermetaphorical motion: in the skeptical denial that restores distinction (that restores our sense of duality where there are two entities), there is an opening outward beyond the miracle (the metaphor, the work, and the world of its words) to the world we know and what that world refuses to permit. An ironic self-doubt arises from the state of dialogue in the work that comes to terms with itself and yet, on the sly, proclaims itself as play; this self-doubt finally can lead even beyond the still-limited visionary dialogue of the single work to the ultimate catholicity of vision that is the proper end of the contemplative life.

The expansion of consciousness I have been urging, the dual awareness, the dialogistic sense that returns with a furtive openness to what has been closed, sealed off, may seem to echo the claims for the anti-poem of neo-romantic critics like Hassan. Let me remind you of this more moderate passage of his which I quoted in the first part of my essay:

> Literature recoils from the withering authority of the new Apollo, but it does not surrender itself wholly to the frenzy of Dionysus. It only *feigns* to do so. It employs self-irony and self-parody, as in the novels of Mann and Camus; it develops, as in the work of Beckett or Genet, forms that are antiforms. . . . Literature, in short, pretends to a wordy wordlessness and participates in the Dionysian denial of lan-

guage not with its own flesh, but with the irony of its divided intelligence.[23]

If Hassan would concede more to what closed form can permit, this might seem a helpful way to indicate the Janus-faced character of the work. Its very closedness, its absolute commitment to its metaphorical reduction, its compression into its constitutive symbol, into its emblem — all are accompanied by its prompting our common-sense denial that dissolves its miracles and drags it to earth. All poems must covertly contain their anti-poems, must transcend themselves and their closed limits, transform themselves into *genera mixta*. I quoted earlier my claim that my argument must reconcile those traditions which characterize poetic form as convergent (as in Aristotelian unity) or as divergent (as in Empsonian ambiguity). The centripetal emphasis on an exclusive unity and the centrifugal emphasis on an inclusive variety, simultaneously asserted, are further reflections of the strange commingling of openness in the aesthetic closedness of the literary object. I mean to remind you here of my discussion of the paradoxical co-existence of openness and closedness in our discrete experience viewed at once as instant and instance.

I move on, in conclusion, to suggest some existential consequences of these claims. The extreme situation is that which, forgoing the ameliorations of the center, forces confrontation at the edge; but the existent who would confront is also the creator of the extreme situation. Buried in this circularity is the notion that the mess in the soft center of our experience is a mess that most of us have to create in order to muddle ourselves and preserve our sanity, to keep going as social animals who do not want to look too deeply into mirrors or into another's eyes. Our pursuit of endlessly diversified experience, veering in its infinitely various and self-aborting directions, our blunting the points we have sharply shaped, our lurching and starting and slowing and gliding and leaping, by turns, all are ways we hide from confrontation of what we dare not confront. As in Kafka's *The Trial* we must accept the ambiguous duality of K.'s having been seized for arrest gratuitously *and* K.'s having chosen the state of being arrested, so in this literature generally we must acknowledge both that extremity is there beckoning for him who would cast off all palliative veils to dare confront it and that extremity is a creation of those so willful as to choose the confrontation. The visionary courage — which is to say, the metaphorical courage — of those whose fear of blindness will not permit the diversion of their confronting impulse must be matched by the self-conscious insanity that forces them to wrestle — and to watch themselves wrestling — with casuistic phantoms instead of joining the rest of us in the center, going round and round in the dizzying dance of life. As we stop to look at them as our surrogates, if we observe

closely enough, we find their struggle — combined with their consciousness of struggle — to have the purity and perfection of ballet. After such
a vision, with what self-consciousness, with what new and corrective
sense of our aimless heavy-footedness, do we return to make our motions?

IV

Notes

Introduction

1. In W. K. Wimsatt, *The Verbal Icon: Studies in the Meaning of Poetry* (Lexington, 1954), p. 21. Cf. Mark Spilka, "The Affective Fallacy Revisited," *Southern
Review: An Australian Journal of Literary Studies,* I (1965), 57–72.
2. In *The Verbal Icon,* p. 33. They have in mind an "affective critic" like I. A.
Richards.
3. Ibid., "Introduction," p. xvii.
4. "History of Ideas Versus Reading of Poetry," *The Southern Review,* VI (1941),
p. 602. See René Wellek, "Leo Spitzer (1887–1960)," *Discriminations: Further
Concepts of Criticism* (New Haven, 1970), p. 202.
5. In *Essays on English and American Literature,* ed. Anna Hatcher (Princeton,
1962), p. 4.
6. In the "Closing Statement" from which Bateson quotes Wellek also said that
the conference had virtually ignored "the enormous labors" and the impressive
achievements of philological or literary stylistics.
7. Quoted by Donald C. Freeman, "Linguistic Approaches to Literature," in
Linguistics and Literary Style, ed. Freeman (New York, 1970), p. 3.
8. "Introduction: Orientation of Critical Theories," *The Mirror and the Lamp:
Romantic Theory and the Critical Tradition* (New York, 1953), p. 21. On "Pragmatic Theories" see pp. 14–21.
9. Energetic efforts have been made to keep classical rhetoric alive in modern
criticism: see Edward P. J. Corbett's Bibliography in *Rhetorical Analyses of Literary
Works,* ed. Corbett (New York, 1969), pp. 233–72. On the New Rhetoric see the
collection *New Rhetorics,* ed. Martin Steinmann, Jr. (New York, 1967). On the
differences between Old and New Rhetoric see Richard Ohmann, "In Lieu of a
New Rhetoric," *College English,* XXVI (1964), 17–22.
10. *The Philosophy of Rhetoric* (New York, 1936), p. 24.
11. "The Main Trends of Twentieth-Century Criticism," *Concepts of Criticism,*
ed. Stephen G. Nichols, Jr. (New Haven, 1963), p. 353.
12. "Philosophy and Postwar American Criticism," *Concepts of Criticism,* p. 325.
13. In *Counter-statement,* 2d ed. (Los Altos, 1953), p. 124.
14. See René Wellek, "The Main Trends of Twentieth-Century Criticism," pp.
348–49. For a bibliography of psychoanalytically oriented criticism see Walter Sutton, *Modern American Criticism: Humanistic Scholarship in America, The Princeton Studies* (Englewood Cliffs, N.J., 1963), pp. 175–218. See also Norman N.
Holland, "The 'Unconscious' of Literature: The Psychoanalytic Approach," in *Con-*

temporary Criticism: Stratford-upon-Avon Studies 12, ed. Malcolm Bradbury and David Palmer (London, 1970), pp. 130–53.

15. An answer to the first question may be found in the actions of the students at Columbia University during 1968. Perhaps the students showed by the upheaval, riots, uprising, or liberation (naming what happened depends on who is looking and for what reasons) that they took what Trilling had been saying about modern literature at his word. Peter Brooks, reviewing, in *Partisan Review,* XXXVII (1970), p. 125, the account of "The Columbia Happenings" in Stephen Spender's *The Year of the Young Rebels* (New York, 1968), goes so far as to suggest that the events were motivated by, or at least a manifestation of, the discontent of the students with the teaching of literature. Brooks says: "Our most persuasive modern theories of criticism suggest that the highest form of human activity is the disinterested contemplation of a fine aesthetic stasis in which every utterance, be it the negations of Ivan Karamazov or the apocalyptic affirmations of Rimbaud, meets its ironic counterpart in a harmonious tension, a reconciliation of opposites. . . . No wonder that the first effort of the students should be directed toward eliciting a response, a connection, and that they sometimes seem willing to trade in their freedom to be rid of their sense of helplessness." For Trilling's view of the events see Stephen Donadio, "Columbia: Seven Interviews," *Partisan Review,* XXXV (1968), 386–92.

16. From "Reflections in a Mirror," addressed to a meeting of the English Institute considering his critical theories, in *Northrop Frye in Modern Criticism: Selected Papers from the English Institute 1965,* ed. Murray Krieger (New York, 1966), p. 138.

17. Quoted by R. P. Blackmur, *A Primer of Ignorance,* ed. Joseph Frank (New York, 1967), p. 76. In 1929 Richards published in *Practical Criticism* the results of what became a famous experiment in reading. He had asked his students at Cambridge University to comment freely on a group of poems, without date or authorship attached, and varying widely in literary quality. The written responses, which Richards called "protocols," were filled with wild misreadings and misinterpretations. Richards tabulated the ten "chief difficulties" in his respondents' readings, and among these he listed: irrelevant associations, stock responses, sentimentality, and inhibition. Richards's experiment has been used by many critics since as an object lesson in the hazards of impressionistic "analysis" and of undisciplined response to literature (see, for example, Northrop Frye, *The Well-Tempered Critic* [Bloomington, 1963], p. 133 ff.), but Richard's intention was to *advance* affective criticism, to distinguish valid from invalid responses, not to discourage it. On this point see Mark Spilka, "The Affective Fallacy Revisited."

18. "Comparative Literature Today," *Discriminations,* p. 50. For Wellek's critique of Richards see "The Revolt Against Positivism in Recent European Literary Scholarship," *Concepts of Criticism,* pp. 265–66.

19. See W. B. Yeats, *Autobiographies* (London, 1956), p. 156. Yeats had been reprimanded by his father for "talking for effect" in trying to make a good impression at a social engagement: "talking for effect was precisely what one must never do; he had always hated rhetoric and emphasis and he made me hate it."

20. Preface, *The Performing Self: Compositions and Decompositions in the Languages of Contemporary Life* (New York, 1971). This answers an objection implicit in the following statement by Wimsatt and Beardsley in their article "The Concept of Meter: An Exercise in Abstraction" (reprinted in W. K. Wimsatt, *Hateful Contraries: Studies in Literature and Criticism* [Lexington, 1965], p. 116): "A performance is an event, but the poem itself, if there *is* any poem, must be some kind of enduring object." Wimsatt and Beardsley are defending the scansion of traditional English syllable-accent meter against the attempt by certain linguists to describe the versification of poetry "as it is actually performed."

21. *The Performing Self,* p. 90. The interview with Frost is in *Writers at Work: The Paris Review Interviews, Second Series,* ed. Van Wyck Brooks (New York, 1963), pp. 7–34.

22. The most famous of these has been Leavis's feud with C. P. Snow, which

began with Leavis's lecture on "The Significance of C. P. Snow" (published in *The Spectator*, 9 March 1962), following Snow's Rede Lectures of 1959 entitled "The Two Cultures and the Scientific Revolution." The battle raged for years and pulled in just about everyone in the British intellectual community before it died down, and it has flared up again with Leavis's lecture " 'Literarism' Versus 'Scienticism,' " published in *The Times Literary Supplement*, 23 April 1970, and Snow's rejoinder, "The Case of Leavis and the Serious Case," 9 July 1970.

23. For a frequent criticism of Leavis's alleged assumption of, as Raymond Williams has put it, "a wholly organic and satisfying past," see A. Alvarez and Donald Davie, "A New Aestheticism?" (p. 650, Part V).

24. In *Northrop Frye in Modern Criticism*, pp. 112–13.

25. In "Criticism, Visible and Invisible," *The Stubborn Structure: Essays on Criticism and Society* (Ithaca, 1970), p. 79.

26. Ibid., pp. 77, 85.

LEO SPITZER, *From "Linguistics and Literary History"*

1. Perhaps the transition from a particular historical line in language, as traced by an etymology, to the self-contained system of a work of literature, may seem violent to the reader: in the first case the "etymon" is the "soul of the nation" at the moment of the creation of the word; in the second, it is the "soul of one particular author." The difference, as Professor Singleton has pointed out to me, is that between the unconscious will of the nation that creates its language, and the conscious will of one member of the nation who creates willfully and more or less systematically. But, apart from the fact that there are rational elements in popular linguistic creations, and irrational ones in those of the creative artist — what I would point out here is the relationship, common to both, between the linguistic detail and the soul of the speaker(s), and the necessity, in both cases, of the to-and-fro philological movement.

Perhaps a better parallel to the system of a work of art would be the system of a language at a definite moment of its evolution. I attempted just such a characterization of a linguistic system in my article on Spanish in *Stilstudien*, I.

2. This study has been published in *Stilstudien*, II. The method I have been describing in the text is, of course, one that is followed by all of us when we must interpret the correspondence of someone with whom we are not well acquainted. For several years I had been in correspondence with a German emigrant in France whom I did not know personally and whose letters had given me the impression of a rather self-centered person who craved a cozy and congenial environment. When she was finally rescued to another country, she published a book of memoirs, a copy of which was sent me. On the cover of the book I saw pictured the window of the room she had occupied in Paris; behind this window, in the foreground, was a great cat looking out upon the Cathedral of Notre Dame. A great part of the book itself was taken up with this cat, and I had not read far before I found — without great surprise — several sentences such as "blottie dans un fauteuil, j'éprouvai un tel bonheur, je me sentis si bien à mon aise sous ce soleil doux qui me faisait ronronner à la manière des chats." Evidently a catlike existence was the deep-felt aspiration of this emigrant who, in the midst of world catastrophe, had lost the feeling of protectedness and had had to seek protection in herself.

3. We could here also be reminded of Goethe's simile (in *Die Wahlverwandtschaften*, II, 2): "We have learned about a special arrangement of the English Navy: all ropes of the Royal Fleet, from the strongest to the thinnest, have a red thread woven into them in such a way that it cannot be taken out without completely raveling the rope, so that even the smallest particle is stamped as the property of the Crown. Similarly, Ottilia's diary is pervaded by a thread of affection and attachment which connects every part and characterizes the whole of it." In this passage Goethe has formulated the principle of inner cohesion as it exists in a sensitive writer. It is

the recognition of this principle which enabled Freud to apply his psychoanalytical finds to works of literature. While I do not wish to disavow the Freudian influence in my earlier attempts at explaining literary texts, my aim today is to think, not so much in terms of the all-too-human "complexes" which, in Freud's opinion, are supposed to color the writing of the great figures of literature, but of "ideological patterns," as these are present in the history of the human mind.

Mr. Kenneth Burke, in his book *Philosophy of Literary Form* (Baton Rouge, La., 1941), has worked out a methodology of what he calls the "symbolic" or "strategic" approach to poetry — an approach which comes very close to the Freudian one (and to my own, as far as it was influenced by Freud), and which consists of establishing emotional clusters. When Mr. Burke finds such clusters in Coleridge, for example, he will claim to have found a factual, observable, irrefutable basis for the analysis of the structure of the work of art in general.

What I would object to in this method is that it can, obviously, be applied only to those poets who do, in fact, reveal such associational clusters — which is to say, only to those poets who do allow their phobias and idiosyncrasies to appear in their writing. But this must exclude all writers before the eighteenth century, the period in which the theory of the "original genius" was discovered and applied. Before this period, it is very difficult to discover, in any writer, "individual" associations, that is to say, associations not prompted by a literary tradition. Dante, Shakespeare, Racine are great literary "individuals," but they did not (or could not) allow their style to be permeated by their personal phobias and idiosyncrasies (even Montaigne, when portraying himself, thought of himself as "l'homme"). When a student of mine, working on the style of Agrippa d'Aubigné, was influenced by Professor Burke's book to apply the method of "emotional clusters" to that sixteenth-century epic poet, and was able, indeed, to find a series of antithetical associations, such as "milk-poison," "mother-serpent," "nature-unnatural" used in reference to pairs represented by the Catholic Catherine de Médicis and her Protestant opponents, I had to point out to him that these particular associational patterns (which had reminded him of Joyce) were all given by classical and Scriptural tradition: D'Aubigné merely gave powerful expression to age-old ideological motifs that transcended his personal, nervous temperament: the starting point for his "mère non-mère" was, obviously, the Greek μήτηρ ἀμήτωρ. Recently, I have had occasion also to point out the same truth in regard to the sixteenth-century poet Guevara, whose style has been explained by Freudian frustration.

4. Under the noble pretext of introducing "history of ideas" into literary criticism, there have appeared in recent times, with the approval of the departments of literary history, academic theses with such titles as "Money in Seventeenth-Century French (English, Spanish, etc.) Comedy," "Political Tendencies in Nineteenth-Century French (English, Spanish, etc.) Literature." Thus we have come to disregard the philological character of the discipline of literary history, which is concerned with ideas couched in linguistic and literary form, not with ideas in themselves (this is the field of history of philosophy) or with ideas as informing action (this is the field of history and the social sciences). Only in the linguistico-literary field are we philologians competent qua scholars. The type of dissertations cited above reveals an unwarranted extension of the (in itself commendable) tendency toward breaking down departmental barriers, to such a degree that literary history becomes the gay sporting ground of incompetence. Students of the department of literature come to treat the complex subjects of a philosophical, political, or economic nature with the same self-assurance that once characterized those Positivists who wrote on "The Horse in Medieval Literature." But while it is possible for the average person to know "what a horse is" (if less so what "a horse in literature" is), it is much more difficult for a student of literature to know "what money is" (and still more so what "money in literature" is). In fact, this new type of thesis is only an avatar of the old positivistic thesis; but, while the original positivism was motivated by a sincere respect for competence, the neopositivists now would administer the death-blow to scholarly competence.

5. Cf. my article in *Modern Philological Quarterly:* "Why Does Language

Change?" and the polemics resulting therefrom in *Language*, XX (1944), 45, 245.
6. Cf. Schleiermacher, *Sämtl. Werke*, III, no. 3, p. 343. "Über den Begriff der Hermeneutik mit Bezug auf F. A. Wolfs Andeutungen und Arts Lehrbuch" — a speech delivered in 1829. Schleiermacher distinguishes between the "comparative" and the "divinatory" methods, the combination of which is necessary in "hermeneutics," and since hermeneutics falls into two parts, a "grammatical" and a "psychological" part, both methods must be used in both parts of hermeneutics. Of the two methods, it is the divinatory which requires the "Zirkelschluss." We have been dealing here with the *Zirkelschluss* in the "divination" of the psychology of authors; as for "grammatical divination," any college student who attempts to parse a Ciceronian period is constantly using it: he cannot grasp the construction except by passing continuously from the parts to the whole of the sentence and back again to its parts.

Dr. Ludwig Edelstein has called my attention to the Platonic origin of Schleiermacher's discovery: it is in *Phaedo* that Socrates states the importance of the whole for the cognition of the parts. Accordingly, it would appear that I err in adopting Schleiermacher's "theological" approach and that I am undiplomatic in asking for an approach so at variance with that which is traditional in the humanities (when Dewey reproved the Humanists for the residues of theology in their thinking, they made haste to disavow any theological preoccupation — while I take the stand of saying: "Yes, we Humanists are theologians!"); would it not, I am asked, be better to show the irrationalism inherent in any rational operation in the humanities, than to demand the overt irrationalism of religion which our secular universities must thoroughly abhor? My answer is that Socrates himself was a religious genius and that, through Plato, he is present in much of Christian thought. As concerns the necessity, for the scholar, of having recourse to religion, cf. the conclusive reasoning of Erich Frank in his book *Philosophical Understanding and Religious Truth* (1945).

The traditional view of the "viciousness" of the philological circle is unfortunately held in an otherwise brilliant attack against "the biographical fashion in literary criticism" (University of California Publications, in *Classical Philology*, XII, 288) by Professor Harold Cherniss: in his argument against the philologians of the Stefan George school who, though not dealing with the outward biography of artists, believe that the inner form of the artist's personality can be grasped in his works by a kind of intuition, Cherniss writes: "The intuition which discovers in the writings of an author the 'natural law' and 'inward form' of his personality, is proof against all objections, logical and philological; but, while one must admit that a certain native insight, call it direct intelligence or intuition as you please, is required for understanding any text, it is, all the same, a vicious circle to intuit the nature of the author's personality from his writings and then to interpret those writings in accordance with the 'inner necessity' of that intuited personality. Moreover, once the intuition of the individual critic is accepted as the ultimate basis of all interpretation, the comprehension of a literary work becomes a completely private affair, for the intuition of any one interpreter has no more objective validity than that of any other."

I believe that the word "intuition" with its deliberate implication of extraordinary mystic qualities on the part of the critic, vitiates not only the reasoning of the Stefan George school but also that of their opponents. The "circle" is vicious only when an uncontrolled intuition is allowed to exercise itself upon the literary works; the procedure from details to the inner core and back again is not in itself at all vicious; in fact, the "intelligent reading" which Professor Cherniss advocates without defining it (though he is forced to grant rather uncomfortably that it is "a certain native insight, call it direct intelligence or intuition as you please") is based precisely on that very philological circle. To understand a sentence, a work of art, or the inward form of an artistic mind involves, to an increasing degree, irrational moves — which must, also to an increasing degree, be controlled by reason.

Heidegger, in *Sein und Zeit*, I, 32, ("Verstehen und Auslegung"), shows that all "exegesis" is circular, i.e., is a catching up with the "understanding," which is nothing else than an anticipation of the whole that is "existentially" given to man: "Zuhandenes wird immer schon aus der Bewandtnisganzheit der verstanden. . . .

Die Auslegung gründet jeweils in einer *Vorsicht,* die das in Vorhabe Genommene auf eine bestimmte Auslegbarkeit hin 'anschneidet.' . . . Auslegung ist nie ein voraussetzungsloses Erfassen eines Vorgegebenen. . . . Alle Auslegung, die Verständnis beistellen soll, muss schon das Auszulegende verstanden haben. . . . *Aber in diesem Zirkel ein vitiosum sehen und nach Wegen Ausschau halten, ihn zu vermeiden, ja ihn auch nur als unvermeidliche Unvollkommenheit 'empfinden,' heisst das Verstehen von Grund aus missverstehen* [the italics are the author's]. . . . Das Entscheidende ist nicht aus dem Zirkel heraus-, sondern in ihn nach der rechten Weise hineinzukommen. . . . In ihm verbirgt sich eine positive Möglichkeit ursprünglichsten Erkennens, die freilich in echter Weise nur dann ergriffen ist, wenn die Auslegung verstanden hat, dass ihre erste, ständige und letzte Aufgabe bleibt, sich jeweils Vorhabe, Vorsicht und Vorgriff nicht durch Einfälle und Volksbegriffe vorgeben zu lassen, sondern in deren Ausarbeitung aus den Sachen selbst her das wissenschaftliche Thema zu sichern. Der 'Zirkel' im Verstehen gehört zur Struktur des Sinnes, welches Phänomen in der existenzialen Verfassung des Daseins, im auslegenden Verstehen verwurzelt ist."

This "Vorsicht," this anticipation of the whole, is especially necessary for the understanding of philosophical writing. Franz Rosenzweig, "Das neue Denken" (in *Kleinere Schriften,* 1937) writes: "The first pages of philosophical books are held by the reader in special respect. . . . He thinks they [such books] ought to be 'especially logical,' and by this he means that each sentence depends on the one that precedes it, so that if the famous one stone is pulled, 'the whole tumbles.' Actually, this is nowhere less the case than in philosophical books. Here a sentence does not follow from its predecessor, but much more probably from its successor. . . . Philosophical books refuse such methodical ancien-régime strategy; they must be conquered à la Napoleon, in a bold thrust against the main body of the enemy; and after the victory at this point, the small fortresses will fall of themselves." (I owe this quotation to Kurt H. Wolf's article, "The Sociology of Knowledge" in *Philosophy of Science,* X; Wolf calls the anticipatory understanding of wholes a "central attitude": "In our everyday social interaction we constantly practice the central-attitude approach without which we could not 'know' how to behave toward other persons, or how to read a book, to see a picture, or to play or listen to a piece of music. . . .") What Heidegger, Rosenzweig, and Wolf describe is the method of the humanities which Pascal has called the "esprit de finesse" (as contrasted to the "esprit géométrique").

For the students in Romance Gröber formulated the idea of the philological circle (without mentioning the "circle" itself) in *Gröber's Grundriss* 1/3 (1888): "Absichtslose Wahrnehmung, unscheinbare Anfänge gehen dem zielbewussten Suchen, dem allseitigen Erfassen des Gegenstandes voraus. Im sprungweisen Durchmessen des Raumes hascht dann der Suchende nach dem Ziel, mit einem Schema unfertiger Ansichten über ähnliche Gegenstände scheint er das Ganze erfassen zu können, ehe Natur und Teile gekannt sind. Der vorschnellen Meinung folgt die Einsicht des Irrtums, nur langsam der Entschluss, dem Gegenstand in kleinen und kleinsten vorsichtigen Schritten nahe zu kommen, Teil und Teilchen zu beschauen und nicht zu ruhen, bis die Überzeugung gewonnen ist, dass sie nur so und nicht anders aufgefasst werden müssen."

It is also true of the comparative linguist who establishes his "phonetic laws" on the basis of "evident etymologies," which themselves are based on those "phonetic laws," that he moves in a circle, in the words of Zupitza, *Zeitschr. f. vergl. Sprachwissenschaft,* XXXVII (1904), 387: "Unsere wissenschaft kommt aus einem kreislauf nicht heraus: sie geht von evidenten gleichungen aus, entnimmt diesen ihre gesetze und prüft an diesen gesetzen jene gleichungen, die ihre grundlage bilden." And even elementary language teaching must move in a circle: R. A. Hall in *Bulletin of the American Association of University Professors,* XXXI, no. 6, advocating the modern "direct method" as preferable to the old "reading method," writes: "When he [the student] has learnt a sufficient number of examples, the linguistic analysis becomes simply a series of obvious deductions from what he has learned;

it helps him to perceive the patterns inherent in what he already knows, and tells him how far he can go in extending these patterns to new material." The inference from "patterns" is nothing but an anticipation of a whole deduced from the known examples.

7. The frequent occurrence, in my text, of quotations in the original foreign language (or languages) may prove a difficulty for the English reader. But since it is my purpose to take the word (and the wording) of the poets seriously, and since the convincingness and rigor of my stylistic conclusions depends entirely upon the minute linguistic detail of the original texts, it was impossible to offer translations.

8. Perhaps I should make it clear that I am using the word "method" in a manner somewhat aberrant from common American use: it is for me much more a "habitual procedure of the mind" (Lalande, *Vocabulaire de la philosophie,* s.v. *méthode* I) than a "program regulating beforehand a series of operations . . . in view of reaching a well-defined result" (ibid. 2). As used by me it is nearly synonymous with *Erlebnis,* and consequently would correspond relatively to what is called in America "approach," were it not for the volitional and even "strategic" nuance, in this word, of military siege or of tracking down a quarry, by which it may be historically explained.

In this connection I may quote a passage from a letter of Descartes to Mersenne (*Oeuvres,* ed. Adam-Tannery, I, 347): "Mais ie n'ay sceu bien entendre ce que vous objectez touchant le titre [Discours de la Méthode]; car ie ne mets pas *Traité de la Methode,* mais *Discours de la Methode,* ce qui est le mesme que *Preface ou Advis touchant la Methode,* pour monstrer que ie n'ay pas dessein de l'enseigner, mais seulement d'en parler. Car comme on peut voir de ce que i'en dis, elle consiste plus en Pratique qu'en Theorie, & ie nomme les Traitez suivans des *Essais de cette Methode,* pource que ie pretens que les choses qu'ils contiennent n'ont pû estre trouvées sans elle, & qu'on peut connoistre par eux ce qu'elle vaut."

9. If I were to give one piece of advice to our students of literary history, it would be substantially the same as that which Lanson, touring the United States forty years ago, gave to the students of his time who were then, as they are now, only too eager to rush to their big libraries to find in the many books of "secondary literature" an alibi for getting away from the "primary" texts they should study: "*Read your texts!*" My "circular method" is, in fact, nothing but an expansion of the common practice of "reading books": reading at its best requires a strange cohabitation in the human mind of two opposite capacities: contemplativity on the one hand and, on the other, a Protean mimeticism. That is to say: an undeflected patience that "stays with" a book until the forces latent in it unleash in us the re-creative process.

10. Sometimes it may happen that this "etymology" leads simply to a characterization of the author that has been long accepted by literary historians (who have not needed, apparently, to follow the winding path I chose), and which can be summed up in a phrase which smacks of a college handbook. But, to make our own way to an old truth is not only to enrich our own understanding: it produces inevitably new evidence, of objective value, for this truth — which is thereby renewed. A *comédie-proverbe* of Musset is based, after all, on a commonplace saying: was it a waste of time to illustrate so wittily "il faut qu'une porte soit ouverte ou fermée"?

11. The requirement at St. John's for the Hundred Great Books is good, I believe, insofar as it may encourage the "click" to repeat itself in an accelerated manner — if, of course, it has come about in the first experiences: to have read these hundred books "without click" would be equivalent to not having read a single book.

F. W. BATESON, *Linguistics and Literary Criticism*

1. I have three recent works particularly in mind: *Style in Language,* ed. Thomas A. Sebeok (Cambridge, Mass.: M.I.T. Press, 1960); *Linguistics and Style,* ed. John Spencer (London: Oxford University Press, 1964); *Essays on Style and Language,*

ed. Roger Fowler (London: Routledge, 1966). *Style in Language* incorporates papers originally read at a conference "to explore the possibility of finding a common basis for discussing and, hopefully, understanding, particularly among linguists, psychologists and literary critics, the characteristics of style in language" (Foreword, p. v). René Wellek contributed a closing statement, "From the Viewpoint of Literary Criticism," which includes a dictum on "the superstition of behaviourism" that may serve as epigraph to this paper: "It [behaviorism] denies the evidence of introspection and empathy, the two main sources of human and humane knowledge" (p. 409).

2. *General Linguistics: An Introductory Survey* (London: Longmans, 1965), p. 368.

3. *New Readings in Shakespeare* (Cambridge: Cambridge University Press, 1956), II, 197.

4. *The Oxford English Dictionary* excludes Old English, except for purposes of etymological explanation, on two grounds: (i) the failure of so large a part of the O.E. vocabulary to survive after ca. 1150; (ii) the O.E. inflections would have meant a wholly different system of entry from that "adapted to the words which survived the twelfth century" ("General Explanations," 1933 ed., I, xxviii).

5. "Place de la langue dans les faits de langage," pp. 27–32 of the 1955 ed.

6. Translation by Sir Robert Phillimore (London, 1874).

KENNETH BURKE, *Rhetoric — Old and New*

1. See the author's *Rhetoric of Motives* (New York: Prentice-Hall, 1949), p. 158.

2. V. 296–97, Loeb ed., trans. W. Rhys Roberts (Cambridge: Harvard University Press, 1946), p. 481.

3. *Rhetoric* 2. 23.

FREDERICK CREWS, *Anaesthetic Criticism*

1. *Anatomy of Criticism: Four Essays* (Princeton, 1957), pp. 6–7; copyright © 1957 by Princeton University Press; reprinted by permission of Princeton University Press.

2. *Fearful Symmetry: A Study of William Blake* (Princeton, 1947).

3. Murray Krieger, "The Critical Legacy of Matthew Arnold; Or, The Strange Brotherhood of T. S. Eliot, I. A. Richards, and Northrop Frye," *Southern Review,* n.s. V (April 1969), 457–74.

4. René Wellek and Austin Warren, *Theory of Literature* (New York, 1949), pp. 75–88. For more up-to-date thinking, purportedly sympathetic, see Lee T. Lemon, *The Partial Critics* (New York, 1965), p. 94: "Neither proper psychological definition of *archetype* nor the relative soundness of Freud's and Jung's views of the content of the unconscious need concern the literary critic directly. The only significant fact is that elements do get into poetry which can best be explained by psychoanalytic theory." The likelihood that *some* theory is potentially useful exhausts the critic's curiosity; since he has no way of choosing between Freud and Jung, he calls them both "psychoanalytic" and drops the subject.

5. See Glover, *Freud or Jung* (London, 1950).

6. On these matters see Louis Kampf's essay-review of three books of literary, history in *History and Theory,* VI (1967), 72–88. See also R. J. Kaufmann, "On Knowing One's Place: A Humanistic Meditation," *Daedalus,* Summer 1969, pp. 699–713, and Allen Grossman, "Teaching Literature in a Discredited Civilization," *Massachusetts Review,* X (Summer 1969), 419–32.

7. Frye's "archetype" is not quite the same as Jung's; it is merely any "typical or recurring image" in literary tradition, and archetypal analysis is consequently "the study of conventions and genres" (Frye, p. 99).

8. It is supremely ironic that some frustrated students, deducing that any intellectual effort must be inimical to their neglected feelings, are now turning against "the mind" and discovering an ally in C. G. Jung — the Jung of numinosity, astrology, numerology, augury, alchemy, and the vulgarized Mysterious East.

9. This point is elaborated by Weston La Barre, "Family and Symbol," in George F. Wilbur and Warner Muensterberger, eds., *Psychoanalysis and Culture: Essays in Honor of Géza Róheim* (New York, 1967), pp. 156–67. La Barre's *The Human Animal* (Chicago and London, 1960) and Alex Comfort's *The Nature of Human Nature* (New York, 1968) are helpful books for the layman.

10. Freud, "Five Lectures on Psycho-Analysis," *The Standard Edition of the Complete Psychological Works of Sigmund Freud,* ed. James Strachey et al. (hereafter abbreviated *S.E.*), 24 vols. (London, 1953–   ), XI, 17.

11. Géza Róheim, *The Origin and Function of Culture* (New York, 1943), p. 100.

12. See especially Erik H. Erikson, *Young Man Luther: A Study in Psychoanalysis and History* (New York, 1958) and *Childhood and Society* (2nd ed.; New York, 1963); and Norman Cohn, *The Pursuit of the Millennium* (Fairlawn, N.J., 1957) and *Warrant for Genocide: The Myth of the Jewish World Conspiracy and the Protocols of the Elders of Zion* (London, 1967). The last of these books may remind us that more than a methodological quarrel stands between those who analyze the projective content of myths and those who celebrate them as awesome powers.

13. See *Psychoanalytic Explorations in Art* (London, 1953).

14. Quoted by Roy P. Basler, *Sex, Symbolism, and Psychology in Literature* (New Brunswick, N.J., 1948), p. 4.

15. Freud, "Repression," *S.E.*, XIV, 149.

16. Indeed, the theoretical difference between Chomsky's linguistic rationalism and Skinner's linguistic behaviorism is entirely parallel to the difference between a psychoanalytic view of literature and an antimotivational view that treats any given work as a product of "influences" derived in an unknown manner from previous works. Like innate linguistic capacity, innate psychic disposition must be posited to account for ascertainable regularities. This is not, of course, to say that Chomsky's refutation of Skinner justifies Freud. The point is that a relatively "constrained" notion of psychic uniformity may prove flexible where a relatively "free" notion breaks down. Skinner's shunning of hypotheses about linguistic capacity leaves him with no choice but to ascribe an incredible causative weight to the mere hearing of words and sentences; so, too, literary theorists who sidestep the unconscious often end by deifying tradition and memory. See Noam Chomsky, "A Review of B. F. Skinner's *Verbal Behavior*," in Jerry A. Fodor and Jerrold J. Katz, eds., *The Structure of Language: Readings in the Philosophy of Language* (Englewood Cliffs, N.J., 1964), pp. 547–79.

17. Introduction to Christina Stead, *The Man Who Loved Children* (New York, Chicago, San Francisco, 1965), p. xl.

18. Academic critics have made characteristic rhetorical use of Ernest Jones's *Hamlet and Oedipus* (New York, 1949), taking its outdated scholarship and its literalism regarding fictional personages as reasons for dismissing the whole relevance of psychoanalysis to Shakespeare criticism. Meanwhile Jones's (and Freud's) central insight about the play has been confirmed and refined by other observers. See Simon O. Lesser, "Freud and *Hamlet* Again," *American Imago*, XII (Fall 1955), 207–20, and the studies summarized in Norman N. Holland, *Psychoanalysis and Shakespeare* (New York, Toronto, London, 1966).

19. On this point see David Rapaport, *The Structure of Psychoanalytic Theory* (New York, 1960), Abraham Kaplan, *The Conduct of Inquiry: Methodology for Behavioral Science* (San Francisco, 1964), and Michael Sherwood, *The Logic of Explanation in Psychoanalysis* (New York and London, 1969).

20. See especially E. Pumpian-Mindlin, ed., *Psychoanalysis as Science: The Dixon Lectures on the Scientific Status of Psychoanalysis* (Stanford, 1952); Helen

D. Sargent, "Intrapsychic Change: Methodological Problems in Psychotherapy Research," *Psychiatry,* XXIV (1961), 93–108; and L. A. Gottschalk and A. H. Auerbach, eds., *Methods of Research in Psychotherapy* (New York, 1966).

21. See *The Sociological Imagination* (New York, 1959).

22. See generally Norman S. Greenfield and William C. Lewis, eds., *Psychoanalysis and Current Biological Thought* (Madison and Milwaukee, 1965). The essays by Herbert Weiner, John D. Benjamin, and Robert R. Holt are especially important.

23. New York, 1968.

24. Quoted by Hanna Segal, "A Psycho-Analytical Approach to Aesthetics," *International Journal of Psycho-Analysis,* XXIII (1952), 206.

25. See *The Nation,* CXCII (1961), 339–41. Holland's chief authority for eschewing value judgments is Northrop Frye, whom he admires for having "cleared the air of a great deal of obscurantist smog" (*Dynamics,* p. xvi; see also pp. 196–97).

26. That this is a consequence of Holland's model and not a personal limitation is apparent from his excellent essay, "H. D. and the 'Blameless Physician,'" *Contemporary Literature,* X (Autumn 1969), 474–506.

27. Alfred North Whitehead, *The Aims of Education* (New York, 1929), p. 139.

28. For a comparable argument from the standpoint of perception psychology, see Morse Peckham, *Man's Rage for Chaos: Biology, Behavior, and the Arts* (Philadelphia, 1965). In excluding psychodynamic factors, however, Peckham overrates the aesthetic importance of sheer perceptual novelty — a flaw of some moment, given the present state of the arts.

29. Certain Freudian romantics, of whom the best known is Norman O. Brown, regard history itself as a gigantic tussle between the psychic forces posited by psychoanalysis. No such "psychologism" is being asserted here. A position like Brown's lends support to the accusation that psychoanalysis wants to replace other styles of observation by collapsing them into a general pathology. This is psychic determinism with a vengeance, but it is not psychoanalysis. Since my own essay may be subject to misunderstanding on this score, let me emphasize that psychoanalytic discourse properly seeks to show how individuals and groups *respond to* a totality of inner and outer conditions, and that for this task an awareness of nonpsychological forces is indispensable. (The point was made most clearly by Otto Fenichel, "The Drive to Amass Wealth," in his *Collected Papers,* Second Series [New York, 1954], pp. 89–108.) As applied to literature, this position not only welcomes but insists upon knowledge of every operative factor, including genre, convention, rhetorical devices, philosophical intent, audience, class, and personal background. What psychoanalysis disputes is not the usefulness of such information, but the equation of it with literary experience.

30. *Beyond Good and Evil,* in *The Complete Works of Friedrich Nietzsche,* ed. Oscar Levy, 18 vols. (New York, 1964), XII, 85.

LIONEL TRILLING, *On the Teaching of Modern Literature*

1. I leave out of my summary account the two supreme virtues that Arnold ascribes to the most successful examples of a "modern" literature. One is the power of effecting an "intellectual deliverance," by which Arnold means leading men to comprehend the "vast multitude of facts" which make up "a copious and complex present, and behind it a copious and complex past." The other is "adequacy," the ability to represent the complex high human development of a modern age "in its completest and most harmonious" aspect, doing so with "the charm of that noble serenity which always accompanies true insight."

MURRAY KRIEGER, *Mediation, Language, and Vision in the Reading of Literature*

1. Geoffrey H. Hartman, *The Unmediated Vision: An Interpretation of Wordsworth, Hopkins, Rilke, and Valéry* (New Haven, 1954), p. 155.

2. See Hassan's "The Dismemberment of Orpheus: Notes on Form and Antiform in Contemporary Literature," in *Learners and Discerners,* ed. Robert Scholes (Charlottesville, Va., 1964), pp. 135–65; "Beyond a Theory of Literature: Intimations of Apocalypse?" *Comparative Literature Studies,* 1 (1964), 261–71 (see Part II, this book); *The Literature of Silence: Henry Miller and Samuel Beckett* (New York, 1967).

3. "The Dismemberment of Orpheus," pp. 148–49.

4. Ibid., p. 162.

5. I expand this idea in my essay "The Ekphrastic Principle and the Still Movement of Poetry; or *Laokoön* Revisited," *The Play and Place of Criticism* (Baltimore, 1967), pp. 105–28.

6. See Sutton's "The Contextualist Dilemma — or Fallacy?" *JAAC,* 17 (1958), 219–29, and "Contextualist Theory and Criticism as a Social Act," *JAAC,* 19 (1961), 317–25. See my comments in "Contextualism Was Ambitious," *The Play and Place of Criticism,* pp. 153–64.

7. I refer to two fine essays in the "Structuralism" double issue of *Yale French Studies,* no. 36–37 (1966): Michael Riffaterre, "Describing Poetic Structures: Two Approaches to Baudelaire's *les Chats,*" pp. 200–42, and Geoffrey Hartman, "Structuralism: The Anglo-American Adventure," pp. 148–68.

8. *Deceit, Desire, and the Novel: Self and Other in Literary Structure,* trans. Yvonne Freccero (Baltimore, 1965), pp. 290–314.

9. In "The Continuing Need for Criticism," *Concerning Poetry,* 1 (1968), 18–20.

10. The role of the veil in medieval and Renaissance theory is usefully and effectively traced in Katherine E. Gilbert and Helmut Kuhn, *A History of Esthetics* (New York, 1939), pp. 149–72.

11. Perhaps it is for this reason an error for me to employ the term "vision," and indeed I might have searched for an alternative had I known when I began *The Tragic Vision* what the contemporary and subsequent use of "vision" was to do to it.

12. Leo Spitzer, *"Explication de texte* Applied to Three Great Middle English Poems," in *Essays on English and American Literature,* ed. Anna Hatcher (Princeton, 1962), pp. 193–247, esp. pp. 216–19.

13. I refer again to that most helpful and precise description of distinctions among critics of this sort in J. Hillis Miller, "The Geneva School," *Critical Quarterly,* VIII (1966), 305–21. Miller carefully traces the differences in the ways they play off the counterattractions of consciousness and of literary forms. Perhaps, in both parts of my essay, I have made my task too easy by choosing as my representative of the Geneva school so extreme a critic as Poulet, whom Miller shows to be the most Cartesian (hence antiphenomenological) and most antiformalistic of the group. The less antiformal, of course, are also less representative of the distinctive character of this critical mode.

14. The most useful statement of the claims which follow occurs in the preface to Poulet's *Interior Distance,* although I believe that, assumed rather than stated, similar claims underlie many writers in this "school." Again I refer the reader to Miller's essay "The Geneva School" for important differences among these critics which I am forced to blur here.

15. I repeat what I said in the first part of my essay: that it is undoubtedly unjust to couple Hassan with the Geneva school and its followers, but the dialectic of my argument calls for them to be seen as united on this issue.

16. I refer once more to my essay "The Ekphrastic Principle and the Still Movement of Poetry," pp. 105–28.

17. In Coleridgean terms, I seek in the work a direct reflection of the secondary imagination, which in its workings with language I must claim to be discontinuous with the primary imagination, "the prime agent of all human perception." Instead of merely being an "echo" of the primary, the secondary "dissolves, diffuses, dissipates" our reality as envisioned for us by our generally constitutive power, the primary. Coleridge uses both descriptions to make up an almost contradictory characterization of the secondary imagination. I choose to see only its character as creator, not that as echo.

18. See *The Tragic Vision* (New York, 1960), pp. 242 ff., for my original definition of *thematics,* together with a discussion of the consequences of that definition.

19. My book *A Window to Criticism: Shakespeare's Sonnets and Modern Poetics* (Princeton, 1964) rests almost wholly on my attempt to demonstrate the contextually sustained metaphor as the secular substitute for a theologically sustained transubstantiation; see especially pp. 200–204.

20. This was the antitragic, anti-Dostoevskian, anti-Kierkegaardian plea which the late Philip Blair Rice saw Thomas Mann making, a plea for experience of the center rather than experience at the polar extremes. See Rice's "The Merging Parallels: Mann's *Doctor Faustus,*" *Kenyon Review,* XI (1949), 199–217.

21. (Princeton, 1964), pp. 209–13.

22. See my discussion of Eliseo Vivas' terms, "subsistence," "insistence," and "existence" (from "The Object of the Poem," *Creation and Discovery* [New York, 1955], pp. 129–43), as I try to relate the poetic context to the existential context in *A Window to Criticism* (pp. 59–63, 214–15). "For it is this metaphor, this total substitution, that allows us to see what an historical moment, in the privacy of hidden, personal inwardness has, in its most daring creations, in the total metaphors of its single, reduced moments of vision, dared to make of its world."

23. "The Dismemberment of Orpheus," pp. 148–49.

Literature's Relation
to the World

Vladimir Nabokov, while teaching at Cornell University, would begin his first lecture of every term by saying, "Great novels are above all great fairy tales . . . literature does not tell the truth but makes it up." [1] This sounds like a joke, and typical of Nabokov's way with an audience, but he always means what he says, and the issue he propounds is perfectly serious. The question is whether literature recreates, renders, mirrors the world, or creates one of its own; whether it makes over or makes up the truth — experience, life, nature, reality, whatever it is we say exists in or constitutes the "world." And if most modern writers share one view on the question, it is, as William H. Gass has said, that "the esthetic aim of any fiction is the creation of a verbal world," and that the worlds literature creates "are only imaginatively possible ones; they need not be at all like any real one." The writer, Gass asserts, "is ceasing to pretend that his business is to render the world; he knows, more often now, that his business is to *make* one." [2] Literature is an activity of radical imaginative construction, not one of reflecting or making replicas of what exists or happens in life.

But how does this view affect literature's role *in* the world? Critics and readers have always liked to believe that literature is the supreme mode for making sense of the world. If now we grant it absolute autonomy, allow it to be isolated from the world, will we not risk losing the saving and redemptive powers by which literature gives meaning or savor or value to life? And will

we not end by handing literature over to all its enemies, fancied
or real, who have made art precarious enough in, as Yeats put it,
"this pragmatical, preposterous pig of a world"? We feel a duty
to protect the vocation, and the mystique attaching to it, which
contemporary writers seem bent on abdicating. Wallace Stevens, echoing the whole grand tradition of apologies for poetry
from Sidney to Shelley, declared that the poet's "role is to help
people live their lives." But if literature is fairy tales, or even
worse, a "game," as Gass calls it, how can the poet possibly perform that function? [3] What can literature do in the world? How
can it change our image of ourselves and the world? What is
left of its relation to politics, history, all the springs of action?
Can literature evade or ignore the existential realities of our personal, social, and cultural histories?

A. Alvarez and Donald Davie address these issues in "A New
Aestheticism?" Davie, who named the program, describes it as an
attempt to explore in poetry "the relation between the man who
makes it and the medium which he uses." Alvarez, while acknowledging the inadequacy of an exclusive concern with "the
relationship between the man and his society rather than his
medium," is afraid that a preoccupation with the medium is only
a dodge for "the medium concerned with itself," something narcissistic or solipsistic, rather than engaging what he thinks to be
the real business of poetry: "all one's anxieties and tensions and
the general mess one has to come to terms with in life." Davie
counters by saying that Alvarez holds that the only reality "is the
human reality, the social reality, the psychological reality,"
whereas he would include other things in or about the world
enjoyed, made over, or made up for themselves.[4] Alvarez keeps
burrowing at the point that literature cannot be about itself, its
own medium of words or literary forms, and he cites as an
example the case of Ezra Pound (the most notorious instance
since Oscar Wilde of the poet who ran afoul of society), who has
been masterful in his command of the medium of poetry, but
whose good poems "are all about literature"; he is a poet "who
reacts to literary occasions" only. The poet must be more than
skillful at his trade. It is absolutely impossible to avoid politics;
"the facts of history are too much." He must grapple with the
very difficult and very destructive forces of social change. Davie
believes, as Yeats said, that the poet has "no gift to set a statesman right." [5] But Alvarez will not be pinned to specific political
action. He wants the poet to be more responsive to the stresses of
the general social situation, serve as an "early warning system" of

impending menace, register the pressure of "things impinging on him as a man moving in society." The poet must make a statement, bear personal witness, reveal and commit himself. Davie, however, argues that the "self" is not something ready made and imposed on the medium; the poet finds himself "in the process of writing the poem." Alvarez agrees, yet he insists that the occasions for this self-discovery must not be strictly literary, but like his own attempt to write a poem about a visit to Auschwitz. Although the poem did not refer to anything specific in history, it did represent his response to the "great ugliness, and pain in the nature of all our experience," the existential agony memorialized forever by the fact of the extermination camp. Davie, on the other hand, wants to relieve the human relation of "all the enormous weight of anxiety and responsibility" that Alvarez wants to put upon it and get into literature.

The argument shuttles back and forth, the two critics defining and qualifying their terms and positions as they go, without coming to any clear conclusion. It is, after all, a conversation, and, more than that, closer to the actual give-and-take of critical argument than the putative model of the adversary proceeding of actions at law, where each advocate offers a measured brief of his position. Alvarez and Davie enact the process of critical exchange F. R. Leavis describes as "This is so, or not so, but . . ." (p. 577). And that may be as valuable to the onlooker as the stands they take. We want to plunge into the talk ourselves, perhaps to ask, as Richard Poirier does of the argument of literature's relevance to historical catastrophes (p. 569), whether Alvarez isn't operatic in his pronouncements; or to ask, following Frederick Crews's discussion of the human relation (p. 533), whether Davie isn't too timid or inhibiting in his sense of a writer's traumatic experiences. Or we may want to ask whether both critics don't assume a conception of the self that the French structuralists have challenged as being a romantic fiction (p. 18). The point is that Alvarez and Davie incite inquiry, as all spirited talk will, and if we are left wondering whether they have settled anything, that may be less important than their having given us a sharper awareness of the complexity of the issues and a livelier sense of the need to scrutinize the assumptions of our assertions about literature's relation to the world.

Frank Kermode, in *Romantic Image* (whose first chapter, "The Artist in Isolation," is included here),[6] traces the origins of the conception of literature as an act of making up worlds to the ideas of certain nineteenth-century writers, artists, and critics. The doctrine, as he calls it, of the Romantic Image had two aspects: a belief in the Image "as a radiant truth out of space and time," and a conception of the artist as "different, isolated from society," but, by virtue of his isolation and his finer aesthetic sensibilities, superior as a prophet, visionary, or magician. These artists disavowed any desire "to instruct or change the world," but they insisted "upon the moral value of what is highly organised and profoundly apprehended, in life and art." Indeed, even in such extreme forms as the aestheticism of Walter Pater, art was not really detached from life; it was thought of as "life at its most intense and significant." Deliberately withdrawing from purposeful action, hostile to science and rational discourse or inquiry, and aristocratic in advocating "the privileged moment" of the aesthetic experience (if not necessarily in their politics, for the writers covered the whole spectrum of political persuasions), they looked on art as the supreme mode of making the world intelligible.

The theory that emerged from these convictions Kermode calls "the Romantic-Symbolist aesthetic," and he argues that it has shaped the main tradition of twentieth-century literature and criticism in English. He has elsewhere described twentieth-century "Symbolist criticism" (and in terms similar to those used by Denis Donoghue in his essay on Yeats in Part III), as comprising the following beliefs: "A poem is an anonymous and autonomous verbal structure; literal meaning cannot be rendered in other words; literary form is spatial; the intention is defined in the text." [7] Kermode attributes these articles of belief directly to "the Romantic-Symbolist heritage" of the nineteenth century.

The Romantic-Symbolist aesthetic Kermode describes is virtually identical with that of the American New Criticism. In fact, the New Critics were bedeviled by the charge of being successors to the "art for art's sake" of Walter Pater and Oscar Wilde. No matter how strenuously they tried to shake the label off, over and over again they had to answer the accusation that, as Joseph Frank has put it, they "were a group of myopic Formalists who wished to remove literature to some ethereal realm unsullied by contact with the grosser realities of life and history." Frank, however, argues that their emphasis on formalism was more a polemical exaggeration than a doctrine held absolutely, the result of their battles with Marxist or Marxist-influenced opponents during the 1930's as well as with the academic champions of historical positivism:

Faced with the attempt to appropriate literature for purely social and propagandistic purposes, it was only natural for the New Critics, defending the autonomy and integrity of art, to exaggerate and overemphasize its purity and independence from immediate social and political concerns.[8]

But the last thing that can be said of the New Critics is that they were "aesthetes" in any strict sense. None of them would ever say as Wilde did, turning the question of literature's relation to the world on its head, that nature imitates art. Although the New Critics shared with critics such as Pater and Wilde a conviction in the autonomy of art and its uniqueness as a mode of knowledge, they had no use for "pure" poetry or exquisite rarefactions of passion. They were sternly cognitive in their conception of poetry.

W. K. Wimsatt, for example, has made the issue of literature's relation to the world principal in his critical theories. He points out that the question begins with the argument between Plato and Aristotle over the conception of poetry, and art generally, as imitation, *mimēsis*. Plato held that literature, by imitating the sensible appearance of things in nature, is at least two removes from the reality of what he called "the Ideas" (so that, in Plato's example, the artist who paints a bed imitates the beds we actually see and sleep in, but these are only copies of the "real" or ideal bed). In return, Aristotle argued that literature is an imitation in words of human action, passion, and character. If a poet utters technical inaccuracies about the pace of a horse or about medicine or any other art, Aristotle says in the *Poetics*, the error is not essential to the poetry, and if he does not know that a doe has no horns, this is less serious than if he portrays the doe "inartistically," "indistinctly," "unimitatively," or "unrecognizably" — *amimētōs*. Wimsatt says that Aristotle is here "defining a circle of paradox (or contradiction) within which literary theory has ever since that time continued to move." This is "the double difficulty," Wimsatt explains,

> of poetry in relation to the world, and of criticism in relation to value — the so-far irreducible critical experiences: that literature is both more lively and less lifelike than the real world (this impossible pig of a world); that criticism cannot demonstrate value but is at the same time inescapably concerned with trying to do so.[9]

Wimsatt's own attempt to contain the paradox and solve its difficulties, and the general attempt of the New Criticism, has been to divide the relation into the "truth of correspondence" and the "truth of coherence," so that while the truth-value of discourses other than literature is measured by the correspondence of its statements to what is verifiable in the external world, the truth-value of literature is measured by the coherence of its words within the particular context established by the containing form of the literary work. In ordinary uses of language, such as talk, as well as in such discursive discourse as philosophical argument, words function as "referential" propositions; they point outward to meanings fixed or identified by some external frame of reference. In literature words function "contextually"; they point inward to the particular significations fashioned by the framing context. In this sense literature is a "closed" rather than "open" form of discourse. Criticism, Wimsatt asserts, is concerned with "saying" and "making," the first of which, with its complementary term "seeing," is Platonic or Romantic and is concerned with meanings; the second is Aristotelian and is concerned with structures. The special character of poetry or imaginative literature, Wimsatt concludes, is "a tensional unity of making with seeing and saying." Art or poetry is the peculiar situation where we perceive each member "only in or through its opposite: making through saying and saying through making." [10]

Any affinities, then, between the New Critics and the nineteenth-century proponents of "art for art's sake" have to be scrupulously qualified if they are not to be pointless or deceiving. (Affinities can be as bewitching as they are easy to manufacture in criticism. Both Kant and Oscar Wilde believed that "all art is quite useless," but there is something funny about placing the two men in the same sentence.) Moreover, there is even less cause for accusing the New Criticism of trying "to isolate the aesthetic fact from its human content" (p. 161). Wimsatt and the New Critics generally have wanted literature to be thought of as a closed rather than open form, not to seal off whatever it is that we call "life," but to seize, shape, and hold the human experience that went into its making (and is released in our reading) in the most meaningful, complex, and enduring "tensional unity."

Contemporary critics have assailed the theory of the New Criticism less for its supposed tendency to aestheticism and "art for art's sake" than its profession of the privileged or unique character of literature. Literature is not the only activity of "making through saying and saying through making." We do that in talk, and, to a degree, in all forms of discourse. Leo Bersani showed in Part I how the French structuralists have been exploring the general process of "making sense" in all modes of verbal activity. William H. Gass says fiction is a game, but so is philosophy, and these are only two of the vast number of "language games." Northrop Frye, even though he conceives of literature as an autonomous order of words, has expanded that order to include all manner of works besides the kinds of poems, plays, or novels to which the New Critics would restrict the privileged status of literature.

Perhaps the most provocative attack on the theoretical foundations of the New Criticism has come from a challenge of its assumption that literature achieves the form and order which is lacking in life. Leo Bersani says that formalist criticism generally holds the view that literature is "a triumph of reason and order over a formless 'source' called life"; life is chaotic and incoherent to our ordinary experience (p. 91). Bersani, however, contends that we all create "intelligible structures as a way of interpreting the world." Many of our activities, dreams for example, we render in "a tautology of beautifully and absurdly intelligible structures." It is, he says, more common and natural than otherwise "to spatialize the world in fixed patterns." Richard Poirier has developed the same notion. "Life," he asserts,

> even before the novelist proposes to represent it, exists, it would seem, in the conditions and shapes imposed upon it by art, by the pastoral, allegorical, epic, narrative, political imaginations, all as much as by the myths and rituals that are the accompaniment of nationality and religion.[11]

Frank Kermode has offered the most ambitious treatment of this idea in his book, *The Sense of an Ending.* He shows "the way we try to make sense of our lives," "the way we make sense of the world," by employing structural devices large and small; plots that give beginning, middle, and end to our lives; metaphorical conceptions, such as "apocalypse," by which we interpret human history and the nature of the external world — in short, the whole repertory of fictions critics ordinarily confine to literature. We all use fictions to confer organization and meaning on the contingencies of experience, Kermode contends; they are anything but unique to literature.

In this view the function of literature is not simply to give order and value to life, to make sense of the world, but to unstabilize and unsettle the fictions and structures by which we ordinarily live; to expose the paucity or falsity of the roles we have chosen to invent (as images of our desires and needs) or have been conditioned to wear; and, more positively, to enlarge our sense of what is imaginatively conceivable. Kermode says of *King Lear* that we are never in danger of thinking that the death of Lear is true. But neither is it just an image of the fiction we make of how we think our lives will or should end. We are shocked by the play. If we respond to it well "the gain is that we shall never quite resume the posture towards life and death that we formerly held." And "in changing ourselves" — for it is ourselves, Kermode says, we are encountering whenever we invent or read fictions — "we have, in the best possible indirect way, changed the world." [12]

Jorge Luis Borges, in "Partial Enchantments of the *Quixote*" in this section, goes as far as possible in collapsing the boundaries between literary fictions and life by saying that if the characters in a story can be readers or spectators, as happens when Don Quixote is made to be a reader of his own novel and Hamlet a spectator of his play, "then we, their readers and spectators, can be fictitious." Borges's verbal magic, like Nabokov's, is not to everyone's taste, and his conundrum may strike some as just juggling words, a studied perplexity not nearly so profound or entertaining as the puzzle cases philosophers have invented, but it makes perfect sense as literary criticism if we take him to mean that such inversions as occur in *Don Quixote* and *Hamlet* unsettle the illusion of fictionality we interpose as a barrier between literature and life.[13] Bersani says that the distinctness of the object in literary criticism is "an illusion created by the distance we arbitrarily put between ourselves and the work, a distance which makes it possible for us to think of our systematic interpretations of life as epistemological certainties." Borges, in this essay and in his own marvelously riddling fictions, confounds both the illusion of distance between life and art and the certainties by which we think we live.

E. H. Gombrich, in his essay, "Meditations on a Hobby Horse or the Roots of Artistic Form," by asking whether we should describe an ordinary hobby horse as the image of a horse or as a substitute of some kind, considers the main theories of the image-making process and of the relation between image and reality in the plastic arts from Plato to the present. He makes it quite clear why any attempt to think of the image as at all like "a photograph of a pre-existing reality is to misunderstand the whole process of image-making." There is, he says, no such thing as "an innocent eye." No painter can look at, and re-create nature directly; he has to work with received images, forms, or schemata that he may then adapt or modify. "Ours is a structured universe," Gombrich contends, "whose main lines of force are still bent and fashioned by our biological and psychological needs." Art reflects these needs and structures rather than the given form of external objects. And a primary source for the invention of the artistic forms that perform these symbolic functions, indeed the very starting point for most artistic creations, is the repertory of basic forms conceived by previous artists. As Heinrich Wölfflin put the principle: "All pictures owe more to other pictures than they do to nature."

This is, as we have seen, the concept on which Northrop Frye has based his theory of the autonomy of literature: Literature is made out of prior literature, not life. One of Frye's most direct treatments of literature's relation to the world is in his essay, "Nature and Homer." The writer, he says, creates "a second nature," which is separate from, rival to, although dependent upon the visible world of nature. A poem is an imitation of other poems rather than of "nature, life, reality, experience, or whatever is being shaped." The relation of art to nature "is not an external relation of reproduction to model, but an internal relation of form to content. Art does not reflect nature; it contains nature, for the essence of content is to be contained." [14] Hence, in literature, nature and Homer are the same.

All the same we find it extremely difficult, as Gombrich acknowledges, "to rid ourselves of the prejudice that all images should be 'read' as referring to some imaginary or actual reality," and we persist in making the kind of "existential projection" Frye has tried to reason us out of — especially in the case of the characters of fiction. No element of literature puts our theories of literature's relation to the world to a harder test. With the novel and with the characters of novels we find we have to grapple with the real complexities and perplexities of that relation (which happens as well when we try to deal with the presence of the human voice in poetry), and these are the problems William H. Gass engages in "The Concept of Character in Fiction."

On one hand, we have been schooled by the American New Critics, by Northrop Frye, by the French structuralists, by just about everyone in modern criticism, to regard a character in a novel as a strictly verbal construction existing in a certain structural field.[15] He has no life apart from the world constituted by the words and verbal actions of the story. The primary requirement is that he satisfy the truth of coherence rather than of correspondence; he must act "in character." Gass shows with elaborate and precise detail why it is impossible to consider a literary character as anything like a real person. And behind his view of the specific functioning of character in fiction is his argument that "the so-called life one finds in novels is nothing like actual life at all." He deplores, in fact, the sentimentalizing of "the supreme values of fiction" insofar as they are based on the belief that literature renders the world. The "tragic view of life" in all, even the greatest, literature, he says brusquely, "is not one jot as pure and penetratingly tragic as a pillow stuffed with Jewish hair."

On the other hand, we stubbornly cling to the conviction that the creation of character, "to fasten in the memory of the reader, like a living presence, some bright human image," is the whole art of fiction. We go on believing, despite the skepticism critics have admonished, that "great character is the most obvious single mark of great literature," or, as Geoffrey H. Hartman puts it (in "Toward Literary History"), that one "function of art is to create character-types of universal or general appeal." We insist on thinking of the human presence as the most compelling of all that the novelist invents with his words.

All very well and good, Gass argues, so long as we do not demand that characters in fiction look, think, and behave as people do in life. He uses the figure of a striding statue in explanation. Our eye travels along its outstretched arm and pointing finger "only to the finger's end," which bids us to stay and "journey slowly back along the tension of the arm," rather than beyond, for what actually surrounds the statue is "empty space and silence." A novelist, unlike the philosopher or any ordinary user of language, does not invite "us to pass through his words to his subject"; "if he is any good, [he] will keep us kindly imprisoned in his language." [16]

Gass's own concept of character is that it is "the primary substance" in the fictional world, whose qualities are verbal rather than existential. "Characters," he says, "are those primary substances to which everything else is attached." They are like the primary substances of the empirical world as the grounds for experience, but because they are different in what they organize and constitute, they achieve quite different effects. And the characters of fiction fascinate us because "unlike ourselves, freed from existence," they "can shine like essence, and purely Be."

Gass is close enough to the conceptions of language, meaning, and being associated with the New Criticism to be open to many of the same misgivings several contemporary critics have registered against it, but when he analyzes how characters are created and the manner of their workings, as in his treatment of Mr. Cashmore in James's *The Awkward Age*, he opens new possibilities for the criticism of "fiction and the figures of life."

Georg Lukács's "The Ideology of Modernism" is the polar opposite to Gass's essay. Lukács treats literature in terms of an adamantine realism. The characters of literature, he says flatly, are "a description of actual persons inhabiting a palpable, identifiable world." And because characters inescapably represent the way the world looks to their creators, it is "the view of the world, the ideology or *weltanschauung* underlying a writer's work, that counts" in literature and in literary criticism. In all great realistic literature the characters "cannot be distinguished from their social and historical environment. Their human significance, their specific individuality cannot be separated from the context in which they were created." They faithfully mirror the objective social and historical reality. The great realist writers portray the world as it actually and truly is. By contrast, the most influential modern writers such as Joyce or Beckett, Lukács argues, have severed the connection between the mind and the world; they are "subjectivistic" and portray their own moods and imaginings. The images of man they represent are alienated, rootless, pathological, antihumanistic, abstractly subjective. Some writers have resisted this tendency and continued the realistic tradition: Mann, Conrad, Shaw, Sholokhov. Lukács has praised Mann, for example, as "an extreme type of the writer whose greatness lies in being a 'mirror of the world' " [17] — the very metaphor, one of the oldest for describing literature's relation to the world, that Gass tries to discredit.

Few literary critics outside of the orbit of Lukács's Marxist ideology would agree with his judgments of the most influential modern writers. Lukács appears to be just the kind of critic the American New Critics battled against in their defense of literature. He seems to exemplify their worst fears of what would happen if modern literature were to be judged and made captive by the criteria of political, social, or philosophical ideologies: the work of art would become nothing in or by itself, only a representative of a *weltanschauung;* its functions would be narrowed to what was acceptable or desirable according to the ideology; its value would be adjudicated by ideologues rather than literary critics. But Lukács was no party hack. Nor were his literary opinions simply crude applications of political dogma. His specifically literary judgments were contained within an overarching political and philosophical system, but he was hardly lacking in literary sensibility and he made many acute critical observations about literature. He was a participant in the business of politics, an ideologist and propagandist for the Communist party, a philosopher whose specialty was aesthetics, as well as a literary critic, and these activities were all of a piece, in the fashion of the Central European intellectual tradition. Hence, it would be misleading to say that one activity presided over and dictated the rest.[18]

The "subjectivist modernism" Lukács condemns so violently in literature he saw as corresponding to the philosophical doctrine of "subjective idealism," originating with Kant and his followers, which spawned the "romantic intuitionism" of Nietzsche and others that led to or became the rationale for the intellectual and political madness of the Third Reich. Realism, Lukács's version of "dialectical materialism," was the only saving alternative to this catastrophic procession of ideas and events. Realism affirms that human thought represents an objective world independent of the mind, not one that is "constituted" by our mental apparatus. As George Lichtheim has explained:

> For Lukács everything turns upon the recognition of one single central truth: realism in art (like realism in philosophy) *portrays* the world, in the sense that — however complex the formal mediations employed in the process — it enables men to perceive their own true nature.[19]

Lukács's realism was not a simple pictorial naturalism — he was never party to the demand for so-called socialist or proletarian realism — for that reflects only surface phenomena. The artistic imagination is creative, autonomous, universal, but it is not self-centered and capricious, except in "subjectivist" writers.

> What the artistic imagination brings forth is not a private world, but an ordered whole ultimately rooted in mankind's collective experience. In this sense art "reflects" a reality, but this reality is not one of "facts"; neither is it one of mere "feelings." Art is the mirror-image of an "objective" realm of values, or in different language, it states a truth about the world.[20]

And more than that: literature can change the world, not in the indirect fashion Frank Kermode mentions in connection with *King Lear*, but immediately, because it has the power to shape the reader's consciousness of what the world ought to be.

Whatever we may think of these ideas, and they are distinctly against the grain of most selections in this anthology, we cannot toss them aside simply for being ideological or doctrinaire. "Ideology" is suspect in the American and English intellectual tradition, but it follows from Lukács's sense of the term that no matter how remote or concealed the ideological bases of criticism may seem, they are there, if not explicitly, then in the assumptions we make of what literature is or should do. The American New Criticism, for example, was constructed on precisely the "subjective idealist" doctrines of Kant, Schiller, and Coleridge (as Murray Krieger points out on pp. 589 ff.) that Lukács so implacably opposed. If Lukács is to be answered on his terms, it must be by attempting to reconcile or dissolve the dichotomy between subject and object by the New Critics and the critics of consciousness; or by using an alternative philosophical tradition, based on the Anglo-American philosophy shaped by Ludwig Wittgenstein, which is behind Gass's essay; or by Frye's attempt to legislate against extraliterary presuppositions; — and so on through all the other attempts by critics represented here to probe the philosophical bases of literature and literary criticism.

But how much business does literary criticism have with issues and arguments of this kind? Is it necessary to meet Lukács on his own ground? Criticism is always in danger of losing its distinction as an activity by being engulfed in matters outside of its scope and competence. The literary critic may be less able than the philosopher, say, to defend or confute what Nabokov and Borges affirm about literature's relation to the world, but he can show, as no one else can so well, how these writers enact their belief in their fiction. How far, then, should he depart from what is observable in the literary performance? John Crowe Ransom, in urging literary critics to master philosophy, said a critic has the advantage of being "intimate with the immediate pulsing fact which is his poem," and any excursion he makes outside his field can never leave "his own experience" of the poem too far behind.[21] What made R. P. Blackmur so profoundly skeptical of systematic criticism, however, was the very seductiveness of "substituting intellectual formulae for experience" in delving into explanations of the being and performance of the poem.[22] From this outlook, the best way to answer Lukács's strictures against the world-view of the characters in Beckett's fiction, for instance, would be to follow Gass's example in attentively and lovingly exploring how a character actually performs in a given novel or play. Bringing the work to full performance in such fashion would be as much as criticism can or needs to show what literature does for us and how it can help us to lead our lives.

Hans Magnus Enzensberger, in "The Aporias of the Avant-Garde," icily dismisses Lukács's judgments about modern writers as "reactionary criticism" — no less so than that of the political Right, and just as menacing when there is a police power to enforce its critical opinions. In totalitarian regimes "the harmless tug of war about the avant-garde . . . assumes murderous traits." But Enzensberger does not spare democratic regimes his recriminations, for in neocapitalist societies, he says, reactionary criticism has its own techniques for exercising censorship, exploiting literature, and making life difficult for writers. All the custodians — Left, Right, and Center — of what is proper in art and good for society, who represent themselves as "the healthy forces of preservation" of the "beautiful, sane, and constructive," Enzensberger declares, are incompetent to criticize the avant-garde: Every work of art "deserves to be defended against its suppressors."

Enzensberger's main purpose, however, is to investigate and expose "the aporias of the avant-garde, its concept, its assumptions, and its postures." He is minute, almost pedantic, in his examination of the term and its doctrines, and he is scathing about what he considers to be the charlatanry of contemporary artists who pass themselves off as avant-garde. What seems to vex him most is that they seek to gain, easily and safely, the rewards and honors, even the profits, of being daring and iconoclastic, which genuine artists earn only by solitary toil, real sacrifice, and unostentatious risk. Indeed, Enzensberger's essay may be seen as a treatment, both literal and figurative, of the *costs* of making art. The concept of experiment, he says for example, "is to insure against the risk of all esthetic production." His concern is less that the avant-garde threatens the formal integrity of art, which is René Wellek's anxiety (p. 21), than that it *cheapens* aesthetic production. Enzensberger is particularly interesting in discussing how "the consciousness industry," as he calls it, exploits, promotes, and manipulates the avant-garde movement, its producers, and its consumers. The effect of these business operations, motivated by the desire of "making it" in the commercial rather than the artistic sense, has been to render literature spurious or at least uniquely problematical for writers and readers alike.

Enzensberger's disparagement of the present-day avant-garde

should be compared with Ihab Hassan's treatment (pp. 149–50). Enzensberger is well aware of the dangers of condemning individual writers by their group affiliations or doctrinal proclamations, but he stoutly urges using critical judgment to unmask the frauds and fakes. Hassan, on the other hand, suggests that critics might be better occupied with trying to understand and catch up with what the avant-garde is doing. Worse than being beguiled would be to miss the real point of their doctrines. Some doctrines of the avant-garde have become the working principles for genuine as well as counterfeit art, and it is next to impossible to separate the idea from the product. The notion, for example, that "modernism means not the enrichment, but the negation of art," which Lukács concludes is what is wrong with literature, has become the positive manifesto of the current avant-garde. The idea that art is "de-creative" is a compelling motive for what is happening in contemporary literature.[23] And as a working principle the negation or de-creation of art has been practiced in varying degrees, modes, and forms, both straight and parodistic, grave and sportive, from Hassan's example of "a novel about a novel which cancels itself in the very act of reading" to Enzensberger's example of the painter who contrived his work as something to be obliterated on the spot. Now it would be easy enough to show the aporias, the muddles or contradictions, of such a credo — for how can something negate what it offers itself as being? — but this kind of analysis, Hassan's argument runs, is less productive than if we take the credo at its face value, try to respond to the art that issues from those who profess it, and investigate the consequences of its view for the aporias, concepts, assumptions, and postures of the art and the criticism against which it is directed.

Lukács and Enzensberger are concerned with literature's relation to history, but their perspective does not differentiate the writer from other men, whereas Geoffrey H. Hartman, in "Toward Literary History," proposes to explore the possibilities of "history from the point of view of the poets." He does not mean to undertake anything like the positivistic literary history that the New Critics deposed: the facts about a poet's life and contacts, or about the provenience and publication of a poet's texts. Nor does Hartman mean to keep strictly to the kind of documentary history that inquires into literature's relation to the contexts of "race, moment, and milieu," to use the famous formulation of Hippolyte-Adolphe Taine's *History of English Literature* (1863), that

is, according to the national character, the character of a particular segment of time, and the general social and cultural
environment. And although Hartman is preoccupied with form
in literature, he does not mean to restrict himself to the history
of the life of forms in art, the progress of such literary conventions or genres as the ode or the pastoral. He is interested in
what poets have made in their poetry of their encounters with
history, and, even more specifically, with "their consciousness
of the historical vocation of art." [24]

But how shall we describe "history," the term on which all
these relations hinge? That is as thorny a question, and as remote
from doing criticism, as the issues of language, meaning, and
being which surround literature's relation to reality, but some
rudimentary observations may help in following the intricate
course of Hartman's argument. We may think of history as the
unfolding of events or phenomena through time in a linear,
continuous, natural fashion; or, alternatively, we may think of
phenomena in history as encapsulated rather than contiguous,
existing, as it were, with a life of their own in spatialized patterns. A basic difference between so-called historicist criticism
(which can range from the positivistic concern with the facts of
literary history to the study of "race, moment, and milieu") and
structuralist criticism (which can range from the practice of
linguistically oriented critics to Roland Barthes and to Northrop
Frye) is that the former is "diachronic" and the latter "synchronic" in its procedures. These are the terms made famous
by the linguist Saussure, and they are discussed by Roland
Barthes (p. 123) and F. W. Bateson (p. 504). Synchronic
modes of criticism isolate certain phenomena from the stream of
history, screening all the other events that act upon them, in
order to study their structural properties. It is not quite that one
is historical and the other ahistorical, one dynamic and dialectical, the other systematic and static. Synchronic criticism
concentrates on the dialectical progress within a specific field of
phenomena.

Northrop Frye's criticism may help to clarify the point. Frye
says in the "Polemical Introduction" (Part I) that *Anatomy
of Criticism* originated as an attempt to annotate T. S. Eliot's
principle that the existing monuments of literature form an ideal
order among themselves, which he announced in his 1919 essay,
"Tradition and the Individual Talent": "The historical sense
compels a man to write . . . with a feeling that the whole of
the literature of Europe from Homer and within it the whole of

the literature of his own country has a simultaneous existence and composes a simultaneous order." [25] In other words, all the important events of literary history are part of a single synchronous totality. Frye explains in "The Critical Path: An Essay on the Social Context of Literary Criticism" that he, too, "wanted a historical approach to literature" — but this approach had to be "a genuine history of literature, and not the assimilating of literature to some other kind of history." Accordingly, he has studied the conventions, genres, and archetypes of literature as generative forms that are, he says, "even stronger than history." These forms change in history, they undergo dialectical development, but they are not determined by history. Literature, Frye affirms, is "a unified, coherent and autonomous created form, historically conditioned but shaping its own history, not determined by any external historical process."

The trouble with Frye's conception of literary history, Hartman contends, is that it excludes too much of the concrete reality of the other kinds of history as they impinge upon the consciousness of writers. Hartman says that Frye's "idea of literary history is certainly abstract: not only less sweaty than Marxist literary history, but also less concrete than most scholarly versions."

Hartman goes on to consider other theories of artistic form, including those of the French structuralists and the American New Critics, and from these he takes what he thinks is useful in developing his own "theory linking the form of the medium to the form of the artist's historical consciousness." His conditions for such a theory are that it respect the autonomy of art; that it be clean of any elitist assumptions about literature of its role in society; that it be responsive to the temper of contemporary art, which seeks "to create a truly iconoclastic art, a structure-breaking art, to change the function of form from reconciliation and conservation to rebellion, and so to participate in the enormity of present experience"; and that it be based on the idea "that literary form is functional, and that its function is to keep us functioning," but at the same time it must be "a theory of *literary* form as well as *functional* form, i.e., one which "makes the theory specifically relevant to literature." Hartman's solution is to encompass literary or cultural history by the relation of the genius of an author and the genius of his particular age to the genius of art. By the genius of art he means the traditions, the whole order of art; all "the past masters" of literature; its synchronous totality. And in Hartman's view, "the artist's struggle with his vocation — with past masters and the 'pastness' of art in modern society" is a version "of a universal human struggle: of genius with Genius, and genius with *genius loci* (spirit of place)." The language of this sentence makes it clear how he differs from Eliot and Frye, though he otherwise appears to be fairly close to them. Hartman wants to bring literature and literary criticism to a more direct, concrete, and dialectical relation with history as poets past and present feel and engage it.

Erich Auerbach's *Mimesis* (whose first chapter, "Odysseus' Scar," is included here) draws together many issues of literature's relation to the world in a memorable critical performance. He revives and gives a new meaning to the concept of imitation, he is concerned with the representation of reality in literature, and he is inspired by a sense of history, literary and other kinds. Auerbach was one of a quartet — along with Karl Vossler, E. R. Curtius, and Leo Spitzer — of great German literary scholars in Romance philology, and one of the best practitioners of philological stylistics, but his formalism was not of the kind contemporary critics have been trying to reach beyond. Indeed, Auerbach approaches as closely as any modern critic has to the ideal of "the great interpreter" Hartman describes in "Beyond Formalism"; in his criticism "the human content of art" and "its formal properties" are "caught and exposited as one thing."

Auerbach's procedure in this chapter is typical. He compares the scene from Book 19 of the *Odyssey* where Euryclea, the old nurse of Odysseus, recognizes him at his homecoming by a scar on his thigh, with the account in Genesis 22:1 of the sacrifice of Isaac by Abraham, and by analyzing the opposed modes of style by which the episodes are rendered, reveals the sense of reality and history each work represents or "imitates."

Auerbach saw history in both its synchronic and diachronic aspects. He examined literature in relation to an idea of history as a kind of eternal Platonic state despite constant change (an idea expressed by the early eighteenth-century Neapolitan philosopher Giambattista Vico, for whose work Auerbach had a special admiration and affection), and at the same time he showed literature responding to social and economic forces in a fashion not that unlike Georg Lukács's historicist criticism.

The same combination, which René Wellek says may in fact have been a contradiction, is evident in Auerbach's conception of realism.[26] On one hand he exhibits a kind of existential realism, the revelation of reality in moments of ultimate risk and choice, as when Abraham is about to sacrifice Isaac. And on the other, Auerbach portrays the reality of a particular culture, time, and place, as when he relates the dramatistic actions of Euryclea in her encounter with Odysseus to her status as a slave in the feudal aristocracy of the world of the Homeric poems.

But more important than these conceptions or contradictions (which may be clarified and, if need be, resolved by consulting *Mimesis*, his study of Dante, and, especially, his essay on "Figura"),[27] and certainly more compelling, is the luminosity and mastery of Auerbach's critical performance — the way he makes the texts come alive in his and our reading, and the dimensions he adds to our understanding of literature's relation to the world.

Walter Benjamin's political imagination was as large, fine, and adventurous as Auerbach's historical imagination — and just as aesthetic. A Marxist critic who shared many of Lukács's ideological views, he was more independent in his political affiliations if not in his political ideas, and he was much more sensitive to the essential ingredients that make ideology "specifically relevant to literature." Like Lukács, Benjamin was troubled by the problematic nature of art, though the reasons for his disquiet are closer to those that are reflected in Hartman's essay than in Lukács's.

Benjamin begins "The Storyteller: Reflections on the Works of Nikolai Leskov," by saying (with the same plaintive note of "Virgilian regret" Hartman remarks in Auerbach's *Mimesis*) that "the art of storytelling is coming to an end," a casualty of all the social, economic, and historical forces that have "diminished the ability to exchange experiences." The dying out of storytelling is, Benjamin suggests,

> a concomitant symptom of the secular productive forces of history, a concomitant that has quite gradually removed narrative from the realm of living speech, and at the same time is making it possible to see a new beauty in what is vanishing.

The beauty of what is vanishing, a love of what is passing away, shapes his musings, and it is almost as if he would fan it back to life by the ardor of his words and the force of his affection. The qualities he attributes to storytelling — handing counsel, sharing companionship, showing the look and feel of experience, staying the nullity of death, keeping memory alive, carrying the

sound and presence of the human voice — are made so immediate and attractive by his critical performance that we are
inspired, better than by any direct exhortation, to preserve
what remnants of storytelling we can and to celebrate any new
writer who tries in his fiction to be faithful to their memory.
Compared to the views of fiction in William H. Gass's essay,
Benjamin's convictions seem old-fashioned, although not, perhaps, sentimental, for he had too tough a sense of the world for
anything softer than tenderness.

Benjamin's essay is probably dullest on the qualities of fiction
where Gass is brightest. Hartman, discussing the French structuralist conception of myth following Lévi-Strauss, says that what
is lacking "are the qualities of storytelling that actually involve
us — tone, rhythm, humor, surprises, and displacements." These
are beautifully exhibited in Gass's criticism. Benjamin exhibits the
less purely formalistic aspects of the qualities essential to storytelling.

Not that Benjamin is indifferent to form in literature. Rather,
he is more interested in the textures of experience, the play of
sense and sense-impression in storytelling, than in the textures
of its language or the structures of its forms. He does make
several observations about genres, conventions, and archetypes,
even about myths and fairy tales, but, compared to Frye, for
instance, his vision is always directed toward the flow of time,
the concrete actions of change, the dialectical relation between
literature and other happenings in history. He has a very firm
and very clear sense of *genius loci*. And that consciousness of
the interanimation between literature and the world, combined
with Benjamin's awareness of the experiential qualities of
storytelling, suggests new possibilities for the criticism of fiction
and for criticism itself. Benjamin may have adumbrated a next
necessary step for criticism — one that may be in advance even
of the formalism beyond formalism that Hartman proposes.

But the authority of Benjamin's criticism derives less from
his ideology or any critical doctrine than from his tone, his own
voice, vibrant with so many of what Frost called "the sentence
sounds" of the imagination. The astonishing thing about Benjamin's essay is that as a critic he almost becomes the very storyteller he celebrates. Just as "a man listening to a story is in the
company of a storyteller," so Benjamin's listeners, his readers,
are caught up in what he tells, raptly attending to his own handing of counsel, sharing companionship, and all the other functions the true storyteller performs. That is only a fancy, of

course. Nothing so ingenious is necessary to appreciate his criticism, and besides it might contradict what he says about storytelling needing no explanation, conveying no information. But it is a pleasant fancy all the same. We have seen literary critics acting many roles in this anthology, each a function of criticism: advocate, judge, connoisseur, impresario, analyst, expositor, interpreter, ideologue — and now a storyteller. As Benjamin plays the part, it is a good role for critics.

A. ALVAREZ
DONALD DAVIE

A New Aestheticism?
A. Alvarez Talks to Donald Davie

ALVAREZ: You wrote recently an article called "Towards a New Aestheticism." I thought it was a very moving piece of prose but I wasn't quite sure in what direction it was moving. I wonder if you would like to explain yourself just a little bit.

DAVIE: Yes, well I hoped it would be moving towards a new aestheticism, since that is what I called it. I'm not really very serious about that, I don't think, but it does seem to me that some of the topics that interest me most in respect of poetry today are blocked because of a built-in prejudice against aestheticism and Art for Art's sake and Walter Pater. It so happens that for some years now I have been able to set my ideas in order about the poems I write and the poems of other people by thinking in terms of analogies between the different arts — how is poetry like music? How is poetry like sculpture? Now I don't argue that this is the one right and proper way to talk about poetry or that this gives you a truer version of poetry than any other. But the climate of literary opinion being what it is I seem to find that people won't even let me begin to talk this way. For this whole way of talking and thinking. . . .

ALVAREZ: I take it that you, at one point or another, came to the conclusion that poetry was an answer in itself and it seems to me that what you are trying to say in this idea of "Towards a New Aestheticism" is that there is no further answer other than the ones you can get in poetry, and the more self-enclosed poetry can be the more likely it is to be effective. Let me tell you a story. When I was an undergraduate at Oxford, an American — who shall be nameless — arrived in Oxford and went around saying "Poetry is the most important thing in the world and one

SOURCE: "A New Aestheticism? A. Alvarez Talks to Donald Davie" is reprinted from *The Modern Poet: Essays from "the Review,"* edited by Ian Hamilton, copyright © 1962 by A. Alvarez. Reprinted by permission of Robert Lantz–Candida Donadio Literary Agency, Inc.

646

must be professional about it." Well now, in the face of the kind of "frou-frou" that passed as a literary life in Oxford at that time this was marvellous. It seemed to me that I wanted to stand on the chairs and cheer. It seemed to me something very good, and almost rather brave to say. Well, I've seen the chap more or less ever since — less more recently. When I went to America about five years later, I found him ravaging around on the literary-political scene, with a wife and two kids, and an ice-box as big as Verlaine's garret, still saying that poetry is the most important thing in the world. It seemed ludicrous. He had simply never grown up. Now you don't mean that.

DAVIE: You've never heard me say that.

ALVAREZ: But you know what I mean. Are you implying that in this idea of a new aestheticism? What is your new aestheticism? Is it simply Walter Pater, or what is it?

DAVIE: No, I said in that article that what I call the new aestheticism is seeing poetry and all the arts — but poetry, since that is the one we are concerned with — in terms of the relation between the man who makes it and the medium which he uses. This — it seems to me — is what was valuable about Walter Pater and that climate of opinion. It seems to me a relation which is now no longer, or very seldom, considered in our talk about poetry.

ALVAREZ: Your implication in the article was that the only relationship which is considered now is the relationship between the man and his society rather than his medium. Well, now I agree with you that this is inadequate too; although I think it is less inadequate than you do. What I'm not sure about is to what extent you want to consider poetry as a relation between the man and his medium and to what extent you want to consider it simply in relation to the medium itself — to the medium concerned with itself.

DAVIE: This comes back to your earlier point which I didn't understand and still don't understand about "poetry is the answer." I ask: "the answer to what?"

ALVAREZ: Well, the answer to all one's anxieties and tensions and the general mess one has to come to terms with in life. . . .

DAVIE: Yes, well of course it isn't the answer for anyone, but in so far as one is a poet (and this, I suppose, is where the professionalism comes in), this is the particular answer that one is concerned with. It seems to me unnecessary, and I should think you'd agree with me, unnecessary and wrong — if this is the job you've taken on, and it's very difficult after all to write good poems — to be worrying all the time about the other answers which can be given in quite different terms from the ones you happen to have chosen. We all have our jobs to do.

ALVAREZ: But the point is that the job is a more complicated and responsible one than simply being a skilful writer. It's the job of living in society and being, as it were, a responsible grown up human being, isn't it? And something that says that the man must be sacrificed to the poem, to the discipline of art, seems to me nonsense, and seems, in a sense, a kind of childishness. To move smack into your domain: there is a kind of double talk that goes on apropos Ezra Pound — where can you separate Pound the craftsman from Pound the political juvenile delinquent? Now, he is a very good test case for he happens to have written some very beautiful poems — when he can forget about everything except poetry; he is very sensitive to language. But his grown-upness, his professionalism, functions on no other level, and as he is always bringing other levels into his poetry I think this is really debilitating.

DAVIE: Yes. Of course, I don't agree with this view of Pound. Here, oddly enough, it is I who am maintaining, as far as I see it, that technique and technical expertise cannot do as much as you claim that it can. You claim that sheer technical expertise in Pound, sheer feeling for the medium of language, can produce beautiful poems. This I would deny, you see.

ALVAREZ: I think he has produced some very beautiful poems but they are all about literature. And I don't just mean "Mauberley"; I mean the early Cantos, the first seven Cantos anyway; I mean "Propertius," where it's feeling for the literature of the past, for literary experience of the past. I mean, there he is, from Idaho — and suddenly literature looms into his life. He has all the reactions of a man from Idaho, except this fantastic enthusiasm and skill and ear, and sheer pleasure in using his ability — on that one subject. He reacts to literary occasions.

DAVIE: I still maintain that with all the skill, with all the delicate ear, with all the pleasure you take in sheer verbal manipulation you do not in this way get good poetry. A good poem is necessarily a response to a human situation. "Propertius," for example. "Propertius" is a response to the British Empire at a certain point of its decline, and all the literary manipulation is there deployed for that specific purpose; to register what it was like to be an American poet living in England at a time when he saw the British Empire tottering to its fall. Or so it seems to me.

ALVAREZ: I see this. But what is also in Pound is not just the pleasure in manipulation — I put that badly — I mean also this involvement with literature, this passion for literature, which is very much a whole passion, in which all his intelligence comes to work.

DAVIE: Well now, perhaps I can come half-way to meet you here, because I would certainly want to maintain very firmly that a man who has this sort of feeling for literature and for a literary use of language can, while operating upon that material, in fact transcend the limitations which he has in other circumstances. That is to say a man who is emotionally immature can, by dint of the passion which he has for literature, transcend his emotional immaturity for the sake of the poem which he is making. If you are going to say this is what Pound does, then I would be near to agreeing with you.

ALVAREZ: I think he does when he is writing well: but I think he only does when he is writing on literature — that's the tragedy of Pound — well, not on literature, but with some kind of literary occasion behind him; when it's a translation, or a reminiscence of classical myth, or something like that.

DAVIE: But why is this a tragedy? This is the way in which the body of achieved literature helps us now.

ALVAREZ: It's a tragedy because one feels that the occasions when you can do this are very rare. The occasions with Pound became rarer — because of the time he was living in — as his political involvements got more urgent. As a result there is a great mass of his writing which is plainly so much below the standard of what he could do.

DAVIE: Well, this is true, no doubt. Perhaps we had better face up quite frontally to this business of Pound's politics, which of course I deplore as much as you do. But don't you see, it seems to me that by and large the English are right not to trust poets and artists when they set themselves up as political sages and pundits. If you tick over on your fingers the political pronouncements of those whom we would agree to be the great poets of the past century, they are nearly all politically remarkably unreliable people; and if when you are asking that a poet should be responsible, you ask that he also be politically responsible then it seems to me you are asking for too much.

ALVAREZ: What you're really trying to say is that by some curious chemistry nearly all of the really important writers of our time, in fact of all times since Shelley anyway, have been on the Right, haven't they? It is almost impossible now for a good poet to be on the Right — since the rise and fall of the Third Reich. What do you get? You get Betjeman.

DAVIE: Yes. Yes. Still, all the same, I wouldn't accept your position on that, it is impossible for a good poet to be on the Right even in this country. I don't think that the history of poetry over the last hundred years gives you any sort of basis at all for the sort of correlation that you are making between political standpoint and poetic achievement. Poets in general do not have political good sense. That's all I'm saying.

ALVAREZ: No, but I think politics is the key issue, because I think that we are living in a kind of society where it is absolutely impossible to avoid them. The facts of history are too much. It's not a question of your having to adopt what Leavis called "cocktail party communism" or anything like that, as they did in the Thirties. It's something much more urgent. You can't just opt out of society like that, because you're in it for better or for worse, and no-one is going to fight your battles for you.

DAVIE: This I agree with, and I'm not in the least arguing that the poet should leave politics alone. In fact, the poems that I'm writing now are semi-political poems. But I wouldn't be able to write them if I felt that a peculiar responsibility was involved for me to be more sensible in the political conclusions I reached than the next man in the street.

ALVAREZ: No, I do agree with you there. But if I had an aesthetic myself — which I suppose I don't — it would be that phrase of Eliot's which I've worked to death: "The only method is to be very intelligent." I think if one goes around in the cloak-and-dagger of the intellectual, one should at least try to live up to it. It's very important to be as intelligent as one can, as tough-minded.

DAVIE: Yes, indeed. I would hope that in the political poems I write, the political issues I discuss are discussed, I hope, with more intelligence and at a deeper level of feeling and with more multifarious human connections, and all that. . . . I think that the quality of the exploration is important. It seems to me not different in fact from the position in respect of ethics too. Leavis and Leavisites are right to demand from writers an unusual degree and quality of moral concern. This is quite a different matter from supposing that the conclusions they come up with will be the right ones.

ALVAREZ: One's own training has been so much involved with Leavis — though he'd be the last person to want to have to claim any of us — nevertheless it seems to me the Leavisite position is no longer wholly tenable because the kind of concern that is involved depends on standards which seem no longer totally relevant in our present society.

DAVIE: Yes, I would agree.

ALVAREZ: Pottel, the Marxist critic in Leeds, or Sheffield, is it . . .?

DAVIE: You mean Kettle, actually.

ALVAREZ: Kettle, yes that's right. Not Pottel's Miscellany, Kettle's Miscellany. Kettle has said that the real trouble with Leavis is that he never came emotionally to recognise that the Industrial Revolution has taken place. This is presumably why there is this huge stress on Lawrence: because Lawrence, in a sense, has roots in pre-industrial revolution England, and wanted — and the older he grew the more exacerbated he grew, as in, you know, Lady Chat. — wanted to return to a world which hadn't been touched by the Industrial Revolution. And in the "Leavisite" — as distinct from Leavis who is very much more intelligent — this becomes a vague invocation of the Wheelwright's Shop and all the rest of the romanticised pre-industrial country. This is nothing to do with our society now. What I would like to do is to get my own position clear; and it is this: twice in the last few months I've been to Auschwitz — and if one had any kind of reaction — well it's a very difficult thing to cope with, as you know, but it gives one a new scale of values. There is a poem by Marianne Moore "On Poetry" which begins "I, too, dislike it. There are things that are important beyond all this fiddle." It seems to me that what happened in Auschwitz, and the other 130 concentration camps that were within the Reich, and that's happening in concentration camps in Russia and presumably in China and so on, is of an order that makes it very very important to, as it were, be sane about one's own identity, to be sure about one's own identity, because the whole movement of the concentration camps is the movement to destroy individuals, and towards the kind of efficiency that destroys art. One has simply got to say that the seeds of the concentration camps are in us all — we've all got these self-destructive tendencies, tendencies to give up, not to give up the fight, but simply to hand over your identity. And you can do it in all sorts of ways; you can do it in your personal life, you can do it in your working life. But to use the immortal words of E. E. Cummings: "There is some shit I will not eat." This is absolutely vital. One has got to be able to cope with one's society — its traps and shams. And one's aesthetics, as you call them, must follow that.

DAVIE: Well, they do more than follow that, they are that. We must be careful not to agree too much. I agree with everything you say and as far as I'm concerned the blank sheet on which I try to write my poems is precisely the battlefield on which I maintain my identity. I find it and maintain it.

ALVAREZ: No, I think we don't really agree, because my feeling is that you would say that the medium is the thing by which you discover your identity, that the medium is the thing on which one imposes or fights out one's identity.

DAVIE: Yes, this is a real difference between us. It seems to me you see the self that one is as something given that one has to fight through the barrier of language on to the paper. For me, I could cite authorities. . . .

ALVAREZ: Something given but at the same time in itself revealing — it's not given, it's not known, it's not worked out beforehand. I don't mean that at all.

DAVIE: Well, yes, this means you are nearer to what I would maintain which is that a dialogue ensues between the self that you are and the medium you are operating with. And what comes out of the marriage between — if you are lucky — the marriage between the self that you are or thought you were and the medium that you are operating with is the self that you truly are, you are finding your self in the process of writing the poem.

ALVAREZ: You are talking about your poetry. Let me do the same. When I went to Auschwitz, it was the most traumatic experience I've ever been though. Even now, it's still appalling. I tried to write a poem about it. I picked up the poem a couple of months later and it started changing, but it didn't come out. I recently drafted some kind of version, and completed it. There is no Auschwitz in it at all. There's nothing about the concentration camps at all. It has become a personal poem about loss. It does seem to me that the self-revealing nature of, you know, "What is the experience?" "How do I cope with it?" goes into the machinery of the self, sure, but it comes out quite different from what you'd expect. Where I think we differ is that I think one has to face that there is a great ugliness, and pain in the nature of all our experience. It's very difficult to go into the ivory tower. I think fundamentally my basic criticism of your attitude towards aestheticism is that — you know — you've got it easy because you are in Cambridge. I'll take this up though, in a moment. What one has to do is to get a language which is tough enough and clear enough, and pure enough. Not tough in an Allen Ginsberg way, but in a sort of unflinching way, in a facing what there is way, in facing what you don't want to have to recognise, which is done superbly by a poet, like, say, Robert Lowell who seems to me very much the best poet now writing. You create this language of the self, and it's a language very disciplined, highly disciplined, and it's got to be because one has not only got to write of oneself, one has also got to be intelligent about it.

DAVIE: Yes, well what I always feel in conversations like this, because this is not the first one we have had, is that in fact we do agree most of the time about the poems that we like. It's only when we try to find reasons that the different vocabularies we use make us seem to disagree, which is odd. I agree for instance that Lowell's poems from *Life Studies* onwards represent the best model in the English language that I know of — of poets roughly of our generation or my generation. All of this I would agree with. It was, oddly enough, in order to explain to myself what I saw as the remarkable distinction of — for instance — Lowell's poem "To the Union Dead" that I found myself going into something that interests me very much — I mentioned it earlier — this business of the analogy there is between poetry and the other arts. It was in relation to that poem that it seemed to me that I understood for the first time something of what is meant by poetry becoming like music. Now this is just my way of explaining to myself the distinction which I feel, the impression which it makes on me. The impression is the same in your case, I'm convinced, but you find a totally different vocabulary for it.

ALVAREZ: I think it's rather more than that. One of the bones of contention there has been between us a good deal is the poetry of Charles Tomlinson which I do not admire nearly as much as you, although I think actually his most recent poems — since his book — show a marked improvement. New depth and all this. You tend, aren't I right, to admire poetry which is concerned with the other arts. I tend

to admire poetry which is concerned with, . . . well . . . let me explain: Sydney Nolan was with me when I was last in Poland. As we
drove away from Auschwitz his comment was: "It's a bastard being human." You feel when you see the conditions — I'm sorry to come back to
this but it's very much on my mind — you see that it would not only be
better to be dead than to live like this but that it would be infinitely better
to be dead. Then you go into the chimney, the incinerator . . . well
. . . it's not simple. . . . It really is a bastard being human. It seems
to me that what one has to cope with in poetry — as I wrote in the introduction to this Penguin anthology, in which I refer to the "new seriousness" — is the ability to express the complexity, the bastardy of being
human and having to face all the pain and . . . remain sane. . . .

DAVIE: Well, I'm entirely with you in this sense of urgency. I haven't
been to Auschwitz, I haven't had an experience quite as traumatic as
that, but I think I know what you mean — as you know I've been to
Eastern Europe. I felt very much the same as you. But to come back to
Tomlinson. What you find suspicious in the admiration I have for Tomlinson's poems is that so many of them are about the other arts. These
aren't, in fact, the poems which I admire most and the difference to me
is that Tomlinson's are as often as not poems about things. What you are
asking for is poems about people — all the time. The only reality which
you really think of as adequate for poetry is the human reality, the social
reality, the psychological reality. That is to say, the reality of the sort of
person I am and the sort of person you are and the sort of relationship
there is between us. I agree that this is very important. Tomlinson most
of the time is talking about the sort of reality which there is in him, the
sort of reality that there is in that stone wall, the relation that is set
up between him and that stone wall. Now I quite see that this might
very well seem to be a less urgent concern than the ones which you prefer. My way of getting round this — and it's more than a way of getting
round, it's what I profoundly feel, would go something like this: I dare-
say that you would agree that the cardinal rule in human relations is for
one partner in the relation to respect the integrity of the other person,
not to attempt to violate it, not to attempt to dominate it, not to attempt
to possess. Well, we've been hearing this from Lawrence and many
others for quite a long time. We ask "How do we learn to do this, how
do we learn not to dominate, not to be aggressive?" Simply a resolution:
"I will not dominate," is not good enough. And it seems to me that the
sort of thing which Tomlinson in certain poems in a sense recommends
— realising this stone wall as different from all other stone walls — in its
otherness, its thusness, its quiddity. To see things in this way, to see a
tree thus, to see a stone wall thus, affords a sort of model which you can
then apply to human relations.

ALVAREZ: Let me take up this image of the stone wall because it seems to be very useful. I think fundamentally the difference is this: all sensitive people nowadays are in the same boat. In the same ghastly position. We are all standing there with our hands against this stone wall against which there presses on the other side, a flood tide of neurosis, both inner and social. What you are saying is "If I keep my hands hard against it and look away or look at the detail of the brick, this is the answer." What I am saying is "Christ, it's hurting my arms." You see the difference? We've all got to deal with the same things. It's going to break down and flood us if we are not damn careful. I don't think this is just a personal paranoia — I think this is the general social situation. That's why, I take it, people sit down in Trafalgar Square. You are saying: "We're here and I'm making the effort, but while I'm making it I might as well describe to you the construction of the wall that is keeping us safe." I am saying: "Look at the difficulty of the situation which we are in."

DAVIE: No, it seems to me something like this. I agree with you that humanity and human relations are under an intolerable strain in our time. An all but intolerable strain. We are all at breaking point. Neurosis is very prevalent indeed and menaces all of us. Now, in such a situation, the principal first requirement is to keep sane, to keep the neurosis at bay as far as possible. . . .

ALVAREZ: Not just to keep it at bay but to learn to know what it is. So you can live despite it. So you can cope with it.

DAVIE: Yes, all right. Well. . . .

ALVAREZ: There's no need to be so defensive about it, is what I mean.

DAVIE: Well. . . .

ALVAREZ: I think that is where we really differ. . . .

DAVIE: I think perhaps it is where we differ. I would say that if human relations are under the intolerable and perhaps unprecedented strain they are under today, one must make what efforts one can to relieve this pressure so that human relations may as far as possible be decent. One does this certainly not by burdening the human relation with all the enormous weight of anxiety and responsibility which it seems to me you want to put upon it.

ALVAREZ: Let me put it in a very vulgar way. I think the difference is that, what you are saying is that "My affair with X was a terrible bloody mistake — not necessarily a mistake — a terrible bloody failure, and brought nothing but pain on us both. So the hell to it. I will, as it were, be content merely with masturbation." My feeling is that "It was a terrible failure but here I go again into exactly the same kind of affair with someone else which will be even worse." But, that's it. That's what I meant by defence, I suppose.

DAVIE: Of course, I refuse the masturbation analogy. Surely the world is full of people who've got themselves into the wrong sort of relationship, which is, all right, a bloody awful mistake for them both.

ALVAREZ: I don't believe in mistakes. . . .

DAVIE: All right then, a failure. But what do they do? Generally what people do is learn to live with it. They make the relationship somehow more viable by taking a lot of the weight off it, by not expecting as much out of that relationship as first they did, by seeing it as part of a much wider pattern of disseminated interests.

ALVAREZ: There is probably a difference in years here. You were in the war, whereas I was a kid in the war. This makes a slight difference. It seems to me a lot of marriages now go straight on the rocks because of a feeling that there is no time to live with a failure. One has to make something of one's life — there's probably not much time. There is that kind of neurosis underneath it now. I think that having come through the war, you've got some slightly larger frame of reference. I'm very pro the frame of reference. But let me again quote Nolan, who has a theory that art doesn't actually mirror the times, but acts as a kind of Early Warning System, and that what you get in art now you are going to get in society in ten, twenty years' time. As it were, the kind of contempt for the human being which one had in Cubism is mirrored in Auschwitz. Auschwitz is full of straight lines. It's very efficient. The good poets to-day, in America say — let's get on to neutral territory — the ones I admire — people like Lowell and Berryman — whom I think we both admire, are poets who are writing about violent neurotic breakdown. Where the English poet used to go on the bottle, the Americans now go into the mental homes. It's a kind of occupational disease for a poet. I think this could be the kind of society we are heading for. If we are heading for a nuclear war it's going to be a bloody great breakdown.

DAVIE: Well if we are heading for that. . . .

ALVAREZ: The thing is to try to cope with these forces and create real poetry out of them. Not just express them as, say, Ginsberg did in that poem "Kaddish," which seems to me a rather heavily edited transcript of what happened between Ginsberg and his psychiatrist when he got on the subject of his mother.

DAVIE: What I find hard to take here is the assumption that poetry lives or falls with society. We all know that if there is a nuclear holocaust, everybody's killed so there are no poets; but I really think that poetry can survive a social breakdown and, we had to come to this sooner or later — I think both of us are more or less infidel, more or less agnostic, more or less unbelieving people.

ALVAREZ: I'm an atheist.

DAVIE: I think, honestly, your being that, and my being pretty much

that, is what leads us naturally to suppose that the only grounds for poetry are therapeutic and social. Of course, in the history of poetry down
the centuries, however much it may embarrass us in fact, the grounds
for poetry have frequently been religious or — this is a new word I've
lately learned (I'm not quite sure what it means) — ontological. It
does seem to me increasingly — though it's embarrassing for me to admit
it because of my own agnosticism — we may be selling the pass on
poetry from the start when we don't allow that it may have metaphysical
or religious sanctions. This is what I meant by respecting the otherness,
the being of a tree, a stone wall, a landscape. Even if there were a complete social breakdown there would still be a poet with a tree in front of
him, a poet with a stone wall in front of him.

ALVAREZ: Now look, that's a terrible piece of emotional muddle. I
remember once when I was about fourteen or fifteen and I was busy discovering literature, and trying to write appallingly bad poems — I read
some article, I can't remember where — maybe I heard it on the BBC or
maybe I read it in some ghastly paper — where a lady writer, of course,
said that, you know "we are all poets: anyone who has stood in front of a
beautiful landscape and felt sort of moved by the landscape is a poet even
though he can't say it." Well, that's rubbish. I don't believe that there
are any specifically poetic emotions to be released by a landscape. There's
a fundamental difference here. I, as you know, climb mountains, but I
can't stand mountain landscape. It bores me starry-eyed.

DAVIE: This seems to me very instructive. The man who climbs mountains in order to conquer them is of course not the man who respects
them for what they are in themselves.

ALVAREZ: This is your aestheticism, fundamentally, isn't it? Or is
your aestheticism concerned with language, the nature of the medium?
The nature of the contemplation or the nature of the medium, that's
what I really want to know.

DAVIE: My aestheticism is designed as purely a short-term manoeuvre
to try to rehabilitate a notion of aestheticism, the notion that poetry is
an art simply in order to break what I see as the constricting climate of
opinion in this country, by which you can only talk about poetry and
justify poetry in social, ethical terms. This seems to me the easiest way
of getting back to realising that possibly it is just as reasonable to talk
about poetry in metaphysical and religious terms.

ALVAREZ: You have a very limited interpretation of the word "art."
At the end of your article, for instance, you say — you are talking about
the difference between art and life and so on and about these young
students of yours who would sooner, you say, read Valéry's poems than
Lawrence's, Charles Tomlinson's sooner than Philip Larkin's or Ted
Hughes's — now I think this is restricting yourself — although I myself

am a great admirer, an enormous admirer of Valéry. But I think there is also considerable art and skill and subtlety in Lawrence's poems when they are good. There is the ability to create objects, so that they're not only out there but they're in here, too.

DAVIE: Lawrence really fits my case extraordinarily well. That famous anthology piece of Lawrence's, "Snake," gives me precisely what I'm asking for. The response of the human to the non-human, splendidly rendered. It seems to me that it is — as I understand it — your programme for poetry rather than mine which would tend to exclude such poems and look on them as necessarily trivial because they are not essentially human, not dealing with human relations.

ALVAREZ: To go back to the written word, I praised "Snake" very highly. I think it is very much one of his best poems, but — as you must know — I don't take what you call the "New Left" line. I don't criticise poetry according to the class it comes from. It seems to me, though, that you can really criticise a poet like Christopher Logue simply because of his almost Fascist fascination with power. The real point that no one has made about Christopher Logue is that something like "The Lily White Boys" might easily have been written, not by Brecht, but by the young Goebbels.

DAVIE: Yes.

ALVAREZ: It seems to me that one should do social analysis of that kind in poetry, but when there is something being said, and where something very original is being done to the language, as with Lawrence, when he is writing well, and as Ted Hughes seems to me to be doing, then I think you have got to break down this distinction which you have made, I think, rather than I, between Art and Life.

DAVIE: But the distinction between art and life is broken down every time one writes a poem. One is forced to talk in these terms because these are the terms that are current. . . .

ALVAREZ: Now I think this is where you fail to rise to the — what do they call it — the challenge? You had this idea once of "The Poet in the Imaginary Museum." Now, I think really what my objection to your idea of aestheticism is — when we talk about it there is very little difference between us — when you actually get down to it, you take what is fundamentally an extremely academic point of view; that is, that there are styles which have been created in the past, they can be more or less tarted up for use now, but they are there and they can only be expanded. Now it seems to me that really new things are happening all the time which have their roots in the past, but they grow a long way from their roots like some — to use that thing I once told you not to write poems about — like some cypress tree. The top is a long way from the bottom.

DAVIE: If in my broadcasts on the Imaginary Museum, I said what you impute me to say now, I now unsay it. I do not believe there is a repertoire of styles from the past which can, as you say, be tarted up. . . .

ALVAREZ: What you are saying is, let's get back to Pater, let's get back to Valéry, and my thing is "let's get forward to something new." I think this is what, say, Robert Lowell has done.

DAVIE: Let's get forward from them to the next thing. Let's not write off our past.

ALVAREZ: Well, let's get back to Charles Tomlinson, who is obviously a serious poet, but about whom we disagree. At the end of Charles Tomlinson's book was a series of poems very closely modelled on early Pound and Eliot — the Laforgue things. Now, there was a review by Hugh Kenner which seemed to be absolutely disingenuous, where he said that English poets have never coped with American poetry, and Tomlinson is the first man to do so, ergo he is the first really good English poet. This seems so stupid. The point is, these poets were writing in 1917. Charles Tomlinson was doing it forty years later at least. Times have changed.

DAVIE: But what's wrong with that argument is precisely the ergo. In fact, you find yourself saying something very near to precisely this in the introduction to your new Penguin Anthology. I was interested to see that you are there, as I think very rightly, lambasting us for our insularity — and this I think is true. We got our peep into Europe and the rest of the world through the work of these two American expatriates, Eliot and Pound, and the Irishman Yeats, and — as you put it in the preface to your anthology — what we have done ever since has been to get our heads back again as quickly as we can to this private island paradise of ours. You analyse, very interestingly and to my mind very justly, the three "negative feed-backs" as you put it, which have enabled us to do this. This analysis of literary history is precisely mine and I don't understand why you don't draw the same conclusions from it as I do. Let's go back then, to them, and go forward from there.

ALVAREZ: You have only read half my introduction, or three quarters of it. What I actually go on to say is that people have gone on from there. People like Lowell and Berryman, the two I quote — they take for granted that a poet doesn't have to be some blindly inspired seer, some Sitwellian fiddler with words or what have you, but he's got to be intelligent and he has got to be very skilful. He has also got to face the fact that he is moved, whether he likes it or not by forces which are very difficult and very destructive. He has to face this in his poetry, and — you know, in England we didn't have any Forties — the Forties were fundamentally the final giving up of all this Eliot stringency and so on, in the face of beer-swilling wartime neurosis. We don't have to go back as far as Eliot or Pound. If you need models there are models. There are a lot of people in their forties writing in America. The thing is to go on from there.

DAVIE: Well, all right. This I agree with. Let us go back to Lowell.

ALVAREZ: Let us, for Christ's sake, face the fact that we live in a pretty complicated thing called Europe and not just a rather less complicated thing called the British Isles.

DAVIE: I entirely agree with your view of the importance of Lowell. And let me remind you — you of all people — that Lowell is a very Poundian poet. He has just published a book of translations, you too have helped to publish his translations of Villon in a newspaper — he is very thoroughly in this Eliot-Pound lineage.

ALVAREZ: He is infinitely better than Pound. I think his translations are better, very much more personal. There is not, in fact, this simply literary involvement. His involvement is so much deeper. His personality is showing so much more. Pound keeps his hemline down.

DAVIE: Yes, indeed, that's perfectly true. It's a matter of Lowell's intention. His intentions are Poundian at any rate. I agree that he doesn't perform as a poetic translator in anything like as good a way as Pound does.

ALVAREZ: Well, well, well . . . as they say in Westerns — prove it. I think the Lowell "Villon" is better than the Pound "Propertius." And I'm an enormous admirer of Pound's "Propertius."

DAVIE: On this then we would differ. But this isn't the central issue. Can I at this stage, as I warned you I would — quote you something?

ALVAREZ: Yes, please do.

DAVIE: This is from Pasternak's *Dr. Zhivago* and Pasternak at this point is talking about Zhivago's experience when writing a poem. I quote: "After two or three stanzas, and several images, by which he was himself astonished, his work took possession of him and he experienced the approach of what is called inspiration. At such moments the correlation of forces controlling the artist is, as it were, stood on its head. The ascendancy is no longer with the artist or the state of mind which he is trying to express, but with language, his instrument of expression. Language, the home and dwelling of beauty and meaning, itself begins to think and speak for man and turns wholly into music, not in the sense of outward audible sounds but by virtue of the power and momentum of its inward flow." Well, that is enough. What I would ask about this, is it a mere gaud of rather windy rhetoric or is it, bearing in mind that it is Pasternak writing it, in fact saying something significant and useful about the act of poetic composition? My point in asking the question is simply that our vocabulary, I believe, prevents us from even beginning to understand what it is that Pasternak may here be saying.

ALVAREZ: I don't agree with you. I should have thought actually that the vocabulary and the concepts he is using are those of the nineteenth century. What he is saying is true. I am sure he is right. One's own experience — in a very much more paltry way, when you and I write, or try to write, poems, bears this out. But the actual way in which it is put is wrong. It's the Aeolian harp thesis all over again, isn't it? It seems to me that nowadays, somehow or other, we know too much. It's very difficult simply when writing about it, not actually writing, but writing about it later, simply to accept this blindness of inspiration; and the whole attempt when writing poetry, when manipulating language, is to understand what is going on as you do it. At no point can you give up the ghost, throw up your hands and say, as Edith Sitwell used to say, "It's all a question of those dark vowels."

DAVIE: I read this not at all for the sake of the inspiration but rather for the sake of the sentence where he says "the ascendancy is no longer with the artist but with language, his instrument of expression" and still more "language itself begins to think and turns wholly into music." Now both of these it seems to me are experiences which I can, in the way you have talked about it, partially confirm from my own experience in writing poems. As you point out, the vocabulary which they use is nineteenth century vocabulary. It is — let's face it — the vocabulary of Water Pater and aestheticism. It is only Pater and his disciples who were the last people to talk of language in poetry turning into music. You know perfectly well that in the give and take of literary talk in this country, as it might be between you and me — I can't even use a phrase like "the music of poetry" or "poetry aspiring to the condition of music."

ALVAREZ: It's like using the phrase "magic," isn't it? The old school mistress line.

DAVIE: Well, precisely. Nonetheless this is talking about a reality which I know and which I think you know and we are absurdly prevented from talking about it simply because the vocabulary which is available for us has been smeared, tainted by association with a man who died sixty or seventy years ago.

ALVAREZ: We won't have to dig his skeleton out of the cupboard, it seems to me. I think, really, I know what the difference is now between us. Let's take Zbigniew Herbert, the Polish poet, whom we both agree is absolutely first-rate — in what he does and in the way he does it. He is a poet who is very much on his own. He lives in a Marxist society and will have no truck with the Marxist tools of translation of experience. He does it very independently but is infinitely a political poet. What I think you have here — when there is this great pressure — unlike most Poles he wasn't in the concentration camps but had a very rough time indeed in the Partisan army; he saw too much too early, if you like — what one has is a kind of insistence on the facts of society, on the hard, resistant things there, so to speak. Things impinging on him as a man moving in society. This kind of factuality is what makes his poetry good and at the same time very involved, committed. He has this ability to re-create rather abstract states of mind, but in terms of these facts all the time. There's something terribly hard about it. This unyieldingness seems to me so much more worthwhile than talking about a stone wall. In *Encounter* last summer there was a very beautiful poem of his called "Fortinbras's Elegy", which is Fortinbras talking about Hamlet. It is the elegy of the political man on the non-political man, the man who couldn't stand the pace. It's marvellous . . . clever, ironic . . . and in it the whole of modern Poland, and the whole of Hamlet seems to be. It does seem to me that he faces the facts; and the facts in Poland are terrible. We don't know what the war was about. When you go over there you realise we had nothing in this country.

DAVIE: I think it is no accident that we find ourselves talking about poets of Eastern Europe. What strikes me about these poets from Eastern European countries is that, having been brought face to face with the agonies of the human condition in our time, this does not make them in the least embarrassed about talking about Art with a capital A, talking about poetry becoming music. This was from *Doctor Zhivago* — here was an Eastern European writer who was certainly brought face to face with the brutalities and atrocities of what the human condition is in the present century. It is only we who have this bad conscience and we have it precisely because we haven't experienced it, and we imagine what it must have been like to be a Pole or a Russian or a Hungarian. As far as I can see, among the acquaintances I made in these countries, it has the effect which is, I should have thought — inspiring, of confirming them more than ever in their values, in the value of the poetic act, of the act of the imagination. They speak with all the less embarrassment, all the more confidence about the creativity of the human imagination, about its indestructibility, its inexhaustibility. . . .

ALVAREZ: I grant that they are very much concerned with aesthetic matters but it seems to me their aestheticism works on a much more serious level. They are not concerned with the minor irritations that plague us, like manners in poetry and so on. They are concerned with getting the poem as perfect as they can, in itself, and at the same time with making it as inclusive as it can be. After all, if poetry is to continue to be worth the effort in the present time, it must be a concentration of experience, not a diffusion of it.

FRANK KERMODE

The Artist in Isolation

Je ne suis pas fait comme aucun de ceux que j'ai
sus. Mais si je ne vaux pas mieux, au moins je
suis autre.

ROUSSEAU

We poets in our youth begin in gladness,
But thereof comes in the end despondency and madness.

WORDSWORTH

As its title is intended to indicate, this essay is primarily concerned with the evolution of assumptions relating to the image of poetry;
it is an attempt to describe this image in a new way, and to suggest new
ways of looking at contingent issues, in poetry and criticism. The main
topic is, in fact, that "esthetic image" explained in Thomist language by
Stephen Dedalus in the *Portrait of the Artist as a Young Man:* it is for
him that beauty which has the three attributes of integrity, consonance
and clarity; which is "apprehended as one thing . . . self-bounded and
self-contained upon the immeasurable background of space or time which
is not it"; apprehended in its *quidditas* by the artist whose mind is arrested in "a luminous stasis of esthetic pleasure."

This is only one famous — and rather obscure — way of putting it,
and the conclusions concerning poetry at which Joyce, starting from this
position, arrives, are characteristic of the whole movement I shall discuss.
One such conclusion is that the artist who is vouchsafed this power of
apprehending the Image — to experience that "epiphany" which is the
Joycean equivalent of Pater's "vision" — has to pay a heavy price in suffering, to risk his immortal soul, and to be alone, "not only to be separate
from all others but to have not even one friend."

These two beliefs — in the Image as a radiant truth out of space and
time, and in the necessary isolation or estrangement of men who can
perceive it — are inextricably associated, and because of their interdependence I find that I must begin this essay on the Image with a few

SOURCE: From *Romantic Image* by Frank Kermode (London: Routledge and Kegan Paul Ltd., 1957), pp. 1–29. Reprinted by permission of Routledge and Kegan
Paul and Chilmark Press.

pages on what is for me the subsidiary theme, this ubiquitous assumption that the artist is cut off from other men; and even these notes will contain some anticipations of later chapters on the Image proper.

The author to whom it would be natural to turn for a fully developed view of both themes is Thomas Mann, who sets them, so to speak, in the full context of modern life and learning. They occur in singular and suggestive purity — if that is the word — in the early stories *Death in Venice* and *Tonio Kröger,* and later receive encyclopaedic enlargement. The first of these stories is nevertheless the most systematic exposition, in art, that I have so far encountered. But for my purposes the topic of isolation is more directly relevant as it occurs in poetry, and more particularly in English poetry, since what I have to say later about Yeats is the heart of this essay. The real difficulty about this topic is to know where to start; the literature of the past hundred and fifty years has millions of texts for discourses upon it, and in any case the "difference" of artists is common ground to the artists themselves and to those who hate them. Perhaps we need an exhaustive study in critical, psychological, and sociological terms; that would be a daunting task, involving the history of the very tools one was using. All I intend here is to recall to mind a few aspects of the subject which seem indispensable to what I have to say about the Image.

Occasionally one encounters the paradox that the artist is magnificently sane, only the quality of his sanity distinguishing him from other men. His *sensibility* (in Henry James's sense, the "very atmosphere of his mind") is more profound, subtle and receptive, and his powers of organizing experience very much greater. His art is not made of stuff inaccessible to them; there is no qualitative difference between his way of knowing and theirs; all depends upon this intensity of organization. Pater said it in his liturgical monotone; Dr. Richards said it in his scientific parables, making the point with the aid of diagrams. (These critics, saying the same thing in their so different ways, span a period in which many voices, proclaiming novelty, seem on analysis to be saying much the same thing.) But Pater also knew the cost of this intensity; the Cyrenaic visions, "almost beatific," of ideal personalities in life and art were "a very costly matter," requiring "the sacrifice of a thousand possible sympathies" and so effectively setting the visionary apart. And this is characteristic of the way in which the paradox of the artist's "normality" melts away into the received opinion: artists are different, isolated.

It is important to distinguish, in passing, between this opinion as a serious belief held by and about artists, and the vulgarized bohemian tradition that the artist is poor, immoral, and marked by an eccentricity of costume. This is really a confused echo from the Paris of Mürger and

Huysmans and the *poètes maudits,* with a few collateral English rumours. As an example (rather a sophisticated one, indeed) of the persistence of the lowbrow version, here is a passage from a notice in a London evening paper of an exhibition of paintings by M. Bernard Buffet (1955):

> Three years ago you could have bought a Buffet for the cost of a meal but now the Buffet price is £300–£500. He has just been voted France's leading young painter in a ballot run by a glossy art magazine . . . which says one of the causes of his success is that he painted the miseries of youth after the war. Only 27 now, he was 18 when the critics first acclaimed him. At the time he was living the real, unglamorised Bohemian life, going without food to buy canvas. . . . He works entirely from memory and imagination, and by electric light. The house he has had built in the Basses Alpes is specially designed to exclude the beautiful views that other people would dote upon. Nothing must disturb his imagination.

An accompanying reproduction of a painting by M. Buffet shows that he takes his isolation as his subject. What is expected to appeal to the public is the "human interest" of such eccentricity. Why build the house there, amid the "beautiful views" (it is "natural" and decent to admire the view, and normal painters, not these modern madmen, would be outside with an easel) if you are going to work out of your own head? "Imagination" is what M. Buffet works by; but "it's all imagination" can mean different things to different people, and the meaning the public is here expected to supply is that which places "imagination" in an antithetical relationship with "reality." The philistines, though they were long ago bludgeoned into accepting "nature" as a mysteriously good thing, cannot see M. Buffet's work as anything but fantastic nonsense, whereas for him their "nature" is dead, and the concern only of a science which specialized in measuring dead things. He is interested in what he has access to, and they have not — the image that is truth *because* he makes it up; *because* it has nothing to do with "nature." There was once a *New Yorker* joke about a haggard genius who said "I paint what I *don't* see." This joke, good as it is, depends on our readiness to think of "modern art" as fantastic nonsense, and the drawing has to show a Simeon Solomon type, garret-dwelling, ragged, pitiable but also odious; for nearly two centuries there have been painters who would not have seen this joke (except by some special effort of sympathy) because the old scarecrow is saying something that has, for them, a great deal of truth in it. For them, and for M. Buffet, these public misunderstandings are merely another aspect of their isolation. For we may roughly distinguish two aspects of the condition. The first is represented by M. Buffet's voluntary, even somewhat ostentatious, retreat to the Alps, his blocking the windows to keep out the normally beautiful views and the normally welcomed daylight; this is the cult of isolated joy, the pursuit of the Image by the specially fated and highly organized artist, a man who gets things out of his own head. He excludes society and its half-baked sensibilities. The second is the reaction of astonishment and contempt in those who "dote upon" beautiful views. Whether he likes it or not, society excludes him.

Each of these aspects is in turn presented (though of course not in this very simple way) as the whole truth about the estrangement of the modern artist, though the second is the more popular. Of course they are really inseparable. The artist's devotion to the Image developed at the same time as the modern industrial state and the modern middle class. From the beginnings of Romantic poetry the artist has been, as M. Béguin says of Lichtenberg, "malade de sa différence avec son temps." The great poet of the modern city, Baudelaire, was a self-confessed "seer." The *frisson nouveau* upon which Hugo congratulated him proceeded from the study of a fallen humanity in the new context; his mythology is of the perversion, the *ennui,* the metaphysical despair of men and women subjected to what Dickens (in this respect Baudelaire's English equivalent — compare *Le crépuscule du matin* with certain passages in *Little Dorrit*) called "the shame, desertion, wretchedness and exposure of the great capital." The poet, though devoted to the Image, belongs to this city, his place in which Baudelaire notoriously compares with that of the prostitute. All men, he says, have an "invincible taste for prostitution," and he calls this the source of man's "horror of solitude"; the poet is different in that he wants to be alone, but this is only "prostituting yourself in a special way"; as Mr. Turnell says in his recent book on Baudelaire, this attempt at unity in solitude fails because of internal stress and division, and the poet can claim not unity but only difference in the manner of his prostitution. Yet Baudelaire, so sensitive to the horror of the modern city, remains true to a central Romantic tradition in abstaining from any attempt to alter the social order, and despises the "puerile Utopias" of some other Romantic poets. And his answer to the question, what has the movement, whose poets find themselves in this dreadful situation, done for us, is striking: it has "recalled us to the truth of the image." The Image is the reward of that agonising difference; isolated in the city, the poet is a "seer." The Image, for all its concretion, precision, and oneness, is desperately difficult to communicate, and has for that reason alone as much to do with the alienation of the seer as the necessity of his existing in the midst of a hostile society.

Baudelaire is a famous case, but there is nothing specifically French about his difficulties, and these notions of Image and isolation developed independently in England, from native Romantic roots. The Symbol of the French is, as we shall see, the Romantic Image writ large and given more elaborate metaphysical and magical support; and, if we go back far enough, we can see that English poets — using the same ultimate sources, Boehme and Swedenborg, the Germans of the later eighteenth century — developed their own way of "recalling us to the truth of the image." This native tradition is in some ways more significant for modern poetry than imported Symbolism; Blake and Pater stand behind Yeats at his most magnificent, and in the thought of Arthur Symons, crucial for the historian, they are at least as important as the French poets. And an awareness of the Image involves, for English poets also, a sense of powerful forces extruding them from the life of their society, a sense of irreconcileable difference and precarious communication. Here too we encounter that ambiguity concerning the degree of responsibility for the poet's estrangement. Obviously it is too simple to say, with the prose Arnold and with Mencken, each criticising the materialism of his own society, that the artist is forced into seclusion; that is where, on his own view, he has to be. The ambiguity is very acutely presented by D. H. Lawrence (who certainly earned the right to understand it) in a comment on Beethoven's letters: "always in love with somebody when he wasn't really, and wanting contacts when he didn't really — part of the crucifixion into isolate individuality — *poveri noi.*" The crux of the matter is in this colloquial "really"; did he or didn't he want such contacts, was he natural man or artist, did he want to "go out of himself" or not? "Crucifixion" (a word that recurs with significant frequency in this context, from Kierkegaard to Yeats and Wilde) does not completely exclude the idea of torment freely though painfully chosen; *poveri noi,* however you look at it we artists are all in the same boat, whether we "really" like it or not. To be cut off from life and action, in one way or another, is necessary as a preparation for the "vision." Some difference in the artist gives him access to this — an enormous privilege, involving *joy* (which acquires an almost technical sense as a necessary concomitant of the full exercise of the mind in the act of imagination). But the power of joy being possible only to a profound "organic sensibility," a man who experiences it will also suffer exceptionally. He must be lonely, haunted, victimised, devoted to suffering rather than action — or, to state this in a manner more acceptable to the twentieth century, he is exempt from the normal human orientation towards action and so enabled to intuit those images which are truth, in defiance of the triumphant claims of merely intellectual disciplines. But that is pushing too far ahead. I have now introduced into the discussion the crucial concept of *joy,* of which the *locus classicus* is Coleridge's Ode; and I now turn more specifically to the English tradition.

The "difference" of some of the English Romantic poets is almost too well known; they were outcast because they had to pay for their joy and their vision. Sometimes they attributed their condition to some malady in themselves, but they also blamed the age in which they lived, as Hazlitt did when he measured the sad alteration of the world by comparing the art of West with that of Raphael, in which "every nerve and muscle has intense feeling." How often are we to hear this repeated! For Yeats the painters to be compared are Sargent and Titian. The alienation of the artist and this despair at the decay of the world are two sides of one coin; the present age is the one that hates art, some earlier age loved the poet without corrupting him. So it was that Hazlitt found in Godwin's *St. Leon* a magician who could stand for the modern artist, and who might just as easily have come from some fantasy after Villiers de l'Isle Adam:

> He is a limb torn off from society. In possession of eternal youth and beauty he can feel no love; surrounded, tantalized and tormented by riches, he can do no good. The faces of men pass before him as in a speculum; but he is attached to them by no common tie of sympathy or suffering. He is thrown back into himself and his own thoughts. He lives in the solitude of his own breast, without wife or child or friend or enemy in the whole world. His is the solitude of the soul, not of woods or trees or mountains — but the desert of society — the waste and oblivion of the heart. He is himself alone.

Keats will show us how this kind of thing gets into poetry. He gave his full and considered approval to these passionate remarks of Hazlitt, and himself undertook to "live like a hermit" in the midst of the world, and "bear anything — any misery, even imprisonment — so long as I have neither wife nor child." He even thanked the "English world" for its cruelty to writers, saying that it "ill-treated them during their lives and fostered them after their deaths" so that "they have in general been trampled aside into the bye paths of life and seen the festerings of Society"; yet this is "one of the great reasons that the English have produced the finest writers in the world." Keats very naturally related the artist's joy to his suffering:

> Ay, in the very temple of Delight
> Veil'd Melancholy has her sovran shrine,
> Though seen of none save him whose strenuous tongue
> Can burst Joy's grape against his palate fine;
> His soul shall taste the sadness of her might,
> And be among her cloudy trophies hung.

This view of melancholy-in-genius probably goes back, through Burton, to an older opinion of the necessity of melancholy in artists: we have a sudden perspective, back to Dürer and Ficino. But it looks forward also, for here, very richly and completely, is the artist as a man of high "sensibility" — *feeling* with remarkable intensity as a necessity of genius; and here too is the artist as victim, that other necessary consequence.

Keats, indeed, seems to me to have been the first to achieve in English a
characteristic poetic statement of the joy and cost of the Image — his is
more central, I think, than Shelley's somewhat similar efforts, more imita-
ble than Coleridge's. I am thinking not of *Lamia* (where the tension is between the luxurious and decorative but still sinister, chthonic, image of
poetry, and "cold philosophy") but to *Hyperion*, and particularly to the
second draft. That version begins with the poet's claim to a higher
dream than the mere fanatic's. He tells his vision: in a sort of earthly
paradise he drank from an enchanted vessel, and this set him apart from
other men, like the touch of the Sidhe in Celtic mythology. He falls into a
sleep within his dream, and awakes in a sanctuary; with terror and anguish he approaches an altar from which issues a voice promising him,
as a reward, a mitigation of mortality. He has, says the voice, "felt What
'tis to die and live again before Thy fated hour"; though some fail in the
ascent to the altar, and "Rot on the pavement where thou rottedst half."
Unlike the normal man, who knows joy and pain "alone, distinct," the
poet "venoms all his days, Bearing more woes than all his sins deserve."
It is to soften this fate that he is admitted to the sanctuary and its altar.
A cut passage in the manuscript, which shows us how Keats's mind was
working, describes how the poet distinguishes himself from mock-artists.
He asks where he is, before whose altar he stands. It is the altar of Moneta,
sole divine survivor of the Saturnian age, Goddess of Memory and Mother
of the Muses. Moneta, I take it, represents the survival of the archaic way
of thought — imaginative rather than discursive ("the large utterance of
the early gods"), *un-dissociated*, mythopoeic; more profound, though certainly, to use the word in a limiting sense, less *human* than the discourse
of "philosophy" which Keats, with his tentative evolutionism, was trying
to accept as a necessary human development. This is the philosophy that
explicates the rainbow in terms of the spectrum, but it also promises a
diminution of human misery; the Lamia of poetry shrivels before it, but
Apollonius is after all only being considerate. Moneta is a painful survival, in a world that has, in its "philosophic" way, disentangled the
dream of imagination from true knowledge. Her children are the patron-
esses of the arts that preserve, in this hostile later world, the old intuitive
knowing that men admired and associated with the angels. It is access to
the knowledge she represents that distinguishes the poet; and this poet is
permitted to see her face, which is described in a very remarkable passage:

> Then saw I a wan face,
> Not pined by human sorrows, but bright-blanch'd
> By an immortal sickness which kills not;
> It works a constant change, which happy death
> Can put no end to; deathwards progressing
> To no death was the visage; it had past

The lily and the snow; and beyond these
I must not think now, though I saw that face.
But for her eyes I should have fled away;
They held me back with a benignant light,
Soft, mitigated by divinest lids
Half-closed, and visionless entire they seem'd
Of all external things; they saw me not,
But in blank splendour beam'd, like the mild moon,
Who comforts those she sees not, who knows not
What eyes are upward cast.

Moneta is full of terrible knowledge, and this knowledge is about to be revealed to the poet; it is the myth of the Titans, and for Keats myth was of the same imaginative order as the poet's knowledge. She is immortal; her face is the emblem of the cost as well as of the benefits of knowledge and immortality. Moneta's face haunts many later poets as well as Keats. It has the pallor and the equivocal life-in-death of Coleridge's spectre — whiter in disease than the hands of Venus and Adonis, which, after the *Biographia Literaria,* were strongly associated with the act of imagination. The face is alive only in a chill and inhuman way. The knowledge it represents is not malign, but it is unrelated to "external things"; the eyes express nothing, looking inward to the "high tragedy In the dark secret chambers of the skull." To prostrate himself before this figure is the privilege of the artist's joy and the reward of his suffering. The face of Moneta is an emblem we shall often encounter again in these pages.

The other version of *Hyperion* has yet more of this association of suffering and joy, in the account of the apotheosis of Apollo. But indeed this association is at the root of Romantic thought.

Joy is the sweet voice, Joy the luminous cloud —
    We in ourselves rejoice!
And thence flows all that charms or ear or sight,
    All melodies the echo of that voice,
    All colours a suffusion of that light.

And Joy cannot be had without anguish. Wordsworth's poet is a "man speaking to men," dealing with "Joy in widest commonalty spread." But already in the Preface of 1800 he allows a difference between poets and other men, though insisting that it is only a difference of degree; this was forced on him by his belief in the uniformity of human personality, which also bred the theory of diction (the language of poets comes not from poets but from men). Yet Wordsworth's belief that the poet is more highly organised, more passionate and subtle, than the peasant, in fact puts as much distance between poet and peasant as between peasant and amoeba. Already the poet is necessarily estranged, and his work may become increasingly unintelligible and offensive to all who cannot share his dream and his persecution, or believe that the grounds of his joy are true.

> What portion in the world can the artist have
> That has awakened from the common dream,
> But dissipation and despair?

This is Yeats, more categorical than Wordsworth. Yet Wordsworth had to admit (thinking of Burns) that the artist's peculiar susceptibility to pleasure made him an easy victim of vicious temptations, and therefore a man especially prone to misery. He feels more pleasure, but also more pain. His difference isolates him; he incurs hatred for all sorts of reasons — for his sinewy thigh, for his claim of agonised privilege; but there is little he can do save to trust in the Image, to weld joy and misery together in some symbolic blaze, some "Leech Gatherer"; and, that victory over, plan another. "Among subjective men," says Yeats, "the victory is an intellectual daily recreation of all that exterior fate snatches away, and so that fate's antithesis. We begin to live when we have conceived life as a tragedy." But even tragedy is a matter of joy; Hamlet and Lear are gay. Wordsworth was always aware of this. All his great solitaries are tragic figures, and he had an extraordinary relish for the appearances of disaster and misery. Leaving the Ruined Cottage, the poet "walks along his road in happiness"; in the drowned man taken from the lake, a "spectre shape of terror," he finds, imagination aiding, "a dignity, a smoothness, like the works of Grecian art." In what is perhaps the most tremendous passage in *The Prelude* he demonstrates the conversion of a "visionary dreariness" — the "naked pool,"

> The beacon crowning the lone eminence,
> The female with her garments vexed and tossed
> By the strong wind —

by the "spirit of pleasure" into profound joy. It is one of Yeats's "victories." What saves the poet here is the symbol-making power; it is not what the Leech Gatherer says, but the fact that Wordsworth could invent him, that saves his joy and his sanity, gives him his victory. But of course there is always a last victory; and that is the Romantic poet's Dejection Ode, which exhausts him.

I dwell on this rather grim emphasis on pleasure (which, as Coleridge and Arnold also believed, must be felt before it can be communicated) because it is vital to the conception of the isolated poet. *Joy* is what they have to communicate, and it is good. They are in no position to teach, and indeed have a great dread of the didactic; but they have redefined the relationship of *utile* to *dulce,* and usually believe in their moral function, so that, in short, the pleasure communicated conduces to morality. That is why George Eliot, in some ways a typical Romantic artist, could

call herself an "aesthetic teacher," and yet protest that she had no desire
to instruct or change the world; that is why, to our great benefit, Pater in
The Renaissance and *Marius the Epicurean,* and James in "The Art of
Fiction" and in his practice, insisted upon the moral value of what is
highly organised and profoundly apprehended, in life and in art.

The position is, of course, easily misunderstood, particularly when expressed by such formulae as "All art is quite useless." "The artist must
serve Mammon," said Keats; this makes it easy to behave like an artist.
We have no space to treat of frauds and misconceptions; but it remains
true that corruption in an artist (a condition perhaps not fully described
before Collingwood's *Principles of Art*) came to be regarded as another
matter from corruption in another man. His purity cannot be judged by
the rough standards that serve in the world; it is primarily an aesthetic
purity. Here we have a situation for Jamesian comedy perhaps; at any
rate, it can be made to seem serious in one way or another by a James
or a Yeats or a Mann. (Yeats said he had seen more artists ruined by
wives and children than by harlots.) Yet a whole gifted generation of
English poets which held these views in an extreme form, and which
Yeats calls a "tragic generation," never seem to be taken seriously at all.
The reason is, partly, that in such extreme formulations as Wilde's, the
doctrine is unpalatable; but it is also, partly, that these poets have come
to be regarded as exotics, outside the main English tradition. Since this is
an important generation of poets for my purposes, I must try briefly to
remedy this by dwelling for a moment on Arnold and Pater, and particularly on Arnold.

Arnold was a very influential transmitter of Romantic thought, and
no one was more fully aware of our problem, under all its aspects, than
he. Unhappily, he himself rejected *Empedocles on Etna,* in this connexion his most important poem; and consequently it is not much read. If
it were, we should be less prone to think of the poets of the nineties as
merely wayward young men who picked up bad habits from the French.
Arnold's attitude to this poem — in some ways a great poem, profound
and finely-designed — is exasperating. We might paraphrase Blake's remark on Wordsworth's criticism, and say of the 1853 *Preface,* "I do not
know who wrote this Preface; it is very mischievous, and directly contrary
to Arnold's own practice." It was written by Arnold's spectre. Or perhaps
we should say that the rejection was the work of Arnold the Critic, who
rightly distrusted poems which were victories to Arnold the poet, but messages of despair to one who saw the need to get poetry usefully working,
leavening the lump. Indeed, his turning away from the poem is in a sense
a personal consequence of the suicide of Empedocles; the poem wrote off
Arnold's main topic. It contains his solution — Empedocles is Arnold's
Leech Gatherer. But there seemed no prospect of indefinitely repeating

this victory (Pyrrhic, because suicide is the least useful of answers in *life*) and so Arnold rejects it in favour of another solution which involves not death but merely poetic extinction, or rather a curiously effective compromise which keeps the poet in a state of suspended animation. At any rate there is no need to accept the dismissal of a poem by its author simply because it happened not to be the kind of poem he liked after he had finished it (though, with his oddly literal acceptance of the Romantic pleasure-principle, Arnold thought his own enjoyment a certain index of other people's).

The gist of his complaint in the Preface — that dry attempt to direct poetry back to its "normal" material, the unchanging human heart — is that in *Empedocles* suffering finds no vent in action, everything is to be endured and nothing to be done. But in fact the poem, designed with extraordinary care, a professional job of architectonics, is a system of tensions which deliberately excludes all movement save the suicide of the hero. Empedocles is the Romantic poet who knows enough; Callicles the Romantic poet who does not know enough. "Wordsworth's sweet calm" is no longer available; it is Sénancour who knows the situation through and through; *Eternité, deviens mon asile!* is his admired epitaph, and Empedocles's "Receive me, save me!" is the same thing. *Greater by far that thou art dead.*

> Ah! two desires toss about
> The poet's feverish blood.
> One drives him to the world without,
>   And one to solitude.

Obermann deals with the privileged moments of the poet driven into solitude, moments when the truth is known to be interior, independent of sensible reality or perceived in that reality by a mystical intuition; there is a momentary euphoria, joy, in this participation of the mind with the perceived harmonious order, which has to be paid for. (Incidentally, the thought of Sénancour, like that of Novalis, Blake, Coleridge and later Romantics, stems in part from the hermetic thought of the sixteenth and seventeenth centuries; the movement, like Kierkegaard's poet, was unhappily in love with God.) Arnold augmented the profound insight into isolation which Sénancour provided, by his reading in Maurice de Guérin, a poet who knew "the freshness of the early world" and was tortured by the rarity and brevity of those moments of imaginative perception he was always seeking to recapture. For him it was the imagination that made truth; "rarement on a fait, autant que lui," says M. Béguin, "confiance à l'efficacité des images; le mot imagination était pour lui 'le nom de la vie intérieure.' " But as a direct consequence of such searching and such confidence in the interior life, he believed that the poet will always be pursued from exile to exile, with no continuing stay; and he meditated upon the permanent and luxurious escape of death. From such sources derives the figure of the Romantic poet which, in his play, Arnold dissociates, so to speak, into the persons of Empedocles and Callicles.

Of course he himself was such a poet; but he had some confidence that the intolerable situation of himself and his like would end when (hastened by Criticism) a new social order would make poetry possible, and a "joy whose grounds are true"; and Sénancour, from his grave, counsels the ageing Arnold to continue the task of Criticism:

> But thou, though to the world's new hour
> Thou come with aspect marr'd,
> Shorn of the joy, the bloom, the power,
> Which best befits its bard —
>
> . . . Though late, though dimm'd, though weak, yet tell
> Hope to a world new-made!

Empedocles abandons contemplation, acts and dies; Arnold acts and lives, as a critic, a disengaged, antididactic critic; still seeing widely and steadily, but talking of society, not so much of the poet in society, seeking to end rather than to analyse that problem by the reform of society; dealing, at any rate, in life, not in art, becoming not being.

But *Empedocles* is about art, or rather about the artist. It is a victory fought over the same ground as "The Strayed Reveller." Empedocles belonged to a great age of poetry, an age of acceptable *Aberglaube,* an age when the poet had a function (specified as therapeutic) in society. But the new age excludes him, or rather he excludes himself from a new society,

> since this new swarm
> Of sophists has got empire in our schools
> Where he was paramount, since he is banish'd
> And lives a lonely man in triple gloom.

To the young Callicles there is nothing genuine in the plight of Empedocles. Callicles has not yet understood. "The sophists are no enemies of his," he says, and prefers what is for himself the more comfortable explanation, that Empedocles has "some root of suffering in himself." More comfortable, but not false; what Callicles does not yet know — it is the first of many ironies in the structure of the work — is that he too must have this "root of suffering." At present, his "tongue outruns his knowledge." He is sent to the lower slope. Callicles has already progressed some way — he has abandoned the sensual feast below; but he has no place as yet on the top of the mountain, the eminence of isolation and self-destruction.

There follows a richly ironical debate between a poet ignorant enough to know joy and an ex-poet who knows that its grounds are not true, who scrabbles prosaically among the rubbish for the ethical fragments of which he must try to build himself a shelter. The great risk Arnold had to take here was, technically, analogous to putting a bore in a play; he may be boring. Arnold's extinct poet has to be flat and joyless; the solution is to make him sing like a tired Browning, and it is perhaps not a good solution. But the failure is not complete, though a line-by-line analysis might suggest that it is. The "poetry," spontaneous, local, charming, "Keatsian," as natural as the leaves on the tree, but fundamentally inept and doomed, flows from the younger poet, who is still in love with his dream, still unaware of its falsity and uselessness, and of the cost of his art; still unbroken by its rigours. Callicles sings the heroic wisdom of Chiron and Peleus; Empedocles replies with a long poem advocating a sober epicureanism which, with traditional anti-intellectualism (different in orientation, it should be noted, from the genuine Romantic variety found in Wordsworth and Coleridge, Rossetti, Pater, Wilde and Yeats) calls the village churl nearer the truth than the poet, with his "estranged eyes." The answering song of Callicles is one of Arnold's most perfect poems, and this not merely in its rich and delicate texture, but in the precision of its structural ironies. He extracts a Wordsworthian joy — the rejected joy — from the tragedy of Cadmus and Harmonia, confidently asserting that happy immortality of the tormented soul which is the lie hidden in the joy. Empedocles, for all his knowledge and experience, cannot resist it; "How his brow lightened as the music rose!" But this is Arnold's act-ending; and immediately the ironies become more conclusive, the situation more explicit.

> No, thou art come too late, Empedocles,
> And the world hath the day, and must break thee,
> Not thou the world. With men thou canst not live,
> Their thoughts, their ways, their wishes, are not thine;
> And being lonely thou art miserable,
> For something has impaired thy spirit's strength,
> And dried its self-sufficing fount of joy,
> Thou canst not live with men or with thyself —
> O sage! O sage! — Take then the one way left; . . .
> Before the soul lose all her solemn joys,
> And awe be dead, and hope impossible,
> And the soul's deep eternal night come on,
> Receive me, hide me, quench me, take me home!

But as he advances to the crater's edge, the voice of Callicles floats up, bearing another lovely fable that mythologizes the mountain's destructive power; he is content with the beauty of the Titan's anguish, and does not comment upon it; it is not for him to draw conclusions. His pleasure is the same, whether he is considering the sufferings of Typho or the "awful

pleasure bland" of Jove, and his unspeakable content under the ministrations of Hebe, whose "flush'd feet glow on the marble floor." The joy of
Callicles turns it all to joy. But Empedocles allegorizes the poet's myth:

> He fables, yet speaks truth!
> The brave, impetuous heart yields everywhere
> To the subtle contriving head;
> Great qualities are trodden down,
> And littleness united
> To become invincible.

"Great art beaten down . . . the best lack all conviction. . . ." All
that has happened, on this view, between Arnold and Yeats, is that the
wicked have discovered the lost intensity of the good; the world has become, as no one could foresee, more murderous as well as darker. At this
latest outburst of false joy, Empedocles resigns the symbols of his wisdom;
at the next he lays aside his laurel bough. The song of Callicles is the
beautiful and ironical song of the flaying of Marsyas at the orders of the
cold and beautiful god — Marsyas, the first victim of that presumptuous
devotion. (Pater thought of Raphael's "Apollo and Marsyas" almost as "a
parable of the contention between classic art and the romantic"; and it is
possible that Arnold felt something of this also, making his god cold and
marmoreal, without Dionysiac elements.) Empedocles is the god's latest
victim:

> And lie thou there,
> My laurel bough! . . .
> I am weary of thee,
> I am weary of the solitude
> Which he who bears thee must abide —
> Of the rocks of Parnassus,
> Of the rocks of Delphi,
> Of the moonlit peaks and the caves.
> Thou guardest them, Apollo!
> Over the grave of the slain Pytho.
> Though young, intolerably severe!
> Thou keepest aloof the profane,
> But the solitude oppresses thy votary!

Cut off from the profane, he is cut off from life, to which he is instinctively propelled; but life is what he cannot live, and he flies from it to
intolerable solitude:

> only death
> Can cut his oscillations short, and so
> Bring him to poise.

A certain action, a violent process of life, is possible to the contemplative
and to the artist; but the cost is extinction. What cannot be had is the

slow economical burning away of life; the damp faggots. Callicles, lower down, does not know this. When young

> we received the shock of mighty thoughts
> On simple minds with a pure natural joy;

but, this stage past, life is "ceaseless opposition," living a doomed attempt to preserve the "dwindling faculty of joy." Thinking of the sweet singing Callicles, the sage adds:

> Joy and the outward world must die to him
> As they are dead to me.

Callicles is given the last word. He is still far from the necessity of saving himself by fire; the outward world and the inward dream are still consistent, orderly and beautiful. Poetry belongs to this apparent joy, not to the truth of disaster:

> Not here, O Apollo!
> Are haunts meet for thee.

But Callicles will learn.

To describe the drama in these terms is like saying that the point of "Resolution and Independence" is:

> I could have laughed myself to scorn to find
> In that decrepit man so firm a mind.

The *rightness* of Callicles is not in question, nor is that of Empedocles; the poem does not offer that kind of answer (what good poem, the tradition has taught us to say, would?). What Callicles says is "wrong," but only by a false abstraction, for his words are part of a larger organization of words and images (in the sense of the word discussed later in this book) and their discursive truth or falsity is simply not the point. The poem is a victory; or, in another legitimate formula, a momentary stasis in an endless process, keeping a marble or a bronze repose. The question for the poet, however, is, where is the next victory to come from? Must he always write to end isolation for a moment? Arnold found this solution intolerable, suppressed *Empedocles* because it had no action, and set out to reform the world that was culpable of this absurd situation; forgetting perhaps, that "root of suffering." He plunged into action, into other people's business; we may remember Yeats's self-criticism: "every enterprise that offered, allured just so far as it was not my business," and the colder self-censure: "I had surrendered to the chief temptation of the artist, creation without toil." For in so far as Arnold was an artist — and he surely was a very considerable one — the answer to his dilemma, in the terms in which he undoubtedly understood it, lay in the cruel effort and continued self-expenditure of a series of Empedoclean victories, not in the carefully qualified betrayal, the compromise of life and art, action and inaction, which his Mask as Critics represents.

To himself, or to his notebook, Arnold would obviously not put it in this way (and of course, in any case, I boldly simplify). Arnold knew all about masks, and he knew about the Image, and what it costs; he abandoned it not only because it seemed to lack utility, but to save his soul. This may seem a dramatic way of putting it, yet not only Yeats but Pope would have understood it. Inert melancholy means self-destruction; hence all the exhortations to *Tüchtigkeit,* the repeated admonitions of the Notebooks: *Ecce labora et noli contristari.* Be known in action, not in suffering; seek light and not shade. Sénancour was seductive, but Sainte-Beuve was sane, and had little time for *poètes maudits.* Perhaps Arnold did alter his world, perhaps he even made it a little more like his dream. At any rate, he acted, and he got out of poetry and the dreadful fate of Empedocles. There is a sharp contrast here with Yeats, who, equally aware of the problem, and seeing it in very similar terms, knew why he wanted the management of men, understood his own guilt and felt conscious of damnation; he did not walk out of his dream, but simply extended it to include everything, and went on being a poet till he died.

It may seem curious that Arnold rather than Pater, who was much less reservedly admired in the nineties, should be the writer who most completely states the nineteenth-century English version of the old problem, how is the artist different, and what is the nature of his special access to truth, provided he has one; but Arnold was steeped in Romantic literature in three languages, and it is the dominance of the critic-school-inspector that precludes our seeing him in the first place as a fully Romantic, though fully critical, poet. Like his contemporaries on the Continent, though in different terms, he was disposed to see the prophetic or rhapsodic element in the poet as antithetical to the cast of mind which succeeded in "science"; but, unlike them, he so far accepted the valuation of scientists as to be content with the identification of poetry and that *Aberglaube* of which scientific criticism was depriving religion. This solution did not recommend itself to later English poets in the tradition; but they were, I think, aware of the importance of Arnold's grasp of the problem, and his influence upon them was more considerable and direct than might easily be believed.

It is nevertheless true that Pater, though equally preoccupied with the problem of incorporating the *utile* into the *dulce,* found answers which were at once more congenial to artists who wanted to go on being artists, and more liable to debasement. Perhaps in his life Pater exhibits, though in a manner peculiar to himself, the stigmata of isolation: without risking

the uncharted portions of his biography we can at least remind ourselves
of the famous and curious visit to London, immediately after the publication of *Marius the Epicurean*, when for a while he stepped out, with every
appearance of determination, in society, but withdrew gratefully to his
Oxford seclusion. For Pater, "sensibility" — the power of profoundly
experiencing what is significant in life and art — does for the artist the
work done by a coarser, apriorist morality in society at large. Art, indeed,
is life at its most intense and significant, "the products of the imagination
must themselves be held to present the most perfect forms of life," we are
told in *Marius;* art is what is significant in life, and so sensibility or insight, corruptible as it is, is the organ of moral knowledge, and art, for all
its refusal to worship the *idola* of vulgar morality, is the only true morality; indeed it is nothing less than life itself. The artist or the "aesthete,"
so elevated above all others, "refines" the instruments of "intuition" till
his "whole nature" becomes "one complex medium of reception"; what he
receives is the "vision" — the "beatific vision," if we cared to make it
such — of our actual experience in the world. To achieve this, which is
"not the conveyance of an abstract body of truths or principles" but "the
conveyance of an art," demands an intense individuality, a cultivation of
difference, and indeed conflict with the world at large. "It was intelligible
that this 'aesthetic' philosophy might find itself . . . weighing the claims
of that eager, concentrated, impassioned realization of experience against
those of received morality," possibly it might even be (and here Pater
could have been less carefully conditional), "as Pascal says of the kindly
and temperate wisdom of Montaigne, 'pernicious for those who have any
natural tendency to impiety or vice.'" Pater returns with some evidence
of anxiety to this possibly dangerous nonconformity; Marius comes to see
the cost of this specialization to its devotees: "if now and then, they apprehended the world in its fullness, and had a vision, almost 'beatific,' of
ideal personalities in life and art, yet these moments were a very costly
matter: they paid a great price for them, in the sacrifice of a thousand
possible sympathies, from which they detached themselves, in intellectual
pride. . . ." If we want to know more about this "vision," we have to
return to the description of art as intensified life — "spirit and matter
alike under their purest and most perfect conditions." At some time in the
past (Pater blames the schoolmen, though there is no good reason for
saddling them with the responsibility) it became habitual to establish a
false opposition between spirit and matter. In the truly apprehended experience they are not dissociated; in the "vision" they are inseparably
fused. The form, in fact, of the work of art is not dissociable from its
matter. "The mind," says Pater in the essay on Winckelmann, "begins
and ends with the first image, yet loses no part of the spiritual motive.
That motive is not loosely or lightly attached to the sensuous form, but

saturates and is identical with it." This, of course, is what gives music its status as the art to which all the others aspire; it resists the separation of matter and form. Pater's thought about his "vision" — it is the Image which is the subject of this essay — is well summed up by Mr. Graham Hough in the chapter on Pater in his book *The Last Romantics:* "His ideal is the kind of art where thought and its sensible embodiment are completely fused." Discourse is purged; the Image is the wisdom of Moneta, and it is a wisdom available only at great cost to the artist. Pater has his emblems of this costly wisdom, as Keats had the face of Moneta; and to him we shall return when such emblems come to be considered in themselves.

Between Wordsworth's account of "sensibility" and Pater's, it will be observed that a far-reaching change has occurred. For Pater the "sensibility" is the organ not merely of fine feeling but of moral discrimination and perception. The metaphysics of Coleridge crosses and diverts the simplicity of what Wordsworth, preceded by the empirical psychologists of the previous century, and succeeded by J. S. Mill, had believed: namely, that the higher degree of sensory organisation which distinguished poets from other men was fundamentally only a way of seeing and feeling *more,* not of seeing and feeling *differently,* and that it was a morally dangerous gift because it made it hard for the artist to be dully cautious about the satisfaction of his sensual appetites. Mill in particular seems to have correlated the necessarily high degree of "sensiblity" in artists with a certain intellectual immaturity, in Shelley for instance. And this, of course, is completely different from Pater's position; he maintains, in effect, that the estranged morality of artists is the only genuine kind. Now it is well known that Pater's account of the tension between the wisdom of the Image and a more utilitarian knowledge, between the artist's and the received morality, were gospel to the "tragic generation"; and for all their perversity, for all their inferiority to these great predecessors, that generation transmitted the doctrine to the twentieth century and fed the imagination of its major poet.

No one has written better than Yeats about that generation of poets who "had to face their ends when young" — about Wilde, who so admired "The Crucifixion of the Outcast," about Dowson, and Johnson, who was to become crucial to Yeats's own developing idea of isolation. When the outcast counts on being crucified, indeed savours the prospect; when, bitter and gay, he abstains from morality for fear, as Yeats put it in a late letter, of losing the indispensable "heroic ecstasy," then we know we are dealing with a tradition which has become fully, not to say histrionically, self-conscious. A movement is strong when a man like Henley throws himself into an antithetical, activist movement, to oppose it. ("To converse with him," said Wilde after Henley had thrown him out of a café, "is a physical no less than an intellectual recreation.")

If we suspect the testimony of those who were all too deeply involved, we may turn to the detached, ironical, adverbial James; who, asked by the *Yellow Book* for a story, immediately began his own investigation into the relation between the quality of the work and the estrangement of its maker. As Mr. Blackmur has said, James saw the artist as an interesting theme for fiction only in his guise as a failure. If *life* is important, why be an artist? "It's so poor — so poor! . . . I mean as compared with being a person of action — as living your works." The young artist in *The Lesson of the Master,* who is in a sense James's Callicles, may protest against this plight; but the Empedoclean Master has his answer ready:

> "What a false position, what a condemnation of the artist, that he's a mere disenfranchised monk and can produce his effect only by giving up personal happiness! What an arraignment of art!" Paul went on with trembling voice.
>
> "Ah, you don't imagine by chance that I'm defending art? 'Arraignment' — I should think so! Happy the societies in which it hasn't made its appearance, for from the moment it comes they have a consuming ache, they have an incurable corruption in their breast. Most assuredly the artist is in a false position! But I thought we were taking him for granted. . . ."

The life these artists want, and which the older of them achieves at the cost of corrupting his art, is appallingly seductive; it is represented by the girl the young man desires and the older man marries, and by "the life she embodied, the young purity and richness of which appeared to imply that real success was to resemble *that,* to bloom, to present the perfection of a fine type, not to have hammered out headachy fancies with a bent back at an ink-stained table." Allowing for the difference of accent, this might be Yeats speaking. A man may choose (if indeed there is a choice) perfection of the life or of the work; and, as Yeats believed, the latter choice meant sacrifice, self-sacrifice. Marchbanks in *Candida* is absurd and embarrassing; but like him, the poet of the nineties was doomed, if not for the sake of the future for which Marchbanks was to legislate, then simply to guarantee his lonely access to the Image.

Lionel Johnson, the friend of Yeats, was in some ways the most distinguished of these poets. Yeats's many accounts of him dwell upon those elements in Johnson's life which he came increasingly to regard as typical. It is of Johnson he thinks first when he considers the dissipation and despair that are the inevitable lot of the modern artist, who must live in a world where what Yeats called Unity of Being is impossible — a world of division, where body and mind work separately, not moving as one, where the artist's motive and subject is his struggle with himself. When

Yeats was young he used to write in autograph albums the famous words of Axel (later he substituted "For wisdom is a butterfly and not a gloomy bird of prey"). In 1899 he admiringly credited Johnson with Axel's attitude. "He has renounced the world and built up a twilight world instead. . . . He might have cried out with Axel, 'As for living, our servants will do that for us.' " It was *Marius,* said Yeats, that had taught Johnson's generation "to walk upon a rope"; for as life demanded extravagant participation, art required isolation. These men, whom he later groups in his lunar system as "belonging by nature to the nights near the full," made, says Yeats, what Arnold called "that morbid effort," and "suffered in their lives because of it." Formerly there had been ways of escape — Yeats's image for one of them is the Christian Thebaid — but these existed no more. Johnson might brood upon sanctity, but the Christian confessor cannot order a man not to be an artist, when "the whole life is art and poetry." "Full of the Image, he could never have that empty heart which calls the Hound of Heaven." And Johnson took pleasure in his doom, and in the torment he experienced because "some half-conscious part of him desired the world he had renounced"; he and Dowson "had the gravity of men who had found life out and were awakening from the dream." Johnson "fell" constantly; not only in the moral sense, but downstairs, off stools, brooding upon sanctity as he did so; but when Yeats calls him "much-falling" he almost certainly has in mind that poem so much admired by Dowson, called "Mystic and Cavalier," which is quoted in the *Autobiographies:*

> Go from me: I am one of those who fall . . .
>
> And in the battle, when the horsemen sweep
> Against a thousand deaths and fall on sleep:
> Who ever sought that sudden calm if I
> Sought not? Yet, could not die.

That such a poem exhausts action, that art exhausts life, was a notion that haunted Yeats: "Exhausted by the cry that it can never end, my love ends," he says magnificently in *A Vision;* and the song in *Resurrection* says the same thing. Johnson drained his life away into art, looking forward, with a kind of tragic irony, to ten years on when he would be ruined, begging from his friends; but he fell once too often before the time was up. What of the artist who continues to exist, preying gloomily upon the substance of his own life? Age merely confirms his abstraction, his exclusion from ordinary vitality, by turning him into a scarecrow. Age is as hateful as the headache and the cough, the inky laborious craft — Adam's curse — whether the artist be young or old. "My first denunciation of old age," said Yeats, "I made before I was twenty." Indeed the antithesis of living man and creator was one of the root assumptions of his life and work; he drew the artist as a tragic hero, proving life by the act of withdrawing from it. He was of the great conspiracy of contemplative men, and had made his choice of "perfection of the work"; but he retained and developed a harrowing sense of the goodness of life and action, and a conviction that "real success was to resemble *that*."

"Art is solitary man," wrote J. B. Yeats to his son, in the midst of their rich wartime correspondence. At that time, the poet was obviously unhappy about his abstinence from the exceptionally violent contemporary life of action; he had a taste for such violence, satisfied later when affable irregulars frequented Thoor Ballylee, and gunfights went on round the offices of Dublin, but in the English war he could not even play a poet's part. At such a time his father's emphasis on the proper detachment of the artist must have been agreeable. "All art is *reaction from life*," said J. B. Yeats, "but never, when it is vital and great, *an escape*. . . . In Michelangelo's time it was not possible to escape for life was there every *minute* as real as the toothache and as terrible and impressive as the judgment day." This is a very Yeatsian formula. Yet, whatever the quality of life he has to deal with, "the poet is the antithesis of the man of action." He does not "meddle in ethics"; he is a magician, "his dreams shall have a potency to defeat the actual at every point" — this is the poet *versus* the universe of death, the world of reason.

> Art exists that man cutting himself away from nature may build in his free consciousness buildings vaster and more sumptuous than these [the "habitations of ease and comfort"] built by science; furnished too with all manner of winding passages and closets and boudoirs and encircled with gardens well shaded and with everything he can desire — and we build all out of our spiritual pain — for if the bricks be not cemented and mortised by actual suffering, they will not hold together. Those others live on another plane, where if there is less joy there is much less pain. . . . The artist . . . out of his pain and humiliations constructs for himself habitations, and if she [Nature] sweeps them away with a blow of her hand he only builds them afresh, and as his joy is chiefly in the act of building he does not mind how often he has to do it.

Here, apart from the dubious connotations of the architectural analogy, we have something close to the essence of the younger Yeats's résumé of the tradition. What, after all, is the *Vision,* but a blueprint of a palace of art, a place in the mind where men may suffer, some less and some more, where the artist explains his joy in making at the cost of isolation and suffering? The joy of building is the same thing as Yeats's brief victory, the creation of an antithesis for fate. The father admitted his intellectual debt to his son; but nobody could have restated the Romantic case so suitably to the son's purposes.

The free, self-delighting intellect which knows that pain is the cost of its joy; the licence to look inward and paint, as Blake and Palmer painted, a symbolic world; to make a magical explanation of a divine order — all this represents the victory of Coleridge, of Blake and the French; it is the heritage, delightful and tragic, to which Yeats was born. Much in his own life made him kick against the pricks; his love of aristocratic skills, of the achievements of others in the sphere of action, of his own successes in the active life. Out of this oscillation between the two states of life came the desire, natural to a magician, to tame by explaining, to answer the question, why are men different, and why are men divided? But long before Yeats ventured on his schematic explanations he had been concerned in a more general way with the justification of the ways of the artist and the defence of poetry.

The development of Yeats's cluster of ideas about the status of the artist in life is complex, and some aspects of it I here almost ignore. But I must say something about it . . . because it is an indispensable preliminary to any discussion of Yeats's conception of the work of art itself. So certain was he that art was not "escape" that he thought of the situation the other way round: art was what you tried to escape from. The failure of Wilde to understand this was, for Yeats, something to be explained only by taking Wilde out of the ranks of the artists altogether. It was because he hated the conventional notion of "escape" that Yeats was early troubled by that dreaminess, that conscientious lack of actuality, which prevailed when he made his début; he was trying to shake it off much earlier than is usually supposed, trying to get strong, living rhythms and a language "as subtle, as complex, as full of mysterious life, as the body of a flower or of a woman." He grew suspicious of a kind of covert sensuality in this Romantic dream. We may be grateful that he did; the extension of his range, the cult of a language of organic rhythms and of great rhetorical variety, are what made him a great poet. But for all that, he never ceased to subscribe to the old doctrine that art is a kind of dream, and that to dream it well is the most difficult and exhausting of all callings. Great art unifies sense and spirit, like the body of a beautiful woman, or like a portrait by Titian, or like Donne's Elizabeth Drury; but the age was unpropitious, the available method faulty and in need of revision. The tradition is not to be sacrificed; all that is potent and valid in it is to be preserved, though in a new form.

In *A Vision*, Yeats wrote of "an early conviction of mine that the creative power of the lyric poet depends upon his accepting some of a few traditional attitudes, lover, sage, hero, scorner of life"; and as early as *The Celtic Twilight* he describes a Symbolist vision, of apes eating jewels in hell, which contains the elements of what later became a powerful and immediate impulse. "I knew that I saw the Celtic Hell, and my own Hell,

the Hell of the artist, and that all who sought after beautiful and wonderful things with too avid a thirst, lost peace and form, and became shapeless and common." Here, in embryo, is the story of the cost to the artist
of what Yeats, in an early essay entitled "Poetry and the Tradition," calls
his unique "continual and self-delighting happiness"; it turns the dedicated, however pretty their plumage, into old scarecrows, and excludes
them from life. Hanrahan, of whom the poet was to speak again in the
isolation of the Tower, — "leave Hanrahan, For I need all his mighty
memories" — is tricked into leaving the dance of life, just as he was coming to where comfort was. Later he composed a great curse on old age; he
had been touched by the Sidhe — a Yeatsian figure for the dedication,
voluntary or no, of the artist — and had to pay the cost. The poet is not
like the others. Joy makes him free for his task of stitching and unstitch-
ing, of labour at the higher reality of the imagination. But this labour is
what ruins life, makes the body shapeless and common. Solitude grows
with what Yeats calls the growing absorption of the dream; the long series
of indecisive victories, "intellectual recreations of all that exterior fate
snatches away," increase it further and torment the poet. His fate is a
ruined life, intermittently illuminated by the Image. Poets and artists,
says Yeats in *Per Amica Silentia Lunae,* "must go from desire to weari-
ness and so to desire again, and live for the moment when vision comes
like terrible lightning, in the humility of the brutes." Tormented by the
necessary failure of his life, appalled in conscience or in vanity, he can
say, "I suffered continual remorse, and only became content when my
abstractions had composed themselves into picture and dramatisation."
This content is impermanent; the poet is thus perpetually divided against
himself. Hence the distinction Yeats makes "between the perfection that
is from a man's combat with himself and that which is from a combat
with circumstance." Behind it lies the hopeless anger of an artist in love
with action, with life. This occupied Yeats incessantly, and it is hardly too
much to say that it informs most of his later poetry as well as his universal history, which is, virtually, an attempt to make all history an explanation of why the modern artist is isolated.

A young poet, encountering for the first time the *fertilisante douleur*
and the massive indifference of the public, might be aware of the pressure
of problems similar to his own in the poetry of Yeats without grasping the
fullness of Yeats's statement, the institutional — one might almost say
apostolic — quality of this poet, which places the enthusiastic anti-
Romanticism of a Hulme as a heresy, the sad heresy of the slightly misin-
formed, who seek a primitive purity with eyes blinded by tradition. The
modern truth about the poet's difference, about that stern injunction,
"No road through to action," about the problem of communication —

how and to whom? — is in Yeats, in a rich and perfected context. He is
the poet in whose work Romantic isolation achieves its full quality as a
theme for poetry, being no longer a pose, a complaint, or a programme;
and his treatment of it is very closely related to his belief in what Pater
called "vision" and the French called Symbol. He does not deny the pain
that is terminated momentarily by the daily victory, permanently by
death; indeed the fascination of this last, fierce solution was as apparent
to him as to Moritz and some of the French writers. He simply understands it more fully than anybody else, in its relation to the Image. That is
why there is so much about Yeats in what follows. The poem that gives us
the best start is his elegy, "In Memory of Major Robert Gregory." . . . .

E. H. GOMBRICH

Meditations on a Hobby Horse or the Roots of Artistic Form

The subject of this article is a very ordinary hobby horse. It is
neither metaphorical nor purely imaginary, at least not more so than the
broomstick on which Swift wrote his meditations. It is usually content
with its place in the corner of the nursery and it has no aesthetic ambitions. Indeed it abhors frills. It is satisfied with its broomstick body and
its crudely carved head which just marks the upper end and serves as
holder for the reins. How should we address it? Should we describe it as
an "image of a horse"? The compilers of the *Pocket Oxford Dictionary*
would hardly have agreed. They defined *image* as "imitation of object's
external form" and the "external form" of a horse is surely not "imitated"
here. So much the worse, we might say, for the "external form," that
elusive remnant of the Greek philosophical tradition which has dominated our aesthetic language for so long. Luckily there is another word in

SOURCE: "Meditations on a Hobby Horse or the Roots of Artistic Form" is from
Meditations on a Hobby Horse and Other Essays on the Theory of Art published by
Phaidon Press, London, and Phaidon Publishers, Inc., New York. Reprinted by
permission of Phaidon Press, Ltd. This essay was originally written as a contribution
to *Aspects of Form: A Symposium on Form in Nature and Art,* edited by L. L. Whyte
(London, 1951).

the *Dictionary* which might prove more accommodating: *representation.* To *represent,* we read, can be used in the sense of "call up by description or portrayal or imagination, figure, place likeness of before mind or senses, serve or be meant as likeness of . . . stand for, be specimen of, fill place of, be substitute for." A portrayal of a horse? Surely not. A substitute for a horse? Yes. That it is. Perhaps there is more in this formula than meets the eye.

I

Let us first ride our wooden steed into battle against a number of ghosts which still haunt the language of art criticism. One of them we even found entrenched in the *Oxford Dictionary.* The implication of its definition of an image is that the artist "imitates," the "external form" of the object in front of him, and the beholder, in his turn, recognizes the "subject" of the work of art by this "form." This is what might be called the traditional view of representation. Its corollary is that a work of art will either be a faithful copy, in fact a complete replica, of the object represented, or will involve some degree of "abstraction." The artist, we read, abstracts the "form" from the object he sees. The sculptor usually abstracts the three-dimensional form, and abstracts *from* colour; the painter abstracts contours and colours, and *from* the third dimension. In this context one hears it said that the draughtsman's line is a "tremendous feat of abstraction" because it does not "occur in nature." A modern sculptor of Brancusi's persuasion may be praised or blamed for "carrying abstraction to its logical extreme." Finally the label of "abstract art" for the creation of "pure" forms carries with it a similar implication. Yet we need only look at our hobby horse to see that the very idea of abstraction as a complicated mental act lands us in curious absurdities. There is an old music hall joke describing a drunkard who politely lifts his hat to every lamp-post he passes. Should we say that the liquor has so increased his power of abstraction that he is now able to isolate the formal quality of uprightness from both lamp-post and the human figure? Our mind, of course, works by differentiation rather than by generalization, and the child will for long call all four-footers of a certain size "gee-gee" before it learns to distinguish breeds and "forms"! [1]

II

Then there is that age-old problem of universals as applied to art. It has received its classical formulation in the Platonizing theories of the Academicians. "A history-painter," says Reynolds, "paints man in general; a portrait-painter a particular man, and therefore a defective model." [2]

This, of course, is the theory of abstraction applied to one specific problem. The implications are that the portrait, being an exact copy of a man's
"external form" with all "blemishes" and "accidents," refers to the individual person exactly as does the proper name. The painter, however,
who wants to "elevate his style" disregards the particular and "generalizes
the forms." Such a picture will no longer represent a particular man but
rather the class or concept "man." There is a deceptive simplicity in this
argument, but it makes at least one unwarranted assumption: that every
image of this kind necessarily refers to something outside itself — be it
individual or class. But nothing of the kind need be implied when we
point to an image and say "this is a man." Strictly speaking that statement
may be interpreted to mean that the image itself is a member of the class
"man." Nor is that interpretation as farfetched as it may sound. In fact our
hobby horse would submit to no other interpretation. By the logic of Reynolds's reasoning it would have to represent the most generalized idea of
horseness. But if the child calls a stick a horse it obviously means nothing
of the kind. The stick is neither a sign signifying the concept horse nor
is it a portrait of an individual horse. By its capacity to serve as a
"substitute" the stick becomes a horse in its own right, it belongs in the
class of "gee-gees" and may even merit a proper name of its own.

When Pygmalion blocked out a figure from his marble he did not at first
represent a "generalized" human form, and then gradually a particular
woman. For as he chipped away and made it more lifelike the block was
not turned into a portrait — not even in the unlikely case that he used a
live model. So when his prayers were heard and the statue came to life she
was Galatea and no one else — and that regardless of whether she had
been fashioned in an archaic, idealistic, or naturalistic style. The question
of reference, in fact, is totally independent of the degree of differentiation.
The witch who made a "generalized" wax dummy of an enemy may have
meant it to refer to someone in particular. She would then pronounce the
right spell to establish this link — much as we may write a caption under
a generalized picture to do the same. But even those proverbial replicas
of nature, Madame Tussaud's effigies, need the same treatment. Those in
the galleries which are labelled are "portraits of the great." The figure on
the staircase made to hoax the visitor simply represents "an" attendant, one
member of a class. It stands there as a "substitute" for the expected guard
— but it is not more "generalized" in Reynolds's sense.

III

The idea that art is "creation" rather than "imitation" is sufficiently familiar. It has been proclaimed in various forms from the time of
Leonardo, who insisted that the painter is "Lord of all Things," [3] to that

of Klee, who wanted to create as Nature does.[4] But the more solemn overtones of metaphysical power disappear when we leave art for toys. The
child "makes" a train either of a few blocks or with pencil on paper. Surrounded as we are by posters and newspapers carrying illustrations of
commodities or events, we find it difficult to rid ourselves of the prejudice
that all images should be "read" as referring to some imaginary or actual
reality. Only the historian knows how hard it is to look at Pygmalion's
work without comparing it with nature. But recently we have been made
aware how thoroughly we misunderstand primitive or Egyptian art whenever we make the assumption that the artist "distorts" his motif or that he
even wants us to see in his work the record of any specific experience.[5]
In many cases these images "represent" in the sense of being substitutes.
The clay horse or servant, buried in the tomb of the mighty, takes the
place of the living. The idol takes the place of the god. The question
whether it represents the "external form" of the particular divinity or, for
that matter, of a class of demons is quite inappropriate. The idol serves as
the substitute of the God in worship and ritual — it is a man-made god in
precisely the sense that the hobby horse is a man-made horse; to question
it further means to court deception.[6]

There is another misunderstanding to be guarded against. We often try
instinctively to save our idea of "representation" by shifting it to another
plane. Where we cannot refer the image to a motif in the outer world we
take it to be a portrayal of a motif in the artist's inner world. Much
critical (and uncritical) writing on both primitive and modern art betrays
this assumption. But to apply the naturalistic idea of portrayal to dreams
and visions — let alone to unconscious images — begs a whole number
of questions.[7] The hobby horse does not portray our idea of a horse. The
fearsome monster or funny face we may doodle on our blotting pad is not
projected out of our mind as paint is "ex-pressed" out of a paint tube. Of
course any image will be in some way symptomatic of its maker, but to
think of it as of a photograph of a pre-existing reality is to misunderstand
the whole process of image-making.

IV

Can our substitute take us further? Perhaps, if we consider how it
could become a substitute. The "first" hobby horse (to use eighteenth-
century language) was probably no image at all. Just a stick which qualified as a horse because one could ride on it. The *tertium comparationis,*
the common factor, was function rather than form. Or, more precisely,
that formal aspect which fulfilled the minimum requirement for the performance of the function — for any "ridable" object could serve as a
horse. If that is true we may be enabled to cross a boundary which is

usually regarded as closed and sealed. For in this sense "substitutes" reach deep into biological functions that are common to man and animal. The cat runs after the ball as if it were a mouse. The baby sucks its thumb as if it were the breast. In a sense the ball "represents" a mouse to the cat, the thumb a breast to the baby. But here too "representation" does not depend on formal similarities, beyond the minimum requirements of function. The ball has nothing in common with the mouse except that it is chasable. The thumb nothing with the breast except that it is suckable. As "substitutes" they fulfill certain demands of the organism. They are keys which happen to fit into biological or psychological locks, or counterfeit coins which make the machine work when dropped into the slot.

In the language of the nursery the psychological function of "representation" is still recognized. The child will reject a perfectly naturalistic doll in favour of some monstrously "abstract" dummy which is "cuddly." It may even dispose of the element of "form" altogether and take to a blanket or an eiderdown as its favourite "comforter" — a substitute on which to bestow its love. Later in life, as the psychoanalysts tell us, it may bestow this same love on a worthy or unworthy living substitute. A teacher may "take the place" of the mother, a dictator or even an enemy may come to "represent" the father. Once more the common denominator between the symbol and the thing symbolized is not the "external form" but the function; the mother symbol would be lovable, the father-imago fearable, or whatever the case may be.

Now this psychological concept of symbolization seems to lead so very far away from the more precise meaning which the word "representation" has acquired in the figurative arts. Can there be any gain in throwing all these meanings together? Possibly: for anything seems worth trying, to get the function of symbolizing out of its isolation.

The "origin of art" has ceased to be a popular topic. But the origin of the hobby horse may be a permitted subject for speculation. Let us assume that the owner of the stick on which he proudly rode through the land decided in a playful or magic mood — and who could always distinguish between the two? — to fix "real" reins and that finally he was even tempted to "give" it two eyes near the top end. Some grass could have passed for a mane. Thus our inventor "had a horse." He had made one. Now there are two things about this fictitious event which have some bearing on the idea of the figurative arts. One is that, contrary to what is sometimes said, communication need not come into this process at all. He may not have wanted to show his horse to anyone. It just served as a focus for his fantasies as he galloped along — though more likely than not it fulfilled this same function for a tribe to which it "represented" some horse-demon of fertility and power.[8] We may sum up the moral of this "Just So Story" by saying that substitution may precede portrayal, and creation communication. It remains to be seen how such a general theory can be tested. If it can, it may really throw light on some concrete questions. Even the origin of language, that notorious problem of speculative history,[9] might be investigated from this angle. For what if the "pow-wow" theory, which sees the root of language in imitation, and the "pooh-pooh" theory, which sees it in emotive interjection, were to be joined by yet another? We might term it the "niam-niam" theory postulating the primitive hunter laying awake through hungry winter nights and making the sound of eating, not for communication but as a substitute for eating — being joined, perhaps, by a ritualistic chorus trying to conjure up the phantasm of food.

V

There is one sphere in which the investigation of the "representational" function of forms has made considerable progress of late, that of animal psychology. Pliny, and innumerable writers after him, have regarded it as the greatest triumph of naturalistic art for a painter to have deceived sparrows or horses. The implication of these anecdotes is that a human beholder easily recognizes a bunch of grapes in a painting because for him recognition is an intellectual act. But for the birds to fly at the painting is a sign of complete "objective" illusion. It is a plausible idea, but a wrong one. The merest outline of a cow seems sufficient for a tsetse trap, for somehow it sets the apparatus of attraction in motion and "deceives" the fly. To the fly, we might say, the crude trap has the "significant" form — biologically significant, that is. It appears that visual stimuli of this kind play an important part in the animal world. By varying the shapes of "dummies" to which animals were seen to respond, the "minimum image" that still sufficed to release a specific reaction has been ascertained.[10] Thus little birds will open their beak when they see the feeding parent approaching the nest, but they will also do so when they are shown two darkish roundels of different size, the silhouette of the head and body of the bird "represented" in its most "generalized" form. Certain young fishes can even be deceived by two simple dots arranged horizontally, which they take to be the eyes of the mother fish, in whose mouth they are accustomed to shelter against danger. The fame of Zeuxis will have to rest on other achievements than his deception of birds.

An "image" in this biological sense is not an imitation of an object's external form but an imitation of certain privileged or relevant aspects. It is here that a wide field of investigation would seem to open. For man is not exempt from this type of reaction.[11] The artist who goes out to represent the visible world is not simply faced with a neutral medley of forms he seeks to "imitate." Ours is a structured universe whose main lines of force are still bent and fashioned by our biological and psychological needs, however much they may be overlaid by cultural influences. We know that there are certain privileged motifs in our world to which we respond almost too easily. The human face may be outstanding among them. Whether by instinct or by very early training, we are certainly ever disposed to single out the expressive features of a face from the chaos of sensations that surrounds it, and to respond to its slightest variations with fear or joy. Our whole perceptual apparatus is somehow hypersensitized in this direction of physiognomic vision [12] and the merest hint suffices for us to create an expressive physiognomy that "looks" at us with surprising intensity. In a heightened state of emotion, in the dark, or in a feverish spell, the looseness of this trigger may assume pathological forms. We may see faces in the pattern of a wallpaper, and three apples arranged on a plate may stare at us like two eyes and a clownish nose. What wonder that it is so easy to "make" a face with two dots and a stroke even though their geometrical constellation may be greatly at variance with the "external form" of a real head? The well-known graphic joke of the "reversible face" might well be taken as a model for experiments which could still be made in this direction. It shows to what extent the group of shapes that can be read as a physiognomy has priority over all other readings. It turns the side which is the right way up into a convincing face and disintegrates the one that is upside down into a mere jumble of forms which is accepted as a strange headgear.[13] In good pictures of this kind it needs a real effort to see both faces at the same time, and perhaps we never quite succeed. Our automatic response is stronger than our intellectual awareness.

Seen in the light of the biological examples discussed above there is nothing surprising in this observation. We may venture the guess that this type of automatic recognition is dependent on the two factors of resemblance and biological relevance, and that the two may stand in some kind of inverse ratio. The greater the biological relevance an object has for us the more will we be attuned to its recognition — and the more tolerant will therefore be our standards of formal correspondence. In an erotically charged atmosphere the merest hint of formal similarity with sexual functions creates the desired response and the same is true of the dream symbols investigated by Freud. The hungry man will be similarly attuned to the discovery of food — he will scan the world for the slightest promise of nourishment. The starving may even project food into all sorts of dissimilar objects — as Chaplin does in *Gold Rush* when his huge companion suddenly appears to him as a chicken. Can it have been some such experience which stimulated our "niam-niam" chanting hunters to see their longed-for prey in the patches and irregular shapes on the dark cave walls? Could they perhaps gradually have sought this experience in the deep mysterious recesses of the rocks, much as Leonardo sought out crumbling walls to aid his visual fantasies? Could they, finally, have been prompted to fill in such "readable" outlines with coloured earth — to have at least something "spearable" at hand which might "represent" the eatable in some magic fashion? There is no way of testing such a theory, but if it is true that cave artists often "exploited" the natural formations of the rocks,[14] this, together with the "eidetic" character of their works,[15] would at least not contradict our fantasy. The great naturalism of cave paintings may after all be a very late flower. It may correspond to our late, derivative, and naturalistic hobby horse.

VI

It needed two conditions, then, to turn a stick into our hobby horse: first, that its form made it just possible to ride on it; secondly — and perhaps decisively — that riding mattered. Fortunately it still needs no great effort of the imagination to understand how the horse could become such a focus of desires and aspirations, for our language still carries the metaphors moulded by a feudal past when to be chival-rous was to be horsy. The same stick that had to represent a horse in such a setting would have become the substitute of something else in another. It might have become a sword, sceptre, or — in the context of ancestor worship — a fetish representing a dead chieftain. Seen from the point of view of "abstraction," such a convergence of meanings onto one shape offers considerable difficulties, but from that of psychological "projection" of meanings it becomes more easily intelligible. After all a whole diagnostic technique has been built up on the assumption that the meanings read into identical forms by different people tell us more about the readers than about the forms. In the sphere of art it has been shown that the same triangular shape which is the favourite pattern of many adjoining American Indian tribes is given different meanings reflecting the main preoccupations of the peoples concerned.[16] To the student of styles this discovery that one basic form can be made to represent a variety of objects may still become significant. For while the idea of realistic pictures being deliberately "stylized" seems hard to swallow, the opposite idea of a limited vocabulary of simple shapes being used for the building up of different representations would fit much better into what we know of primitive art.

VII

Once we get used to the idea of "representation" as a two-way affair rooted in psychological dispositions we may be able to refine a concept which has proved quite indispensable to the historian of art and which is nevertheless rather unsatisfactory: that of the "conceptual image." By this we mean the mode of representation which is more or less common to children's drawings and to various forms of primitive and primitivist art. The remoteness of this type of imagery from any visual experience has often been described.[17] The explanation of this fact which is most usually advanced is that the child (and the primitive) do not draw what they "see" but what they "know." According to this idea the typical children's drawing of a manikin is really a graphic enumeration of those human features the child remembered.[18] It represents the content of the childish "concept" of man. But to speak of "knowledge" or "intellectual realism" (as the French do [19]) brings us dangerously near to the fallacy of "abstraction." So back to our hobby horse. Is it quite correct to say that it consists of features which make up the "concept" of a horse or that it reflects the memory image of horses seen? No — because this formulation omits one factor: the stick. If we keep in mind that representation is originally the creation of substitutes out of given material we may reach safer ground. The greater the wish to ride, the fewer may be the features that will do for a horse. But at a certain stage it must have eyes — for how else could it see? At the most primitive level, then, the conceptual image might be identified with what we have called the minimum image — that minimum, that is, which will make it fit into a psychological lock. The form of the key depends on the material out of which it is fashioned, and on the lock. It would be a dangerous mistake, however, to equate the "conceptual image" as we find it used in the historical styles with this psychologically grounded minimum image. On the contrary. One has the impression that the presence of these schemata is always felt but that they are as much avoided as exploited.[20] We must reckon with the possibility of a "style" being a set of conventions born out of complex tensions. The man-made image must be complete. The servant for the grave must have two hands and two feet. But he must not become a double under the artist's hands. Image-making is beset with dangers. One false stroke and the rigid mask of the face may assume an evil leer. Strict adherence to conventions alone can guard against such dangers. And thus primitive art seems often to keep on that narrow ledge that lies between the lifeless and the uncanny. If the hobby horse became too lifelike it might gallop away on its own.[21]

VIII

The contrast between primitive art and "naturalistic" or "illusionist" art can easily be overdrawn.[22] All art is "image-making" and all image-making is rooted in the creation of substitutes. Even the artist of an "illusionist" persuasion must make the man-made, the "conceptual" image of conventions his starting point. Strange as it may seem he cannot simply "imitate an object's external form" without having first learned how to construct such a form. If it were otherwise there would be no need for the innumerable books on "how to draw the human figure" or "how to draw ships." Wölfflin once remarked that all pictures owe more to other pictures than they do to nature.[23] It is a point which is familiar to the student of pictorial traditions but which is still insufficiently understood in its psychological implications. Perhaps the reason is that, contrary to the hopeful belief of many artists, the "innocent eye" which should see the world afresh would not see it at all. It would smart under the painful impact of a chaotic medley of forms and colours.[24] In this sense the conventional vocabulary of basic forms is still indispensable to the artist as a starting point, as a focus of organization.

How, then, should we interpret the great divide which runs through the history of art and sets off the few islands of illusionist styles, of Greece, of China, and of the Renaissance, from the vast ocean of "conceptual" art?

One difference, undoubtedly, lies in a change of function. In a way the change is implicit in the emergence of the idea of the image as a "representation" in our modern sense of the word. As soon as it is generally understood that an image need not exist in its own right, that it may refer to something outside itself and therefore be the record of a visual experience rather than the creation of a substitute, the basic rules of primitive art can be transgressed with impunity. No longer is there any need for that completeness of essentials which belongs to the conceptual style, no longer is there the fear of the casual which dominates the archaic conception of art. The picture of a man on a Greek vase no longer needs a hand or a foot in full view. We know it is meant as a shadow, a mere record of what the artist saw or might see, and we are quite ready to join in the game and to supplement with our imagination what the real motif undoubtedly possessed. Once this idea of the picture suggesting something beyond what is really there is accepted in all its implications — and this certainly did not happen overnight — we are indeed forced to let our imagination play around it. We endow it with "space" around its forms which is only another way of saying that we understand the reality which it evokes as three-dimensional, that the man could move and that even the aspect momentarily hidden "was there." [25] When medieval art broke away from that narrative conceptual symbolism into which the formulas of classical art had been frozen, Giotto made particular use of the figure seen from behind which stimulates our "spatial" imagination by forcing us to imagine the other side.

Thus the idea of the picture as a representation of a reality outside itself leads to an interesting paradox. On the one hand it compels us to refer every figure and every object shown to that imaginary reality which is "meant." This mental operation can only be completed if the picture allows us to infer not only the "external form" of every object represented but also its relative size and position. It leads us to that "rationalization of space" we call scientific perspective by which the picture plane becomes a window through which we look into the imaginary world the artist creates there for us. In theory, at least, painting is then conceived in terms of geometrical projection.[26]

The paradox of the situation is that, once the whole picture is regarded as the representation of a slice of reality, a new context is created in which the conceptual image plays a different part. For the first consequence of the "window" idea is that we cannot conceive of any spot on the panel which is not "significant," which does not represent something. The empty patch thus easily comes to signify light, air, and atmosphere, and the vague form is interpreted as enveloped by air. It is this confidence in the representational context which is given by the very convention of the frame, which makes the development of impressionist methods possible. The artists who tried to rid themselves of their conceptual knowledge, who conscientiously became beholders of their own work and never ceased matching their created images against their impressions by stepping back and comparing the two — these artists could only achieve their aim by shifting something of the load of creation on to the beholder. For what else does it mean if we are enjoined to step back in turn and watch the coloured patches of an impressionist landscape "spring to life"? It means that the painter relies on our readiness to take hints, to read contexts, and to call up our conceptual image under his guidance. The blob in the painting by Manet which stands for a horse is no more an imitation of its external form than is our hobby horse. But he has so cleverly contrived it that it evokes the image in us — provided, of course, we collaborate.

Here there may be another field for independent investigation. For those "privileged" objects which play their part in the earliest layers of image-making recur — as was to be expected — in that of image-reading. The more vital the feature that is indicated by the context and yet omitted, the more intense seems to be the process that is started off. On its lowest level this method of "suggestive veiling" is familiar to erotic art. Not, of course, to its Pygmalion phase, but to its illusionist applications. What is here a crude exploitation of an obvious biological stimulus may have its parallel, for instance, in the representation of the human face. Leonardo achieved his greatest triumphs of lifelike expression by blurring precisely the features in which the expression resides, thus compelling us to complete the act of creation. Rembrandt could dare to leave the eyes of his most moving portraits in the shade because we are thus stimulated to supplement them.[27] The "evocative" image, like its "conceptual" counterpart, should be studied against a wider psychological background.

IX

My hobby horse is not art. At best it can claim the attention of iconology, that emerging branch of study which is to art criticism what linguistics is to the criticism of literature. But has not modern art experimented with the primitive image, with the "creation" of forms, and the exploitation of deep-rooted psychological forces? It has. But whatever the nostalgic wish of their makers, the meaning of these forms can never be the same as that of their primitive models. For that strange precinct we call "art" is like a hall of mirrors or a whispering gallery. Each form conjures up a thousand memories and after-images. No sooner is an image presented as art than, by this very act, a new frame of reference is created which it cannot escape. It becomes part of an institution as surely as does the toy in the nursery. If — as might be conceivable — a Picasso would turn from pottery to hobby horses and send the products of this whim to an exhibition, we might read them as demonstrations, as satirical symbols, as a declaration of faith in humble things or as self-irony — but one thing would be denied even to the greatest of contemporary artists: he could not make the hobby horse mean to us what it meant to its first creator. That way is barred by the angel with a flaming sword.

JORGE LUIS BORGES

Partial Enchantments of the Quixote

It is probable that these observations have been made before at least once and, perhaps, many times; the novelty of them interests me less than their possible truth.

In comparison with other classics (the *Iliad,* the *Aeneid,* the *Pharsalia,* the Dantesque *Comedy,* the tragedies and comedies of Shakespeare), the *Quixote* is realistic; but this realism differs essentially from the nineteenth-century variety. Joseph Conrad was able to write that he excluded the supernatural from his works, because to include it would seem to be a denial that the quotidian was marvelous. I do not know whether Miguel de Cervantes shared that idea, but I do know that the form of the *Quixote* caused him to counterpose a real, prosaic world with an imaginary, poetic one. Conrad and Henry James incorporated reality into their novels

SOURCE: "Partial Enchantments of the *Quixote*" is from *Other Inquisitions, 1947–1952,* translated by Ruth L. C. Simms (Austin: University of Texas Press, 1964). Copyright © 1964 by the University of Texas Press and reprinted by their permission.

because they deemed it poetic; to Cervantes the real and the poetic are antonyms. To the vast and vague geography of the Amadís, he opposes the dusty roads and sordid inns of Castile; it is as if a novelist of our day were to sketch a satirical caricature of, say, service stations, treating them in a ludicrous way. Cervantes has created for us the poetry of seventeenth-century Spain, but neither that century nor that Spain were poetic for him; men like Unamuno or Azorín or Antonio Machado, whose emotions were stirred by the evocaton of La Mancha, he would have found incomprehensible. The plan of his work precluded the marvelous, but still the marvelous had to be there, if only indirectly, as crime and mystery are present in a parody of the detective story. Cervantes could not have had recourse to amulets or sorcery, but he insinuated the supernatural in a subtle and therefore more effective way. In his heart of hearts, Cervantes loved the supernatural. In 1924 Paul Groussac observed: "With his cursory smattering of Latin and Italian, Cervantes derived his literary production primarily from pastoral novels and novels of chivalry, fables that had given solace to him in his captivity." The *Quixote* is less an antidote for those tales than a secret nostalgic farewell.

Every novel is an ideal depiction of reality. Cervantes delights in fusing the objective and the subjective, the world of the reader and the world of the book. In the chapters that consider whether the barber's basin is a helmet and the packsaddle a harness, the problem is treated explicitly; other parts, as I mentioned before, merely hint at it. In the sixth chapter of Part One the priest and the barber inspect Don Quixote's library; astonishingly enough, one of the books they examine is the *Galatea* by Cervantes. It develops that the barber is a friend of his who does not admire him very much, and says that Cervantes is more versed in misfortunes than in verses. He adds that the book has a rather well-constructed plot; it proposes something and concludes nothing. The barber, a dream of Cervantes or a form of one of Cervantes' dreams, passes judgment on Cervantes. It is also surprising to learn, at the beginning of Chapter IX, that the whole novel has been translated from the Arabic and that Cervantes acquired the manuscript in the marketplace of Toledo. It was translated by a Morisco, who lived in Cervantes' house for more than a month and a half while he completed the task. We are reminded of Carlyle, who feigned that the *Sartor Resartus* was a partial version of a work published in Germany by Dr. Diogenes Teufelsdröckh; we are reminded of the Spanish Rabbi Moisés de León, who wrote the *Zohar* or *Book of the Splendor* and divulged it as the work of a Palestinian rabbi of the third century.

The set of strange ambiguities culminates in Part Two. The protagonists of the *Quixote* who are, also, readers of the *Quixote,* have read Part One. Here we inevitably remember the case of Shakespeare, who includes on the stage of *Hamlet* another stage, where a tragedy almost like that of

Hamlet is being presented. The imperfect correspondence of the principal work and the secondary one lessens the effectiveness of that inclusion. A device analogous to Cervantes' and even more startling, appears in the *Ramayana,* epic poem by Valmiki, which relates the deeds of Rama and his war with the evil spirits. In the last book Rama's children, not knowing who their father is, seek refuge in a forest, where a hermit teaches them to read. That teacher, strangely enough, is Valmiki; the book they study is the *Ramayana.* Rama orders a sacrifice of horses; Valmiki comes to the ceremony with his pupils. They sing the *Ramayana* to the accompaniment of the lute. Rama hears his own story, recognizes his children, and then rewards the poet.

Chance has caused something similar to occur in *A Thousand and One Nights.* That compilation of fantastic stories duplicates and reduplicates to the point of vertigo the ramification of a central tale into subordinate ones, without attempting to evaluate their realities; the effect (which should have been profound) is superficial, like that of a Persian rug. The first story is well known: the desolate oath of the Sultan, who marries a maiden each night and then orders her to be beheaded at dawn, and the courage of Scheherazade, who delights him with fables until a thousand and one nights have gyrated about them and she shows him their son. The need to complete a thousand and one sections obliged the copyists of the work to make all sorts of interpolations. None is so disturbing as that of night DCII, magic among the nights. That is when the Sultan hears his own story from the Sultana's mouth. He hears the beginning of the story, which embraces all the other stories as well as — monstrously — itself. Does the reader perceive the unlimited possibilities of that interpolation, the curious danger — that the Sultana may persist and the Sultan, transfixed, will hear forever the truncated story of *A Thousand and One Nights,* now infinite and circular?

The inventions of philosophy are no less fantastic than those of art. In the first volume of *The World and the Individual* (1899) Josiah Royce has formulated the following one:

> . . . let us suppose, if you please, that a portion of the surface of England is very perfectly levelled and smoothed, and is then devoted to the production of our precise map of England. . . . But now suppose that this our resemblance is to be made absolutely exact, in the sense previously defined. A map of England, contained within England, is to represent, down to the minutest detail, every contour and marking, natural or artificial, that occurs upon the surface of England. . . . For the map, in order to be complete, according to the rule given, will have to contain, as a part of itself, a representation of its own contour and contents. In order that this representation should be constructed, the representation itself will have to contain once more, as a part of

itself, a representation of its own contour and contents; and this representation, in order to be exact, will have once more to contain an image of itself; and so on without limit.

Why does it make us uneasy to know that the map is within the map and the thousand and one nights are within the book of *A Thousand and One Nights?* Why does it disquiet us to know that Don Quixote is a reader of the *Quixote,* and Hamlet is a spectator of *Hamlet?* I believe I have found the answer: those inversions suggest that if the characters in a story can be readers or spectators, then we, their readers or spectators, can be fictitious. In 1833 Carlyle observed that universal history is an infinite sacred book that all men write and read and try to understand, and in which they too are written.

WILLIAM H. GASS

The Concept of Character in Fiction

I have never found a handbook on the art of fiction or the stage, nor can I imagine finding one, that did not contain a chapter on the creation of character, a skill whose mastery, the author of each manual insists, secures for one the inner secrets of these arts: not, mind you, an easy thing: rather as difficult as the whole art itself, since, in a way, it *is* the whole art: to fasten in the memory of the reader, like a living presence, some bright human image. All well and good to paint a landscape, evoke a feeling, set a tempest loose, but not quite good enough to nail an author to his immortality if scheming Clarence, fat, foul-trousered Harry, or sweetly terraced Priss do not emerge from the land they huff and rage and eat in fully furnished out by Being; enough alive, indeed, to eat and huff in ours — dear God, more alive than that! — sufficiently enlarged by genius that they threaten to eat up and huff down everything in sight.

Talk about literature, when it is truly talk about something going on in

SOURCE: From *Fiction and the Figures of Life* by William H. Gass. (First appeared in *New American Review*, No. 7.) Copyright © 1958, 1962, 1966, 1967, 1968, 1969, 1970, 1971 by William H. Gass. Reprinted by permission of Alfred A. Knopf, Inc. and International Famous Agency.

the pages, if it is not about ideas, is generally about the people in it, and ranges from those cries of wonder, horror, pleasure, or surprise, so readily drawn from the innocently minded, to the annotated stammers of the most erudite and nervous critics. But it is all the same. Great character is the most obvious single mark of great literature. The rude, the vulgar, may see in Alyosha nothing more than the image of a modest, God-loving youth; the scholar may perceive through this demeanor a symbolic form; but the Alyosha of the untutored is somehow more real and present to him than the youth on his street whom he's known since childhood, loving of his God and modest too, equally tried, fully as patient; for in some way Alyosha's visionary figure will take lodging in him, make a model for him, so to reach, without the scholar's inflationary gifts, general form and universal height; whereas the neighbor may merely move away, take cold, and forget to write. Even the most careful student will admit that fiction's fruit survives its handling and continues growing off the tree. A great character has an endless interest; its fascination never wanes. Indeed it is a commonplace to say so. Hamlet. Ahab. Julien Sorel. Madame Bovary. There is no end to their tragedy. Great literature is great because its characters are great, and characters are great when they are memorable. A simple formula. The Danish ghost cries to remember him, and obediently — for we are gullible and superstitious clots — we do.

It hasn't always been a commonplace. Aristotle regarded character as a servant of dramatic action, and there have been an endless succession of opinions about the value and function of characters since — all dreary — but the important thing to be noted about nearly every one of them is that whatever else profound and wonderful these theories have to say about the world and its personalities, characters are clearly conceived as living outside language. Just as the movie star deserts herself to put on some press agent's more alluring fictional persona, the hero of a story sets out from his own landscape for the same land of romance the star reached by stepping there from life. These people — Huckleberry Finn, the Snopeses, Prince Myshkin, Pickwick, Molly Bloom — seem to have come to the words of their novels like a visitor to town . . . and later they leave on the arm of the reader, bound, I suspect, for a shabbier hotel, and dubious entertainments.

However, Aristotle's remark was a recommendation. Characters ought to exist for the sake of the action, he thought, though he knew they often did not, and those who nowadays say that given a sufficiently powerful and significant plot the characters will be dominated by it are simply answered by asking them to imagine the plot of *Moby Dick* in the hands of Henry James, or that of *Sanctuary* done into Austen. And if you can persuade them to try (you will have no success), you may then ask how the heroes and the heroines come out. The same disastrous exercise can be given those who believe that traits make character like definitions do a dictionary. Take any set of traits you like and let Balzac or Joyce, Stendhal or Beckett, loose in a single paragraph to use them. Give your fictional creatures qualities, psychologies, actions, manners, moods; present them from without or from within; let economics matter, breeding, custom, history; let spirit wet them like a hose: all methods work, and none do. The nature of the novel will not be understood at all until this is: *from any given body of fictional text, nothing necessarily follows, and anything plausible may.* Authors are gods — a little tinny sometimes but omnipotent no matter what, and plausible on top of that, if they can manage it.[1]

Though the handbooks try to tell us how to create characters, they carefully never tell us we are making images, illusions, imitations. Gatsby is not an imitation, for there is nothing he imitates. Actually, if he were a copy, an illusion, sort of shade or shadow, he would not be called a character at all. He must be unique, entirely himself, as if he had a self to be. He is required, in fact, to act *in character,* like a cat in a sack. No, theories of character are not absurd in the way representational theories are; they are absurd in a grander way, for the belief in Hamlet (which audiences often seem to have) is like the belief in God — incomprehensible to reason — and one is inclined to seek a motive: some deep fear or emotional need.

There are too many motives. We pay heed so easily. We are so pathetically eager for this other life, for the sounds of distant cities and the sea; we long, apparently, to pit ourselves against some trying wind, to follow the fortunes of a ship hard beset, to face up to murder and fornication, and the somber results of anger and love; oh, yes, to face up — *in books* — when on our own we scarcely breathe. The tragic view of life, for instance, in Shakespeare or in Schopenhauer, Unamuno, Sartre, or Sophocles, is not one jot as pure and penetratingly tragic as a pillow stuffed with Jewish hair, and if we want to touch life where it burns, though life is what we are even now awash with — futilely, stupidly drawing in — we ought not to back off from these other artifacts (wars, pogroms, poverty: men make them, too). But of course we do, and queue up patiently instead to see Prince Hamlet moon, watch him thrust his sword through a curtain, fold it once again into Polonius, that foolish old garrulous proper noun. The so-called life one finds in novels, the worst and best of them, is nothing like actual life at all, and cannot be; it is not more real, or thrilling, or authentic; it is not truer, more complex, or pure, and its people have less spontaneity, are less intricate, less free, less full.[2]

It is not a single cowardice that drives us into fiction's fantasies. We often fear that literature is a game we can't afford to play — the product of idleness and immoral ease. In the grip of that feeling it isn't life we pursue, but the point and purpose of life — its facility, its use. So Sorel is either a man it is amusing to gossip about, to see in our friends, to puppet around in our dreams, to serve as our more able and more interesting surrogate in further fanciful adventures; or Sorel is a theoretical type, scientifically profound, representing a deep human strain, and the writing of *The Red and the Black* constitutes an advance in the science of — what would you like? sociology?

Before reciting a few helpless arguments, let me suggest, in concluding this polemical section, just how absurd these views are which think of fiction as a mirror or a window onto life — as actually creative of living creatures — for really one's only weapon against Tertullians is ridicule.

There is a painting by Picasso which depicts a pitcher, candle, blue enamel pot. They are sitting, unadorned, upon the barest table. Would we wonder what was cooking in that pot? Is it beans, perhaps, or carrots, a marmite? The orange of the carrot is a perfect complement to the blue of the pot, and the genius of Picasso, neglecting nothing, has surely placed, behind that blue, invisible disks of dusky orange, which, in addition, subtly enrich the table's velvet brown. Doesn't that seem reasonable? Now I see that it must be beans, for above the pot — you can barely see them — are quaking lines of steam, just the lines we associate with boiling beans . . . or is it blanching pods? Scholarly research, supported by a great foundation, will discover that exactly such a pot was used to cook cassoulet in the kitchens of Charles the Fat . . . or was it Charles the Bald? There's a dissertation in that. And this explains the dripping candle standing by the pot. (Is it dripping? no? a pity. Let's go on.) For isn't Charles the Fat himself that candle? Oh no, some say, he's not! Blows are struck. Reputations made and ruined. Someone will see eventually that the pot is standing on a table, not a stove. But the pot has just come from the stove, it will be pointed out. Has not Picasso caught that vital moment of transition? The pot is too hot. The brown is burning. Oh, not *this* table, which has been coated with resistant plastic. Singular genius — blessed man — he thinks of everything.

Here you have half the history of our criticism in the novel. Entire books have been written about the characters in Dickens, Trollope, Tolstoi, Faulkner. But why not? Entire books have been written about God, his cohorts, and the fallen angels.

II

Descartes, examining a piece of beeswax fresh from the hive, brought it near a flame and observed all of its sensible qualities change. He wondered why he should believe that wax remained. His sensations lent him nothing he could fasten his judgment firmly to. Couldn't he give

that puddle in his hand another name? He might have added that the
sleights of the mountebanks did not bewilder him. Somehow he knew
milady's hanky didn't disappear in a fist to emerge as a rose. It occurred
to Descartes then that perhaps his imagination was the unifying faculty.
But the wax was capable of an infinite number of spills, reaching every
stage of relaxation, and he was unable, he writes in what is now a brilliant phrase, "to compass this infinity by imagination." How then? Some
higher, finer capacity was required. His knowledge of the wax, soft or
hard, sweet or flat, became an intuition of the mind.

Like so many philosophical arguments, this one was erected upside
down, and consequently is a bit unsteady on its head. How, I'd rather ask,
from the idea of wax, can we predict and picture just this sticky mess?
What do we see when we peer through a glass of words?

If we ask this question of Hume, he will give us, as usual, a brilliantly
reasonable, and entirely wrong answer — out of the habit empiricists
have, I suppose, of never inspecting their experience. Nothing is more free
than the imagination of man, he says; "it can feign a train of events with
all the appearance of reality. . . ." *With all the appearance of reality.*
. . . Then we might suppose that it's my imagination which allows me
to descend from a writer's words, like a god through the clouds, and
basket down on sweet Belinda's belly at the moment of her maximum
response (or less excitingly, to picture upon the palm in my mind a slowly
sprawling blob of molten wax).

To imagine so vividly is either to be drunk, asleep, or mad. Such images
are out of our control and often terrifying. If we could feign with *every*
appearance of reality, we would not wish to feign *Nostromo,* or even *Pride
and Prejudice.* Of course, the imagination cannot give us every appearance of reality, and just as well, but perhaps it can give us every appearance of a *faded* reality: the shadow of Belinda's body on the bed (so far
has this theory fallen through the space of a sentence!), an image seen
the way I see this print and paper now, though with the mind's disocular
eye. Or, as Gilbert Ryle writes:

> Sometimes, when someone mentions a blacksmith's forge, I find myself
> instantaneously back in my childhood, visiting a local smithy. I can
> vividly "see" the glowing red horseshoe on the anvil, fairly vividly
> "hear" the hammer ringing on the shoe and less vividly "smell" the
> singed hoof. How should we describe this "smelling in the mind's
> nose"? [3]

Certainly not by explaining that there is a smell in me, a shadow of a
smell, a picture of a smell, an image, and putting to my noseless spirit the
task of smelling it. Not as a bruise to its blow, as Ryle says, are our
imaginings related to our experience. Yet Hume sometimes supposes that

imagination works like madness. If it can give to fiction all the appearance of reality, how is one to know what to believe when an author's words, stirring in us like life, managing our minds with the efficiency of reality, throw Anna Karenina under the train's wheels before our eyes?

Here is the whole thing in a single passage:

> The imagination has the command over all its ideas and can join and mix and vary them in all the ways possible. It may conceive fictitious objects with all the circumstances of place and time. It may set them in a manner before our eyes, in their true colors, just as they might have existed. But as it is impossible that this faculty of imagination can ever, of itself, reach belief, it is evident that belief consists not in the peculiar nature or order of ideas, but in the manner of their conception and in their feeling to the mind.[4]

The name of this feeling is belief, and I am given it by the greater intensity and steadiness with which actual impressions occupy me — a narrow difference, one only of degree. Don't mystery stories make us lock our doors?

But I should suppose that "seeing things" through novels did not involve succumbing to a drunken frenzy, finding animals in walls or naked ladies draped on desert rocks like some long celibate Saint Anthony.

We do visualize, I suppose. Where did I leave my gloves? And then I ransack a room in my mind until I find them. But the room I ransack is abstract — a simple schema. I leave out the drapes and the carpet, and I think of the room as a set of likely glove locations. The proportion of words which we can visualize is small, but quite apart from that, another barrier to the belief that vivid imagining is the secret of a character's power is the fact that when we watch the pictures which a writer's words have directed us to make, we miss their meaning, for the point is *never* the picture. It also takes concentration, visualization does — takes slowing down; and this alone is enough to rule it out of novels, which are never waiting, always flowing on.

> Instantly Hugh's shack began to take form in her mind. But it was not a shack — it was a home! It stood, on wide-girthed strong legs of pine, between the forest of pine and high, high waving alders and tall slim birches, and the sea. There was the narrow path that wound down through the forest from the shore, with salmonberries and thimbleberries and wild blackberry bushes that on bright winter nights of frost reflected a million moons; behind the house was a dogwood tree that bloomed twice in the year with white stars. Daffodils and snowdrops grew in the little garden.[5]

And so forth. Do you have all that? the salmonberries and the thimbleberries? I'm afraid you'll be all day about it. One reason is that our imaginings are mostly imprecise. They are vague and general. Even when colored, they're gray.

> A hare vaguely perceived is nevertheless a specific hare. But a hare which is the object of a vague image is a vague hare.[6]

Consequently, writing which carefully defines its object, however visual its terms, sets the visual successfully aside. It does, that is, if what we see inside us are misty visual schema. But

> Suppose that I have an image of a head that is nonspecific about baldness, is this not rather queer? For presumably this head must be neither bald nor not bald nor even a half-way house with just a few hairs.[7]

Enter Mr. Cashmore, who is a character in *The Awkward Age.*

> Mr. Cashmore, who would have been very redheaded if he had not been very bald, showed a single eyeglass and a long upper lip; he was large and jaunty, with little petulant movements and intense ejaculations that were not in the line of his type.

We can imagine any number of other sentences about Mr. Cashmore added to this one. Now the question is: what is Mr. Cashmore? Here is the answer I shall give: Mr. Cashmore is (1) a noise, (2) a proper name, (3) a complex system of ideas, (4) a controlling conception, (5) an instrument of verbal organization, (6) a pretended mode of referring, and (7) a source of verbal energy.[8] But Mr. Cashmore is not a person. He is not an object of perception, and nothing whatever that is appropriate to persons can be correctly said of him. There is no path from idea to sense (this is Descartes' argument in reverse), and no amount of careful elaboration of Mr. Cashmore's single eyeglass, his upper lip or jauntiness is going to enable us to *see* him. How many little petulant movements are there? Certainly as many as the shapes which may be taken by soft wax. If we follow Hume, we think we picture things through language because we substitute, on cue, particular visual memories of our own, and the more precisely language defines its object, the less likely we are to find a snapshot in our book to fit it. Our visualizations interfere with Mr. Cashmore's development, for if we think of him as someone we have met, we must give him qualities his author hasn't yet, and we may stubbornly, or through simple lack of attention, retain these later, though they've been explicitly debarred. "On your imaginary forces work," *Henry V*'s Prologuer begs. "Piece out our imperfections with your thoughts . . . Think, when we talk of horses, that you see them / Printing their proud hoofs i' th' receiving earth," and then the audience (and the similarly situated novel reader) is praised for having done so; but this is worse than the self-congratulating pap which periodically flows from the bosom of the "creative" critic, because these generous additions destroy the work as certainly as "touching up" and "painting over." The unspoken word is often eloquent.

> *Well, I finally met Mr. Mulholland.*
> *Oh, what's he like?*
> *He has large thumbs.*

Characters in fiction are mostly empty canvas. I have known many who have passed through their stories without noses, or heads to hold them; others have lacked bodies altogether, exercised no natural functions, possessed some thoughts, a few emotions, but no psychologies, and apparently made love without the necessary organs. The true principle is direct enough: Mr. Cashmore has what he's been given; he also *has* what he *hasn't,* just as strongly. Mr. Cashmore, in fact, has been cruelly scalped.

Now, is there a nose to this Mr. Cashmore? Let's suppose it — but then, of what sort? We're not told. He is an eyeglass without eyes, he has no neck or chin, his ears are unexplored. "Large" — how indefinite a word. But would it have been better to have written "sixteen stone"? Not at all, nor do we know how this weight is disposed. If it is impossible to picture Mr. Cashmore, however carefully we draw him, will it be easier to limn his soul? Or perhaps we may imagine that this sentence describes not Mr. Cashmore, out or in, but his impression — what sort of dent he makes in his surroundings. He gives the impression of a man who would have been redheaded if he hadn't been bald. Very well. What impression, exactly, is that? Will it do to think of Mr. Cashmore as a man with red eyebrows and a red fringe above his ears, but otherwise without hair? That would rephrase Mr. Cashmore, and rephrase him badly. The description of Mr. Cashmore stands as James wrote it, even if Mr. Cashmore hasn't a hair on his body. As a set of sensations Mr. Cashmore is simply impossible; as an idea he is admirably pungent and precise.

Similarly, it is not at all correct to infer that because Mr. Mulholland has thumbs, he has hands, arms, torso, self. That inference destroys the metaphor (a pure synecdoche), since his thumbs are all he seems to be. Mr. Mulholland is monumentally clumsy, but if you fill him in behind his thumbs, clumsiness will not ensue.

So sometimes, then, we are required to take away what we've been given, as in the case of Mr. Cashmore's red hair; sometimes it's important to hold fast to what we've got and resist any inclination we may have to elaborate, as in the case of Mr. Mulholland, who I said had thumbs; and sometimes we must put our minds to the stretch, bridging the distances between concepts with other concepts, as in the two examples which follow; or we may be called upon to do all these things at once, as in what I promise will be my final misuse of poor Mulholland.[9]

> *Well, I finally met Mr. Mulholland.*
> *Oh, what's he like?*
> *A silver thimble.*

> *I saw Mr. Mulholland today.*
> *Oh, what was he doing?*
> *Walking his thumbs.*

> *Mr. Mulholland's face had*
> *a watchful look. Although*
> *its features had not yet arrived,*
> *they were momentarily expected.*

To summarize, so far:

1. Only a few of the words which a writer normally uses to create a character can be "imaged" in any sense.

2. To the extent these images are faded sensations which we've once had, they fill in, particularize, and falsify the author's account.

3. To the degree these images are as vivid and lively as reality is, they will very often be unpleasant, and certainly can't be "feigned." Then words would act like a mind-expanding drug.

4. To the degree these images are general schema, indistinct and vague, the great reality characters are supposed to have becomes less plausible, and precise writing (so often admired) will interfere with their formation.

5. Constructing images of any kind takes time, slows the flow of the work; nor can imagining keep up, in complexity, with the incredibly intricate conceptual systems which may be spun like a spiderweb in a single sentence.

6. We tend to pay attention to our pictures, and lose sight of the meaning. The novelist's words are not notes which he is begging the reader to play, as if his novel needed something more done to it in order to leap into existence.

Words in daily life are signposts, handles, keys. They express, instruct, command, inform, exhort — in short, they serve; and it is difficult to think of our servants as kings.[10] But among real things words win the gold medals for Being. Ortega y Gasset asks us to imagine we are looking through a window at a garden.

> The clearer the glass is, the less (of the glass) we will see. But then making an effort we may withdraw attention from the garden; and by retracting the ocular ray, we may fixate it upon the glass. Then the garden will disappear in our eyes and we will see instead only some

confused masses of color which seem to stick to the glass. Consequently to see the garden and to see the glass in the windowpane are two incompatible operations. . . . Likewise he who in the work of art aims to be moved by the fate of John and Mary, or of Tristan and Iseult, and readjusts to them his spiritual perception will not be able to see the work of art. . . . Now the majority of people are unable to adjust their attention to the glass and the transparency which is the work of art; instead they penetrate through it to passionately wallow in the human reality which the work of art refers to. If they are invited to let loose their prey and fix their attention upon the work of art itself, they will say they see nothing in it, because, indeed, they see no human realities there, but only artistic transparencies, pure essences.[11]

Ortega seems to believe, however, that words are windows through which something can be seen, and I have argued that words are opaque, as opaque as my garden gloves and trowel, objects which, nevertheless, may vividly remind me of spring, earth, and roses. Or Uncle Harry, Africa, the tsetse fly, and lovesick elephants.

On the other side of a novel lies the void. Think, for instance, of a striding statue; imagine the purposeful inclination of the torso, the alert and penetrating gaze of the head and its eyes, the outstretched arm and pointing finger; everything would appear to direct us toward some goal in front of it. Yet our eye travels only to the finger's end, and not beyond. Though pointing, the finger bids us stay instead, and we journey slowly back along the tension of the arm. In our hearts we know what actually surrounds the statue. The same surrounds every other work of art: empty space and silence.[12]

III

A character, first of all, is the noise of his name, and all the sounds and rhythms that proceed from him. We pass most things in novels as we pass things on a train. The words flow by like the scenery. All is change.[13] But there are some points in a narrative which remain relatively fixed; we may depart from them, but soon we return, as music returns to its theme. Characters are those primary substances to which everything else is attached. Hotels, dresses, conversations, sausage, feelings, gestures, snowy evenings, faces — each may fade as fast as we read them. Yet the language of the novel will eddy about a certain incident or name, as Melville's always circles back to Ahab and his wedding with the white whale. Mountains are characters in Malcolm Lowry's *Under the Volcano,* so is a ravine, a movie, mescal, or a boxing poster. A symbol like the cross can be a character. An idea or a situation (the anarchist in *The Secret Agent,* bomb ready in his pocket), or a particular event, an obsessive thought, a decision (Zeno's, for instance, to quit smoking), a passion, a memory, the weather, Gogol's overcoat — anything, indeed, which serves as a fixed point, like a stone in a stream or that soap in Bloom's pocket, functions as a character. Character, in this sense, is a matter of degree, for the language of the novel may loop back seldom, often, or incessantly. But the idea that characters are like primary substances has to be taken in a double way, because if any thing becomes a character simply to the degree the words of the novel qualify it, it also loses some of its substance, some of its primacy, to the extent that it, in turn, qualifies something else. In a perfectly organized novel, every word would ultimately qualify one thing, like the God of the metaphysician, at once the subject and the body of the whole.[14] Normally, characters are fictional human beings, and thus are given proper names. In such cases, to create a character is to give meaning to an unknown X; it is *absolutely* to *define;* and since nothing in life corresponds to these Xs, their reality is borne by their name. They *are,* where it *is.*

Most of the words the novelist uses have their meanings already formed. Proper names do not, except in a tangential way. It's true that Mr. Mulholland could not be Mr. Mull, and Mr. Cashmore must bear, as best he can, the curse of his wealth forever, along with his desire for gain. Character has a special excitement for a writer (apart from its organizing value) because it offers him a chance to give fresh meaning to new words. A proper name begins as a blank, like a wall or a canvas, upon which one might paint a meaning, perhaps as turbulent and mysterious, as treacherous and vast, as Moby Dick's, perhaps as delicate, scrupulous, and sensitive as that of Fleda Vetch.

I cannot pause here over the subject of rhythm and sound, though they are the heartbeat of writing, of prose no less than poetry.

> Their friend, Mr. Grant-Jackson, a highly preponderant pushing person, great in discussion and arrangement, abrupt in overture, unexpected, if not perverse, in attitude, and almost equally acclaimed and objected to in the wide midland region to which he had taught, as the phrase was, the size of his foot — their friend had launched his bolt quite out of the blue and had thereby so shaken them as to make them fear almost more than hope.[15]

Mr. Grant-Jackson is a preponderant pushing person because he's been made by *p*'s, and the rhythm and phrasing of James's writing here prepares and perfectly presents him to us. Certainly we cannot think of Molly Bloom apart from her music, or the gay and rapid Anna Livia apart from hers.

If one examines the texture of a fiction carefully, one will soon see that some words appear to gravitate toward their subject like flies settle on sugar, while others seem to emerge from it. In many works this logical movement is easily discernible and very strong. When a character speaks, the words seem to issue from him and to be acts of his. Description first forms a *nature,* then allows that nature to *perform.* We must be careful, however, not to judge by externals. Barkis says that Barkis is willing, but the expression *functions* descriptively to qualify Barkis, and it is Dickens' habit to treat speech as if it were an attribute of character, like tallness or honesty, and not an act. On the other hand, qualities, in the right context, can be transformed into verbs. Later in the book don't we perceive the whiteness of the whale as a design, an intention of Moby Dick's, like a twist of his flukes or the smashing of a small boat?

Whether Mr. Cashmore was once real and sat by James at someone's dinner table, or was instead the fabrication of James's imagination,[16] as long as he came into being from the world's direction he once existed outside language. The task of getting him in I shall call the problem of rendering. But it must be stressed (it cannot be stressed too severely) that Mr. Cashmore may never have had a model, and may never have been imagined either, but may have come to be in order to serve some high conception (a Mr. Moneybags) and represent a type, not just himself, in which case he is not a reality *rendered,* but a universal *embodied.*[17] Again, Mr. Cashmore might have had still other parents. Meanings in the stream of words before his appearance might have suggested him, dramatic requirements may have called him forth, or he may have been the spawn of music, taking his substance from rhythm and alliteration. Perhaps it was all of these. In well-regulated fictions, most things are *over-determined.*

So far I have been talking about the function of a character in the direct stream of language, but there are these two other dimensions, the rendered and the embodied, and I should like to discuss each briefly.

If we observe one of J. F. Powers' worldly priests sharpening his eye for the pin by putting through his clerical collar, the humor, with all *its* sharpness, lives in the situation, and quite incidentally in the words.[18] One can indeed imagine Powers thinking it up independently of any verbal formulas. Once Powers had decided that it would be funny to show a priest playing honeymoon bridge with his housekeeper, then his problem becomes the technical one of how best to accomplish it. What the writer must do, of course, is not only render the scene, but ,render the scene inseparable from its language, so that if the idea (the chaste priest caught in the clichés of marriage) is taken from the situation, like a heart from its body, both die. Far easier to render a real cornfield in front of you, because once that rendering has reached its page, the cornfield will no longer exist for literary purposes, no one will be able to see it by peering through your language, and consequently there will be nothing to abstract from your description. But with a "thought up" scene or situation, this is not the case. It comes under the curse of story. The notion, however amusing, is not literary, for it might be painted, filmed, or played. If we inquire further and ask why Powers wanted such a scene in the first place, we should find, I think, that he wanted it in order to embody a controlling "idea" — at one level of abstraction, the worldliness of the church, for instance. If he had nuns around a kitchen table counting the Sunday take and listening to the Cubs, *that* would do it. Father Burner beautifully embodies just such a controlling idea in Powers' celebrated story "The Prince of Darkness." Both rendering and embodying involve great risks because they require working into a scientific order of words what was not originally there. Any painter knows that a contour may only more or less enclose his model, while a free line simply and completely is. Many of the model's contours may be esthetically irrelevant, so it would be unwise to follow them. The free line is subject to no such temptations. Its relevance can be total. As Valéry wrote: There are no details in execution.

Often novelists mimic our ordinary use of language. We report upon ourselves; we gossip. Normally we are not lying; and our language, built to refer, actually does. When these selfsame words appear in fiction, and when they follow the forms of daily use, they create, quite readily, that dangerous feeling that a real Tietjens, a real Nickleby, lives just beyond the page; that through that thin partition we can hear a world at love.[19] But the writer must not let the reader out; the sculptor must not let the eye fall from the end of his statue's finger; the musician must not let the listener dream. Of course, he will; but let the blame be on himself. High tricks are possible: to run the eye rapidly along that outstretched arm to the fingertip, only to draw it up before it falls away in space; to carry the reader to the very edge of every word so that it seems he must be compelled to react as though to truth as told in life, and then to return him, like a philosopher liberated from the cave, to the clear and brilliant world of concept, to the realm of order, proportion, and dazzling construction . . . to fiction, where characters, unlike ourselves, freed from existence, can shine like essence, and purely Be.

GEORG LUKÁCS

The Ideology of Modernism

It is in no way surprising that the most influential contemporary school of writing should still be committed to the dogmas of "modernist" anti-realism. It is here that we must begin our investigation if we are to chart the possibilities of a bourgeois realism. We must compare the two main trends in contemporary bourgeois literature, and look at the answers they give to the major ideological and artistic questions of our time.

We shall concentrate on the underlying ideological basis of these trends (ideological in the above-defined, not in the strictly philosophical, sense). What must be avoided at all costs is the approach generally adopted by bourgeois-modernist critics themselves: that exaggerated concern with formal criteria, with questions of style and literary technique. This approach may appear to distinguish sharply between "modern" and "traditional" writing (i.e., contemporary writers who adhere to the styles of the last century). In fact it fails to locate the decisive formal problems and turns a blind eye to their inherent dialectic. We are presented with a false polarization which, by exaggerating the importance of stylistic differences, conceals the opposing principles actually underlying and determining contrasting styles.

To take an example: the *monologue intérieur*. Compare, for instance, Bloom's monologue in the lavatory or Molly's monologue in bed, at the beginning and at the end of *Ulysses*, with Goethe's early-morning monologue as conceived by Thomas Mann in his *Lotte in Weimar*. Plainly, the same stylistic technique is being employed. And certain of Thomas Mann's remarks about Joyce and his methods would appear to confirm this.

Yet it is not easy to think of any two novels more basically dissimilar than *Ulysses* and *Lotte in Weimar*. This is true even of the superficially rather similar scenes I have indicated. I am not referring to the — to my mind — striking difference in intellectual quality. I refer to the fact that with Joyce the stream-of-consciousness technique is no mere stylistic de-

SOURCE: From *The Meaning of Contemporary Realism,* trans. John and Necke Mander. Reprinted by permission of The Merlin Press Ltd. Lines from *The Cocktail Party* by T. S. Eliot are reprinted by permission of the publishers, Harcourt Brace Jovanovich, and Faber and Faber Ltd.

vice; it is itself the formative principle governing the narrative pattern and the presentation of character. Technique here is something absolute; it is part and parcel of the aesthetic ambition informing *Ulysses*. With Thomas Mann, on the other hand, the *monologue intérieur* is simply a technical device, allowing the author to explore aspects of Goethe's world which would not have been otherwise available. Goethe's experience is not presented as confined to momentary sense-impressions. The artist reaches down to the core of Goethe's personality, to the complexity of his relations with his own past, present, and even future experience. The stream of association is only apparently free. The monologue is composed with the utmost artistic rigour: it is a carefully plotted sequence gradually piercing to the core of Goethe's personality. Every person or event, emerging momentarily from the stream and vanishing again, is given a specific weight, a definite position, in the pattern of the whole. However unconventional the presentation, the compositional principle is that of the traditional epic; in the way the pace is controlled, and the transitions and climaxes are organized, the ancient rules of epic narration are faithfully observed.

It would be absurd, in view of Joyce's artistic ambitions and his manifest abilities, to qualify the exaggerated attention he gives to the detailed recording of sense-data, and his comparative neglect of ideas and emotions, as artistic failure. All this was in conformity with Joyce's artistic intentions; and, by use of such techniques, he may be said to have achieved them satisfactorily. But between Joyce's intentions and those of Thomas Mann there is a total opposition. The perpetually oscillating patterns of sense- and memory-data, their powerfully charged — but aimless and directionless — fields of force, give rise to an epic structure which is *static*, reflecting a belief in the basically static character of events.

These opposed views of the world — dynamic and developmental on the one hand, static and sensational on the other — are of crucial importance in examining the two schools of literature I have mentioned. I shall return to the opposition later. Here, I want only to point out that an exclusive emphasis on formal matters can lead to serious misunderstanding of the character of an artist's work.

What determines the style of a given work of art? How does the intention determine the form? (We are concerned here, of course, with the intention realized in the work; it need not coincide with the writer's conscious intention). The distinctions that concern us are not those between stylistic "techniques" in the formalistic sense. It is the view of the world, the ideology or *weltanschauung* underlying a writer's work, that counts. And it is the writer's attempt to reproduce this view of the world which constitutes his "intention" and is the formative principle underlying the style of a given piece of writing. Looked at in this way, style ceases to be a formalistic category. Rather, it is rooted in content; it is the specific form of a specific content.

Content determines form. But there is no content of which Man himself is not the focal point. However various the *données* of liteature (a particular experience, a didactic purpose), the basic question is, and will remain: what is Man?

Here is a point of division: if we put the question in abstract, philosophical terms, leaving aside all formal considerations, we arrive — for the realist school — at the traditional Aristotelian dictum (which was also reached by other than purely aesthetic considerations): Man is *zoon politikon,* a social animal. The Artistotelian dictum is applicable to all great realistic literature. Achilles and Werther, Oedipus and Tom Jones, Antigone and Anna Karenina: their individual existence — their *Sein an sich,* in the Hegelian terminology; their "ontological being," as a more fashionable terminology has it — cannot be distinguished from their social and historical environment. Their human significance, their specific individuality cannot be separated from the context in which they were created.

The ontological view governing the image of man in the work of leading modernist writers is the exact opposite of this. Man, for these writers, is by nature solitary, asocial, unable to enter into relationships with other human beings. Thomas Wolfe once wrote: "My view of the world is based on the firm conviction that solitariness is by no means a rare condition, something peculiar to myself or to a few specially solitary human beings, but the inescapable, central fact of human existence." Man, thus imagined, may establish contact with other individuals, but only in a superficial, accidental manner; only, ontologically speaking, by retrospective reflection. For "the others," too, are basically solitary, beyond significant human relationship.

This basic solitariness of man must not be confused with that individual solitariness to be found in the literature of traditional realism. In the latter case, we are dealing with a particular situation in which a human being may be placed, due either to his character or to the circumstances of his life. Solitariness may be objectively conditioned, as with Sophocles' Philoctetes, put ashore on the bleak island of Lemnos. Or it may be subjective, the product of inner necessity, as with Tolstoy's Ivan Ilyitsch or Flaubert's Frédéric Moreau in the *Education Sentimentale.* But it is always merely a fragment, a phase, a climax or anti-climax, in the life of the community as a whole. The fate of such individuals is characteristic of certain human types in specific social or historical circumstances. Beside and beyond their solitariness, the common life, the strife and togetherness of other human beings, goes on as before. In a word, their solitariness is a specific social fate, not a universal *condition humaine.*

The latter, of course, is characteristic of the theory and practice of modernism. I would like, in the present study, to spare the reader tedious excursions into philosophy. But I cannot refrain from drawing the reader's attention to Heidegger's description of human existence as a "thrownness-into-being" (*Geworfenheit ins Dasein*). A more graphic evocation of the ontological solitariness of the individual would be hard to imagine. Man is "thrown-into-being." This implies, not merely that man is constitutionally unable to establish relationships with things or persons outside himself; but also that it is impossible to determine theoretically the origin and goal of human existence.

Man, thus conceived, is an ahistorical being. (The fact that Heidegger does admit a form of "authentic" historicity in his system is not really relevant. I have shown elsewhere that Heidegger tends to belittle historicity as "vulgar"; and his "authentic" historicity is not distinguished from ahistoricity). This negation of history takes two different forms in modernist literature. First, the hero is strictly confined within the limits of his own experience. There is not for him — and apparently not for his creator — any preexistent reality beyond his own self, acting upon him or being acted upon by him. Secondly, the hero himself is without personal history. He is "thrown-into-the-world": meaninglessly, unfathomably. He does not develop through contact with the world; he neither forms nor is formed by it. The only "development" in this literature is the gradual revelation of the human condition. Man is now what he has always been and always will be. The narrator, the examining subject, is in motion; the examined reality is static.

Of course, dogmas of this kind are only really viable in philosophical abstraction, and then only with a measure of sophistry. A gifted writer, however extreme his theoretical modernism, will in practice have to compromise with the demands of historicity and of social environment. Joyce uses Dublin, Kafka and Musil the Hapsburg Monarchy, as the locus of their masterpieces. But the locus they lovingly depict is little more than a backcloth; it is not basic to their artistic intention.

This view of human existence has specific literary consequences. Particularly in one category, of primary theoretical and practical importance, to which we must now give our attention: that of *potentiality*. Philosophy distinguishes between *abstract* and *concrete* (in Hegel, "real") *potentiality*. These two categories, their interrelation and opposition, are rooted in life itself. *Potentiality* — seen abstractly or subjectively — is richer than actual life. Innumerable possibilities for man's development are imaginable, only a small percentage of which will be realized. Modern subjectivism, taking these imagined possibilities for actual complexity of life, oscillates between melancholy and fascination. When the world declines to realize these possibilities, this melancholy becomes tinged with con-

tempt. Hofmannsthal's Sobeide expressed the reaction of the generation
first exposed to this experience:

> The burden of those endlessly pored-over
> And now forever perished possibilities . . .

How far were those possibilities even concrete or "real"? Plainly, they
existed only in the imagination of the subject, as dreams or day-dreams.
Faulkner, in whose work this subjective potentiality plays an important
part, was evidently aware that reality must thereby be subjectivized
and made to appear arbitrary. Consider this comment of his: "They were
all talking simultaneously, getting flushed and excited, quarrelling, making the unreal into a possibility, then into a probability, then into an
irrefutable fact, as human beings do when they put their wishes into
words." The possibilities in a man's mind, the particular pattern, intensity
and suggestiveness they assume, will of course be characteristic of that
individual. In practice, their number will border on the infinite, even with
the most unimaginative individual. It is thus a hopeless undertaking to
define the contours of individuality, let alone to come to grips with a
man's actual fate, by means of potentiality. The *abstract* character of
potentiality is clear from the fact that it cannot determine development
— subjective mental states, however permanent or profound, cannot
here be decisive. Rather, the development of personality is determined by
inherited gifts and qualities; by the factors, external or internal, which
further or inhibit their growth.

But in life potentiality can, of course, become reality. Situations arise in
which a man is confronted with a choice; and in the act of choice a man's
character may reveal itself in a light that surprises even himself. In literature — and particularly in dramatic literature — the denouement often consists in the realization of just such a potentiality, which
circumstances have kept from coming to the fore. These potentialities are,
then, "real" or concrete potentialities. The fate of the character depends
upon the potentiality in question, even if it should condemn him to a
tragic end. In advance, while still a subjective potentiality in the character's mind, there is no way of distinguishing it from the innumerable
abstract potentialities in his mind. It may even be buried away so completely that, before the moment of decision, it has never entered his mind
even as an abstract potentiality. The subject, after taking his decision,
may be unconscious of his own motives. Thus Richard Dudgeon, Shaw's
Devil's Disciple, having sacrificed himself as Pastor Andersen, confesses:
"I have often asked myself for the motive, but I find no good reason to
explain why I acted as I did."

Yet it is a decision which has altered the direction of his life. Of course,
this is an extreme case. But the qualitative leap of the denouement,

cancelling and at the same time renewing the continuity of individual consciousness, can never be predicted. The concrete potentiality cannot be isolated from the myriad abstract potentialities. Only actual decision reveals the distinction.

The literature of realism, aiming at a truthful reflection of reality, must demonstrate both the concrete and abstract potentialities of human beings in extreme situations of this kind. A character's concrete potentiality once revealed, his abstract potentialities will appear essentially inauthentic. Moravia, for instance, in his novel *The Indifferent Ones,* describes the young son of a decadent bourgeois family, Michel, who makes up his mind to kill his sister's seducer. While Michel, having made his decision, is planning the murder, a large number of abstract — but highly suggestive — possibilities are laid before us. Unfortunately for Michel the murder is never actually carried out; and, from the sordid details of the action, Michel's character emerges as what it is — representative of that background from which, in subjective fantasy, he had imagined he could escape.

Abstract potentiality belongs wholly to the realm of subjectivity; whereas concrete potentiality is concerned with the dialectic between the individual's subjectivity and objective reality. The literary presentation of the latter thus implies a description of actual persons inhabiting a palpable, identifiable world. Only in the interaction of character and environment can the concrete potentiality of a particular individual be singled out from the "bad infinity" of purely abstract potentialities, and emerge as the determining potentiality of just this individual at just this phase of his development. This principle alone enables the artist to distinguish concrete potentiality from myriad abstractions.

But the ontology on which the image of man in modernist literature is based invalidates this principle. If the "human condition" — man as a solitary being, incapable of meaningful relationships — is identified with reality itself, the distinction between abstract and concrete potentiality becomes null and void. The categories tend to merge. Thus Cesare Pavese notes with John Dos Passos, and his German contemporary, Alfred Döblin, a sharp oscillation between "superficial *verisme*" and "abstract Expressionist schematism." Criticizing Dos Passos, Pavese writes that fictional characters "ought to be created by deliberate selection and description of individual features" — implying that Dos Passos' characterizations are transferable from one individual to another. He describes the artistic consequences: by exalting man's subjectivity, at the expense of the objective reality of his environment, man's subjectivity itself is impoverished.

The problem, once again, is ideological. This is not to say that the ideology underlying modernist writings is identical in all cases. On the contrary: the ideology exists in extremely various, even contradictory forms. The rejection of narrative objectivity, the surrender to subjectivity, may take the form of Joyce's stream of consciousness, or of Musil's "active passivity," his "existence without quality," or of Gide's *"action gratuite,"* where abstract potentiality achieves pseudo-realization. As individual character manifests itself in life's moments of decision, so too in literature. If the distinction between abstract and concrete potentiality vanishes, if man's inwardness is identified with an abstract subjectivity, human personality must necessarily disintegrate.

T. S. Eliot described this phenomenon, this mode of portraying human personality, as

> Shape without form, shade without colour,
> Paralysed force, gesture without motion.

The disintegration of personality is matched by a disintegration of the outer world. In one sense, this is simply a further consequence of our argument. For the identification of abstract and concrete human potentiality rests on the assumption that the objective world is inherently inexplicable. Certain leading modernist writers, attempting a theoretical apology, have admitted this quite frankly. Often this theoretical impossibility of understanding reality is the point of departure, rather than the exaltation of subjectivity. But in any case the connection between the two is plain. The German poet Gottfried Benn, for instance, informs us that "there is no outer reality, there is only human consciousness, constantly building, modifying, rebuilding new worlds out of its own creativity." Musil, as always, gives a moral twist to this line of thought. Ulrich, the hero of his *The Man without Qualities,* when asked what he would do if he were in God's place, replies: "I should be compelled to abolish reality." Subjective existence "without qualities" is the complement of the negation of outward reality.

The negation of outward reality is not always demanded with such theoretical rigour. But it is present in almost all modernist literature. In conversation, Musil once gave as the period of his great novel, "between 1912 and 1914." But he was quick to modify this statement by adding: "I have not, I must insist, written a historical novel. I am not concerned with actual events. . . . Events, anyhow, are interchangeable. I am interested in what is typical, in what one might call the ghostly aspect of reality." The word "ghostly" is interesting. It points to a major tendency in modernist literature: the attenuation of actuality. In Kafka, the descriptive detail is of an extraordinary immediacy and authenticity. But Kafka's artistic ingenuity is really directed towards substituting his *angst*-ridden vision of the world for objective reality. The realistic detail is the expression of a ghostly unreality, of a nightmare world, whose function is to evoke *angst*. The same phenomenon can be seen in writers who attempt to combine Kafka's techniques with a critique of society — like the German writer, Wolfgang Koeppen, in his satirical novel about Bonn, *Das Treibhaus*. A similar attentuation of reality underlies Joyce's stream of consciousness. It is, of course, intensified where the stream of consciousness is itself the medium through which reality is presented. And it is carried *ad absurdum* where the stream of consciousness is that of an abnormal subject or of an idiot — consider the first part of Faulkner's *Sound and Fury* or, a still more extreme case, Beckett's *Molloy*.

Attenuation of reality and dissolution of personality are thus interdependent: the stronger the one, the stronger the other. Underlying both is the lack of a consistent view of human nature. Man is reduced to a sequence of unrelated experiential fragments; he is as inexplicable to others as to himself. In Eliot's *Cocktail Party* the psychiatrist, who voices the opinions of the author, describes the phenomenon:

> Ah, but we die to each other daily
> What we know of other people
> Is only our memory of the moments
> During which we knew them. And they have changed since then.
> To pretend that they and we are the same
> Is a useful and convenient social convention
> Which must sometimes be broken. We must also remember
> That at every meeting we are meeting a stranger.

The dissolution of personality originally the unconscious product of the identification of concrete and abstract potentiality, is elevated to a deliberate principle in the light of consciousness. It is no accident that Gottfried Benn called one of his theoretical tracts *"Doppelleben."* For Benn, this dissolution of personality took the form of a schizophrenic dichotomy. According to him, there was in man's personality no coherent pattern of motivation or behaviour. Man's animal nature is opposed to his denaturized, sublimated thought-processes. The unity of thought and action is "backwoods philosophy"; thought and being are "quite separate entities." Man must be either a moral or a thinking being — he cannot be both at once.

These are not, I think, purely private, eccentric speculations. Of course, they are derived from Benn's specific experience. But there is an inner connection between these ideas and a certain tradition of bourgeois thought. It is more than a hundred years since Kierkegaard first attacked the Hegelian view that the inner and outer world form an objective dialectical unity, that they are indissolubly married in spite of their apparent opposition. Kierkegaard denied any such unity. According to Kierkegaard, the individual exists within an opaque, impenetrable "incognito."

This philosophy attained remarkable popularity after the Second World War — proof that even the most abstruse theories may reflect social reality. Men like Martin Heidegger, Ernst Jünger, the lawyer Carl Schmitt, Gottfried Benn and others passionately embraced this doctine of the eternal incognito which implies that a man's external deeds are no guide to his motives. In this case, the deeds obscured behind the mysterious incognito were, needless to say, these intellectuals' participation in Nazism: Heidegger, as Rector of Freiburg University, had glorified Hitler's seizure of power at his Inauguration; Carl Schmitt had put his great legal gifts at Hitler's disposal. The facts were too well-known to be simply denied. But, if this impenetrable incognito were the true *"condition humaine,"* might not — concealed within their incognito — Heidegger or Schmitt have been secret opponents of Hitler all the time, only supporting him in the world of appearances? Ernst von Salomon's cynical frankness about his opportunism in *The Questionnaire* (keeping his reservations to himself or declaring them only in the presence of intimate friends) may be read as an ironic commentary on this idelogy of the incognito as we find it, say, in the writings of Ernst Jünger.

This digression may serve to show, taking an extreme example, what the social implications of such an ontology may be. In the literary field, this particular ideology was of cardinal importance; by destroying the complex tissue of man's relations with his environment, it furthered the dissolution of personality. For it is just the opposition between a man and his environment that determines the development of his personality. There is no great hero of fiction — from Homer's Achilles to Mann's Adrian Leverkühn or Sholokhov's Grigory Melyekov — whose personality is not the product of such an opposition. I have shown how disastrous the denial of the distinction between abstract and concrete potentiality must be for the presentation of character. The destruction of the complex tissue of man's interaction with his environment likewise saps the vitality of this opposition. Certainly, some writers who adhere to this ideology have attempted, not unsuccessfully, to portray this opposition in concrete terms. But the underlying ideology deprives these contradictions of their dynamic, developmental significance. The contradictions co-exist, unresolved, contributing to the further dissolution of the personality in question.

It is to the credit of Robert Musil that he was quite conscious of the implications of his method. Of his hero Ulrich he remarked: "One is faced with a simple choice: either one must run with the pack (when in Rome, do as the Romans do), or one becomes a neurotic." Musil here introduces the problem, central to all modernist literature, of the significance of psychopathology.

This problem was first widely discussed in the Naturalist period. More than fifty years ago, that doyen of Berlin dramatic critics, Alfred Kerr, was writing: "Morbidity is the legitimate poetry of Naturalism. For what is poetic in everyday life? Neurotic aberration, escape from life's dreary routine. Only in this way can a character be translated to a rarer clime and yet retain an air of reality." Interesting, here, is the notion that the poetic necessity of the pathological derives from the prosaic quality of life under capitalism. I would maintain — we shall return to this point — that in modern writing there is a continuity from Naturalism to the Modernism of our day — a continuity restricted, admittedly, to underlying ideological principles. What at first was no more than dim anticipation of approaching catastrophe developed, after 1914, into an all-pervading obsession. And I would suggest that the ever-increasing part played by psychopathology was one of the main features of the continuity. At each period — depending on the prevailing social and historical conditions — psychopathology was given a new emphasis, a different significance and artistic function. Kerr's description suggests that in naturalism the interest in psychopathology sprang from an aesthetic need; it was an attempt to escape from the dreariness of life under capitalism. The quotation from Musil shows that some years later the opposition acquired a moral slant. The obsession with morbidity had ceased to have a merely decorative function, bringing colour into the greyness of reality, and become a moral protest against capitalism.

With Musil — and with many other modernist writers — psychopathology became the goal, the *terminus ad quem,* of their artistic intention. But there is a double difficulty inherent in their intention, which follows from its underlying ideology. There is, first, a lack of definition. The protest expressed by this flight into psychopathology is an abstract gesture; its rejection of reality is wholesale and summary, containing no concrete criticism. It is a gesture, moreover, that is destined to lead nowhere; it is an escape into nothingness. Thus the propagators of this ideology are mistaken in thinking that such a protest could ever be fruitful in literature. In any protest against particular social conditions, these conditions themselves must have the central place. The bourgeois protest against feudal society, the proletarian against bourgeois society, made their point of departure a criticism of the old order. In both cases the protest — reaching out beyond the point of departure — was based on a concrete *terminus ad quem:* the establishment of a new order. However indefinite the structure and content of this new order, the will towards its more exact definition was not lacking.

How different the protest of writers like Musil! The *terminus a quo* (the corrupt society of our time) is inevitably the main source of energy, since the *terminus ad quem* (the escape into psychopathology) is a mere abstraction. The rejection of modern reality is purely subjective. Considered in terms of man's relation with his environment, it lacks both content and direction. And this lack is exaggerated still further by the character of the *terminus ad quem*. For the protest is an empty gesture, expressing nausea, or discomfort, or longing. Its content — or rather lack of content — derives from the fact that such a view of life cannot impart a sense of direction. These writers are not wholly wrong in believing that psychopathology is their surest refuge; it is the ideological complement of their historical position.

This obsession with the pathological is not only to be found in literature. Freudian psychoanalysis is its most obvious expression. The treatment of the subject is only superficially different from that in modern literature. As everybody knows, Freud's starting point was "everyday life." In order to explain "slips" and daydreams, however, he had to have recourse to psychopathology. In his lectures, speaking of resistance and repression, he says: "Our interest in the general psychology of symptom-formation increases as we understand to what extent the study of pathological conditions can shed light on the workings of the normal mind." Freud believed he had found the key to the understanding of the normal personality in the psychology of the abnormal. This belief is still more evident in the typology of Kretschmer, which also assumes that psychological abnormalities can explain normal psychology. It is only when we compare Freud's psychology with that of Pavlov, who takes the Hippocratic view that mental abnormality is a deviation from a norm, that we see it in its true light.

Clearly, this is not strictly a scientific or literary-critical problem. It is an ideological problem, deriving from the ontological dogma of the solitariness of man. The literature of realism, based on the Aristotelian concept of man as *zoon politikon,* is entitled to develop a new typology for each new phase in the evolution of a society. It displays the contradictions within society and within the individual in the context of a dialectical unity. Here, individuals embodying violent and extraordinary passions are still within the range of a socially normal typology (Shakespeare, Balzac, Stendhal). For, in this literature, the average man is simply a dimmer reflection of the contradictions always existing in man and society; eccentricity is a socially-conditioned distortion. Obviously, the passions of the great heroes must not be confused with "eccentricity" in the colloquial sense: Christian Buddenbrook is an "eccentric"; Adrian Leverkühn is not.

The ontology of *Geworfenheit* makes a true typology impossible; it is replaced by an abstract polarity of the eccentric and the socially average. We have seen why this polarity — which in traditional realism serves to increase our understanding of social normality — leads in modernism to a fascination with morbid eccentricity. Eccentricity becomes the necessary complement of the average; and this polarity is held to exhaust human potentiality. The implications of this ideology are shown in another remark of Musil's: "If humanity dreamt collectively, it would dream Moosbrugger." Moosbrugger, you will remember, was a mentally retarded sexual pervert with homicidal tendencies.

What served, with Musil, as the ideological basis of a new typology — escape into neurosis as a protest against the evils of society — becomes with other modernist writers an immutable *condition humaine*. Musil's statement loses its conditional "if" and becomes a simple description of reality. Lack of objectivity in the description of the outer world finds its complement in the reduction of reality to a nightmare. Beckett's *Molloy* is perhaps the *ne plus ultra* of this development, although Joyce's vision of reality as an incoherent stream of consciousness had already assumed in Faulkner a nightmare quality. In Beckett's novel we have the same vision twice over. He presents us with an image of the utmost human degradation — an idiot's vegetative existence. Then, as help is imminent from a mysterious unspecified source, the rescuer himself sinks into idiocy. The story is told through the parallel streams of consciousness of the idiot and of his rescuer.

Along with the adoption of perversity and idiocy as types of the *condition humaine,* we find what amounts to frank glorification. Take Montherlant's *Pasiphae,* where sexual perversity — the heroine's infatuation with a bull — is presented as a triumphant return to nature, as the liberation of impulse from the slavery of convention. The chorus — i.e., the author — puts the following question (which, though rhetorical, clearly expects an affirmative reply): "Si l'absence de pensée et l'absence de morale ne contribuent pas beaucoup à la dignité des bêtes, des plantes et des eaux . . . ?" Montherlant expresses as plainly as Musil, though with different moral and emotional emphasis, the hidden — one might say repressed — social character of the protest underlying this obsession with psychopathology, its perverted Rousseauism, its anarchism. There are many illustrations of this in modernist writing. A poem of Benn's will serve to make the point:

> O that we were our primal ancestors,
> Small lumps of plasma in hot, sultry swamps;
> Life, death, conception, parturition
> Emerging from those juices soundlessly.
>
> A frond of seaweed or a dune of sand,
> Formed by the wind and heavy at the base;
> A dragonfly or gull's wing — already, these
> Would signify excessive suffering.

This is not overtly perverse in the manner of Beckett or Montherlant. Yet, in his primitivism, Benn is at one with them. The opposition of man as animal to man as social being (for instance, Heidegger's devaluation of the social as *"das Man,"* Klages' assertion of the incompatibility of *Geist* and *Seele,* or Rosenberg's racial mythology) leads straight to a glorification of the abnormal and to an undisguised anti-humanism.

A typology limited in this way to the *homme moyen sensuel* and the idiot also opens the door to "experimental" stylistic distortion. Distortion becomes as inseparable a part of the portrayal of reality as the recourse to the pathological. But literature must have a concept of the normal if it is to "place" distortion correctly; that is to say, to see it *as* distortion. With such a typology this placing is impossible, since the normal is no longer a proper object of literary interest. Life under capitalism is, often rightly, presented as a distortion (a petrification or paralysis) of the human substance. But to present psychopathology as a way of escape from this distortion is itself a distortion. We are invited to measure one type of distortion against another and arrive, necessarily, at universal distortion. There is no principle to set against the general pattern, no standard by which the petty-bourgeois and the pathological can be seen in their social context. And these tendencies, far from being relativized with time, become ever more absolute. Distortion becomes the normal condition of human existence; the proper study, the formative principle, of art and literature.

I have demonstrated some of the literary implications of this ideology. Let us now pursue the argument further. It is clear, I think, that modernism must deprive literature of a sense of *perspective.* This would not be surprising; rigorous modernists such as Kafka, Benn, and Musil have always indignantly refused to provide their readers with any such thing. I will return to the ideological implications of the idea of perspective later. Let me say here that, in any work of art, perspective is of overriding importance. It determines the course and content; it draws together the threads of the narration; it enables the artist to choose between the important and the superficial, the crucial and the episodic. The direction in which characters develop is determined by perspective, only those features being described which are material to their development. The more lucid the perspective — as in Molière or the Greeks — the more economical and striking the selection.

Modernism drops this selective principle. It asserts that it can dispense with it, or can replace it with its dogma of the *condition humaine.* A naturalistic style is bound to be the result. This state of affairs — which to my mind characterizes all modernist art of the past fifty years — is disguised by critics who systematically glorify the modernist movement. By concentrating on formal criteria, by isolating technique from content and exaggerating its importance, these critics refrain from judgment on the social or artistic significance of subject-matter. They are unable, in consequence, to make the aesthetic distinction between *realism* and *naturalism*. This distinction depends on the presence or absence in a work of art of a "hierarchy of significance" in the situations and characters presented. Compared with this, formal categories are of secondary importance. That is why it is possible to speak of the basically *naturalistic* character of modernist literature — and to see here the literary expression of an ideological continuity. This is not to deny that variations in style reflect changes in society. But the particular form this principle of naturalistic arbitrariness, this lack of hierarchic structure, may take is not decisive. We encounter it in the all-determining "social conditions" of Naturalism, in Symbolism's impressionist methods and its cultivation of the exotic, in the fragmentation of objective reality in Futurism and Constructivism and the German *Neue Sachlichkeit,* or, again, in Surrealism's stream of consciousness.

These schools have in common a basically static approach to reality. This is closely related to their lack of perspective. Characteristically, Gottfried Benn actually incorporated this in his artistic programme. One of his volumes bears the title, *Static Poems.* The denial of history, of development, and thus of perspective, becomes the mark of true insight into the nature of reality.

> The wise man is ignorant
> of change and development
> his children and children's children
> are no part of his world.

The rejection of any concept of the future is for Benn the criterion of wisdom. But even those modernist writers who are less extreme in their rejection of history tend to present social and historical phenomena as static. It is, then, of small importance whether this condition is "eternal," or only a transitional stage punctuated by sudden catastrophes (even in early Naturalism the static presentation was often broken up by these catastrophes, without altering its basic character). Musil, for instance, writes in his essay, *The Writer in our Age:* "One knows just as little about the present. Partly, this is because we are, as always, too close to the present. But it is also because the present into which we were plunged some two decades ago is of a particularly all-embracing and inescapable character." Whether or not Musil knew of Heidegger's philosophy, the idea of *Geworfenheit* is clearly at work here. And the following reveals plainly how, for Musil, this static state was upset by the catastrophe of 1914: "All of a sudden, the world was full of violence. . . . In European civilization, there was a sudden rift. . . ." In short: thus static apprehension of reality in modernist literature is no passing fashion; it is rooted in the ideology of modernism.

To establish the basic distinction between modernism and that realism which, from Homer to Thomas Mann and Gorky, has assumed change and development to be the proper subject of literature, we must go deeper into the underlying ideological problem. In *The House of the Dead* Dostoevsky gave an interesting account of the convict's attitude to work. He described how the prisoners, in spite of brutal discipline, loafed about, working badly or merely going through the motions of works until a new overseer arrived and allotted them a new project, after which they were allowed to go home. "The work was hard," Dostoevsky continues, "but, Christ, with what energy they threw themselves into it! Gone was all their former indolence and pretended incompetence!" Later in the book Dostoevsky sums up his experiences: "If a man loses hope and has no aim in view, sheer boredom can turn him into a beast. . . ." I have said that the problem of perspective in literature is directly related to the principle of selection. Let me go further: underlying the problem is a profound ethical complex, reflected in the composition of the work itself. Every human action is based on a presupposition of its inherent meaningfulness, at least to the subject. Absence of meaning makes a mockery of action and reduces art to naturalistic description.

Clearly, there can be no literature without at least the appearance of change or development. This conclusion should not be interpreted in a narrowly metaphysical sense. We have already diagnosed the obsession with psychopathology in modernist literature as a desire to escape from the reality of capitalism. But this implies the absolute primacy of the *terminus a quo,* the condition from which it is desired to escape. Any movement towards a *terminus ad quem* is condemned to impotence. As the ideology of most modernist writers asserts the unalterability of outward reality (even if this is reduced to a mere state of consciousness) human activity is, *a priori,* rendered impotent and robbed of meaning.

The apprehension of reality to which this leads is most consistently and convincingly realized in the work of Kakfa. Kafka remarks of Josef K., as he is being led to execution: "He thought of flies, their tiny limbs breaking as they struggle away from the fly-paper." This mood of total impotence, of paralysis in the face of the unintelligible power of circumstances, informs all his work. Though the action of *The Castle* takes a different, even an opposite, direction to that of *The Trial,* this view of the world, from the perspective of a trapped and struggling fly, is all-pervasive. This experience, this vision of a world dominated by *angst* and of man at the mercy of incomprehensible terrors, makes Kafka's work the very type of modernist art. Techniques, elsewhere of merely formal significance, are used here to evoke a primitive awe in the presence of an utterly strange and hostile reality. Kafka's *angst* is the experience *par excellence* of modernism.

Two instances from musical criticism — which can afford to be both franker and more theoretical than literary criticism — show that it is indeed a universal experience with which we are dealing. The composer, Hanns Eisler, says of Schönberg: "Long before the invention of the bomber, he expressed what people were to feel in the air raid shelters." Even more characteristic — though seen from a modernist point of view — is Theodor W. Adorno's analysis (in *The Aging of Modern Music*) of symptoms of decadence in modernist music: "The sounds are still the same. But the experience of *angst,* which made their originals great, has vanished." Modernist music, he continues, has lost touch with the truth that was its *raison d'être.* Composers are no longer equal to the emotional presuppositions of their modernism. And that is why modernist music has failed. The diminution of the original *angst*-obsessed vision of life (whether due, as Adorno thinks, to inability to respond to the magnitude of the horror or, as I believe, to the fact that this obsession with *angst* among bourgeois intellectuals has already begun to recede) has brought about a loss of substance in modern music, and destroyed its authenticity as a modernist art-form.

This is a shrewd analysis of the paradoxical situation of the modernist artist, particularly where he is trying to express deep and genuine experience. The deeper the experience, the greater the damage to the artistic whole. But this tendency towards disintegration, this loss of artistic unity, cannot be written off as a mere fashion, the product of experimental gimmicks. Modern philosophy, after all, encountered these problems long before modern literature, painting or music. A case in point is the problem of *time.* Subjective Idealism had already separated time, abstractly conceived, from historical change and particularity of place. As if this separation were insufficient for the new age of imperialism, Bergson widened it further. Experienced time, subjective time, now became identical with real time; the rift between this time and that of the objective world was complete. Bergson and other philosophers who took up and varied this theme claimed that their concept of time alone afforded insight into authentic, i.e., subjective, reality. The same tendency soon made its appearance in literature.

The German left-wing critic and essayist of the Twenties, Walter Benjamin, has well described Proust's vision and the techniques he uses to present it in his great novel: "We all know that Proust does not describe a man's life as it actually happens, but as it is remembered by a man who has lived through it. Yet this puts it far too crudely. For it is not actual experience that is important, but the texture of reminiscence, the Penelope's tapestry of a man's memory." The connection with Bergson's theories of time is obvious. But whereas with Bergson, in the abstraction of philosophy, the unity of perception is preserved, Benjamin shows that with Proust, as a result of the radical disintegration of the time sequence, objectivity is eliminated: "A lived event is finite, concluded at least on the level of experience. But a remembered event is infinite, a possible key to everything that preceded it and to everything that will follow it."

It is the distinction between a philosophical and an artistic vision of the world. However hard philosophy, under the influence of Idealism, tries to liberate the concepts of space and time from temporal and spatial particularity, literature continues to assume their unity. The fact that, nevertheless, the concept of subjective time cropped up in literature only shows how deeply subjectivism is rooted in the experience of the modern bourgeois intellectual. The individual, retreating into himself in despair at the cruelty of the age, may experience an intoxicated fascination with his forlorn condition. But then a new horror breaks through. If reality cannot be understood (or no effort is made to understand it), then the individual's subjectivity — alone in the universe, reflecting only itself — takes on an equally incomprehensible and horrific character. Hugo von Hofmannsthal was to experience this condition very early in his poetic career:

> It is a thing that no man cares to think on,
> And far too terrible for mere complaint,
> That all things slip from us and pass away,
>
> And that my ego, bound by no outward force —
> Once a small child's before it became mine —
> Should now be strange to me, like a strange dog.

By separating time from the outer world of objective reality, the inner world of the subject is transformed into a sinister, inexplicable flux and acquires — paradoxically, as it may seem — a static character.

On literature this tendency towards disintegration, of course, will have an even greater impact than on philosophy. When time is isolated in this way, the artist's world disintegrates into a multiplicity of partial worlds. The static view of the world, now combined with diminished objectivity, here rules unchallenged. The world of man — the only subject-matter of literature — is shattered if a single component is removed. I have shown the consequences of isolating time and reducing it to a subjective category. But time is by no means the only component whose removal can lead to such disintegration. Here, again, Hofmannsthal anticipated later developments. His imaginary "Lord Chandos" reflects: "I have lost the ability to concentrate my thoughts or set them out coherently." The result is a condition of apathy, punctuated by manic fits. The development towards a definitely pathological protest is here anticipated — admittedly in glamorous, romantic guise. But it is the same disintegration that is at work.

Previous realistic literature, however violent its criticism of reality, had always assumed the unity of the world it described and seen it as a living whole inseparable from man himself. But the major realists of our time deliberately introduce elements of disintegration into their work — for instance, the subjectivizing of time — and use them to portray the contemporary world more exactly. In this way, the once natural unity becomes a conscious, constructed unity (I have shown elsewhere that the device of the two temporal planes in Thomas Mann's *Doctor Faustus* serves to emphasize its historicity). But in modernist literature the disintegration of the world of man — and consequently the disintegration of personality — coincides with the ideological intention. Thus *angst,* this basic modern experience, this by-product of *Geworfenheit,* has its emotional origin in the experience of a disintegrating society. But it attains its effects by evoking the disintegration of the world of man.

To complete our examination of modernist literature, we must consider for a moment the question of allegory. Allegory is that aesthetic genre which lends itself par excellence to a description of man's alienation from objective reality. Allegory is a problematic genre because it rejects that assumption of an immanent meaning to human existence which — however unconscious, however combined with religious concepts of transcendence — is the basis of traditional art. Thus in medieval art we observe a new secularity (in spite of the continued use of religious subjects) triumphing more and more, from the time of Giotto, over the allegorizing of an earlier period.

Certain reservations should be made at this point. First, we must distinguish between literature and the visual arts. In the latter, the limitations of allegory can be the more easily overcome in that transcendental, allegorical subjects can be clothed in an aesthetic immanence (even if of a merely decorative kind) and the rift in reality in some sense be eliminated — we have only to think of Byzantine mosaic art. This decorative element has no real equivalent in a literature; it exists only in a figurative sense, and then only as a secondary component. Allegorical art of the quality of Byzantine mosaic is only rarely possible in literature. Secondly, we must bear in mind in examining allegory — and this is of great importance for our argument — a historical distinction: does the concept of transcendence in question contain within itself tendencies towards immanence (as in Byzantine art or Giotto), or is it the product precisely of a rejection of these tendencies?

Allegory, in modernist literature, is clearly of the latter kind. Transcendence implies here, more or less consciously, the negation of any meaning immanent in the world or the life of man. We have already examined the underlying ideological basis of this view and its stylistic consequences. To conclude our analysis, and to establish the allegorical character of modernist literature, I must refer again to the work of one of the finest theoreticians of modernism — to Walter Benjamin. Benjamin's examination of allegory was a product of his researches into German Baroque drama. Benjamin made his analysis of these relatively minor plays the occasion for a general discussion of the aesthetics of allegory. He was asking, in effect, why it is that transcendence, which is the essence of allegory, cannot but destroy aesthetics itself.

Benjamin gives a very contemporary definition of allegory. He does not labour the analogies between modern art and the Baroque (such analogies are tenuous at best, and were much overdone by the fashionable criticism of the time). Rather, he uses the Baroque drama to criticize modernism, imputing the characteristics of the latter to the former. In so doing, Benjamin became the first critic to attempt a philosophical analysis of the aesthetic paradox underlying modernist art. He writes:

> In Allegory, the *facies hippocratica* of history looks to the observer like a petrified primeval landscape. History, all the suffering and failure it contains, finds expression in the human face — or, rather, in the human skull. No sense of freedom, no classical proportion, no human emotion lives in its features — not only human existence in general, but the fate of every individual human being is symbolized in this most palpable token of mortality. This is the core of the allegorical vision, of the Baroque idea of history as the passion of the world: History is significant only in the stations of its corruption. Significance is a function of mortality — because it is death that marks the passage from corruptibility to meaningfulness.

Benjamin returns again and again to this link between allegory and the annihilation of history:

> In the light of this vision history appears, not as the gradual realization of the eternal, but as a process of inevitable decay. Allegory thus goes beyond beauty. What ruins are in the physical world, allegories are in the world of the mind.

Benjamin points here to the aesthetic consequences of modernism — though projected into the Baroque drama — more shrewdly and consistently than any of his contemporaries. He sees that the notion of objective time is essential to any understanding of history, and that the notion of subjective time is a product of a period of decline. "A thorough knowledge of the problematic nature of art" thus becomes for him — correctly, from his point of view — one of the hallmarks of allegory in Baroque drama. It is problematic, on the one hand, because it is an art intent on expressing absolute transcendence that fails to do so because of the means at its disposal. It is also problematic because it is an art reflecting the corruption of the world and bringing about its own dissolution in the process. Benjamin discovers "an immense, anti-aesthetic subjectivity" in Baroque literature, associated with "a theologically-determined subjectivity." (We shall presently show — a point I have discussed elsewhere in relation to Heidegger's philosophy — how in literature a "religious atheism" of this kind can acquire a theological character.) Romantic — and, on a higher plane, Baroque — writers were well aware of this problem, and gave their understanding, not only theoretical, but artistic — that is to say allegorical — expression. "The image," Benjamin remarks, "becomes a rune in the sphere of allegorical intuition. When touched by the light of theology, its symbolic beauty is gone. The false appearance of totality vanishes. The image dies; the parable no longer holds true; the world it once contained disappears."

The consequences for art are far-reaching, and Benjamin does not hesitate to point them out: "Every person, every object, every relationship can stand for something else. This transferability constitutes a devastating, though just, judgment on the profane world — which is thereby branded as a world where such things are of small importance." Benjamin knows, of course, that although details are "transferable," and thus insignificant, they are not banished from art altogether. On the contrary. Precisely in modern art, with which he is ultimately concerned, descriptive detail is often of an extraordinary sensuous, suggestive power — we think again of Kafka. But this, as we showed in the case of Musil (a writer who does not consciously aim at allegory) does not prevent the materiality of the world from undergoing permanent alteration, from becoming transferable and arbitrary. Just this, modernist writers maintain, is typical of their own apprehension of reality. Yet presented in this way, the world becomes, as Benjamin puts it, "exalted and depreciated at the same time." For the conviction that phenomena are *not* ultimately transferable is rooted in a belief in the world's rationality and in man's ability to penetrate its secrets. In realistic literature each descriptive detail is both *individual* and *typical*. Modern allegory, and modern ideology, however, deny the *typical*. By destroying the coherence of the world, they reduce detail to the level of mere particularity (once again, the connection between modernism and naturalism is plain). Detail, in its allegorical transferability, though brought into a direct, if paradoxical connection with transcendence, becomes an abstract function of the transcendence to which it points. Modernist literature thus replaces concrete typicality with abstract particularity.

We are here applying Benjamin's paradox directly to aesthetics and criticism, and particularly to the aesthetics of modernism. And, though we have reversed his scale of values, we have not deviated from the course of his argument. Elsewhere, he speaks out even more plainly — as though the Baroque mask had fallen, revealing the modernist skull underneath:

> Allegory is left empty-handed. The forces of evil, lurking in its depths, owe their very existence to allegory. Evil is, precisely, the non-existence of that which allegory purports to represent.

The paradox Benjamin arrives at — his investigation of the aesthetics of Baroque tragedy has culminated in a negation of aesthetics — sheds a good deal of light on modernist literature, and particularly on Kafka. In interpreting his writings allegorically I am not, of course, following Max Brod, who finds a specifically religious allegory in Kakfa's works. Kafka refuted any such interpretation in a remark he is said to have made to Brod himself: "We are nihilistic figments, all of us; suicidal notions forming in God's mind." Kafka rejected, too, the gnostic concept of God as an evil demiurge: "The world is a cruel whim of God, an evil day's work." When Brod attempted to give this an optimistic slant, Kafka shrugged off the attempt ironically: "Oh, hope enough, hope without end — but not, alas, for us." These remarks, quoted by Benjamin in his brilliant essay on Kafka, point to the general spiritual climate of his work: "His profoundest experience is of the hopelessness, the utter meaninglessness of man's world, and particularly that of present-day bourgeois man." Kafka, whether he says so openly or not, is an atheist. An atheist, though, of that modern species who regard God's removal from the scene not as a liberation — as did Epicurus and the Encyclopedists — but as a token of the "God-forsakenness" of the world, its utter desolation and futility. Jacobsen's *Niels Lyhne* was the first novel to describe this state of mind of the atheistic bourgeois intelligentsia. Modern religious atheism is characterized, on the one hand, by the fact that unbelief has lost its revolutionary *élan* — the empty heavens are the projection of a world beyond hope of redemption. On the other hand, religious atheism shows that the desire for salvation lives on with undiminished force in a world without God, worshipping the void created by God's absence.

The supreme judges in *The Trial,* the castle administration in *The Castle,* represent transcendence in Kafka's allegories: the transcendence of Nothingness. Everything points to them, and they could give meaning to everything. Everybody believes in their existence and omnipotence; but nobody knows them, nobody knows how they can be reached. If there is a God here, it can only be the God of religious atheism: *atheos absconditus.* We become acquainted with a repellent host of subordinate authorities; brutal, corrupt, pedantic — and, at the same time, unreliable and irresponsible. It is a portrait of the bourgeois society Kafka knew, with a dash of Prague local colouring. But it is also allegoric in that the doings of this bureaucracy and of those dependent on it, its impotent victims, are not concrete and realistic, but a reflection of that Nothingness which governs existence. The hidden, non-existent God of Kafka's world derives his spectral character from the fact that his own non-existence is the ground of all existence; and the portrayed reality, uncannily accurate as it is, is spectral in the shadow of that dependence. The only purpose of transcendence — the intangible *nichtendes Nichts* — is to reveal the *facies hippocratica* of the world.

That abstract particularity which we saw to be the aesthetic consequence of allegory reaches its high mark in Kafka. He is a marvellous observer; the spectral character of reality affects him so deeply that the simplest episodes have an oppressive nightmarish immediacy. As an artist, he is not content to evoke the surface of life. He is aware that individual detail must point to general significance. But how does he go about the business of abstraction? He has emptied everyday life of meaning by using the allegorical method; he has allowed detail to be annihilated by his transcendental Nothingness. This allegorical transcendence bars Kafka's way to realism, prevents him from investing observed detail with typical significance. Kafka is not able, in spite of his extraordinary evocative power, in spite of his unique sensibility, to achieve that fusion of the particular and the general which is the essence of realistic art. His aim is to raise the individual detail in its immediate particularity (without generalizing its content) to the level of abstraction. Kafka's method is typical, here, of modernism's allegorical approach. Specific subject-matter and stylistic variation do not matter; what matters is the basic ideological determination of form and content. The particularity we find in Beckett and Joyce, in Musil and Benn, various as the treatment of it may be, is essentially of the same kind.

If we combine what we have up to now discussed separately we arrive at a consistent pattern. We see that modernism leads not only to the destruction of traditional literary forms; it leads to the destruction of literature as such. And this is true not only of Joyce, or of the literature of Expressionism and Surrealism. It was not André Gide's ambition, for instance, to bring about a revolution in literary style; it was his philosophy that compelled him to abandon conventional forms. He planned his *Faux-Monnayeurs* as a novel. But its structure suffered from a characteristically modernist schizophrenia: it was supposed to be written by the man who was also the hero of the novel. And, in practice, Gide was forced to admit that no novel, no work of literature could be constructed in that way. We have here a practical demonstration that — as Benjamin showed in another context — modernism means not the enrichment, but the negation of art.

HANS MAGNUS ENZENSBERGER

The Aporias of the Avant-Garde

To count himself a member of the avant-garde has for several life-times now been the privilege of everyone who covers empty surfaces with paint or sets down letters or notes on paper. Not everyone has availed himself of this opportunity. Whoever undauntedly sticks the label *avant-gardist* on an author like Franz Kafka is already seduced into negligence by that mouthful of a word; it would have stuck in Kafka's craw. Neither Marcel Proust nor William Faulkner, neither Bertolt Brecht nor Samuel Beckett — none of them, as far as we know, has invoked that vocable, which nowadays, to be sure, every laundry list lays claim to, but on whose meaning, as if it were settled once and for all, hardly anyone of the crowd who mouth it stops to reflect.

This is true of the partisans of the avant-garde no less than of its enemies. They differ in their judgments but not in their premises. Both sides help themselves uncritically to a critical concept that struck it rich in Paris over a hundred years ago, and has since passed for a touchstone of which it has not been expected or demanded that it undergo a test it-self. The minds that it separates from one another have a way of lapsing into a permanent debate whose beginnings are lost in a mist and whose end can be held off ad libitum. Names and catch phrases change; the schema remains the same. Since Swift's *Full and True Account of the Battle Between the Ancient and the Modern Books* (1710), this con-troversy has lost some of its originality and brilliance; what remains is that modest abstraction for which, all along, it was willing to settle. The cast-iron stances of the contenders, no matter on which side, are of de-pressing innocuousness; they remind one of the figures of middle-class family drama to whose antiquated conflict between father and son they would reduce the march of history. Commonplaces like the ones about the impetuous youngster whose ears will yet be pinned back, about the excesses of youth and the wisdom of maturity, and about the enlightened traditionalism of age that looks back with a wink on its own rebellious past are characteristic of the entire sphere of such discussions with their lack

SOURCE: Translated by John Simon. First published in *Modern Occasions*, ed. Philip Rahv (New York; Farrar, Straus & Giroux, 1966). Copyright © 1962 Suhrkamp Verlag Frankfurt/Main, 1966 by Hans Magnus Enzensberger.

of a sense of history. Unhistoric, not merely hackneyed, is the blind trust they are happy to put in the threadbare concept of generations, quite as if it were the life of the arts, rather than that of trichinae, that is subject to the biological law of the life cycle; or as if the content of a hymn by Hölderlin or a play by Brecht could be read off the author's "vintage." Whoever distinguishes between old and new, or old and young, in such comfortable fashion, agrees by his very choice of criteria with the philistines. To him, the simplest dialectical propositions must remain inaccessible. That the durability of works is always determined only by their immanence in today's creation, which simultaneously devours and rejuvenates them, remains unfathomed, indeed unfathomable, even though this insight could be gleaned at the starting point of all European thought: "The old, veering round, becomes the new, and the latter, veering back, the former." The statement is to be found in Heraclitus.

The argument between the partisans of the old and those of the new is unendurable, not so much because it drags on endlessly, unresolved and irresoluble, but because its schema itself is worthless. The choice that it invites is not only banal, it is a priori factitious. The semblance of a timeless symmetry with which it surrounds itself is invalidated by history, which has as yet overtaken every unhistoric position and given it the lie. For no sooner do the arts enter the gravitational field of totalitarianism than the harmless tug of war about the avant-garde, or rather what passes for it, assumes murderous traits. The symmetry of the old and the new, that timeless mirror image, is brutally broken in two, and its real substratum becomes manifest. No avant-garde has thus far called for the police to rid it of its opponents. The "healthy forces of preservation" are the ones that have persistently sanctioned censorship, book burning, bans on publishing, indeed murder, as the extension of their criticism to other means; they purport to be liberal only until the political conditions permit, or rather command them to talk of a breach.

Only when it has come to that (but it has always come to that on the other side of the fence) do the categories of Progressive and Reactionary in the arts come into their own. To be sure, they are scarcely less questionable and shabby than those of the Old and the New; moreover, so many cardsharps have been operating with them that there are indelible black marks against them on the books. Nevertheless, they can lay claim to their historicity; they are not suited to the analysis of biological but of historic processes. So long as somewhere in the world esthetic questions are settled by force — so long, indeed, as such a procedure can be reckoned with as a real possibility — they are indispensable; in other words, everywhere and for an unforeseeable length of time. They require no metaphysical foundation. Their usefulness is simply and solely heuristic.[1] They require, therefore, constant reappraisal: like every indispensable device, they imperil the user as soon as he relies on them blindly. What most profoundly distinguishes the progressive attitude from every reactionary one is precisely its relation to doubt. The readiness to revise all solidified theses, to examine endlessly its own premises, is the essence of all progressive criticism. Reactionary criticism, on the contrary, considers itself, so to speak, naturally and everlastingly in the right. It is exempt from reflecting on its presuppositions. As complaisantly as it adapts its judgment, from case to case, to the nature of the powers that be, as unshakably has it established what is to be considered beautiful, sane, and constructive.

Only after coming into power does it reveal its brutal countenance. Until then it operates in the underbrush of conventicles, on the unsurveyable terrain of textbooks and "education in the arts"; in the open, it observes certain precautions. Under democratic conditions, reactionary criticism sees itself constrained to deny its own existence. It even admits tacitly to its canon of imperishables what it previously denigrated: the moment a modern work is no longer new, no longer risky, it is claimed as a "contemporary classic" by that very criticism which for decades tried in vain to strike it dead with its "rigid yardstick." Once annexed to the heritage that must be preserved, it is truly deprived of its life, that is, removed from criticism and exhibited as an embalmed holy relic. Whatever he cannot lick, the reactionary critic will join, and even thinks thereby to demonstrate his magnanimity. As long as he cannot enforce his doctrine with police assistance, he finds himself willing even to sign a truce and passes himself off as a mediator and man of common sense who stands "above the press of things." Social pluralism becomes, for the time being, an esthetic pillow; in the dark of freedom, all cats are gray. Every work has its justification along with every other one, trash "complements" the masterpiece, and with the obligingness of all judgments the critical faculty itself is made to vanish by sleight of hand.

Neutrality of this ilk, which likes to answer to the name of "open-mindedness," condemns itself. At the first sign that esthetic questions are about to be adjudicated by the power of the state, it flaps over into what it has secretly been all along. In the face of a rule of terror, whether exercised by a Goebbels or a Zhdanov, there can be no tolerance; which, for reactionary criticism, means that tolerance for the victims of that terror can be dispensed with. Such criticism rests untroubled on its certitudes as long as it sees to it that the yardsticks of its Beckmesserdom are always calibrated according to regulation.

The prescriptions are always the same: "The emphasis must be placed on questions pertaining to a world view." The work of art is nothing in itself; it functions merely as the "representative" of the currently demanded "Weltanschauung," which it must "adequately reproduce." "What matters is not the specific, artistically formal manner of writing, but this stand in terms of an ultimate world view." Opportunism that makes common cause with the stronger battalions is candidly appealed to: "Affiliation with the determinant tendencies of the times, which, sooner or later, will be the ruling ones," is what the writer must seek, placing himself "on the ground" designated to him by reactionary criticism. He is thus given the "concrete plumb line" by which he can hang himself, and "the justified, world-historic optimism, so extraordinarily fruitful for art" will then come about on its own. The arts are there to supply "lifelike realism" and "all-embracing positivism" and "to fashion man's future from within." "The will and aptitude for the creation of such a positive, new reality" facilitate "the choice between social health and sickness." "From that there follows" — verbatim! — "such a heightening of the watchtower" that it can no longer be doubted what sort of strait jacket the watchman intends for the arts: the avant-garde, or whatever that term means to him, is "decadent," "perverse," "cynical," "nihilistic," and "sickly." This vocabulary will be well remembered from the *Völkische Beobachter,* and that the state of mind it expresses has not died out in our land is demonstrated by every second glance into the newspapers that appear between Bonn and Passau. The quoted phrases did not, however, sprout from fascist dung; they were not culled from the *Neues Deutschland,* either. The man who wrote them passes for the most intelligent, distinguished, and courageous literary critic whom Communism can point to anywhere; they appear in Georg Lukács's book, *Against Misunderstood Realism,*[2] which could not come out on the other side of the Elbe, for to the cultural police that has the word there it seemed still not reactionary enough. To be sure, Lukács objects — in a language that, probably unjustly, claims to derive from Schiller and Goethe — to the "ever more pronounced stepping-into-the-foreground of the pathological" in literature, but he does not opt for the therapy that customarily follows on such pronouncements and consists of liquidating the patient. Lukács does not by any means reach for his gun when he hears the word *culture.* He has kept within him a remnant of that bad conscience that the most intelligent "representatives" of reactionary criticism bring to it as a dowry. It stirs in vain.

The "artistic striving" of such criticism does not manifest itself only in that its language, under whatever party insignia, gets tattered and rotten. This criticism can dispense even with the knowledge of what it defames. The goat turned gardener need not concern itself with botany. It separates herbs from weeds with its horns. What passes for healthy is most likely to be the mediocre: Theodore Dreiser, Sinclair Lewis, Norman Mailer, Romain Rolland, and Roger Martin du Gard are for Lukács the quintessence of modern literature. To what unhappy misconception Thomas and Heinrich Mann may owe their appearance on this roster of those given a clean bill of health remains inscrutable. Sickly and decadent, however, in contradistinction to the apple-cheeked author of *The Black Swan,* are Dos Passos and Beckett, Montherlant and Kafka, Proust and Jens Rehn, Koeppen and Jünger, Gide and Faulkner — about as non-sensical a collocation of names as could possibly be conceived.[3] Tonsure is administered over the self-same unclean comb to heads that, for content and quality, for style and provenance, simply cannot be compared. Lu-kács calls this pocket comb "avant-gardism" — naturally without taking the trouble to analyze the term.[4] Nor have Hanns Johst and Will Vesper made the art of discrimination any harder for themselves.

Neither Western nor Eastern exponents of such criticism, on whatever bastions they may ply their trade, are competent to criticize the avant-garde. Their verdict about what is healthy or sick — about people or the degenerate — must be implemented by the police, or it remains without significance. With every one of their anathemas, they attest to their lack of authority.

In the face of their censure, whose aim is nothing other than censorship, solidarity goes without saying. Every work deserves to be defended against its suppressors: this tenet precedes all esthetic probing, and even the most superfluous "experiment" may have recourse to it. A criticism that considers itself progressive must weigh all the more carefully its rights and duties precisely as regards the most advanced production. If it is content with turning the verdicts of the culture wardens upside down, it thereby makes them seem only more justified. Whoever denies the bailiffs of unjust power their competence cannot simultaneously vindicate himself by reference to their pronouncements. Solidarity can be valid in the arts only as long as it is not used as a carte blanche. What proclaims itself the avant-garde is by no means immune to criticism. There is much evidence for this term's having become nowadays a talisman, which is to make its wearers proof to all objections and to intimidate perplexed reviewers. What is most revealing is that the term, to this day, has not been analyzed. Those who would be happiest to eradicate it have never specially concerned themselves with what the avant-garde actually is. That is understandable. What is queerer is that its followers have hardly contributed more to the definition of that which they admire than have its foes. The concept *avant-garde* is in need of elucidation.

Under that catchword, there appears in all [German] dictionaries, in token of its military derivation, a pair of crossed daggers. Older works of reference do not even recognize the figurative meaning:

> *Avant-garde, advance guard, vanguard,* that segment of a marching troop which the latter (the main body) sends some distance forward. . . . An a. subdivides itself frontward into ever smaller divisions, down to the spearhead marching at the very forefront. Each of these

subdivisions serves the purpose of gaining for the larger one following it more security and time. . . . The flung-out smaller divisions must govern themselves as to their movement according to the larger ones that follow them.[5]

The transfer of this strategic concept to the arts was first effected in the fifties of the past century in France. The metaphor has since dislodged and obscured the original sense of the term; it must, however, accept the fact of being taken at its word. The objection that it wasn't meant that way comes ready to hand but does not matter. The figure of speech preserves what its users have forgotten; analysis merely brings to light what presuppositions it drags along. The concept of the avant-garde is, like the word itself, a composite.

Its first component poses no conundrum. The field in which the avant-garde moves is history. The preposition *avant,* conceived spatially in the technical military sense, returns in the metaphor to its original temporal significance. The arts are regarded not as historically unvarying activities of mankind or as an arsenal of timelessly extant "cultural goods" but as a continually advancing process, as a work in progress, in which every single production participates.

Now, this process has a single direction. Only that makes it possible to differentiate advance guard, main body, and rear guard. Not all works are equally far "forward," and it is by no means a matter of indifference which position they occupy. The pathos of the concept feeds on the notion that the place at the spearhead of the process distinguishes a work, endows it with a rating denied other works. What is being compared is not really present performance with the past. To be sure, the avant-garde metaphor does not exclude the dull and inferior view that whatever came earlier can, for that very reason, be thrown on the junkheap. But it cannot be reduced to vulgar worship of the latest thing. Included in the concept is the nonsimultaneity of the simultaneous: precursors and stragglers are, at every moment of the process, simultaneously present. External and internal contemporaneity fall apart. The *en avant* of the avant-garde would, as it were, realize the future in the present, anticipate the course of history.

This conception has its justification in the fact that art without a moment of anticipation cannot even be thought of. It is contained in the very process of creation: the work is preceded by the design. The design, the project, does not disappear in its realization. Every work of art, and the masterwork in particular, has in it something unfinished; indeed, this necessary residue makes up its durability: only with it does the work fade away. An inkling of it is the prerequisite of all productivity. The idea of fame has its roots here. It has always been the notion of posthumous fame, not to be compared with mere celebrity during one's lifetime. Only subsequent generations can fulfill the work of art that juts, uncompleted, into the future; only they can, so to speak, redeem anticipation through fame. The works of antiquity were created in this confidence. It is stated explicitly in a widespread literary *topos:* the poet's apostrophe to posterity.

With the development of historical consciousness, this faith in posterity begins to decline. No doubt, there opens before any work, even the least significant, a prospect of a new immortality: everything can, indeed must, be preserved in mankind's memory — but as a "memorial," as a relic. That brings up the question of surpassability. Eternal survival in the museum is being bought with the prospect that henceforth the march of history can stride across everything without extinguishing it. Everyone becomes aware of the process of steady advance, and this awareness, in turn, becomes the motor that accelerates the process. The arts no longer find protection in their future: it confronts them as a threat and makes them dependent on itself. Faster and faster, history devours the works it brings to fruition.

From now on, the arts are cognizant of their own historicity as a stimulant and a threat, but this change of consciousness is not all there is to it. The triumph of capitalism turns it into a hard economic fact: it brings the work of art into the market place. It thus enters into a state of competition not only with other merchandise but also with every other work of art. The historic contest for future recognition becomes a competition for present purchase. The mechanics of the market imitates the devouring course of history on a smaller scale: it is geared to a rapid turnover in accord with the scant breath and crude eye of planned economy. The anticipatory moment of art is cut down to a mere speculation; its future is charted like that of stocks and shares. Historic movement is observed, comprehended, and discounted — a market trend upon whose correct prediction economic success depends. In the long run, however, the consciousness industry does not content itself with merely letting its augurs survey the market place of the arts. It attempts to insure itself against changes in the weather by creating it. If it does not exactly invent tomorrow's trend, it certainly proclaims and promotes it. The future of the work of art is sold before it has even occurred. What is steadily being offered for sale is, as in other industries, next year's model. But this future has not only always begun; it is also, when tossed out into the market, always already past. Tomorrow's esthetic product offered for sale today proves, the day after tomorrow, a white elephant and, no longer sellable, wanders into the archives in the hope of the possibility that, ten years later, it might still be palmed off as the object of a sentimental revival. Thus the work of art too is subject to the industrial procedure of built-in obsolescence: its afterlife is immediately cashed in on and cashiered; indeed, it is transmogrified, by way of publicity, into a forelife, which the work inherits before it even appears on the scene. Its afterlife is factory-made. The proposition concerning the nonsimultaneity of the simultaneous is realized by training the clientele to become a vanguard that insists on being served the newest thing and demands the future, so to speak, as consumer goods.

As suppliers of this industry, writers, painters, composers assume, economically speaking, the traits of employees. They must "keep in step with the times" and always nose out the competitors. To keep in the forefront, they must not "fail to connect." This explains why fifty-year-olds let themselves be described as young authors. Such an economic disposition obviously invites contemptible maneuvering. It gives rise to an avant-garde as bluff, as escape forward, with which the main body, for fear of being left behind, falls in. The type of the fellow traveler who would like to pass for a forerunner becomes prominent; in the rush for the future, every ram fancies himself the bellwether. The man on the treadmill remains unremittingly the object of a process that he thinks he is, as subject, in control of.

These economic consequences, however, merely reveal an aporia that is posited with the very concept of an avant-garde in the arts. What is questionable is not just its commercial exploitation but also the very *en avant* with which the avant-garde presents itself. For just who, other than the avant-garde itself, is to determine what at any given time is "to the fore" remains an open question. "The flung-out smaller divisions must govern themselves as to their movement," if we may trust the Brockhaus, "according to the larger ones that follow them"; but that means, as soon as a spatial movement is translated into a temporal one, governing themselves according to an unknown body.

Of course, it is possible to verify without much trouble that there exists at all times a rear guard. It coincides without fail with what reactionary criticism recommends as healthy. Its physiognomy can be described down to its minutest traits, for in them it is only the all-too-familiar that epigonously recurs. An extreme, very-well-explored example is the popular novel, which always reiterates older, exhausted patterns in distorted fashion. This does not actually devaluate what previous epochs have produced; devaluated, rather, are the suppliers of this rear guard, which likes to justify itself — but always unjustly — with reference to tradition. Its unassuming, petty bourgeois wing is shielded from every objection by its stupidity; in Communist countries, it enjoys state protection; in neocapitalist society, it supplies, hardly observed by the public eye, the proletariat, which, by universal demand, has been rechristened "lower middle class." How this majority of the population is being provided for, without dissension, with fifth-hand esthetics, can be studied in the catalogs of the large department stores and mail-order houses. At the forefront of this inarticulate rear guard is to be placed that "elevated" one, which consists of "culture-bearers." Its speciality is the aristocratic gesture with which it purports to "attend to spiritual interests" and defend "values"; its shadowboxing with modernity, of many decades' standing, needs no elucidation, and its points of view have become known *ad nauseam*.

On the contrary, it is not possible to discern a vantage point from which one could determine what is avant-garde and what isn't. All the efforts of the consciousness industry to detect a trend in the historic movement of the arts and elevate its prognostications to the level of a dictate misfire as speculation; at best, it is by chance that it scores any bull's-eyes. The actual process puts to shame not only the impotent attempts of the Communists to plan it but also the cleverer endeavors of capitalist economy, which would steer it by means of advertising and market manipulations. All that can be affirmed is what *was* "out front," not what *is* there. The work of Kleist or Kafka remained invisible to the contemporaries not because they refused to "go with the times" but because they went with the times. This does not mean that, in the arts, what contains futurity must go unrecognized. The notion of the unrecognized has, in any case, taken on an old-fashioned coloring, ever since the capacity of the reproducing apparatus has become greater than existing production, and since, consequently, anything at all that anyone writes or paints is indiscriminately and suspiciously publicized. That in this way every work — let alone one that anticipates the future — is done justice to cannot for a moment be entertained; there is no authority before which such justice can be pleaded or, like a tariff regulation, implemented. Where the word *avant-garde* is being construed in the present tense, a doctrinaire formulation results. Whoever becomes rigid about objective necessity, the demands of the medium, and compulsory evolution is already in the wrong. Every such doctrine relies on the method of extrapolation: it prolongs lines into the unknown. Such a procedure, however, will not get even at a political or economic process, because it is applicable only to linear, not to dialectical operations, to say nothing of an esthetic process, which can be apprehended through no prognosis, not even a statistical one, because its characteristics are determined by leaps. Their spontaneous appearance defies any theory of futurity.

The model according to which the concept of the avant-garde orients itself is invalid. The forward march of the arts through history is conceived of as a linear, perspicuous, and surveyable movement in which everyone can himself determine his place, at the forefront or with the hangers-on. What is overlooked is that this movement leads from the known into the unknown, that, therefore, only the stragglers can indicate where they are. Nobody knows what is up front, least of all he who has reached unknown territory. Against this uncertainty there is no insurance. Only someone willing to suffer the consequences of error can get involved with the future. The *avant* of the *avant-garde* contains its own contradiction: it can be marked out only a posteriori.

The metaphor of the avant-garde, however, contains not only temporal but also sociological determinants. These are expressed in the second component of the compound term.

> *Guards* is the name given, other than to the bodyguards of princes, in many armies, to elite troops distinguished by excellent supplies and especially brilliant uniforms (cf. *Elite*); they are usually garrisoned in capitals and royal residential towns. Guard means originally an enclosure. . . . Napoleon I must be considered the actual creator of the g. Tradition puts into the mouth of its commander, General Cambronne (to be sure, without foundation), the saying, "The guard dies, but does not surrender." [6]

Every guard is a collective; that is the first thing that can be deduced from this word. First the group, and only then the individual, whose decisions are of no consequence in the undertakings of the guard, unless he be its leader. For every guard is most rigorously divided into the one who issues the commands and passwords of the day and the many who receive them, pass them on, and obey them. What all who belong to it have in common is discipline. Without dictates and regulations, it cannot manage. To abide by them is not always easy, but it does relieve the member of the guard of many worries. Along with his freedom, he delegates to the collective body doubt, fear, and insecurity; he feels surer about his cause, which is no longer his concern but that of the whole. The protection that the guard vouchsafes is enjoyed, in the first place, by the guard itself. The guardsman has not only duties but also rights — to be exact, prerogatives. To belong to the guard is a distinction. It is an exclusive league of men; the enclosure keeps others out. Every guard, and so too the avant-garde, considers itself an elite. It is proud not only of being ahead of and further on than the others but also of belonging to a distinguished minority.

The guard's vocation is combat. In it, and only in it, does the guard prove its worth. Not productivity but contest is its *raison d'être:* it is always militant. Here the transfer of the concept to the arts leads into some difficulties. What adversary does the vanguard expect to encounter on the terrain of history if it alone, and nobody else, operates in, or into, the future? What enemy army could it meet there? Enemies should not be lacking to anyone who forsakes the safe, allegedly so "healthy" grounds of mediocrity; but these adversaries seem to be located in back of him rather, and aside from the fact that he will not exactly see his purpose in life as fighting the likes of them, it just will not jibe with the idea of a guard that its only foe should be the tail of that very column it has the privilege of leading.

The concept of the avant-garde was applied not only to the arts but also, over half a century later, more felicitously and sensibly to politics. In 1919, Lenin defined the Communist Party as the avant-garde of the proletariat.[7] This formula became part of the international Communist vocabulary.[8] It pinpoints what the avant-garde metaphor sociologically comprehends, or rather, uncomprehendingly drags along. The role played by Sorel's concept of an elite in the development of Lenin's theories is well known. Very much in Sorel's sense, the party is to Lenin a strictly organized, elite combat unit, where absolute internal discipline is a matter of course; no less obviously, it is entitled to a privileged position vis-à-vis the outsiders, the mass of nonparty members. Here the avant-garde metaphor is thought out with sharp consistency down to its last detail. At one point only does the figurative meaning diverge from the literal one: the Communist avant-garde need not "govern itself as to its movement" according to the main body, but conversely, it is at the same time the general staff according to whose plans the entire operation must proceed: it enforces the dictatorship not only *of* but also *over* the proletariat. Understandably, if the revolution is to be "carried out" in the name of the majority but against its will, what is required is not so much muses as a bodyguard. In all other particulars, however, the Communist concept of an avant-garde is strictly relevant. What is forward is determined once and for all by an infallible doctrine, and the adversary at whom the vanguard action is directed is established and really there.

Beside Lenin's well-defined application of it to politics, the concept of the avant-garde in the arts appears to be somewhat confused. Least convincing it is collective trait. Clearly, a historic process has many collaborators, so many that it would be ridiculous to speculate about just how many individuals at a given period "constitute" a literature. But as much as every literature is a collective effort, as little is it to be visualized as a troop organized along disciplinary lines and sworn to a doctrine. Whoever participates in it enters forthwith into a direct relationship with the process as a whole; he can consign his freedom and risks to no group outside of himself.

The avant-garde metaphor does not contain the slightest reference to a revolutionary or even rebellious intent. Nothing is more glaring than this lack. For as yet every group that made use of the concept, in the arts as in politics, viewed itself as a *Fronde* and proclaimed the overthrow of existing conditions. No avant-garde program but protests the inertia of the merely extant and promises to burst esthetic and political bonds, throw off established rule, liberate suppressed energies. Freedom, gained through revolution, is heralded by all avant-garde movements. It is to this claim, which it does not even express, rather than to its future-orientedness, rather than to its promise to form an elite, that the concept of the avant-garde owes its emotional appeal. This aspect too was thought out more acutely and thoroughly by Lenin than by all the writers and painters. From what the Communist avant-garde would free its partisans and everybody else is made clear beyond any doubt; its revolutionary character will not be denied by its worst enemy. By contrast, it remains vague and blurry just what freedom the manifestoes of the artistic avant-garde have in mind and what the word *revolution,* frequently though it may appear in them, is supposed to mean there. All too often these manifestoes sound both grandiloquent and innocuous, as if they had no other concern than to scare off bourgeois conventions, which, in any case, are nothing more than ghosts. The cry for absolute freedom rings peculiar when the question involved is whether or not fish may be eaten with a knife. The propensity for revolutionary rhetoric may reveal the surface nakedness of the avant-garde; it does, however, cover up its central aporias. Only where it ruthlessly formulates its aims and methods, as with Lenin, do these aporias become apparent.

In much the same way as Communism in society, the avant-garde in the arts would enforce freedom in doctrinaire fashion. Just like the Party, it believes itself to have taken, as a revolutionary elite, which is to say as a collective, a lease on the future. It disposes with the indefinable in the most definite manner. It arbitrarily dictates what will be valid tomorrow and, simultaneously, submits, disciplined and will-less, to the commands of a future of its very own contriving. It proclaims as its goal total freedom, and surrenders, unresisting, to the historic process, which is to relieve it of that self-same freedom.

These aporias lie in the concept *avant-garde* itself. They can be verified empirically in all groups that have had recourse to it, but they have never become more flagrantly apparent than in that which today exhibits itself as the avant-garde: in tachism, in *art informel,* and in monochrome painting; in serial and electronic music; in the so-called concrete poetry; and in the literature of the beat generation.[9] These movements have in common the more or less obstreperously announced conviction of being "out front," their doctrinaire bias, and their collective state. That their names have become, in the course of a few years, catchwords, indeed trademarks, stems not merely from their accord with the consciousness industry; these terms were launched with premeditation as handy slogans. Avant-gardism, nowadays, is brought into currency overnight, as coin of the realm. All the more reason for examining the coinage a little more closely.

It is to Jack Kerouac, the supreme commander of the Beatnik sect, canonized by his partisans as Holy Jack, that we owe the following maxim, which he posited in his "Credo" together with a "List of Indispensable Remedies" for the writer: "Be always idiotically absentminded!" The sentence can serve as motto for the current mass productions of tachism, *art informel,* action painting, concrete poetry *in toto,* as well as for a large part of the latest music. Kerouac goes on: "My style is based on spontaneous get-with-it, unrepressed word-slinging. . . . Push aside literary, grammatical and syntactic obstacles! Strike as deep as you can strike! Visionary spasms shoot through the breast. You are at all times a genius." [10] To be sure, the avant-garde bares its breast with so much naiveté (even if false) only between New York and San Francisco. The harmless simplicity with which it proclaims barbarism has a downright endearing effect in contrast to its European counterpart. Here indeterminacy expresses itself in a petrified academic jargon that dishes out delirium as a seminar report: the proffered texts form "a system of words, letters or signs, which obtain their meaning only through the personal contribution of the reader. . . . They are arbitrarily disposed in the sixteen directions of the quadratic square and alligned in a chance sequence . . . they possess stringency only through the swirls of motion and the assent they evoke in the reader . . . when carried through with rigorous consistency, they debouch into the black stone, the last standstill, as the no-further-enhanceable complex motion. Are, thereby, concrete form, uninterruptedly centered point, objective duration in nature (as materia-l *sine qua non*) guess whyyyy." [11]

That reads like a translation of Kerouac's catechism into occidental culture-gibberish. The translator keeps strictly to the prescriptions of the original, which, to be sure, is garnished with eruditional flotsam, but to whose intellectual exiguity he remains absolutely faithful. Mobility raised to an end in itself reappears as "swirls of the no-further-enhanceable complex motion," and the "visionary spasms" turn into "the black stone guess whyyyy." In both cases, mystification demands "carrying through with rigorous consistency," and the precept "Be always idiotically absent-minded" lays claim to stringency. An idea of the possibilities this avant-garde opens up may be gleaned from the following "text"; [12]

```
ra ra ra ra ra ar ra ra ra ra ar ar er ir
ra ra ra ra ar ar ar ka ra ra ar ar ar er
ra ra ra ar ar ar ak af ka ra ar ar ar ra
ra ra ar ar ar ak af ab af ka ar ar ra ra
ra ar ar ar ak af ab af ab af ak ra ra ra
```

This result does not stand in isolation. Works of the same stamp are available in such quantities that it would be unjust to name the begetter of the specimen, even though he has already made a bit of a name for himself with his output. Since, however, it is hardly distinguishable from the outpourings of his companions, what should, rather, be considered the author, insofar as this word still applies, is the collective: in such texts the guard brings itself into being. It can be seen at a glance (and this in itself justifies the reproduction of a specimen) that the sociological aporias of the avant-garde are repeated in them quite accurately on the formal level; indeed, they perfectly consume themselves in their reproduction. Indeterminacy appears as doctrine, retrogression as progress. The milkman's bill masquerades as inspired madness, quietism as action, chance as prescription.

That these characteristics apply not only to "concrete poetry" and the literature of the Beat Generation but also to the self-declared avant-garde in all the arts is demonstrated by an international album in which it draws its self-portrait and which purports to be "at once account, documentation, analysis and program." It contains a list of basic concepts and categories, which are supposed to be equally valid for literature and painting, music and sculpture, film and architecture (insofar as such distinctions are still permissible). The following should be noted: improvisation, chance, moment of imprecision, interchangeability, indefiniteness, emptiness; reduction to pure motion, pure action, absolute motion, motoricity, *mouvement pur.* Arbitrary, blind movement is the guiding principle of the entire album, as emerges already from its title. That title applies insofar as the avant-garde was all along bent on movement, as conceived not only by the philosophy of history but also by sociology. Each one of its groups not only believed itself to be anticipating a phase of the historic process but also saw itself always as movement, motion. This movement, in both senses of the word, now proclaims itself an end in itself. The kinship with totalitarian movements lies close to hand, their center being precisely, as Hannah Arendt has shown, empty kinetic activity, which spews forth thoroughly arbitrary, indeed manifestly absurd, ideological demands and proceeds to implement them.[13] Kerouac's appeal, "Strike as deep as you can strike!" is so utterly innocuous only because it is directed at literature, and because literature, like all arts, cannot be terrorized by the likes of him. Transposed onto the plane of politics, it could serve as a device for any fascist organization. The impotent avant-garde must content itself with obliterating its own products. Quite consistently, the Japanese painter Murakami contrives a large painted paper screen destined for his work, which is "the piercing of several holes in one instant"; "the work of Murakami made a mighty noise as it was being pierced. Six holes were torn into the strong eightfold paper screen. This was done with such speed, in a single moment, that the cameramen [!] missed the exact instant. When the six holes were there, he had an attack of bloodlessness of the brain. 'I've been a new man ever since,' he later murmured." [14]

All avant-garde groups incline toward the adoption of obscure doctrines of salvation. They are, characteristically, defenseless toward Zen Buddhism, which, within a few years, spread rapidly among writers, painters, and musicians of this cast. In its imported form, Zen Buddhism serves to confer upon blind action an occult, quasi-religious consecration. Its teachings are transmitted in *exempla,* the so-called *mondo.* The punch line of the best-known *exemplum* consists in the master's answering the metaphysical questions of a disciple with a stick or a slap in the face. Murakami's "action" too may be considered a Zen precept. It points to the latent acts of violence in avant-garde "movements," which, to be sure, is directed first against the "materials" with which they are dealing: they blindly toss about paints, tones, or word fragments rather than hurling hand grenades or Molotov cocktails.

The reverse side of this susceptibility to extremely irrational, supposedly mystical teachings is the no less extreme faith in science that the avant-garde proudly sports. The indeterminacy of its "actions" always pretends to be exact. It tries to convey this impression by means of a terminology for which the most diverse disciplines have been ransacked: along with vacuum and absolute motion, there are catchwords like *constellation, material structure, correlogram, coordination, rotomodulation, microarticulation, phase-shift, autodetermination, transformation,* and so on and so forth. A laboratory smock enfolds the breast shot through with visionary spasms; and what the avant-garde produces, whether it be poems, novels, pictures, movies, constructions, or pieces of music, is and remains "experimental."

Experiment as an esthetic concept has long since become part of the vocabulary of the consciousness industry. Put in circulation by the avant-garde, used as an adjuration, worn threadbare and unelucidated, it haunts artistic conferences and cultural panels and reproduces itself through reviews and essays. The obligatory modifier is *bold,* but the choice of the ennobling epithet *courageous* is also permitted. The most modest reflection reveals that it is a case of plain bluff.

Experimentum means "that which has been experienced." In modern languages, the Latin word designates a scientific procedure for the verification of theories or hypotheses through methodical observation of natural phenomena. The process to be explained must be isolable. An experiment is meaningful only when the variables that appear are known and can be controlled. There is the additional requisite that every experiment must be susceptible of rechecking and must at every repetition yield the same unequivocal result. That is to say, an experiment can succeed or miscarry only with regard to a previously exactly defined goal. It presupposes reflection and contains an experience. It can in no way be an end in itself: its intrinsic worth equals zero. Let us also set down that a genuine experiment has nothing to do with boldness. It is a very simple and indispensable procedure for the investigation of laws. It requires, above all, patience, acuteness, circumspection, and diligence.

Pictures, poems, performances do not satisfy these requirements. The experiment is a procedure for bringing about scientific insights, not for bringing about art. (Of course, every publication can be considered an economic or sociological experiment. Under this heading, success and failure can be established quite accurately, and most publishers, art dealers, and theatrical managers do not hesitate to derive from that the theory and practice of their enterprises. To be sure, viewed from this angle, Karl May is every bit as experimental as Jack Kerouac. The difference between the two experiments lies in the result, that is, in the number of copies sold. That such experiments possess esthetic relevance may be doubted.) Experiment as bluff does, indeed, flirt with the scientific method and its demands, but has not the least intention of getting seriously involved with it.[15] It is unconditional "pure action"; intentions of any kind are not to be attributed to it. Method, possibility of proof, stringency have no share in it. The farther removed from any sort of experience they are, the more the experiments of the avant-garde are "experimental."

That proves that this concept is nonsensical and unusable. What has yet to be explained is what makes it so popular. That is not hard to say. A biologist who undertakes an experiment on a guinea pig cannot be held accountable for its behavior. He is answerable only for the irreproachable observance of the conditions of the experiment. The result is out of his hands; the experimenter is literally obligated to interfere as little as possible in the process he is observing. The moral immunity he enjoys is precisely what appeals to the avant-garde. Though it is by no means ready to adhere to the methodical demands to which the scientist submits, it does wish to avoid all responsibility, both for its activities and their results. It hopes to achieve this by referring to the "experimental" character of its work. The borrowings from science serve as an excuse. With the designation *experiment,* the avant-garde excuses its results, takes back, as it were, its "actions," and unloads all responsibility on the receiver. Every boldness suits the avant-garde perfectly as long as it itself remains safe. The concept of the experiment is to insure it against the risk of all esthetic production. It serves both as trademark and as camouflage.

What is under investigation here is the aporias of the avant-garde, its concept, its assumptions, and its postures. Such an analysis reveals the claims made in behalf of concrete poetry, the Beat Generation, tachism, and other present-day avant-garde groupings to be untenable, each and all. On the other hand, it can by no means serve the purpose of condemning the productions of such groups as a whole. It does not unmask doctrinaire fraud only to fall prey to it itself. Not a single work can be dismissed by pointing to the fact that its creator has joined up with such-and-such-a-guard, and even the silliest esthetic program does not *ipso facto* vitiate the potency of those who subscribe to it. The person who demolishes the terminological tricks and doctrinal screens with which today's avant-garde tries to shield itself does not thereby save himself the trouble of critically examining its products: he merely makes such a critical examination possible in the first place. Such examination must be insisted upon all the more determinedly the more advanced a work claims to be; and the more assiduously it appeals to a collective, the more it must affirm its individuality. Every popular movie deserves more leniency than an avant-garde that would simultaneously overpower critical judgment and timorously rid itself of the responsibility for its own works.

The aporias that have rent it and delivered it into the hands of charlatans have always been contained in the concept of the avant-garde. They were not first dragged in by hangers-on and stragglers. Already the first futurist manifesto of 1909, one of the earliest documents of an organized "movement," makes *"dynamisme perpétuel"* into an end in itself: "We live," Marinetti writes, "already in the absolute: we have created permanent and omnipresent speed. . . . We extol aggressive motion, feverish sleeplessness, marching on the double, the slap of the palm and the blow of the fist above all things. . . . There is no beauty but that of battle. . . . Only in war can the world recover its health." (The last sentence in the original: *"La guerre seule hygiène du monde."*) [16]

In futurism, the avant-garde organized itself for the first time as a doctrinaire clan, and already then it lauded blind action and open violence. That in 1924 the nucleus of the movement collectively rushed into the fascist camp is no accident. In formal matters, the futurists, exactly as did their descendants, advocated the removal of all "literary, grammatical and syntactic barriers." Even the disconnected slapping together of pseudo-mathematics and questionable mysticism can already be found among them. The painters of the movement declared in 1912 that they wished to "reinforce the emotions of the viewer according to a law of inner mathematics"; there is talk also of visions and ecstasies. In the futurist texts, mathematical formulas crop up alongside occult incantations and chaotic verbal debris.[17] The catechism of the avant-garde of 1961 contains hardly a sentence that was not formulated fifty years earlier by Marinetti and his circle. Be it mentioned in passing that the few significant authors of the movement left it shortly after the publication of the first manifestoes and that these manifestoes are the only texts futurism has left us.

An extensive survey of the countless avant-gardist collectives of the first half of the twentieth century is neither possible nor called for here. The role of most of them is overestimated. Literary and art historians, who, as is known, enumerate "currents" and isms with passionate fondness because that relieves them of concern with details, have accepted too many such group appellations as gospel truth instead of sticking to the particulars of the given works; indeed, they even, as it were, invented such movements a posteriori. Thus German expressionism became hypostatized into a collective manifestation which, in reality, never existed: many expressionists did not even live to hear the word *expressionism,* introduced into German literature in 1914 by Hermann Bahr. Heym and Trakl died before it came up; as late as 1955, Gottfried Benn declared that he did not know what it was supposed to mean; [18] Brecht and Kafka, Döblin and Jahnn never "joined a movement" that went by that name. Every historian can claim for himself the right to bundle manifestations and lump together the manifold under one heading, but only on the condition of not confusing his auxiliary constructs with reality, whose representation they are meant to subserve.

In contrast to expressionism, surrealism was, from the outset, a collective enterpirse that had at its disposal a well-developed doctrine. All previous and subsequent groupings seem, compared to it, impoverished, dilettantish, and inarticulate. Surrealism is the paradigm, the perfect model of all avant-gardist movements: once and for all it thought through to the end all their possibilities and limitations and unfurled all the aporias inherent in such movements.

"Only the word freedom can still fill me with enthusiasm. I consider it suited to keep the old human fanaticism upright for an indefinite length of time yet to come." With these words, André Breton, in the year 1924, opens the first surrealist manifesto.[19] The new doctrine crystallizes, as always, around its yearning for absolute freedom. The word *fanaticism* is already an indication that this freedom can be acquired only at the price of absolute discipline: within a few years, the surrealist guard spins itself into a cocoon of regulations. The tighter the bond to the collective, the blinder the "pure action": "The simplest surrealist deed consists," we read in Breton, "in walking out into the street with guns in the hand and shooting as long as possible blindly into the crowd." A few years were yet to pass before this maxim was realized in Germany. In any case, even before World War II broke out, Salvador Dali reached the conclusion that "Hitler is the greatest surrealist." [20]

Long before the coming to power of this surrealist, inner aporias had split open the movement. Its sociology would deserve more detailed consideration. At the end of the twenties, the intrigues, declarations of apostasy, bickerings, and "purges" within the group reached their high point. Its development into a narrow-minded sect strikes one as both ridiculous and tragic; yet it cannot be stemmed by the energy and self-sacrifice of the members because it follows of necessity from the presuppositions of the movement.[21] Its commander-in-chief assumes more and more the features of a revolutionary pope; he sees himself compelled solemnly to excommunicate his companions-in-arms one after another. Occasionally this turns into show trials that, in retrospect, seem like bloodless parodies of the later Stalinist purges. At the outbreak of World War II, the surrealist movement lost all its best brains without exception: Artaud, Desnos,

Soupault, Duchamp, Aragon, Eluard, Char, Queneau, Leiris, and many
others turned their backs on it. Since then, the group ekes out a shadowy
existence.

The party-line surrealist literature is faded and forgotten; the above-
named authors have, with the exception of Breton, produced nothing
worth mentioning while submitting to the group's discipline. Surrealism
was destined to have an enormous effect, but it became productive only in
those who freed themselves from its doctrine.[22]

We see no reason for gloating over its foundering. Every backward
glance at an avant-garde whose future is known has an easy time of it.
Everyone today participates in the historical experiences of surrealism. No
one has the right to encounter it with condescension to or pleasure in its
plight; it is, however, our duty to draw the consequences from its downfall. The law of increasing reflection is inexorable. Whoever tries to dodge
it ends up offered for sale at a discount by the consciousness industry.
Every avant-garde of today spells repetition, deception, or self-deception.
The movement as a doctrinairely conceived collective, as invented fifty or
thirty years ago with the purpose of shattering the resistance of a compact
society, did not survive the historic conditions that elicited it. Conspiring
in the name of the arts is only possible where they are being suppressed.
An avant-garde that suffers itself to be furthered by the state has for-
feited its rights.

The historic avant-garde perished by its aporias. It was questionable,
but it was not craven. Never did it try to play it safe with the excuse
that what it was doing was nothing more than an "experiment"; it never
cloaked itself in science in order to be absolved of its results. That distinguishes it from the company of limited responsibility that is its successor; therein lies its greatness. In 1942, when, except for him, nobody
believed in surrealism any more, Breton raised his voice against "all those
who do not know that there is no great departure in art that does not
take place in mortal peril, that the road to be taken quite obviously is not
protected by a breastwork, and that every artist must set out all alone on
the quest for the Golden Fleece."

This is no plea for a "middle way" and no cue for an about-face. The
path of the modern arts is not reversible. Let others harbor hopes for the
end of modernity, for conversions and "reintegrations." What is to be
chalked up against today's avant-garde is not that it has gone too far but
that it keeps the back doors open for itself, that it seeks support in doctrines and collectives, and that it does not become aware of its own
aporias, long since disposed of by history. It deals in a future that does
not belong to it. Its movement is regression. The avant-garde has become
its opposite: anachronism. That inconspicuous, limitless risk, of which the
artists' future lives — it cannot sustain it.

GEOFFREY H. HARTMAN

Toward Literary History

> "Go to Art, and tell him Pop sent you."
> *Chafed Elbows*

I am concerned with the idea of history by which men live, and especially with the idea of history by which poets have lived. No one has yet written a history from the point of view of the poets — from within their consciousness of the historical vocation of art. To write decent literary history is, of course, important in itself: We are all disenchanted with those picaresque adventures in pseudo-causality that go under the name of literary history, those handbooks with footnotes that claim to sing of the whole, but load every rift with glue. Twenty years ago Wellek and Warren were forced to ask, "Is it *possible* to write literary history, that is, to write that which will be both literary [in subject] and a history?" Most histories of literature, the authors continued, "are either social histories, or histories of thought as illustrated in literature, or impressions and judgments on specific works arranged in more or less chronological order." [1]

The dissatisfaction with literary history is not limited to this country. In 1950 Werner Krauss, the distinguished East German scholar, published an essay entitled "Literary History as a Historical Duty" (*Literaturgeschichte als geschichtlicher Auftrag*); and Hans Robert Jauss recently delivered an inaugural lecture at Konstanz on "Literary History as Provocation." [2] American scholars, in fact, have been slower than their European colleagues to shake off that distrust of speculative ideas that came in reaction to the giddy era of *Geistesgeschichte* and the equally dubious if more sober pomps of the History of Ideas. This cautiousness has long degenerated into the positivist's medley of fact and fashionable ideas or into a formalistic kind of literary criticism only vaguely in touch with history writing. [3] Yet if I raise the question of literary history, it is not merely to urge its importance as an intellectual discipline or to deplore the absence of methodological thinking in that area. There are just too

SOURCE: Reprinted by permission from *Daedalus, Journal of the American Academy of Arts and Sciences,* Boston, Massachusetts, Volume 99, Number 2 (Spring 1970), pp. 355–83.

many areas in which one could be thinking more clearly and generously. My argument will be that literary history is necessary less for the sake of intellect than for the sake of literature; it is our "historical duty" because it alone can provide today a sorely needed defense of art.

Since Aristotle, the best defense of art has been to call it "more philosophical" than history. Despite recent advances in sociology, literature continues to escape historical research at some point. To demonstrate, as Lucien Goldmann has done, that the dramas of Racine participate in the public thought of his time, that there is nothing in his plays not illuminated by the conflict within church or state, is a significant authentification of the reality principle guiding even the most abstract or stylized art, and a cogent reminder that literature is never as self-centered as it seems to be.[4] But the influence of Racine, the continuing resonance of his language and form, even for those who do not know of the topical historical issues, remains unclarified. There exists, in other words, a principle of authority in art that is purely authorial: It seems to derive from art alone or from the author's genius rather than from the genius of his age. Werner Krauss, troubled by this characteristic autonomy of literature, by this "capacity of art-forms to outlast the destined hour," admits that Marxist theory has not been able to understand the phenomenon. Whether or not poetry is more philosophical than history, it is more formal: That is the brute yet elegant fact that we must appreciate without falling into idealistic or unhistorical explanations.

Thus the formality of art becomes a central issue in any literary history. How do we ground art in history without denying its autonomy, its aristocratic resistance to the tooth of time? Is it not a monument rather than a document; a monument, moreover, of the soul's magnificence, and so a richly solipsistic or playful edifice?

To understand the "art" in art is always essential. But it is even more essential today, for we have clearly entered an "era of suspicion" in which art seems arty to the artist himself. The artist, indeed, is often the severest critic of his own medium which turns against itself in his relentless drive for self-criticism. Artistic form and aesthetic illusion are today treated as "ideologies" to be exposed and demystified; this has long been true on the Continent, where Marxism is part of the intellectual milieu, but it is also becoming true of America. If literary history is to provide a new defense of art, it must now defend the artist against himself as well as against his other detractors. It must help to restore his faith in two things: in form and in his historical vocation.

TOWARD A THEORY OF FORM

It may seem strange, this suggestion that we suffer at present from a shame of form. But the modern insistence on process, on openness,

on mixed media, and especially on the mingling of personal and technological elements indicates more than the usual difficulty with inherited
patterns or the desire to "make it new." The older way of achieving a form
impersonal enough to allow the new to emerge was to subordinate the
individual talent to the tradition. Eliot still thought it possible. Then what
is wrong with the old forms? Why do they appear less exciting, less viable
— even less "pure" — than mixed or technological forms? Take the example of a man from whom Eliot learned his craft: No one was more interested in purity of form, or form as such, than Ezra Pound. Yet Pound's
Cantos, which ransack the high culture of both West and East, remain a
nostalgic montage without unity, a picaresque of styles.

We look back at Pound and Eliot,[5] at Bridges and Yeats, and we realize that their elitist view of culture is dead. Though their art aimed for the
genuine vernacular, it could not resist the appeal of forms associated with
high culture, forms that remained an "ideological" reflex of upper-class
mentality. To purge this ideological stain, and to rescue art from the imputation of artiness, the writer had to become his own enemy. Today all
art stands in a questionable relation to elite modes of thought and feeling.
But while the artist moves closer to self-criticism, the critic moves closer
to art by expanding the notion of form until it cannot be narrowly linked
to the concerns of a priestly culture or its mid-cult imitations.

I want to examine modern criticism in the light of this tendency. Is
there a larger conception of literary form in the making? There are four
significant theories to be considered: first, Marxist criticism, which raises
explicitly the issue of elitism; then Frye's theory of archetypes; and finally
two kinds of structuralist theory, that of C. Lévi-Strauss, and that of I. A.
Richards and the Anglo-American critics. I hope to persuade you that an
important new theory of form is gradually emerging.

Let me illustrate the Marxist preoccupation with form by a work of art
that provides its own critical perspective. Jean-Luc Godard's *Weekend* is
cinematic self-criticism of an extreme kind. The title of the film points to
the theme of leisure or, rather, of "ignoble leisure"; and Godard engages
in the film in a ruthless violation of taboos, especially the "taboo" of form.
Not only are the unities of time, place, and action killed once again, or
rather parodied to death, but just about every art-movie cliché — from the
films of Antonioni, Fellini, Bunuel, Resnais, Truffaut — and Godard
himself — is exposed to massive lyrical ridicule. The result is strangely
operatic, since opera tends to be pure superstructure, its form having but
an absurd or magical connection with the passions staged. The Antonioni
promenade, the Fellini harlequinade, the Bonnie-and-Clyde relationship,
the Truffaut tenderness, the Bunuelian symbols — everything is mocked
in this bloody, endlessly interrupted pastoral.

What remains? It is the problem of the elitist status of art, expressed in
powerful visual graffiti. One scene shows a truck-driver playing Mozart

on a huge concert-piano that has somehow found its way into a farmyard. Various laborers and old peasant women seem as entranced by that music as the beasts were by Orpheus. It is Godard's gentlest scene, but also the most mocking vis-à-vis the Marxist theory of a proletariat pastoral. What reconciliation is possible between Mozart, the proletariat *régisseur,* and the barnyard setting? "What are the conditions," asks Werner Krauss, "which compel a break-through from the base (*Unterbau*) of society and which might rectify its relation to the superstructure (*Überbau*)? In what way can literature belong to the superstructure of society?" [6] There is nothing that belongs authentically to either the social base or superstructure in Godard's mise-en-scène. We are left with a few lyrical images of old women who seem to listen to the incongruous music and a farmhand walking to its rhythm and yet not to its rhythm. All the rest is — ideology.

If we insert this film into a history of the concept of form, we would have to say that, for Godard, form was less important than its violation. He writes about the problem of form in blood — in the life-blood of his medium. He hopes that by violating all taboos something deeper than the gratuitous values of a leisure class might emerge: real pastoral values, perhaps; something from the *Unterbau* or Marxist "deep structure." Yet this movie, which begins as sophisticated pornography, ends with a totally undelicious scene of anthropophagy: a progress which suggests that to destroy through revolution or some other mode of cleansing the forms of our high culture will simply result in primitivism, in the naked substructure. We are therefore forced to consider a second reason for Godard's violation of taboos. The movie medium, instead of discovering new values, is shown to participate necessarily in the old values, in the capitalistic desire for conspicuous consumption. All the totems of movie culture are therefore offered up to the reluctant viewer in this moveable feast which is like the massacre of matériel in American spectaculars. To go beyond this movie means to go beyond a movie-centered culture and no longer to confuse participation with consumption.

We come away from Godard with two observations about the authenticity of art forms in contemporary society. The first is that the only forms that all classes of society enjoy are primitivistic; the second, that the most we can expect from art is not authenticity but purity — the fissure of the work of art into ideology on the one hand and pure form on the other. Godard's "alienation-effects" are more Mallarmean than Brechtean and substantiate the view that poetry is detachable from a more continuous prose base. Thus form remains a lyrical and dying effect, a falling star in the twilight of taboos.

The theory of form advanced by Northrop Frye is more familiar. He removes the elitism of the art object by pointing to similarities between the structure of primitive myths and the formal principles of all art. The structure of a sophisticated novel by Henry James or Virginia Woolf is like that of any story; and the historical difference between stories is due to what Frye calls the displacement of myth, that is, its accommodation to rules of verisimilitude that differ for different cultures. In a culture, for example, that is "realistic," a writer cannot depict supernatural figures directly, yet he invents characters with daemonic attributes or with the capacity for violating social norms. Thus Frye can talk of the pharmakos or sacred scapegoat in Virginia Woolf and Henry James; and Ihab Hassan expands that insight to cover a broad range of modern works in *Radical Innocence*.

The virtue of Frye's system is that it methodically removes the one barrier that prevents art from exerting wide influence: the distinction of kind between sacred and secular, or between popular and highbrow. His sense for the commonality of art is radically Protestant: Every man is imagination's priest. All art that is good expands imagination; all art that is bad restricts it. Mystery and its brood — secret religion, secret sex, secret government — are simply imagination gone bad. For Frye as for Blake, bad art argues a sick society, one that has the power to block our imagination. And the blocking agent is always a priesthood: some political or religious or artistic elite.

It is clear that Frye's theory has affinities with Marxist thought. But the latter is more dialectical and realistic in its view of history. Where Marxist critics confront the individual work and evaluate it according to its struggle with the proletariat-elite, base-superstructure split, Frye's structural observations are developed for descriptive and not for evaluative purposes. His idea of literary history is certainly abstract: not only less sweaty than Marxist literary history, but also less concrete than most scholarly versions. Though he expands our concept of form and redeems individual works from the isolation imposed on them by cult and culture, he may do so at the cost of a false idea of universality and an elite idea of literary history. The illusion that a world-wide culture is already within reach is fostered by evading the question of national difference and large-scale social (East-West) conflict. I suspect that for the Marxist his vision of cultural dissemination is a technocrat's ideal and betrays an American perspective. Werner Krauss would surely commend Frye, as he does other American scholars, for his "radical break with all monopolistic attitudes in the writing of literary history," but he would also criticize a method that bypasses national or ideological differences till literature becomes an "All-Souls, in which Cervantes and Rabelais, Dante and Voltaire, amicably drink tea together." [7] It is, in short, bad comparative literature.

We return later to this problem of how the nationality of literatures is to be respected; but it is important to add that Frye writes about criticism rather than about literature, and he seems more interested in improving the consumer than in evaluating the product. His whole effort is an attempt to improve the public relations of art. His vision of an expanding cultural universe includes literary works, but they are not the reified apples of his eye. On the contrary, he is less interested in the marmoreal object than in a change of perception from which the object would profit. To Eliot's thesis that the advent of the authentically new work of art revises our view of all preceding works, Frye adds an important footnote: This change is a change in our consciousness of art and can only occur, therefore, if mediated by criticism. Whatever totemic or elitist elements remain in the literary work, this interplay between art and critic, between product and consumer, expands both and anticipates the Marxist hope (itself a version of Christian communism elaborated around the time of Blake, Ballanche, and Saint-Simon) [8] that the forms of social life dissolve into the form of man — into the expanding humanistic consciousness of a classless society.

It is, hence, a question whether Frye is dealing with "form" at all. He seems to approach the concept of "structure" with which structuralism (the third of our theories) is concerned. This structure is a mental fact and supposedly intersubjective: common to every man as man, to priest and peasant, sophisticate and primitive. The shift in linguistics from individual languages (or sign-systems) to language in general (or semeiotics) and from there to structures of the mind parallels Frye's shift from the individual work of art to literature as a totality and from there to a "verbal universe" which exhibits archetypes basic to science as well. Yet the "structures" isolated by Claude Lévi-Strauss differ from Frye's in an essential respect. They are solutions to real social problems — which is why structuralism can call itself a science, a *science humaine*. The principles of structure described by Frye solve a problem only in the sense that they free art from the stigma of archaism or elitism, and so publish it once again. Tradition is extradition; art must become transitive vis-à-vis its original site in history. Frye teaches us a lot about tradition, handing-on, but less about what is handed on. He fails to bring together the form of art and the form of its historical consciousness — which is the ideal of the science we seek.

Claude Lévi-Strauss also fails in this, but he does bring together the form of myth and a kind of *social* consciousness. Myth, according to him, resolves a societal hang-up or articulates its solution. Since every society has conflicts of interest that cannot be resolved without great mental anxiety, every society will have its myths. If all myths use the same basic method to resolve these social conflicts, then a science of myth would be possible. And this possibility is the claim of anthropological structuralism.

Let us look more closely at the structuralist's description of myth. The form of myth is always twofold: Its surface structure reflects local traditions and may be esoteric, but its deep structure is logical and can be formulated in mathematical terms. Myths dealing with the incest taboo, for example, should project in their totality a theory of kinship that makes it clear that the generative problem is how to distribute women fairly — how to pry them loose from father or clan and make them "go around." The incest taboo, therefore, is neither absolute nor eternal, but a humane and logical institution, part of a system of exchange as complex as the monetary system today.

Here, as in Frye, myth is both story and a principle of structure: a primitive narrative and a functional type of logic. Myth and mathematics join in a mysterious way more reminiscent of Plato than Aristotle. What is lacking in this description is precisely the middle-ground between myth and mathematics that art occupies. Where in this description are the qualities of story-telling that actually involve us — tone, rhythm, humor, surprises, and displacements? A sense of hidden structure or a delight in exotic surface is only a part of this involvement. Surely, even if literature proves to be a problem-solving form, it must be of a more liberal and chancy kind than Claude Lévi-Strauss suggests. And since, for Lévi-Strauss, form is totally explained by its social function, we cannot ask which myths are viable universals and which are empty or chauvinistic versions of what Blake called "the Human Abstract." The structuralist science of myth does not allow us to cross over from its theory of form to a descriptive or critical account of the artist's historical consciousness.

Our last theory, and in many ways the one most clearly focused on the literary work, is that of I. A. Richards and the New Criticism. Richards' concept of form is as functional as that of Lévi-Strauss, and it may have a common source with the latter in Malinowski.[9] What ritual, according to Malinowski, does for primitive societies, literary form, in Richards, does for the civilized (and perhaps overcivilized) individual; it reconciles tensions and helps to unify. Richards, however, does not specify what the basic tensions or "hang-ups" are. He is content with the commonsense observation that tensions always exist and that the deeper they are and the more complexly respectful of them the reconciling form, the better the work of art or the harmony of the person. We seem to have a very open theory of form that defines neither the contents reconciled nor the exact, perhaps organic, structure by which they are unified.

This theory is open, except for the very insistence on unity or reconciliation, which has become a great shibboleth developed by the New Critics on the basis of Eliot and Richards. Only Empson tried to escape it by postulating "types" of ambiguity which showed how precarious this unity was, or how rebellious language. It is important not to be deceived by the sophisticated vagueness of such terms as "unity," "complexity," "maturity," and "coherence," which enter criticism at this point. They are code words shored against the ruins. They express a highly neoclassical and acculturated attitude, a quiet nostalgia for the ordered life, and a secret recoil from aggressive ideologies, substitute religions, and dogmatic concepts of order. Out of the passionate intensity of the post-war period, out of the pressures of politics, press, and propaganda comes a thoughtful backlash that attempts to distinguish the suasion of literary statements from more imperative kinds. A poem, we learn, does not "mean," but "is"; art, we are told, is pseudo-statement or pseudo-action. Thus the literary work, though nominally democratic — inclusive of anything —is thought of as exclusive by its structure. Art turns out to be a mental purification of the impulses to action: an idea that has eastern resonances in I. A. Richards, but is associated in Cleanth Brooks with testing the simplifications by which we live.

Richards' concept of the functional unity of the work of art is far from narrow, of course. By modeling it on the psychology of communication, which includes reader or auditor in the aesthetic transaction, he opened a path to a theory of participatory form and helped to revive the academic interest in rhetoric still important today when new and sophisticated notions concerning the "entrapment" of reader by writer are emerging. He may also have influenced Kenneth Burke's refusal to equate rhetorical forms with aristocratic or privileged ideas of order and to examine anew both their psychological function and social-participatory (Burke continues to call it "ritual") aspect. Sigurd Burkhardt's emphasis on the "troth-value" of words is a further echo of these explorations.[10]

There is, nevertheless, the distinct afterglow of an elitist idea of culture in Richards' work. The function of art moves closer to that of ordinary language and normal psychological transactions, but it remains reminiscent of Plato's "dialectic." Art's therapeutic virtue is to Richards what the intellectual virtue of dialectic was to Socrates: Purging fixed ideas, it still leads upward to the one form of truth. The Socratic assumption, moreover, of a basic identity of questioner and questioned evades the issue of class or nationality — it assumes a society of equals whose upward mobility is intellectual in essence. Join Plato's dialectic to communications theory, and you get the idea of art as an elite communications medium. What you do not get is a concrete understanding of how this medium mediates: of how in history it actually reconciles or unifies different persuasions. For this we need quite another kind of dialectic, which Hegel and Marx tried to develop. We still have not found a theory linking the form of the medium to the form of the artist's historical consciousness.

TOWARD A THEORY OF LITERARY VOCATION

It is time I showed my hand and proposed such a theory. Let us construct it on the basis that literary form is functional and that its function is to keep us functioning, to help us resolve certain "hang-ups" and bring life into harmony with itself. But let us also agree that art can divide as well as heal and that its healing power may be complicated by its power to hurt. Wordsworth, in the "Preface to Lyrical Ballads," defines the poet as one who "considers man and the objects that surround him as acting and reacting upon each other, so as to produce an infinite complexity of pain and pleasure." Art cannot be expected to "bring us together again" by metaphysic, by an occult virtue of unification.

Since we are looking for a theory of *literary* as well as *functional* form, the essential ingredient is whatever makes the theory specifically relevant to literature. Otherwise we might quote Housman's "For Malt does more than Milton can/To justify the ways of God to Man," and leave it at that. But are there perhaps specifically *literary* hang-ups? And are we not forced by this question into the psychology of art on the one hand, but also into an analysis of literary history on the other?

Take the contemporary situation. Many artists today doubt art to the point of becoming incapable of it. The reason for their extreme self-questioning has already been suggested. The artist has a bad conscience because of the idea that forms, structures, and so on always reconcile or integrate, that they are conservative despite themselves. To create a truly iconoclastic art, a structure-breaking art, to change the function of form from reconciliation and conservation to rebellion, and so to participate in the enormity of present experience — this is the one Promethean aim still fiery enough to inspire. It is the psychic state of art today. But let us think, in addition, about other periods. Is the problem of the present era unique or a special case of a more inherent, perhaps universal dilemma besetting the writer's consciousness of himself? Were not Keats and Milton, those great formalists, also great iconoclasts, and did they not think about the historical vocation of art?

Pursuing this question we come on the probability that no great writer is without an identity crisis. The shape of that crisis can be generalized. Though we may not always discern what developmental impasse occurs within the poet's private life, we can describe the vocational crisis that occurs in the poet as poet, in his literary self-consciousness. No great artist is without the ambition to seize (and hand on) the flame of inspiration, to identify the genius of art with his own genius or that of a particular age (*genius loci*). But this is the crisis of self-consciousness in its purity: of emergence and commitment to being manifestly what one is. In the modern era with its problem of "legitimacy," the artist is especially aware of the need for self-justification.[11] The basic problem, however, is as old as history: How is spiritual authority to be transmitted if not through an elite of persons or communities? There seems to be no *recorded* greatness without the driving force of an idea of election or the search for evidences of election.

All societies have rituals for the passage out of latency and into the public light. They seek to guide it and to assure the individual a formal maturity. Van Gennep, who studied these ceremonies, called them *"rites de passage."* His findings have a complex but real bearing on the function of literature, whether in society or in the individual consciousness of artists. Take Shakespeare's Hamlet, a figure that has fascinated generations. It is widely agreed that an important function of art is to create character-types of universal or general appeal, and that Hamlet is the type of a man deprived of typical existence: of vocation or role or the possibility of commitment. The paradox, a simple one, is clarified by reference to Van Gennep: Hamlet is *"le seigneur latent qui ne peut devenir"* (Mallarmé) because he cannot assume his real (regal) self by innocent means — by the formal rite. Ceremony itself, in its legal and ludic aspects, in its justifying and mediating functions, is wounded. Deprived of kingship and shunning the outlaw role of avenger, Hamlet is doomed to remain a liminal person in an action (the play) that is an abortive rite of passage. He becomes the "juvenile shadow of us all" in his psychic struggle with *"le mal d'apparaître."* [12]

Yet every artist is like Hamlet. The artist must always find his own way to "appear"; he has no ritual to guide him. The presumption of his act, the daring of his art is all. The conventions at his disposal do not lessen the agony of self-election: If he admires the ancients, he trembles to rival them; if he does not admire, he trembles before a void he must fill. No wonder art continually questions the hopes for art; no wonder also that it endures irony and negativity to the point of substantiating Yeats's comment, so appropriate to Mallarmé: "The last kiss is given to the void."

The plea for literary history merges here with that for phenomenology or consciousness studied in its effort to "appear." Consciousness can try to objectify itself, to disappear into its appearances, or to make itself *as* consciousness the vocation. Social anthropology is involved because rites of acculturation and the structure of public life provide many of the collective forms that could allow self-objectification. Indeed, the very multiplicity of terms used to characterize the dynamics of phenomenology (appearance, manifestation, individuation, emergence, being-in-the-world, and so forth) imply a concern that incorporates the human sciences, or all sciences to the extent that they are humane. This concern centers on the problem of "civilization" and encompasses both nature and nurture, "those frontiers of biology and sociology from which mankind derives its hidden strength." [13] We have only to look at the crisis point in Keats's *Hyperion* to see this struggle for "appearance" accompanied by all the suggestiveness that hidden frontiers bestow.

In the third book of *Hyperion,* Apollo, the young sun-god, attempts to rise — to emerge into himself helped by the memory-goddess, Mnemosyne.

The sun never rises, however; *Hyperion* begins and ends in twilight. While attempting to dawn, Apollo suffers pangs like those accompanying childbirth or sexual climax or the biomorphic passage from one state of being to another. His "fierce convulse" is comparable to that of the snake Lamia in her transformation to womanhood (*Lamia,* Part I, 145 ff.). We expect Apollo to become the sun: "from all his limbs/Celestial" a new dawn will break. But the poem breaks off, as if Apollo's metamorphosis had tied itself into a knot and entered a developmental impasse. Though the impasse cannot be reduced to ego psychology — it is clearly related to the Enlightenment assumption of a "progress" of religion and literature — Apollo, in bringing his identity to light, is also bringing his father to light. In the psychotheology of art, as Keats depicts it here, the ephebe god, under the influence of "knowledge enormous," is about to replace the sun-god Hyperion. To bring his identity to light means to bear a father-god *out of himself.* The poem stops on that uncanny yet familiar truth.

To stress the "phenomenological" dimension is not to transcend the "literary" aspect. Apollo is the god of art by traditional equation. The knowledge that floods him,

> Names, deeds, gray legends, dire events, rebellions,
> Majesties, sovran voices, agonies.
> Creations and destroyings . . .

is "epic" knowledge, mediated by literature or by Mnemosyne as mother of the Muses. It signals the change from a lower to a higher mode of consciousness, from pastoral romance to that kind of heroic verse which *Hyperion* seeks to be. Yet Keats does not succeed in passing from pastoral to epic any more than Apollo does from ephebe state to Phoebus. What he writes is *hot pastoral* rather than epic. The very rituals that wing him into a new sphere prove too literary, too magical-archaic, and do not prevent fresh anxieties about the authenticity of his "passage." The marble steps the dreamer barely ascends in *The Fall of Hyperion* or Moneta's face "deathward progressing / To no death" are images raised up by his anxiety. Literature is breaking with an archaic mode that has been its glory and remains influential; yet the very idea of ritual transition is part of this archaism and makes the poet aware of his lateness or inauthenticity. His art, a new star, finds itself in the arms of the old by a fatal if fine repetition.

The impasse, then, is that Keats believes in poetry, in its "progressive" character, yet cannot see an authentic catena between old and new. In a sense *he* is the catena and his art the "passage." The past masters haunt him: Their glory is his guilt. The burden of *traditio* [14] leads to a preoccupation with *transitio,* and transition has two very different aspects in

Keats. It may infer a real passing-over, a transcendence of past stages enabled by the "grand march of intellect" — Keats's phrase for the Enlightenment. Wordsworth, he speculates, thinks more deeply into the human heart than Milton, whether or not he is a greater poet. Transition can also, however, infer the obverse of transcendence: transience, or abiding the *consciousness* of change by "negative capability." That is the real test of the fallen gods in *Hyperion,* by which they become human. All rites lead only to further "dark passages" and not beyond. "We are in a Mist — *We* are now in that state." If the first aspect of the idea of transition requires a philosophy of history, the second elicits the watchword, "The creative must create itself." "The Genius of poetry," Keats also says, "must work its own salvation in a man."

We are close to the era that makes transition a historiographical concept, as in "The Age of Transition." But this concept is a compromise and belies the rich gloom of Keats's verse. While he fails to place us where we can see the historical vocation of poetry, he does somehow transmit deeply, feelingly, an existential or temporal consciousness. This is not only by the sensuous or empathic highpoints of his art. His famed sensuousness exists as one pole in this temporal rhythm, the other being the mind's irritable, positivistic "reaching after fact and reason." A sharp revolution of tempi or moods, the alternation of an overwrought questing with "silence and slow time," is what catches us. In the odes, which traditionally permit bold transitions, this is less remarkable than in the *Hyperion.* Moments before Mnemosyne brings Apollo to the flood-stage of recollection, he is steeped in forgetful, even indolent sensation. ("Beside the osiers of a rivulet / Full ankle-deep in lilies of the vale. . . .") This direct, precipitous transition from puberty to epiphany, from pastoral to apocalypse — which aborts historical vision proper — puts all progress by "stages" in doubt.

What remains is almost purely existential: a birth which is a forgetting, and a dying into recollection. But the poetry also remains and the question of its relation to this "existential metaphysics." There is a metaphysical element, because Apollo "dies" into an ante-life by a kind of platonic anamnesis. On examination, however, this ante-life proves to be Wordsworth, Milton, Spenser, the Bible, Plato . . . the *paradise of poets.*[15] Keats is not less a humanist for being visionary; what pre-exists is not metaphysical or transcendent of life, but souls that are *logoi,* "sovran voices" mediated by each great poet. So Milton "descends" into Keats: Apollo's birth is predicated on an overcoming of the father-gods just as in *Paradise Lost* (itself "descended" from Biblical tradition) Adam's birth presupposes the fall of the angels. The fledgling god's dying into the life of recollection is, similarly, comparable to Adam's falling into knowledge or the ambiguous career of the soul in Wordsworth's "Intimations Ode," its humanizing passage from a birth that is "a sleep and a forgetting" to the compensating radiance of the philosophic mind. Keats's invention trails clouds of glory. It is itself a recollection, or anamnesis, which either justifies or devours the literary identity of its poet.

GENIUS, GENIUS, AND GENIUS LOCI

On the surface there is some naivete in claiming that literary history should be written from the point of view of the poets or of poetry. It is like saying naval history should be written from the point of view of sailors or ships. Hence it becomes important to stress the relatedness of the literary and the phenomenological points of view, as is implied by the previous section. The artist's struggle with his vocation — with past masters and the "pastness" of art in modern society — seems to be a version of a universal human struggle: of genius with Genius, and of genius with the *genius loci* (spirit of place).

It is always hard to defend the analytic categories one chooses. I have found the above terms useful and flexible. They have some kinship, obviously, with race, milieu, and moment, but they are free of special sociological meaning and may be as old as Western religion. A study of their history and prevalence must still be made,[16] but I would guess that the *genius loci* concept, at least, becomes visible with the nationalization of culture in Roman times and the revival of literary nationalism in the modern period. It also appears, from very preliminary observations, that whatever credence was given to the *genius loci* as a myth, it was an important principle of structure or an informing idea in literature and art from the sixteenth through the nineteenth centuries. One reason for its importance (to which I will return) is that it helped to mediate the conflict between the universal and nationalistic aspirations of art.[17]

In general, the artist's struggle with past masters corresponds to the struggle of genius with Genius, and his anxiety about the outmodedness of art to his anxiety about the genius of his country or time. To begin with the genius / Genius contest: This opposes, or conjoins, the personal "ingenium" in its unmediated, forgetful vigor, and the starry guide whose influence accompanies us from birth,[18] but is revealed mainly at crucial — "historical" or "self-conscious" — junctures. The contest is like that of Jacob with the Angel, which results in a name (or a new name), one that is generic as well as personal. In the Romantic period, Genius appears to genius as Memory: as an internalized guardian self or fateful shadow. This is as true of Hegel as it is of Wordsworth and Keats.[19] But in every period something pre-exists: original sin, or the world of the fathers, or Plato's Ideas or Husserl's *Ideen,* or the mythic forms of *illud tempus.* And in every period there is an *ingénu* to be tested by vision, to be lead out of the state of natural light by a Muse who opens an "everlasting scryne" where the "antique rolles" (rôles and scrolls) lie hidden.

To restrict literary or cultural history to the genius/Genius relation skirts two errors. One is that art is seen as a puberty rite or adolescent crisis, localized in personal time even if recurring periodically. The other is that art becomes the story of Humanity, in which Genius appears as a hero with a thousand faces (and therefore no face, like the ecumenical God), pursuing a gnostic odyssey. Much literary biography or existential criticism falls prey to the first, most myth-criticism to the second error. These errors, however, are fruitful and complementary. We must manage to embrace both; only singly do they lead to an impoverishment in our understanding of art. Apollo's crisis, for example, is clearly that of adolescence. He has left the "chamber of Maiden-Thought" and hovers darkling between ephebic state and godhead. He is at once too young and too old: The middle state is what is obscure, and to emerge from it as a decisive, individuated being, there may have to be something equivalent to infanticide or parricide. His metamorphosis can only be toward pure youth (and the mythic figure of the divine child) or pure eld (the divine *senex*) or theriomorphic (and the figure, for example, of the snake). But these are the very transformations studied by gnostic or myth-critical thought. The philosophers of individuation, from Plotinus through the modern school of Jung and Neumann, reveal how improbable it is for anyone to become truly individual, having wrestled with Genius and received the blessing and curse of identity.

Yet a poet is even more — because more *inobviously* — besieged than they describe. The dramatic encounter of genius with Genius is accompanied by the commonplace quarrel of genius with *genius loci*: of art with the natural religion or dominant myth of its age. To the burden of vision which rouses the poet's sense of his powers is added a combat with insidious habits of thought or perception. "Reasonings like vast Serpents / Infold around my limbs, bruising my minute articulations" (Blake). "A weight / Heavy as frost, and deep almost as life" (Wordsworth). The *genius loci* can rival Genius as an influence, for it suggests the possibility of a more "natural" (unselfconscious) participation in a pre-existent or larger self. England as Gloriana or America as Virgin Land is a visionary commonplace indistinguishable from an "idol of the tribe" or "collective representation." [20] Though bounded by period and place, the *genius loci* is as all-pervasive in its domain as a climate of opinion — which makes it harder to confront than a Mnemosyne. What arms does one take up against a *spirit*? Who will challenge a temperament, tilt with a weather? It is as absurd as the Beatles fighting the Blue Meanies: They try the solvent of music, but their true arms, one suspects, are counter-visionary, obliging the enemy to recrudesce by pop or parody art. One best engages the lurking, many-headed *topoi* or fixed ideas of a culture by sending against them their own image, enlarged and purified. "Bring me my chariot of fire." This is still a *topos,* but more than commonplace. We see the spirited form, not the nebulous. The imagery of the tribe is given bounding outline, the imaginative vigor of national prejudices acknowledged and faced.

Should there be conflict in an artist between *genius loci* and Genius, it takes the form of humanity versus nation or local integrities versus abstract conceptions or art itself versus party allegiance. In the case of Keats, there is evidence that *Hyperion* was meant to depict a geopolitical "progress of poetry" from Antiquity to modern England. The "beautiful mythology of Greece" was to have been revived or rivaled by "home-bred glory" — by the "Sister of the Island," as Keats calls the muse of his native land in *Endymion* IV. This is the context of the poet's famous, formalistic-sounding statement that "English ought to be kept up." A contradiction remained (as also in Blake) between the Genius of Poetry and the national genius. Keats thought Milton had shown the way to their reconciliation, and he began *Hyperion* in that belief, but he eventually put Chatterton's "English Idiom in English words" against Milton's "artful or rather artist's humour." There are always, it seems, two genii fighting for the soul of the artist: two stars or visions of destiny, or Genius and the *genius loci.*

Starry persons, of course, are an inveterate poetical superstition, and the astrology of genius revives explicitly in Yeats' *Vision,* but all literary judgment, insofar as it is historical, adjudicates the claims of Genius and *genius loci.* Here is Michelet on the greatness of Rabelais:

> Rabelais collected wisdom from the old, popular idioms, from sayings, proverbs, school farces in the mouth of fools and clowns. But mediated by follies of this kind the genius of the age and its prophetic power are revealed in their majesty. Where he does not reveal, he glimpses, he promises, he guides. In this forest of dreams, one can see under each leaf fruits which the future will harvest. The entire book is a golden bough.[21]

Compare this with Bronson Alcott, Thoreau's friend, praising *A Week on the Concord and Merrimack Rivers* as "purely American, fragrant with the lives of New England woods and streams, and which could have been written nowhere else," then because "the sod and sap and flavor of New England have found at last a clear relation to the literature of other and classic lands . . . Egypt, India, Greece, England." Alcott seems more interested than Michelet in harmonizing native and classical *genii loci,* but when he adds that "Especially am I touched by this soundness, this aboriginal vigour, as if a man had once more come into Nature," [22] he appeals beyond the *genius loci* to the genius of the artist in its unmediated relation to Nature.

The *genius loci* is especially significant for modern, that is, vernacular art, for it is then that the assertion of a national genius becomes vital, and a Dante, Ariosto, or Milton turn to the "adorning of their native Tongue." Native and national are not always identical, of course; and this, in the Renaissance, is part of the general problem of constructing a "national universal" from the genius of different localities. In Rabelais, Panurge at one point answers Pantagruel in seven languages, two of which are nonexistent; and Bakhtin has shown how this problematic abundance of linguistic "masks" fosters a peculiarly modern awareness of concrete historic space.[23] The literary self-consciousness of the modern era is intimately linked to a reflection on the fall of culture into nationality and its redemption into a new universality.

Finding a more "concrete" universal, one with truly national or native roots, proves to be, in the Renaissance, a highly liberative and creative endeavor. In Rabelais, Cervantes, and Shakespeare, those vernacular giants, popular culture joins the learned muses. The neoclassical or purist reaction merely showed how these giants traumatized later writers. Even before Shakespeare, Gabriel Harvey had doubts about Spenser — hardly a pop artist, yet to the genteel he seemed "hobgoblin run away with the garland from Apollo." With the signal exception of France, which identified culture once more with the purification of language and the achieving of a new latinity — an ideal that dominated Europe from about 1660 to 1760 — Apollo retrieved his garland by hobnobbing with hobgoblin. If literary creativity becomes problematic toward the end of the eighteenth century, it is not because of a sudden mysterious uncertainty about the vocation of the artist, but on the contrary, because that vocation, in the light of the failure of French universalism, is only too clear. An intensely programmatic consciousness arises that defines the vocation of literature as *Art seeking Pop* — art seeking its father-figure in folk culture. Genius merges confusingly with *genius loci* as *Volksboden* or autochthonous art. We see this most clearly among the German and English Romantics. In the 1770's Herder wrote an influential essay attributing his nation's literary poverty to the fact that, unlike England, it had produced no poets to revitalize the learned muse by bringing folklore into the mainstream of art. Where are *our* Chaucer, Spenser, and Shakespeare? he asks. Or, as Keats will say: "Let us have the old poets, and Robin Hood." [24]

There is, then, a model that haunts the consciousness of vernacular artists. The "vegetable gold" of great art is to bring Sancho Panza into relation with Don Quixote. Patrician and plebeian are to be fellow-travellers, part of the same human family. Genius, in expelling a false or discovering a true *genius loci,* discovers itself and enlarges us.

In our own day, this model is often dangerously simplified. Art, we are told, seeks to revitalize, and, if need be, rebarbarize man. There must be contact with devil or drug or forbidden areas. Thomas Mann's *Dr. Faustus* is the definitive expression — and critique — of that simplification. Yet, simplified or not, this model for creativity becomes an animating force, a psychic silhouette with which the artist strives to coincide. There is also a counter-model, inspired by the French tradition, in which art seeks to purify *"les mots de la tribu."* Both models, however, are functions of the rise of the national literatures. The nationalization of art is a cultural analogue of the Fall (perhaps a fortunate Fall) [25]; and true literary history, like true theology, can help to limit the curse and assure the promise. At least it makes us honor the paradoxes of an era in which the tenth Muse is Pop.

MILTON AS EXAMPLE: FORM AND THE HISTORICAL VOCATION OF ART

Milton's *Arcades* is a version of pastoral Empson left unexamined and which Godard might enjoy. It is hard to imagine a piece more elite in conception than this courtly interlude. A pastoral in little, it depicts the unmasking of shepherds as noble primitives. An opera in little, it is all opsis, like the tableaux vivants, the staged devices common from Elizabeth's time. A drama in little, its action is a single recognition, complete in the first stanza of the first song, and confirmed by the Genius of the Wood. As this sophisticated mixture of genres — pastoral, drama, and masque — it tends in its contracted yet leisurely form toward a fourth and undermining genre. Composed of but three songs and the "recitative" of the *genius loci,* the lyrical form of an ode clearly appears. If genres here, in their very multiplicity, their very formality, are the superstructure, the deep structure is nothing less than the spirit of song itself, questing like the "secret sluice" of Arethusa for a new country or local form, which turns out to be England — that is, the possibility of a truly native lyricism.

Arcades begins with the fulfilment of a quest:

> Look Nymph and Shepherds look
> What sudden blaze of majesty
> Is that which we from hence descry
> Too divine to be mistook
> This, this is she. . . .

The cry practically ends the action: "here our solemn search hath end." It is the formal sign of an epiphany or theophany, of a "present deity" being revealed. It is a show-cry, the equivalent of the Lo, Behold, O see. But who is this new god? A lady of seventy, the Countess Dowager of Derby. The whole thing seems to be an extravagant courtly compliment; and after the Genius of the Wood has confirmed the perception of these displaced magi as well as acknowledged their own "bright honour," the piece concludes by inviting us to attest that a new deity has been found, one who makes England a greater Arcady.

Is there in this spectacle more than meets the eye? Is the compliment all that extravagant, the form all that gratuitous? The setting is not only the estate of a noble Lady but the English countryside, and the masque was probably performed in the open air. Although Milton's literary code is classical and the allusions italianate, the plot, what there is of it, depicts a journey from a southern to a northern Arcadia and the discovery that England, despite its dank climate, has deities worth celebrating:

> Who had thought this clime had held
> A deity so unparallel'd?

In the last song of the masque, the Dowager Countess is directly identified with a transcendent nature-spirit, the *genius huius loci:*

> Here ye shall have greater grace
> To serve the Lady of this place.

These words invite the nature-spirits haunting more classical shores to emigrate and grace the English countryside. "A better soil shall give ye thanks." Thus Milton's *Arcades* is really a farewell to Arcades, a "we'll to [Italian] woods no more," or "we'll to Fresh woods, and Pastures new." It is a nativity hymn for English nature-poetry, in which nymphs, shepherds, and the *genius loci* make their formal submission.

Milton's simple sooth is never simple. The real discovery here is that of a pastoral within a pastoral. The old gods, the old forms — the elite superstructure — must serve a "rural Queen" identified with the *genius loci* of England. But is it not ridiculous to make of this septagenarian Dowager a new Gloriana? Is what we find here the authentic expression of a national idea of poetry or its misuse as a courtly compliment? Is not *Arcades* at most *dirigisme, Kulturlenkung,* rather than poetry grappling authentically with the spirit of English history and countryside?

It is a question I want to explore rather than answer. If the Countess of Derby is a personal patron, she is also, not without authority, a patroness of English poetry as a whole, being a distant relative of Edmund Spenser and appearing as Amaryllis in "Colin Clout Comes Home Again." Spenser's homecoming, of course, was bitter: Promises of "chere of court" were not fulfilled. He used the pastoral disguise of Colin Clout as a *topos* of modesty, but also took secret pride in his resumption of vernacular poetry. Milton's version of pastoral foresees Spenser's redemption and a true homecoming of the spirit of poetry to England. He associates the aristocracy with the poet's game: The unmasking of artificial shepherds as guardians of the realm (nobles) also unmasks the simple sooth of his poetry as not so simple, as having a tutelary function and lineage as old as theirs. Poetry's tutelary function appears even more clearly in *Comus,* Milton's second pastoral masque, which introduces young aristocrats both to society and the truth of fable.

Thus, by glorifying the lineage of the Countess, Milton at the same time glorifies the lineage of vernacular poetry. He honors Spenser, all the more so because Spenser had first taught English poets how to transfer the Virgilian genres to England and so to increase the honor of the line, revivified rather than interrupted by national ideals. There was schism in the Church, but there would be no schism in poetry. Spenser had more than imitated Virgil: He had *Englished* him by understanding how the idea of form merged with that of the historical vocation of art.

Artists may always have had a bad conscience, have always felt themselves Colin Clouts; but Virgil gave his feelings direct expression at the end of the *Georgics* where he accused himself of practicing an art of "ignoble leisure" (*ignobile otium*) compared to the victorious military exploits of Caesar Octavianus. Make war, not poetry. Later commentators saw Virgil's poetry as a conscious progression from pastoral to georgic to epic, a movement which is thought to express a mounting sense of vocation. We go from sheep and the man, to tools and the man, to arms and the man: from the silly arts and the competitive songs of rural life to the more cultic, war-like tasks of agriculture, and finally to those martial and political qualities that extend the empire of civilization. The Virgilian progress was a commonplace in the Renaissance: One may refer to the stanzas introductory to the *Faerie Queene* in which Spenser promises to exchange his "oaten reedes" for "trumpets sterne," or to Marvell's ode on Cromwell which begins,

> The forward Youth that would appeare
> Must now forsake his Muses dear
> Nor in the Shadowes sing
> His Numbers languishing.

Here Cromwell is a male debutant: To "appear" or to "come out" — the humanistic equivalent of epiphany — he must leave the pastoral sphere and exchange plow or harp for sword.

The debut of the Countess Dowager of Derby is somewhat belated (she is seventy years old, the span of human life according to the Bible), but then Milton himself is a belated poet, uncertain, despite the greatness of the poetical era just passing, whether there is true public recognition of the poet as a seeing mouth. Though *Arcades* still looks toward the epiph-

772 GEOFFREY H. HARTMAN

any of poetry, the courtly culture that could have recognized it is clearly at the term of its life. Seven years later, in *Lycidas,* Milton almost stages his own debut as a poet-prophet who sings independent of any class but his own, the class of all great poets. But he vacillates, returns to swainishness at the end, and does not "appear" in the Marvellian sense till after Cromwell and the Civil War, when he finally passes from pastoral to epic and to a more than national idea of poetry.

AN OBJECTION

Is not the theory presented here a throwback to nationalistic speculation? That is its danger, yet a lesser danger for us than to remain trapped in the rhetoric of an Esperanto history. Substantive thought about the racial or ideological components in a culture became especially suspect after the Nazis; the American ideal of assimilation then appeared the only pragmatic answer to ethnic stresses in a nation-state. Now that assimilation has proved to be not false, but certainly an imperfect reality, we are facing the agony of pluralism all over again: conflicts of allegiance, cultural transvestism, and a splintered national identity. Most criticism before the present era was a matter of defining the national genius rather than a particular work of art; and literary history established the native or foreign influences carried forward by an artist. Such determinations could be crassly nationalistic, but they acknowledged that the community was struggling for self-definition and that art played its role in that struggle. No one of course, wishes to return to the nineteenth century racial calculus, even when practiced by so sensible a critic as Matthew Arnold:

> Science has now made visible to everybody the great and pregnant elements of difference which lie in race, and in how signal a manner they make the genius and history of an Indo-European people vary from those of a Semitic people. Hellenism is of Indo-European growth, Hebraism is of Semitic growth; and we English, a nation of Indo-European stock, seem to belong naturally to the movement of Hellenism. But nothing more strongly marks the essential unity of man than the affinities we can perceive, in this point or that, between members of one family of peoples and members of another; and no affinity of this kind is more strongly marked than that likeness in the strength and prominence of the moral fibre, which, notwithstanding immense elements of difference, knits in some special sort the genius and history of us English, and of our American descendants across the Atlantic, to the genius and history of the Hebrew people. . . .[26]

It may be needful, however, to take back into consciousness what was too quickly subsumed. "An era comes," said a French contemporary of Arnold's, the philosopher and mathematician Cournot, "which will see the value of ethnic characteristics increase relatively, though decrease in an absolute sense; and Europe seems now [circa 1860] to be entering that era." The *relative* increase in the importance of ethnic distinctions he laid to the very advance of civilization which levels or blunts purely social or historical distinctions and so raises the more ancient or indelible ones. Cournot's anxiety for the organic nurture of cultural forms — an anxiety first arising in the Romantic age — springs from the same insight concerning the advance of civilization. He fears that the expansion and availability of historical forms will burden emerging talents to the point of endangering their growth:

> If it is true that everything living, everything which bears the cachet of native beauty must emerge from a seed . . . how can we conceive of the birth and nurture of a truly original art, a truly innovative style, in an era where all genres, all styles are understood historically, explained, liked, and imitated. . . . When one preserves so well all the dead no place is left for the living. . . . The new type will not be able to sustain the competition with existing types already at a high degree of maturity and evolution. Art will therefore arrive by the very progress of historical criticism at a syncretistic and erudite stage . . . incompatible with conditions favoring its organic development.[27]

A return to Herder and the Romantic historians — or simply to E. R. Curtius [28] — may be painful. We have tended to forget such "unhappy, far-off things" as the birth-struggle of cosmopolitanism, and the foundation of the idea of world literature in the cultural effects of persecution, which made the Muse an émigré many times over. Without "racist" events like the revocation of the Edict of Nantes, which "drove the national genius abroad," [29] we might never have had that cross-fertilization of talents that modernism takes for granted. In re-evaluating the prevalence of so many national, religious, or geopolitical ideals — superstitions we still live with despite the universalisms around us — the *genius loci* concept may help to prevent our collapsing national into nationalistic. It reminds us how flexible, if necessary, the idea of community is.

If art is the offspring of a precarious marriage between genius and *genius loci,* the place of which it is the genius is not necessarily a nation-state. Art can express a people (an emerging class or suppressed majority) or region (a Galilee whose genius becomes triumphant) or speech-community (as large as an Empire, as small as a professional body). Hence literary study often combats the premature universalism that urges the institution of a common tongue or perfect language. This ideal of a *charactéristique universelle* has haunted intellects from Leibnitz to Noam Chomsky. Turning skeptical and sensuous, it ends in the aggressive, ecumenical utopianism that makes the law go forth from the Zion of T-groups. But a pentecostal ideal of the plurality or mingling of tongues seems preferable to a one-dimensional, deracinated language. "Would to God that all the Lord's people were prophets," was Moses's reply to those who urged him to put down rival sayers. At the end of the eighteenth century, Rivarol claimed with elegant contempt that "Leibnitz was seeking a universal language, and we French were creating it all around him," [30] but by the middle of the nineteenth — the great period of philological discovery — even a rationalist could defend the secularity of language against ideals of *une langue bien faite:*

> C'est . . . le langage, dans sa nature abstraite ou dans sa forme générale, que l'on doit considérer comme essentiellement défectueux, tandis que les langues parlées, formées lentement sous l'influence durables de besoins infiniment variés, ont, chacune à sa manière et d'après son degré de souplesse, paré à cet inconvénient radical. Selon le génie et les destinées des races, sous l'influence si diverse des zones et des climats, elles se sont appropriées plus spécialement à l'expression de tel ordre d'images, de passions et d'idées. . . . Ce qui aggrandirait et perfectionnerait nos facultés intellectuelles, en multipliant et en variant les moyens d'expression et de transmission de la pensée, ce serait, s'il était possible, de disposer à notre gré, et selon le besoin du moment, de toutes les langues parlées, et non de trouver construite cette langue systématique qui, dans la plupart des cas, serait le plus imparfait des instruments.[31]

CONCLUSION

"I believe in Eternity. I can find Greece, Asia, Italy, Spain and the Islands — the genius and the creative principle of each and of all eras, in my own mind." This confession of a comparatist is Emerson's. Only a century old, it already seems dated in its optimism and deceptively easy in its transcendence of nationality. Yet some such faith has always governed the study of literature when humanistic in its aim. Some such faith makes each national book a Book of the Nations. Studied this way, literature might do what Seneca attributed only to philosophy. It could open "not some local shrine, but the vast temple of all the gods, the universe itself." [32]

The one literary historian, however, who came closest to Emerson's sense of Eternity or Seneca's of Universality was strangely pessimistic about it. Erich Auerbach's *Mimesis,* written in exile and published after World War II, foresaw the end of western history as we know it — of history as a rich, parti-colored succession of events, with personalities and writers dramatically divided by the pressure of class or conscience. Auerbach looked at this canvas of history, on which he saw consciousness strive with consciousness in the Hegelian manner, with something of Virgilian regret. Like Cournot, he surmised that we were moving toward a *nivellement* that would reduce the autochthonous element and gradually eliminate both local and national traditions; and for him this beginning to conformity augured the end of history. When one sees an airline ad with the motto "Introducing the Atlantic River" or hears André Malraux speak of technology creating an "Atlantic civilization," the forerunner of a world-wide humanistic culture, one is almost inclined to agree with Auerbach that historical time and space may be fading into the uniformity of landscapes seen from the air. But then one remembers the source of Auerbach's own strength as a historian of literature, how he traced the interaction of genius and *genius loci,* of Latin and the *lingua franca,* of the vernacular and the high style. Surely in that dubious cultural millenium, in that predicted mass-cult era, a Gloriana will appear once more to a Colin Clout, like another angel to another Caedmon, and say "Sing to me."

ERICH AUERBACH

Odysseus' Scar

Readers of the *Odyssey* will remember the well-prepared and touching scene in book 19, when Odysseus has at last come home, the scene in which the old housekeeper Euryclea, who had been his nurse, recognizes him by a scar on his thigh. The stranger has won Penelope's good will; at his request she tells the housekeeper to wash his feet, which, in all old stories, is the first duty of hospitality toward a tired traveler. Euryclea busies herself fetching water and mixing cold with hot, meanwhile speaking sadly of her absent master, who is probably of the same age as the guest, and who perhaps, like the guest, is even now wandering somewhere, a stranger; and she remarks how astonishingly like him the guest looks. Meanwhile Odysseus, remembering his scar, moves back out of the light; he knows that, despite his efforts to hide his identity, Euryclea will now recognize him, but he wants at least to keep Penelope in ignorance. No sooner has the old woman touched the scar than, in her

SOURCE: "Odysseus' Scar" is from *Mimesis: The Representation of Reality in Western Literature,* translated by Willard R. Trask (copyright 1953 by Princeton University Press; Princeton Paperback, 1968), pp. 3–23. Reprinted by permission of Princeton University Press.

joyous surprise, she lets Odysseus' foot drop into the basin; the water spills over, she is about to cry out her joy; Odysseus restrains her with whispered threats and endearments; she recovers herself and conceals her emotion. Penelope, whose attention Athena's foresight had diverted from the incident, has observed nothing.

All this is scrupulously externalized and narrated in leisurely fashion. The two women express their feelings in copious direct discourse. Feelings though they are, with only a slight admixture of the most general considerations upon human destiny, the syntactical connection between part and part is perfectly clear, no contour is blurred. There is also room and time for orderly, perfectly well-articulated, uniformly illuminated descriptions of implements, ministrations, and gestures; even in the dramatic moment of recognition, Homer does not omit to tell the reader that it is with his right hand that Odysseus takes the old woman by the throat to keep her from speaking, at the same time that he draws her closer to him with his left. Clearly outlined, brightly and uniformly illuminated, men and things stand out in a realm where everything is visible; and not less clear — wholly expressed, orderly even in their ardor — are the feelings and thoughts of the persons involved.

In my account of the incident I have so far passed over a whole series of verses which interrupt it in the middle. There are more than seventy of these verses — while to the incident itself some forty are devoted before the interruption and some forty after it. The interruption, which comes just at the point when the housekeeper recognizes the scar — that is, at the moment of crisis — describes the origin of the scar, a hunting accident which occurred in Odysseus' boyhood, at a boar hunt, during the time of his visit to his grandfather Autolycus. This first affords an opportunity to inform the reader about Autolycus, his house, the precise degree of the kinship, his character, and, no less exhaustively than touchingly, his behavior after the birth of his grandson; then follows the visit of Odysseus, now grown to be a youth; the exchange of greetings, the banquet with which he is welcomed, sleep and waking, the early start for the hunt, the tracking of the beast, the struggle, Odysseus' being wounded by the boar's tusk, his recovery, his return to Ithaca, his parents' anxious questions — all is narrated, again with such a complete externalization of all the elements of the story and of their interconnections as to leave nothing in obscurity. Not until then does the narrator return to Penelope's chamber, not until then, the digression having run its course, does Euryclea, who had recognized the scar before the digression began, let Odysseus' foot fall back into the basin.

The first thought of a modern reader — that this is a device to increase suspense — is, if not wholly wrong, at least not the essential explanation of this Homeric procedure. For the element of suspense is very slight in the Homeric poems; nothing in their entire style is calculated to keep the reader or hearer breathless. The digressions are not meant to keep the reader in suspense, but rather to relax the tension. And this frequently occurs, as in the passage before us. The broadly narrated, charming, and subtly fashioned story of the hunt, with all its elegance and self-sufficiency, its wealth of idyllic pictures, seeks to win the reader over wholly to itself as long as he is hearing it, to make him forget what had just taken place during the foot-washing. But an episode that will increase suspense by retarding the action must be so constructed that it will not fill the present entirely, will not put the crisis, whose resolution is being awaited, entirely out of the reader's mind, and thereby destroy the mood of suspense; the crisis and the suspense must continue, must remain vibrant in the background. But Homer — and to this we shall have to return later — knows no background. What he narrates is for the time being the only present, and fills both the stage and the reader's mind completely. So it is with the passage before us. When the young Euryclea (vv. 401 ff.) sets the infant Odysseus on his grandfather Autolycus' lap after the banquet, the aged Euryclea, who a few lines earlier had touched the wanderer's foot, has entirely vanished from the stage and from the reader's mind.

Goethe and Schiller, who, though not referring to this particular episode, exchanged letters in April 1797 on the subject of "the retarding element" in the Homeric poems in general, put it in direct opposition to the element of suspense — the latter word is not used, but is clearly implied when the "retarding" procedure is opposed, as something proper to epic, to tragic procedure (letters of April 19, 21, and 22). The "retarding element," the "going back and forth" by means of episodes, seems to me, too, in the Homeric poems, to be opposed to any tensional and suspensive striving toward a goal, and doubtless Schiller is right in regard to Homer when he says that what he gives us is "simply the quiet existence and operation of things in accordance with their natures"; Homer's goal is "already present in every point of his progress." But both Schiller and Goethe raise Homer's procedure to the level of a law for epic poetry in general, and Schiller's words quoted above are meant to be universally binding upon the epic poet, in contradistinction from the tragic. Yet in both modern and ancient times, there are important epic works which are composed throughout with no "retarding element" in this sense but, on the contrary, with suspense throughout, and which perpetually "rob us of our emotional freedom" — which power Schiller will grant only to the tragic poet. And besides it seems to me undemonstrable and improbable that this procedure of Homeric poetry was directed by aesthetic considerations or even by an aesthetic feeling of the sort postulated by Goethe and Schiller. The effect, to be sure, is precisely that which they describe, and is, furthermore, the actual source of the conception of epic which they themselves hold, and with them all writers decisively influenced by classical antiquity. But the true cause of the impression of "retardation" appears to me to lie elsewhere — namely, in the need of the Homeric style to leave nothing which it mentions half in darkness and unexternalized.

The excursus upon the origin of Odysseus' scar is not basically different from the many passages in which a newly introduced character, or even a newly appearing object or implement, though it be in the thick of a battle, is described as to its nature and origin; or in which, upon the appearance of a god, we are told where he last was, what he was doing there, and by what road he reached the scene; indeed, even the Homeric epithets seem to me in the final analysis to be traceable to the same need for an externalization of phenomena in terms perceptible to the senses. Here is the scar, which comes up in the course of the narrative; and Homer's feeling simply will not permit him to see it appear out of the darkness of an unilluminated past; it must be set in full light, and with it a portion of the hero's boyhood — just as, in the *Iliad,* when the first ship is already burning and the Myrmidons finally arm that they may hasten to help, there is still time not only for the wonderful simile of the wolf, not only for the order of the Myrmidon host, but also for a detailed account of the ancestry of several subordinate leaders (16, vv. 155 ff.). To be sure, the aesthetic effect thus produced was soon noticed and thereafter consciously sought; but the more original cause must have lain in the basic impulse of the Homeric style: to represent phenomena in a fully externalized form, visible and palpable in all their parts, and completely fixed in their spatial and temporal relations. Nor do psychological processes receive any other treatment: here too nothing must remain hidden and unexpressed. With the utmost fullness, with an orderliness which even passion does not disturb, Homer's personages vent their inmost hearts in speech; what they do not say to others, they speak in their own minds, so that the reader is informed of it. Much that is terrible takes place in the Homeric poems, but it seldom takes place wordlessly: Polyphemus talks to Odysseus; Odysseus talks to the suitors when he begins to kill them; Hector and Achilles talk at length, before battle and after; and no speech is so filled with anger or scorn that the particles which express logical and grammatical connections are lacking or out of place. This last observation is true, of course, not only of speeches but of the presentation in general. The separate elements of a phenomenon are most clearly placed in relation to one another; a large number of conjunctions, adverbs, particles, and other syntactical tools, all clearly circumscribed and delicately differentiated in meaning, delimit persons, things, and portions of incidents in respect to one another, and at the same time bring them together in a continuous and ever flexible connection; like the separate phenomena themselves, their relationships— their temporal, local, causal, final, consecutive, comparative, concessive, antithetical, and conditional limitations — are brought to light in perfect fullness; so that a continuous rhythmic procession of phenomena passes by, and never is there a form left fragmentary or half-illuminated, never a lacuna, never a gap, never a glimpse of unplumbed depths.

And this procession of phenomena takes place in the foreground — that is, in a local and temporal present which is absolute. One might think that the many interpolations, the frequent moving back and forth, would create a sort of perspective in time and place; but the Homeric style never gives any such impression. The way in which any impression of perspective is avoided can be clearly observed in the procedure for introducing episodes, a syntactical construction with which every reader of Homer is familiar; it is used in the passage we are considering, but can also be found in cases when the episodes are much shorter. To the word scar (v. 393) there is first attached a relative clause ("which once long ago a boar . . ."), which enlarges into a voluminous syntactical parenthesis; into this an independent sentence unexpectedly intrudes (v. 396: "A god himself gave him . . ."), which quietly disentangles itself from syntactical subordination, until, with verse 399, an equally free syntactical treatment of the new content begins a new present which continues unchallenged until, with verse 467 ("The old woman now touched it . . ."), the scene which had been broken off is resumed. To be sure, in the case of such long episodes as the one we are considering, a purely syntactical connection with the principal theme would hardly have been possible; but a connection with it through perspective would have been all the easier had the content been arranged with that end in view; if, that is, the entire story of the scar had been presented as a recollection which awakens in Odysseus' mind at this particular moment. It would have been perfectly easy to do; the story of the scar had only to be inserted two verses earlier, at the first mention of the word scar, where the motifs "Odysseus" and "recollection" were already at hand. But any such subjectivistic-perspectivistic procedure, creating a foreground and background, resulting in the present lying open to the depths of the past, is entirely foreign to the Homeric style; the Homeric style knows only a foreground, only a uniformly illuminated, uniformly objective present. And so the excursus does not begin until two lines later, when Euryclea has discovered the scar — the possibility for a perspectivistic connection no longer exists, and the story of the wound becomes an independent and exclusive present.

The genius of the Homeric style becomes even more apparent when it is compared with an equally ancient and equally epic style from a different world of forms. I shall attempt this comparison with the account of the sacrifice of Isaac, a homogeneous narrative produced by the so-called Elohist. The King James version translates the opening as follows (Genesis 22: 1): "And it came to pass after these things, that God did tempt Abraham, and said to him, Abraham! and he said, Behold, here I am." Even this opening startles us when we come to it from Homer. Where are the two speakers? We are not told. The reader, however, knows that they are not normally to be found together in one place on earth, that one of them, God, in order to speak to Abraham, must come from somewhere, must enter the earthly realm from some unknown heights or depths. Whence does he come, whence does he call to Abraham? We are not told. He does not come, like Zeus or Poseidon, from the Aethiopians, where he has been enjoying a sacrificial feast. Nor are we told anything of his reasons for tempting Abraham so terribly. He has not, like Zeus, discussed them in set speeches with other gods gathered in council; nor have the deliberations in his own heart been presented to us; unexpected and mysterious, he enters the scene from some unknown height or depth and calls: Abraham! It will at once be said that this is to be explained by the particular concept of God which the Jews held and which was wholly different from that of the Greeks. True enough — but this constitutes no objection. For how is the Jewish concept of God to be explained? Even their earlier God of the desert was not fixed in form and content, and was alone; his lack of form, his lack of local habitation, his singleness, was in the end not only maintained but developed even further in competition with the comparatively far more manifest gods of the surrounding Near Eastern world. The concept of God held by the Jews is less a cause than a symptom of their manner of comprehending and representing things.

This becomes still clearer if we now turn to the other person in the dialogue, to Abraham. Where is he? We do not know. He says, indeed: Here I am — but the Hebrew word means only something like "behold me," and in any case is not meant to indicate the actual place where Abraham is, but a moral position in respect to God, who has called to him — Here am I awaiting thy command. Where he is actually, whether in Beersheba or elsewhere, whether indoors or in the open air, is not stated; it does not interest the narrator, the reader is not informed; and what Abraham was doing when God called to him is left in the same obscurity. To realize the difference, consider Hermes' visit to Calypso, for example, where command, journey, arrival and reception of the visitor, situation and occupation of the person visited, are set forth in many verses; and even on occasions when gods appear suddenly and briefly, whether to help one of their favorites or to deceive or destroy some mortal whom they hate, their bodily forms, and usually the manner of their coming and going, are given in detail. Here, however, God appears without bodily form (yet he "appears"), coming from some unspecified place — we only hear his voice, and that utters nothing but a name, a name without an adjective, without a descriptive epithet for the person spoken to, such as is the rule in every Homeric address; and of Abraham too nothing is made perceptible except the words in which he answers God: *Hinne-ni,* Behold me here — with which, to be sure, a most touching gesture expressive of obedience and readiness is suggested, but it is left to the reader to visualize it. Moreover the two speakers are not on the same level: if we conceive of Abraham in the foreground, where it might be possible to picture him as prostrate or kneeling or bowing with outspread arms or gazing upward, God is not there too: Abraham's words and gestures are directed toward the depths of the picture or upward, but in any case the undetermined, dark place from which the voice comes to him is not in the foreground.

After this opening, God gives his command, and the story itself begins: everyone knows it; it unrolls with no episodes in a few independent sentences whose syntactical connection is of the most rudimentary sort. In this atmosphere it is unthinkable that an implement, a landscape through which the travelers passed, the serving-men, or the ass, should be described, that their origin or descent or material or appearance or usefulness should be set forth in terms of praise; they do not even admit an adjective: they are serving-men, ass, wood, and knife, and nothing else, without an epithet; they are there to serve the end which God has commanded; what in other respects they were, are, or will be, remains in darkness. A journey is made, because God has designated the place where the sacrifice is to be performed; but we are told nothing about the journey except that it took three days, and even that we are told in a mysterious way: Abraham and his followers rose "early in the morning" and "went unto" the place of which God had told him; on the third day he lifted up his eyes and saw the place from afar. That gesture is the only gesture, is indeed the only occurrence during the whole journey, of which we are told; and though its motivation lies in the fact that the place is elevated, its uniqueness still heightens the impression that the journey took place through a vacuum; it is as if, while he traveled on, Abraham had looked neither to the right nor to the left, had suppressed any sign of life in his followers and himself save only their footfalls.

Thus the journey is like a silent progress through the indeterminate and the contingent, a holding of the breath, a process which has no present, which is inserted, like a blank duration, between what has passed and what lies ahead, and which yet is measured: three days! Three such days positively demand the symbolic interpretation which they later received. They began "early in the morning." But at what time on the third day did Abraham lift up his eyes and see his goal? The text says nothing on the subject. Obviously not "late in the evening," for it seems that there was still time enough to climb the mountain and make the sacrifice. So "early in the morning" is given, not as an indication of time, but for the sake of its ethical significance; it is intended to express the resolution, the promptness, the punctual obedience of the sorely tried Abraham. Bitter to him is the early morning in which he saddles his ass, calls his serving-men and his son Isaac, and sets out; but he obeys, he walks on until the third day, then lifts up his eyes and sees the place. Whence he comes, we do not know, but the goal is clearly stated: Jeruel in the land of Moriah. What place this is meant to indicate is not clear — "Moriah" especially may be a later correction of some other word. But in any case the goal was given, and in any case it is a matter of some sacred spot which was to receive a particular consecration by being connected with Abraham's sacrifice. Just as little as "early in the morning" serves as a temporal indication does "Jeruel in the land of Moriah" serve as a geographical indication; and in both cases alike, the complementary indication is not given, for we know as little of the hour at which Abraham lifted up his eyes as we do of the place from which he set forth — Jeruel is significant not so much as the goal of an earthly journey, in its geographical relation to other places, as through its special election, through its relation to God, who designated it as the scene of the act, and therefore it must be named.

In the narrative itself, a th:rd chief character appears: Isaac. While God and Abraham, the serving-men, the ass, and the implements are simply named, without mention of any qualities or any other sort of definition, Isaac once receives an appositive; God says, "Take Isaac, thine only son, whom thou lovest." But this is not a characterization of Isaac as a person, apart from his relation to his father and apart from the story; he may be handsome or ugly, intelligent or stupid, tall or short, pleasant or unpleasant — we are not told. Only what we need to know about him as a personage in the action, here and now, is illuminated, so that it may become apparent how terrible Abraham's temptation is, and that God is fully aware of it. By this example of the contrary, we see the significance of the descriptive adjectives and digressions of the Homeric poems; with their indications of the earlier and as it were absolute existence of the persons described, they prevent the reader from concentrating exclusively on a present crisis; even when the most terrible things are occurring, they prevent the establishment of an overwhelming suspense. But here, in the story of Abraham's sacrifice, the overwhelming suspense is present; what Schiller makes the goal of the tragic poet — to rob us of our emotional freedom, to turn our intellectual and spiritual powers (Schiller says "our activity") in one direction, to concentrate them there — is effected in this Biblical narrative, which certainly deserves the epithet epic.

We find the same contrast if we compare the two uses of direct discourse. The personages speak in the Bible story too; but their speech does not serve, as does speech in Homer, to manifest, to externalize thoughts — on the contrary, it serves to indicate thoughts which remain unexpressed. God gives his command in direct discourse, but he leaves his motives and his purpose unexpressed; Abraham, receiving the command, says nothing and does what he has been told to do. The conversation between Abraham and Isaac on the way to the place of sacrifice is only an interruption of the heavy silence and makes it all the more burdensome. The two of them, Isaac carrying the wood and Abraham with fire and a knife, "went together." Hesitantly, Isaac ventures to ask about the ram, and Abraham gives the well-known answer. Then the text repeats: "So they went both of them together." Everything remains unexpressed.

It would be difficult, then, to imagine styles more contrasted than those of these two equally ancient and equally epic texts. On the one hand, externalized, uniformly illuminated phenomena, at a definite time and in a definite place, connected together without lacunae in a perpetual foreground; thoughts and feeling completely expressed; events taking place in leisurely fashion and with very little of suspense. On the other hand, the externalization of only so much of the phenomena as is necessary for the purpose of the narrative, all else left in obscurity; the decisive points of the narrative alone are emphasized, what lies between is nonexistent; time and place are undefined and call for interpretation; thoughts and feeling remain unexpressed, are only suggested by the silence and the fragmentary speeches; the whole, permeated with the most unrelieved suspense and directed toward a single goal (and to that extent far more of a unity), remains mysterious and "fraught with background."

I will discuss this term in some detail, lest it be misunderstood. I said above that the Homeric style was "of the foreground" because, despite much going back and forth, it yet causes what is momentarily being narrated to give the impression that it is the only present, pure and without perspective. A consideration of the Elohistic text teaches us that our term is capable of a broader and deeper application. It shows that even the separate personages can be represented as possessing "background"; God is always so represented in the Bible, for he is not comprehensible in his presence, as is Zeus; it is always only "something" of him that appears, he always extends into depths. But even the human beings in the Biblical stories have greater depths of time, fate, and consciousness than do the human beings in Homer; although they are nearly always caught up in an event engaging all their faculties, they are not so entirely immersed in its present that they do not remain continually conscious of what has happened to them earlier and elsewhere; their thoughts and feelings have more layers, are more entangled. Abraham's actions are explained not only by what is happening to him at the moment, nor yet only by his character (as Achilles' actions by his courage and his pride, and Odysseus' by his versality and foresightedness), but by his previous history; he remembers, he is constantly conscious of, what God has promised him and what God has already accomplished for him — his soul is torn between desperate rebellion and hopeful expectation; his silent obedience is multilayered, has background. Such a problematic psychological situation as this is impossible for any of the Homeric heroes, whose destiny is clearly defined and who wake every morning as if it were the first day of their lives: their emotions, though strong, are simple and find expression instantly.

How fraught with background, in comparison, are characters like Saul and David! How entangled and stratified are such human relations as those between David and Absalom, between David and Joab! Any such "background" quality of the psychological situation as that which the story of Absalom's death and its sequel (II Samuel 18 and 19, by the so-called Jahvist) rather suggests than expresses, is unthinkable in Homer. Here we are confronted not merely with the psychological processes of characters whose depth of background is veritably abysmal, but with a purely geographical background too. For David is absent from the battlefield; but the influence of his will and his feelings continues to operate, they affect even Joab in his rebellion and disregard for the consequences of his actions; in the magnificent scene with the two messengers, both the physical and psychological background is fully manifest, though the latter is never expressed. With this, compare, for example, how Achilles, who sends Patroclus first to scout and then into battle, loses almost all "presentness" so long as he is not physically present. But the most important thing is the "multilayeredness" of the individual character; this is hardly to be met with in Homer, or at most in the form of a conscious hesitation between two possible courses of action; otherwise, in Homer, the complexity of the psychological life is shown only in the succession and alternation of emotions; whereas the Jewish writers are able to express the simultaneous existence of various layers of consciousness and the conflict between them.

The Homeric poems, then, though their intellectual, linguistic, and above all syntactical culture appears to be so much more highly developed, are yet comparatively simple in their picture of human beings; and no less so in their relation to the real life which they describe in general. Delight in physical existence is everything to them, and their highest aim is to make that delight perceptible to us. Between battles and passions, adventures and perils, they show us hunts, banquets, palaces and shepherds' cots, athletic contests and washing days — in order that we may see the heroes in their ordinary life, and seeing them so, may take pleasure in their manner of enjoying their savory present, a present which sends strong roots down into social usages, landscape, and daily life. And thus they bewitch us and ingratiate themselves to us until we live with them in the reality of their lives; so long as we are reading or hearing the poems, it does not matter whether we know that all this is only legend, "make-believe." The oft-repeated reproach that Homer is a liar takes nothing from his effectiveness, he does not need to base his story on historical reality, his reality is powerful enough in itself; it ensnares us, weaving its web around us, and that suffices him. And this "real" world into which we are lured, exists for itself, contains nothing but itself; the Homeric poems conceal nothing, they contain no teaching and no secret second meaning. Homer can be analyzed, as we have essayed to do here, but he cannot be interpreted. Later allegorizing trends have tried their arts of interpretation upon him, but to no avail. He resists any such treatment; the interpretations are forced and foreign, they do not crystallize into a unified doctrine. The general considerations which occasionally occur (in our episode, for example, v. 360: that in misfortune men age quickly) reveal a calm acceptance of the basic facts of human existence, but with no compulsion to brood over them, still less any passionate impulse either to rebel against them or to embrace them in an ecstasy of submission.

It is all very different in the Biblical stories. Their aim is not to bewitch the senses, and if nevertheless they produce lively sensory effects, it is only because the moral, religious, and psychological phenomena which are their sole concern are made concrete in the sensible matter of life. But their religious intent involves an absolute claim to historical truth. The story of Abraham and Isaac is not better established than the story of Odysseus, Penelope, and Euryclea; both are legendary. But the Biblical narrator, the Elohist, had to believe in the objective truth of the story of Abraham's sacrifice — the existence of the sacred ordinances of life rested upon the truth of this and similar stories. He had to believe in it passionately; or else (as many rationalistic interpreters believed and perhaps still believe) he had to be a conscious liar — no harmless liar like Homer, who lied to give pleasure, but a political liar with a definite end in view, lying in the interest of a claim to absolute authority.

To me, the rationalistic interpretation seems psychologically absurd; but even if we take it into consideration, the relation of the Elohist to the truth of his story still remains a far more passionate and definite one than is Homer's relation. The Biblical narrator was obliged to write exactly what his belief in the truth of the tradition (or, from the rationalistic standpoint, his interest in the truth of it) demanded of him — in either case, his freedom in creative or representative imagination was severely limited; his activity was perforce reduced to composing an effective version of the pious tradition. What he produced, then, was not primarily oriented toward "realism" (if he succeeded in being realistic, it was merely a means, not an end); it was oriented toward truth. Woe to the man who did not believe it! One can perfectly well entertain historical doubts on the subject of the Trojan War or of Odysseus' wanderings, and still, when reading Homer, feel precisely the effects he sought to produce; but without believing in Abraham's sacrifice, it is impossible to put the narrative of it to the use for which it was written. Indeed, we must go even further. The Bible's claim to truth is not only far more urgent than Homer's, it is tyrannical — it excludes all other claims. The world of the Scripture stories is not satisfied with claiming to be a historically true reality — it insists that it is the only real world, is destined for autocracy. All other scenes, issues, and ordinances have no right to appear independently of it, and it is promised that all of them, the history of all mankind, will be given their due place within its frame, will be subordinated to it. The Scripture stories do not, like Homer's, court our favor, they do not flatter us that they may please us and enchant us — they seek to subject us, and if we refuse to be subjected we are rebels.

Let no one object that this goes too far, that not the stories, but the religious doctrine, raises the claim to absolute authority; because the stories are not, like Homer's, simply narrated "reality." Doctrine and promise are incarnate in them and inseparable from them; for that very reason they are fraught with "background" and mysterious, containing a second, concealed meaning. In the story of Isaac, it is not only God's intervention at the beginning and the end, but even the factual and psychological elements which come between, that are mysterious, merely touched upon, fraught with background; and therefore they require subtle investigation and interpretation, they demand them. Since so much in the story is dark and incomplete, and since the reader knows that God is a hidden God, his effort to interpret it constantly finds something new to feed upon. Doctrine and the search for enlightenment are inextricably connected with the physical side of the narrative — the latter being more than simple "reality"; indeed they are in constant danger of losing their own reality, as very soon happened when interpretation reached such proportions that the real vanished.

If the text of the Biblical narrative, then, is so greatly in need of interpretation on the basis of its own content, its claim to absolute authority forces it still further in the same direction. Far from seeking, like Homer, merely to make us forget our own reality for a few hours, it seeks to overcome our reality: we are to fit our own life into its world, feel ourselves to be elements in its structure of universal history. This becomes increasingly difficult the further our historical environment is removed from that of the Biblical books; and if these nevertheless maintain their claim to absolute authority, it is inevitable that they themselves be adapted through interpretative transformation. This was for a long time comparatively easy; as late as the European Middle Ages it was possible to represent Biblical events as ordinary phenomena of contemporary life, the methods of interpretation themselves forming the basis for such a treatment. But when, through too great a change in environment and through the awakening of a critical consciousness, this becomes impossible, the Biblical claim to absolute authority is jeopardized; the method of interpretation is scorned and rejected, the Biblical stories become ancient legends, and the doctrine they had contained, now dissevered from them, becomes a disembodied image.

As a result of this claim to absolute authority, the method of interpretation spread to traditions other than the Jewish. The Homeric poems present a definite complex of events whose boundaries in space and time are clearly delimited; before it, beside it, and after it, other complexes of events, which do not depend upon it, can be conceived without conflict and without difficulty. The Old Testament, on the other hand, presents universal history: it begins with the beginning of time, with the creation of the world, and will end with the Last Days, the fulfilling of the Covenant, with which the world will come to an end. Everything else that happens in the world can only be conceived as an element in this sequence; into it everything that is known about the world, or at least everything that touches upon the history of the Jews, must be fitted as an ingredient of the divine plan; and as this too became possible only by interpreting the new material as it poured in, the need for interpretation reaches out beyond the original Jewish-Israelitish realm of reality — for example to Assyrian, Babylonian, Persian, and Roman history; interpretation in a determined direction becomes a general method of comprehending reality; the new and strange world which now comes into view and which, in the form in which it presents itself, proves to be wholly unutilizable within the Jewish religious frame, must be so interpreted that it can find a place there. But this process nearly always also reacts upon the frame, which requires enlarging and modifying. The most striking piece of interpretation of this sort occurred in the first century of the Christian era, in consequence of Paul's mission to the Gentiles: Paul and the Church Fathers reinterpreted the entire Jewish tradition as a succession of figures prognosticating the appearance of Christ, and assigned the Roman Empire its proper place in the divine plan of salvation. Thus while, on the one hand, the reality of the Old Testament presents itself as complete truth with a claim to sole authority, on the other hand that very claim forces it to a constant interpretative change in its own content; for millennia it undergoes an incessant and active development with the life of man in Europe.

The claim of the Old Testament stories to represent universal history, their insistent relation — a relation constantly redefined by conflicts — to a single and hidden God, who yet shows himself and who guides universal history by promise and exaction, gives these stories an entirely different perspective from any the Homeric poems can possess. As a composition, the Old Testament is incomparably less unified than the Homeric poems, it is more obviously pieced together — but the various components all belong to one concept of universal history and its interpretation. If certain elements survived which did not immediately fit in, interpretation took care of them; and so the reader is at every moment aware of the universal religio-historical perspective which gives the individual stories their general meaning and purpose. The greater the separateness and horizontal disconnection of the stories and groups of stories in relation to one another, compared with the *Iliad* and the *Odyssey,* the stronger is their general vertical connection, which holds them all together and which is entirely lacking in Homer. Each of the great figures of the Old Testament, from Adam to the prophets, embodies a moment of this vertical connection. God chose and formed these men to the end of embodying his essence and will — yet choice and formation do not coincide, for the latter proceeds gradually, historically, during the earthly life of him upon whom the choice has fallen. How the process is accomplished, what terrible trials such a formation inflicts, can be seen from our story of Abraham's sacrifice. Herein lies the reason why the great figures of the Old Testament are so much more fully developed, so much more fraught with their own biographical past, so much more distinct as individuals, than are the Homeric heroes. Achilles and Odysseus are splendidly described in many well-ordered words, epithets cling to them, their emotions are constantly displayed in their words and deeds — but they have no development, and their life-histories are clearly set forth once and for all. So little are the Homeric heroes presented as developing or having developed, that most of them — Nestor, Agamemnon, Achilles — appear to be of an age fixed from the very first. Even Odysseus, in whose case the long lapse of time and the many events which occurred offer so much opportunity for biographical development, shows almost nothing of it. Odysseus on his return is exactly the same as he was when he left Ithaca two decades earlier. But what a road, what a fate, lie between the Jacob who cheated his father out of his blessing and the old man whose favorite son has been torn to pieces by a wild beast! — between David the harp player, persecuted by his lord's jealousy, and the old king, surrounded by violent intrigues, whom Abishag the Shunnamite warmed in his bed, and he knew her not! The old man, of whom we know how he has become what he is, is more of an individual than the young man; for it is only during the course of an eventful life that men are differentiated into full individuality; and it is this history of a personality which the Old Testament presents to us as the formation undergone by those whom God has chosen to be examples. Fraught with their development, sometimes even aged to the verge of dissolution, they show a distinct stamp of individuality entirely foreign to the Homeric heroes. Time can touch the latter only outwardly, and even that change is brought to our observation as little as possible; whereas the stern hand of God is ever upon the Old Testament figures; he has not only made them once and for all and chosen them, but he continues to work upon them, bends them and kneads them, and, without destroying them in essence, produces from them forms which their youth gave no grounds for anticipating. The objection that the biographical element of the Old Testament often springs from the combination of several legendary personages does not apply; for this combination is a part of the development of the text. And how much wider is the pendulum swing of their lives than that of the Homeric heroes! For they are bearers of the divine will, and yet they are fallible, subject to misfortune and humiliation — and in the midst of misfortune and in their humiliation their acts and words reveal the transcendent majesty of God. There is hardly one of them who does not, like Adam, undergo the deepest humiliation — and hardly one who is not deemed worthy of God's personal intervention and personal inspiration. Humiliation and elevation go far deeper and far higher than in Homer, and they belong basically together. The poor beggar Odysseus is only masquerading, but Adam is really cast down, Jacob really a refugee, Joseph really in the pit and then a slave to be bought and sold. But their greatness, rising out of humiliation, is almost superhuman and an image of God's greatness. The reader clearly feels how the extent of the pendulum's swing is connected with the intensity of the personal history — precisely the most extreme circumstances, in which we are immeasurably forsaken and in despair, or immeasurably joyous and exalted, give us, if we survive them, a personal stamp which is recognized as the product of a rich existence, a rich development. And very often, indeed generally, this element of development gives the Old Testament stories a historical character, even when the subject is purely legendary and traditional.

Homer remains within the legendary with all his material, whereas the material of the Old Testament comes closer and closer to history as the narrative proceeds; in the stories of David the historical report predominates. Here too, much that is legendary still remains, as for example the story of David and Goliath; but much — and the most essential — consists in things which the narrators knew from their own experience or from firsthand testimony. Now the difference between legend and history is in most cases easily perceived by a reasonably experienced reader. It is a difficult matter, requiring careful historical and philological training, to distinguish the true from the synthetic or the biased in a historical presentation; but it is easy to separate the historical from the legendary in general. Their structure is different. Even where the legendary does not immediately betray itself by elements of the miraculous, by the repetition of well-known standard motives, typical patterns and themes, through neglect of clear details of time and place, and the like, it is generally quickly recognizable by its composition. It runs far too smoothly. All cross-currents, all friction, all that is casual, secondary to the main events and themes, everything unresolved, truncated, and uncertain, which confuses the clear progress of the action and the simple orientation of the actors, has disappeared. The historical event which we witness, or learn from the testimony of those who witnessed it, runs much more variously, contra-dictorily, and confusedly; not until it has produced results in a definite domain are we able, with their help, to classify it to a certain extent; and how often the order to which we think we have attained becomes doubtful again, how often we ask ourselves if the data before us have not led us to a far too simple classification of the original events! Legend ar-ranges its material in a simple and straightforward way; it detaches it from its contemporary historical context, so that the latter will not con-fuse it; it knows only clearly outlined men who act from few and simple motives and the continuity of whose feelings and actions remains unin-terrupted. In the legends of martyrs, for example, a stiff-necked and fanatical persecutor stands over against an equally stiff-necked and fanati-cal victim; and a situation so complicated — that is to say, so real and historical — as that in which the "persecutor" Pliny finds himself in his celebrated letter to Trajan on the subject of the Christians, is unfit for legend. And that is still a comparatively simple case. Let the reader think of the history which we are ourselves witnessing; anyone who, for ex-ample, evaluates the behavior of individual men and groups of men at the time of the rise of National Socialism in Germany, or the behavior of individual peoples and states before and during the last war, will feel how difficult it is to represent historical themes in general, and how unfit they are for legend; the historical comprises a great number of contradictory motives in each individual, a hesitation and ambiguous groping on the part of groups; only seldom (as in the last war) does a more or less plain situation, comparatively simple to describe, arise, and even such a situa-tion is subject to division below the surface, is indeed almost constantly in danger of losing its simplicity; and the motives of all the interested parties are so complex that the slogans of propaganda can be composed only through the crudest simplification — with the result that friend and foe alike can often employ the same ones. To write history is so difficult that most historians are forced to make concessions to the technique of legend.

It is clear that a large part of the life of David as given in the Bible contains history and not legend. In Absalom's rebellion, for example, or in the scenes from David's last days, the contradictions and crossing of motives both in individuals and in the general action have become so concrete that it is impossible to doubt the historicity of the information conveyed. Now the men who composed the historical parts are often the same who edited the older legends too; their peculiar religious concept of man in history, which we have attempted to describe above, in no way led them to a legendary simplification of events; and so it is only natural that, in the legendary passages of the Old Testament, historical structure is frequently discernible — of course, not in the sense that the traditions are examined as to their credibility according to the methods of scientific criticism; but simply to the extent that the tendency to a smoothing down and harmonizing of events, to a simplification of motives, to a static definition of characters which avoids conflict, vacillation, and development, such as are natural to legendary structure, does not predominate in the Old Testament world of legend. Abraham, Jacob, or even Moses produces a more concrete, direct, and historical impression than the figures of the Homeric world — not because they are better described in terms of sense (the contrary is the case) but because the confused, contradictory multiplicity of events, the psychological and factual cross-purposes, which true history reveals, have not disappeared in the representation but still remain clearly perceptible. In the stories of David, the legendary, which only later scientific criticism makes recognizable as such, imperceptibly passes into the historical; and even in the legendary, the problem of the classification and interpretation of human history is already passionately apprehended — a problem which later shatters the framework of historical composition and completely overruns it with prophecy; thus the Old Testament, in so far as it is concerned with human events, ranges through all three domains: legend, historical reporting, and interpretative historical theology.

Connected with the matters just discussed is the fact that the Greek text seems more limited and more static in respect to the circle of personages involved in the action and to their political activity. In the recognition scene with which we began, there appears, aside from Odysseus and Penelope, the housekeeper Euryclea, a slave whom Odysseus' father Laertes had bought long before. She, like the swineherd Eumaeus, has spent her life in the service of Laertes' family; like Eumaeus, she is closely connected with their fate, she loves them and shares their interests and feelings. But she has no life of her own, no feelings of her own; she has only the life and feelings of her master. Eumaeus too, though he still remembers that he was born a freeman and indeed of a noble house (he was stolen as a boy), has, not only in fact but also in his own feeling, no longer a life of his own, he is entirely involved in the life of his

masters. Yet these two characters are the only ones whom Homer brings
to life who do not belong to the ruling class. Thus we become conscious of
the fact that in the Homeric poems life is enacted only among the ruling
class — others appear only in the role of servants to that class. The ruling
class is still so strongly patriarchal, and still itself so involved in the
daily activities of domestic life, that one is sometimes likely to forget their
rank. But they are unmistakably a sort of feudal aristocracy, whose men
divide their lives between war, hunting, marketplace councils, and feast-
ing, while the women supervise the maids in the house. As a social picture,
this world is completely stable; wars take place only between different groups of the ruling class; nothing ever pushes up from below. In the
early stories of the Old Testament the patriarchal condition is dominant
too, but since the people involved are individual nomadic or half-no-
madic tribal leaders, the social picture gives a much less stable impression; class distinctions are not felt. As soon as the people completely
emerges — that is, after the exodus from Egypt — its activity is always
discernible, it is often in ferment, it frequently intervenes in events not
only as a whole but also in separate groups and through the medium of
separate individuals who come forward; the origins of prophecy seem to
lie in the irrepressible politico-religious spontaneity of the people. We
receive the impression that the movements emerging from the depths of
the people of Israel-Judah must have been of a wholly different nature
from those even of the later ancient democracies — of a different nature
and far more elemental.

With the more profound historicity and the more profound social activity of the Old Testament text, there is connected yet another important
distinction from Homer: namely, that a different conception of the elevated style and of the sublime is to be found here. Homer, of course, is
not afraid to let the realism of daily life enter into the sublime and tragic;
our episode of the scar is an example, we see how the quietly depicted,
domestic scene of the foot-washing is incorporated into the pathetic and
sublime action of Odysseus' home-coming. From the rule of the separation
of styles which was later almost universally accepted and which specified
that the realistic depiction of daily life was incompatible with the sublime
and had a place only in comedy or, carefully stylized, in idyl — from any
such rule Homer is still far removed. And yet he is closer to it than is the
Old Testament. For the great and sublime events in the Homeric poems
take place far more exclusively and unmistakably among the members of
a ruling class; and these are far more untouched in their heroic elevation
than are the Old Testament figures, who can fall much lower in dignity
(consider, for example, Adam, Noah, David, Job); and finally, domestic
realism, the representation of daily life, remains in Homer in the peaceful realm of the idyllic, whereas, from the very first, in the Old Testament

stories, the sublime, tragic, and problematic take shape precisely in the domestic and commonplace: scenes such as those between Cain and Abel, between Noah and his sons, between Abraham, Sarah, and Hagar, between Rebekah, Jacob, and Esau, and so on, are inconceivable, in the Homeric style. The entirely different ways of developing conflicts are enough to account for this. In the Old Testament stories the peace of daily life in the house, in the fields, and among the flocks, is undermined by jealousy over election and the promise of a blessing, and complications arise which would be utterly incomprehensible to the Homeric heroes. The latter must have palpable and clearly expressible reasons for their conflicts and enmities, and these work themselves out in free battles; whereas, with the former, the perpetually smouldering jealousy and the connection between the domestic and the spiritual, between the paternal blessing and the divine blessing, lead to daily life being permeated with the stuff of conflict, often with poison. The sublime influence of God here reaches so deeply into the everyday that the two realms of the sublime and the everyday are not only actually unseparated but basically inseparable.

We have compared these two texts, and, with them, the two kinds of style they embody, in order to reach a starting point for an investigation into the literary representation of reality in European culture. The two styles, in their opposition, represent basic types: on the one hand fully externalized description, uniform illumination, uninterrupted connection, free expression, all events in the foreground, displaying unmistakable meanings, few elements of historical development and of psychological perspective; on the other hand, certain parts brought into high relief, others left obscure, abruptness, suggestive influence of the unexpressed, "background" quality, multiplicity of meanings and the need for interpretation, universal-historical claims, development of the concept of the historically becoming, and preoccupation with the problematic.

Homer's realism is, of course, not to be equated with classical-antique realism in general; for the separation of styles, which did not develop until later, permitted no such leisurely and externalized description of everyday happenings; in tragedy especially there was no room for it; furthermore, Greek culture very soon encountered the phenomena of historical becoming and of the "multilayeredness" of the human problem, and dealt with them in its fashion; in Roman realism, finally, new and native concepts are added. We shall go into these later changes in the antique representation of reality when the occasion arises; on the whole, despite them, the basic tendencies of the Homeric style, which we have attempted to work out, remained effective and determinant down into late antiquity.

Since we are using the two styles, the Homeric and the Old Testament, as starting points, we have taken them as finished products, as they appear in the texts; we have disregarded everything that pertains to their origins, and thus have left untouched the question whether their peculiarities were theirs from the beginning or are to be referred wholly or in part to foreign influences. Within the limits of our purpose, a consideration of this question is not necessary; for it is in their full development, which they reached in early times, that the two styles exercised their determining influence upon the representation of reality in European literature.

WALTER BENJAMIN

The Storyteller: Reflections on the Works of Nikolai Leskov

I

Familiar though his name may be to us, the storyteller in his living immediacy is by no means a present force. He has already become something remote from us and something that is getting even more distant. To present someone like Leskov as a storyteller does not mean bringing him closer to us but, rather, increasing our distance from him. Viewed from a certain distance, the great, simple outlines which define the storyteller stand out in him, or rather, they become visible in him, just as in a rock a human head or an animal's body may appear to an observer at the proper distance and angle of vision. This distance and this angle of vision are prescribed for us by an experience which we may have almost every day. It teaches us that the art of storytelling is coming to an end. Less and less frequently do we encounter people with the ability to tell a tale properly. More and more often there is embarrassment all around when the wish to hear a story is expressed. It is as if something that seemed inalienable to us, the securest among our possessions, were taken from us: the ability to exchange experiences.

SOURCE: "The Storyteller: Reflections on the Works of Nikolai Leskov" is from *Illuminations* by Walter Benjamin, edited by Hannah Arendt and translated by Harry Zohn, copyright © 1955 by Suhrkamp Verlag a. M.; English translation copyright © 1968 by Harcourt Brace Jovanovich, Inc., and reprinted with their permission and Jonathan Cape Ltd.

One reason for this phenomenon is obvious: experience has fallen in value. And it looks as if it is continuing to fall into bottomlessness. Every glance at a newspaper demonstrates that it has reached a new low, that our picture, not only of the external world but of the moral world as well, overnight has undergone changes which were never thought possible. With the [First] World War a process began to become apparent which has not halted since then. Was it not noticeable at the end of the war that men returned from the battlefield grown silent — not richer, but poorer in communicable experience? What ten years later was poured out in the flood of war books was anything but experience that goes from mouth to mouth. And there was nothing remarkable about that. For never has experience been contradicted more thoroughly than strategic experience by tactical warfare, economic experience by inflation, bodily experience by mechanical warfare, moral experience by those in power. A generation that had gone to school on a horse-drawn streetcar now stood under the open sky in a countryside in which nothing remained unchanged but the clouds, and beneath these clouds, in a field of force of destructive torrents and explosions, was the tiny, fragile human body.

II

Experience which is passed on from mouth to mouth is the source from which all storytellers have drawn. And among those who have written down the tales, it is the great ones whose written version differs least from the speech of the many nameless storytellers. Incidentally, among the last named there are two groups which, to be sure, overlap in many ways. And the figure of the storyteller gets its full corporeality only for the one who can picture them both. "When someone goes on a trip, he has something to tell about," goes the German saying, and people imagine the storyteller as someone who has come from afar. But they enjoy no less listening to the man who has stayed at home, making an honest living, and who knows the local tales and traditions. If one wants to picture these two groups through their archaic representatives, one is embodied in the resident tiller of the soil, and the other in the trading seaman. Indeed, each sphere of life has, as it were, produced its own tribe of storytellers. Each of these tribes preserves some of its characteristics centuries later. Thus, among nineteenth-century German storytellers, writers like Hebel and Gotthelf stem from the first tribe, writers like Sealsfield and Gerstäcker from the second. With these tribes, however, as stated above, it is only a matter of basic types. The actual extension of the realm of storytelling in its full historical breadth is inconceivable without the most intimate interpenetration of these two archaic types. Such an interpenetration was achieved particularly by the Middle Ages in their trade structure. The resident master craftsman and the traveling journeymen worked together in the same rooms; and every master had been a traveling journeyman before he settled down in his home town or somewhere else. If peasants and seamen were past masters of storytelling, the artisan class was its university. In it was combined the lore of faraway places, such as a much-traveled man brings home, with the lore of the past, as it best reveals itself to natives of a place.

III

Leskov was at home in distant places as well as distant times. He was a member of the Greek Orthodox Church, a man with genuine religious interests. But he was a no less sincere opponent of ecclesiastic bureaucracy. Since he was not able to get along any better with secular officialdom, the official positions he held were not of long duration. Of all his posts, the one he held for a long time as Russian representative of a big English firm was presumably the most useful one for his writing. For this firm he traveled through Russia, and these trips advanced his worldly wisdom as much as they did his knowledge of conditions in Russia. In this way he had an opportunity of becoming acquainted with the organization of the sects in the country. This left its mark on his works of fiction. In the Russian legends Leskov saw allies in his fight against Orthodox bureaucracy. There are a number of his legendary tales whose focus is a righteous man, seldom an ascetic, usually a simple, active man who becomes a saint apparently in the most natural way in the world. Mystical exaltation is not Leskov's forte. Even though he occasionally liked to indulge in the miraculous, even in piousness he prefers to stick with a sturdy nature. He sees the prototype in the man who finds his way about the world without getting too deeply involved with it.

He displayed a corresponding attitude in worldly matters. It is in keeping with this that he began to write late, at the age of twenty-nine. That was after his commercial travels. His first printed work was entitled "Why Are Books Expensive in Kiev?" A number of other writings about the working class, alcoholism, police doctors, and unemployed salesmen are precursors of his works of fiction.

IV

An orientation toward practical interests is characteristic of many born storytellers. More pronouncedly than in Leskov this trait can be recognized, for example, in Gotthelf, who gave his peasants agricultural advice; it is found in Nodier, who concerned himself with the perils of gas light; and Hebel, who slipped bits of scientific instruction for his readers into his *Schatzkästlein,* is in this line as well. All this points to the nature of every real story. It contains, openly or covertly, something useful. The usefulness may, in one case, consist in a moral; in another, in some practical advice; in a third, in a proverb or maxim. In every case the storyteller is a man who has counsel for his readers. But if today "having counsel" is beginning to have an old-fashioned ring, this is because the communicability of experience is decreasing. In consequence we have no counsel either for ourselves or for others. After all, counsel is less an answer to a question than a proposal concerning the continuation of a story which is just unfolding. To seek this counsel one would first have to be able to tell the story. (Quite apart from the fact that a man is receptive to counsel only to the extent that he allows his situation to speak.) Counsel woven into the fabric of real life is wisdom. The art of storytelling is reaching its end because the epic side of truth, wisdom, is dying out. This, however, is a process that has been going on for a long time. And nothing would be more fatuous than to want to see in it merely a "symptom of decay," let alone a "modern" symptom. It is, rather, only a concomitant symptom of the secular productive forces of history, a concomitant that has quite gradually removed narrative from the realm of living speech and at the same time is making it possible to see a new beauty in what is vanishing.

V

The earliest symptom of a process whose end is the decline of storytelling is the rise of the novel at the beginning of modern times. What distinguishes the novel from the story (and from the epic in the narrower sense) is its essential dependence on the book. The dissemination of the novel became possible only with the invention of printing. What can be handed on orally, the wealth of the epic, is of a different kind from what constitutes the stock in trade of the novel. What differentiates the novel from all other forms of prose literature — the fairy tale, the legend, even the novella — is that it neither comes from oral tradition nor goes into it. This distinguishes it from storytelling in particular. The storyteller takes what he tells from experience — his own or that reported by others. And he in turn makes it the experience of those who are listening to his tale. The novelist has isolated himself. The birthplace of the novel is the solitary individual, who is no longer able to express himself by giving examples of his most important concerns, is himself uncounseled, and cannot counsel others. To write a novel means to carry the incommensurable to extremes in the representation of human life. In the midst of life's fullness, and through the representation of this fullness, the novel gives evidence of the profound perplexity of the living.

Even the first great book of the genre, *Don Quixote,* teaches how the spiritual greatness, the boldness, the helpfulness of one of the noblest of men, Don Quixote, are completely devoid of counsel and do not contain the slightest scintilla of wisdom. If now and then, in the course of the centuries, efforts have been made — most effectively, perhaps, in *Wilhelm Meisters Wanderjahre* — to implant instruction in the novel, these attempts have always amounted to a modification of the novel form. The *Bildungsroman,* on the other hand, does not deviate in any way from the basic structure of the novel. By integrating the social process with the development of a person, it bestows the most frangible justification on the order determining it. The legitimacy it provides stands in direct opposition to reality. Particularly in the *Bildungsroman,* it is this inadequacy that is actualized.

VI

One must imagine the transformation of epic forms occurring in rhythms comparable to those of the change that has come over the earth's surface in the course of thousands of centuries. Hardly any other forms of human communication have taken shape more slowly, been lost more slowly. It took the novel, whose beginnings go back to antiquity, hundreds of years before it encountered in the evolving middle class those elements which were favorable to its flowering. With the appearance of these elements, storytelling began quite slowly to recede into the archaic; in many ways, it is true, it took hold of the new material, but it was not really determined by it. On the other hand, we recognize that with the full control of the middle class, which has the press as one of its most important instruments in fully developed capitalism, there emerges a form of communication which, no matter how far back its origin may lie, never before influenced the epic form in a decisive way. But now it does exert such an influence. And it turns out that it confronts storytelling as no less of a stranger than did the novel, but in a more menacing way, and that it also brings about a crisis in the novel. This new form of communication is information.

Villemessant, the founder of *Le Figaro,* characterized the nature of information in a famous formulation. "To my readers," he used to say, "an attic fire in the Latin Quarter is more important than a revolution in Madrid." This makes strikingly clear that it is no longer intelligence coming from afar, but the information which supplies a handle for what is nearest that gets the readiest hearing. The intelligence that came from afar — whether the spatial kind from foreign countries or the temporal kind of tradition — possessed an authority which gave it validity, even when it was not subject to verification. Information, however, lays claim to prompt verifiability. The prime requirement is that it appear "understandable in itself." Often it is no more exact than the intelligence of earlier centuries was. But while the latter was inclined to borrow from the miraculous, it is indispensable for information to sound plausible. Because of this it proves incompatible with the spirit of storytelling. If the art of storytelling has become rare, the dissemination of information has had a decisive share in this state of affairs.

Every morning brings us the news of the globe, and yet we are poor in noteworthy stories. This is because no event any longer comes to us without already being shot through with explanation. In other words, by now almost nothing that happens benefits storytelling; almost everything benefits information. Actually, it is half the art of storytelling to keep a story free from explanation as one reproduces it. Leskov is a master at this (compare pieces like "The Deception" and "The White Eagle"). The most extraordinary things, marvelous things, are related with the greatest accuracy, but the psychological connection of the events is not forced on the reader. It is left up to him to interpret things the way he understands them, and thus the narrative achieves an amplitude that information lacks.

VII

Leskov was grounded in the classics. The first storyteller of the Greeks was Herodotus. In the fourteenth chapter of the third book of his *Histories* there is a story from which much can be learned. It deals with Psammenitus.

When the Egyptian king Psammenitus had been beaten and captured by the Persian king Cambyses, Cambyses was bent on humbling his prisoner. He gave orders to place Psammenitus on the road along which the Persian triumphal procession was to pass. And he further arranged that the prisoner should see his daughter pass by as a maid going to the well with her pitcher. While all the Egyptians were lamenting and bewailing this spectacle, Psammenitus stood alone, mute and motionless, his eyes fixed on the ground; and when presently he saw his son, who was being taken along in the procession to be executed, he likewise remained unmoved. But when afterwards he recognized one of his servants, an old, impoverished man, in the ranks of the prisoners, he beat his fists against his head and gave all the signs of deepest mourning.

From this story it may be seen what the nature of true storytelling is. The value of information does not survive the moment in which it was new. It lives only at that moment; it has to surrender to it completely and explain itself to it without losing any time. A story is different. It does not expend itself. It preserves and concentrates its strength and is capable of releasing it even after a long time. Thus Montaigne referred to this Egyptian king and asked himself why he mourned only when he caught sight of his servant. Montaigne answers: "Since he was already overfull of grief, it took only the smallest increase for it to burst through it dams." Thus Montaigne. But one could also say: The king is not moved by the fate of those of royal blood, for it is his own fate. Or: We are moved by much on the stage that does not move us in real life; to the king, this servant is only an actor. Or: Great grief is pent up and breaks forth only with relaxation. Seeing this servant was the relaxation. Herodotus offers no explanations. His report is the driest. That is why this story from ancient Egypt is still capable after thousands of years of arousing astonishment and thoughtfulness. It resembles the seeds of grain which have lain for centuries in the chambers of the pyramids shut up air-tight and have retained their germinative power to this day.

VIII

There is nothing that commends a story to memory more effectively than that chaste compactness which precludes psychological analysis. And the more natural the process by which the storyteller forgoes psychological shading, the greater becomes the story's claim to a place in the memory of the listener, the more completely is it integrated into his own experience, the greater will be his inclination to repeat it to someone else someday, sooner or later. This process of assimilation, which takes place in depth, requires a state of relaxation which is becoming rarer and rarer. If sleep is the apogee of physical relaxation, boredom is the apogee of mental relaxation. Boredom is the dream bird that hatches the egg of experience. A rustling in the leaves drives him away. His nesting places — the activities that are intimately associated with boredom — are already extinct in the cities and are declining in the country as well. With this the gift for listening is lost and the community of listeners disappears. For storytelling is always the art of repeating stories, and this art is lost when the stories are no longer retained. It is lost because there is no more weaving and spinning to go on while they are being listened to. The more self-forgetful the listener is, the more deeply is what he listens to impressed upon his memory. When the rhythm of work has seized him, he listens to the tales in such a way that the gift of retelling them comes to him all by itself. This, then, is the nature of the web in which the gift of storytelling is cradled. This is how today it is becoming unraveled at all its ends after being woven thousands of years ago in the ambience of the oldest forms of craftsmanship.

IX

The storytelling that thrives for a long time in the milieu of work — the rural, the maritime, and the urban — is itself an artisan form of communication, as it were. It does not aim to convey the pure essence of the thing, like information or a report. It sinks the thing into the life of the storyteller, in order to bring it out of him again. Thus traces of the storyteller cling to the story the way the handprints of the potter cling to the clay vessel. Storytellers tend to begin their story with a presentation of the circumstances in which they themselves have learned what is to follow, unless they simply pass it off as their own experience. Leskov begins his "Deception" with the description of a train trip on which he supposedly heard from a fellow passenger the events which he then goes on to relate; or he thinks of Dostoevsky's funeral, where he sets his acquaintance with the heroine of his story "À Propos of the Kreutzer Sonata"; or he evokes a gathering of a reading circle in which we are told the events that he reproduces for us in his "Interesting Men." Thus his tracks are frequently evident in his narratives, if not as those of the one who experienced it, then as those of the one who reports it.

This craftsmanship, storytelling, was actually regarded as a craft by Leskov himself. "Writing," he says in one of his letters, "is to me no liberal art, but a craft." It cannot come as a surprise that he felt bonds with craftsmanship, but faced industrial technology as a stranger. Tolstoy, who must have understood this, occasionally touches this nerve of Leskov's storytelling talent when he calls him the first man "who pointed out the inadequacy of economic progress. . . . It is strange that Dostoevsky is so widely read. . . . But I simply cannot comprehend why Leskov is not read. He is a truthful writer." In his artful and high-spirited story "The Steel Flea," which is midway between legend and farce, Leskov glorifies native craftsmanship through the silversmiths of Tula. Their masterpiece, the steel flea, is seen by Peter the Great and convinces him that the Russians need not be ashamed before the English.

The intellectual picture of the atmosphere of craftsmanship from which the storyteller comes has perhaps never been sketched in such a significant way as by Paul Valéry. "He speaks of the perfect things in nature, flawless pearls, full-bodied, matured wines, truly developed creatures, and calls them 'the precious product of a long chain of causes similar to one another.' " The accumulation of such causes has its temporal limit only at perfection. "This patient process of Nature," Valéry continues, "was once imitated by men. Miniatures, ivory carvings, elaborated to the point of greatest perfection, stones that are perfect in polish and engraving, lacquer work or paintings in which a series of thin, transparent layers are placed one on top of the other — all these products of sustained, sacrificing effort are vanishing, and the time is past in which time did not matter. Modern man no longer works at what cannot be abbreviated."

In point of fact, he has succeeded in abbreviating even storytelling. We have witnessed the evolution of the "short story," which has removed itself from oral tradition and no longer permits that slow piling one on top of the other of thin, transparent layers which constitutes the most appropriate picture of the way in which the perfect narrative is revealed through the layers of a variety of retellings.

X

Valéry concludes his observations with this sentence: "It is almost as if the decline of the idea of eternity coincided with the increasing aversion to sustained effort." The idea of eternity has ever had its strongest source in death. If this idea declines, so we reason, the face of death must have changed. It turns out that this change is identical with the one that has diminished the communicability of experience to the same extent as the art of storytelling has declined.

It has been observable for a number of centuries how in the general consciousness the thought of death has declined in omnipresence and vividness. In its last stages this process is accelerated. And in the course of the nineteenth century bourgeois society has, by means of hygienic and social, private and public institutions, realized a secondary effect which may have been its subconscious main purpose: to make it possible for people to avoid the sight of the dying. Dying was once a public process in the life of the individual and a most exemplary one; think of the medieval pictures in which the deathbed has turned into a throne toward which the people press through the wide-open doors of the death house. In the course of modern times dying has been pushed further and further out of the perceptual world of the living. There used to be no house, hardly a room, in which someone had not once died. (The Middle Ages also felt spatially what makes that inscription on a sun dial of Ibiza, *Ultima multis* [the last day for many], significant as the temper of the times.) Today people live in rooms that have never been touched by death, dry dwellers of eternity, and when their end approaches they are stowed away in sanatoria or hospitals by their heirs. It is, however, characteristic that not only a man's knowledge or wisdom, but above all his real life — and this is the stuff that stories are made of — first assumes transmissible form at the moment of his death. Just as a sequence of images is set in motion inside a man as his life comes to an end — unfolding the views of himself under which he has encountered himself without being aware of it — suddenly in his expressions and looks the unforgettable emerges and imparts to everything that concerned him that authority which even the poorest wretch in dying possesses for the living around him. This authority is at the very source of the story.

XI

Death is the sanction of everything that the storyteller can tell. He has borrowed his authority from death. In other words, it is natural history to which his stories refer back. This is expressed in exemplary form in one of the most beautiful stories we have by the incomparable Johann Peter Hebel. It is found in the *Schatzkästlein des rheinischen Hausfreundes,* is entitled "Unexpected Reunion," and begins with the betrothal of a young lad who works in the mines of Falun. On the eve of his wedding he dies a miner's death at the bottom of his tunnel. His bride keeps faith with him after his death, and she lives long enough to become a wizened old woman; one day a body is brought up from the abandoned tunnel which, saturated with iron vitriol, has escaped decay, and she recognizes her betrothed. After this reunion she too is called away by death. When Hebel, in the course of this story, was confronted with the necessity of making this long period of years graphic, he did so in the following sentences: "In the meantime the city of Lisbon was destroyed by an earthquake, and the Seven Years' War came and went, and Emperor Francis I died, and the Jesuit Order was abolished, and Poland was partitioned, and Empress Maria Theresa died, and Struensee was executed. America became independent, and the united French and Spanish forces were unable to capture Gibraltar. The Turks locked up General Stein in the Veteraner Cave in Hungary, and Emperor Joseph died also. King Gustavus of Sweden conquered Russian Finland, and the French Revolution and the long war began, and Emperor Leopold II went to his grave too. Napoleon captured Prussia, and the English bombarded Copenhagen, and the peasants sowed and harvested. The millers ground, the smiths hammered, and the miners dug for veins of ore in their underground workshops. But when in 1809 the miners at Falun. . . ."

Never has a storyteller embedded his report deeper in natural history than Hebel manages to do in this chronology. Read it carefully. Death appears in it with the same regularity as the Reaper does in the processions that pass around the cathedral clock at noon.

XII

Any examination of a given epic form is concerned with the relationship of this form to historiography. In fact, one may go even further and raise the question whether historiography does not constitute the common ground of all forms of the epic. Then written history would be in the same relationship to the epic forms as white light is to the colors of the spectrum. However this may be, among all forms of the epic there is not one whose incidence in the pure, colorless light of written history is more certain than the chronicle. And in the broad spectrum of the chronicle the ways in which a story can be told are graduated like shadings of one and the same color. The chronicler is the history-teller. If we think back to the passage from Hebel, which has the tone of a chronicle throughout, it will take no effort to gauge the difference between the writer of history, the historian, and the teller of it, the chronicler. The historian is bound to explain in one way or another the happenings with which he deals; under no circumstances can he content himself with displaying them as models of the course of the world. But this is precisely what the chronicler does, especially in his classical representatives, the chroniclers of the Middle Ages, the precursors of the historians of today. By basing their historical tales on a divine plan of salvation — an inscrutable one — they have from the very start lifted the burden of demonstrable explanation from their own shoulders. Its place is taken by interpretation, which is not concerned with an accurate concatenation of definite events, but with the way these are embedded in the great inscrutable course of the world.

Whether this course is eschatologically determined or is a natural one makes no difference. In the storyteller the chronicler is preserved in changed form, secularized, as it were. Leskov is among those whose work displays this with particular clarity. Both the chronicler with his eschatological orientation and the storyteller with his profane outlook are so represented in his works that in a number of his stories it can hardly be decided whether the web in which they appear is the golden fabric of a religious view of the course of things, or the multicolored fabric of a wordly view.

Consider the story "The Alexandrite," which transports the reader into "that old time when the stones in the womb of the earth and the planets at celestial heights were still concerned with the fate of men, and not today when both in the heavens and beneath the earth everything has grown indifferent to the fates of the sons of men and no voice speaks to them from anywhere, let alone does their bidding. None of the undiscovered planets play any part in horoscopes any more, and there are a lot of new stones, all measured and weighed and examined for their specific weight and their density, but they no longer proclaim anything to us, nor do they bring us any benefit. Their time for speaking with men is past."

As is evident, it is hardly possible unambiguously to characterize the course of the world that is illustrated in this story of Leskov's. Is it determined eschatologically or naturalistically? The only certain thing is that in its very nature it is by definition outside all real historical categories. Leskov tells us that the epoch in which man could believe himself to be in harmony with nature has expired. Schiller called this epoch in the history of the world the period of naïve poetry. The storyteller keeps faith with it, and his eyes do not stray from that dial in front of which there moves the procession of creatures of which, depending on circumstances, Death is either the leader or the last wretched straggler.

XIII

It has seldom been realized that the listener's naïve relationship to the storyteller is controlled by his interest in retaining what he is told. The cardinal point for the unaffected listener is to assure himself of the possibility of reproducing the story. Memory is the epic faculty *par excellence*. Only by virtue of a comprehensive memory can epic writing absorb the course of events on the one hand and, with the passing of these, make its peace with the power of death on the other. It is not surprising that to a simple man of the people, such as Leskov once invented, the Czar, the head of the sphere in which his stories take place, has the most encyclopedic memory at his command. "Our Emperor," he says, "and his entire family have indeed a most astonishing memory."

Mnemosyne, the rememberer, was the Muse of the epic art among the Greeks. This name takes the observer back to a parting of the ways in world history. For if the record kept by memory — historiography — constitutes the creative matrix of the various epic forms (as great prose is the creative matrix of the various metrical forms), its oldest form, the epic, by virtue of being a kind of common denominator includes the story and the novel. When in the course of centuries the novel began to emerge from the womb of the epic, it turned out that in the novel the element of the epic mind that is derived from the Muse — that is, memory — manifests itself in a form quite different from the way it manifests itself in the story.

Memory creates the chain of tradition which passes a happening on from generation to generation. It is the Muse-derived element of the epic art in a broader sense and encompasses its varieties. In the first place among these is the one practiced by the storyteller. It starts the web which all stories together form in the end. One ties on to the next, as the great storytellers, particularly the Oriental ones, have always readily shown. In each of them there is a Scheherazade who thinks of a fresh story whenever her tale comes to a stop. This is epic remembrance and the Muse-inspired element of the narrative. But this should be set against another principle, also a Muse-derived element in a narrower sense, which as an element of the novel in its earliest form — that is, in the epic — lies concealed, still undifferentiated from the similarly derived element of the story. It can, at any rate, occasionally be divined in the epics, particularly at moments of solemnity in the Homeric epics, as in the invocations to the Muse at their beginning. What announces itself in these passages is the perpetuating remembrance of the novelist as contrasted with the short-lived reminiscences of the storyteller. The first is dedicated to *one* hero, *one* odyssey, *one* battle; the second, to *many* diffuse occurrences. It is, in other words, *remembrance* which, as the Muse-derived element of the novel, is added to reminiscence, the corresponding element of the story, the unity of their origin in memory having disappeared with the decline of the epic.

XIV

"No one," Pascal once said, "dies so poor that he does not leave something behind." Surely it is the same with memories too — although these do not always find an heir. The novelist takes charge of this bequest, and seldom without profound melancholy. For what Arnold Bennett says about a dead woman in one of his novels — that she had had almost nothing in the way of real life — is usually true of the sum total of the estate which the novelist administers. Regarding this aspect of the matter we owe the most important elucidation to Georg Lukács, who sees in the novel "the form of transcendental homelessness." According to Lukács, the novel is at the same time the only art form which includes time among its constitutive principles.

"Time," he says in his *Theory of the Novel*, "can become constitutive only when connection with the transcendental home has been lost. Only in the novel are meaning and life, and thus the essential and the temporal, separated; one can almost say that the whole inner action of a novel is nothing else but a struggle against the power of time. . . . And from this . . . arise the genuinely epic experiences of time: hope and memory. . . . Only in the novel . . . does there occur a creative memory which transfixes the object and transforms it. . . . The duality of inwardness and outside world can here be overcome for the subject 'only' when he sees the . . . unity of his entire life . . . out of the past lifestream which is compressed in memory. . . . The insight which grasps this unity . . . becomes the divinatory-intuitive grasping of the unattained and therefore inexpressible meaning of life."

The "meaning of life" is really the center about which the novel moves. But the quest for it is no more than the initial expression of perplexity with which its reader sees himself living this written life. Here "meaning of life" — there "moral of the story": with these slogans novel and story confront each other, and from them the totally different historical co-ordinates of these art forms may be discerned. If *Don Quixote* is the earliest perfect specimen of the novel, its latest exemplar is perhaps the *Éducation sentimentale*.

In the final words of the last-named novel, the meaning which the bourgeois age found in its behavior at the beginning of its decline has settled like sediment in the cup of life. Frédéric and Deslauriers, the boyhood friends, think back to their youthful friendship. This little incident then occurred: one day they showed up in the bordello of their home town, stealthily and timidly, doing nothing but presenting the *patronne* with a bouquet of flowers which they had picked in their own gardens. "This story was still discussed three years later. And now they told it to each other in detail, each supplementing the recollection of the other. 'That may have been,' said Frédéric when they had finished, 'the finest thing in our lives.' 'Yes, you may be right,' said Deslauriers, 'that was perhaps the finest thing in our lives.' "

With such an insight the novel reaches an end which is more proper to it, in a stricter sense, than to any story. Actually there is no story for which the question as to how it continued would not be legitimate. The novelist, on the other hand, cannot hope to take the smallest step beyond that limit at which he invites the reader to a divinatory realization of the meaning of life by writing "Finis."

XV

A man listening to a story is in the company of the storyteller; even a man reading one shares this companionship. The reader of a novel, however, is isolated, more so than any other reader. (For even the reader of a poem is ready to utter the words, for the benefit of the listener.) In this solitude of his, the reader of a novel seizes upon his material more jealously than anyone else. He is ready to make it completely his own, to devour it, as it were. Indeed, he destroys, he swallows up the material as the fire devours logs in the fireplace. The suspense which permeates the novel is very much like the draft which stimulates the flame in the fireplace and enlivens its play.

It is a dry material on which the burning interest of the reader feeds. "A man who dies at the age of thirty-five," said Moritz Heimann once, "is at every point of his life a man who dies at the age of thirty-five." Nothing is more dubious than this sentence — but for the sole reason that the tense is wrong. A man — so says the truth that was meant here — who died at thirty-five will appear to *remembrance* at every point in his life as a man who dies at the age of thirty-five. In other words, the statement that makes no sense for real life becomes indisputable for remembered life. The nature of the character in a novel cannot be presented any better than is done in this statement, which says that the "meaning" of his life is revealed only in his death. But the reader of a novel actually does look for human beings from whom he derives the "meaning of life." Therefore he must, no matter what, know in advance that he will share their experience of death: if need be their figurative death — the end of the novel — but preferably their actual one. How do the characters make him understand that death is already waiting for them — a very definite death and at a very definite place? That is the question which feeds the reader's consuming interest in the events of the novel.

The novel is significant, therefore, not because it presents someone else's fate to us, perhaps didactically, but because this stranger's fate by virtue of the flame which consumes it yields us the warmth which we never draw from our own fate. What draws the reader to the novel is the hope of warming his shivering life with a death he reads about.

XVI

"Leskov," writes Gorky, "is the writer most deeply rooted in the people, and is completely untouched by any foreign influences." A great storyteller will always be rooted in the people, primarily in a milieu of craftsmen. But just as this includes the rural, the maritime, and the urban elements in the many stages of their economic and technical development, there are many gradations in the concepts in which their store of experience comes down to us. (To say nothing of the by no means insignificant share which traders had in the art of storytelling; their task was less to increase its didactic content than to refine the tricks with which the attention of the listener was captured. They have left deep traces in the narrative cycle of *The Arabian Nights.*) In short, despite the primary role which storytelling plays in the household of humanity, the concepts through which the yield of the stories may be garnered are manifold. What may most readily be put in religious terms in Leskov seems almost automatically to fall into place in the pedagogical perspectives of the Enlightenment in Hebel, appears as hermetic tradition in Poe, finds a last refuge in Kipling in the life of British seamen and colonial soldiers. All great storytellers have in common the freedom with which they move up and down the rungs of their experience as on a ladder. A ladder extending downward to the interior of the earth and disappearing into the clouds is the image for a collective experience to which even the deepest shock of every individual experience, death, constitutes no impediment or barrier.

"And they lived happily ever after," says the fairy tale. The fairy tale, which to this day is the first tutor of children because it was once the first tutor of mankind, secretly lives on in the story. The first true storyteller is, and will continue to be, the teller of fairy tales. Whenever good counsel was at a premium, the fairy tale had it, and where the need was greatest, its aid was nearest. This need was the need created by the myth. The fairy tale tells us of the earliest arrangements that mankind made to shake off the nightmare which the myth had placed upon its chest. In the figure of the fool it shows us how mankind "acts dumb" toward the myth; in the figure of the youngest brother it shows us how one's chances increase as the mythical primitive times are left behind; in the figure of the man who sets out to learn what fear is, it shows us that the things we are afraid of can be seen through; in the figure of the wiseacre it shows us that the questions posed by the myth are simple-minded, like the riddle of the Sphinx; in the shape of the animals which come to the aid of the child in the fairy tale it shows that nature not only is subservient to the myth, but much prefers to be aligned with man. The wisest thing — so the fairy tale taught mankind in olden times, and teaches children to this day — is to meet the forces of the mythical world with cunning and with high spirits. (This is how the fairy tale polarizes *Mut,* courage, dividing it dialectically into *Untermut,* that is, cunning, and *Übermut,* high spirits.) The liberating magic which the fairy tale has at its disposal does not bring nature into play in a mythical way, but points to its complicity with liberated man. A mature man feels this complicity only occasionally, that is, when he is happy; but the child first meets it in fairy tales, and it makes him happy.

XVII

Few storytellers have displayed so profound a kinship with the spirit of the fairy tale as did Leskov. This involves tendencies that were promoted by the dogmas of the Greek Orthodox Church. As is well known, Origen's speculation about *apokatastasis* — the entry of all souls into Paradise — which was rejected by the Roman Church plays a significant part in these dogmas. Leskov was very much influenced by Origen and planned to translate his work *On First Principles.* In keeping with Russian folk belief he interpreted the Resurrection less as a transfiguration than as a disenchantment, in a sense akin to the fairy tale. Such an interpretation of Origen is at the bottom of "The Enchanted Pilgrim." In this, as in many other tales by Leskov, a hybrid between fairy tale and legend is involved, not unlike that hybrid which Ernst Bloch mentions in a connection in which he utilizes our distinction between myth and fairy tale in his fashion.

"A hybrid between fairy tale and legend," he says, "contains figuratively mythical elements, mythical elements whose effect is certainly captivating and static, and yet not outside man. In the legend there are Taoist figures, especially very old ones, which are 'mythical' in this sense. For instance, the couple Philemon and Baucis: magically escaped though in natural repose. And surely there is a similar relationship between fairy tale and legend in the Taoist climate of Gotthelf, which, to be sure, is on a much lower level. At certain points it divorces the legend from the locality of the spell, rescues the flame of life, the specifically human flame of life, calmly burning, within as without."

"Magically escaped" are the beings that lead the procession of Leskov's creations: the righteous ones. Pavlin, Figura, the toupée artiste, the bear keeper, the helpful sentry — all of them embodiments of wisdom, kindness, comfort the world, crowd about the storyteller. They are unmistakably suffused with the *imago* of his mother.

This is how Leskov describes her: "She was so thoroughly good that she was not capable of harming any man, nor even an animal. She ate neither meat nor fish, because she had such pity for living creatures. Sometimes my father used to reproach her with this. But she answered: 'I have raised the little animals myself, they are like my children to me. I can't eat my own children, can I?' She would not eat meat at a neighbor's house either. 'I have seen them alive,' she would say; 'they are my acquaintances. I can't eat my acquaintances, can I?' "

The righteous man is the advocate for created things and at the same time he is their highest embodiment. In Leskov he has a maternal touch which is occasionally intensified into the mythical (and thus, to be sure, endangers the purity of the fairy tale). Typical of this is the protagonist of his story "Kotin the Provider and Platonida." This figure, a peasant named Pisonski, is a hermaphrodite. For twelve years his mother raised him as a girl. His male and female organs mature simultaneously, and his bisexuality "becomes the symbol of God incarnate."

In Leskov's view, the pinnacle of creation has been attained with this, and at the same time he presumably sees it as a bridge established between this world and the other. For these earthily powerful, maternal male figures which again and again claim Leskov's skill as a storyteller have been removed from obedience to the sexual drive in the bloom of their strength. They do not, however, really embody an ascetic ideal; rather, the continence of these righteous men has so little privative character that it becomes the elemental counterpoise to uncontrolled lust which the storyteller has personified in *Lady Macbeth of Mzensk*. If the range between a Pavlin and this merchant's wife covers the breadth of the world of created beings, in the hierarchy of his characters Leskov has no less plumbed its depth.

XVIII

The hierarchy of the world of created things, which has its apex in the righteous man, reaches down into the abyss of the inanimate by many gradations. In this connection one particular has to be noted. This whole created world speaks not so much with the human voice as with what could be called "the voice of Nature" in the title of one of Leskov's most significant stories.

This story deals with the petty official Philip Philipovich who leaves no stone unturned to get the chance to have as his house guest a field marshal passing through his little town. He manages to do so. The guest, who is at first surprised at the clerk's urgent invitation, gradually comes to believe that he recognizes in him someone he must have met previously. But who is he? He cannot remember. The strange thing is that the host, for his part, is not willing to reveal his identity. Instead, he puts off the high personage from day to day, saying that the "voice of Nature" will not fail to speak distinctly to him one day. This goes on until finally the guest, shortly before continuing on his journey, must grant the host's public request to let the "voice of Nature" resound. Thereupon the host's wife withdraws. She "returned with a big, brightly polished, copper hunting horn which she gave to her husband. He took the horn, put it to his lips, and was at the same instant as though transformed. Hardly had he inflated his cheeks and produced a tone as powerful as the rolling of thunder when the field marshal cried: 'Stop, I've got it now, brother. This makes me recognize you at once! You are the bugler from the regiment of jaegers, and because you were so honest I sent you to keep an eye on a crooked supplies supervisor.' 'That's it, Your Excellency,' answered the host. 'I didn't want to remind you of this myself, but wanted to let the voice of Nature speak.' "

The way the profundity of this story is hidden beneath its silliness conveys an idea of Leskov's magnificent humor. This humor is confirmed in the same story in an even more cryptic way. We have heard that because of his honesty the official was assigned to watch a crooked supplies supervisor. This is what we are told at the end, in the recognition scene. At the very beginning of the story, however, we learn the following about the host: "All the inhabitants of the town were acquainted with the man, and they knew that he did not hold a high office, for he was neither a state official nor a military man, but a little supervisor at the tiny supply depot, where together with the rats he chewed on the state rusks and boot soles, and in the course of time had chewed himself together a nice little frame house." It is evident that this story reflects the traditional sympathy which storytellers have for rascals and crooks. All the literature of farce bears witness to it. Nor is it denied on the heights of art; of all Hebel's characters, the Brassenheim Miller, Tinder Frieder, and Red Dieter have been his most faithful companions. And yet for Hebel, too, the righteous man has the main role in the *theatrum mundi*. But because no one is actually up to this role, it keeps changing hands. Now it is the tramp, now the haggling Jewish peddler, now the man of limited intelligence who steps in to play this part. In every single case it is a guest performance, a moral improvisation. Hebel is a casuist. He will not for anything take a stand with any principle, but he does not reject it either, for any principle can at some time become the instrument of the righteous man. Compare this with Leskov's attitude. "I realize," he writes in his story "À Propos of the Kreutzer Sonata," "that my thinking is based much more on a practical view of life than on abstract philosophy or lofty morality; but I am nevertheless used to thinking the way I do." To be sure, the moral catastrophes that appear in Leskov's world are to the moral incidents in Hebel's world as the great, silent flowing of the Volga is to the babbling, rushing little millstream. Among Leskov's historical tales there are several in which passions are at work as destructively as the wrath of Achilles or the hatred of Hagen. It is astonishing how fearfully the world can darken for this author and with what majesty evil can raise its scepter. Leskov has evidently known moods — and this is probably one of the few characteristics he shares with Dostoevsky — in which he was close to antinomian ethics. The elemental natures in his *Tales from Olden Times* go to the limit in their ruthless passion. But it is precisely the mystics who have been inclined to see this limit as the point at which utter depravity turns into saintliness.

XIX

The lower Leskov descends on the scale of created things the more obviously does his way of viewing things approach the mystical. Actually, as will be shown, there is much evidence that in this, too, a characteristic is revealed which is inherent in the nature of the storyteller. To be sure, only a few have ventured into the depths of inanimate nature, and in modern narrative literature there is not much in which the voice of the anonymous storyteller, who was prior to all literature, resounds so clearly as it does in Leskov's story "The Alexandrite." It deals with a semiprecious stone, the chrysoberyl. The mineral is the lowest stratum of created things. For the storyteller, however, it is directly joined to the highest. To him it is granted to see in this chrysoberyl a natural prophecy of petrified, lifeless nature concerning the historical world in which he himself lives. This world is the world of Alexander II. The storyteller — or rather, the man to whom he attributes his own knowledge — is a gem engraver named Wenzel who has achieved the greatest conceivable skill in his art. One can juxtapose him with the silversmiths of Tula and say that — in the spirit of Leskov — the perfect artisan has access to the innermost chamber of the realm of created things. He is an incarnation of the devout. We are told of this gem cutter: "He suddenly squeezed my hand on which was the ring with the alexandrite, which is known to sparkle red in artificial light, and cried: 'Look, here it is, the prophetic Russian stone! O crafty Siberian. It was always green as hope and only toward evening was it suffused with blood. It was that way from the beginning of the world, but it concealed itself for a long time, lay hidden in the earth, and permitted itself to be found only on the day when Czar Alexander was declared of age, when a great sorcerer had come to Siberia to find the stone, a magician. . . .' 'What nonsense are you talking,' I interrupted him; 'this stone wasn't found by a magician at all, it was a scholar named Nordenskjöld!' 'A magician! I tell you, a magician!' screamed Wenzel in a loud voice. 'Just look; what a stone! A green morning is in it and a bloody evening. . . . This is fate, the fate of noble Czar Alexander!' With these words old Wenzel turned to the wall, propped his head on his elbows, and . . . began to sob."

One can hardly come any closer to the meaning of this significant story than by some words which Paul Valéry wrote in a very remote context. "Artistic observation," he says in reflections on a woman artist whose work consisted in the silk embroidery of figures, "can attain an almost mystical depth. The objects on which it falls lose their names. Light and shade form very particular systems, present very individual questions which depend upon no knowledge and are derived from no practice, but get their existence and value exclusively from a certain accord of the soul, the eye, and the hand of someone who was born to perceive them and evoke them in his own inner self."

With these words, soul, eye, and hand are brought into connection. Interacting with one another, they determine a practice. We are no longer familiar with this practice. The role of the hand in production has become more modest, and the place it filled in storytelling lies waste. (After all, storytelling, in its sensory aspect, is by no means a job for the voice alone. Rather, in genuine storytelling the hand plays a part which supports what is expressed in a hundred ways with its gestures trained by work.) That old co-ordination of the soul, the eye, and the hand which emerges in Valéry's words is that of the artisan which we encounter wherever the art of storytelling is at home. In fact, one can go on and ask oneself whether the relationship of the storyteller to his material, human life, is not in itself a craftsman's relationship, whether it is not his very task to fashion the raw material of experience, his own and that of others, in a solid, useful, and unique way. It is a kind of procedure which may perhaps most adequately be exemplified by the proverb if one thinks of it as an ideogram of a story. A proverb, one might say, is a ruin which stands on the site of an old story and in which a moral twines about a happening like ivy around a wall.

Seen in this way, the storyteller joins the ranks of the teachers and sages. He has counsel — not for a few situations, as the proverb does, but for many, like the sage. For it is granted to him to reach back to a whole lifetime (a life, incidentally, that comprises not only his own experience but no little of the experience of others; what the storyteller knows from hearsay is added to his own). His gift is the ability to relate his life; his distinction, to be able to tell his entire life. The storyteller: he is the man who could let the wick of his life be consumed completely by the gentle flame of his story. This is the basis of the incomparable aura about the storyteller, in Leskov as in Hauff, in Poe as in Stevenson. The storyteller is the figure in which the righteous man encounters himself.

V

Notes

Introduction

1. Alfred Appel, Jr., *The New York Times Book Review,* May 4, 1969, p. 1.
2. "Philosophy and the Form of Fiction," *Fiction and the Figures of Life* (New York, 1970), pp. 7, 9, 24.
3. Ibid., p. 4. T. S. Eliot said that poetry is "the game we play with reality," and W. H. Auden has expanded this notion to "poetry as a game of knowledge" in his essay "Squares and Oblongs" (in *Poets at Work,* ed. Charles D. Abbott [New York, 1948], pp. 171–81), but both of these statements use "game" in an ordinary, i.e., nontechnical, sense, whereas Gass's statement derives from the philosophical concept of "language games" of Ludwig Wittgenstein, *Philosophical Investigations* (London, 1953; 2d ed., 1958).
4. Davie here is close to the view that was basic to John Crowe Ransom's poetics: that poetry is different from other modes of knowledge or apprehension because it has no imperial design on the things of the world. In *The World's Body* (New York, 1938), for example, Ransom says, "a naturalist is a person who studies nature not because he loves it but because he wants to use it."
5. Conor Cruise O'Brien notes in "Passion and Cunning: An Essay on the Politics of W. B. Yeats," *In Excited Reverie,* ed. A. Norman Jeffares and K. G. W. Cross (New York, 1965), p. 209, that Yeats's statement, from "On Being Asked for a War Poem," is "particularly popular because it sets a neat and memorable dividing line between literature and politics," but O'Brien argues that Yeats was very much a political poet, and in this instance he "was exercising a political choice" by refusing to write a poem for a cause that did not move him.
6. For different views of the "romantic image" and "the artist in isolation" see *Romanticism Reconsidered: Selected Papers from the English Institute 1962,* ed. Northrop Frye (New York, 1963); Erich Heller, "The Artist's Journey into the Interior," *The Artist's Journey into the Interior and other Essays* (New York: Vintage Books, 1968), pp. 99–170; *Romanticism and Consciousness: Essays in Criticism,* ed. Harold Bloom (New York, 1970).
7. From a review by Kermode of Northrop Frye's *Anatomy of Criticism,* reprinted in *Puzzles and Epiphanies* (London, 1962), p. 72.

8. "R. P. Blackmur: The Later Phase," *The Widening Gyre* (New Brunswick, 1963), p. 230.

9. "Northrop Frye: Criticism as Myth," in *Northrop Frye in Modern Criticism: Selected Papers from the English Institute 1965*, ed. Murray Krieger (New York, 1966), p. 79.

10. "Epilogue," *Literary Criticism: A Short History*, by Wimsatt and Cleanth Brooks (New York, 1957), p. 753. Cf. the title essay in Wimsatt's *Hateful Contraries: Studies in Literature and Criticism* (Lexington, 1963).

11. "The Politics of Self-Parody," *The Performing Self: Compositions and Decompositions in the Languages of Contemporary Life* (New York, 1971), p. 36.

12. *The Sense of an Ending: Studies in the Theory of Fiction* (New York, 1967), p. 40.

13. See Richard Poirier's discussion of Borges in "The Politics of Self-Parody," and Gass's essay, "Imaginary Borges and his Books," *Fiction and the Figures of Life*, pp. 120–33.

14. In *Fables of Identity: Studies in Poetic Mythology* (New York, 1963), p. 41.

15. Actually, this is an old issue in Shakespearean criticism, especially in the controversy occasioned by A. C. Bradley's "character analysis" of *Hamlet*. For a summary of the arguments between Bradley and his successors, as well as a convenient bibliographical listing, see Morris Weitz, *Hamlet and the Philosophy of Literary Criticism* (Chicago, 1964).

16. "Philosophy and the Form of Fiction," p. 8. This passage refers explicitly to the figure of the statue in "The Concept of Character in Fiction."

17. *Essays on Thomas Mann*, trans. Stanley Mitchell (London, 1964), p. 16.

18. Lukács's activities have been clouded by controversy. He was accused even by certain left-wing critics of hewing to the Stalinist line in order to save his skin or position, but the charge needs careful discrimination if it is to be meaningful. To say that he was "no party hack" is not to exonerate him from moral culpability, or to recommend that judgment be suspended in order to make him more acceptable, but only to say what there is ample evidence to prove: that he was frequently at odds with the Communist party bureaucracy on many issues. Nothing shows this better, perhaps, than the fact that the ultra-Stalinist József Révai, once Lukács's pupil, delivered a famous diatribe against Lukács's "deviationism." Any moral judgment of Lukács's actions is pointless without informed discernment. For an excellent guide through the labyrinthine world of Lukács's politics and ideology, and from a point of view that is hardly sympathetic to the Communist party line, see George Lichtheim, *George Lukács*, in the series *Modern Masters*, ed. Frank Kermode (New York, 1970). See also Fredric Jameson, "The Case for George Lukács," *Marxism and Form: Twentieth-Century Dialectical Theories of Literature* (Princeton, 1971), pp. 160–205, for a discussion of Lukács in the context of "Hegelian Marxism" rather than local factional disputes.

For other views, both pro and con, see George Steiner, "Georg Lukács and his Devils's Pact," *The Kenyon Review*, XXII (Winter 1960), 1–18; Alfred Kazin, "Introduction," to Lukács's *Studies in European Realism* (New York, 1964); Susan Sontag, "The Literary Criticism of Georg Lukács," *Against Interpretation and Other Essays* (New York, 1965), pp. 82–92; Harold Rosenberg, "The Third Dimension of Georg Lukács," *Dissent*, XI (1964), 404–14; Alasdair MacIntyre, "Marxist Mask and Romantic Face," *Encounter*, XXIV (April 1965), 64–72; G. H. R. Parkinson, ed., *Georg Lukács: The Man, His Work, and His Ideas* (New York: Vintage Books, 1970).

Lukács's acuteness as a critic can be seen in the passage from his *Theory of the Novel* that Walter Benjamin quotes in "The Storyteller," p. 806. Cf. Paul De Man, "Georg Lukács's *Theory of the Novel*," *Modern Language Notes*, 81 (1966), 527–34.

Lukács is often referred to as the leading Marxist literary critic of the twentieth century, but the ideological orientation of his criticism has been assailed by the so-called Frankfurt School, the leading figure of which was T. W. Adorno. As René Wellek points out in "A Map of Contemporary Criticism in Europe," *Discrimina-*

tions: Further Concepts of Criticism (New Haven, 1970), p. 355, Adorno "sets himself off sharply from eastern Marxism, chiding Lukács for his old-fashioned realist and bourgeois taste, and emphasizes the difference between art and reality." The work of Adorno and the other members of the Frankfurt School is only recently beginning to be translated into English, but some of their views are reflected in Hans Magnus Enzensberger's essay. For an introduction to Adorno's theories, see Jameson, op. cit., pp. 3–60.

19. *George Lukács*, p. 118.

20. Ibid., p. 137.

21. "The Concrete Universal: Observations on the Understanding of Poetry," *Poems and Essays* (New York, Vintage Books, 1955), p. 160.

22. In *A Primer of Ignorance*, ed. Joseph Frank (New York, 1967), p. 78. It should be clear from the selections included here that Blackmur is hardly guilty of "the naïve indifference to theory" that Leo Bersani says is one fault of Anglo-American criticism (p. 102).

23. See Richard Poirier, "The Literature of Waste: Eliot, Joyce, and Others," *The Performing Self*, pp. 50 ff.

24. For a bibliography of some recent studies in literary history, besides the items cited by Hartman, see Hans Galinsky, "Literary Criticism in Literary History," *Comparative Literature Studies*, I (1964), 31–40. See also Phillip Damon, ed., *Literary Criticism and Historical Understanding: English Institute Essays 1966* (New York, 1967).

25. *Selected Essays 1917–1932* (New York, 1932), p. 4. The passage Frye cites from Eliot's "The Function of Criticism," which was published in 1923, is actually a quotation by Eliot from "Tradition and the Individual Talent."

At first glance Eliot's statement may seem directly opposite to Enzensberger's "dialectical proposition" that "the durability of works is always determined only by their immanence in today's creation, which simultaneously devours and rejuvenates them," but the difference may be more one of phrasing and accent than of principle, because Eliot makes it quite clear that a new work of art alters, however slightly, the whole existing order of art. See Jameson, *Marxism and Form*, p. 314.

26. See René Wellek, "Auerbach's Special Realism," *The Kenyon Review*, XVI (1954), 299–307. Cf. Wolfgang Bernard Fleischmann, "Erich Auerbach's Critical Theory and Practice: An Assessment," *Modern Language Notes*, 81 (1966), 535–41.

27. *Dante: Poet of the Secular World*, trans. Ralph Manheim (Chicago, 1961); "Figura," trans. Manheim, in *Scenes from the Drama of European Literature: Six Essays* (New York, Meridian Books, 1959), pp. 11–76.

E. H. GOMBRICH, *Meditations on a Hobby Horse or the Roots of Artistic Form*

1. In the sphere of art this process of differentiation rather than abstraction is wittily described by Oliver Wendell Holmes in the essay *"Cacoethes Scribendi,"* from *Over the Teacups* (London, 1890): "It's just the same thing as my plan . . . for teaching drawing. . . . A man at a certain distance appears as a dark spot — nothing more. Good. Anybody . . . can make a dot. . . . Lesson No. I. Make a dot; that is, draw your man, a mile off. . . . Now make him come a little nearer. . . . The dot is an oblong figure now. Good. Let your scholar draw an oblong figure. It is as easy as to make a note of admiration. . . . So by degrees the man who serves as a model approaches. A bright pupil will learn to get the outline of a human figure in ten lessons, the model coming five hundred feet nearer each time."

2. *Discourses on Art* (Everyman Edition, p. 55). I have discussed the historical setting of this idea in "Icones Symbolicae," *Journal of the Warburg and Courtauld Institutes*, XI (1948), p. 187, and some of its more technical aspects in a review

of Charles Morris, *Signs, Language, and Behavior* (New York, 1946) in *The Art Bulletin*, March 1949. In Morris's terminology these present meditations are concerned with the status and origin of the "iconic sign."

3. Leonardo da Vinci, *Paragone*, edited by I. A. Richter (London, 1949), p. 51.

4. Paul Klee, *On Modern Art* (London, 1948). For the history of the idea of *deus artifex* cf. E. Kris and O. Kurz, *Die Legende vom Künstler* (Vienna, 1934).

5. H. A. Groenewegen-Frankfort, *Arrest and Movement: An Essay on Space and Time in the Representational Art of the Ancient Near East* (London, 1951).

6. Perhaps it is only in a setting of realistic art that the problem I have discussed in "Icones Symbolicae," loc. cit., becomes urgent. Only then the idea can gain ground that the allegorical image of, say, Justice, must be a portrait of Justice as she dwells in heaven.

7. For the history of this misinterpretation and its consequences cf. my article on "Art and Imagery in the Romantic Period," in *Meditations on a Hobby Horse and Other Essays on the Theory of Art* (London, 1963).

8. This, at least, would be the opinion of Lewis Spence, *Myth and Ritual in Dance, Game, and Rhyme* (London, 1947). And also of Ben Jonson's Busy, the Puritan: "Thy Hobby-horse is an Idoll, a feirce and rancke Idoll: And thou, the *Nabuchadnezzar* . . . of the *Faire*, that set'st it up, for children to fall downe to, and worship." (*Bartholomew Fair*, Act III, Scene 6).

9. Cf. Géza Révész, *Ursprung und Vorgeschichte der Sprache* (Berne, 1946).

10. Cf. Konrad Lorenz, "Die angeborenen Formen möglicher Erfahrung," *Zeitschrift für Tierpsychologie* V (1943), and the discussion of these experiments in E. Grassi and Th. von Uexküll, *Vom Ursprung und von den Grenzen der Geisteswissenschaften und Naturwissenschaften* (Bern, 1950).

11. K. Lorenz, loc. cit. The citation of this article does not imply support of the author's moral conclusions. On these more general issues see K. R. Popper, *The Open Society and Its Enemies*, esp., I, pp. 59 ff. and p. 268.

12. F. Sander, "Experimentelle Ergebnisse der Gestaltpsychologie," *Berichte über den 10. Kongress für Experimentelle Psychologie* (Jena, 1928), p. 47, notes experiments that show the distance of two dots is much harder to estimate in its variations when these dots are isolated than when they are made to represent eyes in a schematic face and thus attain physiognomic significance.

13. For a large collection of such faces cf. Laurence Whistler, *Oho! The Drawings of Rex Whistler* (London, 1946).

14. G. H. Luquet, *The Art and Religion of Fossil Man* (London, 1930), pp. 141 ff.

15. G. A. S. Snijder, *Kretische Kunst* (Berlin, 1936), pp. 68 ff.

16. Franz Boas, *Primitive Art* (Oslo, 1927), pp. 118–28.

17. E.g., E. Löwy, *The Rendering of Nature in Early Greek Art* (London, 1907), H. Schaefer, *Von aegyptischer Kunst* (Leipzig, 1930), Mr. Verworn, *Ideoplastische Kunst* (Jena, 1914).

18. Karl Bühler, *The Mental Development of the Child* (London, 1930), pp. 113–17, where the connection with the linguistic faculty is stressed. A criticism of this idea was advanced by R. Arnheim, "Perceptual Abstraction and Art," *Psychological Review*, LVI, 1947.

19. G. H. Luquet, *L'Art primitif* (Paris, 1930).

20. The idea of avoidance (of sexual symbols) is stressed by A. Ehrenzweig, *Psycho-Analysis of Artistic Vision and Hearing* (London, 1953), pp. 22–70.

21. E. Kris and O. Kurz, loc. cit., have collected a number of legends reflecting this age-old fear: thus a famous Chinese master was said never to have put the light into the eyes of his painted dragons lest they would fly away.

22. It was the intellectual fashion in German art history to work with contrasting pairs of concepts such as haptic-optic (Riegl), paratactic-hypotactic (Coellen), abstraction-empathy (Worringer), idealism-naturalism (Dvořák), physioplastic-ideoplastic (Verworn), multiplicity-unity (Wölfflin), all of which could probably be expressed in terms of "conceptual" and "less conceptual" art. While the heuristic

value of this method of antithesis is not in doubt it often tends to introduce a false dichotomy. In my book *The Story of Art* (London, 1950) I have attempted to stress the continuity of tradition and the persistent role of the conceptual image.

23. H. Wölfflin, *Principles of Art History* (New York, 1932).

24. The fallacy of a passive idea of perception is discussed in detail by E. Brunswik, *Wahrnehmung und Gegenstandswelt* (Vienna, 1934). In its application to art the writings of K. Fiedler contain many valuable hints; cf. also A. Ehrenzweig, loc. cit., for an extreme and challenging presentation of this problem.

25. This may be meant in the rather enigmatic passage on the painter Parrhasius in Pliny's *Natural History*, XXXV, 67, where it is said that "the highest subtlety attainable in painting is to find an outline . . . which should appear to fold back and to enclose the object so as to give assurance of the parts behind, thus clearly suggesting even what it conceals."

26. Cf. E. Panofsky, "The Codex Huygens and Leonardo da Vinci's Art Theory," *Studies of the Warburg Institute*, XIII (London, 1940), pp. 90 ff.

27. Cf. J. v. Schlosser, "Gespräch von der Bildniskunst," *Präludien* (Vienna, 1927), where, incidentally, the hobby horse also makes its appearance.

WILLIAM H. GASS, *The Concept of Character in Fiction*

1. This has already been discussed in "Philosophy and the Form of Fiction." In "Mirror, Mirror," I complain that Nabokov's omnipotence is too intrusive. [References by the author to his own essays are to other selections in *Fiction and the Figures of Life*.]

2. I treat the relation of fiction to life in more detail in "In Terms of the Toenail: Fiction and the Figures of Life." The problem is handled in other ways in "The Artist and Society," "Even if, by All the Oxen in the World," and "The Imagination of an Insurrection."

3. In *The Concept of Mind* (New York: Barnes & Noble, 1950).

4. Hume, *An Enquiry Concerning Human Understanding* (New York: Oxford University Press). There is reason to suppose that Hume thinks the imagination plays with ideas only after they have lost all vivifying power. Then, however, their arrangement could satisfy only our conceptions of things, not our perceptions of them.

5. Malcolm Lowry, *Under the Volcano* (New York: Reynal and Hitchcock, 1947).

6. Sartre, *Psychology of Imagination* (New York: Citadel, 1961).

7. J. M. Shorter, "Imagination," in *Mind*, LXI.

8. (1) He is always a "mister," and his name functions musically much of the time. "He was an odd compound, Mr. Cashmore, and the air of personal good health, the untarnished bloom which sometimes lent a monstrous serenity to his mention of the barely mentionable, was on occasion balanced or matched by his playful application of extravagant terms to matters of much less moment." What a large mouthful, that sentence. His name (2) locates him, but since he exists nowhere but on the page (6), it simply serves to draw other words toward him (3), or actualize others, as in conversation (7), when they seem to proceed from him, or remind us of all that he is an emblem of (4), and richly interact with other, similarly formed and similarly functioning verbal centers (5).

9. The entire matter is far more complicated than I have indicated. Not only is there a linear order of apprehension (the reader is first told Mr. Mullholland has been seen, then that he was walking his thumbs), but also an order, in depth, of implications. Analysis, in searching out these implications, frequently upsets this order, bringing the bottom to the top. Meanings, uncovered, must be put back as they were found. It is a delicate operation.

10. See "Gertrude Stein: Her Escape from Protective Language," and "The Medium of Fiction."

11. Ortega y Gasset, *The Dehumanization of Art* (New York: Anchor Books, 1956).

12. The way in which both the reader and the world are drawn into the novel is discussed in "In Terms of the Toenail: Fiction and the Figures of Life."

13. Of course nothing prevents a person from feeling that life is like this. See "A Spirit in Search of Itself."

14. There is no reason why every novel should be organized in this way. This method constructs a world according to the principles of Absolute Idealism. See "Philosophy and the Form of Fiction."

15. Henry James, "The Birthplace."

16. Some aspects of this imagination are dealt with in "The High Brutality of Good Intentions," and "In the Cage."

17. See "Philosophy and the Form of Fiction."

18. I enlarge on this aspect of Powers' work in "The Bingo Game at the Foot of the Cross."

19. See "The Medium of Fiction."

HANS MAGNUS ENZENSBERGER, *The Aporias of the Avant-Garde*

1. Where obscurity is mistaken for profundity, the elegant modifier *shallow* is usually held in readiness to describe enlightenment. In such a climate of thought, it may be needful to note that the concept of the progressive can do without any kind of roseate halo. It does not in the least presuppose optimism or the conviction that man strives — perhaps even under constraint! — for perfection. Whoever clings to such a belief is merely negating a negation whose real effects can scarcely be denied in the teeth of the universally planned return to the Stone Age. Even the person who would stick to his guns and refuse to join the general regression seems to be straining forward against an escaping multitude: he functions as a trouble-maker. Thus the concept of progress is an obstacle to those who practice regression.

2. *Wider den missverstandenen Realismus* (Hamburg, 1958).

3. That all classical writers, without any exception, bask in "health" goes without saying. The "heritage" from Homer to Tolstoy must serve as a bludgeon with which modern literature is given whatfor. But not only the illustrious writers of the past are recruited as witnesses for the prosecution; Lukács does not hesitate to put into the witness box the American popular novelist Louis Bromfield, who is good enough for him to testify against Proust.

4. This negligence takes its toll when Lukács writes, "Lenin repeatedly criticizes the sectarian point of view, as if something of which an avant-garde has become fully conscious could be taken over by the masses without further ado." So quickly, then, can a concept be cured of its ills, if party discipline demands it.

5. Brockhaus, *Konversations-Lexikon*, vol. II (14th ed.; Berlin, 1894).

6. Ibid., vol. VII.

7. Vladimir I. Lenin, *Works*, vol. XXXI (Berlin: 1958), pp. 28 ff. Later incessantly reiterated.

8. Hence the amusing terminological difficulty that presents itself to all Marxists when they write about esthetic matters: avant-garde in the arts is to be damned, but avant-garde in politics is to be respected as authoritative.

9. This assertion is not a wholesale dismissal of whatever counts itself a part of the above groups, or is so counted by others. In this essay, the assertion can be elaborated only with regard to certain literary phenomena; an analysis of corresponding conditions in painting and music would go beyond its competence. Theodor W. Adorno has written about *"Das Altern der neuen Musik"* ("The Aging of New Music"). The essay stands completely by itself in contemporary music criticism for its acuteness and uncompromisingness. It is reprinted in the volume *Dissonanzen*.

Musik in der verwalteten Welt (Dissonances: Music in the Bureaucratic World) (Göttingen, 1956). For the questions of nonobjective art, cf. Hans Platschek's excellent *Versuche zur modernen Malerei: Bilder als Fragezeichen (Essays on Modern Painting: Pictures as Question Marks)* (Munich, 1962).

10. *On the Road* (novel) (Hamburg, 1959) jacket copy; also *The New American Poetry, 1945–1960*, Donald M. Allen (ed.) (New York, 1960), p. 439. The sociological equivalent of esthetic indeterminacy is blind mobility, which is expressed already in the title of Kerouac's novel: change of locale as an end in itself; furthermore, a programmatically fostered promiscuity and obsession with the use of narcotics. The reverse side of this anarchic attitude is the strict code to which the members of the group must submit. There is stern differentiation between them and the outsiders, the so-called squares. To Norman Mailer, who has joined the movement, we owe a repertory of its principal rules in the form of a handy tabulation. These rules extend, among other things, to articles of clothing, philosophers, eating places, and jazz musicians that the hipster must favor. This code is meant in utter earnest; Mailer will not be found guilty of the slightest irony. With equal determination, the group celebrates the secret language of its own invention, whose expressions act as passwords. Here no swerving is allowed, and "uninhibited word-slinging" becomes fixed ritual.

11. *material I* (Darmstadt, 1958). [The last two words in the German text are *ahne warumbe.*]

12. Ibid.

13. Hannah Arendt, *Elemente und Ursprünge totaler Herrschaft* (Frankfurt, 1958); Amer. ed.: *Origins of Totalitarianism*.

14. *Movens. Dokumente und Analysen zur Dichtung, bildenden Kunst, Musik, Architektur (Movens: Documents and Analyses of Poetry, Plastic Arts, Music, Architecture)*, edited in collaboration with Walter Höllerer and Manfred de la Motte, by Franz Mon (Wiesbaden, 1960).

15. Exception must be made of the experiments Max Bense and his students have conducted by means of electronic computers. These experiments do meet scientific requirements. Concepts derived from combination and probability theories are here put to meaningful use. Whether the "stochastic texts" thus derived can be valid esthetic objects is a question of definition. Cf. *Augenblick (Instant)*, vol. IV, no. 1 (Siegen, 1959).

16. Reprinted in A. Zervos, *Un Demi-siècle d'art italien* (Paris, 1950).

17. Cf. *Poeti futuristi*, Filippo Tommaso Marinetti (ed.) (Milan, 1912).

18. In his introduction to the anthology, *Lyrik des expressionistischen Jahrzehnts (Poetry of the Expressionist Decade)* (Wiesbaden, 1955).

19. Quoted from *Surrealismus. Texte und Kritik*, Alain Bosquet (ed.) (Berlin, 1950).

20. Hannah Arendt comments, in the work cited above, *Origins of Totalitarianism*, and particularly in the chapter on the mob and the elite, on the latent totalitarian strains in avant-garde movements. Of course, the occasional sympathies of the avant-garde with the totalitarian movements were thoroughly one-sided, as the example of the futurists in Italy and Russia demonstrates. Their love was not requited, and modern art, avant-gardist or not, was promptly lumped together and put on the index.

21. The details of this development are related by Maurice Nadeau in his *Histoire du surréalisme* (Paris, 1948); Amer. ed.: *The History of Surrealism* (New York, 1965).

22. Cf. Maurice Blanchot's "Réflexions sur le surréalisme," in *La Part du feu* (Paris, 1949).

GEOFFREY H. HARTMAN, *Toward Literary History*

1. Wellek and Warren, *Theory of Literature* (New York, 1948), chap. 19.

2. Krauss, *Studien und Aufsätze* (Berlin, 1959), pp. 19–72; Jauss, *Literatur-*

geschichte als Provokation der Literaturwissenschaft (Konstanz, 1966); also Max Wehrli, "Sinn und Unsinn der Literaturgeschichte," *Neue Zürcher Zeitung* (February 26, 1967), no. 813, blatt 5.

3. There are honorable exceptions. American Studies, strongly in touch with the idea of national character, has Howard Mumford Jones' *Theory of American Literature* (1948), the product of a cosmopolitan mind working in a national context. See also Charles Feidelson, *Symbolism and American Literature* (New Haven, 1953), antithetical yet complementary, the product of a cosmopolitan mind working in a specifically literary context. The call for an "inside history" was revived by Roy Harvey Pearce, *The Continuity of American Poetry* (Princeton: Princeton University Press, 1961). Renato Poggioli engages the subject through Pareto's theory of history in *The Spirit of the Letter* (Cambridge, Mass., 1965), and Claudio Guillén has recently remarked that "To explore the idea of literary history may very well be the main theoretical task that confronts the student of literature today."

4. Lucien Goldmann, *Le Dieu Caché* (Paris, 1955).

5. Eliot's dictum in *Notes Towards the Definition of Culture* (London, 1948), "civilization cannot simultaneously produce great folk poetry at one cultural level and *Paradise Lost* at another," is examined by Raymond Williams in *Culture and Society* (London, 1958), pp. 231–32. He points to the contemporaneity with *Paradise Lost* of *Pilgrim's Progress*.

6. "Was sind die Bedingungen die einen Durchschlag aus den Unterbau der Gessellschaft erzwingen und damit das Verhältnis zum Überbau richtigstellen? In welcher Weise gehört überhaupt die Literatur zum Überbau der Gesellschaft?" Werner Krauss, *Perspektiven und Probleme* (West Berlin: Luchterhand Verlag, 1965), p. 19.

7. Ibid., p. 372, translated freely. "Weltliteratur ist dann zu einem Pandämonium geworden, in dem sich Cervantes und Rabelais, Dante und Voltaire zunicken." The specific context is Krauss' attack on a concept of world literature as superliterature or metahistorical assemblage of masterpieces.

8. See, for example, P. J. Ballanche, *Essais de Palingénésie Sociale* (1827).

9. Cf. Malinowski, "The Problem of Meaning in Primitive Languages" in C. K. Ogden and I. A. Richards, *The Meaning of Meaning* (London, 1923).

10. Sigurd Burkhardt, *Shakespearean Meanings* (Princeton, 1968).

11. Cf. Hans Blumenberg, *Die Legimität der Neuzeit* (Frankfurt am Main, 1966); William Collins, "Ode on the Poetical Character" (1747); Otto Rank, *Art and Artist* (New York, 1932), especially the chapter on "Creative Urge and Personality Development"; and Erik Erikson, *Young Man Luther* (New York, 1958).

12. A. Van Gennep, *Les Rites de Passage* (Paris, 1907; English translation, Chicago, 1961); Victor W. Turner, *The Ritual Process* (Chicago, 1969); and Mallarmé, "Hamlet," *Crayonné au Théâtre* (1886).

13. Philip Aries, *Centuries of Childhood* (London, 1962), p. 11. Cf. the tendency of Elizabeth Sewell's *The Orphic Voice* (New Haven, 1960).

14. Cf. W. J. Bate, "The English Poet and the Burden of the Past, 1660–1820," in *Aspects of the Eighteenth Century*, ed. E. R. Wasserman (Baltimore, 1965); Harold Bloom, "Keats and the Embarrassments of Poetic Tradition" in *From Sensibility to Romanticism*, ed. H. Bloom and F. Hilles (New York, 1965); and G. H. Hartman, "Romanticism and Anti-Self-Consciousness," *Centennial Review* VI (1961), pp. 553–65.

15. Cf. H. Bloom, op. cit., p. 517.

16. See Edgar Zilsel, *Die Entstehung des Geniebegriffes* (Tübingen, 1926); W. Lange-Eichbaum and Wolfram Kurth, *Genie, Irrsinn und Ruhm* (Sixth ed., Munich, 1967), chap. 1; and sources cited in note 1 to my "Romantic Poetry and the Genius Loci," in P. Demetz et al., eds., *The Disciplines of Criticism* (New Haven, 1968).

17. "Romantic Poetry and the Genius Loci," loc. cit.; also my "Blake and the 'Progress of Poesy,' " in A. Rosenfeld, ed., *William Blake* (Providence, 1969).

18. "Natale comes qui temperat astrum" (Horace). The Genius-genial-genital link, common from Roman times in which Genius personified the male procreative power, apparently helped to establish, in the Renaissance, the connection between

Genius and ingenium. (See, for example, Otto Rank, *Art and Artist,* chap. 2.) Zilsel, op. cit., concludes that genius, in the modern sense of the term ("Sondergift der Natur," "Personifikation der Eigenart"), became prevalent toward the middle of the sixteenth century as the *learned* revival of astrological and demonological symbolism joined with a surviving *popular* belief in genii and guardian spirits. (But J. Burckhardt, *The Civilization of the Renaissance in Italy,* describes astrology influencing the higher classes as early as the thirteenth century.) On the relation between "ingenium" and "vocatio," see Richard M. Douglas, "Talent and Vocation in Humanist and Protestant Thought," in T. K. Rabb and J. K. Seigel, eds., *Action and Conviction in Early Modern Europe* (Princeton, 1969).

19. Cf. H. Marcuse, *Eros and Civilization* (new ed., Boston, 1966), p. 232. The modernist conflict between historical memory and "the temptation of immediacy" is scrupulously analyzed by Paul de Man in the Spring 1970 issue of *Dædalus* 99.

20. Myth is expressive of Genius in Northrop Frye, but of the *genius loci* in Henry Nash Smith's *Virgin Land* (1949). The difference, though significant, is not absolute and shows the need for a unified theory. Is the Old Man of Wordsworth's "Resolution and Independence" a Genius or a *genius loci?* We have only the sparsest beginnings of a literary iconography on the subject of Genius. See, for example, C. S. Lewis, "Genius and Genius," in *Studies in Renaissance Literature* (New York, 1966), pp. 169–74. Also the analysis of the relation between sense of place and sense of self in my *Wordsworth's Poetry* (New Haven, 1964), especially pp. 211–19.

21. Michelet, *Histoire de France* X, p. 58.

22. Odell Shepard, ed., *The Journals of Bronson Alcott* (Boston, 1938), pp. 213–14.

23. M. M. Bakhtin, *Rabelais and His World* (Cambridge: M.I.T. Press, 1968), especially pp. 465 ff. on the birth of modern literature "on the boundaries of two languages" (that is, Latin and the vernacular). Borges, from this perspective, is a modern Rabelais with a significantly different space-language relation. For remarks on the birth of a more contemporary literature, cf. Octavio Paz, "A Literature of Foundations," *Triquarterly* XII–XIV (1968–69), pp. 7–12.

24. Herder, "Von Ähnlichkeit der Mittlern Englischen und Deutschen Dichtkunst" (*Deutsches Museum,* 1777). Keats, Letter to J. H. Reynolds, February 3, 1818. The idea survives into the present: ". . . the English language — that was Shakespeare at the beginning of the seventeenth century — the English language grew up through the brains and the mouths of English people as such; I mean the nobility and the common people as well. But here, here in our country, the educated people and nobility spoke German, and just the people spoke Czech . . ." Jan Werich in A. Alvarez, *Under Pressure: The Writer in Society* (Pelican Books, 1965). These remarks differ vitally from an absolutist perspective of popular culture. ("Let us have pop art and *not* the old poets.") For a critique of the educational importance of popular culture, see G. H. Bantock, *Culture, Industrialization and Education* (New York: Humanities Press, 1968).

25. Cf. "The presupposition of *Weltliteratur* is a *felix culpa:* mankind's division into many cultures," Erich Auerbach, "Philologie und Weltliteratur" (1952), translated by M. and E. Said, *Centennial Review* XIII (1969), p. 2.

26. Matthew Arnold, *Culture and Anarchy* (London, 1869). Cf. E. Renan, *De la Part des Peuples Sémitiques dans l'Histoire de la Civilisation* (Paris, 1862).

27. A. Cournot, *Traité de l'Enchaînement des Idées Fondamentales dans les Sciences et dans l'Histoire* (Paris, 1861), section 543, and *Considérations sur la Marche des Idées* (Paris, 1872), book 5, chap. 4.

28. "Es wäre eine wichtige Aufgabe der vergleichenden Literaturgeschichte, den Entwicklungsgang der einzelnen Literaturen und ihre Selbstinterpretationen herauszuarbeiten. Was ich das französische Literatursystem nannte, ist eine solche Selbstinterpretation und d.h. eine Ideologie, die bewusst gemacht werden kann. Die Literaturvergleichung würde, wenn sie die bezeichnete Aufgabe ergreift, einen wichtigen Beitrag zur Analyse der modernen Nationalideologien leisten. Diese sind nicht

weniger bedeutsam und wirksam als die Klassenideologien." E. R. Curtius, *Gesammelte Aufsätze zur Romanischen Philologie* (Bern and Munich, 1960), pp. 20–21.

29. Joseph Texte, *Jean-Jacques Rousseau and the Cosmopolitan Spirit in Literature*, tr. J. W. Matthews (London, 1899), p. xiii. Texte, one of our first scholarly comparatists, sees the cosmopolitan spirit founded not by an abstraction from nationality, but a convergence of the "Germanic" (northern) and "Latin" (southern) genius in Rousseau, who consolidated the eighteenth century influence of England on France.

30. Rivarol, *De l'Universalité de la Langue Française* (Berlin and Paris, 1784).

31. A. Cournot, *Essai sur les Fondements de la Connaissance et sur les Caractères de la Critique Philosophique* (Paris, 1851).

32. Ralph Waldo Emerson, *Complete Works* (Boston, 1903–04), vol. II, p. 9. Seneca, *Ep.* 90.28.

ABOUT THE AUTHORS

M[EYER] H[OWARD] ABRAMS, born in 1912, is Professor of English at Cornell University, where he has taught since 1945. He is the author of *The Milk of Paradise* (1934), *The Mirror and the Lamp: Romantic Theory and the Critical Tradition* (1953), *Natural Supernaturalism: Tradition and Revolution in Romantic Literature* (1970), and the editor of *English Romantic Poets: Essays in Criticism* (1960).

A[LFRED] ALVAREZ, born in 1929, is a free-lance critic and literary journalist whose articles have appeared most frequently in *The Observer*, the *New Statesman*, and *The Spectator*. He has been a Visiting Professor at several American universities, including Princeton, Brandeis, and the State University of New York, Buffalo. He is the author of *The Shaping Spirit: Studies in Modern English and American Poets* (1958), *The School of Donne* (1961), *Beyond All This Fiddle: Essays 1955–1967* (1968), *The Savage God: A Study of Suicide* (1972), and the editor of *The New Poetry* (1962) and *Under Pressure: The Writer in Society* (1965).

ERICH AUERBACH, born in Berlin in 1892, was Professor of Romance Philology at the University of Marburg from 1929 until 1935 when he was dismissed by the Nazi government. He went to the Turkish State University at Istanbul, and then in 1947 to the United States, where he held successive posts at Pennsylvania State University, the Institute of Advanced Study at Princeton, and, from 1950 until his death in 1957, Yale University. Of his works the following are available in English: *Dante: Poet of the Secular World* (1929, translated 1961), *Introduction to Romance Languages and Literature* (1943, translated 1961), *Mimesis: The Representation of Reality in Western Literature* (1946, translated 1953), *Literary Language and Its Public in Late Latin Antiquity and in the Middle Ages* (1958, translated 1965), and *Scenes from the Drama of European Literature* (1959).

GASTON BACHELARD (1884–1962) was Professor of the History and Philosophy of Science at the Sorbonne. Of his works the following have been translated into English: *Psychoanalysis of Fire* (1938, translated 1964), *The Poetics of Space* (1957, translated 1964), *The Poetics of Reverie* (1961, translated 1969), and a volume of selections, *On Poetic Imagination and Reverie* (translated 1971).

ROLAND BARTHES, born in France in 1915, is a Director of Studies at the École Pratique des Hautes Études at the University of Paris. He was a Visiting Professor in 1967–1968 at The Johns Hopkins University. Of his works the following have been translated into English: *Writing Degree Zero* (1953, translated 1967), *On Racine* (1963, translated 1964), *Elements of Semiology* (1965, translated 1967), *Mythologies* (1957, translated 1972), and *Critical Essays* (translated 1972).

F[REDERICK] W[ILSE] BATESON, born in 1901, is Emeritus Fellow of Corpus Christi College at Oxford University, where he has taught since 1946. He has been a Visiting Professor at several American universities, including Minnesota, Cornell, California at Berkeley, and Pennsylvania State. He is the author of *English Comic Drama 1700–1750* (1929), *English Poetry and the English Language* (1934), *English Poetry: A Critical Introduction* (1950), *Wordsworth: A Reinterpretation* (1954), and *The Scholar-Critic: An Introduction to Literary Research* (1972). He is the founder of *Essays in Criticism,* and the editor of *The Cambridge Bibliography of English Literature* (4 volumes, 1940) and *A Guide to English Literature* (1965).

MONROE C. BEARDSLEY, born in 1915, has taught at Swarthmore College since 1947, where he is presently Professor of Philosophy. He is the author of *Aesthetics: Problems in the Philosophy of Criticism* (1958), *Classical Aesthetics from Greece to the Present: A Short History* (1966), and *The Possibility of Criticism* (1970).

WALTER BENJAMIN was born in Berlin in 1892, emigrated to Paris in 1933, and committed suicide there in 1940. In 1925 his dissertation for qualification as a faculty member at the University of Berlin had been rejected, so he became a free-lance literary critic and an essayist for several newspapers. Aside from a collection of his aphorisms and an anthology, none of his works were published in book form during his lifetime. A two-volume selected edition of his writing, *Schriften,* was edited and introduced by Theodor W. Adorno in 1955. A volume of Benjamin's essays, *Illuminations,* was edited by Hannah Arendt and translated into English by Harry Zohn in 1968.

JOHN BERRYMAN (1914–1972), a renowned contemporary poet, was, at the time of his death by suicide, Regents Professor at the University of Minnesota and had taught at Wayne State University, Harvard

University, Princeton University, the University of Cincinnati, the University of Washington, the University of California at Berkeley, and Brown University.

LEO BERSANI, born in 1931, is Professor of Romance Languages at Rutgers University. He is the author of *Marcel Proust: The Fiction of Life and of Art* (1965) and *Balzac to Beckett: Center and Circumference in French Fiction* (1971).

R[ICHARD] P[ALMER] BLACKMUR (1904–1965) taught at Princeton University from 1948 until his death. Besides several volumes of poetry, he wrote *The Double Agent: Essays in Craft and Elucidation* (1935), *The Expense of Greatness* (1940), *Language as Gesture: Essays in Poetry* (1952), *The Lion and the Honeycomb: Essays in Solicitude and Critique* (1955), *Eleven Essays in the European Novel* (1964), and *A Primer of Ignorance,* edited by Joseph Frank (1967).

MAURICE BLANCHOT, born in France in 1907, has been a reviewer and columnist for such journals as *Les Temps Modernes* and *La Nouvelle Revue Française*. He is the author of several novels and *récits,* and the following books of criticism: *Faux-pas* (1943), *La Part du feu* (1949), *Lautréamont et Sade* (1949, rev. ed. 1964), *L'Espace littéraire* (1955), *Le Livre à venir* (1959), *L'Attente l'oubli* (1962), and *L'Entretien infini* (1969).

JORGE LUIS BORGES, the celebrated Argentine writer of fiction, was born in Buenos Aires in 1899 and is the Director of the National Library of Argentina. He held the post of Professor of English and North American Literature at the University of Buenos Aires for many years, and in 1968–1969 he was Charles Eliot Norton Visiting Professor of Poetry at Harvard University. His collection of literary essays *Other Inquisitions, 1947–1952* (1952) was translated into English in 1964.

KENNETH BURKE, born in 1897, has taught at the University of Chicago, Syracuse University, the New School for Social Research, and Bennington College. Besides several works of fiction, he has written *Counter-Statement* (1931), *Permanence and Change* (1935), *Attitudes Toward History* (1937), *The Philosophy of Literary Form* (1941), *A Grammar of Motives* (1945), *A Rhetoric of Motives* (1950), *A Rhetoric of Religion* (1961), and *Language as Symbolic Action: Essays on Life, Literature, and Method* (1966).

FRANK CIOFFI, born in 1928, is Senior Lecturer in Philosophy at the University of Kent, England. He has taught at the University of Singapore and the University of California at Berkeley. He is the editor, with Robert Borger, of *Explanation in the Behavioural Sciences* (1970).

FREDERICK CREWS, born in 1933, is Professor of English at the University of California at Berkeley, where he has taught since 1958. He is the author of *Tragedy of Manners: Moral Drama in the Later Novels of Henry James* (1957), *E. M. Forster: The Perils of Humanism* (1962), *The Pooh Perplex: A Freshman Casebook* (1963), *The Sins of the Fathers: Hawthorne's Psychological Themes* (1966), *The Patch Commission* (1968), and the editor of *Psychoanalysis and Literary Process* (1970).

DONALD DAVIE, born in 1922 in York, England, has taught at Trinity College, Dublin, Cambridge University, the University of Essex, and is presently Professor of English at Stanford University. He is the author of, besides several volumes of poetry, *Purity of Diction in English Verse* (1952), *Articulate Energy: An Inquiry into the Syntax of English* (1955), *Ezra Pound: Poet as Sculptor* (1964), the editor of *Russian Literature and Modern English Fiction* (1965), and one of the editors of *Poetics. Poetyka. Poetika* (1961).

DENIS DONOGHUE, born in 1928, is Professor of Modern English and American Literature at University College, Dublin. He is the author of *The Third Voice: Modern British and American Verse Drama* (1959), *Connoisseurs of Chaos: Ideas of Order in Modern American Poetry* (1965), *The Ordinary Universe: Soundings in Modern Literature* (1968), *Jonathan Swift: A Critical Introduction* (1969), *Emily Dickinson* (1969), *Yeats* (1971), and the editor of *The Integrity of Yeats* (1964) and, with J. R. Mulryne, *An Honoured Guest: New Essays on William Butler Yeats* (1965).

HANS MAGNUS ENZENSBERGER, born in 1929, is a distinguished German poet and the editor of the review *Kursbuch*. He is a founder of the literary movement "Group 47," and has compiled an anthology *Museum der modernen poeisie* (1960). A collection of his poems has been translated into English, *Poems for People Who Don't Read Poems* (1968), but the several volumes of his literary and political essays are still largely unknown to English readers.

ROBERT FROST (1874–1963) taught English at Amherst College, starting in 1917, was a poet-in-residence at the University of Michigan from 1921 to 1923, and Charles Eliot Norton Professor of Poetry at Harvard University in 1936. In the last years of his life, he lectured and gave readings of his poetry in colleges and universities across the country.

NORTHROP FRYE, born in 1912, is University Professor at the University of Toronto, where he has taught since 1939. He is the author of *Fearful Symmetry: A Study of William Blake* (1947), *Anatomy of*

Criticism: Four Essays (1957), *The Well-Tempered Critic* (1963), *The Educated Imagination* (1963), *T. S. Eliot* (1963), *Fables of Identity: Studies in Poetic Mythology* (1963), *A Natural Perspective: The Development of Shakespearean Comedy and Romance* (1965), *The Return of Eden: Five Essays on Milton's Epics* (1965), *Fools of Time: Studies in Shakespearean Tragedy* (1967), *The Modern Century* (1967), *A Study of English Romanticism* (1968), *The Stubborn Structure: Essays on Criticism and Society* (1970) and *The Critical Path* (1971).

WILLIAM H. GASS, born in 1924, is Professor of Philosophy at Washington University. He is the author of the novels *Omensetter's Luck* (1966) and *In the Heart of the Heart of the Country* (1968), and a collection of essays, *Fiction and the Figures of Life* (1970).

E[RNST] H[ANS] [JOSEPH] GOMBRICH, an eminent British art historian, was born in Vienna in 1909 and is the Director of the Warburg Institute of the University of London as well as Professor of History of the Classical Tradition. He is the author of *Caricature,* with E. Kris (1940), *The Story of Art: A Study in the Psychology of Pictorial Representation* (1950), *Art and Illusion* (1960), *Meditations on a Hobby Horse and Other Essays on the Theory of Art* (1963), *Norm and Form: Studies in the Art of the Renaissance* (1966), and *In Search of Cultural History* (1969).

GEOFFREY H. HARTMAN, born in 1929, is Professor of English and Comparative Literature at Yale University. He is the author of *André Malraux* (1960), *The Unmediated Vision: An Interpretation of Wordsworth, Hopkins, Rilke and Valéry* (1954), *Wordsworth's Poetry 1787–1814* (1964), *Beyond Formalism: Literary Essays 1958–1970* (1970), and the editor of *Hopkins: A Collection of Critical Essays* (1966).

IHAB HASSAN, born in 1925, is Research Professor of English and Comparative Literature at the University of Wisconsin at Milwaukee. He is the author of *Radical Innocence: Studies in the Contemporary American Novel* (1961), *The Literature of Silence: Henry Miller and Samuel Beckett* (1967), and *The Dismemberment of Orpheus: Toward a Postmodern Literature* (1971).

ROMAN JAKOBSON, born in 1896 in Moscow, is Emeritus Professor of Slavonic Languages, Literature, and General Linguistics at Harvard University, and Institute Professor at the Massachusetts Institute of Technology. His *Selected Writings* are being published in seven volumes by Mouton (1962–).

FRANK KERMODE, born in 1919, is Professor of Modern English Literature at University College, London. He has taught and lectured at Wesleyan, Princeton, and many other American universities. He is the author of *English Pastoral Poetry* (1952), *Romantic Image* (1957), *Wallace Stevens* (1960), *Puzzles and Epiphanies: Essays and Reviews 1958–1961* (1962), *William Shakespeare, The Final Plays* (1963), *The Sense of an Ending: Studies in the Theory of Fiction* (1967), *Continuities* (1968), and the editor of *The Living Milton* (1960), *The Metaphysical Poets* (1969), and the series *Modern Masters* (1970–).

MURRAY KRIEGER, born in 1927, is Professor of English and Comparative Literature and Director of the Program in Literary Criticism at the University of California at Irvine. He is the author of *The New Apologists for Poetry* (1956), *The Tragic Vision* (1960), *A Window to Criticism: Shakespeare's Sonnets and Modern Poetics* (1964), *The Play and Place of Criticism* (1967), *The Classic Vision* (1971); the co-editor, with Eliseo Vivas, of *The Problems of Aesthetics: A Book of Readings* (1953); and the editor of *Northrop Frye in Modern Criticism: Selected Papers from The English Institute 1965* (1966).

F[RANK] R[AYMOND] LEAVIS, born in 1895, is now retired after many years of teaching at Downing College, Cambridge University. He was the founder and editor of the literary journal *Scrutiny*. He is the author of *New Bearings in English Poetry* (1932), *Revaluation* (1936), *For Continuity* (1933), *Education and the University* (1948), *The Great Tradition: George Eliot, James, and Conrad* (1948), *The Common Pursuit* (1952), *D. H. Lawrence: Novelist* (1955), *Two Cultures* (1963), *Anna Karenina and Other Essays* (1967), *English Literature in Our Time and the University* (1969), *Dickens* (1970), and, with Q. D. Leavis, *Lectures in America* (1969).

CLAUDE LÉVI-STRAUSS, born in 1908, the founder of structural anthropology, has since 1959 held the Chair of Social Anthropology at the Collège de France. Of his books the following have been translated into English: *Race and History* (1952, translated 1958), *Tristes Tropiques* (1955, translated 1961), *Structural Anthropology* (1958, translated 1963), *The Savage Mind* (1962, translated 1966), and *The Raw and the Cooked: Introduction to a Science of Mythology* (1964, translated 1969).

ROBERT LOWELL, the distinguished contemporary poet, was born in 1917 and has taught at Harvard University, Kenyon College, and Boston University.

GEORG LUKÁCS (1885–1971) was widely reputed to be the leading modern Marxist critic. He was Minister of Culture in Hungary in

1919 and in 1956. He held the Chair in Aesthetics at the University of Budapest from 1945 to 1956. Of his works the following have been translated into English: *The Historical Novel* (1936, translated 1962), *Goethe and His Time* (1947, translated 1968), *Studies in European Realism* (1948, translated 1964), *Essays on Thomas Mann* (1949, translated 1964), *The Meaning of Contemporary Realism* (1956, translated 1964), and *Writer and Critic and Other Essays* (translated 1970).

LOUIS T. MILIC, born in 1922, is Professor of English and Chairman of the Department at the Cleveland State University. He is the author of *A Quantitative Approach to the Style of Jonathan Swift* (1967), the compiler of *Style and Stylistics: An Analytical Bibliography* (1967), and the editor of *Stylists on Style: A Handbook with Selections for Analysis* (1969).

J. HILLIS MILLER, born in 1928, is Professor of English at Yale University, and formerly Professor of English at The Johns Hopkins University. He is the author of *Charles Dickens: The World of His Novels* (1958), *The Disappearance of God: Five Nineteenth-Century Writers* (1963), *Poets of Reality: Six Twentieth-Century Writers* (1965), *The Form of Victorian Fiction* (1968), *Thomas Hardy: Distance and Desire* (1970), and the editor of *William Carlos Williams: A Collection of Critical Essays* (1966).

JOHN FREDERICK NIMS, born in 1913, is a noted poet and translator of poetry. He is Professor of English at the University of Illinois at Chicago and has taught at the University of Notre Dame, the University of Toronto, and several European universities, including those of Milan, Florence, and Madrid.

RICHARD OHMANN, born in 1931, is Professor of English at Wesleyan University and former Associate Provost and Chancellor. He is the editor of *College English* and the author of *Shaw: The Style and the Man* (1962).

RICHARD POIRIER, born in 1925, is Professor of English and Chairman of the Federated Departments of English at Rutgers University. He is the author of *The Comic Sense of Henry James: A Study of the Early Novels* (1960), *A World Elsewhere: The Place of Style in American Literature* (1966), and *The Performing Self: Compositions and Decompositions in the Languages of Contemporary Life* (1971); a co-editor, with Reuben A. Brower, of *In Defense of Reading: A Reader's Approach to Literary Criticism* (1962); and an editor of *Partisan Review*.

GEORGES POULET, born in Belgium in 1902, has taught at the University of Edinburgh, The Johns Hopkins University, the University of Zurich, and is presently a professor at the University of Nice. Of his works the following have been translated into English: *Studies in Human Time* (1949, 1950, translated 1956), *The Interior Distance* (1952, translated 1959), and *The Metamorphoses of the Circle* (1961, translated 1966).

SUSAN SONTAG, born in 1933, has taught at Harvard University, Oxford University, the University of Connecticut, the City College of New York, and Columbia University. She is the author of, besides several novels and a film, *Against Interpretation and Other Essays* (1965) and *Styles of Radical Will* (1969).

MARK SPILKA, born in 1925, is Professor of English and Chairman of the Department at Brown University and is the managing editor of *Novel: A Forum of Fiction.* He is the author of *The Love Ethic of D. H. Lawrence* (1955), *Dickens and Kafka: A Mutual Interpretation* (1963), and the editor of *D. H. Lawrence: A Collection of Critical Essays* (1963).

LEO SPITZER, born in Vienna in 1887, taught at the Universities of Vienna, Bonn, Marburg, and Cologne before he had to leave Germany in 1933. After a period at Istanbul he joined the faculty of The Johns Hopkins University, where he taught until his death in 1960. Of his works the following are available in English: *Linguistics and Literary History: Essays in Stylistics* (1948), *A Method of Interpreting Literature* (1949), *Essays on English and American Literature,* edited by Anna Hatcher (1962), and *Classical and Christian Ideas of World Harmony: Prolegomena to an Interpretation of the Word "Stimmung,"* edited by Anna Hatcher (1963).

JEAN STAROBINSKI, born in Geneva in 1920, is Professor of French Literature at the University of Geneva. From 1954 to 1956 he taught at The Johns Hopkins University. He is the author of *Jean-Jacques Rousseau, la transparence et l'obstacle* (1957), *L'Oeil vivant* (1961), *Invention of Liberty 1700–1789* (1964), *Portrait de l'artiste en saltimbanque* (1970), and *La Relation critique* (1970).

LIONEL TRILLING, born in 1905, is Professor of Literature and Criticism at Columbia University, where he has taught since 1932. He is the author of, besides several works of fiction, *Matthew Arnold* (1939), *E. M. Forster* (1943), *The Liberal Imagination: Essays on Literature and Society* (1950), *The Opposing Self: Nine Essays in Criticism* (1955), *A Gathering of Fugitives* (1957), *Beyond Culture: Essays on Literature and Learning* (1965), and the editor of *The Experience of*

Literature (1967) and *Literary Criticism: An Introductory Reader* (1970).

IAN WATT, born in 1917, is Professor of English and Chairman of the Department at Stanford University. He is the author of *The Rise of the Novel: Studies in Defoe, Richardson, and Fielding* (1957).

RICHARD WILBUR, born in 1921, is a distinguished contemporary poet. He is Professor of English at Wesleyan University and has taught at Harvard University and Wellesley College.

W[ILLIAM] K[URTZ] WIMSATT, born in 1907, is Professor of English Literature at Yale University, where he has taught since 1939. He is the author of *The Prose Style of Samuel Johnson* (1941), *Philosophic Words* (1948), *The Verbal Icon: Studies in the Meaning of Poetry* (1954), *Hateful Contraries: Studies in Literature and Criticism* (1965), and, with Cleanth Brooks, *Literary Criticism: A Short History* (1957).